Developmental Psychopathology

Sixth Edition

Sixth Edition

Developmental Psychopathology

From Infancy through Adolescence

Patricia K. Kerig
Amanda Ludlow
Charles Wenar

The **McGraw-Hill** Companies

London Boston Burr Ridge, IL Dubuque, IA Madison, WI New York San Francisco
St. Louis Bangkok Bogotá Caracas Kuala Lumpur Lisbon Madrid Mexico City
Milan Montreal New Delhi Santiago Seoul Singapore Sydney Taipei Toronto

Developmental Psychopathology 6th Edition
Patricia K. Kerig, Amanda Ludlow and Charles Wenar
ISBN-13 9780077131210
ISBN-10 0077131215

McGraw-Hill Higher Education

Published by McGraw-Hill Education
Shoppenhangers Road
Maidenhead
Berkshire
SL6 2QL
Telephone: 44 (0) 1628 502 500
Fax: 44 (0) 1628 770 224
Website: www.mcgraw-hill.co.uk

British Library Cataloguing in Publication Data
A catalogue record for this book is available from the British Library

Library of Congress Cataloging in Publication Data
The Library of Congress data for this book has been applied for from the Library of Congress

Executive Editor: Natalie Jacobs
Marketing Manager: Kevin Watt
Production Editor: Alison Davis

Text Design by Hardlines
Cover design by Ego Creative
Printed and bound in the UK by Bell and Bain Ltd, Glasgow

ISBN-13 9780077131210
ISBN-10 0077131215

To Philip Cowan for setting me on the pathway to developmental psychopathology, and to Charles Wenar for showing me how to follow it.

Patricia K. Kerig

To Roberto Gutierrez for all your support and being you, and to the amazing children and their families who I have had the pleasure to meet along the way. You truly are an inspiration!

Amanda Ludlow

Brief Table of Contents

Detailed Table of Contents

About the Authors

Patricia K. Kerig received her PhD in clinical psychology from the University of California at Berkeley with a specialization in children and families. After completing an internship at Stanford Children's Hospital and a postdoctoral fellow in clinical child psychology at the University of Colorado Health Sciences Center, she held faculty positions at Simon Fraser University, the University of North Carolina at Chapel Hill, and Miami University. Currently she is a Professor and the Director of Clinical Training in the Department of Psychology at the University of Utah, as well as being a licensed clinical psychologist. Her research honours include the Brodsky/Hare Mustin Award from Division 35 of the American Psychological Association and the New Contribution Award from the International Society for the Study of Personal Relationships. She is a member of the editorial boards of the *Journal of Family Psychology*, *Journal of Child and Adolescent Trauma* and *Journal of Maltreatment, Aggression, and Trauma* and is the author of numerous scholarly works on the topics of risk and resilience in children and adolescents exposed to interparental conflict, violence, maltreatment and traumatic stress. Her current interests focus on understanding and intervening with traumatized youth and families involved in the juvenile justice system.

Amanda Ludlow received her PhD in developmental psychology from Goldsmiths College, University of London, with a specialization in children with atypical development. She completed a postdoctoral position on a multidiscipli-nary European project looking at the Stages and Evolution and Development of Sign Usage (SEDSU). Following completion of this project she held the position of lecturer in psychology at Anglia Ruskin University, Cambridge, where she was director of the Master's programme in Clinical Child Psychology. She has recently joined the University of Birmingham as a lecturer in psychology, as well as being an external examiner for Middlesex University. She is author of numerous scholarly works focusing on the development of children with autism spectrum disorders. Her current interests focus on the impact of sensory deficits (e.g., blindness and deafness) on children's social development and its impact on the family.

Charles Wenar, the progenitor of the first edition of this textbook, was professor emeritus of psychology at Ohio State University. He headed both the developmental area and the clinical child programme in the department of psychology there. A graduate of Swarthmore College and State University of Iowa, Dr Wenar was both a clinician and a researcher at Michael Reese Hospital, the Illinois Neuropsychiatric Institute and the University of Pennsylvania. His many books and articles, as well as his research on autism and on negativism in healthy toddlers, attest to his long-standing interest in both normal and disturbed children. In 1986, Dr Wenar received the Distinguished Professional Contribution Award of the Section on Clinical Child Psychology of Division 12 of the American Psychological Association for his meritorious contribution to the advancement of knowledge and service to children.

Acknowledgements

Author acknowledgements

We appreciate the help of many colleagues who contributed information, encouragement and clarification to the text. We are also indebted to many individuals at McGraw-Hill whose names appear on the copyright page. Mary Looser of the University of Utah provided invaluable assistance in compiling the references and keeping us on track.

Finally, we are grateful to the reviewers of this edition. We were impressed by their thoroughness and we profited greatly from their comments.

Publisher's acknowledgements

We would like to thank the following people for their comments and reviews of this edition:

Patricia Bijttebier, *Katholieke Universiteit Leuven*

Cristina Colonnesi, *Universiteit van Amsterdam*

Prof. dr M Dekovic, *Universiteit Utrecht*

Yvette Dijkxhoorn, *Universiteit Leiden*

Dr E S Kunnen, *Rijksuniversiteit Groningen*

Annette Mahoney, *Bowling Green State University*

Peter Musaeus, *Aarhus University*

Elia Psouni, *Lund University*

Anja Rutten, *Staffordshire University*

Peter van den Berg, *Universiteit Leiden*

Dr J J van der Meere, *Rijksuniversiteit Groningen*

We would also like to thank those people who reviewed to the previous edition:

Mary Katherine Weibel-Duncan, *Bloomsburg University*

Patricia Metz, *School of Social Work, University of Michigan*

Gregory P. Hickman, *Penn State University, Fayette*

George W. Ledger, *Hollins University*

Annette Mahoney, *Bowling Green State University*

Jennifer Langhinrichsen-Rohling, *University of South Alabama*

Virginia Powers-Lagac, *Westfield State College*

Azmaira Maker, *Marquette University*

Jeanine Vivona, *The College of New Jersey*

Mikal Galperin, *University of Texas, Dallas*

We would like to thank the following for permission to reprint images:

The Prader Willis Syndrome Association

Nancy J. Price

World Health Organization

Unicef

Getty Images

Harvard University Press

PhotoEdit

Photo Researchers, Inc.

Every effort has been made to trace and acknowledge ownership of copyright and to clear permission for material reproduced in this book. The publishers will be pleased to make suitable arrangements to clear permission with any copyright holders whom it has not been possible to contact.

Preface

The Developmental Approach

The unifying theme in all editions of this text is that childhood psychopathology should be regarded as normal development gone awry. Thus, normal development becomes the point of departure for understanding childhood disturbances. The basic challenge is that of discovering what forces divert development from its normal course and what forces either sustain the deviation or foster a return to normality. Because of this unifying theme, an entire chapter (Chapter 2) is devoted to the contributions made by the biological, family, social and cultural contexts as well as the normal development of six processes in the individual context: cognition, emotion, attachment, the self, moral development, and gender and sexuality. The roots of a given disturbance in normal development are then presented; for example, autism is related to the normal development of infants, and reading disability is related to the normal process of learning to read. A pedagogical advantage of Chapter 2 is that students from diverse backgrounds in areas such as education or social work can all be equally well informed concerning the development of the 10 crucial variables. Another consequence of the developmental approach is that, with some exceptions, the psychopathologies can be arranged in a rough chronological order rather than in the usual descriptive categories such as 'behavioural disorders' or 'emotional disorders'. Autism originates in infancy; anxiety disorders, in middle childhood; and eating disorders, in adolescence. This arrangement, in turn, is another way of helping students to 'think developmentally'.

Not everyone agrees with the developmental approach used here. For some, developmental psychopathology consists of describing a given psychopathology and then dealing with the issues of etiology and prognosis. However, even though such an approach may involve charting the 'developmental pathways' of various disturbances, it is basically the same as that used in descriptive psychiatry. In both instances the *crucial connection to normal development* is neglected.

Changes for the Current Revision

1 The most profound change for the current edition of this textbook is that it is now *international* in scope. In every chapter, we include information derived from around the world, and represent important research findings based upon cross-national samples and/or conducted by international researchers. The result is a textbook that represents the true state of knowledge in the field of developmental psychopathology even more completely and accurately.

2 Each chapter has been extensively revised in the light of *new research* on the prevalence, origins, consequences and treatment of each of the disorders. In particular, the developmental psychopathology perspective has alerted researchers to the crucial need for *longitudinal research* that allows us to observe patterns of continuity and change over the lifespan (see Chapter 1). The dilemma, however, is that a lifespan study requires the entire lifespan of the investigator! Nonetheless, the harvest of a number of long-term longitudinal studies is now being reaped. Important new research is emerging about the etiology and course of many disorders, including depression (see Chapter 9) and conduct disorder (see Chapter 10).

3 Given that developmental psychopathology comprises the study of both normative and pathological development, we now include

consistently in each chapter a section on *resilience* and the *protective processes* that allow some youth to experience positive outcomes despite being 'dealt a poor hand' in life.

Pedagogical Features

The overall organization in terms of *contexts* – specifically, biological, individual, family, social and cultural – provides a consistent framework for ordering the sprawling research literature. In addition, each psychopathology is systematically presented in terms of a set *organizational framework*, namely, definition and characteristics (including prevalence, gender, and socio-economic and ethnic differences), comorbidity, developmental course, etiology and intervention. *Key terms* appear in bold in the text and are included in a glossary at the end of the book. There are frequent *summaries* throughout each chapter, presented either in written form or as figures. Such summaries have the advantage of being more detailed and relevant than an overall, global summation at the end of the chapter.

In each chapter, *boxes* are used to highlight issues of theoretical interest, to illustrate debates and controversies in the field, or to provide greater depth in our coverage of the relevant research.

Further, in each chapter, a *case study* is presented in the form of a vignette or box to illustrate the disorder under investigation. Wherever possible, the case studies used are real-life cases, many of which are derived from autobiographical material. By the same token, Chapter 17 includes transcripts of actual therapy sessions to illustrate each of the intervention modalities described. Consistent with the developmental psychopathology perspective of a continuum between the normative and the psychopathology, our goal is to put a human face on the disorders and to increase our readers' empathy and understanding for those who experience them.

For the Instructor

An *Instructor's Manual*, originally prepared by Patricia Kerig, and updated by Patricia Kerig and Amanda Ludlow, is available on the text's companion website (www.mcgraw-hill.co.uk/textbooks/kerig). It includes additional references for case studies, films, discussion/study questions and suggested examination questions.

PowerPoint presentation slides, created by Leslie Zeigenhorn (University of San Diego and San Diego State University) and updated by Patricia Kerig, are also available to instructors on the companion website.

For the Student

The goal of the present edition has not changed – namely, to enable the student to 'think developmentally' about psychopathology as it unfolds from childhood through adolescence. A number of features of the new edition have been designed to provide students with a clearer pathway through the material. For example, more figures have been included in order to illustrate research findings and conceptual models, the visual appeal of the book has been increased and key terms have been put in bold print. In addition, boxes have been added in order to provide more detailed information, to explore issues and questions raised by the research, or to bring the material alive through case studies. Review articles are often cited so that students can have access to more detailed presentations of research than is possible within a given chapter. Also there are references to literature on topics that, while important, had to be excluded because of space limitations.

The Developmental Psychopathology Approach

Overview

The three vignettes in Box 1.1 illustrate the key hypothesis that informs this text: that child psychopathology can be understood as *normal development gone awry*. Psychopathology is behaviour that once was, but no longer can be, considered appropriate to the child's level of development. Whether the described behaviours are regarded as normal or pathological depends on when they occur in the developmental sequence. All three of the behaviours in the vignettes presented in Box 1.1 are to be expected in toddlers and preschoolers but would be concerning at later ages. In the first example, it is not unusual for a docile infant to become a wilful, negativistic, temperamental tyrant during the 'terrible twos'. If the child were 10, however, his attack on his brother might represent a serious lapse in self-control. Likewise, in the second example, it is not unusual for preschool boys to believe that they can grow up to be women, because they have not grasped the fact that gender remains constant throughout life. And finally, ideas of omnipotence

and a failure to clearly separate fantasy from reality are part of normal cognitive development in toddlers and preschoolers; their presence from middle childhood on suggests the possibility of a serious thought disturbance and an unhealthy lack of contact with reality.

This *developmental framework* informs the response of the child clinician who reassures a parent, 'There's nothing to worry about – most children act that way at this age, and your child will probably outgrow it'; or the one who warns, 'This behaviour is unusual and should be attended to, since it suggests something is seriously awry'. A good understanding of normal development must be achieved before one can judge whether the behaviour at hand is age-appropriate or whether a suspect behaviour is likely to disappear in the course of a child's progress from infancy to adulthood. Further, knowledge of development alerts us to the fact that some problem behaviour is *normal* in the course of life. (See Fig. 1.1.) In fact, the absence of misbehaviour might constitute a reason for worry. The 2-year-old who is not distressed by

Box 1.1 What Is the First Question You Ask?

You are a clinical child psychologist. A mother telephones your office frantic over the sudden personality change in her boy. 'He used to be so sweet and then, out of the clear blue sky, he started being sassy and sulky and throwing a fit if anybody asked him to do the least little thing. What really scared me was last night he got so mad at his brother, he ran at him and started hitting him with all his might. His brother was really hurt and started screaming, and my husband and I had to pull them apart. I don't know what would have happened if we hadn't been there. I just never saw anybody in a rage like that before.'

What is the first question you ask?

You are at a cocktail party and, after learning that you are a clinical child psychologist, a former star-quarterback-turned-successful-business-executive takes you aside. After some rambling about 'believing in sexual equality as much as the next fellow', he comes to the point. 'Last week my son turned to his wife and announced that when he got old enough, he was going to become a girl. When my wife asked him where he got a crazy idea like that, he said that he thought boys were too rough, and he liked to be with girls more. I know he's always been a "mama's boy", but I'll be darned if I want any son of mine to have one of those sex changes done on him.'

What is the first question you ask?

You are a clinical child psychologist conducting an initial interview with a mother who has brought her daughter to a child guidance clinic. 'She has always been a sensitive child and a loner, but I thought she was getting along all right – except that recently she has started having some really strange ideas. The other day we were driving on the highway to town, and she said, "I could make all these cars wreck if I just raised my hand". I thought she was joking, but she had a serious expression on her face and wasn't even looking at me. Another time she wanted to go outside when the weather was bad, and she got furious at me because I didn't make it stop raining. And now she's started pleading and pleading with me every night to look in on her after she has gone to sleep to be sure her leg isn't hanging over the side of the bed. She says there is some kind of crab creature in the dark waiting to grab her if her foot touches the floor. What worries me is that she believes all these things can really happen. I don't know if she's crazy or watching too much TV or what's going on.'

What is the first question you ask?

The first question is the same in all three cases: *how old is your child?*

separation from the mother, the 3-year-old who never says no, the adolescent who never experiments with new roles – children such as these might warrant a second look.

Before we set out to understand child psychopathology as normal development gone awry, we first must set the stage. First, we will present a general *developmental framework* in order to examine various characteristics of development itself. Then we will identify those *developmental processes* that are particularly important to the understanding of childhood psychopathology and trace their normal

FIGURE 1.1 Development is Lifelong and Problems are a Part of Normal Development.

Source: PEANUTS © United Feature Syndicate, Inc.

Guided Tour

Glossary

accelerated longitudinal approach (Also known as the longitudinal, cross-sectional approach.) A research technique in which data on the origins of a psychopathology are obtained from different age groups that are subsequently followed until the children in the younger groups are the same age as those in the next older group.

accommodation In Piaget's theory, the process of changing an existing cognitive schema in order to take into account new information from the environment.

adaptational failure A conceptualization of psychopathology in which disorder is viewed as stemming from the child's inability to adapt to the expectations of the environment.

alternates between dieting and binge eating, followed by self-induced vomiting or purging.

anxiety disorders A group of disorders characterized by intense, chronic anxiety. Formerly called psychoneurotic disorders.

assimilation In Piaget's theory, the process of transforming information so as to make it fit with an existing cognitive schema.

asynchrony Disjointed or markedly uneven rates of progression among developmental variables.

attention deficit hyperactivity disorder Developmentally inappropriate inattention accompanied by motor restlessness and impulsivity.

Glossary

All key terms are identified in the text and then defined in the glossary at the end of the book, to assist you in learning the important terms as you go through the course.

Figures and Tables

Figures and tables draw out key concepts in a more accessible format or to aid understanding through diagrammatic representation. Key models are displayed in this way, as well as reference tools for DSM/ICD criteria.

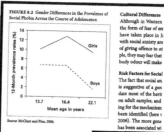

FIGURE 8.2 Gender Differences in the Prevalence of Social Phobia Across the Course of Adolescence.

Source: McClure and Pine, 2006.

TABLE 5.2 DSM-IV-TR Criteria for Asperger's Disorder

A. Qualitative impairment in social interaction, as manifested
   1. Marked impairment in the use of multiple nonverbal beh postures, and gestures to regulate social interaction
   2. Failure to develop peer relationships appropriate to devel
   3. A lack of spontaneously seeking to share enjoyment, inte showing, bringing or pointing out objects of interest to o
   4. Lack of social or emotional reciprocity
B. Restricted repetitive and stereotyped patterns of behavior, i following:
   1. Encompassing preoccupation with one or more stereotyp either in intensity or focus
   2. Apparently inflexible adherence to specific, nonfunction
   3. Stereotyped and repetitive motor mannerisms (e.g., hand movements)
   4. Persistent preoccupation with parts of objects
C. The disturbance causes clinically significant impairment in functioning
D. There is no clinically significant general delay in language (phrases used by age 3 years)
E. There is no clinically significant delay in cognitive developr skills, adaptive behavior (other than in social interaction), a

Source: Reprinted with permission from the Diagnostic and Statistical Manu by the American Psychiatric Association.

Summary

Although frequently overlooked by child protection agents and psychological investigators alike, psychological maltreatment is embedded in the experience of all other forms of abuse and may even account for many of their effects (Hart et al., 2011). However, psychological maltreatment has *unique effects*, with pervasive and insidious consequences for development. While aggression is seen increasingly over the course of development, *depression* and *internalizing disorders* appear to be most strongly related to psychological maltreatment. The resulting negative views of self and others – feelings of worthlessness, self-loathing and insecurity – compromise the ability to get emotional needs met in current or future relationships.

Summary

Summaries are included at key points in the chapter to help you digest the content that has just been presented.

Case Studies

In each chapter, case studies are presented as vignettes or boxes to illustrate the particular disorder under investigation. A number of these are real-life case studies, sometimes drawn from biographical material. The cases will help give a feel for the pathology and for an individual's difficulty.

Box 6.3   Case Study in Oppositional Defiant Disorder: Joseph 8 Years

'I hate this place, no one tells me what to do any more,' 8-year-old Joseph screams at his teacher, 'You always tell me I am naughty but I ain't, I only get in trouble because of stupid you. It's not my fault that I am sat next to Amy, she makes me do stupid things. I hate you all!' He heads for the door knocking books off shelves, and tears down some of his peers' work off the wall before eventually kicking the classroom door open to mount his escape. He eventually turns around and looks back at the teacher, willing a final standoff between him and the teacher.

Joseph is notorious for getting in trouble and has a school record with extreme violent outbursts over the duration of a year. This particular episode erupted simply following a teacher's request for him to be quiet in class. This demonstrates his overreaction to small events, violent outbursts and extreme frustration as well as his willingness to disobey authority. Joseph has suspected ODD.

Behavioural characteristics duration. Pattern of ODD than 6 months and he woul out of the following: (1) ofte refuses to comply with adu rules; (4) deliberately annoy for his mistakes; (6) easily a and resentful; (8) is often 2000, p. 70).

It is important to estab Children who are at high r have parents with some typ ily members who might be Other factors that may inc include, although not an es rejection, separation from alternative caregiver, family

Box 10.2   A Developmental Dilemma: When

During the past decades, spurred by concerns about youth violence, legal reforms in the US lowered the age at which adolescents could be tried as adults in criminal court. For example, in 2006, 200 000 youths under the age of 18 were tried as adults. However, developmentally, are adolescents ready to be held to the same standards as adults? Are they competent to participate in the legal process, assist in their own defence and comprehend the nature of the charges laid against them? To answer these questions, Steinberg and his colleagues (2009) administered a structured interview to nearly 1000 juveniles aged 11 to 17, and 500 young adults aged 18 to 24, half of whom were incarcerated and half of whom were drawn from the community. Their results showed significant age differences in children's ability to comprehend their rights, understand courtroom procedures, and reason about the information relevant to launching their legal defense. Approximately one-third

Other Boxes

Other boxes in the chapter highlight theoretical issues, illustrating debate and controversy within the field.

course. Our vignettes, for example, suggest that the variables of self-regulation, gender identity and cognition should be included in the list. We also will evaluate *theoretical models* that contribute most to the developmental approach. As we examine various disorders, we shall discover that there are many variations on this theme of psychopathology as developmentally inappropriate behaviour; therefore, we shall constantly be seeking the specific developmental scheme that best fits the data at hand. Lastly, we shall examine the **developmental psychopathology** approach, which attempts to integrate these different perspectives.

A General Developmental Framework

Our general developmental framework includes the time dimension along with five *contexts* of development: the biological, individual, family, social and cultural.

The Biological Context

The biological context involves a number of organic influences that are relevant to understanding deviant development: *genetics, biochemistry, brain structure, neurological* and *neuropsychological* functioning, and innate characteristics that are involved in the development of individual differences, such as *temperament*. Research in the neuropsychology of childhood disorders has been burgeoning in recent years, and we will consider this work in our exploration of each of the psychopathologies. The effects of psychological disturbances on biology will be central to our examination of certain disorders, such as bulimia and anorexia nervosa. Reversing the direction of influence, we will also consider the psychological consequences of biological problems, such as physical illness and brain damage. Further, throughout the text, we will explore the role that genetic factors play in various psychopathologies.

The Individual Context

The individual context concerns psychological variables within the person – personality characteristics, thought processes, emotions and internalized expectations about relationships. This context will figure prominently in our discussions of psychopathology, since it is so clearly concerned with developmental factors. We also will consider how different theories would direct us to focus on one of these aspects of development over others. For example, traditional behaviourists would urge us to focus on observable behaviour and avoid 'mentalistic' constructs; cognitive psychologists would persuade us to focus on the child's ways of thinking about and interpreting events; psychoanalyst self psychologists would have us examine the child's unconscious internalizations; attachment theorists would remind us of the importance of internal working models of the relationship between self and other.

Because our primary goal here is to understand the individual context rather than to champion a particular conceptualization of it, we use various theories to the extent that they throw light on the psychopathology at hand. No single theory offers a satisfactory account of all of childhood psychopathology, while various individual theories may offer conflicting but useful accounts of specific disturbances. Nonetheless, as we will review in detail in Chapter 2, our understanding of normative and pathological development leads us to focus on six psychological processes that have been implicated as playing a key role in the emergence of the disorders that will concern us in all the chapters to come: these are *cognitive* development, *emotional* development, the *attachment* system, *moral* development, the *self* and, lastly, *gender and sexuality*.

The Family Context

The family provides an important – perhaps the most important – context for child development. Among family influences, the greatest amount of attention has been paid to the parent–child relationship. However, it is important to note that most parents in research have been mothers. Fathers have been relatively neglected in child development research, with notable exceptions (Lamb, 2010; Phares et al. 2010). We will consider different normative patterns of parenting and the child behaviours associated with them, as well as such pathological extremes as neglect and physical and sexual abuse. In addition, we will look at the family systemic perspective, which highlights qualities of the whole family that influence child development.

The Social Context

Broadening our scope, we move from the intimate family context to the world of social relations outside the family, a world that widens incrementally over the course of development. *Peer relations* play a significant role in normal and deviant development and have been given increasing attention in recent years. In our discussions we explore positive peer relations, such as popularity and friendship, and also their negative counterparts, such as rejection and encouragement of antisocial behaviour. We also will consider the role of *extra-familial adults* such as teachers or coaches who might provide children with positive role models and mentorship or, on the negative side, with maltreatment or discouragement.

The Cultural Context

In considering the cultural context, we will discuss the role of the larger social and cultural factors that might increase the risk of, or protect against, psychopathology. We will consider *social class* in general and *poverty* in particular. We will also incorporate into our discussions considerations related to *race and ethnicity*, issues related to *immigration* and *acculturation*, and will take into account *cross-cultural* and *cross-national* differences where the data allow. Cultural background is a superordinate variable that significantly affects all other contexts. Culture may affect the risk for becoming disturbed and, moreover, may even affect whether a given behaviour is considered to be psychopathological. Thus, in some cultures obedience and conformity in children are valued, while self-assertiveness and independence are valued in others; in some cultures beliefs in malevolent spirits are normative, while in others such

ideas would be considered to be a sign of serious disturbance.

Interactions

We have been discussing these contexts of development as if they were static entities, but in fact, they are in constant *interaction* with one another. For example, the context of time interacts with all other contexts, which in turn interact with one another. Parents who are 25 years old when their daughter is born are not at the same stage in their development as they will be at 40 when she enters adolescence. In a like manner, the casual, improvised peer group of the preschool period differs from the adolescent clique, which begins to surpass the parents as the major influence on dress, music, language and social behaviour.

In sum, our developmental framework entails the interaction of variables both at a given point in time and over time. The framework itself is presented schematically in Fig. 1.2.

Models of Child Psychopathology

The developmental framework we have presented is designed to be general and comprehensive. It is intended to serve as a means of organizing what might otherwise be a bewildering array of variables used to account for a given psychopathology. It also is sufficiently general to embrace the specific theories of psychopathology that we are about to present.

A variety of theories provide models of the **etiology** (origins or cause) of childhood psychopathology. While they each have distinctive features, the models are not necessarily incompatible. Some share common features. Others are complementary. Still others have irreconcilable differences. Each has merit; none is totally satisfactory. Therefore, we must reconcile ourselves to living with diversity and partial truths. In our own presentation of models, we concentrate on those features that will be relevant to our subsequent discussion of various psychopathologies.

FIGURE 1.2 A Developmental Framework.

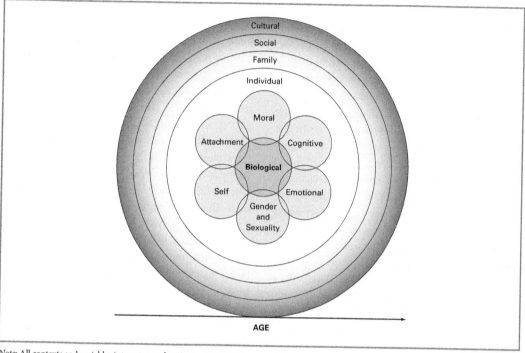

Note: All contexts and variables interact at each point in time as well as over time.

The Medical Model

There are two essential components to the tradi-tional medical model. The first involves the gen-eral hypothesis that psychopathologies result from *organic dysfunctions*. The second characteristic of the medical model is its penchant for classifying psychopathological behaviour in the same way as physical diseases – namely, in terms of *diagnoses*. Emil Kraepelin, who published a landmark classi-fication of adult psychopathologies in the late 1800s, set the stage by assuming a biological etiol-ogy for each disorder in his list. Attempts to con-strue child behaviour problems in medical terms have resulted in some odd classifications indeed, such as the eighteenth-century concept of 'mastur-batory insanity', which posited that excessive self-stimulation was the cause of mental problems in children. More modern perspectives hold that the body and mind are part of a system, such that each influences the other. While psychopathology may arise out of organic disturbances – whether as a function of neurochemistry, brain structure or neuropsychological functioning – it is also the case that psychological processes – such as strong emo-tions, stress and exposure to trauma – can affect biology.

In Chapter 3, we will take a detailed look at the major classification systems used to diagnose disor-ders in children, the *Diagnostic and Statistical Manual of Mental Disorders* (*DSM-IV-TR*; American Psychiatric Association, 2000) and the International Classification of Diseases (ICD-10; World Health Organization, 2007). Although these classification systems remain neutral on the ques-tion of etiology – biological origins of the disorders are not assumed – the *DSM* in particular retains the medical model's tendency to view psychopathology as an illness residing within the person, rather than as a product of dynamic interactions between the child and the environment.

The Behavioural Model

Three characteristics distinguish behavioural psychology. First is the assertion that scientific psychology must be based only on *observable behaviour*. Radical behaviourists would limit psychology to the study of responses organisms make to environmental stimuli, excluding all 'mentalistic' variables such as thoughts, images, feelings and memories, since these cannot be observed. More moderate theorists include non-observable concepts under two conditions: that such terms can be defined behaviourally and that their inclusion assists us to meet the goals of predicting and modifying behaviour. Next, behaviourists base their evidence on *empirical research* conducted under highly controlled conditions, with the laboratory experiment being the ideal method for studying the behaviour under investigation. Third, behaviourists believe that the acquisition, maintenance, change or elimination of much of human and animal behaviour can be adequately and concisely accounted for in terms of *learning principles*.

Learning Principles

The three principles of learning that form the basis of the behavioural approach are respondent conditioning (also called classical or Pavlovian conditioning), operant conditioning (also called instrumental conditioning) and imitation (also called modelling or observational learning).

In **respondent conditioning** a stimulus that innately elicits a response (e.g., a snarling dog will elicit fear in a child) is paired with a neutral stimulus (e.g., the sound of a bell). After a given number of pairings, the previously neutral stimulus comes to elicit the response, such that the child begins to experience fear upon first hearing the sound of the bell. Such associations may explain the origins of phobias (i.e., irrational fears related to an object that is not in and of itself threatening).

In **operant conditioning** the organism operates upon or does something to the environment in order to achieve a given result. In essence, this is a process by which an organism learns to associate certain consequences with certain actions it has

taken. These consequences may serve to increase or decrease the likelihood of the behaviour's being repeated. The consequence that increases the likelihood of occurrence is termed **reinforcement**. In *positive reinforcement*, behaviour is followed by a reward; for example, the father of an 8-year-old treats his daughter to an ice-cream cone after she has completed her chores. In *negative reinforcement* an aversive stimulus is removed; for example, a 10-year-old boy is excused from mowing the lawn for a month after improving his grades. The two methods used to decrease the likelihood of a behaviour's being repeated are extinction and punishment. In **extinction** the reinforcement maintaining a response is removed; for example, upon her therapist's advice, a mother no longer gives in to her 4-year-old's demands every time he has a temper tantrum, and the tantrums disappear. In **punishment** a response is followed by an aversive stimulus; for example, a 3-year-old must sit in the time-out chair when she colours the walls with her crayons.

One consequence of punishment is particularly relevant to our interest in psychopathology. Once exposed to an aversive stimulus, an organism will try in the future to avoid re-exposure, a process called **avoidance learning**. Avoidance learning is a double-edged sword. It protects the organism from a repeated encounter with a possibly harmful situation; for example, once burned, a 2-year-old is not likely to touch again the burner of a stove. But avoidance learning also can lead to unrealistic avoidance of situations after they are no longer noxious; for example, an adult may be terrified of his reasonable, benevolent boss because, as a child, he was brutally criticized by his father. Thus, avoidance prevents the individual from adopting new behaviours that are appropriate to changed circumstances.

The third learning principle is **imitation** or modelling, which involves learning a new behaviour by observing and imitating another person's performance of that behaviour. Thus, without being directly taught to do so, preschoolers will pretend to clean the house or hammer a nail as their parents do or will answer the phone with the exact words and intonation they have heard adults use. Unfortunately, children whose parents, peers and communities model non-constructive behaviour are likely to develop antisocial ways of behaving.

Behavioural Perspectives on Psychopathology

The behaviourists believe that – once allowance has been made for genetic, maturational and temperamental factors – all behaviour conforms to the basic principles of learning just described.

How does psychopathology develop in this perspective? Some children grow up with the kinds of learning experiences that maximize their chances of making a successful adaptation to environmental demands. For these children, positive behaviours have been rewarded and modelled, and negative consequences have been appropriate and clear. For other children, however, *maladaptive* behaviours may be the ones that are rewarded and modelled, and positive behaviours have been punished or extinguished through lack of reinforcement. An important consideration, however, is the context in which those behaviours take place: what is adaptive in one society or at one point in history may be maladaptive in another.

Using cultural standards as their guide, behaviourists define psychopathology as deviations in the *frequency or intensity* of behaviour. According to such a definition, psychopathologies can be grouped in terms of behavioural deficit or excess. In **behaviour deficit**, behaviours occur at a lower frequency or intensity than is expected within society, so the child's social, intellectual or practical skills are impaired. Autism, learning disabilities and mental retardation are examples of disorders in which children do not evidence age-appropriate behaviours such as sociability, reading ability or cognitive skills. In **behaviour excess**, behaviour occurs at a higher frequency or intensity than is adaptive to the standards of society. The hyperactive child who is in a continual state of activity, the obsessive-compulsive child who repeatedly washes his hands, and the anxious child who is constantly terrified by real and imagined dangers all show signs of behaviour excess.

The *developmental dimension* in the behavioural model refers to age-related changes in societal expectations for behaviour. In Western societies generally, a child should be toilet trained towards the end of the preschool period, should be able to cope with school by the beginning of middle childhood, should be able to control his or her behaviour independently of parents by the end of adolescence, and so on. Other societies have different requirements and different timetables.

Social Learning Theory

Social learning theorists such as Bandura (1986) expanded the scope of behaviour theory in a number of ways. For one, Bandura countered the radical behavioural assumption that the individual is a mere reactor to environmental stimuli. He proposed a process of **reciprocal determinism**, by which the person and the environment come to influence one another. He also views individuals as having an active role in determining their responses to the environment. Whereas radical behaviourists focused on the stimulus → response relationship, terming what went on between these two events in the person's mind the 'black box', Bandura invited us to open that box and peer inside.

Bandura's most significant contribution was to expand behavioural theory to include attention to *cognitive processes*, such as internal representations of experiences, expectancies and problem solving. Cognitive processes determine how external events will affect behaviour by influencing 'which external events will be observed, how they will be perceived, whether they leave any lasting effects, what valence and efficacy they have, and how the information they convey will be organized for future use' (Bandura, 1977, p. 160). Bandura also introduced the concept of **self-efficacy**, which reflects the fact that individuals come to anticipate not only that a given behaviour will produce a given outcome, but more importantly, whether or not they can successfully execute such a behaviour. Thus, people fear and avoid situations they believe exceed their coping skills, and they behave with confidence in those situations which they believe themselves capable of handling. Therefore, self-efficacy influences both the choice of action and persistence in the face of obstacles.

Whereas the cognitive dimension to social learning theory is an important contribution, one significant limitation is the lack of attention to developmental differences. Thus, we must turn to cognitive developmental theory – exemplified by the work of Piaget – to further understand childhood psychopathology.

Cognitive Models

Cognitive Developmental Theory

Piaget is one of the major figures in developmental psychology. Although much of his work focused on the development of cognition, Piaget and others that followed him have applied his research to the understanding of psychopathology. (See Cowan, 1978, and Piaget, 1981.)

Piaget makes the assumption that cognitive development proceeds in a series of orderly, fixed stages. Each stage is qualitatively distinct, and no higher type of thinking can evolve until the child has gone through all the preceding stages. The timetable may differ from child to child, but the order can never vary. (One of the clearest and most succinct expositions of Piaget's theory is found in chapters 1 and 2 of Piaget, 1967.)

One of the significant contributions Piaget made to our understanding of development is the concept of the schema. A **schema** is a model or blueprint that helps the child to understand and predict the environment. The schema also is the fundamental building block of change over the course of development, as the child's capacity to reason becomes more sophisticated, complex and abstract. What causes schemas to change? According to Piaget, development is fuelled by the child's attempts to adapt to the environment and adaptation takes place through two psychological processes: assimilation and accommodation. **Assimilation** refers to the incorporation of new information into an existing schema. For example,

the boy accustomed to playing with his affectionate siblings may approach the first child he encounters in preschool with an enthusiastic hug, assuming this new child fits his schema of 'kids just love me!'. **Accommodation** refers to the alteration of a schema to take into account new information. Thus, if the new child backs away in alarm at the unexpected hug, the exuberantly affectionate boy may adjust his schema to a more realistic one of '*some* kids just love me'.

In general, cognitive development is characterized by a balance, or **equilibration**, of assimilation and accommodation. Assimilation gives the world some predictability and provides the child with some context in which to place new experiences so that they are not bewildering. Accommodation allows the child to take in new information and expand his or her understanding of the world. In Chapter 2 we will detail Piaget's cognitive developmental stages and explore the implications of assimilation and accommodation for understanding how psychopathology develops.

Piaget's theory has generated an impressive body of research that confirms some aspects and disconfirms others. More sophisticated experimental techniques show that Piaget underestimated the infant's cognitive capacities: for example, object permanence is possible earlier in infancy than Piaget postulated. By the same token, when researchers alter tasks to make them more familiar, preschoolers can produce higher levels of reasoning than Piaget would predict. Piaget's concept of stages also is hotly debated. For example, there are those who maintain that cognitive development is gradual and continuous rather than marked by qualitative advances (see R. L. Campbell, 2006).

Social Cognitive Theory

More recently, *social cognitive theorists* (also called social information processing theorists) have expanded Piaget's concepts in important ways. For example, Dodge and his colleagues (Dodge and Petit, 2003) use the concept of the *schema* to study children's behaviour in the interpersonal domain, termed *social information processing*.

Dodge emphasizes the fact that schemata are stable mental structures that incorporate children's perceptions of self, their experiences in the past and their expectations for the future. Therefore, based on the lessons they draw from past experiences, schemata colour children's perceptions of new events and thus their response to those events. For example, depressed children display a pessimistic cognitive style that draws their attention to all that is negative and consistent with their low expectations. Consequently, they may behave towards others in ways that promote rejection, fulfilling their worst prophecies; for example, the child who enters the classroom the first day of school expecting to be friendless and rejected may isolate herself and display a scowling affect, thus contributing to her own friendlessness. In a similar manner, conduct-disordered children display a *hostile attribution bias* that leads them to perceive others as ill intentioned towards them and thus as deserving a response in kind. For example, the child who accidentally bumps into another in a rush to the water fountain might be perceived as 'mean' and deserving of punishment by the child with conduct problems. In turn, when conduct-disordered children's aggression does in fact inspire peers to respond negatively to them, their hostile schema is confirmed. As we shall see, the social cognitive perspective makes an important contribution to the understanding of the development of psychopathology, particularly depression and conduct disorder, and has informed a number of highly effective interventions for children.

Psychoanalytic Models
Classical Psychoanalysis
Classical psychoanalysis, also known as drive theory, is concerned with discovering the dynamics – the basic motives, the prime movers – of human behaviour. This concern with intrapersonal forces clearly sets psychoanalysts apart from the behaviourists, with their concern for the environmental factors that shape behaviour, and cognitive psychologists, who focus primarily on conscious processes and reason. As with the other approaches discussed so far, our coverage of Freud's work

will not be comprehensive; instead, we will concentrate on the two aspects of classical psychoanalysis most relevant to understanding childhood psychopathology – the structural model and the psychosexual stages.

The Structural Model
Freud's tripartite conceptualization of the human psyche – id, ego and superego – is known as the *structural model*. (For an interesting overview of Freud's theory and how it was lost in the translation from the original German to American English, see Bettelheim, 1983.)

According to classical Freudian theory, originally the human psyche consists of the **id** ('it') which is the source of all biological drives. The drives of the id are primitive, demanding immediate and complete satisfaction, and its thought processes are irrational and magical. At about 6 months old, the **ego** ('me') arises from the id's need to balance gratification with reality. Unlike the id, the ego is endowed with *ego functions*, such as perception, memory and reasoning, which enable it to learn realistic means of satisfying the id. The ego also is the source of the **defence mechanisms** that help a child tolerate intense emotions and cope with anxiety, in part by keeping unacceptable thoughts and feelings out of consciousness.

The third structure, the **superego** ('over-me'), comes into its own at about 5 years of age. Also a part of the unconscious, the superego contains the moral standards that the preschooler takes over from his or her parents and that become an internalized judge of right and wrong behaviour. When the child misbehaves, the superego punishes the child with guilt feelings. The superego can be absolutist and implacable, demanding strict obedience to its standards of proper behaviour. From middle childhood on, then, the ego must find ways of obtaining as much id gratification as reality will allow without arousing the superego, which in its way is as irrational and demanding as the id.

In structural terms, therefore, psychopathology is a matter of *internal conflict* and imbalance between id, ego and superego. If the id is excessively strong, the result is impulsive aggressive or sexual behaviour. If the superego is excessively strong, the result is overly inhibited behaviour in which the child is tortured by guilt feelings for the slightest transgression, real or imagined.

The Psychosexual Theory

Freud's *psychosexual theory* assumes that there is an inevitable progression in the parts of the body that predominate as sources of pleasure. Equally important, each progression of libido is accompanied by a psychological change in the intimate relations with the parents or primary caretakers.

During the initial **oral stage**, feeding is associated with the first emotional attachment or *object relation*. Sensitive, loving caretaking engenders a positive image both of mother and of self; caretaking marked by distress and frustration will engender an image in which love is mixed with anxiety and rage. In the **anal stage**, conflicts over autonomy and parental control of behaviour are primary. If parental discipline is punitive, unloving or coercive, the toddler may become rebellious and oppositional or anxious and overly compliant. The **phallic stage** in boys is associated with the wish to be the exclusive love object of the mother, which results in rivalry towards the father. This is referred to as the **Oedipus complex**. Resolution of the Oedipus complex requires that the child relinquish this infantile wish for exclusive love and, through identifying with the same-sex parent, content himself with the idea that 'I am not your rival; I am like you'. (Freud's explanation of female development was never satisfactory, even to himself; see Chodorow, 1989.) The **latency stage** offers a period of relative calm in which attention is turned to mastery of developmental accomplishments other than sexuality. In the **genital stage** of adulthood, mature sexuality entails a mutuality and appreciation of the partner's point of view that is counter to the egocentricism of the early stages.

Although much of the content of Freud's assumptions about psychosexuality is not now generally accepted, the theory has contributed valuable ideas to the developmental processes by which psychopathology might come about. **Fixations** in development lay the groundwork for psychological disturbances either because they hamper further development or because they increase the possibility that, under stress, the child will return to the fixated, less mature stage. This latter process is called **regression**. Excessive fixations can result either from inadequate gratification, such as inadequate love during the oral period, or excessive gratification, such as an overly involved parent during the Oedipal phase. The stage at which fixation occurs determines both the severity and the kind of psychopathology. In general, the earlier the fixation, the more severe the psychopathology, so a child who is either fixated at or regresses to the oral stage is more disturbed than one who is fixated at or regresses to the anal stage.

Ego Psychology

Ego psychology made a major revision in the classical theory by arguing that the ego initially is endowed with its own energy and can function autonomously rather than being subservient to the id. The emphasis of ego psychologists such as Erikson (1950) is the reality-oriented, adaptive functions of the psyche. In addition, Erikson enlarges the interpersonal context of development from the nuclear family to the larger society.

Briefly, Erikson's developmental model focuses on stages of *psychosocial* development, which closely parallel Freud's stages of psychosexual development. Each of these stages represents a crisis, the resolution of which sets the individual on a particular developmental trajectory.

During the first year of life, the quality of the caregiving environment contributes to the child's sense that the world is either a safe and loving place or a disappointing and dangerous one. This is the crisis of *trust versus mistrust*. In the second year, conflicts with caregivers over such emotionally charged issues as toilet training can lead children to develop a sense of either self-pride or self-doubt; this is the crisis of *autonomy versus shame*. In the fourth to fifth year, the way in which the Oedipus complex is resolved can contribute to children's comfort with their own impulses or else the sense that they are fundamentally 'bad' for having such desires. This is the crisis of *initiative versus guilt*. At age 6, children begin to confront the tasks of school and socialization with peers, contributing to a sense of either competence or inadequacy; this is the crisis of *industry versus inferiority*. The last stage of Erikson's we will describe is associated with adolescence, in which the tasks are to form a clear sense of identity and a purpose in life. This is the crisis of *ego identity versus role confusion*.

Erikson's framework enhances our understanding of psychodynamic development by laying out a clear progression of stages and the tasks that must be accomplished for the child to proceed through them apace, as well as by pointing out the social context in which child development takes place. We will refer to his work particularly when we consider the developmental challenges associated with adolescence.

Object Relations Theory

A 'third revolution' in psychoanalytic thinking is represented by **object relations** theory. Object relations actually refers to a diverse collection of psychoanalytic perspectives that share an emphasis on the importance of affectionate *attachments* in human development. In contrast to Freud, who posited that infants attached to their parents initially because their parents gratify their drives, for object relations theorists it is relatedness – in essence, love – that is the primary motivator of human behaviour. The label 'object relations' refers to the relationships with people – the objects of our affections – that determine what kind of individuals we become. (For more detail, see Blanck and Blanck, 1992.)

A major figure in this tradition is the British psychiatrist John Bowlby (1988b) whose theory of attachment has had a powerful influence on the conceptualization of normal and deviant development and has generated considerable research. We will refer to his work in subsequent discussions, and we will describe the development of attachment in more detail in Chapters 2 and 6.

A second important figure is Margaret Mahler, whose theory provides a bedrock for object relations theory (Mahler et al., 1975). Over the course of the first three years of life, Mahler proposes, the 'psychological birth' of the child takes place through a series of stages called the **separation-individuation** process.

Initially, at birth, the infant does not distinguish between the self and other (*normal autism*). During the first two months of life, however, there is a dawning recognition that there is a caregiver who responds to the infant's needs. Initially, the infant perceives the self and caregiver as two parts of one organism (*symbiotic phase*). Inevitably, however, there are moments when caregiver and child are not in perfect synchrony. By about 4 months of age, such experiences – of delay, frustration, mismatched goals – help the child to recognize that the caregiver is a separate person with her or his own feelings and intentions (*differentiation phase*). At about 8 months of age, the infant begins crawling and is able to move under his or her own steam. The infant explores in ever-widening circles around the caregiver, returning to this 'safe base' at regular intervals in order to 'emotionally refuel', actively experimenting with separation versus closeness (*practising phase*). As toddlers advance to the second year of life, the beginnings of symbolic thought provide them with a growing awareness of the vulnerability associated with being separate (e.g., 'If I wander too far, I might get lost'). At the same time, the child craves independence, and the parent–child relationship is marked by ambivalence as the infant alternates between clinging to the caregiver and pushing her away (*rapprochement phase*). It is as though the child experiences the caregiver as two separate beings – the 'good' mother who is loving and kind and the 'bad' mother who is frustrating and disappointing.

The final stage in the separation-individuation process is ushered in by the achievement of emotional **object constancy**; the ability to integrate both positive and negative feelings into a single representation. Thus, it is possible to be angry with the mother and yet still love her, to be disappointed with oneself and yet still believe one is a worthwhile human being. Like Piaget's concept of object permanence, object constancy depends on the *cognitive* capacity to recognize that an object out of sight still exists. However, object constancy requires the recognition that an *emotion* we are not currently experiencing – for example, affection for someone who has just enraged us – still exists. In summary, object constancy allows us to experience ourselves and others as fully fleshed, whole persons, complete with both good and bad qualities.

Central to object relations theory is that the child's sense of self develops in the context of the relationship with the caregiver. The quality of that relationship communicates important messages about the child's own worth and the trustworthiness of others. Thus, through his or her experiences with the caregiver, the child comes to develop an *internal representation* of the relationship. Children who experience warm and sensitive care internalize an image of the loving parent – the 'good object' – and of themselves as lovable. In contrast, children who experience poor parenting internalize an image of their caregiver as angry and rejecting – the 'bad object' – and perceive themselves as unworthy and incapable of inspiring love.

A criticism of Mahler's work, as indeed of most psychoanalytic theory, is that it is based on clinical observation and speculation rather than objective data. Most recent work on self-development in infancy suggests that revision of this formulation may be in order. For example, evidence suggests that normal infants do not lack a sense of separation between self and other. Rather, from the very beginning of life, infants demonstrate emergent capacities for self-organization and for engaging in the complex choreography of interpersonal relationships (Stern, 1985). While Mahler's theory may not be an accurate depiction of *normal* infant development, it may be a useful way of describing the origins of some forms of *psychopathology* (Greenspan, 2003).

In conclusion, the psychoanalytic models are among the most developmentally oriented of all the theories of psychopathology. Among the most significant contributions they make to our understanding of normal and pathological development is the uncovering of *unconscious* representations and motives that underlie human behaviour, a supposition that modern research supports (Fonagy and Target, 2000). The concept of ego *defence mechanisms* is another important contribution that psychoanalytic theory makes to our understanding of development. The nature of the defences used to ward off anxiety – whether primitive or sophisticated, rigid or flexible, brittle or robust – gives us important clues about the person's emotional maturity and level of functioning.

However, among the weaknesses of psychodynamic concepts is a tendency to narrowly focus on the first five years of life, without attention to later developmental stages. Psychoanalysis is also mentalistic, inferential, exceedingly complex and riddled with inconsistencies; and its assumptions are difficult to test with the tightly controlled research that behaviourists believe is essential to a scientific psychology. But to conclude that psychodynamic concepts cannot be tested empirically is unjustified. Psychoanalytic theory has generated more research than any other personality theory, and empirical support has been found for some of its key assumptions (Fonagy et al., 2006; Westen, 1998). Modern psychoanalytic theory, integrated with the cognitive perspective, also has inspired a new generation of clinical child psychology researchers (Mayes et al., 2007).

Family Systems Models

The last major theoretical orientation we describe is the family systemic perspective. Although many other theories acknowledge the importance of family relationships, what sets the systemic model apart is that it views the entire family as the unit of analysis. The family is conceptualized as a *system*, a dynamic whole that is greater than the sum of its parts. Systems have certain characteristics. For example, they are coherent and stable, and they have a self-righting tendency, termed *homeostasis*, that allows them to maintain their structure even in the face of change. Like psychoanalytic theory, the systemic perspective is composed of many different schools of thought, but in this case the core idea that unites them is that individual personality is a function of the family system. We will concentrate on the work of the Argentinian-born psychiatrist Salvador Minuchin (Minuchin, 1974; Minuchin et al., 2006), whose perspective is called *structural family theory*.

According to Minuchin, one of the ways in which being part of a family helps us to develop is by allowing us to participate in a number of different relationships simultaneously. Within the larger family system, there are naturally occurring *subsystems* that join some family members and differentiate them from others. For instance, the parents form a *marital* subsystem, which is based on the complementary roles that husbands and wives fulfil: to be a romantic couple, to raise their children and to play a leadership role in the family. *Parent–child* relationships comprise another subsystem, based on the non-reciprocal needs and responsibilities that parents and children fulfil for one another; for example, while children turn to their parents for comforting and advice, and parents expect their authority to be respected, the reverse usually is not the case. *Siblings* form yet another subsystem, based on their shared status as the children in the family. Yet siblings, too, are differentiated from one another; for example, special privileges might be granted to the eldest child and extra latitude to the youngest. Thus, through the various roles they play, family members simultaneously experience feelings of belonging and feelings of independence from others.

What allows these subsystems to function well are the **boundaries** that separate them. Clear boundaries differentiate the subsystems from one another, define the roles of individuals, and allow family members opportunities to meet their appropriate developmental needs. Clear boundaries are also permeable and adaptable; that is, they allow both emotional contact and independence, and change as the needs of family members change over development. For example, the parent–child relationship should become more reciprocal and egalitarian as children enter young adulthood.

Failure to maintain appropriate boundaries can cause families to become confused and dysfunctional. For example, overly *rigid* boundaries foster separation between family members or maintain strict role differentiation among them: 'Father knows best'; 'Children should be seen and not heard'. While rigid boundaries can foster a sense of independence and self-sufficiency, they can also make it difficult for family members to reach across barriers to communicate their feelings or obtain emotional support. Individuals may feel lonely and unsupported in rigidly structured families and may lack a sense of belonging.

At the other extreme, absent or unclear boundaries result in **enmeshment**. Family members who are enmeshed do not differentiate between one another, even between parent and child. Mutuality and togetherness are emphasized at the expense of individuality and separateness. Whereas family members may enjoy the feelings of belonging and sharing that ensue, extreme enmeshment may interfere with individuals' freedom to have their own autonomous thoughts and wishes. An attempt by a family member to individuate may be perceived as a threat to the harmony of the family system and thus may arouse anxiety or resistance. For example, the youth in an enmeshed family who expresses a desire to go away for college may precipitate a family crisis.

In Minuchin's view of family structure, the heart of the family is the *marital subsystem*. The kind of intimacy, emotional support and mutuality that characterize a healthy couple's relationship is unique; for example, the emotional needs that an adult romantic partner fulfils are different from those fulfilled by parent–child and sibling relationships. Therefore, Minuchin especially emphasizes a need for clear boundaries around the marital dyad. When this boundary is violated, children become involved in their parents' marital relationship in inappropriate ways, and psychopathology may develop. Minuchin describes the different problematic family systems as *rigid triangles*, which may take one of three general forms, described next (Kerig, 1995).

First, a **parent–child coalition** arises when one parent involves the child in an alliance that excludes the other parent. Such a relationship occurs when a parent encourages the child to behave disrespectfully to the other parent, or it may take the form of an overly intimate and enmeshed relationship between one parent and the child. This family dynamic may create a *parentalized child* who is burdened by the assumption of such developmentally inappropriate tasks as offering emotional support and acting as an intimate confidante to a parent (Kerig, 2005). Minuchin gives the example of a family in which the unhappily married mother becomes depressed. The 10-year-old eldest daughter takes over preparing meals and caring for her younger siblings, covering for the mother so the father will not know the extent of her dysfunction. A number of negative consequences follow from this scenario. Because the daughter has taken on responsibilities beyond her years, she begins to feel stressed and overwhelmed. In addition, because the younger siblings do not have direct access to their mother and cannot receive the care and attention they need from her, they begin to misbehave. Further, because the parents are not communicating directly with each other, they cannot resolve their marital problems. In sum, while the intentions of the parentalized child are good and her self-sacrifice might help the family to cope in the short term, in the long term the family is an increasingly distressed and unhappy one.

In the second type of rigid triangle, called **triangulation**, the child is caught in the middle of the parents. In this case the child attempts to maintain a coalition with each parent, either to be a peacemaker or go-between or in response to pressure from parents to side with one or the other. Minuchin describes this as the most stressful family dynamic for the child, whose attempts to be close to either parent may be interpreted as disloyalty by the other.

The third kind of triangle, **detouring**, is the most subtle of the triangular family forms because there may be no apparent conflict between the parents. Instead, they may insist that their marriage is perfect and that the only problem in the family is their child's disobedience or delicate nature. As Minuchin got to know this kind of family better, however, he noticed that the parents never spent any time together as a couple but rather devoted all their time and energy to caring for their child. Then he began to observe covert ways in which the parents supported and encouraged their child's problems. Further, the only time the parents acted conjointly was when they were responding to their child's 'special needs'. It became apparent to Minuchin that in such cases having a troubled child was meeting some need for the parents.

Minuchin concludes that some unhappily married couples attempt to avoid acknowledging their marital problems because they do not know how to resolve them; instead, they try to deflect attention from them or detour around them. Having a troubled child, therefore, serves a function in the family by providing the parents with a problem external to their relationship on which to focus their attention. Because they are united when attempting to respond to their 'problem child', detouring allows the couple to maintain an illusion of harmony. Further, detouring couples are motivated to covertly reinforce children's behaviour problems in order to maintain the homeostasis in the family system. The detouring may take two forms: *detouring-attacking* when the child is viewed as troublesome or 'bad' and *detouring-supportive* when the child is viewed as needy or delicate (Carlson, 1990). (See Fig. 1.3.) The child caught in the family triangle is called the *identified patient* because he or she is the one who is overtly symptomatic.

Minuchin's perspective widens our scope of vision to include the larger context in which child development takes place. Not only is the individual psychology of the child important, as well as his or her relationship with parents, but the entire family *system* must be taken into account. Another important implication of the family systemic approach is that the location of psychopathology is not in the child, or even in the parents, but in the *relationships among them*. Lastly, the systemic perspective reminds us to take a *functional* approach to interpreting problem behaviour. An aggressive, acting-out child may appear to be disturbed. However, another possibility

FIGURE 1.3 Pathological Triangles.

A set of three lines indicates an enmeshed relationship; a broken line indicates a conflictual relationship.

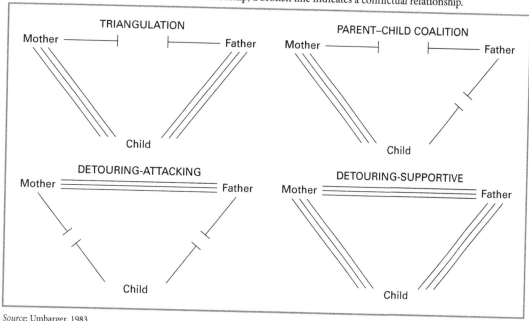

Source: Umbarger, 1983.

is that the child's misbehaviour serves a function in the family system, perhaps representing an attempt to meet appropriate developmental needs in a pathological environment. Thus, the family systems perspective fits well with our definition of psychopathology as normal development gone awry.

Comparing and Integrating Models

There are many points of *divergence* among the models we have presented. (See Table 1.1.) Freud was primarily concerned with drives, the unconscious and mental events, whereas ego psychologists concentrate on psychosocial adaptation and object relations theorists emphasize the primacy of interpersonal relations. Traditionally, behaviourists wanted to banish the intrapersonal context with all of its mentalistic baggage, substituting an environmentally oriented objective psychology. Cognitive psychologists reintroduce mental terms such as schemata in order to understand how children interpret their experiences with the environment. The choice among these theoretical conceptualizations also has important clinical

implications. The behavioural viewpoint leans towards a definition of psychopathology based on social norms – since there is nothing in behaviour itself that designates it as abnormal, such a judgement must be based on the behaviour's infrequency or on the fact that a given society chooses to label certain behaviours as psychopathological. In another society the same behaviour might go unnoticed or even be regarded as a special gift, such as the accepting attitudes displayed towards psychotic behaviour in certain African cultures. The psychoanalysts' approach, on the contrary, maintains that behaviour is important only as it furnishes clues to the child's inner life; psychopathology is not a matter of behaviour per se, but of the meaning of such behaviour. The frequency of daydreaming in adolescence, for example, is not as important as the stage-appropriateness of the fantasies that accompany the behaviour.

There are also some points of *convergence*. For example, even such apparently opposing models as object relations and family systems theories agree

TABLE 1.1 Comparing and Integrating Models of Development

	What Develops?	**What Are the Processes of Development?**	**What Is Psychopathology?**	**How Does Psychopathology Develop?**
Medical Model	Biology	Maturation	Mental illness	Organic dysfunction
Social Learning	Behaviour	Rewards, punishment, imitation of models	Inappropriate behaviour	Reinforcement or modelling of maladaptive behaviour
Cognitive Developmental	Schemata	Assimilation, accommodation	Imbalance between assimilation-accommodation	Overstimulation or understimulation
Classical Psychoanalysis	Ego/superego, psychosexuality	Clashes between drives and reality, transfer of libido	Fixation or regression	Conflicts among parts of psyche
Ego Psychology	Ego strengths	Interactions with social world	Inability to resolve stage-related issues	Failures at mastery experiences
Object Relations	Self-other relationships	Separation-individuation	Failure to progress in development	Affective splitting, internalization of bad relationships
Family Systems	Adaptivity	Belonging and separateness	Maladaptive family structure	Boundary dissolution, triangulation
Developmental Psychopathology	The whole child	Hierarchization, organization, integration, adaptation	Development gone awry	Risks, vulnerabilities; potentiating, transactional, and protective processes

that relationships are central to personality development. Further, each of these models has undergone its own developmental process, which in many cases has led to an expansion of common ground shared with other theories. The medical model no longer couches issues dichotomously as, for example, heredity versus environment. Instead, there is a recognition that organisms develop in an environmental context that interacts with and affects organic variables. The psychoanalytic model has shifted from emphasizing the intrapersonal to appreciating the interpersonal context, while the behavioural model has changed in the opposite direction. With the increasing overlap and convergence among the different models of psychopathology, the possibility of – and need for – a unified model emerges. Developmental psychopathology represents the beginning steps towards creating such an integrative model.

Developmental Psychopathology

Developmental psychopathology is not a theory in and of itself; rather, it is an approach to understanding how psychopathology emerges over the life span. (Our review follows Cicchetti and Toth, 2009, and Cicchetti, 2006, except where noted. The classic paper that launched the field, still well worth reading, is Sroufe and Rutter, 1984.) Developmental psychopathology is an *integrative* and *unified* approach that incorporates different theoretical perspectives under one umbrella to produce an understanding of the development of the whole person as she or he interacts with the environment (Achenbach, 1990; Sameroff, 2010). (See Fig. 1.4.) Instead of focusing only on biology, behaviour, cognition, unconscious processes, social forces, and so on, the developmental psychopathologist pays attention to each of these variables in order to understand how they contribute to the formation of psychopathology – or of emotional health. Although a number of definitions of developmental psychopathology have been offered, they often overlook the latter point, that both adaptive and maladaptive development are relevant to the field (Cicchetti and Toth, 2009). Therefore, we offer the following as a concise definition:

> Developmental psychopathology is the study of developmental processes that contribute to, or protect against, psychopathology.

Now we turn to the specific principles that define the developmental psychopathology approach.

The Organizational Perspective

Although developmental psychopathology does not follow any unitary theoretical model, it is guided by an *organizational perspective*. First, the organizational perspective views the human organism in an *integrative way*, as a holistic and dynamic system in which all domains of development – the cognitive, social, emotional and biological – are in continual interaction with one another. Second, development itself is considered to be *hierarchical*; psychological growth is a process of increasing complexity and organization, such that new structures emerge out of those that have come before.

The key to understanding development in this perspective is to attend to the tasks at each stage of development – termed *stage-salient issues* – that must be confronted and mastered. Whether these issues are resolved in adaptive or maladaptive ways influences future development. Erikson's (1950) ego theory provides a good example of this construct; for example, whether the infant resolves the first developmental crisis by forming an attitude of trust or mistrust towards the world will influence his or her capacity to satisfactorily resolve the salient issues of the next stage.

The implication of the organizational perspective is that stage-salient issues affect the individual in such a way that their effects are carried forward into the next stage of development. Thus, previous

FIGURE 1.4 The 'Umbrella' of Developmental Psychopathology.

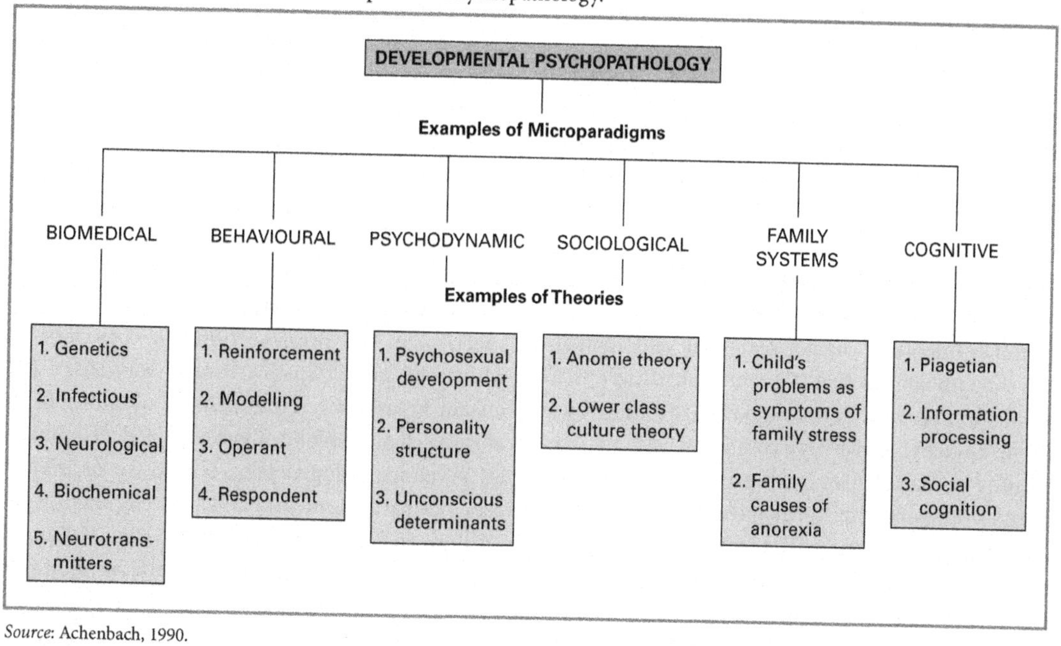

Source: Achenbach, 1990.

areas of vulnerability or strength may influence the way in which individuals handle stress and crisis and may shape the way in which they adapt to future life challenges. However, the consequences of previous stage-salient resolutions are *probabilistic* rather than *deterministic*. In other words, whereas previous development might have a shaping or constraining effect on subsequent development, such that it tends to increase or decrease the likelihood of psychopathology, such an effect is not predetermined. Many individual, social or environmental factors might intervene in order to change the course of development. What happened before does not doom us, and what is to come is not written in stone. A nice illustration of this is provided by Bowlby (1988b), who argues that, although the quality of attachment between an infant and caregiver has an important influence on child development, it is not an immutable one. A secure attachment may set the child on the pathway to healthy development, but other stresses and traumas might intervene that deflect that child from that course. In turn, and on a hopeful note, the child with a disrupted attachment who gets a poor start in life still has many opportunities to be nudged back towards a healthy pathway, such as by forming a relationship with a loving step-parent or a caring teacher. Pathways might be particularly amenable to change during key turning points of development, when young people are striving to understand and make choices about their place in the world.

The Continuum between Normal and Abnormal Development

Another important characteristic of developmental psychopathology is that it assumes that there is a *continuum* between normal and abnormal development. Underlying every life course – whether it is a healthy or maladaptive one – are the same fundamental developmental principles. Therefore, it is important to have a clear conceptualization of adaptive development in order to understand how development might go awry (Sroufe, 1997). The challenge is to understand *why* development takes one path

rather than the other. Further, as we will see in Chapter 2, it is *normal* to have some problems in the course of development. In sum, unlike the medical model, developmental psychopathology views psychological problems not as disease processes resident within the individual, but as significant deviations from a healthy developmental course.

Risk, Vulnerability, Potentiation and Protection
Risk Factors and Risk Mechanisms

A **risk factor** is any condition or circumstance that increases the likelihood that psychopathology will develop. The list of potential risk factors is extensive and they span all contexts. (See Table 1.2.) In the biological context risk may involve birth defects, neurological damage, inadequate nutrition or a parent who has a disorder with a known genetic component. In the individual context, risk may be in the form of cognitive deficits, low self-efficacy or poor self-control. In the family context, risk may take the form of parental neglect and, in the interpersonal context, antisocial peers may present a risk. In the cultural context risk may arise from poverty. While single risks have limited predictive power, multiple risks have a cumulative effect; for example, children with two alcoholic parents are more than twice as likely to develop problems as are children with one alcoholic parent.

However, the developmental psychopathology framework goes beyond viewing risks as static causal agents. Simple cause-and-effect relationships (e.g., physical abuse causes depression) do not capture the complex nature of child development. (Consider the lampooning of this simplistic perspective in Mel Brooks's film *High Anxiety*, in which the protagonist's neurosis was cured the instant he uncovered the memory of falling from his high chair in infancy.) Instead, the developmental psychopathologist asks, If poverty or intelligence or parental neglect affect development, *how* do they do so? To answer this question, we must look beneath these one-dimensional variables to uncover the *mechanisms* by which these risks exert their negative effects. In Chapter 2, we will detail a

TABLE 1.2 Examples of Risks, Risk Mechanisms, Vulnerabilities, Protective Factors and Protective Mechanisms

Context	Risk Factors: What adverse events have impinged on this child's development?	Risk Mechanisms: Through what developmental processes do these adverse events affect the child?	Vulnerabilities/ Potentiating Factors: What characteristics of the child or environment increase the likelihood that risk factors will negatively affect development?	Protective Factors: What characteristics of the child or environment decrease the likelihood that risk factors will negatively affect development?	Protective Mechanisms (Across All Contexts) Through what developmental processes do protective factors help the child to be resilient?
Biological	Genetic disorders Prenatal injury Inadequate nutrition	Neurological damage Impaired executive functioning	Difficult temperament High vagal tone HPA axis dysregulation	Easy temperament Regulated vagal tone Long allele of 5-HTTLPR gene	← Reduction of risk impact Reduction of negative chain reactions Self-efficacy and coping skills Opening of opportunities →
Individual	Cognitive deficits Low self-esteem Poor behavioural control	Emotion dysregulation Maladaptive appraisals	Gender Poor planning ability Lack of sociability	Intelligence Competence Ego resilience Engaging personality Self-efficacy	
Family	Interparental conflict Abuse Neglect Domestic violence Parental psychopathology	Boundary dissolution Insecure working models of attachment	Family isolation/lack of social support Lack of community cohesion	Positive, stable care Family cohesiveness Competent adult role models Parental supervision and monitoring Parental valuing of child attributes	
Social	Bullying Harsh teachers	Poor social skills Perceived rejection	Friendlessness Exposure to antisocial peers	Positive peer relationships Adult mentors	
Cultural	Poverty Racism Prejudice Community violence	Institutionalized racism Futurelessness	Personal characteristics that clash with societal ideals/ expectations	Positive cultural values Positive ethnic identity Cultural tolerance for diversity Ability to navigate and negotiate across cultures	

Source: Curtis and Cicchetti, 2007; Fergusson and Horwood, 2003; Luthar, 2003, 2006; Masten et al., 1999, 2009; Rutter, 1990, 2000; Spencer et al., 2006; Szalacha et al., 2003; Ungar, 2010; von Soest et al., 2010.

number of potential **risk mechanisms** that underlie psychopathology, including insecure attachments, dysregulated emotions, and distorted schemas.

Vulnerabilities and Potentiating Factors

Whereas a risk is a factor that would be expected to negatively affect any child exposed to it, a **vulnerability** increases the likelihood that a *particular* child will succumb to risk. In other words, a vulnerability intensifies the child's response to risk. For example, although frequent family relocations are significant events in a child's life, not all children will be stressed by them – it is the child with an anxious temperament who is most likely to be negatively affected by disruptions in the home. A helpful way to distinguish between risks and vulnerabilities is in terms of the statistical concepts of main effects versus interactions (Zimmerman and Arunkumar, 1994). A risk factor is associated with an increased likelihood of psychopathology for *all* children exposed to it; thus, it emerges as a main effect in statistical analyses. (See Fig. 1.5.) A vulnerability, in contrast, increases the likelihood of psychopathology *particularly* for those children who are susceptible to it; thus, it emerges as an interaction effect. Rutter (1990) identifies a number of vulnerability factors that act in this way. Gender is one; for example, whereas both boys and girls are adversely affected by family stress, boys react with a higher rate of behaviour problems than do girls. Temperament is another vulnerability factor; children who are difficult to soothe are more reactive to stress and also are more likely to frustrate and irritate their caregivers, thus increasing the family's stress level. Rutter's list also includes the absence of a good relationship with parents, poor planning ability, a lack of positive school experiences, lack of affectionate care, and poor social skills. Further, at the sociocultural level, children whose personal characteristics do not match societal expectations – such as the shy child in a culture that values boldness – may be the most vulnerable to risk.

In a similar vein, a **potentiating factor** is one that exacerbates the impact of a risk. For example, exposure to community violence and being a 'latchkey' child who comes home to an empty house each day are both potential risks for the development of child behaviour problems. However, the child most likely to be negatively affected is the one living in a neighbourhood without a strong sense of community, who has no friendly or caring neighbours to go to when the sound of gunshots rings out while she is alone at home during the evening. Thus, social isolation may potentiate the effects of other environmental stressors.

Protective Factors and Resilience

Since not all children who are at risk become disturbed, the challenge for researchers is to discover the factors that promote or maintain healthy development. These are called **protective factors**, and the children who make a good adjustment in spite of being at high risk are deemed to show **resilience**. Protective factors within children might include intelligence, an easygoing disposition, and the presence of competencies valued by themselves or society, whether they be academic, athletic, artistic or mechanical. Protective factors in the family might include the presence of a loving, dependable parent; a parenting style characterized by a combination of warmth and structure; socio-economic advantage; and social support from an extended family network. Peers can have a protective influence through providing emotional support and encouragement for pro-social behaviour. Protective factors in the cultural context might include involvement with pro-social institutions, such as the church or school (Wadsworth and Santiago, 2008) and, for ethnic minorities, may involve skill in navigating the complexities of dual participation in both the majority and minority culture (Ungar, 2008). (See, for example, Ungar's, 2010, description of cross-cultural resilience in the case of African-Canadian youth.)

For example, a classic in-depth study of resilience was conducted on the Hawaiian island of Kauai. Werner and Smith (1992) evaluated 505 individuals in infancy, early and middle childhood, late adolescence and early adulthood. True to the developmental psychopathology model, the authors conceptualized resilience as the balance between risk and protective factors. Risk factors included poverty,

FIGURE 1.5 Risk Factors and Vulnerabilities.

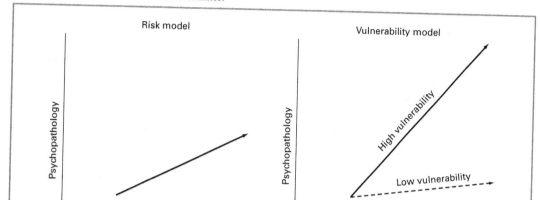

perinatal stress and parental psychopathology or discord. Most of the low-risk participants became competent, confident, caring adults, while two-thirds of the high-risk participants had delinquency records or mental health problems or were divorced. The authors were particularly interested in the remaining third of the high-risk group who became competent, confident, caring adults.

The authors were able to isolate three clusters of *protective factors*: (1) at least average *intelligence* and *personal attributes* that elicited positive responses from family members and other adults, such as robustness, vigour and a sociable temperament; (2) *affectionate ties* with parent substitutes such as grandparents or older siblings, which encouraged trust, autonomy and initiative; and (3) an external *support system* in church, youth groups or school, which rewarded competence. In more recent research, these factors were nicely confirmed in a study using data from a national survey conducted in Norway involving 9085 high school students (von Soest et al., 2010). Individual characteristics (e.g., perceived competence, playfulness, a positive social orientation), qualities of family relationships (e.g., shared values, emotional supportiveness), and the availability of resources in the larger social environment (e.g., availability of support, encouraging and positive role models in peer, school, neighbourhood and extra-familial relationships) were found to differentiate those youth who were functioning adaptively from those who demonstrated mental health problems.

Protective Mechanisms

Rutter (1990) proposes that we go beyond listing protective factors and instead attempt to understand what *accounts* for the protective power of such variables; for example, what is it about intelligence or socio-economic advantage that protects against psychopathology? The term he uses for these processes is **protective mechanisms**, and he has identified four of them on the basis of theory, observations and empirical research.

The first mechanism, *reduction of risk impact*, suggests that some variables intervene to buffer a child from exposure to risk. For example, negative peer influences are powerful risk factors for children growing up in gang-ridden neighbourhoods. However, parents who monitor their children's peer group activities and who guide them in their choice of friendships can reduce the likelihood of delinquency.

The next mechanism is *reduction of negative chain reactions*. These protective factors may provide their effects through their influences on relationships. For example, a temperamentally easy child is less likely to be the target of his stressed parent's anger; consequently, the child is less likely to develop behaviour problems, thereby de-escalating the parent's stress and lessening the anger. Thus, a vicious cycle of negative reaction from parent to child is averted.

Next, factors that *promote self-esteem and self-efficacy* help children feel they can cope successfully with life's problems. These qualities are enhanced by secure and supportive personal relationships and by task accomplishments, such as school achievement, that foster self-confidence.

The fourth protective mechanism is *opening of opportunities*. Development involves many turning points that offer a chance to reduce the impact of risk factors, and the resilient child is the one who takes advantage of these opportunities. Thus, adolescents who choose to stay in school allow themselves more opportunities for growth and achievement than dropouts do, and those who pursue their unique artistic talents or interests have more opportunities for personal fulfilment than do those who deny their talents and follow the crowd.

Table 1.2 provides examples of risks, vulnerabilities, protective factors and protective mechanisms derived from the literature. However, it is important to keep in mind that no variable *inherently* falls into one category or another. A particular variable can be construed in different ways, depending on how its effects unfold. For example, although poverty acts as a general risk factor for many forms of psychopathology, it may also play the role of a vulnerability factor by increasing the likelihood that a child will react negatively to a stressor: children whose families have few economic resources may be the most negatively impacted by certain stressful life events, such as a house fire in which all their possessions are lost.

Research in resilience is hopeful and inspiring. However, Luthar (2006) urges a cautionary note. Whereas earlier work referred to resilient children as *invulnerable*, this term implies an imperviousness to harm that does not characterize them accurately. For example, in her own research Luthar observed subtle ways in which resilient children still carried a legacy of their adverse upbringing. Although resilient individuals were less likely to behave in ways that labelled them as troublesome to others, they still showed signs of being inwardly troubled; for example, 85 per cent had significant symptoms in the areas of anxiety and depression. By the same token, many resilient adults in Werner and Smith's (1992) sample had stress-related health problems such as migraines and backaches, as well as feelings of dissatisfaction with their lives. In many cases they reported feeling burdened by the expectation that they care for their non-resilient parents and siblings. Thus, even resilient children are not armour plated and their good social functioning may come at some personal cost (Curtis and Cicchetti, 2007; Luthar et al., 2000).

Developmental Pathways

The emergence of psychopathology over the life course is conceptualized in terms of **developmental pathways**, or trajectories (Pickles and Hill, 2006). The initial question in constructing a pathway is this: At what point in time and for what reasons does development begin to be diverted from its normal course? Not all at-risk children become disturbed; therefore, both the factors that make children more vulnerable to risk *and* the factors that protect them from risk must be uncovered. In those cases in which protective factors are outweighed by risk and vulnerability, the question becomes, How do the latter two factors work their mischief over time in order to produce a full-blown psychopathology?

Finally, since children grow out of disturbances as well as grow into them, charting developmental pathways involves understanding the factors leading to extinction as well as those leading to persistence of psychopathology; this is the question of *continuity versus discontinuity*. The final challenge is to explain the data in terms of developmental principles and to understand the mechanisms and processes responsible for propelling the child from one step to the next along the path to a particular disorder (Sroufe, 1997). For example, Mulvey and colleagues (2010) used data gathered over a period of three years to investigate trajectories among youth who had become involved in the juvenile justice system. Which variables predicted patterns of desistance from delinquency, and which predicted continuity in antisocial behaviour? We will revisit the results of this study in Chapter 10.

In addition, sometimes pathways cross to produce **comorbidity**, or the co-occurrence of two psychopathologies. In the past, clinicians tended to focus on a single disturbance and researchers tried to study 'pure' cases, regarding the existence of other psychopathologies as potential confounds. However, it has become increasingly clear that certain disturbances, such as anxiety and depression or conduct disorders and hyperactivity, frequently occur together.

The implications of developmental pathways for prevention and intervention are significant. The more we learn about the earliest risk factors, the better able we will be to design effective preventive programmes. And at least for those psychopathologies showing a progression in seriousness of disturbance, earlier intervention is likely to result in more effective treatment. In our subsequent examinations of specific psychopathologies in the chapters ahead, we will chart developmental pathways and give more detailed accounts of the examples cited above.

Although the terms are not used consistently in the literature, we will reserve *developmental pathways* to refer to research that charts the journey children travel to a disorder; for example, how does a child come to be depressed? In contrast, the term *developmental course* will be used in reference to the progression of the disorder once it has developed; for example, what does the future hold for the child who is depressed? Developmental course is also referred to as *prognosis*; however, *prognosis* is a term derived from the medical model that implies that disorder is a fixed and static state. Because the

developmental psychopathology literature suggests that there is much variability and diversity of outcome, we have chosen developmental course as a preferable term.

Equifinality and Multifinality

Equifinality refers to the idea that a number of different pathways may lead to the same outcome (Cicchetti, 2006). For example, a variety of factors may lead to the development of depression, including genetics, environmental stress, and cognitive style. In contrast, **multifinality** states that a particular risk may have different developmental implications, depending on such contextual and individual factors as the child's environment and his or her particular competencies and capacities. For example, loss of a parent may result in depression in a child whose previous relationships with caregivers have been marked by insecurity, but it may result in conduct disorder in a child who faces additional environmental stress such as exposure to community violence.

Multideterminism

Following from the notions of equifinality and multifinality, developmental psychopathology proposes that the etiology of any psychopathology is *multidetermined*. The search for a single cause – as in 'juvenile delinquency results from neglectful parents' – is simplistic and erroneous. Rather, psychopathologies have multiple causes.

Continuity and Discontinuity

As we follow children along their unique developmental journeys, we find that, while some stay on a disordered course (continuity), others are deflected onto more healthy pathways (discontinuity).

Continuity in psychopathology has been found in studies following individuals from early childhood through adolescence (Costello et al., 2003). The evidence is particularly strong in the case of aggressive behaviour. For example, Fergusson and Horwood (2003) followed a sample of 1265 children in New Zealand from age 3 through adolescence and into adulthood. Children with early disruptive behaviour were 16 times more likely to develop later conduct problems than other children, while only 12 per cent showed a discontinuous history.

Discontinuity can occur in a number of ways. The first of these is as a function of *development* itself. Problem behaviour in the toddler and preschool period tends not to be a good predictor of subsequent disturbances, which is not surprising given the inconsistency of behaviour in early development. Around 6 or 7 years of age predictability increases, with children who have many symptoms at one age tending to have many symptoms later as well.

Sometimes the behaviour associated with a disturbance changes with age, a phenomenon termed **developmental transformation** (Sroufe, 1990). This means that there is continuity in the underlying disorder while its behavioural manifestations change over time. For example, insecure attachment is evidenced by precocious independence from the mother in infancy but excessive dependence on the teacher in preschool (Carlson and Sroufe, 1995). The underlying insecurity is consistent but is expressed differently at different ages. Similarly, in the New Zealand study cited early (Fergusson and Horwood, 2003), only 10 per cent of children who were diagnosed with attention problems were given the same diagnosis in adolescence. However, only 25 per cent of these children were problem-free in adolescence, as compared to 75 per cent of their peers. Thus, while there may be discontinuity in a *specific* disorder, continuity may be expressed in terms of an underlying vulnerability to psychopathology.

Discontinuity in Well-Functioning Children

If disturbed children can 'outgrow' their psychopathology, can normal children 'grow into' disturbances as adults? The idea that certain well-functioning children are at risk for becoming disturbed is a perplexing but important one. Just what are the telltale signs indicating that all is not as well as it appears to be? Some insight into this kind of discontinuity can be gleaned from Fergusson and Horwood's (2003) longitudinal study. Those without behaviour problems in childhood who went on to develop later conduct disorder were

more likely to associate with delinquent peers in adolescence. Therefore, just as with the transition from a pathological to a normative course, unexpected negative outcomes may be accounted for by *mediating factors* within or external to the child.

The Question of Specificity

As we have noted, developmental psychopathology models have become increasingly complex, recognizing the interactions amongst multiple factors in the origins of a disturbance. However, the multiplicity of factors implicated in each psychopathology creates a new problem, that of *specificity*. The specificity question refers to whether a particular risk factor is *specific* to the development of a particular disorder, as opposed to increasing the likelihood of some sort of *global* psychopathology. As we will see, certain risk factors – such as insecure attachment – may be precursors to such various forms of child psychopathology as depression, suicide, anxiety, conduct disorder and substance abuse. Therefore, the question remains whether knowing about a given risk factor, such as a history of broken parent–child bonds, is helpful in predicting a child's specific developmental outcome beyond a rough notion of 'bad input, bad output'.

One of the snarls we encounter in attempting to untangle the specificity question is that most of the research devoted to identifying risk factors has focused on only one individual disorder; for example, a particular study might ask, is insecure attachment a risk factor for childhood depression? The problem with this strategy is that it does not tell us whether that same risk factor might predict other forms of psychopathology equally well. Thus, one researcher's discovery of a relationship between insecure attachment and depression needs to be interpreted in the light of other research demonstrating that insecure attachment is a risk factor for conduct disorder. There is a need for studies that look at multiple risk and protective factors, as well as multiple outcomes, in order to discriminate between specific and general effects. This is rarely done, since most researchers focus on one particular disorder or predictor at a time. This strategy leaves us vulnerable to either overestimating – or underestimating – the extent to which knowledge about the past can help to predict a child's developmental outcome.

Transactions

An additional concept that helps us to understand how multideterminism in psychopathology comes about is that of transactions. A **transaction** can be defined as a series of dynamic, reciprocal interactions between the child and his or her social context (Sameroff, 2010). Rather than viewing etiology as a matter of simple linear cause and effect – due to organic factors such as genetics, or family variables such as parenting style – developmental psychopathology views development as a function of a complex interplay between the child and the environment over time (Cicchetti, 2006).

Let us look at an example. A young mother gives birth to a delicate and premature son, which is a source of some anxiety. Her anxiety during the first few months of the child's life causes her to be hesitant and inconsistent in her parenting. Subsequently, the child develops some irregularities in his sleeping and eating habits, making him more difficult to soothe. This difficult child taxes the mother's parenting skills even more, and she begins to withdraw from interaction with him. As he enjoys less interaction and verbal stimulation with his caregiver, the child develops language delays that affect him when he enters preschool, impacting both his academic success and social

relations with peers. Thus, a complex developmental sequence can be seen, in which parent and child both influence one another's behaviour. (See Fig. 1.6.)

Three important features of transactions help to define them. The first is that the nature of the transaction *changes over time*. Any particular relationship, such as that between the parent and child, is the product of a series of exchanges during which they gradually shape one another's behaviour over the course of development. Thus, the observation the clinician makes at any given moment – that the mother responds with helpless distress to her youngster's oppositionality, for example – is the product of a long history of their influence on one another. The second feature of transactions is that they are *reciprocal*, which means that development is a function of the way in which child and environment influence one another, each changing as a function of the other. The third feature of transactions is that they are *dynamic*. There is a live quality to them in that something new happens in the chemistry of the relationship. In the case of parent behaviour, for example, Sameroff (1995) states, 'In order for a genuine transaction to occur, the parents must be influenced by the infant's behavior to do something they would not have done if the child had behaved otherwise' (p. 7).

Transactional processes do not always lead to negative developmental outcomes. Consider the following clinical scenario concerning a severely depressed mother and her young child: when initially observed, this girl had a tendency to be

FIGURE 1.6 An Example of a Transactional Process.

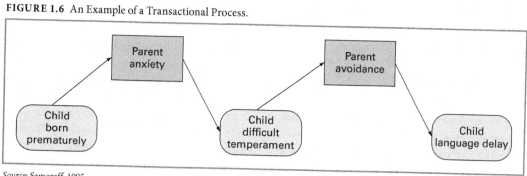

Source: Sameroff, 1995.

sombre and reserved, showing some signs of emerging depression as is often the case in a child of a depressed parent. However, during her early struggles to learn to dress herself, the toddler discovered that there were behaviours she could perform that could coax a smile from her mother. For example, when her mother was distressed, the child might come into the room in outlandish get-ups – her father's boots on her feet, her mother's panties on top of her head. The mother began to respond more warmly and positively to the child, who in turn began to increase her repertoire of 'silly' yet heart-warming behaviours. The feeling that she was a successful parent helped to lift the mother's depression, while the experience of being 'mother's little sunshine' brightened the child's affect. Thus, through the transactions between them, mother and daughter shaped one another's behaviour in more adaptive ways. Despite all the risks associated with maternal depression, the mother and child developed a positive relationship, which decreased the mother's depression and increased the daughter's chances of staying on a healthy developmental course.

In sum, like the family systems approach, developmental psychopathology perceives psychopathology not as something a person 'has' but rather as the result of a series of successive adaptations to the environment (Sroufe, 1997). Because transactions are observable and malleable, they can provide a powerful tool for intervention.

Conceptualizing Relationships between Development and Psychopathology

Stages of Development

Piaget's cognitive theory and Erikson's ego psychology are two good examples of theories that associate psychopathology with stages of development. Typically, stage theories make two assumptions: (1) stages represent significant *qualitative* reorganiza-tions of behaviour rather than mere *quantitative* changes or 'more of the same', and (2) the sequence of stages is unalterable. Thus, something new emerges at each stage and the order of emergence is fixed. For both Piaget and Freud, the question 'How old is the child?' is not as important as 'What stage is the child in?'

A characteristic of stage theories is that they often regard the *transition between stages* as a time of increased tension, unrest, and even regression to less mature behaviours. Freud's psychosexual stages have this characteristic, and Piaget describes the child's return to immature ways of thinking during cognitive transitions. Stage conceptualizations stand in contrast to radical behaviourism, which claims that stability or instability is primarily the consequence of the experiences the child is having. The important idea here is that normal development may entail built-in times of stress and upset; for example, the transitions from infancy to the preschool period and from middle childhood to adolescence are two potentially stressful periods. Knowing when disturbed behaviour is part of normal growth helps the clinician decide when to tell a parent, 'Most children act like that and yours is likely to outgrow it'.

There is another aspect of stage theories that informs our approach in this text. Our developmental framework implies that in order to evaluate the meaning and import of an event in a child's life, it is essential to know not only what happened but also at *which stage of development* it happened. A lengthy separation from the mother, for example, may have few negative effects in early infancy before an attachment to the mother has developed but may trigger a dramatic reaction in a 3-year-old who has formed a secure attachment. Being hospitalized becomes progressively less upsetting for children between 2 and 12 years of age and also may have different meanings, with the younger children being distressed over separation, for example, and the 4- to 6-year-olds fearing mutilation or death or viewing hospitalization as punishment.

Earlier perspectives on development proposed that there were *critical periods* during which negative effects have pervasive and irreversible effects. For example, it was once believed that infants needed to bond with the mother within the first hours after birth or the relationship would be irrevocably damaged. However, current theories are less deterministic and foreboding. Now it is believed that there are *sensitive* periods during which particular **stage-salient issues** come to the fore and when they are both most vulnerable to disruption and most open to change.

How Might Development Go Awry? Conceptualizations of Psychopathology

If psychopathology is normal development gone awry, in what ways might development be disrupted? There are several ways in which psychopathology might relate to stages of development: delay, regression, deviation, asynchrony and precocity. There also are two non-stage-related conceptualizations of psychopathology that we will encounter in the chapters to come: developmental deviation and adaptational failure. Next we define these terms and provide some concrete examples.

In **developmental delay** development proceeds at a pace significantly slower than normal, such as the 3-year-old who has not yet learned to talk. **Regression** involves falling off the course of normal development, such as when a formerly articulate 8-year-old suddenly begins to refuse to talk, termed selective mutism. We also might see in a regressed child a return to developmentally early forms of behaviour that are no longer appropriate, such as bed-wetting or temper tantrums.

Next, in **asynchrony** there are markedly uneven rates of progress among processes of development. This unevenness may result from maturational *delays* in particular developmental variables; for example, children with Asperger's disorder may be on track in the verbal realm and yet far behind their peers in social development. Alternatively, unevenness may result from emotionally painful experiences that cause *fixation* at the stage of development in which the trauma or conflict occurred. For example, the otherwise bright and well-functioning child who, at the end of elementary school, reacts

with distress rather than pleasure to the idea of graduation may be one who has had repeated experiences with traumatic separations.

In turn, **precocity** involves an accelerated rate of development that might be associated with psychopathology. Examples of precocity include the attempt by substance-abusing youths to take on adult roles and responsibilities before they are developmentally prepared for them, or the way in which children with generalized anxiety disorder worry excessively about grown-up matters, carrying the weight of the world on their shoulders.

The foregoing definitions of psychopathology are basically *quantitative*; that is, compared to others at this age, is this child displaying too much or too little of the behaviour in question? In contrast, a **developmental deviation** involves the emergence of a function that is so *qualitatively* different from normal that it would be considered inappropriate at any stage of development. An example of this is the echolalic speech of the autistic child who monotonously repeats back what others have said to him or her.

Finally, there is a very different conceptualization of psychopathology that does not concern developmental processes within the child, but rather the goodness of fit between the child and the environment. The concept of **adaptational failure** concerns the child's ability to adapt to the expectations of the environment. When the environment exerts demands that tax the capacities of the child – for example, the adolescent with low verbal abilities who is required to perform in school – dysfunction might be apparent. Should the youth find a better fitting niche – a vocational training programme that capitalizes on his or her non-verbal intelligence, for example – good adaptation is possible nonetheless.

Research Strategies in Developmental Psychopathology

We have discussed how the developmental psychopathology framework views the origins of psychopathology as *multiply determined*, incorporating variables within the person, the social environment and the transactions among them. Consequently, research designs that capture such models must be complex and sophisticated. The two essential techniques of the developmental psychopathology researcher are longitudinal designs and multivariate statistical techniques. To accomplish the task of determining what risks and protective factors lead to disorder or resilience, we need to follow children over time; hence, longitudinal research is essential. Further, in order to assess which variables are significantly related to children's outcomes over time, we need statistical techniques that are able to tease apart their effects; to this end, we use multivariate analytic strategies. Let us take a closer look at the tools in the developmental investigator's toolbox.

Longitudinal Research Designs
The Retrospective Strategy

A time-honoured method of gathering developmental data is the **retrospective strategy**, in which inquiry is made about the past history of a disturbed child or adult in order to reconstruct the origins of the psychopathology. For example, Fitzgerald and colleagues (2008) asked college students to reflect back on the experiences they had in childhood, including sexual abuse, interparental violence and role-reversal with their parents, in order to determine how these adversities were related to their functioning as young adults. Although either self-report or interview measures may be used in retrospective research, both of these sources of data may be coloured by the subjective judgements of the respondents and subject to the limitations of human memory for events that happened far in the past. Therefore, although retrospective data may offer initial leads about which intra-personal and interpersonal variables may be fruitful to study, questions about their reliability and validity suggest that they should be used with due caution.

The alternatives to retrospective designs are those that are *prospective*; that is, they follow children over time. The interval between assessments should be sufficient to capture general developmental trends, and the evaluations should be independently conducted by individuals who are more objective than parents. Three of the most popular strategies are the follow-back, the follow-up and the cross-sectional models, all of which eliminate a number of the deficiencies of retrospective data, although they have limitations of their own.

The Follow-Back Strategy

Like the retrospective approach, the **follow-back strategy** begins with a population of disturbed children or adults but obtains data from a previous time period via data kept by observers, such as school records, teachers' assessments, child clinic files and court records. An example of this is Best and Hauser's (2011) examination of archival records documenting the early histories of adolescents who were psychiatrically hospitalized. In order to organize the data, the investigators created a 'life chart' for each youth, tracking the occurrence and timing of stressful and unusual life events from birth to the time of hospital admission, which allowed them to assess the interrelations of these events and the onset of youth symptoms.

Advantages of the follow-back design include that it allows the investigator to focus on a specific target population and it is flexible enough to permit the investigator to pursue new leads as they emerge. However, the follow-back strategy has a number of limitations. The data may be *uneven* in quality and availability, with some records being comprehensive and clear, and others being skimpy and inconsistent. The data also tend to be very *general* – for example, number of arrests, decline in school grades, intact or broken family, number of job changes – lacking both the detail and the potential subtlety of variables found in an in-depth evaluation.

Other problems concern *population bias*. Clinical populations may not be representative of disturbed children in general. Parents who seek professional help for a child with a school phobia, for example, may be different from those who do not, so findings from a clinical population cannot be generalized to all parents of anxious children. Likewise, children who are arrested may not be a representative sample of all youthful offenders, because police officers have their own biases about whom they arrest and whom they let go.

More important, reliance on data such as child guidance and court records biases the data in terms of *accentuating pathology* and *exaggerating relationships* found at time 1 and time 2. To illustrate, let us say that one follow-back study indicated that 75 per cent of substance-abusing adults had dropped out of high school, compared with 26 per cent of healthy individuals – a highly significant difference – but a follow-up study revealed that only 11 per cent of high school dropouts and 8 per cent of graduates become substance abusers. Thus, dropping out of school can have a variety of outcomes, and its particular association with substance abuse is too weak for predictive purposes. In general, follow-back studies, which select individuals who have already developed a particular disturbance, tend to show stronger relations between time 1 and time 2 variables than do follow-up studies, the design we turn to next.

The Follow-Up Strategy

The ideal method of charting children's development is the **follow-up strategy**, in which children enter into the study in their early years and are followed into the next developmental period – or even into adulthood. The resulting longitudinal data can reveal which children develop what psychopathologies, together with how they fared with and without intervention. Instead of being at the mercy of whatever records exist, as with follow-back studies, the investigator can ensure that data will be gathered by well-trained investigators using the best available methods. Collishaw and colleagues (2007a) provide an example of this kind of research in their 20-year follow-up of a sample of youth originally recruited for a large-scale longitudinal

project conducted on the Isle of Wight in the UK. In adulthood, those participants who had reported severe physical or emotional abuse during childhood were at substantially increased risk for psychopathology. However, among this group was a minority who were described as resilient: these were the adults who had enjoyed a higher quality of parental care and peer relationships in their teenage years, and as adults had developed loving relationships with their life partners.

A major advantage of the follow-up study is that prospective longitudinal data allow the researcher to sort out the relationships among variables. For example, evidence that psychopathology in children of divorce was present *before* the breakup would indicate that the divorce alone was not the cause; rather, the more likely culprit would be the long and bitter process of marital dissolution that leads up to divorce. Although no longitudinal design can demonstrate *causal* relationships – a true experiment in which variables are controlled and manipulated is necessary for that – prospective data allow investigators to test the plausibility of hypotheses about antecedent and consequent relationships.

Despite its advantages, the follow-up study has a number of limitations. Such research is extremely *costly* in terms of money and expenditure of effort. A major problem is that of *time*: the investigator ages at the same rate as the participants, and therefore one must live to a ripe old age indeed in order to reap the rewards of a lifespan longitudinal study. On the other side of the equation, participants are difficult to retain in a study for such long periods of time. **Attrition** occurs when investigators lose track of participants; worse, participants may drop out selectively, with the most disturbed children and unstable families tending to be the ones who become uncooperative and move without leaving a forwarding address. Thus, researchers may be faced with a dwindling number of people in the very population they are most interested in studying. Population *selectivity* is another problem. Because most psychopathologies are rare, large numbers of children must be evaluated at time 1 to ensure a reasonable number of disturbed ones at time 2. As one solution, many investigators begin with a disturbed population or with a population at risk for developing a given psychopathology, such as infants of mothers with schizophrenia, who have a greater likelihood of developing schizophrenia than do infants from an unselected population. However, such selectivity may introduce the same population bias we noted in the follow-back design.

Moreover, the follow-up study is *rigid*. Once having selected variables to study, the design does not allow the investigator to drop some and add others as results from relevant studies come in or as new theories and concepts come to the fore. Moreover, new measurement techniques may be devised that are superior to the ones in use; however, the researcher cannot use them without losing comparability to the old data in the data-set.

One final problem with the follow-up studies is the so-called **cohort effect**; one cannot assume that groups born in different eras are equivalent, since the time of birth may significantly affect development. Children born in times of war or depression are not necessarily comparable to those born in times of peace and prosperity, just as children born before the advent of television or the Internet grew up in an environment very different from that of those born afterwards. Thus, the results of a 30-year longitudinal study may or may not be applicable to the current population of children.

The Cross-Sectional Strategy

The **cross-sectional approach** to gathering developmental data consists of studying different age groups (cohorts) at one point in time. For example, a researcher interested in the effects of exposure to stress on children of various ages might collect samples of 8-year-olds, 10-year-olds, 14-year-olds, and so forth. The chief advantage of this approach is that of time in that age-related differences can be studied without waiting for participants themselves to age. However, among its disadvantages is, again, the cohort effect. Although these groups may be equated for all the variables thought to be important, they cannot be equated for differential experiences they might have had because of their time of birth. For example, in a sample of military families, the parent–child relationships of a group of 14-year-old boys who grew up during wartime might differ significantly from those of a group of 7-year-old boys who grew up after the war. Thus, age and environmental events are confounded. The cross-sectional design is not truly developmental in that we do not know whether two years from now the 8-year-old participants will respond in the same way as those who are currently 10-year-olds; we can only assume that differences between them are due to age.

The Accelerated Longitudinal Approach

One solution to the confounding of developmental effects with cohort effects is the **accelerated longitudinal approach**, also known as the longitudinal, cross-sectional approach. In this design children at different ages are studied as in the cross-sectional approach but then are subsequently followed over time. In this design, several age cohorts of children are followed up for the same number of years until the children in the younger groups are the same age as those in the next older groups. Thus, the length of time needed to carry out a study spanning a long developmental period is reduced significantly. This strategy was used by Bongers and colleagues (2003), who assessed seven cohorts of Dutch children ages 4, 5, 6, 7, 8, 9 and 10 every two years for a period of 10 years. In this way, both within-cohort and between-cohort differences could be assessed. For example, the 4-year-old girls were compared with 6-year-old girls at time 1 and then again at time 2 to assess between cohort differences, and the girls' scores at age 4 were compared to their own scores at age 6 to assess within-cohort differences.

Among its advantages, such a design allows researchers to compare the age trends obtained cross-sectionally with longitudinal data. The saving in time is obvious: a longitudinal study that would have had to follow the 4-year-olds for 14 years can now be accomplished in half the time. However, as with any design, this one has limitations. These include the difficulty in equating groups and the likelihood of selective loss of participants across groups.

Evaluation of Research Strategies

Whereas the follow-up and follow-back strategies are an improvement over the retrospective approach, neither is a panacea. Because of its flexibility, the follow-back strategy is most suited to generating hypotheses. Leads as to possible significant antecedents can subsequently be accepted or rejected as they are put to further tests. However, follow-up studies, because of their ability to monitor the child's development while it actually occurs, provide the most convincing data concerning change. This strategy also comes closest to testing causal relations among variables, although, because it is correlational rather than experimental, it cannot actually establish causation.

One final cautionary note: the designs of follow-up and follow-back studies have only recently received the attention they deserve. Consequently, our reviews of longitudinal research will include studies using varying degrees of methodological sophistication and thus generating results with varying degrees of conclusiveness. While containing important leads about the developmental course of childhood psychopathology, many of the findings reviewed should be regarded as tentative.

Multivariate Research

Without going too far afield into the realm of statistics, we will briefly describe some essential techniques that are used to test the complex designs that are generated by multifaceted, longitudinal research. This will be helpful given that these methods are the ones used to construct the integrative developmental frameworks that we will feature in our discussions of each of the psychopathologies.

Moderators and Mediators

Research in developmental psychopathology, as we have seen, goes beyond the simple questions of 'bad input → bad output' and attempts to discover how the input variable and the output variable are related. For example, a large body of literature has established that childhood maltreatment increases the risk for adolescent delinquency (Kerig and Becker, 2010). But *how* and *why* do these effects take place? In other words, we want to identify the mechanisms – such as risk or protective processes – that account for the effects of maltreatment (the *independent variable*, or IV) on delinquency (the *dependent variable*, or DV). These linking mechanisms come in two types. A **mediator** is a *causal* variable; it is through the mediator that the IV affects the DV (MacKinnon, 2008). For example, perhaps children exposed to maltreatment develop a hostile attribution bias towards others, and it is this distorted cognition that accounts for their poor adjustment (Dodge et al., 1995). In contrast, a **moderator** is a variable that *affects* the strength or direction of the relationship between the IV and DV, but does not cause it. A vulnerability is a good example of a moderator, in that children who are at low levels of the moderator variable will be affected differently from children who are at high levels. For example, perhaps self-blame moderates the effects of maltreatment on children, such that it is only those who are perceive themselves to be at fault for the abuse who will go on to act-out antisocially (Feiring et al., 2007).

Moderator and mediator effects may well co-occur and Salzinger and colleagues (2007) provide a relevant example of this in their study of the relationship between abuse and delinquency. Using a matched sample of 100 physically abused youth and 100 non-abused classmates, the investigators assessed youths' quality of attachment to parents, their friendships, and their engagement in antisocial behaviour. Whereas attachments to parents mediated the relationship between childhood physical abuse and adolescent delinquency, peer relations moderated this relationship such that, for abused youth only, associations with delinquent peers and abusive behaviour towards best friends increased the risk for violent behaviour.

The search for moderators and mediators helps us to create some powerful models of how psychopathology comes about. These linking mechanisms also allow us to identify possible targets for intervention. Because we cannot simply assign children to 'happy families', we cannot eradicate family stress from their lives. But if we can interrupt the process by which hostility in the home is carried over into hostility with peers, for example, we can help children to stay on a healthy developmental pathway.

Structural Equation Modelling

Testing complex moderational and mediational models requires sophisticated analytic strategies. We will not attempt to describe them all here, but we will introduce one technique that we will see many times as we review integrative developmental models. Structural equation modelling (SEM) is a method of evaluating how well a complex theoretical model fits the actual relationships among a set of observed variables (Kline, 2011). Rather than examining these relationships one at a time as a correlation does, the advantage of SEM is that it simultaneously assesses the interrelationships among multiple variables, taking each association into account when considering the others.

To make the model more robust, instead of relying on a single measure, the investigator may select a number of different measures of a construct. To avoid biases, ideally these measures involve dissimilar methods and come from diverse sources. For example, a researcher interested in child anxiety disorders might interview teachers, provide parents with a questionnaire to complete, and observe children in the laboratory in order to come up with a set of measures for the construct 'anxiety'. The individual measures are termed *observed variables* and the theoretical construct they are assumed to tap is the *latent variable*. If the observed variables indeed relate to one another consistently so as to form a latent construct, the investigator may then proceed to the next step of testing his or her hypothesis regarding the relationships among the constructs.

For example, Willgerodt (2008) was interested in the interplay among family factors, peer relations and emotional distress as they predict risky behaviour among youth from different subcultures in the USA. Using two waves of data from the National Longitudinal Study on Adolescent Health, she gathered a sample of 194 Chinese, 345 Filipino and 395 White adolescents. To test her model, she wanted to assess four constructs, or latent variables: family bonds, peer problem behaviour, emotional distress and risky behaviours. *Family bonds* were assessed through three self-report measures: emotional bonds (perceptions of encouragement, and emotional availability), instrumental bonds (frequency of engaging in activities with the parent) and family closeness (perceptions that the family is close to and attentive to one another). *Peer antisocial activity* also was assessed with three measures (how often their best friends drink alcohol without parental supervision, smoke cigarettes or use illegal substances). *Emotional distress* was assessed through a measure of physical symptoms and two subscales derived from a standardized measure of depression. Finally, the latent variable of *risky behaviour* was assessed through three observed measures, including self-reported substance use and two delinquency scales.

Results of the SEM analyses indicated that, over time, family bonds were associated with a decrease in both emotional distress and risky behaviour for all youth in the study. (See Fig. 1.7.). However, whereas for Filipino and White adolescents peer antisocial activity was associated with increased risky behaviour over time, this effect did not hold for the Chinese youth. To explain these results, Willgerodt proposes that because of the 'strong and enduring emphasis on maintaining family honor' (2008, p. 404) in Chinese culture, Asian American youth who hold to these traditional values might be more influenced by their parents than by the behaviour of their peers.

To make matters even more complex, developmental psychopathology models require that we test the interactions among multiple variables over time. Thus, we need techniques that allow us to assess not only whether variables are related to one another, but also whether those relations emerge developmentally in patterns consistent with the theory. Additional techniques such as growth curve

FIGURE 1.7 Structural Equation Model Showing the Links Among Family Bonding, Peer Activity, Emotional Distress and Risky Behaviour for Chinese Youth.

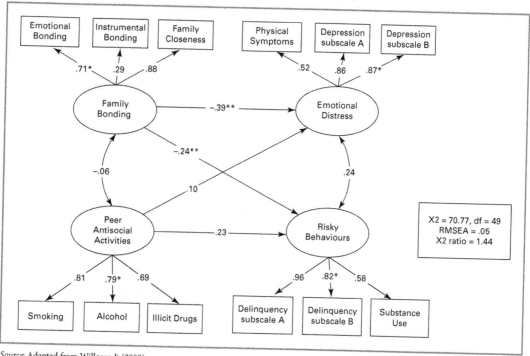

Source: Adapted from Willgerodt (2008).

modelling and hierarchical linear modelling also allow for testing models of change over time in longitudinal research.

Having outlined our general developmental framework and the methods used in its study, we are now ready to describe the normal development of the intra and interpersonal variables that will have a bearing on our subsequent discussions of the

various childhood psychopathologies. Then, in Chapter 3, we will build a bridge to the psychopathologies themselves.

(It would be helpful for the reader to have the kind of general familiarity with the major developmental theories that can be gained from a general text in child development. For example, see Bornstein and Lamb, 2010.)

Normative Development

If we are to understand childhood psychopathology as normal development gone awry, we must first chart normative development. Although development occurs across all psychological and biological processes, we have chosen a few key developmental lines that are so crucial to a child's well-being that, should anything go radically wrong with any one of them, we should seriously consider the possibility that the child will become disturbed.

First, there is a *biological* context to development. The child with a difficult temperament, or whose brain or neurochemistry has gone awry, is vulnerable to the development of psychopathology.

Within the psyche of the child, there are a number of developmental processes in what we term the *individual* context. First, it is essential for the child to understand the physical and social environment as well as himself or herself; thus *cognitive development* comes into play. Reality can be distorted by magical ideas in the first few years of life because of cognitive immaturity. It is essential that these distortions be replaced by realistic understanding; the persistence of bizarre, magical ideas – such as a 10-year-old's belief that he can control television pictures by his thoughts – is a sign of disturbed development.

In addition, *emotional* development is essential to our understanding of the boundary between the normative and psychopathological. Pivotally related to emotional development are *attachment* and the development of the *self-system*. From the earliest years, when young children are buffeted by the effects of emotional storms over which they can exert little control, responsive environments and sensitive care assist the child to develop the capacity to regulate emotions and engage in increasing degrees of self-control. In addition, throughout childhood and life the ability to feel deeply about and become attached to another individual lies at the core of the human experience and the sense of self. As children form important relationships with others, they are also forming a conceptualization of who they themselves are: am I loved and therefore lovable? Am I able to win friends and influence people and therefore likely to be able to achieve whatever I set out to do? Thus attachment and the self are pivotal to many developmental variables that might be related to psychopathology and health, including self-esteem, perceived self-efficacy, mastery motivation, identity and the ego functions that allow for successful coping with internal and external stress.

In addition, socialization often involves curbing children's behaviours; with time, children take over these monitoring and controlling functions themselves. *Moral development* therefore comes into play by guiding the child in regard to the rightness or wrongness of behaviour. Morality and self-control also involve the development of defence mechanisms, which help to manage anxiety and serve as one of the principal deterrents to performing socially disapproved actions.

Gender differences interact with all of the other processes we have mentioned, as biology and sex-role socialization affect self-perceptions and behaviour to a significant degree. With the advent of *sexuality* later in development, erotic attachments and truly intimate relationships are formed. If something goes radically awry with any of these bonds – if, for example, the loving overtures of a parent are met with rage or profound indifference, if sexual intimacy is a source of terror rather than pleasure, if the child is socially isolated and friendless – we would rightfully be concerned.

A critical context for us to consider is that of the *family*. The quality of the parenting the child receives, the structure of the family system, and the extent to which the parent–child relationship is warm and kind versus harsh and rejecting will affect susceptibility to negative developmental outcomes.

As development advances, children and youth expand their social horizons to form increasingly meaningful and significant *social relations* with peers and adults outside the family. Last, but not least, children develop in a larger *cultural* context that must be considered. Cultural attitudes and values, social class and ethnicity are all variables that affect the child by shaping his or her physical and psychological environment.

In sum, in our developmental approach to childhood psychopathology, we will discuss contributions made by the biological, family, social and cultural contexts. In addition, we will focus on six processes in the individual context: cognition, emotion, attachment, the self, moral development, and gender and sexuality.

Development in the Biological Context

Genetics

As we discuss each of the specific disorders in the chapters to follow, we will make note of whether there is evidence of genetic transmission within families. Models of genetic heritability involve the *genotype* – the genetic material that is passed on; the *phenotype* – the way the genes are expressed in physical characteristics and behaviour; and the *environment* – aspects of the surroundings that might compete with genes as the explanation for behaviour. (See Rende and Waldman, 2006.) *Epigenetics*, in turn, refers to the way in which genes and the environment interact to create individual variations in phenotype that reflect the influence of environmental conditions (Meaney, 2010). Just as biology affects our behaviour, our experiences in life have the power to affect our biology. As Fox and colleagues (2010) state, 'Although our genetic code provides an important foundation for early development, it must be understood as a framework upon which many environmental factors influence future structure and function' (p. 31).

Therefore, instead of engaging in an old-fashioned either-or debate regarding nature versus nurture, the modern field of behavioural genetics assumes that all behaviour arises as a function of an interaction between genetic and environmental factors. *Heritability* is estimated as the proportion of variability in a given trait within a group of individuals that is attributable to their shared genes, in contrast to variability that is attributable to *shared environments* (e.g., experiences all the siblings in a family share, such as being parented by a stressed mother) and *non-shared environments* (e.g., experiences that are unique for each sibling, such as parents' differential treatment of the youngest and eldest child).

There are three ways in which genes and the environment might interact and reciprocally influence one another over the course of development (Scarr and McCartney, 1983). First, *passive* gene-environment interactions may occur when biological families share both genes and environments. For example, children of depressed mothers are recipients not only of a genetic predisposition for depression but also a caregiving environment shadowed by the mother's depressive parenting style. *Evocative* gene-environment interactions take place when genetic propensities cause others to elicit or evoke certain kinds of responses from their environments. For example, children with a difficult temperament might elicit negative reactions from caregivers, and thus evoke less ideal parenting from them. Third, *active* gene-environment interactions occur when individuals select, create or modify their environments on the basis of their genetic predispositions. In a process known as *niche-picking*, children increasingly engage actively in shaping their environments by choosing activities, friends and experiences according to their own individual attitudes and interests (Reiss et al., 2000). Therefore, through the ways in which children select and modify their interpersonal spheres, over the course of development there is a decline in the extent to which siblings in the same family share the same environment.

The strongest evidence for genetic influences comes from studies of twins, which compare those who share 100 per cent of their genes in common (identical or monozygotic twins) to those who share only 50 per cent of their DNA (fraternal or dizygotic twins). The investigator determines the *concordance rate*, the percentage of cases in which a characteristic displayed by one child is also displayed by his or her twin. The ideal behavioural genetics study is one that compares twins reared in the same family to those reared apart. If twins reared apart are more alike then different, this suggests that genes rather than environmental influences are affecting their behaviour. For example, the Minnesota Study of Twins Reared Apart (Markon et al., 2002) sheds light on the genetic contributions to personality development. The investigators evaluated the adaptive and maladaptive personality traits of 122 monozygotic and dizygotic twin pairs who had been reared in different households. Overall, the data suggested that identical twins were more similar than fraternal twins; thus, the contribution of genetics was significant. However, environment still made a significant contribution to personality phenotype.

Another innovative research strategy that allows for the comparison of genetic and environmental effects is a 'prenatal cross-fostering' design. In such a study, mothers who are biologically related to their children are compared to those who received a donor egg via *in vitro* fertilization and thus did not contribute to their child's genetic make-up. Using this design, Rice and colleagues (2010) in the UK studied the relationships among maternal prenatal stress and the development of children's antisocial behaviour, anxiety and attention problems. The findings showed links between prenatal stress and children's antisocial behaviour in both genetically related and unrelated mother–child pairs, suggesting an environmental link. In contrast, the association between prenatal stress and child attention problems was only present in biologically related pairs, indicating that this link can be attributed to inherited factors.

In general, the weight of the research suggests that about 50 per cent of personality is attributable to genetics (Plomin et al., 2008). Therefore, there still is much room for psychological and environmental processes to exert their influences. In particular, there is increasingly recognition of the ways that genetics, behaviour and environmental influences affect one another dynamically and reciprocally (Moffit, 2005). For example, one study evaluated adopted children's genetic risk for aggression by assessing their biological parents' antisocial behaviour, and then investigated the relationship between the adoptive parents' discipline styles and the children's subsequent conduct problems (Riggins-Caspers et al., 2003). The results showed that adopted children at high genetic risk for aggression received more discipline and control from their adopted parents than did low-risk children, and that the link between the genetic risk and the adoptive parents' parenting behaviour was mediated by the child's aggression. Thus, the children's genetics affected their behaviour, which then evoked a specific response from the caregiving environment – in this case, an adaptive one designed to set limits on the child's misconduct.

Neuropsychology

The field of child neuropsychology has been making rapid and exciting advances in recent years, and it will be beyond our scope to review it in its entirety here. But, briefly, important dimensions of neuropsychological development that will concern us include brain structure, function and chemistry. (For a basic overview of neuropsychological development, see Kolb and Whishaw, 2003; for excellent reviews of neuropsychology and psychopathology, the reader is referred to Cicchetti and Walker, 2003, and Romer and Walker, 2007.)

Regarding *brain structure*, or neuroarchitecture, we will make note of whether research shows that various disorders are linked to malfunctions or disconnections among the parts of the developing brain. Next, we want to consider *brain function*, or how differences in brain anatomy are displayed in behaviour. In the realm of *brain chemistry*, we will be concerned with the **neurotransmitters** that communicate between nerve cells (neurons) in the brain, including dopamine, serotonin, GABA, and norepinephrine. When these transmissions are disrupted, or they are excessive or deficient in quantity, psychopathology might develop. In addition, stressful experiences overstimulate the release of certain **neuroendocrines** that, in excessive quantity, have toxic effects on the developing brain. For example, in our investigations of anxiety, trauma (Chapter 8) and maltreatment (Chapter 14), we will encounter the *hypothalamic-pituitary-adrenal (HPA) axis*, which plays an important role in the response to stress by regulating the production of the hormone cortisol and stimulating the familiar 'fight, flight or freeze' response. Children who are exposed to excessive amounts of cortisol in the context of prolonged or repeated trauma may become locked in a state of heightened fear and arousal, with resulting pernicious effects on the developing brain (Gunnar, 2007).

Brain Development

The development of the infant's brain parallels the advance of evolution in that the first structures to develop are the most primitive. For example, the lowest part of the brain, the brain stem, connects to the spinal cord and regulates autonomic functions such as breathing, heartrate, motor co-ordination, and arousal. (See Fig. 2.1.) Behind this sits the *cerebellum*, which is responsible for coordination and

FIGURE 2.1 Map of the Human Brain.

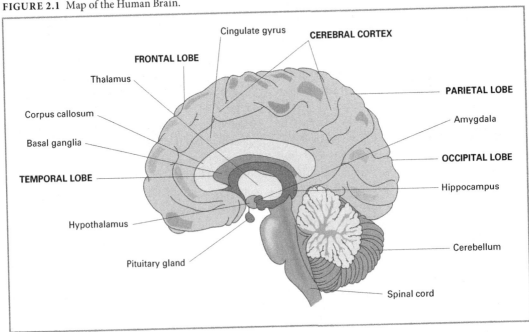

balance. Atop the brain stem is the *limbic system*, which incorporates structures such as the *hippocampus, cingulate gyrus* and *amygdala*. This collection of structures governs the basic drives of sex, aggression and satiety, and plays an important role in the regulation of emotion and impulse control. Next, the *basal ganglia*, including the *caudate nucleus*, are involved in the organization and integration of information regarding thoughts, feelings and behaviour.

The last part of the brain to develop is the *cerebral cortex*, which is involved in the most complex human operations of reasoning and creativity. The cortex comprises two hemispheres that are specialized for certain functions, a characteristic of the human brain termed *lateralization*. The *left hemisphere* (dominant in most right-handed people) is involved in the processing of verbal information and linear forms of logic, such as reading and mathematics, while the *right hemisphere* specializes in visual and holistic processing, such as that involved in spatial and social perception. However, despite this bilateral specialization, the two sides of the brain are highly integrated and both are involved to some extent in most tasks, with communication taking place through the *corpus callosum*, a bundle of fibres that connects the two hemispheres.

The cerebral cortex is further divided into four areas, or *lobes*: occipital, parietal, temporal and frontal. The *occipital* lobe, at the very rear of the cortex, is largely involved in visual processing. Above this, the *parietal* lobes are responsible for perception of sensory information, including the recognition of pain, pressure, touch and the movement of the body through space. The *temporal* lobes, in the temple area on either side of the cortex, are important for memory, auditory perception and facial recognition.

At the very forefront of the brain lie the *frontal lobes*, which are central to the higher mental operations. These include the **executive functions**, so named because they act like executives in a corporation and oversee such tasks as planning, problem solving, decision making and organization.

Although it was once assumed that the process of brain development was complete around 12 years of age, recent research has revealed that significant changes in the cerebral cortex continue to occur well into adolescence, and even into early adulthood (Giedd, 2003). Two important developmental processes are myelination and pruning. **Pruning** involves the brain's ridding itself of unnecessary redundant or non-functional cells. The first wave of pruning occurs in the final months before birth, following an explosive growth in prenatal neural development. There is a second, critical, pruning stage that begins later in childhood and culminates in the late teens. This second wave involves reducing not only the number of cells but also the number of connections between neurons.

The brain consists of two types of neural tissue, grey matter and white matter. White matter gets its colour from the *myelin sheath* that surrounds the axon of the nerve cell and serves much the same function of insulation on a wire, increasing the speed and efficiency of the transmission of information. Increasing **myelination** of the neurons begins around puberty (age 11 for girls and age 12.2 for boys) and continues at least into the twenties and perhaps even into the forties. Myelination proceeds in the same manner as brain development in general: from the rear portions of the brain, where basic and primitive functions are housed, to the front of the brain, where more advanced functions lie. The last part of the brain to be pruned and myelinated is the prefrontal cortex, which is responsible for such higher mental functions as planning, decision making, organization and weighing alternatives. Therefore, investigators propose that some of the risky behaviour and illogical thinking associated with the 'storm and stress' of adolescence may have a biological basis (Steinberg, 2010).

Temperament

Each infant appears to be born with a particular *temperament* – a characteristic tempo and activity level, a particular mood and adaptability, a special set of vulnerabilities and resiliencies. (See Rothbart, 2011; Rothbart and Bates, 2007.) As Nigg (2006) describes it, temperament at its essence reflects the biological reactivity of the child to the environment, but has its expression in many facets of development: behavioural (is the child inhibited or bold): psychological (is the child anxious or confident); neural (is the limbic system reactive or well modulated); physiological (is the autonomic nervous system aroused or stable); genetic (are the genes that modulate the neurotransmitters responsible for emotional reactivity turned 'off' or 'on').

Temperament Types

The pioneers in the study of temperament are Alexander Thomas and Stella Chess (1977), who distinguished among three types of infants: difficult, easy and slow-to-warm-up. *Difficult* infants are fussy, irregular in their eating and sleeping habits, easy to upset and difficult to soothe. *Easy* infants, in contrast, generally display positive affect, react in a mild manner to frustration and are easily soothed by parental comforting. *Slow-to-warm-up* or shy infants have a generally low activity level and, while they may show an initially negative reaction to new stimuli or change, they will adapt over time and begin looking more like the easy infants.

Using data from the New York Longitudinal Study, Thomas and Chess (1977) followed 133 people from infancy into adulthood. While they found no correlation between any single temperamental trait and early adult adjustment, difficult temperament at 3 years of age was negatively correlated with overall ratings of emotional adjustment in adulthood. Further, children who developed psychiatric problems were overwhelmingly more likely to have shown a difficult temperament in infancy.

Another set of temperament researchers used data from the Berkeley Guidance Study, which began in 1928 and followed 214 people from early childhood through adulthood (Caspi, 1987). Based on parent report, young children were classified as temperamentally *dependent, ill-tempered* or *shy*; and when the participants were 40 years of age, they were interviewed by members of the research team. (Although the term 'dependent' sounds negative, keep in mind that dependency on caregivers is normative for young children; therefore, this was the most adaptive temperament pattern.) Inspired by the personality typology developed by their theorist Karen Horney, the investigators described the children who exhibited these three temperamental patterns as, respectively, moving *towards, against* or *away* from the world. They found remarkable continuities in temperamental patterns as well as interesting gender differences regarding the consequences of particular temperaments for adults in the 1950s. For example, childhood ill-temper was associated with hostility and irritability in both men and women (Caspi et al. 1987). On the other hand, whereas shy men had difficulty with life transitions throughout adulthood, delaying marriage, childrearing and the establishment of their careers, shy women's temperament was not associated with a problematic developmental course (Caspi et al. 1988). Whereas shy girls grew up to be reticent women, their preference for a quiet, domestic lifestyle fits well with the stereotypical expectations for women of their era.

Subsequently, Caspi and colleagues followed a sample of over 900 children from age 3 to age 21 (Caspi and Shiner, 2007). The investigators identified five distinct temperamental types: *well adjusted, reserved, confident, inhibited* and *undercontrolled*. Whereas the first three groups displayed a range of interpersonal behaviours in adulthood, their adjustment was generally good. Inhibited children, in turn, grew up to be adults who experienced lower levels of social support than others, but still enjoyed adaptive relationships with romantic partners and workmates. The undercontrolled preschoolers, however, were significantly more likely than others to display significant adjustment problems across all interpersonal relationships in adulthood. We will revisit the finding from these studies when we discuss psychopathologies of anxiety and aggression in Chapters 8 and 10.

Rothbart (2011), in turn, has conducted extensive research on temperament across the lifespan and has used factor analyses to derive three broad factors underlying temperamental types. (See Table 2.1.) The first factor, termed *surgency*, concerns the child's activity level and engagement with the environment. The second factor, *negative affectivity*,

TABLE 2.1 Rothbart's Three-Factor Model of Temperament

Surgency	Activity level (e.g., 'Tends to run rather than walk from room to room')
	Approach towards others, positive anticipation (e.g., 'Shows great excitement when opening a present')
	High-intensity pleasure (e.g., 'Likes to go fast and high when pushed on a swing')
	Impulsivity (e.g., 'Often rushes into new situations')
	Lack of shyness (e.g., 'Prefers to join other children playing rather than stand on the sidelines')
	Smiling and laughter (e.g., 'Smiles when looking at a picture book')
Negative affectivity	Anger/frustration (e.g., 'Gets angry when told s/he has to go to bed')
	Discomfort in reaction to sensory stimulation (e.g., 'Is bothered by light or colour that is too bright')
	Slow rate of recovery from distress or arousal, difficult to soothe (e.g., 'Cries for a long time once s/he starts')
	Fearfulness, unease, worry, nervousness (e.g., 'Is afraid of the dark')
	Sadness in response to disappointment (e.g., 'Cries sadly when a favourite toy gets lost or broken')
Effortful control	Ability to maintain attentional focus (e.g., 'When drawing or colouring in a book, shows strong concentration')
	Able to inhibit or suppress responses (e.g., 'Can easily stop an activity when s/he is told "no"')
	Pleasure or enjoyment in response to low-intensity stimuli (e.g., 'Enjoys sitting on parent's lap')
	Perceptual sensitivity to low-intensity stimuli (e.g., 'Notices even little specks of dirt on objects')

Source: Adapted from Rothbart (2011).

reflects the child's tendency to react negatively to frustrations and to be difficult to soothe once aroused. The third factor, *effortful control*, describes the child's ability to intentionally maintain focused attention and control impulses.

Research from Rothbart's laboratory shows stability of these temperamental dimensions from infancy to 7 years of age. Longitudinal research also has confirmed the relations of these temperament factors to the development of psychopathology. For example, Komsi and colleagues (2006) followed a sample of Finnish children from infancy to age 5. years and a half. Children deemed overcontrolled showed internalizing problems and were high in fearfulness, low in surgency and high in effortful

control. In contrast, undercontrolled children with externalizing problems were high in negative emotion, high in surgency and low in effortful control. In turn, children deemed *resilient* were without mental health problems and were high on surgency, low on negative affect, and high in effortful control. Research from other laboratories also has indicated that the temperamental dimension of effortful control may be related to **resilience**. For example, Gardner and colleagues (2008) have found that effortful control protects youth from the negative effects of exposure to antisocial peers, and Lengua and Long (2002) report that family stress is related to lower levels of internalizing problems when children are high in effortful control. Thus, whereas a difficult temperament might comprise a vulnerability to the development of psychopathology, adaptive temperamental qualities might confer protection against risk (Nigg, 2006).

In summary, despite their use of different terminologies and classification systems, temperament studies consistently show that extremely shy/inhibited temperaments and their opposite, extremely difficult/aggressive/undercontrolled temperaments, increase children's vulnerability to the development of psychopathology. The remarkable continuity of child temperament from infancy to adulthood also emerges as a consistent theme. In their attempt to explain the mechanism by which childhood temperament affects adult behaviour, Caspi and Shiner (2007) proposed two valuable concepts. The first of these is *interactional continuity*. For example, they proposed that because shy boys were timid and lacking in social skills, they tended to be neglected by other people: They were overlooked, ignored, the last picked when teams were being formed. We would term this a *transaction* (see Chapter 1): through the way that shy boys interacted with others, they inspired others to respond to them in ways that exacerbated their shyness and, consequently, led them to want to withdraw even more. The second concept is a *historical* one. As Caspi and colleagues argue, every culture at every historical epoch defines a set of roles that have to be fulfilled by individuals – these identify the competencies individuals are expected to have and specify which behaviours are deemed appropriate to display. Therefore, individual development is in part influenced by how the person negotiates the agenda provided by his or her culture at his or her time in history.

Another valuable contribution that Chess and Thomas have made to our understanding of developmental psychopathology is their observation that temperamental characteristics alone do not determine a child's outcome. Instead, it is the *fit* between the child and environment that determines whether development took a healthy or a pathological course (Chess and Thomas, 1999). Next we look at this concept in more detail.

Goodness of Fit

Chess and Thomas (1990) were struck by the individual differences in their longitudinal sample in that some children stayed on a consistent pathway from infancy to adulthood while others ended up at quite a different destination. Given that Chess and Thomas are clinicians who are interested in how their research can be used to enhance the outcomes of the children in their samples, the investigators became intrigued with the question of why one child shows a consistent temperamental course whereas another shows great variability over time. Chess and Thomas proposed that the explanation lay in the **goodness of fit**: the meshing between the child's temperamental style and the demands the environment places on the child. When the environment's expectations, demands and opportunities are compatible with the individual's temperament, the child is able to master environmental challenges effectively. When there is a poorness of fit, the demands from the environment exceed the child's capacities and the ensuing stress leads to an unhealthy developmental course. As Chess and Thomas (1990, p. 211) state:

> Goodness of fit does not imply an absence of stress or conflict: quite the contrary. Stress and conflict are inevitable during development, as new expectations and demands for ever-higher levels of functioning occur continuously as the child grows older. Demands, stresses, and conflicts, when they are consistent with the child's developmental potentials and capacities for mastery, will be constructive in their consequences. The issue involved in disturbed functioning is rather one of excessive stress resulting from poorness of fit between environmental demands and the capacities of the child at a particular stage of development.

Two case examples from Chess and Thomas' longitudinal research are presented in Box 2.1.

More recently, in a longitudinal study of over 2000 early adolescents in the Netherlands, Sentse and colleagues (2009) assessed two dimensions of temperament, fearfulness and frustration. Youth's perceptions of the quality of parenting were

Box 2.1 Case Studies in Temperament and Goodness of Fit: Norm and Carl

Stella Chess and Alexander Thomas describe two young people who participated in their longitudinal study of temperament and developmental psychopathology, Norm and Carl.

In infancy, Norm showed temperamental traits of shyness, distractibility and low persistence. However, he was intelligent and did well in school. Norm's father was of a different temperamental type: he was focused and hard-driving and he did not tolerate well Norm's hesitancy and dreaminess. While the investigators did their best to provide the parents with insight into the temperamental basis for Norm's behaviour, the father preferred to interpret it as 'irresponsibility' and 'lack of character', opinions that he expressed openly to his son. Norm grew to recognize that he did not have his father's drive, but he also accepted his father's negative judgement about his character. By adolescence he was very self-critical and he told Dr Chess, 'My father doesn't respect me, and let's face it, why should he?' His introspectiveness only increased his negative self-image and led to further discouragement and hopelessness. He dropped out of several colleges for lack of effort and went from job to job without motivation enough to continue with any one of them. He tried psychotherapy but was not helped by it, because his self-defeating tendencies would not allow him to see the possibility that he could make any positive changes.

Carl also had been an infant in the longitudinal study, and when he was 19 years old, he requested an interview with Dr Chess. He had just finished his first semester in college and was experiencing feelings of depression and inability to cope with the new academic and social demands pressing on him. He had not been able to make any new friends and was having trouble studying, problems that he had not experienced before in his life. He did not understand what was happening to him: 'This just isn't me!'

Looking back at his research profile, Dr Chess noted that, as an infant, Carl had shown a very difficult temperament pattern, with intense negative reactions to new situations and slow ability to adapt. His mother had worried that she must be doing something wrong as a mother; otherwise, why would Carl behave so differently from other children? Happily, his father was a very patient person who saw Carl's behaviour as challenging but not abnormal and reassured his wife that they could cope with their demanding infant. Dad interpreted Carl's loud shrieking as 'lustiness' and viewed his son's boldness as admirable in comparison to the father's own mild temper. Consequently, the parents handled Carl's tantrums with a patient, consistent and low-key approach.

Throughout his childhood, Carl lived in the same community. He went through school with the same group of friends and had no major disruptions or stressors in his life. Any changes he experienced were slow to occur and he had time to adapt to them. In contrast, college was an abrupt change that simultaneously confronted him with a whole series of stressors: new surroundings, a strange peer group and a variety of different academic pressures. He experienced an intense negative emotional reaction and fell back on his temperamental pattern of withdrawal from these new stimuli.

Sitting down with Carl, Dr Chess reviewed the evidence regarding his temperamental pattern. She also gave him some behavioural strategies to help him cope, such as limiting the number of new academic subjects he took per semester and becoming involved with a peer activity group and attending it regularly so that he could develop a consistent set of friends. After this consultation, Carl expressed appreciation and went on his way. Seven years later Carl, now age 26, made another appointment to see Dr Chess. He was extremely cheerful and talked about the many activities he had under way. He was enjoying a successful career in computers and was planning to start his own business, while at the same time he wanted to take a year off and study music. He was also in an intense relationship and was trying to decide whether to get married, was learning photography and was actively involved in athletics. She joked with him, 'When do you sleep?' He replied, 'That's one of my problems. I don't get enough sleep and I'm always tired. But I really came to ask you why I have all these tics.' Dr Chess laughed to herself and pointed out that all these activities, dilemmas and decisions must be causing tension and fatigue. Carl responded by limiting his activities and, upon returning for a check-up three years later, was doing well.

Source: Adapted from Chess and Thomas, 1990.

obtained, including measures of **overprotectiveness**, rejection and emotional warmth, and an interview was used to assess parent psychopathology. Finally, family socio-economic status (SES) was noted and youth externalizing and internalizing problems were rated. The investigators found interesting patterns of interactions between temperament and family factors. For example, frustration predicted the development of externalizing problems in adolescence, but this effect was buffered by parental emotional warmth and high SES. In turn, the negative effects of frustration were exacerbated by the presence of parental rejection. In short, temperament appears to provide a biological predisposition upon which the environment acts in order to moderate or potentiate the development of psychopathology. As Nigg (2006) phrases it, 'in some instances … temperament alone is insufficient to account for the full emergence of psychopathology. Rather, vulnerable temperament plus unfortunate experiences in development appear to account for etiology' (p. 19).

Biological Processes and Developmental Psychopathology

To summarize, there are several processes by which biology might contribute to the development of psychopathology: (1) genetically inherited traits; (2) abnormalities in brain structure; (3) dysfunctions in brain function or miscommunication among parts of the brain; (4) imbalances in brain chemistry; (5) inadequate myelination; (6) dysfunctions of the pruning process that rids the brain of redundant and non-functional pathways; and (7) difficult temperament. Each of these biological processes evolves in interaction with the environment, and therefore our consideration of organic factors will be conducted with the concept of *transactions* in mind.

Development in the Individual Context

Cognitive Development

As we noted in Chapter 1, Piaget (1967) outlined a series of orderly, fixed stages that children progress through in the process of cognitive development.

During the first two years of life the child is in the **sensorimotor stage**, so called because the vehicles for understanding are sensation and motor action. When presented with a novel object such as a rattle, an infant may determine its properties by placing it in the mouth or shaking it. Incapable of symbolization, except towards the end of the period, infants and toddlers must explore and learn by acting directly on the environment and by using their senses. A significant development in this period is that of **object permanence**. For the first few months, infants give no evidence of missing an object they can no longer see or hold. Thus, the world exists only when they are acting upon it or perceiving it. Only gradually do infants come to realize that objects exist regardless of their own actions or perceptions – objects exist 'out there' as part of the environment, while actions exist 'in here' as part of the self. This represents a giant step toward separating 'me' from 'not me'.

The **preoperational stage** lasts from approximately 2 to 7 years of age and marks the appearance of *symbolic functions*. The most obvious manifestation of symbolization is language, which develops rapidly in this period. However, the preschooler tends literally to believe what he or she sees. Consequently, something that *looks* different *is* different. Piaget's well-known documentation of this thesis is the *conservation* experiment. If, before their very eyes, water is poured from a wide, squat glass into a tall, narrow glass, preschool children will claim that there is now more water. It looks like more, so it must be more. Lack of conservation also contributes to erroneous beliefs we explored earlier, such as the young child's conviction that by changing her clothes she can change her gender. Preoperational children also are known for magical thinking, also termed **omnipotent thinking**. Because their understanding of causality is limited, they tend to view themselves as the agents causing the events around them.

The **concrete-operational stage** extends from approximately 7 to 11 years of age. The triumph of middle childhood is that children are capable of understanding the world in terms of reason rather than in terms of naive perception. They grasp the notion that objects conserve or maintain their identity despite changes in appearance. Although realistic, the child's thinking is still tied to concrete reality and bound to the here and now.

The **formal-operational stage** begins around the twelfth year and lasts into adulthood. In this period the youth is able to generalize ideas and construct abstractions. The ability to draw conclusions from hypotheses rather than relying totally on actual observation is called *hypothetical-deductive* thinking. Adolescents can go wherever their thoughts lead them. They discuss, they write, they ruminate. They create a philosophy of life and explain the universe. They are also capable of being truly self-critical for the first time because they can reflect on and scrutinize their own ideas.

Cross-cultural research has confirmed that children from diverse societies typically perform at the stages proposed by Piaget's theories, and at the ages he would predict, as long as the stimuli used to assess their cognitive functioning are culturally relevant and involve objects, concepts and language that children have encountered in their daily lives (Maynard, 2008).

Cognitive Processes and Developmental Psychopathology

Assimilation-Accommodation Imbalance

In order to understand the origins of psychopathology in Piaget's scheme, we must consider the processes that account for cognitive growth and progression through these stages. According to Piaget, development is fuelled by the child's attempts to adapt to the environment. As we noted in Chapter 1, adaptation occurs through two psychological processes: assimilation and accommodation. **Assimilation** refers to the incorporation of new information into an existing schema and **accommodation** refers to the alteration of a schema to take into account new information. Whereas normative development is characterized by a balance, or **equilibration**, of assimilation and accommodation, problems may arise when accommodation and assimilation are used to the exclusion of one another.

Exclusive use of assimilation, for example, might interfere with new learning, leading the child to make erroneous assumptions and to distort information so that it fits with pre-existing notions. At the extreme, the child who is overly reliant on assimilation may be lost in fantasy, trying to bend the world to his or her own wishes. On the other hand, exclusive use of accommodation would result in the child's constantly changing his or her schema to fit with new stimuli. In the extreme, the overly accommodating child may lack a cohesive sense of self (Cowan, 1978).

Magical Thinking

An adolescent girl who will not speak for fear that faeces would come out of her mouth, or a young man who always sleeps on his back in the belief that, if he did not, he would turn into a woman, would be regarded as psychopathologically disturbed because they are convinced that they can cause events, which, in reality, are beyond their control. While in normal development magical ideas and omnipotence begin to give way to logic during middle childhood, remnants of preoperational thinking may be seen in children whose development is delayed or children who are undergoing regression due to traumatic stress. Omnipotent thinking is problematic particularly for those traumatized children who misattribute to themselves causality – and blame – for their abuse.

Egocentrism

Piaget defines **egocentrism** as conceiving the physical and social world exclusively from one's own point of view. Consequently, characteristics of the self are used to define or interpret characteristics of the objective environment: the me is confused with the not-me. Egocentric thinking appears at all stages of cognitive development. The infant believes the very existence of objects depends on his or her actions. For preschoolers, egocentrism has an important social consequence in that it prevents them from understanding that each person has his or her own point of view. The ability to view the same situation from multiple vantage points – for example, to see an episode of classroom cheating from the viewpoint of the boy who cheated, the boy who was pressured into helping him cheat and the teacher responsible for disciplining the classroom – represents a giant step forward in co-operative social interactions.

Social perspective-taking has its own progressive stages; for example, 3- to 6-year-olds seldom acknowledge that another person can interpret the same situation differently from the way they interpret it, whereas 7- to 12-year-olds can view their own ideas, feelings and behaviours from another person's point of view and realize that other people can do the same in regard to them. As we shall see, social perspective-taking enters into the discussion of a number of psychopathologies, including conduct disorder (Chapter 10) and borderline personality (Chapter 17), but most especially autism (Chapter 5) in which the absence of social perspective-taking is so profound that the child fails to comprehend the fact that other people have mental states, thus lacking what is termed a *theory of mind*.

Egocentrism makes its last childhood stand in early adolescence. Piaget assumed that times of cognitive transition are times when primitive modes of thought are apt to reappear. One aspect of egocentrism may be expressed as *self-consciousness*; if someone laughs on the bus while the adolescent boy is fumbling to find the correct change for the fare, he is certain that he is being laughed at. Another aspect of the adolescent's egocentrism is the belief that ideas alone will win the day and that his or her ideas hold the key to solving the world's problems – if only the world would listen!

Cognitive Delays and School Failure

Whereas formal operations are considered a characteristic of adolescence, not all youths achieve this advanced stage of reasoning. In fact, children with severe cognitive delays may not even progress to concrete operations. There are also learning-disabled children with different learning styles that interfere with their ability to fulfil their potential and achieve in school (see Chapter 7). The child's general level of cognitive functioning has important implications for his or her functioning throughout development. School failure figures prominently in discussions of psychopathology. Both the future delinquent and the future schizophrenic might be variously described as disruptive and inattentive in class, defiant and truant, for example, while the devaluing of achievement in school is an important factor determining drug use in adolescence (see Chapter 12).

Cognitive Distortions

The social information-processing model we encountered in Chapter 1 also provides leads about how cognition can influence psychopathology. When solving social problems, children go through a series of steps: encoding social cues, interpreting those cues, searching for possible responses, deciding on a particular response from those generated and, finally, acting on that response (Crick and Dodge, 1994). The second step of cue interpretation involves the important psychological process of *attribution*. An attribution is an inference about the causes of behaviour. Dodge's thesis is that in disturbed children the cognitive process is either distorted or deficient. Aggressive children, for example, are predisposed to attribute malicious intent to the behaviour of others even when such behaviour is benign or accidental. This distorted appraisal is termed a *hostile attribution bias*. We will return to this concept when we discuss aggression in Chapter 10.

Emotional Development

The development of emotions has important implications for our understanding of both psychopathology and normalcy. Although emotions have important adaptive functions, they also might have maladaptive consequences when emotions are not integrated with other systems of development. (Here we follow Izard et al., 2006, except where otherwise noted.)

Emotion Expression

A number of processes are involved with emotional development, one of which is *emotion expression*. At the very beginning of life, the newborn is capable of displaying a wide variety of emotions, including interest, smiling, disgust and pain. As early as 2 or 3 months of age, infants exhibit sadness and anger, whereas fear emerges at 6 or 7 months. With increasing cognitive advances after the first year of life, children are able to express more complex emotions such as contempt, shame, shyness and guilt. The emergence of emotion expression is highly influenced by caregivers. Infants directly imitate their caregiver's affect and caregivers, in turn, selectively reinforce the infant's facial expressions.

By 10 to 12 months of age, the role of emotional expression is increasingly social and has an important function in organizing behaviour. The 1-year-old judges the meaning of events through studying the caregiver's emotional reaction to them, a phenomenon known as *social referencing*. For example, in a classic study, Klinnert and her colleagues (1983) placed infants on a 'visual cliff', a glass sheet underneath which a vividly patterned chasm appeared. The mother stood on one side of the cliff and beckoned the infant to crawl across to her. When the mothers beckoned with a smile, almost all of the infants crossed the cliff, whereas when mothers displayed a fearful expression, none of the infants ventured out.

As children progress through the second year of life, emotional expression becomes increasingly stable and integrated with cognitive development. In the third year, as self-awareness and representational thought emerge, we begin to see the emergence of *self-conscious emotions*, such as shame, guilt, embarrassment and pride (Tracy et al., 2007). Preschoolers evaluate their performance and react emotionally to success and failure, appearing to experience pleasure or dissatisfaction not just with the task, but with *themselves*.

In middle childhood, children demonstrate an increasing capacity to determine the *social appropriateness* of emotional expressions and to suppress or disguise their emotional reactions when the situation and social standards warrant. For example, when given yet another used video game at her birthday party, the 10-year-old is better able to smile nonetheless and say thank you than the 5-year-old would be. True to stereotype, research suggests that adolescence actually does bring with it an increase in emotional intensity and ability. Larson and Richards (1994) asked adolescents and

their parents to carry pagers and to report their emotions when beeped at random intervals throughout the day. Adolescents were five times more likely to report being 'very happy' than their parents but were also three times more likely to report being 'very unhappy'. While adolescents' emotions were more extreme, they were also more fleeting, suggesting that teenage moodiness is real. On the other hand, their cognitive development provides adolescents with awareness of the social impact of their emotional displays as well as increasing skill at managing them, allowing youths to suppress affects when they might harm relationships or to communicate feelings when they might enhance connections with others (Saarni, 2006).

Emotion Recognition

Klinnert and colleagues' visual cliff experiment also reveals the emergence of another important process in emotional development, that of *emotion recognition*. Children scan the faces of their caregivers in order to obtain clues about the meaning of events going on around them: is it safe or is it dangerous? Young children often look to the emotional expressions of those around them to interpret even the children's *own* internal experiences: take, for example, the toddler who takes a fall and, depending on whether the parent's affect expresses alarm or calm, either begins to cry or blithely goes on playing. Emotion recognition plays an important role in the development of healthy social relations and is a prerequisite for the acquisition of empathy and prosocial behaviour.

Emotion Understanding

Nowhere is the interplay between cognitive and emotional development as important as in the emergence of children's *emotion understanding* (Dunn, 2000). A crucial task for development is to be able to identify, understand and reason about emotions in oneself and others. Emotion understanding is central to development in the individual context, including the self-concept, and has a central place in interpersonal and moral development, including the emergence of empathy and social competence. Just as emotional expression comes under increasing conscious control over the course of development, the older child is able to reflect on and understand her or his emotions with greater complexity and depth. For example, the school-aged child understands that it is possible to experience more than one emotion at a time ('double-dip feelings', Harter and Whitesell, 1989), that emotions arise out of specific situations and that the same experience might evoke different emotions in different people.

Emotion Regulation

Emotion regulation, also termed *affect regulation*, is the ability to monitor, evaluate and modify one's emotional reactions in order to accomplish a goal (Gross, 2010). Emotion regulation requires the capacity to identify, to understand, and, when appropriate, to moderate one's feelings. Emotion regulation might involve *inhibiting* or subduing emotional reactions; for example, children might breathe deeply or count to 10 in order to calm themselves in the face of distressing feelings. But emotion regulation also may involve *intensifying* emotional arousal in order to meet a goal. For example, children might 'pump up' their anger in order to gather the courage to stand up to a fearsome bully; or children might enhance positive emotions by recalling or re-enacting a pleasant experience. In essence, emotion regulation allows the child – in the words of one child client – to be 'boss of my own self'.

Parents contribute to children's emotion regulation skills by responding sensitively to children's distress and keeping affect at tolerable levels so that it is manageable (Kopp, 2002). Over the course of development, children are able to take over these regulatory functions themselves in order to engage in *self-soothing* and regulation of their own affect. As with other forms of self-regulation, the functions that children initially rely on parents to provide become internalized so that the child is able to perform those skills for himself or herself.

Emotion Processes and Developmental Psychopathology

Inaccurate Emotion Expression, Recognition or Understanding

In our discussions of the psychopathologies, we will encounter children who have deficits in some of the basic emotion functions. For example, with autism (Chapter 5) children may express emotions inappropriately and fail to accurately read and understand them in others. In other cases, the child's ability to develop emotion recognition skills is hampered by a social environment that offers mixed or unclear signals, as we will discover in our discussions of insecure attachment (Chapter 6) and maltreatment (Chapter 14). In other cases, children may hold distorted beliefs that colour their ability to interpret emotions in others, as is the case in conduct disorder (Chapter 10). Consequently, when the development of emotion expression, recognition or understanding goes awry, we will see a major effect on psychological adjustment.

Emotion Dysregulation

A pre-eminent risk mechanism in emotional development is poor emotion regulation (Keenan, 2000). Emotion regulation can go awry in two ways: through *under-regulation* or through *over-regulation*. In other words, the inability to express one's feelings can be as problematic as the inability to control them. Whereas under-regulation is related

Dysregulated emotion.
© Rebecca Ellis

to externalizing disorders associated with poor impulse control, acting-out and aggressive behaviour, over-regulation may be related to the development of internalizing problems associated with anxiety, depression and internal distress.

Emotion regulation is an essential component of many forms of psychopathology that we will discuss. For example, emotion regulation is central to coping with anxiety as well as a key to moderating anger so that it does not give rise to aggression. Similarly, the child's ability to control extreme states of negative and positive emotional arousal allows peer relations to go smoothly. Consequently, we will encounter the concept of emotion regulation in our review of the literature regarding several manifestations of psychopathology, including depression (Chapter 9), conduct disorder (Chapter 10), eating disorders and substance abuse (Chapter 12), as well as the consequences of maltreatment (Chapter 14).

As we noted previously, parent–child relationships play an important role in scaffolding the child's ability to manage upsetting emotions. However, increasingly over the course of development children need to be able to become self-reliant and govern their own emotions in settings where their parents are not available to help them, such as in school and in the peer context. Perhaps the best window into this process – by which children shift from reliance on parents to internalized emotion regulation – is provided by the construct of parent–child attachment.

Attachment

We do not usually think of radical behaviourism and classical psychoanalysis as compatible points of view but, when it comes to parent–child attachment, it seems they are. Both of these perspectives assume that human infants form affectionate ties with their caregivers secondary to those caregivers meeting the child's biological needs. The parent who provides for the infant's primary necessities, such as food, becomes associated with the positive feelings that result from being fed. In essence, this is a classical conditioning paradigm: food is an unconditioned reinforcer that is paired with the presence of the caregiver. After a number of such pairings, the caregiver comes to be associated with positive feelings and acquires the properties of a conditioned reinforcer.

However, research on primate behaviour suggests that there is a fundamental need for affection that is independent of other biological drives and may even supersede them. The pre-eminent examples of this are the classic experiments conducted by Harry Harlow (1958). Harlow demonstrated that infant macaque monkeys raised in isolation preferred a soft terry-cloth-covered 'mother' to the wire-mesh 'mother' that fed them. While experiments such as Harlow's certainly are not conducted on human infants, in Chapter 6 we will explore the effects of deprivation of care such as is suffered by children who are raised in bleak, impersonal institutions.

Attachment Theory

Attachment theory originates with Bowlby (1982a, b), who took an ethological perspective on human behaviour. Bowlby argued that, given the extreme helplessness of the human infant, it is highly adaptive to remain in close contact with the caregiver early in life. By attaching to the caregiver, the child is assured of safety, food and, ultimately, survival.

Thus, the 'set-goal' of attachment is to maintain proximity to the caretaker. The child's behaviour is organized around this goal and is designed to enhance the probability that the relationship with the caretaker will be a strong one. The attachment system becomes activated by distress, either in the form of internal needs, such as hunger, or external stressors, such as danger.

Stages of Attachment

The development of attachment follows a series of clearly identifiable stages over the first three years of life. (Our review follows Kobak et al., 2006, and Cassidy and Shaver, 2008.) Newborns arrive in the world oriented towards and responsive to other people. By 2 weeks of age they prefer the human voice over other sounds, and by 4 weeks they prefer the mother's voice over any other. In the second month, eye contact is established and precursors of attachment are seen as the infant orients towards the caregiver and signals his or her needs. During the next phase, from ages 3 to 6 months, infants begin to express and elicit delight in human interaction through the *social smile*. The fact that adults go through all kinds of antics to elicit such a smile shows just how adaptive and valued this behaviour is, as it assures not only that a strong attachment will be formed but that it will be reciprocal. Between the sixth and nineth month, infants increasingly discriminate their own caregiver from other adults and reward this special person with a *preferential smile*. Both *separation anxiety* and *stranger anxiety* signal that the infant is aware that the caregiver has a unique value and function. From 12 to 24 months of age, crawling and walking allow children to regulate their closeness or distance to the caregiver. *Proximity-seeking*, also known as safe base behaviour, is seen as infants turn to the caregiver for comforting, assistance, or simply 'emotional refuelling'.

Around 3 years of age, the goal of attachment expands beyond the infant's safety and comfort and becomes more reciprocal. In the preschool years, attachment is oriented towards establishing a *goal-directed partnership* with the caregiver, in which the needs and feelings of both participants in the relationship are taken into account.

Patterns of Attachment

Our understanding of variations in attachment relationships has been advanced by the work of Mary Ainsworth and her colleagues (1978). Ainsworth began by observing infants and their mothers in Uganda and noticed that there were distinct differences in the quality of their relationships. Back home in Boston she set up a laboratory for conducting observations of parents and infants. Her observations allowed her to identify three types of attachment relationships that have held up well over 30 years of research, with the more recent addition of a fourth pattern.

First, however, we should understand the ingenious method that Ainsworth developed in order to study attachment. So as to activate the attachment system without unduly distressing the infant, Ainsworth created a protocol called the *Strange Situation*. The laboratory itself is a new and truly strange situation for the child and, first, the parent and child spend time together there while the investigator observes the quality of their interaction. Of particular interest is how the child uses the mother as a source of security in the presence of a new person and as a secure base from which to explore the unfamiliar toys. Subsequently, the mother is asked to leave the room and the infant's reaction to her departure is observed, as is the child's ability to settle and engage in play in the mother's absence. The most powerful variable in determining attachment, however, is how the child responds to the mother when being reunited after a separation. Next, we take a closer look at these four variations in attachment.

Secure Attachment

Securely attached infants explore the environment freely and interact well with the unfamiliar adults when in the caregiver's presence. They may be distressed by separation and, if so, will protest and limit exploration in the caregiver's absence. Upon reunion, they greet the caregiver positively and seek contact with her, are readily soothed and can return to play after a period of emotional refuelling. Cross-cultural research shows that between 56 and 80 per cent of infants in normative samples are securely attached (van IJzendoorn and Sagi-Schwartz, 2008).

The caregiver's behaviour is marked by *sensitivity* to the infant's needs. Specifically, the caregiver correctly reads the infant's signals and responds quickly, appropriately and with positive affect.

Insecure-Avoidant Attachment

In cases of **avoidant attachment** the infants seem to be precociously independent. They do not seem to rely on the caregiver for security when she is present, exploring the room very independently and responding with equal interest to the parent or the stranger. They react minimally to the caregiver's absence, sometimes not even looking up from their play as she leaves. Upon reunion, these infants avoid proximity with the caregiver; they may turn away, avoid eye contact and ignore her. Although they appear indifferent, physiological measures show that they are in fact distressed. With the exception of some samples where it is rarely seen, such as Israeli kibbutzim and Javanese children, around 16 to 28 per cent of infants in cross-cultural research show this avoidant pattern (van IJzendoorn and Sagi-Schwartz, 2008).

The caregiver's behaviour is marked by *distance* and an absence of comforting combined with irritability and anger during closeness. Avoidance is believed to be the infant's attempt to cope with the parent's need for distance by keeping a low profile and suppressing emotional displays that might trigger parental rejection (Main and Weston, 1982).

Insecure-Resistant Attachment

In contrast with the avoidant infants, those with **resistant** (also called ambivalent) **attachment** are preoccupied with the caregiver. They tend to be clingy and inhibited from exploring the room or interacting with the stranger even when the caregiver is present. They are highly distressed by separation but, upon reunion, angrily resist attempts at closeness and are not easily soothed. They respond to the mother with an ambivalent pattern of proximity-seeking and rejection. For example, they may demand to be picked up and then angrily push the caregiver away, or cling to her while arching away and refusing to accept her caresses. The percentage of infants from normative samples showing this resistant pattern varies widely cross-culturally, from 6 per cent in Northern Europe, to 12 per cent in the USA, to as many as 37 per cent of Israeli kibbutzim (IJzendoorn and Sagi-Schwartz, 2008).

The caregiver's behaviour is marked by *unpredictability* – the caregiver is excessively close at some times and uninvolved or irritable at others. Resistance is viewed as infants' attempts to capture the attention of the caregiver, while anger results from the frustration of inconsistent care.

Insecure-Disorganized Attachment

The fourth category, which was added more recently to the typology, is the **disorganized**

attachment pattern (Main and Solomon, 1986). Disorganized infants act in an inconsistent or odd manner. They may have a dazed expression or wander around aimlessly or seem to be fearful and ambivalent in the presence of the caregiver, not knowing whether to approach for comfort or avoid for safety. If they seek proximity, they do so in distorted ways such as approaching the caregiver backwards, or suddenly freezing and staring into space. Unlike infants with avoidant and resistant attachments, these infants do not seem to have developed a consistent strategy for dealing with the caregiver.

The caregiver's behaviour is marked by the use of *confusing cues*, such as the caregiver's extending her arms to the infant while backing away. Caregivers of disorganized infants also are observed to behave in strange and frightening ways. Disorganized attachment, therefore, appears to represent a collapse of any kind of systematic strategy in the face of an unpredictable and threatening environment (Lyons-Ruth and Jacobvitz, 2008). In a meta-analysis of 55 studies including over 4000 children, a team of international researchers confirmed that the risk for attachment disorganization is highest in maltreating families (Cyr et al., 2010).

To summarize, the quality of the caregiving relationship – whether it is warm and reliable or erratic and harsh – influences the kind of attachment that will develop. If parents are sensitive in their caregiving, if they are alert to the infant's needs and react quickly and appropriately, the infant is more likely to develop a *secure* attachment. A securely attached infant responds positively to his or her caregivers and, because of their consistency, is confident they will be there when needed. Such infants develop a loving, trusting relationship. Closeness does not result in dependency and clinging, however; on the contrary, securely attached infants explore the environment confidently. Well-cared-for infants are also apt to develop a positive self-image and confidence in their ability to cope successfully with problems as they arise. There is evidence, for example, that the securely attached infant becomes the effective problem solver as a toddler and the flexible, resourceful and curious preschooler who is enthusiastically involved with school tasks and peers (Weinfield et al., 2008). Thus, through their experiences with the caregiver, children develop a schema about relationships and about the self in those relationships. This **internal working model** of attachment acts as a template or guide for the child's interpersonal behaviour and expectations of the self and other (Bretherton and Munholland, 2008).

Transactional Processes

It is important to examine attachment relationships in the context of a host of other relational variables that affect the parent–child bond and interact with one another over time. Take, for example, child temperament. The child with a difficult temperament is negative, unpredictable and difficult to read, which might impede even the best-intentioned parent's ability to provide sensitive care. On the other hand, the child who is securely attached expresses positive affect and responds positively to the parent's discipline techniques, setting off a positive chain reaction in which both parent and child are increasingly rewarding to one another (Cummings and Cummings, 2002).

Therefore, attachment should not be regarded as a quality inherent in the parent or the child, but as the product of *transactions* that change over time. Thus, the patterns of attachment are not permanently fixed nor are they due exclusively to the parent's contribution to the relationship. While the various kinds of attachment show stability, for example, they also may change, especially as environmental conditions change. Or again, whereas there is a relation between attachment security and sensitivity of caregiving, there is still room for the influence of other variables such as infant temperament, parenting style, and socio-economic and cultural variables (Kobak et al., 2006).

Continuity of Attachment over the Lifespan

Many short-term longitudinal studies have provided evidence that the quality of infant attachment is related to functioning in preschool, middle childhood, adolescence and even into adulthood. (These studies are reviewed in Cassidy and Shaver, 2008.)

Recently, a number of prospective longitudinal studies have emerged that explore the question of whether attachment is continuous over the lifespan. These data are impressive and virtually unprecedented in the developmental psychopathology literature. For example, Sroufe and colleagues (2005) conducted a study spanning over 20 years, in which they investigated the relationship between attachment in infancy and adult functioning in a sample of children born to at-risk mothers. Although these investigators found consistency across time points, the results of other studies do not concur.

However, the fact that attachment at time 1 does not predict attachment at time 2 is not necessarily evidence against the validity of attachment theory. What we need to look for is whether attachments are merely discontinuous or whether they show *lawful discontinuities* – that is, do attachment relationships change with circumstances in ways that attachment theory would predict (Kobak et al., 2006)? For example, one prospective longitudinal study found no continuity in attachment patterns from infancy to adulthood. However, changes in attachments were linked in 'lawful' and predictable ways to negative interpersonal events, such as maternal depression and family adversity (Weinfield et al., 2000). In another example, Lewis and colleagues (2000) assessed attachment patterns at 12 months and 18 years of age but also investigated other dimensions of family functioning in the intervening period. Whereas attachment classifications at 1 year and 18 years were not continuous, parental divorce during childhood was predictive of insecure attachment in late adolescence. In other words, the loss of a secure family environment was associated with the development of a less secure internal working model of attachment, as the theory would suggest.

Cross-Cultural Diversity in Attachment

An impressive body of research has investigated the validity of the attachment construct in diverse cultures, including several African countries, Canada, China, Columbia, Germany, Indonesia, Israel, Japan, the Netherlands, Puerto Rico, Sweden, the

UK and the USA. On the side of universality, investigators find the same patterns of attachment across samples and are able to link attachment security to sensitive caregiving and good child adaptation, as attachment theory would predict (van IJzendoorn and Sagi-Schwartz, 2008). However, on the side of cultural diversity, evidence suggests that the proportion of children in each of the classifications differs across societies, as we have noted.

Differences in attachment may be in keeping with cultural styles of caregiving. For example, in Japanese samples, when children are rated insecure, it is almost always with the resistant type; the avoidant type is rarely seen. Presumably, this occurs because in Japanese culture, where young children rarely attend day care, mother–child togetherness is emphasized to the extent that the child would react with outrage to the unexpected and unwelcome event of her leaving (Dennis et al., 2002). A similar finding emerges in studies of infants among the Dogon tribe of West Africa, who are breast-fed until their second year and thus typically remain in very close proximity to the mother, where the Strange Situation appears to be a highly rather than a mildly stressful experience (see van IJzendoorn and Sagi-Schwartz, 2008).

In addition, as Rosen and Rothbaum (2003) point out, the meaning that is associated with child attachment behaviours might vary as a function of culture. For example, in their research in Japan, they find that parents view autonomy and self-assertion in young children as a sign of developmental immaturity. Therefore, the investigators argue, attachment researchers must be careful not to impose Western ideals of self-reliance and self-sufficiency on other cultures nor assume that these behaviours are universally signs of a secure attachment.

Attachment Processes and Developmental Psychopathology

It is important to remember that the patterns of attachment described previously represent variations in *normal* patterns of the parent–child relationship. Insecure attachment is not equivalent to psychopathology. However, as we will review in detail in Chapter 6, a wealth of research suggests that a secure attachment starts the child off on the right road in life, while insecure attachment increases vulnerability to the development of disorder. Therefore, rather than viewing insecure attachment as psychopathology, attachment relationships are viewed as a *general* risk associated with a host of psychopathologies, including the entire spectrum between internalizing (e.g., Colonnesi et al., 2011) and externalizing (e.g., Allen et al., 2007) problems.

Risk Mechanisms Associated with Insecure Attachment

Let us take a closer look at the mechanisms by which insecure attachment increases the risk for psychopathology.

Insecurity   The affective heart of attachment is *felt security* (Cassidy, 2008). Our evolutionary history has programmed infants to associate proximity to the caregiver with safety and security and separation from the caregiver with danger and anxiety. The child whose parent reliably provides the child with such security instils in the child the belief that the interpersonal world is a trustworthy place and the self is lovable. As Erikson's theory suggests, basic trust is an important prerequisite to healthy social and psychological development. (See Chapter 1.)

Inhibited Mastery Motivation   Whereas motor skills enable the toddler physically to explore the environment, attachment makes it possible for the child to explore from a secure emotional base. With a home port to return to, the child may venture out while being confident that, in times of danger, distress and fatigue, the caregiver will be available for protection and comfort. In contrast, insecurely attached infants either are hesitant and uncertain or defensively avoidant of the environment, thereby depriving themselves of many learning opportunities (Schölmerich, 2007). This willingness to engage with and explore the world is linked to **mastery motivation**, the child's drive to interact with the environment for the intrinsic satisfaction of learning about it. Thus, through affecting exploration and mastery motivation, insecure attachment deflects the child from a healthy path of cognitive and emotional growth.

Emotion Dysregulation   The ability to rely on the caregiver as a secure base allows the child to cope successfully with the stresses and frustrations of childhood. Even when the parent is absent, the child can call on the image of the loving caregiver to soothe himself or herself. In early childhood, when children are still developing their representational skills, a physical prop can help; for example, to ease a preschooler's distress at her leave-taking, a sensitive mother may leave her keys with the child if his or her favourite cuddly blanket is not available. As we have seen, over the course of early life, children who have experienced secure attachments are increasingly able to internalize the caregiver's comforting functions, modulate their own emotions, and cope self-sufficiently and autonomously with stressful situations (Allen and Miga, 2010).

Internal Working Models   As symbolic skills develop, the young child internalizes the attachment relationship in the form of an *internal working model*. The model represents not only an image of the caregiver as loving, but also of the self as lovable and love-worthy. Like any other schema, the internal working model reflects past experiences and guides expectations as to future intimate relationships. Thus, for example, the preschooler with a secure attachment will tend to be open and trusting; one with an avoidant attachment will tend to be guarded and standoffish; and one with a resistant attachment will tend to be clingy, demanding and petulant – not just with the caregiver, but with other adults and children (McElwain et al., 2003). Transactionally speaking, these behaviours are likely to bring about just the kind of negative relationship that the insecurely attached child expected. In each case past experiences with caregiving have left their imprint on the children's mental life, and this imprint produces different expectations concerning what future close relations will be like and, consequently, different interpersonal behaviour. In later life internal working models of self and other

play a part in the quality of friendships (Berlin et al., 2008) and adult romantic partnerships (Feeney, 2008).

In sum, attachment involves core affective and cognitive variables in both the intrapersonal and interpersonal contests. It is therefore reasonable to assume that, if the process goes awry, the child's development might be at risk for being diverted from its normal course. Given the importance of attachment relationships to the child's core sense of identity, we turn next to the development of the self.

Self-Development

As we turn from attachment to the development of the self-system, remember that the internal working model of attachment is a model not only of the relationship with the caregiver, but of the self. Over the course of childhood, children develop increasingly complex and differentiated models of the self and of relationships. Through their interactions with caregivers, children develop a sense of who they are and what value is placed on their unique personhood and qualities. As the philosopher George Herbert Mead (1932) suggested, 'Selves can only exist in definite relationship to other selves' (p. 285).

The Emergence of Self

Sroufe (1990) defines the self as 'an inner organization of attitudes, feelings, expectations, and meanings' (p. 281), which arises in the context of the caregiving relationship. The emergence of self over the course of childhood is characterized by increasing organization and increasing agency, as the child becomes a more active participant in the process of development, a process proceeding through a series of phases over the course of childhood.

In the first 6 months of life (the *pre-intentional self*), infants become increasingly socially interactive and aware of their surroundings. They are dependent on their caregivers to modulate states of arousal and provide them with regulation of their inner states. However, they also begin to adapt their behaviour to that of their caregivers and can respond to complex patterns of interaction, resulting in mutual delight.

During the next stage, from 6 to 12 months (*the intentional self*), infants are more intentional and goal directed in their behaviour and can now coordinate, initiate and direct exchanges with the caregiver. For example, the infant now engages in a greeting response (smiling, cooing, bouncing and raising both arms) at the sight of the caregiver while showing negative reactions to strangers. Towards the end of this stage, as we know from attachment research, the infant's emotions, cognitions and social behaviour are organized around the caregiver and the caregiving relationship.

From ages 12 to 24 months (*the separate, aware self*) toddlers increasingly actively pursue their own goals and plans, even when these are contrary to the caregiver's. They initiate separations both physically and psychologically, practising their independent skills, while still orienting around the caregiver as a 'safe base'. This phase marks a development shift toward the emergence of self-awareness and agency, the self as the author of its own actions.

The next period, from ages 24 to 60 months (*the self-monitoring self*), is marked by a new level of awareness of both self and other. This change is ushered in with the capacity for representational thought as well as an increasing ability to modulate and regulate their own emotions and behaviour. These symbolic capacities allow the child to recognize internal states in the self and others as well as the boundaries between them. For example, not only are children aware of their own plans and intentions, but they are aware that the caregiver is aware of their plan and has opinions about it. The most important attainment here is a sense of **self-constancy**, the recognition that the self is an organized whole that 'goes on being' even with shifts in mood and in the relationship with the caregiver.

These processes of internalization, stability and self-directedness continue to direct self-development over the next years of life. Middle childhood, according to Sroufe, is the era of the *consolidated self*, as the child's internal working model leads to consistency in representations of self and other. In adolescence, we see the emergence of the *self-reflective self*, as formal operations allow the youth to observe and reflect on his or her own perspectives and capacities.

At the core of self, in Sroufe's perspective, is ownership of one's own experience. The mechanism by which children learn that they are the authors of their own actions is *internal regulation* of emotions and behaviour. In other words, children initially develop a sense of self through experiencing their actions as effective or ineffective in managing internal and external demands and maintaining equilibrium. 'The core of self', states Sroufe, 'lies in patterns of behavioral/affective regulation, which give continuity to experience despite development and environmental change' (Sroufe, 1990, p. 292).

Self-Regulation

As we have seen, normal development involves the increasing organization and self-directedness of behaviour. In short, the child is increasingly in his or her own driver's seat and able to initiate and regulate behaviour and emotions. **Self-regulation** is defined as the exercise of control over oneself, which involves efforts to regulate one's own inner states or responses, including thoughts, feelings, impulses, desires or attention (Carver and Scheier, 2010). Thus, children who are self-regulated are intrinsically motivated, not requiring parents to control and structure their behaviour. They are also able to make independent choices and think for themselves without being unduly vulnerable to peer pressure.

Self-regulation has two components: *emotion regulation*, which we introduced previously, and *behavioural self-regulation* or *effortful control* (Eisenberg et al., 2010). Place an attractive toy in front of a young child and say, 'Now don't touch until I come back', and you will see how difficult it is for children to control their impulses and delay gratification. Self-regulation emerges in the second year of life and is observed when children display self-control and act socially appropriately even in the absence of parental monitoring. In the preschool years, the child's representational capacities allow for increasingly adaptive and flexible self-regulation.

The origins of self-control
© *Elizabeth Crews*

Language development assists this process, enabling children to engage in self-talk to cope with temptation. For example, it is not unusual to see the young child look at the desirable toy and repeat aloud the adult's prohibition ('Mustn't touch!'). Over the course of childhood, the capacity for effortful control is related to a number of aspects of competence, including positive social, emotional and behavioural development (Eisenberg et al., 2003). In turn, as Jucksch and colleagues (2011) find in their laboratory in Germany, a pattern of severe self-dysregulation in children is associated with a history of psychosocial adversity and underlies the development of significant impairments in behavioural and emotional functioning. Althoff and colleagues (2010) found the same effect in a longitudinal study of 2076 Dutch children ages 4 to 16 followed every two years for 14 years. Behavioural dysregulation in childhood was associated with increased rates of anxiety, depression, disruptive behaviour, and substance abuse in adulthood.

Self-Concept

Self-concept comprises two components. The first of these concerns the *content* of the self-concept (e.g., 'What am I like?'). The second involves *valence*, that is whether those self-perceptions are positive or negative (e.g., 'Do I like who I am?'), also termed *self-esteem* or *perceived competence*. Children's self-concept emerges through a series of stages that parallel their cognitive and emotional development.

Development of the Self-Concept

Infancy and Toddlerhood (Our review follows Harter, 2012, except where otherwise noted.) The infant's dawning recognition of self arises out of experiences of effectiveness in the world: I smile and people smile back; I cry and the food I need appears. Thus, in the earliest years the infant's sense of self is termed the *self-as-agent*. By 2 years of age, children respond with recognition to their reflection in a mirror and are able to pick themselves out of an array of photographs. Perhaps the clearest expression of a sense of self is evident during the 'terrible twos' when the toddler asserts his or her own wants, needs and opinions in sometimes strident tones.

Preschool In the preschool years, generally viewed as ranging from ages 3 to 5, children's conceptions of self are focused on concrete observable characteristics such as their physical appearance ('I'm tall'), play activities ('I play baseball'), preferences ('Pizza is my favourite food') or possessions ('I have a bike'). This is the time of the *behavioural self*. These concrete descriptors represent discrete behaviours rather than higher-order categories (e.g., 'I can run really fast' does not generalize to 'I'm good at sports'). Thus, the self-concept of the preschool child is not organized in a particularly logical or coherent way, and contradictory evaluations of the self can coexist quite comfortably. Further, young children are likely to evaluate themselves in unrealistically positive ways, confusing their hopes and desires with their actual competencies. Children at this age also engage in all-or-none thinking about the self, based on the affective states they are experiencing at the moment ('I'm always happy'; 'I'm never scared').

Cognitive limitations also make it difficult for children to understand that they can experience two different feelings at the same time, a phenomenon termed affective *splitting* (Fischer and Ayoub, 1994).

Early to Middle Childhood   Children aged 5 to 7 still show some of the characteristics of the early stage, including a tendency towards unrealistically positive self-perceptions (e.g., 'I can also throw a ball real far; I'm going to be on some kind of team when I am older. I can do lots of stuff real good. Lots! If you are good at things you can't be bad at things, at least not at the same time. I know some other kids who are bad at things, but not me!' [Harter, 2006, p. 381]). All-or-nothing thinking persists in the form of thinking in terms of opposites and *over-differentiating* – that is, a child whose learning disability results in low achievement may come to the conclusion that she is 'all dumb'. In middle childhood, children's self-descriptors focus on specific competencies and skills they have mastered. These now begin to be interrelated and organized into general categories, but these tend to be compartmentalized on the basis of positive and negative valence, and the child still cannot integrate both positive and negative attributes with one another. Although before middle childhood children do not have a general self-concept, they do differentiate two sources of self-esteem, one deriving from being socially acceptable; the other from being competent.

Middle to Late Childhood   By age 8 to 11, children's concepts of self involve generalizations that integrate a number of characteristics of the self (e.g., 'I'm pretty popular, at least with the girls. That's because I'm nice to people and helpful and can keep secrets' [(Harter, 2006, p. 348]). In late childhood, children view the self not in terms of observable behaviours they perform but in terms of personality characteristics they hold – this is the *psychological self*, which is increasingly stable and integrated. The new ability to form higher-order concepts allows the school-age child to develop a representation of his or her overall self-worth. In addition to a *global* sense of self-esteem, children evaluate themselves in terms of three specific areas of competence: *academic, physical* and *social*. From middle childhood on, self-evaluation is also closely related to behaviour: academic self-esteem predicts school achievement, curiosity and motivation to take on challenges, while social self-esteem is related to confidence with peers. In this period, children also engage in *social comparison*, evaluating their competencies and worth in comparison to others'.

Adolescence   The formal operational skills of adolescence allow the youth to think about the self in increasingly abstract and multifaceted terms based on not only what is but what could be. This is the *abstract, future-oriented self*. The adolescent's representational abilities also can be a source of vulnerability, as egocentricity and increasing self-consciousness lead adolescents to become preoccupied with what (they assume) others must be thinking of them (e.g., 'I'm an extrovert with my friends. I'm talkative, pretty rowdy, and funny ... I can be an introvert around people I don't know well. I'm shy, uncomfortable, and nervous. Sometimes I act really dumb and say things that are just plain stupid. Then I worry about what they must think of me, probably that I'm a total dork. I just hate myself when that happens' [Harter, 2006, p. 391]). In adolescence, the self also becomes more complex as, in addition to the global, academic, physical, and social dimensions of self-concept, adolescence brings the additional areas of *close friendship, romantic appeal* and *job competence*. However, whether any of these areas affect general self-worth depends on their *salience* or importance to the youth. Making all As or being good-looking may mean everything to one youth but be a matter of indifference to another. Consequently, while children with low self-worth believe they are incompetent in areas that are important to them, children with high self-worth can tolerate perceiving themselves as less competent in areas that are unimportant to them. For example, African American youths who perceive their school achievement to be devalued may cope by simply de-identifying with the academic domain and minimizing its importance (Wong et al., 2003). Thus, how the self is valued depends on the discrepancy between the *real self* – how one believes one is – and the *ideal self* – how one feels one should be.

Identity

Although the process of self-concept formation is ongoing throughout childhood, Erikson (1950) proposed that in adolescence the youth confronts a crisis of *identity versus identity confusion*. As confirmed by more recent work on this topic by the Norwegian researcher Jane Kroger (2007), the youth who has successfully navigated this process is termed *identity achieved*. Adolescents in this category have explored their options and developed a coherent sense of identity and are more socially mature and motivated to achieve than their peers. However, the identity formation process might go awry in different ways. One relates to *precocious* development (see Chapter 1): the youth who precipitously declares an identity without exploring the options is termed *identity foreclosed*. Research shows that foreclosed youths are rigid and authoritarian in their attitudes. Another deviation relates to *developmental delay*: youths who are confused and uncertain about their identity and are making no progress toward establishing one are termed *identity diffuse* and tend to be socially isolated, unmotivated and attracted to substance abuse. In contrast, youths who are in *moratorium* are engaged in actively exploring their options but have not yet made a commitment to any of them. Whereas they are also likely to have experimented with drugs and show some anxiety, they also are high in self-esteem.

Ethnic Identity

Another important task in the process of identity formation is the inclusion of ethnicity into the self-concept. Ethnic identity involves not only membership in an ethnic group and participation activities related to one's ethnic heritage, but also attitudes involving ethnic pride and perceiving one's ethnic-

ity as central to one's sense of self (Phinney, 2003). By around age 7, children identify themselves as a member of their ethnic group and by about 10 they understand that their ethnicity is constant (Marks et al., 2007). Parents and community members make an important contribution to children's understanding of and pride in their culture; however, as youth enter the adolescent years, they are increasingly aware of prejudice and racism in the society around them (Szalacha et al., 2003). Ethnic minority youths also might experience conflict between their family's values and those shared by their peers from the dominant culture. For the growing population of immigrant families around the world, *acculturative stress* may be present when children struggle to adapt to a culture that is much different from that of their parents. (See Serafica and Vargas, 2006.)

Research on ethnically diverse samples also raises an important question as to whether the identity status presumed to be ideal in Western society is a culturally specific one. Youths who are raised in cultures that emphasize maintaining traditional values, such as a communal or familial orientation, might not aspire to the same kind of individual identity formation that characterizes Erikson's ideal. Research confirms that youth in cultures as diverse as India (Graf et al., 2008) and Sweden (Stegarud et al., 1999) are disproportionately represented among those classified as identity diffused and foreclosed. However, for these young people it may be adaptive to commit themselves early on to membership in a cohesive, supportive community rather than undergoing a long process of self-discovery or estranging themselves by attempting to individuate in a Western fashion which clashes with their own culture's values.

The task of identity formation is complex for ethnic minority and immigrant youth. It involves forging an identity that incorporates a sense of the self as a member of a unique subgroup as well as a member of the larger culture. Some research supports the notion that the achievement of a *bicultural identity* is associated with the best psychological health (Vargas-Reighley, 2005). For example, ethnic self-esteem was found to buffer youth from the effects of ethnic discrimination in a sample of over 2600 Turkish, Moroccan, Surinamese and Dutch youth in the Netherlands (Verkuyten and Thijs, 2006), just as strong cultural involvement was found to buffer Latino adolescents from negative effects of acculturation stressors in the USA (Smokowski et al., 2009).

Ego Development and the Self

In Chapter 1, we described the evolution of psychoanalytic theory from its early focus on primitive drives to its more modern attention to the adaptive aspects of the person. Two legacies of ego psychology have proven especially helpful to our attempts to understand psychopathology of the self. The first concerns the concepts of ego resilience and ego control. The second concerns the development of ego defences.

Ego Resilience and Ego Control

To set the stage, let us imagine the scene that Jeanne and Jack Block created in their own developmental laboratory. To assess individual differences in children's response to challenge, they brought a series of young children into their laboratory and presented them with a puzzle to solve that was beyond the child's developmental level. One group of children gave up easily: some with indifference, some with tears and others with rage. Yet other children persisted at the task despite their frustration and inability to solve it. Some persisters demonstrated a grim, driven style, repeating the same strategy over and over despite its ineffectiveness, while others displayed a scientist-like curiosity and creative problem-solving style. At the end of the day, some children appeared dejected and some angry, while others declared the study 'fun'.

To explain these individual differences, the Blocks proposed the constructs of ego resilience and ego control (Block and Block, 1980). **Ego control** refers to the degree to which individuals give free expression to their impulses; and, at moderate levels, it is associated with spontaneity, emotional expressiveness and socially appropri-

ate behaviour in research conducted in the USA, France (Hofer et al., 2010) and Sweden (Chuang et al., 2006). In addition, children higher in ego control also appear to be more resilient in the face of maltreatment (Cicchetti and Rogosch, 2009). However, as has been shown in a series of longitudinal studies conducted in the Netherlands, at extreme levels, children who are ego overcontrolled are inhibited, reluctant to express their feelings, and vulnerable low self-esteem and peer victimization (Overbeek et al., 2010). In turn, ego undercontrol is related to conduct problems in children and adolescents (Kim et al., 2009; Van Leeuwen et al., 2004).

Ego resilience, in contrast, is defined as 'resourceful adaptation' to a changing environment (Block and Block, 1980). Ego resilient individuals are able to analyse situations and flexibly choose from an array of strategies the problem-solving approach that best fits the circumstances. In contrast, *ego brittleness* involves inflexibility and 'an inability to respond to the dynamic requirements of the situation, a tendency to perseverate or become disorganized ... when under stress, and a difficulty recouping after traumatic experiences' (p. 48). Research has linked ego resilience to lower emotional and behavioural problems and better adaptation to school in the transition from childhood to adolescence whereas ego brittleness is related to childhood disorders such as anxiety and depression (Chuang et al., 2006; Overbeek et al., 2010).

Ego Defences

Freud stated that internal conflicts can become so painful that we develop strategies to defend ourselves against awareness of them. For example, one such defence mechanism is **repression**, in which both the dangerous impulse and the ideas and fantasies associated with it are banished from consciousness. In essence, the child says, 'What I am not aware of does not exist'; for example, a girl who is frightened of being angry with her abusive mother no longer is aware of such feelings after repression. If repression is insufficient, **reaction**

formation might be called into play so that the child thinks and feels in a manner diametrically opposed to the anxiety-provoking impulse. Continuing our example, the girl now feels excessively loving toward her mother and would not dream of being angry. In **projection**, the forbidden impulse is both repressed and attributed to others; the little girl might be upset that 'all of the other girls' she knows are sassy and disrespectful to their mothers. In **displacement**, the impulse is allowed expression but is directed towards a different object; for example, our little girl becomes angry with her babysitter.

The danger of defence mechanisms is that they might distort an individual's perceptions of the self, the other or reality in general. The child who represses her hostility towards her parents is as convinced as if, in reality, the relationship were an unusually blissful one. If defence mechanisms prevent reality testing by protecting the child from facing his or her fears, are they then inherently pathological? Not so, said Anna Freud (1965), who extended her father's work on the understanding of defence mechanisms. Defences are a necessary and normal part of psychological development. The healthy child can use defences flexibly, relying on them to manage a particularly painful episode in development but relinquishing them when they are no longer needed. When defences become *rigid*, *pervasive* and *extreme* and when the child's repertoire is unduly *limited*, defences are in danger of jeopardizing future growth.

Recently, research has documented the emergence of the defence mechanisms over the course of development, from preschool to adulthood (Cramer, 2009) and across different levels of psychological maturity in adolescents and adults (Bond, 2004). Taken together, this research suggests that defences can be construed along a *developmental continuum*, ranging from those that are primitive – and associated with poor adaptation if used exclusively and rigidly – to those that are mature and associated with high adaptive levels. This continuum is represented in the Defensive Functioning Scale, one of the Axes Provided for Further Study in DSM-IV-TR (APA, 2000). (See Table 2.2.) Defences at the *high adaptive level* are those that allow for a balance between conflicting thoughts and feelings and maximize their access to conscious awareness. An example of an adaptive defence is humour, which allows a person to acknowledge something painful without being devastated by it. At the *low adaptive level* are those defences that interfere with the child's perception of objective reality, such as psychotic denial.

Self-Processes and Developmental Psychopathology

To summarize, a number of aspects of self are implicated in psychopathological development.

Low Self-Esteem

A *negative self-concept* is a risk mechanism for a number of disorders, most obviously depression and suicide. The child who perceives himself or herself as defective, unworthy or unable to achieve the cultural ideal is vulnerable to feelings of sadness, hopelessness and futurelessness. A poor self-concept may also be the product of societal attitudes, such as racism, homophobia or religious intolerance. Disturbances in self-esteem may take the opposite form as well. Some disturbed children evidence unrealistically *high* self-esteem, claiming that they are the 'best at everything' (Baumeister et al., 2000). However, in contrast to normal, healthy self-esteem, exaggerated self-importance tends to be brittle and easily threatened (Witt et al., 2010).

Identity Confusion

As we have seen, youths who have difficulty resolving the crisis of identity are more vulnerable to risk in adolescence. For many youths, this process also involves the task of incorporating ethnicity and/or sexuality into the identity concept. One form identity confusion takes is a lack of *self-continuity*, when youths 'lose the thread that tethers together their past, present, and future' (Chandler et al., 2003, p. 2). As we will discuss in Chapter 9, such youths are highly vulnerable to suicide.

TABLE 2.2 DSM-IV-TR Defensive Functioning Scale and Definitions of Defences

> 1 **High adaptive level**: allowing conscious awareness of feelings and ideas and promoting a balance between conflicting motives
>
> **Humour** – emphasizing the amusing or ironic aspects of a conflict or stressor
>
> **Sublimation** – channelling potentially maladaptive feelings or impulses into socially acceptable behaviour
>
> 2 **Mental inhibitions or compromise level**: keeping potentially threatening ideas and feelings out of awareness
>
> **Isolation of affect** – separating ideas from the feelings originally associated with them
>
> **Repression** – expelling disturbing wishes, thoughts or experiences from conscious awareness
>
> 3 **Minor image-distorting level**: distorting one's image of self or others in order to allow one to maintain self-esteem
>
> **Devaluation** – attributing exaggerated negative qualities to others in order to minimize their importance
>
> **Omnipotence** – perceiving self as being superior to others in order to fend off feelings of vulnerability
>
> 4 **Disavowal level**: keeping unpleasant or unacceptable impulses, ideas, affects or responsibility out of awareness
>
> **Denial** – refusing to acknowledge some painful aspect of external reality or subjective experience
>
> **Projection** – falsely attributing to another one's own unacceptable feelings, impulses or thoughts
>
> 5 **Major image-distorting level**: creating gross misattributions or distortions in the image of self or other
>
> **Projective identification** – falsely attributing to another one's own unacceptable thoughts or feelings and behaving in such a way as to engender in the other person those very thoughts or feelings
>
> **Splitting** – compartmentalizing positive and negative experiences in order to block one side of ambivalence from awareness
>
> 6 **Action level**: dealing with stress by acting or withdrawing
>
> **Acting out** – giving vent to conflicts through action in order to avoid experiencing upsetting feelings
>
> **Passive aggression** – presenting a facade of overt compliance that masks covert resistance, resentment or hostility
>
> 7 **Defensive dysregulation**: using defences involving a pronounced break with objective reality
>
> **Delusional projection** – forming a fixed delusional belief system revolving around one's own projections
>
> **Psychotic denial** – engaging in extreme denial of perceived external reality resulting in gross impairment in reality testing

Source: Adapted from *DSM-IV-TR*. Copyright 2000 American Psychiatric Association.

Disruptions in Self-Organization

Whereas identity confusion represents a delay in normal development, lack of self-organization is a severe deviation from the norm that is associated with some of the most serious psychopathologies we will cover in this text.

Disruptions in self-organization are associated either with profound mental illnesses, such as autism and schizophrenia, or with extremes of pathological caregiving. For example, as we saw earlier, severely traumatized adolescents with disorganized attachment histories lack a cohesive sense of self (Lyons-Ruth, 2008). Instead, their self-image vacillates with their moods and they have difficulty maintaining the boundaries that separate themselves and others – in other words, they have trouble recognizing where the self ends and others begin. These youths also engage in the use of primitive defences that distort their perceptions of self and other. Such disruptions in self-organization are associated with the development of borderline personality disorder, a deviation in self-development that we will describe more fully in Chapter 15.

Ego Brittleness

In Chapter 1, we introduced the concept of resilience, the remarkable ability to emerge as a psychologically healthy individual despite negative circumstances. The concept of ego resilience describes protective factors that are incorporated into the self. The ego resilient youth is able to 'play a bad hand well', while the ego brittle youth has rigid defences, lacks adaptibility and is discouraged by obstacles rather than challenged by them.

Poor Self-Regulation

Another accomplishment of normal development is the ability to regulate one's own behaviour, emotions and relationships with others. When this process goes awry, the child is highly reactive, impulsive and unable to adapt smoothly to changing environmental demands. One of the important developmental processes that contributes to self-regulation is the *internalization* of parental values. Internalization and self-regulation are also directly related to another important developmental task, moral development; we will next turn to that topic.

Moral Development

Under the heading of moral development, we are integrating research on a number of different themes, including conscience, guilt and moral judgement. In particular, we are concerned with the question of how children come to *internalize* their parents' values and teachings. Over the course of development, children's prosocial behaviour comes to be governed less by fear of punishment and more by self-generated moral standards and ideals. First, however, we should look at how children's reasoning about right and wrong progresses as a function of their cognitive development.

The Development of Moral Reasoning

Elaborating on Piaget's (1932) earlier work on children's thinking about moral issues, Lawrence Kohlberg constructed a theory of the development of moral reasoning. By presenting children with classic moral dilemmas, such as that of Little Hans, who must decide whether it is right to steal to provide his mother with life-saving medication, Kohlberg determined that children's moral judgement advances through a series of stages (Kohlberg, 2008).

At the *pre-conventional* level, during the early preschool years, children evaluate actions in terms of whether they lead to pleasure or punishment.

Those resulting in rewards are good; those resulting in punishment are bad. ('He better not or the store owner might get mad at him.') During the *conventional* morality stage, in middle childhood, the child adopts the conventional standards of behaviour to maintain the approval of others or conform to some moral authority such as religion. Thinking is absolutist and inflexible – right is right, wrong is wrong, and there are no extenuating circumstances or mitigating considerations. ('It is wrong to steal; it's the law.') In the *post-conventional* or principled stage, older children and adolescents judge behaviour in terms of the morality of contract and democratically accepted law, of universal principles of ethics and justice, and of individual conscience, holding themselves personally accountable for moral decisions. ('Some things have a higher priority than others – like human life is more important than money. So saving his mother's life is more important than obeying rules about property.') Between 6 and 16, the pre-conventional level gradually declines while the other two levels increase, although only about one-quarter of 16-year-olds achieve the highest level.

One of the shortcomings of research on moral reasoning is that it is not always predictive of moral behaviour. Therefore, children's ability to think in sophisticated ways about hypothetical dilemmas is not necessarily linked to the choices they make in real life. Some youths, as we will see in Chapter 10, are perfectly aware of the higher moral principles that they 'should' follow, and yet they behave otherwise. What differentiates children who behave prosocially or antisocially is more than a matter of cognition; it also involves emotion – particularly the emotions of guilt and empathy. Before we explore the role of these emotions, let us look at the context in which they emerge: the parent–child relationship.

Internalization

Ultimately, the goal of socialization is that children be guided not merely by concern for external rewards and punishment but rather that they come to *internalize* parental values and therefore be intrinsically motivated to behave in prosocial ways.

Internalization leads directly to the development of *conscience* and therefore is an important developmental process underlying moral behaviour. In short, through the process of internalization, morality comes to be something that is intrinsic to the self, not something imposed from without.

Kochanska and Aksan's (2007) line of research on internalization teaches us a great deal about the process by which behavioural regulation is transferred from the parent to the child over the course of development. The standard scenario is to expose the child to temptation – to provide the child with opportunities to cheat on a task or to ignore a parental command or prohibition – and to observe how the child behaves in the parent's absence. Internalization is inferred when the child complies with parental expectations even when the parent is not there to monitor his or her behaviour. (See Fig. 2.2.)

The first stage in the process of internalization is *committed compliance* – that is, rather than complying solely on the basis of the immediate consequences of behaviour, the child appears to share the parent's values and to be as committed as the parent to the goal of good behaviour. The committed child not only behaves appropriately without prompts and reminders, but does so enthusiastically. Research confirms that committed compliance is a precursor to internalization: committed compliance in toddlerhood predicts internalization and self-regulation in the preschool years (Kochanska and Aksan, 2006).

Kochanska and colleagues' research also reveals the qualities of parenting that are most likely to foster internalization. First, observations show that *shared positive affect* is key. Committed compliance is related to shared positive affect between parents

FIGURE 2.2 Internalization, 'For Better or Worse'.

and children during free play in the laboratory, presumably via increasing the child's motivation to share the parents' values and goals. Second, internalization is related to a quality of *mutual responsiveness* between parent and child (Aksan et al., 2006). Mutual responsivity is a transactional process in which children who experience their parents as responsive and caring respond in kind by showing consideration for the parents' feelings and wishes. Over time, mothers who engage in mutually responsive relationships with their toddlers have less need to be directive and controlling when the children are preschool age, and in the school-age years their children are less likely to give in to the impulse to cheat (Kochanska et al., 2008).

Kochanska's research points to the importance of the quality of the parent–child relationship for moral development. When the relationship is marked by parent sensitivity and responsiveness – qualities that are also related to a secure attachment – the child is motivated to please the parent as well as to adopt the parent's goals and values. Thus, love plays a role in morality. Three other emotions come into play and deserve our attention: shame, guilt, and empathy.

Emotional Dimensions of Morality: Shame, Guilt and Empathy

The Emergence of Shame and Guilt

In our previous discussion of emotional development, we mentioned that self-conscious emotions emerge after the third year of life. Among these are the two emotions of shame and guilt. While the terms are often used synonymously, research shows that they have different origins and functions. The experience of *shame* is other oriented, focusing on public disapproval and involving a negative evaluation of the entire self (e.g., 'I'm bad'). In contrast, *guilt* is inner oriented, focusing on failure to meet one's own internalized standards and involving a negative evaluation of the behaviour (e.g., 'I did a bad thing') (Tracy et al., 2007).

Again, parental socialization is key. Parents who are *coercive* – that is, those whose reprimands focus on children's failures and make the children feel badly about themselves – are likely to produce children who are prone to experiencing shame, whereas parents whose discipline calls children's attention to the effect they have on others are likely to help engender guilt. While guilt might sound like an unpleasant emotion from which we would want to spare the child, in fact it is linked with prosocial behaviour and consideration for others. In contrast, shame is linked to antisocial behaviour and destructiveness (Tracy et al., 2007).

An integrative study by Kochanska and colleagues (2002) establishes the links among parenting, self, guilt and moral development. In their laboratory, children were observed after having been told that they had damaged a valuable toy – in fact, the experimenters had rigged the toy to fall apart as soon as the child handled it. Children whose self-concepts were more developmentally advanced at 18 months displayed more guilt for their 'transgression' at 22 months of age and, in turn, engaged in more prosocial behaviour and exhibited higher levels of moral reasoning at 56 months. Coercive maternal discipline was related to lower levels of guilt in children; however, the relationship was a curvilinear one: the highest levels of guilt were displayed by children whose mothers were either very high or very low in coerciveness.

Empathy

Empathy refers to an emotional reaction to another's experience. A distinction is often made between *empathic concern*, which involves caring about others' welfare and being motivated to help them, and mere *empathic distress* (Hoffman, 2010). For example, if two children observe another child crying, the empathically concerned child may ask what is wrong, whereas the empathically distressed child may simply start crying as well. As early as 6 months of age children respond to emotional distress in peers, but it is not until the preschool years that children display true empathy, in which they clearly distinguish their own experience from the other person's (Siegler et al., 2003). Research shows that empathy in children evokes feelings of guilt which, in turn, motivate prosocial behaviour (Kochanska et al., 2009a).

Research also shows gender differences in the emergence of empathy over the course of childhood. Generally, at every age, girls score higher on measures of empathy (Brody and Hall, 2008). However, there are also gender-related differences related to the *recipient* of empathy. For example, Endresen and Olweus (2001) found that as boys approach adolescence, they tend to become increasingly more empathic towards females. The authors suggest that sex-role socialization comes into play, because an acceptable part of masculinity entails being protective and caring towards females but not towards other males.

Moral Processes and Developmental Psychopathology

Relational Deficits

The context in which all the dimensions of morality previously described develop is a caring relationship. When caregivers are harsh and unresponsive, children have little motivation to comply with their expectation or to internalize their parents' values. Similarly, children who experience shaming forms of discipline grow to be deficient in empathy and the appropriate guilt that motivates prosocial behaviour. In Chapter 10, we will describe a possible exception to this, a group of children whose callousness towards others does not appear to be a product of poor parenting practices.

Cognitive Deficits

Children who are not able to reason about moral problems are likely to respond merely on the basis of immediate rewards and punishments. Social cognitive variables we discussed earlier are important to understanding how moral judgement results in prosocial or antisocial behaviour. Children who engage in distorted cognitions about others may perceive their own aggression not as bad behaviour but as justifiable self-defence – even as an act of heroism (Caprara et al., 2001).

Cultural Expectations

Cultural expectations also come into play. As we will discuss in Chapters 10 and 14, children growing up surrounded by brutality learn that this behaviour is normative and acceptable. Societal forces also arise in the form of sex-role stereotyped expectations for the display of such qualities as kindness, caring and empathy in males and females.

Let us now turn to look in greater detail at the developmental variables of sex and gender.

Sex and Gender

First, some terminology is in order. While *sex* and *gender* are both used to refer to biological maleness or femaleness, the child's awareness of his or her sex is called **gender identity**. In addition, society prescribes which behaviours and feelings are appropriate for boys and which are appropriate for girls, and children must learn such appropriate **gender-role** behaviour. Finally, *sexuality* involves sexual feelings and behaviour, while **sexual orientation** refers to the choice of partner, whether same or other sex.

Gender Identity

The typical 2- to 3-year-old male child has grasped the idea that 'boy' applies to him, and he can correctly answer the question 'Are you a boy or a girl?' However, he does not comprehend the real meaning of the label, nor has he grasped the principle of categorizing people by sex, relying instead on external cues of size, clothing and hairstyle (Blakemore et al., 2008). Remember that preschoolers are still cognitively in the preoperational stage, literally believing what they see, so their categorizations by sex are on the basis of manifest differences. Because children of this age are incapable of conservation (understanding that objects remain the same even when their appearance changes), they also believe that as appearances change so do essences – things that look different are different. Consequently, for a child this age it seems perfectly possible for boys to change into girls and vice versa just by altering their clothes, hairstyle and behaviour to that of the other sex. To the boy in our third vignette in Chapter 1, it seems perfectly possible for a child to grow up to be a 'mummy' or a 'daddy' regardless of his or her present status. Only around age 6 or 7, when conservation is cognitively possible, do children achieve **gender constancy**, grasping the idea that gender is permanent and immutable. They also come to realize that the genitals are the crucial factor determining gender.

Gender Roles

Every society prescribes behaviours and feelings appropriate and inappropriate to males and females.

Traditionally in Western society, boys should be dominant, aggressive, unsentimental, stoic in the face of pain and pragmatic; girls should be nurturing, sociable, non-aggressive and emotionally expressive. The essential differences between these prescriptions for the masculine and feminine role have been defined as *agency* versus *communion* (Block, 1983). Despite changes in the roles of men and women in Westernized societies, gender stereotypes have remained remarkably consistent over the past three decades (Cook and Cusack, 2010). Children as young as 3 years of age can classify toys, clothes, household objects and games according to social stereotypes; and preschoolers do the same with adult occupations. As thinking becomes less concrete and more inferential in middle childhood, children are able to associate gender roles with more subtle psychological characteristics such as assertiveness and nurturance.

In addition to knowing the stereotypes, very early in development children also show a preference for engaging in gender-stereotypical behaviour. Children aged 2 to 3 prefer stereotyped toys (trucks for boys, dolls for girls) and would rather play with same-sex peers (Ruble et al., 2006). In middle childhood boys increasingly prefer gender-typed behaviour and attitudes, while girls shift to more masculine activities and traits. This is an example of boys being more narrowly gender-typed than girls. 'Sissies' are teased, whereas 'tomboys' are tolerated.

Social learning theorists point to the many ways culturally prescribed gender-typed behaviour is reinforced. For example, fathers play more vigorously with their infant sons than with their infant daughters. In the toddler and preschool periods boys receive more physical punishment, are rewarded for playing with gender-typed toys and are encouraged to manipulate objects and to climb. In middle childhood parents interact more with the same-sex child. Also, boys are reinforced for investigating the community and being independent, while girls are supervised more and rewarded for being compliant. In general fathers are more narrowly stereotyped in their behaviour than are mothers, which is one reason boys are punished for deviations more than girls are (Lamb, 1997). Finally, both teachers and peers, in numerous overt and subtle ways, exert pressure on children to conform to social stereotypes.

Sexuality

Our understanding of normal childhood sexuality is surprisingly limited (Sandfort, 2000). Since Freud first opened the Pandora's box of childhood sexuality, many have expressed shock and discomfort with the idea of the child as a sexual being. Moreover, it has been difficult for us to arrive at an understanding that is based on empirical research. If parents are uncomfortable with the idea that children have sexual feelings, they are hardly likely to allow them to participate in a study that enquires about these. Childhood sexuality is not only sensitive to study but methodologically difficult. Children's capacity to understand their private experiences is limited, as is their ability to put those experiences into words. And even young children are aware that certain topics are not appropriate for discussion with a strange adult. However, an understanding of normative sexual development is valuable to us. Sexual feelings are a part of life and a motivator of behaviour. Further, as we consider the continuum between normal and abnormal development, we will want to know what sexual behaviours in a child are signs of psychopathology and which are part of normal childhood sexual exploration.

For example, age-inappropriate sexual knowledge is often used as evidence that a child has been molested. Therefore, it is important to know what children of various ages normally understand about sex (Friedrich et al., 2001). Before the age of 4 girls tend not to have a specific term for their genitalia, referring generally to that entire region of their body as their 'bottom'. Before the age of 7 children generally do not report a sexual function for their genitalia beyond a vague notion that 'babies are made there'. It is only by the age of 9 that children normally begin to associate procreation with the sex act. Volbert (2000) conducted one of the rare studies of young children's knowledge of sexuality by interviewing a sample of 147 2- to 6-year-old children in Germany. Until the age of 5, no children demonstrated knowledge of adult sexual behaviour, and only three of the older children described overtly sexual actions, the most knowledgeable boy revealing that he had seen this activity in a movie.

Children's understanding of sexuality also is a function of their level of cognitive development. True to Piaget, children will transform the facts they are taught to fit with the schemas they already have. Therefore, when children provide wild explanations about where babies come from, Bernstein and Cowan (1975) argue, the source may not be misinformation but the process of assimilation at work on information that is too complex for the child to understand. Children's knowledge about sex also varies across cultural contexts, determined by norms for adult openness about sexual matters and how accessible sex-related information is to children.

Other research focuses on what kinds of sexual behaviours children display in the course of normal development. Curiosity about their own and others' genitals is quite common in children in the pre-school years, notes the German researcher Schuhrke (2000). Beginning in the second year, children look, play with, expose and comment on their bodies, and invite caregivers to do the same, while the object of their interest begins to shift from parents to peers in the school-age years. Sandfort and Cohen-Kettenis (2000) asked a group of Dutch mothers about the behaviours they observed in their own children, including 351 boys and 319 girls ranging in age from 0 to 11. Mothers reported that 97 per cent of children touched their own genitals, 60 per cent played 'doctor' with friends, 50 per cent masturbated, 33 per cent touched others' genitals, 21 per cent displayed themselves to others, 13 per cent drew sex parts, 8 per cent talked about sex acts and 2 per cent imitated sexual behaviour with dolls. A number of these behaviours increased in frequency across the child's age, whereas some were more common in boys (e.g., masturbating) and others in girls (e.g., sex play with dolls).

Cross-cultural research also suggests, as we might expect, that differences in cultural attitudes and socialization of sexuality are related to children's sexual behaviour. For example, in a comparison of parent reports obtained regarding Dutch and US preschoolers, Friedrich and colleagues (2000) found a consistent pattern of parents reporting higher levels of sexual behaviours in the Netherlands, consistent with the more accepting attitudes about sexuality in Dutch society.

Despite the interest children show in learning about sex throughout development, normally it is not until adolescence that sexuality takes centre stage. *Puberty* ushers in dramatic changes in physiological maturation, with an onset ranging from 8 to 13 years for girls and 9 to 14 for boys. For reasons that are not fully understood, in recent decades the age of puberty onset has been decreasing in Western and developing countries, particularly among girls. The effects of nutrition, health status and socioeconomic advantage generally have been suspected as the explanation. However, a team of international researchers reviewed data suggesting an increase in sexual precocity for youth migrating from non-deprived developing countries. The investigators propose instead that a complex interaction among genetic, endrocrinological and environmental factors may be implicated, including the effects of hormone-dysregulating chemicals in the environment (Parent et al., 2003).

Ideally, for those youth who reach full sexual maturity in their teens, new biological urges arrive in tandem with the advances in cognitive, emotional and social development that will allow them to successfully navigate the stage-salient issues of adolescence. In turn, youths whose sexual development is premature, whether spurred on by precocious hormones or inappropriate sexual stimulation, will not be ready to face the complex challenges and responsibilities of burgeoning adult sexuality (Gaffney and Roye, 2003). Ultimately, in late adolescence sexuality is part of the questions 'Whom can I love?' and 'With whom can I share my life?' and the search for a physically and psychologically fulfilling relationship with another person.

Sexual Orientation

The issue of sexual orientation is bound up in important ways with the process of identity development that we described earlier. Although some gay, lesbian, bisexual and transgendered youths report having known their orientation from an early age, it is in adolescence that most grapple with the question of whether to confirm or closet these feelings and whether to incorporate them into their image of 'who I am'.

Estimates of the proportion of youth who identify themselves as gay, lesbian, bisexual or transgendered are hard to obtain reliably. This not only is because studies generally are conducted on small convenience samples rather than representative populations, but also because the definitions of what constitute sexual minority status are inconsistent and may not correspond to participants' own categorizations. In particular, many youth acknowledge same-sex attractions and behaviour without identifying themselves as homosexual. For example, the most recently published results from the Youth Risk Behavior Study (Pathela and Schillinger, 2010), which involved over 17000 high school students in New York City, indicate that among the 6.9 per cent of boys and 11.9 per cent of girls who have had sex with same-sex partners, 38.9 per cent reported that they considered themselves 'heterosexual or straight'.

Overall, the US National Longitudinal Survey of Adolescent Health finds that approximately 6 per cent of boys and 15 per cent of girls identify themselves in some way other than strictly heterosexual (Savin-Williams and Ream, 2007). Among these youth, 3.2 per cent of boys and 10.7 per cent of girls described themselves as 'mostly heterosexual'; 2.4 per cent of boys and 3.8 per cent of girls identified as bisexual, mostly homosexual or homosexual; and approximately 0.5 per cent of boys and girls stated that they were attracted to no gender. Moreover, over the course of the six years that youth were followed in the study, there were significant shifts both towards and away from same- and other-sex attractions and behaviour, a phenomenon known as 'sexual fluidity' (Diamond, 2008). However, in general, the prevalence rates in this US sample are similar to those obtained in cross-cultural research in Norway, New Zealand, Australia, Great Britain and Thailand (Savin-Williams and Ream, 2007).

The process of sexual minority identity development has been studied by Savin-Williams (2001), who conducted a series of interviews with youth who identified themselves as gay, bisexual or transgendered. The first step, *recognition*, involves the realization that one is different, sometimes accompanied by feelings of alienation and fear of discovery. On average, youths come to label themselves as gay, lesbian or bisexual around 15 to 18 years of age. Recognition is followed by a phase of *test and exploration*, marked by ambivalence and curiosity. The third phase is *acceptance*, which is evidenced by a positive attitude and openness about one's sexual orientation. The final stage, *integration*, involves a firm commitment to a sexual object choice, accompanied by pride and open identification with one's community.

Not all individuals progress through all the stages, particularly when negative attitudes in the larger culture make the process of coming out uncomfortable – or even dangerous. After revealing their sexual orientation, many sexual minority youth report feeling rejected by family members (Ryan et al., 2009) and bullied by peers (Birkett et al., 2009).

Gender and Sexual Processes Involved in Developmental Psychopathology
Exaggerated Sex-Role Characteristics

In Bakan's (1966) original formulation, healthy psychological development requires a balance between the opposite poles of *agency* and *communion*. The agentic, or masculine, side of human nature is competitive, aggressive and egocentric, while the communal, or feminine, side is empathic, altruistic and interpersonally oriented. Unmitigated agency, in Bakan's view, may lead to self-serving destructiveness. Unmitigated communality is problematic as well because it fails to equip the person to meet the developmental challenges of individuation. Assertiveness, a sense of self-esteem and a willingness to defend oneself when wronged all are essential to the development and protection of the self. Therefore, whereas agency must be tempered with considerations of 'mutuality, interdependence, and joint welfare', communality also must be amended to 'include aspects of agentic self-assertion and self-expression – aspects that are essential for personal integration and self-actualization' (Block, 1973, p. 515).

Bakan's theory suggests that a *hypermasculine* identification, an exaggerated notion that being unemotional and dominant in every situation is endemic to what it means to be a 'real man', might contribute to a propensity for antisocial behaviour. As we will see in Chapter 10 when we discuss conduct problems, this idea has garnered some support (e.g., Majors et al., 1994). Similarly, exaggerated notions of *femininity* might increase the risk of certain disorders, given that the individual's focus is on accommodating to others at the expense of the self. In Chapter 12, we will review evidence for the role of sex-role socialization and feminine identification in the development of eating disorders.

Precocious Sexuality

Mature sexuality involves not only physical intimacy, but also interpersonal sensitivity and self-understanding. Children who engage in sexual behaviour precociously – those whose cognitive, emotional and interpersonal development does not keep pace with their physical development or life experience – are at risk for maladjustment. We will encounter at least two examples of this: the increase in inappropriate behaviour associated with early maturation in girls (Chapter 10) and the negative effects of sexual abuse on children (Chapter 14).

Sexual-Minority Orientation

Gay, lesbian, bisexual and transgendered youths who are developing in a culture that is judgemental or hostile to their orientation may face additional stresses that affect the process of identity formation as well as family and peer relations (Meyer, 2003). Feelings of isolation and lack of acceptance may increase the risk of maladaptation in sexual-minority youth. For example, a group of researchers in the UK performed an exhaustive review of studies conducted in seven countries in North America, Europe and Australasia, and found that around the globe, gay, lesbian and bisexual youth have disproportionate rates of suicide and deliberate self-harm (King et al., 2008; see Chapter 9) and

substance abuse (see Chapter 12). Further research suggests that suicidal feelings and drug use among sexual minority youth are linked to perceived rejection and harassment, whereas a positive school climate and absence of homophobic teasing can buffer youth from these negative effects (Birkett et al., 2009).

Development in the Family Context

The Development of the Family

When we consider development, we often only think of it as relevant to children. However, all members of a family are in the process of development throughout the lifespan, as is the family as a system (McGoldrick and Carter, 2003). For example, at the first stage of the family life cycle, adults must individuate from their families of origin and form a new marital partnership. As children are born, the couple relationship must adjust to make room for these new members. Next, as children advance into the teenage years, the parent–child relationship must become more flexible in order to allow adolescents to move in and out of the family system. The next stage of family development involves launching children into the world as well as realigning the family in order to include children's significant others and in-laws and, ultimately, the grandchildren. The developmental tasks for parents at the stage of middle adulthood are complex because, just when their own children have achieved adult status, they often become caregivers to their own ageing parents.

Appreciation of family developmental processes suggests an important insight, that the parenting strategies that are most adaptive at one time in development (e.g., the close supervision of a 2-year-old) are not ideal at another stage (e.g., consider the average adolescent's reaction to such monitoring). Thus, parenting strategies must be flexible as well as developmentally sensitive. Let us take a look at the major dimensions of parenting that are implicated in healthy and pathological development.

Parenting Style

One of the most influential typologies of parenting style is the one developed by Baumrind (1991a, 1991b). She views two independent dimensions of parenting as essential: *warmth/support* and *control/structure*. By assessing parents on these two dimensions, she derives four parenting styles.

The **authoritarian parent** is high on structure but low on warmth; consequently, this parent is demanding, controlling and unreasoning. The implicit message is 'Do what I say because I say so'. If parents discipline in a punitive, rejecting manner, their children tend to become aggressive, uncooperative, fearful of punishment, and low on initiative, self-esteem and competence with peers. The **permissive/indulgent parent** is high on warmth without accompanying structure. This parent is undemanding, accepting and child centred, and makes few attempts to control. The result may be a dependent, irresponsible, aggressive, spoiled child. **Authoritative parents**, in contrast, are high on both warmth and structure. They set standards of mature behaviour and expect the child to comply, but they are also highly involved, consistent, loving, communicative, willing to listen to the child and respectful of the child's point of view. Their children tend to be self-reliant, self-controlled, secure, popular and inquisitive. Lastly, the **neglectful parent** rates low on both warmth and structure; consequently, this parent is described as indifferent, uninvolved or self-centred. Lax, unconcerned parenting is the breeding ground for antisocial behaviour. Self-centredness on the parents' part is associated with child impulsivity, moodiness, truancy, lack of long-term goals, and early drinking and smoking.

For example, Steinberg and colleagues (1994) used Baumrind's system to assess parenting style in families of over 4000 14- to 18-year-olds. Adolescents from authoritative homes were better adjusted than the others on measures of psychosocial development, school achievement, internalized distress and problem behaviours, while youths from neglectful families fared the poorest. Youths from authoritarian families were doing fairly well in school and were refraining from delinquency, but their self-concepts and self-reliance were poor. In turn, adolescents from indulgent homes engaged in misconduct, achieved poorly in school and abused drugs, but tended to perceive themselves positively. One year later, the investigators reassessed 2000 of the youths and found that differences accounted for by parenting style were generally maintained or even increased. Youths from authoritative homes continued to outshine their peers, while youths from authoritarian homes not only showed continued poor self-image but increasing internalized distress. Adolescents from indulgent homes presented a mixed picture. Although their self-concepts were positive, their school behaviour and achievement had worsened. Youths from neglectful families showed continued significant declines in functioning over the year, including disinterest in school, drug and alcohol use, and delinquency.

Although research conducted in white, middle-class US samples consistently shows that authoritative parenting is associated with the best child outcomes, the cross-cultural universality of this finding is called into question by research showing that in other cultures, authoritarian parenting also is associated with good child adjustment (Pomerantz and Wang, 2009). Thus, parenting style may need to be understood from within the perspective of a given culture and the ways in which that culture's values affect the goals of parenting and the child outcomes that are prioritized. For example, Chao (2001) argues that Chinese parenting involves an overarching goal of training children to become members of a collective society, a goal that requires not only control but also high levels of parental involvement that are not well captured by the concept of authoritarianism. By a similar token, culturally appropriate styles of conveying warmth may be demonstrated through the parent's high investment and support for the child's achievement rather than via the physical demonstrations of affection and unconditional acceptance that characterize Western samples. Thus, both structure and warmth are present in the parents' behaviour, but are expressed differently in the Chinese style of parental training.

Overall, when the constructs are evaluated in culturally appropriate ways, the cross-cultural comparisons conducted to date do suggest that controlling parenting in the absence of warmth is associated with more negative child outcomes in both collectivist and individualist societies (Chan and Koo, 2010; Sorkhabi, 2005). However, these effects may be moderated by the extent to which the parenting practices in question are culturally normative. For example, Lansford and colleagues (2005) interviewed mother–child dyads in China, India, Italy, Kenya, Philippines and Thailand, and found that corporal punishment was less strongly associated with children's aggression and anxiety in contexts in which this was perceived as a normative and accepted parenting strategy. In a subsequent cross-cultural study, Gershoff and colleagues (2010) found that it was children's perceptions of normativeness in particular that buffered the effects of harsh parenting on children's emotional well-being.

Parental Sensitivity

When we discussed attachment, we saw the importance of parental sensitivity to the child's signals, emotions and developmental needs. Sensitive parents engage in a careful choreography with the child, providing structure and guidance when needed and stepping back and allowing children the pleasure of doing for themselves those things that they have mastered. Following from the work of the Russian psychologist Vygotsky (1978), this process is known as *scaffolding*. Like the scaffold that is erected to support a building under construction, parental support should be available but non-intrusive, allowing the child to grow strong and resourceful under its protection – it would be a poor scaffold indeed that never could be removed without collapsing the building underneath. On the contrary, in Vygotsky's view, development is essentially a process of internalization in which the child is increasingly able to take over for himself or herself competencies that parents have scaffolded for them. For example, mothers' scaffolding of children's problem solving leads to greater self-regulation and competence (Neitzel and Stright, 2003).

Sensitive caregiving involves stimulation as well as comforting.
© Elizabeth Crews

Parent–Child Boundary Dissolution

According to Minuchin's (1974) family systems theory, clear boundaries in the family are crucial to healthy psychological development. While in Chapter 1 we described the pathological triangles that might result when children are inappropriately involved in the marital subsystem, here we will describe three forms of boundary problems that may arise in parent–child relationships. (Here we follow Kerig, 2005, and Kerig and Swanson, 2010).

Enmeshment

At the extreme end of boundary dissolution is *enmeshment*, characterized by a lack of acknowledgement of the autonomy or separate selfhood of the child. The enmeshed parent and child are 'two halves of the same person', at least as far as the parent is concerned. Children from enmeshed families exhibit increasing anxiety over the course of childhood (Sturge-Apple et al., 2010) and, as developmental theory would predict, children with enmeshed parent–child relationships have difficulty individuating in adolescence (Allen and Hauser, 1996). They also are more depressed in comparison with youths whose parents allow psychological autonomy (Jewell and Stark, 2003).

Intrusiveness

Intrusive, or *psychologically controlling*, parenting (Barber, 2002) is characterized by the parent who is overly controlling, not of the child's behaviour, but of the child's thoughts and feelings. In short, a psychologically controlling parent strives to manipulate the child's thoughts and feelings in such a way that the child's inner life will conform to the parent's wishes. The parent may use subtle techniques such as indirect hints, guilt induction and withdrawal of love to coerce the child into complying. Cross-cultural research including samples from 11 nations (including South Africa, Bangladesh, China, India, Bosnia, Germany, Palestine, Columbia and the USA) provides evidence that children of intrusive parents demonstrate problems in academic, social, behavioural and emotional adjustment (Bradford et al., 2003).

Role-Reversal

Role-reversal, also termed *parentification*, refers to a relationship in which a parent relies on the child for emotional support and care, rather than providing it (Jurkovic, 1997). A parent engaged in role-reversal may be ostensibly warm and solicitous, but the relationship is not a truly nurturing one because the parent's emotional needs are being met at the expense of the child's. Children who fulfil their parents' emotional needs exhibit more internalizing, behavioural and social problems in the early years (Jacobvitz et al., 2004; MacFie et al., 2005), as well as depression, anxiety, low self-esteem (Kerig and Swanson, 2010) and eating disorders (Rowa et al., 2001) in later development.

Spousification

Spousification occurs when a parent turns to a child for an adult-like intimate partnership that is inappropriate for the child's years (Jacobvitz et al., 1999). Longitudinal research shows that children of parents who engage in spousification are inattentive and overactive in kindergarten, violate boundaries with peers in middle childhood and exhibit more behaviour problems in adolescence (Shaffer and Sroufe, 2005). Spousification also might take a hostile form, when marital tensions spill over onto the parent–child relationship (e.g., 'You're just like your father!'). Research shows that parental hostile spousification is related to internalizing, externalizing and relational difficulties with dating partners among emerging adults (Kerig et al., in press).

Interparental Conflict and Divorce

Whereas in the early 1960s almost 90 per cent of US children spent their childhood in a home with two biological, married parents, the stereotypical nuclear family is a reality for only 40 per cent of those children today (Amato et al. 2007). Although less common than in the USA, rates of divorce also have risen among all European countries during this same period (Dronkers et al., 2006). Cross-cultural research confirms that children are negatively affected by family dissolution and are at increased risk for a variety of behavioural and emotional problems over the course of development, including low self-esteem, poor academic achievement, conduct problems and difficulties in interpersonal relationships (Amato and James, 2010) – including the dissolution of their own marriages (Wagner and Weiß, 2006). However, other investigators have noted that there is great diversity in children's reactions to parental divorce. For example, the majority of children cope with the stress of family disruption without developing significant mental health problems. Therefore, research needs to be directed towards uncovering the risk and resiliency factors that account for the variability in children's reactions (Hetherington, 2006).

Risk Factors for Children of Conflictual Marriages

Divorce is not a discrete event in the life of a child; it is the culmination of a long process. The majority of couples report years of marital acrimony leading up to the decision to divorce. The children, therefore, are exposed to significant levels of *interparental conflict*, sometimes even interparental violence. As we saw in Chapter 1, evidence is strong that children are affected by quarrelling between their parents even in the absence of divorce (Cummings and Davies, 2010) and that it is this conflict rather than the act of divorce per se that accounts for the deleterious effects on children (Kelly, 2003). Divorce even may benefit children when it results in relief from exposure to marital hostilities. However, counterintuitively, children are highly distressed by divorce when there have been *low* levels of interparental conflict during the marriage, presumably because the divorce is a surprising and unwelcome change in a family that seemed to the child to be 'not so bad' (Strohschein, 2005). Moreover, unfortunately, divorce does not necessarily bring an end to interparental conflict and may even increase it. The separation process itself brings up many heated issues (e.g., child custody, visitation, alimony and child support) that spark parental hostilities. Children may feel 'caught in the middle' when they are asked to take sides with one parent against the other, to inform parents of one another's activities, or to act as a messenger between parents who are not on speaking terms (Amato and Afifi, 2006). As we saw in our discussion of family systems theory in Chapter 1, this kind of *triangulation* is highly stressful for children. Exposure to these stressful family processes may last far longer than the divorce. For example, Maccoby and colleagues (1992) found that even as long as 31 years after their marriage ended, 26 per cent of the parents in their sample experienced ongoing hostilities.

Divorce also is accompanied by a number of *life stresses*: children may have to move, change schools, separate from friends, lose contact with grandparents and suffer many other disruptions. For the vast majority of children who live primarily with their mothers after divorce, it is a significant decline in economic circumstances that is observed across studies in the USA and Europe (Andreß et al., 2006; Sayer, 2006); in fact, divorce is one of the principal ways by which children enter poverty.

In addition, for many parents divorce represents a painful failure at one of life's most important accomplishments, that of sustaining a love relationship. All of the life changes and stresses that affect children are felt keenly by parents. Consequently, divorce is associated with a number of signs of *parental distress*, including depression, anxiety, irritability and substance use (Braver et al., 2006).

When parents' emotional difficulties spill over into the *parent–child relationship*, parents may become emotionally unavailable to children and their parenting skills may be disrupted, with subsequent negative consequences for children's development. Relationships between children and their fathers may be particularly vulnerable to these effects (Amato and Dorius, 2010).

Further complicating the picture, for many families divorce is merely a transitional stage in a process that leads to the formation of a new family. Step-families, also termed blended families, are common among those who divorce. For example, in the USA, approximately 69 per cent of women and 78 per cent of men will remarry after a divorce and many of these parents will bring children with them from a previous marriage; in fact approximately 12 per cent of children in the USA live in a household with a half-sibling or step-sibling (Sweeney, 2010). Unfortunately, it also is the case that these remarriages are highly vulnerable to dissolution as well and therefore the children will have the challenge of navigating multiple family transitions and resolving the ensuing ambiguity about who is still and who is not a member of their 'family' (Brown and Manning, 2009).

Protective Factors for Children of Conflictual Marriages

Despite the risks and emotional distress accompanying divorce, within two to three years most children are able to adapt successfully. What protective factors account for this? Hetherington and Elmore (2003) review the existing research and note that many of the *individual characteristics* related to resilience in other contexts also emerge as protective factors in studies of divorce: intelligence, easy temperament, and perceived competence. Young *age* may also be protective, particularly when parents remarry; whereas adolescents do not adapt easily to remarriage, younger children benefit from the return to an intact family structure. Children's own *coping strategies* also can serve to exacerbate or alleviate divorce-related stress. For example, children of divorce who use distraction or active coping strategies such as seeking social support demonstrate fewer internalizing or externalizing problems than those who cope through passive withdrawal. Further, as children approach adolescence, they increasingly are able to look outside the family to peers and other adults as sources of *social support*. Young people's finding prosocial support systems to turn to can be beneficial. However, many adolescents of divorce precociously seek independence and disengage from their families, increasing the risk of involvement in antisocial activities.

Just as parent–child conflict and poor parenting are risk factors for maladjustment, a *positive parent–child relationship* and *authoritative parenting* style can help to buffer children from family stress. Children in joint custody arrangements especially benefit when they are able to enjoy positive involvement with both parents. Finally, despite their difficulty in getting along with one another, many parents are able to set aside their differences when it comes to raising their children. Consequently, *co-parenting co-operation* buffers children from the negative effects of interparental conflict in both divorced and intact marriages. Informed by this research, and in an effort to increase co-parental co-operation and prevent children from being inveigled in interparental conflicts, many jurisdictions mandate that divorcing parents work with a mediator to resolve any potential custody disputes.

Single-Parent- and Grandparent-Headed Homes

It is increasingly being recognized that the term 'family' refers to a diversity of forms and members. The stereotypical 'nuclear family' comprised of a father, a mother and 2.2 children is far from the norm for many children around the world. Rising rates of divorce and teenaged pregnancy have resulted in an increase in *single-parent families*, most of which are mother-headed. Single-parent families are, on average, economically more stressed and the children are vulnerable to a number of negative behavioural and emotional outcomes (Sayer, 2006). Moreover, this is not the only

commonly seen alternative to the nuclear family. Grandparent-headed households are becoming increasingly prevalent; for example, the number of grandparents with sole responsibility for raising grandchildren has increased by 30 per cent in the USA in the past decade. Grandparents often step in when a parent dies, is incarcerated, loses employment, is too young to assume responsibility for child rearing or simply abandons the child to the grandparents' care. In our reviews of the disorders to come, we will be attendant to the risks associated with the financial and emotional stresses associated with single-parent- and grandparent-headed homes, but we also will be sensitive to the sources of resilience and strength that nonetheless can lead to positive development for children raised in these alternative family forms (Murry et al., 2001).

Yet another growing phenomenon is that of child-headed households, particularly among war-torn countries and the impoverished African nations that have been devastated by the HIV/AIDS epidemic (Richter and Desmond, 2008). Some of these children are caring for ageing and ill parents whereas others are orphans who have assumed responsibility for their younger siblings. Among these children, food security, social welfare grants and access to schooling help to buffer them from the significant effects of their traumatic lives on their psychological well-being (Cluver et al., 2009).

Maltreatment and Family Violence

Children do not need to grow up in an ideal family to emerge as psychologically healthy persons. The 'average expectable environment' (Cicchetti and Valentino, 2006) for infants includes protection and nurturance from adult caregivers, whereas older children require a supportive family as well as opportunities to relate to peers and master the environment. Families can meet those needs of children in a variety of ways without impeding their development, as long as the home environment falls within the range of expectable conditions. In contrast, home environments that are violent, abusive or neglectful fall outside this range and send the child on a pathological developmental course.

Maltreatment is implicated in the development of many of the psychopathologies that we will investigate (Cicchetti and Valentino, 2006) and is such an important issue that it will receive extensive coverage as a topic of its own in Chapter 14. Moreover, maltreatment can take many forms. Children do not have to be the direct victims of abuse in order to be negatively affected by family violence. Consequently, in Chapter 14 we will review research regarding the experience of children who are innocent bystanders to violence between the adults in the home.

Family Processes and Developmental Psychopathology

To review, in this section we have uncovered several processes by which family relationships may contribute to the development of psychological health or pathology: (1) overly harsh or lax parenting; (2) parental insensitivity; (3) inappropriate parent–child boundaries; (4) interparental conflict and family dissolution; and (5) victimization or exposure to violence in the home. Given its importance, in the chapters to follow we will many times return to consider the quality of the family context in which child development takes place.

Development in the Social Context

Peer Relations

Peer relations are a potent predictor of subsequent psychopathology (here we follow Parker et al., 2006). As with all of the aspects of development we discuss in this chapter, there are major milestones and transformations in peer relations that occur across the various ages of children's lives. An exploration of these developmental changes in the quantity, quality and context of children's peer relationships will help us to better recognize and understand patterns of maladaptation when they emerge.

Infancy to Preschool

From the very beginning of life, children show an emerging interest in their peers. Two-month-old infants are interested in looking at one another, and by 10 months of age there are more varied and sustained reactions expressed in mimicking, patting, hitting and imitating one another's laughter. By 15 months of age affection appears, and by age 2 increased locomotion and communication skills allow for mutual participation in games, although the toddler's short attention span and limited ability to control the behaviour of others gives sociability a fleeting, improvisational quality.

Clearly, early peer relations are less stable and intense than parent–child attachments, and for good reason. Young children have no interest in assuming the caregiving roles of relieving distress and providing stimulation, nor do they have the caregiver's skill in responding quickly and appropriately to needs. However, they have one inherent advantage over adults in that, being at comparable developmental levels, they are naturally attracted to one another's activities. Whereas a parent may love a child for what he or she is, peer attraction is based on mutual interests. Peer relations are important not because they represent diluted versions of attachment but because they add a new dimension of mutuality to development.

A number of changes take place in the preschool period. The ability to engage in social pretend play emerges, allowing children to work through fears and worries, as well as to use fantasy to establish and maintain social relationships with peers. Children begin to organize materials for socio-dramatic play and to assign social roles and scripts (e.g., doctor, mother, police officer) which call for a new level of organization, communication and social skill in conscripting peers to join the game. Specific friendships also begin to be observed, with children showing distinct preferences for play with particular peers based upon shared interests and shared affect. Even in these early years, it is rare to see children without friends, and these young friendships provide children with important social competences that predict positive, adaptive behaviour later in childhood. Empathy, sharing and helping also are on the rise and are linked to peer acceptance during the preschool period. On the less positive side, there also are

Peer relations are an important influence on children's development.
© *Image Source*

increases in conflict, competition and rivalry. However, learning to manage aggression is one of the most important developmental tasks of the pre-school period. Therefore, dealing with challenging peers in preschool provides children with important opportunities to develop the conflict resolution skills which will lead to good social-cognitive functioning later in development.

Middle Childhood

Friendships and positive peer experiences in preschool predict a smooth transition into the greatly enlarged sphere of peer relations that opens up upon a child's entry into school and enrolment in extra-curricular activities. In fact, spontaneous and unstructured play largely disappears during this period and is replaced by adult-organized structured activities, such as sports or games with formal rules.

Among the developmental advances that contribute to children's peer relationships in this period are increases in capacities for *social perspective-taking* and *social problem solving*, which involve a number of social-cognitive skills: perceiving others' point of view, encoding and accurately interpreting social cues, generating possible problem-solving strategies and evaluating their probable effectiveness, and, finally, enacting the most effective strategy. Consequently, older children take the needs of others into account and are inclined towards persuasion and compromise rather than brute force. Although there is no evidence that children's

empathic behaviour increases with age, there is an increase in the complexity and contextuality of children's responses to the dilemmas that arise when self-interest must be balanced with fairness and reciprocity. In particular, children's understanding of friendship significantly changes during middle childhood as they are increasingly insightful into the subjective experiences of their peers and recognize that friendship requires co-ordinating and adjusting to the needs of both parties in a mutually satisfying way. Children more clearly differentiate true friends from others during this period and explicitly identify loyalty, trust and self-disclosure as the ingredients of friendship.

However, despite the opening up of these new worlds of peer exposure, children in middle childhood demonstrate a tendency to sort, label and segregate themselves from one another on the basis of observable characteristics: most notably gender, but also race, ethnicity and social class. Stable cliques begin to form in this period and provide both a source of protection, in the form of a sense of belonging and acceptance for children who have found their place within the group, but also a source of vulnerability by threatening children who are 'outsiders' with a sense of insecurity. Research shows that children in middle childhood spend a significant amount of time, energy and thought worrying about their social status and the possibility of rejection.

Studies of children's *sociometric status* focus on the extent to which children are nominated as 'liked' or 'disliked' by peers. Generally, four types of children emerge: accepted, rejected, neglected and controversial. The child who is *accepted* by other children is resourceful, intelligent, emotionally stable, dependable, co-operative, and sensitive to the feelings of others. *Rejected* children are aggressive, distractable and socially inept in addition to being unhappy and alienated. Moreover, they are at risk for being school dropouts and for having serious psychological difficulties in adolescence and adulthood. *Neglected* children, who are neither liked nor disliked by peers, tend to be anxious and lacking in social skills. Finally, *controversial* children are perceived both positively and negatively by others. These children may be troublemakers or class clowns, yet they possess interpersonal skills and charisma that attract or impress other children. Some recent evidence suggests that another category of children, those who are perceived as *popular*, are not in fact those who are more liked by others but rather are those who are seen as socially powerful – thus, they may be closer to the controversial than the accepted children. We will encounter these 'popular' youth again in Chapter 10 when we discuss the role that charismatic ringleaders play in orchestrating bullying in the social circle.

There is another important dimension of peer relationships that adds to the child's development. Whereas unconditional positive regard may be at the heart of the affection that the child experiences at home, with peers the child must be respectworthy, which is a matter of proven *competence*. Children must expose themselves to comparisons with other children in regard to athletic ability, manual skills, resourcefulness in suggesting and implementing interesting activities, and so on. They are admired in terms of their actual contributions to the activities that peers themselves value. Thus, children at this stage are concerned with mastery, not only in the spheres that matter to parents and teachers, but in the skills and attributes that are considered 'cool' among their peers.

Adolescence

The importance of peer relationships reaches a high point in adolescence. Some studies show that adolescents in the USA spend over twice as much time with their peers as they do with parents and other adults. Increasingly age-mates are perceived as primary sources of social support and advice. Levels of intimacy and self-disclosure increase, with the long, emotional and psychologically deep conversations of teenagers playing an important role in the development of their understanding of themselves and others.

In addition to increasing participation in cliques and friendship groups, participation in which is associated with a sense of well-being and successful coping with stress, adolescence also heralds youths' identification with a 'crowd'. The term crowd refers to a designation that a group of youth might share based on similar interests, attitudes or styles, rather than on mutual affiliation: for example, youth might be identified as 'jocks', 'nerds', 'preps', 'geeks', 'Goths' or 'emos'. Although bearing a reputation associated with one of these designations might seem to constrain youth's identity exploration, in fact there is significant mobility that allows youth to enter and exit membership in these crowds across the high school years.

In early adolescence, youth generally socialize in mixed-sex groups in which flirtation and experimentation with sexuality is fleeting and non-committal. One of the most significant shifts in adolescence is towards romantic relationships that comprise stable and heartfelt alliances. According to Brown (1999) the development of romantic relationships emerges as a function of advances in individual identity as well as youth's sensitivity to the peer context. In the initiation phase, youth are primarily concerned with keeping up with their peers and demonstrating their own efficacy in the dating arena. Consequently, their choices of dating partners are highly influenced by peer perception. In the affection stage, dating relationships are more of a personal matter and are characterized by heightened emotional intensity and desire for intimacy. Lastly, the bonding stage involves continued emotional investment and commitment to a long-term relationship.

Adolescents' peer relationships provide an important bridge to the future. They provide a sense of belonging, which is especially important during the period of transition between being a child and being an adult. They help adolescents to master uncertainty by prescribing behaviour, right down to what clothes to wear, what music to listen to and what language to use. They provide both provocation and protection in the process of transitioning towards sexual relations. Finally, they support youth in individuating from their parents by providing an alternative world with its own rules, values and language. Along with these sources of protection, however, adolescent peer relationships also involve certain risks, such as the promotion of risktaking and participation in precocious sexual behaviour and substance use. In addition, the keen importance placed on success in the social arena creates a vulnerability for those youth who are late to develop, not accepted by the group, or feel left behind by their peers.

As we shall see, disturbances in peer relations play a prominent role in many of the childhood disorders we will discuss, including pervasive developmental disorders (Chapter 5), attention deficit (Chapter 7), anxiety (Chapter 8), depression (Chapter 9), conduct disorder (Chapter 10), schizophrenia (Chapter 11), substance abuse (Chapter 12), personality disorders (Chapter 15) and the consequences of maltreatment (Chapter 14). Consequently, we will also see how attention to peer relations contributes to our understanding of children during the process of clinical assessment (Chapter 16) and helps to inform the development of effective treatments for child psychopathologies (Chapter 17).

Extra-Familial Adults

As children move through the school years into adolescence, adults outside the family increasingly play a role in shaping their behaviour and attitudes about themselves. Potential mentors and sources of support outside the family include teachers, coaches, tutors, school counsellors, camp leaders, clergy, godparents, neighbours and other adult friends of the family. The quality of children's relationships with *teachers* contributes in important ways to children's sense of well-being. For example, teachers who blatantly treat differently the students they perceive as high and low achievers inculcate in children not only perceptions of low self-efficacy but actual lowered school performance, the so-called Pygmalion effect (Weinstein, 2008). Peers also are sensitive to differential teacher treatment and are likely to reject the child they perceive as ill-favoured (McKown and Weinstein, 2008). On the other hand, teachers who relate to children with warmth, structure and personal interest increase children's well-being and

sense of security as well as children's capacity to cope with stress (Pianta, 2006). Similarly, *school environments* that are perceived as dangerous, unsafe or uncaring contribute to student maladjustment; in contrast, as was confirmed in a recent study in Australia (Shochet et al., 2008), children who feel a positive attachment to their school evidence better socio-emotional functioning.

Social Processes and Developmental Psychopathology

To review, the social context involves several processes that might influence psychopathology. These include (1) peer rejection, (2) poor social skills, (3) social problem-solving deficits, (4) negative peer influences and (5) weak or negative attachments to schools and extra-familial adults.

Development in the Cultural Context

Poverty and Social Class

The most extensive data available on children living in poverty comes from the Luxembourg Income Study (www.lisproject.org), in which government statistics were gathered from Australia, Canada, 12 Western and East European nations (Belgium, Estonia, Finland, France, Germany, the Netherlands, Norway, Poland, Russia, Slovenia, Sweden and the UK), as well as the USA. Heuveline and Weinshenker's (2008) analyses of these data show that children are more likely to be poor in the USA than in any other Western society with the exception of Russia. (See Table 2.3.) Children living with married parents are the least likely to experience poverty in all countries, and those living with a single mother have the highest poverty rates around the globe.

Children growing up in impoverished families are at increased risk for a wide range of behavioural, emotional, health and academic problems (Edin and Kissane, 2010). For example, low household income has emerged as a predictor of both internalizing and externalizing problems in the Avon Longitudinal Study conducted in the UK

TABLE 2.3 Child Poverty Rates (%), by Household Type

Country	Overall	Married Couple	Cohabiting Couple	Single Male Head	Single Female Head, No Other Adults	Single Female Head and Other Adults
United States	22.0	13.9	29.7	25.6	55.4	36.9
Australia	16.0	12.1	—[a]	25.8	51.6	27.2
Belgium	7.7	7.0	10.9	19.0	9.3	12.2
Canada	14.9	10.4	14.4	13.3	48.3	16.8
Estonia	13.6	10.2	15.5	10.9	27.3	15.2
Finland	2.8	1.9	3.0	2.1	9.0	0.0
France	7.9	5.2	11.7	13.3	27.3	19.0
Germany	9.0	4.1	12.0	10.0	42.1	11.3
Netherlands	9.8	6.6	15.9	11.0	38.4	16.0
Norway	3.4	2.1	1.6	5.4	11.6	8.6
Poland	12.7	12.2	—[a]	10.5	20.1	15.1
Russia	23.4	20.7	30.6	16.6	41.0	24.9
Slovenia	6.9	5.6	7.4	16.8	28.8	14.4
Sweden	4.2	2.3	2.3	4.2	13.5	7.1
United Kingdom	15.3	9.2	15.0	21.4	37.3	9.8

[a]Married and cohabiting couples are grouped together in the data for Australia and Poland.

Source: Heuveline and Weinshenker (2008).

and the Tracking Individual Lives Survey in the Netherlands (Huisman et al., 2010). Poverty may exert its effects on child development through a number of mechanisms. Some of these are *environmental*; for example, economically deprived neighbourhoods are bleak and unattractive, lacking in child-friendly amenities such as yards and playgrounds; and marked by high rates of violence, drug-dealing and models of antisocial behaviour (Evans, 2004). The homes of children reared in poverty are crowded, noisy, unsafe and poorly maintained; the air they breathe and water they drink are more polluted. Children from poor families also have less access to cultural amenities and cognitively stimulating activities than do children from more privileged backgrounds. Low SES, moreover, may exert its effects indirectly through the *parent–child relationship*. For exam-

ple, poverty is associated with lower levels of warmth and parental responsiveness and increases in interparental conflict, which in turn are associated with child behaviour problems (Conger et al., 2010).

A compelling study conducted in Finland demonstrated the effects of economic stress on children and their families. Solantaus and colleagues (2004) began studying a sample of 527 families at the time the children were 8 years of age, shortly before a severe economic recession hit the country. Following the children into their twelfth year, the investigators found that the economic downturn was associated with increased parent distress, interparental conflict and negative parenting, which, in turn, were associated with a significant rise in youth depression, aggression and oppositional behaviour. These data replicate previous findings reported in European American and African American samples (Conger et al., 2010), pointing to their cross-cultural relevance.

Other neighbourhood characteristics frequently associated with poverty also may affect child development. One of these is a lack of *community cohesion*: neighbourhoods in which neighbours do not know one another and do not provide mutual support and a sense of belonging are not the villages in which one would wish to raise a child. A second risk factor is *community violence*, to which children in poverty are exposed to an alarming degree and which is associated with significant levels of aggression, posttraumatic stress disorder and depression (Fowler et al., 2009; Zinzow et al., 2009b).

Whereas poverty may increase the risk for psychopathology, it far from ensures it. Therefore, we must be careful not to rush to pathologize children and families on the basis of their social class. There are many sources of strength and resilience among economically challenged families that can protect children from the risks (Felner, 2006; Wadsworth and Santiago, 2008). In the family system, nurturant parenting, a positive parent–child relationship and a harmonious home act as buffers. For youth themselves, good intelligence and the use of adaptive coping strategies are associated with greater resilience in the face of economic adversity (Vanderbilt-Adriance and Shaw, 2008).

Ethnic Diversity

Although the terms are not used consistently in the literature, the American Psychological Association (2003) defines *race* as a 'category to which others assign individuals on the basis of physical characteristics, such as skin color or hair type, and the generalizations and stereotypes made as a result' whereas *ethnicity* is used to refer to 'the acceptance of the group mores and practices of one's culture and the concomitant sense of belonging' (p. 380). Whichever of these terms is used, there is no doubt that many nations in our increasingly mobile world are becoming more diverse. To take the USA as an example, the most recent census data available indicate that approximately 40 per cent of the US youth population belongs to a racial or ethnic minority group; further, the proportion of American youth from non-European descent is projected to increase to 50 per cent by the year 2022 (US Census Bureau, 2010). Twenty-three per cent of US children are of Hispanic origin, 14.7 per cent are African American, 4.4 per cent are Asian American and 1.6 per cent are Native American (American Indian or Alaska Natives). An additional 4.1 per cent belong to more than one ethnic group, termed *biracial* or multiracial.

However, these statistics obscure the great diversity within ethnic and racial categories. For example, the label Hispanic includes many races (White, Black and Indian) and such divergent families as Mexican Americans whose ancestors' residence in California pre-dates European Americans, recent poor immigrants fleeing from political strife in Central America, and upper-class Cuban Americans who fled that country's regime change a generation ago (McGoldrick et al., 2005). Similarly, the term African American overlooks the fact that Black Americans' origins include other continents than Africa and that their families range widely in income levels, religiosity and the extent to which they adopt majority cultural values.

Thus, there are two additional dimensions that must be considered when we discuss ethnicity. First, within ethnic groups there are important differences related to *social class*. Members of minority groups are disproportionately likely to live in poverty, which increases the risk for a variety of negative outcomes, including school dropout, substance use and delinquency (Edin and Kissane, 2010). However, there also exist middle- and upper-class minority families to whom these stressors do not apply. Second, there are significant differences in the level of *acculturation*, or adoption of the values of the majority culture. Acculturation is related to language use, customs and ties to the community outside the ethnic enclave. Because of such differences, first- and third-generation Chinese Americans, for example, may have less in common with one another than do middle-class, acculturated

Chinese and European Americans (Gibbs and Huang, 2003).

Racism and Prejudice

According to the *International Convention on the Elimination of All Forms of Racial Discrimination* adopted by the United Nations, racial discrimination involves 'any distinction, exclusion, restriction or preference based on race, color, descent, or national or ethnic origin which has the purpose or effect of nullifying or impairing the recognition, enjoyment or exercise, on an equal footing, of human rights and fundamental freedoms in the political, economic, social, cultural or any other field of *public life*' (Part 1 of Article 1 of the UN International Convention on the Elimination of All Forms of Racial Discrimination). Further, under Article 21 of the *Charter of Fundamental Rights of the European Union* adopted in 2001, the EU 'prohibits discrimination on any ground such as race, colour, ethnic or social origin, genetic features, language, religion or belief, political or any other opinion, membership of a national minority, property, disability, age or sexual orientation and also discrimination on the grounds of nationality'. Nonetheless, as Spencer and colleagues (2006) point out, 'Racism is omnipresent, though often subtle' (p. 643). The experience of systematic, chronic racism has been identified as a significant risk factor for child and adolescent physical and mental health, including psychological distress, depression, anxiety, and physiological reactions such as elevated blood pressure (Paradies, 2006). Coker and colleagues (2009), drawing upon a sample of over 5000 fifth-graders drawn from three large urban areas in the USA, found that children who reported perceived racial discrimination rated higher than their peers on measures of depression, attention deficit, oppositionality and conduct disorder – in other words, all four of the mental health outcomes measured by the investigators.

Children appear to have some awareness of racial differences in physical appearance as early as 6 months of age. (See Katz, 2003, for an overview of longitudinal research on the topic.) However, the valence associated with perceived difference is influenced in major ways by parental attitudes. Attitudes about race may be conveyed through direct instruction or more subtle behaviours (Spencer et al., 2006). Between the ages of 21 to 31 months, young children demonstrate knowledge of prevailing stereotypes associated with race. Young children may shy away from those with a different skin colour or refuse to play with a peer who has a physical disability or speaks a different language. By the time they are in preschool, children have labels for ethnic groups and can express their own theories about what causes racial differences. In the early school years, children have formed a core sense of individual ethnic identity and actively seek out information about their own group. Moreover, by middle childhood, attitudes about other races tend to have consolidated and are unlikely to change without a significant influential event or intervention. Throughout childhood and into adulthood, individuals receive messages from peers, family members and the media that reinforce already formed attitudes and beliefs (Aboud and Amato, 2001).

Racism is not the only form of *prejudice* that increases the risk of psychopathology. Misogyny, nationalism and religious intolerance – the list of forms that hatred takes is vast. Prejudiced attitudes are held not only by bigoted individuals but may be socially sanctioned by belief systems that place certain outsiders beyond the pale. As we have seen, one particular form of prejudice that presents a risk to some developing adolescents is *homophobia* (King et al., 2008). In sum, any form of hatred and intolerance directed at a child might increase the risk for the development of psychopathology.

Sources of Risk and Resilience in Ethnically Diverse Families

We have reviewed a number of increased risks and vulnerabilities associated with ethnic minority status, particularly due to its overlap with poverty. However, one of the significant shifts in recent thinking about the roles of race and ethnicity in developmental psychopathology is the shift from a deficit/pathology perspective to one of strength and resilience (Murry et al., 2001; Spencer et al., 2006). For example, an important advance has been the recognition of context, in that various parenting strategies are most effective and associated with more youth resilience when they are responsive to the environment. The fact that more highly controlling and authoritarian ('no-nonsense') parenting practices predict better adjustment in African American youth growing up in dangerous urban environments provides one example. Cultural values such as familism and the closeness of large, extended families also provide sources of resilience for ethnically diverse families.

In regard to coping with racism, as Szalacha and colleagues (2003) note, an important buffer against the effects of discrimination is the child's recognition of it as such – in other words, if someone is saying bad things about them they should 'consider the source'. The ability to correctly attribute negative feedback to others' prejudice or ignorance, therefore, may serve as a source of resilience. However, a sophisticated set of cognitive skills is needed for children to correctly attribute negative events to prejudice and discrimination. These include the ability to classify the self and other on multiple dimensions, perspective-taking skills, moral judgement and formal operational reasoning. In addition, in their research involving Turkish, Moroccan and Surinamese immigrant children and their Dutch peers in the Netherlands, Verkuyten (2002) found that shared beliefs about power differentials were important as well. Among all children, discrimination was more likely to be recognized when the victim was a minority child and the perpetrator a member of the majority.

Ethnic Processes and Developmental Psychopathology

Ethnicity is a crucial variable for us to consider as we attempt to chart a pathway of normative development. First and foremost, ethnicity influences *norms* for child development: what is normative in one ethnic group may not be in another and may even be an indication of psychopathology. We will need to keep

in mind that race is not a sufficient index of *ethnic identity*, which is also a product of *social class* and *acculturation*. Perhaps one of the most significant differences we will need to keep in mind is that of the *parenting styles* that are prevalent and considered appropriate in various ethnic groups, driven as they are by different philosophies and values regarding child-rearing, family and attitudes towards the larger society. Overt *racism* and *prejudice*, the regrettable accompanying overlap between ethnic minority status and *poverty*, as well as simple *ignorance* about minority groups' norms and belief systems also at times will complicate the process. For example, although we will strive to consider issues of diversity in all of the disorders we will study, in many cases the relevant research has not been done and therefore few if any studies have paid attention to race, ethnicity or social class in the prevalence, etiology, course or treatment of the disorder under question.

Cross-Cultural Norms and Expectations

In addition to attending to ethnic subgroups within the USA, we also will be interested in exploring how psychopathology might develop in different cultures around the globe. (See Bornstein, 2010.) Beliefs about what constitutes psychopathology and how it arises vary across cultures. Some conceptualizations are quite unique to their context. For example, consider the concept of *zar*, or spirit possession, found in North Africa and the Middle East; *amok*, a Malaysian dissociative experience involving a period of brooding followed by an outburst of violence; or *taijin kyofusho*, the Japanese fear that one's body or bodily functions are offensive to others. (A further list of culture-bound syndromes is given in *DSM-IV-TR*.) In other cases, culturally specific syndromes have clear relationships to those that are defined by Western taxonomies such as *DSM-IV-TR*, but cross boundaries in ways that reflect a different underlying meaning. For example, consider the Latin American syndrome of *ataque de nervios*, a syndrome that is conceptualized as resulting from a loss of significant personal relationships and which is characterized by a generalized sense of emotional distress and physical symptoms, including heart palpitations and body aches, irritability, insomnia, nervousness, inability to concentrate, trembling and dizziness (Varela and Hensley-Maloney, 2009). Although this syndrome includes features of Western diagnostic entities such as anxiety, depression and somatoform disorder, applying to a child these multiple diagnoses would not do justice to the larger gestalt of symptoms and the meaning that they have within the culture.

Cross-cultural research also teaches us that whether a child's behaviour is considered normal or disordered depends on parental *expectations* about appropriate behaviour, which vary across societies (Bornstein and Lansford, 2010). For example, an oft-cited cultural distinction is the one between an emphasis on *individualism*, the promotion of self-expression, independence and individual achievement in children, and *collectivism*, the valuing of social relations, interdependence and the placement of one's own interests second to those of the larger group (Kitayama, 2000). Precociously independent behaviour, for example, may earn a child delighted praise in one context and parental disapproval in another. A crucial factor is the *fit* between the child's characteristics and those the culture values. Consider the expectation that a 6-year-old child sit quietly and attentively in the classroom for six hours a day. Some would criticize this expectation as a developmentally inappropriate one, fostered by a culture that is in a rush to 'hurry' us through childhood (Elkind, 1981). However, because certain cultures expect this behaviour, those children whose activity level is on the high end of the normal continuum are at risk for being labelled as hyperactive (Timimi and Taylor, 2004).

Cultures collide in the case of recent *immigrant families*, a growing group that has been relatively neglected in the research literature. Spurred by the upheavals brought by war, terrorism, ecological problems and the search for economic betterment, our world is an increasing mobile one. For example, in the USA, nearly one in six children has a parent who was born in another country (Federal Interagency Forum on Child and Family Statistics, 2010). Effects of immigration on children vary as a function of social class and circumstance. For impoverished immigrants fleeing economic hardship or war or civil unrest, the process may be fraught with danger and peril, resulting in trauma for parents and children alike (Wadsworth, 2010). The process of immigrating itself may expose children and families to further terrors and degradations. Once settled in their new country, children of immigrant families may be exposed to new stresses and developmentally taxing expectations, such as the children's translating for their parents and helping their elders navigate social service bureaucracies. Generational strains may develop when parents hold to the cultural beliefs and values of the home country while their children are being exposed to and adopting the values of the new country, particularly as adolescence approaches and American norms of freedom and experimentation for youth challenge the old ways.

The individual family's level of *acculturation* plays a role, as does whether the immigrant culture values assimilating into the new home country versus maintaining its distinct identity. Such values and practices vary. For example, Bornstein (2010) conducted a study in which they examined the parenting beliefs and practices of immigrant Japanese American and South American mothers and compared them with those of European American mothers as well as those in the home countries of Japan and Argentina. Consistent with previous research, the investigators found that Japanese American immigrant mothers tended to maintain traditional values and beliefs, with their ratings closely corresponding to those of mothers in the home country. In contrast, South American immigrant mothers' attitudes were closer to those of European Americans than to those of Argentinians.

Cultural Processes and Developmental Psychopathology

According to Castillo (1997), culture influences psychopathology in five key ways. The first of these is *culture-based subjective experience*, the way in which culture influences one's view of psychopathology and one's perceptions of self. For example, cultures that emphasize internal processes as causal in psychopathology might lead depressed persons to perceive themselves as ill, whereas, in contrast, non-Western conceptualizations might locate the problem in a misconnection between the self and others and therefore construe depression as a family or interpersonal issue. Second are *culture-based idioms* of psychological distress, which refer to the ways in which psychopathology is evidenced in behaviour. Culture may influence the symptoms that individuals exhibit as well as those that others focus on in determining mental health or illness. For example, Asian beliefs regarding the interconnectedness of the mind and body may contribute to the expression of emotional distress in the form of physical ailments (Ryder et al., 2002). Third, *culture-based diagnosis* involves the categories and language that people use to understand and explain psychopathology. For example, we described earlier several examples of culturally specific syndromes that have meaning only within their unique context. Fourth, *culture-based treatments* determine who are the potential healers and what are the mechanisms through which healing takes place: for example, whether a psychiatrist is sought for medication, a faith healer is visited to reconnect the spirit to the body, or the symptom is hidden to protect the honour of the family. Fifth are *culture-based outcomes*, the results that ensue when a psychopathology has been conceptualized and treated in a particular way. For example, the child's response to treatment may be influenced by the degree to which society emphasizes the need to provide familial support to the individual who is suffering from mental illness.

As Serafica and Vargas (2006) point out, culture provides an important context for child development, influencing the physical and interpersonal settings, the styles of child rearing, the psychology of parenting and the social relations that the child will need to adapt to over the course of childhood.

Developmental Integration

Now we will integrate the information about developmental pathways presented in Chapter 1 with the 10 developmental processes just discussed. To do this we use the case of a hypothetical girl named Zoey. (See Fig. 2.3.)

Zoey is an African American, lower-middle-class child growing up in a suburban area in the south-eastern USA. Zoey's mother went through a postpartum depression when Zoey was born; consequently, Zoey's attachment to her mother was tainted by insecurity (*attachment, slight deviation*). While this did not constitute a major problem, she tended to react strongly to changes in her environment (*temperament, vulnerability*). She showed some anxiety about beginning school and struggled academically throughout her elementary school years (*cognitive development, deviation*). When Zoey was 8 years of age, she experienced an increase in familial disharmony when her parents began arguing heatedly (*interparental conflict, risk*). However, her good relationship with her father enabled her to take the stress in her stride (*parent–child relationship, protective factor*).

When she was 10 years old, Zoey's parents divorced (*family dissolution, risk*), and she was placed in her mother's custody. Mother and child moved from the family home to a small apartment closer to the inner city. The two spent more time apart as the mother returned to the workforce, sometimes working two jobs because the pay her unskilled labour earned was poor (*socio-economic disadvantage, risk*). At this point, a number of behaviour problems began to develop. Zoey's principal problems were angry outbursts and argumentativeness with the teacher (*emotion regulation, severe deviation*). Although initially a friendly child, Zoey began to be regarded as a troublemaker by peers. As peers rejected her, Zoey began acting out in an increasingly hostile manner towards other children (*transactional process*). Consequently, her popularity declined (*peer relations, moderate deviation*). However, two positive events occurred when Zoey was age 12. First, a hitherto undiagnosed learning disorder in reading was uncovered by a perceptive and supportive school psychologist, and Zoey was made eligible for special educational services. As a consequence, Zoey was transferred to the

FIGURE 2.3 Zoey's Developmental Pathway.

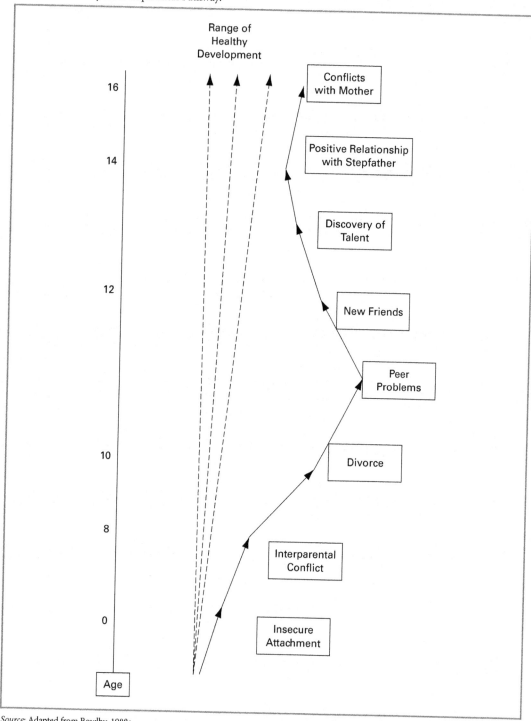

Source: Adapted from Bowlby, 1988a.

special education classroom where she made friends with two other girls who formed a special clique of 'outsiders' (*social relations, protective factor*).

As a pre-teen, Zoey was chronically sullen with her mother (*attachment, continued moderate deviation*), although there were outbursts of more serious temper tantrums and name-calling, especially after she came home from visits with her father. Her angry outbursts usually were overreactions to ordinary frustrations of everyday life. She was not spoiling for a fight by imagining everyone else was against her (*cognition, adaptive*). She went from being a B student to being a C student at school but, while she acted bored and sardonic, she did not give up on school entirely (*mastery motivation, moderate deviation*). Rather than doing homework, she concentrated on drawing and sketching, a hobby she had shared with her father, becoming quite skilled and covertly enjoying being praised (*self-esteem and self-efficacy, protective mechanisms*). She and her friends talked about sex, masturbation and other pubertal changes, and, while wary of boys, she was no more so than a number of other shy pre-adolescent girls (*sex and gender, adaptive*). She was properly but not excessively troubled over her outbursts (*moral development, adaptive*). Finally, whereas her self-regulation had declined significantly, it had not deflated altogether. She was not an impulse-ridden child, driven to strike out at the slightest provocation; rather, she was basically a good kid in the grips of a problem too big for her to handle (*emotional development, moderate deviation*).

When she was 14 years old, her mother remarried and, after some initial storminess, Zoey established a good relationship with her stepfather (*protective factor*). Her problem behaviours gradually subsided and her development began to shift towards a more healthy pathway. However, she continued to be cool and standoffish towards her mother and made a point of finishing high school early so that she could move away from home as soon as possible (*attachment, continued deviance*).

This vignette suggests that the degree of deviation from normative development is a function of the *severity* of the disturbance both within and across the developmental variables and the *duration* of the disturbance. It is also a function of the *balance* between risk, vulnerability and protective factors. Zoey's story also demonstrates that a disturbance may not envelop all of the child's personality – or even all of a given developmental process. As we have noted, it is important for the child clinician to assess areas of competence and resilience as well as deviations, especially when planning interventions.

Our challenge in the coming chapters is to construct developmental pathways for the various classifications of childhood psychopathologies. First, for a given classification we must discover which of the developmental and contextual variables have been adversely affected and to what degree of severity. Then we must discover both the balance between risk, vulnerability and protective factors that produces psychopathology and the balance that enables the child to overcome the disturbance.

Before doing this, however, we must become acquainted with the psychopathologies themselves and develop a general understanding about which are apt to continue into adulthood and which are apt to be outgrown. These are the matters that will occupy us next.

CHAPTER 03

The Bridge to the Psychopathologies

Chapter Contents

In Chapters 1 and 2 we established a general developmental framework and provided a working knowledge of the variables we will use to investigate psychopathology as normal development gone awry. In this chapter we begin to focus on the psychopathologies themselves. We first discuss the way normality shades gradually into psychopathology both conceptually and empirically, then discuss the major psychopathologies of childhood, and finally summarize longitudinal studies of normal and disturbed children to show which psychopathologies tend to persist and which tend to be outgrown. In Chapters 4 through 15 we go on to explore selected psychopathologies.

First, however, we must investigate the methods that are used to determine whether a child should receive the psychopathological labels we are about to describe.

Diagnosis and Classification

Any group is able to be divided into more than one category so a classification system provides rules in which to divide groups. They can use a *categorical* approach to classifying whether a disorder is present or not. Alternatively they can use a *dimensional approach* that represents intensity of a child's symptoms along a continuum. The two main classifications systems which exist, The World Health Organization International Classification of Disorders-10 (hereafter ICD-10; WHO, 1996) a clinical version of which is widely used in a day-to-day practice in UK and Europe, and the APA Diagnostic Statistic Manual-IV (hereafter DSM-IV; APA, 1994), rely on a categorical approach for symptoms that frequently lie along a continuum. Some children who are diagnosed with a disorder may experience symptoms that are only somewhat more severe than those of children who are not diagnosed with the disorder. It should be highlighted that while in clinical practice the DSM-IV is viewed as the US alternative to European ICD-10, the ICD-10 is in fact not exclusively European. It is the instrument through which the WHO, a UN agency, collects data and compiles statistics on all diseases in all UN countries.

Before we address each classification system in turn we need to consider the purpose of a classification system. For example, an important question which relates to the role of any classification system is *whether or not to diagnose a child*. If the sole purpose of any system is to improve an individual's ability to function in daily life, then why not address the specific problems a child appears to be having and eliminate them without developing a classification system for disorders? Also, as we will address later in the chapter, any diagnosis itself will bring its own problems.

Classification systems are believed to have a series of functions. For example, they aim to organize a myriad of descriptors and observations into meaningful units. However, they do more than help place a given child in a given category: they are points of departure for exploring *etiology*, on the one hand, and *prognosis*, on the other. Thus, the diagnosis of adolescent schizophrenia should carry with it implications about causative factors and consequences, both in regard to the chances of outgrowing the disturbance and the effectiveness of therapeutic intervention. At present, we are far from realizing such an ideal goal.

Another goal of classification systems is *differential diagnosis* – that is, deciding which disorder best captures the child's presentation and which alternative disorders should be ruled out. The correct diagnosis is invaluable in determining how treatment should proceed; for example, the child whose inattentiveness is a product of attention-deficit hyperactivity disorder (ADHD) needs a very different intervention from the child whose inattentiveness is due to anxiety. However, children rarely fit neatly into a single diagnostic category. Disorders in children are often *comorbid*; that is, they occur together. Consequently, multiple diagnoses are often used rather than a single diagnostic label. The clinician also should take into account acuteness or chronicity based on the history of the disturbance, evaluate the severity of disturbance, specify the developmental period the child is in and describe the specific behaviours that comprise the psychopathology.

A classification system also allows for the *development of epidemiological information* about incidence and prevalence of various problems. Incidence refers to the risk of developing a disorder within a specific timeframe whereas prevalence can be defined as a measure of how frequently the condition occurs in a population at a particular point in time. Knowledge of these factors can be hugely beneficial in providing possible markers for at risk children and identifying key developmental milestones which may be problematic. It also provides a *language* through which clinicians and researchers communicate with each other. Using the classification systems the same labels should reflect the true condition of the child. A child labelled ADHD by one clinician should be the same as another. A team of researchers who are investigating genetic basis of ADHD should be testing a group of children who

TABLE 3.1 Common Problems Seen in Routine Clinical Practice

Domain	Problem Area
Early childhood	Sleeping problems Toileting problems Learning disabilities Pervasive developmental disorders
Middle childhood	Conduct disorder ADHD Anxiety problems Repetition problems Somatic complaints
Adolescence	Drug abuse Depression Eating disorders Schizophrenia
Child abuse	Physical abuse problems Emotional abuse and neglect-related problems Sexual abuse-related problems
Major developmental transitions	Substitutive childcare-related problems Separation and divorce adjustment problems Grief associated with bereavement and life-threatening illness

Source: Adapted from Carr (2006).

others would identify with this condition. Otherwise any information those researchers gain about the genetic basis of ADHD will be meaningless if they cannot be sure the group of children tested actually have the condition.

A clear diagnosis and understanding implies sorting through a great amount of information, a process that can be daunting and confusing especially for a parent seeking to understand their child's condition. For parents, the realization that their child may not develop typically is a distressing time. Ideally, parents should be told about their child's condition as early as possible, as delays in this process could lead to dissatisfaction. Unfortunately discrepancies among professional opinions over the complexity of the syndrome can often result in a professional reluctance to diagnose until they are certain.

Receiving a diagnosis for their child represents a crisis for parents as they enter a period of mourning a loss of the 'hoped for' child. Accepting a diagnosis and resolving themselves to the implications and possible outcomes is an extremely difficult process for most parents. Milshtein et al. (2010) identified that resolution involves parents coming to terms with and accepting their child's diagnosis. Resolved parents acknowledge difficulties associated with receiving a diagnosis as well as identifying the positive changes it might bring. They are more likely to focus on the present and future rather than dwelling on questions of causality. A diagnosis can also often remove feelings of blame and bring about a sense of relief, that the child's behaviour is not related to problems at home or shortcoming of the parents (Isaksson et al., 2010).

We will start by reviewing the traditional method of diagnosis used in the USA, the DSM. However, clinicians concerned with the adequacy of traditional systems for diagnosing children have raised a number of criticisms, particularly in regard to whether such systems pay sufficient attention to developmental considerations. As part of our discussion we will examine alternative strategies for clinical diagnosis.

The DSM

The various editions of the *Diagnostic and Statistical Manual of Mental Disorders* (**DSM**) are in the tradition of classification based on naturalistic observation. The tradition has primarily been carried on by psychiatrists and relies heavily on the observational skills of the clinician for its implementation. The current version of the DSM is the fourth, with a recent text revision: DSM-IV-TR (American Psychiatric Association, 2000).

Features of DSM-IV-TR
The Development of the DSM-IV-TR
As with all the editions of the DSM, the selection and definitions of the disorders to be included in DSM-IV-TR were the product of 13 work groups, each of which took responsibility for revising a section of the manual. The work groups were composed of at least five members and often more. For example, the group that developed the section on Disorders Usually First Diagnosed During Infancy, Childhood or Adolescence included 12 medical doctors and four psychologists. Their recommendations in turn were critiqued by 50 to 100 advisers, selected to represent diverse nationalities and diverse disciplines, including both clinicians and researchers. The work groups were charged with conducting comprehensive and objective reviews of the relevant literature on each of the disorders under their purview and, where empirical research was lacking or contradictory, to conduct reanalyses of existing data or to carry out field trials to determine the reliability and utility of the diagnosis in the real world. As might be expected, this was a lengthy process. The DSM-IV (American Psychiatric Association, 1994) was 12 years in the making, and the current text revision took three years to produce. The DSM-V is expected to take even longer than its predecessors, and therefore the text revision was undertaken to bridge the gap by updating the manual in the light of more recent research findings. The most recent version of the DSM also was developed in close collaboration with the developers of the *International Statistical*

Classification of Diseases and Related Health Problems (ICD-10; World Health Organization, 1996), in order to increase compatibility between the two systems.

Definition of Psychopathology

There is no generally accepted definition of psychopathology, as our survey of models has shown. The authors of the DSM do not pretend to resolve the knotty issue of conceptualizing psychopathology but settle for stating their own criteria for what is termed a mental disorder. According to DSM-IV-TR, a mental disorder is a

> clinically significant behavioural or psychological syndrome or pattern that occurs in an individual and that is associated with present distress (e.g., a painful symptom) or disability (i.e., impairment in one or more areas of functioning) or with a significantly increased risk of suffering death, pain, disability, or an important loss of freedom. (p. xxxi)

The authors of DSM-IV-TR are careful to state that disorders, not individuals, are being classified. Thus, the manual never refers to 'a schizophrenic' or 'an alcoholic', as if the psychopathology were the person; instead, it uses such phrases as 'a child with schizophrenia' or 'an adult with alcohol dependency'. The distinction is a simple but a significant one, which we also have adopted in this text.

Objectivity and Behavioural Specificity

DSM-IV-TR strives to avoid the use of terms that are inferential, theoretical and open to multiple interpretations. Instead, *behaviourally specific* terms are used that can be objectively described and operationally defined. For example, 'Fights more frequently than agemates' is more specific than 'Has destructive impulses'. To take only one example, separation anxiety disorder is defined in terms of 10 behavioural criteria, including unrealistic worry about possible harm befalling major attachment figures, repeated nightmares involving the theme of separation and persistent reluctance to be separated from major attachment figures.

Reliability

Reliability refers to the consistency of results obtained from using a diagnostic instrument. An instrument that would place the same child in different categories when used by two different clinicians would not be very useful. One criterion of reliability is the consistency with which a diagnostic instrument functions at two points in time, or *test–retest reliability*. More frequently, however, diagnostic systems use *inter-observer agreement*, in which two experts are asked to evaluate the same child at the same point in time.

In his review of reliability studies of DSM-IV, Cantwell (1996) concludes that acceptable reliability has been demonstrated for most of the major diagnostic categories. However, reliability is greater for more general categories, such as anxiety disorder, than for more narrowly defined subcategories such as social phobia or generalized anxiety disorder. There is also evidence that clinicians are less reliable than are researchers who undergo specific training to use the diagnostic system in a standardized way. One reason for poorer reliability in practice is that while DSM provides lists of various criteria that must be met to diagnose a particular disorder, there are no precise rules for determining when a criterion is met, nor are there guidelines for how to evaluate and integrate various sources of information. Thus, if one clinician uses a parent report to judge whether a symptom is present, another interviews the child, and a third relies on a score on a formal psychological test, they might well reach different conclusions.

Validity

Validity is crucial to the utility of a measure. It indicates the extent to which the measure assesses what it claims to assess or, in this case, the extent to which a diagnostic system does, in fact, correctly classify disturbed children. There are a number of different ways in which evidence for validity might be demonstrated. There is *content* or *face* validity, which is the degree to which the content of a diagnostic category has an obvious relation to what is being evaluated. In the case of separation anxiety disorder, the three behavioural criteria mentioned make sense on the face of it. Ideally, the criteria should also be analysed statistically to test whether they do, in fact, cluster together. *Concurrent* validity compares the current evaluation with some other contemporary criterion; for example, the diagnosis of a reading disability based on parental report could be compared with scores on a reading achievement test. *Predictive* validity compares current evaluations with some future criterion; for example, children diagnosed with schizophrenia in middle childhood should continue to be more disturbed as young adults than children diagnosed with school phobia. *Construct* validity is the relationship between a diagnostic category and other variables that should be related to it theoretically; for example, children diagnosed with conduct disorder should perform poorly on measures of self-control, such as the ability to delay gratification. And, finally, *discriminative* validity is the extent to which clinical features are unique to the disorder in question and differentiate it from other similar disorders. For example, the diagnostic criteria should help to distinguish children with separation anxiety disorder from those who are depressed. This corresponds to the important clinical task of *differential diagnosis*, and the *DSM-IV-TR Handbook of Differential Diagnosis* (Frances and Pincus, 2002) is available to assist the clinician with this process.

Validity is difficult to establish, given that there are few independent criteria that can be used for predictive or concurrent validation studies. However, Cantwell (1996) notes that advances have been made in the attempts to obtain external validation of the DSM-IV disorders, although the study of child psychopathology has lagged behind that on adults in this regard. DSM-IV has a stronger *empirical basis* than its predecessors and thus corresponds better to the research evidence regarding different forms of psychopathology. This evidence was obtained from comprehensive reviews of published literature, from reanalysis of studies containing information concerning diagnosis, and from field trials in which data on 6000 participants were analysed in terms of reliability and validity of diagnostic criteria. The resulting five-volume DSM-IV sourcebook provides documentation of the decisions reached concerning the classifications and their behavioural components.

Other evidence for external validity is suggested by the fact that there are different predictors and correlates of certain syndromes of disorders, as well as studies demonstrating continuities over time. For example, research has shown that the three kinds of depression described in DSM-IV-TR – Major Depression, Dysthymia, and Adjustment Disorder with Depressed Mood – have a different age of onset, course and recovery during childhood. In addition, the fact that individuals diagnosed with a particular disorder respond differentially to treatments designed specifically for that disorder lends credibility to the system used to diagnose them.

Comprehensiveness

DSM-IV is substantially more comprehensive than previous versions in its coverage of childhood disorders. In addition, DSM-IV-TR supplies updated information concerning a host of characteristics of a given disorder where such information is available: for example, prevalence; age of onset; course; predisposing factors; differential diagnosis; laboratory findings; and specific age, cultural or gender-related features.

Multiaxial Classification
Five Dimensions

Instead of assessing only in terms of the presenting problem, DSM-IV-TR uses a **multiaxial classification** system to evaluate the child comprehensively in terms of five dimensions.

Axis I: Clinical Disorders; Other Disorders That May Be a Focus of Clinical Attention

This axis contains most of the disorders with which we will be concerned. The DSM criteria for those disorders will always be included in our discussions.

Axis II: Personality Disorders; Mental Retardation

This axis is concerned with conditions that affect functioning in a pervasive manner, including personality disorders and mental retardation. It can also be used to indicate problematic personality characteristics that do not meet the criteria for a full-blown personality disorder, such as maladaptive and rigid use of defence mechanisms.

Axis III: General Medical Conditions
This axis includes general medical conditions that are potentially relevant to the understanding or management of cases: for example, injuries and infectious diseases, diseases of the nervous system or digestive system, and complications of pregnancy and childbirth.

Axis IV: Psychosocial and Environmental Problems
This axis includes negative life events, stresses, and environmental deficiencies that provide the milieu within which the child's problems developed. Categories include problems related to the *primary support group* (e.g., death of a family member, divorce, abuse); the *social environment* (e.g., inadequate social support, acculturation difficulties, discrimination); *education* (e.g., illiteracy, discord with teachers or classmates); *occupation* (e.g., stressful work schedule, discord with boss or co-workers); *housing* (e.g., homelessness, unsafe neighbourhood); *economics* (e.g., poverty, insufficient welfare support); *health care* (e.g., transportation difficulties, inadequate health insurance); *legal system* (e.g., arrest, criminal victimization); and *other psychosocial and environmental problems* (e.g., exposure to natural disaster or war).

Axis V: Global Assessment of Functioning
This is the clinician's judgement of the overall level of functioning. Such information is useful in planning treatment and measuring its impact. The judgement is made in terms of a Global Assessment of Functioning (GAF) Scale, which goes from superior functioning (100 points) to persistent danger of hurting self or others or persistent inability to maintain minimal personal hygiene (1 to 10 points). (See Table 3.2 for a condensed version of the GAF adapted for children.)

Strengths and Limitations of DSM from a Developmental Psychopathology Perspective
In many ways DSM-IV-TR represents an impressive accomplishment. However, as its authors note, it is difficult to accurately place individuals into discrete diagnostic categories. Even individuals with the same disorder present in slightly different ways, and there is some fuzziness to the boundaries between the different classifications. Consequently, the DSM requires a high level of clinical judgement and is vulnerable to the subjectivity of the diagnostician. Classification systems such as DSM also have not coped well with the *comorbidity* problem that frequently arises in studies of childhood psychopathology (Cantwell, 1996). It is difficult to know whether multiple diagnoses are accurate – whether they result from a lack of clear distinctions between diagnostic categories or whether they arise from different early expressions of various forms of psychopathology during development.

The Heterogeneity Dimension
One of the reasons why it is difficult to place individuals into discrete diagnostic categories is that they do not fit very neatly. The children who are categorized within a given disorder may be extremely heterogeneous. Take for example two children given the diagnosis of conduct disorder: one is a 7-year-old who engages in cruelty to animals, fighting and bullying peers, while the other is a 17-year-old boy who engages in vandalism, truancy and theft. Although the symptoms and their behavioural manifestations differ, both children receive the same DSM code – and by implication, according to the medical model, should receive the same treatment (Douchette, 2002).

The Developmental Dimension
Another significant shortcoming of the DSM is its failure to acknowledge the *developmental dimension* within disorders. With some exceptions, DSM-IV-TR assumes that the diagnostic criteria are essentially identical across development, whereas research increasingly indicates that this is not the case (Silk et al., 2000). Evidence suggests that the

TABLE 3.2 Selected Levels of the Children's Global Assessment Scale for DSM-IV Axis IV

100–91	Superior functioning in all areas (at home, at school, and with peers); involved in a range of activities and has many interests (e.g., has hobbies or participates in extra-curricular activities or belongs to organized groups such as Scouts). Likable, confident, 'everyday' worries never get out of hand. Doing well in school. No symptoms.
80–71	No more than slight impairment in functioning at home, at school, or with peers. Some disturbance of behaviour or emotional distress may be present in response to life stresses (e.g., parental separations, deaths, birth of a sibling), but these are brief and interference with functioning is transient. Such children are only minimally disturbing to others and are not considered deviant by those who know them.
50–41	Moderate degree of interference in functioning in most social areas or severe impairment of functioning in one area, such as might result from, for example, suicidal preoccupations and ruminations, school refusal and other forms of anxiety, obsessive rituals, major conversion symptoms, frequent anxiety attacks, frequent episodes of aggressive or other antisocial behaviour with some preservation of meaningful social relationships.
30–21	Unable to function in almost all areas (e.g., stays at home, in ward, or in bed all day without taking part in social activities) OR severe impairment in reality testing OR serious impairment in communications (e.g., sometimes incoherent or inappropriate).
10–1	Needs constant supervision (24-hour care) due to severely aggressive or self-destructive behaviour or gross impairment in reality testing, communication, cognition, affect, or personal hygiene.

Source: Rapoport and Ismond, 1996.

symptom picture of a disorder changes with age. For example, younger children with separation anxiety disorder worry excessively about separation from their attachment figure and have nightmares, while older children primarily have physical complaints and are reluctant to go to school. Motor disturbances are more characteristic of younger boys with attention-deficit hyperactivity disorder, while older boys with the disorder are characterized by inattention.

Developmentally oriented clinicians have been offering similar criticisms across several generations of DSM revisions. As long ago as 1965, Anna Freud observed that the two criteria fundamental to diagnosing clinical disorders in DSM – *subjective distress* and *impairment of functioning* – are not appropriate for children. The most seriously disturbed children – for example, those with autism, schizophrenia or conduct disorder – may be oblivious to the fact that they have problems and may experience no subjective distress. Instead of being disturbed, such children are better characterized as disturbing to others. Regarding the second crite-

rion, children do not have a consistent level of functioning. Given that they are still in the process of developing, it is normal for their abilities to wax and wane and fluctuate significantly. Therefore, Anna Freud proposed that only one criterion could help to determine whether a particular behaviour or symptom was an indication of psychopathology in a child: *whether it interferes with the child's capacity to move forward in development*.

A classic paper by Garber (1984) proposes a developmental framework for the classification of psychopathology in childhood, arguing against the 'adultomorphism' inherent in DSM's tendency to apply adult categories to the problems of children. In attempting to avoid all theory, the authors of DSM also ignore the developmental perspective, overlooking the point that development is not a theory but a basic fact (Bemporad and Schwab, 1986). Further, not only do children change over time, but one of the child's tasks throughout development is to respond in age-appropriate ways to a changing environment. By focusing on superficial descriptions of behaviour, DSM ignores the complex nature of the transactions and adaptations that affect individuals as they move through development (Jensen and Hoagwood, 1997).

Cantwell's (1996) conclusion echoes that of Garber 12 years earlier: 'Developmental aspects of child and adolescent psychopathology will have to be given much greater consideration in future classification systems' (p. 9).

The Transactional Dimension

Given how dependent children are on their caregivers, the interpersonal context needs must play a significant role in childhood psychopathology. However, problems arising from troubled relationships are not considered clinical disorders in the DSM (Volkmar and Schwab-Stone, 1996). Although DSM avoids taking any overt stand on etiology, by focusing on the disorder as something the child 'has', it reveals that an underlying assumption is a static and undetermined one. This is a far cry from the transactional perspective of developmental psychopathology, in which problems arise in the context of relationships and are a product of reciprocal influences of individuals on one another (Jensen and Hoagwood, 1997). Consequently, some of the most significant concerns that bring children to the attention of mental health professionals – abuse, family conflict, bereavement, family dissolution – are placed in DSM-IV-TR in a somewhat vaguely defined category of V-Codes, which may not be seen as priorities for treatment.

In a move towards acknowledging the significance of relationships for psychopathology, DSM-IV-TR includes the Global Assessment of Relational Functioning (GARF) Scale in the Axes Provided for Further Study. Like the GAF, the GARF allows the clinician to rate the overall adaptive functioning of a relationship on a scale of 0 to 100. The ability of the family to meet the instrumental or emotional needs of its members is rated by consideration of the three following areas: *problem solving* (e.g., adaptability to stress, ability to resolve conflicts and negotiate), *organization* (e.g., maintenance of appropriate boundaries, appropriate distribution of control and responsibility) and *emotional climate*

(e.g., empathy, attachment, mutual affection, and respect). Although not yet widely used, the GARF has shown promise as a strategy for assessing the ways in which psychopathology affects relationships and the ways in which relationships elicit and maintain psychopathology (Yingling, 2003).

Family systems-oriented clinicians also have proposed alternative ways to conceptualize and classify psychopathologies as *relational disorders* (Kaslow, 1996). To date these intriguing ideas have not been incorporated into the DSM system, although a working group currently is in the process of developing a Classification of Relational Diagnoses (CORE) that it hopes to see included in the next version of the DSM (Group for the Advancement of Psychiatry Committee on the Family, 1996).

Cross-Cultural and Ethnic Diversity

In response to calls that the field of mental health be more culturally informed and sensitive to ethnic diversity, DSM-IV-TR attempts to deal with *multicultural* considerations in several ways. Cautions appear throughout the DSM that behaviours or emotions that are culturally sanctioned are not symptoms of a disorder. For example, if a child is quiet and withdrawn behaviours would not be considered symptoms if a child's culture expects a child to be quiet and withdrawn. First, there is a section describing culturally specific symptom patterns, prevalence and preferred ways of describing or exhibiting distress; for example, in certain cultures depressive disorders are characterized by a preponderance of somatic symptoms rather than by sadness. Next, there is an index of culture-bound syndromes that are found in one or only a few of the world's societies. The index includes the name of the condition, the cultures in which it is found, a brief description of the psychopathology, and a list of possibly related DSM-IV-TR disorders. Examples include *brain fog*, a West African condition primarily experienced by male high school or university students, in which a feeling of mental fatigue is accompanied by neck pain and blurring of vision; *falling out*, a Caribbean and Southern American phenomenon characterized by a sudden collapse, loss of vision, and an inability to move; and *taijin kyofusho*, a Japanese phenomenon involving intense fear that one's body or bodily functions are displeasing, embarrassing or offensive to others.

Nonetheless, it is the case that the diagnostic categories contained within DSM are creations of a particular Western cultural perspective, and it is far from certain that they are universally valid. There are a number of ways in which culture might affect diagnosis. A particular concern is that a culturally naive diagnostician may perceive as pathological behaviour that is normative in the context of the child's culture. For example, Tharp (1991) describes the preferences of certain Native American children for allowing time to pass before responding to a question as well as for avoiding direct eye contact with the speaker: a clinician who did not understand the meanings of these behaviours in their cultural context might make the error of assuming that the child is anxious or depressed. (We will revisit this issue in Chapter 16 on psychological assessment.) Another example is that styles of child rearing in the African American community that involve physical discipline and sharp verbal admonitions have historically been interpreted as abusive by investigators lacking in cultural understanding. (We will explore this issue in more detail in Chapter 14 when we discuss child maltreatment.)

Fundamentally, there is the inescapable problem that all diagnostic systems call for clinical judgement, judgement that might be coloured by issues of race, social class, ethnicity, religion, and the personal characteristics and predilections of the diagnostician. The developers of the DSM have made efforts to ensure that clinicians remain cognizant of these issues just as the American Psychological Association (2003) mandates that all psychologists should be clinically competent. Nonetheless, prejudices often are hidden, even from those who hold them (McIntosh, 1998), and so we will need to take care in our review of the psychopathologies to take into account ethnic and cultural considerations, wherever the data exist that allow us to do so. (see Box 3.2 on p. 105.)

The ICD-10

The (ICD-10) *Classification of Mental and Behavioural Disorders in Children and Adolescents* (World Health Organization, 1996) is based on the International Classification of Diseases, a diagnostic system that is widely used outside the USA. Like the DSM, it is multiaxial; however, the child is assessed on six axes in the ICD-10 system.

Axis One: Clinical Psychiatric Syndrome
Like the DSM's Axis I, this axis includes the major mental and behavioural disorders that may be seen in either children or adults.

Axis Two: Specific Disorders of Psychological Development
In a departure from the DSM, the ICD-10 separately assesses the extent to which the child experiences delays in development. These may occur in areas such as speech and language, scholastic skills (reading, spelling, arithmetic, etc.), and motor functions.

Axis Three: Intellectual Level
This axis provides a rating of the person's general level of intellectual functioning on an 8-point ordinal scale, ranging from very high intelligence to profound mental retardation. The extent of impairment in the child's functioning associated with intellectual deficits is also noted, whether minimal or significant.

Axis Four: Medical Conditions
Similar to DSM's Axis III, current non-psychiatric medical conditions, illnesses or injuries are coded here.

Axis Five: Associated Abnormal Psychosocial Situations
This axis includes situations in the child's psychosocial environment that might have implications for understanding the origins of the child's clinical psychiatric syndrome or that might be relevant for treatment planning. Unlike DSM's Axis IV, the list here is extensive and specific to the kinds of deficiencies in family life that are likely to affect children's development. A closer look is provided in Table 3.3. Each category is rated for severity from 2 to 0, with 2 at the highest level, 1 for situations that occurred but whose

TABLE 3.3 ICD-10 Axis Five: Associated Abnormal Psychosocial Situations

00 No significant distortion or inadequacy of the psychosocial environment
1 Abnormal intrafamilial relationships
  1.0 Lack of warmth in parent–child relationships
  1.1 Intrafamilial discord among adults
  1.2 Hostility toward or scapegoating of the child
  1.3 Physical child abuse
  1.4 Sexual abuse (within the family)
2 Mental disorder, deviance, or handicap in the child's primary support group
  2.0 Parental mental disorder/deviance
  2.1 Parental handicap/disability
  2.2 Disability in sibling
3 Inadequate or distorted intrafamilial communication
4 Abnormal qualities of parenting
  4.0 Parental overprotection
  4.1 Inadequate parental supervision/control
  4.2 Experiential deprivation
  4.3 Inappropriate parental pressures
5 Abnormal immediate environment
  5.0 Institutional upbringing
  5.1 Anomalous parenting situation
  5.2 Isolated family
  5.3 Living conditions that create a potentially harzardous psychosocial situation
6 Acute life events
  6.0 Loss of a love relationship
  6.1 Removals from home carrying significant contextual threat
  6.2 Negatively altered pattern of family relationships
  6.3 Events resulting in loss of self-esteem
  6.4 Sexual abuse (extrafamilial)
  6.5 Personal frightening experience
7 Societal stressors
  7.1 Persecution or adverse discrimination
  7.2 Migration or social transplantation
8 Chronic interpersonal stress associated with school/work
  8.0 Discordant relationships with peers
  8.1 Scapegoating of child by teachers or work supervisors
  8.2 Unrest in the school/work situation
9 Stressful events/situations resulting from the child's own disorder/disability
  9.0 Institutional upbringing
  9.1 Removal from home carrying significant contextual threat
  9.2 Events resulting in loss of self-esteem

severity was mild and falls short of the criteria guidelines, and 0 when no such clinically significant situations have arisen in the child's life.

Axis Six: Global Assessment of Psychosocial Disability

As with the DSM, the clinician is asked to rate the young person's overall psychological, social and occupational functioning at the time of the evaluation. A 9-point ordinal scale is used, ranging from 0 = superior social functioning to 9 = profound and pervasive social disability. Consideration is given to psychiatric, developmental or intellectual deficits and excludes problems that are related to physical or environmental limitations.

Strengths and Limitations of the ICD-10

Like the DSM, the ICD-10 retains the medical model and requires that children be classified into discrete categories, subject to all the limitations of clinical judgement discussed earlier. The fact that the ICD-10 asks the clinician to consider separately the child's developmental level suggests that this classification system is more developmentally friendly than the DSM. However, the focus of the developmental axis in ICD-10 is cognitive and motor development, to the exclusion of the other psychological variables we examined in Chapter 2, such as emotional and self-development. Thus, the developmental psychopathologist is unlikely to feel that either of these systems has yet captured the 'whole child'. On the other hand, a particularly valuable contribution of the ICD-10 is that it calls to the diagnostician's attention a comprehensive list of problems in the child's psychosocial environment that may have an impact on functioning. The clinician who is reminded to consider whether the child's peer relations are contributing to the problem (8.0; see Table 3.3), whether conflicts between adults are creating a stressful home life for the child (1.1), or whether the child's own behaviour problems generate stress and rejection (9.2) is taking a step further towards a transactional approach to understanding childhood psychopathology.

Now that we have addressed the strengths and limitations of each of the two core classification systems, it is important to return to the core question regarding any diagnosis: whether to diagnose or not. Collectively the two systems have been shown to have both strengths and weaknesses. Below we sum up the key overall issues which need to be weighed up when considering the use of classification systems in the process of diagnosis.

General Strengths and Limitations of Classifications Systems

There are clear positives to classifications systems, many of which have already been covered. The most important one is that it acts as a *guide* to a set of particular behaviours which may *inform* others about the *etiology, maintenance, protective and risk factors* of the disorders as well as *treatment* options. *Clear and specific* diagnostic criteria allow different researchers to gather and study samples of children or adults. Importantly, both DSM and ICD are open to revisions in the light of new information. For example, ICD-10 made a distinction between Oppositional Defiant Disorder and Conduct Disorder, whereas its precursors, such as ICD-9, did not make this distinction. The differentiation of the two disorders is based on research which shows that the two disorders have different correlates and prognoses. Box 3.1 demonstrates the case of when research has informed diagnosis.

Additionally classification systems provide an important platform for researchers and clinicians to communicate from. On the flip side there are limitations which need to be taken into consideration when using classification systems. For example, both ICD-10 and the DSM-IV have problems – technical problems that include *low reliability, poor coverage, high comorbidity* and *low validity*. The ICD and DSM systems have both been shown to have *poor reliability*. Clinicians who interviewed the same cases frequently reached different conclusions about the most appropriate diagnosis. These classification systems can also give limited *coverage* of different disorders. Along with the use of diagnostic criteria, there had been a gradual narrowing of definitions of disorders to reduce within-category heterogeneity and improve reliability. Many cases typically cannot be classified into clearly defined categories. To account for this, in the DSM individuals who fall outside a category are referred to as 'Pervasive Developmental Disorder Not Otherwise Specified; PDD-NOS' and in the ICD the term 'unspecified' is used. *Comorbidity* where more than one diagnosis may be given is also problematic in the two systems. The *validation* of diagnostic categories within the DSM and ICD systems involves demonstrating that cases which meet the diagnostic criteria for a particular category share common critical characteristics. These include predisposing risk factors, precipitating factors that trigger the onset of the disorder; maintaining factors that lead to persistence or exacerbation of the disorder; and protective factors that modify the impact of aetiological factors. The course of disorder and treatment should also be shared. However, there exists high variability within disorders and there are many cases of misdiagnosis.

It is important to note that there are also pragmatic and ethical concerns relating to diagnosis (Carr, 2006). There are clear ethical issues diagnosing youngsters and/or those with mental problems who are relatively powerless to resist this process. That is, diagnoses focus on weakness of a child rather than their actual strengths. Thus the process of traditional diagnosis may lead youngsters, their families and the community to view diagnosed children as defective. The same occurs for how the family is viewed by others. Some diagnoses have more negative connotations than others. For example, a label such as 'ADHD' or an 'attachment disorder' may level the label of 'dysfunctional' at the child's family. In the case where labelling leads to stigmatization, then it may only be justifiable to the extent that the diagnoses given lead to treatment which ameliorates the problems described by the labels. At the pragmatic level, there is some debate as to the usefulness of classification systems. Many clinicians argue that they offer very limited guidance on how to proceed clinically and, particularly in the case of the DSM, are fairly open to the clinician's integrity. In the majority of cases, no child is likely to match the profile perfectly due to many factors including severity, comorbidity and the

Box 3.1 Case Study: Early Infantile Schizophrenia

Sam is 12 years old and is described as an unusual boy. His mother had been aware of his difficulties relating to peers and being in a group situation since he was aged 2 years when he started to receive negative reactions from other toddlers. Despite repeated visits to professionals to express her concerns, no diagnosis was suggested as an explanation of his difficulties. During his years at primary school, teachers frequently called his mother to complain about his antisocial behaviour. Sam was regarded as rude and spoilt as he would not share or take turns with other children. When teachers asked him, 'What have I just been talking about?', he would imitate word for word what they had said. One professional suggested that Sam was emotionally disturbed. Sam was actually diagnosed late with an autism spectrum disorder (ASD); however, had he been diagnosed in the early 1970s he could well have received a diagnosis of early infantile schizophrenia.

Careful work by Kolvin in the late 1960s showed that the category of childhood schizophrenia included several disorders that could be distinguished from each other based on their patterns of symptoms and the timing of their onset (Kolvin, 1971). He argued that children with autism, who were then diagnosed as having childhood schizophrenia, had a unique disorder because it began earlier in life and had a unique pattern of symptoms. The work by Kolvin then paved the way for the creation of

several disorders that differed from those that had previously been combined as childhood schizophrenia, beginning in the DSM-III. For example, autism and other severe disorders that always begin in childhood were listed in a new pervasive developmental disorders category (American Psychiatric Association, 1980). Children who met the diagnostic criteria for schizophrenia continued to be given that diagnosis.

Over the years other cases were identified, while many were misdiagnosed (frequently as infantile schizophrenia). In the 1940s, Leo Kanner and Hans Asperger developed the foundation for the modern diagnosis of autism by laying out a clearer description of the disorder. Interestingly, Kanner was disturbed by how quickly the rate of diagnosis of new cases of autism rose after his paper was published. This was in the 1950s. Since then, of course, the diagnosis has been refined and subsequently broadened, resulting in the class of ASDs we are familiar with today. In many ways, the history of autism up to this point is not so different from the history of other debilitating disorders, like schizophrenia, in that it consists of slow acknowledgement of a unique set of symptoms, followed by attempts at classification and an increase in the number of diagnoses due to clearer diagnostic criteria. Only through the process of research are we able to refine and classify different disorders.

many complex interactions between risk and protective functions. Sadly, in practice many clinicians view the process of giving a DSM diagnosis as an administrative chore since in the USA insurance companies often link payment to the presence of the DSM diagnoses. The same is thought to occur in parts of Europe, particularly in the public health services, where funding may be linked to the completion of administrative forms on each patient seen and these forms include a requirement to give an ICD diagnosis (Carr, 2006).

Differences in the ICD-10 and DSM-IV definitions for the same disorder impede international communication and research efforts. Some of the criteria-set differences in DSM-IV and ICD-10

are substantive and reflect different conceptual approaches to classification. Work is under way on revising DSM-IV-TR1 and ICD-10 with plans for DSM-V to be published in 2012 and for ICD-11 to be completed by 2014. The forthcoming parallel development of DSM-V and ICD-11 offers an opportunity to harmonize the two classifications (First, 2009). The World Health Organization (WHO) has put these recommendations into practice by forming a DSM-ICD Harmonization Coordinating Group comprised of members of the DSM-V Task Force and the International Advisory Group for the Revision of ICD-10 with the charge to 'facilitate the achievement of the highest possible extent of uniformity and harmonization'.

The DSM-PC

An alternative diagnostic system that even better captures the developmental psychopathology approach is the DSM-PC, the *Diagnostic and Statistical Manual for Primary Care – Child and Adolescent Version* (Wolraich et al., 1997). The DSM-PC was developed by a consortium of pediatricians, child psychiatrists and child psychologists expressly to help primary care clinicians identify psychosocial factors that might be affecting the children who come to their consulting rooms. Because paediatricians and family doctors are often the professionals who first come into contact with children and adolescents with behavioural and emotional problems, it was deemed essential that they have a basis on which to evaluate whether the child's problems are part of the normal spectrum or whether they represent deviations that warrant a mental health referral.

The developers of the DSM-PC wanted to create a system that was clear, concise, objective and organized in order to facilitate revision in the light of new empirical evidence, as well as one that would be compatible with existing systems. In particular, the DSM-PC integrates aspects of both the DSM and the ICD, as we shall see now.

In addition, the DSM-PC makes two key assumptions about the nature of childhood psychological problems that are familiar to developmental psychopathologists. The first assumption is that *children's environments have an important impact on their mental health*. As the authors state:

A critical influence on children's general well-being – including behavioural and cognitive functioning and physical health – is the quality of the environment in which the child lives. A basic tenet of this manual is the central importance of the transaction over time between the child and the environment in which the child lives and grows. (p. 31)

The second assumption is that the *symptoms children display lie along a continuum ranging from normal variations to disorders*.

In order to take into account the transactional and developmental perspectives, the DSM-PC asks the clinician to evaluate the child on two dimensions:

Situations This section contains a list of potentially adverse situations that might affect a child's mental health, as well as descriptors of common behavioural responses that are indicative of the child's distress. Among the wide range of potentially stressful situations listed are disrupted attachment relationships, domestic violence, psychiatric disturbance in a parent, sexual abuse, social discrimination and/or family isolation, inadequate school resources, homelessness, unsafe neighbourhood, and natural disaster. For each situation, the clinician is provided with a developmentally sensitive list of protective and potentiating factors that might moderate the child's response to the stressor.

Child Manifestations The second section contains the classifications of child behaviour problems, divided into 10 categories. The disorders generally follow the DSM-IV-TR; however, because the DSM-PC includes behaviours that are on the normative spectrum, the terminology differs and additional distinctions are made:

1 *Developmental competency* (e.g., mental retardation; difficulties acquiring motor, speech or academic skills).

2 *Impulsive, hyperactive, inattentive behaviours* (e.g., overactivity, difficulty sustaining attention).

3 *Negative/Antisocial Behaviours* (e.g., negative emotional behaviours, aggressive/oppositional behaviours, secretive antisocial behaviours).

4 *Substance-Related Behaviours* (e.g., substance use or abuse).

5 *Emotions and Moods* (e.g., anxiety, sadness, obsessive-compulsive behaviours, suicidal ideation).

6 *Somatic Behaviour* (e.g., pain, daytime sleepiness, sleep problems).

7 *Feeding, eating and elimination* (e.g., soiling, purging-binge eating, body image dissatisfaction, irregular eating).

8 *Illness-related behaviours* (e.g., excessive fearfulness of medical procedures, non-compliance with medical regime, denial of physical illness).

9 *Sexual behaviours* (e.g., wishing to be, or believing one is, the other gender; crossdressing; discomfort with one's own sexual anatomy).

10 *Atypical behaviours* (repetitive or bizarre behaviours, absence of normal social relatedness).

Within each of these classifications, child behaviour problems are further subdivided into three levels of severity: developmental variations, problems, and disorders. The *developmental deviations* include behaviours that may concern parents but that are still within the normal range of age expectations. For example, an 18-month-old who still speaks in one-word sentences is by no means precocious but is still within the normal range. Often such variations are brought to the paediatrician's attention by parents who lack accurate information about normal child development, and their concerns are quickly resolved with a consultation and parent education. In contrast, a *problem* refers to behaviour that is significant enough to disrupt the child's functioning in school, family or peer relationships, but is not serious enough to warrant the diagnosis of a disorder. For example, a developmental/cognitive problem would be coded when a preschooler evidences a mild delay in acquisition of speech and language skills. Generally, such problems can be treated with a short-term intervention. Lastly, the *disorders* are those defined by DSM and represent clinically significant behaviour problems that are distressing and disruptive to functioning, such as the child whose stuttering interferes with school performance. The disorders generally require referral to a child mental health professional. The DSM-PC manual also describes how problems at each level of severity would present in infancy, early childhood, middle childhood or adolescence. An example of classifications related to sadness is provided in Table 3.4.

Strengths and Limitations of the DSM-PC

The DSM-PC has not taken us far afield from the medical model, given that it retains the focus on classifying the disordered behaviour with which children present. However, DSM-PC offers a number of advantages to the clinician with a developmental psychopathology perspective. First, the DSM-PC is *transactional*, viewing problems as arising from the relationship between the child and the environment. Consequently, the diagnostician is asked to consider a host of environmental, social and interpersonal factors that might have affected this child's development. Risks, vulnerabilities and protective factors are to be weighed. Second, the DSM-PC appreciates the *continuum* between normal and abnormal development and provides the diagnostician with guidelines for determining when development is slightly deviant or has indeed fallen off the normal course. Third, the DSM-PC is explicitly *developmental*, placing its definitions of variations, problems and disorders in the context of age-appropriate norms and behavioural manifestations. On the other hand, this diagnostic system also requires even more complex clinical judgements than the other two systems. The boundaries between the categories of deviation, problems and disorder are often fuzzy; and, because normal development is so varied, there can be no firm criteria for deciding whether behaviours exceed the normal range. Finally, data on its reliability and validity are not yet available.

The Empirically Based Approach

In contrast to the top-down approach exemplified by systems based on the medical model, such as the DSM and ICD, the empirically based approach can be termed 'bottom up' (Achenbach, 2000). (See

TABLE 3.4 Example of DSM-PC Categories: Sadness

Classification	Common Developmental Presentations
V65.49 Sadness Variation: Transient depressive responses to stress are normal in an otherwise healthy population. **V62.82 Bereavement:** Sadness related to a major loss that typically persists for less than 2 months after the loss. Children in hospitals or institutions often experience some of the fears that accompany a death or separation. These fears may be demonstrated in actions that mimic normal grief responses.	**Infancy:** Brief expressions of sadness, which normally first appear in the last quarter of the first year of life, manifest by crying, brief withdrawal and transient anger. **Early Childhood:** Transient withdrawal and sad affect occur after losses; bereavement due to the loss of a parent, pet or treasured object. **Middle Childhood:** Transient loss of self-esteem after experiencing failure and feelings of sadness with losses. **Adolescence:** Similar presentation to that of middle childhood but may also include fleeting thoughts of death. Bereavement includes loss of a boyfriend or girlfriend, friend or best friend.
V40.3 Sadness Problem: Sadness or irritability that begins to include some symptoms of major depressive disorders in mild form: • Depressed/irritable mood • Diminished interest or pleasure • Weight loss/gain or failure to make expected weight gains • Insomnia/hypersomnia • Psychomotor agitation/retardation • Fatigue or energy loss • Feelings of worthlessness or guilt • Diminished ability to think/concentrate These symptoms are more than transient and have a mild impact on the child's functioning. However, the behaviours are not sufficiently intense to qualify for a depressive disorder.	**Infancy:** Developmental regressions, fearfulness, anorexia, failure to thrive, sleep disturbances, social withdrawal, irritability and increased dependency, which are responsive to soothing and engagement by caregivers. **Early Childhood:** Sad affect becomes more apparent. Temper tantrums may increase, as well as physical symptoms such as soiling, constipation, bedwetting and nightmares. **Middle Childhood:** Some sadness that results in brief suicidal ideation with no clear plan of suicide, some apathy, boredom, low self-esteem, and unexplained physical symptoms such as headache and abdominal pain. **Adolescence:** Some disinterest, decrease in motivation, and daydreaming in class may lead to deterioration of schoolwork. Hesitancy in attending school, apathy and boredom may occur.
300.4 Dysthymic Disorder: Depressed/irritable mood for most of the day, for more days than not, for at least 1 year. Also the presence of two or more of the following: • Poor appetite/overeating • Insomnia/hypersomnia • Low energy or fatigue • Poor concentration/difficulty making decisions • Feelings of hopelessness Because of the chronic nature of the disorder, the child may not develop adequate social skills.	**Infancy:** Not diagnosed. **Early Childhood:** Rarely diagnosed. **Middle Childhood and Adolescence:** Feelings of inadequacy, loss of interest/pleasure, social withdrawal, guilt/brooding, irritability or excessive anger, decreased activity/productivity. May experience sleep/appetite/weight changes and psychomotor symptoms. Low self-esteem is common.

Table 3.5.) Instead of starting with a theoretical construct, such as Oppositional Defiant Disorder, and then collecting data to determine how well the label applies to children, the empirical approach starts by collecting data in the real world. The empiricist begins by measuring a large number of specific behaviours exhibited by disturbed children; eliminates those that are infrequent, redundant and obscure; and subjects the rest to statistical techniques designed to determine which are highly related to one another. The statistical technique employed is called *factor analysis*, and the behaviour

TABLE 3.5 Comparison of DSM and Empirically Based Approaches

Similarities Between Paradigms	
Explicit statements of problems to be assessed Some DSM categories and empirically based syndromes describe similar problems Statistically significant agreement between some diagnoses and syndromes	
Differences Between Paradigms	
DSM	**Empirically Based**
Categorical	Dimensional
Problems judged present or absent.	Problems scored on a continuum.
'Top-down' approach: Categories and criteria are chosen by committees.	'Bottom-up' approach: Syndromes are derived from empirical data.
Clinical cutpoints are identical for both genders, all ages and all informants.	Clinical cutpoints and norms are derived separately by gender, age and informant.
Individual clinician chooses sources of data, data to obtain and assessment procedures to use.	Standardized procedures for obtaining data.
No procedures specified for comparing data from different sources.	Statistical methods available for comparing scores across informants.
End products are diagnoses.	End products are syndrome scores and profiles compared against norms for age and gender.
Many separate diagnostic categories.	Specific problems are grouped into a smaller number of statistically robust syndromes.

Source: Achenbach, 2000.

items that relate to one another form *factors*. After examining the content of the interrelated items, the investigator assigns each factor a label. Such labels may resemble the theoretical constructs used in traditional diagnosis, such as 'oppositionality' or 'neurosis'; however, what the factors actually mean is a question that can only be answered by further empirical research.

Another important difference between the empirical approach and DSM is that, while DSM is *categorical*, classifying children in terms of whether or not they 'have' a disorder, the empirical approach is *dimensional*, rating children on the extent to which they show symptoms or problem behaviour consistent with a particular diagnosis. One objection to categories is their all-or-none quality; for example, a child either is

or is not depressed; and if he or she is, the clinician must decide whether the degree of disturbance is mild, moderate or severe. The dimensional approach is compatible with the idea of continuity between normality and psychopathology, with the number of symptoms providing a measure of the severity of the deviation from the norm.

The pre-eminent proponent of the empirically based approach is Thomas Achenbach. His Achenbach System of Empirically Based Assessment (ASEBA) (Achenbach and Rescorla, 2001) consists of a set of carefully developed measures to assess children's behaviour problems from the perspectives of parents, teachers/caregivers and, in the case of adolescents, the youths themselves. Here we will focus on the parent report measure, the

Child Behaviour Checklist (CBCL) (Achenbach, 1991).

Achenbach's first step was to collect descriptions of pathological behaviour from psychiatric case histories and from the literature. Through a series of preliminary studies these were reduced to 112 items that form the current CBCL. Here are some examples of items on the checklist: argues a lot, complains of loneliness, does not eat well, runs away from home, has strange ideas. To obtain norms, the CBCL was filled out by parents of 4994 children derived from a national survey encompassing 40 US states, as well as Australia and England. The analyses yielded both narrow-band and wide-band factors. The narrow-band factors included specific **syndromes**, or behaviour problems, such as Withdrawn/Depressed, Somatic Complaints, Social Problems, Attention Problems and Aggressive Behaviour. The Withdrawn/Depressed syndrome contains the following behavioural items: would rather be alone than with others, secretive, shy, sad, and withdrawn. The Aggressive Behaviour scale includes these behavioural items: destroys own and others' things, disobedient in home and school, argues, fights, and threatens others.

Several of the narrow-band syndromes were grouped together to form two wide-band factors. The **internalizing** factor comprises Anxious/Depressed, Withdrawn/Depressed, and Somatic Complaints, and the **externalizing** factor comprises Rule-Breaking Behaviour and Aggressive Behaviour. The internalizing–externalizing distinction describes two very different symptom pictures. Anxious children, for example, generally are well behaved but are tormented by fears or guilt. They suffer inwardly, internalizing their distress. On the other hand, some children act out their problems in relation to others, thereby externalizing their distress. It is important to note, however, that internalizing–externalizing is a dimension of behaviour, not a typology of children. While some children fall at either extreme, many of them demonstrate mixtures of both elements; that is, children can be both sad and aggressive or have a 'nervous stomach' and steal.

By comparing data from normal and clinical populations, it is possible to determine cut-off scores, below which the child is considered within the normal range and above which the child would be considered disturbed. Children whose scores are higher than those of 98 per cent of children in the normative population are considered to be above the clinical cut-off. These norms differ by age and gender. For example, girls generally are rated lower than boys on aggressiveness and therefore the cut-off score for girls is lower.

After scoring all eight narrow-band scales, the clinician can obtain a profile indicating which scales are within normal limits and which exceed them. A hypothetical child might be within the normal limits for the internalizing scales of Anxious/Depressed, Withdrawn/Depressed and Somatic Complaints, while exceeding the norm in the externalizing scales of Rule-Breaking Behaviour and Aggressive Behaviour. Figure 3.1 presents the profile of a 15-year-old boy's behaviour based on the parent-report version of the CBCL.

In an innovation for the most recent version, Achenbach has included profiles that relate children's CBCL scores to DSM-oriented categories: affective problems (items reflecting depression and suicidality), anxiety, somatic problems, attention deficit/hyperactivity, oppositional defiance and conduct problems. Thus, the CBCL can be used to assist the clinician in determining whether one of the subjective DSM categories actually fits the data.

Limitations of the Empirical Approach

The empirical approach offers significant advantages over more subjective diagnostic systems, including increased precision, reliability and behavioural objectivity. However, those benefits come at some cost. One of the prices paid is in comprehensiveness. For example, Achenbach's system provides us with eight narrow-band and two broad-band dimensions for rating children's problems, and these map onto six DSM-oriented diagnoses. In contrast, DSM-IV-TR and ICD are more differentiated; for example, they distinguish between degrees of depression (e.g., major depression and dysthymia) and have separate diagnoses for subtypes of anxiety disorders such as separation anxiety and phobia.

FIGURE 3.1 CBCL Profile of a 15-Year-Old Boy.

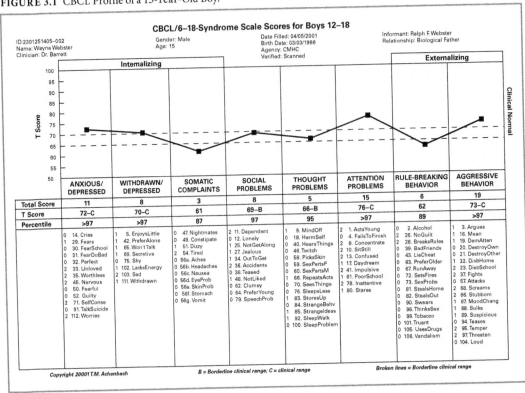

Source: From Achenbach and Rescorla, 2001.

DSM-IV-TR and ICD also contain diagnoses not found among Achenbach's syndromes, most notably anorexia nervosa, bulimia, specific learning disabilities and autism. Because the empirically based approach starts with descriptors that occur frequently in clinical populations, it has difficulty capturing rare but important disturbances.

Further, while the empirical approach is more behaviourally specific and objective, subjective judgements still enter into informants' ratings (Drotar et al., 1995). While it is true that the statement 'Is disobedient at home' is more objective than 'Has a problem with authority figures', the former still requires a judgement. Thus, the same behaviour a mother might regard as disobedient in her son might be dismissed by the father as being 'just the way boys are'. Behavioural ratings depend on who does the rating and the situation in which the behaviour occurs. Parents, teachers

and professionals may disagree in rating a particular child either because they evaluate the same behaviour differently or because they observe the child in different settings. An oppositional girl may respond to the teacher's firm discipline and thus not display the problem behaviour she does at home, while the inattentive child's problems may emerge in the school setting but not be noticeable to parents. Achenbach's system takes into account the perspective of different raters by providing methods for integrating and comparing scores across informants. However, when raters disagree, clinical judgement is needed in order to interpret the meaning of these discrepancies. Are the mother's ratings high due to the fact that she is stressed and intolerant of even ordinary misbehaviour, or are the father's low ratings due to the fact that the child indeed behaves differently when he is present?

Box 3.2 Case Study: Comparing Diagnostic Systems

In Chapter 2, we introduced the case of Zoey, whose development we tracked from birth to age 14. Recall that when Zoey was age 10, after experiencing her parents' divorce, a move to the inner city and her mother's return to the workforce, Zoey began exhibiting a number of behaviour problems. These included angry outbursts and argumentativeness with the teacher, poor peer relationships and sullenness with her mother. Further, she was struggling with school, hampered by a reading difficulty that had long gone undiagnosed. While our knowledge of Zoey's eventual good outcome points out one of the major limitations of diagnosis – it takes a static snapshot of a child whose developmental trajectory is still in motion – let us look at how different diagnostic systems might have classified her 10-year-old behaviour.

DSM-IV-TR

Axis I (Clinical Disorder): 313.81 Oppositional Defiant Disorder; 315.00 Reading Disorder

Axis II (Personality Disorder/Mental Retardation): V71.09 No diagnosis

Axis III (General Medical Conditions): None

Axis IV (Psychosocial and Environmental Problems): Parent–Child Problem (divorce, mother–child conflict); Educational Problems (conflict with teachers and classmates); Economic Problems (inadequate finances)

Axis V (Global Assessment of Functioning): 65

DSM-PC

Axis I (Clinical Disorder): 313.81 Oppositional Defiant Disorder; 315.00 Reading Disorder; V40.3 Sadness Problem; V65.49 Hyperactive/Impulsive Variation

Axis II (Personality Disorder/Mental Retardation): V71.09 No diagnosis

Axis III (General Medical Conditions): None

Axis IV (Psychosocial and Environmental Problems): V61.20 Challenges to Attachment Relationship; V61.0 Divorce; V60.2 Inadequate Financial Status; V62.3 Discord with Peers/Teachers

Axis V (Global Assessment of Functioning): 65

ICD-10

Axis One (Clinical Psychiatric Syndrome): F92.8 Mixed Disorder of Conduct and Emotions; Rule out F91.3 Oppositional Defiant Disorder

Axis Two (Specific Disorders of Psychological Development): F81.0 Specific Reading Disorder

Axis Three (Intellectual Level): 4

Axis Four (Medical Conditions): None

Axis Five: (Associated Abnormal Psychosocial Situations):

1.0 Lack of warmth in parent–child relationships

1.5 Intra-familial discord among adults

5.4 Living conditions that create a potentially hazardous psychosocial situation

6.6 Negatively altered pattern of family relationships

8.0 Discordant relationships with peers

Axis Six: Global Assessment of Psychosocial Disability: 5

Achenbach System of Empirically Based Assessment
(Based on Teacher Report Form)

Syndrome Scale Scores

Anxious/Depressed:	Normal
Withdrawn/Depressed:	Borderline
Somatic Complaints:	Normal
Social Problems:	Clinical
Thought Problems:	Normal
Attention Problems:	Borderline
Rule-Breaking Behaviour:	Normal
Aggressive Behaviour:	Clinical

Factor Scores

Internalizing:	Normal
Externalizing:	Borderline

DSM-Oriented Scales

Affective Problems:	Borderline
Anxiety Problems:	Normal
Somatic Problems:	Normal
Attention Deficit/ Hyperactivity Problems:	Borderline
Oppositional Defiant Problems:	Clinical
Conduct Problems:	Borderline

FIGURE 3.2 Abnormally Normal Behaviour?

The fact that information providers often have discrepant views of the same child is not a problem confined to multivariate statistical assessment but is present in all assessment procedures that rely on multiple sources of information. However, we do have a few leads about what sources would be most valid for some particular psychopathologies. There is some evidence that parents and teachers are better informants in regard to *externalizing* symptoms, such as disruptive behaviour, hyperactivity, inattentiveness and oppositional-defiant disorders than are children, who tend to under-report them. In turn, children's own reports are more informative about *internalizing* symptoms such as anxiety and depression (Cantwell, 1996). This is an issue we return to in Chapter 16, when we discuss strategies for coping with multiple sources of data and divergent information about the same child.

Normal Problems and Normal Problem Behaviour

If we are to treat psychopathology as normal development gone awry, we must anchor our thinking in a definition of normality. Moreover, we must have an idea of the problems and problem behaviours inherent in normal development, since normality never means problem-free.

Normal development involves both problems and problem behaviours (see Fig. 3.2). To take one example of the latter: one study found that about half the children in kindergarten through to grade 2 were described as 'restless', while another study found that a similar per cent of 6- to 12-year-olds were described as 'overactive'. While both of these behaviours are part of the syndrome of hyperactivity, it would be incorrect to assume that half the children were hyperactive, since they have neither the clustering nor the intensity and chronicity of problems that would interfere with adaptive functioning. On the other hand, it would be equally foolish to deny that restlessness and overactivity constitute a problem both at home and in school. (See Box 3.3.)

S. B. Campbell (1989, 2006) outlines some typical non-psychopathological developmental problems during the infancy and preschool period:

The 'Difficult' Infant
Studies of individual differences in infants, or infant temperament, have shown that some infants are easy to care for while others are difficult. The latter tend to be irritable, slow to adapt to change in routine, intense and negative in their reactions, and irregular in their biological functioning. If cared for sensitively, infants can outgrow this difficult phase; however, if caretakers are impatient and intolerant,

Box 3.3 Are the Problems of America's Children Getting Worse?

Attention deficit hyperactivity disorder (ADHD), a condition characterized by inattention, restlessness and impulsivity, is commonly diagnosed in early childhood and affects between 3 and 5 per cent of American children, according to the National Institute of Mental Health. This means that 'in a classroom of 25 to 30 children, it is likely that at least one of them will have ADHD'. Some studies – and some school teachers – will tell you that is a conservative estimate. While in statistical terms there *appears* to have been an increase in ADHD cases, whether that means an actual rise in the number of children born with the condition or a perceived increase due to better recognition and more frequent diagnosis is not entirely clear. In most of Europe, the disorder is commonly dismissed 'as simply a behavioural problem', which can trivialize the contributing neurological factors.

The predominance of American research in this field and apparent differences in the prevalence of ADHD, or hyperkinesis, as defined by the World Health Organization ICD, has also led to the impression that this is largely an American disorder and is much less prevalent elsewhere. The question still remains, however, whether ADHD is largely an American disorder, perhaps stemming from social and cultural factors which are more common in American society. Alternatively, is this behavioural disorder common to children worldwide, or to a large number of races and societies, but not recognized by the medical community, perhaps due to confusion regarding its diagnosis and/or misconceptions regarding its adverse impact on children and their families and society as a whole, or persistent concerns regarding its treatment with stimulant drugs?

Factors affecting prevalence rates include terminology used to define ADHD, characteristics of the sample population, and methods of diagnosis. Prevalence is further complicated by differences in how rigorously all the elements of the DSM-IV definition are applied. For example, some researchers omit the requirement for symptoms to be present in at least two settings such as home and in a school environment (e.g. Magnusson et al., 1999), while others omit the requirement for functional impairment resulting from the symptoms (e.g. Gadow et al., 2000). Other factors which affect the diagnosis of ADHD in different studies are the informants used to assess symptoms, e.g. whether parents and/or teachers and/or subjects; and whether the diagnosis is based on scores on behaviour checklists or from direct interviews or both (e.g. Graetz et al., 2001).

It is generally agreed that the prevalence of ADHD is significantly greater in boys than girls, especially in children. Thus the ratio of males to females in the sample population can affect the apparent prevalence and may need to be taken into account. Similarly, the prevalence of ADHD is known to vary with age. These confounding factors make it difficult to compare the prevalence data for ADHD from one study and from one country to another. It is necessary to take all these factors into account when comparing data from different studies. Other possible factors for the general increase in ADHD prevalence include advances in behavioural disorder classification, efficacy of clinical and behavioural treatments for ADHD and improvement in clinical, parental and societal recognition of disorders. The past decade has also seen an increase in prenatal risk factors for any developmental disability, such as older parental age, pre-term birth and the use of hormonal infertility treatments.

---

or change routines abruptly and often, the chances of behaviour problems in the toddler period are increased.

The Defiant Toddler

Disciplinary problems and uncertainty about when and how to set limits are the major concerns of parents of toddlers. In most instances the problems are stage-specific, leaving no residue. However, paren-

tal mismanagement, say in the form of overcontrol, may increase the likelihood that problems will develop and persist.

The Insecurely Attached Child

We have already described the concept of secure and insecure attachment and reviewed the evidence that the insecurely attached infant may be at risk for problems in the area of initiative and social relations. However, such problems are not inevitable and can be minimized by sensitive caregiving. In Chapter 6, we will review the evidence.

The Aggressive or Withdrawn Preschooler

Aggressive behaviour towards peers is a common complaint of parents and teachers of preschoolers, with boys being more aggressive than girls. However, as with other behaviour problems, there is no need to read ominous portents into such aggressiveness unless it is coupled with mismanagement by parents or a discordant family situation. Social withdrawal, unlike aggression, is relatively rare and has not been satisfactorily studied. There is tentative evidence that the shy, quiet child is less at risk for developing behaviour problems than is the disruptive one, but such risk may be increased in extreme cases when combined with other internalizing problems such as separation anxiety or dysphoric mood.

Next, at the other end of our developmental spectrum the American Psychological Association (2002a) outlines some normal behaviour problems of adolescence.

The Oppositional Adolescent

Adolescents often practise their new higher reasoning skills by engaging adults in debates, arguing persistently and taking an oppositional stance over matters that may seem trivial to their parents. By the same token, they are often highly critical of the adults around them, seeming to intentionally search for discrepancies, contradictions or exceptions to what adults say. Parents who take personally this excessive fault-finding might experience raising an adolescent as a highly frustrating experience. However, the teenager's argumentativeness is best viewed as a form of cognitive exercise that helps adolescents to develop their critical thinking skills.

The Overly Dramatic/Impulsive Youth

The teenage years are a time of heightened emotionality and, sometimes, rash thinking. Adolescents may appear to jump to conclusions, stating extreme opinions that startle and concern the adults around them. Such bravado, however, may be an attempt to cover anxiety and uncertainty. By the same token, adolescents may have a ten-dency towards overexaggeration and dramatics because they are experiencing their world in a particularly intense way. While adults may complain that everything seems to be a big deal to teens, to the youths themselves, what is happening in the moment indeed appears dire.

The Egocentric Teenager

As adolescents focus inwards in order to explore such stage-salient issues as identity, gender role and sexuality, they may appear to adults to be excessively 'me-centered'. With time, they can be expected to develop a more reciprocal orientation. Where perspective-taking abilities do not develop naturally, these skills can be taught.

The DSM-IV-TR Disorders

While keeping in mind its limitations, throughout this text, we will be utilizing the DSM-IV-TR classifications of the disorders. Here we provide summaries only of those specific psychopathologies that we will subsequently discuss in detail in later chapters.

Adjustment Disorders

We describe **adjustment disorders** first because they form a link between the normal problems just described and the more serious psychopathologies to come. The symptoms of an adjustment disorder emerge in reaction to a recent identified stressor. The symptoms are significant enough to interfere with social, academic or occupational functioning and are in excess of the normal expected reaction. Adjustment disorders may occur with *depression* (sadness, hopelessness), *anxiety* (nervousness, separation fears), disturbance of *conduct* (aggression, truancy), or a combination of these. However, the symptoms do not persist longer than six months after the termination of the stressor, thus marking the boundary between adjustment disorders and other more persistent disorders.

Disorders Usually First Diagnosed in Infancy, Childhood or Adolescence

As for the more serious psychopathologies, DSM-IV distinguishes between disturbances that are specific to children and those that are essentially the same for children and adults. We present those in the former category first.

Mental Retardation

Mental retardation is defined as significantly below-average intellectual functioning (i.e., an IQ of 70 or below) combined with deficits in adaptive functioning such as self-care, social skills and personal independence.

Learning Disorders

Learning disorders include *reading disorder, mathematics disorder* and *disorder of written expression*. In each instance, the academic ability is substantially below what is expected given the child's chronological age, measured intelligence or age-appropriate education.

Pervasive Developmental Disorders

The primary disorder here is **autism**, which is marked by a qualitative impairment in social interaction (e.g., lack of social or emotional reciprocity, impaired use of non-verbal behaviour such as eye contact and gestures to regulate social interaction); gross and sustained impairment in communication (e.g., delayed or total absence of spoken language, stereotyped language, absence of imaginative play); and restricted, repetitive and stereotyped patterns of behaviour, interests and activities.

Attention Deficit and Disruptive Behaviour Disorders

The disorders included here were formerly listed under separate categories. They have been subsumed under a single classification because of the frequency with which they overlap.

Attention deficit hyperactivity disorder is characterized by a number of inattentive behaviours (e.g., being easily distracted, having difficulty in following through on instructions, frequent shifting from one uncompleted activity to another) and/or by hyperactivity-impulsivity (e.g., acting before thinking, fidgeting, having difficulty waiting in line or taking turns).

Conduct disorder is characterized by repetitive and persistent patterns of behaviour in which either the basic rights of others or major age-appropriate societal norms or rules are violated (e.g., initiating fights, using weapons that can cause serious physical harm, stealing, setting fires, truancy).

Oppositional defiant disorder is marked by a pattern of negativistic, hostile, defiant behaviour (e.g., loses temper, argues with adults and defies their requests, deliberately annoys others, lies, bullies).

Elimination Disorders

In this category we will only be discussing **enuresis**, which is defined as repeated voiding of urine into bed or clothes at a chronological age of at least 5 years, and **encopresis**, which involves soiling.

Other Disorders of Infancy, Childhood or Adolescence

Separation anxiety disorder is characterized by excessive anxiety concerning separation from those to whom the child is attached; for example, unrealistic worry about harm befalling an attachment figure, refusal to go to school in order to stay with an attachment figure, refusal to go to sleep without being near an attachment figure.

Reactive attachment disorder is characterized by disturbed social relatedness (e.g., excessive inhibition or ambivalence, or diffuse attachments manifested by indiscriminate sociability with relative strangers) due to grossly pathogenic care, such as neglect or frequent change of caretakers.

Disorders Diagnosed in Children, Adolescents and Adults

The following disorders either have the same manifestations in children as in adults or can be made applicable to children with a few specific modifications.

Substance-Related Disorders

Substance-related disorders are specific to a specific substance (alcohol, cocaine, cannabis, amphetamines, etc.) and involve clinically significant distress or impairment of function relating to its use. The classifications involve substance use disorders, including **substance abuse** and **substance dependence** or **substance-induced disorders** that

TABLE 3.6 The Relationship Between Psychopathology and Normal Development

Developmental Process	Infancy (0–12 months)	Toddlerhood (1–2½ years)	Preschool-Age (2½–6 years)	
Stage-salient issues	Biological regulation, secure attachment	Affect regulation, autonomous self-hood	Self-regulation, formation of interpersonal relations outside family	
Psychosexual development (Freud)	Oral	Anal	Phallic → Oedipal	
Ego development (Erikson)	Trust *vs* mistrust	Autonomy *vs* shame and doubt	Initiative *vs* guilt	
Separation individuation (Mahler)	Normal autism → Symbiosis	Differentiation → Practising	Rapprochement → On the road to object constancy	
Cognitive development (Piaget)	Sensorimotor		Preoperational	
Attachment	Preferential smile → Separation reactions	Caregiver as secure base	Goal-directed partnership	
Self-development	Self-as-agent	Self-constancy emerges	Behavioural self: defined 'all-or-none' by abilities and actions	
Emotional development	Emotions driven by immediate experience; labile, primary and intense	Emotion language expands, displays heightened (temper tantrums, fears)	Emotions viewed as caused by external events; emotion regulation increases	
Moral development			Preconventional: absolute, rigid, literal	
Gender and sexuality		Gender identity Curiosity about own body	Gender constancy; stereotyped interests Curiosity about others' bodies	
Peer relations	Focused on relations with caregivers, egocentric	Recognition of others' emotions, empathy	Increasing peer interactions, social comparison; co-operative play	
Family relations	Dependent on parents to define meaning of events and provide safety	Parents must tolerate vacillation between dependency and independent strivings		
Emergence of psychopathologies	Autism	Reactive attachment Attention deficit hyperactivity disorder	Separation anxiety disorder Oppositional defiant Enuresis/encopresis	

	Middle Childhood (6–11 years)	Pre-Adolescence (11–13 years)	Adolescence (13–17 years)	Late Adolescence-Young Adulthood (17–20 years)
	Mastery of academic and social environments	Individuation, identity, sexuality	Independence from family, formation of intimate relationships	Work, purpose and meaning in life, formation of lifelong romantic attachments
	Latency		Genital	
	Industry *vs* inferiority		Identity *vs* role diffusion	Intimacy *vs* isolation
	Concrete operations	Formal operations begin	Metacognition and abstraction continue to develop	
	Internal working model of self and other guides relationships	Re-emergence of conflict over closeness *vs* independence	Formation of new attachments opens opportunities for the reworking of old ones	
	Psychological self: stable internal representation	Abstract, future-oriented self	Self increasingly stable, integrated, self-reflective	
	Affects more stable, affective 'style' emerges, capacity for internally generated emotions	Labile emotions, negative affect common	Stable affect regulation, capacity for full range of emotions and defences against them	
	Conventional: rule-bound, right *vs* wrong	Perspective taking; considerations of mutuality	Post-conventional: self-determined moral principles	
	Sex-segregated play Understanding of relationship between genitals and procreation	Increasing flexibility of gender roles Knowledge of adult sexuality, combined with misinformation	Gender stereotyped behaviour re-emerges Sexual experimentation, awareness of sexual preference	Stable gender role adherence Commitment to sexual preference and intimate partner
	Sustained friendship; relations with adults outside family; social perspective taking	Group-oriented relationships with peers increasingly important, social problem-solving	Peers have increasing importance over family	Stable, deep, meaningful friendships and romantic relationships
	Family's functioning viewed in increasingly public realms	Boundaries must become more flexible to allow adolescent independence	Realignment of relationships to allow adolescent to function as young adult	
	Conduct disorder Social/school phobia Learning disorders Anxiety disorders	Substance abuse Depression bipolar Disorder gender Identity disorder	Eating disorders Schizophrenia	Personality disorders

are caused by ingestion (e.g., intoxication, anxiety, mood disorder, psychosis).

Schizophrenia

Schizophrenia is a severe, pervasive disturbance consisting of delusions, hallucinations, disorganized speech, bizarre behaviours, and the so-called negative symptoms of flat affect, avolition and alogia. Among the different types of schizophrenia are the *paranoid type*, marked by delusions or hallucinations, and the *disorganized type*, marked by disorganized speech and behaviour and inappropriate affect.

Mood Disorders

Major depression is defined in terms of a depressed mood, weight loss, insomnia, psychomotor agitation or retardation, feelings of worthlessness or guilt, indecisiveness, recurrent thoughts of death, and markedly diminished interest or pleasure in activities. It occurs in single or repeated episodes. **Dysthymic disorder** designates a chronic state of depression lasting at least one year. The third major category, **bipolar disorder**, is characterized by mood swings from depression to mania.

Anxiety Disorders

There are many anxiety disorders, but here we describe only those we will be discussing in later chapters.

Specific **phobia** is a fear provoked by the presence or anticipation of a specific object or situation (e.g., flying, heights, animals). The phobic stimulus is avoided or endured with marked distress. While adults recognize the unreasonable nature of the fear, this is not true of children.

Social phobia, also known as social anxiety disorder, involves excessive anxiety and avoidance of situations in which one might be exposed to unfamiliar people or required to perform in front of them. Typically, the child fears that he or she will be embarrassed or negatively evaluated in a public setting.

Obsessive-compulsive disorder is characterized either by obsessions, defined as recurrent thoughts, impulses or images that are intrusive and inappropriate and cause marked anxiety or distress, or by compulsions, defined as ritualistic behaviours (e.g., hand washing) or mental acts (e.g., counting, repeating words silently) that a person feels driven to perform in response to an obsession or according to rigidly applied rules.

Posttraumatic stress disorder results when a person has experienced an event involving actual or threatened death or injury to the self or others. Among the many symptoms are persistent re-experiencing of the traumatic event (e.g., through recurrent, intrusive, distressing recollections), persistent avoidance of stimuli associated with the trauma (e.g., inability to recall aspects of the trauma or a diminished range of interests or activities) and persistent symptoms of increased arousal (e.g., difficulty falling asleep, irritability, difficulty concentrating).

Generalized anxiety disorder involves excessive worry and tension that is uncontrollable and pervasive across stimuli and situations.

Eating Disorders

Anorexia nervosa is an intense fear of gaining weight even though the individual is underweight, an undue influence of body weight on self-evaluation or denial of the seriousness of current low body weight, and a body weight less than 85 per cent of that expected. **Bulimia nervosa** is marked by recurrent episodes of binge eating along with a sense of lack of control over eating during the episode. Self-valuation is unduly influenced by body shape and weight, while weight is often normal.

Gender Identity Disorders

Gender identity disorder is evidenced by a strong and persistent desire to be, or insistence that one is, a member of the other sex. The child displays an intense discomfort with the gender roles and anatomical features associated with his or her own biological sex.

Personality Disorders

Personality disorders are inflexible patterns of behaviour and inner experience that deviate significantly from social expectations and lead to distress or impairment. Their onset is seen in adolescence and early adulthood and they are rarely applied to children. However, increasing attention has been drawn to a particular personality disorder whose precursors appear to manifest themselves early enough in life to warrant diagnosis in young persons. **Borderline personality disorder** involves a pervasive instability in interpersonal relationships, self-image and affect. We will explore its manifestations as we discuss the transition from late adolescence to adulthood.

Integration of Normal Development and Psychopathology

In Table 3.6, we present an outline of the developmental variables associated with each developmental period, as described in Chapter 2, and show how these are related to the emergence of the various psychopathologies. This developmental time line is approximate. With some exceptions, most of the disorders can be seen in children of any age. Even infants, for example, can exhibit symptoms of depression. However, what we have done is to display the age that is associated with an increased *prevalence* of the disorder, since this indicates that the risk of developing this psychopathology is associated with this developmental stage. Consequently, we place depression in the early adolescent period, given that this age is associated with a dramatic increase in the diagnosis of mood disorders, particularly for girls.

We are now ready for a detailed exploration of selected psychopathologies. As much as possible we will take them in chronological order from a development standpoint. In all cases we will use the information about normal development provided in Chapter 2 to answer the question, How can this psychopathology be understood in terms of normal development gone awry? How deviations from normality at one point in time affect future development will also be discussed. This dual concern requires reconstructing the natural history of the psychopathology. Finally, the issue of the efficacy of psychotherapeutic measures in curtailing further deviance will be addressed. However, a systematic examination of psychotherapy will come only after we conclude our exploration of the psychopathologies.

CHAPTER 04

Infancy: The Developmental Consequences of Mental Retardation

In this chapter, we have our first encounter with a disorder that is not coded with the other Clinical Disorders on Axis I of the DSM-IV-TR (see Chapter 3). Mental Retardation is coded on the DSM Axis II, reflecting its pervasive effect on functioning and the need to take its presence into account when considering any other diagnosis that might be present for the individual.

Is Mental Retardation a Psychopathology?

Why include *mental retardation* (MR) in a discussion of psychopathology? Just because a child has a low score on an IQ test, should he or she be placed in the company of children who have a conduct disorder or a phobia or attention deficit hyperactive disorder? On the surface, such a child does not seem to be 'troubled' in the way those other children do – he or she is just cognitively slower than others. As we shall soon see, this question has been of concern to the experts, who have made the definition of MR increasingly contingent upon factors other than intelligence quotient (IQ) scores alone.

On the other hand, MR indeed may be related to psychopathology. It was once believed that mental retardation excluded an individual from a psychiatric diagnosis, under the misapprehension that an individual with a low IQ score was not capable of developing a full-fledged neurosis. Consequently, the emotional problems of those with MR were dismissively attributed to their cognitive limitations or to underlying medical problems. However, we now know that not only may individuals with MR develop the full range of psychopathologies, but they are at three to four times the risk for developing psychological disturbances when compared with members of the general population.

Returning to the question that opened our discussion, the answer is clearly no; MR is not a psychopathology. However, MR should be considered a deviation in development that increases the risk for psychopathology (Einfeld et al., 2011). All the factors that come into play in the developmental psychopathology of disorder – biology, emotion, cognition, family relationships, peers and sociocultural factors – also affect the developing individual with an MR diagnosis.

Definition

Historical Background

Prior to 1959, the original definition of MR was in terms of *subaverage intelligence*, as measured by a standardized **intelligence test**. Numerically, an IQ (**intelligence quotient**) score that is more than two standard deviations below the mean is regarded as a significant deviation from average intelligence, which means that an IQ of 70 was considered to be the cut-off score for the MR range.

In 1959, **adaptive behaviour** was added as a criterion. If a person were adapting adequately to the environment, why regard him or her as dysfunctional or abnormal just because the score on a cognitive test was below a given cut-off point? For example, there is a group called '6-hour retardates' who do poorly in school (which is approximately 6 hours per day) but function well, say, in a rural or inner-city environment. Thus, the key to MR became not a test score but the way an individual *functioned*.

The American Association of Mental Retardation (AAMR) Adaptive Behavior Scale (Nihira et al., 1974) is an example of an instrument that assesses adaptive behaviour. Factor analyses showed that the scale contains three dimensions: personal self-sufficiency, community self-sufficiency and personal-social responsibility (Nihira, 1976). *Personal self-sufficiency* is found at all ages and involves the ability to satisfy immediate personal needs such as eating, toileting and

dressing. *Community self-sufficiency* involves independence beyond immediate needs, along with self-sufficiency in relation to others: for example, using money, travelling, shopping and communicating adequately. *Personal-social responsibility* involves initiative and perseverance – the ability to undertake a task on one's own and see it through to completion. These last two factors represent higher-level behaviour than the mere satisfaction of immediate needs and emerge at around 10 years of age.

A Controversial Revision

Mental retardation is not something you have, like blue eyes or a bad heart. Nor is it something you are, like being short or thin. It is not a medical disorder ... nor is it a mental disorder.... Mental retardation is present when specific intellectual limitations affect the person's ability to cope with the ordinary challenges of everyday living in the community. If the intellectual limitations have no real effect on functioning, then the person does not have mental retardation. (American Association on Mental Retardation, 1992, pp. 9, 13)

These statements represent the latest in a series of reconceptualizations by the AAMR. In 1992 the AAMR proposed a new definition of MR that takes the concept of adaptation further than had been done in the past. Adaptation itself is not some kind of trait or absolute quality individuals possess. Rather, adaptation is always *in relation to an environment*. Therefore, the characteristics of the environment to which the individual is adapting must be scrutinized before one can determine whether that individual is mentally retarded.

The new conceptualization of MR is represented schematically in Fig. 4.1. Note that the criterion of *functioning* is at the base of the triangle, signifying that it is the basic, or fundamental, construct. Thus, how well or how poorly a child can function in a given environment is more important than intellectual level. Functioning, in turn, is determined by two factors: *capabilities* and *environments*.

FIGURE 4.1 General Structure of the Definition of Mental Retardation.

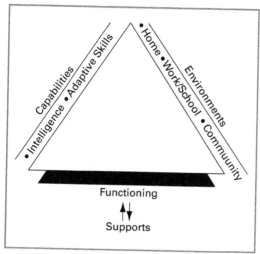

Source: American Association on Mental Retardation, 1992.

Capabilities (or competencies) are variables in the intra-personal context. There are two kinds of capabilities: intelligence and adaptive skills.

1 *Intelligence* encompasses both cognition and learning. The AAMR identified an IQ of 75 or lower as the cut-off criterion for MR.

2 *Adaptive skills* are made up of practical and social intelligence. *Practical* intelligence involves the skills needed to maintain one's independence in managing the ordinary activities of daily living (e.g., bathing, dressing or feeding oneself). *Social* intelligence involves the ability to comprehend appropriate social behaviour, social skills and good ethical judgement in interpersonal situations.

Environments are conceptualized as the *specific settings* in which the person lives, learns, plays, works, socializes and interacts. The environment must be typical of the child's same-age peers and appropriate to the child's socio-economic background. Mental retardation quite literally does not exist when the individual is able to function well in the community without special support services. However, if the individual requires special supports

or services, such as a sheltered workshop or institutional care, that person can be considered mentally retarded.

The AAMR further requires that the diagnosis specify the child's *level of impairment* by indicating the extensiveness of the *support services* that would be needed to allow the child to function in the environment. There are four such levels: intermittent, limited, extensive and pervasive. For example, one child might only need special tutoring in academic courses, while another might need 24-hour custodial care.

According to the AAMR revision, duration of MR need not be lifelong. If the environment becomes less demanding – say, in the case of a child's leaving school – and the child adapts to it, then MR is 'outgrown'. Here it is important to note that intellectual functioning as measured by an IQ score is fairly stable from childhood on; however, it is the impact of intellectual limitations on functioning that may change over the course of development. An adult may find his or her niche and function well in a job that does not require the same kinds of skills that caused that person to fail in school. Therefore, the individual may not be limited or handicapped in any identifiable way despite a low IQ.

Finally, the AAMR conceptualization explicitly states that MR is *not* a psychopathology. In addition, the definition in no way implies that MR places the child at risk for behaviour problems. The essence of the definition is the child's adapting or failing to adapt to the environment. This definition also offers a new way of conceptualizing psychopathology, as an *adaptational failure*.

Change in Terminology Used by the AAMR

Mental retardation and *intellectual disability* are two names for the same thing. But intellectual disability is gaining favour as the preferred term. In fact, the American Association on Mental Retardation changed its name in 2007 to the American Association on Intellectual and Developmental Disabilities (AAIDD) (Schalock et al., 2007). This word change has occurred for various reasons amongst which include being *less offensive* and being more consistent with *internationally* used technology, and it emphasizes the sense that intellectual disability is no longer considered an absolute, invariable trait of a person. It also aligns with current professional practices that focus on providing support tailored to individuals to enhance their functioning within particular environments.

Importantly for the next editions of both DSM and ICD, the term 'mental retardation' is expected to be universally replaced by 'intellectual disability'. However, because at the time of writing this chapter both the current ICD and DSM refer to MR still, this is the term that will be continually adopted throughout the text.

DSM-IV-TR Criteria

The DSM-IV-TR (American Psychiatric Association, 2000) criteria include three features: (1) sub-average intelligence defined as an IQ score below 70, (2) deficits in adaptive behaviour and (3) early onset typically defined as below 18 years of age. (See Table 4.1.)

Intellectual Deficits

The first criterion for MR involves significantly sub-average general intellectual functioning. The DSM establishes an IQ cut-off score of 70 to define intelligence that is in the mentally retarded range.

The DSM also uses IQ scores to make finer classifications according to levels of retardation (see Box 4.1 for more detailed information):

1 *Mild* mental retardation: IQ 55 to 70. This level comprises as many as 85 per cent of all persons with retardation. These individuals acquire academic skills up to approximately the sixth-grade level by their late teens and can live successfully in the community either independently or in supervised settings. Speech problems that interfere with the development of independence may persist into adult life. An organic aetiology is identifiable in only a minority of subjects. Associated conditions such as autism, other developmental disorders, epilepsy, conduct disorders or physical disability are found in

TABLE 4.1 DSM-IV-TR Criteria for Mental Retardation

A. Significantly sub-average intellectual functioning: an IQ of approximately 70 or below on an individually administered IQ test (for infants, a clinical judgement of significantly sub-average intellectual functioning).
B. Concurrent deficits or impairments in present adaptive functioning (i.e., the person's effectiveness in meeting the standards expected for his or her age by his or her cultural group) in at least two of the following areas: communication, self-care, home living, social/interpersonal skills, use of community resources, self-direction, functional academic skills, work, leisure, health and safety.
C. Onset is before age 18 years.
Code degree of severity reflecting level of intellectual impairment:
Mild Mental Retardation: IQ level 50–55 to approximately 70
Moderate Mental Retardation: IQ level 35–40 to 50–55
Severe Mental Retardation: IQ level 20–25 to 35–40
Profound Mental Retardation: IQ level below 20 to 25

Source: Adapted from DSM-IV-TR. Copyright 2000, American Psychiatric Association.

varying proportion. If such disorders are present, they should be coded independently.

2 *Moderate* mental retardation: IQ 40 to 54. While some of these individuals require few supportive services, most require some help throughout life. They adapt well to community life in supervised settings, with some individuals achieving higher levels in visuospatial skills than in tasks dependant on language, while others are markedly clumsy but enjoy social interaction and simple conversation. The level of development of language is variable: some of those affected can take part in simple conversations while others have only enough language to communicate their basic needs. Some never

learn language because of their speech disabilities. An organic etiology can be identified in the majority of moderately mentally retarded people.

3 *Severe* mental retardation: IQ 25 to 39. These individuals have limited ability to master academic skills, although they can learn to read certain 'survival' words. As adults they may perform simple tasks under supervision and adapt to the community by living with their family or in group homes. The IQ is under 20. Comprehension and use of language is limited to, at best, understanding basic commands and making simple requests. Most people in this category suffer from a marked degree of motor impairment or other associated deficits, indicating the presence of clinically significant damage to or maldevelopment of the central nervous system.

4 *Profound* mental retardation: IQ below 25. These individuals require lifelong care and assistance and intensive training is needed to teach basic eating, toileting and dressing skills. Almost all show organic causes for their retardation. The most basic and simple visuospatial skills of sorting and matching may be acquired, and the affected person may be able with appropriate supervision and guidance to take a small part in domestic and practical tasks. An organic etiology can be identified in most cases. Severe neurological or other

physical disabilities affecting mobility are common, as are epilepsy and visual and hearing impairments. Often this includes pervasive developmental disorders in their most severe form, especially atypical autism.

Adaptive Behaviour

The second criterion in the DSM-IV-TR requires that the individual be unable to function according to the age-appropriate norms of his or her cultural group in areas such as communication, self-care and social skills.

In general there are few differences between the ICD and DSM and IQ classifications (see Table 4.2). The ICD has a slightly more stringent approach then the DSM. Those individuals with IQ of 75 are more likely to be given a classification of mild retardation using the DSM classification but this would not be the case using the ICD. Similar to the DSM, the ICD also includes adaptive behaviour and states that the diagnostic category chosen for any individual should be based on global assessments of ability and not on any single area of specific impairment or skill. Importantly, the IQ levels given are solely provided as a guide in both classification systems.

The ICD states that other forms of mental retardation should only be used when assessment of the degree of intellectual retardation is rendered particularly difficult or impossible by associated sensory or physical impairments. Unspecified mental retardation is used when there is evidence of mental

TABLE 4.2 Comparison of IQ Criteria for ICD-10 and DSM Classifications

	Mild Retardation	Moderate Retardation	Severe Retardation	Profound Retardation
DSM-IV (1994)	50 to 55–70	35–40 to 50–55	20–25 to 35–40	Below 20–25
DSM-IV-TR (2000)*	50–75*	35–55	20–40	Below 25
ICD-10 (1992)**	50–69	35–49	20–34	Below 20

*The boundary for Mild Retardation was raised in the DSM text version.

**ICD also includes two other categories – Other mental retardation and Unspecified mental retardation.

retardation but insufficient information is available to assign the patient to one of the categories.

Comparison of the AAMR and DSM Approaches

The AAMR's 1992 revision was controversial from the start and to this date has not been universally accepted by other organizations nor by practitioners and researchers. We can see that not all of its recommendations were adopted by the DSM-IV-TR.

The first difference we should note is the defining score used to establish MR in the two definitions. AAMR's decision was a highly contentious one in that, when determining the level of intelligence that defined MR, the AAMR raised the cut-off IQ score from 70 to 75. This may seem to be a slight adjustment; however, because IQ scores form a bell curve, it actually doubles the number of individuals in the MR category. The developers of the DSM-IV-TR, like most clinicians and researchers in the field, have ignored this recommendation.

Box 4.1 Developmental Differences in Mental Retardation and Down Syndrome

Level	Preschool Age (birth to 5 years)	School Age (6 to 21 years)	Adult (over 21 years)
Mild Retardation (IQ of 50–70)	Can develop social and language skills; less retardation in sensorimotor areas; seldom distinguished from normal until older	Can learn academic skills to approximately sixth-grade level by late teens; cannot learn general high school subjects; needs special education, particularly at secondary school levels	Capable of social and vocational adequacy with proper education and training; frequently needs guidance when under serious social or economic stress
Moderate Retardation (35–49)	Can talk or learn to communicate; poor social awareness; fair motor development; may profit from self-help; can be managed with moderate supervision	Can learn functional academic skills to approximately fourth-grade level by late teens if given special education	Capable of self-maintenance in unskilled or semi-skilled occupations; needs supervision and guidance when under mild social or economic stress
Severe Retardation (21–34)	Poor motor development; speech is minimal; generally unable to profit from training in self-help; little or no communication skills	Can talk or learn to communicate; can be trained in elemental health habits; cannot learn functional academic skills; profits from systematic habit training	Can contribute partially to self-support under complete supervision; can develop self-protection skills to a minimal useful level in controlled environment
Profound Retardation (20 or below)	Gross retardation; minimal capacity for functioning in sensorimotor areas; needs nursing care	Some motor development present; cannot profit from training in self-help; needs total care	Some motor and speech development; totally incapable of self-maintenance; needs complete care and supervision

Source: Adapted from Sattler, 1992.

Another criticism of the AAMR's definition is that, while it requires deficits in 2 of 10 domains of adaptive behaviour, these were not identified on any empirical basis and no norms and standardized scales exist that measure these particular domains (State et al., 1997). Also problematic is the AAMR's elimination of the usual classifications of levels of retardation (mild, moderate, etc.) and substitution of *levels of impairment* as defined by the need for support services. While there are criteria listed for defining these levels, there are no objective ways of measuring them. Since assigning levels depends on clinical judgement, the chances of unreliability and misdiagnosis are increased. Moreover, there is evidence that levels of retardation and need for supportive services *cannot* be equated, especially for mildly retarded children who vary in their need for support across different contexts.

On the other hand, the AAMR's attempts have been lauded as an attempt to reduce the stigma associated with mental retardation.

Some other conceptual issues have arisen since either of these diagnostic systems were developed and with which neither has yet grappled. Increasingly, models of intelligence are becoming multifaceted, requiring the assessment of cognitive abilities in a multidimensional framework for which a single summary score may not be a reliable index. The concept of IQ itself has been called into question, in part because of the popular misinterpretation that this number is immutable and sets an absolute limit on an individual's potential. Indeed, a recent version of one of the commonly used intelligence tests for children – the *Stanford-Binet, Fourth Edition* (Thorndike et al., 1986) – abandoned the term IQ entirely. While the most recent Weschler Intelligence Scale for Children-IV (2003) retains an overall IQ score, its developers advocate focusing more on domain-specific index scores.

Intelligence has played a fairly controversial role in diagnosis of mental retardation since it was first conceptualized and remains so to this day. Critics argue that the definition of mental retardation varies depending also on the type of intelligence used. Silverman and colleagues (2010) have recently added to this debate. They compared Stanford-Binet and Wechsler Adult Intelligence Scale (WAIS) IQs in a group of 74 adults with intellectual disability (ID). In every case, WAIS Full Scale IQ was higher than the Stanford-Binet Composite IQ, with a mean difference of 16.7 points. These differences did not appear to be due to the lower minimum possible score for the Stanford-Binet. Additional comparisons with other measures suggested that the WAIS might systematically underestimate severity of intellectual impairment. We will have more to say about both of these tests and the reconceptualizations of intelligence from which they derive when we discuss assessment in Chapter 16. In the meantime, it is interesting to speculate about how the definition of MR might have to be revised in the light of newer conceptualizations of multiple intelligences.

Characteristics

Prevalence

Mental retardation is the most *common* developmental disability in many countries around the world and is estimated to be occurring in around 1–3 per cent of general population (Maulik et al., 2011). In the USA, the prevalence rate is estimated to be around 1 per cent in the population and ranks first among chronic conditions causing major activity limitation. On the other hand, *developmental delay* (DD) is a term that is commonly applied to a preschool child whose development is substantially behind the average expectations of children of the same age in two or more developmental domains. Very often, DD represents an early warning sign of later developmental problems, such as MR and other developmental disorders.

The question of how many children fall into the MR category depends, of course, on how MR is defined. Using IQ scores alone as the criterion, prevalence changes significantly if one raises the cut-off score from 70 to 75, as we have seen. Using the DSM criterion of 70 and below, 3 per cent of the population can be classified as in the mentally retarded range of intelligence. This is an important point to consider given that the ICD and DSM differ here, with individuals more likely to gain a diagnosis according to the DSM.

However, IQ scores ignore other factors critical to the diagnosis of MR, the most important of which is adaptive behaviour. Particularly at the level of mild retardation, IQ and adaptive behaviour are not highly correlated, so IQ scores alone would overestimate the prevalence of MR. In turn, overestimation might occur due to the instability of IQ scores, since some children who now are in the mildly retarded range will, upon retesting, score in the lower bound of average intelligence.

Our ability to detect MR is related to children's age, and may become more sensitive and accurate later in development. In particular, children with mild mental retardation are less likely to be identified until the school years when academic performance serves to highlight their limitations. Therefore, the prevalence rate tends to be low in the preschool years, then gradually rises in the school years, peaks in early adolescence and declines subsequently.

Finally, prevalence may change depending on the comparison groups used. Comparing a child with MR to a group of chronological age-matched controls is not without controversy. The problem with this approach is that retarded individuals across a broad range of syndromes would differ from controls on virtually all measurable characteristics, therefore making it difficult to extrapolate the strengths and weaknesses of MR. A more sophisticated solution is to include a comparison group that controls for developmental level, often referred to as mental age controls. Mental age is a concept in relation to intelligence, expressed as the age at which a child is performing intellectually. The mental age of the child that is tested is the same as the average age at which normal children achieve a particular score. However, a mental age result on an intelligence test does not mean that children function at their 'mental age level' in all aspects of life.

Gender

As many as three times more boys than girls qualify for a label of mental retardation (Stromme and Hagberg, 2000). The gender difference is probably largely due to the fact that genetically linked disorders, in general, affect males more than females. There is also a substantial body of research showing that boys tend to be over-represented relative to girls for many categories of special education needs (SEN). In England in January 2005, the incidence of pupils with a formal statement of SEN was twice as high for boys as it was for girls (Department for Education and Skills, 2005). Similarly in the USA substantial gender differences have been reported. For example, Coutinho and Oswald (2005) report US national data indicating that boys were 1.3 times more likely than girls to be identified with mental retardation.

Socio-economic Status and Ethnicity

In defining and assessing MR, AAIDD stresses that professionals must consider such factors as *community* environment typical of the individual's peers and culture, linguistic *diversity* and *cultural* differences in the way people communicate, move and behave. Mental retardation could also be caused by social factors, such as the level of child stimulation and adult responsiveness, and educational factors, such as the availability of family and educational supports that can promote mental development and greater adaptive skills. Therefore it is particularly important to see how MR is distributed across cultures, races and social economic status.

While MR is more prevalent among socio-economically disadvantaged samples, which disproportionately include ethnic minorities and single-parent families (Emerson, 2007), this is true only for those children with mild MR. The more severe levels of MR occur about equally in different economic and racial groups (Hodapp and Dykens, 2003). With regard to social class, genetic and environmental effects probably contribute to the fact that parents with low socio-economic status tend to have lower IQs, as do their children. Poverty and gender have been found to have stronger associations than ethnicity with the overall prevalence of special education needs (Strand and Lindsay, 2009).

Explanations for racial differences include cultural factors (e.g., a relative lack of emphasis on individual achievement) and environmental factors (e.g., poverty and lack of access to resources; Turkheimer et al., 2003). For example, Brooks-Gunn and colleagues (2003) found that the effects of economic deprivation, an under-stimulating home environment, and maternal youth and lack of education accounted for 71 per cent of the difference in IQ between European American and African American children.

In addition, there is concern that standardized IQ tests might be biased in ways that underestimate the intelligence of children from minority backgrounds. In recognition of this possibility, some school systems have moved away from the use of IQ tests in evaluating children's needs for educational support services. For example, in the 1970s, parent advocates brought a suit against the San Francisco school system, arguing that the use of culturally biased IQ tests was resulting in an over-representation of minority children in special education. The suit was successful, and California school systems are now prohibited from using IQ tests for educational placement decisions involving minority students.

Differential Diagnosis

Children with MR must be differentiated from those who have *low intellectual abilities* but no deficits in adaptive skills. Indeed, as some higher-functioning children with MR learn to care for themselves and perform tasks independently, they may lose their MR label as they advance in development. Similarly, MR is differentiated from simple *learning disorders* that are confined to a specific academic skill (see Chapter 7); the deficits in MR are more pervasive. Lastly, although MR may co-occur with *autism* (see Chapter 5), the two can be distinguished primarily because of the limited social interest and odd repetitive behaviours of the autistic child; children with MR are often quite sociable and friendly (First et al., 2002).

With regard to MR, pervasive and significant deficit (> 2 S.D.) in general intellectual functioning and significant limitations in adaptive functioning are expected and form part of the definition of the syndrome. This is in contrast to the disorders that fall under the umbrella of pervasive developmental disorders (PDD), where at least half have intellectual impairment (Yeargin-Allsopp and Boyle, 2002).

Comorbidity

There is good evidence that MR increases the risk of developing psychological disturbances. Both the prevalence of physical disorders (Van Schrojenstein Lantman-de Valk et al. 1997) and of mental health problems (Emerson and Hatton, 2007) is higher in people with MR than in people without MR. Estimates of comorbidity in the MR population range from 30 per cent to 50 per cent (Einfeld et al., 2011). Studies find that, among those in the MR range, the risk of developing a psychiatric disorder is three to four times that in the typically modifying developing population (Sachs and Barrett, 2000). Recent studies (Emerson et al., 2010) have even found that those with 'borderline' intellectual functioning, commonly defined as scoring between 1 and 2 standard deviations below the mean on standard tests of intelligence or IQ < 85, show increased psychological problems. Comorbid disorders in MR include a wide spectrum, among them: *aggression, inattention/hyperactivity, schizophrenia, autism, depression* and *anxiety*.

Among the most common behavioural disorders in children with mental retardation are *attention deficit hyperactivity disorder* (ADHD) and *conduct problems* (Emerson, 2003). Attention deficit hyperactivity disorder is three to five times more prevalent among children with mental retardation than among typically developing children. Children with mild MR are more likely to meet the diagnostic criteria for ADHD (Lindblad et al., 2011).

However, the likelihood of comorbidity is related to the *degree of retardation* (Einfeld and Tonge, 1996). Those in the profoundly retarded group have considerably lower rates of comorbidity, probably because their behavioural repertoire is more limited, as is their capacity to communicate emotional problems. Level of retardation also affects the kind of disturbance seen, with those in the mildly retarded range having a predominance of disruptive and antisocial behaviour, and the severely retarded group being characterized by withdrawn and autistic-like behaviour.

Einfeld and Aman's (1995) summary of factor analytic studies is instructive in regard to how comorbidity differs in the MR and typically developing populations. While both groups develop withdrawal, aggression and hyperactivity, *anxiety* is less common in children with MR than the typically developing population. In addition, *stereotypic and self-injurious* behaviours are often seen in children with MR but are rare in those who do not have MR. Consequently, withdrawal in children with MR generally is not accompanied by anxiety as it is in other children, while aggression is more often accompanied by self-injurious behaviour in those with MR. In short, there seems to be a different mix of problems in children with MR.

Difficulties in Detecting Psychopathology in MR

Hodapp and Dykens (2003) point out that the nature of MR makes it difficult to detect and measure psychopathology. For example, while certain behaviour problems are common to children with MR, such as temper tantrums, overactivity and withdrawal from others, they may not reflect psychiatric illness per se. Limitations in the ability of individuals with MR to reflect on and articulate internal emotional states particularly hinder the diagnosis of internalizing disorders such as depression, which often rely on self-reports of subjective experience. In turn, observers' ratings usually require a judgement about the appropriateness of behaviour for a person of this individual's chronological age, when the individual with MR might display behaviour that actually is appropriate for his or her mental age. For example, an adolescent functioning at a preschool level could be expected to show some of the magical reasoning and poor reality testing that are typical of the preoperational period. Future work in this area will benefit from the development of measures that are designed for and provide norms on the MR population.

The vast numbers of causes attributed to the development of MR not only contributes to problems in diagnosing children, but also in determining risk factors for children. Anything that damages and interferes with the growth and maturation of the brain can lead to MR, and this might happen before, during or after the birth of the child (complications of pregnancy/birth, toxics, malnutrition, trauma, infections, under-stimulation). Genetically determined MR aetiology (comprising chromosomal aberrations, single-gene disorders and other genetic conditions) accounts for only 17 to 41 per cent of cases, depending on the different techniques of analysis (Bernardini et al., 2010).

The Biological Context: Organic MR

Mental retardation comes in two general types with two distinct etiologies. The first, **organic MR**, which will be our focus in this section, comprises a mixed group. It is estimated that there are over 1000 different biological causes of mental retardation. These include genetic anomalies, prenatal insults and neuropsychological abnormalities. Most children with organic MR are severely impaired; for example, 77 per cent of cases in the moderate-to-profound range are due to organic factors.

Genetic Factors

Many genetic anomalies result in mental retardation – over 750, in fact – each of which may be associated with a different phenotype consisting of a unique set of physical, cognitive and behavioural features. (Here we follow Hodapp and Dykens, 2003.) Next we describe three of the more commonly seen syndromes. However, a consistent percentage of children with genetic MR do not present a recognizable phenotype striking of a well-recognizable syndrome.

Down Syndrome

Down syndrome is the most common of the genetic birth defects related to MR, with a prevalence of 1 to 1.5 per 1000 births. Children with the disorder have three number 21 chromosomes instead of the normal two; hence, the condition is also called trisomy 21. Recently, a critical region on chromosome 21 has been identified, and the available markers for this and flanking regions have enabled clinicians to confirm cases of Down syndrome in the context of subtle translocations and chromosomal abnormalities other than trisomy (King et al., 1997). Thus, the genetic basis for the syndrome has been expanded.

This disorder was originally called mongoloidism because of the characteristic facial features of wide face, slanted eyes and flattened nose. They often have

A child with Down syndrome can be an enjoyable playmate
© *Lauren Shear/Photo Researchers Inc.*

Box 4.2 Case Study: Down Syndrome

Dan's mother was 37 and his father was 40 when he was born in an isolated, rural area of the mountains. At the birth, the midwife immediately recognized Dan's physical characteristics – disproportionate and odd-appearing eyes, ears, hands and feet – and suggested that Dan's mother have him checked out at the Mountain Medical Clinic. There, the doctors diagnosed Dan with Down syndrome.

While most parents would have been very upset at having a Down syndrome child, Dan's parents were surprisingly unmoved by it all. They did not especially value intellectual achievement, and Dan, like many Down syndrome children, did not have behavioural problems. Dan was generally content to play in the woods behind their house, and when inside was content to sit with his toys in front of the television set for hours. Also, fortunately, Dan did not have many of the medical handicaps from which most other Down children suffer. He did have some liver problems that were not too severe, and he also seemed prone to respiratory problems.

He was never enrolled in day care or kindergarten. When he was brought to school for the first grade, his intellectual deficiency was quickly evident to the teacher. She immediately referred Dan to the school psychologist for testing. The psychologist administered

a Wechsler Intelligence Scale for Children, and Dan attained an IQ score of 61. This score would place him in the 'mild' level of mental retardation and is a higher score than would be attained by the average Down syndrome child. However, it was clear he could not compete in the standard classroom, so he was placed in special education classes. Dan enjoyed the school and made reasonable progress, although he never made it beyond the second grade in any academic skill area, in part because his parents never really encouraged him at home in academic work.

By the time he was 14, he was 40 pounds overweight. He was put on a strict diet and exercise plan that was way overdue. His health was obviously declining. However, when Dan lost weight and became more active, his health improved. Dan made it through his school years and on into young adulthood without major difficulty, and he was even doing some easy part-time work for some neighbours.

Dan continued to live at home. When he was about 30, he started showing signs of emotional deterioration. He became irritable and had tantrums for no reason that he could explain. Other times he would not communicate at all. He was also having more medical problems and, at 36 years of age, Dan succumbed to a bout of pneumonia.

Source: Adapted from Meyer, 1989.

poor physical health, such that approximately half of infants with Down syndrome show congenital heart defects, and hospitalizations of infants with the syndrome (often for respiratory problems) are common in the first year of life (So et al., 2007). The cognitive picture of children with Down syndrome includes a decelerating rate of mental growth, and the mean IQ of the group as a whole is around 50. Their social intelligence tends to be high, but their speech and comprehension of grammar are low.

In regards to behaviour, the typical Down syndrome child is friendly and sociable, although some studies suggest that this picture becomes less positive with age, with aggression sometimes emerging in adolescence. People with Down syndrome have varying degrees of learning disability, which may range from moderate to severe. They also experience premature ageing. However, generally, the children tend to have a low level of behavioural disturbance. (See Box 4.2.)

Fragile X Syndrome
The prevalence of this syndrome is 0.73 to 0.92 per 1000 births. Fragile-X syndrome is caused by a change in the size of the FMR1 gene, which is on the X chromosome, and occurs more often in males than in females (Tassone et al., 2007). Normally, the FMR1 gene makes a protein needed for the brain to grow properly. A defect in this gene makes the body produce too little of the protein, or none at all. At a particular point on the FMR1 gene everybody has a

© *The Fragile X Society*

repeat of the chemical sequence CGG. In the typically developing population this is usually between 6 and 50. The full mutation of fragile X (usually associated with learning difficulties) is defined as those with a repeat sequence of more than 200 CGG repeats. The more repeats, the more likely there is to be a problem. However, the actual repeat number appears not to correlate to the level of learning difficulty.

The main problem in fragile X is intellectual impairment. This can range from very minor, so that the person has a normal IQ and shows no sign of fragile X, to severe learning difficulties. How badly someone is affected depends on the degree of change in the gene. Cognitively, boys show a moderate level of retardation, with development slowing from puberty on, whereas when girls are affected, there may be no MR apparent. The children do well on tasks requiring the processing of holistic, gestalt-like information, such as picture recognition, but do poorly on those requiring linear reasoning, such as auditory short-term memory. Behaviourally, the children tend to be hyperactive or to show autistic-like features, such as stereotyped behaviours, social withdrawal and gaze avoidance.

Prader-Willi Syndrome
This condition is due to anomalies in a region of chromosome 15 and occurs in 1 per 15 000 births.

© *The Fragile X Society*

In 70 per cent of cases those with the syndrome have a microscopic or submicroscopic deletion on the paternal chromosome 15, while the remaining cases have two copies of the maternal chromosome and no paternal contribution. In either case, the child is missing genetic material from the father.

The cognitive picture of children with Prader-Willi syndrome (PWS) involves a mild degree of retardation. However, the deficits are largely in the verbal realm while some non-verbal skills are left intact. For example, a peculiar characteristic of children with the disorder is a remarkable facility with jigsaw puzzles, which they can complete more quickly than even typically developing children of the same age (Dykens, 2007).

Behaviourally, the picture changes with age. In infancy, children may show significant developmental delays and problems with feeding that can lead to failure to thrive. Beginning at ages 2 to 6, children begin to become preoccupied with eating (termed *hyperphagia*) and are vulnerable to obesity. While earlier in development, young children with the syndrome generally were described as affectionate and pleasant, the onset of hyperphagia is associated with increasing behaviour problems, including stubbornness, temper tantrums, impulsivity and underactivity. *Obsessive-compulsive* symptoms also are often seen, including hoarding, compulsive talking or questioning, excessive ordering and rearranging, and repeating rituals (Dykens et al., 1996).

Recent evidence suggests that the two different genetic mechanisms underlying Prader-Willi syndrome have different behavioural phenotypes. Those with the deletion on the paternal chromosome 15 tend to have more maladaptive behaviour and cognitive deficits than those with the duplicate maternal chromosome. It also turns out that only children in the former category have the unique splinter skill of solving jigsaw puzzles so adeptly (Verdine et al., 2008).

As these descriptions illustrate, different genetic origins result in a different kind of MR, complete with relative strengths and weakness in various areas of functioning. As Hodapp and Dykens (2003) argue, the advancement of research in the field will require that investigators acknowledge that there are various types of MR rather than treating the disorder as a single entity.

Prenatal and Post-natal Factors

A host of prenatal and post-natal factors can damage the central nervous system and result in MR. Rubella (German measles) contracted by the mother during the first trimester of pregnancy can cause a number of impairments, MR being one. Syphilis is another cause of MR. Exposure to massive doses of radiation in the first few months of pregnancy, chronic alcoholism, age (35 years or older) and severe emotional stress throughout pregnancy are among the numerous maternal factors that increase the risk of MR in the infant. There is also an increased risk for MR in offspring of mothers with health conditions such as asthma and diabetes, which is a particularly important risk factor for disadvantaged or ethnic populations, for whom these conditions are more prevalent and

© Courtesy of PWSA UK and Katrina Hardy and family

Box 4.3 Case Study: Prader-Willi Syndrome

Kate Haggarty describes her child who was diagnosed with Prader-Willi syndrome. (www.pwsa.co.uk)

To start at the beginning – 13 years ago, when Ollie was born and we received the shattering news that he had PWS. I remember quite clearly amongst the myriad of emotions that we experienced at the time, a determination that, with the benefit of an early diagnosis (three weeks), it would surely be possible to teach Ollie not to take food. We could train him – we could educate him as he became older about the importance of not overeating and if we were disciplined and consistent, then perhaps we might succeed.

Looking back, this seems extremely naive, and no doubt was part of a denial about Ollie's condition, but at the time it felt good to have something positive to aim for – to feel that there was a way forward when we felt so overwhelmed. It was with a real sense of failure initially then, when about seven years ago I fitted the first cupboard lock. As Ollie became taller and more physically able it was becoming increasingly difficult to rely on my vigilance and to trust him not to take food that he was not allowed. Ollie knew then, as he knows now, why his food intake must be controlled – he can and does talk knowledgeably about a healthy diet and is far more informed than many adults! However, the reality is that the obsession is so innate that all the theorizing in the world counts for nought if the opportunity for Ollie to take food (without being caught!) presents itself. Although there are times when he will proudly bring me some food that has been

left lying around inadvertently by the girls or a visitor, on most occasions, the temptation to eat it is too great.

And so the number and type of locks multiplied! I realized that, in fact, rather than being a failure, this was a more effective way of managing life with a PWS child – to rely on his willpower and the vigilance of the girls and myself was unfair to him and unrealistic for us. However, the locks were certainly not a problem-free solution. They are designed to make access to food difficult, but not impossible, and the very fact that it is possible to overcome them provides a temptation. As he has grown, it has proved increasingly difficult to find any that are totally Ollie-proof! Even the magnetic ones present him with the challenge of finding the magnetic key to unlock them. An alarm in the hallway, covering internal access to the kitchen was successful briefly until Ollie discovered that he could crawl under the sensor! Bolting the kitchen door was fine until he tried climbing out of the window of another room into the garden and through the back door. And of course, one of the big downsides of all these locks and alarms is that they restrict life for everyone in the household and simple tasks become major exercises; popping upstairs to put washing away involves checking where everyone is (particularly Ollie), locking all necessary doors and windows to the kitchen, making sure that noone is locked outside etc.!

Nonetheless, despite all the difficulties Ollie has done extremely well – he weighs approximately 45 kg and, with the help of growth hormone, is 151 cm tall.

---

may be less well managed (Leonard et al., 2006). Paediatric AIDS, foetal alcohol syndrome, and exposure to substances in utero also may be associated with MR.

Camp et al., (1998) found a series of maternal and neonatal risk factors for mental retardation age 7. They found low socio-economic status of the family accounted for 44–50 per cent of mental retardation and a low level of maternal education accounted for 20 per cent. Other prenatal factors included maternal age, weight gain in pregnancy

less than 10 pounds and multiple births. Relative risk was also significantly increased with low 1 minute APGAR, primary apnea, and head circumference and length more than 2 SD below average.

Prematurity and prenatal anoxia (oxygen deprivation during or immediately after delivery) are hazards of birth that can lead to MR. Post-natal causes of MR include encephalitis and meningitis (inflammations of the brain resulting from infections by bacteria, viruses or tuberculosis organisms), particularly if they occur during infancy.

Throughout childhood, head injuries (most commonly resulting from automobile accidents and child abuse), infections, seizure disorders and exposure to toxic substances may contribute to mental retardation. These risk factors are summarized in Table 4.3.

Examining the Phenotype

The diagnosis of a child with MR requires exhaustive and comprehensive evaluations of the patient. Investigation of family history is an initial first step as is a detailed pre-, peri- and post-natal history. A dysmorphic child may be at risk from the stress of birth, and later delay may be erroneously attributed to birth injury (Hall, 1989). A careful developmental history, with emphasis on milestones, formal assessments and behaviour, is also required. Medical records should be sought or requested to validate any diagnosis of malformations. An accurate EEG study and/or brain MRI are sometimes sufficient to be able to identify or rule out some relatively common disorders (such as Rett syndrome) (Battaglia and Carey, 2003).

The degree of MR is an important indicator for the so-called 'chromosomal' phenotype. The behavioural phenotype is also distinctive for several well-known syndromic conditions, such as Williams syndrome (Cassidy and Morris, 2002). Finally, the physical examination of the child is crucial.

Unfortunately, in many cases the MR is the unique and unspecific sign present in the patient, with lack of major hallmarks. When present, minor anomalies of the face (such as hypo-hypertelorism, unusual ear conformation, multiple hair whorls, etc.), hands, genitalia and skin should be noted and supplemented by objective measurements.

TABLE 4.3 Some Causes of Mental Retardation/Intellectual Disability

Before or at Conception	*Inherited disorders (such as phenylketonuria, Tay-Sachs disease, neurofibromatosis, hypothyroidism and fragile X syndrome)
	*Chromosome abnormalities (such as Down syndrome)
During Pregnancy	*Severe maternal malnutrition
	* Infections with HIV, cytomegalovirus, herpes simplex, toxoplasmosis, rubella virus
	*Toxins (such as alcohol, lead and methylmercury)
	*Drugs (such as phenytoin, valproate, isotretinoin and cancer chemotherapy)
	*Abnormal brain development (such as porencephalic cyst, grey matter heterotopia and encephalocele) *Pre-eclampsia and multiple births
During Birth	*Extreme prematurity
	*Insufficient oxygen (hypoxia)
After Birth	*Brain infections (such as meningitis and encephalitis)
	* Severe head injury
	* Malnutrition of the child
	*Severe emotional neglect or abuse
	*Toxins (such as lead and mercury)
	*Brain tumours and their treatments

Abnormalities in head size, growth parameters and neurologic signs should be carefully investigated. The MR phenotype can also vary over time and it should be useful to collect photos and/or videos of patients at different ages to gain a developmental perspective.

Neuropsychological Factors

Studies of brain structure and development are beginning to pinpoint various anomalies in the different types of MR. For example, in Down syndrome, neuroimaging studies indicate a normal-appearing brain at birth with a declining brain volume over the course of development. (Here we follow Pennington, 2002.) In the first few months of life, children with Down syndrome evidence delayed myelination and reduced growth in the cerebellum and frontal lobes. By adulthood, the brain appears microcephalic, with many of the features of Alzheimer's disease.

In contrast to the microcephaly seen in Down syndrome, children with fragile X have a large brain volume, which suggests a failure of the brain to 'prune' redundant and inefficient neuronal connections as it does in normal development. Interestingly, this is also a feature of the autistic brain, and children with fragile X often show autistic like behaviours. Fragile X also is associated with decreased size of an area of the posterior cerebellum, which may be related to impairments in sensory motor integration, as well as ventricular enlargements that could be the result of oversecretion of cerebrospinal fluid.

Genetic Factors

Many genes on the X chromosome are now associated with mental retardation (Tarpey et al., 2009). The current estimate is that > 70 genes on the X chromosome when mutated give rise to a syndrome with associated MR or a non-syndromic form of the disease. This represents approximately 10 per cent of the genes on the X chromosome.

There are many benefits of identifying genes that cause mental retardation. From the family's perspective the identification of a genetic cause of disease can often give a final explanation for why their son or daughter has a disability. Parents often feel partially responsible for what has happened to their child and question whether the disability was due to something they did or did not do during pregnancy or during the early years of parenting. For most, just knowing that there is a gene mutation that causes the disease is of some therapeutic benefit. It can also help the wider family come to terms with the diagnosis. For some family members the identification of a mutation in an affected individual means that the risk to other family members can be accurately assessed. For X-linked conditions predictive testing can be made available to female relatives to determine their carrier status. Since the identification of a number of genes that cause MR, we have observed significant changes in the reproductive habits of families who have had the genetic cause identified in their family. Turner et al. (2008) observed that when families know they are at risk of having a child with an X-linked intellectual disability syndrome, the women at risk have fewer children than predicted based on the population rate of reproduction.

The Individual Context

Answering the question, 'What has gone awry with normal development in the case of mental retardation?' has resulted in an impressive body of research addressing both the cognitive and the personality motivational factors involved.

Cognitive Factors

Two different questions have been raised concerning the cognitive factors involved in MR. One is a general question: is the *development* of intelligence in children with MR the same as or different from its development in children with normal intelligence? This is known as the *difference versus development* issue. The second question is a specific one: what *particular deviations* underlie the subnormal intellectual functioning of individuals who are retarded?

Social Cognition

The lack of peer acceptance is usually attributed to a low level of social competence in children with MR. While social competence has been conceptualized in a variety of ways and involves a number of variables, research has primarily been concerned with the variable of social cognition, which lies at the juncture between intelligence on the one hand and adaptive behaviour on the other. There is evidence that children with MR, as compared with those who are not retarded, have less developed perspective-taking, are less skilled in interpreting social cues, and have less advanced social strategies for dealing with problem situations (e.g., joining a group or responding to provocative behaviour). (See Leffert and Siperstein, 1996.)

Siperstein and Leffert (1997) also studied the difference between mildly retarded fourth and sixth graders who were socially accepted and those who were socially rejected. The findings concerning social behaviour and social cognition seem paradoxical. Accepted children favoured submissive goals and generated few positive, outgoing strategies. In contrast, the rejected children favoured assertive goals and positive, outgoing strategies. One explanation for this unexpected finding is that low-key, deferential and accommodating goals and strategies protect children against being rejected by making them 'blend in' with the others, whereas socially assertive and intrusive goals and strategies do not. Since peer rejection and indifference are more likely than acceptance, children with MR have more to lose if assertiveness goes wrong than do children without MR.

The Difference Versus Development Issue

Historically, there have been two points of view concerning the nature of MR. One is that MR is due to a *basic cognitive deficit* that results in thinking that is *fundamentally different* from that found in typically developing populations. The term 'mental *deficiency*' epitomizes this view. The second point of view is that thinking in mental retardation is the

same as it is in normal intelligence, the only difference being a *developmental* one, which results in *slower progress* and a *lower level of final achievement*. (See Fig. 4.2.) There are data supporting both sides of the controversy.

Zigler has been the principal advocate of the developmental approach, proposing two hypotheses to test it. One is concerned with similar sequencing of cognitive development; the other with similar structure. (A detailed account of these hypotheses and the research testing them can be found in Hodapp and Zigler, 1995.)

The Similar Sequencing Hypothesis

This hypothesis states that children with MR will proceed through the same *stages* of cognitive development and in the same *order* as do children who are not retarded. For example, children with MR will go through the same Piagetian stages in the same invariant order from sensorimotor to preoperational to concrete operational thought. (They rarely reach the final level of formal operational thinking.) Retardation is the result of slower progress and a lower level of achievement.

A considerable body of research supports the similar sequence hypothesis, which holds for retardation due to both organic and non-organic (or familial) causes. Thus, the same sequential development has been found in Piagetian tasks, moral reasoning, symbolic play, geometric concepts and language, to name some of the specific areas. Moreover, when strict sequencing does not hold for the retarded population, as in the more advanced stages of moral reasoning, it tends not to hold for typically developing populations as well.

Finally, there is suggestive evidence that children with some kinds of retardation exhibit a less solid grasp of the kinds of thinking involved at the higher levels. Thus, they are more apt to show a mixture of higher and lower levels of thinking than are their typically developing counterparts. This variability can be evidenced from month to month or even within a single testing session (Hodapp and Zigler, 1995).

FIGURE 4.2 Developmental Model of Cognitive Growth.

The single vertical arrow represents the passage of time. The horizontal arrows represent environmental events impinging on the individual, who is represented as a pair of vertical lines. The individual's cognitive development appears as an internal ascending spiral, in which the numbered loops represent successive stages of cognitive growth.

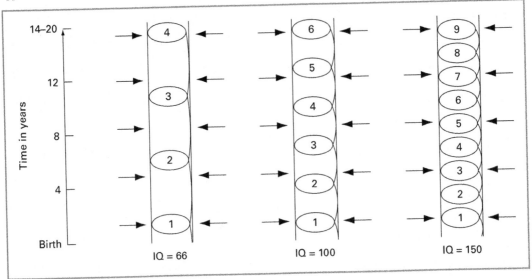

Source: Hodapp and Zigler, 1990.

The Similar Structure Hypothesis

This hypothesis states that, when matched for overall mental age, children who are retarded will be at the same level of functioning on a variety of intellectual tasks (other than those used to measure intelligence) as are children who are not retarded. Thus, this hypothesis is concerned with *inter-task* functioning. It runs counter to the idea that there are specific areas of deficit in thinking in MR.

The support for the similar structure hypothesis is more qualified than that for the similar sequencing hypothesis. When they are doing Piagetian-based tasks, the performance of children with familial (i.e., non-organically determined) retardation is comparable to mental-age-matched typically developing children. However, in performance on information-processing tasks of learning, memory, learning set formation, distractibility and selective attention, the MR group tends to be inferior. The reason for this puzzling finding is not clear.

The performance of children whose retardation is due to organic factors does *not* support the similar structure hypothesis. Not only is such performance worse than matched mental-age controls, but there are also specific areas of deficit. For example, children with Down syndrome have deficits in grammar relative to other abilities, while boys with fragile-X syndrome are particularly weak in sequential thinking such as remembering a sequence of digits. (See Hodapp and Zigler, 1995, for details.)

In sum, there is good support for the similar sequencing hypothesis, but the support for the similar structure hypothesis is limited to Piagetian tasks in children with non-organically determined retardation. The similar structure hypothesis is not supported when information-processing tasks are used and retardation is due to organic factors.

Specific Deviations in Thinking

Having discussed the general developmental question concerning cognitive factors involved in MR, we now turn to the research on specific deviations underlying subnormal intellectual functioning. The findings can be grouped under five categories.

1. Attention to Relevant Cues

The basic research paradigm here is called *discrimination learning*. The child is presented with a succession of stimuli, such as objects differing in colour, shape and size, two or three at a time, and is asked to choose one. On the basis of being told that a choice is either right or wrong, the child must learn what dimension – colour, shape or size in this instance – is the key to making a correct choice. To illustrate: a girl is presented with a red circle and a blue square. Guessing that 'circle' is the correct response, she chooses the first figure and is told she made a correct choice. Next time a green circle and a blue triangle are presented and she is told her choice of the circle is incorrect. She must now change her hypothesis. If she remembers that the original circle was also red, she strongly suspects 'red' to be the solution, which she verifies when another red object is shown. If she does not remember, she must adopt another hypothesis such as 'triangle' or 'green'. In discrimination learning situations, the learning curve for children of normal intelligence rises quickly at first and then levels off. For children who are retarded, choices are no better than chance for a number of trials, but then there is rapid improvement.

Further investigation reveals that children with MR often do not attend to relevant aspects of the situation; for example, they are not asking themselves, is it colour or shape or size? On the contrary, they have a strong initial preference for position, such as the first object, which they persist in using despite being told that their choice is frequently incorrect. Once they can break this irrelevant set, they learn rapidly. Given a task in which position is the relevant cue, they learn as fast as or faster than children with normal intelligence. Thus, in a special sense they are not slow learners, but they are slow to catch on to the relevant question. (See Hale and Borkowski, 1991.)

The preference for position responses seen in children who are retarded has its counterpart in normal development, since position habits have been observed to interfere with discrimination learning in 1-year-olds. Such habits no longer seem to affect discrimination learning in the toddler and preschooler, although the evidence is not conclusive on this point. If the preference in children who are retarded does in fact represent a fixation, it is one that goes back to earliest childhood and may significantly interfere with subsequent learning.

2. Attention

Children who are mentally retarded may have a basic attentional deficit. For example, they have slower reaction times in simple reaction-time experiments. These experiments involve a preparatory signal, such as a buzzer, followed by a stimulus, such as a light, to which the subject must respond as quickly as possible (e.g., by pressing a button).

3. Memory

There is no evidence that children who are retarded have a deficit in short-term memory, as tested in tasks involving repeating back digits. The findings concerning a possible deficit in long-term memory are contradictory and inconclusive because it is exceedingly difficult to control all the prior processes in order to obtain an unconfounded evaluation of this one alone. The situation is also complicated by the fact that long-term memory depends on the use of a number of *strategies* designed to aid retention and organize the incoming information. Such strategies include rehearsal, clustering and mediation.

3a. Rehearsal

Rehearsal typically consists of repeating each new item along with all the prior ones; for example, in remembering a series of numbers, a child may think, 'six, six-three, six-three-eight', and so forth. Rehearsal is clearly evidenced by the third grade in children who are not retarded. Research indicates that children who are retarded are deficient in rehearsal. If they are trained, their performance improves, but in most cases they will not spontaneously use such aids. As with discrimination learning, they fail to do what they are capable of doing. And again, as with discrimination learning, this failure has its counterpart in normal development, since first-graders also make no use of their ability to rehearse.

3b. Clustering

Remembering improves if incoming information is organized in a meaningful manner, a strategy called *clustering*. Present the average child with, say, a list comprised of three categories of words arranged in random order, and the child will tend to recall them by categories; for example, the words the child remembers and says following 'dog' will tend to be other animal words in the list, and those following 'apple' will be the other food words. Both children who are retarded and young children of normal intelligence show little evidence of using the strategy of clustering. While children who are retarded can be taught to do so, once again they fail to use this aid spontaneously.

3c. Mediation

Memory is also facilitated by mediation strategies. The research paradigm here is paired-associate learning. Initially, two stimuli are presented, and subsequently only the first is shown, and the child is asked to recall the second. Paired associate learning can be facilitated if the child ties the two stimuli together in a meaningful manner; for example, 'sun' and 'bird' are more readily associated if related by something such as 'The sun shines on the bird'. While 5- to 6-year-olds can produce and use mediational strategies, younger children and those who have mental retardation do not use them. If the latter children are provided with mediators or even instructed to generate them, their learning is significantly improved. However, if the experimenter no longer instructs the children, they may fail to continue using mediators on their own. Training them to get into the habit has met with only limited success, being effective primarily with the mildly retarded. Thus, it is not that children with MR are deficient in the sense that they are incapable of grasping higher-level strategies; rather, for some unknown reason, they fail to use spontaneously the abilities they possess.

3d. Retrieval

There is evidence that the same deviation in categorization that hampers memory also adversely affects the retrieval of information that has been learned. It makes sense to assume that items stored singly in memory would be more difficult to retrieve than items stored by categories that represent superordinate organization of the individual items. As was the case in regard to rehearsal and clustering, the deficit seems to be one of lack of *use* of category knowledge rather than lack of category knowledge itself.

3e. Metamemory

Metamemory refers to children's understanding of how memory works, such as knowing it takes more time and effort to memorize a long list of words than a short one. While metamemory improves dramatically with age in children of normal intelligence, the rate of improvement is variable in populations with MR. For example, their understanding of the relation between amount of study time and remembering or the effect of delay of recall on performance is commensurate with mental-age-matched peers; however, even children with higher levels of intellectual functioning lack awareness of the fact that it is easier to relearn old material than to learn new material.

4. Problem Solving

Problem solving typically requires attention, abstraction, planning and logical thinking. The same failure to generate relevant hypotheses that mars discrimination learning in children with MR also affects the more complex task of solving problems. For example, even when the classic '20 questions' task has been modified so that, in the simplest case, only one question is sufficient to supply the information necessary to make a correct choice, children who are retarded ask non-critical questions as frequently as critical ones. Once the information is supplied, they can use it effectively, however.

5. Generalization

Finally, while children with MR can be trained to do a specific problem successfully, they characteristically do not generalize to similar problems. It is as if each task is a new one that must be mastered in its own right. The impediment to learning is obvious.

Summary

Children with MR perform poorly on discrimination learning tasks, although once their position set is broken, they learn as fast as typically developing children. The same failure to generate relevant hypotheses that hampers discrimination learning also adversely affects problem solving. Children with MR have a basic deficiency in attention and generalization, but their short-term memory is intact. While they are not incapable of grasping the strategies of rehearsal, mediation and clustering that facilitate long-term memory, they neither spontaneously generate such strategies nor assimilate them to the point of habitually using them after being instructed or taught to do so. In a similar manner, children with MR do not use their categorizing ability to facilitate the retrieval of information. For unknown reasons, their performance in regard to metamemory tasks is variable, being a mixture of adequate and low-level functioning.

Personality-Motivational Factors
The Similar Reaction Hypothesis

Zigler's third hypothesis, called the *similar reaction hypothesis*, states that there is no basic difference between children who are and are not retarded when it comes to their reactions to life experiences. However, since these experiences might well be different for children who are retarded, such as repeated failure or institutionalization, the children with MR may have special motivational and personality characteristics. A number of these characteristics have been investigated. (Our presentation follows Hodapp and Zigler, 1995.)

Dependency and Outerdirectedness

Children with MR are more attentive to and dependent on adults. For example, because of their need to gain positive reinforcement from adults, institutionalized children will play a boring, repetitious game longer than will non-institutionalized children matched for mental and chronological age. Zigler calls this need for positive reinforcement the *positive reaction tendency*. Along with this tendency goes outer-directedness, or *an exaggerated need to look to others* for clues about how to solve problems. Such clues will subsequently be used even when they are extraneous or misleading. Outer-directedness contrasts with the behaviour of children who are not retarded, who are more self-reliant and use their own judgement more.

Lower Expectancy of Success

Because of repeated experiences with failure, children who are retarded have a lower expectancy of success that makes them give up more readily than children who are not retarded. In certain instances this can lead to a vicious cycle, with the self-protective need to avoid yet another failure experience, resulting in a premature abandoning of the attempt to solve problems – which in turn further reduces the likelihood of success.

Lower Mastery Motivation

Finally, there is a decrease in mastery motivation, or initiative, in children who are retarded. There is less interest and pleasure in tackling new tasks or meeting new challenges, and less intrinsic reward in achievement for its own sake.

The Self

In regard to personality, the self of a child with MR is less differentiated than it is for children in the typically developing population. Recall that, while there is a generalized self-concept, it is also divided into various domains such as intellectual, social and athletic. Thus, a child might say, 'I don't do well in school, but I have lots of friends'. Compared with children matched for chronological age, those with MR have fewer specific domains and a more impoverished concept of the self.

Individuals also have an ideal self and a real self – a 'me as I would like to be' and a 'me as I am'. Compared with typically developing children, those with MR have a lower ideal self, perhaps due to their greater number of failures and to their being treated as incompetent. (See Hodapp and Zigler, 1995.)

We now see that the child with MR has two handicaps – one intellectual, the other motivational. The problem may further be compounded in institutional settings where docility and conformity to a drab routine are rewarded, while assertiveness and initiative are punished. The challenge to researchers is to disentangle basic intellectual handicaps from those that result from motivational and environmental influences. The therapeutic challenge is to find ways our society can accommodate the realistic limitations while maximizing the assets of the child who is retarded. Meeting this challenge will result in a more balanced mixture of successes and failures for those with MR than presently exists. It is helpful to remind ourselves that in certain societies MR is not stigmatized or even viewed as a problem that needs to be corrected. Our achievement-oriented society might profit from such examples of acceptance.

The Family Context

Parent–Child Relationships

Recent studies of parents of a child with MR have shifted from a focus on pathology to a *stress and coping* orientation. For example, parental reactions used to be described in terms of depression and mourning. Currently, researchers regard retardation as an added stressor on the family system and explore the coping techniques used by parents. This new approach allows for positive as well as negative consequences, such as parents being brought closer together or siblings developing an empathy with and concern for children with handicapping conditions. (Here we follow Hodapp, 2002.)

A model for conceptualizing this approach is called the *Double ABCX* (Minnes, 1988). *X* represents the *stress* of having a child with MR, and that stress is a function of the *specific characteristics* of the child, or *A*; the family's internal and external *resources*, or *B*; and the family's *perception* of the child, or *C*. *Double* refers to the *developmental* dimension that takes account of the fact that all

the components may change with time. It will be worthwhile to examine this model in greater detail.

Child Characteristics (A)

As we have seen, children with different types of MR can behave differently and, in keeping with the developmental psychopathology concept of *transactions*, these differences can affect parental behaviour. In families of children with Prader-Willi syndrome, for example, parental stress is related to such syndrome-specific behaviours as overeating, sleeping more than usual, and hoarding objects (Hodapp et al., 1997). Initially, investigators believed that families of children with Down syndrome were more cohesive and harmonious than families of children with other kinds of MR, with the mother experiencing less stress and having a more satisfactory social network. However, there is evidence that, when methodological flaws in previous studies are eliminated, the stress related to rearing children with Down syndrome is no different from that of rearing children with other disabilities (Cahill and Glidden, 1996). Importantly, this study also found that the average adjustment of all families was quite good, being at or near the norm for families with children who were not retarded. Specific characteristics of the Down syndrome phenotype – including a happy disposition, affectionate nature and sociability – may contribute to positive parent–child relationships and, in turn, to a lower incidence of family stress.

Internal and External Resources (B)

Some of the factors enabling parents to cope are obvious: affluent parents cope better than do poor ones, two-parent families cope better than single-parent families, and mothers in harmonious marriages cope better than those in conflicted marriages. More interesting are the findings that parents differ in the kinds of support they find helpful. Mothers request more social-emotional support along with more information about the child's condition and help in child care, while fathers are more concerned with the financial cost of rearing the child. Mothers are helped by a close, supportive social network, while fathers cope better when they have an extended, non-critical social network.

Perception of the Child (C)

Although mothers of children with or without disabilities typically tailor their language to match their child's mental age, data are scarce on how children's cognitive strengths or weaknesses influence parental behaviour. Both mothers of children with MR and mothers of typically developing children shorten their sentences and emphasize and repeat key words when the children are learning to speak. However, unlike their counterparts, mothers of children with MR are more directive, initiating bids more often and overriding the child's speech. By contrast, the interaction between mothers and children without MR is more playful and spontaneous and is less goal oriented. The behaviour of mothers of children with MR is motivated by their perception of the child as needing to be taught, along with their anxiety concerning the child's ability to learn to speak. Ironically, the mother's intrusiveness runs the risk of further increasing the child's communicative difficulties. In fact some intervention programmes aim at helping the mothers to become less directive and to imitate the child more, thus allowing the child to take a more active role in learning to speak.

The Developmental Dimension (Double)

Development of an individual with mental retardation depends on the type and extent of the underlying disorder, the associated disabilities, environmental factors, psychological factors, cognitive abilities and comorbid psychopathological conditions.

Parents' reactions and successful adaptation to parenting a child with MR may change over the course of development. Parents may go through a phase of mourning at each developmental transition, when they are struck anew with a sense of loss when the child fails to achieve a significant developmental milestone. For example, depression

may appear in a mother of a child with Down syndrome when the child is about 4 months old, at which time the child's inconsistent smiles and dampened affect contrast with the vigorous and gleeful responses of the typical infant (Hodapp and Zigler, 1995). A depressive reaction may appear again in the parent when the child is 11 to 15 years of age (entering puberty) or at 21 years of age (entering adulthood). Parents also may begin distancing themselves from the child from middle childhood on in order to prepare the child for becoming independent.

The Social Context

Social development means acquisition of the ability to behave in accordance with social expectations (Pati and Parimanik, 1996). Becoming socialized involves three processes: (1) learning to behave in socially approved ways, (2) playing approved social roles, and (3) development of social attitudes (Hurlock, 1967). For people with mental retardation, their eventual level of social development has implications for the degree of support needed in their literacy arrangement and their integration in the community with increasing emphasis on mainstreaming the attainment of skills in personal, domestic and community functioning. It also contributes considerably to quality of life.

There is evidence that children with MR often are not accepted by their typically developing peers, although they tend to be ignored rather than actively rejected (Nabors, 1997). Their friendship patterns in pre-adolescence also differ. Friendships among typical pre-adolescents are marked by a high level of engagement, evidenced by frequent verbal communication, shared decision making, and mutual responsiveness at a high affective level such as laughing together. Friendships between a pre-adolescent who is typically developing and one who has mild retardation have a low level of engagement, with the children often working independently and rarely laughing together. In short, the children look more like acquaintances than friends (Siperstein et al., 1997).

The Cultural Context: Familial MR

Familial Mental Retardation

In contrast to the organically derived types of MR described in the foregoing section, approximately half of all cases of MR have no clear biological cause and are called **familial or familial-cultural retardation**.

The characteristics of this kind of MR include a level of retardation that is usually mild, with IQs rarely lower than 45 to 50. Individuals are likely to blend into the general population before and after they reach school age. Familial retardation is more prevalent among minorities and individuals of low socio-economic status, and one or both parents are likely to qualify for a diagnosis of MR.

However, the causes of familial retardation are hotly debated. On the biological side, it is hypothesized that these individuals have minor, difficult-to-detect neurological problems that have not yet been identified. In contrast, environmentalists emphasize the features of low socio-economic status that place intellectual growth in jeopardy – prenatal and post-natal risk, inadequate health care, large families, and a disorganized home environment lacking in personal attention and growth-promoting objects such as books and school-readiness games. Finally, statisticians claim that familial retardation simply represents the lower end of the bell-shaped curve of intelligence. However, the prevailing wisdom suggests that both environmental and genetic factors are involved, the contribution of each being about equal (Pennington, 2002).

Whatever its true origins, familial MR clearly can be contrasted with organic MR. Children with organically based MR tend to be moderately to severely retarded and come from all ethnic groups and socio-economic levels, while those in the familial-cultural category tend to be mildly retarded and come from minority groups and low socio-economic levels. Further, the mental retardation of children in the genetic category has a clear organic etiology, whereas for children in the familial-cultural category both organic and environmental factors are involved.

Risk Factors

While the causes of familial retardation are not known, there are data concerning environmental variables that place children at risk for MR. Sameroff (1990) hypothesized that it was not the kind but the number of risks that determined intellectual functioning in children of comparable biological status. He extracted 10 such risk factors from previous research, including maternal mental illness, rigid values in regard to child development, large family, and minimal education. Using longitudinal data, he found that, when they were 4 years old, children with no risks scored more than 30 IQ points higher than children with eight or nine risks. In general, IQ declined as risk factors increased; for example, in multiple-risk families, 24 per cent of the children had IQ scores below 85, while none of the children in the low risk families did.

Further analysis of Sameroff's (1990) data revealed that no single risk variable and no one pattern of variables reduced intellectual performance; rather, different families had different constellations of risk factors. While the low socio-economic status group had more high-risk families, high-risk middle-class and upper-class families were equally damaging to their children's intellectual growth. Finally, Sameroff found that the same lack of environmental support that undermined the children's competence at an early age would continue to do so when they were 13 years old.

The picture was not totally pessimistic, however, since 20 per cent of the high-risk children escaped the fate of the group at large. The variables responsible for a more favourable outcome were parental restrictiveness, clarity of rules and emotional warmth. This pattern of authoritative parenting was sufficiently potent to counteract environmental risks.

Developmental Course

The potential developmental outcomes associated with MR are as diverse as are the causes of the disorder (see de Ruiter et al., 2007 for a review). While children with more profound levels of retardation may need 24-hour supervision and care, requiring them to live their lives in an institutional setting, children with mild MR may lead adaptive and successful lives in the mainstream.

Stability and Change

First, any generalizations about the developmental course of MR must be tempered by the recognition that their functioning may wax and wane over time, depending on the level of retardation and the type. Regarding level, while severe MR is relatively stable from childhood to adulthood, children with mild MR may show IQ changes in an either upward or downward direction. Developmental course is also affected by the type of MR. For example, the IQ of children with Down syndrome continues to develop, but at a decelerating rate, making smaller and smaller gains over time, while children with fragile-X syndrome, show a steady or near-steady gain in IQ until they are 10 to 15 years old, at which point the development slows considerably. (See Hodapp and Dykens, 2003).

Type of retardation also affects the developmental trajectory of adaptive behaviour. Children with Down syndrome reach a plateau during middle childhood, making few advances between 7 and 11 years of age. A longitudinal, cross-sectional study of boys with fragile-X syndrome, on the other hand, showed the most striking gains in the toddler and preschool periods, less marked but still significant gains up until 11 years of age, and no age-related gains into early adulthood (Dykens et al., 1996).

Stage-Salient Issues
Infant Development

Mental retardation may affect the child's accomplishment of the major stage-salient issues of infancy, namely attachment, self-regulation, and exploration of the environment. (Here we follow Sachs and Barrett, 2000.) Many children with MR show delayed or absent eye contact, cooing and social smiling, all of which may interfere with the development of a secure attachment relationship, as may the frequent hospitalizations of children who have accompanying physical disabilities. By a similar token, on the parents' side, attachment may be complicated by grieving in the parent whose child has received the MR label or frustration and irritation in the parent whose child's more subtle deficits have not yet allowed the diagnosis to be made.

The Bayley scales of infant development, BISD-II and its predecessor (Bayley, 1969, 1993), are probably the best known and most widely used of all infant development tests. The Bayley scales are used with infants and children between 1 and 3 years of age, and are generally used to assess children who are suspected to be at risk for abnormal development. Because these tests were designed to be used with very young children, their non-verbal test items were chosen for their ability to measure specific developmental milestones. For example, the Bayley mental scale includes such things as looking for a hidden object and naming pictures, whereas the motor scale includes such items as grasping ability. It provides invaluable information about patterns of mental retardation in the child's early development (Matson, 2007).

Early Childhood

Mental retardation also runs the risk of interfering with the child's development of mastery, self and peer relationships in early childhood. By this point in development, most children's developmental delays have been identified. Parental reactions play a crucial role in the child's outcome and may range from mobilization of resources in a campaign to 'beat the odds', to denial and unrealistic expectations at one extreme, or sadness and resignation at the other. Early and intensive intervention is important at this stage in order to assist the child with language and communication skills, which are strongly predictive of the development of behaviour problems. Children who are unable to communicate their needs or desires are at risk for becoming aggressive, destructive or withdrawn.

Self-care skills may be disrupted by MR, interfering with the child's capacity to participate in mainstream activities unless intervention is initiated. Mental retardation similarly might interfere with the child's ability to engage in meaningful play behaviour and communicate socially with peers. Self-esteem, interpersonal trust and perceived competence all emerge from the successful mastery of these tasks.

Middle Childhood

In the school-age years, mainstreaming, particularly of children with mild mental retardation, introduces a new set of challenges. Many have difficulty adapting to the transition from the supportive, flexible, child-focused day at home to the more structured school setting. For the first time, children may have to cope with interacting with non-developmentally disabled peers and with hearing labels applied to them such as 'retarded', 'slow learner', or 'special ed'. Unfortunately, one of the downsides of mainstreaming is the too-frequent incidence of teasing and rejection by peers. The self-aware child with MR may respond with withdrawal, isolation and depression, or begin to act out his or her frustration in the form of externalizing behaviour. Similarly, as school progresses and subjects become more abstract and complex, children with MR begin to fall further behind and to recognize their differences from others. The physical disabilities that often accompany MR also interfere with the child's ability to participate in important socializing activities, such as sports and scouts. A protective factor, however, is the parent who has access to and knowledge about special activities for developmentally disabled children, such as Special Olympics or community programmes.

Adolescence

The strivings for independence, self-esteem and social awareness that preoccupy adolescents are additionally challenging for the child with MR. Poor social skills and lack of adherence to social norms, such as a lack of attention to personal hygiene, can contribute to peer rejection. The emphasis on physical appearance in adolescence is a further challenge to the self-esteem and social acceptance of the youth with physical anomalies. The youth with MR also is likely to have difficulty keeping up with the verbal repartee, changing styles and complexities of social relationships in the peer group. Friendships with typically developing peers may languish as those peers begin dating, working, driving and engaging in more independent behaviours. Youths with mild MR may have the same dreams and aspirations as their peers, but be unable to reach these goals. Consequently, depression and withdrawal may emerge. Suicidal ideation is not uncommon.

Sexuality is another developmental challenge for the adolescent with MR. Girls with moderate to severe levels of retardation may have difficulty comprehending menstruation and engaging in appropriate self-care. Youths who do not comprehend rules related to sexual touching may engage in inappropriate physical behaviour. However, it is important to note that youths with MR are not likely to be perpetrators of sexual abuse but rather to be the victims of sexual mistreatment by others. This is a particular risk for those who are living in institutional settings, such as group homes.

The academic realm brings further challenges and potential protective factors. In adolescence, youths with MR are likely to be routed out of the academic mainstream and into vocational classes, a boon to the youths who find their niche, but a bane to the youths who feel stigmatized and bored by the repetitive tasks such training often involves.

Finally, adolescence brings a new set of challenges to the family system, which must cope with weighing the developmentally appropriate needs of the youth for independence with the needs for structure and, in some cases, lifelong care. Youth with MR are also characteristically less able to move around independently compared to those without, as carers tend to keep a closer eye on them. This has been speculated as leading to increased negative externalizing behaviours in MR such as stealing.

Intervention

Prevention efforts are typically categorized as 'primary', 'secondary' and 'tertiary' (Kasten and Coury, 1991). Primary interventions concentrate on the prevention of health problems linked to the development of mental retardation; among these interventions are the provisions of good prenatal care, providing routine health care, preventing accidents and preventing maternal drug and alcohol use during pregnancy. Secondary interventions are attempts to correct situations that are likely to lead to mental retardation. These efforts include amniocentesis, chorion villus sampling, genetic counselling, newborn screening for phenylketonuria (PKU) and subsequent treatment if required, surgical placement of a shunt to treat hydrocephaly treatment for congenital hypothyroidism, and the development of an effective rubella vaccine. In addition, the provision of services such as Head Start or other efforts to prevent developmental delays falls under the category of secondary prevention. Finally, tertiary prevention involves treatment of already existing mental retardation. This might include corrective surgery for a congenital heart defect for a child with Down syndrome (which could prevent functional impairment later in life).

Government Regulations

One unique aspect of programmes for the mentally retarded is the involvement of the federal government. PL 94-142, known as the Education for All Handicapped Children Act of 1975, assures that all handicapped children have a free public education tailored to their unique needs, assures the rights of handicapped children and their parents or guardians, assists states in providing education, and assesses and assures the effectiveness of efforts towards education.

Two specific requirements have had far-reaching effects. The first is that an *individualized education programme (IEP)* must be devised for each child with special needs. Implementing an IEP involves assessing the child's present level of functioning, setting goals, and providing educational services and procedures for evaluating educational progress. Parents as well as various professionals participate in the decision-making process.

The second requirement is that handicapped children be educated in the *least restrictive environment*. This requirement reversed the 75-year-old tradition of placing children who are retarded in self-contained special settings, such as special classrooms for the educable mentally retarded (EMR). The contention was that such classes were ineffective in helping many EMR children learn basic academic and occupational skills, that minorities were over-represented, and that advances in education have made individualized instruction in regular classes feasible (Beyer, 1991).

The health sector has a key role to play in the promotive, preventive and curative aspects concerning mental retardation. It is a well-known fact that strong and adequate maternal and child health services in a community can decrease the prevalence of mental retardation. Its essential components are health education, spacing of pregnancies, improving the nutritional status during pregnancy, screening in pregnancy for conditions such as syphillis and Rh incompatibility, detection of and obstetric care for high-risk pregnancy, proper nursing and medical care during labour, nutritional supplementation and proper immunization of young children. In addition, primary health care personnel could carry out other services such as early detection and intervention for developmental delay, guidance and counselling for families and referral to appropriate agencies for rehabilitation.

Special Education

Children classified as *educable mentally retarded* have IQ scores between 55 and 80 and are expected to perform at least at a third-grade level and occasionally as high as a sixth-grade level by the time they finish school. The *trainable mentally retarded (TMR)*, who have IQ scores between 25 and 55, are taught to function in a restricted environment and are not expected to master traditional academic skills.

In special education classes, EMR pupils are taught academic subjects as tools to enhance social competence and occupational skills. Small classes with individualized attention are recommended. Between 6 and 10 years of age, the EMR child, whose mental age is between 3 and 6 years, is given the kind of readiness programmes usually found in kindergarten: the emphasis is on language enrichment and self-confidence, along with good health, work and play habits. EMR children between 9 and 13 years of age, whose mental age is about 6 to 9 years, can master the basic academic skills involved in the three Rs. At the junior and senior high school levels the applied emphasis continues; for example, the children are trained to read the newspaper and job application forms and to make correct change. Occupational education stresses appropriate work habits such as punctuality and following directions, since most vocational failures are due to poor adjustment rather than low mental ability. After formal schooling, sheltered workshops and vocational rehabilitation centres help the mildly retarded adjust to our complex society.

The curriculum for TMRs emphasizes self-care and communication skills, work habits, following directions and rudimentary social participation. Reading instruction, for example, is likely to include recognizing signs such as 'Stop', 'Men' and 'Women', while arithmetic is limited to making change. The majority of these children do not achieve social or economic independence as adults, although they can engage in useful work and adjust well in the protective setting of the family.

However, there have been many concerns raised surrounding the disproportionate number of children from certain ethnic groups and poor socioeconomic backgrounds who are in special education. Both over- and under-representation are problematic if they are associated with reduced access to the most appropriate forms of education, whether by inappropriate placement in special education programmes for students who do not need such support and who may then miss out on a mainstream curriculum, or lack of support for students who would benefit from special education provision. This issue stills needs addressing as to whether this is truly the case. Invalid evidence of over-representation of minority ethnic groups is also problematic as it is associated with inappropriate, negative value judgements about the groups specified (Reid and Knight, 2006).

Mainstreaming

Educating children with MR in regular classrooms is called *mainstreaming*. In keeping with the civil rights movement in the 1960s and 1970s, special classes were labelled another form of discrimination and segregation. The majority of children and adults appear to benefit from inclusion into mainstream educational settings (Freeman and Alkin, 2000).

A current ethic assumption is the right to inclusive education for persons with disabilities: inclusive education means that all students in a school, regardless of their strengths or weaknesses in any area, become part of the school community. Students with special needs, who are not responsive to typical regular education, have also the right to specialized educational programmes.

Studies concerning mainstreaming practices have revealed that support services for the student and the classroom teacher often result in better student academic and social achievement. Salend and Duhaney (2007) claim that mainstreamed students communicated more with others, received social support more often from other students and that their friendships lasted longer compared to students in segregated educational settings. They also show greater social development (Frederickson, 2010). Despite the positive consequences of mainstreaming, mainstreamed students have known to experience difficulties in peer relations such as being accepted less and being rejected more (Luciano and Savage, 2007). Studies have also found that students with special needs as well as low academic achievement show higher levels of loneliness compared to students without special needs (Bakkaloğlu, 2010).

Pavri (2001) has suggested certain critical student and teacher-generated interventions that can increase social support and reduce feelings of loneliness in students. These approaches to working with students who are lonely include (a) social skills training, (b) creating opportunities for social interaction, (c) creating an accepting classroom climate, (d) teaching adaptive coping strategies, and (e) enhancing student's self-esteem.

Behaviour Modification

By far the most successful and widely used therapeutic technique for children with MR is behaviour modification. This technique involves the operant principles of changing undesirable behaviours by altering the specific consequences that reinforce them and by reinforcing new, more socially acceptable responses. It has been used to increase a wide array of behaviours: self-help behaviours (toileting, feeding, dressing), work-oriented behaviours (productivity, task completion), social behaviours (co-operation, group activities), non-academic classroom behaviours (attending, taking turns, talking at appropriate times), academic learning (arithmetic, sight vocabulary), as well as decreasing undesirable behaviours such as attention-getting and aggressive or self-injurious behaviours. An important benefit is that parents can actively participate in the therapeutic programme in the home setting. Most important of all, more than any other single therapeutic technique, behaviour modification has been responsible for changing the prevailing attitude of hopelessness among professional and non-professional caregivers. (See Carr et al., 1999.)

Didden et al. (1997) carried out a meta-analysis of 482 published studies covering a period of 26 years which provides some specific details in regard to treatment outcomes. As to overall effectiveness, 26.5 per cent of all behaviours can be treated quite effectively, 47.1 per cent can be treated fairly effectively, while treatment effectiveness of the remaining 26 per cent is questionable or poor. In regard to kinds of treatment, response contingent procedures (i.e., those based on the operant principle of immediate reinforcement) are significantly more effective than are other techniques.

Prevention

The most challenging population to involve in prevention consists of mothers who have mental retardation, 40 per cent of whose children will

FIGURE 4.3 Growth Curves in Reading Achievement for Groups from the Abecedarian Project.

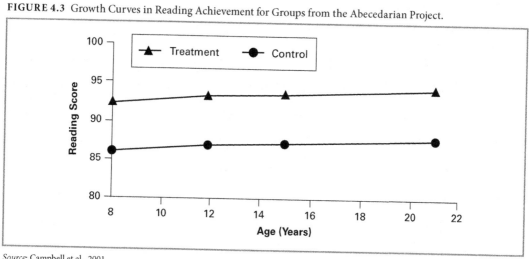

Source: Campbell et al., 2001.

develop familial MR. While most of these mothers are socio-economically deprived, the basic problem is not so much poverty itself but impaired parenting skills. This group has been the target of myriad preventive programmes, including parent education or placing the child in a more stimulating environment, or both.

One of the more successful and better designed prevention programmes was initiated by Ramey and Campbell (1991). Called the Abecedarian Project, the intervention took its name from a term referring to the literate individual – the abecedarian is one who knows his or her ABCs. Evidence shows that, without early intervention, infants of mothers with low IQs are particularly at risk for poor intellectual outcomes. The lower the mother's IQ, the greater the risk. The Abecedarian Project was designed to counter the early decline in infant IQ by placing preschoolers in a special early childhood education programme. The preschool was intensive, involving a full day five days a week for 50 weeks a year for the first five years. Each child received an individualized programme of educational activities that addressed cognitive, social and emotional development but emphasized language most of all.

By the time the children were 3 years old, those receiving the educational intervention scored 20 IQ points higher than children in the control group, putting 95 per cent of them in the average range as compared with 49 per cent of the control children.

Moreover, the programmes had a particularly powerful preventive effect on children whose mothers had the lowest IQs – the group most at risk for developing mental retardation.

To date, follow-up analyses have been conducted on the children at ages 12, 15 and 21. In contrast to an untreated control group, the children who received the intervention had higher reading achievement scores throughout their school years (see Fig. 4.3). In addition, they had higher intelligence test scores and better academic achievement, and were significantly more likely to attend a four-year college course (Campbell et al., 2002). The intervention also had positive benefits for the mothers. Because their children were in the preschool programme, the mothers were able to work at higher-paying jobs and to better their own life situations.

The development of more acceptable terminology for mental retardation is necessary. In clinical practice, it is generally the interaction with other categories – CMDs and psychoses – that leads to the necessity for assessment and intervention. An intellectual ability specifier would enable children with MR to be identified more easily.

Our next topic involves another disorder with its roots in the infancy period. However, unlike organically based mental retardation, which usually is apparent right from birth, autism is an insidious disorder whose effects begin at birth but may not reveal themselves until much later in development.

Infancy: Disorders in the Autistic Spectrum

What lies at the heart of human development in the first two years of life? The establishment of the bond of love is certainly important, as are curiosity and symbolic communication culminating in speech. But what if all were wrenched from their normal course? We would rightly predict severe psychopathology. One such psychopathology that could result is one of the pervasive developmental disorders, the subject of this chapter. In this chapter, we will concern ourselves with two of these profound psychopathologies, both of which are in the *autistic spectrum*. We will first outline *autistic disorder*'s behavioural manifestations and effects on subsequent development, and then we will describe the related disorders of *Asperger's disorder and PDD-NOS*. After that we will raise the seemingly simple question mentioned in previous chapters – how can this psychopathology be understood in terms of normal development gone awry? – and find out how complex the answers are. As we shall see, the study of disorders in the autistic spectrum also illustrates one of the other important issues in developmental psychopathology that we have been considering throughout this text – the continuum between normal and pathological development.

Autism

Definition

Early Descriptions

The term *autism* derives from the Greek word *autos*, meaning self. The term was first coined by the psychiatrist Eugen Bleuler at the beginning of the twentieth century to refer to an extreme withdrawal from social life into the self that he saw in some of his severely disturbed patients. In a classic paper, Leo Kanner (Kanner and others, 1943), a Baltimore psychiatrist, used the term to refer to an unusual group of patients who shared several essential features.

The first feature identified by Kanner was *autistic aloneness*:

There is from the start an extreme autistic aloneness that, whenever possible, disregards, ignores, shuts out anything that comes to the child from the outside.... He has a good relation to objects; he is interested in them, can play with them happily for hours. [But] the child's relation to people is altogether different.... Profound aloneness dominates all behavior. (1943, pp. 242, 246)

The social imperviousness and manneristic behaviour of the autistic child.

© LaraJo Regan/Liaison/Getty

The second characteristic of autism identified by Kanner was a pathological *desire for sameness*:

> The child's noises and motions and all his performances are as monotonously repetitive as are his verbal utterances. There is a marked limitation in the variety of his spontaneous activities. The child's behavior is governed by an anxiously obsessive desire for the maintenance of sameness. (1943, p. 245)

Third, Kanner noted that these children evidenced significant language problems characterized by delayed language development, echolalia, pronoun reversals and extreme literalness.

A fourth observation made by Kanner was that these children exhibited what he termed *islets of ability*. That is, in spite of severe overall deficits in their functioning – particularly in the area of communication, which was often severely impaired – specific skills might be preserved or even enhanced. Among these, he noted, were the 'astounding vocabulary of the speaking children, the excellent memory for events of several years before, the phenomenal rote memory for poems and names, and the precise recollection of complex patterns and sequences' (1943, p. 247).

Kanner proposed that deficits so profound must be the signs of an inborn disturbance, the core of which is a failure of normal attachment: 'We must, then, assume that these children have come into the world with innate inability to form the usual biologically provided affective contact with people, just as other children come into the world with innate physical or intellectual handicaps' (1943, p. 250). Interestingly, he later abandoned this view in favour of a theory that attributed autism to psychodynamic factors, a wrong turn that the field took with him for several generations, as we shall see. (See Box 5.1.)

DSM-IV-TR Definition

The DSM-IV-TR places autistic disorder in the category of the pervasive developmental disorders (PDDs), a group of syndromes characterized by severe and pervasive impairment in several areas of development. Three subtypes of autism are identified in this group, autistic disorder, asperger disorder and pervasive developmental disorder not otherwise specified (PDD-NOS). The group of PDDs also includes Rett syndrome, and childhood disintegrative disorder, which have similar autistic-like behaviours. However, the latter two differ from the other three in several aspects. They are degenerative conditions, with a later onset and different course and outcome, and therefore not considered to be forms of autism. Although there are some differences of detail and terminology in the classifications in the DSM-IV and ICD-10, there are more similarities than differences. For example the ICD-10 also separates autism into three autism subtypes but uses different labels – childhood autism, atypical autism (the same as DSM-IV PDD-NOS) and Asperger's. They list other PDDs as including other childhood disintegrative disorder, Rett syndrome and overactive disorder associated with mental retardation and stereotyped movements.

Importantly, autism is characterized by both classification systems as having deficits in social interaction, communication and the presence of stereotyped behaviours, interests and activities. These three core deficits are often referred to as the 'Triad of Impairments' (Wing and Gould, 1979).

Table 5.1 summarizes the basic diagnostic features of autism. Note that three of Kanner's observations – social isolation, impaired speech

Box 5.1 The 'Refrigerator Mother': Theories of Autism Take a Wrong Turn

Although Kanner (1944) originally proposed that autism was a biologically based disorder, he later revised his theory in favour of a psychodynamic one, in keeping with the tenor of the times. He was the first to call attention to what he saw as a lack of parental warmth and attachment to their autistic children. In his 1949 paper, he attributed autism to a 'genuine lack of maternal warmth' and was instrumental to the formation of 'Refrigerator Mother' theory. The belief that autism was caused by maladaptive parenting caught hold with clinicians as well as the general public. The parent of the autistic child was described as cold, rejecting and emotionally absent: the 'refrigerator mother'.

It was Bruno Bettelheim who gave the theory widespread popularity. For example, in his book *The Empty Fortress* (1967), Bruno Bettelheim wrote, 'Throughout this book I state my belief that the precipitating factor in infantile autism is the parent's wish that his child should not exist' (p. 241). He described one mother as follows:

About other people she spoke with animation and clarity. But when the conversation turned to Joey, she immediately became impersonal, detached, and was soon unable to keep her mind on him, switching to other topics. When she told us about his birth and infancy, it was as if she were talking about some vague acquaintance, some person or event she had heard about and noted without interest. Soon her thoughts wandered away to other people, or herself. It seemed that Joey simply never got through to his mother. (p. 241)

Viewed through a critical lens, the behaviour of a mother or father trying to parent an unresponsive child indeed might look less than ideal. Yet, both Kanner and Bettelheim consistently ignored the fact that the autistic children had non-autistic siblings who were, presumably, exposed to the same parents and their warmth or lack of it. However, the refrigerator parent theory quickly gained momentum and represented a tragic wrong turn in the study of autism, which a growing volume of data supporting a biological cause now clearly refutes. Many generations of parents bore the burden, not only of parenting an extremely disabled child, but of misplaced guilt for causing the problem. Research has shown that mothers of children with autism are not significantly different in their personality characteristics and attitudes towards their children from mothers of children with other handicaps (Griffith et al., 2010). Further, despite the indifference and lack of reinforcement with which their overtures are met, mothers of children with autism are observed to be highly adept at adjusting their behaviour in order to socially engage their children (Doussard-Roosevelt et al., 2003). Therefore, in contrast to other attachment disorders that are secondary to pathological caregiving that we discuss in Chapter 6, autism can be considered a *primary* attachment disorder in that the child comes into the world lacking in normal response to others.

and a pathological need for sameness – have stood the test of time. Next, we describe the deficits characteristic of autism in each of these areas of functioning.

Impairment in Social Interaction

Children with autism exhibit extreme *social isolation* and an inability to relate to people. For example, in a face-to-face situation a girl with severe autism will not look at you or even away from you; rather, she will look *through* you. If you put her on your lap, her body will not accommodate to yours; instead she will sit as if you were a chair. If she needs you to do something, say, open a door, she will take your hand (rather than taking *you* by the hand) and bring it in contact with a doorknob. It is as if you do not exist as a person but rather as a thing. She will be unable to request an object by directing her gaze and will also be unable to follow where you are looking. In fact combined impairments in *joint attention* and *social orienting* have been found to distinguish young children with ASD from those without ASD and are important early diagnostic markers (Dawson et al., 2004).

Wing and Attwood (1987) described the social impairments of the children with autism in their

TABLE 5.1 DSM-IV-TR Criteria for Autistic Disorder

A. A total of six or more items, with at least two from category 1.

   1. Qualitative impairment in social interaction, as manifested by at least two of the following:

      a. Marked impairment in the use of multiple nonverbal behaviors such as eye-to-eye gaze, facial expression, body postures, and gestures to regulate social interaction

      b. Failure to develop peer relationships appropriate to developmental level

      c. A lack of spontaneous seeking to share enjoyment, interests, or achievements with other people (e.g., by a lack of showing, bringing, or pointing out objects of interest)

      d. Lack of social or emotional reciprocity

   2. Qualitative impairments in communication as manifested by at least one of the following:

      a. Delay in, or total lack of, the development of spoken language (not accompanied by an attempt to compensate through alternative modes of communication such as gesture or mime)

      b. In individuals with adequate speech, marked impairment in the ability to initiate or sustain a conversation with others

      c. Stereotyped and repetitive use of language or idiosyncratic language

      d. Lack of varied spontaneous make-believe play or social imitative play appropriate to developmental level

   3. Restricted repetitive and stereotyped patterns of behavior, interests, and activities, as manifested by at least one of the following:

      a. Encompassing preoccupation with one or more stereotyped and restricted patterns of interest that is abnormal either in intensity or focus

      b. Apparently inflexible adherence to specific, nonfunctional routines or rituals

      c. Stereotyped and repetitive motor mannerisms (e.g., hand or finger flapping or twisting, or complex whole body movements)

      d. Persistent preoccupation with parts of objects

B. Delays or abnormal functioning in at least one of the following areas, with onset prior to age 3: (1) social interaction, (2) language as used in social communication, or (3) symbolic or imaginative play

Source: Reprinted with permission from the *Diagnostic and Statistical Manual of Mental Disorders*, Fourth Edition Text Revision. Copyright 2000 by the American Psychiatric Association.

study as falling into one of three types (see Fig. 5.1). The first includes *aloof* children, who seem to be isolated in their own bubble. These children are withdrawn and do not respond to the social overtures of others. They do not seek eye contact and often actively attempt to avoid it. They also dislike physical contact, refusing to be cuddled, and do not respond to caregivers with interest or excitement. While they will approach others, it is only to get instrumental needs met, such as to be fed, and not to meet emotional needs, such as for comfort or affection. The second group includes the *passive* children, who accept others' social overtures but in a submissive and indifferent manner. While they interact with others, they do so as a matter of daily routine rather than as a source of spontaneous pleasure. They also are compliant and even overly so; for example, they may be easily led into mischief by peers because they do whatever they are instructed to do. The third group includes the *odd* children, more commonly referred to as the *active but odd group*, who are very interested in other people but are lacking in social comprehension and appreciation for the norms of behaviour. They might approach strangers and indiscriminately touch them or ask inappropriate questions, without registering the feedback that their behaviour is discomfiting to others.

Wing (1991) observed the children over the next 16 years of their lives and found that many

FIGURE 5.1 Three Types of Social Impairment.

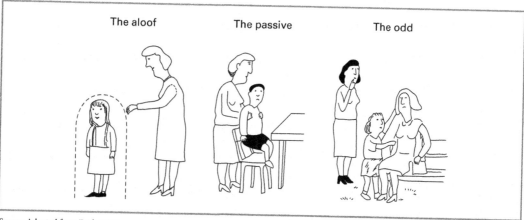

Source: Adapted from Frith, 2003.

changed from one category to another. In particular, there was a strong tendency for children in the aloof group to become passive or odd over the course of development, probably as a result of interventions that encouraged socialization. Wing (1996) has further identified a fourth type, the *'overly formal, stilted group'* referring to a group of highly able adolescents or adults who are excessively polite and formal, and try very hard to behave well. They are believed to cope in social situations by sticking rigidly to the rules of social interaction.

The descriptions of social interaction impairments are important, because it counteracts the myth that all individuals with ASD are completely asocial. Anyone who has spent time with individuals with ASD will know that this is not the case. Importantly, Wing's terminology for the four different social groups did not express these groupings as constituting discrete, clear-cut subtypes of ASD if only to reflect the fact the individual's social interaction often changes over time.

Impairments in Communication

Communicative deficits are commonly seen in autism and often are severe. They may range from *mutism* – as many as half of children with autism will never learn to speak – to *non-communicative* speech. Characteristics of non-communicative speech may include *echolalia*, the exact repetition of words or phrases spoken by others with no

effort to comprehend their meaning (e.g., a child who had been scolded for eating butter out of the butter dish repeatedly stated, 'Don't do that, Gregory'). Speech also may be used *idiosyncratically*, such as the utterance of phrases or sentences that are irrelevant to the situation (e.g., while repeatedly flushing the toilet, a girl with autism suddenly said, 'The hamburgers are in the refrigerator!').

The speech of autistic children is often extremely *literal* and *pedantic*, with speech used in an overly formal and stilted manner as if they had memorized by rote phrases in a foreign language (e.g., one British child always requests, 'May I extract a biscuit from this tin?'; another young man, each time he telephones his favourite aunt, announces himself by saying, 'This is J. M. Wright, your nephew, speaking'). Children with autism also tend to comprehend speech in an overly literal way. Such literalism can be scary: a girl with autism was terrified when a nurse asked her to 'Give me your hand' because she thought the nurse literally wanted her to remove her hand (Frith, 2003).

Children with autism often have difficulty understanding the correct use of first and third person. They may engage in *pronoun reversal*, using 'you' instead of 'I' (e.g., 'You want to go out') or referring to themselves by name (e.g., 'Jack wants to eat' rather than 'I want to eat').

Another commonly seen characteristic of autistic speech is that it lacks *prosody*, the changes in rhythm and intonation that gives normal speech its melody. Instead, the child with autism speaks in a monotone without the proper stress on words or rise and fall in tone that help to convey emotion and meaning. Correspondingly, children with autism also seem to lack an understanding of what others are communicating through the prosody of their speech. Consider how comprehension of humour, irony or sarcasm relies on attention to the *way* something is said (e.g., imagine that an exasperated parent walks into a room strewn with toys and says, 'Well, thanks very much for cleaning up in here!'). While the typically developing child would likely pick up on the dripping sarcasm – and respond by beginning to pick up the toys – the child with autism is likely to be bewildered, unable to grasp that the literal meaning is not the intended one.

Children with autism show severe deficits in the development of *gesture* communication (Stieglitz et al., 2008). *Imitation* of gestures, body movement and pantomime is significantly impaired. Deficits in gesture are more pronounced for those involving joint attention or those involving expressing affectionate states as opposed to instrument needs. For example, they fail to make requests for objects of actions via distal gestures, such as pointing, showing, offering/giving and ritualized requests. They also fail to demonstrate *spontaneously* many *descriptive* gestures; these may be *conventional* (e.g. struggling to indicate 'I don't know'), *affective* (e.g. hands on hips to indicate 'angry'), or *gestures and gestural description* of objects attributes and actions (e.g. holding arms apart to indicate 'big').

Play is another modality through which children communicate. However, unlike typically developing children, the play behaviour of those with autism is lacking in social and symbolic functions. In particular, children with autism do not tend to initiate make-believe play. For example, when given blocks to play with, a typically developing preschooler might use them to represent a car ('Vroom! Vroom!') or to create an airport landing strip. The child with autism, in contrast, is more likely to become fixated on lining the blocks up in a precisely straight row or, if they are striped or brightly coloured, spinning them and staring as they whirl. However, most of this research has required children with autism to produce pretend play spontaneously. When they are provided with prompts, such as the investigator's asking, 'What can you do with these [toys]?' or 'Can you pretend to give dolly a drink [from an empty cup]?' the performance of children with autism is comparable to that of children with mental retardation (Charman and Baron-Cohen, 1997). These findings suggest that there is not a basic inability to pretend in children with autism but rather that they are not as *motivated* to pretend as are other children.

A child with autism has little or *no flexibility* of thinking or behaviour. A perfect illustration is given by Hart (1991) when describing the behaviour of his autistic son, Ted, during a birthday party when ice-cream cones were served. He reports that while the other children immediately began to lick them, his son just stared at his and appeared to be afraid of it. He did not know what to do, because in the past he had eaten ice cream with a spoon.

Another serious problem is that autistic individuals lack *common sense*. They can easily learn how to get on a bus to go to school, but have no idea what to do if something interrupts the routine. Any disruption of routine causes a panic attack, anxiety or a flight response, unless the person is taught what to do when something goes wrong. *Rigid thinking* makes it difficult to teach the subtleties of socially appropriate behaviour (Grandin, 2006).

Restricted and Stereotyped Interests and Behaviour

The *need for sameness* applies both to the child's own behaviour and to the environment. Often the child's activities are simple, such as sitting on the floor and *rocking* back and forth for long periods of time, or *twirling* his or her shoelaces, or obsessively *lining* toys up. The need for sameness can be expressed in a number of other ways; for example, the child must have the exact same food and plate and utensils, or wear the same article of clothing, or have the furniture arranged in a specific way. The intensity of the need is evidenced not only by the **rigidity** of the behaviour but also by the child's panic and rage when attempts are made to alter the environment even in minor ways, such as providing a different food or moving a chair to a different part of the room.

A child obsessively ordering toys
© *Nancy J. Price*

Associated Features
Sensory Processing

Abnormal responses to *sensory* stimuli were omitted from DSM-III (1980) because of confusion over the interpretation of such symptoms and also because of the poverty of systematic empirical research in this domain. Since DSM-IV was published in 1994 there has been increasing awareness that sensory processing difficulties may be an important symptom in the clinical picture for many, if not most, individuals with autism. In fact the appearance of these sensory behaviours often precedes diagnosis. Tomchek and Dunn (2007) recently found that as many as 95 per cent of children with ASD denote some degree of sensory processing dysfunction.

Children with autism often respond to sensory *stimulation* in unusual ways. They may smell every object that comes into their hands, even an inert object, or place it in their mouths. Children with autism can be either *hypersensitive* or *hyposensitive* to stimuli, often with an unpredictable fluctuation between the two. For example, they may be *hypersensitive* to touch and find unbearable the feel of certain fabrics on their skin. *Hyposensitivity* may take the form of an unusual tolerance of cold or imperviousness to pain, which may be related to the fact that many children with autism engage in self-injurious behaviour such as head banging or hitting, slapping, scratching or biting themselves. Hyposensitivity to sound may be so profound that the child is mistakenly thought to be deaf. In fact, this hyporeactivity (e.g. diminished response to name) has even been considered an early diagnostic marker in that children who appeared to be deaf early in life have subsequently been diagnosed with autism (Wing, 1996). Peculiar hyposensitivity may exist for some sounds at the same time that the child is hypersensitive to others. Thus, the same child who shrieks in fear and rage at the sound of the telephone may be entirely unresponsive to the sound of a fire alarm.

Autobiographical accounts of adults with autism also contain references to a generalized sensory *overload*, such as feeling *bombarded* by bright lights and unpredictable movement or being overwhelmed by the noise and confusion of large gatherings. It may be that, when faced with such an environment, the children seek the safety of repetitive, low-intensity sensory stimulation, such as humming the same note over and over or concentrating their attention on the movement of a spinning coin. In short, the pathological need for sameness may provide a defence against being *overwhelmed* by ordinary environmental stimuli.

Autistic Savants

A common *misconception* surrounding autism, made famous by Dustin Hoffman in the film *Rain Man*, is the popular image of all individuals being *savants* – a rare condition in which people with developmental disorders have one or more

FIGURE 5.2 A Drawing by Nadia at 3 Years 5 Months.

Source: Selfe, 1977.

areas of *expertise*, ability or brilliance which are in contrast with the individual's overall limitations. For example, possessing a rare talent or the ability to perform remarkable feats can include memorizing the telephone book, calculating complex equations, knowing the day of the week on which any date ever fell or learning foreign languages. Sometimes referred to as **savantism**, such splinter skills are in fact seen in only about 10 per cent of children with the disorder (Hermelin, 2001).

Kim Peek was the real Rain Man whose almost unimaginable powers of memory were coupled with severe disabilities. He showed an amazing ability to read and memorize books before he reached the age of 2. If a city was named to him, he could list roads, businesses, postal/zip codes and historical data from the area. This was in stark contrast to the difficulty he had buttoning up his shirts and he failed to master walking up stairs until he was 16 years of age.

Another stunning example of a savant is the case of Nadia (Selfe, 1977). Between the ages of 4 and 7, Nadia produced drawings admired by professionals and compared with the beauty of cave paintings from 30000 years ago (Humphrey, 1998). An example of a drawing done by Nadia is shown in Fig. 5.2.

Sadly, while these cases provide a fascinating insight into the world of savants they are under-representative of autism. Much of what society at large learns of disorders on the autism spectrum is produced by representations of autism in novels, television series, movies or autobiographies, and therefore it is important that they do not misrepresent such cases. Media representations of talent and special abilities, such as those shown in *Rain Man*, can be said to have contributed to a harmful divergence between the general image of autism and the clinical reality of the autistic condition (Draaisma, 2009). For most children with autism, the disorder is associated with significant cognitive deficits in all areas. (See Box 5.2.)

Box 5.2 Conceptualizations of Psychopathology: Qualitative Differences and Asynchrony

Note that DSM-IV uses the term 'qualitative' when describing impairment in social interaction and communication (see Table 5.1). Whether psychopathology represents a quantitative or a qualitative difference from normality is a perennial question. Generally speaking, the *quantitative* view is more prevalent: phobias are regarded as extremes of normal fears; delinquency is viewed as an exaggeration of normal adolescent rebelliousness. The three major developmental models of psychopathology – fixation, regression and developmental delay – are quantitative. DSM-IV's description of autism in terms of *qualitative* impairments implies that autistic behaviour has no counterpart even in the behaviour of younger normal children and that the developmental sequencing of behaviour does not follow that charted for normal children.

To evaluate the quantitative versus qualitative issue, Wenar and colleagues (1986) compared the development of 41 children with autism between 5 and 11 years of age with that of 195 normal children between 3 months and 5 years of age, using a standardized observational technique called the Behavior Rating Instrument for Autistic and Other Atypical Children (BRIAAC). The investigators found that severely autistic children's obliviousness to caretaking adults, their minimal expressiveness, their disinterest in or fleeting exploration of objects, their unresponsiveness or negative reaction to sound, and their indifference to social demands all indicated an imperviousness to the social and physical environment that had little counterpart in normal behaviour and development. In a like manner Dawson (1991), in discussing early socio-emotional development, concludes that in certain cases both the surface behaviour and the function or need it fulfils may be unique to the autistic child, and parallels in normal developmental patterns may be difficult to find.

Our review of research on autism also suggests another new conceptualization of normal development gone awry. In autism, deviance lies in the relationships among variables rather than within a single variable itself. We will call this deviation *asynchrony*. Progress among variables is disjointed, with some variables proceeding at a normal pace while others lag or follow an idiosyncratic course. While asynchrony has been noted in the clinical literature (see Freud, 1965), it is now being verified in objective studies of language development in children with autism (e.g., in the discrepancy between understanding of syntax and language semantics).

Characteristics

Age of Onset

According to the DSM-IV-TR criteria, autistic behaviour must be present before the third year of life in order for the diagnosis to be valid. Although the disorder is believed to be present at birth, the diagnosis is complicated by the fact that many of the diagnostic criteria concern functions that emerge later in development. For example, it is not until 18 months that we would expect a typically developing child to demonstrate the first rudiments of pretend play. The timing of the diagnosis also is likely to be related to the degree of deficit. Children with autism are sometimes divided into low-, medium- or high-functioning autism (LFA, MFA and HFA), based on intelligence quotient thresholds (Baron-Cohen, 2006) or on how much support the individual requires in daily life. Generally children with IQs below 70 are considered to be low functioning, and those whose IQs are within the normal range of typical development are classed as high functioning. However, these subdivisions are not standardized and are controversial. The diagnosis of autism might come later for the child who is higher functioning, because the disparity between the child and his or her normally developing peers only becomes apparent as development proceeds. A diagnostic dilemma also exists for the low-functioning child, who might languish with an incorrect diagnosis of mental retardation.

However, just because adults did not notice or label the child's autism, that does not mean it was not present throughout infancy. Geraldine Dawson and her colleagues (Osterling and Dawson, 1994) came up with the ingenious idea of watching old family videos of the first birthday parties of children who later were diagnosed with autism.

Comparing 11 typically developing infants with 11 infants with autistic disorder, the investigators found that children with autism engaged consistently less in several behaviours, including looking at the faces of others, showing or pointing to objects of interest, or orienting to their names when called. These behaviours allowed raters to correctly classify 91 per cent of the children as being in the autistic or non-autistic group.

In a subsequent study, Dawson and colleagues (Werner et al., 2000) found that they could reliably detect oddities in behaviour even earlier in development. At 8 to 10 months of age, infants later diagnosed with autism were less likely than a matched cohort of typically developing children to orient to the speaker when their names were called and were slightly less likely to look at another person while smiling. Interestingly, developmental paediatricians performed no better than chance when attempting to classify the 8- to 10-month-olds as autistic or non-autistic. However, the raters were able to place children in the correct group 78 per cent of the time when provided with videotapes made when the children were 12 months of age, a mere few months later. Consequently, the investigators conclude, autism may be extremely difficult for observers to detect prior to 1 year of age even though subtle signs of the disorder are emerging.

Prevalence

Officially, DSM-IV-TR places the median prevalence rate at 5 per 10000 individuals but notes that there is wide variation from study to study. While earlier reports suggested that autism was an extremely *rare* phenomenon, more recent surveys have revealed a surprising increase (Baird et al., 2006). Statistics compiled in the USA show that autism is 10 times more prevalent now than it was 20 years ago (Yeargin-Allsop et al., 2003) a pattern which is reflected across both continental Europe and the UK. Wing and Potter (2002) reviewed 39 population-based studies derived from a dozen different countries and found that, in the past decade, prevalence rates for autistic disorder ranged between 3.8 and 60 per 10000 children.

If rates of autism are *increasing*, does this signify an *epidemic* or is it merely a product of changes in diagnostic circumstances affecting assessment of outcome or enhanced ascertainment of those at risk? Experts in the field generally believe that the rise in prevalence is due to an increase in *improved* clinical and public awareness, leading to earlier diagnosis and inclusion of mildly affected cases. It also reflects the changing diagnostic trends, overlay of symptoms and awareness across different conditions. In addition, there has been a *widening* of the diagnostic criteria. For example, Frith (2003) notes that a survey in California reported a 250 per cent increase in the diagnosis of autism between 1987 and 1994, while rates of the diagnosis of mental retardation decreased by exactly that amount in the same time period. Rather than indicating an increase in the prevalence of autism, a more likely explanation of these data is that, as the accuracy of the diagnostic system increases, more children with autism are being correctly diagnosed.

There may also have been an increase in the use of autism spectrum disorder (ASD) as a diagnostic label to obtain early intervention funding (Prior, 2003). Diagnosis as a 'ticket' for services is a problem referred to as diagnostic substitution. For example, children are recognized to have a non-ASD condition but may be given a primary diagnosis of ASD, influenced by awareness but also the support benefits associated with them. Where resources are being directed towards ASD greater incidence is associated with declines in other diagnostic categories indicating that clinicians prefer to label children with ASD in order to allow them access to greater resources (Shattuck, 2006).

Another common misdiagnosis substitution is when children are labelled ASD as their primary diagnosis instead of the other comorbid condition. For example, Bishop et al. (2008) investigated diagnosis substitution between developmental language disorder and autism, applying contemporary criteria for autism to adults diagnosed with developmental language disorder during the 1980s and early 1990s. Just over 20 per cent (8/38) of individuals met full criteria while a further four (10 per cent) met criteria for milder forms of ASD.

Gender

The sex difference in autism is significant. On average across studies, boys outnumber girls at a ratio of 4 to 1, a ratio that has not changed significantly from the time of Kanner (Fombonne, 1999). However, the ratios change when we look at children with varying levels of cognitive ability: boys predominate less at the lower end of the IQ range. For example, in a large-scale study conducted in the UK, Wing (1991) found that at the lowest IQ levels, the ratio of boys to girls was 2 to 1, whereas at the highest levels it was 15 to 1. The explanation for this gendered pattern is not yet known.

The high incidence of autism found in males has led to the development of an idea first postulated by Hans Asperger (1944) who said that 'autistic personality is an extreme variant of male intelligence'. Today this is more commonly referred to as the 'Extreme Male Brain Theory of Autism' (Baron-Cohen, 2002) and implies that autism is resultant of overdeveloped 'male' characteristics. This claim has been supported by a wealth of findings tracking the autistic profile of strengths in visuospatial analysis, in which men are often found to be superior, and weaknesses in social judgement, where women are more superior. Happé et al. (2001) have also given more weight to this theory by demonstrating characteristics associated with autism to be more common in first degree male relatives (brother, fathers).

Social Class, Ethnicity and Culture

In the earliest clinical descriptions of children with autism, Kanner noted a preponderance of 'highly intelligent parents'. A belief which was reiterated in some of the earlier studies is that autism was in fact more prevalent among the upper classes. However, more recent research shows that this may simply be due to a sampling bias in the populations that made their way to diagnostic clinics. For example, it has been suggested that 'more parents of high social class families have the necessary information and financial resources to find their way to the specialized facilities' (Tsai et al., 1982, p. 212) and 'a knowledgeable and determined parent of an autistic child is more likely to obtain an informed decision' (Wing, 1980, p. 410).

Ethnicity and socio-economic status do not consistently influence the prevalence of autism. For example, there are no known differences by race and ethnicity in epidemiology of autism (Fombonne, 2003). Studies conducted in many different nations reveal a similar picture of the disorder (Schreibman and Charlop-Christy, 1998). For example, North American studies tend to conclude that neither maternal ethnicity nor immigrant status are related to the rate of autism spectrum disorders. However, this is in contrast to a growing number of European studies, particularly from Nordic countries, which suggest an increased frequency of autism in children of immigrant parents. A recent retrospective case note analysis of 428 children diagnosed with ASD, and referring to child development services in London during a six-year period, found mothers born outside Europe to have a significantly higher risk of having a child with autism compared to those born in the UK, with the highest risk observed for the Caribbean group. Mothers of black ethnicity were also found to have a significantly higher risk than white mothers (Keen et al., 2010).

One thing that is clear is that ethnic minority groups seem under-represented in mental health institutions that focus on the treatment of autism. It has been speculated that professionals screen for autism spectrum (ASD) less often in children from minority than majority groups (Mandell et al., 2009). Language and social problems related to immigrant and ethnic status may be partly to blame, as these hamper proper detection of autistic features.

Cultural factors may also affect parents' recognition and interpretation of symptoms adding to differences in age of diagnosis. For example, Daley (2004) found Asian-Indian parents were more likely to first notice social difficulties in their children with autism, attributed to the value Indian culture place on social conformity, while studies in the USA have found parents to first identify more general developmental delay or regression in language skills in their children with autism.

Comorbidity

Many children with autism also qualify for a diagnosis of *mental retardation.* (However, mentally retarded children without autism differ in numerous and profound ways from children with the disorder, as we shall see, and thus the two clearly are distinct disorders.) Whereas earlier studies reported that 75 per cent of children with autism were mentally retarded, with IQ scores falling below 70, these studies were based on clinical populations and included only the most severely disturbed. A population-based study in the UK, which sampled the entire range of the autistic spectrum, found that only 35 per cent of children affected by autistic spectrum disorders had cognitive skills in the mentally retarded range (Baird et al., 2000).

Psychiatric disorders appear to be prevalent: the most commonly reported are disruptive, mood and anxiety disorders (De Bruin et al., 2007) and nearly half of all youngsters with ASD are administered psychotropic medicines to stabilize their behaviour. *Anxieties* are evident in 7 to 84 per cent of autistic children (Lainhart, 1999), particularly related to stimuli to which they are hypersensitive. At times, these may reach phobic proportions, interfering with the child's ability to function. For example, Klinger et al. (2003) describe the child afraid of tarmac who consequently was unable to walk across the parking lot, street or school playground. Autism also coexists with *seizure disorders* in 11 to 39 per cent of cases. Those most likely to be affected are females and those with mental retardation (Ballaban-Gil and Tuchman, 2000).

Asperger's Disorder

Definition

Early Descriptions

Unbeknown to Kanner, at the same time that he was studying autism in Baltimore, Hans Asperger was writing about a similar group of children in Vienna. Asperger's classic paper, published in 1944, was long forgotten until it was reintroduced to the profession by Lorna Wing (1981). Asperger's words were translated by Frith (1991) as follows:

> In what follows I will describe a type of child which is of interest in a number of ways: the children have in common a fundamental disturbance which manifests itself characteristically in all behavioural and expressive phenomena. This disturbance results in considerable and typical difficulties of social integration. In many cases, the failure to be integrated in a social group is the most conspicuous feature, but in other cases this failure is compensated for by a particular originality of thought and experience, which may well lead to exceptional achievement in later life. (p. 37)

Asperger noted a number of features these children had in common: they avoided eye contact, their speech lacked melody and was often monotone or sing-song, they engaged in odd stereotypic movements and they did not respond to positive emotional displays from others.

Although Asperger in fact described children whose symptoms ranged widely, his name became associated with a particular subset of children in the autistic spectrum. Currently, the label Asperger's disorder is reserved for children whose deficits are more subtle and whose intellectual and language functioning is higher than that of those children who fit the autistic disorder label.

DSM-IV-TR Definition

The separate diagnostic category of Asperger's disorder (AD; also known as Asperger syndrome) was first added to the DSM-IV in 1994. The DSM-IV-TR criteria are listed in Table 5.2. As we see, the key difference with autism is that children with AD show no delays in language development and no significant cognitive deficits. It must be said that even though the diagnosis is part of the official nomenclature, experts disagree about whether AD truly represents a different category of disorder

TABLE 5.2 DSM-IV-TR Criteria for Asperger's Disorder

A. Qualitative impairment in social interaction, as manifested by at least two of the following:

    1. Marked impairment in the use of multiple nonverbal behaviors such as eye-to-eye gaze, facial expression, body postures, and gestures to regulate social interaction

    2. Failure to develop peer relationships appropriate to developmental level

    3. A lack of spontaneously seeking to share enjoyment, interests, or achievements with other people (e.g., by a lack of showing, bringing or pointing out objects of interest to other people)

    4. Lack of social or emotional reciprocity

B. Restricted repetitive and stereotyped patterns of behavior, interests, and activities as manifested by at least one of the following:

    1. Encompassing preoccupation with one or more stereotyped and restricted patterns of interest that is abnormal either in intensity or focus

    2. Apparently inflexible adherence to specific, nonfunctional routines or rituals

    3. Stereotyped and repetitive motor mannerisms (e.g., hand or finger flapping or twisting, or complex whole-body movements)

    4. Persistent preoccupation with parts of objects

C. The disturbance causes clinically significant impairment in social, occupational, or other important areas of functioning

D. There is no clinically significant general delay in language (e.g., single words used by age 2 years, communicative phrases used by age 3 years)

E. There is no clinically significant delay in cognitive development or in the development of age-appropriate self-help skills, adaptive behavior (other than in social interaction), and curiosity about the environment in childhood

Source: Reprinted with permission from the *Diagnostic and Statistical Manual of Mental Disorders*, Fourth Edition Text Revision. Copyright 2000 by the American Psychiatric Association.

from autism (Volkmar and Klin, 2000). Many in the field tend to the view that the two are variants of the same underlying developmental disorder, with AD at the less severe end of the autistic spectrum (Frith, 2003).

Associated Features

Although not part of the DSM-IV-TR criteria, there are a number of other characteristics often seen in children with AD. For example, they frequently show a number of *obsessive-compulsive* tendencies, including behavioural and verbal rituals such as the accumulation and recitation of facts.

While children with AD may be highly verbal, they show a number of deficits in the social use of language, or *pragmatics*. For example, their communications with others may be restricted to monologues in their *narrow* specific area of interests, not including the other as an active participant in the conversation; and they lack the social niceties of

turn-taking, sharing the floor and using *appropriate* non-verbal communication such as eye contact and facial expression.

Although children with AD are intact cognitively and their verbal skills are preserved, they still may have difficulties in the area of *non-verbal intelligence* (Lincoln et al., 1988). Indeed, children with AD are remarkably similar to those with non-verbal learning disabilities (Rourke and Tsatsanis, 2000).

Characteristics
Prevalence

Because AD has only recently been officially recognized, less is known about its prevalence. It is often the case that because of their good intelligence, children with AD may long go *undetected*. In fact, many Asperger individuals *never* get formally diagnosed, and they often hold jobs and live independently. Children with AD have more *normal* speech

Box 5.3 Case Study: An Autobiographical Account of Asperger's

Kenneth Hall, a 10-year-old boy, was diagnosed with Asperger syndrome when he was 8 years old. He wrote about his experiences in his autobiography: Asperger Syndrome, The Universe and Everything.

It is hard for me to know for sure what is different about me because I just feel normal to myself. I think there are some differences about how I feel and learn things. Some things are easier and some are harder. I always try to work very hard at the things that are difficult for me. This is a very important thing to do.

My difficulties

Crowds

One thing I don't like is crowds. For example, I just hated the classroom. The noise annoyed me. At the time the sound of the children's chatter was like dynamite going off in my ears.

Concentrating

I find it impossible to concentrate on more than one thing at a time. And sometimes I find it hard to stop and move onto the next task. I don't like being asked something when I am already concentrating on something else. Sometimes I find it hard to start concentrating or remembering what I have been asked to do. Like most nights, when Mum asks me to get on my jammies I have to come and ask her ten minutes later what I am supposed to be doing!

Being patient and understanding others

Sometimes I find it difficult to be patient and small things might still upset me like someone leaving a drawer open. I try to understand how other people feel but sometimes I find it extremely difficult to know.

Usually I find it hard not to get attention. Sometimes I like to talk and be listened to a lot and I get really upset when I am ignored. I hate it when Mum starts to talk on the phone. Then she might chat on and on and on for ages. Or if I am out with my Mum and she meets a friend. Sometimes the person talks to me too or asks me questions, but I usually just ignore them. The reason I do this is because it is so boring. It makes me act very restless so I complain loudly and try to pull Mum away. Other times I can't stand to have any attention at all and I need to be ignored and left in peace. When I feel like this I usually tell people to go away. It is cosy then to be in my room, curled up in my sleeping bag. I love my sleeping bag. I love it when Mum lets me stay in my sleeping bag in the kitchen or the hall. Or during the tutoring when Julie May lets me have it at break time.

Being part of a group

This is another thing which is extremely difficult for me. In groups I behave differently. I can't concentrate or be friendly at all. I get distracted easily. The first time I meet someone I usually put them into one of two categories, friend or not, and then I don't like to change my mind about my decision. I have a lot of trouble when there are about four or more other children around. I don't know what causes this problem but I think it is something to do with AS. It is easiest to be with one other child at a time. This can make it difficult to have friends. But any friends that I make are very good friends and I would do my best to never let them down.

Staying still instead of twirling and leaping

I often find it hard to stay still and I have a lot of energy. I do stunts in the hall which I am quite good at.

development and much better *cognitive* skills than those diagnosed with autism and tend to be described as extremely *clumsy*. The diagnosis of Asperger's is often confused with PDD, a label that is applied to children with mild symptoms which are not quite serious enough to call for one of the other labels.

In addition to the criterion of *no significant delay* in language skills, the issues to explore in

seeking a diagnosis of AD include the level of self-help skills, adaptive behaviour and the degree to which these aspects are inconsistent with general intellectual development in the first three years. However it is very difficult to quantify these measures. Recent studies using good diagnostic criteria suggest that AD appears in a larger segment of the population than previously thought. For example, studies of children in the mainstream school system

Quite often I don't stop jumping and twirling around and pummelling my cuddly toys, especially Leo. I also love leaping around the furniture. I like to do this approximately every half hour, or even every fifteen minutes if I can manage it. I also enjoy making noises like 'Zzzhhh Zzzhhh' quite a lot. I like doing that. Sometimes I get dizzy which can be a nice feeling. Another thing I love is running along the side of the ocean and throwing stones into the water, or playing with the sand. I love rough and tumble play and climbing on Chris's shoulders. It is a bit strange but I also love being squashed tight. Once we went to see a lady who told us a lot about the importance of relaxation. Then we got a Peanut Roll. Its proper name is a Physiotherapy Roll but we call it a Peanut Roll because it looks like an huge peanut. It is good fun. You can use it for squashing games or else you can just lie under it and have someone roll it right over you and squash you. This is very relaxing for me.

Making decisions and changes

Sometimes I find it very difficult making decisions. Then I might toss a coin – heads one choice; tails the other. Sometimes the coin gives me the wrong answer and I say 'best of three' or 'best of five'. It's funny how sometimes I don't really know what decision I want till after the coin has been tossed. I prefer it when some things don't change too much. Lunch works best when it is the exact same each day. When I take grated cheese for lunch each day then I know where I stand. I like it to be with the proper grater – my own grater– that is, because it is horrible when it is grated too coarsely. I just can't take it. There is a perfect texture for cheese. I am not at all keen on changes of plan. Especially if it is something like Mum promising me a jammie day and then trying to get me to do something else. Or someone coming to visit when I wasn't expecting them.

How I feel things

Senses help people feel and learn about things. Some people think there are only five senses but there are more than five. For example there is intuition. I know a lot of things with my mind or spirit alone, not my body. Another one is the heavenly sense. This one is the most important. It tells us about God, but some people throw it away. God is like the stars, always there even if we don't see Him. He gives people special tasks and missions. I think my special mission might be to do with helping other kids with AS.

Pain

I think AS people sometimes feel things differently. They might be very sensitive. For me, one weird thing is I seem to be immune to certain pains. Like recently I was sick during the night without knowing it till the morning. Other times I feel things very intensely.

Noise

I like peaceful noises best. Like birds singing. Noises I absolutely hate are the hoover and the liquidizer.

Taste and food

Another unusual thing about me is that I definitely can't take most foods. Eating is one of my biggest difficulties. I can't explain why I have this difficulty, but for me this is the worst thing about AS. The thing I absolutely hate most is trying anything new. There are hardly any foods I eat at all. I especially hate any food with bits in it, or things mixed together with each other, like cheese mixed with bread in a cheese sandwich, or mixed colours of foods.

in Sweden have estimated the prevalence between 36 and 48 per 10000, amounting to 0.4 per cent of the child population (Kadesjö et al., 1999).

As Frith (2003) notes, if these initial investigations of the prevalence of autism and AD are replicated across cultures and stand the test of time, we may be looking at a prevalence rate of disorders in the autistic spectrum that is near 1 per cent of the total population, akin to the prevalence of schizophrenia.

Gender

As we noted in our description of autism, boys are disproportionately represented among those with high cognitive abilities. Consequently, we would expect to see more boys than girls with AD and this

Box 5.4 Case Study: To Diagnose or not to Diagnose

Luke Jackson, a 13-year-old diagnosed with Asperger syndrome, describes in his autobiography 'Freaks, geeks and Asperger syndrome: A user guide to adolescence' the importance of having a diagnosis.

A label or a signpost? A lot of people worry about whether it is a good thing to actually give someone's problems a name (and I don't mean Bob or Fred!). By this I mean actually getting a proper diagnosis of Asperger syndrome or autism or whatever someone has, instead of it just being called complex difficulties or global developmental delay or something like that.

Many doctors and a lot of people seem to think that if someone's difficulties actually have a name, then they become a reality and people might actually start to live up to them. I think a lot of Asperger syndrome and the Autistic Spectrum 25 people also think a label is a bad thing and will make others automatically conjure up negative ideas if they hear the word 'autistic'. It is possible that these doctors and therapists may have the person's best interest at heart and think that maybe as they get older people might not want to give them a job if they have a syndrome or a 'disability'. Even if doctors are being well meaning, I still think that is wrong. If someone got a job

and behaved oddly or could not cope with some things, they would get the sack (isn't that a strange expression?), but if someone knew that it was part of a problem they could just help them to overcome it and realize they were still capable of good work.

The Disability Acts now mean that employers are not allowed to discriminate against disabled people, and AS is counted as a disability even though lots of us (I am throwing in a dash of arrogance and including myself in that category!) are more than able in many ways. Hands up those of you reading this who have been called a freak or a geek or a boffin or a nerd? (Or any variation on this theme!) I am pretty sure that would be the majority of AS kids, probably adults too. Do any of you actually feel freaky on the inside? Here, I will raise my hand and sing out a resounding 'Ay' (that means yes in old English). Doctors, therapists and professionals in general, this is how we feel when we do know what the reason is. When we didn't know and didn't have a diagnosis (or weren't told about it) it was a million times worse than you can ever imagine. If the child you are seeing has one or two boxes of the checklist you are working from still unchecked, then please for the sake of their sanity, tell them or their parents if you have any suspicion that they

---

is the case. Based upon the available studies, Frith (2003) estimates that the gender ratio in AD is approximately 15 boys for every girl. However, it is predicted that the prevalence may be higher in girls than is typically reported. Diagnosing the disorder in girls is problematic as the symptoms of Asperger's in girls are thought to be more passive in nature, which makes them more difficult to notice. Also because the symptoms are milder, parents are often more reluctant to bring their daughters in for a diagnosis.

Age of Onset

For many with AD, the disorder is not detected until late in development because recognition of their deficits is obscured by their *good* cognitive and verbal skills. Far from being seen as disordered, these precocious children may have even delighted the adults around them with their 'little professor'

demeanour, their lack of interest in peers shrugged off as an eccentricity. Some with AD are not assessed until adolescence, when stage-salient tasks begin to demand just those abilities that the youth has failed to develop. For example, the young person's social difficulties may begin to interfere with the development of *normal intimacy* to a degree that they no longer can be explained away. Yet others with AD are not diagnosed until adulthood, in part because the disorder simply was not known when they were children. However, AD is believed to be an innate disorder that is present from birth, just as is autism.

Comorbidity

Particularly in adolescence and adulthood, mood disorders such as *anxiety* and *depression* frequently are seen in individuals with AD (Howlin, 2000). Clinical reports recount that young persons with have AS. After all, as we get older and understand ourselves better, then maybe more and more bits of the AS are not so glaringly obvious.

The problems affect us and a good doctor or therapist must surely be one who realizes that. If someone is older then they must be quite sure themselves that there is something different about them and the doctors should listen very carefully. If the parent is telling a doctor that they think their child has AS or autism, then there must be a very good reason for this. Why would any parent want their child to have anything wrong with them? Of course a lot of people will not have heard of AS so cannot possibly decide that their child or themselves have it. Even with much more use of the Internet, there will still be people without and people who do not read much. So here the problem lies. If the doctor doesn't know enough to diagnose properly and the parent or person doesn't know at all, then everyone is left scratching their heads and wondering why they or their child are having so many problems. The answer to this is that doctors need to learn in more detail about the Asperger syndrome and autism and listen to those of us who actually live with it.

I think what we have here is a Catch-22 situation – if the world in general does not understand or accept that people are all different, then people with AS are reluctant to tell others about it for fear of being considered a freak. After all, no one wants to be treated as if they have some contagious disease. These things then go unmentioned and people stay nervous and uncomfortable around someone who is seen to have a disability, especially when it is an invisible one. The people with the disability learn to keep quiet and struggle on; the doctors and the rest of the world therefore learn nothing – and so it goes on!

This is rather like the last episode of Star Trek Voyager, 'Endgame', in that when the future version of Captain Janeway went back into the past to save the past version of Captain Janeway from the Borg and near the end got herself assimilated by the Borg queen herself. This episode had a strange twist to it – the future version of Captain Janeway would grow up, go into the past, save the past version of Captain Janeway from the Borg and then get assimilated herself and so it would go on in a never-ending cycle. I would like to think that this circle of silence and lack of understanding could be broken by a few people and then more setting the ball rolling and talking about the real stuff that goes on in the mind of someone with Asperger syndrome, and making others, especially doctors, realize that we don't all fit into a carefully planned set of rules. To me that is rigid thinking on the doctor's part!

AD may become painfully self-aware of their social deficits and exclusion from the mainstream of human society. These negative appraisals may lead to dysphoria and hopelessness. Dyspraxia, otherwise known as motor planning disorder, is seen in a large majority of individuals with AD. In fact motor clumsiness is so common that one diagnostic model for AD, Gillberg's Criteria for Asperger's Disorder, includes motor clumsiness as a symptom which must be present in order for an individual to receive an AD diagnosis.

Is Asperger's *Necessarily* a Disorder?

One of the implications of the idea of an autistic spectrum is that children may be placed at various places on the continuum – in other words, some might have 'just a touch' of autism. This is most clearly seen in the case of high-functioning individuals with AD, who, despite their social oddities, may never be considered disabled in any significant way. Characteristics of AD might be subtly present in many individuals who are able to function in the mainstream at school, at work and in the community.

For example, Baron-Cohen and his colleagues (2001a) developed a screening tool for Asperger's disorder, which they administered to four groups: 58 adults diagnosed with AD or high-functioning autism, 174 randomly selected adults from the community, 840 Cambridge University students, and 16 winners of the UK Mathematics Olympiad. They found that, overall, males scored higher than females and that students studying mathematics and the physical sciences scored higher than those studying humanities or social sciences. Award-winning mathematicians evidenced the most

Asperger-like symptoms, replicating an earlier study that showed a tendency in individuals with AD to show an interest in and penchant for mathematics, physics and engineering (Baron-Cohen et al., 1998).

One of the implications of the finding that AD may be found among university students and award-winning mathematicians is that AD need not be an impediment to very high achievement in life (Baron-Cohen et al., 2001a). Many of those who study and treat individuals with AD are struck with the myriad strengths those with the disorder exhibit. Indeed, Baron-Cohen (2000) has argued that we should consider AD a 'difference' rather than a 'disability'. For example, he argues, consider the child who prefers to remain in the classroom poring over the encyclopedia instead of playing outside with the other children at recess: just because this child is doing something different, who are we to assume it is less legitimate or valuable?

Researchers in the field have used psychobiography to retrospectively diagnose a number of famous high achievers throughout history, including Isaac Newton and Albert Einstein (Baron-Cohen, 2003). More currently, we have the benefit of autobiographical accounts from such remarkable individuals as Temple Grandin (1996), who went on to earn a PhD in the study of animal behaviour. Her specialization, designing facilities for livestock, is greatly assisted by her ability to visualize complex systems, a talent that she calls 'thinking in pictures'.

However, Frith (2003) counters that it is important not to paint too optimistic a picture. A lack of social awareness can affect a person's ability to function in many spheres. Many adults with AD never leave the family home and, if they work, end up in careers that are far below their intellectual ability (Barnhill, 2007).

As we have noted, researchers in the field are not in agreement about whether autism and AD represent truly distinct disorders as both disorders look almost identical. Importantly the current diagnostic difference has failed to be clinically useful. For example, while the provision of a diagnosis of autism versus Asperger's may lead to different political/personal/social consequences, clinically the current DSM-IV distinction between these two conditions, and the research that has come out of this distinction, has not informed or improved our clinical practice (e.g., selection of treatment, assessment, prognosis, etc.). This has led to the proposed change in the DSM-V of a merger between AD and autism.

Many clinicians believe the merger of the two conditions would better reflect the true nature of the conditions as variations within a single spectrum (Bennett et al., 2008). However, opponents of the merger believe the DSM-IV criteria for Asperger's simply do not reflect the true disorder and argue strongly for a redefinition of Asperger's instead. For example, Mazefsky and Oswald (2006) found differences between the disorders when using new suggested diagnostic criteria for AD (Klin et al., 2005), criteria which are not that dissimilar to those proposed in Asperger's (1944) original observations. Using this system, the disorders would then differ on three specific domains:

1   Nature of social impairments: autism would be characterized by self-isolation and lack of interest while Asperger's would be characterized by interest in social relations and 'seeking others' but in a socially insensitive or atypical manner.

2   Nature of language impairment: autism would be characterized by delayed, echolalic and stereotyped language while Asperger's would be characterized by adequate or precocious language but with difficulties in the use of language (pragmatics).

3   Asperger's diagnosis would include one-sided verbosity and the presence of factual, circumscribed interest that interferes with daily living.

Pervasive Developmental Disorder Not Otherwise Specified

It is important to briefly mention finally the last subtype of autism-pervasive developmental disorder not otherwise specified (PDD-NOS). This is also known as atypical autism in the ICD-10 and sometimes is referred to as pathological demand avoidance syndrome (PDA). The diagnosis of PDD-NOS is appropriate when some but not all of the core features of an autistic disorder are present. For example, there is severe and pervasive impairment in the development of reciprocal social interaction, or verbal and non-verbal communication skills, or when stereotyped behaviour, interests and activities are present. It is also deemed an appropriate diagnosis when the child presents with all characteristics associated with autism but that these characteristics are atypical in some way, are mild or of late onset, although late onset autism is more commonly referred to as regressive autism.

PDD-NOS often has been seen as an afterthought or grab-bag diagnosis when compared to ASD in general, and autism in particular (Matson and Boisjoli, 2007). Therefore PDD-NOS definitions tend to be more about what it is not versus the symptoms that define the condition. Not surprisingly then, correct identification of PDD-NOS by clinicians is thought to be very low (Matson and Kozlowski, 2010).

Relatively little is known about PDD-NOS, and research has largely addressed PDD-NOS in children and not adults. However, it is viewed as being caused by neurological abnormalities and generally will be identified when the child is around the age of 3 or 4. Importantly, symptoms of PDD-NOS are thought to fluctuate across the lifespan. Symptoms related to repetitive behaviours have poorer prognosis compared with social and communication domains within these children (Charman et al., 2005).

DSM-V

At the time of writing this book, there are several proposed changes to the diagnostic criteria that the Neurodevelopmental Disorders work group is currently proposing. They believe pervasive developmental disorders should be replaced with the category Autism Spectrum Disorders. This would entail a single diagnosis for the disorders currently entitled: Autism, Asperger and PDD-NOS. The rationale for doing this includes the following:

1 A single spectrum better reflects the pathology and symptoms.

2 Separation of ASD from typical development is reliable and valid, while separation of disorders within the spectrum is variable and inconsistent.

3 Individuals with autism, PDD-NOS or Asperger disorder often are diagnosed by severity, rather than unique, separate criteria defining the three diagnoses.

They propose that symptom severity for ASD could be defined along a continuum that includes normal traits, subclinical symptoms and three different severity levels for the disorder. They are also considering changing the three current symptom domains (social deficits, communication deficits and fixated interests/repetitive behaviours) to two (social communication deficits and fixated interests and repetitive behaviours).

Etiology of Disorders in the Autistic Spectrum

In the review that follows, we will describe research exploring the origins of both autism and AD. Perhaps reflecting the belief of many researchers that the two are manifestations of the same underlying disorder, as already discussed, studies do not always differentiate the two. Additionally, researchers have just begun to turn their attention to AD, and so most of the evidence is based on studies of autism. Therefore, in each section we will begin with a description of research on autism and/or the autistic spectrum and will end with a description of the research specific to AD, where it is available.

The Biological Context
Environmental Factors

In recent years, a number of environmental factors have been posited to play a causal role in autism. One of these involves birth complications. However, recent investigations have found birth complications to be either minor or no greater than those found in non-autistic infants with congenital anomalies. A second proposed environmental factor was congenital rubella. Initial studies suggested that rubella in pregnant mothers increased the incidence of autism in their infants. However, further research indicated that both the clinical description and the course of the children's disturbance were atypical; for example, such children tended to outgrow their presumed autism.

One alarming suggestion was that the combined measles, mumps and rubella (MMR) vaccine was a culprit. Because the media subsequently gave equal coverage to opposing views surrounding the link between MMR and autism, parents understandably thought this meant that the scientific evidence for and against a link with autism was equally weighted. Many parents responded by declining to have their children immunized against these devastating diseases (Frith, 2003). The findings triggered a public health crisis. In Britain, immunization rates collapsed from 92 per cent before the findings were published, to 80 per cent at the peak of Britain's alarm (Bedford and Elliman, 2010). However, investigators have assessed the association between the incidence of autism and the introduction of the vaccine in several different countries and at several different time points and, to date, have found no discernable pattern (de los Reyes, 2010). However, it remains possible that the vaccine potentiates the onset of autistic spectrum disorders in children who are genetically vulnerable to them (Wing and Potter, 2002).

Increased paternal or maternal age has been associated with an increased risk for ASD (Croen et al., 2007) with a greater than twofold risk with each 10-year increase in paternal age. Women in general are now having children at an older age; this may be a factor also contributing to the higher prevalence rate.

Genetic Factors

There is little doubt that genetics plays an etiological role in autism. Although it is rare for parents to have two children with autism, the risk of having a second child with the disorder is 15 to 30 times higher for parents with an autistic child versus those with a typically developing youngster. (Here we follow Rutter, 2000, 2011).

As is always the case, the most convincing genetic data come from comparing monozygotic (MZ) with dizygotic (DZ) twins, one of whom has autism. General-population twin studies yield concordance rates ranging from 36 per cent to 91 per cent for the MZ twins and from 0 to 5 per cent for DZ twins. Further evidence for a strong genetic component in autism comes from the finding that the non-autistic MZ twins have some autistic characteristics but to a lesser degree, termed the *broader autism phenotype*. Characteristics of the phenotype include some type of cognitive deficit, usually involving language delay, and persistent social impairment. Only 8 per cent of the MZ co-twins were without such cognitive or social disorders compared with 90 per cent of the DZ pairs. These studies suggest that the autistic phenotype extends well beyond the traditional diagnosis, involving characteristics similar to autism but markedly different in degree.

Because of its complexity it is not likely that autism is caused by a single genetic abnormality, but is more likely due to *genetic heterogeneity* – that is, different genetic abnormalities that all lead to the same clinical picture. The model of transmission, therefore, would involve multiple interacting genes rather than a single gene operating in a Mendelian fashion.

The search for genetic factors in AD is only beginning and the number of available studies is small (Folstein and Santangelo, 2000). In one of the larger investigations to date, Volkmar and colleagues (1997) surveyed 99 families of individuals with AD. The investigators found that 46 per cent of the families reported symptoms consistent with AD in first degree relatives, generally male family members. Rates of autism also were higher among the siblings and cousins of children with AD (2 to 6 per cent; Rutter et al., 1999) than would be expected in the normative population (1 per cent according to highest estimate), suggesting a genetic link between autism and AD, if indeed they are separate disorders.

Neuropsychological Factors

The task of bridging the gap between brain and behaviour is easiest when there is a circumscribed disturbance in behaviour that can be related to a known characteristic of brain structure or functioning. Autism is a far cry from this model of simplicity. Autism is a pervasive disorder and the many psychological functions are affected. In light of this complexity, we cannot expect simple and certain answers to the question of the relation between brain and behaviour, but many suggestive leads are emerging.

Neurochemical Findings

Neurochemical studies of autism search for abnormalities in **neurotransmitters** (the 'chemical messengers' responsible for communication among nerve cells). Findings in regard to serotonin, dopamine, norepinephrine and endorphins have been suggestive but inconsistent and inconclusive. Studies using **positron-emission tomography (PET) scans** have identified higher brain glucose metabolism of individuals with autism (Luat and Chugani, 2010).

Neuroanatomical Findings

Neuroimaging studies of the brains of individuals with autism have been inconsistent to date. Many different structures have been implicated in the different studies. Many investigators have found abnormalities in the temporal lobe and cerebellum, but these findings have not been replicated in all studies (Dawson et al., 2002). Interestingly, even when the *specific* brain areas differ, studies have converged on the finding that there are abnormalities in the various parts of the brain involved in social cognition. In particular, several neuroimaging studies have found that individuals with autism have an abnormally large *amygdala*, an area of the medial temporal lobe that is linked to processing information about emotions (Schultz, 2005). Further, the extent of the abnormality in the amygdala is directly proportional to the degree of impairment in recognition of facial expressions and joint attention, two of the social cognitive functions that are most affected by autistic disorder (Sparks et al., 2002).

Much of the available evidence suggests that there is diffuse damage to widespread parts of the brain rather than one localized deficit (Johnson et al., 2002). One consistent finding is that individuals with autism have a larger cerebral volume or brain weight than those who are typically developing. Interestingly, this increased volume is not present at birth but is observed later on in development. The larger size is due to an excess of *white matter* in the brain (Filipek, 1999), which consists of connective tissue involved in the communication between areas of the brain. Normally, the connections proliferate early in development only to be pruned later, eliminating redundant or inefficient pathways and making for quicker and more efficient connections. Therefore, the deficits in autism may have less to do with any specific area of the brain and more to do with abnormalities in *pruning* and the development of connections between the parts of the brain.

Researchers have only begun to investigate whether there are differences in neuroanatomy that are specific to AD. So far findings are preliminary and only suggestive. One speculation has been that **brain lateralization** – the differentiation of function between the left and right hemispheres – differs between AD and autism. Schultz and colleagues (2000) note that there are two areas of functioning – motor skills and visuospatial abilities – that differentiate AD from autism. Because these are functions related to the right side of the brain, as are socio-emotional processes and facial recognition, some in the field have speculated that AD is related specifically to a right hemispheric dysfunction. However, autistic children, too, evidence right hemispheric deficits, just as children with AD evidence left hemispheric deficits (Ozonoff and Griffith, 2000), so the answer may not lie in brain lateralization alone.

As in those with autism, individuals with AD are found to have increased brain size associated with abnormal white cell growth. Neuroimaging also shows that those with AD typically have abnormalities in two other areas of the brain, the limbic-temporal lobe system (which includes the amygdala) and the frontal lobes (Schultz et al., 2000). In one of the rare neuroanatomical comparisons of autism and AD, Lincoln and colleagues (1998) found that individuals with AD had less pathology in the cerebellar region, a thinner posterior (at the back of the head) corpus callosum, and a larger anterior (at the front of the head) corpus callosum.

Clearly, more research is needed in the neuropsychology of autism. Future research will benefit from the newer imaging technologies that allow us to watch the brain in action, such as functional MRI and positron-emission tomography.

The Intrapersonal Context

What Is the Essential Deficit?

One of the conundrums in the study of autism has been arriving at a clear understanding of what the disorder essentially *is*; that is, what is the core deficit that underlies this extreme deviation from normal development? As we review studies that have examined developmental processes within the child – attachment, emotions, cognitive development, joint attention, theory of mind – consider how each of these reflects a different emphasis, even a different construal of the essential nature of autistic disorder.

Attachment

Because the lack of affectionate ties to caregivers is such a core feature of autism, it stands to reason that a fundamental disorder of attachment might lie at the heart of autistic disorder. Indeed, attachment took centre stage in Kanner's (Kanner and others, 1943) original depiction of autism.

However, it is an exaggeration to say that children with autism are incapable of forming an attachment. Studies using Ainsworth's Strange Situation paradigm (see Chapter 2) show that 40 to 50 per cent of children with autism were securely attached, which comes close to the 65 per cent found in the typical population (Capps et al., 1994).

Rutgers et al. (2004) carried out a meta-analysis of studies on attachment in children with autism and found that while children with autism were less securely attached to their parents/caregivers compared with children without autism, these differences disappeared when children with autism had higher level of functioning. It may be that attachment-related behaviours, such as seeking proximity during times of stress, are so critical to the survival of the species that they have been programmed into the infant by evolution. Thus, they are preserved even in the most psychopathologically disturbed infants.

Nonetheless, there are qualitative differences between autistic and typically developing children in regard to attachment. Attachment-related behaviours are not accompanied by the same kind of emotional pleasure and reciprocity as they are in typically developing children. Behaviourally, attachment in children with autism is interspersed with characteristic repetitive motor movements such as hand flapping, rocking and spinning. Their attachment-related behaviour is also more variable over time than it is in other children (Dissanayake and Sigman 2001).

Further, attachment involves more than behaviour aimed at maintaining a secure base. It also involves an *internal working model*, or mental image, of the parent and of the parent–child relationship. This kind of complex mental image is probably not existent in young children with autism (Capps et al., 1994). Thus, while the child with autism may have a working model of mother as someone who is a source of security and fulfilment of concrete needs, it is doubtful that this child can evolve an image of the mother as a person in her own right, with her own unique thoughts, motives, desires and personality.

Emotional Development

A number of deficits in the area of emotional development point towards this as a potential key to the mystery of autism.

Emotion Recognition

Children with autism, in contrast to typically developing children or those with mental retardation, have difficulty decoding the basic emotions as they are displayed on the human face (Baron-Cohen et al., 2001b). They particularly have difficulty discriminating negative emotions, such as fear (Pelphrey et al., 2002). The problem is not with processing visual information – they are as adept as others at recognizing objects – but is specific to the human face. This is a significant deficit given that the recognition of emotions is essential to forming meaningful relationships with others, which is the ability that is most absent in autism.

Further, detailed studies of gaze patterns show that even individuals with autism who *can* discern emotional expressions do not look at faces in the same way that others do. Normally, when looking at a human face, people's gaze first focuses on the eyes of the other person. This is a good strategy, given the amount of social information that is presented in the facial expressions of the eyes – it is for good reason that they are known as the windows of the soul. Studying someone's affect can give us clues about their inner state, just as following someone's gaze can alert us to their intentions (Emery, 2000). Individuals with autism, however, spend as much time looking at others' chins as at their eyes (Pelphrey et al., 2002). It is as if they do not perceive that any useful information is to be obtained from reading others' facial expressions. The lack of interest in faces appears to be peculiar to disorders in the autistic spectrum, in that it sets apart these children not only from typically developing children but also from those with mental retardation or other disorders of brain development. (See Fig. 5.3.)

A central feature of autism is an impairment in 'social attention' – the prioritized processing of socially relevant information, e.g. the eyes and face. Infants with autism spectrum disorders (ASD) tend to be less attentive to people – especially their faces – and many other social cues in their environment (Dawson et al., 2004; Swettenham et al., 1998).

Deficits in face perception may even be hardwired into the autistic brain. Osterling and colleagues (2002) compared the eventual-related potential (ERP) responses to visual images of 4-year-old typically developing children, those with

FIGURE 5.3 Facial Processing in Autism.

Sample scanpaths from Phase II of the experiment for three autistic participants (first column) and three control participants (second column).

Participants were instructed to identify the emotion portrayed in each face.

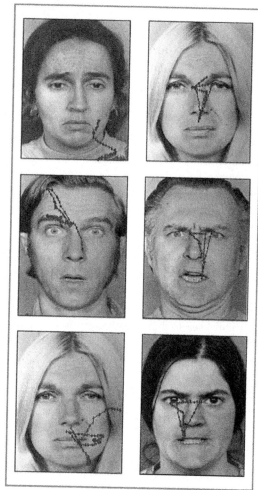

Source: Pelphrey et al., 2002. Reprinted with permission from Kluwer Academic/Plenum Publishers.

autistic spectrum disorders and those with developmental delays. Both typically developing and developmentally delayed children showed different responses when viewing their mother's face versus that of a stranger, as well as when observing their favourite toy versus an unfamiliar one. Children with autism, in contrast, showed no difference in responding to their mother's face versus a stranger's face, but did respond differently when viewing their favourite toy versus an unfamiliar toy. Further, Schultz and colleagues' (2000) functional MRI studies indicate that the part of the brain that is specialized for facial recognition in typically developing people is not so specialized in those with autism or Asperger's syndrome. While most individuals use the fusiform gyrus when perceiving faces, those in the autistic spectrum show activity in the inferior temporal gyrus, the area of the brain usually used for the perception of objects.

Emotional Expression

While children with autism are less affectively communicative than other children, careful observation has shown that the stereotype of the autistic child as flat, wooden and without emotional expression is incorrect. They giggle when happy, throw temper tantrums when angry, express delight when tickled or bounced, and in fact are capable of displaying quite intense emotions – frenetic glee, distress, frustration, fury and panic. However, what differentiates them from typically developing children is that children with autism are more likely to show negative emotions and odd blends of affect (Kasari et al., 1993). Children with autism also are less likely to direct affect at a partner or to reciprocate it, such as by mirroring another's social smile. Therefore, what is missing is not emotion expression per se, but the expression of emotions that would be expected as part of a reciprocal interaction. For example, one study showed that children with and without autism alike displayed pleasure at learning a new task; however, the typically developing children displayed their pride in a way that was uncharacteristic of those with autism: typical children turned around to check their observer's reaction (Kasari et al., 1993). In short, children with autism do not *share* emotions with others.

Joint Attention

Another feature of autism that has been proposed as the core of the disorder is a deficit in shared or *joint attention*. The typically developing 6- to

9-month old will look between an object and the caretaker, as if to say, 'Look what I am looking at'. This is called *referential looking*. Towards the end of the first year of life, the infant starts using *referential gestures*, such as pointing to an object when a caregiver is present or holding an object up for the caregiver to see. Rather than attending to the object alone, the infant now tries to attract the adult's attention so that the interest can be shared. Note that the goal is a social one, to share a feeling or interest, rather than merely an instrumental one, such as to meet a concrete need. The infant is not signalling in order to get an adult to do something the infant cannot do, such as bring a toy that is out of reach, but rather to share with the parent the infant's delight in the toy. When the adult responds with interest, the interaction is a highly rewarding one.

In children with autism, shared attention behaviours are deficient or even absent, as the home video studies reported earlier illustrated (Osterling et al., 2002). While children with autism may point to objects when they want them, or show that they need a toy mended, these *instrumental* gestures are not accompanied by the *expressive* gestures that communicate the desire that the parent join them in appreciating or recognizing the toy. Such deficits in shared attention are seen in all developmental periods. For example, Attwood, Frith and Hermelin (1988) found that adolescents with autism were no different from normal and retarded children matched for mental age in regard to using or understanding instrumental or action-oriented gestures. However, they never used gestures expressing *feelings* concerning the self or others, such as hugging and kissing another child, putting an arm around another to console or as a sign of friendship, or putting the hand over the face to express embarrassment. Such social gestures, unlike instrumental ones, require knowledge of how another person feels along with an expression of one's own feelings and desires.

By the same token, when shared attention behaviour occurs in children with autism, it is not accompanied by the sharing of positive affect as it is in typically developing children or those with Down syndrome (Roeyers et al., 1998). Thus, autism robs shared attention behaviours of the affective signals of smiling and laughter that play such an important role in reinforcing the social interplay.

Language Development

We have described a number of qualities that differentiate autistic speech from normative language development; for example, autistic speech tends to be echolalic, literal and lacking in prosody. We also know that there is great variation, ranging from mutism to speech that is odd in content. We also know that language development is a defining distinction between autism, in which language development is delayed, and Asperger's disorder, in which language skills are preserved.

Tager-Flusberg (2000) and her colleagues carried out a longitudinal study of language development in which they compared children with autism, children with Down syndrome, and typically developing children. As the toddlers were just learning to talk, the investigators found that syntax and grammar developed similarly across the three groups. While their results showed no deficits in the formal *structure* of language, there were significant differences in the way in which children with autism *used* language. Specifically, children with autism appear to talk *at* rather than *with* their listeners, seeming to lack the interest or need to share communication with others. They are prone to using bizarre idiosyncratic phrases and language that reflect their own private meaning and associations, to which they are not concerned about cluing in the listener. Children with autism also have difficulty differentiating between the information that is relevant or irrelevant for the listener and determining whether their meaning has been comprehended by others (Frith, 2003).

Even when children with high-functioning autism or AD have adequate language development, they have difficulty with *language pragmatics*, the social rules of communication that require understanding the point of view of the speaker (Landa, 2000). For example, typically we learn to mark a change in topic ('Well, anyway…'; 'Oh, speaking of that….') so that our listener is not confused. However, the subtleties in communication that assist others to understand our meaning are not available to individuals with autism or AD. They are likely to interpret and respond in literal ways that make for awkward conversation, to miscommunicate and misinterpret the intended meaning of utterances, and to fail to provide the cues and references that will keep the listener oriented to the topic.

However, it is interesting to note that even among those children who never speak, there is evidence of written language development. For example, Frith (2003) describes a case of a young man who had been mute all his life but who quickly mastered the use of a computerized communicator. Many individuals in the autistic spectrum are able to read fluently even when they display delays in spoken language. However, their processing of the information they read is unusual. Typically developing children read for the gist, or meaning, of a sentence or passage, while children with autism focus on the individual words. Therefore, children with autism are unable to recognize when silly words or nonsense phrases have been inserted into a passage (e.g., 'The hedgehog could smell the scent of the *electric* flowers' [Frith, 2003, p. 125]).

Perspective-Taking

Many of the deficits seen in autistic language appear to reflect a deficit in *perspective-taking*. Language pragmatics are a prime example of the way in which good communication requires understanding the perspective of the listener. For another example, take the confusion of pronouns 'you' and 'me' in autism and the tendency to refer to the self in the third person. While this might seem to signify a deep confusion of personal identity, a lack of a sense of self, in fact, children with autism recognize their own names and identify others by name. The key to the riddle is that, while names are constant, pronouns change. The person called 'I' by Charles is not the person referred to as 'I' by Patricia. The use of pronouns is a matter of *perspective*: the correct pronoun depends on who is the speaker and who is the listener, and it is just this ability to shift perspective that is absent in autism.

Echolalia offers yet another example. While echoing another's speech is a highly socially awkward form of communication, it has a certain logic for the child focused only on his or her own perspective. The child with autism is essentially a behaviourist – his or her knowledge of others is acquired through observing cause and effect. When the mother asks, 'Do you want a cookie?' and one is given to the child, a logical conclusion is that those words are the magic spell for making another treat appear.

Cognitive Development

As we have seen, children with autism range widely in intelligence, with scores in the average to the severely mentally retarded range. One concern about these data is that IQ tests may not be sensitive to measuring non-standard forms of intelligence, some of which may be intact in autism (Frith, 2003). In contrast, children with AD have average to superior cognitive abilities. However, a concern is that these data do not accurately reflect whether this intelligence is *functional*. For example, a savant with an extraordinary memory who is able to memorize and recite the bus schedules of every route in London may still have difficulty finding the way to the bus stop or negotiating a ticket purchase with the conductor.

Even when intelligence is intact, children in the autistic spectrum tend to show a particular *pattern* of scores that is consistent across different ability levels. Generally, children with autism score low on tests that assess their *social reasoning*, such as is assessed by the Comprehension subtest on the Wechsler Intelligence Scale for Children, which asks children questions such as what they should do if they find a lost wallet. In contrast, children with autism perform best on tasks that assess reasoning about *concrete* objects, such as on the Block Design subtest, which requires children to solve a visual puzzle (Frith, 2003).

An interesting cognitive difference between typical children and those in the autistic spectrum is in their use of *context* to solve a problem. Generally, people find it useful to place a problem in a real world context: for example, to translate the arithmetic equation $5 - 4$ into a word problem ('If you have 5 cents and spend 4 cents, how much will you have left?'). In contrast, individuals with autism do not benefit from contextual information. In fact, they perform better than their peers on tasks that require ignoring the context. An example of this is an embedded figures task, in which the image of a common form or object is embedded in a complex geometric display. (See Fig. 5.4.) While typically developing children have trouble ignoring the context in order to pick out the object, children with autism do quite well at the task. These data, as Happé (1999) points out, show us that differences in autistic thinking do not necessarily represent deficits.

This characteristic of autistic thinking, of focusing on details and ignoring the big picture, is termed a *lack of central coherence* (Frith, 2003). While ordinarily humans strive to generalize across contexts, make associations, extract underlying meanings, and otherwise integrate the information they receive into a coherent whole, this propensity is lacking in the child with autism. It is as though the child is detached cognitively in the same way that he or she is detached socially (see Happé and Frith, 2006, for a review). In their recent review it is proposed that individuals with autism have a cognitive style which is characterized by preference for seeing the parts, a localized processing style, rather than deficit to see the whole, a global processing deficit. This is commonly referred to as the Weak Central Coherence theory (WCC).

Executive Functions

Children in the autistic spectrum also have difficulties in the area of *executive functions* involving planning, organization, self-monitoring and cognitive flexibility. For example, one task assessing executive functions is the Wisconsin Card Sorting Test (WCST), in which the child first learns by feedback from the experimenter whether colour, shape or number is the 'correct' criterion on the

FIGURE 5.4 Examples from the Children's Embedded Figures Test.

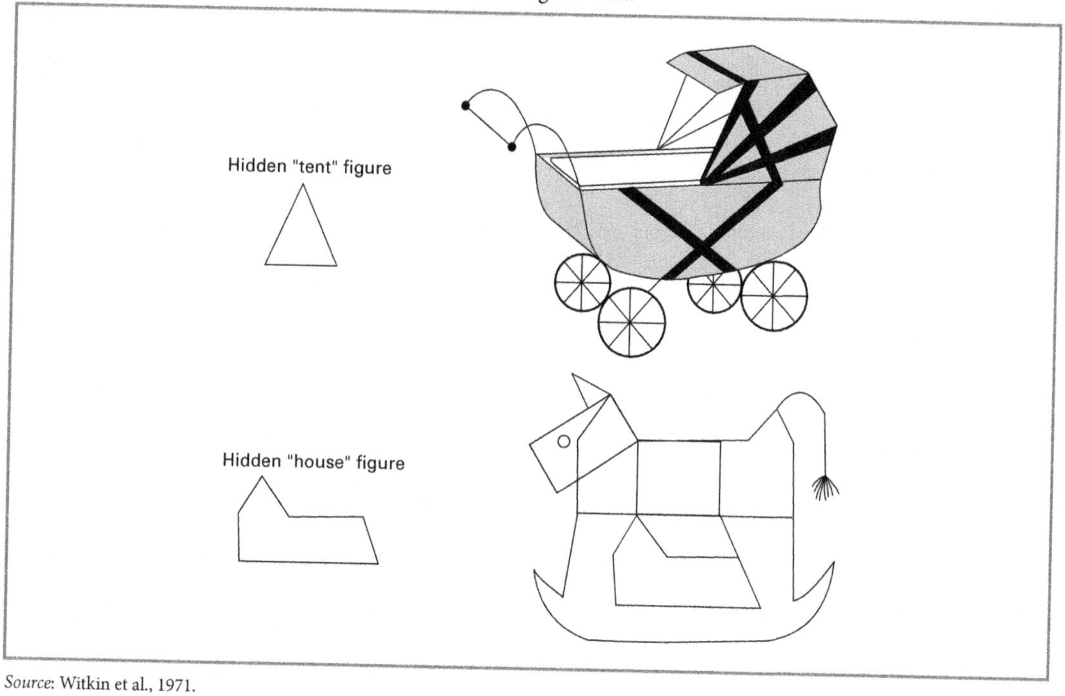

Hidden "tent" figure

Hidden "house" figure

Source: Witkin et al., 1971.

basis of which to sort 10 cards into piles. Then the experimenter changes the 'correct' category without telling the child. The critical measure is how long the child persists in the incorrect sorting when it is no longer accurate. For example, after the child has learned that colour is the 'correct' way to sort the cards, the experimenter shifts to shape as the 'correct' sort and records how many sorts it takes the child to make the shift. The WCST is regarded as a measure of set shifting or flexibility. Another executive functions task is the Tower of Hanoi, a measure of planning ability. This is a ring transfer task requiring children to plan a sequence of moves transferring an initial configuration of rings on a peg into a tower of rings of decreasing size on another peg. When the rings are moved, larger ones cannot be placed on top of smaller ones. A third task, the Stroop Colour-Word Test, assesses inhibition by requiring the child to ignore the colour in which a word is printed: for example, to read as 'blue' the word 'blue' that is coloured in red ink.

At all ages and levels of severity, children with autism consistently show deficits in performing executive functions tasks assessing set-shifting and planning. Children with autism make more perseverative mistakes than do children with conduct disorder or attention deficit hyperactivity disorder (ADHD), even though these two groups are also deficient in executive functions. Ozonoff et al. (1991) found that children with mental retardation and autism had more difficulty with the WCST and the Tower of Hanoi when compared with learning disabled children with the same IQ level. At a three-year follow-up, the investigators found that learning disabled children's performance on the executive functions tasks improved, whereas the children with autism did not change over the course of development (Ozonoff and McEvoy, 1994).

While executive functions deficits also are seen in a number of other disorders, there are some qualitative differences that are specific to individuals in the autistic spectrum (Ozonoff and Griffith, 2000).

Box 5.5 Case Study: An Autobiographical Account of Autism

Jim, a university student studying anthropology, was diagnosed with autism in his childhood but was only informed by his parents when he was 19 years old. He agreed to tell his story in a remarkable collection of autobiographies written by college students with autism and compiled by Dawn Prince-Hughes (2002), a university professor diagnosed with Asperger's disorder.

Autism, for me, is just the way things are. It means I don't receive and process information in the same manner as other people, not that I am stupid. It means that I don't share the general neurotypical population's innate receptive and expressive communication skills; it doesn't mean I am unable to have feelings and emotions or am unable to share those emotions with others.

Let me give some examples here. As a child, I didn't understand the terms used to describe emotions. For the first seven years of my life, 'happy' meant my blue toy truck. 'Afraid' meant the Wizard of Oz poster on the wall of my bedroom that I was unable to ask to have removed; 'sad' meant rainy weather. I didn't generalize that the emotion I felt when I was playing with my blue truck was the same as when my father came home.

Sometime – before I had a sense of time – I learned to read. I read the cards I received for my birthday. When I was five and six years old I read the *Encyclopedia*

Britannica in hopes of understanding why I was not like everyone else. I read a lot of interesting facts, but found no explanation. When I was seven years old, on a visit to see a great-aunt, I discovered a collection of about fifty years of *National Geographic* in her basement. I spent most of the summer reading them. The articles described strange cultures and far-away lands in terms very similar to the way I thought about the world around me ... I can remember thinking that the worlds they studied were as strange to them as the world around me was to me – so the same methodology should teach me about my world ...

What was 'weird'? Let me just say that at age 10 I had a list of several pages of areas of behavior where I differed substantially from the norms I had identified around me. And I had no idea why ... I considered a lot of approaches to dealing with the differences ... The first idea that came to mind was suicide. In retrospect, I can understand the discomfort people have when they consider that a ten-year-old boy actually did a cost/benefit analysis on suicide ... One of the positive benefits of suicide was that I would no longer have to deal with a world I couldn't understand. It was outweighed by my curiosity about the world around me. The next possibility was to change myself to better fit into the society around me. Anyone who has ever dieted or tried to stop smoking has an idea how difficult it is to institute permanent changes

---

For example, while individuals with autism show deficits in flexibility and planning, they do not evidence the difficulties in inhibition that are seen in children with ADHD. However, research to date has not been consistent, especially in identifying executive functions deficits in preschoolers with autism.

Theory of Mind

On the cover of her classic text on autism, Uta Frith (2003) reproduces a painting that depicts a scene in which, with gestures and significant glances, a group of card players convey to the observer that one of their members is cheating. In the text, Frith explains the many clues to the painting's meaning and what intuitive knowledge is required of the

viewer to extract their meaning. However, not everyone is able to interpret this social information. A. C., a young woman with high-functioning autism, sent Frith an e-mail in which she commented on the cover of the book, stating,

I remember looking at the picture for something like an hour, figuring out how smooth the pigments of the paints the artist [used] had to be, and the quality of brushes ... and of reproduction of the actual textures of the fabrics in the character's clothes, and of course this is the most obvious thing about the painting, the realism and the skill of the artist, and then I read inside the book, and I was like, What the ... There's this whole in one's behavior – imagine changing literally everything about your behavior, when you don't understand any of it. I actually tried to do this for about a year.

While I was busy trying to institute permanent changes in my behavior, I developed an interest in lithic technology – stone tools. Writers spoke of 'tool kits'; ... I began to consider adapting this to my needs. Such a 'tool kit' would consist, for my purposes, of a package of cognitive skills and behaviors to meet the needs of a situation ... This was a real breakthrough for me, but it was obvious that it would take me forever to gain the skills and understanding I would need. I realized this after my first attempt at developing a behavior module failed miserably. My first attempt was at developing a module that would allow me to participate in recess activities with my peers.

I was playing basketball with my classmates at noon recess. Someone shot the ball and missed. I moved for the rebound. I was focused on the ball in typical autistic fashion and injured one of the other players – I just ran him over. I didn't understand why the others were upset. By my understanding of 'success' in this situation, I succeeded – I had recovered the ball for my team. In study hall after lunch, I asked a classmate what I had done wrong. She said I should have apologized to the student I had injured. After a bit, she said, 'You don't understand – you really don't understand, do you?' (This was the first time any of my classmates directly asked me about my differences.)

I told her what I was doing. She sat down and helped me develop what has evolved into the most suc-cessful of my behavior modules – ethics. Under this heading, we classified things that most would consider 'manners'. None of it made any sense to me, despite her attempts to explain, so we set some tentative rules and some default modes. If I'm unsure how to behave, I can follow those rules. I may seem strange, but I won't be breaking any of the formal rules of society. I tend to be very polite with strangers, that way I won't offend people. Regardless of responsibility, I apologize. (I do realize that many people find these habits annoying, but I consider that better than to be seen as incredibly rude.) ...

Emotionally, I get by. I realize that isn't very descriptive, but I am still working on correlating the vocabulary with the actual emotions. Most of the time I can pass as normal, when I am under stress people begin to notice I am not. If I am happy or excited, my body rocks and my voice changes but very few people know what this means. If I am really stressed I try to escape to someplace safe, usually home. I live alone so no one is bothered if I pace for 36 hours ... As time goes on the times when I engage in self-injurious behavior grow farther and farther apart.

I realize my life is not what a lot of parents would want for their children, but it's a life. I have my studies, my work and a few friends. I have a degree of satisfaction in life. It's important to remember that while my mind is different from the neurotypical population around me, it's my mind – and it's the only thing I know.

'soap opera' that the 'normal' person is supposed to pick [up] on first, and this person cheating, and that person knows, and that other person doesn't, etc. It's nuts! (Frith, 2003, pp. 78–9).

In a similar vein, Sir Michael Rutter (1983) describes a young man with autism who

> complained that he could not mind-read. Other people seemed to have a special sense by which they could read other people's thoughts and could anticipate their responses and feelings; he knew this because they managed to avoid upsetting people whereas he was always putting his foot in it, not realising that he was doing or saying the wrong thing

until after the other person became angry or upset. (p. 526)

One of the most profound deficits in autistic spectrum disorders – and one that some experts believe underlies and integrates all the others we have described – is what Baron-Cohen (1995) has referred to as 'mind-blindness': the lack of recognition of mental states in oneself and others. The formal name for this important human function is **theory of mind (ToM)**. It is called a theory because, while we cannot feel, smell or otherwise directly observe the minds of other people, we *believe* they have one. How do we prove our theory is correct – that other people have minds?

Well, for one thing, we can play tricks on them. A key element for successful interaction in social situations is the understanding of other people's intentions, emotions and actions. Throughout childhood, an understanding of ToM is fundamental to skilled communication and social interaction, especially in complex situations including sarcasm, deception and humour (e.g. Harris, 2006).

For example, Baron-Cohen and colleagues (1985) created the 'Sally-Anne' scenario in which dolls act out the following sequence: Sally and Anne are in a room together; Sally puts a marble in a basket and leaves the room; Anne transfers the marble to a box; Sally returns. The experimenter then asks the child the crucial question: 'Where will Sally look for the marble?' The child must understand that Sally will act on her belief that the marble is in the basket even though the child knows it is no longer valid. A correct answer indicates that the child has distinguished what he or she knows from what the doll knows. This test of theory of mind is called a *false belief* task and requires the child to infer what another person knows and does not know and to predict his or her behaviour accordingly. Significantly, while typically developing children *and* those with Down syndrome are able to perform the task correctly, children with autism cannot, no matter how high their intelligence. Similar results are found with another task, the 'Smarties' scenario, in which children are shown a candy box with a pencil inside and are asked to predict what another child would expect to find inside the box.

Since these classic experiments were conducted, more recent research has not been quite as clear-cut (Yirmiya et al., 1998). It appears that, later in development, many children with autism may be able to solve false belief tasks correctly. Frith and Happé (1995) found that the majority of typically developing children were able to pass false belief tests by age 5, as were learning disabled children by a mental age of 5. However, children with autistic spectrum disorders typically could not pass false belief tasks until age 10, if at all. This may suggest that, in autism, there is a five-year developmental delay in the understanding of mental states in others. However, it is also possible that children arrive at the correct answer to these questions via two different routes. The first way, available to typically developing children, is an intuitive theory of mind. The second way, available to the bright autistic child, is to compensate for a lack of intuitive understanding by learning about mental states through observing and applying logic. (See Box 5.5.)

Happé (1994) supposed that the compensatory theory of mind – one that is acquired the hard way, so to speak – might be fragile and prone to error. To test this hypothesis, she constructed scenarios that required more sophisticated understanding of others' mental states than the Sally-Anne task. These included scenarios depicting sarcasm, white lies, pretence and other forms of social communication that require inferring another's intentions, perceptions or feelings. As predicted, individuals with autism struggled to comprehend these more advanced theory of mind tasks even when they were able to correctly respond to the Sally-Anne scenario.

Ozonoff and Miller (1995) investigated whether they could directly teach individuals with autism about theory of mind. They devised an intervention that, in addition to teaching specific social communication skills, directly instructed average-IQ adolescents with autism in the social cognitive skills needed to understand mental states in others. For example, they taught perspective-taking by having participants walk a blindfolded leader through a maze, describing obstacles to be avoided along the way, and had children engage in role-plays modelled after the false belief tasks on theory of mind measures such as the Sally-Anne scenario. Following the intervention, participants performed better on laboratory tasks assessing theory of mind. However, no meaningful change was seen in their social competence as rated by parents and teachers. Therefore, while children with autism can be taught theory of mind, just as they can be taught social skills, they may continue to lack an intuitive grasp of others' mental states and be unable to apply their acquired knowledge in a flexible and socially adept manner.

The implications of a lack of theory of mind are profound. It will affect children's social relationships and language development, given the lack of interest and motivation in sharing their experience with others. It will affect their emotional development, given the lack of understanding of the correspondence between inner states and affective expressions. It will affect their ability to communicate, given their difficulty adjusting their perspective to that of the listener. In short, as we ourselves seek central coherence in our study of autism, we see that many of the core features of the disorder can be organized under the concept of theory of mind.

On the other hand, while her review of the research evidence suggests much merit to the theory of mind hypothesis of autism, Tager-Flusberg (2007) points out that there remain features of the disorder that are not well explained by the model. For example repetitive behaviours, stereotyped and limited interests, and superior visual spatial skills also are seen in the disorder and are not clearly linked to the absence of theory of mind. Again, the complexity of autism defies simple explanations. Most likely, there are a series of deficits – perhaps linked to different genes – that combine to create the autistic phenotype.

Systematizing

A remarkable new theory about the essential deficit in autism has been proposed by Simon Baron-Cohen (2003, 2008). Baron-Cohen follows up on a suggestion that Asperger (1944) had made 60 years ago, in which he likened autistic intelligence to an extreme masculine turn of mind. Developing this theme, Baron-Cohen states that those with autism (who, he reminds us, are mostly male) are specifically lacking in just those characteristics that are associated with stereotypical femininity – empathy and sensitivity to relationships – and have strengths in those tasks that require skills associated with stereotypical masculinity – objectivity and systematic analysis. He calls this masculine form of intelligence *systematizing*.

Systematizing requires a drive to understand the laws that govern cause and effect relationships, as well as detachment, attention to details and deductive thinking. Baron-Cohen is careful to point out that, in the normative population, the differences between males and females are small and there is a large overlap in their distributions. However, he proposes, at the greatest extremes of the continuum we may see individuals who exemplify one characteristic to the exclusion of the other. Extreme systematizers he describes as follows:

> These are the people (mostly men) who may talk to others only at work, for the purposes of work alone, or talk only to obtain something they need, or to share factual information. They may reply to a question with the relevant facts only, and they may not ask a question in return because they do not naturally consider what others are thinking. These are the people who are unable to see the point of social chit chat ... Why bother? And what on earth about? How? For these people it is both too hard and pointless ... The object or system in front of them is all that is in their mind, and they do not stop for a moment to consider another person's knowledge of it. These are the people with the extreme male brain. (Baron-Cohen, 2003, p. 133)

To illustrate his theory, Baron-Cohen points to the autistic preference for attending to things rather than relationships, particularly things that are orderly, predictable and controllable. Individuals with autism are fascinated and even obsessed with mastering closed systems, such as understanding computers or collecting facts on obscure topics such as the pressure points of the human body or the mathematics of juggling. However, when they are required to deal with the unpredictable and less controllable social world, they are out of their element and may attempt to impose order through rigid insistence on sameness, the use of repetition and rituals, or, ultimately, temper tantrums.

As evidence for this *extreme male brain* theory of autism, Baron-Cohen cites evidence from studies assessing empathy and the reading of facial expressions, which show that on average females score higher than males, while individuals with high-functioning autism or AD score lower than the average male. A similar pattern of results is found for tasks assessing language pragmatics, theory of mind, and interpersonal sensitivity. By the same token, on tests assessing systematizing, such as one devised by Baron-Cohen (e.g., 'When I look at an animal, I like to know the precise species it belongs to'; 'When I cook, I think about exactly how different methods and ingredients contribute to the final product'), males on average score higher than females, while those with AD score higher than the average male.

This is a provocative proposal and one that is sure to generate much discussion and research.

Developmental Course

Initial Detection

As we noted previously, data on age of onset reveal a great deal of variability in the time when the symptoms are first detected. Interestingly, there are two different pathways to detection. (Here we follow Klinger et al., 2003.) In the majority of cases, there is a clear developmental *delay*. Symptoms appear in the child's first year of life, although parents may only retrospectively recognize them as signs of the disorder. The most common first symptoms to be noticed include the child's failure to look at others' faces, to share his or her interests by looking or gesturing, or to engage in pretend play. The second route to detection involves *regression*. In 20 to 47 per cent of cases, parents report that the child's development was initially on track until some point – generally 16 to 24 months of age – when the child suddenly loses previously attained developmental achievements. Most commonly, it is language development that is gained and then lost. It appears, however, that in at least half the cases, there were pre-existing deficits that were simply not noticed by the parents.

As Zelazo (2001) notes, our knowledge of the developmental unfolding of autistic spectrum disorders is hindered by the fact that developmental psychologists have rarely identified the children during the critical first years of life.

Developmental Outcome

The developmental course of autistic spectrum disorders was investigated in a large-scale study conducted in Japan that followed 197 individuals with autism who were treated in childhood (Kobayashi et al., 1992). When the individuals with autism reached adulthood, the investigators found that 27 per cent were living independently (i.e., had employment) or were on their way to doing so (i.e., they were enrolled in a college or technical school). Approximately 47 per cent had developed good language skills and were able to communicate verbally with others. However, 73 per cent required close supervision and were not able to function on their own. Further, adolescence was a time of transition, for better or worse. While about half showed a deterioration of functioning in adolescence, almost half showed a marked improvement.

The developmental outcome for individuals with autism depends greatly on how many cognitive deficits are present and how much language development is affected. A lack of communicative speech by 5 years of age and an IQ below 70 are poor prognostic signs, as is the presence of a seizure disorder (Gillberg, 1991). Another major factor influencing outcome is whether early intervention was initiated. As we will see when we discuss treatment, there is hope for significant gains for children who receive intensive intervention in the first few years of life.

Only a small minority of high functioning people with ASDs find paid employment in jobs for which they are well qualified. However, it has been shown that supported employment schemes for more able individuals can achieve a high level of success with significant benefits to individuals themselves and society in general in terms of cost savings (Howlin et al., 2005).

The prognosis for children with AD is generally more favourable, although again this depends on the degree of dysfunction. Even among high-functioning individuals with AD, only between 5 to 44 per cent are employed and only 16 to 50 per cent live independently (Howlin, 2000). One study of 20 adolescents with AD found that, according to parent report, only 50 per cent performed daily self-care activities (e.g., washing, grooming, eating) independently, only 15 per cent used the phone without assistance, and only 5 per cent planned their activities without guidance and supervision. None had a social life outside the home and 90 per cent had difficulty making friends (Green et al., 2000).

Integrative Developmental Model

Given the many different deficits associated with autistic spectrum disorders, and the many different tacks that researchers have taken in describing them, it can be no surprise that there is as yet no holistic integrative model to account for the development of autism. Therefore, it is impossible to discern whether any *specific* area of development is more centrally causal than the others.

For example, according to Happé and Frith (2006), co-occurring atypicalities in Theory of Mind (ToM), Executive Function (EF) and Central Coherence (CC) are independent in autism. These authors have hinted at the possibility that there might be interactions between cognitive functions but do not discuss the extent or nature of potential interactions. This view sharply contrasts with the developmental approach championed by several authors (Karmiloff-Smith, 2009; Klinger et al. 2003), which stresses the fluidity of developing systems, where the profile of cognitive atypicalities, and of the associations or dissociations between them, may change over time within individuals with autism. They make the important point that

affective development, social development, cognitive development and language development are all intrinsically linked during early development. Impairment in one area is thus likely to have significant consequences for all the others.

Addressing this further, Pellicano (2010) carried out a three-year study looking at the relationship between EF, CC and ToM. The results of the longitudinal findings suggested that functioning in EF and CC potentially contributes to the emergence of ToM in children with autism. These results reinforce the view that early executive skills are an essential ingredient in children's developing understanding of mind – a pattern common to both typically and atypically developing children. Moreover, her results suggest that the presence of an additional and especially pronounced atypicality early in development (in the case of her study, weak CC) might have damaging effects on ToM in children with autism.

Intervention

In view of absence of a definitive cure, many treatment programmes have gradually been developed over the world. In fact, a great diversity of treatment has been utilized including some somatic treatments, drugs, psychotherapy, behaviour modification, nutritional treatments and education interventions. However, it has proved difficult to assess the treatment effects systematically.

Social Skills

Children with autism show deficits in social skills such as initiating conversation, responding in social situations, social problem-solving, and others. These deficits are targeted through the use of social skills interventions, some of which use a technology-based approach as a resource-efficient alternative to common forms of instruction. The majority of social skills training makes use of video or DVD to deliver the intervention (modelling or feedback), usually conducted in school settings, and targeting more than one social skill. (See DiGennaro Reed et al., 2011.) Social skills groups have also been found to be an effective intervention. (See Reichow and Volkmar, 2010 for a recent review of social interventions.)

Other interventions have focused on more individualized deficits. For example, deficits in imitation of gestures often contribute to the difficulty children have in social situations. Interventions focusing on teaching children spontaneous use of gesture through modelling (Charlop et al. 2010) have so far shown promising results.

Cognitive Behavioural Therapy (CBT)

Individuals with autism who have acquired functional communication strategies – particularly more cognitively able individuals – may be candidates for talk-based therapies such as CBT. While talk-based therapies are widely used in community settings for school-aged youth and adults with autism (Hess et al., 2008), the evidence base for using many such treatments is surprisingly weak. Compared to other types of intervention in autism (e.g., applied behaviour analysis for young children) and interventions for other types of neurodevelopmental disorder (e.g., attention deficit hyperactivity disorder, ADHD), there are very few well-designed studies of CBT and other talk-based therapies for individuals with autism. (See Wood et al., 2011.)

Behavioural Modifications

Interventions for children with autism mainly come in two types. The first involves focal interventions designed to address specific deficits, such as social interaction or symbolic play skills, reports of which abound in the literature. The second type involves comprehensive programmes designed to increase the child's general level of functioning in all areas, which have the greatest likelihood of making a significant difference in the life of a child with autism (Rogers and Vismara, 2008).

All the programmes have five particular features in common (Dawson and Osterling, 1997):

1 Treatment focuses on a broad range of autistic behaviours, including attention and compliance, motor imitation, communication, appropriate use of toys, and social skills.

2 In light of the difficulty children with autism have with generalization, specific strategies are needed for generalizing newly acquired skills to a wide range of situations; for example, skills learned with the therapist would be implemented by the parent at home and then by the teacher in school.

3 The teaching environment is highly structured with a low staff-to-student ratio. In addition, the daily schedule is highly predictable. This emphasis on structure and predictability is necessary because of the children's stormy affective reactions to novelty and change.

4 There is a high level of family involvement, with parents serving as therapists or co-therapists.

5 Particular attention is paid to developing the skills needed to make the transition from the programme to a regular preschool or kindergarten classroom.

Lovaas's Behaviour Modification Programme

Among the comprehensive programmes, Lovaas and his colleagues (see Lovaas and Smith, 2003) pioneered the use of intensive behaviour modification in the treatment of autism. This focused on using the augmentative and alternative communication (AAC) systems (i.e. systems used by persons with disabilities in order to replace or supplement insufficient communication skills) (Mirenda and Erikson, 2000). Treatment in the Lovaas model is both intensive and extensive. Children enter the programme in the preschool years and remain for two years or longer, receiving 40 hours a week of intensive behavioural therapy. Initially, treatment takes place mostly in the home, with parents trained to use operant conditioning to reinforce children for demonstrating appropriate social, cognitive and language skills. Later in treatment, the investigators strive for generalization by shifting the treatment into community and typical pre-school settings.

In order to empirically demonstrate the effectiveness of their treatment, Lovaas and colleagues (McEachin et al., 1993) compared the outcomes achieved by 19 treated children with those in two control groups. The first control group consisted of children who were eligible for services in the clinic but for whom there were no available therapists; consequently, these children received a minimal exposure to the treatment, consisting of less than 10 hours per week of individual therapy and community services. The second control group consisted of children who received interventions solely from the community. All children were matched on chronological and mental age, and their autism diagnoses were confirmed by independent clinicians. The treatment was manualized and close supervision was provided to the university students who directly implemented it in order to assure treatment fidelity. At the end of two years, 47 per cent of the treated group were functioning well in a regular school setting, with no need for special services, in contrast to 2 per cent of children in the control groups. Further, intelligence tests revealed a huge 30-point difference in IQ between the treated and control groups. Only 10 per cent of the treated children had IQs in the mentally retarded range, whereas 53 per cent of children in the control groups had IQs in the mentally retarded range.

At a follow-up conducted when the children were in adolescence, the investigators found that 47 per cent of the treated children were performing well in regular schools, while this was true of none of the control children. The 30-point IQ difference remained stable and similar gains emerged for the treated group on measures of adaptive behaviour. Overall, the children who benefited most from the intervention were those whose mental ages were higher before the treatment began. While a number of independent replications of Lovaas's treatment have been published, they are plagued by methodological limitations and, in many cases, have failed to obtain results quite as dramatic or long lasting as those reported by Lovaas and his colleagues (Rogers, 1998).

TEACCH

Another well-respected comprehensive treatment program is TEACCH (Treatment and Education of Autistic and Related Communication Handicapped Children), which was developed 30 years ago at the University of North Carolina at Chapel Hill for the treatment of children at all points along the autistic continuum. The core element of TEACCH's approach is called Structured Teaching (Mesibov et al., 2004). In recognition of the significant deficits that children in the autistic spectrum demonstrate, the TEACCH programme highly structures the child's environment in order to build on strengths and minimize deficits. For example, because of their receptive verbal communication problems, children with autism and AD are presented with visual information whenever possible (e.g., chores may be presented as pictures, or as a written list; choices of strategies for self-calming may be written on a cue card). Another structuring technique used is the 'social story', in which a series of brief, written sentences is developed to explain situations that are puzzling or upsetting to the child. Examples include 'Why we put on different clothes each day', and 'What happens at a birthday party', and 'Why we sometimes have substitute teachers'. Structuring of the environment also helps individuals with autism to cope with their hypersensitivity to sensory stimulation, and reduces the emotional distress and tantrums that arise out of cognitive confusion and anxiety. Further, TEACCH's interventions are developmentally sensitive, focusing on stage-salient issues such as social skills in the school-age years and vocational issues in late adolescence.

Although the TEACCH programme has not yet published empirical data from its preschool intervention research, clinicians who have used aspects of the TEACCH curriculum have reported good results in well-controlled studies. For example, Ozonoff and Cathcart (1998) added a daily TEACCH home-teaching session to their intervention for preschoolers with autism and found significant gains in comparison to a group of control children.

Comparing the Programmes

While having a number of features in common, Lovaas's programme and TEACCH use different techniques. For illustration, we describe here two contrasting methods of remedying the language deficiencies in autism, both of which have an impressive record of success.

Lovaas (1977) employs an operant conditioning model that relies heavily on imitation and reinforcement. For example, the therapist models and reinforces words and phrases until the child gradually acquires a repertoire of language. The meaningful use of language is accomplished by two techniques. In *expressive discrimination* the child is reinforced for making a verbal response to an object, such as correctly labelling a cup when it is presented. In *receptive discrimination* the stimulus is verbal and the response non-verbal, such as correctly responding to 'Give me a cup'. Sequences are carefully graded so that new sequences are based on mastered material.

By contrast, TEACCH's interventions are based on principles of normal language acquisition and development. The motivational aspect of teaching is handled by making language relevant to the children's own interests and showing them that words are powerful means for getting people to act in a desired way. For example, 'ride' is taught as a means of obtaining a favoured bicycle, *not* as a rewarded label to a picture, as it would be in the Lovaas programme. Comprehension is aided by teachers simplifying their language and supplementing it with gestures. Finally, as is done with normal children, language is integrated into ongoing activities and is supported by as many contextual cues as possible rather than being taught as an isolated skill.

Pictures Exchange Communication System (PECS)

The Picture Exchange Communication System (PECS) (Bondy and Frost, 1994) has been developed for non-verbal children with ASD. The aim of PECS is to teach spontaneous social communication skills by means of symbols, namely pictures, in order to request desired objects.

A child can be trained in PECS by a parent, caregiver or therapist who has learned about the method. This also incorporates applied behaviour analysis (ABA) approach, in which prompts are given to guide the picture exchange. Further, in the early phases of PECS training, the child chooses a picture of a desired food, and receives the food in exchange for the picture. Getting the food is the positive reinforcement for using the picture to communicate. Although PECS enjoys widespread use, there are not enough empirically controlled investigations that support it (Charlop-Christy et al. 2002; Yarnall, 2000).

An autistic child using the PECS
© *Kim Gunkel*

The Son-Rise Programme

The Son-Rise Programme (SRP; also known as the option method) is another home-based intervention treatment which was developed in the USA in the late 1970s (Kaufman, 1981). It is an individual child-led treatment, so that the parent joins the child in the activity, even when it is somewhat stereotypical or repetitive. When the child becomes attentive and interacts with the adult, the latter attempts to expand the shared activity, to promote communication and social skills. Some parents recruit volunteer helpers to assist in providing the treatment, because of its intensity. The SRP is usually described as a very intensive approach with parents implementing the programme for most of the child's waking hours (Jordan and Powell, 1995).

The SRP uses a loving and non-judgemental educational approach to help parents and caregivers connect with children with ASD. The emphasis is on joining the child in its ritualistic behaviour and engaging in interactive play in order to establish rapport. There are families that use the programme on an intensive basis, in some cases even up to 80 hours per week, with the help of volunteers (Kaufman, 1981). In a small number of case studies on the use of SRP, some families have reported that it has helped them develop a more positive attitude towards their child's disability (Williams, 2006). However, the underlying principle of the SRP method is for the adult to imitate the child in order to engage with the child and critics argue that continuing in this way throughout therapy may not be conducive to long-term behaviour (Smith et al., 2007).

While this concludes our discussion of autism, we are not ready to conclude discussion of the infancy period as yet. A considerable body of research deals with attachment disturbances as a risk factor for psychopathology. We need to examine this research before going on to disorders of the toddler and preschool periods.

Infancy through Preschool: Insecure Attachment, Oppositional Defiant Disorder and Enuresis

Chapter Contents

As noted in the previous chapter, we have more to explore concerning the infancy period in order to do justice to the literature on **insecure attachment**, a topic that has generated an impressive body of research. While there is one attachment disorder listed in DSM-IV-TR, we will also consider the ways in which insecure attachment alone is a risk factor for other disorders.

Later in the chapter we will turn to the toddler period, first presenting an overview of normal developments that will be germane to understanding the psychopathologies that follow – namely, **oppositional defiant disorder** and **enuresis**.

Attachment Disorders

In Chapter 2, we described the development of normal attachment and reviewed the ways in which secure attachment provides a basis for healthy cognitive, emotional, social and self-development. Attachment is such an important evolutionary adaptation that, as we saw in Chapter 5, it is seen even in some of the children who are most psychopathologically disturbed, albeit in distorted forms. Attachment is thought to derive from an absence of opportunities for normal attachments to development. Much of the theory surrounding attachment concerns the nature and origins of individual differences in *qualities* of attachment, along a dimension of *security* and *insecurity*. Whether or not a child developed a secure or insecure attachment presupposed that there were adequate opportunities to form a selective discriminating attachment and, indeed, all of the attachment measures (e.g., strange situation) are conducted on the assumption that there is an attachment relationship between the child and his or her caregiver. Therefore, while many troubled children may show signs of *insecure* attachment, *absence* of attachment is very rare. In the case of attachment disorder, there is a presumption that the child did not have the opportunities to form a selective attachment to his or her current caregiver.

Reactive Attachment Disorder

The DSM-IV-TR bounds the essence of reactive attachment disorder (RAD) as 'markedly disturbed and developmentally inappropriate social relatedness in most contexts that begins before the age of 5 years and is associated with grossly pathological care' (APA, 2000, p. 127). Reactive attachment disorder is diagnosed when the child shows a markedly disturbed and developmentally inappropriate pattern of social relatedness. (See Table 6.1.) The child's disturbed relatedness may take two forms: (1) the *inhibited type*, in which the child persistently fails to initiate and respond to social interactions; and (2) the *disinhibited type*, in which the child is indiscriminately sociable and is not selective in the choice of attachment figures. The key to the diagnosis is that the relational problems are the result of severely inadequate caregiving; hence, the disorder is a *reaction* to a pathological emotional environment. Pathogenic care is evidenced either by significant emotional neglect of the child or by repeated changes of caregivers, either of which interferes with the child's ability to form a secure, deep and abiding attachment relationship.

For almost 20 years the disorder of RAD has attracted very little attention. In fact, the first study directly addressing the validity of the criteria did not appear until Boris et al. (1998). However, despite the limited amount of empirical data relating to the disorder, it was maintained in the DSM-IV primarily because it appeared to encompass a unique set of signs and symptoms not explained by other disorders.

A long history of research and clinical reports of young children who experience institutional rearing

TABLE 6.1 DSM-IV-TR Criteria for Reactive Attachment Disorder of Infancy or Early Childhood

---

A. Markedly disturbed and developmentally inappropriate social relatedness in most contexts, beginning before age 5 years, as evidenced by either:

  (1) Persistent failure to initiate or respond in a developmentally appropriate fashion to most social interactions, as manifest by excessively inhibited, hypervigilant, or highly ambivalent and contradictory responses (e.g., the child may respond to caregivers with a mixture of approach, avoidance, and resistance to comforting, or may exhibit frozen watchfulness)

  (2) Diffuse attachments as manifest by indiscriminate sociability with marked inability to exhibit appropriate selective attachments (e.g., excessive familiarity with relative strangers or lack of selectivity in choice of attachment figures)

B. The disturbance is not accounted for solely by developmental delay (as in Mental Retardation) and does not meet criteria for a Pervasive Developmental Disorder

C. Pathogenic care as evidenced by at least one of the following:

  (3) Persistent disregard of the child's basic emotional needs for comfort, stimulation, and affection

  (4) Persistent disregard of the child's basic physical needs

  (5) Repeated changes of primary caregiver that prevent formation of stable attachments (e.g., frequent changes in foster care)

D. There is the presumption that the care in Criterion C is responsible for the disturbed behavior in Criterion A.

Specify Type:

Inhibited Type: if Criterion A1 predominates in the clinical presentation

Disinhibited Type: if Criterion A2 predominates in the clinical presentation

---

Source: Reprinted with permission from the *Diagnostic and Statistical Manual of Mental Disorders*, Fourth Edition Text Revision. Copyright 2000 by the American Psychiatric Association.

provided the basis for what eventually became known as reactive attachment disorder in both the DSM and ICD. The DSM-IV and ICD-10 agree on several features of the disorder, such as it being linked with severe early caregiving disturbance and the existence of two forms of the disorder: the disinhibited (indiscriminantly friendly) and inhibited (withdrawn, hypervigilant) forms (O'Connor and Spagnola, 2009). Both classification systems state for a diagnosis of RAD, behaviours cannot be categorized as a mental deficiency or developmental disability (MR or PDD). In fact the APA (2000) warns the clinician to be wary of confusing RAD with the following: MR, autism, pervasive development disorder, attention deficit hyperactivity disorder, conduct disorder and oppositional defiant disorder. Importantly RAD is usually found in homes where there is a persistent disregard for the

child's basic emotional needs for comfort, stimulation and affection (APA, 2000). However, there are significant differences in how the ICD classify the disorder. The ICD has more specific disorder-focused criteria whereas the DSM classification leaves more room for the clinician's discretion.

Key Characteristics
The key similarities and differences between the two types of RAD are illustrated in Table 6.2. This also provides an overview as to how each type develops.

Prevalence and Characteristics
The diagnosis of reactive attachment disorder is *rarely* given, due to the extremely pathological care associated with it, which happily is rare. Children with reactive attachment disorder often first come to the attention of their paediatrician because of

TABLE 6.2 Similarities and Differences between Two Types of RAD

Types of RAD	Inhibited/Emotionally Withdrawn	Disinhibited/Indiscriminately Social
Etiology	Linked etiology to social deprivation and neglect	Linked etiologically to social deprivation and neglect (but also may have biological etiology, e.g., Williams syndrome)
Maltreated children	Readily identifiable in maltreated children	Readily identifiable in maltreated children
Children being raised in institutions	Readily identifiable in some young children being raised in institutions	Readily identifiable in some young children being raised in institutions
Children adopted out of institutions	Not identified in studies of young children adopted out of institutions	Readily identifiable in a substantial minority of young children adopted out of institutions
Relationship to selective attachment	Present only in children who lack attachments	Present in children with and without selective attachments
Interactions with adults	Limited interest in interaction and passively acquiescent	Interested and willing to approach and interact with familiar and unfamiliar adults without distinction
Quality of caregiving	Related to quality of caregiving	Not related to quality of caregiving
Relationship to internalizing problems	Moderate convergence with depressed mood	No relationship with depressed mood
Relationship to externalizing problems	No relationship	Moderately associated with measures of inattention/overactivity inconsistent relation to aggressive behaviour
Response to intervention	Very responsive to enhanced caregiving	Marginally responsive or not responsive to enhanced caregiving

Source: Adapted from Zeanah & Smyke (2008).

failure to thrive, a term that describes an infant or child who is failing to develop physically. The differential diagnosis is made when physical causes for the child's growth deficiency are ruled out and observations of parenting behaviour reveal *disregard* for the child's *basic physical and/or emotional needs*. However, historically the one caregiving environment that significantly increases the risk of reactive attachment disorder is the *cold*, impersonal institution that we will describe later.

Most reviewers view RAD as a disorder found in the foster care system, therefore the majority of research follows from that population. The overall prevalence of mental health problems in foster or residential care children in 2006 was 45 per cent; however, with the ambiguity of current criteria, the prevalence of RAD in this percentage is still unknown (Minnis et al., 2006). While many researchers use RAD solely as an issue for adopted children, there may be more cases of RAD and attachment disorders in the general population than the current diagnostic criteria allows (Wimmer et al., 2009). For example, other groups of children that may also be at risk for RAD are children whose parents have alcohol, substance and mental health problems. These children may experience a chaotic and, at times, dangerous home environment with unavailable parents who do not respond to the child's psychological or physical needs.

Gender, Race and Social Status
Because the disorder is so rare, very limited information exists about ethnic, gender or cultural differences in its prevalence or manifestations. Javier et al. (2007) have carried out an important study to address gender difference in adopted children diagnosed with RAD aged 12 to 15. They found that boys were more likely to steal, lie, cheat, participate in vandalism, etc. In contrast, they found that adopted girls tend to be more cruel and aggressive against people and objects. Ten per cent of children included in the study, who were adopted at later ages and in the foster care system longer, were diagnosed with RAD. However,

another study found boys struggling more with hyperactivity and aggressiveness, attention and thought problems as well as with anxious and withdrawn depressive tendencies. Girls on the other hand, only outperformed boys in antisocial behaviours of somatic issues and rule breaking (Cappelletty et al., 2005).

Course
Again, due to its rarity and the lack of research attention given to it, there are limited data available on the developmental course of reactive attachment disorder. It has been shown to affect the *emotional functioning* and *well-being* of the middle childhood to adolescent years, but has not been researched beyond this point and no longitudinal studies have been made to see effects into later adulthood (Millward et al., 2006). Of the research that has been done, conflicting results seem to be all that is yielded (Javier et al., 2007). However, data from Rutter et al.'s (2007) English Romanian adoptee study has been key in showing that the *disturbance* in attachment can be *persistent*. Here children aged between 6 months and 2 years, from Romanian orphanages, were adopted into English families, and were reassessed at 4, 6 and 11 years of age. The findings indicated considerable stability in individual differences and a persistence of disinhibited behaviour found in the 11-year-old children.

When considering the developmental course it is important to also mention how it has been viewed in relation to other psychopathologies. For example, various researchers have seen RAD within current criteria as a possible first step to conduct disorder (Minnis et al., 2006). Other researchers take a more scientific biopsychosocial model of RAD, believing that traumatic experiences may have physiological effects on biological and neurochemical structures in the brain. Here it is the neurobiological effects of neglect that are thought to be more detrimental to the child than the impact of abuse and related trauma (Corbin, 2007). Reactive attachment disorder is also being studied from a systematic perspective for links between

Posttraumatic stress disorder and borderline personality disorder (Kasenchak, 2003).

Etiology

In contrast to other disorders, the DSM makes an explicit statement about the origins of reactive attachment disorder. The definition specifies that the disorder is caused by pathogenic care; therefore, the culprit clearly is in the interpersonal context.

Institutionalized Children

The concept of reactive attachment disorder emerged from studies of the effects of maternal deprivation on children raised in institutions. For example, in the 1940s, Rene Spitz began studying infants separated from their parents and raised in what were then termed foundling homes. In one such orphanage in Mexico, Spitz discovered that 37 per cent of the infants died within a few weeks of admission. These children were given proper nutrition and were fed and bathed and clothed – there was no physical reason for them to fail to thrive. Spitz made careful observations of these children and described a clinical picture characterized by loss of interest in their environment, poor weight gain, rocking and stereotypic behaviour, and extreme listlessness. He made a film of his observations, heart-rending to watch, which is entitled simply *Grief.* Spitz termed this disorder in children *anaclitic depression*, a term that refers to the loss of that on which one depends – for the young child, this traumatic loss was the loss of loving care (Spitz, 1946a). Spitz argued that, if children do not receive human affection, despite adequate food and shelter, they literally wither away and die.

Further evidence for the importance of attachment came after the Second World War, when there was a great problem with orphaned and homeless children throughout the world. In the 1950s John Bowlby worked on a World Health Organization report on the mental health of these orphans. His report made a resounding impact on the world community. He argued that in the first three years of life even the most clean, well-run institution would increase the risk for physical and mental illness and could possibly damage children irreparably. His classic work is the three-volume series entitled *Attachment, Separation, and Loss.* Bowlby (1982) identified three stages of grief and mourning in young children undergoing separation.

The first was *protest*, as the child vigorously attempts to elicit a response from a caregiver with tears and cries. The second stage, *despair*, was characterized by sadness and grief and appeared to be akin to mourning in adults. The third stage, *detachment*, is evidenced by a kind of learned helplessness as the child becomes passive and unresponsive even to adults who attempt to engage the infant.

More recently, studies of children raised in large, impersonal, depriving institutions in Romania have confirmed the relationship between lack of *affectionate care* and developmental psychopathology. While, generally, children *recover* when placed in a more nurturing environment, previously institutionalized children often *continue* to show odd social behaviour. In Rutter et al.'s (2007) English Romanian longitudinal study which began in 1998, Rutter wanted to see if good care could compensate for the privation the children had suffered before the overthrow of the communist dictator Ceaucescu. Rutter addressed three groups of children: those adopted before the age of 6 months, those between 6 months and 2 years and a later group of those after two years. By the age of 6, children were making a very good recovery; however the children adopted at an older age had a much higher level of disinhibited attachment. In 2007, Rutter returned (the children then aged 11 years) and found that some of the children had made a full recovery, but about half of those diagnosed with the condition at the age of 6 still had it at the age of 11.

Hawk and McCall (2011) have also found extreme behaviours of post-institutionalized Russian adoptees. Behavioural problems reported by parents on the child behaviour checklist (Achenbach and Rescorla, 2001) were studied in 316 children adopted from social-emotionally depriving Russian institutions as a function of age at adoption (18 month cut-off), age at assessment (6–11; 12–18) and gender.

Children adopted after 18 months have higher problem scores when assessed first at 12–18 years of age. A significant proportion of them (59 per cent) were found to have particular difficulties in later life relating to antisocial behaviours, social difficulties and withdrawal.

A particular behaviour problem that persists is *indiscriminate friendliness*, a component of the disinhibited type of reactive attachment disorder described earlier. For example, in a longitudinal study of children adopted from Romania into Canadian families, investigators found indiscriminately friendly behaviour was evident both 11 months and 39 months post adoption (Chisholm et al., 1995). In a more recent study, Groark et al., (2011) addressed children's general behavioural development and problem behaviours from three different institutions for young children in central America. While the institutions were clean they were physically sparse. Caregivers provided routine caregiving with *limited emotion*, responsiveness, support empathy or guidance. Caregivers tended to work long hours and then were off for two to three days, and children periodically graduated to new wards, so there was very limited stability of caregivers in the children's lives. These children displayed high frequencies of indiscriminate friendliness, non-compliance and provocative and aggressive/violent behaviours. These data and those of a few studies represent the only comprehensive, empirical description of institutions for young children. Results are consistent with the hypothesis that a lack of warm, sensitive, contingently responsive interactions with relatively little consistency of available caregivers may be a major contributor to *delayed* contemporary developmental and *persistent deficits* and *problems* observed in some post-institutionalized children and adolescents.

Fortunately, the kind of complete loss of a nurturing relationship that institutionalization represents is a relatively rare occurrence. Instead, the bridge from attachment to psychopathology most often takes the form of *variations* in the quality of relationships between parents and children. The DSM-IV classification refers to an extremely impaired subgroup of infants whose insecure attachments are due to neglect or frequent changes in caregiving. However, as we will see next, most insecure attachments are not so extreme in their manifestations nor are they a product of such deviant caregiving (Shorey and Snyder, 2006).

Insecure Attachment and Psychopathology

As we explored in Chapter 2, a secure attachment provides children with a sense of comfort, self-worth and self-reliance. Securely attached children are emotionally *expressive* and *responsive* to others, are flexible and resourceful in response to challenges, and are able to cope with distressing emotions. In contrast, avoidantly attached children display *brittle independence* and *affective overcontrol* while resistantly attached children are *dependent*, *fearful* and *angry*. Another piece of evidence confirming the relationship between attachment and psychopathology is that insecurely attached children are more prevalent in clinical populations.

In summary, although insecure attachment is not in itself a form of psychopathology, it can be considered to be a risk mechanism for psychological disturbance. The DSM and ICD criteria of RAD seem to form from severely pathological, insecure types. However, no studies have directly categorized RAD diagnosable criteria into Bowlby's attachment types. Next, we consider whether there is evidence that attachment patterns are related to specific psychopathologies.

Limitations to Continuity

First, we need to make some comments on the methods we use to investigate the relationship between attachment and the development of specific disorders. One of the factors that complicates the attachment–disorder link is that attachments themselves are not always *stable* across development. One longitudinal study, for example, found that only half the infants maintained the same classification by 4 years of age (Goldberg, 1997). Therefore, whether an avoidant attachment in infancy predicts school-age anxiety depends on whether the child's attachment pattern is continuous across that developmental period. This is the *continuity–discontinuity* distinction we introduced in Chapter 1. What the research evidence suggests is that, when the family environment is stable, so is attachment. But when the family environment changes, for better or worse, so may the quality of the child's attachment. (See Chapter 2.)

Further, and in keeping with the multi-determined, transactional developmental psychopathology model, it is unlikely that one variable alone – even one so significant as attachment – can predict the complex etiology of a disorder. Radke-Yarrow and co-workers' (1995) research nicely illustrates this point. First, they found that insecure attachment at 1.5 and 3.5 years of age *alone* was not directly related to disturbance when the children were 6 and 9 years of age; however, it was related *in interaction* with other variables – in this case, the mothers' depression. Further, styles of attachment could serve either as risk or protective factors depending on how they interacted with other variables. Interestingly, secure attachment in the context of severe maternal depression predicted the child's developing a depressive disorder; *insecure* attachment to a depressed mother was associated with an *absence* of child anxiety at 6 years of age. Thus, while in general security and insecurity can be regarded as protective and risk factors, respectively, under special circumstances their roles may be reversed.

Cross-Cultural Differences

Cross-cultural research on attachment has shown that culture plays a significant role in parenting behaviours and infant attachment (van IJzendoorn and Sagi-Schwartz, 2008). As we reviewed in Chapter 2, although the central tenets of attachment theory appear to hold up well across diverse cultures, the proportions of securely attached children do vary. In addition, there is as yet little research to confirm that the implications of insecure attachment are consistent across these different cultures. For example, while almost half of the children in samples taken in certain countries are judged to be insecurely attached (Ein-Dor et al., 2011), we do not yet have evidence that their rates

of psychopathology are higher. Also it is important to note that behaviour that is considered maladaptive and indicative of insecure attachment in a US sample may be viewed as adaptive in another cultural context.

Empirical Evidence

Evidence concerning the relation between insecure attachment and subsequent disorders is beginning to emerge from a series of longitudinal studies. Table 6.3 summarizes the findings on the relationship between attachment types and psychopathology.

Resistant Attachment

One study confirming a relation between infant attachment and subsequent psychopathology was conducted by Warren and colleagues (1997). They hypothesized that resistant attachment in infancy would predict subsequent *anxiety disorders* since inconsistent caregiving would result in a chronic concern about whether needs would be met. In addition, this anxiety would be more overtly displayed by resistant children than it would be by those with an avoidant attachment. The data confirmed the hypothesis. Resistant attachment at 12 months of age was significantly related to anxiety disorders at 17.5 years of age. Moreover, the relation was a specific one. Resistant attachment predicted anxiety disorders in particular rather than a variety of other disturbances while, on the other hand, avoidant attachment did *not* predict later anxiety problems.

Avoidant Attachment

Infants classified as avoidant have learnt that overt displays of need, anxiety and fear do *not* bring protective or comforting responses from caregivers. They learn that the way to maintain proximity to people is to remain fairly *expressionless* and *not* too demanding. The nature of this type means that their insistence for independence and self-sufficiency, and lack of admission of distress often linked to dissociation, minimize the need to seek treatment. For this reason the description of the case of avoidant attachment in a clinical setting is

TABLE 6.3 Developmental Findings Regarding Attachment and Psychopathology

	Secure	Avoidant	Resistant	Disorganized
Infancy				
With caregiver	Uses caregiver as secure base from which to explore	Precociously independent	Clingy, inhibited exploration	Inconsistent
During separation	If distressed, protests	Minimal reaction	Highly distressed	Odd behaviours
Upon reunion	Seeks contact, easily soothed	Avoids proximity	Hard to soothe, seeks and rejects proximity	Distorted attempts at proximity seeking
Caregiver behaviour	Responsive, non-intrusive	Unresponsive, rejecting	Inconsistent	Coercive, frightening behaviour, mixed signals
Preschool	Competent with peers	Unempathic and negative with peers	Passive, immature, easily victimized by peers	Aggressive, oppositional
School age	Socially skilled, self-confident, harmonious friendships	Interpersonally insensitive, more likely to be alone	Dependent on teachers, negative biases toward peers	Externalizing problems
Adolescence	Sociable, insightful, ego resilient	Hostile towards peers, low in social support	Anxious, distressed, poor self-concept	Personality disorganization, dissociation
Adulthood	Autonomous	Dismissing	Preoccupied	Unresolved

extremely rare. (See Silverman, 2011.) An avoidantly attached child appears to be particularly resistant to change (Haggerty et al., 2010) and their new interactions with people are often incorporated into avoidant schema for *fear* of rejection and ridicule. A recent study found that the maladaptive schema regarding rejection and disconnection may partially mediate the relationship between avoidant attachment and later psychopathology (Bosmans et al., 2010).

Disorganized Attachment

Research on disorganized attachment yields mixed results, perhaps because this is the newest and least well-studied classification. The essence of disorganized attachment is fright without solution (Main and Hesse, 1990). The best example of disorganized attachment is the relationship between the abused child and the abusive parent. In fact behaviours that are described as the 'disorganized pattern' have been

shown to be present in 80 per cent of abused children and to be highly correlated with childhood aggression (Minnis et al., 2006). The abusive parent fulfils two incompatible roles. On the one hand he or she is the child's attachment figure and the only potential source of safety in an uncharted threatening world. On the other hand, the abusive parent is the stressor who can suddenly and unexpectedly threaten the child with physical or psychological violence. The child is placed in an irresolvable paradoxical situation in which the only possible base from which to explore the world is at the same time the source of unpredictable abusive threat. Disorganized attachments has been found to carry an increased risk for externalizing problems particularly in boys, whereas no such risks were found for the other insecure attachment types (Fearon et al., 2010).

A much earlier study by Lyons-Ruth and colleagues (1993) found that disorganized attachment in infancy predicted *aggressive behaviour* in kindergarten. The relationship was especially strong when the mother evidenced psychiatric problems such as depression, which increased her hostility and intrusiveness with the child. Further, another longitudinal study found that disorganized attachment in infancy predicted clinical levels of *externalizing* behaviour problems in elementary school (Rutter et al., 2009b, for a review).

Shaw and co-workers' (1996) longitudinal study also found that disorganized/disoriented attachment in infants differentially predicted *aggression* at 5 years of age. However, this risk was not sufficient in itself but had to be potentiated by the mother's perception of the child as being difficult to cope with. In fact, disorganized/disoriented attachment, child-rearing disagreements between parents, maternal personality (aggression, depression and suspiciousness), and child aggression at 3 years of age were *equally* predictive of aggression at 5 years of age.

Finally, studies of adolescents with disorganized attachment patterns show that they are vulnerable to severe forms of psychopathology involving *personality disorganization* and *dissociation*. These effects also were linked to a history of traumatic abuse in the home (Sarkar and Adshead, 2006).

Given the pervasive and wide-ranging effects of attachment, we will return to the relation between insecure attachment and specific psychopathologies many times in subsequent chapters.

Inter-generational Transmission of Insecure Attachment

In Chapter 2, we described the different behaviours exhibited by parents of securely and insecurely attached infants. Interest in understanding what accounts for these different parenting styles has led to a body of research on the parents' own internal working models of relationships. The method used is an interview that asks parents to reflect on their own childhood attachment experiences. The Adult Attachment Interview classifies mothers into four types that parallel the child attachment categories (see Table 6.3): autonomous, preoccupied, dismissing and unresolved (Main and Goldwyn, 1988). Prospective studies conducted before the birth of

the child show that mothers' internal working models of attachment predict their 1-year-old children's attachment security with uncanny accuracy. This has also been identified in other cultures, such that in a Japanese study a mother's attachment style has been shown to predict their children's (Behrens et al., 2007). A meta-analysis of 18 separate studies found a 75 per cent correspondence rate between mother and child security/insecurity. Further, across studies, mothers with insecure attachments are highly prevalent among those whose children develop psychopathology: among mothers of children being treated for psychiatric disorders, only 14 per cent had secure internal working models (van IJzendoorn, 1995).

Continuity in attachment patterns has been observed even into the third generation. One study interviewed pregnant women and their mothers and then later observed the new mothers with their infants in the strange situation. The investigators found that, in 64 per cent of the families, mothers, grandmothers and children were classified into the same attachment pattern (Benoit and Parker, 1994). However, the results are qualified by the fact that most of the individuals in this well-functioning, middle-class sample were securely attached; dismissing or preoccupied mothers often had children with a different attachment pattern than theirs. Also when a single mother lives with her own mother, the child's grandparents may influence the child's attachment not only indirectly through the mother's attachment history but also directly through the grandmother's involvement in caregiving (Cook and Roggman, 2010).

Proposed Disorders of Insecure Attachment

Research indeed suggests that, over time, insecure attachment is a significant risk factor for psychopathology. However, most of this work is not reflected in the DSM-IV-TR. Charles Zeanah (1996, 2000) argues that the DSM diagnosis of reactive attachment disorder describes only the extreme end of a clinically significant continuum. These authors characterize the current diagnostic systems as 'oddly detached' from the extensive research literature on insecure attachment and developmental psychopathology. Therefore, based on their observations and clinical work with disturbed children, they propose an alternative classification of attachment disturbances that integrates the DSM-IV and ICD classifications with the research evidence (Zeanah and Gleason, 2010). The disorders are of three general types: non-attachment, distortions and disruptions.

Disorders of Non-attachment

In keeping with the DSM and ICD, Zeanah and colleagues propose two disorders in which there is an absence of a preferred attachment figure: (1) non-attachment, evidenced by emotionally withdrawn and inhibited behaviour towards the caregiver; and (2) indiscriminate sociability, in which the child seeks comfort and affection from strangers, without demonstrating developmentally appropriate discrimination of the attachment figure from others. Children who display these patterns are likely to have serious problems with self-regulation and self-protection.

Secure Base Distortions

What distinguishes the disorders in this category is that the child has a preferred attachment figure, but the relationship is severely disturbed. Moreover, these disturbances are specific to a *particular* relationship, in keeping with research evidence that children form different kinds of relationships with different caregivers.

Attachment Disorder with Self-Endangerment

The child boldly and uninhibitedly explores the environment without seeking proximity or reassurance from the safe haven of the attachment figure. The child may engage in dangerous or provocative behaviour such as running into traffic, running away in crowded places or climbing on ledges. The child may also engage in aggression that is directed towards self or the caregiver, particularly in the context of comfort-seeking.

Attachment Disorder with Clinging/Inhibition

At the opposite extreme, the child does not venture away from the attachment figure in order to explore the environment in an age-appropriate fashion, instead clinging and showing extreme dependence. Just like aggression in the first child, the inhibition

in this child is seen only in relation to the caregiver. There may be no such anxiety or inhibited behaviour in other contexts, such as when the child is with another familiar trusted adult.

Attachment Disorder with Vigilance/Hypercompliance

Like the aforementioned child, this child is inhibited from exploring the environment while in the caregiver's presence. However, rather than clinging, this child appears emotionally constricted, hyperattentive and overly compliant with the caregiver, seeming to fear the caregiver's displeasure. All spontaneity is gone from the child's behaviour. This is similar to the pattern of 'compulsive compliance' observed in children of harsh, intrusive parents (Crittenden, 1988).

Attachment Disorder with Role Reversal

In this pattern the child, rather than seeking emotional support, nurturance and caregiving, provides it to the parent. 'Children often try to control the caregiver's behaviour, either punitively, over solicitously, or in some other role-inappropriate manner' (Zeanah, 2000, p. 300). This behaviour is often seen in children who are either caring for an ill relative or have experienced a loss of a parent through bereavement or a divorce. Consequently, the child bears a developmentally inappropriate burden of responsibility for the caregivers' well-being and is deprived of having his or her own emotional needs met.

Disrupted Attachment Disorder

This category is reserved for cases in which the child experiences the sudden loss of the attachment figure. Following from Bowlby, the child evidences the reaction sequence of protest, despair and detachment. Although not well studied due to its rarity, case reports paint a compelling picture of the distress exhibited by children who lose their attachment figures through death, illness or foster care placement (Dann, 2011). (See Box 6.1.)

Because these categories are still in the proposal stage, we do not yet have evidence for their reliability, validity or clinical utility. As Zeanah (2000) notes, more research is needed to clarify how

Box 6.1 Case Study in Attachment Disorder: John at 17 Months

In the 1950s it was not thought unusual to place a child in an institution when the mother went into hospital to give birth to a sibling. While this may have been accepted practice, two colleagues of John Bowlby, James and Joyce Robertson, thought differently. They requested permission to observe a group of five children who were placed either with foster families or in a residential nursery (i.e., an orphanage). One child in the latter group was John, who at 17 months was a bright and happy child with an easy temperament. He slept and ate well and was developing normally in all spheres. His father was a young professional man at a crucial point in his training, and it was considered impractical for him to care for John on his own. So, on their family doctor's advice, the parents dropped John off at the nursery the night his mother went into labour.

On the first day, John woke in a strange setting, surrounded by the clamour of other children. When a nurse approached him with a smile, he responded in a friendly way and interacted as she dressed him. At breakfast a different nurse fed him and he was friendly to her as well as to the two others who cared for him in the course of the day. When his father came to visit, he was slow to respond but finally blossomed into a smile of recognition.

While John continued to cope well on the second day, by the third day he was visibly distressed. He cried little, but sat forlornly at the end of the room or played with his back to the group. He made tentative approaches to the various nurses but was often overlooked in the noisy bustle. By the fourth day, he had ceased to eat and drink and was listless, with lengthy spells of sad crying. On the fifth day, the nurses noticed his constant misery but were not able to comfort or distract him. He continued to refuse to eat and cried in quiet despair, sometimes rolling about and wringing his hands. He made fewer attempts to get close to the nurses and lay on the floor, burrowed under a giant teddy bear. While Nurse Mary tried to make herself more consistently available to him, she came and went with the duty roster and not according to John's need of her.

On the sixth day, John was miserable and inactive. He cried a great deal. When his father came to visit, John pinched and smacked him. Then his face lightened and he went to the door, gesturing his wish to go home. He fetched his outdoor shoes and when his father humoured him by putting them on, John broke into a little smile. But when his father did not move, John returned to the nurse and gave his father an anguished expression. He then turned away from the nurse and sat forlornly in a corner.

On the seventh day, John cried weakly but continually all day long. He did not play, did not eat, and did not respond for more than a few seconds to the attempts of the nurses to cheer him. His expression was dull and blank and he stumbled when he walked. Towards the end of the day, he would walk towards an adult, then either turn away to cry in a corner or fall on his face on the floor in a gesture of despair. On the eighth day, John was even more miserable. For long periods he lay in apathetic silence on the floor. When his father tried to feed him, John was so distraught that he could neither eat nor drink.

On the ninth day John cried from the moment he awoke. He was slumped motionless on a nurse's lap when his mother came to take him home. His response was immediate and dramatic. He threw himself about, crying loudly and, after stealing a glance at his mother, looked away from her. Several times he looked and then turned away with loud cries and a distraught expression. After a few minutes, his mother took him in her arms, but John continued to struggle and scream, arching his back away from his mother. Eventually, he got down and ran crying to Joyce Robertson, who calmed him down and passed him back to his mother. John then cuddled into his mother, clutching his blanket but not looking at her.

When the father entered the room, John struggled away from his mother and into his father's arms. His crying stopped and for the first time he looked at his mother directly. It was a long hard look. His mother said, 'He has never looked at me like that before'.

After returning home (and remember that home now included a new sibling who shared his mother's attention), he had more frequent temper tantrums, went through periods of refusing food, slept badly and was more clingy. Seven weeks after he returned home, Joyce Robertson visited and John reacted strongly to her presence – he began refusing food, rejecting his parents' attention, and aggressing against his mother, an episode that lasted for five days. Even three years later, when John was 4½, his parents worried that they could see some long-lasting effects of the separation. Although he was generally a happy and competent child, he was very fearful of losing his mother and became extremely upset any time she was out of sight. Also, every few months he had bouts of aggression against her that seemed to come out of the blue and lasted for several days.

Source: Adapted from Robertson and Robertson, 1971.

different types of relational disturbances relate to psychopathology.

Intervention
Parent–Child Therapies

A characteristic of attachment interventions is that it is neither the child nor the parent but their *relationship* that is the 'identified patient' (MacMillan et al., 2009). Examples of this approach include the Steps Toward Effective and Enjoyable Parenting (STEEP) programme developed by Egeland and colleagues (2000) and the Infant–Parent Programme developed by Lieberman and Pawl (1993). The majority of the families in these programmes are considered high risk, due to socio-economic disadvantage, cultural uprooting, mental illness and/or substance abuse. Many times the mothers have a history of being abused as children. The focus of the intervention is on changing the parent's internal working model of relationship through changing her relationship with her child.

Components of the intervention include weekly home-based visits in which the therapist provides the parent with gentle guidance and information about normal development, as well as fostering a trusting and close relationship in which the parent is encouraged to reflect on her own childhood experiences and how they influence her interactions with the child. The therapist also helps the mother to become a more developmentally sensitive and empathic observer of the child, expanding the parents' understanding of attachment-related behaviour, separation anxiety and the centrality of the parent–child relationship in the infant's world. (We will take a closer look at this intervention in Chapter 17.)

A review of attachment-based interventions found that, while they were effective overall, the best results were obtained for studies that focused on increasing *parental sensitivity* towards the child (Kalinauskiene et al., 2009). Further, although change in the parent's behaviour was seen, this was not always accompanied by a change in her internal working model. (See also Bakermans-Kranenburg et al., 2003.)

Child Therapies

Sometimes the focus of intervention is on the individual child, especially in the case of children in foster care or group homes whose connections to attachment figures may have been severed. Unstructured *play therapy* may be used to provide the child with a safe environment in which to explore his or her thoughts and feelings and to experience a positive relationship with a caring therapist. (We will describe play therapy more fully in Chapter 17. For more information on interventions for attachment disorders, see Brisch, 2002, and Box 6.2.)

In summary, as we have seen, the origins of attachment disorders are clearly in the family context, particularly the quality of caregiving received in the first three years of life. However, the *consequences* of attachment disorders span all developmental contexts and place the child at risk for taking a deviant pathway in development. Attachment is a crucial stage-salient issue of the toddler years that affects the child's ability to master developmental issues at each subsequent stage. Attachment is concerned with balancing between the need to cling and the need to let go. When the child has difficulty resolving that dilemma, one possible consequence is the development of an overly rigid, controlling and oppositional stance toward the world.

Oppositional Defiant Disorder

The toddler period is a time of increased expansiveness on the child's part and increased restrictions on the part of the socializing adults. It is natural that these two should go hand in hand. Toddlers who are now physically able to explore vast new regions of the environment inadvertently damage valued household items, leave chaos in their wake, and occasionally endanger themselves. Such unfettered initiative must be limited by 'No' and 'Don't'. Socializing parents want to teach their toddlers control of unacceptable behaviour while the enterprising toddlers brazenly assert their autonomy. The

Box 6.2 Controversies in the Diagnosis and Treatment of Reactive Attachment Disorder

In recent years, clinicians and researchers have seen a dramatic increase in the number of children diagnosed with reactive attachment disorder. On the one hand, this may reflect greater awareness and sensitivity to the devastating effects on pathological caregiving and may serve children well by placing the blame or their disturbed environments rather than labelling the children themselves as 'bad seeds' or 'defectives'. Correct diagnosis also is helpful because it can lead to the proper treatment to alleviate the child's difficulties. But when is the diagnosis correct and what is the proper treatment? Investigators in the field are far from unified on these points (Hanson and Spratt, 2000).

In regard to diagnosis, perhaps the most thorny issue is that, unlike almost every other disorder in DSM, the criteria for the diagnosis of reactive attachment disorder are specific as to etiology: the disorder must arise as a function of pathological caregiving. This requires a high level of inference on the part of the diagnostician, who must determine not only that inadequate care has been given to the child, but that it is this care – and no other cause – that is responsible for the disorder. While child maltreatment may result in a number of pathological disturbances, as we will discuss in Chapter 14 – including

such suggestive symptoms as withdrawal, passivity and the avoidance of attachment figures – not all young children who receive inadequate parenting develop reactive attachment disorder. However, in actual practice, Hanson and Spratt find in their review, clinicians concerned to highlight the issue of maltreatment and avoid pathologizing the child frequently apply the reactive attachment disorder label to children who have been abused but whose symptoms go far beyond the criteria specified in the diagnostic criteria.

What harm is there, really, in erroneously diagnosing a child with reactive attachment disorder? The other controversy in the field concerns the treatment of the disorder. Many alternative therapies that have been developed for this disorder are theoretically ungrounded and lacking in empirical support. Further, some of these treatments may be damaging or traumatizing for children. They may even be fatal. For example, 'rebirthing' is a technique used to simulate the physical and psychological birth of the child in order to foster the development of attachment afresh. In one widely publicized case in Colorado, a child died during the process. She suffocated when wrapped in a blanket and held down by the rebirthing therapists, while her foster mother looked on unawares.

ensuing battles are fought over the issue of who is going to control whom. The sometimes stormy confrontations are responsible for the entire period being humorously called the terrible twos.

If all goes well in the confrontations between expansive toddlers and the restricting parents, the toddlers will emerge as socialized preschoolers who can both control themselves and be assured of their autonomy. In short, they are both self-controlled and self-reliant.

However, there is also the possibility that this normal development will go awry, resulting in psychopathological deviations. The healthy need for self-assertion evidenced in negativism can be carried to an extreme of *oppositional defiant* behaviour, which disrupts relations with caregiving adults while blocking the child's own growth.

Definition and Characteristics
Definition
The essential features of oppositional defiant disorder (ODD) are a recurrent pattern of negativistic, defiant, disobedient and hostile behaviour towards authority figures. Manifestations of the disorder include outbursts of temper; arguing; defying and deliberately annoying others and blaming others for the child's own mistakes; and being touchy, angry and spiteful (see Table 6.4 for the DSM-IV-TR criteria). However, unlike conduct disorder (CD), there are no violations of the basic rights of others or of major societal norms and rules, such as persistent lying, aggressiveness and theft. ODD has often been regarded as a milder form of CD and forms an early stage in the CD development.

TABLE 6.4 DSM-IV-TR Criteria for Oppositional Defiant Disorder

A. A pattern of negativistic, hostile, and defiant behavior lasting at least six months, during which four (or more) of the following are present:

   (1) often loses temper

   (2) often argues with adults

   (3) often actively defies or refuses to comply with adults' requests or rules

   (4) often deliberately annoys people

   (5) often blames others for his or her mistakes or misbehavior

   (6) is often touchy or easily annoyed by others

   (7) is often angry and resentful

   (8) is often spiteful or vindictive

   NOTE: Consider a criterion met only if the behavior occurs more frequently than is typically observed in individuals of comparable age and developmental level.

B. The disturbance in behavior causes significant impairment in social, academic, or occupational functioning.

C. The behaviors do not occur exclusively during the course of a psychotic or mood disorder.

D. Criteria are not met for Conduct Disorder.

Source: Reprinted with permission from the *Diagnostic and Statistical Manual of Mental Disorders*, Fourth Edition Text Revision. Copyright 2000 by the American Psychiatric Association.

Oppositional defiant disorder was introduced as a separate diagnosis in the DSM-III (APA, 1980). Initially concerns were expressed over its distinctiveness from normal behaviour on the one hand and from a mild form of conduct disorder on the other. Progressive tightening of ODD criteria in DSM-III (APA, 1980) and DSM-IV (1994) has classified the distinction between normal and disordered behaviour, but evidence of the distinctiveness of ODD and CD remains quite limited. CD will be addressed in the later chapter but because of its interplay with the symptoms of ODD will also be addressed in part in this chapter.

Prevalence and Characteristics

Costello and colleagues (2003) gathered data from a representative community sample of 1420 children assessed annually from ages 9 to 16 in one of the most frequently reported problems of clinically referred children in the USA; for example, one-third of all clinically referred pre-adolescent and adolescent children are diagnosed as ODD (Nock et al., 2007). Moreover, rates of oppositional behaviour increase in youths as they enter adolescence (Keenan et al., 1999). Using a standardized diagnostic interview, the authors found that the prevalence of the ODD diagnosis ranged from 2.1 per cent at age 9 to 4.1 per cent at age 15 to 2.2 per cent at age 16. Across the age range, overall prevalence rates were 2.1 per cent for girls and 3.1 per cent for boys. Lifetime prevalence of ODD was estimated to be 10.2 per cent (males = 11.2 per cent; females = 9.2 per cent). Of those with lifetime ODD, 92.4 per cent meet criteria for at least one other

Oppositional defiant behaviour
© *Judith D. Sedwick /PictureCube*

lifetime DSM-IV disorder, including: mood (45.8 per cent), anxiety (62.3 per cent), impulse control (68.2 per cent) and substance use (47.2 per cent) disorders.

Although the fundamental conceptualization of both ODD and CD have remained constant over the past decades, the criteria for diagnosing these disorders have undergone considerable changes across various iterations of the DSM. For example, symptoms of the disorder have been added and removed, symptoms have been modified, diagnostic thresholds have been changed and various subtyping for CD has come and gone. There is also a major concern that limited empirical evidence has been used to justify continuing changes to the diagnostic criteria for ODD and CD. These changes to the criteria have lead to difficulties in trying to ascertain the prevalence of the disorder.

Prevalence is heavily influenced by the diagnostic classification criteria used, the measurement instrument and the time window involved. Even minor changes in diagnostic criteria can produce large differences in prevalence. A comparison of DSM-III and DSM-III-R diagnoses, on the same sample of children, found cases of ODD became 25 per cent less prevalent and CD became 44 per cent less prevalent using the earlier version (Boyle et al., 1996). Furthermore, Costello and Angold (unpublished data, 1998) showed that the prevalence of DSM-IV CD was slightly lower than that of the DSM-III-R CD but no differences occurred for ODD.

Differences in Diagnostic Classification Systems

The difficulty in specifying the relationship between ODD and CD is reflected in the contrasting nosological approaches taken by the DSM-IV and ICD-10. In DSM-IV, CD and ODD are specified in separate disorders with exclusive symptom lists. The assumption that ODD is however a less severe manifestation of CD is built into DSM-IV through the requirement that ODD is not diagnosed in the presence of CD. ODD by contrast is treated as a subtype of CD in the ICD-10.

As a result all children who receive a diagnosis on the DSM-IV scheme also receive a diagnosis on the ICD-10, but a number of children who meet the ICD criteria for CD would not receive a diagnosis in the DSM. This happens with children who have two ODD symptoms and two CD symptoms or three ODD symptoms and either one or two CD symptoms. These children are often referred to as the 'gap group' because they fall in the gap between the CD and ODD diagnosis (Rowe et al., 2005).

Concern has also been raised about the four symptom threshold for diagnosing ODD in DSM-IV. Many have found no difference between 'subthresholds' cases and children who met full DSM-IV criteria and suggested that diagnostic criteria should be expanded to include them. Further weight is given to this argument as many of these 'subthreshold children' would obtain a diagnosis under the ICD-10.

Gender, Ethnicity and Social Status

Regarding *gender*, ODD appears at similar rates in boys and girls in early childhood with perhaps a slight male majority (Nock et al., 2007). However, by late childhood, ODD is overwhelmingly more predominant in boys. Importantly, very limited research has been carried out addressing ODD in girls so it is likely that its prevalence in girls is far higher than is currently estimated. The question has also been raised as to whether the diagnostic criteria for ODD has the same clinical applications across both boys and girls and whether gender specific diagnosis criteria and thresholds should be used (Keenan et al., 2008).

It is also not clear why an increase in ODD occurs in adolescence for boys but not girls. For example, both sexes seem largely similar in their sensitivity to psychosocial risk factors for antisocial behaviour and are also similarly exposed to potential family and environmental correlates (see Boden et al., 2010, for a review). *Social class* is an important factor; data consistently show that living in impoverished or adverse socio-economic conditions during childhood is associated with increased risk of ODD in later life and is found to be more prevalent in groups who are socio-economically disadvantaged (Collishaw et al., 2007b). *Racial and ethnic differences* are not consistently examined; when they are, they are found in some studies but not others (Lahey et al., 1999). Further, seldom have the effects of social class been controlled in studies of the ethnic diversity of ODD, making these data difficult to interpret.

Comorbidity and Differential Diagnosis
ODD and Conduct Disorder

Both in the descriptive psychiatric literature and in objective studies there is a strong association between ODD and conduct disorder (CD). The DSM-IV states that 'all of the features of ODD are usually present in CD' (APA, 1994, p. 93) and precludes a diagnosis of ODD if full criteria of CD are met. The DSM-IV organized ODD, CD and antisocial personality disorder (ASPD) hierarchically and developmentally 'as if they reflect age dependent expressions of the same underlying disorder' (Moffitt et al., 2008, p. 22). ODD is assumed to constitute a development precursor to CD in a significant proportion of cases (APA, 1994) and it is noted that childhood onset subtypes of CD (though not adolescent) may have ODD during early childhood. In clinical samples, rates of ODD have been reported to be as high as 96 per cent (Frick et al., 1992).

Research has consistently shown that there is a common developmental progression from ODD to CD. Youth with ODD begin showing mild oppositional problems early in development, around the ages of 3 and 4 years. These disruptive behaviours tend to increase in rate and severity over the course of development, gradually progressing into increasing severe types. In one recent study, as many as 80 per cent of boys with childhood onset CD have been shown to have previously diagnosed with ODD; however, it is important to note that a proportion of children with ODD (40 per cent) never progress to more severe CDs (Kimonis and Frick, 2010).

DSM-IV-TR groups them under the more general rubric of *disruptive behaviour disorders* just as the empirical approach classifies both as *externalizing disorders*. In fact, some have argued that the overlap is so extensive that ODD should be regarded as a mild form of CD rather than being a psychopathology in its own right.

However, there are a number of reasons why ODD is regarded as a separate disturbance from CD. (For a detailed discussion see Hinshaw and Lee, 2003.) As we have seen, DSM-IV-TR differentiates the disorders on the basis that children with ODD do not violate the basic rights of others or major societal norms. Moreover, in ODD the deviant behaviours are more commonly, although not exclusively, limited to parents and the home environment, whereas in CD deviant behaviours frequently involve peers, teachers and others outside the home. While both ODD and CD are related to antisocial behaviour and adverse events in the family, the severity of such problems is less in ODD children (Walker et al., 1991). In general, children with ODD are less disturbed than those with CD.

Developmental data provide additional reasons for regarding ODD as being independent of CD. ODD emerges in the preschool period, whereas CD typically does not appear until middle childhood. While it is true that in the majority of cases CD is preceded by ODD, longitudinal research shows that approximately two-thirds of children do *not* go on to develop CD (Kimomis and Frick, 2010).

There are some data on why certain oppositional children develop the more serious psychopathology of CD while others do not. A high level of *aggression* seems to be the most important determinant of subsequent CD. However, family variables such as parental antisocial behaviour, neglect, lack of parental monitoring and father separation also play a role (Burt et al., 2005). In a data-set of 1420 individuals (56 per cent male) covering ages 9–21 years, ODD was a significant predictor of later CD in boys but not girls. Key differences have also been identified in their outcomes such that CD largely was found to predict behavioural outcomes, whereas ODD was found to be a stronger predictor of emotional disorders in early adult life.

ODD and Attention Deficit Hyperactivity Disorder

There is considerable overlap between ODD and attention deficit hyperactivity disorder (ADHD), with comorbidity rates of 30–90 per cent. ADHD increases the risk of early onset of ODD and, in children with *both* ADHD and CD, there is an increase in the severity of ODD symptoms (Gadow and Nolan, 2002).

Oppositional defiant disorder is thought to mimic ADHD symptoms (Furman, 2008). For example, studies linking ADHD and ODD symptoms provide ample evidence of relations between impulsivity (a deficit in behavioural inhibition) and externalizing behaviours (oppositionality, aggressions) in childhood. Impulsivity is recognized as the underlying core behavioural deficit of ADHD (Barkley, 2006) and often co-occurs with ODD (Sprafkin et al., 2011). Importantly, ADHD combined subtype (hyperactivity-impulsivity and inattentive components) are more likely to meet diagnostic criteria for ODD than children with ADHD or those diagnosed with predominantly inattentive type.

Thus, ADHD appears to potentiate ODD. This ODD–ADHD comorbidity is also associated with numerous maladaptive correlates and outcomes, including higher levels of aggression, attention problems, internalizing behaviours, peer and family difficulties, and academic problems. Factors that decrease the association between child impulsivity and ODD symptoms could act as protectors against the emergence of ODD symptoms.

ODD and Learning Disabilities

Oppositional defiant disorder *by itself* is not associated with learning disabilities (LD). When such a relationship is found, it is due to the presence of ADHD as a comorbid disturbance (Hinshaw and Lee, 2003).

ODD and Internalizing Disorders

Interestingly, ODD also is prevalent in children diagnosed with anxiety and depression (Hinshaw and Anderson, 1996). One explanation for this may lie in the irritability and bad temper that accompany internalizing disorders, which lead children to respond in a negativistic manner to their parents. However, clinical observations suggest that anxious children often attempt to bind their anxiety by controlling the world around them (Lieberman, 1992). Therefore oppositional behaviour may be the child's method of trying to make the interpersonal world less intrusive and unpredictable. Follow-up of a sample of children into early adulthood showed that ODD in adolescence was independently associated with increased risks of anxiety and depression in early adult life (Copeland et al., 2009).

Etiology

Oppositional defiant disorder remains a controversial diagnosis (Moffitt et al., 2008). Many critics argue that ODD resembles normal 'rebellious' behaviour and that it might be more useful to treat oppositional as a temperamental dimension rather than as a categorical defined disorder (Loeber et al., 2009a). There is certainly general agreement that ODD is on a continuum with normal behaviour. In fact, normal children fail to comply with parental commands about one-third of the time (Webster-Stratton and Herbert, 1994). Thus, normal problem behaviours in toddlers include disobedience, defiance, tantrums and negative mood. (See Chapter 1.) The terrible twos are aptly named except that the behaviours can also extend into the preschool period. Psychopathology enters the picture when there is an increase in *frequency* and *intensity* of such behaviours or when they *persist* into later periods (Gabel, 1997).

The Individual Context

Oppositionality in Normal Development

If psychopathology can be understood as normal development gone awry, then it is reasonable to look to studies of normal development for clues to answering the etiological question of why it becomes diverted. The relevant literature concerns negativism, or non-compliant behaviour.

In their longitudinal study of toddlers and preschoolers, Kuczynski and Kochanska (1990) conceptualize negativistic behaviour in terms of *social strategies*. Direct defiance is the least skilful strategy because of its openness and aversiveness to parents. Passive non-compliance is also considered unskilful but not so aversive to parents. Negotiation, which attempts to persuade parents to modify their demands, is relatively indirect and non-aversive, so it is the most skilful. The investigators found that direct defiance and passive non-compliance decreased with age, while negotiation increased, reflecting a more active and adroit way of expressing resistance to parental requests. Of particular interest to us is the finding that only the least skilful forms of resistance were predictive of externalizing problem behaviours at 5 years of age.

Kuczynski and Kochanska also make a point concerning compliance that clinical child psychologists should note. Although non-compliance may be problematic, *excessive compliance* is of concern as well. A rigid and compulsive form of compliance develops among infants of abusive parents, with fear of the parent's reaction inhibiting the child from normal expressions of self-will and spontaneity. In their study, these investigators found that overly compliant young children were at risk for the development of internalizing problems.

Oppositionality in Clinical Populations

Recently there has been some interest in studying the association between ODD and attachment. DeKlyen (1996) found more *insecure attachment* in a group of 25 preschool boys referred for disruptive behaviour disorder than in normal controls. Speltz and co-workers (1995) also found that attachment classification discriminated clinically referred ODD preschoolers from normal controls better than measures of maternal behaviour such as the number of commands and criticisms. In particular, prospective studies show that *avoidant* attachment in infancy is linked to oppositional-defiant behaviour in the preschool years (Nordahl et al., 2010). The authors of all these studies are careful to point out that attachment should not be regarded as the sole cause of ODD but rather as a factor that interacts with other risk variables.

There is also some evidence that a *difficult temperament* predicts ODD in adolescence (Singh and Waldmen, 2010). However, as is the case with attachment, temperament should be regarded as one of many risk factors producing ODD.

The Family Context

The family environment has often been identified as particularly important to the development of ODD. Evidence suggests that exposure to parental *maladaptive* behaviour, including parental alcoholism, illicit drug use and criminality, is related to increased risk of ODD (Marmorstein et al., 2009). *Family stability* is also a common risk factor during childhood with children living in less stable family environment at particular risk for developing disruptive behaviours (Afifi et al., 2009).

Research on the characteristics of parents of ODD children describes them as more negative towards, and more critical of, their children than are mothers of other children. They also engage in more threatening, angry and nagging behaviours. Both parents give their children significantly more commands and instructions while not allowing enough time for the child to comply. (See Webster-Stratton and Hancock, 1998, for a summary of the research.) As is always true of interactional studies, there is the 'chicken and egg' problem of the direction of causation. Parents either may be generating or reacting to their children's behaviour, and only additional studies can help distinguish the direction of effects.

Looking at more specific parental behaviours, McMahon and Frick (2005) found that noncompliant behaviour is maintained by parental attention. Attention serves as a reinforcer even when it is negative and takes the form of anger and punitiveness. In addition, McMahon and Forehand (2003) discovered the types of parental commands that are most apt to elicit non-compliance. The so-called *alpha commands* are specific and clear and are less likely to produce non-compliance. They include commands that have a clear, explicitly stated objective: for example, 'Eat your peas or there will be no dessert' or 'You may finish watching this programme, but then the TV goes off'. The so-called *beta commands* are vague and interrupted. They are difficult or impossible to obey, either because of their ambiguity or because the parent issues a new command before the child has a chance to comply: 'Do you think that you might want to do something not so noisy – or not?' or 'Quit picking on your .... Now help Mommy find her pocketbook'. Beta commands are more characteristic of parents of non-compliant children than are alpha commands.

Parents' *attributions* for their children's non-compliance also influence their parenting behaviour and, subsequently, the likelihood that the child will respond positively to discipline. Parents who view their children's misbehaviour as intentional and malicious – or view themselves as helpless and incompetent to manage it – respond more harshly to their children and thus engender more misbehaviour (Geller and Johnston, 1995).

New research looking at multiple risk factors suggests that ODD is a product of interactions among a number of factors in both the intra-personal and family contexts, including child temperament as well as poor attachment, family conflict and low SES (Campbell, 2006). But again, we are left with the question of how these general risk factors *specifically* result in the ODD diagnosis. We turn next to a model that attempts to address this question.

Integrative Developmental Model

In a thoughtful review paper, Greene and Doyle (1999) propose that there are multiple developmental pathways to ODD. While the social learning model focuses on faulty parenting practices as the major determinant, children bring to the interaction their own characteristics that can contribute to the problem. The proof is in the pudding, the authors suggest, when one considers the limited effectiveness of treatments that focus only on changing the parents' behaviour. Therefore, their model incorporates both child characteristics and

parent–child transactions that may increase the risk of oppositional defiant behaviour.

Child Characteristics that Contribute to ODD

Poor Self-Regulation

Children with problem behaviour are generally found to be impulsive and reactive and to have poor control over their emotions and behaviour. This poor self-regulation underlies both ADHD and ODD and may in fact account for the comorbidity between them. As Greene and Doyle point out, compliance is a skill that is acquired over the course of development. In order for the child to be able to delay gratifying his or her own goals in response to a caregiver's goals or standards, the child needs the capacity to adapt, internalize, self-regulate and modulate his or her emotions. Deficits in self-regulation, therefore, might lead to ODD. Poor self-regulation occurs frequently in the face of cues for rewards and punishment, with individuals with ODD focusing readily on rewards, whilst ignoring signals of punishment. Experimental findings with a task in which the rate of winning decreased and the rate of reward of losing increased, confirmed that children with ODD keep responding for reward, irrespective of increasing punishment (Matthys et al., 2004). Psycho-physiological findings also show this pattern, with individuals with ODD displaying a reduced cardiac response to aversive outcomes and an increased cardiac response to reward (Luman et al., 2010). If children with ODD focus on reward whilst being less sensitive to (infrequent) penalty, then using large and infrequent punishments to shape children with ODD behaviour would appear to be ineffective.

Executive Functions

Another deficit that ADHD and ODD may share is in the area of executive functions: cognitive skills that are necessary for planning, monitoring and correcting one's own performance; adapting and shifting set; and flexible problem solving. Children who are lacking in these capacities may have difficulty, for example, reflecting on previous experiences and anticipating the likely consequences of further non-compliance, or shifting quickly from one mindset to another as is required by the parental command, 'Turn off that video game and get ready for bed'. Indeed, children with these kinds of deficits may appear intentionally defiant to parents, when the actual culprit is their inability to process information and choose a response pattern in an organized, adaptive manner.

Mood and Anxiety Disorders

As noted previously, ODD is comorbid with depression as well as some anxiety disorders, particularly obsessive compulsiveness (Garland and Weiss, 1996). The underlying mechanism here again may be poor emotion regulation. Children who are not able to modulate their reactions to affectively charged situations are likely to become overaroused and respond with emotion rather than reason in what are termed 'affective storms'. Thus, irritability, mood instability, anxiety and obsessiveness can compromise the child's capacity to respond adaptively to adult commands.

Language Processing Problems

Language is crucial to development in many ways, including the emergence of self-regulation. The toddler's language skills enable him or her to label, categorize and communicate needs, and to identify appropriate behavioural responses. Language also allows children to receive feedback about the behaviours they choose and to reflect and consider their actions. Oppositional behaviour may ensue when a child with language problems has difficulty labelling and communicating about feelings, engaging in co-operative give-and-take interactions, and developing a flexible repertoire of problem-solving skills.

Cognitive Distortions

Children with poor emotion regulation skills are vulnerable to interpreting social information in biased, inaccurate, incomplete or distorted ways that are coloured by the affect they are experiencing

in the moment. This sets the stage for the child's viewing the parent's limit-setting in a hostile light – and responding in kind.

Transactional Patterns in ODD

Children's self-control, emotion regulation and cognitive capacities do not develop in a vacuum; parents are pivotal to the acquisition of these skills. Parents model and teach, but also may elicit compliant or non-compliant behaviour from children by the tone of their commands and the harshness of their responses to child disobedience. The quality of parent–child transactions is particularly crucial during the stage of development when oppositional behaviour begins to emerge. As Greene and Doyle state, 'It is at this point in development where two important forces – a child's capacity for compliance and adults' expectations for compliance – are thought to intersect' (1999, p. 137). In sum, if the parent responds to the child in a way that exacerbates the child's frustration and cognitive and emotional difficulties, a maladaptive transactional pattern will ensue. Quoting DSM-IV-TR, there may develop 'a vicious cycle in which the parent and child bring out the worst in each other' (p. 100).

Therefore, in the transactional approach, no one characteristic of the child or parent accounts for ODD. Rather, the problem arises out of what the authors term *parent–child incompatibility*, akin to the concept of goodness of fit we discussed in Chapter 2. For example, if a boy whose language-processing problems interfere with his ability to express frustration in a socially appropriate manner were paired with a parent who lacked understanding and attempted to motivate the child by offering rewards for behaviours of which the boy was incapable, frustration and oppositionality might develop. Or, to take another example, if a parent with poor emotion regulation skills were paired with a child with similar temperamental deficits, their incompatibility might also increase the risk of ODD.

Developmental Course

The onset of ODD is usually gradual, emerging over the first eight years of life. There is evidence that ODD declines in frequency during middle childhood but increases again in the adolescent period (Lahey et al., 2000). Prognostically, ODD is one of the most stable diagnoses and one with the poorest rate of recovery. And, as we have seen, ODD is associated with the development of other disorders, notably conduct disorder, attention deficit hyperactivity disorder and learning disorders. Early onset (before age 8) and comorbidity predict slow speed of recovery of ODD (Nock et al., 2007). See Box 6.3 for a case study.

Intervention

Behavioural strategies for the treatment of ODD are the most widely used and researched. For example, McMahon and Forehand (2003) focus first on improving the quality of the relationship between parent and child by helping parents to attend to children's behaviour and interact with them in a warm, non-coercive manner. They then teach parents specific behavioural skills, such as to replace their vague, interrupted beta commands with firm, specific alpha commands; to shift from punishing non-compliant behaviour to rewarding compliance with praise, approval and positive physical attention; and to employ a 'time-out' procedure of isolating the child for a brief period after non-compliance. It is also helpful to teach parents the general principles of operant conditioning rather than providing them solely with techniques for handling specific problems. Modification of one behaviour tends to affect other behaviours within the home; for example, one girl who was reinforced for picking up her toys spontaneously began to keep her clothes tidy. Moreover, there is evidence that the compliance of untreated siblings undergoes the same positive change, since the parents alter their behaviour to them as well.

Box 6.3 Case Study in Oppositional Defiant Disorder: Joseph 8 Years

'I hate this place, no one tells me what to do any more,' 8-year-old Joseph screams at his teacher, 'You always tell me I am naughty but I ain't, I only get in trouble because of stupid you. It's not my fault that I am sat next to Amy, she makes me do stupid things. I hate you all!' He heads for the door knocking books off shelves, and tears down some of his peers' work off the wall before eventually kicking the classroom door open to mount his escape. He eventually turns around and looks back at the teacher, willing a final standoff between him and the teacher.

Joseph is notorious for getting in trouble and has a school record with extreme violent outbursts over the duration of a year. This particular episode erupted simply following a teacher's request for him to be quiet in class. This demonstrates his overreaction to small events, violent outbursts and extreme frustration as well as his willingness to disobey authority. Joseph has suspected ODD.

Case questions: What factors need to be taken into consideration before a diagnosis of ODD is pursued? Remember both genetic and environmental factors may play a part in his diagnosis.

Behavioural characteristics Joseph displays and their duration. Pattern of ODD needs to persist for no less than 6 months and he would need to show at least four out of the following: (1) often loses temper; (2) defies or refuses to comply with adult's rules; (3) actively defies rules; (4) deliberately annoys people; (5) blames others for his mistakes; (6) easily annoyed by others; (7) angry and resentful; (8) is often spiteful or vindictive (APA, 2000, p. 70).

It is important to establish Joseph's family history. Children who are at high risk from ODD are likely to have parents with some type of conduct disorder, or family members who might be suffering severe depression. Other factors that may increase the chances of ODD include, although not an exhaustive list, early maternal rejection, separation from parents without adequate alternative caregiver, family neglect, abuse or violence, parental marital discord or poverty.

Source: Adapted from Timothy Wagner, *Handout for Professionals.*

Suggestions also are made for including teachers in the behavioural programme in order to generalize successes from home to school. Finally, there is evidence that gains made in middle childhood are sustained in adolescence.

Webster-Stratton (1998) has adapted these methods and introduced the innovation of including videotapes that provide parents with models of both adaptive and maladaptive techniques. The empirical support for this approach is strong and has been established in studies of ethnically diverse, low SES populations. We will describe her intervention in more detail in Chapter 17.

Over a period of two decades, the behavioural approach has proven effective, although, as Greene and Doyle (1999) point out, not for all children. Instead, Greene and Doyle suggest that we move to designing treatments that are tailored toward the *specific* mechanisms that are driving oppositional behaviour in each individual child and family who present to the consulting room.

Comprised sensitivity to early reinforcement information in the orbitofrontal cortex and caudate and to reward outcome information in the orbitofrontal cortex suggest that integrated functioning of the amydala, caudate and orbitofrontal cortex may be disrupted. This not only provides a functional neural basis for why such youths are more likely to repeat disadvantageous decisions but also raised new treatment possibilities, as pharmacological modulations of serotonin and dopamine can affect this form of learning (Finger et al., 2011).

The disorders of attachment and oppositionality we have just discussed arise from normal developmental challenges that children face in the period from infancy through preschool. Among the other developmental tasks the child must accomplish in this period, those that concern bodily functions are particularly important – not only to the child but to the caregiver. We turn to these next.

Enuresis

While the requirements for self-control affect many aspects of the toddler's life, they are keenly felt when they intrude upon bodily functions. The young child lives close to his or her body, and eating and elimination hold special pleasures and special fascinations. The socializing parents' demands can, therefore, trigger some of the most intense conflicts of early childhood. We will be exploring a major disturbance in regulating elimination – namely, enuresis.

Definition and Characteristics
Definition
Enuresis has a long history: it was mentioned in Egyptian medical texts as early as 1550 BC (Thompson and Rey, 1995). In current usage *enuresis* is defined as repeated involuntary or intentional discharge of urine into bed or clothes beyond the expected age for controlling urination. According to DSM-IV-TR, this age is 5 years or a comparable developmental level. The behaviour is clinically significant if it occurs twice a week for at least three consecutive months. However, it may also be regarded as significant if there is considerable distress or impairment in important areas of functioning. Another qualification is that enuresis is not due to a general medical condition or to drugs that affect urination. (See Table 6.5.)

There are three different types of enuresis. In *nocturnal* enuresis passing urine occurs only during nighttime sleep. In *diurnal* enuresis urine is passed during waking hours. In *mixed*, or nocturnal and diurnal enuresis, urine is passed during both waking and sleeping hours. These three distinctions are not always made in the research literature, however, resulting in a certain ambiguity in the findings.

There is another important classification. *Primary enuresis* refers to children who have never been successfully trained to control their urination. *Secondary enuresis* refers to children who have been successfully trained but revert back to wetting after a six-month or greater period of dryness – for example, in response to a stressful situation in the family. In our developmental terminology, primary enuresis represents a *fixation*, whereas secondary enuresis represents a *regression*.

TABLE 6.5 DSM-IV-TR Criteria for Enuresis

A. Repeated voiding of urine into bed or clothes (whether involuntary or intentional)

B. The behavior is clinically significant as manifested by either a frequency of twice a week for at least 3 consecutive months or the presence of clinically significant distress or impairment in social, academic (occupational), or other important areas of functioning

C. Chronological age is at least 5 years (or equivalent developmental level)

D. The behavior is not due exclusively to the direct physiological effect of a substance (e.g., diuretic) or a general medical condition (e.g., diabetes, spina bifida, a seizure disorder)

Specify Type:

Nocturnal Only: passage of urine only during nighttime sleep
Diurnal Only: passage of urine during waking hours
Nocturnal and Diurnal: a combination of the two subtypes above

Source: Reprinted with permission from the *Diagnostic and Statistical Manual of Mental Disorders*, Fourth Edition Text Revision. Copyright 2000 by the American Psychiatric Association.

Prevalence and Characteristics

In the USA, it is thought that approximately 15 to 20 per cent of 5-year-old children will develop symptoms of enuresis. Fischel and Liebert (2000) summarize prevalence rates across several studies and find that the prevalence of enuresis changes significantly with *age*. It is found in 33 per cent of 5-year-olds, 25 per cent of 7-year-olds, 15 per cent of 9-year-olds, 8 per cent of 11-year-olds, 4 per cent of 13-year-olds and 3 per cent of 15- to 17-year-olds. Of these children, 75 per cent showed only nocturnal enuresis; diurnal enuresis is much less common. However, the prevalence estimates of enuresis are highly variable worldwide with a range of 3.8 per cent to 24 per cent. There is a *gender difference*: overall, it is approximately twice as common in boys as in girls (Tai et al., 2007). However, this gender difference may change with age. Between ages 4 and 6 years the number of boys and girls with enuresis is about equal. However, the ratio changes so that by 11 years of age there are twice as many boys as girls. There is evidence that the incidence of enuresis varies with *social class*; more prevalent among those who are socio-economically disadvantaged (Hazza and Tarawneh, 2002) and of black race (Shreeram et al., 2009), and is also more common in those with a family history of enuresis (Bayoumi et al., 2006).

The wide differences found in prevalence rates may be accounted for primarily by the differences in the definitions of enuresis in the International Classification of Diseases (ICD-10) and the DSM-IV. The ICD-10 requires a bed-wetting frequency of twice per month in the past three months for children aged 5 and 6 years and once per month in the past three months for children aged 7 years or older than 7 years, whereas the DSM-IV requires a bed-wetting frequency of twice per week for three consecutive months or the presence of clinically significant distress or impairments. Higher prevalence rates have been shown when using the ICD-10 criteria (Srinath et al., 2005).

Comorbidity

Attention problems and hyperactivity co-occur frequently with enuresis (Shreeram et al., 2009). A recent study has estimated as many as 30 per cent of children with ADHD suffer an enuretic event (Graham and Levy, 2009). Children with enuresis also are more likely to display behaviour problems such as misconduct, anxiety, immaturity and underachievement in school. Enuresis also has been implicated in studies of encopresis (faecal soiling), learning disabilities and developmental delays in intelligence (Biederman et al., 1995).

Developmental Course

Both noctural and diurnal enuresis appear to be self-limiting; that is, children tend to outgrow them even without treatment. There is some evidence that remission rates for girls may be higher than those for boys: 71 per cent of girls and 44 per cent of boys between the ages of 4 and 6 spontaneously stop wetting themselves (Harbeck-Weber and Peterson, 1996). Since there are also effective treatments, as we shall see, the prognosis is quite favourable for enuresis.

Etiology

The Biological Context

Enuresis can be caused by a number of purely medical problems such as anomalies of innervation of the bladder that result in an inability to empty it completely, illnesses such as diabetes insipidus or urinary tract infections, and drugs such as diuretics. The clinical child psychologist should make sure that these factors have been ruled out by a medical examination.

There are two leading contenders in biologically focused theories of etiology. The first involves deficiencies in the night-time secretion of antidiruetic hormone, which normally reduces the amount of urine produced at night. However, evidence in support of this hypothesis is questionable, since not all enuretic children produce excessive urine, and not all children who produce excessive urine are enuretic (Ondersma and Walker, 1998). The other leading theory involves the absence of learned muscle responses that inhibit urine flow during sleep (Mellon and Stern, 1998). Children who have nocturnal enureris have been shown to have smaller than normal functional bladder capacities at night, and urodynamic studies have demonstrated high bladder instability at night compared with during the day (Graham and Levy, 2009).

There appears to also be a strong *genetic* component to enuresis. For example, when both parents have a childhood history of enuresis, the risk of the child's developing the disorder is estimated to be 80 per cent. In contrast, if one parent had the disorder, the risk for the child is 45 per cent, whereas if neither parent were enuretic, the child's risk is only 15 per cent (Fischel and Liebert, 2000). Furthermore, there is a 68 per cent concordance rate for monozygotic twins and only a 36 per cent concordance rate for dizygotic twins (Harbeck-Weber and Peterson, 1996).

The Individual Context
Developmental Status

Although we might tend to take toilet-training for granted, it is actually quite a developmental accomplishment. Communication skills are needed to convey to the parents that the toilet is needed, social and emotional development must have advanced to the point that the child recognizes the importance of adhering to social expectations, fine and gross motor skills are needed to accomplish the physical tasks involved, and cognitive skills are needed to engage in planning and self-control. Therefore, a child whose overall development is delayed in any of these areas may be more vulnerable to enuresis (Fritz and Rockney 2004). Research also indicated that children with nocturnal enuresis are more difficult to waken from sleep (Neveus, 2003), which suggests a possible correlation between sleep arousal and nocturnal enuresis.

Psychosocial Stress

For the majority of children, primary enuresis is not caused by psychological factors. Instead, the literature indicates that children with enuresis are generally well adjusted (Friman, 2008). On the one hand for a minority of children, especially those who have secondary enuresis, it may be a response to stress such as parental divorce, neglect, abuse or other stressors (Fritz and Rockney, 2004). On the other hand, studies have failed to find a relation between enuresis and a variety of psychosocial factors such as economic background, family intactness and the quality of the family environment (Biederman et al., 1995).

An Integrative Developmental Study

A rare longitudinal study was conducted by Kaffman and Elizur (1977), set in a kibbutz in

Israel. In the kibbutz, four to six infants are cared for by a trained caretaker, or *metapelet* (plural, *metaplot*), in a communal children's house. Each child spends four hours daily with his or her parents. Generally speaking, the children's development and the parent–child relationships are similar to those in traditional Western families. Toilet training in particular is non-punitive and child centred.

Kaffman and Elizur assessed 153 children on a number of physiological, interpersonal and intrapersonal variables from infancy to 8 years of age. The investigators regarded enuresis as beginning at 4 rather than 5 years of age. While they found the usual genetic and physiological predisposing factors in the 4-year-olds with enuresis (siblings with enuresis, smaller functional bladder capacity, impaired motor co-ordination), the intra-personal and interpersonal factors are of greater interest.

In the *individual context*, the children with enuresis had a significantly greater number of behaviour symptoms than the non-enuretic ones, indicating that they were more disturbed. Within this general context, two high-risk personality patterns could be distinguished. Around 30 per cent of the children were hyperactive, aggressive, negativistic in response to discipline, had low frustration tolerance and resisted adjusting to new situations. One can imagine how difficult it must have been for these children to sit or stand still when being potty trained! A smaller group of children with enuresis were dependent and unassertive, had low achievement and mastery motivation, and masturbated frequently, perhaps to compensate for their lack of realistic pleasures. In contrast, the children who were *not* enuretic were self-reliant, independent and adaptable; and they had a high level of achievement motivation.

In the *family context*, the clearest relation was between parental disinterest and enuresis. In addition, temporary separation from the parents was the only stress related to increased bed-wetting, for the kibbutz children took in stride the stresses of a sibling's birth, hospitalization and, even, war. Interestingly, absence of the *metapelet* produced

no such reaction, suggesting that the parent–child relationship was central. While not statistically significant, a relationship between bed-wetting and the *metapelet*'s behaviour was suggested. Permissiveness, low achievement demands and insecurity on the part of the metapelet tended to be related to enuresis, whereas structured, goal-oriented and directive toilet training in the context of a loving relationship enhanced early bladder control.

The authors draw some general conclusions from the data. For low-risk children the *timing* of toilet training does not matter. In the high-risk group, *delayed* training *increases* the likelihood of enuresis in the motorically active, resistive and aggressive infant. Such an infant is difficult enough to socialize, but the difficulties are compounded during the terrible twos and threes. In the interpersonal realm, a *permissive* attitude, combined with non-involvement or uncertainty, tends to perpetuate bed-wetting, since there is neither sufficient challenge nor sufficient support for the child to take this particular step towards maturity. Such a finding is congruent with studies of normal development that show that a child's competence is maximized when parental affection is combined with challenges and an expectation of achievement. Overall, the children's *personality characteristics* were more highly correlated with enuresis than were interpersonal variables.

In the longitudinal phase of their study, Kaffman and Elizur (1977) found that 50 per cent of the children with enuresis were identified as problem children when they were 6 to 8 years of age, in contrast to 12 per cent in the non-enuretic group. Learning problems and scholastic underachievement were the most frequent symptoms, although some of the children also lacked self-confidence and felt ashamed, guilty or depressed. Unfortunately, Kaffman and Elizur did not analyse their data further to determine *which* children were more apt to develop problems.

These longitudinal findings have important implications for developmental course. Looking at a graph showing the progressive decline of enuresis, one would opt for the prediction that children would outgrow their problem. Such graphs are based on cross-sectional data. But longitudinal studies that include intra-personal and interpersonal variables alert the clinician to the possibility that enuresis in some 4-year-olds may be the first sign of other problems that will persist and perhaps escalate. In short, while most children may 'grow out of' a psychopathology, a substantial subgroup might 'grow into' other problems.

It is essential for the clinical child psychologist to have a good understanding of such longitudinal information when helping parents decide whether or not their child with enuresis is in need of intervention. After all, why subject a child to treatment for a problem that is apt to disappear? Parents should be made aware that the prognosis is not so favourable when the focus shifts from enuresis alone (which is apt to be 'outgrown') to problem behaviour in general, so they can then make an informed decision about treatment by considering both sets of information.

Intervention

Active treatment should usually not be started before the age of 6 years. It is important that any treatment should also consider the beneficial effects of advice on general lifestyle for the families concerned. The family should be talked through what is considered to be normal bladder function as well as the pathogenesis of enuresis. An individualized programme with a series of goals between appointments and monthly follow-ups is also important to sustain motivation.

The *urine alarm* is a behavioural treatment that has a proven record of effectiveness and of superiority to drug treatments. Essentially, this is a classical conditioning paradigm. A device the size of a stick of gum is worn on the child's body and an attached urine-sensitive probe is placed in the child's underwear. This device activates a buzzer when the child wets, awakening the child, who then goes to the bathroom to finish voiding. Eventually, the child begins to awaken in *anticipation* of the alarm, allowing the child to get up before urinating.

(See Fig. 6.1.) Studies have shown the urine alarm to be effective in the majority of cases: 65 to 75 per cent of bedwetters are able to stay dry within 3 months, especially those of the primary enuretic type. However, the alarm takes 12 weeks or more to achieve an effect, and the patience and compliance of parents with the treatment is not always high (Fischel and Liebert, 2000). In addition, there is a significant relapse rate within the year after treatment.

Full Spectrum Home Training (Houts, 2003) combines the urine alarm with three other interventions: cleanliness training, retention control training and over-learning. In *cleanliness training*, the child is provided with a wall chart with which to track 'wet' and 'dry' nights. The child is rewarded with a sticker each time the child wakens in response to the alarm. To ensure that the child fully awakens, parents are encouraged to have the child wash his or her face and hands or work on some arithmetic homework. *Retention control training* involves rewarding the child over a two-week period for holding his or her urine for incrementally large periods of time, up to 45 minutes. Finally, *over-learning* is designed to prevent relapse. After the child has enjoyed 14 consecutive dry nights, he or she is required to drink a gradually increasing amount of water each night before bedtime. For every two nights the child remains dry, the amount of water increases by 2 ounces a night until the maximum amount for that child's age is reached. Again, this procedure continues until 14 consecutive dry nights are achieved. This procedure has reduced relapse rates up to 50 per cent, with 45 per cent of children showing a lasting benefit (Mellon and Stern, 1998).

Some medications have also been suggested to be effective. Desmopressin is considered to be the most effective in children. An estimated 30 per cent of children with enuresis are full responders and 40 per cent have partial response. However, there is a safety concern, as if combined with an excessive fluid intake, despmopressin can cause water intoxication with hyponatremia and convulsions (Glazener and Evans, 2002). Tricylic antidepressant imipramine has

FIGURE 6.1 Anticipatory Awakening.

also frequently been used for enuresis. Approximately 50 per cent of selected children with enuresis respond to the drug and the response rate seems to be the same in children with therapy resistant enuresis (Gepertz and Neveus, 2004). However, due to side effects it is usually only considered as a third-line therapy at tertiary care facilities.

Recently, cognitive techniques have been added to the clinician's repertoire for treating enuresis. For example, children are encouraged to make self-efficacious statements, such as 'When I need to urinate, I will wake up all by myself, urinate in the toilet, and return to my nice, dry bed' (Miller, 1993). Additionally, visualization techniques may be used such as teaching children to picture themselves as if they are on videotape as they sleep, feel their bladders filling and wake to use the bathroom. They may also be encouraged to visualize their bladders as they expand and fill, sending 'beeper signals' to the brain and triggering the brain to wake the child (Butler, 1993).

Finally, recent research using hypnotherapy (Diseth and Vandvik, 2004) and acupuncture (Honjo et al., 2002) as a treatment protocol for enuresis have so far produced encouraging preliminary results.

Our presentation of various psychopathologies will now move from the preschool years to disorders that are risks for the child entering the school years. From regulating bodily functions and the relationship with the caregiver, the focus will shift to the ability to pay attention and to work up to one's academic potential. As we will explore in Chapter 7, both of those can go awry, producing hyperactivity on the one hand and learning disabilities on the other.

The Preschool Period: The Emergence of Attention Deficit Hyperactivity Disorder and Learning Disorders

Chapter Contents

As we have just explored in Chapter 6, when the development of self-regulation goes awry in the toddler period, the child may start down the pathway to an oppositional defiant disorder. However, adaptive development involves not only self-reliance and autonomy but also curiosity and exploration. As Piaget has taught us, even infants are problem solvers, implicitly asking, 'What is that?' and 'How does it work?' until, by the end of the first year, they are actively experimenting with the physical and social environment. In a like manner, toddlers have a remarkable ability to give their undivided attention to the tasks involved in exploration. In the preschool period, children begin to experience the academic setting that channels intrinsic curiosity into the work of learning specific subjects.

Yet this ability to concentrate on school work in the preschool period can be seriously curtailed by hyperactivity and inattention, which prevent children from keeping their minds on the task at hand. When schooling begins in earnest, a different deviation can appear in intelligent, motivated children: the inability to achieve at an appropriate level in one or another academic subject such as reading or arithmetic. In this chapter we will first discuss attention deficit hyperactivity disorder (ADHD) and then consider learning disorders and their consequences for development.

Attention Deficit Hyperactivity Disorder

History

Over the past 50 years the concept of ADHD has developed from the notion of a specific form of brain dysfunction to that of a heterogeneous set of related behaviours (Taylor, 2009). The concept of what is known as 'ADHD' today, grew in climate of professional thought based on a psychoanalysis and social learning 'Minimal brain dysfunction' war. It was not until 1960s and 1970s that a more crystallized and recognizable behavioural syndrome was constructed as researchers began to realize that brain damage (whether minimal or not) could not usually be inferred simply from the behaviour presentation. A quest for more reliable diagnoses led to focusing on a clearer description of key psychological profiles, leading diagnostic schemes such as the DSM and the ICD to define a disorder marked by inattentiveness, overactivity and impulsiveness.

Definition and Characteristics

Definition

We will begin by presenting and discussing the DSM-IV-TR criteria for attention deficit hyperactivity disorder because they capture the restless history of the attempt to define this psychopathology. (See Table 7.1.)

Note that there are three major types of ADHD: one featuring inattention, one focusing on hyperactivity/impulsivity, and one based on a combination of the two. Children with the *inattentive* type are unable to sustain attention at an age-appropriate level. Parents and teachers might complain that the children cannot concentrate, are distractible, go from one activity to another, are disorganized, and are forgetful and prone to daydream. With *hyperactivity*, children are continually 'on the go' as if 'driven by a motor'. This drive to move may be evidenced by their climbing or running about, excessive talking or continually and inappropriately leaving their seats during class. *Impulsivity* is 'acting without thinking'. Children may blurt out answers rather than taking time to think a problem through, they may interrupt or intrude on others by butting into conversations and games, or they may have difficulty waiting for their turn. Many of these behaviours can be found in typically developing young children, and therefore the diagnosis requires that the child demonstrate them at a level

that is significantly age-inappropriate. (See Box 7.1.)

Historically, diagnoses have emphasized the most obvious manifestation of the disturbance, which is hyperactivity. For example, DSM-II (American Psychiatric Association, 1968) labelled the condition 'hyperkinetic reactions of childhood', characterizing it by overactivity, distractibility, restlessness and a short attention span. Subsequent research, particularly that conducted by Virginia Douglas (1983), suggested that attention, rather than motor activity, was the crucial deficit. This research led to the primary diagnosis of attention deficit disorder (ADD) in DSM-III (American Psychiatric Association, 1980), which could be either with or without hyperactivity. Thus, we now have DSM-IV-TR's tripartite diagnosis of ADHD predominantly inattentive type, ADHD predominantly hyperactive-impulsive type, and ADHD combined type, which includes both behaviours.

Importantly in contrast to the DSM, the world health organization (WHO) International Classification of Diseases ICD-10 which is primarily used in Europe, has traditionally used the narrower category of hyperkinetic disorder. While this lists similar operational criteria, diagnosis is dependent on the presence of hyperactive, impulsive and inattentive symptoms. This point will be returned to later in the chapter when discussing prevalence and key differences in the two classifications systems.

Three other features of the DSM-IV classification deserve further comment: (1) the specific times defining age of onset, (2) duration of symptoms, and (3) the importance of setting.

Age of Onset

Age of onset of symptoms is defined as before 7 years in DSM-IV-TR. However, a study of a clinical sample of 380 youths, 4 to 17 years of age, showed that children who met criteria for ADHD before the age of 7 were predominantly the hyperactive-impulsive type. Forty-three per cent of the inattentive type and 18 per cent of the combined type did not

TABLE 7.1 DSM-IV-TR Criteria for Attention Deficit Hyperactivity Disorder

A. Either (1) or (2):

   (1) *Inattention:* Six (or more) of the following symptoms of inattention have persisted for at least 6 months to a degree that is maladaptive and inconsistent with developmental level:

   (a) Often fails to give close attention to details or makes careless mistakes in schoolwork, work, or other activities

   (b) Often has difficulty sustaining attention in tasks or play activities

   (c) Often does not seem to listen when spoken to directly

   (d) Often does not follow through on instructions and fails to finish schoolwork, chores, or duties in the workplace (not due to oppositional behavior or failure to understand instructions)

   (e) Often has difficulty organizing tasks and activities

   (f) Often avoids, dislikes, or is reluctant to engage in tasks that require sustained mental effort (such as schoolwork or homework)

   (g) Often loses things necessary for tasks or activities (e.g., toys, school assignments, pencils, books, or tools)

   (h) Is often easily distracted by extraneous stimuli

   (i) Is often forgetful in daily activities

   (2) *Hyperactivity/Impulsivity:* Six (or more) of the following symptoms of hyperactivity/impulsivity have persisted for at least 6 months to a degree that is maladaptive and inconsistent with developmental level:

   Hyperactivity

   (a) Often fidgets with hands or feet or squirms in seat

   (b) Often leaves seat in classroom or in other situations in which remaining seated is expected

   (c) Often runs about or climbs excessively in situations in which it is inappropriate (in adolescents and adults, may be limited to subjective feelings of restlessness)

   (d) Often has difficulty playing or engaging in leisure activities quietly

   (e) Is often 'on the go' or often acts as if 'driven by a motor'

   (f) Often talks excessively

   Impulsivity

   (g) Often blurts out answers to questions before the questions have been completed

   (h) Often has difficulty awaiting turn

   (i) Often interrupts or intrudes on others (e.g., butts into conversations or games)

B. Some hyperactive-impulsive or inattentive symptoms that caused impairment were present before 7 years

C. Some impairment from the symptoms is present in two or more settings (e.g., at school and at home) Code based on type:

Attention Deficit Hyperactivity Disorder, Combined Type: If both Criteria A1 and A2 are met for the past 6 months

Attention Deficit Hyperactivity Disorder, Predominantly Inattentive Type: If Criterion A1 is met but Criterion A2 is not met for the past 6 months

Attention Deficit Hyperactivity Disorder, Predominantly Hyperactive-Impulsive Type: If Criterion A2 is met but Criterion A1 is not met for the past 6 months

Source: Adapted from DSM-IV-TR. Copyright 2000 by the American Psychiatric Association.

manifest symptoms until after 7 years of age (Applegate et al., 1997). Thus, the age of onset appears to differ with the type of ADHD. The hyperactive-inattentive type emerges in the pre-school years, the combined type emerges in the early primary school years (ages 5 to 8), while the primarily inattentive type emerges later (ages 8 to 12) (Barkley, 2003). Whether these age effects reflect true differences in onset or merely recognition of the disorder is not clear. Certainly hyperactive and impulsive behaviours are more disruptive to the family and the classroom and are therefore more readily identified than the more subtle symptoms of inattentiveness.

Subsequent research has failed to consistently show differences between children with early onset versus late onset of the disorder, although there is some evidence that the earlier the symptoms manifest themselves, the more severe the developmental consequences (McGee et al., 1992).

Box 7.1 Case Study in Attention Deficit Disorder

Ricky S. is a 7-year-old African American boy referred by his school psychologist to an outpatient mental health clinic. At the time of the assessment, Ricky was in second grade. During her initial call to the clinic, Mrs S. stated that her son was 'out of control'. When asked for specifics, she said that Ricky was 'all over the place' and 'constantly getting into trouble'. As a single mother, she felt overwhelmed by his behaviour and was unable to manage him.

As part of the evaluation, Ricky and his mother were interviewed separately by a doctoral intern in clinical psychology. Ricky was interviewed first and presented as polite, reserved and a little socially anxious. He reported having difficulty adjusting to his new school and especially to his new teacher, Mrs Candler, who was always yelling at him and sending notes home to his mother. When asked why the teacher was yelling at him, Ricky said at first that he did not know, but then admitted that it was mostly about not paying attention or following class rules. Ricky said he was often 'on red'; the classroom had a discipline system in which students had to change their name card from green to yellow to orange to red for each infraction of the rules. A red card meant an automatic call home to the child's parents. In the past month alone, Ricky had accumulated five red and seven orange cards.

When asked if he liked school, Ricky shrugged and said that he liked science, especially now when the class was studying the growth of tadpoles. He said he had a few friends but often he had to keep to himself because Mrs. Candler had him spend so much time in a corner of the classroom in order to complete his work. Ricky said he felt bored, sad, tired and angry in the classroom. He felt happiest in the afternoons after school when he would go riding his bicycle for hours. 'Then nobody yells at me and I can go wherever I want.' Ricky denied other emotional or behavioural problems, but did acknowledge that he felt bad about being 'a pain to my mom' and was confused about why he was doing so poorly in school.

A subsequent interview with Mrs S. confirmed most of Ricky's report, with added detail. For example, Mrs S. revealed that Ricky was almost intolerable in the classroom, in that he often threw tantrums or cried when forced to do his work and was even disrespectful to the teacher, which resulted in many of the calls home. At home he was fidgety and disorganized and tended to lose things, and either did not listen to or did not understand some of what was said to him. Mrs S. had already attended four conferences with the teacher at school, including one with the principal and school psychologist. Ricky had recently undergone cognitive and educational testing, which revealed an average level IQ and achievement scores commensurate with his abilities. The teacher wanted to refer Ricky to a classroom for behaviourally and emotionally handicapped children, but Mrs S. opposed this and came to the clinic in order to seek an independent evaluation.

After carrying out a classroom observation, obtaining parent and teacher behavioural ratings, and conducting more detailed neurocognitive testing of Ricky's attentional skills, the intern came to the conclusion that he fit the criteria for a diagnosis of attention deficit hyperactivity disorder. His mother was introduced to the idea of multimodal treatment and, after some hesitation, agreed to give stimulant medication a try. Ricky's teachers also were trained to implement a behaviour modification programme in which they rewarded successively longer periods of time of on-task behaviour by allowing Ricky to participate in an enjoyable activity, including playing a new video game on the classroom computer. Next, attention and self-monitoring were targeted, with rewards given when Ricky made eye contact, listened to Mrs Candler's instructions and repeated them to himself. As he mastered these skills, the goals of treatment shifted to organizational and study skills, such as keeping his desk neat, handing his homework in on time, raising his hand to ask questions and telling his mother what supplies he needed for school. Although Ricky benefited from treatment, showing less disruptive behaviour and increased attention over the next six months, his mother discontinued abruptly, saying that she felt he had improved enough to be maintained only on drug treatment. Telephone contact a year later revealed that Ricky's misbehaviour was still manageable but that his school performance remained mediocre to poor.

Source: Adapted from Kearney, 2009.

The DSM-V looks to be revising the current age-of onset criterion, extending the current requirement that symptoms associated with impairment must be present before the age of 7 years to 12 years (McGough and Barkley, 2004). However, concerns have been raised as to whether this would increase the prevalence of the disorder or even change the clinical profile and risk factors associated with ADHD.

Duration of Symptoms

In regard to duration of symptoms, the DSM-IV-TR requires that the symptoms be present for the duration of a six-month period. This time frame was created to prevent diagnosing ADHD in children whose symptoms simply reflect time-limited situational factors, e.g., psychosocial stress or settling into a new classroom. However, there is evidence that the six-month period required by DSM-IV-TR is too short, particularly for young children. Concern has also been expressed that the six-month time frame may not span successive school years and therefore children could meet full ADHD diagnostic criteria based on symptoms reported by a single teacher. For example, Rabiner et al. (2010) found in three independent samples that children rated by their teachers as highly inattentive in one year group were not considered to demonstrate these problems the following year, even children with a confirmed ADHD diagnosis. The instability in clinically elevated teacher ratings highlights the importance of annual re-evaluations to avoid treating children for problems that may no longer be present. Expanding the six-month symptom duration requirement may help prevent diagnosing with ADHD children whose school attention problems have a good probability of being transient. Research has also shown a 12-month period to be a more appropriate duration of symptoms for preschoolers (Barkley, 2003).

Setting

Although the DSM-IV-TR criteria specify that the symptoms of ADHD must be present in two or more settings, for some children they may be evident only in one, such as the home or at school, while for other children they may be pervasive across environments. For example, a clinical child psychologist, after having read the referral on a hyperactive child, may be braced to deal with the 'holy terror' the mother described, only to find the child to be a model of co-operativeness in the consultation room. Research suggests that the children's ability to sustain attention and control their impulses is more problematic (1) later in the day; (2) when tasks are more complicated and require more organizational skills; (3) when behavioural restraint is required, such as sitting in church or a restaurant; (4) when levels of stimulation are low; (5) when there is a delay in feedback or reward for task completion; (6) in the absence of adult supervision; and (7) when the task requires persistence. Children with ADHD also tend to show fewer behavioural problems when their fathers are at home, perhaps because of the additional structure that fathers' presence provides. Taking all these factors into account, it is no surprise that the classroom is the single most problematic setting for children with ADHD, given that it requires all of the skills and aptitudes that are most challenging for the child with the disorder (Barkley, 2003).

The inconsistency of the child's behaviour from setting to setting also might mislead adults about the wilfulness of the child's inattentiveness and overactivity. For example, because children with ADHD may demonstrate relatively few behavioural problems in unstructured or stimulating settings, such as during the lunch period, free play, playing computer games or during novel events such as field trips, adults may erroneously assume that the children's behaviour is a matter of choice and that ADHD is within their control: 'He can behave when he wants to!'

Prevalence

There is high variability in the rates of ADHD reported worldwide, ranging from as low as 1 per cent to as high as nearly 20 per cent among school-age children (Faraone et al., 2003). Prevalence rates differ between cultures but this may be attributed to cultural norms (Lovecky, 2004) and to the interpretation of symptoms provided by others (Barkley, 2003). There is also evidence of a decline with age, especially for boys. However, it is not clear whether this is a true decline or an artefact of the developmentally insensitive assessment techniques used; for example, the diagnostic criteria might not be as appropriate for adolescents as they are for those in middle childhood (Barkley, 2003). There are also age dependent changes in the presentation of symptoms. For example, hyperactivity and impulsivity become less obvious in adulthood.

It remains a possibility that the apparent increase in number of children diagnosed with ADHD may be attributable to changes in recognition and diagnostic practice rather than a true increase in the disorder. Alternatively it is possible that there is an increase in the number of cases or even in those involving misdiagnosis. During childhood as many as 65 per cent of children with ADHD have one or more comorbid conditions.

Other factors which affect prevalence rates include characteristics of the sample population, methods of diagnosis, and how rigorously diagnostic criteria are applied. Whilst both the DSM-IV and ICD-10 provide similar lists of symptoms they recommend different ways of establishing a diagnosis with the ICD being more stringent in its recommendations. For example, the ICD-10 requires a minimum number of symptoms in all three dimensions (inattention, overactivity and impulsivity). In contrast, the DSM-IV defines only two dimensions (with hyperactivity and impulsivity symptoms included in the same dimension), and a diagnosis can be made if there is a minimum number of symptoms in only one dimension. The ICD-10 requires that all criteria be met in at least two different situational contexts, whereas DSM-IV requires the presence of some impairment in more than one setting. The ICD-10 includes mood, anxiety and developmental disorders as exclusion diagnoses, whereas in the DSM-IV these diagnoses may be classified as comorbid conditions. Therefore, ADHD prevalence rates based on DSM-IV are expected to be higher than those based on ICD-10, which has consistently been

demonstrated by individual studies (Goodman et al., 2005).

While the WHO ICD-10 definition is still used in some countries, mainly in Europe, there is now a general move to using the DSM-IV definition of ADHD, which should make comparison of data between studies much easier in the future.

Gender Differences

Determining the extent of sex differences in ADHD is complicated by referral bias. Since more boys than girls have the comorbid conditions of oppositional defiance and conduct problems, boys are more likely to be referred for an evaluation. For example, the ratio of boys to girls in the clinical population is 6:1 to 9:1, while the ratio ranges between 2:1 to 3:1 in non-clinical samples. Further, the behavioural criteria used to diagnose ADHD appear to be more relevant to boys than girls; consequently, girls must meet a higher threshold in order to qualify for the diagnosis (Barkley, 2003). Therefore, there is some question about the true nature and extent of the gender difference in ADHD.

The public perception that boys are the only ones with ADHD can partly be attributed to the way ADHD is inaccurately portrayed in the media (Barkley et al., 2002). It seems that ADHD in girls often remains undetected and these girls tend to be invisible to many professionals, parents and society in general. Perhaps part of the problem is the difficulty of recognizing girls with hyperactivity (Dray et al., 2006).

Hyperactive-impulsive behaviour problems arise earlier than problems associated with inattention in children diagnosed with ADHD (Barkley, 2003). ADHD hyperactive-impulsive subtype is more easily recognized than the inattentive subtype because of the observable excessive motor symptoms. However, there are differences in how girls and boys exhibit these symptoms. While in severe cases the behaviours in girls are similar to that of boys (Lovecky, 2004), some typical hyperactive-impulsive behaviours in girls are excessive talking, being silly, tomboyish behaviours and displaying emotional reactivity (Quinn, 2005). Teachers may perceive these behaviours as negative or immature rather than oppositional in girls. In addition, adults appear to be more tolerant of girls' hyperactive behaviour than of boys' hyperactive behaviour (Wicks-Nelson and Israel, 1997). It is possible that the lack of knowledge about hyperactive behaviour in females as well as adult attitudes may contribute to the under-identification of girls with ADHD. In support of this, the gender ratio becomes equal during the middle school years (Solanto, 2004), which is when ADHD inattentive subtype is usually diagnosed and thus more girls are included.

In clinical samples, when girls are diagnosed with the disorder they show a similar level of impairment as boys and the same pattern of comorbidity, but even greater deficits in intelligence. However, samples drawn from the community show that girls with ADHD are less likely to have comorbid conduct problems and oppositionality but are as socially and academically impaired as boys (Gershon, 2002).

Socio-economic Status, Ethnicity and Culture

There is some evidence that ADHD is more prevalent in *socio-economically disadvantaged* groups; however, the data are not consistent and the association seems to disappear when comorbid disorders are taken into account (Barkley, 1998). Similarly, while some studies show a disproportionate percentage of ADHD in lower-SES African American and Hispanic children, this may be due to the increase in the comorbid conditions of aggression and conduct problems in these populations rather than to ADHD itself (Szatmari, 1992).

Ethnic differences in the prevalence of ADHD are unclear and a topic of some debate. While disconcertingly few studies have included ethnically diverse samples, one finding of note is that teachers tend to rate African American children higher on symptoms of ADHD than they do European American children (Epstein et al., 1998). In contrast, studies based upon parental reports suggest higher prevalence rates in whites (Pastor and Reuben, 2005). Whether these ratings are related to

actual behavioural differences or biased perceptions is an important question for future research.

Looking *cross-culturally*, we find that discrepant prevalence rates are reported in international studies comparing samples derived from diverse cultures, including the USA, Germany, New Zealand, Canada, Japan, India, China, the Netherlands, Brazil, Columbia, the United Arab Emirates and Ukraine. Rates have been found ranging from a high of 29 per cent in India to a low of 2 per cent in Japan (see Barkley, 2003). Several investigators have suggested that prevalence rates found in Europe were significantly lower than in North America (Timimi and Taylor, 2004). However this has been found to be largely dependent upon case definitions and that no prevalence difference exists when case definitions are the same (L.A. Rohde et al., 2005).

Polanczyk et al., (2007) reviewed literature from the period 1978–2005 and found the overall pooled prevalence rate was 5.29 per cent worldwide. Despite the higher number of studies conducted in North America and Europe, their searches showed similar prevalence rates has been estimated in several different countries. Any variability that existed was found to be explained primarily by the methodological characteristics of studies (i.e. impairment criterion, diagnostic criteria and sources of information). For instance, applying the same methodological procedures and diagnostic criteria, very similar rates of ADHD/HD were found in Russia (Goodman et al., 2005) and Britain (Ford et al., 2003) (1.3 per cent and 1.4 per cent respectively) However, when the diagnosis of ADHD/HD was made in the same geographic location but according to a different methodological criterion (i.e., with or without the requirement of functional impairment) estimates ranged from 3.7 per cent to 8.9 per cent (Canino et al., 2004).

While much of the variability probably is due to differences in the diagnostic criteria, measures and sampling methods used, culturally derived differences in expectations for children's behaviour and the interpretation of symptoms also may contribute to these discrepancies. For example, while Chinese children in Hong Kong were found to have higher rates of hyperactivity than comparison children in the USA and the UK, Chinese parents appeared to be less tolerant of a high activity level in children, and therefore might have been more inclined to rate their children's behaviour as troublesome (Evans and Lee, 1998). In fact, some critics have questioned whether ADHD is anything *but* a culturally derived disorder. (See Fig. 7.1 and Box 7.2.)

Comorbidity and Differential Diagnosis

The clinical picture of ADHD has been somewhat clouded by the high levels of comorbidity found across other childhood disorders. In fact this has led many researchers to question whether it should be considered an identifiable disorder, particularly given that inattention, hyperactivity and impulsive symptoms underlie most medical, emotional and psychosocial conditions in children (Furman, 2008).

For example Posttraumatic stress disorder (PTSD), attachment disorder or even attachment disorganization show similar profiles to ADHD. While the DSM-IV (APA, 1994) rules out a diagnosis of autistic disorder with ADHD, a large percent-

age (65–80 per cent) of children with ADHD portray symptoms in the autistic spectrum (Gillberg et al., 2004). Other disorders frequently observed in patients with ADHD are dyslexia (25–40 per cent), motor co-ordination problems (50 per cent), dyscalculia (10–60 per cent), sleep disorders (25–50 per cent) and enuresis and/or encopresis (30 per cent). However these are just a few of the comorbid conditions. Let us briefly consider those conditions which have been shown to have a more severe impact on both the symptoms of ADHD and in children's day-to-day functioning.

ADHD/Disruptive Behaviour

There is a strong association between ADHD and disruptive behaviour disorders. By 7 years of age, 54 to 67 per cent of clinically referred children with ADHD will also be diagnosed as having oppositional defiant disorder (ODD). From 20 to 50 per cent will develop comorbid conduct disorder (CD) in middle childhood and 44 to 50 per cent will be diagnosed with CD in adolescence. Conduct problems persist into adulthood in as many as 26 per cent of cases (Fischer et al., 2002). Hyperactivity specifically is more likely to be comorbid with CD.

ADHD/CD has an earlier onset than ADHD alone and a higher ratio of boys to girls. In general, the combination results in a more severe and persistent disturbance, adversely affecting a wide array of developmental variables within the children, in their relations with parents, and in their performance at school and in other settings (Kuhne et al., 1997). They are also reported to have poorer prognosis, and show a stronger association with cognitive deficits and low verbal abilities than when they occur alone (Thapar et al., 2007).

ADHD/Anxiety Disorder

There is an overlap between ADHD and anxiety disorders in 10 to 40 per cent of the clinical population (Tannock, 2000). The presence of an anxiety disorder, unlike that of conduct disorder, tends to diminish rather than intensify the negative effects of the disturbance. Specifically, children with comorbid ADHD and anxiety demonstrate lower

FIGURE 7.1

Source: TOLES Copyright © 2000 *The Washington Post*. Reprinted with permission of UNIVERSAL PRESS SYNDICATE. All rights reserved.

Box 7.2 Is ADHD a 'Real' Disorder? The International Consensus Statement

In the history of clinical child psychology, perhaps no disorder has been more challenged and subject to scrutiny than ADHD. Indeed, the very existence of the disorder has been called into question by some who dismiss it as a myth or even a fraud. As the cartoon in Fig. 7.1 suggests, some critics have argued that the mental health establishment is quick to label as psychopathological exuberant and energetic behaviour in children merely because it is inconvenient to the adults around them. Further, it is argued, earlier in human evolution, impulsive thinking, snap judgements and vigilance to every distraction in the environment were adaptive traits for human beings (Hartmann, 1997) – and perhaps still are in our fast-paced world of quick sound bites and instant gratification (Hallowell and Ratey, 1994). Critics have even suggested it to be considered largely an American disorder, perhaps stemming from social and cultural factors which are more common in American society (Timimi and Taylor, 2004). For example, as pointed out by Taylor and Sandberg (1984), data from studies in the late 1970s give a twenty-fold greater prevalence of childhood hyperactivity in North America compared with England.

In response to these challenges, an international consortium of 70 ADHD investigators, spearheaded by Russell Barkley (Barkley et al., 2002), published an international consensus statement to counter media dismissals of the authenticity of the ADHD diagnosis. They argue that it is not merely a social construct, because of the growing links of neurological and genetic components with ADHD. Furthermore, studies from numerous countries consistently indicate that the behaviour pattern of ADHD is worldwide, although the diagnostic label varies (Barkley, 2003) and is dependent on cultural norms (Lovecky, 2004). Excerpts from the statement will best illustrate the urgency of their argument and the heat the controversy has generated:

- 'We cannot overemphasize the point that, as a matter of science, the notion that ADHD does not exist is simply wrong. All of the major medical associations and government health agencies recognize ADHD as a genuine disorder because the scientific evidence indicating it is so overwhelming … As attested to by the numerous scientists signing this document, there is no question among the world's leading clinical researchers that ADHD involves a serious deficiency in a set of psychological abilities and that these deficiencies pose serious harm to most individuals possessing the disorder' (Barkley et al., 2002, p. 89).

- 'ADHD is not a benign disorder. For those it afflicts, ADHD can cause devastating problems … Yet, despite these serious consequences, studies indicate that less than half of those with the disorder are receiving treatment. The media can help substantially to improve these circumstances. It can do so by portraying ADHD and the science about it as accurately and responsibly as possible while not purveying the propaganda of some social critics and fringe doctors whose political agenda would have you and the public believe there is no real disorder here' (p. 90).

- 'To publish stories that ADHD is a fictitious disorder or merely a conflict between today's Huckleberry Finns and their caregivers is tantamount to declaring the earth flat, the laws of gravity debatable, and the periodic table in chemistry a fraud' (p. 90).

- 'ADHD should be depicted in the media as realistically and accurately as it is depicted in science – as a valid disorder having varied and substantial adverse impact on those who suffer from it through no fault of their own or their parents and teachers' (pp. 90–91).

externalizing behaviours and less impulsivity (Pliszka, 2006). In this way, anxiety appears to act as a buffer against ADHD symptoms. The primarily inattentive children are the most likely to have comorbid anxiety disorders (Milich et al., 2001).

While anxiety disorders may be comorbid with ADHD, *differential diagnosis* is important in the case of Posttraumatic stress disorder. (See Chapter 8.) ADHD and PTSD have in common a number of symptoms such as distractibility, inattentiveness and difficulty concentrating. However, the origins, implications and interventions for the symptoms are significantly different for the two disorders. Therefore, it is important to assess for the presence of trauma in the lives of children who are suspected of having ADHD (Kerig et al., 2000).

ADHD/Mood Disorders

ADHD also tends to co-occur with depression, both in its mild and severe forms (Spencer et al., 2000). Both disorders share many characteristics: impulsivity, inattention, hyperactivity, physical energy, and behavioural and emotional lability (behaviour and emotions change frequently). Family histories in both conditions often include mood disorder, and psychostimulant/antidepressants have been shown to reduce symptom logy of both disorders. While the prevalence range differs from study to study, most find rates of comorbidity to be between 20 and 30 per cent. There is also significant overlap between ADHD and bipolar disorder (manic depression), but there is a question about whether this is an artefact of the similarity in the symptoms used to diagnose the two disorders (Kim and Miklowitz, 2002).

ADHD/Learning Disorders (LD)

The majority of clinically referred children with ADHD have difficulty with school performance, which can be detected as early as the preschool years (Barkley et al., 2002). From 19 to 26 per cent of children with ADHD have difficulties severe enough to qualify for a diagnosis of learning disorder, and as many as 80 per cent have learning problems significant enough to cause them to lag two years behind their peers in school (Barkley, 2003). Low academic achievement seems to be a natural consequence of children with the inattentive type of ADHD because of the difficulty in sustaining attention on tasks, distractibility, failure to follow through on instructions and problems with organization. There is also a small but significant relation between lower IQ and the hyperactive-impulsive type of ADHD, which in turn plays a role in lower academic achievement.

Rapport et al. (1999) proposed two pathways by which ADHD might be linked to academic underachievement. In one pathway, ADHD symptoms increase the risk of conduct problems in the classroom that lead to academic problems. In the other pathway, cognitive deficits associated with ADHD, including poor attention, lower general intelligence and deficits in executive function, directly affect academic achievement.

Associated Developmental Problems

Frequently, children with ADHD demonstrate problems in a wide number of areas of development. For example, they often have difficulties with fine and gross motor co-ordination, non-verbal reasoning, executive functions such as planning and organization, verbal fluency and emotion regulation. They also often evidence social problems and present teachers, parents and peers with a difficult interactional style characterized by intrusiveness, demandingness, negativism and excessive emotionality (Barkley, 2003). While not disorders in and of themselves, these associated characteristics increase the risk for negative transactions, maladaptation and the development of comorbid psychopathology.

So far we have considered what ADHD is and outlined some of the key characteristics as well as some of the reasons why many people question the diagnosis of ADHD. So assuming ADHD is a psychopathological condition in its own right, what are the likely causes and how does it develop?

Etiology
The Biological Context
Unsupported Hypotheses

We will note here a number of biological hypotheses that were once popular but have failed to stand up under the scrutiny of objective studies.

An influential etiological hypothesis around 50 years ago was that ADHD was due to *brain damage*. This is understandable given that attention problems are a frequent consequence of traumatic brain injury (see Chapter 13). However, subsequent research using more advanced technology for exploring the brain showed that fewer than 5 per cent of the children with ADHD have suffered neurological injury or seizure disorders, and therefore brain injury is not implicated in most of the children with the disorder (Barkley, 1990).

Some studies have targeted *diet* and *neurotoxins* as causes of ADHD. Sugar and food additives such as artificial colouring have been regarded as the culprits by some researchers, and special diets have been devised as treatment. However, when randomized blind trials have been carried out, the conclusion on the whole is that additives in food are not a major influence on most symptoms of ADHD (Conners, 1980), but that they do appear to have a small effect in increasing hyperactive behaviour in the population (Bateman et al., 2004).

Elevated blood lead levels have been implicated as causing ADHD, but studies relating lead poisoning to the symptoms of ADHD have yielded conflicting results. While it is clear that lead blood level is not a primary etiological agent for ADHD, there is a small but significant relation between the two; for example, one estimate is that lead poisoning accounts for approximately 4 per cent of the variance in ADHD symptoms (Fergusson et al., 1988).

Genetic Factors

There is compelling evidence that heredity plays a major role in causing ADHD. Twenty per cent of parents of children with ADHD will have ADHD themselves (Faraone et al., 2000). Results from studies of twins provide the most convincing evidence (Greven et al., 2011). In such studies the heritability for symptoms ranges from .75 to .97, meaning that approximately 75 to 97 per cent of the observed population is due to genetic variability (Levy and Hay, 2001). For example, Levy and colleagues (1997), using a cohort of 1938 families with twins and non-twin siblings ages 4 to 12, found a heritability quotient of .75 to .91. The finding was robust, holding across familial relations (i.e., between twins, between siblings, and between twins and other siblings) as well as across definitions of ADHD. Estimates of the contribution of non-shared environmental (nongenetic) factors is around .53.

Twin and adoption studies indicate that the familiarity of ADHD symptoms results from genetic factors rather than shared environmental risks, providing a further rationale for considering ADHD as a lifelong condition (Faraone et al., 2001).

Neuropsychological Factors

A host of characteristics of ADHD implicate impairment within the brain: the early onset and persistence of symptoms, the dramatic improvement with medication, deficient performance on neuropsychological tests such as working memory and motor co-ordination, and the genetic risks just described. Data from direct examination of the brain have yielded suggestive findings. For example, there is increasing agreement on the role of prefrontal-striatal-thalamocortical circuit in attention deficit hyperactivity disorder (ADHD), with a preponderance of evidence suggesting that the right-sided circuit is primary, at least at the level of the basal ganglia (Filipek, 1999).

Studies using EEGs have found a consistent pattern of increased slow-wave activity in the frontal lobes, suggesting underarousal and underreactivity in children with ADHD. (Here we follow Barkley, 2003.) Further, stimulant medication directly corrects these abnormalities.

Investigations of cerebral blood flow using single-photon emission computed tomography (SPECT) show decreased blood flow to the prefrontal regions, particularly the right frontal area, as well as to pathways connecting these areas to the limbic system, particularly an area known as the caudate nucleus, and the cerebellum. The frontal and frontal-limbic areas are of special interest because one of their functions is the inhibition of motor responses. The prefrontal lobes also are suspected to be involved in ADHD because this is the area of the brain that is primarily involved with the executive functions of planning, organization, self-regulation and impulse control that are so lacking in the child with ADHD. The degree of blood flow in the right frontal area can be directly correlated with the severity of the disorder, just as that in the cerebellum is related to motor problems in children with ADHD (Gustafsson et al., 2000).

Magnetic resonance imaging (MRI) techniques have revealed that children with ADHD have a smaller splenium, which is the posterior portion of the corpus callosum (the structure connecting the two hemispheres of the brain). In addition, studies have also found a smaller left caudate nucleus, consistent with the blood flow studies described earlier. This latter finding is particularly interesting given that it represents a reversal of the usual asymmetry of the caudate, in which the right side is generally smaller.

It has even been suggested that the ADHD brain is wired differently (Konrad and Eickhoff, 2010). For example it has been proposed that ADHD may be dysfunction of or disconnection between brain regions that support the 'default network'. The default network is a network of brain regions that are active when the individual is not focused on the outside world and the brain is at wakeful rest. Such misconfiguration of the default-mode network (DMN) may result in a reduced capability for modulation of its activity, which in turn may interfere with task relevant attentional networks. With respect to the involvement of the DMN in ADHD pathophysiology, two perspectives have been developed. On one hand, different models conceptualize ADHD as a disorder driven by either a hyper (Tian et al., 2006) or a hypoconnectivity of the DMN (Castellanos et al., 2008). On the other hand, it has been suggested that DMN activity is undisturbed at rest but fails to be attenuated during the transition from rest to task in ADHD patients. This persistent DMN activity then intrudes into and interferes with the neuronal circuits underlying active task performance (i.e., the default-mode interference hypothesis; Sonuga-Barke and Castellanos, 2007).

Advances in methodology have allowed us a peek into the brain at work. Studies using functional MRI (fMRI) show that, when asked to do tasks requiring attention and inhibition, children with ADHD show abnormal patterns of activation in the right prefrontal region, the basal ganglia (that includes the striatum), and the cerebellum. Speculatively, the observed gender differences in incidence, age of onset and symptom profile of ADHD could arise from the complex interactions between gender-specific differences in brain development and the child's environment. For example, the lower incidence of attention deficit hyperactivity disorder (ADHD) in girls might be related to them having a relatively larger caudate nucleus than boys (Santosh, 2000).

There also has been interest in investigating central nervous system neurotransmitters, particularly dopamine and norepinephrine, which are thought to be important to the functioning of the frontal-limbic area of the brain (Antshel et al., 2011). (See Box 7.3.)

The Developmental Dimension

Seidman and associates (1997), who conducted one of the few studies yielding developmental data, were concerned with changes in neuropsychological functioning as assessed by tests of attention and executive functions. The 118 ADHD and control male participants, who were between 9 and 22 years of age, were divided into two age groups, one younger than 15, the other older. The investigators found both ADHD groups to be neuropsychologically impaired, attesting to the enduring nature of such deficits. In regard to development, older boys with ADHD performed better than younger ones did; however, this improvement was seen in normal controls as well. Consequently, while older boys with ADHD become less impaired, they still are not able to catch up with the normal group, which also has improved over time.

The Family Context

DSM-IV-TR classifies ADHD as a *disruptive behaviour disorder*, signifying that its symptoms of aggression, oppositionality, intrusiveness and disorganization interfere with the normal give-and-take of social interaction. As might be expected, such negative behaviour has a transactional effect on family relations, bringing out the worst in both parent and child. Parents of ADHD children report more stress and maladaptive strategies for

Box 7.3 Neurotransmitters: What Can They Tell Us?

Researchers at Vanderbilt University Medical Center have found evidence that genetic variations affecting three different brain chemicals may contribute to the three types of attention deficit hyperactivity disorder (English et al., 2009). Specifically, variations on the transporter genes, which allow drugs to enter cells or, in some cases, act to keep them out, have been shown to differentiate the three different ADHD subtypes, Transporters regulate the supply of these and other brain chemicals in the synaptic gap to ensure proper signalling

Children with predominantly inattentive ADHD have changes to their norepinephrine transporter gene, which affects norepinephrine levels in their brains. Those with predominantly hyperactivity-impulsive ADHD have changes to their dopamine transporter gene, thus affecting dopamine levels in the brain. In support of these findings, medications on the market for ADHD, both stimulant [Ritalin] and non-stimulant [Strattera], target these particular neurotransmitters blocking its transporter. For example, hyperactivity is often treated with drugs like Ritalin, which are thought to act primarily by blocking the dopamine transporter to increase the supply of dopamine in the synapse.

A variation in the choline transporter gene is associated with the 'combined' type, characterized by both inattention and hyperactivity/impulsivity. Choline is the precursor to acetylcholine, which, along with norepinephrine and dopamine, transmits messages across the synapse, or gap between nerve cells. Importantly, no medication exists for this specific neurotransmitter, which may go some way to explaining why medication is less effective in those with the combined type.

Nikolas et al. (2010) note that dopamine and norepinephrine are associated with reward processing behaviours seen in ADHD, but not the emotional dysregulation seen in ADHD. Therefore, another gene linked to attention deficit disorder is 5HTTLPR, a serotonin transporter gene. Two variants of 5HTTLPR, the 'short' allelic variant and the 'long' allelic variant, have been linked to ADHD and to disorders that often occur along with attention deficit disorder, such as conduct disorder and mood problems. These 5HTTLPR alleles result in either low or high serotonin transporter activity.

Neurotransmitters may not only identify the cause ADHD but may also be crucial in identifying the most appropriate medication to manage symptoms. However, it is important to highlight that genetics are not the only factor involved in the onset of ADHD. The environment (individual, social, family and cultural) all have also been shown to have an impact. (See Stannard Gromisch, 2010, for additional reviews.)

---

coping with the demands of parenting and tend to respond more negatively to their children than do parents of control children (DuPaul et al., 2001). Parents' difficulties in following and reading the children with ADHD often serve to increase the child's frustration and negative affect, and are thought to lay the foundations for the child learning coercive and oppositional behaviours (Johnston and Jassy, 2007).

Johnston and Mash (2001) reviewed the literature on the family relationships of children with ADHD and found that, although the research is often mixed and complicated by comorbidity with conduct problems, several trends emerge consistently. One is that parents and children with ADHD engage in more negative and coercive behaviour with one another, a dynamic that is particularly salient when observations are made of mothers' interactions with young boys. Parents of ADHD children also report higher levels of stress and psychological symptoms across numerous studies. Another consistent theme is that parents' attributions for their children's behaviour differ as a function of ADHD. Parents of children with ADHD are more likely to view the child's behaviour as caused by uncontrollable and stable factors within the child, while they perceive their child's positive behaviour as less dispositional, and the parents themselves as having less responsibility for how their child behaved. On the other hand, the available research does not support the assumption that parents of children with ADHD have more marital problems or are more likely to divorce than parents of typically developing children.

Given the heritability of ADHD, we also must keep in mind that many of the parents also struggle with ADHD, which might interfere with their ability to consistently implement good parenting techniques. Mothers of ADHD children who themselves have ADHD also report more personality and psychiatric problems, including depression, anxiety, low self-esteem and poor coping, than do mothers of ADHD children who do not themselves have ADHD (Weinstein et al., 1998).

There also is strong evidence that it is not the presence of ADHD per se but of the comorbid ODD and CD that it is associated with problematic family relations. This same comorbidity is associated with a greater degree of parental psychopathology, marital discord and divorce than is found in ADHD alone (Loeber et al., 2000).

Protective Factors

On the side of protective factors, research shows that among children at high risk for ADHD, positive parenting can provide a buffer. Tully and colleagues (2004) conducted a study of 2232 5-year-old twins, half of whom had low birth-weight. Using a measure of expressed emotion (EE), in which mothers were tape-recorded while they answered open-ended questions about their children, raters coded parental warmth as a function of mothers' tone of voice, empathy and positive feelings expressed toward the child. While low birth-weight children of mothers high in warmth were less likely to exhibit ADHD symptoms on scales completed by teachers and parents, low maternal warmth appeared to exacerbate the effects of low birth-weight on children's attention.

Positive parenting has also been found to be a protective factor for the developmental course of conduct problems among children with ADHD. Chronis et al. (2007) followed for 2–8 years following initial assessment a large sample of children with ADHD. Maternal positive parenting was found to negatively predict conduct problems whereas maternal depression was highlighted as being a particular risk factor.

The Social Context

The annoying, intrusive and insensitive behaviours of children with ADHD significantly increase the chances of peer rejection and social isolation. They interact with peers in a more negative and socially unskilled way than do control children (DuPaul et al., 2001). Moreover, when introduced to a peer with ADHD, children take only minutes to notice and react negatively to the ADHD child's behaviour. Kindergarten children with ADHD have been found to be especially lacking in social co-operation skills, the ability to follow rules, structure and social expectations of both children and adults (Merrell and Wolfe, 1998). Children with ADHD are more likely to affiliate with deviant peer groups if social rejection continues into adolescence (Barkley, 2006).

Parental behaviour also plays a role in the peer status of children with ADHD. Hinshaw et al. (1997) found that authoritative parenting, with its combination of firm limits, appropriate confrontations, reasoning, warmth and support, promoted social competence in children with ADHD. The social problems are more serious in the subgroup with comorbid ODD and CD. In addition, adolescents with ADHD begin sexual activity at an earlier age and are at a greater risk of being involved in teenage pregnancies, and the ratio for the number of births before the age of 20 years is markedly greater (37:1) (Barkley, 2006).

The Cultural Context
Television Viewing

For some time, concerns have been raised in the professional and popular media about the potential effects of *television* and *video games* on children's attention. In contrast to the natural pace of life, Christakis and colleagues (2004) point out, television presents children with a rapidly changing series of images, scenes and events that can be interesting and stimulating but requires only a limited span of attention. The investigators set out to determine whether television viewing in the early years, when the brain is developing in crucial ways, increases the risk of ADHD symptoms. The researchers followed a group of 1345 children from age 1 to age 7 and asked parents to report on the number of hours a day children spent in front of the television screen. Among 1-year-olds, 36 per cent watched no television while 37 per cent watched 1 to 2 hours daily and 14 per cent watched television for 3 or more hours. The risk of attention problems by age 7 increased directly as a function of the number of hours spent in front of the television during the preschool years. Two hours daily was associated with a 10 to 20 per cent increased risk, and 3 to 4 hours daily was associated with a 30 to 40 per cent increased risk when compared to the children who watched no television at all. In contrast, researchers who analysed data collected in the 1990s found no relation between kindergarteners' television viewing and symptoms consistent with attention deficit hyperactivity disorder when the children entered first grade (Stevens and Mulsow, 2006), nor was infants' television exposure associated with behaviour problems during the preschool years in a sample of Danish children (Obel et al., 2004).

Box 7.4 Case Study in Attention Deficit Hyperactivity Disorder

The social deficits of an 8-year-old child with ADHD.

Amy exhibits symptoms of ADHD, such as having difficulty in situations controlled by others – difficulty sitting still, waiting, not talking, listening, paying attention, not focusing on work. Symptoms also include nervously dropping things, and starting several projects and not completing them.

Although Amy is drawn to people of all kinds, the interactions usually deteriorate for various reasons which Amy does not understand. People think her unpredictable and strange even though kind at heart and well-meaning. Amy exhibits many relationship problems when in the presence of other people. She is constantly aware of others and how they are seeing her, trying to get some kind of attention from them. She seems to be worried about what impression is being made by her on others. She is constantly 'on stage', trying to get a person to like her, and if this doesn't work, to get them angry at her – pushing the limits to see just how mad the person will get.

She often will be 'well behaved' in the presence of the authority figure, but rude and annoying to a child in the next moment – almost as a release of the strain of pretending to be perfect for the adult. I have seen a lot of lying, tattling, annoying on purpose, interrupting, and a void of good manners. For example she will walk up to a man who was in conversation with another woman, and blurt out a comment on what he was saying, completely interrupting the conversation.

Sometimes a person Amy approaches is flattered by such attention from a young girl, and sometimes by a spontaneous hug, but soon tires of the constant, not very polite, chatter, and becomes uncomfortable. Even if the conversation starts on a successful basis, Amy sometimes gets excited about her seeming success and starts acting silly, talking in a high, silly voice, saying things that are not appropriate to the conversation and laughing nervously. Amy talks so constantly sometimes that I thought this was a case of needing to verbalize in order to process information.

Amy shows a wonderful natural curiosity and excitement for any new experience. Part of this enthusiasm is a natural need to move. She almost explodes into a happy, cheerful verbosity and movement at times, usually from a natural healthy pleasure, which can be annoying to those around her, or can incite a matching hyperactivity in other children who are not aware of what is happening. This gets her into trouble.

Amy seems to feel very good about herself when she has had some time alone to work. She comes out of a period of time like this happy, smiling and helpful. Also whenever she is around an adult alone she seems fine. But when there is another person present, child or adult, her self-image plummets. She seems to get jealous, or get into competition with one of the people in a subtle way, or find herself lacking. Then she revs up and starts talking.

While the data by Christakis and colleagues are suggestive, the investigators acknowledged that they did not track the kinds of television programmes the children were watching. Recent findings suggest attention problems at 4 years of age are linked only to adult directed television and not to child directed television (Barr et al., 2010). Another limitation of their study concerns other possible differences among the families and households in which young children were protected from television viewing: these might have been more highly educated parents or affluent families who had access to alternative activities in which to engage their young children. Indeed, reanalysis of the data-set (National Longitudinal Survey of Youth) used by Christakis and colleagues (2004) indicates that only the top 10 per cent of the sample were negatively affected by very high levels of television exposure at ages 1 and 3, and this effect was eliminated when two additional covariates (poverty status and a measure of maternal skills) were added to the analysis (Foster and Watkins, 2010).

An Integrative Developmental Model: The Hyperactive-Impulsive Type

Russell A. Barkley (1997, 2003) has developed a model that integrates research findings concerning the hyperactive-impulsive type of ADHD. (See Fig. 7.2.)

The cornerstone of Barkley's model is *behavioural inhibition* or the ability to delay motor response. There are two component processes to behavioural inhibition: (1) the capacity to delay an initial response (response inhibition), and (2) the capacity to protect this response delay from interference by competing events that might tempt the child to become disinhibited (interference control).

Behavioural inhibition, in turn, allows for the adaptive development of *executive functions*. There are four such functions. The first of these is *nonverbal working memory*, which allows the child to hold information 'online' while performing an operation on it, such as by comparing it to previously learned information. Working memory is

essential for planning in that it allows the child to activate past images ('hindsight') in order to guide a future response ('foresight'). Working memory also has a role in sustained attention in that it allows the child to keep in mind an intention or plan in order to engage in goal-directed activity in the face of distractions, obstacles or, even, boredom. Impairments in working memory may be a culprit in many of the deficits that are characteristic of ADHD, including forgetfulness, poor time management, reduced hindsight and forethought, and problems with sustaining long chains of organized behaviour. To date, research has confirmed that children with ADHD have difficulties with working memory, temporal sequencing and forethought, although the model's predictions regarding sense of time have yet to be tested.

The second executive function is *internalized speech*, which is related to verbal working memory. As children enter the preschool years, language becomes a vehicle not only for communicating with others, but for communicating with the self. Young preschoolers often provide a running commentary about their own activities, for the edification both of themselves and others. By the time they enter first grade, for most children self-talk becomes more quiet and private and is used specifically for the purposes of self-instruction and self-control. For example, children might repeat aloud to themselves the rules of a game or their parents' inhibitions about touching a fragile object. However, Barkley proposes that children with ADHD exhibit a delay in the internalization of speech, resulting in excessive talking in public, less mental reflection before acting, poorer self-control, and difficulty following rules and instructions.

The third executive function necessary for adaptive development is *self-regulation of affect*, which involves the ability to moderate the expression of feelings and to delay responding in reaction to them. Such self-regulation occurs internally, moderating the intensity of the emotional experience, as well as externally, allowing the child control over the public display of emotion. As we know

FIGURE 7.2 An Integrative Model of Hyperactivity-Impulsivity.

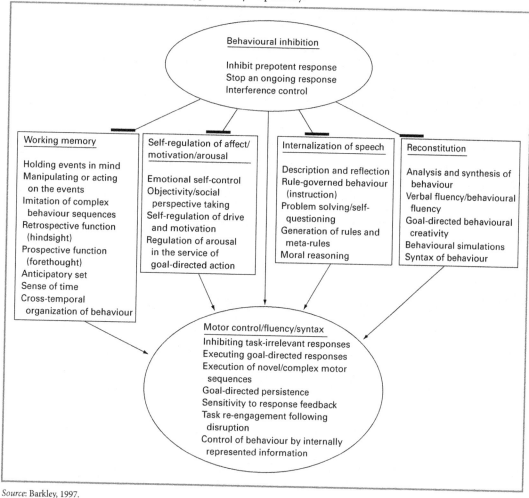

Source: Barkley, 1997.

from our discussion of emotion regulation in Chapter 2, the child who is able to regulate emotions can dampen as well as heighten them as needed. Therefore, affect regulation allows children to 'psych up' and increase arousal as needed, such as to motivate themselves in order to keep working on a tedious task. The child with ADHD, in contrast, lacks this kind of emotional self-control, Barkley posits, leading to greater emotional reactivity to events, less objectivity and poorer perspective-taking in that their perceptions are coloured by their immediate emotional reactions, and depend-

ence on external motivators to sustain their efforts to meet a goal. Research has demonstrated that children with ADHD have poorer emotion regulation, but this appears to be true particularly of those children who have comorbid oppositional defiant disorder.

The fourth executive function is *reconstitution*, which involves high-level mental operations, such as analysis, synthesis and creative thinking. The child who can delay responding long enough to sustain a mental image of a problem is a child who is better able to study it, explore its component pieces, and perhaps even put it together in a different way. Barkley surmises that these higher-level mental processes arise out of the internalization of play: just as internalization of language goes from overt (talking aloud) to covert (thinking it through in one's mind), so does mental play. The capacity for reconstitution is essential to the child's ability to shift set and engage in flexible problem solving in order to overcome obstacles. In contrast, the model suggests that children with ADHD would have difficulty with analysis and synthesis, verbal and non-verbal fluency, and strategy development. To date, little research is available on this facet of Barkley's model.

The final outcome of executive functions is *motor control and fluency*, which relates to the planning and carrying out of actions. Given that Barkley's model assumes that the deficits in behavioural inhibition arise in the brain's motor system, the executive function dysfunctions described previously should show their effects in developmental difficulties in motor co-ordination and the planning and execution of complex chains of goal-directed behaviour.

Barkley believes that the primary deficit in ADHD is the weakened ability to *inhibit behaviour*. All other deviations characteristic of ADHD are secondary to this reduced capacity for behavioural control. Thus, when the development of behavioural inhibition goes awry, this deficiency is primarily responsible for the deficits in the subsequent executive functions that emerge later over the course of development. Further, Barkley's model assumes that the primary deficit in behavioural inhibition arises as a product of biological factors, whether genetic or neuropsychological. While interpersonal factors may influence the expression of the disorder, they do not cause it.

Barkley's is a complex model that integrates many of the findings regarding children with the hyperactive-impulsive type of ADHD. One of its particular strengths is that it accounts for many of the associated characteristics that reflect underlying cognitive, social and emotional developmental problems in ADHD beyond simple inattention or

disinhibition. The model also has a developmental component that helps to explain the temporal ordering of the emergence of ADHD symptoms. On the other hand, many of the elements of the model have yet to be tested, and so it remains a promising hypothetical construction of the developmental psychopathology of ADHD.

The Dual Pathway Model

Several alternatives to the integrative model have since been put forward, with current research favouring a dual pathway model (see Sonuga-Barke et al., 2010 for a review) as being a better model in explaining the etiology of ADHD. As acknowledged by the integrative developmental model, ADHD is characterized by symptoms of inattention and/or hyperactivity/impulsivity that produce impairments across cognitive, behaviour and interpersonal domains of function. However, there is increasing evidence that there is also a dysfunction of reward and motivation (Johansen et al., 2009). For example, children with ADHD require stronger incentives to modify their behaviour than those without ADHD. They also show a failure to delay gratification, have impaired response to partial schedules of reinforcement and a preference for small immediate rewards over larger delayed ones (Sonuga-Barke, 2003).

The dual pathway model (Sonuga-Barke, 2003, 2005) explains neuropsychological heterogeneity in ADHD in terms of two dissociable cognitive and motivational deficits, each affecting some but not all patients. One of these deficits is grounded in dorsal mediated by inhibitory based executive dysfunction, the other underpinned by ventral fronto-striatal circuits and linked to altered signalling and delayed rewards. Thus, problems children with ADHD experience in daily life are thought to be either the result of deficits in executive functioning or motivational dysfunctions. The strengths of the model include accounting for key behaviour characteristics of ADHD while factoring in individual variability in characteristics displayed. The model also presents specific areas of brain to test these claims.

Developmental Course

In keeping with our thesis that psychopathology is normal development gone awry, we will first present relevant material on normal development. This material, in turn, will serve as a point of departure for presenting the deviations evidenced by the symptoms of ADHD.

The Toddler/Preschool Period

Campbell (2002) makes the point that normal development shades imperceptibly into ADHD, especially in the first six years of life. One expects toddlers to be 'all over the place and into everything', for example, and if they have a high energy level along with a determination to do what they want to do when they want to do it, it may not be easy to decide whether or not they are disturbed because these are age-appropriate behaviours. In addition, the fluidity of early development makes it difficult to predict if a child will outgrow the behaviour when it is deviant.

Normal preschoolers are expected to be sufficiently task oriented to complete what they start and monitor the correctness of their behaviour. They are also sufficiently co-operative to accept tasks set by others and participate in peer activities. As in the toddler period, deviations from expectation may be part of normal development, perhaps because of temporary difficulties in adjustment or temperament or unrealistic adult requirements. The main clues to disturbance lie in the severity, frequency, pervasiveness and chronicity of the problem behaviours.

Now we consider ADHD itself. Before 3 years of age, toddlers evidence an undifferentiated cluster of behaviours that has been called an *undercontrolled* pattern of conduct. However, at around 3 years of age this pattern becomes differentiated, making it possible to distinguish between hyperactive and impulsive behaviour on the one hand and aggressive and defiant behaviour on the other. Thus, at age 3 to 4 years we are able to detect ADHD properly (Barkley, 2003).

Hyperactive and impulsive preschoolers who continue to be difficult to control for a year or more are highly likely to have ADHD in middle childhood (Campbell, 2002). This persistence of ADHD, in turn, is more apt to occur if parent and child are locked into a pattern of negativism and over-controllingness on the mother's part and defiance on the child's. In fact, parental stress is at its highest during the preschool period (Campbell et al., 1991).

Middle Childhood

By middle childhood the standards for self-control, task orientation, self-monitoring of appropriate and inappropriate behaviour, and co-operation in family and peer groups are sufficiently clear that the difference between typical variability of behaviour and ADHD is more readily apparent. Thus, a persistent constellation of disruptive behaviour at home and in the classroom, along with disorganization and inability to follow routines, raises serious questions of psychopathology (Campbell, 2002).

Hyperactive-impulsive behaviour is likely to persist throughout middle childhood. In addition, there are two new developments. One is the appearance of problems with sustained attention, or the ability to continue a task until completed. These problems appear at around 5 to 7 years of age (Loeber et al., 1992). *Inattention*, in turn, gives rise to difficulties with work completion, forgetfulness, poor organization and distractibility, all of which may adversely affect the children's functioning at home and at school.

There is evidence that inattention remains stable through middle childhood whereas hyperactive-impulsive behaviour declines (Hart et al., 1995). As has been noted, it is not clear whether the latter effect represents a true developmental phenomenon or whether it is an artefact of increasingly inappropriate behaviours used to define hyperactivity/impulsivity (e.g., inappropriate running around and climbing) (Barkley, 2003).

The second important development in middle childhood is the increased prevalence of comorbid conditions (Barkley, 2003). Early in the period ODD may develop in a significant number of children, and by 8 to 12 years of age such early forms of defiance and hostility are likely to evolve into symptoms of CD in up to half of the children (Hart et al., 1995). Comorbid disruptive behaviours are most likely to develop among the children whose ADHD symptoms are more pervasive across situations (McArdle et al., 1995).

Adolescence

The previously held idea that ADHD is outgrown in adolescence has proved to be incorrect. From 50 to 80 per cent of clinically referred children will continue to have ADHD into adolescence. While it is true that adolescence marks a decline in the symptoms of hyperactivity and inattention, the same decline is noted in normal controls. There may also be a change in the expression of symptoms; for example, driven motor activity may be replaced by an inner feeling of restlessness, or reckless behaviour such as bicycle accidents may be replaced by automobile accidents (Cantwell, 1996).

Perhaps because of the cascading effects of previous developmental failures in school and peer relations, adolescents with ADHD engage in a number of problem behaviours. Klein and Mannuzza (1991), in their review of longitudinal studies, found that a substantial subgroup (25 per cent) of adolescents with ADHD engaged in antisocial activities such as stealing and fire setting. Between 56 and 70 per cent were likely to repeat grades, and the group as a whole was more likely to be expelled or drop out of school, as compared with controls. In addition, Whalen et al. (2002) found that higher levels of ADHD symptoms were related to increasingly negative moods in adolescents, less time spent on achievement-oriented tasks, and more tobacco and alcohol use.

A substantial amount of research has been conducted on the occurrence of ADHD in children with language difficulties (Snowling et al., 2006). The prevalence of language difficulties in ADHD is thought to be as high as 45 per cent. Language difficulties in ADHD are thought to be persistent, and young adults with ADHD are 1.9 times more likely to meet the diagnostic criteria of DSM-IV language disorder (Bierdeman et al., 2006). Deficient language functions include pragmatics, verbal fluency, verbal intelligence and reading. Language comprehension has also been found to be impaired.

In sum, adolescents with ADHD are significantly more disturbed than those without ADHD and must face the normative adolescent challenges of physiological changes, sexual adjustment, peer acceptance and vocational choice burdened by the cascading deficits arising from poor resolution of stage-salient issues in past developmental periods.

Adulthood

In the majority of cases ADHD persists into adult life where it is associated with a range of clinical and psychosocial impairments. In a recent meta-analysis carried out by Faraone and colleagues (2006) concluded that 15 per cent of adolescents retain full diagnosis by age 25 years, with a further 50 per cent in partial remission, indicating that around two-thirds of children with ADHD continue to have impairing levels of ADHD symptoms as adults. In a study from the World Health Organization Mental Health Survey, it was found that childhood predictors of adult ADHD in childhood included symptom severity, the presence of comorbid depression, high rates of other comorbidities, social adversity and parental psychopathology (Lara et al., 2009). Nevertheless, all forms of ADHD are known to persist into adulthood including ADHD with predominantly inattentive symptoms and ADHD associated with milder levels of impairment and comorbidity.

The *continuity* of ADHD across the lifespan is addressed by four large-scale studies that followed children with ADHD into adulthood. For example, in a study based in Montreal, Weiss and Hechtman (2003) found that 67 per cent of their now 25-year-old sample reported that symptoms of the disorder continued to interfere with their functioning. Thirty-four per cent reported moderate to severe hyperactivity, inattention and/or impulsivity. Similar results were obtained in Sweden by Rasmussen and Gillberg (2001), who found that 49 per cent of those diagnosed with

ADHD in childhood had symptoms of the disorder at age 22, in comparison to 9 per cent of controls. Both of these studies were based on symptom rating scales rather than official DSM criteria. A more exacting methodology was used in a study based in New York (Mannuzza et al., 1998) that found that 31 to 43 per cent of their sample met DSM-III criteria for ADHD in adolescence, whereas 4 to 8 per cent met the newer DSM-III-R criteria in adulthood eight years later. A possible reason for this remarkable disparity is that, as the research participants reached adulthood, the source of information about symptoms shifted from parents and teachers to the individuals themselves. (See Box 7.5.)

Longitudinal studies of children with ADHD indicate that as adults they have a higher prevalence of ADHD, antisocial behaviour and substance abuse than do other adults (Klein and Mannuzza, 1991). However, while the risk for criminal behaviour

---

Box 7.5 Dilemmas in the Assessment of ADHD: Whose Report Is Valid?

The attentive reader will have noted that at a number of junctures we offered cautions regarding the possibility that some findings may in fact be artefacts of problems with the measures used to assess and diagnose ADHD. These include the fact that measures are generally developmentally insensitive and thus do not capture well the differential appropriateness of the relevant behaviours across the lifespan; in addition, the measures are not sensitive to gender differences in the ways that girls and boys display symptoms of the disorder. Research suggests that an expectation that a child has ADHD can bias perceptions negatively (e.g. Harris et al., 1998). Negative ascriptions about children from adults may have a powerful biasing effect and children's behaviour may align accordingly with the label levelled on them. Children may become increasing disruptive if they are expected to behave in such a way. Barkley (2003) adds to these concerns the fact that the diagnostic criteria do not require the clinician to obtain information from reporters who know the child's behaviour well.

This can lead to erroneous assumptions, such as that ADHD symptoms decrease over the course of late adolescence and adulthood. For example, Barkley and his colleagues (2002) conducted a follow-up study of adults who had been diagnosed with ADHD in childhood. Based upon self-reports of behaviour, the investigators found that only 5 per cent of these individuals still met DSM criteria for the disorder. Does this mean that they had outgrown their ADHD? It depends on whom you ask. When the interviewers asked parents to provide ratings, the number of adults who still met DSM criteria for ADHD rose to 46 per cent – a ninefold increase.

Whose report is the most valid? To answer this question, the investigators compared how well self-reports and parent reports predicted individuals' educational, social and occupational functioning, as well as their antisocial behaviour. The results showed that parents' reports made a larger contribution to predicting almost all domains of functioning than did self-reports, suggesting that parents' ratings might indeed be more valid.

Another diagnostic dilemma results from DSM-IV-TR's requirement that the child exhibit symptoms in at least two of three settings, in which his or her behaviour is likely to be rated by different observers. The perspectives of teachers, parents, paediatricians, employers, and so forth often do not agree, precisely because they are seeing the individual in different environments. What draws the observer's attention to the child and raises his or her concern also might differ according to setting. For example, parents might be more reactive to disruptive behaviour, whereas teachers might be more sensitive to inattentiveness that interferes with school performance. The type of behaviour the child demonstrates may also underlie differences in prevalence rates across gender, such that disruptive behaviour is expected more in boys. Further, observers' ratings might be coloured by comorbidity of the child's ADHD with other disorders that call attention to themselves, particularly conduct problems and ODD (Costello et al., 1991). Ideally, the clinician will seek multiple sources of information, 'triangulating' them the way that a surveyor does (Cowan, 1978).

increases in adulthood, this holds only for those who have both ADHD and CD or other antisocial behaviours; there is no direct connection between ADHD and criminality.

While no cognitive deficits have been documented in adults, academic achievement and educational history both suffer. Children with ADHD complete about two years less schooling than do controls. As can be expected, when they enter the work world in adulthood, they have lower-ranking occupational positions (Mannuzza et al., 1998).

Since the recognition of ADHD is relatively recent through much of Europe there are many adults with ADHD who were never diagnosed or treated for ADHD when they were children. Recent national guidelines now recommend that ADHD should be recognized and appropriately treated throughout the lifespan (NICE, 2008). Despite this, across much of Europe many professionals remain unaware that ADHD persists into adulthood and has consequences across the lifespan. The European Network Adult ADHD was founded in 2003, with the aim of increasing awareness of the disorder to improve knowledge and patient care for adults with ADHD across Europe (Kooij et al., 2010).

Summary of Developmental Course

In the preschool period hyperactive-impulsive behaviour and aggressive and defiant behaviour become differentiated out of a generalized pattern of uncontrolled behaviour. Consequently, children begin to clearly exhibit behaviour that allows for the diagnosis of ADHD at around 3 to 4 years of age. Persistent ADHD in the preschool period is predictive of its continuation into middle childhood. Early middle childhood sees the addition of the inattentive type of ADHD. Moreover, comorbid ODD emerges early in the development, while CD emerges later on. Whereas inattention remains constant throughout middle childhood, hyperactivity/impulsivity declines.

Attention deficit hyperactivity disorder persists into adolescence and adulthood. While hyperactivity may decline in those with ADHD, it is still significantly greater than in non-ADHD controls, with impulsive behaviour being replaced by feelings of restlessness. The adolescent with ADHD may engage in antisocial behaviour and do poorly academically. Adults may have problems with alcoholism and drug abuse, as well as with antisocial behaviour. However, antisocial behaviour is related to comorbid CD rather than to hyperactivity itself. While the rate of employment for ADHD adults is no different from that of non-ADHD adults, those with ADHD have lower-ranking occupational positions. There is also ample evidence that ADHD is a strong predictor of psychiatric comorbidity in both males and females. Importantly, a two-year study of 1478 children with ADHD across 10 European countries found no difference in ADHD symptomatology and psychiatric comorbidity (Novik et al., 2006).

The Inattentive Type

Comparatively little is known concerning the predominantly inattentive type of ADHD. The diagnosis itself was not established as a separate type until DSM-III, and systematic etiological research has been conducted only recently. Perhaps the fact that the symptoms are relatively subtle and unobtrusive has made the study of the disorder seem less urgent than in the case of the obstreperous hyperactive-impulsive type. However, the emerging evidence suggests that the inattentive subtype has different correlates and consequences than the hyperactive impulsive or combined subtypes.

Descriptive Characteristics

In contrast to their hyperactive peers, who are described as noisy, messy and disruptive, children with the inattentive type of ADHD are described in terms such as dreamy, 'in a fog', 'spaced out', passive, withdrawn or lethargic (Barkley, 2003). The primary difficulties of children with inattentive type are non-disruptive in nature and are related to planning and organizing actions (DuPaul and Stoner, 2003). Compared with typical children they are more often 'off task', are less likely to complete their work, are less persistent in correctly performing boring assignments, procrastinate, work more slowly and are less likely to return to an interrupted task (Barkley, 1997). With peers, inattentive children are withdrawn, shy and apprehensive rather than aggressive (Milich et al., 2001).

Speculation has been increasing that the inattentive type actually represents a separate disorder from the hyperactive-impulsive type. In contrast to their hyperactive peers, the inattentive children exhibit a sluggish cognitive style, poor *selective* rather than sustained attention, less comorbidity with ODD and CD, more passivity in social relationships, and, as we will discuss in more detail next, a more benign developmental course (Milich et al., 2001). In addition, inattentive children appear to have more problems with verbal memory and visual-spatial processing than do children with the hyperactive-impulsive type.

As was true of the hyperactive-impulsive children described earlier, questions have arisen about the accuracy of the DSM criteria for describing the inattentive subtype. In particular, the sluggish cognitive tempo characteristic of children with the inattentive subtype is not well captured in the DSM description of inattentiveness. Carlson and Mann (2002) identified a subset of inattentive children who exhibited this slow cognitive tempo and found that, in comparison with other inattentive children, they were more likely to have problems with anxiety, depression and social withdrawal. Therefore, it is possible that future diagnostic systems will need to take into account the possibility of a separate disorder – inattention – with two subtypes: slow and fast cognitive tempo (Barkley, 2003; Milich et al., 2001).

Prevalence and Gender Differences

The inattentive type of ADHD appears to be less prevalent than the hyperactive-impulsive type, at least during the school-age years. For example, one epidemiological study (Szatmari et al., 1989) found that 1.4 per cent of boys and 1.3 per cent of girls had the inattentive type (in contrast to 9.4 per cent of boys and 2.8 per cent of girls with the hyperactive-impulsive type). There was a shift in adolescence, however, with 1.4 per cent of boys and

1 per cent of girls having the inattentive type (in contrast to 2.9 per cent of boys and 1.4 per cent of females with the hyperactive-impulsive type). Diagnosis and treatment rates remain much higher in boys (Quinn and Wigal, 2004). Interpretation of this difference remains open to interpretation. It may reflect absolute differences in prevalence in males versus females, or it might stem from perceived less urgency of the problems ADHD-diagnosable girls face, or less trouble that diagnosable females cause those around them. A relationship often exists between the impact of gender of children with ADHD and teachers' perceptions of impairment and referral (Coles et al., 2010).

A recent US national epidemiological study of 8- to 15-year-old children found an 8.7 per cent prevalence of ADHD with the predominantly inattentive type most prevalent (4.4 per cent) among the ADHD subtypes (combined type, 2.2 per cent; predominantly hyperactive-impulsive type, 2 per cent) (Froehlich et al., 2007).

Developmental Course of the Inattentive Type

While the majority of preschool children with ADHD are diagnosed with the hyperactive-impulsive type, it is in the school-age period that both the inattentive type and the combined hyperactive-inattentive type of ADHD begin to emerge. Thus, the age of onset is later for disorders involving primarily inattention. The reasons for this developmental difference are unclear. Whether the later emergence of attention problems is due to the increasing developmental demands for attentiveness in school, because these represent two different developmental stages of the disorder, because these in fact represent two different disorders, or whether the explanation lies in the natural unfolding of the developmental variable of attention is not yet known.

What is clear, however, is that the developmental consequences differ for children whose ADHD is not accompanied by hyperactivity-impulsivity. Inattentiveness alone is not related to antisocial behaviour, as is hyperactivity; but inattentiveness is predictive of poor academic achievement, particularly in reading. Symptoms of inattention also are more stable over the course of development, whereas hyperactivity and impulsivity decline in the transition from middle childhood to adolescence. However, Barkley (2003) offers a caveat: the behavioural measures used to assess hyperactivity-impulsivity appear to be more appropriate for younger children, whereas the measures used to assess inattention appear relevant across the age span. Therefore, it is possible that the stability of inattentiveness is an artefact of the methods we use to assess it.

Intervention

The behavioural difficulties of patients with ADHD inattentive type may be markedly different from those of children with combined hyperactive/impulsive type and the targets of treatment will therefore need to be tailored accordingly. While behavioural interventions targeting organization, planning and time management cannot be classified as 'well-established', they have shown considerable promise for those with inattentive type (Langberg and Epstein, 2009). Currently treatment of ADHD has failed to consider the separate subtypes but instead treated them all under the umbrella term of ADHD.

Pharmacotherapy

Medication is considered by many to be the most powerful and best-documented intervention for ADHD (e.g. Hinshaw, 2007), leading influential guidelines (e.g. American Academy of Child and Adolescent Psychiatry, 1997) to suggest pharmacology to be the first intervention to be used to treat ADHD.

Stimulants

Stimulants are the first choice for medication and the literature on them is voluminous. Stimulants are clearly effective, the onset of their action is rapid, and the side effects generally considered mild. The most popular stimulant is methylphenidate (Ritalin) followed by amphetamines (e.g., Dexedrine) and Pemoline (e.g., Cylert). Methylphenidate is estimated to be used in 2.8 per cent of school-aged children (DuPaul and Volpe, 2009). Despite being considered the most effective treatment for ADHD across the lifespan, their use in some parts of Europe remains controversial in both children and adults (Kooij et al., 2010). Stigma and myths continue to surround the condition and its treatment, particularly with stimulant medication.

Stimulants not only affect the major symptoms of ADHD but also affect a host of social, cognitive and academic problems. In regard to interpersonal problems, stimulants improve the mother–child and family interactions, reduce bossiness and aggression with peers, and increase the ability to work and play independently. Cognitively, short-term memory is improved along with the use of strategies already in the children's repertoire. Academically, classroom talking and disruptions decrease, while both the amount and accuracy of academic work completed increase. Incidentally, improvement is not specific to ADHD, since normal children given these stimulants improve as well. While most children with ADHD improve on stimulants, with the percentages ranging from 70 per cent to as high as 96 per cent, most reviews on this topic have found limited evidence to suggest a direct impact of stimulant medication on academic achievement (Raggi and Chronis, 2006).

In regard to comorbid conditions, stimulants are as effective in children with ADHD and aggression as with those who have ADHD alone. Evidence concerning the effectiveness of stimulants in ADHD with comorbid anxiety is mixed and research on other comorbid conditions, such as ODD and CD, is sparse.

In general, stimulants have an extremely high margin of safety, and there is little evidence of increased tolerance that would necessitate increased dosage. However, there are side effects. Mild appetite suppression is almost universal, while individual children might also respond with irritability, headaches and abdominal pains. Proponents of stimulants argue that concern about other side effects are exaggerated (Barkley, 2003). Children do not become 'zombies' when medicated; on the contrary, they are alert and focused. Adverse effects on height and weight are rarely large enough to be clinically significant, although prolonged appetite suppression may be associated with delayed growth. Nor is there an increased risk of substance use or abuse later in development (Biederman, 2003). However, a general problem with all stimulant medications is that their positive effects are not sustained after they are withdrawn.

Non-Stimulants

Some children do not respond or may even not tolerate stimulants due to side effects. Several non-stimulant medications such as Modafinil and Reboxetine have been found to be effective in the treatment of ADHD (Antshel et al., 2011). The most commonly used is atomoxetine, a selective non-repinephrine reuptake-inhibitor (SNRI). While atomoxetine rarely normalizes behaviour, symptom improvement is often reflected in gains in social and behavioural function.

Tricyclic Antidepressants

While far less studied than stimulants, tricyclic antidepressants (TCSs) have demonstrated effectiveness in treating children and adolescents with ADHD. They are second-line drugs for children who do not respond to stimulants or who develop significant depressive or other side effects. Children with comorbid anxiety disorders, depression or tics may respond better to TCSs than to stimulants.

However, there are drawbacks to TCSs. Efficiency in improving cognitive symptoms is not as great as for stimulants; there is a potential for cardiac side effects, especially in pre-pubertal children; and there is a possible decline in effectiveness over time.

Variation in the Use of Medication

About half of US children and adolescents diagnosed with ADHD receive stimulant medications or related agents. Despite major differences from the US health care system and considerable regulation of pharmaceutical prices, Canada also exhibits high usage of ADHD medications. It is possible that this pattern reflects its proximity to the USA, with exposure to US advertisements and cultural norms. Within other countries (such as Sweden

and France), strict governmental regulation against the prescription of ADHD medications might also explain some of the variations in use (Frances et al., 2004; Sizoo et al., 2005). For example, in France, use of methylphenidate, the only approved ADHD medication, requires a hospital-initiated prescription from a neurology, psychiatry or paediatric specialist. British national guidelines have recommended that only professionals in specialist health services should make a diagnosis of ADHD and initiate medication. Medication use is likely to decrease further after national recommendations that parent education and training should be a first-line treatment for ADHD (NICE, 2008).

Limitations to Medication
Scope of Research

While the quantity of research on medication is impressive, its scope is limited. Most of the research consists of short-term studies of European American boys in middle childhood. Relatively little is known about long-term effects or about possible gender and ethnic differences. Comorbidity has also been neglected, as was noted. The few studies of other age groups suggest that adolescents and children in middle childhood respond well but that preschoolers do not (Spencer et al., 1996). Research has also failed to consider what type of life impairments are most affected by continued ADHD symptoms that occur despite medication treatment.

Non-Medical Dangers

The twin dangers of pharmacotherapy for treating ADHD are the belief that drugs are a cure-all and that 'one size (dosage) fits all'. These dangers have little to do with the positive effects of the drugs themselves, but they can significantly obstruct progress in helping the children.

As we have seen, ADHD is accompanied by a wide variety of comorbid problems. Medication, in spite of its effectiveness, does not solve them all. It cannot magically produce the social and academic skills that the children have failed to acquire, it leaves learning disorders untouched, and it does not resolve all the difficulties arising from the attempts of parents (who themselves often have ADHD) to deal with their disturbed children. Moreover, the illusion of the pill-as-cure-all provides an excuse for parents and professionals alike not to undertake the often arduous demands of other forms of treatment.

The 'one size fits all' illusion ignores the fact that, while medication is generally effective, individual children vary widely in their response. For a particular child some symptoms and some attendant problems may improve while others are not helped at all. In addition symptoms often return once medication is discontinued.

There is also variability in compliance. Parents may be resistant to using medication and adolescents in particular may fear stigmatization by peers. For physicians there is the danger of over-prescribing medication and a subsequent failure to conduct the necessary but time-consuming monitoring of effectiveness of dosage.

Medication without Assessment

One of the other concerns about the way in which medications are used to treat children with ADHD is that too often they are prescribed by paediatricians or psychiatrists without a thorough assessment to confirm the diagnosis. Because ADHD is such an eminently treatable problem, it may be tempting for a physician to view all child behaviour problems in its light and to prescribe the cure. However, it is important to first determine that it is in fact this disorder that is causing the parents' or teachers' complaints of poor school work, inattentiveness, uncontrolled behaviour, and so forth, rather than a competing explanation such as a learning disorder, anxiety or parenting problem. In response to this concern, the American Academy of Pediatrics (Overturf, 2000) has issued a set of guidelines requiring that physicians conduct a careful assessment of ADHD before a prescription is written, including gathering information from parents, ruling out other conditions, and inquiring directly of teachers regarding the child's behaviour in the classroom – the

setting, which we know, in which ADHD is most likely to evidence itself.

Medication-Related Attributions

What do children with ADHD make of the fact that they must take medication in order to be able to function in structured settings? Some critics have suggested that these children are being set up to become substance abusers in that they are being given the message that drugs can solve their problems, although the weight of the evidence has not supported this supposition (Barkley, 2003). However, the attributions that children make about medication can have an impact on their developmental outcomes. For example, Treuting and Hinshaw (2001) presented children with ADHD with a series of hypothetical scenarios involving a boy who has good and bad experiences during his school day. In some of the stories, the boy receives his medication and in other stories his mother forgets to give it to him. Their results showed that children largely gave medication the credit for the boy's good outcomes, more so than the boy's own efforts or abilities. Moreover, children with ADHD were highly likely to ascribe bad outcomes to a lack of medication, even when the mother in the story *had* remembered to give it (e.g., 'His medication wore off'; 'He needs a higher dose'). Further, children who gave medication-related attributions for good outcomes in the story gave significantly higher self-reports of depression and low self-esteem. Thus, it appears that it is important for children with ADHD to have perceived self-efficacy and an internal locus of control in regard to their disorder and not to credit all their successes to medication. The investigators suggest that clinicians and parents think carefully about how to introduce children to the idea of medication treatment, and emphasize the role of medication as a *facilitator* rather than a determinant of good behaviour, one that will allow the child's true potential to shine through.

Psychosocial Interventions

As we have seen, medication does not remedy all the problems that beset children with ADHD.

Specifically, it may not affect comorbid conditions, parental psychopathology, academic and social skills, and peer popularity. Therefore, other remedial measures are needed. We will describe some of these briefly.

Behaviour Management

In the operant approach, environmental rewards and punishments along with modelling are used to decrease problem behaviours and increase adaptive ones. In the short term, behavioural interventions improve social skills and academic performance in the setting in which they are implemented. There is evidence that the operant approach in the classroom significantly improves the behaviour of children with ADHD (Pelham et al., 1998). The greatest weakness of behaviour modification is that gains often are not maintained over time and do not generalize to other situations.

There has been only one published study that has systematically examined treatment sequence (Döpfner et al., 2004) comparing medication and behavioural modification interventions. This study found approx two-thirds of children with ADHD were adequately treated with behaviour modification (average 17 sessions) when it was used as the first treatment option, whereas 82 per cent of those treated first with medication needed additional behavioural modification afterwards. Recent studies have in fact shown many positive effects of behavioural interventions for ADHD (Pelham and Fabiano, 2008).

Cognitive Behavioural Therapy

Cognitive behavioural interventions were developed to remedy the previously mentioned shortcomings of behaviour modification. In order to increase the transfer of learning to new situations, children are taught cognitive strategies that they can take with them wherever they go, such as stepwise problem solving. This has recently been applied to working memory training, with positive results found in children with ADHD (Beck et al., 2010).

Interventions that combine cognitive techniques with behavioural techniques, such as contingency management, have also proven very effective. *Contingency management* involves helping children to evaluate their own behaviour and to apply the appropriate consequences. For example, in order to shape and reward children's ability to monitor their own behaviour, Hinshaw (2000) utilizes the 'Match Game' in which children are asked to rate their behaviour on a skill or concept that needs to be learned or practised, such as paying attention or cooperating. (See Fig. 7.3.) The adult also rates the child and the two discuss the reasoning that went into their ratings, giving specific examples of desirable or undesirable behaviour. The child receives points based on how high the adult's ratings were, but the points are *doubled* if the

FIGURE 7.3 The Match Game.

Source: Hinshaw, 2000.

child's ratings agreed with the adult's – in other words, if there was a match. Over time, children not only become more accurate in their self-evaluations, taking over the monitoring required by the supervising adult, but also come to require less external reinforcement as self-monitoring becomes a reward unto itself.

Neurofeedback

Neurofeedback works by retraining the brain's electrical activity (EEG) by using operant conditioning of brain activity for self-regulation of attentional processes and states (Heinrich et al., 2007). Sensors are attached to the child's head in order to detect the electrical activity (EEG) from the brain. This is then amplified and converted into an image of brain waves on the therapist's computer screen. The therapist sets the targets – i.e. the specific brain-waves that the child needs to enhance or reduce. The principle behind this, is that through changing their brain waves to a more normalized state and through reinforcement the child will have more control over their behaviour. A recent meta-analysis (Arns et al., 2009) concluded that neurofeedback treatment of ADHD improved behaviour in open trials with medium to large effect sizes when compared to passive, or to some active control treatments, while the beneficial effects of non-pharmacological treatment of ADHD with its long-lasting effects are obvious. The complexity and length of neurofeedback is difficult to test under double blind placebo trials.

Anger Management Training

Because of the high comorbidity with conduct disorder, children with ADHD often benefit from cognitive behavioural training in anger management to provide them with alternatives to aggression (Hinshaw, 2000). (These are described in more detail in Chapter 10.)

Social Skills Training

Children with ADHD often have interpersonal problems and could benefit from learning better social skills (Hinshaw, 2000). One empirically supported social skills intervention was developed by Pfiffner and McBurnett (1997), in which girls and boys with ADHD meet in groups of 6 to 9. Groups are designed to systematically address (1) children's social knowledge, (2) performance deficits, (3) recognition of verbal and non-verbal social cues, (4) adaptive responding to problem situations, and (5) generalization, including bringing parents into the treatment in order to promote and support children's use of their newfound skills in other settings.

Parent Training

Parent training aims at substituting adaptive for maladaptive ways parents deal with their children. The parents are trained to focus on specific problematic behaviours and to devise strategies for changing them. Behavioural parent training (BPT) is documented to be effective in improving parent–child relations, altering parenting practices, and reducing child symptoms and impairment (see Fabiano et al., 2009). However, there are limitations to this treatment option as rates of parent treatment non-acceptance and non-adherence are relatively high for behavioural interventions. Furthermore, even for families who consistently attend treatment sessions and implement recommended strategies, immediate treatment-related effect sizes generally are small to moderate in magnitude (Hoza et al., 2008) and often decrease after active treatment ceases (Molina et al., 2009).

Academic Skills Training

Academic skills training involves specialized individual or group tutoring that teaches children to follow direction, become organized, use time efficiently, check their work, take notes and, more generally, to study effectively. Remediation of comorbid learning disorders may also be necessary. The effectiveness of academic skills training for children with ADHD has received little systematic evaluation.

Comparison of Treatment Effects

One of the most comprehensive treatment effectiveness studies was carried out by the Multimodal Treatment (MTA) Cooperative Group (1999), a consortium of prominent ADHD researchers at several different sites who pooled their resources in order to provide a more definite answer to the question, What works for ADHD? The study involved a sample of 579 children aged 7 to 9.9 years, all of whom were diagnosed with ADHD combined type. Children were randomly assigned to one of four treatments, each of which lasted 14 months: (1) medication with stimulants; (2) intensive behavioural treatment, involving the child, the parent and the school; (3) a combination of medication and behavioural treatment; or (4) standard community care provided by outpatient mental health agencies. The design allowed the investigators to answer a number of specific questions:

Which is more effective, medication or behavioural treatment? Results strongly indicated that medication resulted in a more significant improvement in ADHD symptoms, according to parents' and teachers' reports of inattention and teachers' ratings of hyperactivity/impulsivity. (See Fig. 7.4.)

Does the combination of medication and behavioural treatment result in increased effectiveness? Somewhat surprisingly to many in the field, the multimodal treatment was not superior to medication alone. The combined treatment showed no difference in effectiveness when compared to medication alone, but was superior to behavioural treatment alone in reducing parents' and teachers' ratings of inattention, parents' reports of hyperactivity/impulsivity, as well as parents' reports of oppositional/aggressive behaviour, internalizing symptoms and reading difficulty.

FIGURE 7.4 Results of the MTA Co-operative Study Comparing Treatments for ADHD.

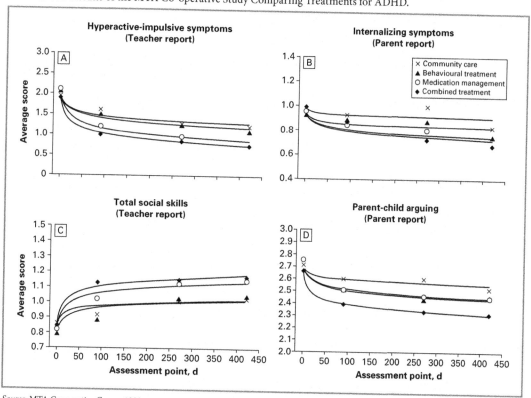

Source: MTA Cooperative Group, 1999.

Are the three MTA treatments superior to traditional community care? Again, the addition of medication to the mix generated the best results. Children who received medication alone or the combined treatment improved more than those in traditional community care, according to both parents' and teachers' reports, whereas children who received behavioural treatment alone did not.

Conclusions

The most parsimonious conclusion from these data is that medication is the treatment of choice for ADHD. However, to determine any longitudinal effects, children in the MTA were followed 6 and 8 years following enrolment on the study. The results revealed that the type or intensity of 14 months of treatment for ADHD in childhood (at age 7.0–9.9 years old) did not predict functioning six to eight years later. Rather, early ADHD symptom trajectory regardless of treatment type was prognostic (Molina et al., 2009). The result of the follow-up clearly demonstrates, in stark contrast to the original findings, that medication did not show the greatest benefits. It also highlights the importance and need for more longitudinal studies in gaining evidence about the effectiveness of treatment in ADHD.

DSM-V

Finally before we leave our review of ADHD, it is important to reflect on how this knowledge is being fed in to clinical practice. The next edition of the DSM now in preparation is due to be published in 2013 and the revised ICD (version 11) in 2015. The revised DSM-V criteria are expected to follow similar lines to the current criteria with the expected changes listed in Table 7.2.

These changes are expected to be incorporated to reflect that impairment from the symptoms of ADHD may develop later in life. The reduction in the symptom threshold for adults as compared to children recognizes the age-dependent changes in the course of the disorder, since the lower threshold in adults is still clinically significant where there is clear evidence of impairment from the symptoms of ADHD, and better reflects the characteristics and natural course of the disorder. However, those in the medical profession have raised some concern already about these potential changes as it means that many people who previously met the 'in partial remission criteria' would then meet full criteria.

Learning Disorders

Definition and Diagnosis

As we turn our attention to *learning disorders* (LD), we must consider the two questions basic to understanding any psychopathology: How should LD be defined? and How should the definition be operationalized?

Conceptualizing Learning Disorders

In regard to conceptualizing LD, matters got off on the wrong foot in the first widely adopted legal

TABLE 7.2 Proposed / Expected DSM-V Changes for ADHD

	The following changes are expected.
1	Symptom thresholds: For older adolescents and adults (aged 17 and above) only 4 symptoms in either the inattentive or hyperactive-impulsive domain are required
2	The list of hyperactive-impulsive symptoms has been increased to 13 to include 'uncomfortable doing things slowly or carefully', 'is often impatient', 'difficult to resist temptations or opportunities' and 'tends to act without thinking'
3	Descriptions of symptom items have been elaborated to include more specific descriptions of behaviour, some of which are more applicable to adults
4	The age of onset criteria has been broadened to include 'noticeable inattentive or hyperactive-impulsive symptoms by the age of 12 years'
5	Autism spectrum disorder is no longer listed as an exclusion criterion

Source: Kooij et al., 2010, p. 67.

definition. In the Education for All Handicapped Children Act of 1977 (PL 94-142), LD was defined as a disorder in one or more of the *basic psychological processes* involved in understanding and using spoken or written language. It may manifest itself in a severe *discrepancy between age and ability levels* in one or more of the following areas of academic achievement: oral expression, listening comprehension, reading, writing or arithmetic. According to this definition, LD does not include children who have learning problems that are primarily the result of visual, hearing or motor handicaps, mental retardation, emotional disturbances, cultural or economic disadvantage, or limited educational opportunities. This definition is reflected in the federal law currently governing special education, the Individuals with Disabilities Education Act (IDEA), which was most recently re-authorized in 1997.

A core problem with this definition is that the 'basic psychological processes' are not specified, and, indeed, it is only now becoming clear what some of these processes might be. The exclusion of a number of other groups of disturbed and deprived children has been criticized on two counts: first, LD can co-occur with conditions excluded from the definition, such as physical handicaps or emotional disturbances, and second, it is not always possible to disentangle LD from these excluded conditions. (See Shaw et al., 1995.)

Definitions prepared subsequently by the National Joint Committee on Learning Disabilities (NJCLD) and DSM-IV-TR come closer to hitting the mark, although they are not without problems. The NJCLD (1988) defines LD as a heterogeneous group of disorders manifested by significant difficulty in the acquisition and use of listening, speaking, reading, writing, reasoning, or mathematical abilities. The specification of 'underlying processes' has been deleted. The NJCLD also states that the disorder can occur concomitantly with other handicapping conditions, such as sensory impairment, emotional disturbance, cultural differences or insufficient instruction, but that LD is not the result of these conditions. The disorder is presumed to be due to a central nervous dysfunction.

DSM-IV-TR does not have a general definition for LD, which it calls learning disorders; rather it lists the diagnostic criteria for three such disorders: reading disorder, mathematics disorder and disorder of written expression. Since the criteria are essentially the same for all three, we will present only those for reading disorder (see Table 7.3).

DSM-IV-TR's definition is more precise in that it substitutes discrepancies between objective measures of achievement on the one hand and IQ, age and grade on the other for NJCLD's somewhat nebulous 'significant difficulty in acquisition and use' of an academic skill. DSM-IV-TR is also more concerned with the effects of LD on the child's adjustment. However, NJCLD has a broader spectrum of concurrent conditions than does DSM-IV-TR.

Assessing and Diagnosing Learning Disorders

Satisfactorily assessing LD has proved to be an even more thorny undertaking than conceptualizing it. At the heart of the matter is the use of the **discrepancy model** – the difference between what students should be able to do (ability) and how they actually are performing in school (achievement). Typically, children's ability is operationalized by their score on a standardized intelligence test, while their achievement is measured by an educational test battery, such as the Woodcock-Johnson-III tests of achievement (Woodcock et al., 2001b). A learning disorder is indicated when a child's achievement

TABLE 7.3 DSM-IV-TR Criteria for Reading Disorder

A. Reading achievement, as measured by individually administered standardized tests of reading accuracy or comprehension, is substantially below that expected given a person's chronological age, measured intelligence, and age-appropriate education.
B. The disturbance in Criterion A significantly interferes with academic achievement or activities of daily living that require reading skills.
C. If a sensory deficit is present, the reading difficulties are in excess of those usually associated with it.

Source: DSM-IV-TR. Copyright 2000 by the American Psychiatric Association.

falls significantly below what would be expected on the basis of his or her intelligence test score. Generally, children with LD are found to have low average to superior intelligence, which clearly differentiates them from the children with mental retardation whom we encountered in Chapter 4.

However, a basic practical problem is that there is no general agreement about how large a discrepancy should be in order to classify children as LD. Because local criteria differ, a child can change from being LD to being non-LD simply by moving from one state to another. Moreover, professionals differ among themselves about what scores on achievement and IQ tests constitute a significant discrepancy.

Another problem with the discrepancy model that particularly concerns clinicians is that it requires the children to fail academically before being diagnosed. This requirement impedes early detection and intervention. It is not unusual, for example, for children to be in the third grade before explanations other than LD are exhausted; for example, 'He doesn't like the teacher' or 'Girls just don't do well in math'. The delay is important because the longer it persists the less amenable the child is to remedial measures (Lyon et al., 2003a).

A final limitation of the discrepancy model is that, at least in the case of reading, it does not serve the basic diagnostic function of differentiating a unique population of children. For example, there is evidence that children classified as LD in reading because their achievement is lower than their IQ are no different from children who are classified as 'slow readers' because their poor achievement in reading is congruent with their IQ level. This lack of differentiation of the two groups applies to a number of variables: information processing, response to instruction, genetic variability and neurophysiological markers (Lyon et al., 2003a).

Even with all its shortcomings and with the at times heated controversies that the concept of LD has sparked, it also has had a number of positive consequences. It has called attention to a population of children who are neither 'stupid' nor 'lazy' in regard to schoolwork, as they tended to be regarded in the past. The concept of LD has also stimulated research into cognitive skills involved in learning specific subjects, the possible biological roots of such cognitive processes, and the consequences of LD for general adjustment.

Race, Social Class and Lack of Opportunity

There are two ways in which considerations of ethnic diversity and social class complicate our understanding of learning disorders. Interestingly, these lie at opposite ends of a continuum: one argument is that minority children might be *under-represented* among those identified as LD, whereas the other suggests that they might be *over-represented*.

Under-identification

DSM-IV-TR stipulates that learning disorders must not be due to other factors, including economic disadvantage, race, ethnicity, lack of opportunity or other cultural characteristics. However, this creates a diagnostic dilemma. These factors may well co-occur with learning disorders and even have a contributing influence on them. For example, children who grow up in economically deprived circumstances often are behind their peers in language development when they enter school, which in turn will interfere with their mastery of reading and math skills. Further, parents who are under-educated or who themselves have reading problems will find it difficult to foster their children's literacy. While learning disorders occur in children from all social classes, the exclusionary criteria may have the undesirable effect of depriving under-privileged children of the special education services that would help to remediate their difficulties.

Over-identification

At the opposite end of the spectrum are those who argue that, in fact, children from ethnic minority and lower SES families are over-represented among those in special education classrooms, which suggests some bias in the identification and referral process. At the centre of this debate is the question of whether standardized intelligence and achievement tests – which were developed by and often normed on middle-class European Americans – might underestimate the abilities of minority, disadvantaged or immigrant children (Kaminer and Vig, 1995; Valencia and Suzuki, 2000). (See Chapter 16.) Children who have not had the same sorts of cultural experiences as those from the majority culture, as well as those whose language skills are limited or whose use of English simply differs from the standard, might be unfairly assessed by the very instruments that are key to identifying LD. Unfortunately, there has been little research to inform us about the extent to which the LD label is applied in a biased or inequitable manner. However, we should keep this possibility in mind as we review the available literature.

Alternative Models

Response to Intervention

Currently, efforts are under way to modify the IDEA, with bills placed before both the US Senate and the House of Representatives that would change the language in the federal law governing the LD designation. Rather than focusing on the IQ–achievement discrepancy as the main method of identification, advocates are promoting an alternative model called 'response to intervention' (RTI). In this model, which is used in a handful of school systems nationwide, children with academic difficulties are routed through a series of levels of intervention before being diverted to special education. First, children are given the opportunity to succeed in the regular classroom. Those who struggle are offered a secondary intervention, generally utilizing intensive, small-group instruction that is individualized to each student's needs; and in some school systems an even more intensive tertiary intervention is offered. Only those students who fail to respond to each successive level of intervention are placed in special education.

Advocates argue that this system increases the likelihood that scarce special education resources will be reserved for those truly in need of them and that the continual assessment of the child provided in the model will provide a more accurate and competency-based index of the child's abilities. However, critics argue that such a system requires

the child to fail at multiple levels before special education services are offered. Further, critics point out that RTI does not specify how assessments are to be conducted in order to identify the cognitive processes that might be interfering with an individual child's classroom learning (Bailey, 2003).

Empirically Derived Learning Disorders

Other experts in the field of learning disorders who question the basis for the DSM and federal definition's categorizations of LD offer a different typology based on empirical research. Table 7.4 lists the learning disorders that have emerged from empirical investigations. These include three separate disorders of reading, involving word recognition, comprehension or fluency; two of mathematics, depending on the presence or absence of word recognition problems; and one of written expression, which includes difficulties with spelling, handwriting or expression of ideas.

Reading Disorder

The recent trend in research is to study specific learning disorders rather than the heterogeneous population that makes up LD as a whole. This approach is proving fruitful in uncovering core etiological variables and, in the case of reading disorders, in forcing a rethinking of the nature of LD itself. We will concentrate on reading disorder (RD) because it is the most frequent of the various disorders and because the research findings are particularly substantial and revealing.

TABLE 7.4 Subtypes of Learning Disorders Supported by Empirical Research

Reading Disorder: Word Recognition
Reading Disorder: Comprehension
Reading Disorder: Fluency
Mathematics Disorder
Mathematics Disorder – Reading Disorder
Disorders of Written Expression: Handwriting, Spelling, and/or Expression of Ideas

Source: Adapted from Lyon et al., 2003a.

Definition and Characteristics

Definition

Most definitions of RD utilize the discrepancy model. In the case of reading this means a significant discrepancy between reading accuracy, speed or comprehension and chronological age or measured intelligence. (Our presentation follows Lyon et al., 2003a, unless otherwise noted.) Children with RD are assumed to be different from children whose reading, while significantly below average, is in keeping with their lowered IQ. This latter group is sometimes called 'garden variety reading disordered', and we will designate it as GRD.

Reading disorder was thought to be different from GRD for another reason. A number of years ago data showed that performance in reading, rather than being normally distributed, has a 'hump' at the lower end of the curve. This hump was believed to be due to the addition of a group of children with a special kind of reading problem. It was further assumed that these children with RD were qualitatively different from children with GRD.

Recent studies have cast doubt on the validity of the discrepancy model, as we have seen. For example, studies show that there is no difference between RD and GRD in the reading skills of word recognition and knowledge, on nine cognitive variables such as vocabulary and memory that are related to reading proficiency, and on teachers' behavioural ratings. Moreover, subsequent population studies of school children have failed to find the hump at the lower end of the distribution of the reading curve. Rather than indicating a qualitatively different group, the data show that performance in reading is continuously distributed throughout the school population. On a practical level this means that trying to establish a cut-off point that will distinguish the RD population from other slow readers is doomed to fail.

Traditionally, dyslexia has been primarily assessed with measures of single word decoding; however, difficulty with reading fluency has been increasingly acknowledged as a significant aspect of reading disabilities. Reading fluency was added to the federal definition of a specific learning disability in the reauthorization of the Individuals with Disabilities Education Improvement Act (IDEA, 2004). Recent conceptualizations by the International Dyslexia Association (Lyon et al., 2003b) also include reading fluency as an area of difficulty for individuals with dyslexia. This definition refers to the fact that many adult dyslexics experience difficulties with reading fluency even after becoming accurate word readers (Lefly and Pennington, 1991; Shaywitz, 2003). Furthermore, intervention research has shown that it is harder to attain improvements in reading fluency compared to improvements in reading comprehension, decoding and word identification skills (Torgesen et al., 2001).

Empirically Derived Types of Reading Disorder

Although they are lumped together in DSM-IV-TR, research suggests that there are two distinct types of reading disorder: one involving problems with *word recognition* (commonly termed dyslexia; see Box 7.6) and the other involving *reading comprehension*. Most of the research has been devoted to the first type of reading disorder, while relatively little is known about the latter.

Prevalence

Reading disorder affects approximately 10 to 15 per cent of the school-age population. It also is the most common form of learning disability, comprising 80 per cent or more of children served in special education programmes. While schools tend to identify more boys than girls, epidemiological and longitudinal studies show no *gender differences*. Boys tend to demonstrate comorbid externalizing problems, which cause them to be referred at a greater rate than girls (Lyon et al., 2003a).

The question of whether there are *social class* or *ethnic differences* in the prevalence of LD is an important one to which, unfortunately, little attention has been given. While children from lower-income and minority groups are disproportionately assigned to special education classrooms, it is not clear whether this is a product of a true higher prevalence of learning disorders or whether these differences reflect biases in identification and

Box 7.6 Case Study in Learning Disorders

When University of Rochester basketball player Todd Rosseau opens his political science textbook, the first line looks something like this: 'We hop thes turths to be sefl eivdent'.

But this is not just another 'jock' who cannot read. Rosseau in fact is very bright. But he suffers from a reading disorder that does not discriminate between the mentally gifted and the disabled.

'When I was growing up, I used to think I was just dumb,' the college senior said. 'I thought that for a long time. I didn't know I was different from anyone else. I just wondered why my sister was so much smarter than I was. It was all so confusing.'

The first hint that something was wrong came in a kindergarten play group. 'It was on my report card,' he recalled. 'The teacher wrote, "Good with blocks and not much else".' By fourth grade, Todd was leaving class for special tutoring in language arts several times a week. When that did not help, he went to Massachusetts General Hospital in Boston to be tested for learning disorders. 'The tests showed that I had a superior IQ, but I was severely dyslexic,' he said. 'I see what everyone else sees on the paper, but somehow in the translation to the mind, it shows up wrong. And it's a random thing. I can read the same sentence perfectly the second time.'

Todd attended seventh and eighth grades at the Carroll School in Lincoln, Massachusetts, a special facility for children with reading disorder. He went on to a private high school in Cambridge, Massachusetts, which was founded as a prep school for Harvard but offered extensive assistance for youths with learning problems. The University of Rochester was a good college choice in that it too offers special assistance to students with special needs – as well as an excellent basketball programme. 'School never was as easy for me as other people. There were times when I worked real hard with no results. It would be easy to say, "There's no point in trying, I'm dyslexic". But basketball has helped,' he said. 'It gave me something to work for outside school.' Todd's talent in basketball is one source of his resilience, but so is his stick-to-itiveness when it comes to overcoming his difficulties with reading. 'I'm learning the ropes and getting better at it. As a matter of fact, I even read for pleasure, something I didn't do much in high school.'

Source: Adapted from Meyer, 1989.

---

referral (Sattler, 2002). More research is clearly warranted on this given the recent research showing that children from higher socio-economic background tend to have higher initial reading scores and show faster rates of growth compared with children from lower backgrounds (Aikens and Barbarin, 2008). Additionally, initial rates of reading performance and subsequent growth are higher when parents show high levels of educational involvement (Cheadle, 2008).

Comorbidity and Differential Diagnosis
RD and Other Learning Disorders

While some children have difficulty only in the domain of reading, other children evidence multiple learning disorders, including difficulties with oral language, written expression or mathematics. Children with more pervasive learning problems may comprise a different subtype with a different etiology (Lyon et al., 2003a).

RD and ADHD

Around 20 to 25 per cent of students with RD also have ADHD (Beitchman and Young, 1997). However, the reasons for this overlap are not known. There is evidence suggesting a shared genetic variation between the two conditions. One can also argue that problems with attention along with restlessness interfere with learning to read. It is equally plausible to argue that persistent academic failure can lead to restlessness and inattention in the classroom. However, it is important to tease apart the difference between these two disorders to ensure that both diagnoses are warranted. While some children do experience both a reading disability and ADHD, there are others whose symptoms may not fit.

RD and Behaviour Problems

Three longitudinal studies throw light on the relation between RD and behaviour problems: Sanson et al.'s (1996) study going from infancy to middle childhood; Smart et al.'s (1996) study of the middle childhood period; and Maughan and colleagues' (1996) study going from adolescence to early adulthood.

In general, the results indicate a lack of any direct causal relation between RD and behaviour problems. For example, there was no evidence that RD in middle childhood was the precursor of behaviour problems in general or externalizing problems in particular in adolescence and adulthood. In addition, adolescents who had RD had no higher rates of alcohol problems, antisocial personality disorders or crime when they became adults. While there was an increase in delinquency in teenagers, this was due to poor school attendance (and, inferentially, increased opportunities for delinquent behaviour) rather than to RD itself. Thus, whatever relation exists between RD and behaviour problems is due to the comorbid condition of ADHD.

Reversing the direction of causation, we can ask whether behaviour problems and ADHD can be precursors of RD. The longitudinal data indicate that they can. For example, there was evidence that problem behaviour in the period of infancy through the preschool increased the likelihood of RD plus behaviour problems in middle childhood. Moreover, while behaviour problems in general were not a precursor of RD in the middle-childhood period, hyperactivity in particular was.

The developmental data also indicate that there were important sex differences. Boys followed a different developmental course from girls, evidencing more externalizing problems such as hyperactivity, which, as we have seen, can be a precursor of RD. However, girls develop RD in the absence of behaviour problems in general and hyperactivity in particular.

More recent studies have investigated whether the relationship between RD and problem behaviour might be due to the contribution of a third variable: ADHD. Indeed, Willcutt and Pennington (2000) found that the comorbidity of RD and ADHD explained the association between externalizing behaviour and reading problems. Once ADHD was accounted for, the association between RD and misbehaviour was no longer significant.

RD and Social Skills Deficits

The relation between learning disorders and social skills deficits has been well established empirically. In a meta-analysis of 152 studies over the past 15 years, Kavale and Forness (1996) found that 75 per cent of students with LD manifested significantly greater social skills deficits than did comparison groups. The finding was robust, being consistent across different evaluators (teachers, peers, and the students themselves) and across most of the major components of social skills.

In terms of peer evaluations, children with LD were considered less popular and cooperative, were selected less often as friends and were avoided more than non-LD peers. These negative evaluations, in turn, were attributed to a perceived lack of communicative competence and reduced empathetic behaviour. LD students themselves, like their peers, perceived their social functioning as adversely affected by a lack of competence in communication as well as deficient social problem-solving skills. There were two pervasive attitudes underlying their perceptions. The first was a general feeling of inferiority due to a poor self-concept and a lack of self-esteem. The second was an external locus of control that made them view success and failure as due to luck or chance rather than to their own effort.

RD and Internalizing Problems

Children with RD are vulnerable to the development of internalizing problems, including low self-esteem, social isolation, anxiety and depression, many of which can be attributed directly to their frustrations and failure experiences in school. Internalizing problems are a particular risk for girls with RD (Willcutt and Pennington, 2000).

The Direction of Effects

Do behavioural and emotional problems co-occur with learning disorders, or are they causally related to them? Evidence suggests that the direction of effects is from learning problems to socio-emotional problems. For example, large-scale clinical trials show that effective interventions for reading and math difficulties in first grade are associated with lower levels of behavioural and emotional problems in middle school (Kellam et al., 1994). In short, children who fail in school are likely to act out or to feel badly about themselves, but remediation of their academic problems can moderate the risk.

Etiology: The Biological Context
Genetic Influences

There is a strong genetic component in reading achievement (Kovas et al., 2007). Grigorenko's (2001) review of this research shows that 25 to 60 per cent of parents of RD children also have reading difficulties, and this is more true of the fathers than the mothers. However, children's reading growth is often dependent on being provided a rich home literacy experiences (Aikens and Barbarin, 2008) and thus there also exists a strong overlap with environmental factors. Further, twin studies find that concordance rates are high for monozygotic twins (80 per cent) versus dizygotic twins (50 per cent). More complex statistical analysis estimates that 50 to 60 per cent of the variance in reading achievement is attributable to genetic factors. Advances in genetic research are beginning to allow investigators to locate the area of dysfunction. Currently, the best evidence implicates an area of chromosome 6, a finding that has been replicated in several different laboratories.

Neuropsychology

As our techniques for viewing the brain in action advance, so does our understanding of the neuropsychology of reading disorders.

For example, studies using technology that measures magnetic activity in the brain have found consistent differences in the activation patterns of children with and without RD. For example, Simos and colleagues (2000) observed brain activity while children completed tasks in which they listened to words or were asked to recognize either real words or nonsense syllables. Both groups of children showed activation primarily in the left hemisphere when listening to words, as would be expected. However, on the word recognition tasks, brain activation patterns were remarkably different for the two groups. Typically developing children showed activation in the occipital lobes, which are specialized for visual recognition, followed by activation of the left temporoparietal region (including the angular gyrus, Wernicke's area, and the superior temporal gyrus). In children with RD, however, the temporoparietal region of the *right* hemisphere was activated. This altered pattern of lateralization is consistent with findings based on other brain-imaging methodologies, including positron-emission tomography and functional MRI.

Etiology: The Individual Context
Normal Reading Development

Before discussing the etiology of RD it is essential to present the normal process by which children learn how to read. Reading is obviously a complex skill involving the entire gamut of psychological processes, from visual and auditory perception to the higher-order thinking processes of abstraction and conceptualization. Our discussion will concentrate on the very early stages of learning to read, since these will be the most germane to our interest in the etiology of RD. (A more comprehensive presentation can be found in Lyon et al., 2003a.)

Consider this hypothetical situation: a friend shows you, a non-Arabic reader, a sentence in Arabic and challenges you to find the name David, which is pronounced 'Dah-oo-dah' in the Arabic language. (See Fig. 7.5.) Confronted with a swirl of graceful lines, dashes, dots and curlicues, how would you go about it? One way is to assume that Arabic uses a phonetic alphabet as does English. Analysing the sound of the word, you note that it begins and ends with the same sound, 'dah'. Next, you assume that the written Arabic reflects the sounds of the oral language on a one-to-one basis. Consequently, you look for a visual pattern that

FIGURE 7.5   Find the Name David.

لما كنا في كندا قابلنا داوود في شلالات نياغرا.

begins and ends with the same squiggle, with a different squiggle in between. While any or all of your assumptions may be wrong, you are using a process of reasoning that serves you well in comprehending your native written language. What you are doing is proceeding from the known oral word to the unknown written representation of that word and trying to 'break the code' of the latter. ('Dah-oo-dah' are the letters of the word on the far right.)

Many psychologists regard *breaking the code* as an essential first step in learning to read; specifically, the preschooler must find the relation between the *meaningless visual pattern* of the written language and the *meaningful auditory patterns* of words and sentences.

The major problem in breaking the written code is that spoken words are directly perceived as units; for example, 'cat', when spoken, registers as a whole. The fact that 'cat' is really made up of three separate sounds, or *phonemes*, does not occur to children. Written language is different. Written words do not register as wholes. Understanding that individual words are composed of units – the letters – and understanding that different letters represent different phonemes is crucial to learning how to read. Awareness of and access to the sound structure of language is called *phonological awareness*, which, stated simply, is the awareness that words are made up of separate sounds, or phonemes.

Identification of the individual phonemes in words is called *phonological analysis*, while combining a sequence of isolated speech sounds in order to produce a recognizable word is *phonological synthesis*. One measure of phonological analysis involves orally presenting children with words containing two to five blended phonemes and asking them to tap out the number of phonemic segments. One measure of synthesizing skills is a word-blending task that consists of presenting individual phonemes at half-second intervals and asking the child to pronounce the word as a whole.

Phonemic awareness shows a developmental trend. At age 4 years few children can segment by phonemes, although half can segment by syllables. By 6 years of age 90 percent can segment by syllables and 70 per cent can segment by phonemes. By 7 years of age 80 per cent can segment syllables into their component phonemes, but between 15 and 20 per cent still have difficulty understanding the alphabetic principle underlying the ability to segment words and syllables into phonemes – which is approximately the same percentage of children manifesting difficulties in learning to read.

Phonological Processing and RD

A deficit in phonological processing is the major culprit that impedes learning how to read (Lyon et al., 2003a). Approximately 80 to 90 per cent of children with RD have a defect in phonological processing, with the gender ratio being no different from that in the population as a whole. For example, studies show that children with RD have difficulty with segmenting phonemes, storing phonological codes in short-term memory, categorizing phonemes and producing some speech sounds. Moreover, the research indicates that the relation is a causal one; that is, there is evidence that the deficit precedes the difficulty in learning to read.

There are two cautions in regard to the research findings. First, all of the studies used single words or word recognition as the measure of reading, and it remains to be seen whether differences exist on other measures of reading disorder such as comprehension or response to instructions. Second, we are dealing with the weight of evidence rather than with universal findings, since there are some contradictory data and some support for alternative etiological hypotheses.

Locating the origin of RD in the ability to decode and read single words runs counter to the idea that RD represents a defect in reading comprehension. However, comprehension itself is dependent on the ability to decode single words rapidly and automatically. If words are not rapidly and accurately processed, children's ability to understand what they read is likewise hampered.

Emotional Development and School Achievement

While we tend to focus on cognitive factors when we think about the skills and qualities needed for school achievement, the child involved in the learning process is engaged emotionally as well. When the task is difficult, is the child intrigued by the challenge, driven to overcome it, or humiliated by failure and easily discouraged? For all children, and even for adults, learning requires some ego resilience in that we may well feel 'dumb' while we are struggling to master a new task. For children with learning disabilities, the challenges to self-esteem and motivation are amplified, as they watch their age-mates surpass them; and they may even suffer the wounds of teasing by peers and the stigmatization of placement in the special education classroom. For some LD children, such negative experiences may turn them off the learning process entirely. (See Box 7.7.)

Another important contribution to children's attitudes toward school and the learning process is made by teachers. Children as young as first grade appraise the way that teachers behave toward them and their classmates and learn to differentiate themselves according to who is a high and low achiever. (See Fig. 7.6.) *Differential teacher treatment* (Weinstein, 2002) subsequently affects children's self-image, their choice of which peers to play with and study with, and how receptive or responsive they are to future teachers' attempts to educate them. Further, children who are turned off to learning, dislike school and react as if the teacher is torturing them are, in the transactional model, not going to inspire her to do her best teaching.

Grade retention is another consequence of poor school achievement that has a significant effect on children's socio-emotional functioning. For example, in a longitudinal sample of children

---

Box 7.7 A Piagetian Approach to Understanding Underachievement

Philip Cowan (1978), in his pioneering book on developmental psychopathology, *Piaget with Feeling*, describes his experience offering consultation to teachers regarding children who had been identified as underachievers. A good Piagetian, he began by interviewing the children in order to gain their perspective on just where the problem lay. He discovered that the children were able to articulate quite clearly that they had made a conscious decision to disengage from the learning process, and they were very aware of their motivations for doing so.

Some wanted to win a power struggle with their parents and teachers – whether or not the child learned was something the child alone had control over.

Some avoided learning because they wanted to reject adults' expectations of what they should be like, or to avoid being ridiculed by their classmates for being 'nerds' or 'teacher's pets' if they did well in school.

Others Cowan described as having a 'Peter Pan' syndrome: with increased learning comes increased responsibilities and expectations from others, and the best way to avoid these unwanted demands is to fail to achieve or to deliberately give the wrong answers on tests.

Yet another group wanted to avoid the experience of failure and therefore did not want to risk trying to succeed for fear that they would feel badly about themselves if they made an effort that missed the mark. As long as they did not try, their failures could be chalked up to being 'too cool to care'.

FIGURE 7.6 Differential Teacher Treatment.

followed from kindergarten to age 12 in Quebec, Pagani and colleagues (2001) found that children's academic performance worsened, and their anxiety, inattention and disruptive behaviour persisted or even increased after being held back a grade. Boys were more vulnerable than girls to the negative effects of grade retention on achievement and externalizing behaviour, but both long- and short-term negative effects were striking for all children. Indeed, Stipek (2001) points to the pernicious effects of unsupportive school environments that 'demoralize and discourage children' (p. 228), leading to negative attitudes towards the self and others.

Rethinking LD

Let us review certain relevant findings concerning RD.

1 Children with RD do not form a distinct qualitatively different group of readers. Rather, performance in reading is normally distributed with children with RD and children with GRD at the lower end of the continuum. Moreover, children with RD do not differ from children with GRD in regard to numerous cognitive dimensions.

2 Accurate, fluent reading, with appropriate comprehension, depends upon rapid and automatic recognition and decoding of the printed word – in short, on phonological processing. The basis of RD is a specific defect in this processing.

3 Phonological defects impede the normal progress of learning to read *regardless of the children's level of general intelligence* – that is, regardless of whether they have adequate intelligence and are labelled RD or whether their intelligence is below average and they are labelled GRD.

It is this last point that hides a demon. If the core difficulty in learning how to read exists regardless of IQ level, what happens to the concept of LD as a discrepancy between achievement and ability? In regard to reading, at least, the disorder has little to do with phonological defects. In short, the discrepancy model is invalid. At the very least, the conceptualization of LD must be broadened to recognize the fact that the discrepancy model is not universally applicable. Instead, there may be core deficiencies that impede academic progress regardless of children's general ability.

Developmental Course

A number of well-designed longitudinal studies attest to the continuity of RD from childhood into adulthood. (Our presentation follows Maughan, 1995). Not all aspects of reading are equally affected, however. Comprehension continues to improve well into adulthood, for example, while phonological processing (i.e., understanding the sound structure of words) is highly resistant to change.

A number of factors determine the developmental course of RD. As might be expected, initial severity of RD and general intelligence are the most potent predictors of progress; however, context factors also play an important role. Socially advantaged children who are given special attention at school and support at home can make good progress even though they take longer to achieve a given level of competence and they tend to avoid reading-intensive courses. However, school systems are inequitable and there are significant differences between schools in affluent and impoverished neighbourhoods in terms of the length of waiting lists for LD assessments, classroom size, resources for special education, and the like. Consequently, the picture of the disadvantaged student with RD is a bleak one characterized by early dropout along with a negative attitude towards formal schooling. For example, one study showed that 40 per cent of poor readers remained without any academic or vocational qualifications in their twenties. Educational attainment, in turn, is the strongest predictor of occupational outcome, so it is not surprising that disadvantaged students with RD experience more unemployment, tend to work at semi-skilled or unskilled tasks, and have lower vocational aspirations. (See Maughan, 1995.)

In terms of adult self-perception, childhood reading problems adversely affect only the specific area of literacy, where adults tend to blame themselves for their problem. The level of overall self-esteem of such adults, however, is on a par with that of their more literate peers. In terms of general psychological well-being, the functioning of young adults shows little traces of the problems that had formerly characterized their behaviour. Where problems exist, they seem to be related to other difficulties, such as immaturity or personality disturbances, rather than to RD per se.

Summary

The severity of children's RD and their general intellectual level are the most powerful predictors of RD's developmental course. Advantaged children who receive support at home and special education at school and who, as adults, select vocations that maximize their strengths and minimize their limitations can have a positive view of their general self-worth (although still blaming themselves for their reading failure) and tend to outgrow their childhood problems. On the negative side, being disadvantaged increases the likelihood of dropping out of school at an early age, which, in turn, limits vocational choice and increases the likelihood of unemployment.

Intervention

Assessment and the Educational Plan

Intervention with learning disorders begins with a careful educational assessment that details the child's deficits as well as strengths that might be capitalized on to help the child overcome the challenges. Next, the parents, teachers and school psychologist meet to discuss the findings and devise an Individualized Educational Plan that will provide the least restrictive and most supportive educational modifications that will increase the child's chances of success in school.

Mainstreaming

Increasingly, due to the Individuals with Disabilities Act (IDEA, 1997), children with special educational needs are mainstreamed with other children. Mainstreaming, also known as inclusion or regular education, is intended to reduce stigma or the denial of educational opportunities that might result from segregation in a separate classroom. Instead, children either receive specialized tutoring in the regular classroom or are pulled out for part of the day in order to receive services.

Educational Interventions

Educational interventions utilize a number of modalities, including the following (here we follow Elliott et al., 1999, except where otherwise noted).

Instructional Interventions

Instructional interventions include the use of specially designed educational materials that are devised to target the specific deficits that are interfering with the child's ability to perform in school. For example, in the case of reading disorder, the child might be provided with exercises and practice with letters, words and a variety of specialized reading materials. Other interventions attempt to maximize children's ability to learn by presenting information in the children's preferred sensory modality, such as vision or hearing, or presenting material in a multisensory manner that combines sight, touch, hearing and kinesthetic cues.

Phonological Training

Phonological training that specifically helps children with word identification is particularly helpful in the case of reading disorders and has been proven effective (Lovett et al., 2000). Remarkably, Simos and colleagues (2002) demonstrated that an eight-week intensive course of phonologically based intervention was successful in changing patterns of brain activation. Children with severe word recognition difficulties, ranging in age from 7 to 17 years, received an intense phonologically based intervention for two hours a day, five days a week, over an eight-week period. While prior to treatment all of the children exhibited the atypical pattern of activation in the right hemisphere, after the intervention not only were their reading scores in the average range, but their brain images had shifted to the more typical left-dominated activation pattern. (See Fig. 7.7.) Clearly, this is a powerful intervention. While special phonological instructional materials have been developed for the classroom, parents also are able to work on these skills with home-based programmes. Materials are presented in an attractive and game-like way, including opportunities for hands-on manipulation of objects, such as using coloured alphabet blocks to break words up into their constituent sounds.

Behavioural Strategies

Classroom contingency management involves teachers providing children with rewards for adaptive learning behaviours such as completing work, handing in assignments on time, and checking work for accuracy. The focus may be specifically academic, such as increasing the legibility of handwriting, or it may be a more general academic one such as increasing on-task behaviours. *Performance feedback* involves providing children with frequent direct feedback about their task performance, in order to increase awareness and self-monitoring.

Cognitive Interventions

Cognitive strategies include *self-instruction* to help children to talk themselves through problem-solving steps. For example, in the case of reading, young children might be encouraged to remind themselves to sound out the words, while more advanced readers might be provided with a series of questions with which to quiz themselves on the text (e.g., 'What is the main point here? How does this sentence follow from the one that came before?'). Another cognitive technique is *self-monitoring*, which, as we saw in the treatment of ADHD, helps children to learn to monitor, regulate and reward their own academic efforts.

Computer-Assisted Learning

Children find computers inherently interesting and rewarding and therefore may benefit from special computer programs for reading, mathematics and spelling. Such programs may keep children engaged in the sometimes tedious processes of decoding speech and learning word-attack skills, for example.

Peer Interventions

Peer interventions include: *peer tutoring*, in which children help one another on academic tasks; *cooperative learning*, in which students complete assignments together; and *group contingencies*, in which the entire class is rewarded for good effort by all class members.

Collaborative Partnerships with Parents

At a minimal level, teachers may utilize *school-to-home journals* in order to maintain good communication with parents. Teachers may use the journals to keep parents aware of what work needs to be

FIGURE 7.7 Brain Activation Patterns in Reading Disorders Before and After Phonological Training.

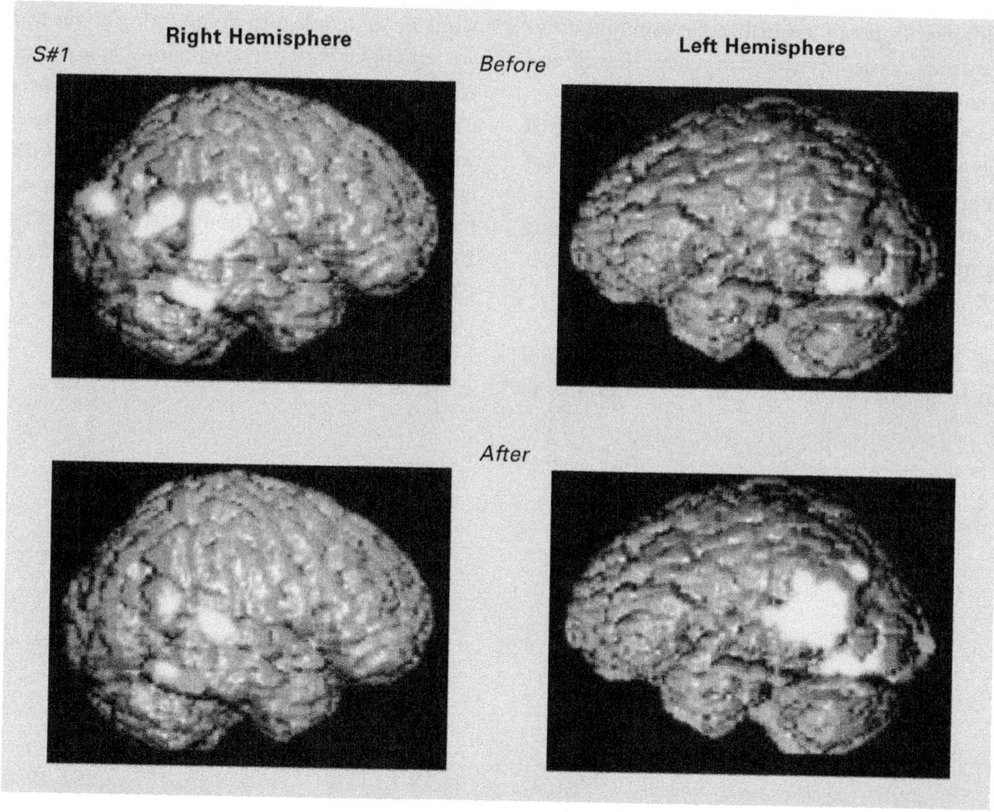

Source: Simos, et al., 2002.

done, and parents may use them to alert teachers to areas of homework in which children particularly are struggling.

However, even more active involvement of parents in their children's education has been touted as a strategy for remediating or even preventing early learning problems from developing into full-blown disorders. The goal of this movement is for parents and teachers to work together as collaborative *educational partners* (Christenson and Buerkle, 1999), who meet together to discuss problems as they emerge and to arrive at mutually agreed goals and means for meeting them. Empirical support for collaborative partnerships is promising. Results are particularly good when

efforts are made to reach out to and empower low income parents, some of whom may feel intimidated by or disengaged from official institutions such as schools.

Effectiveness of Interventions

Despite their appeal and the good intentions behind them, the empirical evidence for learning disorders interventions is only modest to date. In a review of dozens of educational intervention studies, Kavale and Forness (2000) found that most yielded only medium to small effect sizes. Further, there is considerable debate about whether children with special needs are best served by inclusion in mainstream classrooms, where they still may be stigmatized by other students, and where teachers might not have the training or time to provide the children with the individualized accommodations they need in order to succeed in school (Kavale and Forness, 2000).

One thing is certain, however, and that is that early assessment and intervention are key. For example, children at risk for reading problems benefit most when they receive phonological training beginning in the preschool period (Foorman et al., 1997).

One consequence of various psychopathologies may be feelings of anxiety. Consider children with LD, who are forced to go to school every day and face failure in reading or mathematics or spelling while being helpless to do anything about it; who are unpopular with peers; who must face parents or teachers who might regard them as 'just lazy' – all of these are enough to make any child feel tense and worried. However, such natural reactions are different from the psychopathology of anxiety, which is more than worrying about worrisome things. Exploring anxiety disorders will be our concern in Chapter 8.

CHAPTER 08

Middle Childhood: The Anxiety Disorders

Chapter contents

In the course of his psychoanalysis, a middle-aged man recalls, 'When I acted up as a kid my grandmother would scold me, saying, "You're too young to have nerves!" For a long time after that I kept wondering, "Am I old enough now?" like having nerves was one of the signs of being grown up.' Grandmother, unknowingly, was a good Freudian. According to classical psychoanalytic theory, excessive anxiety is a hallmark of neurosis and neurosis itself is a developmental achievement. However, both modern research and theory belie this. Anxiety is an experience that is normative and moreover serves a function in development. But, when development goes awry, even preschoolers can suffer from debilitating anxieties that interfere with their functioning and cause them significant emotional distress.

In our presentation of the anxiety disorders, we proceed as follows. First we describe the characteristics of anxiety and fears as they are manifest over the course of development. Then, we describe general features common to the anxiety disorders before exploring several specific anxiety disorders in turn: generalized anxiety disorder, specific phobias, social anxiety, separation anxiety disorder, obsessive-compulsive disorder and Posttraumatic stress disorder. For each disorder, we offer a clinical vignette that will help to inform differential diagnosis. After that we raise the question that lies at the heart of developmental psychopathology: why does normal development go awry and produce anxiety disorders? To answer this question, we consider an integrative developmental model that integrates the major research findings concerning etiology.

The Nature of Anxiety

Fears in Normal Development

Fear is usually defined as a normal reaction to an environmental threat. It is adaptive and even essential to survival because it warns the individual that a situation may be physically or psychologically harmful. In the early years of life, infants learn to anticipate when a noxious stimulus is imminent and experience *signal anxiety*, an internal red flag that warns, 'Danger ahead!' With such warning, the child can take steps to avoid the feared situation, including crying out to the parent for help.

Fears are common in childhood. For example, Muris and colleagues (2000) found that 71 per cent of preschoolers acknowledge having fears, whereas fears peak between the ages of 7 to 9 (87 per cent of children), and then decline from age 10 to 12 (68 per cent of children). There also are age differences in the content of children's fears. (See Table 8.1.) Preschoolers are most likely to report fears of ghosts and monsters, while in middle childhood these imaginary fears begin to be replaced by more realistic fears, such as the fear of bodily injury and physical danger. However, school-aged children continue to show some irrational fears, such as fears of snakes and mice, as well as nightmares. Adolescence brings with it a new set of age-appropriate fears, such as social anxieties, concerns over money and work, and fear of war or destruction of the environment. The fear of failure looms particularly in the teenage years. Irrational fears are less frequent but do not disappear altogether; teenagers also can be afraid of the dark, of storms, of spiders, or of cemeteries (Vasey et al., 1994).

From Normal Fears to Anxiety Disorders

In the process of normal development, children are able to master their fears by the use of increasingly adaptive defence mechanisms (see Chapter 2) and sophisticated coping strategies. For example, as

TABLE 8.1 Common Fears in Childhood

Age Range	Worries and Fears
0–12 months	Loud noises, looming objects, loss of support.
12–24 months	Separation, strangers.
24–36 months	Separation, animals, dogs.
3–6 years	Separation, strangers, animals, darkness, imaginary beings.
6–10 years	Darkness, injury, being alone, animals.
10–12 years	Injury, school failure, ridicule, thunderstorms.
12–18 years	Social failure, peer rejection, war, natural disasters, the future.

children enter concrete operations, they are able to use logic and reasoning to calm their fears, as exemplified by the coping strategy of positive cognitive restructuring (e.g., 'I'll remind myself that it is just a dream; it's not real.' 'Even if I goof up, it really isn't the end of the world; I'll do better next time'). By the same token, with age children increasingly are able to 'dose' their exposure to a feared stimulus until they feel ready to approach it (e.g., 'That makes me too nervous, so I'm not going to think about it right now').

However, the overwhelming nature of pathological anxiety suggests a failure in these adaptational mechanisms. Anxiety disorders are distinguished from normal fears on the basis of their *intensity*, which is out of proportion to the situation; their *maladaptiveness* and their *persistence*. They are also *beyond voluntary control* and cannot be explained or reasoned away. Ultimately, our task will be to understand how it is that development goes awry and leaves some children unable to master their fears.

The Anxiety Disorders
Common Features

As the name implies, **anxiety disorders** are a group of disturbances characterized by intense, persistent anxiety. They also have other characteristics in common: the symptoms are distressing and unwanted, reality testing is relatively intact, the disturbance is enduring, and the symptoms do not actively violate social norms. Descriptively, Freud was correct in locating the origins of anxiety disorders in middle childhood, for the most part.

Children with anxiety disorders are **internalizers**; that is, their suffering is turned inward. Recall that in Chapter 3 we described Achenbach's (2000) factor analysis of a symptom checklist for children, which yielded a principal factor that he labelled 'internalizing–externalizing'. Among internalizing symptoms were phobias, worrying, stomach aches, withdrawal, nausea, compulsions, insomnia, seclusiveness, depression, crying – all indicating an inwardly suffering child.

In terms of *prevalence*, anxiety disorders are among the most common disorders of childhood and adolescence. In the National Comorbidity Survey of 10 123 adolescents in the USA, anxiety disorders were found among 31.9 per cent of community youth (Merikangas et al., 2010). Among the 2942 German children included in the BELLA study (Ravens-Sieberer et al., 2008), 16.5 per cent of girls and 12.3 per cent of boys in the 7- to 10-year-old age-range reported symptoms of anxiety that were significant enough to interfere with functioning. Other large-scale international studies of children report rates of anxiety disorders ranging from 3.3 in the UK to 9.5 in Puerto Rico (Merikangas et al., 2010).

In clinical samples, prevalence rates are much higher: as many as 45 per cent of children undergoing treatment in mental health clinics are diagnosed with an anxiety disorder (Last et al., 1992). In addition, the median age of onset for anxiety disorders – 6 years of age – is substantially earlier than for any other mental health disorder (Merikangas et al., 2010). However, these overall figures mask a developmental trend of increased prevalence. For example, one prospective study found an increase in prevalence from 7.5 per cent of 11-year-olds to 20 per cent of 21-year-olds (Kovacs and Devlin, 1998).

There also are *gender differences* in the prevalence of anxiety disorders in general (although, as we shall see, these gender differences do not hold for all the anxiety disorder subtypes). In Rescorla and colleagues' (2007) comparison of Youth Self-Reports obtained from adolescents in 24 countries around the world, girls consistently reported higher rates of internalizing symptoms. Similarly, Lewinsohn and colleagues (1998) found a predominance of females in their study of 1079 US adolescents with anxiety disorders. Although there was no sex difference in *age of onset*, by the age of 6 females were already twice as likely as males to have experienced an anxiety disorder. As age increases, so does the gender gap. Girls are increasingly more likely than boys to become diagnosed with anxiety disorders throughout childhood and into adolescence and early adulthood (Roza et al., 2003).

Anxiety disorders are unlikely to occur alone. Some studies show *comorbidity* rates as high as 65 and even 95 per cent (Kovacs and Devlin, 1998). While externalizing disorders such as ADHD and conduct disorders can also be present, they are relatively infrequent. Most commonly, anxiety disorders occur with another type of anxiety. Depression is the next most frequently seen comorbid condition.

Finally, anxiety disorders are unlikely to be outgrown: there is significant evidence for **continuity**. For example, in a longitudinal study conducted in the Netherlands of a sample of over 2000 children, parents' reports of children's anxiety were predictive of anxiety disorders in these individuals according to clinical interviews conducted 24 years later (Reef et al., 2010).

Are Anxiety Disorders and Depression Distinct?

Because of the close relation between anxiety and depression and their high degree of comorbidity, researchers have wrestled with the question of whether they are distinct disorders or whether they are accounted for by an underlying common factor. In particular, Clark and Watson's (1991) **tripartite model of emotion** proposes that there is a general factor, **negative affectivity** – a propensity towards negative mood states such as fear, sadness, anger and guilt – which contributes to the development of both anxiety and depression. In turn, their model proposes two additional factors that differentiate the disorders: *physiological hyperarousal*, which is specific to anxiety, and *low positive affect*, which is specific to depression. The tripartite model has received accumulating support in research conducted within adult, adolescent and child samples. For example, in a large ethnically diverse sample of schoolchildren in Hawaii, Chorpita (2002) demonstrated that negative affectivity was positively related to both anxiety and depression, whereas low positive affect was related only to depression and physiological arousal was related only to the anxiety symptoms of panic.

The implications of this model for the classification of disorders, Watson (2005) argues, are profound. Although the developers of DSM have not yet adopted the approach this empirically based structural model would lead the field towards, the research suggests that certain anxiety disorders should be grouped with depression on the basis of an underlying dimension of *distress* (i.e., major depression, dysthymic disorder and generalized anxiety disorder), whereas others should be grouped separately on the basis of an underlying dimension of *fear* (i.e., panic disorder, agoraphobia, social anxiety disorder and simple phobia).

Nonetheless, whereas negative affectivity is a common element in both anxiety and depression, disturbances in either category also have distinctive features that require our attention. For example, Lonigan and colleagues (1994) found that depressed children were more likely to report problems related to loss of interest, low motivation and a negative view of themselves, whereas anxious children reported more worry about the future, their well-being and others' reactions to them.

Next, we turn to a detailed consideration of several of the specific forms that anxiety disorders take in childhood: generalized anxiety disorder, specific phobia, social anxiety, separation anxiety disorder, obsessive-compulsive disorder and Posttraumatic stress disorder.

Generalized Anxiety Disorder

Eleven-year-old Arantxa's parents say that she is a child who 'always worries about everything'. She does not like to try new things and will 'work herself into a state' for weeks before a special event, ruminating about all the things that might go wrong. At school, her teachers report that she repeatedly asks for reassurance about whether her answers are correct and she worries excessively about making mistakes, being late or breaking a rule. Even though she often knows the right answer, she seldom raises her

hand in class because she worries that it will 'come out wrong'. However, her schoolwork often is just as 'perfect' as Arantxa wants it to be, given that she hits the books as soon as she gets home from school and does her work extremely neatly, even if that means tearing up the paper and starting again several times. At night, she frequently has difficulty falling asleep, spending as long as two hours fretting about the events of the day that has passed and worrying about the day ahead. She worries about robbers getting into the house at night and trying to hurt her family, and she will often get up at night to investigate noises and to check that her little brother is okay.

Definition and Characteristics

Definition

In previous editions, the DSM provided a separate category of Overanxious Disorder of Childhood. However, in the most recent edition, the DSM-IV-TR includes both children and adults in the diagnosis of generalized anxiety disorder (GAD). (See Table 8.2.) The hallmark of GAD is *worry*. Unlike other anxiety disorders, in which the worry is related to a specific situation (such as separation) or a specific object (such as a phobia of snakes), the child with GAD can turn anything into an occasion for worry. (See Fig. 8.1.)

The worries of children with GAD focus particularly on their competence and the quality of their performance in activities such as in school or sports. These worries are present even when they are not being evaluated by others – children with GAD are their own worst critics. They tend to perfectionism and self-judging, redoing tasks over and over in order to get them 'just right'. They also may worry excessively about catastrophes, such as the possibility of a natural disaster or war, and seek reassurance repeatedly without benefiting from it. Small imperfections, such as not being punctual, may be raised to the level of catastrophe in their minds.

Observable manifestations of generalized anxiety include: muscle tension; trembling; feeling

TABLE 8.2 DSM-IV-TR Criteria for Generalized Anxiety Disorder

A. Excessive anxiety and worry (apprehensive expectation), occurring more days than not for at least 6 months, about a number of events or activities (such as work or school performance).
B. The person finds it difficult to control the worry.
C. The anxiety and worry are associated with three (or more) of the following six symptoms (with at least some symptoms present for more days than not for the past 6 months). **Note:** Only one item is required in children.
  (1) restlessness or feeling keyed up or on edge
  (2) being easily fatigued
  (3) difficulty concentrating or mind going blank
  (4) irritability
  (5) muscle tension
  (6) sleep disturbance (difficulty falling or staying asleep, or restless, unsatisfying sleep)
D. The focus of the anxiety and worry is not confined to a particular situation or event (as in other anxiety disorders).
E. The anxiety, worry, or physical symptoms cause clinically significant distress or impairment in social, occupational, or other important areas of functioning.

Source: Reprinted with permission from the *Diagnostic and Statistical Manual of Mental Disorders*, Fourth Edition Text Revision. Copyright 2000 by the American Psychiatric Association.

shaky; somatic symptoms such as stomach aches, nausea or diarrhoea; nervous habits, such as nail biting or hair-twirling; and a tendency to startle easily. Younger children may find it difficult to make the connection between these physical sensations and their emotional state. Further, very young children may not yet have a verbal label for such feelings as 'anxiety' or 'worry'. Thus, it may be left to the astute adult to infer what it means when a physically healthy preschooler frequently declines to go out to play because she or he is 'feeling sick'.

Cultural Variations

Symptoms of anxiety also may vary across cultures. For example, whereas individuals from Western cultures may express more *cognitive* symptoms (e.g., excessive worrying), individuals with GAD from Asian cultures may evidence anxiety more in *somatic* forms (e.g., muscle tension) (APA, 2000).

Characteristics
Prevalence

The best and most recent prevalence data in the USA come from the National Comorbidity Study

FIGURE 8.1 A Child with Generalized Anxiety Disorder Can Transform Any Event into an Occasion for Worry.

Source: CALVIN AND HOBBES Copyright © 1988 Watterson. Distributed by Universal Press Syndicate. Reprinted with permission. All rights reserved.

(Merikangas et al., 2010) which indicates that, among US adolescents, 3 per cent of girls and 1.5 per cent of boys meet criteria for a diagnosis of GAD. In turn, rates among community children are 0.8 in the UK and 2.4 in Puerto Rico (Merikangas et al., 2010).

Comorbidity and Differential Diagnosis

Whereas GAD is characterized by a global and diffuse state of anxiety, children with GAD also are vulnerable to developing other *anxiety disorders*, such as specific phobias. Although the disorders are distinct, GAD also often co-occurs with *depression* (APA, 2000). It is easy to see why. The mind of the child who is worrying about his or her performance ('I'm not going to do it right. I'm gonna mess up') is teeming with negative thoughts and self-doubt. Chronic perfectionism and self-criticism can lead to a sense that one is not and never will be 'good enough'. Similarly, excessive worry about bad things that might happen contributes to a child's sense of hopelessness and helplessness.

Developmental Course

The majority of adults with GAD report that they have been anxious all their lives (APA, 2000). Many remained undiagnosed until they sought help in adulthood, suggesting that anxiety symptoms in children are difficult to detect or that they are easy to chalk up as being 'just a stage'. However, the truth of the matter is quite the opposite, given that the course of generalized anxiety disorder tends to be chronic. However, the severity of symptoms is variable over the course of the lifespan, diminishing at some points only to flare up again in times of stress.

Intervention

Cognitive behavioural treatments have proven effective for relieving children of the symptoms of generalized anxiety disorder (Silverman et al., 2008). One of the most well established of these is Kendall's (2006) Coping Cat programme, which we will explore in greater detail in Chapter 17. The essential features of the programme include teaching children to recognize the physiological cues that indicate that they are becoming anxious, identify maladaptive appraisals that turn a neutral event into an anxiety-arousing one, and develop cognitive restructuring and active coping strategies to counter their fears. Children practise their new skills during exposure tasks, in which contact with the anxiety-arousing situation takes place in a series of graduated steps according to the child's pace and comfort level. As a graduation project, children create a picture, videotape or performance that teaches other children what they have learned about conquering anxiety.

A series of randomized clinical trials have established the effectiveness of the intervention (Kendall et al., 2010). Coping Cat also has been adapted successfully cross-culturally, with good results reported by clinicians in the Netherlands, Ireland, Canada (where it was renamed Coping Bear) and Australia (where it was renamed Coping Koala) (Kendall et al., 1998). Its effects over the long term appear to hold. In a longitudinal study, Kendall and colleagues (2004) found that children who successfully completed the treatment for anxiety disorders during childhood had maintained their gains 7.4 years later and were significantly less likely to engage in substance abuse.

Specific Phobias

Twelve-year-old Mei's soccer team is having such a successful year that they have been invited to participate in an exhibition match in another state. It is a three-hour plane ride away and Mei is devastated because she knows she cannot go. The very thought of being in a plane makes her feel shaky, begin to sweat, and fear that she is going to be sick. She is so terrified of planes that she dreads the part of the drive to school that takes her past the airport, where the sound of the jets roaring past sends a shot of anxiety running through her like an electric current. Mei is bewildered by this fear and critical of herself for being unable to 'just get over it'. In fact, she has ridden on a plane before, when the family took a vacation in Vancouver two years ago, and nothing bad happened. Now, however, her mind paints horrific images of the jet falling through the sky, the oxygen failing or terrorists taking over the plane.

Definition and Characteristics
Definition

According to DSM-IV-TR, the defining feature of a specific **phobia** is a marked and persistent fear that is excessive or unreasonable, cued by the presence or anticipation of a specific object or situation. Table 8.3 provides a listing of the major symptoms. Phobias may develop in relation to many different objects or situations, such as fear of snakes, enclosed places, water or flying on aeroplanes. *School phobia* is a common example, although the diagnosis is a controversial one, as we will see.

Common phobias among clinically referred children include the dark, school and dogs (Strauss and Last, 1993). However, childhood phobias sometimes take forms that are bewildering to adults, such as a fear of clowns or people wearing masks. Imagine the dismay of a parent at Disney World whose daughter reacts to Mickey Mouse's greeting with shrieks of terror, or the parent of a son who hides in his room every Halloween because he is horrified by the sight of trick-or-treaters wearing costumes.

Developmental Considerations

It is not uncommon for young children to have transient fears and phobic reactions. For example, a 3-year-old boy was in the car with his father when a blowout forced his father to pull over to change a tyre on the freeway. Although the boy expressed no fear at the sound of the tyre bursting, at the erratic swerving of the car or the sight of his father kneeling on the verge with cars whizzing past him inches away, the boy was startled when, as they pulled away, he spied a lit flare continuing to burn at the side of the road. For several days after the event he reacted fearfully to flames and repeatedly requested reassurance that the 'fire had gone out'. Such fearful reactions may come and go in childhood and, for this reason, the DSM criteria for phobias specify that in children the duration must be at least six months.

Characteristics
Prevalence

In regard to the *prevalence* of phobias, estimates range from 2 to 9 per cent in community samples

TABLE 8.3 DSM-IV-TR Criteria for Specific Phobia

A. Marked and persistent fear that is excessive or unreasonable, cued by the presence or anticipation of a specific object or situation (e.g., flying, heights, animals, receiving an injection, seeing blood).

B. Exposure to the phobic stimulus almost invariably provokes an immediate anxiety response which may take the form of a situationally bound or situationally predisposed panic attack. **Note:** In children, the anxiety may be expressed by crying, tantrums, freezing, or clinging.

C. The person recognizes that the fear is excessive or unreasonable. **Note:** In children, this feature may be absent.

D. The phobic situation(s) is avoided or else is endured with intense anxiety or distress.

E. The avoidance, anxious anticipation, or distress interferes significantly with the person's normal functioning, social activities, or relationships, or there is marked distress about having the phobia.

F. In individuals under age 18 years, the duration is at least 6 months.

Specify type:

Animal Type
Natural Environment Type (e.g., heights, storms, or water)
Blood-Injection-Injury Type
Situational Type (e.g., airplanes, elevators, enclosed places)
Other Type (e.g., fear of choking, vomiting, or contracting an illness; in children, fear of loud sounds or costumed characters)

Source: Reprinted with permission from the *Diagnostic and Statistical Manual of Mental Disorders*, Fourth Edition Text Revision. Copyright 2000 by the American Psychiatric Association.

and 30 to 40 per cent in clinical samples of children (Weiss and Last, 2001). Large-scale studies of children from the UK find prevalence rates of 0.8 (Merikangas et al., 2010), whereas data from the National Comorbidity Study (Merikangas et al., 2010) indicate that, among US adolescents, 22.1 per cent of girls and 16.7 per cent of boys meet criteria for a diagnosis of specific phobia. Thus, as with most of the anxiety disorders, there is evidence for *gender differences*, with girls tending to outnumber boys. Almost no research has been conducted to investigate *social class*, *racial* or *ethnic* differences (Silverman and Ginsburg, 1998).

Comorbidity and Differential Diagnosis

Comorbidity with both *internalizing* and *externalizing* disturbances is high, as is the comorbidity among specific types of phobias (Weiss and Last, 2001). Phobias are specific to a particular stimulus, clearly distinguishing them from the more generalized anxiety of GAD. A separate disorder, which we will review next, is specific to children whose phobias are focused on social relationships.

School Phobia

A common example of a specific phobia is school phobia, which is estimated to occur in 1 per cent of the general population and 5 to 7 per cent of clinically referred children. In school phobia, a child experiences an irrational dread of some aspect of the school situation accompanied by physiological symptoms of anxiety or panic when attendance is imminent, resulting in a partial or total inability to go to school. School phobia in childhood is associated with increased risk of anxiety and depressive disorders in adulthood. For example, approximately a third of such children will need additional treatment for these disorders as adults (Blagg and Yule, 1994).

However, it is important to differentiate true school phobia from the many different disorders that might result in the unwillingness to attend school, known as *school refusal*. For example, children may refuse to attend school due to depression or disturbances that have little to do with

anxiety, such as oppositional defiant disorder. For children with these non-anxious disorders, the reaction lacks the intensity necessary to be a truly phobic response and is mixed with other negative affects such as sadness and low self-esteem. The most common disturbance that may masquerade as school phobia is separation anxiety disorder (Albano et al., 1996). Nonetheless, it is possible to distinguish between the two. Children who fear separation are generally female (when gender differences are found), younger than 10 years of age, and from families of low socio-economic status, whereas children with a school phobia tend to be male, older than 10 years, and of a high socio-economic status (Blagg and Yule, 1994). Children with SAD are more severely disturbed in that they have more additional symptoms and their overall functioning is more disrupted. Children with SAD always remain at home with an attachment figure when not in school, whereas children with a school phobia are comfortable in many settings, as long as it is not the school. Finally, there is evidence that mothers of children with SAD have more emotional problems, particularly in the form of depression (Last and Francis, 1988). (See Box 8.1.)

Developmental Course

Specific phobias have different *ages of onset*. Evidence suggests that animal phobia begins around 7 years of age, blood phobia around 9 and dental phobia around 12. Fear of enclosures and social phobias begin in adolescence or early adulthood (Silverman and Rabian, 1994). Over the course of childhood, specific phobias show a modest level of continuity across intervals varying from two to five years. This finding contradicts a previously held view that they were outgrown for the most part.

Intervention

In their review of research on treating specific phobias, Silverman and colleagues (2008) list a number of methodological limitations: a predominance of single-case studies, research conducted on children

Box 8.1 School Refusal in Japan

Kameguchi and Murphy-Shigetmatsu (2001) discovered that there is a pervasive problem of school refusal among Japanese youths and set about to discover why. Following Minuchin's (1974) structural family theory, they believe that a strong boundary or 'membrane' around the parental subsystem is essential to the healthy organization of the family. However, among Japanese families of school refusing youths, Kameguchi and his colleagues observed a common pattern of excessive closeness between mother and child and disengagement in both the marital and father–child relationships. These patterns, the authors argue, are promoted by features of Japanese society, including the demanding work lives of men that often require them to spend their evenings and vacations with their colleagues rather than their families, and the expectation that women will devote themselves exclusively to the care of their children. Kameguchi and his colleagues propose that 'vague generational boundaries between a parental dyad and a child interfere with the developmental tasks of adolescents... The child is thus deprived of experiences that accelerate his or her psychological separation from the parents and that also assist the parents in separating from the adolescent' (p. 68). Ultimately, both parent and child collude in behaviours – such as the child's staying home from school – which interfere with individuation.

with situational fears such as dental fears rather than on clinical populations of phobic children, lack of formal diagnosis, lack of adequate assessment and lack of follow-up data. Such inadequacies make it impossible to determine which is the treatment of choice or even to judge the merits of a given treatment beyond saying that it shows promise. However, the authors also conclude that *exposure* to the fear stimulus is essential for a successful fear-reduction programme. There are a number of ways in which this exposure can be achieved.

Systematic Desensitization

Systematic desensitization involves substituting the incompatible response of relaxation for the response of anxiety. The therapist helps the child to rate anxiety-arousing experiences on a gradient from the most intense (e.g., riding on a bus) to the least (e.g., walking along the street where the bus stop is). After undergoing relaxation training, the children are instructed to relax after they imagine each successive step in the gradient until they eventually can do so at the point of highest anxiety. When practical considerations allow, the procedure can also be done using the actual feared object or situation, such as a dog or a dark room. In such cases, the procedure is called *in vivo* ('real life') desensitization.

Prolonged Exposure

Prolonged exposure takes the opposite tack from progressive desensitization by exposing children to the full intensity of the feared stimulus and reinforcing them for remaining in its presence for a prolonged period of time. This *'flooding'* with anxiety prevents children from being reinforced by escape and also triggers a physiological reaction involving a return to normal functioning. The exposure itself can be imaginary or *in vivo*.

Modelling

In modelling, the child observes another person interacting adaptively with the feared object. More effective is participatory modelling in which the child, after the observation period, joins the model in gradually approaching the feared object.

Cognitive Self-Management

Cognitive self-management strategies emphasize 'self-talk' to counteract the effects of phobic ideation. There is some evidence that self-statements emphasizing competence (e.g., 'I'm brave and can take care of myself') are more effective than those countering the fear-producing properties of the stimulus (e.g., 'Riding on the bus is fun'). This finding raises the more general question about whether the effective mechanism in treatment is reduction of anxiety or an increase in feelings of mastery or both. (For a comprehensive review of behavioural treatment of specific phobias, see King and Ollendick, 1997.)

Social Phobia (Social Anxiety Disorder)

According to his mother, 9-year-old Devonte has always been an extremely shy child. Although his mother used to attribute his dislike of going out to play to the fact that they lived in a rough neighbourhood, and she was secretly relieved that he preferred to stay home, he also has difficulty making friends with the children in other settings such as his church group. When interacting with peers, Devonte generally keeps his head down, avoids eye contact and mumbles his speech. In school, when asked to give a presentation in front of the class, Devonte becomes extremely nervous and sweats profusely, dreading to have all the eyes in the room turned to him. In fact, he often complains of vague aches and pains in order to avoid going to school on days when he might have to perform in public. Currently, he has one or two boys he talks with at church, but he never asks them to play at his house, and he has refused their invitations to come over so many times that they have stopped asking. He often worries about what others will think of him and assumes that, when peers are laughing, they must be laughing at him. His mother finally realized that there was a problem that needed attention when Devonte, for the fourth time in a row this year, made excuses not to attend a social event at school. Devonte complains that parties are 'no fun' because he never knows what to say and he worries that the other kids will think him 'dumb' or 'uncool'.

Definition and Characteristics
Definition

Perhaps one of the most painful forms that childhood anxiety disorders take is social phobia, also termed social anxiety disorder. Children with social phobia are agonizingly self-conscious and avoidant of social situations, fearing that they will do something that will cause embarrassment or humiliation. (See Table 8.4.) The very thought that their anxiety will show ('My face will turn red'; 'They'll notice my hands are shaking') is a source of significant distress.

Children with social phobia experience uncomfortable physical symptoms in social situations (increased heart rate, tremors, sweating, gastrointestinal upset, diarrhoea, blushing, their minds 'going blank') that further contribute to their fears

TABLE 8.4 DSM-IV-TR Criteria for Social Phobia (Social Anxiety Disorder)

A. A marked and persistent fear of one or more social or performance situations in which the person is exposed to unfamiliar people or to possible scrutiny by others. The individual fears that he or she will act in a way (or show anxiety symptoms) that will be humiliating or embarrassing. **Note:** In children, there must be evidence of the capacity for age-appropriate social relationships and the anxiety must occur in peer settings, not just in interactions with adults.

B. Exposure to the feared social situation almost invariably provokes anxiety, which may take the form of a panic attack. **Note:** In children, the anxiety may be expressed by crying, tantrums, freezing, or shrinking from social situations with unfamiliar people.

C. The person recognizes that the fear is excessive or uncontrollable. **Note:** In children, this feature may be absent.

D. The feared social or performance situations are avoided or else are endured with intense anxiety or distress.

E. The avoidance, anxious anticipation, or distress interferes significantly with the person's normal functioning, social activities, or relationships, or there is marked distress about having the phobia.

F. In individuals under age 18 years, the duration is at least 6 months.

Source: Reprinted with permission from the *Diagnostic and Statistical Manual of Mental Disorders*, Fourth Edition Text Revision. Copyright 2000 by the American Psychiatric Association.

('What if I need to use the bathroom suddenly and can't get there in time?'). These anxiety symptoms may at times reach the level of panic, in which the child feels like she or he is about to faint, lose bowel control or 'die'. Children with social anxiety also tend to be unassertive and overly sensitive to criticism.

In early childhood, social anxiety generally takes the form of excessive *shyness*. Children may react with extreme distress to the presence of unfamiliar adults and peers, crying, clinging, having tantrums and showing inhibition to the point of mutism. They typically refuse to engage in group play, staying on the periphery of social activities and preferring the company of adults to that of peers. In middle childhood, school becomes the focus of fear (Rapee and Sweeney, 2001), which is not surprising given the many social interactions and performance demands that are placed on the child in the school setting.

Sadly, the very activities that are fun for most children – birthday parties, recess, play dates – are for these children sources of intense discomfort. For example, one 15-year-old boy began experiencing nervousness weeks before a school dance and, by the time the date had arrived, had wound himself up into such a state of anticipatory anxiety that he could not attend. Because anxious children determinedly avoid that which they fear, socially phobic children are caught in a vicious cycle (APA, 2000). Their avoidance of social situations prevents them from honing and practising their social skills, leading to a lack of social poise. In turn, their social awkwardness confirms their negative view of themselves and contributes to further social avoidance. Moreover, peers are less attracted to the child who is tense and standoffish, and the socially anxious child may in fact become rejected and friendless. Low self-esteem and feelings of inferiority may result.

Developmental Considerations

Given that many children are shy and reticent around adults, the DSM-IV-TR criteria specify that the social discomfort must be evident in relationships with *peers*. Another development consideration is that the child must show the capacity for *age-appropriate social relationships* but be unable to engage in them because of the intense anxiety they engender. As with most anxiety disorders, children are not expected to have insight into their difficulties; thus, the requirement that the person recognize the unreasonableness of the fear is not applicable to children.

Furthermore, DSM-IV-TR cautions that brief episodes of transient social anxiety are common in childhood and adolescence. Adolescents in particular are vulnerable to social discomfort and the feeling that 'everyone is looking at me'. Therefore, in young people, symptoms must be present for at least *six months* before the diagnosis could be considered.

Characteristics
Prevalence

Although the rates vary widely in individual studies, the prevalence of social phobia in the general child population is about 1 to 2 per cent in the USA (Rapee and Sweeney, 2001), 0.3 per cent in the UK and 2.8 per cent in Puerto Rico (Merikangas et al., 2010). Among US adolescents, social phobia is found in 11.2 per cent of girls and 7.0 per cent of boys (Merikangas et al., 2010). An increasing *gender difference* across the course of adolescence is a strikingly consistent finding across studies and samples (McClure and Pine, 2006). For example, Pine and colleagues (1998) found that rates of social phobia for girls remained failure stable from ages 13 to 22, whereas rates for boys dramatically decreased. (See Fig. 8.2.)

In contrast to community samples, rates of social phobia are substantially higher among children who present to mental health clinics, ranging from 27 to 32 per cent (Weiss and Last, 2001). Unlike community samples, in which females outnumber males, in clinical populations there are no gender differences in prevalence rates. It is possible that when boys are excessively shy, adults become sufficiently concerned to seek treatment, whereas they find such behaviour less concerning in girls (Rapee and Sweeney, 2001).

FIGURE 8.2 Gender Differences in the Prevalence of Social Phobia Across the Course of Adolescence.

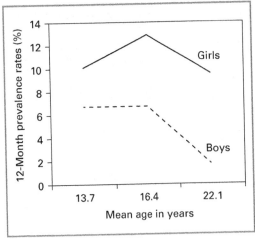

Source: McClure and Pine, 2006.

The little data on *ethnic differences* indicate that social phobia is more prevalent in European American than African American youths.

Comorbidity

Children rarely present with social phobia in the absence of other disorders. For example, Last and colleagues (1992) found that 87 per cent of children with social phobia met criteria for another *anxiety disorder. Depression* is also often seen, but comorbidity is not limited to other internalizing disorders. In one study of 25 children diagnosed with social phobia, Beidel and colleagues (1999) found that 20 per cent met criteria for a specific phobia, 16 per cent for GAD and 8 per cent for depression. However, another 16 per cent had ADHD and an additional 16 per cent had learning disorders.

Differential Diagnosis

Unlike *GAD*, social phobia is specific to the context of social relationships and, unlike other *phobias*, has its own diagnostic criteria. Social phobia can best be differentiated from *separation anxiety* by virtue of the fact that if the separation anxious child is accompanied by the attachment figure, there is no fear of other persons. In addition, the quality of fear of evaluation by others is unique to social phobia.

Cultural Differences

Although in Western cultures social anxiety takes the form of fear of embarrassment, in studies that have taken place in Japan and Korea, individuals with social anxiety are more likely to express a fear of giving offence to *others* (APA, 2000). For example, they may fear that their blushing, eye contact or body odour will make others uncomfortable.

Risk Factors for Social Phobia

The fact that social anxiety tends to run in families is suggestive of a *genetic component*, although to date most of the heritability research has focused on adult samples, and the candidate gene accounting for the mechanism of effect has not consistently been identified (here we follow McClure and Pine, 2006). The more general characteristic of shyness has been associated with the long form of the serotonin transporter gene 5-HTTLPR; however, whether there is a link between behavioural inhibition/shyness and the social evaluative concerns that predominate in social anxiety disorder is not clear. Similarly, studies on the role that parental anxiety or overly critical behaviour have on the development of child social phobia have yielded only mixed results.

Developmental Course

Social phobia generally is first diagnosed in the early teenage years (Weiss and Last, 2001). However, individuals with the disorder often report an *age of onset* of social inhibition and shyness prior to age 10 (APA, 2000). The earlier the onset, the more likely that social phobia will lead to intractable anxiety in adulthood (McClure and Pine, 2006).

Over childhood, social anxiety affects the trajectory of development in many contexts. The child may perform more poorly in school due to frequent absences, avoidance of participation in the classroom, fear of evaluation, or test anxiety. Further, the child who is chronically worrying is simply not able to give academic work his or her undivided attention. In college and adult life, individuals with social anxiety may underachieve due to fear of speaking in public or to supervisors and colleagues.

In adulthood, those who suffer from social anxiety report having fewer friends and support networks and being less likely to marry. Severe social anxiety may be linked to school dropout and social isolation, with some adults never being able to live apart from their family of origin. Depression and substance abuse may ensue (McClure and Pine, 2006).

A compelling picture of the pernicious effects of childhood social anxiety was painted by Caspi and his colleagues (1988). As we described in Chapter 1, these investigators followed individuals throughout the life course, from childhood through their entry into adulthood in the 1950s. Their findings showed that childhood shyness had its most marked effects on the developmental trajectories of men. Just as they were reticent and slow to warm up in childhood, shy men were described in adulthood as aloof, lacking social poise, reluctant to act and tending to withdraw in the face of obstacles. And just as they were reluctant to enter new situations as children, they found it hard to make transitions to new roles in adulthood. As a result, they were delayed in marrying, having children, and establishing their careers. In attempting to understand the life stories of these men, Caspi and colleagues proposed the concept of 'interactional continuity'. Because these men were timid and lacking in social skills, they tended to be neglected, overlooked and ignored by others – the last picked for anyone's ball team. In what we now would term a *transactional* process, they brought their shyness into interactions in ways that caused others to respond to them negatively, thereby exacerbating their shyness and causing them to withdraw further.

For females, there was not such a clear relationship of childhood shyness to adult personality. In late adolescence, they were described as quietly independent, interested in intellectual matters, with high aspirations and a quality of inner-directedness. However, like their male peers, they tended to withdraw in the face of frustration and to be reluctant to act. As adults, women who were shy as children were less likely than others to work outside the home, preferring a domestic-centred lifestyle. Taking a historical perspective, the authors proposed that consequences of shyness for women were modest for women reaching adulthood in the 1950s, given that they could adhere to the traditional feminine social clock of marriage, family, and homemaking.

In a second study, Caspi and colleagues (1996) followed a sample from age 3 to age 21 and found that anxious and inhibited toddlers were more likely than others to have developed anxiety disorders, depression, substance abuse or suicidal ideation in adulthood. Clearly then, social anxiety can have a powerful and pernicious effect on subsequent development.

Intervention

As with other anxiety disorders, the treatments with the most proven effectiveness for social anxiety are cognitive behavioural (Silverman et al., 2008). For example, based on established interventions for socially phobic adults, Beidel and colleagues (2000) developed a programme called Social Effectiveness Treatment for Children. Each week, children receive two treatment sessions, the first focused on exposure to the feared situations and the second focused on social skills training. An innovation of this programme is the inclusion of a generalization session, in which children with social phobia are paired with non-anxious peers for a 90-minute outing in which they practise their newly developed skills. In a carefully controlled study, the investigators found that 67 per cent of the social phobic children who received the treatment no longer met criteria for the diagnosis, whereas this was true of only 5 per cent of children who participated in a control group. Gains were still evident six months after treatment had ended.

In another study, Spence and colleagues (2000) investigated the effectiveness of a group treatment for children that combined exposure therapy and social skills training with relaxation, problem solving and cognitive restructuring. The authors also assessed whether treatment was more effective when parents were involved. Children aged 7 to 14 were assigned either to a waiting list, or the child group alone, or the child group plus parental involvement. In the latter group, parents received training in management of child social anxiety and observed their children's sessions while the therapists modelled and reinforced the treatment goals. The results showed that children in both treatment groups benefited significantly. Eighty-seven per cent of those in the child plus parent group were free of their diagnosis at follow-up, whereas this was true of 58 per cent of those in the child-only group and 7 per cent of those on the waiting list. Although the difference between the two treatments was not significant, it may be that parental involvement is important particularly for younger children (Sweeney and Rapee, 2001) or in families in which the parents themselves are anxious (Cobham et al., 1998).

Separation Anxiety Disorder

Seven-year-old Lili has always had difficulty separating from her parents. When her parents go out to run even a brief errand, Lili begs them to take her or asks repeated questions about where they are going, what route they will take to get there and when they will return. When it is Lili who needs to leave the house in order to go to school or attend an activity, she frequently reports 'feeling funny' and pleads to be allowed to stay home. At times, she becomes so distressed by impending separation that she clings to her parents, cries and has to be dragged kicking and screaming to the car. When she is at home, she does not like to be alone in any room of the house, preferring to follow her mother around and play in whatever room her mother is in. While her parents try to be understanding, they find this clinginess to be exasperating ('I can't move without finding her underfoot!') but, if they do not give in to it, the intensity of Lili's tantrums is unnerving. Consequently, her parents vacillate between pushing her to 'be a big girl' and giving in to her neediness in order to avoid a battle. Lili is able to play comfortably with peers – as long as they play at her house – and can even participate in activities such as

dance class – as long as one of her parents is with her. She has never been willing to spend a night away from home and tends to have trouble sleeping, waking from nightmares in which she has got lost or something bad has happened to her parents.

As we have seen, the development of the bond of love to the caregiver and the fear of loss of the loved one go hand in hand in normal infant development. Normally, separation anxiety emerges between 9 and 12 months, peaks at 13 to 20 months, and then declines. Although a number of factors are responsible for the mastery of this separation anxiety in the toddler period, for some children the panic over separation returns from the preschool period through adolescence, producing separation anxiety. Separation fears may present themselves as school phobia; however, careful evaluation of the child reveals that it is not a pathological fear of school that is the problem, but rather that the child's school avoidance is motivated by fear of being away from the caregiver.

Definition

The core characteristic of Separation Anxiety Disorder (SAD) is excessive anxiety over separation from people to whom the child is attached, typically the parents. The DSM-IV-TR criteria provide a comprehensive listing of symptoms. (See Table 8.5.)

Characteristics
Prevalence

SAD is found in 2 to 12 per cent of the general population of children in the USA and in 29 to 45 per cent of the clinical population (Weiss and Last, 2001). Studies of children in the UK find prevalence rates of 0.4 per cent. Among US adolescents in the general population, SAD is seen in 9 per cent of girls and 6.3 per cent of boys (Merikangas et al., 2010).

The evidence is conflicting in regard to *gender differences*, with some studies finding no evidence of difference and others finding that girls outnumber

TABLE 8.5 DSM-IV-TR Criteria for Separation Anxiety Disorder

> A. Developmentally inappropriate and excessive anxiety concerning separation from home or from those to whom the individual is attached, as evidenced by three (or more) of the following:
>   (1) recurrent excessive distress when separation from home or major attachment figures occurs or is anticipated
>   (2) persistent and excessive worry about losing, or about possible harm befalling, major attachment figures
>   (3) persistent and excessive worry that an untoward event will lead to separation from a major attachment figure (e.g., getting lost or being kidnapped)
>   (4) persistent reluctance or refusal to go to school or elsewhere because of fear of separation
>   (5) persistently and excessively fearful or reluctant to be alone or without major attachment figures at home or without significant adults in other setting
>   (6) persistent reluctance or refusal to go to sleep without being near a major attachment figure or to sleep away from home
>   (7) repeated nightmares involving the theme of separation
>   (8) repeated complaints of physical symptoms (such as headaches, nausea, or vomiting) when separation from major attachment figures occurs or is anticipated
> B. The duration of the disturbance is at least 4 weeks
> C. The onset is before the age of 18 years
> *Specify* If:
> **Early Onset:** if onset occurs before age 6 years

Source: Reprinted with permission from the *Diagnostic and Statistical Manual of Mental Disorders*, Fourth Edition Text Revision. Copyright 2000 by the American Psychiatric Association.

boys. However, Last et al. (1992) found that in a clinical sample of children with anxiety disorders, 48 per cent diagnosed with SAD were boys. SAD is more prevalent in low-income samples and among children whose parents have lower-than-average education (Silverman and Ginsburg, 1998). The families tend to be caring and close, but the incidence of SAD appears to be higher in children of mothers with anxiety disorders (Crowell and Waters, 1990).

Although data concerning *ethnicity* are limited, in studies of US sample, symptoms of SAD tend to be higher in African American (Compton et al., 2000), Hispanic (Silverman and Ginsburg, 1998) and Native American children (Costello et al., 1997) as compared to European American children.

Comorbidity and Differential Diagnosis

One-third of the children with SAD have a secondary diagnosis of *GAD* while, later in development, another third also will be diagnosed with *depression*. The child with SAD fears separation from the caregiver as opposed to fearing other people, as in the case of social phobia, or fearing going to a specific place, as in the case of school phobia. See Box 8.2 for a case requiring a differential diagnosis of separation anxiety, school phobia and GAD.

Developmental Considerations

SAD appears more often in the preschool period than in adolescence, as one would expect. Certain symptoms of separation anxiety show a developmental progression. Symptoms characteristic of 5- to 8-year-olds are excessive worry about harm befalling an attachment figure, nightmares involving separation themes, and school refusals because of separation anxiety; 9- to 12-year-olds are distressed at separation itself; and somatic complaints such as headaches and stomach aches and school refusals are characteristic of 13- to 16-year-olds (Albano et al., 1996).

Developmental Course

The average *age of onset* ranges from 7.5 to 8.7 years, although the mean age at which children with SAD are presented for treatment is 10.3 years, suggesting a delay in the recognition of the disorder (Weiss and Last, 2001).

Box 8.2 Case Study: Separation Anxiety, School Phobia or Generalized Anxiety Disorder?

Leilani Greening, a psychology intern at the UCLA Neuropsychiatic Institute, and her supervisor, Dr Stephen Dollinger, describe the case of Bradley A., a 9-year-old European American boy. Bradley's parents brought him to a university psychology clinic due to their concerns about his fears of the dark and unwillingness to sleep alone in his bedroom. According to his mother, Bradley's fears first emerged when he was 6 years old. Mrs A. had brought Bradley and his sister Janet, 3 years his elder, to see the movie *Jaws*. Bradley was very frightened by the movie and refused to sleep alone in his bedroom that night. His sleep problems continued intermittently over the next several months and intensified in the following summer when he began to complain about monsters in his room and people trying to kill him. He began to refuse to go to sleep unless there was a light left on in his room. Bradley's parents attributed his fears to the movie he had seen and believed that his anxieties would fade over time. While Bradley's symptoms indeed did lift when he returned to school in the fall, they recurred in an even more intense form the next summer. He frequently woke during the night crying out for his parents because he was scared. His parents would comfort Bradley until he fell asleep and return to their bedroom only to be awakened again a few minutes later by his screaming.

Bradley's problems continued with intermittent remissions and relapses over the next three years. The family tried a number of solutions, including reassuring Bradley, having a family member sleep in his room, and praying for guidance. At the time they sought professional help, Bradley's mother was sleeping in a cot in his room. The entire family's functioning was organized around appeasing Bradley's anxiety, and each episode would inevitably end up with everyone yelling at each other. The family conflicts were so stressful that one night Bradley cried and said, 'I would do anything in the world not to be like this!' It was then that Bradley's mother determined to seek professional help.

After evaluating Bradley and his family, the clinicians working on the case were struck by two things. One was Bradley's high level of overall anxiety. The other was his parents' anxiety. In an interview, Bradley's parents described him as a fearful child who often worried about harm befalling his family. He fretted about burglars and was particularly afraid that his father, who worked the night shift at a dangerous manual labour job, would be killed at work or during the long drive home. What was interesting, however, was that Bradley's parents shared his fears. Mrs A. too worried that her husband would be hurt at work and related a number of stories about co-workers who had been killed on the job. Furthermore, she kept a loaded pistol in the house because she and her husband were fearful of robbers coming into the house at night while Mr A. was working. To cope with their anxiety, family members had developed a number of rituals. Both Bradley and his father reported that each time Mr A. left for work they felt that they would never see each other again and engaged in long goodbyes as though each were their last. The parents worried about their children's safety to the extent that they were not allowed to ride their bikes outside of the yard. Later, Mr A. provided the basis for this fear when he related his feelings of guilt following the death of his younger brother, who died in childhood after being hit by a truck while riding Mr A.'s bicycle.

As an initial step, the clinicians worked to increase Bradley's sense of self-mastery by teaching him relaxation exercises to counter his anxiety. When these interventions were only moderately successful, they turned to working with the whole family in order to help the parents cease from reinforcing Bradley's anxiety with their own. One of the family's strengths turned out to be their sense of humour, and they were able to recognize and ultimately to change their patterns of interaction.

Source: Greening and Dollinger, 1989.

There are few studies of the developmental course of SAD, although there is some evidence that the course is a variable one. Periods of remission often are followed by recurrences either in response to stressors or 'out of the blue'. Finally, there is evidence that SAD increases the risk of anxiety or depressive disorders in adulthood and, for females, increases the risk of panic disorder or agoraphobia in adulthood (Albano et al., 1996).

Intervention

Kendall's (2000) cognitive-behavioural Coping Cat programme, which we described under 'Generalized Anxiety', is also a treatment of choice for SAD (Kendall et al., 2003). For example, Levin and colleagues (1996) describe the case example of Allison, a 9-year-old girl whose parents brought her for treatment because she insisted on sleeping in their bed every night. Her need to sleep with her parents was interfering with her social development, because she was unable to tolerate attending sleepovers with her friends. The therapist was able to help Allison connect her 'fidgety' behaviour (nail biting, chewing on her hair) to the emotional experience of anxiety. The therapist also attempted to help Allison counter her negative cognitions with more adaptive ways of thinking. However, although Allison was able to identify her negative thoughts, she became so overwhelmed by them that she could not consider alternative ideas. Therefore, using the treatment manual flexibly, the therapist shifted the focus in treatment to actions ('What can you do to feel better?') rather than cognitions. For her homework, Allison was assigned a series of graduated tasks, beginning with spending time alone in her room every day. Her parents were given tasks of their own, including redecorating Allison's room so that it was comfortable, pleasant and safe, and rewarding her for making attempts – even if unsuccessful – to master her fears. At the end of treatment, Allison no longer met criteria for the SAD diagnosis.

Obsessive-Compulsive Disorder

For the past four months, 10-year-old Oskar has been late for everything. It is not that he does not care about being on time, but there is so much to do before it is safe to leave the house. First, the toys on his shelf have to be exactly right, arranged by height and lined up straight. Then, he has to check that the lights are off in every room and then go back and check them a second time – but, of course, the third time is the charm. Although Oskar's teachers had previously described him as a 'joy', the most neat and well-organized child in the classroom, recently they have been complaining that Oskar is turning his homework in days late, if at all. Oskar's parents are bewildered, given that he spends several hours a night working intently on his homework. When asked to describe his homework strategy, Oskar explains that he gets three sheets of lined paper, three sheets of unlined paper, three newly sharpened pencils and his textbook. Everything has to be placed in exactly the right spot on his desk before he can begin. When he writes his answers, the letters have to be exactly the same size and the distance between the lines of writing exactly the same height. If he makes the smallest mistake, he has to tear up the paper and start over from scratch. When asked why he cannot simply erase the error and continue on, Oskar becomes visibly upset and states, 'I could never do that. I just couldn't stand it.'

Definition and Characteristics
Definition

Obsessive-compulsive disorder (OCD) is marked by intrusive ideas (**obsessions**) and behaviours (**compulsions**). Further, these thoughts and actions (1) arise from sources over which the child has no control, (2) are irresistible, and (3) are often recognized as irrational. (The DSM-IV-TR criteria are presented in Table 8.6.)

The most frequent *obsessions* involve fear of germs or contamination, fears of harm to the self or someone else and excessive religiosity (Chang and Piacentini, 2002). Not all obsessions are related to anxiety. Children might complain of intrusive thoughts, feelings of disgust or discomfort, or a vague sensation that something is just not right, termed the *just-right phenomenon*. (See Table 8.7.)

The most common *compulsions* in children include handwashing, repetitive checking (such as continually checking the doors to make sure they are locked), preoccupation with orderliness and

TABLE 8.6 DSM-IV-TR Criteria for Obsessive-Compulsive Disorder

A. Either obsessions or compulsions:
Obsessions as defined by:
  (1) recurrent and persistent thoughts, impulses, or images that are experienced, at some time during the disturbance, as intrusive and inappropriate and that cause marked anxiety or distress
  (2) the thoughts, impulses, or images are not simply excessive worries about real-life problems
  (3) the person attempts to ignore or suppress the thoughts, impulses, or images, or to neutralize them with some other thought or action
  (4) the person recognizes that the obsessional thoughts, impulses, or images are a product of his or her own mind (not imposed from without as in thought insertion)

Compulsions as defined by:
  (1) repetitive behaviors (e.g., hand washing, ordering, checking) or mental acts (e.g., praying, counting, repeating words silently) that the person feels driven to perform in response to an obsession, or according to rules that must be applied rigidly
  (2) the behaviors or mental acts are aimed at preventing or reducing distress or preventing some dreaded event or situation; however, these behaviors or mental acts either are not connected in a realistic way with what they are designed to neutralize or prevent or are clearly excessive
B. At some point during the course of the disorder, the person has recognized that the obsessions or compulsions are excessive or unreasonable. **Note**: This does not apply to children.
C. The obsessions or compulsions caused marked distress, are time consuming (take more than 1 hour a day), or significantly interfere with the person's normal functioning, social activities, or relationships.

Source: Reprinted with permission from the *Diagnostic and Statistical Manual of Mental Disorders*, Fourth Edition Text Revision. Copyright 2000 by the American Psychiatric Association.

repeatedly counting to a particular number or touching objects a given number of times (Chang and Piacentini, 2002). It is not unusual for a child to combine a number of rituals. An 11-year-old boy who was terrified of germs used his magic number four for protection in a variety of ways: he touched his fork four times before eating, counted to four when entering the locker room in the school gym, got in and out of bed four times before going to sleep, and lined up his perfectly sharpened pencils in groups of four. When he became worried that a ritual might not have worked, he repeated it four times.

It is easy to see how crippling OCD can become; the disorder interferes with children's personal, social and academic lives as well as becoming burdensome to their families. For example, Chang and Piacentini (2002) found that, among 162 children with OCD, parents reported that symptoms interfered with functioning in a number of areas: completing assigned chores at home (78 per cent of children), settling to bed at night (73 per cent), concentrating on schoolwork (71 per cent) and getting along with family members (70 per cent). Over 85 per cent of children reported that OCD impaired their ability to function in all three areas of school, home and peer relations.

TABLE 8.7 Common Obsessions and Compulsions in Childhood OCD

Obsessions	Compulsions
Contamination	Washing
Harm to self or others	Repeating
Aggression	Checking
Sex	Touching
Religion, morality	Counting
Forbidden thoughts	Ordering/arranging
Symmetry	Hoarding
Need to tell, ask, confess	Praying

Source: March and Mulle, 1998.

Children's symptoms are likely to increase at times of stress, such as at the beginning of the school year, moving to a new home or separation from a family member. With great effort, children with OCD are able to control their behaviour for short periods in specific situations, such as the classroom or social situations, and therefore teachers and others may remain unaware of the difficulty for quite some time.

Characteristics

Prevalence

In regard to lifetime prevalence, rates of 1 to 3 per cent have been reported in the general population of US children, consistent with rates for adults (Leckman et al., 2009), while 15 per cent of the child clinical population is affected (Weiss and Last, 2001). Large-scale studies of children in the UK report prevalence rates of 0.2 per cent (Merikangas et al., 2010). However, these prevalence rates might be underestimates – OCD in children appears to be difficult to detect. For example, one epidemiological survey of high school students found that few of the children who had OCD were in treatment and, most remarkably, *none* of the children with the disorder, including those in treatment, had been correctly diagnosed with OCD (Flament et al., 1988).

There is a *gender difference* in childhood, with boys starting earlier than girls and outnumbering girls (Rapoport et al., 2000). However, by adolescence this difference has all but disappeared.

Ethnic and Social Class Differences

Although *ethnic minorities* and children from *disadvantaged social classes* are underrepresented among those treated for OCD (Rasmussen and Eisen, 1992), these statistics may be a result of the fact that children from these communities are referred less often to clinicians. March and Mulle (1998) confirm this, reporting that large-scale epidemiological studies find no differences in prevalence rates based on race and ethnicity, while European American children are disproportionately more likely to receive treatment than are African American children. Strikingly, native Hawaiian adolescents are diagnosed with OCD at rates that are twice as high as those from other ethnicities, a finding that appears to be related to both environmental and genetic factors (Guerrero et al., 2003).

Comorbidity

The comorbidity rate of OCD is high. In community samples, around 84 per cent of the children with OCD have comorbid conditions (Douglass et al., 1995), whereas in clinical samples the figure is around 41 per cent. Common comorbid conditions are *depression* and other *anxiety disorders*, particularly social phobia, *tics* and habit disorders (e.g., nail biting or hair pulling), as well as *substance abuse*. *Learning disorders* also are common among children with OCD, particularly those involving problems with non-verbal reasoning.

Recent speculation about OCD is that it belongs to a family of disorders which includes various subtypes involving child versus adult onset, sporadic versus chronic symptoms and the presence or absence of tic disorders. (For further information on tic disorders and Tourette's Syndrome, see Spessot and Peterson, 2006.) Children whose OCD is accompanied by tic disorders have higher rates of comorbidity with disruptive behaviour disorders, including ADHD, ODD and other developmental disorders. Non-tic-related OCD in children, in turn, is often accompanied by other anxiety disorders (GAD, panic, separation anxiety) and mood disorders (major depression) (Leckman et al., 2009). In addition, there is a proposed subtype of OCD whose onset is believed to follow from an autoimmune disorder, a syndrome known as PANDAS (paediatric autoimmune neuropsychiatric disorders associated with streptococcal infections) (Leckman et al., 2009). (See Fig. 8.3.)

Differential Diagnosis

Whereas ruminative thinking and rigid behavioural patterns might be seen in children with other anxiety disorders, what characterizes OCD is a debilitating level of obsessive thinking and compulsive behaviour that dominates the child's life, interfering with other more adaptive activities.

FIGURE 8.3 Obsessive-Compulsive Subtypes.

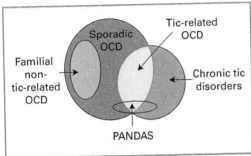

Source: Leckman et al., 2009.

Developmental Considerations

Early in development, some obsessiveness or compulsiveness is commonly seen in children as they attempt to navigate stage-salient issues involving mastery and control. For example, preschoolers frequently want things done 'just so' or insist on elaborate bedtime rituals to help them to sleep (March and Mulle, 1998). Fondness for rituals, repetition and arranging objects until they are 'just right' are behaviours commonly reported by parents of young children and seem to peak at about 24 months of age (Leckman et al., 2009). True OCD is distinguished by the fact that it is not time limited or developmentally appropriate behaviour and that the obsessions and compulsions result in significant distress or dysfunction rather than mastery.

When the disorder does develop, the symptoms generally look the same in children and adults. However, Geller and colleagues (1998) found that there also are a number of differences. For example, although some studies show that males predominate among children, there are no gender differences among adults with the disorder. Child OCD is comorbid for disruptive disorders such as ADHD, which is not true for adults. Finally, children with OCD perform more poorly on intelligence tests than do adults with the disorder, and there is a stronger genetic loading. The authors suggest that childhood OCD might be a developmental subtype rather than being essentially the same as the adult disturbance. As we know, behaviours that look the same in children and adults might, in fact, represent different underlying processes.

Developmental Course

The *age of onset* can be as early as 7 years, although the mean age is approximately 11 years (Nestadt et al., 2000). In one study, more than 75 per cent of those who would go on to develop the disorder had done so by age 14, and 90 per cent had an onset of symptoms by age 17 (Nestadt et al., 2000). Once OCD develops, there is no doubt concerning its *chronicity*. Follow-up studies have found that 43 to 68 per cent of young people treated for OCD continued to meet criteria for the disorder two to 14 years after the initial diagnosis, while 32 per cent had some other comorbid condition (Bolton et al., 1995).

Developmental Pathways to OCD
Early Onset OCD

Research suggests that a strong genetic component can be seen in OCD, but most particularly among those in whom the disorder's onset is in the early years of life (Leckman et al., 2009). For example, one study found that the prevalence of OCD in the relatives of research participants was 13.8 per cent among those with early onset OCD (those whose symptoms started between ages 5 to 17) and 0 per cent among those with late onset OCD (those whose symptoms started between ages 18 to 41) (Nestadt et al., 2000). A review of the existing research on twins suggests heritability in the range of 45 per cent to 65 per cent for childhood onset OCD (van Grootheest et al., 2005). However, environmental factors also may increase the likelihood of childhood OCD, including perinatal problems (maternal illness during pregnancy, difficult delivery), psychosocial adversities and psychological stress (Geller et al., 2008; Leckman et al., 2009).

Adult Onset OCD

Using data from the Dunedin Multidisciplinary Health and Development study, which evaluated a large cohort of New Zealand children every two years from age 3 to 18, Douglass and colleagues (1995) investigated the childhood predictors of

OCD in a sample of 933 young adults. They found no evidence that OCD was predicted by perinatal problems or abnormal birth events, by poor performance on neuropsychological tests, by eating disorders, or by tics. However, the researchers did find that, when they were 11 years old, those who went on to develop OCD in adulthood had been significantly more *depressed* than the healthy group; and when these individuals were 15 years old, they had been significantly more *anxious* than the healthy group and had a higher level of *substance abuse*. Eighty-four per cent never sought help for their psychological difficulties. Although this study is valuable in focusing on the pathways that lead to OCD, it still leaves unanswered the question of how depression, anxiety and substance abuse lead to OCD specifically rather than any other disturbance.

Intervention
Pharmacotherapy
Among medications used to treat OCD, selective serotonin reuptake inhibitors in particular have been found to be effective. Although response rates are positive, with as many as 55 per cent of children reporting some symptom relief, the reduction in symptom severity is only 20 to 50 per cent, and many children continue to experience a significant disruption in functioning due to their OCD (Grados et al., 1999). Accordingly, medication is considered an adjunct rather than the sole treatment for OCD.

Cognitive Behavioural Treatment
Cognitive behavioural treatment has proven to be a highly effective treatment for OCD in children (Barrett et al., 2008). Treatment takes place in five steps. First, the therapist provides *psychoeducation* regarding OCD, firmly framing the problem as the disorder rather than the child. Child-friendly metaphors are introduced, such as the idea that obsessions are 'brain hiccups', and children are invited to externalize their symptoms by giving it a name, such as 'Germy' (March and Mulle, 1998). In the second step, the therapist introduces the child to cognitive strategies for 'bossing back' OCD, such as constructive self-talk. The third step involves 'mapping' the child's symptoms by identifying situations in which the child feels he or she 'wins' against OCD or those in which OCD renders the child helpless. The middle zone, in which the child has partial success against the symptoms, becomes the work zone in which the therapist will stand side by side with the child to increase his or her ability to resist the obsessions and compulsions. At the fourth step comes the core of the intervention, exposure with response prevention, or ERP. *Exposure*, as the term implies, involves exposing the child to the feared stimulus. This is usually done gradually, with the child moving stepwise through a symptom hierarchy, but sometimes it is done abruptly in a variant termed *implosion therapy*. For example, a child who fears contamination may be required to remain in contact with a 'germy' object until the anxiety decreases. In *response prevention*, the compulsive ritual is blocked so that, for example, this same child would be prevented from washing his or her hands. While children benefit from graduated exposure in therapy, the most significant gains from treatment come from practising in the natural environment. Research on the effectiveness of this treatment has yielded impressive results, with positive response shown by 60 to 100 per cent of children (Franklin et al., 2010).

Posttraumatic Stress Disorder

Although it has been a year since her family fled from their war-torn homeland, 16-year-old Radmila still awakens frequently from nightmares about the time that soldiers, looking for an escaped prisoner, hammered down the door of her home. Screaming threats and imprecations, the soldiers forced the family members to the floor and, holding guns to their heads, threatened to shoot if the family did not reveal the location of the prisoner. Radmila's memories converge on a particular image: the smudge on the boot of the soldier who stood at her head as she cowered on the floor. Her mind frequently went back to that detail and she wondered, was that blood or dirt? Although her parents report that Radmila's older brother was dragged away by the soldiers, screaming and begging for his life, Radmila insists she has no memory of this and holds her hands over her ears if anyone tries to speak to her about it. Since the incident, Radmila has been more withdrawn and irritable and appears to take no joy in the artwork that once gave her such pleasure. She is extremely reactive to whatever is going on in her environment and startles at loud, unexpected sounds.

Definition and Characteristics
Definition
Traumatic Event

The first criterion for the diagnosis of **Posttraumatic stress disorder** (PTSD) is that the child has experienced a *traumatic event*, which DSM-IV-TR defines as an event involving actual or threatened death, serious injury or a threat to the self or others. Further, the individual's reaction to that event is one of intense fear, helplessness or horror or, in children, agitation or disorganized behaviour. (See Table 8.8.) The fact that the precipitant is such a clearly anxiety-arousing event points to one respect in which PTSD differs from all other anxiety disorders – it lacks the element of irrationality. If a boy is terrified of riding the school bus when nothing out of the ordinary has happened, we are puzzled; however, if a boy is terrified of riding a school bus after being in one that has skidded off the road and turned over, we might say, 'Of course!' However, in PTSD, the child's reaction persists much longer than would be reasonable, and has become generalized to events and stimuli that are even vaguely reminiscent of the traumatic experience.

However, in order for an event to be traumatic, it must be perceived as such (Pynoos et al., 1995). In other words, the child's *appraisal* of the event is important to determining whether it results in PTSD. A boy who views a car accident as a thrilling adventure with which to regale his friends, for example, is not likely to be traumatized no matter how real the actual threat of harm. By the same token, the child whose cognitions about an event involve negative appraisals, such as shame, helplessness and self-blame, is likely to experience a more severe post-traumatic reaction.

Traumatic events can be of two types (Terr, 1991). *Type I* traumas involve sudden, anticipated single events – 'short, sharp, shocks' such as car accidents, natural disasters, house fires or school shootings. *Type II* traumas, in contrast, involve long-standing, repeated exposure to horrific events, such as those experienced by children who are victims of chronic child abuse. We will focus here on Type I traumas and in Chapter 14 we will return to the study of Type II PTSD in the context of child maltreatment.

Symptom Clusters

Three clusters of symptoms define the disorder: reexperiencing, avoidance and arousal (APA, 2000).

First, children who develop PTSD following a traumatic experience exhibit persistent *reexperiencing* of the event, characterized by intrusive, distressing recollections of the incident. Reexperiencing may occur at unexpected moments throughout the day, but often occurs when the child is exposed to traumatic reminders. For example, while in a restaurant three weeks after undergoing a series of extremely painful treatments for a burn on her chest, a 5-year-old girl erupted in tears upon spying the white latex gloves on the hands of a food service worker replenishing a salad bar, because the gloves reminded her of those that the doctor had worn during the medical procedure. Sometimes the traumatic reminders are so subtle that their connection to the distressing event is hard to discern. Sounds, colours and the quality of the light at a certain time of day all might act as triggers for emotions of distress that, to the child and others, seemingly come out of nowhere. Reexperiencing also might take the form of dreams about the traumatic event or, in children, night-

TABLE 8.8 DSM-IV-TR Criteria for Posttraumatic Stress Disorder

A. The person has been exposed to a traumatic event in which both of the following were present:
   (1) the person experienced, witnessed, or was confronted with an event or events that involved actual or threatened death or serious injury, or a threat to the physical integrity of self or others
   (2) the person's response involved intense fear, helplessness, or horror. **Note:** In children, this may be expressed instead by disorganized or agitated behavior

B. The traumatic event is persistently reexperienced in one (or more) of the following ways:
   (1) recurrent and intrusive distressing recollections of the event, including images, thoughts, or perceptions. **Note:** In young children, repetitive play may occur in which themes or aspects of the trauma are expressed
   (2) recurrent distressing dreams of the event. **Note:** In children, there may be frightening dreams without recognizable content
   (3) acting or feeling as if the traumatic event were recurring (includes a sense of reliving the experience, illusions, hallucinations, and dissociative flashback episodes, including those that occur on awakening or when intoxicated). **Note:** In young children, trauma-specific reenactment may occur
   (4) intense psychological distress at exposure to internal or external cues that symbolize or resemble an aspect of the traumatic event
   (5) psychological reactivity on exposure to internal or external cues that symbolize or resemble an aspect of the traumatic event

C. Persistent avoidance of stimuli associated with the trauma and numbing of general responsiveness (not present before the trauma) as indicated by three (or more) of the following:
   (1) efforts to avoid thoughts, feelings, or conversations associated with the trauma
   (2) efforts to avoid activities, places, or people that arouse recollections of the trauma
   (3) inability to recall an important aspect of the trauma
   (4) markedly diminished interest or participation in significant activities
   (5) feeling of detachment or estrangement from others
   (6) restricted range of affect (e.g., unable to have loving feelings)
   (7) sense of a foreshortened future (e.g., does not expect to have a career, marriage, children, or a normal life span)

D. Persistent symptoms of increased arousal (not present before the trauma) as indicated by two (or more) of the following:
   (1) difficulty falling or staying asleep
   (2) irritability or outbursts of anger
   (3) difficulty concentrating
   (4) hypervigilance
   (5) exaggerated startle response

E. Duration of the disturbance (symptoms in Criteria B, C, and D) is more than 1 month.

Specify If:
Acute (duration of symptoms less than 3 months)
Chronic (duration of symptoms is 3 months or more)
Delayed Onset (onset of symptoms is at least 6 months after the stressor)

Source: Reprinted with permission from the *Diagnostic and Statistical Manual of Mental Disorders*, Fourth Edition Text Revision. Copyright 2000 by the American Psychiatric Association.

mares with non-event-related content such as getting lost or being attacked by monsters. Particularly in younger children, reexperiencing takes the form of post-traumatic play in which aspects of the event are reacted. Although 'playing it out' can be therapeutic for children, post-traumatic play is differentiated by the fact that it is repetitive, compulsive and anxiety arousing rather than relieving. For example, a 5-year-old girl who was attacked and

bitten by a monkey at the zoo repeatedly played out this theme with her dolls, although the play did nothing to help her master her fright.

The second cluster of symptoms involves persistent *avoidance* of stimuli associated with the trauma or numbing of general responsiveness. Children with PTSD may actively avoid thoughts or activities and people that arouse recollections of the trauma. For example, the girl who had been burned covered her ears whenever her mother attempted to talk to her about the scar on her chest and insisted, when mention was made of it by curious peers, 'I don't know what you're talking about'. Avoidance may also take the form of numbing, which is evidenced by a markedly diminished interest in activities that previously were pleasurable. The child with PTSD may no longer show enjoyment of play.

The third cluster of symptoms is characterized by increased *arousal*. Heightened emotional arousal in children may take such forms as sleep disturbance, irritability, difficulty concentrating, heightened physiological reactivity and hyper-vigilance. The hypervigilant child is overly sensitive to the environment, scanning constantly for signs of danger and reacting intensely to unexpected stimuli. A classic sign of post-traumatic arousal is the *exaggerated startle response* – for example, the boy who jumps out of his skin and begins to tremble when a door slams suddenly down the hallway.

Characteristics

Prevalence

First, how prevalent are the kinds of traumatic events that might result in PTSD? In the USA, it is estimated that 25 per cent of children will be exposed to at least one 'high magnitude' traumatic event by the age of 16 (Costello et al., 2002). Nonetheless, it is estimated that only approximately 36 per cent of those children who experience a traumatic event go on to develop PTSD (Fletcher, 2003), suggesting that there is substantial resilience in the face of traumatic stress. For example, data from the National Comorbidity Study (Merikangas et al., 2010) indicate that, among US adolescents in the general population, PTSD is seen in 8 per cent of girls and 2.3 per cent of boys. However, many children who do develop symptoms of PTSD are never identified and do not receive treatment, despite experiencing significant distress. One reason for this is that children frequently only meet partial criteria for a diagnosis of PTSD – for example, they may display symptoms of reexperiencing and arousal, but

not avoidance – and thus they are not formally diagnosed with the disorder even though they may have symptoms that are severe enough to interfere with functioning (Cohen and Scheeringa, 2009).

The data in regard to *gender differences* are contradictory. A number of studies with large samples have found girls exposed to trauma to be more symptomatic than boys, but other studies have found the opposite (Pfefferbaum, 1997).

Ethnic and Cultural Factors

Data on ethnic differences are very sparse but indicate that, among those referred to clinics, African American children are more likely to have a history of PTSD when compared to European American children (Last and Perrin, 1993).

Studies of refugee populations, who commonly suffer the stresses of political violence, displacement and immigration, suggest the importance of cultural factors in symptom *expression*. Cambodian refugee children, for example, while suffering from PTSD and comorbid anxiety and depression, do not show the increase in conduct disorders or substance abuse seen in European American samples. They are respectful of authority, have a positive view of school and function at a high level (Pfefferbaum, 1997).

Comorbidity and Differential Diagnosis

Comorbid conditions are common, with PTSD significantly increasing the risk of *depression*, *anxiety* and *disruptive behaviour disorders* (Amaya-Jackson and March, 1995). PTSD can be differentiated from other anxiety disorders by virtue of the fact that there is a specific precipitating event, a unique symptom constellation, including such symptoms as reexperiencing, and a definitive time line.

Developmental Considerations

The kinds of symptoms children manifest after being exposed to traumatic events vary with age (Kerig et al., 2000). Young children may regress to a previous level of functioning, such as losing bowel and bladder control, collapsing into tears at small frustrations, sucking their thumbs, and developing fears and eating problems. Separation anxiety is apt to reappear. Avoidance and numbing may lead children to become inattentive, 'spaced out', quiet and withdrawn.

While children rarely exhibit total amnesia for traumatic events, preschoolers are particularly vulnerable to cognitive distortions that exacerbate their distress. For example, one young boy was distressed by the memory of the SWAT team members who came to rescue him and his classmates during a sniper attack, because he misperceived these booted, weapon-carrying men as a second wave of assailants. Young children may also confuse the ordering of events. The reversal of cause and effect can result in *omen formation*, the mistaken belief that they could have predicted and therefore prevented the catastrophe.

For school-aged children *fears and anxieties* are the predominant symptoms. These children also more often complain of headaches and visual and hearing problems, fight with or withdraw from peers, and have sleep disturbances such as nightmares and bed-wetting. Younger children re-experience through *behaviour*, such as by engaging in elaborate re-enactments of the traumatic event, while older children might re-experience in *thoughts*. For example, they may have repetitive fantasies of being rescued or avenging themselves against the perpetrator (Terr, 1988).

Pre-adolescents and adolescents, like school-age children, may develop various physical complaints, become withdrawn, suffer from loss of appetite and sleep, and become disruptive or fail at school. Numbing may result in a feeling of estrangement from others, leading to withdrawal, truancy and even aggression.

Although listed as criteria for both children and adults, some symptoms of PTSD are particularly evident in children. For example, children and adolescents may exhibit a sense of *futurelessness*, or foreshortened future, in that they do not expect to grow up, marry, or achieve happiness in adulthood (Saigh, 1992).

Developmental Course

The meagre prospective data suggest that the developmental course depends on the chronicity of trauma. Children tend to outgrow their reactions to single-occurrence stressors, but (not surprisingly) continue to be disturbed by exposure to repeated, multiple stressors.

Risks, Vulnerabilities and Protective Factors

Characteristics of the child as well as the nature of the traumatic event help to determine whether PTSD will develop and whether it will take a prolonged course (Kerig et al., 2000). *Risk* is increased when traumas are intense and repeated and involve human aggression, particularly when violence is perpetrated toward the child or a person to whom the child looks for security, such as a parent. The events with the most impact also will be those experienced directly by the child. Although vicarious traumatization does occur, the child most likely to be distressed is the one who actually witnessed a family member being shot, for example, rather than the child who merely heard about it. On the other hand, the risk is reduced when the event is an acute one with a specific end point so that, once life has returned to normal, the child will have the opportunity to outgrow its effects. Factors that increase a child's *vulnerability* to trauma include previous traumatization, a difficult temperament and poor emotional adjustment. *Protective factors* include a resilient temperament, affect regulation skills, internal locus of control, a history of learning how to cope with and master stressful events, as well as a supportive family environment (Pynoos et al., 1995).

Intervention

'*Psychological first aid*' for children and families exposed to disasters is described in the field guide for mental health workers created by the National Child Traumatic Stress Network and National Center for PTSD (Brymer et al., 2006). By taking the treatment directly to community settings that have been impacted by traumatic events, the clinicians are able to reach children early in the process and act quickly in order to prevent psychopathological reactions from forming. Although the first priorities are to establish the safety and comfort of family members and to help them to reunite with their sources of social support, psychological first aid also provides children and parents with age-appropriate psychoeducation regarding PTSD so as to normalize their reactions, to minimize confusion and the fear that they are 'going crazy', to enhance their coping ability, and to help them recognize if further intervention might be needed. For example, youth are provided with child-friendly language regarding common physical and emotional reactions to trauma:

> When something really bad happens, kids often feel funny, strange, or uncomfortable, like their heart is beating really fast, their hands feel sweaty, their stomach hurts, or their legs or arms feel weak or shaky. Other times kids just feel funny inside their heads, almost like they are not really there, but like they are watching bad things happen to someone else.
>
> Sometimes your body keeps having these feelings for a while even after the bad thing is over and you are safe. These feelings are your body's way of telling you again how bad the disaster was.
>
> Do you have any of these feelings, or other ones that I didn't talk about? Can you tell me where you feel them, and what they feel like? Sometimes these strange or uncomfortable feelings come up when kids see, hear, or smell things that remind them of the bad thing that happened, like strong winds, glass breaking, the smell of smoke, etc. It can be very scary for kids to have these feelings in their bodies, especially if they don't know why they are happening or what to do about them. If you like, I can tell you some ways to help yourself feel better. Does that sound like a good idea? (p. 47)

For children and adolescents who have developed PTSD in the aftermath of trauma, the most empirically well-supported treatment to date is Trauma-Focused Cognitive Behavioural Therapy (TF-CBT; Cohen et al., 2006). Treatment using TF-CBT is brief and strategic, averaging 12 to 18 sessions, and unfolds in a series of components. As a first step, psychoeducation is provided to help normalize the symptoms of PTSD. The next components focus on helping children to develop skills for recognizing, expressing and regulating difficult emotions. Children also learn to understand the connections among thoughts, feelings and behaviours and to develop coping strategies such as positive self-talk. With these cognitive and affect regulation 'tools' in their 'toolboxes', children are then engaged in the process of creating a narrative of the traumatic event which serves to desensitize them to trauma reminders, to separate thoughts about the event from distressing emotions, and to uncover unhelpful cognitions that contribute to post-traumatic reactions. Behavioural components include *in vivo* exposure to feared stimuli related to the traumatic event and completing exercises designed to foster mastery and self-efficacy. Throughout the process of TF-CBT, parents are engaged as active participants in the therapy. Specific parenting components focus on providing parents with strategies for responding to their child's trauma, improving parent–child communication, supporting the child in practising new skills and assisting parents with managing their own post-traumatic reactions when appropriate (Cohen et al., 2006). A series of randomized clinical trials have demonstrated the effectiveness of TF-CBT over non-directive and supportive therapies with traumatized children, and the treatment has been adapted successfully to a variety of different kinds of traumatic events and cultural groups (Cohen et al., 2010).

Developmental Pathways to Anxiety Disorders

Until recently it was erroneously believed that childhood anxiety need not be taken seriously because the symptoms were 'just a phase' and liable to be outgrown. As we have seen in our discussion of each of the DSM-IV-TR categories of anxiety, data using diverse methods and populations show that, on the contrary, having an anxiety disorder increases the risk for future anxiety disorders or related disturbances. Moreover, anxiety disorders in childhood can be the beginning of a longtime pattern of disturbance.

An Integrative Developmental Psychopathology Model

Vasey and his colleagues (Vasey and Dadds, 2001; Vasey and Ollendick, 2001) developed a dynamic, transactional model that integrates the research on the etiology of anxiety disorders. This integration involves four elements:

   i. Predisposing factors.

   ii. Two pathways to the onset of anxiety disorders.

   iii. Factors maintaining or intensifying anxiety.

   iv. Factors contributing to desistance.

The model is presented schematically in Fig. 8.4. We will now discuss it, point by point.

I. Predisposing Factors
The Biological Context

Genetic Risk There is good evidence that anxiety disorders run in families – that is, that there is *genetic risk*. The most convincing data come from twin studies, which show that the risk of developing anxiety disorders is higher for monozygotic twins than it is for other siblings due to the greater similarity of genetic material. Evidence for a genetic link is particularly strong in the case of childhood onset OCD, as we have seen. However, for anxiety disorders in general, the studies show that heritability accounts for only about one-third

FIGURE 8.4 Integrative Model of the Development of Anxiety Disorders.

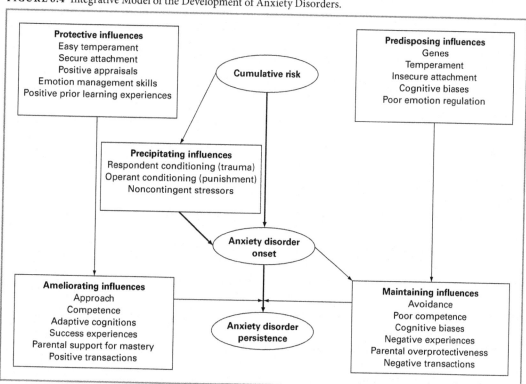

Source: Vasey and Dadds, 2001.

of the variance, whereas there is still a significant role played by the shared environment (Eley, 2001).

Further, it is important to note that what is inherited is not a specific anxiety disorder per se but rather a *predisposition* to develop disorders in the anxiety spectrum. For example, the Virginia Twin Study of Adolescent Behavioral Development (Eaves et al., 1997; Hewitt et al., 1997) assessed 1412 twin pairs aged 8 to 16 years. The authors found that separation anxiety and generalized anxiety disorder were genetically linked, but each disorder showed a specific time course: the same child might be vulnerable to developing separation anxiety disorder in the early years and generalized anxiety disorder in adolescence.

Temperament. Currently, one of the most promising leads concerning the biological precursors of anxiety disorders is the temperament variable of **behavioural inhibition** (Rothbart and Bates, 2007). (See Chapter 2.) Because inhibited infants are characterized by high motor activity and irritability, they also react to novelty with restraint, withdrawal, avoidance or distress. In addition they are shy, withdrawn and fearful, and they avoid challenges. Research suggests that around 20 per cent of children inherit the inhibited temperament type.

However, not all infants with inhibited temperament are 'doomed' to develop anxiety disorders. It is only among the approximately 10 per cent of children whose inhibition is *stable* from the early years into middle childhood that the risk for developing anxiety disorders is heightened (Turner et al., 1996). These are the children whose behavioural inhibition is most extreme. They also tend to develop two or more anxiety disorders; for example, they are more likely than other children to have phobias such as the fear of being called on in class or the fear of strangers or crowds.

Neurobiological factors. Evidence is beginning to emerge pointing to neurobiological processes underlying the development of anxiety-proneness (McClure and Pine, 2006). During moments of fear, stress hormones are released and lead to enhanced excitability of the HPA (hypothalamic-pituitary-adrenocortical) brain circuit associated with fear-

fulness. When these brain circuits are habitually excited, the child develops an increased susceptibility to anxiety (Gunnar et al., 2001). In support of this idea, studies show that children with a stable inhibited temperament have a lower threshold of arousal in the HPA circuit and react with an activated sympathetic nervous system (Oosterlaan, 2001). However, research support is mixed, with some studies showing that shy and anxious children evidence *suppressed* levels of cortisol in response to threat.

Other evidence of neuropsychological factors comes from studies of PTSD, which show that exposure to extreme levels of anxiety affects brain chemistry, which in turn affects the interconnections among neurons, brain structure and brain functioning (De Bellis, 2001).

The Family Context

Attachment   There are a number of reasons for hypothesizing that an *insecure attachment* increases the probability of developing an anxiety disorder (McClure and Pine, 2006). Recall that insecure infants have caregivers who are either insensitive or non-responsive to their needs. This, in turn, engenders a view of the world as unreliable and unpredictable and a view of the self as helpless to control the ensuing anxiety. Secure attachment also is fundamental to the development of such important capacities as emotion regulation, which allows children to approach new situations with confidence in their ability to cope and manage any strong emotions that might arise.

Research shows that insecure infants are more fearful than secure ones in free-play situations and in exploring the environment and are also more shy and withdrawn with peers. Evidence also suggests that insecure attachment is predictive of the development of anxiety disorders. In a prospective study of 172 children, Warren and colleagues (1997) found that of those who had been rated as insecurely attached in infancy, 28 per cent reported having either current or past problems with anxiety at age 17. In contrast, only 13 per cent of those in the securely attached group reported such symptoms. The insecure-resistant and insecure-disorganized attachment patterns in particular have been found to increase the risk of anxiety disorders – in some studies, by as much as 100 per cent (see Manassis, 2001).

The Individual Context

Cognitive Biases Children with anxiety disorders display a number of *information processing biases* (Vasey and MacLeod, 2001). First, there is an *attentional* bias in that children with anxiety disorders are particularly sensitive to potentially threatening events; for example, they selectively attend to threatening versus non-threatening words in an experimental task, as compared with non-anxious children. Children with anxiety disorders also interpret ambiguous situations as *threatening*; for example, they are more apt to interpret a noise in the house as an intruder than as an unlatched window rattling. Lastly, children with anxiety disorders show *unrealistic cognitive beliefs* such that they perceive the world as a dangerous place and perceive themselves as incompetent to deal with its threats. Thus, they are lacking in a sense of self-efficacy.

While these cognitive distortions may arise from the child's negative experiences in the environment, they also lead children to shape their own environments in maladaptive ways. Children with low self-efficacy and perceived powerlessness give up more quickly when faced with obstacles and thus bring about the very failure experiences they fear.

Emotion Regulation Deficits. Not only do anxiety-prone children believe they cannot control threatening situations, but they also believe they cannot control their own anxious responses. Thus, they have poor *emotion regulation* skills (McClure and Pine, 2006). Because they lack the ability to soothe themselves in the face of distress, they develop a 'fear of fear itself'. The fact that they find anxiety to be so overwhelming and intolerable may lead to their attentional bias and hypersensitivity to threatening situations. Metaphorically speaking, it is as if every flame were viewed as a potential firestorm so that the slightest smell of smoke is cause for alarm.

II. Two Pathways to the Onset of Anxiety Disorders

Vasey and colleagues describe two major pathways to the onset of anxiety disorders.

Cumulative Risk Pathway

The first pathway involves the gradual, insidious effects of the various predisposing factors, resulting in the development over time of clinically significant levels of anxiety. An example of this pathway is the child with an inhibited temperament who is permitted to shrink from exposure to fear-arousing stimuli and consequently never learns that his or her fears can be overcome, leading to appraisals of anxiety as unbearable and uncontrollable and increasing avoidance. A disorder evolves over time as the child's temperamental and cognitive biases intensify in transaction with other risks.

Precipitating Event Pathway

The second pathway to anxiety disorders involves the influence of a specific precipitating event. There are three different mechanisms by which anxiety disorders can be acquired along this pathway: first, via respondent conditioning, second by operant conditioning, and third, by a noncontingent exposure to stressful events.

Respondent Conditioning. The simplest case of anxiety acquisition is traumatic conditioning, such as a case in which a child injured in a car accident subsequently becomes terrified of riding in cars. The most familiar example is the classic case of 11-month-old 'Little Albert' (Watson and Rayner, 1920), who, after being exposed to a number of pairings of a white rat (conditioned stimulus – CS) with a loud, frightening noise (unconditioned stimulus – US), became frightened by the sight of the rat alone (conditioned response – CR).

Whether through direct experience, observation or hearsay, respondent conditioning produces in the child an *expectation* that a previously neutral stimulus will result in a negative consequence. Although traumatic conditioning does occur, it is also true that not every child who experiences a trauma becomes phobic nor has every phobic child experienced a trauma. When stressful events interact with other predisposing factors, such as *temperament* and prior *learning history*, traumatic reactions are likely to develop.

However, prior learning also may act as a protective factor against the development of a conditioned response. For example, if a child has had many pleasurable experiences with dogs, a single incidence of being bitten by a dog may not be sufficient to negate past expectations. Therefore, a positive learning history with a stimulus may actually inhibit fear conditioning, a process called *latent inhibition* (Menzies and Clarke, 1995).

Operant Conditioning. The operant conditioning pathway holds when the child learns that a behaviour (such as approaching a feared stimulus) is followed by an aversive consequence. In turn, the punishment intensifies the child's anxiety and increases his or her avoidance of the object. An example is the anxious girl who approaches peers on the playground in an awkward manner and whose bids to play are accordingly rejected. Consequently, the child will view further social encounters as discriminative stimuli signalling that punishment is nigh, and the child will even more studiously avoid exposure to them.

Non-contingent Exposure. Some anxiety disorders appear to arise in reaction to unrelated stressful events. For example, as we have seen, separation anxiety sometimes develops following a major stressor that is unrelated to separation per se, such as a long illness or change of schools. One possibility is that these unrelated stressors exert their effects by *dishabituating* or reinstating a previously mastered fear of normal childhood. In other words, children may regress in the face of stress and lose the developmental attainments that helped them overcome their earlier fears. For example, an 11-year-old boy stressed by a move to a new city may lose his hold on the cognitive skills that allowed him to conquer his preschool-age fear of the dark. Alternatively, the stressful event may contribute to the onset of anxiety by interfering with an important *protective factor*. For example, a girl who missed school due to a long illness may return to the classroom behind her peers academically, losing the protective effect that her previous high achievement had conferred.

III. Factors Maintaining or Intensifying Anxiety

Once they have arisen, anxiety disorders persist in part due to effects that children have on their environments. According to Vasey and Dadds (2001), anxiety is maintained and intensified by five main factors: (1) the child's own tendency to avoid anxiety-arousing situations; (2) poor academic, social and emotion regulation skills; (3) cognitive biases; (4) negative experiences; and (5) responses by parents and other adults.

The Consequences of Avoidance

If mastery of anxiety typically involves facing a frightening situation and learning to cope with it constructively, *avoidance* prevents mastery and ensures perpetuation. Avoidance is a seductive trap because it reduces anxiety temporarily. A shy child may be relieved when she avoids participating in a feared group game during recess, but, at the same time, she is deprived not only of learning the social skills necessary for group participation but also of a chance to correct her unrealistic beliefs concerning what group activity really involves. Thus, children who are inhibited behave in ways that serve to increase their own exposure to risk. By avoiding the situations that discomfort them, inhibited children limit their opportunities to habituate to and master them.

Poor Competence

As the preceding example shows, avoidance can result in the failure to master situations and develop *competencies*. Children who shy away from social interactions lack practice and poise and are therefore more vulnerable to experiencing social failure. Habitual avoidance may result in skills deficits that can have an adverse effect on both academic achievement and social relations. For example, there is evidence that social anxiety and withdrawal lead to peer rejection and unpopularity in middle childhood and to loneliness and depression in adolescence (Rubin, 1993). Avoidance also prevents children from developing the very emotion regulation skills that would allow them to tolerate and conquer their fears.

Cognitive Biases

Avoidance can also produce cognitive biases or distortions that serve to maintain anxiety. By their attentional bias to anxiety-arousing cues, interpretation of ambiguous information as threatening, and avoidance of the very situations that might provide corrective information, anxious children construct a world in which anxiety is perpetuated. Clark (2001) provides an illustrative model of the role of cognitions in the development of social anxiety. (See Fig. 8.5.) First, negative thoughts about feared outcomes in a situation arise, due to assumptions that anxious children make about themselves and others. These assumptions are divided into three categories: *excessively high expectations* of the self (e.g., 'I must always look perfectly cool and confident'; 'I should always have something interesting to say'); *conditional beliefs* about feared consequences ('If I blush, people will make fun of me'; 'If I don't say anything, they'll think I'm boring'); and *negative beliefs about the self* ('I'm weird'; 'I'm incompetent'). These assumptions lead the person to appraise social situations as threatening, to anticipate negative consequences, and to construe others' behaviour as indicating a negative evaluation of themselves. These kinds of thoughts lead socially phobic youths to focus excessively on themselves, with the belief that 'all eyes are on me'. As somatic and cognitive symptoms of anxiety intensify, the child is motivated to seek safety through avoidance.

Negative Experiences

As noted in the previous section, anxious children's cognitive biases and avoidant tendencies interfere with their ability to master many important developmental contexts (Vasey and Dadds, 2001). Consequently, their lack of competence is likely to lead to actual negative experiences and failure in the social world, including criticism from adults and rejection from peers.

Parental Responses

In the interpersonal context, there is evidence that *overprotectiveness* on the part of parents or teachers contributes to the maintenance of anxiety. Ironically, by reducing the child's exposure to anxiety-provoking situations, the parent prevents the child from mastering them. There is also evidence that parents may actually reinforce avoidance on the child's part; for example, a mother might say her child does not have to go to a party if it upsets her so. Parents of anxious children may also be more *controlling* and directive of children. By their well-meaning attempts to solve problems for the child, they interfere with the child's development of perceived competence and confidence in his or her ability to solve problems independently (Dadds and Roth, 2001).

Major contributors to our understanding of family process in the development of anxiety disorders are Mark Dadds and colleagues (1996), who developed strategies for evaluating the family interactions of non-clinical and anxious children. In their laboratory in Australia, they videotaped discussions between parents and children about a range of potentially threatening situations, such as a boy approaching a group of children who laugh as he asks to join their game. Using a detailed observational coding system, they found that, although the parents of non-clinical children were most likely to reinforce children's prosocial problem-solving strategies, parents of anxious children were more likely to *encourage avoidant strategies*. Not only did parents of anxious children fail to agree with and listen to their children's proactive plans for solving the problem, but they tended to keep prompting and questioning the child until he or she proposed an avoidant strategy. Not surprisingly, at the end of the discussion, the anxious children were reliably more likely to choose an avoidant strategy rather than a competent one. (See Table 8.9 for an example of a transcript from their laboratory.)

Although many parents of anxious children appear to be overly sensitive and emotionally reactive to their child's anxiety, at the other

FIGURE 8.5 Cognitive Processes in Anxiety.

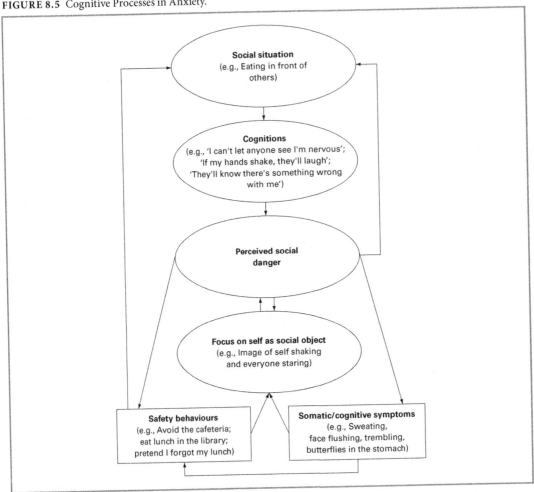

Source: Clark, 2001.

extreme, parents may contribute to child anxiety by *insensitivity* and under-responsiveness. The parent who demeans the shy child's behaviour as 'foolish nonsense' or who angrily forces the child into fear-inducing situations fails to provide adequate emotional support and burdens the child with an additional source of distress (Vasey and Ollendick, 2001). As Dadds and Roth (2001) state, 'Pushing children too forcefully toward challenge, or alternatively being overly protective, both appear to enhance fearful responding' (p. 286).

Transactional Processes

As we know, the concept of transactions suggests that anxious children also affect their parents' behaviour. For example, children who present themselves as reticent and helpless 'pull for' and elicit the very kind of overprotective behaviour in adults that will serve to reinforce the child's withdrawal and perceived incompetence. Moreover, the distress of the overanxious child who screams and tantrums when encouraged to approach a feared object effectively punishes the parents' attempts to help the child overcome his or her

TABLE 8.9 Family Process and Childhood Anxiety Disorders

In Mark Dadds' laboratory at the University of Queensland, a boy and his parents are asked to come up with a solution to a situation in which other children laugh at the boy when he approaches them to play. In coding the interaction, the investigators are particularly interested in whether the parents reinforce the child's tendency toward avoidance as opposed to supporting and guiding the child toward proactive problem-solving strategies. How would you rate these parents?	

Father:	So there's a bunch of kids playing a game and you want to go over and play but as you go over there, they're laughing. What would you do?	*Boy:*	No.
Mother:	Why do you think they're laughing?	*Father:*	They wouldn't?
Boy:	Because they've done something in the game and they thought it was silly and they're laughing at each other.	*Mother:*	Would you be brave enough to go and ask them in the first place?
Mother:	But how would you ask them if you could play with them?	*Boy:*	I wouldn't bother.
Boy:	I'd just ask them; just go up and say 'Can I please join in?'	*Mother:*	No?
Mother:	Do you reckon maybe they'd let you?	*Father:*	Why wouldn't you bother? Because…?
Boy:	Maybe.	*Boy:*	Because I know what the answer would be. Cause I always ask and it's, always 'No'.
Mother:	What sort of games do they usually play?	*Father:*	Do they?
Boy:	Tiggy or handball.	*Boy:*	Yes.
Father:	What's tiggy?	*Mother:*	You don't think they would be laughing at you before you even turned up, thinking, 'He's going to ask again'.
Boy:	Tiggy's tag.	*Boy:*	Oh yes.
Father:	Do you think they would let you if it was handball?	*Mother:*	They might do that?
Boy:	No.	*Boy:*	Yes.
Father:	Why?	*Mother:*	So what do you think you would do – just avoid these situations or would you really like to play?
Boy:	Because I'm not that good at it.	*Boy:*	Handball – I'd like to play.
Father:	You any good at tiggy?	*Mother:*	But you've just got to learn more ball skills.
Boy:	No.	*Boy:*	Yes.
Mother:	Why is this?	*Mother:*	It's hard isn't it?
Boy:	Because I can't run fast enough.	*Boy:*	Yes.
Mother:	So do you think they would let you play or you don't think they would let you play?		

Source: Dadds et al., 1993.

anxieties. All parents want to protect their children from the experience of intense fear, and the termination of a child's distress is a powerful negative reinforcer for the parent (Calkins, 1994). Therefore, through a process of *aversive conditioning*, the anxious child trains the parent to accommodate the child's fearfulness and to aid and abet the child's tendency toward avoidance. Interestingly, this kind of coercive control was first observed in interactions between conduct disordered children and their parents, as we will explore in Chapter 10; but it provides an important insight into the family dynamics of internalizing disorders, as well.

Further, because anxiety tends to run in families, it is highly likely that the parents of anxious children are anxious themselves. There are three potential processes by which parental anxiety might influence the child. First, children might learn to be anxious by imitating the *models* that their anxious parents provide. Second, anxious parents may react to the child's anxiety in ways that perpetuate it, particularly due to a mutual preference for *avoidance* as a coping strategy. For example, while any parent would find it challenging to deal with a fearful and inhibited child, anxious parents may find this behaviour particularly upsetting due to the parents' lack of mastery over their *own* anxiety. Therefore, because of the discomfort that child distress engenders in the parent, anxious parents may be particularly reluctant to expose the child to fear-arousing situations and incur the risk of an emotional 'melt down'.

Third, while the concept of 'goodness of fit' might suggest that an anxious parent would be particularly empathic and supportive of an anxious child, in fact this matching may increase the likelihood of *negative affect* in the parent–child relationship. Because anxious parents lack good affect regulation skills and have difficulty calming themselves in the face of the child's distress, they may find parenting their child to be particularly stressful. Thus, the anxious parent may become irritable with the inhibited child, with the unfortunate effect of further exacerbating the child's anxiety. Support for

this transactional process was found by Hirshfeld and colleagues (1997), who observed a reciprocal interaction among maternal anxiety, maternal criticism and inhibited behaviour in children. Anxious mothers became increasingly harsh and critical as child inhibition increased, whereas no such relationship was found for non-anxious mothers.

IV. Resilience and Anxiety Disorders: Factors Contributing to Desistence

The series of cascading failures presented in the previous section has been humorously termed the 'Temple of Doom' scenario of anxiety disorders (Rubin and Mills, 1991). However, in developmental psychopathology we know that there are many turning points in development and many intervening factors that might deflect a child onto a healthy course. Therefore, Vasey and Dadds's (2001) model provides for *ameliorative* factors that lead to *desistance*, such that each of the five factors listed previously is replaced with its opposite. The child who avoids may learn to approach, perceived incompetence may be replaced with self-efficacy, failure experiences may be transformed into success and parental overprotection may be tempered with encouragement of mastery.

Consistent with this model, one study investigated resilience in the face of childhood trauma among school children in Cape Town, South Africa (Fincham et al., 2009). The investigators asked children to respond to a self-report questionnaire that assesses a cluster of factors associated with the construct of resilience (ability to cope with negative emotions, adaptivity in the face of change, perceived social support and self-efficacy). Resilience served to buffer children from the effects of traumatic stress, with those highest in resilience the least likely to develop symptoms of PTSD. (See Fig. 8.6.)

The Cultural Context

Our multicontextual developmental psychopathology approach also requires that we consider the possibility of cross-cultural differences in the origins, expression, recognition and developmental course of anxiety. Some data suggest that cultural differences

FIGURE 8.6 Resilience as a Moderator of the Relationship between Childhood Traumatic Stress and PTSD among South African Schoolchildren.

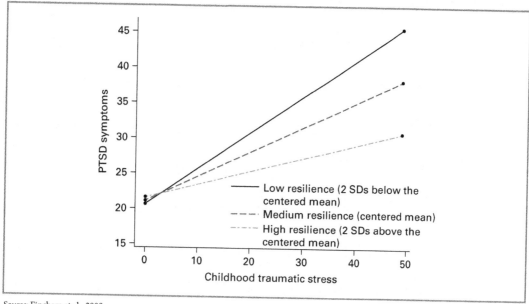

Source: Fincham et al., 2009.

in *child-rearing techniques* might affect the occurrence of anxiety disorders in children. Rates of anxious behaviours such as shyness, inhibition and somatic complaints are elevated in children living in societies that emphasize inhibition, compliance and social evaluation, as is the case in Asian cultures such as Thailand (Weisz et al., 2003). However, whether such child behaviour is problematic and whether it is associated with psychological maladaptation depends on the *cultural interpretation* of it, or as Weisz and colleagues (2003) put it, the lens through which it is viewed. Children who are well-socialized into their culture's values and who exemplify its

ideals and expectations may suffer no ill-consequences. Shyness and reticence, therefore, may be disadvantages only for those youth whose culture rewards boldness and intrepidation.

In our discussions of anxiety we have been dealing with children who are internalizers in the sense that their disturbances are marked by various degrees of internal distress and suffering. We now turn to another form of internalizing disorder in our consideration of children and adolescents who struggle with the 'black dog' of depression.

CHAPTER 09

Middle Childhood to Adolescence: Mood Disorders and Suicide

Chapter contents

In this chapter we will cover a spectrum of disorders related to mood, ranging from the darkest depths of major depression – what Winston Churchill called his 'black dog' (Storr, 1989) – to the 'slow, black, oily anger' (Godwin, 1994) of dythymia and the 'giddy, intoxicating highs' (Redfield-Jamison, 1995, p. 54) of bipolar disorder. As we shall see, depression may emerge in children at any age, even during infancy. However, we have placed our coverage of depression during the transition to adolescence because of an extraordinary increase in prevalence during this period of life. Our task is to identify what in the context and stage-salient tasks of adolescence acts on vulnerable youths to bring about this increased risk. In this chapter we will also discuss the risks associated with child and adolescent suicide, which, we will discover, is related to but independent of depression in some surprising ways.

Depressive Spectrum Disorders

Most of us have times of experiencing something we call depression – being in low spirits, feeling 'down', having 'the blues'. It is even appropriate to feel dejection or despair in response to loss of a loved one or another painful life event. Thus, depression as a *symptom* is relatively common, even normative. Depression as a *syndrome* is a constellation of symptoms that co-occur, including feelings of sadness and loneliness, as well as worry and nervousness. Depression as a *disorder* (sometimes referred to as 'clinical depression') refers to profound levels of these symptoms and has a specific etiology, course and outcome. As with all disorders defined by the DSM, the key is that the combination of symptoms is significant enough to cause distress and/or to interfere with functioning.

In decades past, professionals did not believe that depression existed in childhood, partly because it was assumed that children did not have the cognitive complexity required for depression. This idea also had credibility because of the wide range of non-depressive responses children show in reaction to traumatic losses, such as rebelliousness, restlessness and somatic symptoms. Such behaviours were thought to be 'masking' an underlying depression. However, whereas the concept of **masked depression** was once widely accepted, investigators find that child depression shares many of the same

TABLE 9.1 DSM-IV-TR Criteria for Adjustment Disorder with Depressed Mood

A. The development of symptoms (depressed mood, tearfulness, or feelings of hopelessness) in response to an identified stressor(s) occurring within 3 months of the onset of the stressor(s).

B. These symptoms or behaviors are clinically significant as evidenced by either of the following:
   (1) Marked distress that is in excess of what would be expected from exposure to the stressor
   (2) Significant impairment in social, occupational, or academic functioning

C. The stress-related disturbance does not meet the criteria for another specific mental disorder and is not merely an exacerbation of a preexisting disorder.

D. The symptoms do not represent bereavement.

Source: Adapted from the *Diagnostic and Statistical Manual of Mental Disorders*, Fourth Edition Text Revision. Copyright 2000 by the American Psychiatric Association.

characteristics as adult depression and can emerge at any point in the lifespan. Rather than *masking* depression in childhood, therefore, behaviour problems actually *accompany* the symptoms of depression (Luby, 2010). In recognition of this fact, ICD-10 includes a specific category of depressive conduct disorder and mixed disorder of conduct and emotions within the disorders with onset in childhood.

Definitions, Characteristics and Differential Diagnosis

DSM-IV-TR provides us with four major categories for diagnosing depression, which can be viewed as lying along a continuum of severity. The least severe form of a depressive spectrum disorder is **adjustment disorder** with depressed mood (see Table 9.1). The essential feature of adjustment disorders (see Chapter 3) is the development of short-term emotional or behavioural problems – in this case, sadness, tearfulness and hopelessness – in reaction to a recent identified stressor. ICD-10 includes a similar category for adjustment disorders, but does not classify separately those that feature depressed mood. (See Box 9.1.)

Dysthymic disorder is characterized by the presence of depressed mood that has persisted for at

Box 9.1 A Case Study in Adjustment Disorder with Depressed Mood

Yasmin was a 9-year-old girl about to start fourth grade when her parents suddenly announced that they were separating. There had been no warning. Her parents never raised their voices to one another and she had never seen them fighting. She simply awoke one day to her mother telling her that her father was gone, that he had moved back to their home country to live with his family and it might be a long time until Yasmin could see him again. Yasmin's mother seemed more tired than upset but her eyes were red and Yasmin wondered if she had been crying. Yasmin had never seen her mother cry before and the thought of it scared her. When Yasmin herself began to cry, her mother put her arm around her and encouraged her to 'Be brave. You are my little help-mate now'.

Yasmin began to have trouble sleeping at night and, although she wanted to ask to join her mother, was afraid that her mother would scold her for not being a 'big girl'.

Nonetheless, despite her efforts to appear helpful and confident, she also began wetting the bed. She rises early each day to try to strip the sheets and launder them before her mother finds out what has happened. She frequently feels tired and sad and has little appetite, even though she helps her mother to prepare the meals each evening for herself and her two younger brothers. Although previously a warm and generous big sister, she has begun to respond irritably and with increasing frustration to her younger brothers' boisterous behaviour. Yasmin's teachers approached her mother with their concerns as they noticed Yasmin's school performance declining and her lack of interest in joining her schoolmates in play during recess. A clinical social worker began meeting with Yasmin individually at her school to help her to verbalize and normalize her feelings and sadness and loss, and she also met with Yasmin's mother to help her foster her daughter's ability to cope with this difficult transition.

least one year in children (as opposed to two years in adults). Although the disorder is not described in ICD-10 in ways that differentiate between the symptoms of children and adults, DSM-IV-TR specifies that in children and adolescents negative mood may take the form of *irritability* rather than depression. At least two specific symptoms must accompany the periods of depression, such as loss of pleasure in activities, feelings of worthlessness and fatigue. (See Table 9.2 and Box 9.2.) Dysthymia has an earlier onset than other forms of depression and also has a more protracted course.

Major depression is a more debilitating disorder. It requires the presence of five or more symptoms during a two-week period (see Table 9.3), one

TABLE 9.2 DSM-IV-TR Criteria for Dysthymic Disorder

A. Depressed mood for most of the day, for more days than not, as indicated either by subjective account or observation by others, for at least 2 years. **Note:** In children and adolescents, mood can be irritable and duration must be at least 1 year.
B. Presence, while depressed, of two (or more) of the following:
  (1) poor appetite or overeating
  (2) insomnia or hypersomnia
  (3) low energy or fatigue
  (4) low self-esteem
  (5) poor concentration or difficulty making decisions
  (6) feelings of hopelessness
C. During the 2-year period (1 year for children or adolescence) of the disturbance, the person has never been without the symptoms for more than 2 months at a time.
D. No Major Depressive Episode has been present during the first 2 years of the disturbance (1 year for children and adolescents), unless that episode was in full remission with no signs or symptoms for 2 months before the development of the Dysthymic Disorder.
E. There has never been a Manic Episode or Hypomanic Episode.

Specify If:
Early onset: if onset is before age 21 years
Late onset: if onset is age 21 years or older

Source: Adapted from the *Diagnostic and Statistical Manual of Mental Disorders*, Fourth Edition Text Revision. Copyright 2000 by the American Psychiatric Association.

of which must be depressed mood or irritability in children. Major depression is an acute condition in that the onset is relatively sudden and, while recovery is more likely than from dysthymia, recurrence is likely as well. In the ICD-10, recurrent major depression is diagnosed when an individual suffers from multiple repeating episodes. Severe depressive episodes may even be accompanied by psychotic symptoms, such as auditory hallucinations, which are seen in one-third to one-half of pre-adolescents diagnosed with major depression (Mitchell et al., 1988). *Double depression* is a term used for individuals who experience chronic dysthymia punctuated by periods of major depression. (See Box 9.3 for a case example.)

Virtually none of the literature on the developmental psychopathology of depression addresses adjustment disorders. Therefore, we will focus our discussion on dysthymic disorder and major depression. Distinctions between the two disorders will be made whenever possible, although much of the research literature is based on studies of *symptoms* of depression (e.g., a significant score on a measure of depressive symptoms), rather than those children who meet full criteria for a psychiatric *diagnosis*.

Prevalence

Prevalence estimates vary widely, depending on the criteria and assessment instruments used. Many epidemiological studies only index whether children score above a certain point on a depression rating scale, failing to differentiate amongst the various diagnostic categories.

When viewed as a *symptom*, large-scale studies in the USA and Canada have found that, according to parent reports, 10 to 20 per cent of boys and 15 to 20 per cent of girls in the general population go through periods of depressed mood. Among adolescents, from 20 to 46 per cent of boys and 25 to 59 per cent of girls report experiencing depressed mood.

When depression is viewed as a *disorder*, prevalence rates are lower. Depressive disorders are rare in the preschool period, more frequent in middle childhood, and most prevalent in adolescence.

Box 9.2 A Case Study in Dysthymia

Marta, a 14-year-old girl, was referred for an evaluation by her school counsellor because of her many absences and concern on the part of her teachers about her increasingly poor grooming, withdrawal and sad affect in class. Marta is the youngest of three daughters born to a single mother who was divorced from her second husband – Marta's father – when Marta was 6 years of age. Although the two elder girls enjoy a warm relationship with their biological father, the breakup of Marta's parents was acrimonious and bitter. Consequently, Marta's father keeps his distance and focuses his attention on his new wife and two children. Both Marta's maternal grandfather and her mother report times of having 'blue moods' and there is a history of substance abuse on both sides of the family that has all the earmarks of 'self-medication'.

Although Marta's early history is generally unremarkable, with only the usual childhood illnesses, her mother reports that Marta always has been an anxious and difficult child, who was 'clingy' and coped poorly with changes and new situations. She particularly had difficulty adjusting when her mother returned to work full-time after her parents' divorce, and the stress of having to repeatedly leave work to bring her child home from school with various vague ailments almost cost Marta's mother her job. She acknowledges that she responded irritably to Marta's neediness and sought consultation from her own mother, who suggested strategies for setting more firm limits with her child. Otherwise, her mother describes Marta as a 'good' child who was generally obedient and content to play quietly in her room at home.

In the waiting room, Marta presents with downcast eyes, her sweatshirt hood pulled over her head and her unkempt hair partly covering her eyes. At a time when most teenagers are highly conscious of their appearance,

she is dressed in baggy and unbecoming clothes that seem designed to swallow up and hide her small frame. Marta describes herself as a 'weirdo' and says that she has never felt like she fitted in, either at school or in her family. She believes that she is a 'disappointment' to her mother and that she cannot blame her father for ignoring her. 'After all,' she says, 'what do I have to offer?' She has few friends and describes lunchtime as the most stressful and humiliating part of her day, as she attempts to avoid the teasing and ridicule of the girls who belong to the popular clique when they loudly point out the fact that Marta has no one to sit with in the cafeteria. Consequently, she has taken to leaving school as soon as the lunch bell rings and increasingly has been getting to stay home from school entirely by complaining of the same kinds of vague headaches and stomach aches that troubled her when she was in elementary school. She spends much of her time online chatting with a group of other youth who identify themselves as 'Outsiders'. Although she reports that it relieves her to know that she is not the only one who has such dark thoughts about herself and about life, she also admits that she comes away from these online conversations feeling even more depressed.

Although Marta actually does well at her schoolwork, her academic achievements rarely increase her confidence. Instead, Marta interprets her good grades as a sign that her teachers are being nice to her out of pity, and she worries that her peers will dislike her for getting better grades than they do. Therefore, she has stopped turning in assignments and has let her grades drop. She admits that part of the problem is that her motivation and ability to concentrate also have declined. Marta acknowledges that she often is preoccupied with unhappy thoughts and worries a great deal about her future, fearing that life does not hold much for her.

A distinction is made between point prevalence (how many children in the population are depressed) and lifetime prevalence (how many children will become depressed at some time in their lives). Regarding *point prevalence*, studies generally find that depression occurs in 1 to 2 per cent of preschoolers, 1 to 3 per cent of school-age children, and 5 to 6 per cent of adolescents. Regarding *lifetime prevalence*, estimates rise sharply for adolescents, with a range of 15 to 20 per cent (Klein et al., 2008). However, as we will discuss in detail, much of that rise is accounted for by a marked increase in depression among adolescent girls (Merikangas and Knight, 2009).

TABLE 9.3 DSM-IV-TR Criteria for Major Depressive Episode

A. Five (or more) of the following symptoms have been present during the same 2-week period and represent a change from previous functioning; at least one of the symptoms is either (1) depressed mood or (2) loss of interest or pleasure.

(1) depressed mood most of the day, nearly every day, as indicated by either subjective report (e.g., feels sad or empty) or observation made by others (e.g., appears tearful). **Note:** In children and adolescents, can be irritable mood

(2) markedly diminished interest or pleasure in all, or almost all, activities most of the day, nearly every day (as indicated either by subjective account or observation made by others)

(3) significant weight loss or weight gain when not dieting (e.g., more than 5 per cent of body weight in a month), or decrease or increase in appetite nearly every day. **Note:** In children, consider failure to make expected weight gains

(4) insomnia or hypersomnia nearly every day

(5) psychomotor agitation or retardation nearly every day (observable by others, not merely subjective feelings of restlessness or being slowed down)

(6) fatigue or loss of energy nearly every day

(7) feelings of worthlessness or excessive or inappropriate guilt (which may be delusional) nearly every day (not merely self-reproach or guilt about being sick)

(8) diminished ability to think or concentrate, or indecisiveness, nearly every day (either by subjective account or as observed by others)

(9) recurrent thoughts of death (not just fear of dying), recurrent suicidal ideation without a specific plan, or a suicide attempt or a specific plan for committing suicide

B. The symptoms are not better accounted for by bereavement and are not due to the effects of a substance or medical condition.

Source: Adapted from the *Diagnostic and Statistical Manual of Mental Disorders*, Fourth Edition Text Revision. Copyright 2000 by the American Psychiatric Association.

When clinical populations are studied, studies show that 10 to 57 per cent of children in mental health centres have a depressive disorder. School-aged children referred to treatment have higher rates of major depression (about 13 per cent) when compared with younger children (about 1 per cent) (Hammen and Rudolph, 2003).

Age Differences in Prevalence: The Dramatic Increase in Adolescence

Although depression may be seen in children at any age, most typically the onset for major depression is in mid to late adolescence. There also are differences related to the type of depression shown. Large-scale epidemiological studies show that the mean *age of onset* of the first major depressive episode is 15 years, while the onset of dysthymic disorder is in younger children, beginning at about age 11 (Lewinsohn et al., 1994). In fact, the marked increase in prevalence that comes with *puberty* is probably the most significant developmental trend in the phenomenon of depression. There is a dramatic rise in depression

between the ages of 13 and 15, a peak at ages 17 and 18, and a subsequent decline to adult levels.

Why the increase in depression in adolescence? Part of the explanation may lie with the biological, cognitive, emotional and social factors that come into play during this developmental period. *Biologically*, puberty brings with it profound changes in circulating hormones, and maturation of the brain brings online some of the higher cognitive processes that influence both affect and cognition. *Cognitively*, adolescents can think in terms of generalizations about themselves and their circumstances and can project these negative expectations into the future. They can consciously evaluate the self and judge it as helpless or inept. *Emotionally*, adolescents are capable of experiencing intense sadness and of sustaining this experience over time.

In addition, the *social context* of adolescence differs from that of childhood. Ordinarily, young children have the basic security of knowing they are an integral part of the family unit. By contrast, adolescents are faced with the task of moving beyond the

Box 9.3 A Case Study in Major Depression

Only in the 1980s did it become widely accepted that teenagers could experience major depression; by the 1990s mental health professionals recognized that depression could occur in children in the school-age years. But to this day, there is resistance to the idea, even though well supported by research such as that of Dr Joan Luby's (2010), that preschoolers can be seriously depressed. One such boy is 4-year-old Azdin, whose parents reported that he 'simply didn't seem like the kind of kid to worry about'. They described him as an 'easy' child who rarely disobeyed his parents or acted out, responding quickly to the slightest change in the tone of their voice that indicated they were about to scold him. He also was caring and kind towards other children; if any child in his preschool class began to cry, Azdin began to cry, too.

But, unlike the typical 4-year-old, Azdin did not seem to laugh or play or have times when he was joyful or care-free. He did not run and play on the playground like other children, and generally complained that 'nothing is fun' and that he felt 'bored'. When his parents tried to excite him about an upcoming visit to EuroDisney, Azdin responded in a downbeat manner that he did not care about the trip, and that 'Mickey is dumb. And Jimminy Cricket lies. Dreams don't come true'.

Azdin's parents also began to become concerned about how preoccupied their son was with worry and guilt. They had to take special care any time they scolded him because he took their disapproval so deeply to heart. 'I am bad,' he said after a minor incident in which he was reprimanded for leaving his toys out. 'I should be thrown in the trash can.' Azdin also was highly perfectionistic and easily frustrated by anything he could not do perfectly the first time. When his aunt bought him a challenging puzzle that Azdin struggled to put together, he threw the puzzle away and stated, 'I can't do puzzles, I'm too stupid. I never will do puzzles again.'

His parents finally realized that they needed to seek consultation after a day on a family vacation when Azdin responded with listless indifference to a full roster of child-centred activities the parents had lined up to please him and with his special interests in mind. Azdin merely slumped against the wall of every amusement park, children's museum and sweet shop, complaining that he was 'tired' and 'bored'. At home that evening, he curled up with his security blanket and whined. 'It was as if he was in pain,' his mother said, 'but I could tell it wasn't a physical pain.'

After discussion with his teachers and a thorough evaluation from his paediatrician, Azdin's family visited a clinical child psychologist who conducted a careful assessment and diagnosed him with early onset depression. Luckily, a university clinic was nearby at which a clinical study was being conducted on the treatment of depression in preschool children, and Azdin's family was able to quickly enrol him in the treatment protocol.

Source: Adapted from Pamela Paul, Can Preschoolers be Depressed? *New York Times Magazine*, 29 Aug. 2010, pp. 50–55.

---

family and developing a new status as independent persons. In turn, the increasing salience of the peer group introduces new sources of vulnerability for youth who have not developed strong friendships and social supports among their age mates. Even in a healthy adolescent, therefore, one might expect to see some transitory depressive states when dependence on the family is taboo but alternative sources of a 'secure base' have not yet been found. Thus, vulnerability to depression may arise as a function of difficulties in the normal separation-individuation process of adolescence (Weiner, 1992).

Gender Differences in Prevalence

Although prior to adolescence sex differences in depression are small and not reliably found, between the ages of 12 and 15 there is a dramatic increase in the prevalence, severity and recurrence of depression among girls (Hilt and Nolen-Hoeksema, 2009). For example, using large-scale longitudinal samples gathered in Canada, the UK and the USA, Wade and colleagues (2002) found higher rates of depression among girls overall, with the gender gap in depression emerging by age 14 in all three national samples. Another longitudinal study conducted in Canada of youth ages 12 to 19 found that girls experienced more episodes of major depression than boys at each wave of data collection, at a ratio of 2 to 1 (Galambos et al., 2004). In short, by the time they reach mid-adolescence, girls are twice as likely as boys to be diagnosed with depression. The differential burden of depression for girls also emerges in data collected cross-nationally by the World Health Organization (Sabaté, 2004). (See Fig. 9.1.)

Why are more girls depressed? This is a question that has been given substantial attention in the literature and has spawned important developmental models that integrate biology, emotion and cognition (Hilt and Nolen-Hoeksema, 2009; Mezulis et al., 2011). Therefore, we will first attend to these building blocks for constructing our developmental model of depression and then

we will return to this question later in the chapter.

Ethnicity, Culture and Socio-economic Status

Cross-national differences have emerged, both in the prevalence of depression, and its associated features. For example, Dmitrieva and colleagues (2004) found significantly higher rates of depressed mood among Korean and Czech youth than those from the United States or China. In turn, Ruchkin and colleagues (2006) found similar rates of depressive symptoms in a sample of 3300 14- to 17-year-olds drawn from the USA, Belgium and Russia. However, within-country differences showed that levels of depression were higher among girls than boys in the USA and Russia, where 16–18 per cent of girls and 10–13 per cent of boys met the clinical cut-off for significant levels of

FIGURE 9.1 Prevalence Rates of Major Depressive Disorder by Gender.

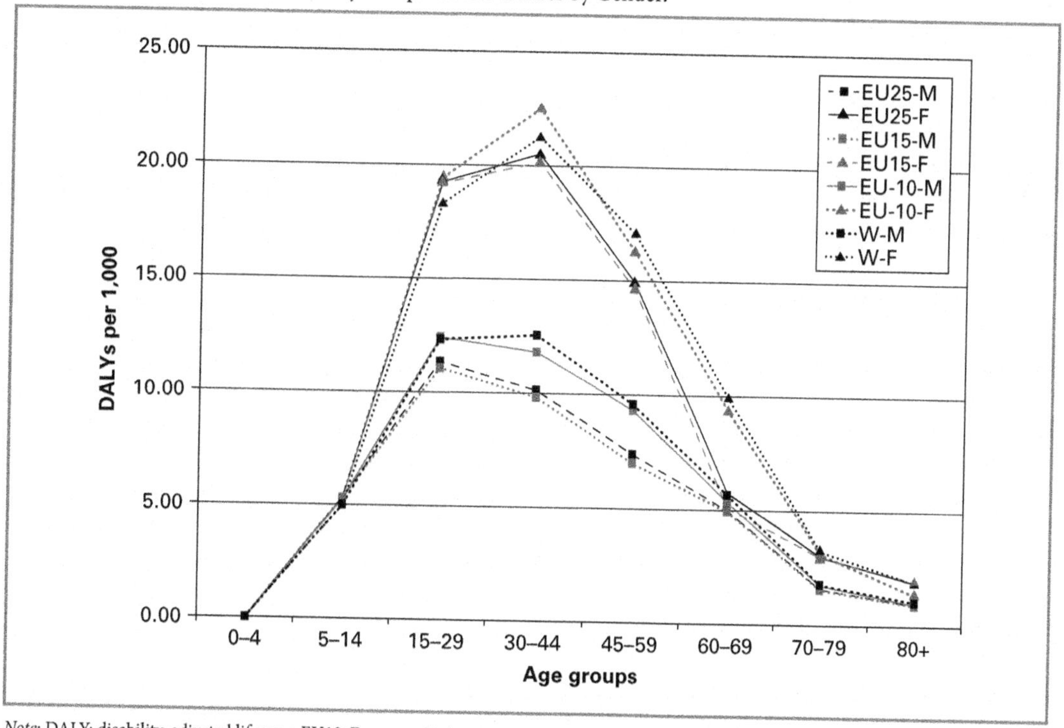

Note: DALY: disability-adjusted life year; EU10: European Union new accession countries; EU15: European Union countries; EU25: Expanded European Union.
Source: Sabaté, 2004.

distress, but not in Belgium, where similar numbers of boys and girls (10 and 12 per cent, respectively) met clinical criteria.

Intriguingly, culture may influence the factors that contribute to depression. For example, Chen and colleagues (2006) found that, consistent with the values of an individualist culture, low self-efficacy was strongly associated with depression for US youth, but not for youth from the more collectivist culture of Hong Kong. However, non-harmonious relationships in the family were significantly related to depression for both groups of youth, suggesting the importance of attending to the quality of family relationships, as we will do when we construct our developmental model.

Among the limited number of studies that have directly investigated *ethnic* differences in the prevalence of depression, results have been inconsistent. Whereas some studies in the US find higher rates among youth of African versus European American descent, others report the opposite. In a large-scale study of a sample of 5423 schoolchildren in grades 6 through 8, Roberts and colleagues (1997a) investigated ethnic differences while controlling for effects associated with social class. These authors found comparable rates of depression among European American and African American children; however, the rates for Hispanic children were higher. Twenge and Nolen-Hoeksema's (2002) meta-analysis of US studies including over 61 000 8- to 16-year-olds also found the highest rates of depressive symptoms were among the Hispanic children, as did Guiao and Thompson (2004) in their study of over 23 000 12- to 19-year-old girls. In one of the few studies to include American Indian youth, Saluja and colleagues (2004) found in a large national sample that American Indian sixth, eighth and tenth graders reported the highest rates of depressive symptoms of any ethnic group.

Although an association between *low SES* and depression has been found for adults, the research involving children also has yielded inconsistent results (Merikangas and Knight, 2009). An exception are those studies that have included the most seriously impoverished families, where differential rates of childhood depression are found (Allen and Astuto, 2009). Stressors associated with low SES, including family disruption, low income, lack of access to educational and cultural resources, unsafe and unattractive neighbourhoods, and other forms of adversity, potentially contribute to the risk.

The Developmental Dimension

The question has been raised as to whether depression in children can be regarded as the same disorder as that in adults, or whether developmental differences necessitate modifications in our diagnostic criteria (Weiss and Garber, 2003). If this is so, age-related differences in reported prevalence rates could be an artefact of the use of developmentally insensitive measures and conceptualizations of depression. Given that children's cognitive, language and emotional functioning is different from that of adults, it would be reasonable to assume that the way depression is expressed by children might be distinct. However, there is some evidence that there are core similarities in the manifestations of depression across development. For example, even as early as preschool (Luby, 2010), a comparable set of symptoms are displayed by both depressed children and adults. They are *emotional* (e.g., feels sad, cries, looks tearful), *cognitive* (e.g., anticipates failure, expresses excessive guilt, says 'I'm no good'), *motivational* (e.g., achievement declines, shows no interest in pleasurable activities) and *physical* (e.g., loss of appetite, somatic complaints).

In general, the weight of the research supports a middle position such that, although there is a significant correspondence between adult and childhood depression, children also have certain unique characteristics. Integrating findings from Luby (2010), Hammen and Rudolph (2003) and Weiss and Garber (2003), we can summarize the findings to date regarding developmental differences in the symptoms of depression.

Infancy and Toddlerhood

Signs of depression in very young children might include delays or losses of developmental accomplishments, such as toilet training, good sleeping habits and intellectual growth. A sad facial expression and gaze aversion may be seen. Children may engage in self-harming behaviour such as head banging and self-biting, as well as self-soothing behaviour such as rocking or thumb sucking. Clinging and demanding behaviour may alternate with apathy and listlessness.

Preschool

As Luby (2010) points out, early studies of depression in preschoolers missed seeing the diagnosis because care was not taken to adjust the DSM symptom definitions in ways that would make them more appropriate for very young children. For example, young children may not verbalize negative thoughts and feelings but might display these preoccupations through the themes of their play. *Anhedonia* (loss of pleasure in previously enjoyed activities) is displayed not as a loss of libido as it is in adults but as an inability to enjoy play activities or to take pride in developmental achievements, such as learning to tie their own shoes. Developmental backsliding may be evident, such as loss of cognitive and language skills, social withdrawal and excessive anxiety about separation from the caregiver. Vague somatic complaints, irritability, and sleep problems and nightmares also are seen.

School Age

As children approach school age, their symptom picture is increasingly similar to that of adults. Depressed mood becomes evident, as do expressions of low self-esteem, self-criticism and guilt. Loss of motivation may affect the child's interest in participating in social or school-related activities. In addition, depressed school-aged children may engage in disruptive and aggressive behaviour that negatively affects their peer relationships and academic performance. Eating and sleep disturbances may be seen, as well as developmental delays. As children advance in age, symptoms become more severe, there is a greater loss of interest or pleasure in previously enjoyed activities, and suicide is a possibility.

Adolescence

Adolescents are the most likely to directly verbalize their sad feelings and distress. Other symptoms of depression prevalent in adolescence include sharp mood swings and negativity, frequently accompanied by truancy, misbehaviour and a drop-off in academic achievement. Hypersomnia (sleeping too much) is another symptom seen more frequently in adolescents than in younger children. Changes in eating behaviour and resulting weight gain also increase with adolescence. Adolescents also display more anhedonia, hopelessness and social withdrawal than younger children.

To summarize, although developmental trends in depressive symptoms exist, age-related differences are not absolute. Studies generally find that depression can be reliably assessed in young children using criteria consistent with DSM-IV and ICD-10. Therefore, despite some age-related differences in symptoms, the existing criteria for depression appear to be valid for use with children. What is striking, and calls for closer attention, is the dramatic increase in the prevalence of depression among adolescents and, more specifically, adolescent girls.

Comorbidity

From 40 to 70 per cent of depressed children and adolescents have at least one other disorder as well (here we follow Rohde, 2009, unless otherwise indicated). Symptoms of *anxiety* and depression are highly correlated, with 25 to 50 per cent of depressed children having comorbid anxiety disorders, and 10–15 per cent of anxious children having comorbid anxiety. As we learned in Chapter 8, the **tripartite model of emotions** explains this comorbidity as being a function of underlying negative affectivity (Clark and Watson, 1991; Watson, 2005). However, developmental data suggest that the disorder still can be conceptualized as distinct. Anxiety symptoms typically predate depression, suggesting a developmental relationship between these two forms of internalizing such that early onset anxiety acts as a risk for later depression. For example, in a large-scale study conducted in Germany, Essau

(2003) found that, among adolescents with comorbid anxiety and depression, 72 per cent developed the anxiety disorder first.

Depressive disorders also may be comorbid with one another, with some children developing 'double depression'. Dysthymia also may increase the risk of developing a future episode of major depression, and the combination of dysthymia and major depression is associated with the most severely negative outcomes.

Anger and aggression also play a significant role in childhood depression, especially among boys. Rates of comorbid disruptive behaviour disorders and depression range from 17 to 82 per cent in community samples and 14 to 25 per cent in clinic samples. Although this observation is compatible with the idea of masked depression described earlier, again these misbehaviours are in addition to, rather than instead of, the symptoms of depression. There also is a gender difference found in most of these studies, such that depressed boys are more likely to demonstrate disruptive behaviour disorders than are girls. Comorbid conduct disorder and aggression are associated with a more negative outcome and are cause for particular concern. Indeed, the International Classification of Diseases (ICD-10) (see Chapter 3) includes a specific category of depressive conduct disorder (DCD). In a test of its validity, Simic and Fombonne (2001) found that among in-patient children and adolescents in the UK, those with the DCD diagnosis had lower levels of depression and anxiety than the depression-only group, but were more likely to engage in self-harming behaviour. In turn, children with DCD were more depressed and less overtly aggressive than the conduct disorder-only group and were more likely to have been abused.

Whether depression leads to problem behaviour, or whether problem behaviour leads to depression, has been the subject of debate and widely divergent findings. Several speculations have been offered to explain the link between depression and conduct problems: (1) the two disorders may be brought about by shared risk factors and genetic vulnerabilities; (2) both disorders may

arise from a single general underlying developmental deficit, such as in emotion regulation; (3) depression may arise as a consequence of the negative events, stresses and disruptions that conduct disorders generate in a child's life; or (4) conduct problems may arise as a consequence of irritability and/or failures to successfully navigate stage-salient issues due to depression (Hammen and Rudolph, 2003). More recent research suggests that the direction of effects may be bidirectional in adolescence, at least for girls, with each disorder in turn exacerbating the risk factors for the other (Measelle et al., 2006).

In contrast to conduct disorder, which is the more common comorbid syndrome for boys, for adolescent girls *eating disorders* often co-occur with depression. For example, Blinder and colleagues (2006) found that 94 per cent of adolescent girls being treated for an eating disorder also met criteria for a diagnosis of mood disorder.

For all youth, one of the most concerning forms of comorbidity is that of depression and *substance abuse*. As we will explore in greater detail, this combination is potentially lethal, contributing the single greatest risk factor for adolescent suicide (Vermeiren et al., 2003). Co-occurring depression and substance abuse also is associated with significant functional deficits and academic impairment. It is estimated that 20 to 30 per cent of community youth who experience depression also have a substance use problem, with some studies showing that this risk is even higher among adolescent girls (Costello et al., 2003). Some studies suggest that substance use contributes to the development of depression. For example, using data from 85 088 individuals drawn from 17 countries gathered as part of the World Health Organization World Mental Health Survey Initiative, de Graaf and colleagues (2010) found that early onset cannabis use was modestly but statistically associated with later depression. However, other research indicates that depression leads to substance use, particularly for girls (Measelle et al., 2006). As Rohde (2009) suggests, the co-occurrence of the two disorders may be a function of (1) substance use as a form of self-medication against depression; (2) depressive affect as a result of substance abuse; or (3) reciprocal relationships such that each disorder contributes to the exacerbation and maintenance of the other.

Etiology
The Biological Context
Genetics

Familial concordance rates provide evidence for a *genetic* component in depression. (Here we follow Lau and Eley, 2009, unless otherwise noted.) Children, adolescents and adults who have close relatives with depression are at higher risk for developing depression themselves, with a genetic component generally estimated at about 20 to 45 per cent. Parent depression is a particular risk factor for the development of child depression, as we will explore in more detail later. The familial loading is higher for those whose depression began before the age of 20; therefore, it is proposed that childhood onset depression is a variant with a particularly strong genetic component.

However, simply showing that depression runs in families fails to disentangle the relative influence of heredity and environment. For this, twin and adoption studies are needed. In one large-scale study, O'Connor and colleagues (1998) compared MZ and DZ twin pairs and reported an overall heritability estimate of 48 per cent. Another study, the Virginia Twin Study of Adolescent Behaviour Development, obtained interviews and self-report ratings of depression from both parents and children (Eaves et al., 1997). The correlations between MZ twins were .66 while those for DZ pairs were less than half as large, suggesting a genetic contribution. A puzzling finding emerging from this study was that estimates varied as a function of whose report was used. Whereas the genetic component was estimated to be 54 to 72 per cent when findings were based on parent interviews, it shrank to 11 to 19 per cent when children's reports were used. The reasons for these discrepancies are not clear.

In contrast, some adoption studies have found *no* genetic component to depressive symptoms in middle childhood, which may reflect the significant effects of environmental factors on the unfolding of depression (Eley et al., 1998). For example, one study of adolescents compared monozygotic and dizygotic twins, biological siblings, half-siblings and biologically unrelated step-siblings, and found significant genetic influences for those with low levels of depression, but significant environmental influences for those with high levels of depression (Rende et al., 1993).

Silberg and colleagues (1999) used the Virginia twin data to attempt to tease out the relative contributions of nature (genes) and nurture (environmental stress) to the developmental psychopathology of depression. Using two waves of data collection conducted 19 months apart, they found that genetic factors contributed to the consistency of depression over the course of the study, and that life stress also had a direct effect on depression, but particularly for adolescent girls. About 30 per cent of the variance in adolescent girls' depressive symptoms was attributable to genetics, with the remainder attributable to environmental factors. In addition, genetic effects tended to increase the likelihood of experiencing negative life events. In conclusion, the authors suggest that an increased genetic liability to depression emerges in adolescence, particularly for girls, which interacts with the experience of life stress in order to produce the disorder.

Lau and Eley (2008) also attempted to tease apart the contributions of genetics and the environment over time in a study of three groups of adolescents assessed at ages 14, 15 and 17 years. Their results showed consent contribution of genetics at each time period (45, 40 and 45 per cent, respectively), decreasing shared environmental effects (19, 9 and 0 per cent, respectively) and increasing non-shared environmental effects (36, 51 and 55 per cent, respectively). The investigators summarize their results as showing that genes contribute primarily towards the continuity of depression over time, whereas non-shared environmental factors increasingly enter the picture over the course of adolescence and contribute to the prediction of change. As we know from our study of *epigenetics* and *gene-environment interactions* in Chapter 2, with age children are increasingly able to select, modify and create their own interpersonal environments by gravitating towards and away from particular people and activities, and by evoking responses in others that might maintain or exacerbate a genetic predisposition toward depression. For example, children who have inherited the genetic predisposition for depression may evidence a difficult temperament which elicits negative reactions from their caregivers, and thus potentiates further adversity and stress in the social environment.

Eley and colleagues (2004a) report findings that further illustrate the way in which genes and environments interact in depression. Their study focused on one genetic marker that might increase the vulnerability to depression, and that is the possession of the *short allele of the 5-HT transporter gene*. This gene is involved in the regulation of the brain's response to stress and the short form of the allele is less efficient than the long form, thus allowing less serotonin to be available in the brain. In a study of female adolescents who had been exposed to significant environmental risk (including psychosocial adversity, stressful life events and family economic strain), the investigators found environmental factors increased the risk of depression significantly more for those girls who had at least one short form of the 5-HT allele (see Fig. 9.2). A similar pattern was reported in data gathered from the Dunedin, New Zealand, longitudinal study (Caspi et al., 2003), in which the relationship between cumulative life stress and depression was amplified by possession of the short form of the allele: those with two short forms were the most sensitive, followed by those with one short form; in turn, those with two long forms were the least likely to develop depression in response to negative life events.

Further insight into the mechanism by which this effect takes place is offered by Goodyer and colleagues (2009), who gave consideration to the fact that the promoter region of the 5-HTT gene, 5HTTLPR, is involved in the neurochemistry underlying the processing of social cognitive information. As we will discuss in more detail later, an

FIGURE 9.2 Interaction of Environmental Risk and Genotype in the Prediction of Depression in Adolescence.

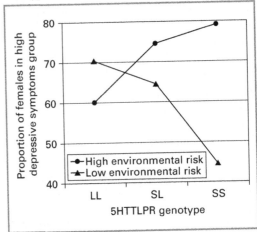

Note: LL = two long alleles; SL = one short allele; SS = two short alleles.
Source: Eley et al., 2004b.

important characteristic of depression is a negative attributional style. Could the short allele be related to the development of such depressogenic cognitions? In a prospective longitudinal study of adolescents at high risk of depression, the investigators found preliminary support for this theory. Among youth with a history of adverse life events, those who were carriers of the short allele reported more negative appraisals of recent events in their lives.

A limitation of much of the research on genetics is that it often does not consider the issue of *specificity*. In fact, the genetic liability appears to be not specific to depression, but to all internalizing disorders, including anxiety and phobia. It may be that what is inherited is an underlying trait such as *negative emotionality*. Further, as we have seen, depression and conduct problems frequently co-occur in families as well as in children, again suggesting a non-specific factor that the two disorders have in common.

Neurochemistry

As our review of the genetics research has made evident, a likely culprit in the neurochemistry underlying depression is the *serotonin* (5HT)

system. Serotonin is involved in the regulation of a wide variety of physiological, behavioural and psychological processes, including mood, sleep, appetite, activity level and sexual arousal, all of which are affected by depression. (Here we follow Goodyer, 2009.) However, although a connection between diminished serotonin functioning in the brain and unipolar depression has been well established, the chain of events linking the two is complex and so it cannot be said that low levels of serotonin 'cause' depression. Serotonin depletion is related to an increased sensitivity of the brain to developing psychiatric disorders generally, rather than to depression specifically.

Another promising hypothesis focuses on corticosteroids, the hormones that are released in response to stress. Cortisol also is involved in the regulation of the HPA axis. Ordinarily, circulating cortisol reaches receptors in the hippocampus which signal back through the HPA axis that sufficient levels have been reached. When this feedback system is interrupted, excessive levels of cortisol are released, which can have a negative effect on the developing brain. Once sensitized to cortisol, the brain is overreactive to further stress, thus increasing the vulnerability to psychopathology in general and perhaps depression in particular. Research by Goodyer and others finds that adolescents diagnosed with, and at risk for, depression have dysregulated HPA activity, demonstrating higher levels of morning cortisol than those of their nondepressed peers.

Brain Structure and Function

Brain-imaging research with adults suggests that depression is related to low levels of activation of the left hemisphere. Interestingly, the left hemisphere appears to be involved in the processing of positive affect; when it is underactivated, the right hemisphere may become more active, generating excessive negative affect (Pliszka, 2004). This pattern of left hemispheric hypoactivation also has been found in infants and toddlers of depressed mothers (Dawson et al., 1997). Whether this intergenerational transmission is a function of genetics,

or of the depressed children's greater experience of life stress and exposure to maternal negative affect, remains to be determined (Hammen and Rudolph, 2003).

The Individual Context
Attachment

A wealth of evidence has accumulated regarding a link between *internal working models of attachment* and depression in infants, children and adolescents (Allen et al., 2007; DeKlyen and Greenberg, 2008). Children who internalize an image of themselves as unworthy and others as unloving are more vulnerable to the development of the cognitive, emotional and biological processes that are associated with depression.

Blatt (2004) relies on attachment theory for his model, which distinguishes between two different kinds of depression. The first, *dependent* or *anaclitic* depression, is characterized by feelings of loneliness and helplessness as well as fear of abandonment. Individuals with dependent depression cling to relationships with others and have unmet longings to be cared for and nurtured. Thus, they have difficulty coping with separation and loss and are uncomfortable expressing anger for fear of driving others away. In contrast, *self-critical* or *introjective* depression is characterized by feelings of unworthiness, inferiority, failure and guilt. Individuals with self-critical depression have extremely high internal standards, resulting in harsh self-scrutiny and evaluation. They have a chronic fear of others' disapproval and criticism, and they worry about losing the regard of significant others. They are driven to achieve and to attain perfection and thus make excessive demands on themselves. While they may even accomplish a great deal, they do so with little experience of lasting satisfaction or pleasure.

Blatt and Homann (1992) hypothesize that these different kinds of depression are due to particular kinds of attachment experiences affected individuals have in early childhood. The quality of their relationships with caregivers leads to the development of internal working models of self and others that leave these individuals vulnerable to depression. Inconsistent parental availability, associated with the *resistant/ambivalent* attachment pattern, may be more likely to result in depression related to issues of dependency, loss and abandonment. In contrast, controlling and rejecting parenting associated with *avoidant* attachment would lead to self-criticism and low self-worth, as angry feelings about the caregiver are redirected against the self.

To date, research has offered some support for the model. Much of the research has focused on adults; however, Blatt and associates (1996) were able to differentiate the two types of depression in a sample of adolescents. Further tentative support for the dual model of depression in children comes from Harter's (1990) research, which revealed two groups of depressed children and adolescents. In the larger group depression was due to low self-esteem, whereas in the smaller group it was due to the loss of a significant person. However, the necessary developmental research – showing that dependent depression and self-critical depression in childhood are predicted from different kinds of attachment relationships in infancy – has not yet been conducted.

Cognitive Perspectives

The Cognitive Triad   Beck's (2002) classic model of depression centres on the **cognitive triad**, which consists of attributions of *worthlessness* ('I am no good'), *helplessness* ('There is nothing I can do about it') and *hopelessness* ('It will always be this way'). The contribution of each of these dimensions to childhood depression has found support in the research to date.

First, evidence regarding the *worthlessness* dimension comes from extensive research documenting the relationship between childhood depression and feelings of low self-worth or perceived competence (see Harter, 2006). Moreover, children's negative view of the self leads to a biased interpretation of information in such a way that it 'confirms' their belief in their inadequacy and depressed youth attend differentially to information that validates their negative view of themselves. For

example, in a study conducted in the Netherlands, depressed children recalled more negative adjectives describing themselves on a memory test while non-depressed children recalled more positive traits (Timbremont and Braet, 2004). In another study, daughters who were at risk for depression by virtue of having a depressed mother selectively attended to negative expressions during a facial recognition task (Joormann et al., 2007). Thus, it appears that depression 'primes' children to attend to whatever is depressing in their interpersonal environments.

Second, Bandura's (1986) concept of **self-efficacy** provides us with insight into the *helplessness* dimension. Perceived self-efficacy refers to children's belief in their ability to affect the world around them in order to obtain a desired result. Without a sense that they can produce effects by their actions, children have little incentive to take action or to persevere in the face of challenges. Bandura and colleagues (1999) propose that a low sense of self-efficacy contributes to depression via three pathways. The first involves feelings of self-devaluation and despondency that arise when children perceive themselves as being unable to live up to their expectations and fulfil their aspirations. The second involves perceived social inefficacy, which arises when children believe they are unable to form satisfying relationships, leading children to withdraw from others and be deprived of the social support that could help to buffer them from stress. The third mechanism involves perceived inability to control depressive thoughts themselves. In a prospective study of 282 middle-school students, Bandura and colleagues (1999) confirmed that perceived social and academic inefficacy influenced children's depression over a period of two years. As expected, depressed children had more non-efficacious beliefs about their skills than their actual performance warranted.

The third dimension of the cognitive triad, *hopelessness*, is supported by research on children's **causal attributions** (Abela and Seligman, 2000). Three dimensions are involved in the causal attributions leading to depression: they are *internal* ('It is because of me'), *stable* ('I will always be like this') and *global* ('Everything about me is this way'). When negative events are attributed to characteristics of the individual rather than to external agents, self-esteem diminishes as helplessness increases. When the negative events are attributed to factors that persist over time, then helplessness is stable. And when negativity is generalized to a host of situations, helplessness is global. Stable and global negative attributions are clearly linked to the cognition of hopelessness, which has a significant role in child and adolescent depression (Abela and Hankin, 2009).

How do these attributional styles develop? According to Rose and Abramson (1991), negative events during childhood – such as traumatic loss, maltreatment or a guilt-inducing parenting – set in motion a vicious cycle. As the child attempts to interpret these events and find meaning in them, cognitions are generated related to the events' causes and solutions. When events are negative, uncontrollable and repeated, hopelessness-inducing cognitions are likely. A number of other factors might facilitate or interfere with the development of negative cognitions, including the extent to which the negative events challenge the child's self-esteem, and the reactions and interpretations of events offered by parents.

These negative cognitive *schemata* affect not only the child's present state of mind but also the child's future orientation toward the world. Schemata are stable mental structures that incorporate children's perceptions of self, their experiences in the past, and their expectations for the future (Dodge, 1993). Therefore, based on the lessons they draw from past experiences, children's perceptions of present and future events are coloured by depressive schemata as if by a pair of grimy grey glasses. Children who look at the world through the lens of depression focus their attention on whatever is negative and consistent with their pessimistic point of view, ignoring the disconfirming evidence offered by positive events. As children develop negative patterns of thinking and engaging with the world, as well as a stable negative cognitive style, the likelihood increases that depression will emerge.

One of the strengths of the cognitive triad model is that these negative attributional styles appear to be specific to the development of internalizing disorders, including anxiety and depression, and are not characteristic of child psychopathology in general (Hankin and Abramson, 2002). However, there are some important limitations to cognitive models of child depression. Some studies of children's attributional styles have produced mixed results; for instance, some longitudinal research has found negative attributions to be *correlates* of youth depression rather than *predictors* of it (Abela and Hankin, 2009). In addition, much of the research is cross-sectional rather than longitudinal, and so the direction of effects cannot be determined. There is still much to be learned about the causal role of the cognitive triad in the etiology of depression.

Another limitation of the cognitive model is a *developmental* one. Whereas depression can be detected in very young children, not all the cognitive markers theoretically associated with depression can be. Not only do the research methods for assessing the cognitive triad require children to understand complex language in interviews or questionnaires, but the constructs themselves require more advanced cognitive development than is usually attributed to young children. In particular, our understanding of normative cognitive development makes it difficult to imagine complex cognitions involving worthlessness, helplessness and hopelessness in infancy, even though the markers of depression can be seen at that early age. In an attempt to resolve this developmental dilemma, Rose and Abramson (1991) offer an intriguing speculation. Although the onset of a depressive attributional style may indeed develop in early childhood, the cognitive components of depression may not become evident until years later. The authors theorize that negative experiences only result in the cognitive triad of depression *if* those stressors persist into the period of concrete operations when the child is able to make causal inferences that are stable and global in nature. In other words, although a negative attributional style indeed may underlie the development of depression from an early age, investigators may only be able to detect the underlying cognitive components of helplessness, hopelessness and worthlessness later in childhood.

Rumination   Research also has suggested that a **ruminative** cognitive style is implicated in the development of depression. Rumination involves dwelling on negative thoughts and feelings as is indicated by a youth's endorsement of items on a questionnaire such as, 'When I feel sad or down, I think about how alone I feel' and 'When I feel sad or down, I think about how hard it is to concentrate' (Nolen-Hoeksema and Morrow, 1991).

To demonstrate the role of rumination in depression, Mezulis and colleagues (2011) followed a sample of children from infancy into adolescence. The investigators found that whereas negative emotionality increased the risk for depression at age 15, this effect was accounted for by the development of a ruminative cognitive style during early adolescence. Moreover, comparisons by gender showed that overall girls were more likely than boys to develop a ruminative cognitive style, and it was only for the girls in the sample that rumination led to depression. The investigators speculate that one possible explanation for this finding might be gender socialization in that parents may attend, respond to and encourage discussion of negative emotions such as fear, distress and sadness when interacting with daughters and thus may inadvertently contribute to a tendency to ruminate on such feelings.

Subsequent research has clarified that the culprit in depression is rumination on *sadness* (Peled and Moretti, 2007), whereas youth who ruminate on angry thoughts and feelings are more likely to show aggression than depression. In turn, other researchers have investigated the concept of *co-rumination*, the tendency of friends to engage in repetitive talk about problems and negative emotions. As Tompkins and colleagues (2011) found, co-rumination is more common among girls and is a unique predictor of internalizing problems among adolescents.

Emotional Development

One of the underlying developmental processes that contributes to child depression is difficulty with *emotion regulation*. Not only do depressed children have poor general skills for coping with life challenges, including interpersonal problems, but they have more difficulty moderating their emotions in the face of stress (Compas et al., 2009). For example, Zeman and colleagues (2002; Suveg and Zeman, 2004) found that depression in adolescents and school-aged children was predicted by difficulty identifying their emotional states, suppression of angry emotions, and dysregulation of anger and sadness. In face of poorly regulated emotional distress, depressed children respond in ineffective ways, such as withdrawal or excessive reassurance seeking, that alienate them from their peers and further exacerbate their difficulties (Joiner et al., 1999). Although emotion dysregulation may arise as a function of temperamental qualities of the child, family patterns of interaction also are implicated, particularly for children of depressed mothers, as we discuss in more detail in the next section.

The Family Context
Families of Depressed Children

An emotionally aversive family environment predicts the development of depression in children and adolescents (Harkness and Lumley, 2008). Families of depressed children report experiencing more acute and chronic stressors than do others, and they have fewer supportive social relationships to buffer them. In a 15-year longitudinal study conducted in New Zealand, children of disadvantaged, dysfunctional and disorganized home environments were at increased risk of depression as well as other behaviour problems (Fergusson et al., 2006). Sagrestano and colleagues (2003) found a similar pattern of results in a two-year longitudinal study of 302 low-income African American school-aged children. Interestingly, their data showed that increases in family conflict and decreases in parental involvement were associated with increases in *both* child and parent depression. Further, Ge and colleagues (2006) found in an 11-year longitudinal study of mostly European American families in the USA, increased *interparental conflict* and family stress subsequent to parental divorce also increases the likelihood of depression, particularly among adolescent girls.

Observations of the interactions of depressed children and their parents confirm that the families are characterized by low levels of cohesion, support, and parental warmth and involvement, along with high levels of conflict, harsh discipline, parental rejection and excessive control (Kaslow et al., 2009). Observational studies of *expressed emotion* indicate that mothers of depressed children are more critical than are mothers of non-depressed children, and that maternal criticism predicts children's relapse into another episode of major depression within a five-year period (Silk et al., 2009). Further, not surprisingly, depression is linked to child *maltreatment* (Cicchetti and Toth, 2009, and see Chapter 14). A dysfunctional family environment may undermine the child's self-worth, which in turn contributes to a sense of failure and depression. All these negative childhood events also interact with the other risk factors we have identified, such as by generating the attributional style of helplessness, hopelessness and worthlessness that is characteristic of depression (Rudolph, 2009).

It is worth noting that the previously cited research shows that children become depressed specifically in relation to *interpersonal stressors*, rather than to other kinds of negative events that might affect adults, such as achievement-related failures (Rudolph, 2009). Perhaps the single most traumatic interpersonal stressor for children is the loss of a parent, which we consider next.

Parental Loss

Our review of the concept of attachment in Chapter 5 demonstrated that adequate caregiving in infancy is not a sentimental luxury but an absolute necessity for optimal development. Although relatively rare, complete loss of a parent is an experience with dramatic effects on child functioning and clear links to depression.

The classic research on *maternal deprivation* was conducted by Spitz (1946b) and Bowlby (1960), who studied infants in institutional settings such as hospitals, orphanages and foundling homes. Despite the fact that their physiological needs were met – they received adequate food, warmth and hygiene – these infants lacked any kind of affectionate care. As a consequence, many wasted away and even died – as many as 37 per cent in one orphanage. Spitz termed these infants' reaction **anaclitic depression** (meaning, essentially, loss of that on which one depends) and believed that it represented a prototype of adult depression. Bowlby (1960) asserted that the loss of this important relationship – the infant's secure base – is so profound that it should be viewed on the same level as war and natural disaster.

An important fact to keep in mind, however, is that Spitz's and Bowlby's research confounds loss of a parent with *institutionalization*. These variables were teased apart in a series of studies conducted by Joyce and James Robertson (1971). They observed young children who had been temporarily separated from their mothers and found that the ill effects of parental loss were more severe for children who were placed in institutions as opposed to those who were placed in foster families. While large, impersonal orphanages provided children with minimal care and attention from an ever-changing series of nurses, children in loving foster families had available to them surrogate caregivers with whom they readily formed attachments. Children in foster care also demonstrated significantly less distress about the separation from their mothers, and they overcame their distress more readily when reunited with their own families. Therefore, it is not separation per se that is so devastating, but rather the extended stay in a strange, bleak or socially insensitive environment with little or no contact with the mother or other familiar figures.

Bifulco (2008) examined other factors that can mediate the effect of loss of the mother. In two large-scale studies conducted in the UK, these investigators studied women who were bereaved as children and also those who underwent a significant period of separation from the mother. Loss of the mother before the age of 11, whether by death or separation, was associated with subsequent depression for most women. Thus, maternal deprivation acted as a *vulnerability factor*. However, loss of the mother had no effect in the absence of a *provoking event*, such as poverty or life stress. Further research from these investigators uncovered additional moderators. The rate of depression was twice as high in women who had experienced *traumatic* separations from their mothers, such as being neglected, abused or abandoned, than it was in women separated by death or by other causes such as maternal illness or divorce. Further, the rate of adult depression was particularly high in women whose mother died before they were 6 years old and even greater if death occurred before they were 3 years old. However, it was not the early timing of the death per se that was important. Rather, it was the fact that the death came at the end of a long sickness, which, the authors infer, prevented the development of a secure *attachment*.

Although most of the research on parental loss has focused on mothers, Jacobs and Bovasso (2009) used data gathered from a large-scale study of 3481 individuals in Baltimore to investigate the impact of *paternal* loss. Their data showed no relationship between experiencing the death of a mother in childhood and later depression, while the death of a father increased the risk of major depression more than twofold. The investigators speculated that the adverse effects of loss of the father on family income and financial stability created stresses that extended throughout childhood and into adulthood.

In sum, both in infancy and childhood, the idea that loss of a caregiver per se leads to depression is too simplistic to be accurate. Rather, depression is contingent on the interaction of a host of factors, including the *individual* (e.g., perceived helplessness), *interpersonal* (e.g., lack of social support), *sociocultural* (e.g., socioeconomic level) and *developmental* (e.g., the child's level of cognitive sophistication). Therefore, the task of investigators is to tease out the interactions among variables and to examine the ways in which such interactions change as loss occurs at different points in development.

Children of Depressed Parents

In a major review article published over a decade ago, Peterson and colleagues (1993) stated that 'the need for services for children of depressed parents as closely approximates a prescriptive recommendation as can be found in the mental health professions' (p. 163). *Maternal depression* more than doubles the risk of a child's developing depression across the life course, and children with two depressed parents are even more significantly at risk. (Here we follow Joormann et al., 2009, unless otherwise noted). Approximately 40 per cent of children of depressed mothers will themselves come to be diagnosed with depression; moreover, these children are particularly at risk for early onset depression, which has the most devastating effects on development. In fact, longitudinal research by Hammen and colleagues (1990) showed that children of depressed mothers had a worse outcome than children of bipolar, medically ill, well or even schizophrenic mothers. Perhaps, in contrast to the guilt-inducing qualities of parental depression, children readily understand that the overtly bizarre behaviour associated with mania and psychosis is not under their control and not of their doing.

Paternal depression affects children's development as well. In a meta-analysis, Kane and Garber (2004) reviewed the available albeit limited research and found that paternal depression was associated with significant increases in children's internalizing and externalizing symptoms as well as father–child conflict.

The Developmental Dimension There also is a developmental dimension to consider regarding the ways in which depressed parents might affect children. In the *preschool* years, we might expect that depression in a primary caregiver would have particularly negative effects, given the extent to which young children are dependent on the parent–child relationship and the critical role that caregiving plays in the mastery of stage-salient tasks such as attachment security, emotion regulation, and the self. In turn, in the *school-age* years, parental depression might interfere most with the stage-salient issues of self-regulation and formation of social relationships. In *adolescence*, autonomy seeking may be compromised in ways that are particularly difficult for the teenage daughters of depressed mothers. In Table 9.4, we present Goodman's (2003) outline of the ways in which depressed parenting might interfere with the child's mastery of stage-salient issues through the course of childhood.

A significant literature confirms that there are negative effects of parental depression on children across developmental stages. For example, a meta-analysis of studies conducted in the USA and the UK (Martins and Gaffan, 2000) confirms the

increase in anxious attachment among preschool children parented by depressed mothers. In the *school-age* years, among mothers seeking treatment for depression, one third of their 7- to 17-year-old children currently had a psychiatric disorder and nearly half had a lifetime history of psychopathology (Pilowsky et al., 2006). In *adolescence*, the evidence is strong that both maternal and paternal depression are highly predictive of the occurrence, recurrence, chronicity and severity of youth depression (P. Rohde et al., 2005) as well as other disorders such as anxiety, as was found in a 13-year longitudinal study conducted in the UK (Halligan et al., 2007).

How Does the Intergenerational Transmission of Depression Take Place? It is not clear how the intergenerational transmission of depression from parent to child takes place. Although the link may be a genetic one, another likely explanation is *parenting style*. Two dimensions of depressed parenting have

TABLE 9.4 Effects of Depressed Parenting on Stage-Salient Issues Across Development

Developmental Stage	Depressed Mothers[1]
Infancy • Fostering an attachment relationship • Facilitating the development of emotional self-regulation	• Less sensitive • Less responsive (slower and less contingent) • Less reciprocal vocalization and affectionate contact • Lower amounts and quality of stimulation
Toddlers and preschool-aged children Providing the external support necessary for children to develop: • An accurate understanding of social and emotional situations • Effective autonomous functioning • The ability to manage emotionally arousing situations • The ability to organize and coordinate environmental resources	• Spend less time mutually engaged with their children in a shared activity • Terminate their children's attention to objects more frequently (rather than encouraging sustained attention) • Respond to children's resisting their influence by dropping their demands or persisting less effectively or engaging in coercive mutual influence
School-aged children and adolescents • Providing general social support or stress buffering • Helping children to maintain their focus on the cognitive intellectual and social environment • Monitoring children's behaviour • Providing consistent discipline	• Reinforce children's misbehaviour by suppressing their dysphoric affect in response to children's aggressive affect • More critical, more negative appraisals, and lower tolerance of their children's behaviour

Note: [1] Compared with non-depressed controls.
Source: Goodman, 2003.

been identified: withdrawal and intrusiveness (Malphurs et al., 1996). In terms of *withdrawal*, depressed mothers are observed to be less psychologically available to their children: they offer less positive affect, warmth, praise and positive feedback. Regarding *intrusiveness*, depressed mothers also are more likely to be controlling, impatient and irritable; to use coercive discipline techniques; to make more negative attributions about child behaviour; and to be less accurate in reading children's affect.

The clearest evidence for the effects of maternal withdrawal comes from studies in which mothers' affect has been experimentally manipulated, a rare thing in the literature on psychopathology. While playing with their toddlers, non-depressed mothers were asked to simulate depressed affect by keeping a 'still face' and remaining emotionally inexpressive, uninvolved and unresponsive to their children. Children reacted to their mothers' emotional unavailability with clear distress, physically withdrawing, making more negative bids for attention, and becoming disorganized and oppositional (Seiner and Gelfand, 1995).

What is the underlying developmental process by which children of depressed parents become depressed? Insecure working models of attachment have provided one rich conceptual model (Toth et al., 2009). Another proposal is that coping with a depressed parent prevents children from developing the biological and psychological capacities for *emotion regulation* (Joormann et al., 2009). Emotion regulation, as we saw in Chapter 2, allows children to calm themselves in the face of upsetting circumstances. Healthy mothers aid the development of emotion regulation by soothing their children and helping to build their competency to soothe themselves. However, depressed mothers' inability to modulate their own negative feeling states interferes with the ability to modulate their children's moods. Thus, children of depressed mothers are exposed to chronically high levels of negative affect and fail to develop effective strategies for managing these distressing feelings (Garber et al., 1995).

Alternatively, there is evidence that *cognitive* factors come into play. As young as 5 years of age,

children of depressed mothers express depressive cognitions such as hopelessness, pessimism and low self-worth when observed responding to a mild stress in the laboratory, such as the threat of losing at a card game (Murray et al., 2001). Similarly, children of depressed mothers are more likely than other children to show a poor self-concept and to focus more on negative words and emotions when their depressive cognitive schemas are primed (Joormann et al., 2007). Depressed mothers may model such depressed cognitive styles for their children as well as reinforce them through maladaptive parenting styles. For example, Langrock et al. (2002) found that children of depressed mothers engaged in maladaptive strategies for coping with stress that were reminiscent of depressive thinking (e.g., rumination and intrusive thinking).

Clinical observations of depressed mothers and toddlers also demonstrate *transactional* processes through which they exert negative influences on one another's behaviour. For example, children of depressed mothers are more irritable and difficult to soothe and exhibit more negative affect, anger, sadness and distress, thus taxing the mother's parenting skills and increasing her stress and irritation (Radke-Yarrow, 1998). Children of depressed mothers, in turn, are highly attuned to their mother's negative affect and may attempt to comfort and nurture the parent, engaging in a process of role reversal or parentification (Kerig, 2005). As we have learned, parentified children are burdened by the developmentally inappropriate expectation that they meet the parents' emotional needs at the expense of their own. In these ways, children's attempts to cope with and respond to their mothers' depression might perpetuate problematic cycles of interaction. Over the long term, maternal depression and child depression have been shown to mutually affect one another, as research shows significant relationships between the onset and succession of depressive mood in at-risk mothers and their children (Hammen and Brennan, 2003).

There is also research to indicate that the effects of maternal depression vary as a function of *gender*;

when the mother is depressed, the risk of developing depression appears to be higher for girls than for boys. For example, a seven-year longitudinal study shows stronger relationships between mother and daughter depressed mood than exists among other family members (Sheeber et al., 2002). For example, a well-replicated finding across cultures recently reported in a Hong Kong sample is that maternal depression is differentially associated with subsequent depression in daughters as compared to sons (Leung et al., 2009). The emotional closeness of mother–daughter relationships may place girls at particular risk for the effects of maternal depression.

As Joormann and colleagues (2009) argue, the transmission of depression from parent to child may occur as a function of a number of processes: (1) genetic vulnerability; (2) a shared underlying neurological dysfunction in emotion regulatory mechanisms; (3) exposure of the child to the parent's maladaptive cognitions, behaviour and affect; and (4) the larger context of stress and family conflict with which both parent and child must cope. As a consequence of these mechanisms of risk, children of depressed parents may experience difficulty with the mastery of many developmental tasks, including attachment security, emotion regulation, interpersonal relationships and problem solving.

Moreover, many confounding factors conspire to prevent simplistic explanations about the intergenerational transmission of depression. First, parent depression occurs in combination of a number of other forms of psychopathology that might affect children, including parental anxiety and personality disorders, as well as family stressors such as marital conflict and economic distress, many of which have similar effects on children's development. Thus, it is hard to tease apart the effects of parental depression alone. In addition, parental depression is associated with the development of disorders in children other than depression, including ADHD, anxiety, substance abuse, bulimia and conduct disorder. Therefore, the concept of **multifinality** applies here; maternal depression is a risk factor not specific to child depression, but rather predictive of a variety of poor outcomes.

The Social Context

Parents are not the only sources of negative evaluation that can result in depressed mood. Peers can be relentless in their taunting of the child who is different or socially awkward. Therefore, it is no surprise that low social support from peers, lack of perceived social competence and loneliness are significant predictors of child and adolescent depression, as was found in Zimmer-Gembeck and colleagues' (2009) study in Australia and Conley and Rudolph's (2009) in the USA. Children who are victims of peer teasing and aggression score higher on measures of depression and low self-esteem, although positive relationships with close friends can help to buffer them from the risk (Prinstein et al., 2001).

Consistent with cognitive models, depressed children have negative perceptions of their social competence. However, evidence also suggests that this is not *entirely* a matter of distorted self-perception: depressed young people actually are less socially skilled than other children. Teachers, peers and parents report that depressed children are less prosocial and more aggressive and withdrawn, and increases in depressed symptoms over time are predictive of increased social incompetence (Rudolph et al., 2008). Whereas good interpersonal skills act as a protective buffer against the impact of negative life events, depressed youths are less able to generate effective solutions to social problems. In sum, although poor peer relationship may contribute to depression, a transactional process may take place by which depression contributes to further interpersonal problems (Rudolph, 2009).

Are depressed children the *victims* or the *initiators* of negative social relationships? An ingenious study by Altmann and Gotlib (1988) investigated the social behaviour of depressed school-aged children by observing them in a natural setting: at play during recess. The authors found that depressed children initiated play and made overtures for social contact at least as much as did non-depressed children and were approached by other children just as often. Yet depressed children ended up spending most of their time alone. By carefully observing the sequential exchanges between children, the researchers discovered the reason for this. Depressed children were more likely to respond to their peers with what was termed 'negative/aggressive' behaviour: hitting, name-calling, being verbally or physically abusive. In this way, depressed children may be generating some of their own interpersonal stress.

Interactions and Transactions

Depressed children evidence a number of interpersonal skill deficits, but are these causes or consequences of depression? The longitudinal research available to date supports both sides of the transactional equation. On the one hand, social difficulties lead to increased depression over time and depression in turn predicts increases in social difficulties (Rudolph, 2009). For example, Steele and Forehand (2003) found that increases in depression predicted decreased social competence over a three-year period in a sample of African American boys. As Hammen (2009) suggests, the social difficulties of depressed children generate negative interpersonal experiences, such as peer rejection, which exacerbate the symptoms of depression.

The Cultural Context
Poverty

Widening our scope to include the larger context of child development, we find that depression has been linked to a number of variables in the socio-cultural context, including economic disadvantage (Allen and Astuto, 2009). For example, using data from the Add Health study of over 13 000 US adolescents, Goodman and colleagues (2003) found that one-third of the depression in the sample could be accounted for by low household income and lack of parental education. Other community characteristics associated with poverty, such as neighbourhood violence and criminal victimization, may contribute to both parents and children feeling anxious and depressed.

Life Stress

In addition to poverty as a specific stressor, there is abundant evidence that general *life stress* has an important role in depression. Longitudinal data show that stress exposure precedes the development of depression in children and exacerbates the severity of depressive symptoms (Hammen, 2009). Although the data are mixed, some studies suggest that girls are more vulnerable to developing depression in reaction to stress, particularly interpersonal stress (Hankin et al., 2007).

However, evidence is accumulating that the children most negatively reactive to stress are those who are cognitively vulnerable to it. The vulnerable children are those with negative attributional styles, maladaptive beliefs about the self and dysfunctional problem-solving orientations (Hammen, 2009). Stressful events, in turn, contribute to the development and consolidation of negative cognitive styles. Again, we need to keep transactional, multidimensional models in mind.

Ethnicity

As Allen and Astuto (2009) note, research on ethnic differences in rates of adolescent depression needs to attend carefully to the overlap between ethnic minority status and *SES*, given that the two are rarely disentangled.

However, one stressor unique to ethnic minority youths that is associated with increased depression is *racial discrimination*. Simons and colleagues (2002) note that middle childhood is a crucial time for the development of perceptions of the self and the social world. Further, during the school years children begin to turn their attention to the world outside their family and are affected increasingly by the community in which their development is embedded. Racism might interfere with healthy development by negatively affecting children's self-esteem and leaving them with a sense of helplessness and discouragement about their ability to redress the inequities they experience. With these considerations in mind, Simons and colleagues (2002) compiled a list of factors in the family and community contexts that might increase the risk for depression in all children – such as low social support, family poverty, neighbourhood crime and lack of parental involvement – as well as processes that are unique to children of colour – such as racial discrimination and lack of ethnic identification. In a sample of 810 African American children, they confirmed that, at the individual level, uninvolved parenting, racial discrimination and being the victim of crime were associated with increased depression, while, at the community level, high rates of racial discord and low levels of pride and identification within the ethnic group also contributed to youth depression.

On the positive side, evidence also suggests that a *positive ethnic identity* and *social support* can act as protective factors that buffer ethnic minority children from becoming depressed, even in the face of the negative effects of poverty, community violence and neighbourhood dysfunction (Allen and Astuto, 2009).

Developmental Course

Although it was once believed that depression was a transitory phenomenon, certainly in contrast to the stability seen in externalizing behaviour problems (see Chapter 10), evidence is accumulating regarding the *continuity* of depression. Depression is predictive of depression 24 months later in samples ranging from preschoolers in the USA (Luby et al., 2009) to mid-adolescents in Finland (Ritakallio et al., 2008). Over the longer term, ratings of childhood depression in normative samples predict suicidal ideation and the likelihood of a diagnosis of major depression in adolescence (Ialongo et al., 2004) and young adulthood (Copeland et al., 2009). In prospective studies of clinical samples, childhood depression has been found to increase the likelihood of depression as much as 15 years later (Weissman et al., 1999).

On an encouraging note, evidence suggests fairly high rates of *recovery* from a given episode of depression. Kovacs and colleagues (1994) followed a group of children diagnosed with depression, assessing them every few years until late adolescence or early adulthood. Most children rebounded

from their initial depressive episode. Rates of recovery were highest from a major depressive episode, second highest from adjustment disorder with depressed mood, and lowest from dysthymia. Children took longest to recover from dysthymia, while adjustment disorder required the shortest time for recovery.

However, the news is not as good as it looks at first glance. Although youths are likely to recover from an episode of depression, *relapse* rates are also high, with about 40 per cent of children and adolescents experiencing another depressive episode over the course of the next three to five years (Asarnow et al., 1988; Lewinsohn et al., 2000a). For example, in Kovacs and colleagues' (1994) study, within a period of five years, children with major depression or dysthymia had a high probability of suffering a new depressive episode. About two-thirds developed a new episode of depression while they were still in their teens. Early onset dysthymia was a particularly negative indicator, with 76 per cent of the children in this category going on to develop a major depressive disorder.

In another large-scale prospective study, Weissman and colleagues (1999) followed a group of 108 clinically depressed children over the course of a decade. About one-third of those with recurrent childhood depression continued to have major depressive episodes in adulthood. Among the adolescents in the study, continuity was even stronger, with 63 per cent experiencing at least one major depressive episode over the next 10 years. Similar results concerning continuity have been reported in other longitudinal studies. For example, Harrington and his colleagues (1996) followed 80 children diagnosed with depression into adulthood and compared them to community children matched for age and sex. Those depressed as children were at significantly greater risk for developing affective disorder in adulthood: 84 per cent of those depressed as children were depressed in adulthood, as opposed to 44 per cent of those who had not had childhood depression. The prospects for later onset depression may be somewhat less grim, but still are negative. Lewinsohn and colleagues (2000a) found that over half of those who were depressed in adolescence met criteria for major depression at some point over the next five years.

Early *age of onset* also is a negative prognostic sign. Onset of depression prior to puberty is associated with more severe dysfunction in general and an even greater likelihood of continuity to adult depression (Goodyer, 2009). This likelihood is the result of the cumulative effects of recurrent depressive episodes, of which more will be experienced by children who are early starters on the developmental pathway to depression. For example, Lewinsohn and colleagues (2003) found that a bout of major depressive disorder in adolescence is associated with pervasive deficits in adult psychosocial functioning, including job performance, relationship functioning, physical well-being and life satisfaction. Remarkably, these negative effects pertained even when the depression did not extend into adulthood. The authors liken the experience of early onset depression to a 'scar' that has a pernicious impact on later development.

Some forms of depression might be precursors to others. Dysthymic disorder is an antecedent to major depression for many youths, with the course of dysthymia often punctuated by episodes of major depression. In addition, a significant number of depressed children and adolescents are later diagnosed with bipolar disorder, as we will soon investigate in greater detail.

A key reason for the continuity of depression is that mood disorders have the potential to interfere with the child's mastery of developmental tasks in a number of spheres, including the capacity to perform at school, to form satisfying relationships at school, and to form secure bonds within the family (Hyman, 2001). Thus, the effects are cumulative and interact with all other contexts of development.

Resilience and Depression

On the positive side, additional research points toward potential *protective mechanisms* and sources of resilience. For example, even among children of depressed mothers, low levels of parental over-involvement and high levels of parental warmth are associated with resilient youth outcomes (Brennan et al., 2003a) as is mother–child closeness (Ge et al., 2009). Thus, for the parent who is sensitive to the child's needs, depression does not necessarily spill over onto child development. In addition, Halligan and colleagues (2007) found in their 13-year longitudinal study in the UK that maternal post-partum depression only increased the risk for adolescent depression when mothers experienced another depressive episode subsequently: there was no increased risk for depression among adolescents whose mother's depression remitted or was successfully treated. Children's own coping strategies also can be protective; for example, Jaser and colleagues (2007) found that adolescents who utilized adaptive strategies such as positive thinking, acceptance and distraction were those least likely to be rated as depressed or anxious.

Integrative Developmental Model

A comprehensive developmental psychopathology model of depression has been put forward by Hammen (2009; Hammen and Rudolph, 1996, 2003) and is presented in Fig. 9.3.

Although acknowledging that there are many pathways to depression, Hammen's model places *dysfunctional cognitions* at the forefront. First, however, the stage for the development of these negative cognitions is set by *family factors*, such as a depressed parent, insecure attachment and insensitive or rejecting caregiving. Adverse interpersonal experiences contribute to the child's development of negative schemata: of the self as unworthy, others as undependable and uncaring, and relationships as hurtful or unpredictable. The depressive cognitive style also involves the belief that others' judgements provide the basis for one's self-worth, as well as a tendency to selectively attend only to negative events and feedback about oneself.

Further, Hammen highlights the fact that the relationships among affect, cognition and behaviour are dynamic and transactional. For example, negative cognitive styles lead to problems in *interpersonal functioning* that act both as vulnerabilities to depression and as stressors in their own right.

FIGURE 9.3 Hammen's Multifactorial Transactional Model of Child and Adolescent Depression.

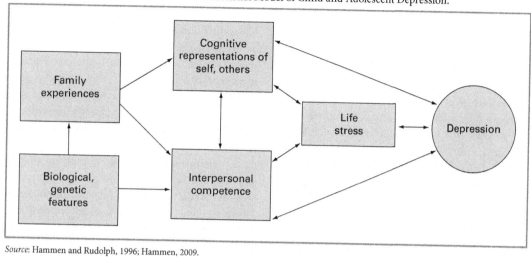

Source: Hammen and Rudolph, 1996; Hammen, 2009.

For example, the negative attributions of depressed children interfere with the development of adequate coping and social skills, and the children respond to interpersonal problems through ineffective strategies such as withdrawal or acquiescence. These strategies not only fail to resolve interpersonal problems but even exacerbate them, increasing the likelihood of experiencing victimization, rejection and isolation. Therefore, the negative cognitive styles and poor interpersonal problem-solving skills associated with depression further disrupt social relationships, undermine the child's competence, induce stress and confirm the child's negative beliefs about the self and the world.

As development proceeds, life *stress* comes into play. These aforementioned cognitive and interpersonal vulnerabilities increase the likelihood that individuals will respond to stress in negative ways. Hammen's model describes three aspects to the role of stress in depression. First, individuals vulnerable to depression may actually generate some of their own stressors, for example by withdrawing from interpersonal relationships, as described previously. In this way they contribute to the aversiveness of their social environments, as well as consolidate their negative perspectives on the world. An illustration of this kind of process later in development

is 'assortative mating', the tendency of individuals to choose partners who mirror or act on their vulnerabilities. For example, Hammen and colleagues find that depressed women are more likely than others to marry men with a diagnosable psychopathology and, in turn, to experience marital problems that contribute further to their depression.

Second, the association between stress and depression is mediated by the individual's cognitive style and interpretation of the meaning of stressful events. While life stress increases the likelihood of psychopathology in general, it is the tendency to interpret negative events as disconfirmations of one's self-worth that leads to depression in particular. Third, certain groups of children are at high risk because they are exposed to the specific kinds of stressors that increase depression. These include maltreated children, those whose parents are emotionally disturbed, those in families with high levels of interparental conflict or those who live in situations of chronic adversity that diminish the entire family's morale and sense of well-being.

Biological factors can come into play at any point in the cycle. For example, individual differences in temperament, such as negative emotionality, may contribute to problems in children's relationships with parents and others. Biological factors can affect children's ability to cope with stressful circumstances, as well as increase their vulnerability to depression as a reaction to stress.

Developmental influences also enter into the picture in a number of ways. First, difficulties that occur earlier in development may have particularly deleterious effects, diverting children to a deviant pathway from which it is difficult to retrace their steps. Once on a deviant trajectory, children become increasingly less able to make up for failures to develop early stage-salient competencies. There may be biological roots to this tendency for pathways to become entrenched, in that accumulated stress may alter the biological processes underlying depression, especially in young children, whose systems are not yet fully matured. Second, cognitive developmental factors may contribute to depression. As we have seen, young children's thinking tends to be undifferentiated and extreme, contributing to an 'all or nothing' kind of reasoning. A negative cognitive style formed at an early age, therefore, may be particularly difficult to change once consolidated. Third, the organizational view of development argues that the connections among cognition, affect, behaviour and contextual factors strengthen over time. Thus, over the life course, depressive patterns are integrated into the self-system, become increasingly stable, and require lower thresholds for activation.

Gender and Adolescent Depression

Having investigated the building blocks that lead to adolescent depression, we are prepared to return to the question that intrigued us early on in this chapter: why the strikingly higher prevalence among teenage girls? Hyde and colleagues (Hyde et al., 2008; Mezulis et al., 2011) propose that to understand adolescent girls' depression from a truly integrated developmental perspective, we need to know our ABCs, by which they mean Affect, Biology and Cognition.

One of the unique features of the ABC model is that it is truly developmental. Rather than simply positing that various negative factors accumulate in order to cause disorder, the ABC model proposes

that there are specific developmental relationships among affective, biological and cognitive vulnerabilities that create a kind of cascade effect leading to adolescent depression. Specifically, the model holds that biological vulnerabilities (genetics, temperament) contribute to affective vulnerabilities (negative emotionality) in childhood, which in turn contribute to the emergence of cognitive vulnerabilities (negative attributions, rumination) in adolescence. (See Fig. 9.4.)

Up to this point, the theory proposes, the development of depression in girls and boys has similar predictors and takes a similar path. However, something happens in adolescence that is different for girls and adds a new element to the model: gender-specific forms of life stress. Girls' biology comes back into play when early-developing girls experience interpersonal stressors such as peer teasing and sexual harassment. For girls with an underlying propensity towards depression, these negative experiences can tip the balance and act on their emotional and cognitive vulnerabilities so as to create a perfect breeding ground for depression.

The way in which this model pulls together the threads of these diverse vulnerabilities into an integrative framework helps us to make sense of the inconsistent findings of those studies that have focused on only one or another element of the model. For example, early maturation has been associated with girls' depression in some studies, but not others. This inconsistency may reflect the different meanings that precocious development has for youth: for those who are self-confident and welcome the changes, the effects may be positive. However, for youth with negative self-perceptions or poor body image, the unwanted attention of peers may be accompanied by painful self-consciousness. Cultural attitudes toward puberty, especially its association with the filling out of the female form, also may influence whether these changes are welcome or unwanted by a youth. For example, pubertal status better predicts depression among Caucasian youth in the USA than among African American or Hispanic adolescents whose

FIGURE 9.4 The ABC Model of Depression.

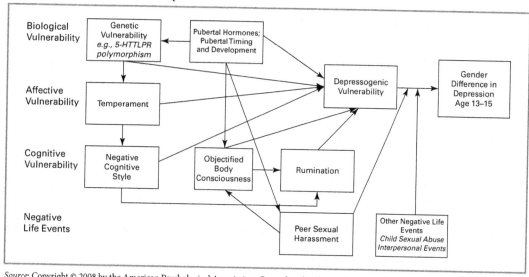

cultures are more accepting of a full female form (Hayward et al., 1999).

Hilt and Nolen-Hoeksema (2009) similarly argue that adolescence is a developmentally sensitive period that has different implications for males and females. First, whereas both boys and girls undergo significant biological changes, girls are more likely to evidence dislike of the changes they are going through and dissatisfaction with their bodies (see Chapter 11). Second, social relationships are particularly important to girls, who have higher needs for affiliation with others and are more attuned and sensitive to the opinions of peers. Therefore, girls may be more reactive to some of the ordinary stressors associated with adolescence, such as increasing peer pressure and the dynamics of social inclusion and exclusion. Moreover, as they move into mid-adolescence, girls are more sensitive than boys to interpersonal stressors in the home, such as maternal distress and interparental conflict, to which they are more likely to react with depressed mood. Third, as Hyde and colleagues (2008) would agree, adolescent girls are more likely than boys to experience certain kinds of psychosocial stressors, including

unwanted sexual attention and sexual assault (see Chapter 14). Fourth, because gender roles and the expectation that one will conform to them increase in adolescence, girls may believe that they will be disliked if they act in ways counter to their gender-role stereotype, such as by being assertive and independent minded or by beating a boy in a competition. Therefore, girls also are more likely than boys to hide their competence in order to avoid others' negative opinions, a phenomenon termed 'silencing the self' (Jack and Ali, 2010). Research has indicated that silencing the self and adherence to a traditional feminine gender role are associated with increased risk for depression among adolescent girls (Aube et al., 2000). In summary, biology, cognition, affect, peer relations, gender role and developmental stage all come into play in girls' depression.

Intervention
Pharmacotherapy

Antidepressant medications that act to increase serotonin availability include the selective serotonin reuptake inhibitors (SSRIs), such as fluoxetine (Prozac) and sertraline (Zoloft), as well as serotonin-norepinephrine reuptake inhibitors (SNRIs), such as venlafaxine (Effexor). Evidence is accumulating that SSRIs are effective in reducing depressive symptoms in children and adolescents (Hetrick et al., 2007). However, controlled clinical trials including children are few and far between and often lag behind the development of new medications. Therefore paediatricians and child psychiatrists frequently prescribe these medications 'off-label' – that is, without official approval based on evidence for their effectiveness and tolerability in young people. Another controversial methodological issue in the research on the effectiveness of antidepressant medications is that many of the studies are sponsored by the pharmaceutical industry, indeed the very manufacturers of the medications under investigation. Ethical questions have been raised about the ability of researchers to remain blind to the interests of their funding sources, and increasingly scientific journals are requiring authors to disclose such ties and possible conflicts of interest.

Other concerns about the use of SSRIs with children include the occurrence of undesirable side effects, such as restlessness and irritability, insomnia, gastrointestinal discomfort and mania. There also are reports of increased suicidal thoughts, which are estimated to occur in 2 to 3 per cent of youth taking antidepressants (US Food and Drug Administration, 2004). In response to this, in 2004 the US Food and Drug Administration decided to require that drug manufacturers place on prescription bottles a 'black box' warning about the risk of suicide in children who take antidepressants. Medical authorities in the UK already had gone a step further, declaring several antidepressant medications to be unacceptable for use with children. (See Box 9.4.)

As with adult depression, the experts' recommendation (if not the usual practice) is to use antidepressant medication as an adjunct to psychotherapy rather than as the sole method for treating child and adolescent depression (Emslie et al., 2000). Many factors that contribute to depression – stressful life circumstances, poor parent–child relationships, family conflict and dissolution, low self-esteem, and negative cognitive biases, for example – cannot be changed by psychopharmacology and might be more effectively addressed by psychotherapy with the child or family. One controlled clinical trial in particular, the Treatment for Adolescents with Depression Study (TADS), has demonstrated the superiority of combined treatment that includes both psychotherapy and medication (TADS Team, 2007). Clinical researchers from 13 geographically diverse sites teamed together for this project, which enrolled 327 youth aged 12 to 17, all of whom were diagnosed with major depression. Youth were randomly assigned to one of three conditions: cognitive behavioural therapy (CBT), fluoxetine, or a combination of the two. Eighteen weeks into the treatment, a positive response to therapy was shown by 69 per cent of those who received medication alone, 65 per cent of those who received CBT only, and 85 per cent of those who received the combination. After 36 weeks of treatment, rates of treatment response were 81 per cent, 81 per cent and 86 per cent, respectively, suggesting that the therapies were equivalently effective at the end of the day. An important caveat, however, was that suicide attempts were more prevalent among the youth receiving fluoxetine (14.7 per cent) than those receiving combination therapy (8.4 per cent) or CBT (6.3 per cent), and that fluoxetine alone was associated with less decline in suicidal thinking than were the conditions that included CBT. The authors of the study concluded that, whereas fluoxetine can help to accelerate a youth's response to psychotherapy, cognitive behavioural psychotherapy enhances the safety of medication treatment.

Psychodynamic Psychotherapy

Psychodynamic treatments for depression focus broadly on problems in underlying personality organization, tracing these back to the negative childhood experiences from which depression emerges. The goals of therapy are to decrease self-criticism and negative self-representations and to

Box 9.4 The 'Black Box' Controversy in the Treatment of Adolescent Depression – Do Antidepressants Cause Suicide?

In 2004, the US Food and Drug Administration required that all antidepressant medications come with a 'black box' warning about the potential risk of increased suicidal thinking and behaviour in children, adolescents and emerging adults (http://www.fda.gov/downloads /Drugs/DrugSafety/InformationbyDrugClass /UCM173233.pdf). Liliana Cordero and colleagues (2008) set out to investigate the research evidence on the basis of which this decision was made, as well as the positive or negative consequences that have ensued since the label was instituted.

First, regarding the research evidence, the investigators note that the concerns about negative effects of antidepressant medications were based on the data arising from clinical trials including only 4400 children (the available clinical trials for adults included 77 000 patients), a small sample in the larger scheme of things. Second, there were no completed suicides among any of the children and adolescents involved in the clinical trials. Although 4 per cent of the youth who received antidepressant medications showed an increase in suicidal thinking, so did 2 per cent of those in the control group – therefore, any increased suicidality that can be associated with antidepressant use was seen in only 2 per cent of the youth treated. Third, a major methodological weakness of the studies was their very short duration, and therefore the longer-term effects of providing or withholding medication treatment could not be evaluated.

Is there evidence that the black box has had unintended consequences? Ample evidence suggests that the black box has had an effect: rates of antidepressant prescriptions for children and adolescents have declined at least 20 per cent since the warning was implemented, with 70 per cent of physicians reporting that they have changed their clinical practice such that they would be less likely to be willing to prescribe and monitor antidepressants for young people. Although these physicians indicated that they would prefer to refer youth to a qualified psychiatrist, child psychiatrists are difficult to access and often have long waiting lists; further, such referrals frequently do not result in treatment: between 30 and 75 per cent of patients fail to show for their initial appointment with a mental health professional (Westra et al., 2000). Consequently, 'the FDA advisories may have had the unintended effect of discouraging the prescription of antidepressants for

pediatric patients and pediatric utilization of antidepressants without compensatory increases in other specific treatments' (Pfeffer, 2007, p. 843). Consistent with this concern, Gibbons and colleagues (2007) observed a 22 per cent drop in SSRI prescription rates for children and adolescents in both the Netherlands and the USA after implementation of the warning label, with an increase in the youth suicide rate during the same time period of 49 per cent in the Netherlands and 18 per cent for the USA. This pattern was confirmed by Katz and colleagues (2008) in a Canadian sample, in which a threefold increase in child and adolescent suicide occurred simultaneously with a decline in both rates of antidepressant prescriptions and the frequency of outpatient visits for the treatment of depression. Finally, Cordero and colleagues (2008) investigated whether prescribing professionals actually understood the information on the black box label. Ninety one per cent did not, with the majority reporting the mistaken belief that the label warned of an increased risk of death for children and adolescents who take antidepressants.

In contrast to these frightening statistics, the investigators also point to accumulating empirical evidence that treatment with SSRIs is associated with a decreased risk of suicide. Although most of the research is focused on adult samples, there are some with adolescents. For example, Valuck and colleagues (2004) studied a sample of over 24 000 youth and found that six months of antidepressant treatment was associated with a significant decline in suicidality, in comparison to treatment that lasted only two months, and that there was no increased risk for suicide associated with treatment with SSRIs as opposed to other antidepressants.

In addition to making sure that professionals and the general public alike have accurate information about what the black-box label actually warns of, and the thin evidence on which that warning is based, the investigators express the hope that those who are convinced by the label to avoid antidepressant treatment will nonetheless avail themselves of some treatment. 'In addition to correcting misunderstandings about the label, psychologists can also make sure patients and parents are aware of all treatment alternatives, including psychosocial ones, that have been proven effective. Psychotherapy is a proven alternative for the treatment of depression in children and adolescents' (p. 324).

help the child to develop more adaptive defence mechanisms in order to be able to continue on a healthy course of emotional development. With younger children, the therapist may use play as a means of bringing these issues into the therapy room, with the focus shifting to discussion as children become more cognitively mature.

Psychodynamic approaches rarely provide outcome studies beyond individual case reports. However, Fonagy and Target (1996) investigated the effectiveness of a developmentally oriented psychoanalytic approach with children. (This is described in more detail in Chapter 17.) Results showed that the treatment was effective, particularly for internalizing problems such as depression and anxiety. Younger children (i.e., under 11 years) responded best. However, the treatment was no quick cure; the best results were found when treatment sessions took place four to five times per week over a period of two years.

Cognitive Behavioural Therapy

Cognitive behavioural therapies for child depression are the most extensively researched, and, overall, findings concerning their effectiveness are positive (David-Ferdon and Kaslow, 2008). One example of a cognitive behavioural approach is the Coping with Depression Course for Adolescence (Clarke et al., 2003), a downward extension of a treatment programme originally designed for adults. This intervention includes role playing to teach interpersonal and problem-solving techniques, positive cognitive restructuring to counter maladaptive cognitions (see Fig. 9.5) and self-reinforcement techniques. Studies of the effectiveness of this approach show that, for the 80 per cent of adolescents who improve, treatment gains are lasting.

Interpersonal Therapy

Interpersonal approaches are predicated on the assumption that relationship dysfunctions are at the core of depression, which much of the developmental psychopathology research would confirm. Interpersonal therapy (IPT) aims to assist depressed individuals to develop better skills for interpreting and coping with interpersonal problems in a brief, focused intervention. Mufson and colleagues (2011) have adapted interpersonal therapy to address the particular social and developmental issues relevant to adolescents, including role transitions, interpersonal conflicts, social skills deficits, grief and coping with family problems. Randomized controlled studies have shown the efficacy of the treatment in a clinic-referred sample of adolescents with major depression. Rossello and Bernal (1999) further modified the IPT approach to increase its relevance to the treatment of depressed

FIGURE 9.5 Positive Cognitive Restructuring.

Source: Copyright © Zits Partnership. Reprinted with special permission of King Features Syndicate.

Puerto Rican teens and found it to be successful in increasing self-esteem and social competence.

Family Therapy
Given the important role that family relationships play in the developmental psychopathology of depression, it is not surprising to learn that the Coping with Depression Course developers found that the effectiveness of their cognitive behavioural intervention for depressed children was enhanced by the addition of interventions with the parents (Lewinsohn et al., 1996). In this addition to the child treatment, group sessions are held in which parents are given the opportunity to discuss issues related to depression and to learn the same inter-personal communication and conflict resolution skills being taught to their children.

An even more explicitly family-focused inter-vention for adolescent depression has been devel-oped by Diamond and his colleagues (2003). Attachment based family therapy (ABFT) focuses on helping to repair the 'relational ruptures' that have led to adolescents feeling hopeless, alone and alien-ated from their parents. By fostering the parents' ability to provide a secure base by being emotionally available, accepting and validating of the youth, the therapist strives to help revise negative internal working models of both self and other. The first ses-sion includes the entire family unit and focusing on reframing the problem from one of individual blame to negative interaction cycles. For example, parent and youth might be helped to see their process as one in which the parent reaches out, the adolescent rejects help, the parent expresses frustration or criti-cism, and the adolescent withdraws and feels rejected. The second session is conducted with the adolescent alone, and focuses on helping the adoles-cent to express his or her feelings and building a therapeutic alliance by empathizing with the youth's experiences. The third meeting involves the parents alone, and focuses on preparing them to listen to and respond to their child's concerns with empathy. The remaining sessions involve various combinations of family members but the overarching goal is to set up a context in which communication can take place openly and competencies on the part of both the parent and the youth can be supported.

In a randomized controlled trial, Diamond and colleagues (2010) offered ABFT to 66 12- to 17-year-old youths, most of whom were African American. At post-treatment 12-month and 24-month follow-ups, youth who received ABFT demonstrated lower rates of depression and sui-cidal ideation in comparison to youth who received referrals for 'treatment as usual' from other mental health providers.

Prevention
Efforts to prevent the development of childhood depression are of two types: targeted programmes for those most at risk (Garber et al., 2009) and universal programmes delivered to all youth (McLaughlin, 2009). As an example of the former, one intriguing project by Malphurs and colleagues (1996) targeted a particularly high-risk sample – depressed teenage mothers. Mothers were observed interacting with their infants and were differenti-ated in terms of whether they demonstrated a with-drawn or an intrusive parenting style. Specific types of interventions were designed to help counter these problematic patterns. For example, intrusive mothers were coached to imitate their children's behaviour, thus giving children more opportunities to initiate and influence the flow of the interaction. In contrast, withdrawn mothers were coached to keep their infant's attention, thus increasing the level of mutual interest and engagement. Results suggest that each specific coaching strategy improved the interactional behaviour of the type of depressed mother for whom it was developed.

One of the most well-respected school-based prevention programmes is the Penn Resiliency Project (Gillham et al., 2008). Teachers and counsel-lors present 12 group sessions with a curriculum focusing on countering the appraisals that con-tribute to a depressive cognitive style. Children are taught to understand how emotions and behaviours follow from our beliefs about adverse events, to rec-ognize unhelpful thinking styles, such as 'catastro-phizing', and to use effective counters to such maladaptive cognitions, such as positive cognitive restructuring. In addition, children learn positive problem-solving strategies such as assertiveness, emotion regulation and interpersonal skills. The empirical support for the programme is extensive and involves studies conducted in the USA, Australia and China.

Another impressive universal effort to prevent depression in adolescents was launched in Australia by Shochet and colleagues (2009). The investigators developed an 11-session intervention called RAP (Resourceful Adolescent Program) that incorporates many of the elements of proven cognitive behavioural therapies (e.g., positive cognitive restructuring, affirmation of existing strengths) as well as targeting interpersonal and family risk and protective factors. A second treatment condition combined RAP with three parent sessions intended to reduce family conflict and increase parental warmth and responsiveness. Eighty-eight per cent of all eligible students in the school participated in the study. To avoid contamination, for the first year of the study, the investigators merely administered measures to all of the ninth graders. The second year, all ninth graders participated in the intervention. After the

intervention and at 10-month follow-up, youth in the two treatment conditions reported lower levels of depression and hopelessness than the control children. An adaptation of the program, RAP-Kiwi, was implemented in New Zealand (Merry et al., 2004).

Resilience and Depression

Martin Seligman, a former president of the American Psychological Association and originator of the *learned helplessness* theory of depression, has devoted his more recent work to the promotion of *positive psychology* and enhancing children's resistance to depression. One of his pivotal publications is a manual for parents entitled *The Optimistic Child: A Proven Program to Safeguard Children against Depression and Build Lifelong Resilience* (Seligman et al., 2007). Since it is not possible to shield children from experience disappointments and stresses in life, the key to his approach is to teach children explanatory styles that help to inoculate them against depression: specifically, to think of bad events as temporary rather than permanent and as specific rather than global. The Penn Resiliency Program (Gillham et al., 2008) is one of the universal prevention programmes that have

TABLE 9.5 DSM-IV-TR Criteria for Manic Episode

A. A distinct period of abnormally and persistently elevated, expansive, or irritable mood, lasting at least a week (or any duration if hospitalization is necessary).
B. During the period of mood disturbance, three or more of the following symptoms have persisted and have been present to a significant degree:
  (1) inflated self-esteem or grandiosity
  (2) decreased need for sleep (e.g., feels rested after only 3 hours of sleep)
  (3) more talkative than usual or pressure to keep on talking
  (4) flight of ideas or subjective experience that thoughts are racing
  (5) distractability
  (6) increase in goal-directed activity or psychomotor agitation
  (7) excessive involvement in pleasurable activities that have a high potential for painful consequences (e.g., engaging in unrestrained buying sprees, risky sexual behaviour)
C. The mood disturbance is sufficiently severe to cause marked impairment in occupational or academic functioning or in usual social activities or relationships with others.
D. The symptoms are not due to the effects of a substance (e.g., drug or medication) or a general medical condition (e.g., hyperthyroidism).

Source: Adapted from the *Diagnostic and Statistical Manual of Mental Disorders*, Fourth Edition Text Revision. Copyright 2000 by the American Psychiatric Association.

accumulated considerable empirical support based upon these ideas.

In a longitudinal, community-based study of adolescents at risk for depression, Carbonell and colleagues (2002) found the key protective factors to be *family cohesion, positive self-appraisals* and *positive interpersonal relationships.*

Bipolar Disorder

Definition and Characteristics

Bipolar disorder, commonly known as manic depression, is defined by both DSM-IV and the ICD-10 as a severe form of psychopathology in which periods of depression alternate with manic episodes involving expansive mood, overactivity, irritability or increased risk-taking behaviour (see Table 9.5).

Bipolar disorder is further differentiated according to type. Type I involves the presence of manic episodes, with or without periods of depression. Type II involves depression interspersed with periods of *hypomania*, a milder form of euphoria or overactivity that is below the threshold for the diagnosis of a mania. Because it is at a lower level of intensity, hypomania is defined as causing a *change* in functioning in contrast to the severe *impairment* in functioning associated with full-blown mania. A third type of bipolar disorder, termed *cyclothymia*, is characterized by small, rapidly shifting changes in mood during which the individual experiences hypomania punctuated by depressive symptoms. (See Fig. 9.6 for a graphic comparison of the different mood disorder diagnoses.)

Prevalence and Age of Onset
Diagnostic Dilemmas

Although the diagnosis of bipolar in children is relatively rare, with increasing recognition of the

FIGURE 9.6 Patterns of Mood Disorder.

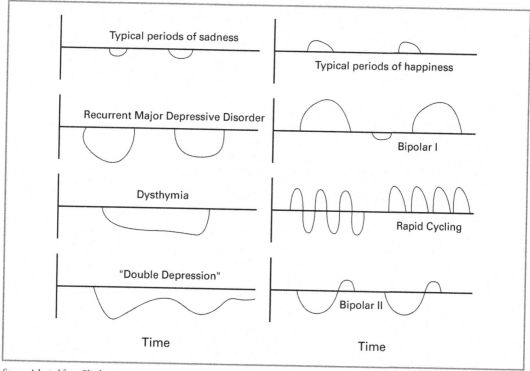

Source: Adapted from Pliszka, 2002.

existence of the disorder in children and adults, investigators are beginning to suspect that it is more prevalent than previously thought. For example, retrospective reports from the USA, France, Switzerland, Italy and Germany find that as many as 60 per cent of adults with bipolar recalled experiencing symptoms of the disorder in childhood or adolescence (see Diler et al., 2010). (See Box 9.5 for a case example.)

As Meyer and Carlson (2010) point out, there are a number of impediments to the diagnosis of bipolar disorder in children and to the compilation of accurate estimates of its prevalence. First, the symptoms are easily misidentified and may even be shrugged off as mere exaggerations of the typical adolescent moodiness and behavioural dysregulation, especially when they are obscured by comorbid disorders such as substance abuse,

---

Box 9.5 Case Study in Bipolar Disorder: Kay Redfield-Jamison Writes

Kay Redfield Jamison, a professor of psychiatry at Johns Hopkins school of medicine, is one the most respected authorities on bipolar disorder – and for good reason. Not only has Dr Jamison made the study of the disorder her life's work, but she has lived personally with its devastating effects. Although in her autobiography she recalls experiencing the crushing lows and giddy highs of the disorder throughout her childhood, it was only when she became a faculty member at the UCLA Neuropsychiatric Institute that she sought professional help and became properly diagnosed and treated.

There is a particular kind of pain, elation, loneliness, and terror involved in this kind of madness. When you're high it's tremendous. The ideas and feelings are fast and frequent like shooting stars, and you follow them until you find better and brighter ones. Shyness goes, the right words and gestures are suddenly there, the power to captivate others a felt certainty … Feelings of ease, intensity, power, wellbeing, financial omnipotence, and euphoria pervade one's marrow. But, somewhere, this changes. The fast ideas are far too fast, and there are far too many; overwhelming confusion replaces clarity. Memory goes. Humour and absorption on friend's faces are replaced by fear and concern. Everything previously moving with the grain is now against – you are irritable, angry, frightened, uncontrollable, and enmeshed totally in the blackest caves of the mind. You never knew those caves were there. It will never end, for madness carves its own reality.

It goes on and on, and finally there are only others' recollections of your behavior – your bizarre, frenetic, aimless behavior – for mania has at least some grace in partially obliterating memories. What then, after the medications, psychiatrist, despair, depression, and over-doses? All those incredible feelings to sort through. Who is being too polite to say what? Who knows what? What did I do? Why? And most hauntingly, will it happen again? Then, too, are the bitter reminders – medicine to take, resent, forget, take, resent, and forget, but always to take. Credit cards revoked, bounced checks to cover, explanations due at work, apologies to make, intermittent memories (what *did* I do?), friendships gone or drained, a ruined marriage. And always, when will it happen again? Which of my feelings are real? Which of the me's is me? The wild, impulsive, chaotic, energetic, and crazy one? Or the shy, withdrawn, desperate, suicidal, doomed, and tired one? Probably a bit of both, hopefully much that is neither …

At this point in my existence, I cannot imagine leading a normal life without both taking lithium and having had the benefits of psychotherapy. Lithium prevents my seductive but disastrous highs, diminishes my depression, clears out the wool and webbing from my disordered thinking, slows me down, gentles me out, keeps me from ruining my career and relationships, keeps me out of a hospital, alive, and makes psychotherapy possible. But, ineffably, psychotherapy heals. It makes some sense of the confusion, reins in the terrifying thoughts and feelings, returns some control and hope and possibility of learning from it all … Psychotherapy is a sanctuary; it is a battleground; it is a place I have been psychotic, neurotic, elated, confused, and despairing beyond belief. But, always, it is where I have believed – or have learned to believe – that I might someday be able to contend with all of this.

Source: Reprinted from Redfield-Jamison, 1995.

conduct problems or ADHD. Second, bipolar disorder often first evidences itself as depression, and therefore youth must be followed over time for the true nature of their disorder to reveal itself. Third, adolescent bipolar disorder often presents with a rapid onset mania, sometimes with psychotic features, that may be confused with schizophrenia or other severe forms of psychopathology. In addition, assessment of key features of BD, such as mania, is neglected in most diagnostic interviews and questionnaires administered to children and their parents.

Comorbidity and Differential Diagnosis

Misdiagnosis of bipolar disorder is a serious matter because improper diagnosis can lead to improper and even damaging treatment. Medications used to treat ADHD may increase irritability in bipolar children, and psychostimulants and antidepressant medications both may potentiate mania. In turn, the major tranquillizers used to treat schizophrenia will negatively impact the functioning of children who are not correctly diagnosed. Therefore, careful attention to *differential diagnosis* is needed

For example, children with bipolar disorder often are diagnosed with ADHD – more than 80 per cent in some studies (Diler et al., 2010; Luby et al., 2010). The overlap is not surprising given that the two disorders share similar symptoms of overactivity, heightened energy, distractibility and impulsivity. However, 'pure' ADHD can be distinguished from bipolar by virtue of the fact that children with ADHD show a *consistent* pattern of overactivity or distractibility, in contrast to the *change* from usual behaviour that is typical of bipolar children. Children with bipolar also often are diagnosed with conduct disorder or oppositional defiant disorder, which share features of irritability and dysregulated behaviour. However, the misbehaviour of the 'pure' conduct disordered child is more likely to be vindictive, intentional and without guilt, whereas the child in a manic state acts more out of impulsivity and a sense of omnipotence: 'Nothing can hurt me!' Further, children with conduct disorder or ODD do not display the

psychotic symptoms, such as delusions, pressured speech and flight of ideas, that frequently are seen in mania. In turn, children with schizophrenia present with an insidious onset of their illness, in contrast to the more acute onset of mania, and are less likely to show the pressured speech and flight of ideas that are typical of the bipolar child.

However, despite the fact that differential diagnosis is needed to eliminate invalid diagnoses, it is possible for children to suffer genuinely from comorbid disorders, including ADHD, conduct disorder and oppositional defiant disorder. There also is a population of children with comorbid bipolar disorder and pervasive developmental disorder (National Institute of Mental Health Roundtable on Prepubertal Bipolar Disorder, 2001). Depression and anxiety also are commonly seen in children with bipolar disorder (Diler et al., 2010). Substance abuse often is seen among adolescents with the disorder and in fact is the most prevalent comorbid diagnosis (Blader and Carlson, 2007). Youth who truly suffer from these comorbid disorders present particular challenges to intervention and the combined diagnoses are associated with more severe functional impairments and resistance to treatment.

The Developmental Dimension

As implied in the previous section, there appear to be developmental differences in the symptoms of bipolar disorder in childhood and adulthood. We should be cautious in interpreting this literature, given that there remains considerable debate over whether and how bipolar disorder should be diagnosed in young people. In addition, whereas evidence that BD presents differently in children than in adults has led some investigators to propose developmental modifications of the diagnostic criteria, yet other researchers insist that the adult criteria are appropriate to children (see Luby et al., 2010). In sum, this is a controversy that has not yet been resolved. However, we can summarize the available evidence to date.

First, unlike adult bipolar, manic episodes in children are not usually so distinct, nor are episodes characterized by an acute onset with intermittent periods of good functioning. Instead, children tend to show a history of chronic mood symptoms that include extremely rapid shifts, known as *rapid cycling*. For example, Geller and colleagues (2000) found that 77.4 per cent of children and early adolescents with bipolar disorder demonstrated mood cycles that vacillated many times a day, while this is a phenomenon seen in only 20 per cent of bipolar adults. Children also are more likely than adults to have mixed episodes, in which both depression and mania occur simultaneously (National Institute of Mental Health Roundtable on Prepubertal Bipolar Disorder, 2001). In turn, Wozniak and colleagues (2001) argue that severe irritability and mood lability are the key features that should be used to determine the presence of BD in children over and above the other DSM-IV criteria. In turn, Geller and Tillman (2005) suggest that developmental modifications need to be made to the DSM duration criterion which requires a week-long episode of mood shift, given that children are likely to show very rapid, continuous cycling of mood within a briefer period. In addition, in comparison to adults, children are more likely to evidence mixed mania and depressed mood. Luby and colleagues (2010) find that, among preschool children, elation, grandiosity, hypertalkativeness, flight of ideas and hypersexuality in the absence of a history of sexual abuse are the most discriminating features that allow for the differential diagnosis to be accurately made between BD and other disorders.

Prevalence Estimates

The caveats we have noted regarding the recognition, assessment and differential diagnosis of bipolar in children make it difficult to glean clear information about the prevalence of the disorder among children. In addition, the large epidemiological studies of the prevalence of childhood disorders to date rarely have included bipolar disorder. However, an exception was a school-based survey of 1700 adolescents in Oregon conducted by Lewinsohn and colleagues (1995) that found a lifetime prevalence rate of 1 per cent, mostly comprised of Bipolar II and cyclothymia. An additional 5.6 per cent of the youths reported subclinical levels of hypomania that negatively affected their functioning.

In contrast to studies that follow the strict DSM criteria, researchers who expand their search to include subthreshold criteria or 'soft signs' of BPD find prevalence rates around 5 per cent (Lewinsohn et al., 2003). Brotman and colleagues (2006) used a broader, more encompassing syndrome they labelled severe mood dysregulation (SMD), the hallmark of which is extreme, impairing and chronic irritability, accompanied by hyperarousal symptoms. In the Great Smoky Mountains Study, a longitudinal epidemiologic study of 1420 children in the American Southeast, the investigators found the prevalence of SMD in children ages 9–19 to be 3.3 per cent. Most (68 per cent) of the youth with SMD youth had an axis I diagnosis, most commonly ADHD (27 per cent), conduct disorder (26 per cent), and/or oppositional defiant disorder (25 per cent). In addition, the youth who met criteria for SMD in the first wave of date collection were seven times more likely to be diagnosed subsequently with a depressive disorder than youth who never met criteria for SMD.

Blader and Carlson (2008) provide an overview of the available *cross-cultural* data on prevalence and note that rates are consistently higher in studies conducted in the USA than in East Asia or Europe. Whether those differences reflect a tendency towards over-diagnosis in the USA or under-diagnosis in other countries remains to be determined (Meyer et al., 2004). What is clear is that rates of diagnosis in clinical settings in the USA have been rising sharply over the course of the past decade. (See Fig. 9.7.) In a review of hospital records from 1996 to 2004, Blader and Carlson (2007) found that rates of hospitalization for BD increased fivefold in children, from 1.3 to 7.5 per 10 000, and increased fourfold in adolescents, from 5.1 to 20.4 per 10 000. Moreover, bipolar disorder was one of the least frequent psychiatric diagnoses recorded for child inpatients in 1996 but the most common in 2004. Differences associated with *race*

FIGURE 9.7 Child Hospitalizations for Bipolar Disorder.

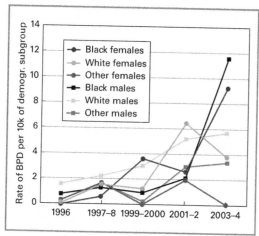

Source: Blader and Carlson, 2008.

also emerged, with rates increasing at a much elevated slope for African American youth, especially boys. Although this shift may represent increasing appreciation for the role of mood disorders in the disruptive behaviours shown by children, the investigators also expressed concern that an unwanted effect may be the 'up-coding' of childhood emotional problems to disorders with more severe and stigmatizing labels.

Regarding *gender* differences, although studies do not indicate a sex difference among adolescents, boys predominate among those with the early onset form of the disorder.

Etiology
The Biological Context
Genetic studies estimate that the heritability of bipolar disorder is high, with estimates in the 20 to 45 per cent range, although the search for the candidate gene is still elusive (see Willcutt and McQueen, 2010). The siblings and parents of children with the disorder are three to 10 times more likely to also have BD than are the family members of children referred for other psychiatric disorders. Evidence further suggests that early onset BD has an even stronger familial component. Given this, a number of studies have focused on high-risk

children – those whose parents are diagnosed with bipolar disorder. (For a moving account of growing up with a bipolar parent, see the reflections offered by the eminent developmental psychopathologist Stephen P. Hinshaw, 2010). For example, Birmaher and colleagues (2010) currently are in the process of conducting a longitudinal study of the offspring of 83 parents with bipolar disorder and comparing their outcomes to those of two groups of matched controls: those whose parent had a non-bipolar psychiatric diagnosis and those whose parent had not history of mental illness. At the most recent assessment, when the children were 2 to 5 years of age, only three of the offspring of bipolar parents evidenced any form of mood disorder. However, this does not mean that they were doing well. Offspring of bipolar parents were eight times more likely to develop ADHD and were at significantly higher risk for being diagnosed with two or more disorders than the comparison children. In addition, those offspring of bipolar parents who met criteria for ADHD or oppositional defiant disorder had significantly more severe current manic and depressive symptoms than comparison children, even if these symptoms did not reach the level of qualifying for a mood disorder diagnosis.

Limitations to our ability to recognize and assess bipolar in such young children may contribute to the fact that studies involving youth at later developmental periods find even stronger familial effects. For example, in a study conducted in the Netherlands, Hillegers and colleagues (2005) followed adolescent offspring of bipolar parents over the course of five years and found that the lifetime prevalence of BD increased from 3 to 10 per cent from the first year to the five-year follow up.

Neuropsychological factors also have been implicated, with particular focus on the *anterior limbic network* responsible for emotional and cognitive regulation (Fleck et al., 2010). In addition, early onset BD is associated with an increased likelihood of adverse perinatal events and developmental delays (Blader & Carlson, 2008).

The Individual Context

Alloy and colleagues (2006) review the available research on *cognitive style* among individuals with bipolar disorder and argue that the weight of the evidence suggests that cognitions are implicated as powerfully in bipolar as in unipolar depression. Maladaptive cognitions associated with bipolar disorder include *perfectionism* (high self-standards and self-criticism) and *excessive goal-striving*. For example, in a study of 2875 German adolescents, Meyer and Krumm-Merabet (2003) found that hypomania was associated with higher expectations for academic success. In addition, individuals with bipolar disorder characteristically demonstrate problematic cognitive strategies for regulating attention, including both *ruminating* on negative experiences and the opposite, termed '*basking*', which is the tendency to mentally perseverate and repetitively dwell on the positive aspects of events (Segerstrom et al., 2003).

These cognitive styles, Alloy and colleagues (2006) hypothesize, inflate the significance of even ordinary events to a youth's sense of his or her self, future and world. In this way bipolar-prone cognitions increase a youth's vulnerability to reacting to life stressors – and even to unusually positive events – with excessively low or high mood. As Depue and colleagues (1987) phrase it, these dysfunctional cognitive styles 'transform the normally mild effects of [daily] events into periods of dysregulation' (pp. 118–19).

The Family Context

As we have seen, children with bipolar disorder are disproportionately more likely to come from families in which at least one parent also suffers from the disorder. However, the heritability quotients are less than 100 per cent, and therefore other aspects of the family environment may affect children's development, as well. Sullivan and Miklowitz (2010) obtained ratings of family functioning from the parents and youth in 58 families in which the adolescents had been diagnosed with BD. In comparison to the scores generally found in healthy families, families of BD youth were lower in cohesiveness and adaptability and were higher in conflict. In addition, parents' *expressed emotion* – criticism, over-involvement and high negative affect – predicts relapse in adolescents with bipolar disorder (Yan et al., 2004).

Furthermore, a large-scale study in Denmark utilized national population data to identify 2299 individuals with bipolar disorder and to retrospectively examine family factors associated with the diagnosis (Mortensen et al., 2003). Not surprisingly, bipolar disorder or schizophrenia in parents or siblings increased the risk thirteenfold. The only other factor that was associated with bipolar disorder was an unexpected one – *parental loss*, particularly of the mother. Children who, prior to their fifth birthday, experienced the loss of their mothers had a fourfold risk of developing bipolar disorder. Loss of the mother may reflect a shared genetic vulnerability – these mothers may have suffered from mood disorders that contributed to their deaths, such by increasing their involvement in unsafe behaviours or suicide – but also may comprise a severe psychosocial stressor that acts upon the vulnerable child and potentiates the disorder.

Another source of childhood adversity that may be predictive of bipolar disorder is parental *maltreatment*. Although the data are not entirely consistent, and the majority rely on retrospective reports, some studies show higher levels of physical and emotional abuse experienced by individuals with the bipolar diagnosis in comparison to controls (Alloy et al., 2006). Intriguingly, Grandin and colleagues (2007) further found that only those childhood adversities that occurred prior to the onset of the first bipolar episode were related to the diagnosis. In addition, the research suggests that maltreatment is associated with an earlier age of onset, more rapid cycling, and a more negative course in those who develop bipolar disorder (Alloy et al., 2005).

Developmental Course
Pathways to Bipolar Disorder

Among youth who come to earn the BD label, symptoms related to mood appear to emerge earlier in development than other disorders in the depressive spectrum. For example, while adolescents in Lewinsohn and colleagues' (1995) study reported a mean *age of onset* of 15 years for major depression, those with bipolar disorder reported a mean age of onset of 11.8 years.

In addition, the available research suggests that there are at least two distinct pathways to bipolar disorder in children. On the one hand, many children initially present with symptoms of *ADHD*. For example, in one follow-up study, Tillman and Geller (2006) found that over a period of six years, 28.5 per cent of children diagnosed with ADHD developed a bipolar disorder diagnosis. The investigators speculate that ADHD might be a developmental precursor to bipolar disorder, with both disorders arising from an underlying excessive level of energy that is expressed in its true bipolar form only later in development.

The second pathway is through *depression*. Longitudinal data from a number of different laboratories show that children and adolescents with unipolar depression are at significant risk for developing bipolar disorder, and that unipolar depression is the disorder most often first demonstrated by those who go on to develop BP. For example, Hillegers and colleagues' (2005) study in the Netherlands found that, except for one participant, all offspring of bipolar parents who developed a BD disorder were diagnosed initially with a unipolar mood disorder that debuted an average of five years prior to the first manic episode. A similar finding is reported by Duffy and colleagues (2009) from their 15-year follow-up of a Canadian sample, in which BD only emerged during adolescence, and the first disorder was always depressive. It is possible that for some youth depression may represent a protracted dysphoric phase in a bipolar cycle that has yet to reveal itself.

The Course of the Disorder Across Development

There are few longitudinal data on the course of childhood bipolar disorder, but the evidence to date suggests that the course is protracted and chronic. For example, Lewinsohn and colleagues (2000b) followed a subset of youth from their study from adolescence into early adulthood. Self-report data indicated significant *continuity* of bipolar symptoms across development, as well as their association with significantly negative outcomes. The most extensive study to date is the Course and Outcome of Bipolar Youth (COBY) study (Birmaher et al., 2009) which has followed a sample of 413 youth ages 7 to 17 over a period of four years. Although youth were highly likely to recover from the bipolar episode that led to their initial diagnosis, 62.5 per cent had a recurrence of mood disorder, particularly depression. Moreover, during the four-year follow-up, youth suffered some level of distressing psychological symptoms 60 per cent of the time, including depression and mood swings. Twenty-five per cent of youth given a diagnosis of Bipolar II converted to Bipolar I, and 38 per cent of those with Bipolar Disorder NOS converted to Bipolar I or II. Early onset, long duration of the disorder, low socio-economic status and family history of mood disorders were associated with poorer outcomes

Diler and colleagues (2010) review the accumulated evidence regarding the long-term course of bipolar disorder, including studies conducted in the USA, Canada and India, which suggest that early onset BD is a more severe, persistent and treatment resistant form than adult onset BD. Once a youth has experienced a bipolar episode, it is speculated that the brain is altered in such a way that it is sensitized and more likely to react with mood disturbance to increasingly milder stressors, a phenomenon termed 'kindling' (Post, 1992). Consequently, each subsequent episode over the lifespan will be more easily triggered but more intractable and harder to treat. In order to attempt to stave off this cascading effect, some clinicians recommend beginning treatment with mood stabilizers as soon as bipolar disorder is even suspected (Hammen and Rudolph, 2003).

As development proceeds, youth with bipolar disorder are at increased risk for maladaptation in all areas of functioning, including school, peer and family relationships, substance abuse, legal problems, and suicide attempts and completions (Diler et al., 2010). Clearly, this is a disorder with devastating effects on development.

Intervention
Pharmacotherapy

Given the assumption that bipolar is a biologically based disorder, medication is usually the first line of treatment. Generally, children are prescribed the same medications that are effective in adults, such as lithium carbonate, which is derived from a naturally occurring salt. Although moderate levels of effectiveness and safety of lithium have been reported in a number of clinical trials with children and adolescents, carefully conducted, double-blind, controlled studies are extremely rare and significant side-effects are reported that may be particularly problematic for young persons, including nausea, excessive thirst and urination, tremulousness, acne and weight gain. (Here we follow Kowatch et al., 2010, except otherwise noted.)

Frequently prescribed alternatives to lithium include anticonvulsant medications, with the strongest evidence to date for the use of valproic acid (Depakote) with children. Increasingly, prescribers are turning to atypical antipsychotic medications such as Risperidone (Risperdol), olanzapine (Zyprexa), and ziprasidone (Geodon), all of which have received approval from the US Food and Drug Administration for use in the treatment of adolescent BD. To date, five large, carefully designed, placebo-controlled studies have been conducted that indicate the effectiveness of these medications for the treatment of symptoms of bipolar and mania. However, grave concerns have emerged about the significant levels of unwanted side-effects experienced by the youth in these studies, including extrapyramidal symptoms (tremor, difficulty controlling speech), tardive dyskinesia (involuntary, repetitive movements), excessive serum prolactin levels, cardiac arrhythmias, and excessive weight gain and its accompanying effects of blood lipid levels, all of which may have deleterious effects on the developing body and brain.

Family Therapy

As we have seen, increased conflict and negative expressed emotion characterize the families of bipolar youth and increase the likelihood of relapse. Therefore, interventions that focus on improving family relations are likely to be of benefit. To this end, Miklowitz and colleagues (2008) developed and tested a family intervention for adolescents with bipolar disorder. Family-Focused Therapy (not to be confused with Functional Family Therapy) includes all available family members (the youth, parents and siblings) and provides psychoeducation about bipolar disorder as well as training in communication and problem-solving skills. In a controlled clinical trial, 58 adolescents with BD were randomly assigned to the treatment condition or to a brief family educational intervention, while all received pharmacological treatment from a study psychiatrist. Over the course of two years, adolescents in the treatment condition showed the most improvement in levels of depression, although improvements in mania were seen only among those youth in family-focused therapy whose families were high in expressed emotion. Currently, a multi-site trial of the intervention involving 150 youth is ongoing, as is an investigation of its effectiveness as a preventative measure for children at risk for BD (Miklowitz and Goldstein, 2010).

In addition, Fristad and colleagues (2009) have developed a multi-family psychoeducational group intervention that is designed to increase social skills and the ability to manage symptoms, increase hope and social support, and improve family members' understanding about mood disorders. Parents and children meet in separate groups that run concurrently for eight highly structured 90-minute sessions, each of which ends in a joint wrap-up activity. In a large-scale randomized controlled trial involving 165 families, the investigators found that parents in the treatment group reported increased knowledge about mood disorders and changed beliefs about their treatment, and that these mediating variables led to better utilization of clinical services, which in turn accounted for the beneficial effects of the treatment on children's mood symptoms.

Child and Adolescent Suicide
Definitions and Prevalence

As we begin our discussion of suicide, we must immediately distinguish among five categories: suicidal thoughts, suicidal intent, suicidal gestures, suicide attempts and completed suicide.

Suicidal thoughts, once considered to be rare in childhood, are in fact disconcertingly prevalent. According to the most recent Youth Risk Behavior Survey (Centers for Disease Control [CDC], 2010), a nationally representative sampling of 16 460 US high school students, 17.4 per cent of girls and 10.5 per cent of boys had 'seriously considered' suicide in the past year.

Suicidal intent is more serious in that it involves not just a thought (e.g., 'I wish I were dead') but a specific plan and the motivation to carry it out. Results of the Youth Risk Behavior Survey (CDC, 2010) indicate that 13.2 per cent of US girls and 8.6 per cent of boys report that in the past year they had made a specific suicide plan.

Suicidal gestures, also known as **parasuicidal behaviour** or non-suicidal self-injury, involve nonlethal self-harming actions such as making cuts on the arms or legs that are not accompanied by a conscious intent to die from the act. Parasuicidal behaviour often is motivated by a desire to communicate one's distress to others and acts as a red flag that help is needed. But self-injury also is characteristic of severely disturbed youths who use physical pain as a method of affect regulation – we will encounter these individuals in Chapter 15 when we explore borderline personality disorder. Moreover, suicidal gestures may represent 'practice runs' that are precursors of more serious attempts and so remain cause for concern.

Suicide attempts vary by lethality. *Low-lethality* attempts typically involve using a slow-acting method under circumstances in which discovery is possible, such as a youth who ingests drugs at home.

Because of the length of time needed for the method to take effect, the likelihood is greater that someone will find the attempter before it is too late to resuscitate. The act most often is in reaction to an interpersonal conflict or significant stressor and, even though the attempt is unsuccessful, it may nevertheless be serious. *High-lethality* attempts involve a potentially deadly method (e.g., a gun) that is quick acting and utilized under conditions in which it would be difficult for others to intervene, such as when the youth is alone. In the USA, 8.1 per cent of high school girls and 4.6 per cent of boys report having made one or more suicide attempts in the past year (CDC, 2010). Further, as few as 2 per cent of attempters seek medical or psychological help. Consequently, since many suicide attempts go unreported, it is likely that our prevalence statistics are underestimates of the actual rates.

Completed suicide is a significant problem among adolescents. In the USA, suicide is the third leading cause of death among 15- to 19-year-olds and the fourth leading cause of death among 10- to 14-year-olds, in line behind accidents and homicides (CDC, 2010). However, one positive note is that rates of youth suicide have decreased over the past decade. Rates for younger children are lower than for adolescents. According to the latest data available, the suicide rate (per 100 000) is 0.7 for children 5–14 years old and 10.0 for those 15–24 years old (Kung et al., 2008). A protective factor for younger children may be that they have more difficulty accessing lethal means; consequently, there are more attempts than completions in children age 10 and below. Firearms are the most frequent method used by both males and females, followed by hanging for males and drug ingestion for females. (See Box 9.6.)

Gender Differences

In all age groups, females are more likely than males to *attempt* suicide, while males are more likely to *succeed*. Females attempt suicide at least three times more often than males do, whereas males age 15 to 19 complete suicide almost six times as often as females (CDC, 2010). Over the

Box 9.6 Youth Suicide: Why the Changes over Time?

Data from across the world show a marked rise in youth suicide over the course of the past few decades, whereas rates have declined significantly in recent years. The Centers for Disease Control and Prevention's (CDC) latest statistics show that, through 2010, suicide rates among US children and adolescents declined 25 per cent. What accounts for these changes over time? In their review of the literature, Gould and colleagues (2003) find that many factors have been implicated, but chief among these are changes in the rates of substance abuse and accessibility of firearms. For example, as rates of youth suicide grew, suicides involving firearms increased at a disproportionate rate; tellingly, guns were twice as likely to be found in the homes of suicide victims as compared to the homes of youths with other kinds of psychiatric disorders. In turn, in the past few years there have been more efforts to restrict firearms in the USA, and the recent decrease in youth suicide appears to largely be accounted for by a decrease in suicide by firearm, according to the CDC. However, Gould and colleagues find these explanations unconvincing for a number of reasons. They point out that youth suicide rates have recently decreased 20 to 30 per cent in other countries in the world where guns are rarely used, including England, Germany and Sweden. Moreover, the decline in youth suicide has not actually been accompanied by a reduction in substance use. Instead, Gould and colleagues propose, a more likely explanation is improvement in availability and effectiveness of treatments for depression. For example, during the period in which youth suicide has declined, prescriptions for the newer class of antidepressants have risen. Exceptions to this expanded availability of treatment, however, include populations such as the African American and Native American communities that have more difficulty accessing mental health services.

course of adolescence, the ratio of males to females steadily increases. The explanation for this appears to lie in the choice of method. In contrast to male suicides, two-thirds of whom die by self-inflicted gunshot wounds, the typical young female attempter utilizes low-lethality methods, such as drug overdose. It should not be assumed, however, that young women necessarily are less serious about wanting to die. Females are more likely to have an aversion to violent methods, and sometimes young people's understanding of how deadly a drug can be is simply inaccurate. Further, suicide statistics often come from mental health clinics and ignore one very important group: incarcerated males. If we included males in juvenile detention facilities in these statistics, the gender differences in suicide attempts might not be so great.

Cross-Cultural Differences

The most recent global data on youth suicide from the World Health Organization's Global Burden of Disease Study were published by an international team of researchers (Patton et al., 2009). The investigators grouped the 192 WHO member states by region (Africa, Americas, European, Mediterranean, Western Pacific and Southeast Asian) and by income level (high income and middle-low income). (See Fig. 9.8.) Overall, suicide increased among both sexes of people aged 15–24 years and was the second-most leading cause of death among young persons worldwide, with striking differences by age, gender and income level. Self-inflicted injuries accounted for 6 per cent of youth deaths overall. However, in high income countries, suicide accounted for 15 per cent of males' mortality and 12 per cent of females'. In contrast, in low and middle income countries in the American region, there was a ninefold increase in suicide for males from early adolescence to young adulthood.

Ethnic Differences

Since 1999 the USA has gathered detailed statistics for *completed suicide* in a national database including many of the ethnic groups that comprise the

FIGURE 9.8 Causes of Death by Violence Stratified by Sex, Age-Group and Region.

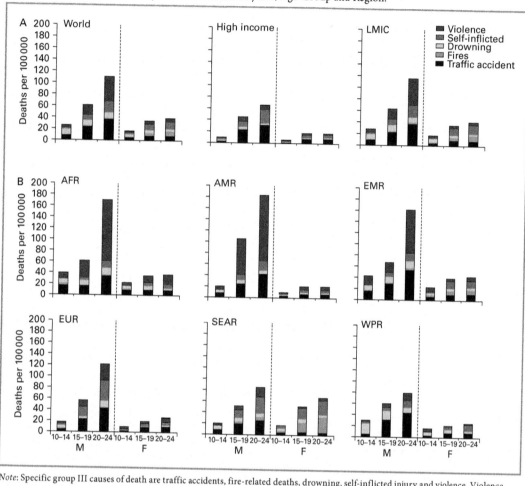

Note: Specific group III causes of death are traffic accidents, fire-related deaths, drowning, self-inflicted injury and violence. Violence refers to deaths from both violence in and outside of war. M = male deaths. F = female deaths. (A) Data for world, high-income countries, and low-income and middle-income countries (LMICs). (B) LMICs grouped by WHO region. AFR = African region. AMR = region of the Americas. EMR = eastern Mediterranean region. EUR = European region. SEAR = Southeast Asia region. WPR = Western Pacific region.

Source: Patton, et al., 2009.

US population (National Center for Health Statistics, 2010). As displayed in Table 9.6, the highest rates are found for Native American youths. European American males far surpass males from other ethnic groups, while females, particularly African American girls, have the lowest rates.

As the data show, the prevalence rates of suicide completion are lower for African American than for European American youth. Nonetheless, suicide rates for African American boys have been increasing at an accelerated pace. Between 1980 and 1999 suicide among European American boys aged 10 to 14 increased 86 per cent, whereas for African American boys in that age group rates increased 300 per cent, while in the 15- to 19-year-old cohort the rates of increase were 22 per cent for European American boys and 164 per cent for African

TABLE 9.6 US Youth Suicide Rates for 15- to 19-Year-Olds by Race and Gender

Race	Sex	Number of Deaths	Population	Rate
White	Males	5208	129 343 347	4.03
	Females	1069	122 426 576	0.87
African American	Males	650	26 508 871	2.45
	Females	110	25 707 856	0.43
Am Indian/ AK Native	Males	171	2 286 736	7.48
	Females	46	2 209 384	2.08
Asian/Pac Islander	Males	145	7 021 385	2.07
	Females	55	6 732 289	0.82
Total		**7454**	**322 236 444**	**2.31**

Source: National Center for Health Statistics, 2010.

American boys. This striking ethnic difference did not emerge for girls (CDC, 2010).

In contrast to the CDC data concerning suicide completion, some individual studies have found that youth from Hispanic families are twice as likely as other youths to make suicide *attempts* serious enough to require medical attention. Finally, one study investigated suicide attempt rates among a more diverse sample of US adolescents, including 5000 youths of European, Mexican, Vietnamese and Pakistani extraction (Roberts et al., 1997b). Pakistani youths were twice more likely than European Americans to engage in suicidal ideation, to have made suicidal plans or to have made a suicide attempt in the past two weeks. Youths of mixed ancestry also were at elevated risk for suicidal thoughts or plans. The findings were unexpected and the reasons for these ethnic differences were not evident; however, both racial discrimination and cultural beliefs regarding the acceptability of suicide might come into play.

Etiology
The Individual Context
Depression

Jacobson and Gould (2009) review the available research on psychological autopsies of suicidal adolescents, which show that the majority – as many as 90 per cent – have a diagnosable psychopathology. *Depression* is the most common diagnosis for both completers and attempters, increasing the odds of suicide by 11 to 27 times, with even higher risks of depressed girls than boys. Many depressed children and adolescents experience suicidal ideation – as many as 60 per cent in some samples. Further, suicide attempts occur at a higher rate among depressed youth than depressed adults. (For a case example, see Box 9.7.)

Aggression and Impulsivity

However, there are other significant predictors of youth suicide besides depression. In particular, *anger and aggression* emerge as an important part of the suicide constellation (Apter and Wasserman, 2003; Wolfsdorf et al., 2003). Conduct disorder is present in approximately one third of boys who die by suicide (Jacobson and Gould, 2009) and childhood conduct disorder has been shown to predict adult suicide independently of depression (Harrington et al., 1994). In fact, Achenbach and colleagues' (1995) six-year longitudinal study shows that suicidal ideation is predicted not by depression but by earlier signs of externalizing disorders: for boys, in the form of aggressiveness and, for girls, in the form of delinquent behaviour. The link between conduct disorder and suicide may also be strongest for boys, with the combination of depression and conduct problems particularly toxic (Apter and Wasserman, 2003). Thus, conduct problems – which often are associated with poor relationships, emotion dysregulation and disinhibition of aggression – are highly related to suicide. Conduct problems also may contribute to suicidality through increasing peer rejection, association with antisocial peers, substance abuse and school dropout, as well as precipitating legal problems that often are a catalyst for suicide (Gould et al., 2003).

Box 9.7 Case Study: A Suicide Attempt

Dr Anthony Spirito and his colleagues (2003) at Brown Medical School in Rhode Island present the case of Amy, a 13-year-old girl who was evaluated in the emergency room following a suicide attempt in which she overdosed on 20 over-the-counter medications she found in her medicine cabinet at home. When interviewed, Amy said that she made the attempt on the spur of the moment, without premeditation. After taking the pills, she secreted herself in her room until she began to feel nauseated, at which time she told her mother what she had done. Amy reported that she truly wanted to die and that she believed that the overdose she had taken was genuinely lethal. She further stated that the stressor that led to her suicide attempt was an argument with her mother. Although they generally got along well, in recent weeks Amy and her mother had been arguing more, particularly in regard to Amy's poor grades and increasing irritability. Amy also acknowledged long-term stressors, including rejection by peers and falling school performance. The purpose of her suicide attempt, she stated, was to escape from the stressors she was experiencing.

Upon obtaining Amy's history, the assessment team learned that she had made two previous suicide attempts, neither of which were viewed as serious by her parents, given that they did not require medical attention. Consequently, the family had never sought professional help. Amy reported that she was exposed to models of suicidal behaviour in her environment, including classmates who had attempted suicide in the previous year. There was a family history of depression in her father and paternal grandmother.

The team asked Amy to complete a number of measures. These included a measure of suicide intent, on which she scored above the norm for other suicide attempters, indicating the sincerity of her wish to die. On a measure of suicidal ideation, her score was in the 85th per centile, reflecting a high frequency of thoughts about ending her life. The team was most struck by Amy's scores on measures of depressed mood and hopelessness, on which her scores were extremely elevated. A structured clinical interview showed that Amy met criteria for a major depressive episode, including symptoms of dysphoric mood and irritability, sleep disturbance, change in appetite, psychomotor slowness, fatigue and loss of energy, and feelings of worthlessness. She met criteria for no other psychiatric diagnosis and scored within the average range on measures of anxiety, anger and substance abuse.

The assessment team concluded that Amy was an adolescent who had been suffering for some time with an undiagnosed major depression. Her irritability and the increased conflicts with parents were obscuring the family's recognition of her underlying deep unhappiness and were contributing to their escalating negativity toward her.

At the end of the evaluation, Amy remained quite depressed and hopeless. She continued to express a wish to be dead and was not able to guarantee that she would not attempt suicide again. Similarly, when asked how she would handle any future stressors that might result in suicidal ideation, she was not able to report any adaptive coping strategies and at one point said that she might simply use a more lethal method. Consequently, an inpatient hospitalization was recommended.

Initially, Amy reacted negatively to being in the hospital, and after several days her parents removed her against medical advice. She agreed to outpatient therapy, however, as well as a trial of antidepressant medications. Nonetheless, within a month she was again threatening suicide and was re-hospitalized. During this second hospital stay, Amy was more amenable and engaged more actively in her treatment. The dosage of her antidepressant medication also was adjusted. At a three-month follow-up, Amy's mood was more positive. In addition, her school performance had improved, she had become involved with previously enjoyable activities, and she had developed relationships with some same-age peers. She continued to attend outpatient psychotherapy and receive careful monitoring of her medications. There were no repeated suicide attempts.

Second, *impulsivity* is implicated in suicide (Esposito et al., 2003). Impulsivity may be seen in many ways, including low frustration tolerance and lack of planning, poor self-control, disciplinary problems, poor academic performance and risk-taking behaviour. *Substance abuse* is second only to depression as the most common disorder among youth who commit suicide (Moskos et al., 2005), with suicidal thoughts increasing after the onset of substance use (Mehlenbeck et al., 2003). Substance abuse may play a role in suicide by increasing impulsivity, clouding judgement and disinhibiting self-destructive behaviour. *Personality disorders* also are associated with an increased risk of adolescent suicide, particularly those associated with impulsive-dramatic or avoidant-dependent traits (see Chapter 15; Brent et al., 1994).

Cognitive Factors

Among cognitive variables related to suicidal behaviour, *hopelessness* and *poor interpersonal problem-solving skills* emerge as major contributors to both suicidal ideation and attempts (Jacobson and Gould, 2009). However, hopelessness does not predict suicide independent of depression. A better predictor of suicide than hopelessness is the youth's lack of endorsement of *reasons for living* (Gutierrez et al., 2000).

Disinhibition of Suicidal Behaviour

Once a youth has crossed the line dividing suicidal thoughts/intentions from actions, inhibitions against reattempting suicide appear to decrease. Consequently, previous suicide attempts are a strong predictor of future suicide. Between one-fourth to one-third of youth suicide completers have made a prior attempt (Jacobson and Gould, 2009).

The Family Context

The family context also is important, although, as is often the case, a significant weakness of many family studies is that they are *retrospective* rather than *prospective*. An assessment of the family after a suicide attempt has taken place cannot provide convincing evidence that family factors led to the suicide.

Parent psychopathology is associated with increased risk of youth suicidal ideation, attempts and completions. Among the most potent risk factors are parent substance abuse and depression (Jacobson and Gould, 2009). Perhaps as a consequence of parental dysfunction, a number of studies have confirmed that suicidal youths experience *poorer parent–child relationships* (Gould et al., 2003; Hollenbeck et al., 2003). Prospective studies show that suicidal ideation and suicide attempts are predicted by low levels of parent warmth, communicativeness, support and emotional responsiveness, and high levels of violence, disapproval, harsh discipline, abuse and general family conflict. Retrospective studies show that attempters, ideators and their parents describe the family as more globally dysfunctional (Prinstein et al., 2000), with lower cohesion, less support and poorer adaptability to change.

Perceived *lack of support* from parents also has been implicated as a significant predictor of adolescent suicidal thinking (Harter and Marold, 1994). Further, Harter and Whitesell (1996) found that the depressed youth exhibiting the least suicidal ideation were those who perceived themselves to have more positive relationships with parents and more parent support. Thus, supportive parent–child relationships may provide a buffer against suicidality in at-risk children. *Parental loss* before the age of 12 also increases the risk of suicide (Brent and Mann, 2003).

Within the family system, suicidal children are more likely to be exposed to *interparental conflict, family violence* and *abuse* (Brent and Mann, 2003). The link between physical or sexual abuse and serious suicidality has been confirmed in a host of studies using diverse cross-cultural samples (de Wilde et al., 2001), with one Belgian study finding that the risk is greatest for those abused during adolescence (Bruffaerts et al., 2010). Other investigators find that childhood maltreatment does not increase the risk of suicide directly, but potentiates the effects of other risk factors, such as interpersonal problems (Johnson et al., 2002).

Finally, a very strong risk factor for suicide in children is a family history of suicidal behaviour (Jacobson and Gould, 2009). This relationship may be due to heritable factors; however, another mechanism of effect may be what has been referred to as *contagion* – youth who are exposed to suicide, especially in those in their immediate social network, are at significantly greater risk for suicide (Gould et al., 2003). It is estimated that every year as many as 12 000 children and adolescents in the USA experience the suicide of a close family member (Gallo and Pfeffer, 2003). Although there is some inconsistency among studies showing that youths exposed to the suicidal behaviour of a family member are more likely to attempt it themselves (Brent and Mann, 2003), the data are consistent in showing the profoundly negative psychological effects of suicide exposure (Gallo and Pfeffer, 2003). Such exposure should be regarded as accelerating the risk factors already present rather than being a sufficient cause of suicide.

The Biological Context

The fact that suicide runs in families may not be solely a function of parent–child relationships or imitation. Some have proposed that suicide has genetic roots, based on studies showing higher concordance rates in twin, adoption and family studies (Brent and Mann, 2003). For example, a large meta-analysis of twin studies estimates the heritability quotient to be 43 per cent (McGuffin et al., 2001). Attempts to identify the mechanism through which genes affect suicidal behaviour have focused on serotonin metabolism and receptivity, which is linked to an increased risk of both depression and impulsivity/aggression (Jacobson and Gould, 2009).

The Social Context

Perceived *lack of peer support* (Harter and Marold, 1994) and *poor interpersonal skills* (Asarnow et al., 1987) have been identified as risk factors. Suicidal youths are more likely than others to feel ignored and rejected by peers and to experience victimization (Prinstein, 2003). They also report having fewer friends and are concerned that their friendships are *contingent* – that they must behave a certain way in order to be accepted by agemates. *Interpersonal stresses*, such as being rejected by peers or breaking up with a boyfriend or girlfriend, are common catalysts for suicide in youths at risk (Jacobson and Gould, 2009). Perceived social failures, rejection, humiliation and romantic disappointments are common precipitants of youth suicide.

Bullying is a specific interpersonal stressor that is strongly predictive of suicide in cross-cultural research conducted in the USA, Finland and the Netherlands. In a major review of these studies, Klomek and colleagues (2010) found that bullying and being bullied were both associated with an increased risk of suicidal thoughts and attempts, especially for girls. In particular, being a bully-victim increased the likelihood of suicide by 10 times among girls. Cyberbullying – using the Internet to harass a victim – also is associated with increased suicidal ideation and behaviour (Hinduja and Patchin, 2010).

The Cultural Context
SES

Socio-economic disadvantage has also been associated with suicide, with youth growing up in poverty being at greater risk for suicidal thoughts and attempts, although the data linking poverty to suicide completion are mixed (Jacobson and Gould, 2009).

Ethnicity

The prevalence rates cited earlier point to important inter-ethnic differences in the risk for suicide, which may be the consequence of different developmental influences. Cultural factors have been cited to explain lower rates of suicide among *African American* youth, such as an increased role of religion in African American families, support provided by extended family networks, and a tendency to direct aggression outward rather than towards the self (Gould et al., 2003). On the other side of the coin, Zayas and colleagues (2000) point to social and cultural factors that might contribute to suicidal behaviour among *Hispanic* youths, including socio-economic disadvantage, restrictiveness of the traditional authoritarian family, conflicts between parents and children related to differences in acculturation, and loss of extended family support due to immigration.

The extraordinary rates of suicide among *Native American* youth have been the source of great concern and research attention (Chandler et al., 2003). Rates vary enormously across tribes and geographic locations (CDC, 2010) but poverty, substance abuse, cultural disenfranchisement, the legacy of forced internment of children in residential schools – and the accompanying high rates of sexual and physical abuse – are all important to understanding the context in which Native American children develop (Malley-Morrison and Hines, 2004). In general, cross-cultural data suggest that suicide is a greater risk for those minority youths whose connections to traditional values and sources of support have been severed.

Sexual Orientation

Youth with alternative sexual orientations also are at increased risk for suicide (Jacobson and Gould, 2009). In a 21-year prospective longitudinal study conducted in Christchurch, New Zealand, Fergusson and colleagues (1999) found that *gay*, *lesbian* and *bisexual* adolescents had higher rates of both suicidal ideation and attempts. Further, in a large epidemiological study in the USA, an increased risk of suicidality for sexual minority youth remained even when the effects of depression, alcohol use, family history of attempts and victimization were accounted for (Russell and Joyner, 2001). However, those who are suicidal also have more mental health problems than other gay and lesbian youth, as well as having higher rates of life stress and substance abuse (Savin-Williams and Ream, 2003). Many also attribute their suicidality to a lack of acceptance by others following disclosure of their sexual orientation, with reactions ranging from rejection to verbal harassment and even violent assault.

The Media

Evidence has accumulated that media reports of suicides are followed by a significant upsurge in suicidal behaviour, particularly among young people (Jacobson and Gould, 2009). Given concerns about the contagion effect and the possible glamorizing of suicide in media reports of pop stars whom youths identify with and idolize, the Centers for Disease Control (O'Carroll and Potter, 1994) called together a panel of experts to compile a list of recommendations for the reporting of suicide. First, the panel points out that overly simplistic explanations of suicide are misleading and do not accurately portray the serious and cumulative psychological and social problems that lead individuals to make this terrible choice. Second, repetitive and inflated media coverage of a suicide may contribute to youths' becoming preoccupied with the issue; and third, sensationalized reporting should be avoided for the same reason. Fourth, reportage needs to avoid presenting suicide as a problem-solving strategy, but instead to highlight the psychopathology that triggers it. A fifth danger is the glorification of those who commit suicide such as through eulogies and public memorials that suggest that the act is honourable and admirable. Sixth, excessive praise for suicide completers' positive characteristics, unless balanced by a portrayal of their psychological troubles, similarly may make suicide attractive to youths who are longing for admiration and attention.

Modernization

At a larger societal level, rising rates of suicide in the developing world have led some to implicate *modernization*, which brings with it increasing social fragmentation, individualism, and loss of traditional values and support systems. Such values may undermine a youth's sense of belonging and meaning, leading to a state of existential despair (Kelleher and Chambers, 2003).

Developmental Course

The question often arises about whether young children who attempt suicide really are trying to kill themselves and, therefore, whether their attempts warrant serious concern or presage future suicidality.

Doubt about whether young children really intend to die is supported by cognitive developmental research on children's limited understanding of the concept of death, as well as studies showing that suicidal children have a limited understanding of the permanency of death (Cuddy-Casey and Orvaschel, 1997). However, longitudinal research is consistent in showing that childhood suicide attempts are a strong predictor of subsequent attempts and completions. For example, eight years after their first attempt, suicidal children were six times more likely than other children to have made another suicide attempt (Pfeffer et al., 1984). As many as one third of adolescent suicides have a history of at least one previous attempt and a previous attempt increases the odds of suicide completion by as much as 30 times (Jacobson and Gould, 2009). Most subsequent attempts occur within two years of the initial attempt, and over half of those who continue to be suicidal made multiple attempts. Therefore, suicide attempts in children should not be dismissed as mere attention-getting behaviour, since those who engage in them are at risk for more serious attempts and possible completions in the future.

Although little prospective research is available regarding the long-term outcome for adolescent suicide attempters, Boergers and Spirito's (2003) review of the literature indicates that these youth are at risk for continued psychological problems and subsequent repeated suicide attempts. One 11-year follow-up found that 29 per cent of adolescent attempters and their parents reported improved adjustment, whereas 22 per cent were unchanged and 33 per cent were rated as more psychologically maladjusted than at the time of the attempt. Not surprisingly, the most improvement is seen in youths whose family relationships and living conditions change for the better following the attempt. School dropout, 'drifting' and engagement in violent and risk-taking activities also are seen over the longer term.

Integrative Developmental Models
Suicidal Ideation

A comprehensive account of the development of suicidal ideation is offered by Susan Harter (Harter and Marold, 1991, 1994; Harter et al., 1992), who integrates her own research with that of others. Her model reconstructs the successive steps that ultimately eventuate in suicidal ideation in a normative sample of 12- to 15-year-olds. (See Fig. 9.9.)

Immediately preceding and highly related to suicidal ideation is what Harter calls the *depression composite*, which is made up of three interrelated variables: low global self-worth, negative affect and hopelessness. The first two are highly correlated – the lower the perceived self-worth, the greater the feelings of negative mood.

Moreover, the depressive composite is rooted both in the adolescents' feelings of *incompetence* and in their *lack of support* from family and friends. These two variables of competence and support are, in turn, related in a special way. In regard to competence, physical appearance, peer likeability and athletic ability are related to peer support, while scholarly achievement and behavioural conduct are related to parental support. Finally, adolescents identify more strongly with peer-related competencies, with the others being regarded as more important to parents than to themselves.

Analyses of the data revealed that peer-related competencies and support were more strongly related to the depressive composite than were parental-related competencies and support, perhaps because the former are more closely connected with the adolescents' own self-concept. However, parental support was important in differentiating the adolescents who were only depressed from those who were depressed and had suicidal ideation. Further, the *quality* of support was crucial. Regardless of the level, if adolescents perceived they were acting only to please parents or peers, their self-esteem decreased and depression and hopelessness increased. On the other hand, unconditional support helped adolescents minimize the depressive composite.

In regard to the question of which came first, lowered self-worth or depression, the data indicate that causation can go in either direction. Some adolescents become depressed when they experience lowered self-worth, while others become depressed over other occurrences such as rejection or conflict or failure, which in turn lower self-worth.

FIGURE 9.9 Risk Factors for Adolescent Suicidal Ideation.

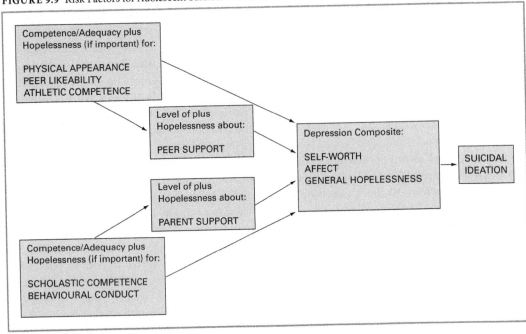

Source: Harter et al., 1992.

To answer the question *Why adolescence?* Harter and colleagues (1997) marshal a number of findings concerning this period. In adolescence, self-awareness, self-consciousness, introspection and preoccupation with self-image increase dramatically, while self-esteem becomes more vulnerable. Peer support becomes significantly more salient, although adolescents still struggle to remain connected with parents. For the first time, the adolescent can grasp the full cognitive meaning of hopelessness, while affectively there is an increase in depressive symptomatology. Suicidal ideation is viewed as an effort to cope with or escape from the painful cognitions and affects of the depressive composite.

Suicide Attempts

A classic reconstructive account is provided by Jacobs (1971), who investigated 50 14- to 16-year-olds who attempted suicide. A control sample of 31 youths, matched for age, race, sex and level of mother's education, was obtained from a local high school. Through an intensive, multitechnique

investigation, Jacobs was able to reconstruct a five-step model of the factors leading up to suicidal attempts:

1　*Long-standing history of problems from early childhood.* Such problems included family instability, death of a family member, serious illness, parental alcoholism and school failure.

2　*Acceleration of problems in adolescence.* Far more important than earlier childhood problems was the frequency of distressing events occurring within the last five years for the suicidal youths; for example, 45 per cent had dealt with divorce in the previous five years as compared to only 6 per cent of the control group. Termination of a serious romance was also much higher among the suicidal group, as were arrests and jail sentences. Recent school failure and parent–child conflicts were other precipitants.

3　*Progressive failure to cope and isolation from meaningful social relationships.* The suicidal and control groups were equally rebellious in terms of becoming disobedient, disrespectful of authority and defiant. However, the coping strategies of suicidal adolescents were characterized much more by withdrawal, including avoiding others and engaging in long periods of silence. The isolation in regard to parents was particularly striking. For example, while 70 per cent of all suicide attempts took place in the home, only 20 per cent of those who reported the attempt had informed their parents about it. In one instance an adolescent telephoned a friend who lived miles away, and the friend, in turn, contacted the parents who were in the next room.

4 *Dissolution of social relationships.* In the days and weeks preceding the attempt, suicidal adolescents experienced the breaking off of social relationships, leading to the feeling of hopelessness.

5 *Justification of the suicidal act, giving the adolescent permission to make the attempt.* This justification was reconstructed from 112 suicide notes of adolescents and adults. The notes contain certain recurring themes; for example, the problems are seen as long standing and unsolvable, so death seems like the only solution. The authors of such notes also state that they know what they are doing, are sorry for their act, and beg indulgence. The motif of isolation and subsequent hopelessness is prevalent. More recently, Overholser and Spirito (2003) note that most suicidal adolescents are ambivalent. They would prefer to go on living, but feel unwilling or unable to endure the pain that they are experiencing.

Jacobs' model was replicated in a study conducted in Sweden (Hultén et al., 2001). The stage for suicide is set by long-standing suffering and lack of support, which produce hopelessness and ineffective coping strategies. Recent stressors resonate with these earlier losses and disappointments, leading to suicide.

Intervention

The vast majority of suicidal adolescents provide clues about their imminent behaviour; one study found that 83 per cent of completers told others of their suicidal intentions in the week prior to their death (Berman and Jobes, 1991). Most of the time such threats are made to family members or friends, who do not take them seriously, try to deny them or do not understand their importance. Friends, for example, might regard reporting the threats as a betrayal of trust. Thus, not only do adolescents themselves not seek professional help, but those in whom they confide tend to delay or resist getting help. Consequently, an important goal of prevention is to educate parents and peers concerning risk signs.

Once an adolescent comes for professional help, the immediate therapeutic task is to evaluate the risk of suicidal behaviour and to protect the youth from self-harm through *crisis intervention* (Van Orden et al., 2008). This might involve restricting access to the means of committing suicide, such as removing a gun from the house or pills from the medicine cabinet; having the adolescent make a 'commitment to treatment' contract (Rudd et al., 2006); decreasing isolation by having sympathetic family members or friends with the adolescent at all times; giving medication to reduce agitation or depression; or, in more serious cases, hospitalization.

Psychotherapy

Many different types of intervention have been developed for suicidal youth, although few have undergone the most rigorous forms of empirical validation (Van Orden et al., 2008). Those that have mustered empirical support include cognitive behavioural (Rudd et al., 2004) and family therapies (Donaldson et al., 2003). Cognitive approaches focus on altering pathogenic ways of thinking such as catastrophizing, whereas family therapy works to increase family communication and support. An alternative approach is dialectical behaviour therapy (DBT, see Chapter 15), which recently has been applied to suicidal and parasuicidal adolescents (Miller et al., 2006). DBT targets important skills such as emotion regulation and stress tolerance, interpersonal problem solving and impulse control. The practice of mindfulness, derived from mediation techniques, is at the core of the intervention.

Suicide Prevention

Unfortunately, two of the most commonly used suicide prevention efforts – suicide hot lines and media campaigns – are only minimally effective (Van Orden et al., 2008). Communities with suicide hot lines have slightly reduced suicide rates; however, hot lines tend to be utilized by only one segment of the population, Caucasian females. Even less helpful, well-meaning efforts to call media attention to the problem of suicide among teenagers may have the reverse effect. Several studies have shown increased suicide rates following television or newspaper coverage of suicide, particularly among teenagers.

School-based suicide prevention programmes are extremely popular, with the number of schools implementing them increasing 200 per cent in recent years. The goals of these programmes are to raise awareness of the problem of adolescent suicide, train participants to identify those at risk and educate youths about community resources available to them. However, a number of problems have been identified with school-based suicide prevention efforts. First, they may never reach the populations most at risk because incarcerated youths, runaways and school dropouts will never attend the classes. Even when students do attend the programmes, there are questions about their benefits. The programmes tend to exaggerate the prevalence of teenage suicide, while at the same time de-emphasizing the fact that most adolescents who attempt suicide are emotionally disturbed. Thus, they encourage youths to identify with the case studies presented, ignoring evidence for the contagion effect. By trying not to stigmatize suicide, these programmes may inadvertently normalize suicidal behaviour and reduce social taboos against it.

Large-scale, well-controlled studies provide some basis for these concerns. For example, one study of 1000 youths found no positive effects on attitudes towards suicide. In fact, participation in the programme was associated with a small number of students responding that they now thought suicide was a plausible solution to their problems. The students most at risk for suicide to begin with (those who had made previous attempts) were the most likely to find the programme distressing (Shaffer et al., 1991). However, subsequent research has indicated that there are no negative effects associated with straightforward presentation of the warning signs for suicide and information regarding how to seek help (Van Orden et al., 2008).

Another recommended strategy is to focus school-based suicide prevention programmes not on suicide per se, but on the risk factors that lead to suicide. While suicide is rare, the stressors and life problems that may lead some youths to it are not. Therefore, successful prevention programmes might be aimed towards such risk factors for suicide as substance abuse, impulsive behaviour, depression, lack of social support, family discord, poor interpersonal problem-solving skills, social isolation and low self-esteem, as well as critical underlying developmental capacities such as insecure working models of relationship, self-identity, emotion dysregulation, ego brittleness and maladaptive coping (Orbach, 2003).

Resilience and Suicide

Three key protective factors have emerged in the research concerning buffers against suicidality among teenagers (here we follow Jacobson and Gould, 2009). The first of these is **family cohesiveness**, defined as mutual involvement, shared interests and emotional support, which is associated with a decreased likelihood of suicide even among youth who are depressed and suffer from high levels of life stress. The second is **religiosity**. The lower incidence of suicide among youth who identify themselves as highly religious may be associated with the increased support gleaned from the community, a sense of hopefulness or with religions' proscriptions against suicide. A third protective factor is having *reasons for living*. Using an inventory developed by Linehan and colleagues (1983), Pinto et al. (1998) found that survival and coping beliefs (e.g., 'I believe I have control over my life and destiny'), moral objections (e.g., 'It would not be fair to others') and fear of suicide (e.g., 'I am afraid of the unknown') were associated with lower likelihood of suicidal ideation among youth, whereas responsibility to family, fear of failure and social disapproval were not.

Our previous two chapters have described children who internalize their distress in such forms as anxiety and depression. Next, we will encounter children who are externalizers in the sense that they act out their problems via antisocial behaviour. We have already discussed externalizers in earlier chapters in conjunction with oppositional-defiant disorder and attention deficit hyperactivity disorder; in the next chapter we will focus on the development of antisocial behaviour. Far from the excessive self-control of depressed and anxious children, here we will see the re-emergence in middle childhood of an issue we encountered earlier in the toddler-preschool period – inadequate self-control, which lies at the heart of conduct disorder.

Middle Childhood to Adolescence: Conduct Disorder and the Development of Antisocial Behaviour

Conduct disorder has a unique place among the psychopathologies. Not only is the development of the individual with this disorder disrupted, but along the way enormous costs are borne by society and the victims of antisocial acts. (See Box 10.1.) Therefore, it is not surprising that more attention has been paid to understanding the development of aggression and antisocial behaviour than any other childhood psychopathology. In this chapter, we will review conduct problems across the life span and their various manifestations, ranging along the continuum from exaggerations of normal misbehaviour to the extremes of cold-blooded murder and violence.

Definition and Characteristics

DSM-IV-TR defines **conduct disorder** (CD) as 'a repetitive and persistent pattern of behaviour in which either the basic rights of others or major age-appropriate societal norms or rules are violated'. (See Table 10.1.) Conduct problems may occur in four categories: *aggression to people and animals, destruction of property, deceitfulness or theft* and *serious violations of rules.*

Severity is specified as *mild* (few conduct problems beyond those necessary to make the diagnosis, and those present cause only minor harm to others); *moderate* (an intermediate number and

Box 10.1 Case Study: The Columbine Killers

At 11:21 a.m., 20 April 1999, two teenagers pulled out sawn-off shotguns and fired on their classmates in the library at Columbine High School in Littleton, Colorado. Even though the homemade pipe bomb they left in the cafeteria did not go off, 15 minutes later, 21 people were wounded and 15 were dead – including the shooters, Eric Harris and Dylan Klebold, who had turned their guns on themselves.

Little forewarning was given for this horrific attack, although in hindsight perhaps some indicators were there. Rewinding the videotape, so to speak, we can see a number of foreboding signs. Both boys were widely known to harbour animosity towards their school and to express alienation from their classmates. Eric often complained that a group of 'jocks' were bullying him – pushing him into lockers, throwing things at him, calling him rude names – while school authorities looked the other way. Both he and Dylan emulated a group of boys, the Trench Coat Mafia, who had banded together to counter the social system by wearing combat boots and thrift store grunge. However, Eric and Dylan remained only on the fringes of this group of self-proclaimed outcasts. A year before the massacre, bored with their usual pastimes of breaking bottles and setting off firecrackers, the two had broken into a vehicle and had been caught with the items they stole. The boys were sentenced to 45 hours of community service, anger management classes and regular drug screens, but they so positively impressed their juvenile diversion counsellor that they were released a month early. This was despite the fact that, days before their court hearing on the theft charges, the concerned parent of a classmate had presented detectives with excerpts from Eric's web

blog that revealed that he and Dylan were sneaking out at night to set off homemade bombs. 'You all better hide in your (expletive) houses because I'm coming for EVERYONE soon and i WILL be armed to the (expletive) teeth and i WILL shoot to kill and i WILL (expletive) KILL EVERYTHING!' Eric had written. 'I am the law, if you don't like it you die. If I don't like you or I don't like what you want me to do, you die. God I can't wait til I can kill you people.'

Are there clues in the boys' childhood histories? Were they subject to psychological or physical abuse, or were they witnesses to violence in their homes or communities? Bartels and Crowder (1999) did some investigative reporting and here is what they found.

Dylan had grown up in Littleton, a quiet residential community. Both of his parents hailed from Ohio, his mother from a privileged family and his father from a tragic childhood: he suffered the death of his mother at age 6 and the loss of his father at age 12. Dylan's parents fell in love as undergraduates, married and determined to raise their two sons in a home that stressed non-violence – the boys were not even allowed to play with toy guns. When the family moved into a new home in a canyon near to wildlife, little Dylan worried that the cougars would eat his beloved cats. The family honoured the mother's heritage by observing Hanukkah and the father's family background by celebrating Christmas, but struggled to find an organized religion that fitted their beliefs. As a child, Dylan was described by neighbours as a 'gawky,' 'nerdy' kid, who was marked as a gifted student, particularly in mathematics. In his first year in high school, Dylan drifted towards a new set of friends who devoted hours of their time to watching violent

severity of problems); and *severe* (many conduct problems *or* their effect causes considerable harm to others). DSM-IV-TR further differentiates between conduct problems with a *childhood onset* (prior to age 10) or *adolescent onset* (absence of criteria characteristic of CD prior to age 10), which is an important distinction, as we shall see.

ICD-10, in contrast, provides a more elaborated differentiation of subtypes of conduct disorder. (See Table 10.1.) Although the overarching criteria are

quite consistent with those of DSM-IV, the ICD also provides for the possibility that conduct disorder might be *confined to the family context* and the youth's interactions with parents or siblings. In addition, reference is made to a distinction that has a long history in the study of antisocial behaviour, although it has been dropped from the most recent DSM, and that is the contrast between unsocialized and socialized aggression. In the case of *unsocialized conduct disorder*, the youth displays significant deficits in computer games and revelled in their capacity to surreptitiously ridicule their teachers and classmates. Dylan even used his computer skills to hack into the school's computer system to learn the locker combination of a disliked peer so that he could leave a nasty note inside. In his sophomore year, he briefly found acceptance with a group of non-conformists who were passionately involved in theatre. However, Dylan showed a melancholy side. He continued to express his hatred of the school and took up a new interest in drinking alcohol. He rarely dated. Still, he was described as 'shy but nice'. As a senior in high school, Dylan often returned home in the afternoons to spend time with his father, who thought that he and his son had become very close. Dylan had been accepted to the University of Arizona to study computer science in the fall.

Eric, in contrast, grew up in a military family and moved many times until his seventh-grade year, when his father decided to retire and return to his native state of Colorado. A much decorated Air Force test pilot, Eric's father spent long hours at his new job while his mother worked as a caterer. Both parents emphasized to their sons the value of hard work and education. As a child, Eric was described by the girl next door as 'preppy and a dork', but otherwise nice and extremely polite. Eric loved the family dog and would take time away from other activities to care for Sparky when he got sick. In high school, he began to favour music with brooding and violent lyrics, which he copied out and sent to his friends; and he retained a fascination with violent video games long after his friends had outgrown them. Eric began taking anger out on those around him, with friendship turning to hate for no reason the other boys could discern. He began dressing all in black

and complained that he was being harassed for it. In a psychology class, he reported a dream in which he and Dylan retaliated against someone who 'dissed' them in a mall by firing guns and spilling blood. For an economics project, Eric created a marketing video for the 'Trench Coat Mafia Protection Service', which, for $10, would kill someone for the consumer. Concerned about their son, his parents sent Eric to a psychiatrist who prescribed an antidepressant. Nevertheless, his supervisor at the fast-food restaurant raved about Eric, calling him a 'real nice kid … kind of quiet but everyone got along with him'. After he and Dylan went to court on their theft charge, Eric began keeping a journal that he kept hidden from his parents. Reading the journal after Eric's death, investigators learned that for a year Eric had been mulling plans to blow up his high school on 20 April, Adolph Hitler's birthday. Finally, on 15 April 1999, five days before the massacre, Eric had learned that his psychiatric history would prevent his acceptance into the Marines, his lifelong ambition. He had been rejected and had no plans for the future.

Of grave concern following Columbine were similar threats from other youth wanting to emulate the killers, not only in the USA but elsewhere around the world. Some of the most infamous of these events include the 2009 Jokela school shooting in Finland in which an 18-year-old youth killed nine people, the 2009 Winneden massacre in Germany in which a 16-year-old shot 16 individuals, and the 2004 Islas Malvinas Middle School event in which a 15-year-old opened fire on his classmates, killing three and wounding five others.

How well do our theories of the developmental psychopathology of conduct disorder help us to explain the Columbine massacre and the copycats who followed?

interpersonal relationships. The youth may be solitary and antisocial, or merely so aggressive that peer relations are impossible to sustain. *Socialized conduct disorder*, in contrast, involves antisocial behaviour that is exhibited in the context of a cohesive peer group, and may involve formal gang activity or merely participating in informal group misbehaviour such as truancy or shoplifting. We will return to this distinction, as it is one that recent research is bearing out as an important one to consider.

Problem Behaviour Versus Conduct Disorder

Misbehaviour is part of normal development, as we know. Therefore, our first task is to determine when behaviour problems warrant a diagnosis of CD. DSM-IV-TR specifies that the category should be used only in cases in which the behaviour is symptomatic of an *underlying dysfunction in the person* rather than being a reaction to the immediate social environment. DSM-IV-TR suggests that

TABLE 10.1 Comparison of DSM and ICD Criteria for Conduct Disorder Diagnosis

DSM-IV-TR Criteria for Conduct Disorder	ICD-10 Criteria for Conduct Disorders

A. A repetitive and persistent pattern of behavior in which either the basic rights of others or major age-appropriate societal norms or rules are violated, during which at least three of the following are present in the past 12 months:
 	
Aggression to people and animals
  (1) often bullies, threatens, or intimidates others
  (2) often initiates physical fights
  (3) has used a weapon that can cause serious physical harm to others (e.g., a bat, brick, broken bottle, knife, gun)
  (4) has been physically cruel to people
  (5) has been physically cruel to animals
  (6) has stolen while confronting a victim (e.g., mugging, purse snatching, extortion, armed robbery)
  (7) has forced someone into sexual activity
 	
Destruction of property
  (8) has deliberately engaged in fire setting with the intention of causing serious damage
  (9) has deliberately destroyed others' property (other than by fire setting)
 	
Deceitfulness or theft
  (10) has broken into someone else's house, building, or car
  (11) often lies to obtain goods or favors or to avoid obligations (i.e., 'cons' others)
  (12) has stolen items of nontrivial value without confronting a victim (e.g., shoplifting, but without breaking and entering; forgery)
 	
Serious violations of rules
  (13) often stays out at night despite parental prohibitions, beginning before 13 years of age
  (14) has run away from home overnight at least twice while living in parental or parental surrogate home (or once without returning for a lengthy period)
  (15) is often truant from school, beginning before 13 years of age
 	
B. The disturbance in behavior causes clinically significant impairment in social, academic, or occupational functioning.
	Disorders characterized by a repetitive and persistent pattern of dissocial, aggressive, or defiant conduct. Such behaviour should amount to major violations of age-appropriate social expectations; it should therefore be more severe than ordinary childish mischief or adolescent rebelliousness and should imply an enduring pattern of behaviour (six months or longer). Features of conduct disorder can also be symptomatic of other psychiatric conditions, in which case the underlying diagnosis should be preferred.
	
	Examples of the behaviours on which the diagnosis is based include excessive levels of fighting or bullying, cruelty to other people or animals, severe destructiveness to property, fire-setting, stealing, repeated lying, truancy from school and running away from home, unusually frequent and severe temper tantrums, and disobedience. Any one of these behaviours, if marked, is sufficient for the diagnosis, but isolated dissocial acts are not.
	
	Conduct disorder confined to the family context
	Conduct disorder involving dissocial or aggressive behaviour (and not merely oppositional, defiant, disruptive behaviour), in which the abnormal behaviour is entirely, or almost entirely, confined to the home and to interactions with members of the nuclear family or immediate household. The disorder requires that the overall criteria for conduct disorder be met; even severely disturbed parent-child relationships are not of themselves sufficient for diagnosis.
	
	Unsocialized conduct disorder Disorder characterized by the combination of persistent dissocial or aggressive behaviour (not merely comprising oppositional, defiant, disruptive behaviour) with significant pervasive abnormalities in the individual's relationships with other children.
	    Conduct disorder, solitary aggressive type
	    Unsocialized aggressive disorder
	
	Socialized conduct disorder Disorder involving persistent dissocial or aggressive behaviour (not merely comprising oppositional, defiant, disruptive behaviour) occurring in individuals who are generally well integrated into their peer group.
	
	    Conduct disorder, group type
	    Group delinquency
	    Offences in the context of gang membership
	    Stealing in company with others
	    Truancy from school

Source: (L) Reprinted with permission from the *Diagnostic and Statistical Manual of Mental Disorders*, Fourth Edition Text Revision. Copyright 2000 by the American Psychiatric Association. (R) Reprinted with permission from *The ICD-10 Classification of Diseases (2010 Version)*. Copyright 2010 by the World Health Organization.

in order to make this judgement the clinician should consider the *social and economic context* in which problem behaviour occurs. For example, aggressive behaviour may arise out of a need to protect oneself in a high-crime neighbourhood or out of a need for survival among immigrant youths from war-torn countries. Therefore, some youths' misbehaviour might represent an adaptation to a deviant environment, rather than a mental disorder.

Some concern has been expressed about whether this guideline is sufficient to prevent misdiagnosis of behaviourally troublesome but otherwise normal youths. For example, Richters and Cicchetti (1993) remind us to be cautious about the ease with which the CD criteria can be applied to children who do not fit the norm. They point out that some of the best-loved characters in fiction, such as Huckleberry Finn – and even such real-life characters as Huck's creator, Mark Twain – could be considered deserving of the CD label. Clearly it is important to identify those youths who are emotionally disturbed and whose behaviour presages more trouble to come. However, it is equally important not to pathologize youths who might get into trouble because of characteristics – such as being non-conforming, independent-minded and 'mischeevous' – that represent potential sources of resiliency in the long term.

However, evidence is mounting that a large proportion of youth who engage in antisocial behaviour have significant mental health problems. For example, according to statistics compiled by the National Center for Mental Health and Juvenile Justice (Skowyra and Cocozza, 2007), large-scale studies show that 65 to 70 per cent of US youth involved in the juvenile justice system have a diagnosable mental health problem, and approximately 27 per cent have a serious psychological disorder that places them in need of mental health treatment. Rates of mental health disorders among juvenile-justice involved girls are even higher than those among boys (Kerig and Becker, 2012; Marston et al., 2012). (See Box 10.2.)

Prevalence

Lahey and colleagues (1999) did an impressive job of compiling statistics on *prevalence* derived from 39 population studies from around the world, 22 of which were conducted in the USA. They report a wide range of prevalence estimates, ranging from 0.0 to 11.9 per cent, with a median of 2.0 per cent. The data are complicated by the fact that different definitions and criteria were used to establish the diagnosis of CD. Using a more standardized diagnostic assessment, Nock and colleagues (2006b) collected retrospective data from a nationally representative sample of 3199 individuals in the USA and found that the lifetime prevalence of the CD diagnosis ranged from 12 per cent of males to 7 per cent of females. In contrast, in a nationally representative sample of 10 438 children ages 5 to 15 collected in the UK, Maughan and colleagues (2004) found prevalence rates of 2.1 per cent for boys and 0.8 per cent for girls.

In large representative samples focused on adolescents specifically, such as the National Comorbidity Study in the US (Merikangas et al., 2010), CD is found among 5.8 per cent of girls and 7.0 per cent of boys, with over twice as many youth meeting criteria at the upper end of the age range (18 years) as at the lowest end (13 years).

Conduct disorder is even more prevalent in *clinical samples*: referrals for conduct problems, aggressiveness and antisocial behaviour make up about one-third to one-half of all child and adolescent treatment cases (see, for example, Döpfner and his colleagues' work with the German CBCL Study Group; Döpfner et al., 2009). Because they are observable, disturbing to others and difficult to ignore, conduct problems are among the most 'referable' of childhood disorders.

Gender differences are significant and are consistently found across cultures, as Rescorla et al. (2007) report in their comparison of data from 24 nations. The diagnosis of CD is about four times more common in boys than in girls, although the gap may begin to narrow in later adolescence (Lahey, 2008). For example, in the US arrest rates

Box 10.2 A Developmental Dilemma: When Should Children Be Held Legally Responsible?

During the past decades, spurred by concerns about youth violence, legal reforms in the US lowered the age at which adolescents could be tried as adults in criminal court. For example, in 2006, 200 000 youths under the age of 18 were tried as adults. However, developmentally, are adolescents ready to be held to the same standards as adults? Are they competent to participate in the legal process, assist in their own defence and comprehend the nature of the charges laid against them? To answer these questions, Steinberg and his colleagues (2009) administered a structured interview to nearly 1000 juveniles aged 11 to 17, and 500 young adults aged 18 to 24, half of whom were incarcerated and half of whom were drawn from the community. Their results showed significant age differences in children's ability to comprehend their rights, understand courtroom procedures, and reason about the information relevant to launching their legal defense. Approximately one-third of the 11- to 13-year-olds and one-fifth of the 14- to 15-year-olds scored in the *impaired* range on these variables. Further, young offenders' immaturity influenced their behaviour in other ways that might negatively affect a legal defence. They were more likely to recommend confessing to the police rather than waiting for the advice of an attorney and to accept a plea bargain rather than standing up for themselves in court. In subsequent research, the investigators found significant differences between adults and youths on measures of ability to engage in impulse control, resistance to peer pressure, future orientation and logical reasoning.

Consequently, the investigators came to the conclusion that adolescents have limited capacity to make the kinds of informed choices that qualify them as 'criminally responsible' for their behaviour, and that youths' ability to

participate in legal proceedings was diminished by virtue of their deficient decision-making skills, heightened vulnerability to being coerced and reactivity to their environments. As the authors state, the results of their study confront lawmakers with 'an uncomfortable reality': under the constitutional restrictions that prevent the state from adjudicating those who are incompetent to stand trial, many young offenders are not equipped to participate effectively in their own defence. Further, the authors note that the characters of youthful offenders are still in the process of being formed. In contrast to adult criminals, the antisocial behaviour of adolescents may be limited to that time period and shaped by environmental and developmental forces, rather than by immutable and fixed personality characteristics. Thus, even though both the adult and adolescent criminal may be characterized by immaturity and poor decision making, these are developmental deficits that the adolescent might have the capacity to grow out of. Given these factors, the authors raise serious concerns about the application of the death penalty to youthful offenders. In response to these concerns, expressed forcefully to jurists by the researchers in an amicus curiae (friend of the court) brief, in March 2005, the United States Supreme Court ruled that the Constitution's Eighth Amendment, which prohibits 'cruel and unusual punishment', precluded the use of capital punishment for crimes committed before the age of 18. With that ruling, the USA finally joined the rest of the nations in the developed world that bar the death penalty for children. The researchers continue their efforts to help courts make developmentally sound policy by presenting reasoned arguments against the practice of trying teenagers in adult court or imposing draconian sentences such as life without parole (Steinberg, 2009).

for female juveniles have increased 7.4 per cent over the past decade even while arrest rates for male juveniles decreased almost 18.9 per cent (Schwartz and Steffensmeier, in press). Girls and boys also tend to display different symptoms: boys are more likely to engage in overt aggression while girls earn the CD label through more covert antisocial behaviour such as skipping school, running away and abusing substances (Loeber et al., 2009a).

Ethnicity and Social Class

Consistent evidence is found that CD is more prevalent among youths from economically underprivileged groups, particularly those who live below the poverty line; however, overall the effects of SES are relatively small (Loeber et al., 2008a). Once social class is controlled, there is no consistent evidence for ethnic or racial differences in the prevalence of CD. We will have much to say about the risks associated with growing up in an impoverished neighbourhood when we explore the cultural context later in this chapter.

Typologies of Conduct Disorder

Childhood Onset versus Adolescent Onset

As noted previously, DSM-IV-TR distinguishes between two types of CD. *Childhood onset* CD, also termed 'life-course persistent' CD (Moffitt, 2006), 'aggressive-versatile' CD (Loeber et al., 2008b) or the 'early starter pathway' (Shaw et al., 2000) begins prior to age 10, is associated with overt aggression and physical violence, and tends to be accompanied by multiple problems, such as neuropsychological deficits, inattention, impulsivity and poor school performance. It occurs most often in males and is predicted by antisocial behaviour in parents and disturbed parent–child relationships. The childhood onset type is the one most likely to show persistence across the life span.

Adolescent onset CD, also termed 'adolescence-limited' CD (Moffitt, 2006), 'non-aggressive-antisocial' CD (Loeber et al., 2008b), or the late-starter pathway, is characterized by normal early development and less severe behaviour problems in adolescence, particularly in the form of violence against others. Fewer comorbid problems and family dysfunctions are seen in comparison to the childhood onset type.

Moffitt and colleagues (Lahey et al., 2003) have demonstrated that there are different developmental predictors and consequences of these two subtypes. Longitudinal data were obtained in New Zealand from a representative sample of males who were assessed every two years from ages 3 to 18. The investigators were able to establish a number of ways in which youths with childhood onset CD could be distinguished from their 'late-blooming' peers. A *difficult temperament* at age 3 was a predictor of childhood onset CD, as was an early history of *aggressiveness* and antisocial behaviour. In adolescence, in contrast to other youths, the early starters were more likely to describe themselves as *self-seeking, alienated, callous* towards others and *unattached* to families. They were also more likely to have committed a *violent crime*: early starters were disproportionately convicted of such offences as assault, rape and use of a deadly weapon. Further, few of those on the childhood onset pathway evidenced recovery – less than 6 per cent avoided developing conduct problems in adolescence.

Moffitt (2003) has argued that the majority of those with adolescent onset CD do not deserve a diagnosis at all. In longitudinal research in Dunedin, New Zealand, which has been replicated in several different cultures, late-starting youths can be clearly distinguished from their early-starting peers by virtue of the lack of significant psychopathology or violent offending, and the absence of the neuropsychological, cognitive, familial and temperamental factors that predict early onset CD (Dandreaux and Frick, 2009). Instead of being viewed as psychopathological, Moffitt (2003) proposes that the behaviour of late onset youths is best conceptualized as an 'exaggeration' of the normal adolescent developmental process of rebellion and independence seeking or as a product of '*social mimicry*', in that they imitate the antisocial actions of others in order to gain status in the peer group. As they reach adulthood and have more opportunities to gain status in legitimate ways, their conduct problems generally desist. As Dishion and Patterson (2006) state: 'It seems that early- and late-onset delinquents may come from two different worlds' (p. 527).

However, longer-term follow-up data from the Dunedin longitudinal study, which assessed men at age 26, are not so reassuring (Moffitt et al., 2002). Adult males with adolescent onset CD (who were matched with the early onset group in terms of rates of offending) were, overall, functioning better in life than their early-starting peers. They were less likely to engage in seriously violent behaviours, including spousal battering and child abuse, and exhibited fewer psychopathic traits and better overall adaptation. Nonetheless, the late starters differed from their non-CD peers on a number of variables, including higher rates of substance abuse, impulsivity, poor employment histories and psychological problems.

Borrowing a concept from one of Rutter's (1990) protective mechanisms (see Chapter 1), involvement in an antisocial lifestyle, even when it begins later in adolescence, may have the effect of *closing down opportunities* and ensnaring young men in a network of maladaptive influences from which it is difficult to disentangle themselves. Although certainly of a different character than their childhood onset peers, current thinking is that adolescent onset CD is neither normative nor neutral (Roisman et al., 2010).

An additional note: our understanding of child onset CD versus adolescent onset CD in girls has been hampered by the fact that so many of the earlier studies focused on boys. Although there has been speculation that girls' delinquency was more often of the adolescence limited version, recent large-scale longitudinal studies suggest that adolescent onset CD is in fact rare in girls (Keenan et al., 2010).

Callous/Unemotional Traits and Juvenile Psychopathy

One of the most important changes being considered for the DSM-5 is the inclusion of a specific modifier for the subset of conduct disordered youth who demonstrate callous-unemotional (CU) traits (Frick and Moffitt, 2010). (See Table 10.2.) The study of CU traits was originally inspired by Robert Hare's (1996) pioneering research on adult **psychopathy**. In his studies of criminal populations, Hare found that, among those with antisocial behaviour, there is a subset who exhibit psychopathic personality traits. These traits include *callousness* (a lack of remorse, empathy or guilt), *egocentricity, superficial charm, impulsivity, shallow emotions, manipulativeness* and *an absence of meaningful relationships*. Psychopaths are individuals who commit antisocial acts against others, not out of necessity – they do not rob because they are poor or strike out at others to defend themselves – but because they have no compunction against hurting or manipulating other people. They exhibit a lack of awareness of other people as fellow human beings deserving of consideration or compassion. They are, in short, 'without conscience' (Hare, 1993).

For example, after the Columbine shootings, Robert Hare was one of the experts the FBI called upon to help perform a 'psychological autopsy' of the killers (Cullen, 2004). Although the media were quick to characterize the boys as victims of bullying, Hare's analyses of Eric's private journal showed that the 'jocks' were not the only people Eric held in contempt: 'YOU KNOW WHAT I HATE!!!? STUPID PEOPLE!!! Why must so many people be so stupid!!? ... YOU KNOW WHAT I HATE!!!? When people mispronounce words! Learn to speak correctly you morons ... YOU KNOW WHAT I HATE!!!? STAR WARS FANS!!! GET A FaaaaaaRIGIN LIFE YOU

TABLE 10.2 Proposed DSM-5 Specifier for Callous-Unemotional Traits

1. Meets full criteria for Conduct Disorder.
2. Shows 2 or more of the following characteristics persistently over at least 12 months and in more than one relationship or setting. The clinician should consider multiple sources of information to determine the presence of these traits, such as whether the person self-reports them as being characteristic of him or herself and if they are reported by others (e.g., parents, other family members, teachers, peers) who have known the person for significant periods of time.
   - *Lack of Remorse or Guilt:* Does not feel bad or guilty when he/she does something wrong (except if expressing remorse when caught and/or facing punishment).
   - *Callous-Lack of Empathy:* Disregards and is unconcerned about the feelings of others.
   - *Unconcerned about Performance:* Does not show concern about poor/problematic performance at school, work, or in other important activities.
   - *Shallow or Deficient Affect:* Does not express feelings or show emotions to others, except in ways that seem shallow or superficial (e.g., emotions are not consistent with actions; can turn emotions 'on' or 'off' quickly) or when they are used for gain (e.g., to manipulate or intimidate others).

BORING GEEEEEKS!' Far from expressing a sense of victimization, Eric's journal writings suggest *grandiosity* – someone who is out to punish the entire human race for its appalling inferiority.

Another characteristic consistent with psychopathy was Eric's *deceitfulness*. 'I lie a lot,' he wrote to his journal. 'Almost constantly, and to everybody … Let's see, what are some of the big lies I told? … No I haven't been making more bombs. No I wouldn't do that. And countless other ones.' Lying for the pleasure of manipulating others is a key characteristic of the psychopathic profile.

Eric also evidenced a total *lack of remorse or empathy* – another distinctive quality of the psychopath. Hare and his team were solidly convinced of his diagnosis when they read Eric's response to being punished after being caught breaking into a van. After participating in a diversion programme involving counselling and community service, both killers feigned regret to obtain an early release. However, Eric seemed to relish the opportunity to perform. While Eric wrote an ingratiating letter to his victim offering empathy, remorse and understanding, at the same time he wrote down his real feelings in his journal: 'Isn't America supposed to be the land of the free? How come, if I'm free, I can't deprive a stupid **** from his possessions if he leaves them sitting in the front seat of his **** van out in plain sight and in the middle of **** nowhere on a Fri****day night. NATURAL SELECTION. **** should be shot.'

In summary, Eric's pattern of grandiosity, glibness, contempt, lack of empathy and superiority read like the bullet points on Hare's Psychopathy Checklist.

Although the idea of extending the concept of psychopathy downward to children originally was somewhat controversial, a decade of research spearheaded by Frick and Moffitt (2010) has demonstrated that such traits can and should be detected in children. First, the researchers developed a child version of Hare's device for detecting psychopathic traits, the Psychopathy Checklist. Just as with Hare's studies of adults, the investigators found two separate dimensions of behaviour, one concerned with

antisocial behaviour, termed *impulsivity/conduct problems* (e.g., 'acts without thinking', 'engages in risky or dangerous behaviours') and the other reflecting *callous-unemotional* (CU) traits (e.g., 'does not show emotions,' 'is not concerned about the feelings of others', 'does not feel bad or guilty'). They also identified a third factor that was labelled *narcissism* (e.g., 'brags excessively', 'thinks he or she is more important than others'). A large body of research exists now to show that, consistent with the adult research, CU traits in children and adolescents are related to the violence of their offences and are predictive of the likelihood that they will reoffend (Salekin and Lynam, 2010).

Subsequent studies in clinical samples have shown that, while children with 'garden variety' CD tend to have cognitive deficits, particularly in verbal intelligence, this is not true of conduct-disordered children with CU traits. Children with CU traits also score higher than their non-CU peers on measures of thrill- and sensation-seeking, are less anxious, and show a decreased sensitivity to punishment (see Frick, 2009; Frick and White, 2008). They are lower in empathy and are less distressed by the negative effects of their behaviour on others, have lower levels of moral reasoning, expect to gain more benefits from their aggressive acts and engage in more proactive, predatory forms of aggression (Frick et al., 2003). While all children with CD are characterized by emotional and behavioural *dysregulation*, Frick and his colleagues conclude, what sets apart the conduct disordered children with CU traits from their peers is behavioural *disinhibition*.

In the light of this research, Frick and Moffitt (2010) argue persuasively that the childhood onset CD type should be further differentiated into two groups: those with and without CU traits. They suggest that the different developmental pathways underlying these two types of aggression warrant their being considered separate disorders. Whereas most children's misbehaviour develops as a function of high emotional reactivity and poor verbal intelligence, and arises in the context of dysfunctional parenting, the callous-unemotional child's misbehaviour arises as a function of low emotional reactivity, particularly to the distress of others. A next stage in this programme of research will be to look at the unfolding of CU traits over the life course in order to establish whether CU traits in children truly represent a precursor to the development of adult psychopathy.

Destructive/Non-destructive and Overt/Covert

Another line of research has pointed to a distinction based not on age of onset or underlying personality but on the kinds of acts perpetrated by the youth. Frick and colleagues (1993) conducted a meta-analysis of data from 60 factor-analytic studies involving more than 28 000 children. They identified two dimensions on which children's behaviour could be distinguished. One dimension concerned whether misbehaviour was *destructive* (cruelty to others, assault) or *non-destructive* (swearing, breaking rules). The second dimension concerned whether behaviour problems were *overt* (hitting, fighting, bullying) or *covert* (lying, stealing, destroying property), a distinction that has reliably been made in a number of studies.

Taking these two dimensions into account, the investigators were able to identify four subtypes of conduct-disordered youths, depending on the kind of misbehaviour in which they engaged (see Fig. 10.1). These were labelled *oppositional* (overt and non-destructive), *aggressive* (overt and destructive), *property violators* (covert and destructive) or *status violators* (covert and non-destructive).

Frick and colleagues (1993) also found that these types could be differentiated in terms of *age of onset*. Those who were primarily oppositional were identified by parents as early as 4 years of age. Aggressive children, in contrast, demonstrated problems after their sixth year. Those who engaged in property violations showed an average age of onset of about 7.5, while those whose misbehaviour took the form of status violations had an average age of onset of about 9. Interestingly, the status violations are reminiscent of the kinds of behaviours we noted earlier that tend to earn girls the CD label, and girls tend to be later starters than boys,

suggesting that there may be an unexamined gender dimension to the typology.

Proactive versus Reactive Aggression

Although not part of the diagnostic criteria, the distinction between proactive and reactive aggression has emerged as very important in studies of children's interpersonal behaviour. *Reactive*, or retaliatory aggression, is a defensive reaction to perceived threat and is accompanied by anger and hostility. *Proactive*, or instrumental aggression, is unprovoked, cold-blooded and generally used for personal gain or to influence and coerce others (Dodge et al., 1990). Research demonstrates that there are different predictors and consequences for the two forms of aggression. Reactively aggressive children are more likely to come from physically abusive families, to be temperamentally irritable and dysregulated, to have poor interpersonal problem-solving skills, to misperceive others' motives as hostile and to be socially rejected than their proactive peers. Proactively aggressive children, in contrast, expect more positive outcomes to their aggression, are less anxious, are more likely to engage in delinquency in adolescence, and are higher in callous unemotional traits (Kerig and Stellwagen, 2010).

Bullying

The study of proactive aggression is important for understanding the development of one kind of miscreant who has made miserable the lives of many throughout childhood: the *bully*. As many as 50 per cent of schoolchildren report experiencing some form of bullying or teasing (Finkelhor et al., 2005), and 17 per cent report cyberbullying or Internet harassment (Wolak et al. 2008). The victims of bullying suffer from more than hurt feelings: as large-scale studies in the USA and Finland have shown in particular, significant anxiety, somatic problems, low self-esteem, substance abuse and even suicide can result (Klomek et al., 2007, 2009; Tharp-Taylor et al., 2009). Whereas in some cases there is validity to the stereotype of the lone bully as a 'social oaf' – socially unskilled,

FIGURE 10.1 Meta-Analytic Factor Analysis of Child Conduct Problems.

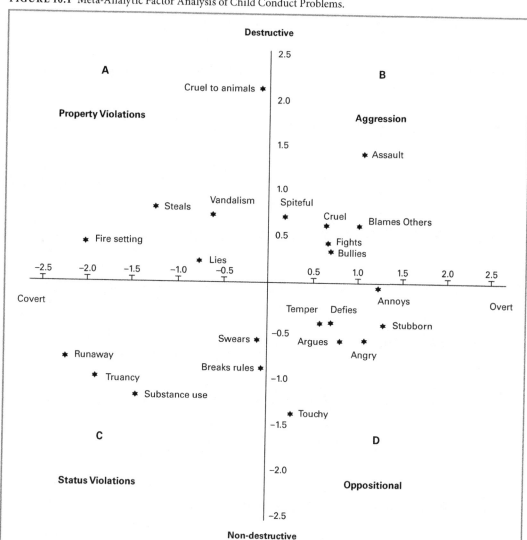

Source: Frick et al., 1993.

verbally limited and alienated from peers – that is not the only kind of bully on the playground. Investigators have identified a second type of bully who is in fact socially and cognitively skilled (Kerig and Sink, 2010). The socially adept bullies are more likely to be identified as *ringleaders*, whose cruelty to victims serves to secure their status and popularity within the peer group (Sutton et al., 1999). In fact, one of the most frequent reasons eighth-grade boys give for bullying is to achieve status with other children such that they will 'respect and admire' them (Sijtsema et al., 2009). The tactic may work. Indeed, Rodkin and Berger (2008) find that boys who bully are among the ones with the highest social status in their samples. These data suggest that the dynamics of the peer group have an important role in the development of bullying; therefore, bullying must be understood not just as a function of intrapersonal variables but also as a social process. Where the peer group rewards bullying with admiration, victimization will flourish.

Comorbidity and Differential Diagnosis

Conduct disorder frequently co-occurs with other disturbances. (Here we follow McMahon and Kotler, 2006, except where noted.) *Attention deficit hyperactivity disorder* (ADHD) and *oppositional defiant disorder* (ODD) are the diagnostic categories most commonly associated with CD. Youth with comorbid ADHD and CD also are among the most disturbed. They display higher rates of physical aggression, more persistent behaviour problems, poorer school achievement and more rejection from peers than the 'pure' CD type. In a longitudinal study following a sample of mostly African American, inner-city boys from first to seventh grade, Schaeffer and colleagues (2003) found that attention/concentration difficulties were one of the most powerful predictors of persistent or increasing levels of aggression. These data are consistent with the speculation that CD is related to the same underlying neurodevelopmental deficits that are responsible for inattention.

Learning disorders are associated with CD, particularly reading disorder. In some youths, learning problems may lead to frustration, oppositional attitudes and misbehaviour in school, and thus to a diagnosis of CD. However, as we saw in Chapter 7, the weight of the evidence argues that learning disorders do not lead to CD, but rather that a third variable accounts for the relationship between them. Youths with *ADHD* are overrepresented among those who have both conduct and learning disorders, and it may be the overlap of these disorders with ADHD that accounts for their co-occurrence. A third variable that may account for the association is socio-economic disadvantage. CD also co-occurs with *substance abuse* and may be a precursor to it, as was found in the National Comorbidity Study (Nock et al., 2006b). This is an issue we will discuss further in Chapter 12.

Although internalizing disorders might seem to be diametrically opposed to externalizing problems, *depression* is highly correlated with CD. As we saw in Chapter 9, longitudinal research suggests that antisocial behaviour in boys leads to academic failures and peer rejection, which lead, in turn, to depression. This was confirmed in the National Comorbidity Study, where Nock and colleagues (2006b) found that the onset of mood disorders most often was subsequent to the onset of CD. Comorbid depression and CD are of particular concern because they are disproportionately associated with suicide and substance abuse in later adolescence (Loeber et al., 2008b).

The relationship between CD and *anxiety* is a complex one. Whereas anxiety of a fearful/inhibited type appears to protect children against the development of externalizing problems, anxiety that is characterized by social isolation and withdrawal is associated with an intensified risk of aggressive behaviour. As the National Comorbidity Study found (Nock et al., 2006b), when the two co-occur, CD comes first about 32 per cent of the time for the majority of anxiety disorders, but follows after the onset of social phobia.

There is a *gender difference* in that comorbidity is most common in girls. Although girls develop CD less often than boys overall, when they do, it is more likely to take a comorbid form (Loeber et al., 2008b). In particular, whereas *depression and anxiety* frequently occur in conduct-disordered youths, girls demonstrate higher rates of comorbidity with these internalizing problems. As we saw in our discussion of depression (Chapter 9), these different comorbidities might in fact represent different subtypes of CD.

Developmental Course
Continuity

There is a high degree of *continuity* in conduct disordered behaviour. Large-scale epidemiological studies in the USA, the UK, New Zealand and other countries have established stability from preschool age to middle childhood (Kim-Cohen et al., 2009), from childhood to adolescence (Lahey et al., 2002), from adolescence to adulthood (Zara and Farrington, 2009) and, most strikingly, from infancy to adulthood (Newman et al., 1997). Thus, the developmental course is a persistent one and the prognosis poor. Youth with CD are at risk for a broad range of negative outcomes, ranging from involvement in the criminal justice system to lower educational and occupational status to poorer physical and psychological health (Maughan and Rutter, 2001). The increased likelihood of teen parenthood among CD youth also amplifies the risk of intergenerational transmission of antisocial behaviour (Zoccolillo et al., 2005).

One of the most impressive data sets on the continuity of conduct problems comes from a large, multinational collaboration (Broidy et al., 2003). This group compiled data derived from studies based in Quebec, Canada (1037 boys followed from ages 6 to 17); Montreal, Canada (1000 boys and 1000 girls assessed from ages 6 to 15); Christchurch, New Zealand (635 boys and 630 girls studied from birth to age 18); Dunedin, New Zealand (535 boys and 502 girls followed from ages 3 to 26); and two

US samples: one based in Pittsburgh (1517 boys followed for 12 years, half of whom were African American); and the Child Development Project (CDP), a multisite collaboration based in Tennessee and Indiana (304 boys and 280 girls followed from kindergarten to age 13).

Overall, the data revealed significant differences in the levels and trajectories of aggressive behaviour across sites and developmental periods. For boys, there was a trend towards increasing aggression in the US samples, stability in the New Zealand samples, and decline in the Canadian samples (see Fig. 10.2). Even within the group patterns of change, however, there was individual stability: within each cohort, even though the absolute level of aggression might change over time, the relative ranking of individuals tended to stay the same. (So, for example, even though Alain is less physically violent at age 16 than he was at age 6, he is still the most aggressive child in his Montreal classroom.) The investigators also were able to identify individual trajectories of aggressive behaviour, with some youths evidencing moderate levels of aggression that desisted over

FIGURE 10.2 Multinational Data on Aggression in Boys.

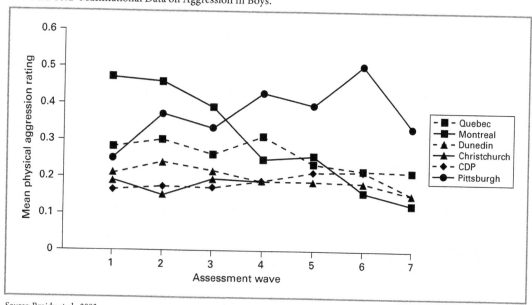

Source: Broidy et al., 2003.

time, and others – the majority in all samples – rarely being aggressive. Only in the USA samples a subset of about 10 per cent of the boys followed a course of increasing aggression over the course of childhood. Finally, childhood aggression was the most powerful predictor of adolescent violent and non-violent delinquency. This prediction held true even when the investigators accounted for the influence of other kinds of disruptive behaviour, such as oppositionality, ADHD and non-aggressive conduct problems. Thus, childhood aggression begets adolescent violence.

Results for *girls* were quite different. Patterns of trajectory were more difficult to discern in girls and were more variable across the samples than they were for boys. Overall, girls' levels of physical aggression were lower than boys' across all four of the sites that included females (see Fig. 10.3). However, in three of the samples, a small group of girls were chronically aggressive over the life course (3 per cent in Quebec, 10 per cent in Christchurch and 14 per cent in the CDP sample), and some of these girls exhibited higher mean levels of aggression than their male peers! But, in contrast to that of boys, girls' adolescent delinquency was not better predicted by childhood aggression than by other forms of disruptive behaviour. Thus, despite the fact that the relation between physical aggression and later offending was strong and consistent for boys, it was weak and inconsistent for girls. Although part of the problem may be a statistical one – rates of violent delinquency in girls were so low that there was little variability to predict – the data also suggest that there may be a different pathway to female adolescent offending. As we shall see later in this chapter, other investigators agree.

Interestingly, there was no evidence of a sudden, late onset type in these studies of the emergence of physical aggression. Does this suggest that the late onset type does not exist? Probably not. Another interpretation is that while *some* forms of delinquent behaviour may emerge only in adolescence in previously well-functioning youths – for example, stealing, truancy or experimentation with drugs – the propensity to be physically *violent* has its roots in childhood aggression.

FIGURE 10.3 Multinational Data on Aggression in Girls.

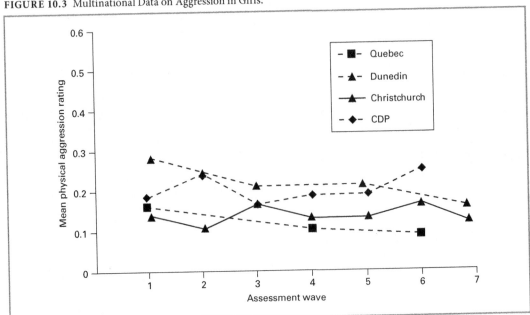

Developmental Pathways

Researchers also have looked more closely at the developmental unfolding of problem behaviour. Generally, a sequential progression is found such that one form of problem behaviour virtually always occurs before the emergence of another. In an exhaustive review of the available longitudinal research, Loeber and Burke (2011) find an '*invariant sequence*' across development: from *hyperactivity-inattention* to *oppositional* behaviour, and then to *conduct problems*. Combining Loeber's research with other work on the precursors and sequelae of conduct problems, we can construct a developmental model tracing the sequencing of behaviour problems from difficult temperament in the early years to antisocial personality in adulthood. (See Fig. 10.4.)

As youth progress through this sequence, they tend to maintain their prior antisocial behaviours; therefore, because behaviours are retained rather than replaced, the developmental progression is better described as one of *accretion* rather than succession. However, the fact that this sequence exists does not mean that all individuals are fated to go through all the steps. On the contrary, whereas most individuals progress to different stages of increasing seriousness of antisocial behaviour, few progress through all of them.

On the side of *discontinuity*, some studies show desistance rates from preschool to school age of about 25 per cent (Loeber et al., 2008b). Although it appears that these are youth with less serious behaviour problems, little is known about the factors that account for their ceasing their antisocial behaviour. However, as longitudinal research on the precursors and consequences of CD has emerged, distinct developmental pathways have been identified over the life span, which we describe next.

Early Childhood: Pathways from ADHD to Conduct Disorder

As noted in the previous section, a number of studies have confirmed the link between CD and ADHD (McMahon and Kotler, 2006). Symptoms of ADHD appear to increase the risk for childhood onset CD, to be associated with more severe behaviour problems, and to result in greater resistance to change. Thus, ADHD propels youths to an earlier onset of behaviour problems, which is predictive, in turn, of a longer-lasting antisocial career.

Attention deficit hyperactivity disorder does not lead irrevocably to CD, however. Only those children whose ADHD symptoms are accompanied by *antisocial behaviour* such as aggression and non-compliance are at risk for future CD (Loeber et al., 2008b). Thus, in this case it appears that ADHD potentiates early conduct problems, hastening them on the way to full blown CD.

Middle Childhood: Pathways from Oppositionality to Conduct Disorder

Oppositional defiant disorder, as described in Chapter 6, is characterized by persistent age-inappropriate displays of anger and defiance. While ODD and CD share some similar behavioural

FIGURE 10.4 Developmental Transformations in Antisocial Behaviour from Infancy to Adulthood.

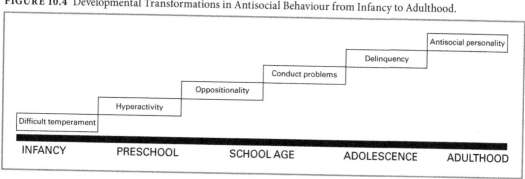

features and risk factors, the two syndromes can be distinguished from one another. As we saw in Fig. 10.1, large-scale meta-analyses of children's problem behaviour reveal a unique factor comprising the kind of overt, non-destructive behaviours that define ODD. ODD also emerges earlier in development than CD, with an average age of onset of six years for oppositionality compared with nine years for conduct problems (Loeber et al., 2008b).

As Loeber and Burke (2011) point out, in all the multinational research conducted to date, CD almost universally is preceded by ODD. In addition, the most severely disturbed children are likely to retain features of oppositionality in addition to acquiring CD symptoms. However, more recent research suggests that this progress may not be as invariant as once thought. In a longitudinal study of 1420 children followed from age 9 to 21, Rowe and colleagues (2010) found that although ODD was a strong predictor of CD, nearly half the children who developed a CD diagnosis exhibited no previous ODD. This finding was confirmed by Burke and colleagues (2010) in a study combining three longitudinal data sets. Therefore, there is convincing evidence that children who develop ODD are at a considerable risk for progressing to CD. However, for other children, the pathway to CD is a more direct one.

Late Childhood and Adolescence: Divergent Pathways

An impressive body of research from Fergusson and his colleagues in Christchurch, New Zealand, informs us of the risk factors that lead to antisocial behaviour in the adolescent years (Boden et al., 2010). Using a longitudinal birth cohort of 926 children, the investigators examined the variables assessed in the first 14 years of life that were predictive of a conduct disorder diagnosis at age 14 to 16: maternal smoking during pregnancy; exposure to socio-economic adversity; parental maladaptive behaviour; childhood exposure to abuse and interparental violence; gender; cognitive ability; and affiliation with deviant peers in early adolescence.

In turn, Loeber and his colleagues (2009a) in the USA have been using prospective data from a longitudinal study of high-risk boys in order to investigate diverse *developmental pathways* predictive of later problem behaviour. Basing their thinking on previous research differentiating CD along the dimensions of overt/covert and destructive/non-destructive, they derived three distinct types (see Fig. 10.5).

The first identified was the *authority conflict* pathway. The behaviour of these youths was characterized by defiance, stubborn and oppositional behaviour, and rule violations such as truancy and running away. While disruptive, these behaviours were considered to be less serious because they did not inflict direct harm on others. Those whose behaviour escalated in the authority conflict pathway tended to have continual conflicts with adults, but they were not likely to develop other forms of aggressive and antisocial behaviour. They also were the least likely to become labelled delinquent.

The second was termed the *covert* pathway. These youths engaged in minor and non-violent acts such as shoplifting, joyriding and vandalism. Escalation in this pathway involved progressing to more serious forms of property crime and theft in later adolescence, but was rarely associated with violence or more severe kinds of antisocial behaviour.

The third, the *overt* pathway, was composed of children who exhibited aggression early in childhood. Escalation in this pathway was associated with progression from aggression to fighting to more serious assaults and violence against others. The overt pathway was linked to high rates of criminal offences in adolescence. In addition, these youths were likely to add covert forms of aggression to their repertoire as their careers proceeded. *Dual overt/covert* pathway youths were more likely to become delinquents; however, the worst outcomes were seen in *triple pathway* youths – those who showed a combination of overt and covert aggression as well as authority conflict.

Patterson and Yoerger (2002) raise an interesting question about how the kinds of misbehaviour that characterize childhood conduct disorder

FIGURE 10.5 Developmental Pathways to Conduct Disorder.

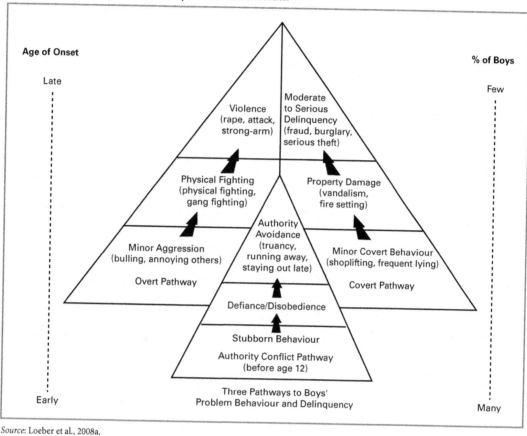

Source: Loeber et al., 2008a.

transform into the kinds of delinquent acts that are described in adolescents' police reports. Breaking into a house is different than taking money from a mother's purse, they suggest, just as physical assaults seem to belong to a different class from temper tantrums. What explains this metamorphosis? During the transition from late childhood to early adolescence, they point out, there is a developmental shift in the importance of peer relationships to youths. Noting that involvement in deviant peer relationships is a powerful predictor of antisocial behaviour, and that the vast majority of juvenile crimes are committed in groups, the authors argue that peer group processes contribute to the *developmental transformation* of childhood misbehaviour into adolescent delinquency.

Finally, Moffit (2003) points out that not all adolescents who demonstrate conduct problems have a childhood history of aggression or antisocial behaviour. Thus, in this developmental period arises the *adolescent onset*, or late onset, type, which we will focus on in greater detail later in this chapter.

Late Adolescence: Pathways to Antisocial Personality and Criminality

Two conclusions can be drawn from the research linking CD to adult *antisocial personality disorder* and criminal behaviour. First, *looking backward*, we find that antisocial adults almost without exception met the criteria for CD earlier in their development. However, one of the criteria for the diagnosis of antisocial personality disorder is onset of problem behaviour before age 15, so this is a link that is structured into the diagnostic criteria. Secondly, *looking forward*, we find that only a minority of conduct disordered youths go on to develop the chronic and disabling patterns characteristic of the adult diagnosis.

The characteristics predictive of those who do go on to develop antisocial personality disorder are early age of onset and diverse, persistent conduct problems in childhood, including aggression and antisocial behaviour. As we have seen previously, *age of onset* is one of the most significant predictors of the subsequent seriousness of antisocial behaviour. Children with early onset both have a higher level of disruptive behaviour and progress more rapidly to more serious problems (Loeber and Burke, 2011; Reid et al., 2002). There is clear evidence that those who begin their antisocial activities before the teenage years will continue to commit a large number of offences at a high rate over a long period of time. Further, *association with antisocial peers* contributes to the continuation of adolescent delinquency into young adulthood. Using longitudinal data from the Oregon Youth Study, Shortt and colleagues (2003) showed that adult antisocial behaviour was predicted by adolescents' involvement, not only with deviant friends, but also with antisocial siblings and romantic partners.

Resilience, Discontinuity and Protective Factors

Not all aggressive youth go on to become antisocial adults. While most adult antisocial behaviour is rooted in childhood, only half of the at-risk children grow up to be antisocial men and women (Loeber et al., 2008b). It is important to understand the factors that account for this discontinuity. To this end, Shaw and colleagues (2003) identified factors that contributed to desistance of aggression in children between the ages of 2 and 8. Specifically, high levels of child *fearfulness* and low levels of *maternal depression* differentiated children whose levels of aggression remained low or did not persist. Although fearfulness may reflect a

temperamental variable that the child brings to the equation, it is worth noting that the investigators measured fearfulness as a function of toddlers' expressions of fear and hesitancy to approach a cabinet in which played a tape recording of gorillas howling in a threatening manner. Recalling our earlier reviews of research on the strange situation (Chapters 2 and 6), a 2-year-old's clinging to the mother and requesting reassurance in this context also might reflect security of attachment.

Subsequently, Veenstra and colleagues (2009) initiated the Tracking Adolescents' Individual Lives Survey (TRAILS) study in the Netherlands to investigate the factors that differentiate youth who persist and those who desist from delinquency. In the first wave of data collection, the investigators followed 2000 youth from age 11 to 13.5 and differentiated between those whose antisocial behaviour was stable and high, versus those whose problem behaviour was limited to childhood. Characteristics that distinguished the 'stable highs' included lower levels of *effortful control* as well as higher levels of *parental overprotection*, *familial vulnerability* to externalizing disorders and *family instability*. Furthermore, the children who desisted from problem behaviour were more likely to receive assistance from *special education* services. Significantly, not only did the desisters show less antisocial behaviour over the course of the study, but they also experienced less *academic failure*, *peer rejection* and *internalizing problems*. Thus, a negative cascade of problems in multiple spheres of development was averted.

Gender Differences in Developmental Pathways

It is notable that almost all of the longitudinal studies cited have been based exclusively on males. What about *female* developmental trajectories? Because most CD is diagnosed in boys, the greater attention focused on males is justified to some extent. However, only by including girls in the research can we determine whether or not they are at reduced risk or have a different developmental course (Miller et al., 2012).

Although most studies agree that the development of CD in girls is more heterogeneous than that of boys, boys and girls tend to go through the same sequence of behaviour problems in the progression toward CD (Fontaine et al., 2009; Gorman-Smith and Loeber, 2005). However, these misbehaviours generally have a later onset in girls than in boys. Antisocial behaviour usually starts at age 8 to 10 for boys, while for girls it generally does not appear until age 14 to 16. One possibility is that this delayed onset represents a 'sleeper effect': perhaps girls with CD have the same underlying temperamental and cognitive deficits as boys, but do not manifest these problems until adolescence (Silverthorn and Frick, 1999).

However, as we saw in the multinational data compiled by Broidy et al. (2003), girls exhibit lower levels of aggression in nearly all studies, and models of CD need to be able to account for this. Perhaps the explanation lies in the developmental mechanisms underlying conduct disorder. Of interest is the fact that girls are under-represented among virtually all of the disorders that co-occur with – or are precursors to – CD, including oppositional defiance, attention deficit and learning disorders. Various theoretical perspectives have been offered to explain this gender difference (Eme, 2007; Eme and Kavanaugh, 1995). Some have argued that males are more biologically vulnerable to the neuropsychological deficits that underlie all these disorders. Others point to socialization factors, including parental reinforcement of aggressive behaviour in boys and nurturance in girls, same-sex role modelling of aggression, and the influence of the peer group, which enforces sex-role stereotypic behaviour such as an assertive-dominant style in males.

Others hypothesize that we simply are not doing a good enough job of catching girls in the act: girls might misbehave in less overt ways than those that are captured by the measures used routinely in our investigations. For example, conduct-disordered girls and boys tend to be identified on the basis of different kinds of behaviour problems. Fighting and theft are the most frequent reasons for referring boys, while *covert antisocial activities* such

as truancy are more often the cause for concern about girls (Chesney-Lind and Belknap, 2004). Another line of research has focused on gender-differentiated expressions of aggression. Whereas boys are more likely than girls to display physical aggression, girls are more likely to be characterized by *relational or social aggression*: attempting to hurt others by ridiculing them, excluding them from the peer group, withdrawing friendship or spreading rumours (Crick and Rose, 2000; Underwood, 2003). Over the course of development, such behaviours may lend themselves to hidden forms of cruelty – such as the teenaged mother who psychologically abuses her child in the privacy of the home – that are not routinely captured by measures of antisocial behaviour.

Despite the gender differences in prevalence, there is evidence that for those girls who do develop CD, the consequences are as negative as those for boys (McCabe et al., 2004). For example, Fergusson and Woodward (2000) found that among girls conduct problems at age 13 predicted later adolescent association with deviant peers, substance use, academic problems and risky sexual behaviour, which in turn predicted antisocial behaviour, mental health problems and sexual victimization, as well as poor achievement in young adulthood.

Etiology

The Biological Context

Recent attention has been drawn to the possibility of uncovering neurodevelopmental factors underlying the emergence of CD. Although much of this research is still in progress, and little of it is definitive, a number of suggestive leads have been identified.

Temperament may reflect a biological underpinning to CD. For example, Frick and Morris (2004) propose that underlying the development of disruptive behaviour disorders are neuropsychological dysfunctions associated with a difficult temperament, which predisposes children to impulsivity, irritability and overactivity. Consistent with this, Newman and colleagues (1997) found that children who showed a difficult, undercontrolled temperamental type at age 3 were more likely to be rated as antisocial in adulthood. However, other longitudinal research indicates that the link between aggression and difficult temperament is not a direct one; instead, it is moderated by family factors. For example, in the Dutch TRAILS study, Sentse and colleagues (2009) found that children who showed a temperamental style characterized by irritability and frustration proneness were particularly susceptible to the risk-buffering effects of parental warmth as well as to the risk-enhancing effects of parental rejection.

Genetics also have been considered, particularly for the childhood onset version of the disorder. One of the best predictors of conduct problems in children is parental criminality or antisocial behaviour, especially when research focuses on fathers and sons. In a meta-analytic review of twin adoption studies, Rhee and Waldman (2002) found that the amount of variance in the diagnosis of CD that could be accounted for by genetics was 50 per cent. A further 11 per cent of the variance could be accounted for by shared environmental factors (e.g., family social class), whereas 39 per cent could be attributed to non-shared environmental influences (e.g., differential parental treatment of the youngest and oldest child).

The search for the specific genetic mechanism of effect has focused in particular on the gene that encodes the enzyme monoamine oxidase-A (MAO-A), which plays an important role in the regulation of neurotransmitters, including serotonin, dopamine and norepinephrine, which are implicated in aggression (Lahey, 2008). Research also has implicated another enzyme, catechol-O-methyltransferase (COMT), which is involved in the synaptic breakdown of the neurotransmitters dopamine, epinephrine and norepinephrine which play a role in the functioning of the frontal cortex (Thapar et al., 2005). Other findings point towards a relationship between conduct problems and the gene that encodes the dopamine transporter, D4, which is involved in the reuptake of

dopamine from the synapse (Haberstick et al., 2006; Lee et al., 2007).

As we have seen, however, genetic influences do not operate outside of the environmental context. In the developmental psychopathology literature, there is increasing interest in the study of the more complex processes represented by *genotype x environment interactions*. For example, in one test of this model, Leve and colleagues (2010) observed 9-month-old infants at genetic risk for externalizing disorders and their adoptive parents. The investigators were particularly interested in the infants' heightened attention to frustrating events (having a toy placed out of reach but not out of sight) during the laboratory task, a tendency which is a known precursor to externalizing problems. Their results showed that infants at genetic risk for conduct disorder responded with heightened attention to frustrating events only when the adoptive parent exhibited high levels of anxious and depressive symptoms. Thus, parent affect dysregulation acted as a *potentiator* (see Chapter 1) of child genetic risk.

Exposure to *toxins* also is implicated in the development of conduct problems. Foetuses exposed to opiates *in utero* are at increased risk for aggressive behaviour 10 years later, as are those exposed to alcohol, marijuana, cigarettes and lead poisoning (see Lahey, 2008).

Psychophysiological indicators also differentiate early onset youths from their peers. These children demonstrate overall lower autonomic arousal, demonstrated by low heart rate and galvanic skin response. Youth with low heart rates are likely to fight and bully others at school and are more likely to become violent adults. Low autonomic arousal leads to stimulation-seeking and behavioural undercontrol on the one hand, and diminished reactivity to punishment on the other. Investigators concerned with the callous-unemotional subtype have been particularly interested in uncovering a physiological basis, given that this form of CD is not well predicted by environmental factors. For example, Frick and colleagues (2010) hypothesize that the behavioural disinhibition seen in these children arises from an *underreactive sympathetic nervous system*, leading to impulsive responding, heightened reactivity to reward and insensitivity to negative feedback – such as the cry of another's distress – that might curb the aggressive impulses of others.

A number of *biochemical* correlates have also been investigated (Hinshaw and Lee, 2003). Testosterone is a likely candidate because of its relation to aggression in animals. However, research on humans indicates that hormone levels do not account for aggressive and antisocial behaviour, although they may serve a mediating role in individual responses to environmental circumstances. Low levels of serotonin and cortisol also have been linked to aggression in children, although it is worth noting that these deficits have also been identified as factors in the development of a quite different disorder, depression (see Chapter 9).

Those pursuing research in the biological domain argue that the existence of organic factors in no way rules out or discounts the importance of social and psychological influences. In fact, there is a general appreciation of the complex interplay between psychology and biology. For example, Brennan and colleagues (2003) investigated the combined and interacting effects of biological and social processes in the development of aggression in an Australian sample of 370 children, followed from 6 months to 15 years of age. Consistent with other researchers, the investigators identified three pathways: early onset persistent, adolescent onset and non-aggressive. For the early onset boys, biological risks (perinatal and birth complications, maternal illness during pregnancy, difficult infant temperament, and neuropsychological defects such as poor executive functioning) predicted aggression only in *interaction* with high social risk (parental rejection, harsh discipline, poor monitoring, parent–child conflict, family poverty and divorce). In turn, the adolescent onset aggressive boys differed from their non-aggressive peers by virtue of being exposed to a greater number of cumulative social risks. Gender differences once again raised their heads, in that biological risk factors did not significantly differentiate the aggressive patterns in girls.

The Individual Context

As we have seen, there is a continuum between normalcy and psychopathology, and deviations in fundamental developmental processes underlie many disorders. Indeed, aggression is part of normal development, and there is no reason for assuming that a 'hotheaded' or a 'hair-triggered' youth has CD if other aspects of his or her personality are proceeding apace. Therefore, to better understand what has gone awry in the development of those children who come to be labelled 'conduct disordered', it will be helpful to review what is known about some of the major developmental variables underlying problem behaviour: *self-regulation*, emotion regulation, empathy and social cognition.

Self-Regulation

Self-regulation is essential to adaptive functioning, and society's expectations that children control their impulses increase with age. Whereas we might not be surprised to see a 4-year-old have a temper tantrum on the floor of the grocery store when denied a candy bar, such behaviour in a 14-year-old would raise a few eyebrows. However, the 4-year-old is still expected to refrain from attacking a sibling in a rage, masturbating in a restaurant or trying out a new toy hammer on the computer screen. Early socialization of self-control is particularly important because toddlers and preschoolers have a strong desire for immediate gratification of their aggressive, sexual and exploratory urges; and they tend to be egocentric and self-seeking.

However, objective studies confirm that conduct-disordered children evidence problems in self-regulation. These include *biological processes*, such as vagal regulation of heart rate and the ability to modulate physiological arousal, *emotion regulation* and the ability to manage negative affective states and *cognitive control processes* such as the ability to regulate attention, inhibit impulses and engage in effortful control (Calkins and Keane, 2009).

Kochanska and her colleagues (Kochanska and Aksan, 2007; Kochanska et al., 2008, 2009a) have conducted studies devoted to uncovering the roots of self-control in young children, which they view as an outgrowth of the internalization of parental values (see Chapter 2). The researchers placed young children in a laboratory situation in which they were given time alone in a room with an attractive toy that their mothers had forbidden them to touch; self-control was indicated by their ability to resist the temptation. Those children who showed *'committed compliance'* – an eager and wholehearted endorsement of their mother's values, as opposed to mere obedience – were those who had experienced the most *mutually positive affect* in the parent–child relationship.

Further, Kochanska's research team has shown that specific parenting styles are optimal for promoting self-control in children with different temperaments. Using longitudinal data, they found that for children assessed as fearful in toddlerhood, a gentle maternal discipline style was most effective (Barry et al., 2008; Kochanska et al., 2009b). However, for children assessed as fearless, gentleness was not sufficient. Instead, mothers needed to heighten their emotional bond with children in order to foster the motivation to accept and internalize parental values. Therefore, the development of self-regulation in temperamentally difficult children, who are at risk for CD, may require the most *intensely involved* and *emotionally available* parenting – the kind they are least likely to receive.

Emotion Regulation

Emotion regulation is a specific aspect of self-control that has been implicated in the development of CD (Eisenberg et al., 2010). Children chronically exposed to family adversity, poor parenting and high levels of conflict are overwhelmed by strong emotions and receive little help in managing them from stressed and unskilled parents. Therefore, they are at risk for failing to develop adequate strategies for coping with their negative emotions and regulating their expression. Consistent with this idea, research has shown that conduct-disordered children have difficulty managing strong affects, particularly anger, and that children with poor emotion regulation skills are more likely to respond aggressively to interpersonal problems (Eisenberg et al., 2010).

Prosocial Development: Perspective-Taking, Moral Development and Empathy

Piaget (1967) observed that one of the pivotal developments in the transition to middle childhood is decentring: that is, shifting from cognitive egocentrism – in which the world is viewed primarily from the child's own vantage point – to cognitive perspectivism – in which a situation can be seen from the diverse views of the individuals involved and their rights and feelings taken into account. *Perspective-taking*, the ability to see things from others' point of view, is fundamental to the development of moral reasoning and empathy, both of which can counter the tendency to behave in antisocial and aggressive ways.

Research attests to the fact that aggressive and conduct-disordered youths are delayed in the development of these cognitive and affective variables. In contrast to their non-delinquent peers, delinquent youth are more cognitively immature in their *moral reasoning* (Barriga et al., 2009; Stadler et al., 2007). In addition, conduct disordered youths are less *empathic*, as well as being less accurate in reading the emotions of others when compared to their non-antisocial peers (Sterzer et al., 2007). Happé and Frith (1996) go so far as to propose that a conduct-disordered youth's lack of social insight and understanding of other people's mental states is akin to the deficits in *theory of mind* seen in autistic children (see Chapter 5). Accordingly, conduct disordered youths tend to misperceive the motives of others and to exhibit distortions in their reasoning about social situations, both of which increase the likelihood that they will respond in an aggressive manner. We next turn to these social cognitive dimensions underlying problem behaviour.

Social Cognition

Eron and Huesmann (1990), in musing about the stability of aggression across time and generations, state: 'The frightening implication of this intractable consistency is that aggression is not situation specific or determined solely by the contingencies. The individual carries around something inside that impels him or her to act in a characteristically aggressive or nonaggressive way' (pp. 152–3). In other words, underlying aggressions are *cognitive schemata*: scripts for interpreting and responding to events that are derived from past experiences and are used to guide future behaviour (Huesmann and Reynolds, 2001).

In particular, evidence suggests that children with CD have distinctive *social-information processing styles* (Dodge and Pettit, 2003). For example, aggressive children misattribute aggressive intent to others when in an ambiguous situation, termed a *hostile attribution bias*. They also are insensitive to social cues that might help them more correctly interpret others' intentions and respond impulsively on the basis of their faulty assumptions. In this way, they are ripe for misinterpretation and overreaction to seeming slights. In addition, these children are able to generate few alternatives for solving interpersonal problems, and they have positive expectations of the outcomes of aggression. Therefore, aggression is their preferred option.

These social-information processing patterns have also been shown to account for the relationship between early experiences of maltreatment and later childhood aggression (Dodge, 2010). Harsh and abusive parenting appears to instil in children a generalized belief that others are hostile and have malicious intent towards them, an assumption that is verified each time they engage in negative exchanges with parents, peers and others. Therefore, children come to internalize their experiences of family mistreatment in ways that are deeply ingrained in their personalities and behavioural repertoires, replete with cognitive rationales that ensure consistency in their behaviour.

Substance Abuse

Involvement in *substance abuse* also may contribute to the onset of serious criminal behaviour (see Chapter 12). For example, the National Center on Addiction and Substance Abuse (2004) reported that four out of every five youths currently in the US juvenile justice system had a prior history of substance offences or were under the influence of drugs or alcohol while committing their crimes. The relationship between CD and substance abuse is likely to be complex and transactional. On the one hand, youths who are behaviourally and emotionally dysregulated may be more attracted to the thrills and sensations accompanying substance use. Once involved with illicit substances, the youth is increasingly likely to engage in illegal activities in order to obtain the drugs and to be a part of the antisocial subculture that surrounds their use. Further, alcohol and drug substances have a disinhibiting effect that increases the likelihood of engagement in risky and illegal behaviour.

The Family Context
Attachment

The idea that conduct problems are linked to troubled attachment relationships is not new. In fact, John Bowlby himself raised this possibility in his seminal 1944 paper on 'forty-four juvenile thieves'. Since that time, a number of studies have shown that insecure attachment is associated with youth aggression, antisocial behaviour, poor interpersonal relationships, use of hard drugs and involvement in the juvenile justice system (see Kerig, 2012; Kerig and Becker, 2010). For example, in a longitudinal study of 125 at-risk youth, Allen and colleagues (2002) found that youth with an anxious attachment style evidenced increasing rates of delinquency from the ages of 16 to 18. In another study of at-risk youth, Egeland and colleagues (2002) construed alienation as a form of insecure attachment that may develop when there is a 'lack of trust in the caregiver's availability, support, and guidance, particularly in stressful situations in which the child needs support and assistance from the caregivers to cope effectively' (p. 251). The investigators found that alienation helped to account for the relationship between childhood maltreatment and externalizing behaviours in adolescence.

On the other hand, secure attachments can act as buffers against risk. For example, following a sample of 100 physically abused children and 100 matched controls from age 10 to 16, Salzinger and colleagues (2007) found that secure attachment to parents mediated the relationship between childhood maltreatment and adolescent violent delinquency.

Parent Psychopathology

Parent psychopathology has been linked to child conduct problems, particularly *maternal depression* (Crockenberg et al., 2008) and *maternal anxiety* (Meadows et al., 2007). As our discussion of transactional models suggests, parental internalizing disorders also are exacerbated by children's behaviour problems. However, the most powerful parent-related predictor of CD in children is parent *antisocial personality disorder*, which increases both the incidence and the persistence of the CD. For example, Lahey and colleagues (2005) conducted a four-year prospective study of 171 boys diagnosed with CD. Parental antisocial personality disorder was correlated with CD at the first assessment and, in combination with boys' verbal intelligence, predicted the continuation of conduct problems in later development. How does parent personality translate into child behaviour problems? This question concerns us next.

Harsh Parenting and the Inter-generational Transmission of Aggression

There is strong evidence for the *inter-generational transmission* of aggression. Aggression is not only stable within a single generation but across generations as well. Eron and Huesmann (1990) conducted a classic 22-year prospective study, compiling data on 82 participants when they were 8 and 30 years of age, as well as collecting information from their parents and 8-year-old children. Strong associations were seen between grandparents', parents' and children's aggressiveness. The correlation between the aggression that parents had shown at age 8 and that was displayed by their

children was remarkably high (0.65), higher even than the consistency in parents' own behaviour across the lifespan.

Whereas the mechanisms responsible for the continuity of this behaviour are not clear, Eron and Huesmann believe it is learned through *modelling*. As noted before, children who have antisocial parents are exposed to models of aggressive behaviour. However, the aggression need not be so extreme in order to provide a model. For example, adult antisocial behaviour is predicted by *harsh punishment* received as a child (Dishion and Patterson, 2006). In adulthood, those punished harshly as children are more likely to endorse using severe discipline in child rearing – in fact, their responses to parenting style questionnaires are strikingly similar to the ones given by their own parents.

As meta-analyses of a host of studies show, corresponding results have been obtained regarding the relationship between *spanking* and child aggression (Straus et al., in press). For example, Gershoff and colleagues (2010) found a correspondence between the use of physical punishment and children's aggressive behaviour in an international sample of families from China, India, Italy, Kenya, Phillipines and Thailand. Similar results have been found in clinical populations, establishing a link between corporal punishment and the development of externalizing disorders (Mahoney et al., 2003). Later in development, childhood corporal punishment also increases the risk that males will grow up to become spousal batterers (Straus, 2010). In sum, through their observations of their own parents, children learn that the rule governing interpersonal relationships is 'might makes right'.

Parenting Inconsistency and Lack of Monitoring

Other research indicates that it is not only the severity of parental discipline but also a pattern of *parental inconsistency* – an inconsistent mix of harshness and laxness – that is related to antisocial acting out. Laxness may be evidenced in a number of ways, particularly lack of parental *monitoring*: failing to provide supervision, to stay knowledgeable about the children's activities and whereabouts, and to enforce rules concerning where the children can go and whom they can be with. These are parents who, when phoned by researchers and asked, 'It is 9 p.m.; do you know where your child is right now?' do not know the answer. Patterson and his colleagues (Dishion and Patterson, 2006) refer to the unsupervised behaviour of youths as *wandering* and find that it is a strong predictor of involvement in delinquent activities. Indeed, in a meta-analysis of 161 studies conducted across North America, Europe and Australia, the Dutch research team of Hoeve and colleagues (2009) examined the effects of parenting behaviours on children's delinquency. The strongest links were found for lack of *parental monitoring*, along with high levels of *psychological control, rejection* and *hostility*.

Coercion Theory

Patterson and his colleagues (Dishion and Patterson, 2006; Reid et al., 2002) have carried out an important programme of research on the family origins of conduct disorder. Based on social learning theory, they set out to investigate the factors that might train antisocial behaviour in children. They found that parents of antisocial children were more likely than others to *positively reinforce* aggressive behaviour – for example, by regarding it as amusing. They also observed that these parents exhibited inconsistent outbursts of anger and punitiveness and made harsh threats with no follow-through, both of which

were ineffectual in curbing negative behaviour. On the other side of the coin, children's prosocial behaviour was either ignored or reinforced non-contingently. Therefore, the investigators conclude that CD is initiated and sustained in the home by maladaptive parent–child interactions.

Patterson's most important contribution was to analyse the interactions of antisocial children and their parents in terms of what he calls coercive family processes. By **coercion**, Patterson means negative behaviour on the part of one person that is supported or directly reinforced by another person. These interactions are transactional and reciprocal; they involve both parent and child, whose responses to one another influence each other's behaviour as part of a dynamic system (Granic and Patterson, 2006). For example, Patterson notes that the families of typical and CD children have different ways of responding to each other. When punished by parents, CD children are twice as likely as normal children to persist in negative behaviour. This is because their family members tend to interact through the use of *negative reinforcement*. Unlike punishment, in which an unpleasant stimulus is applied in order to decrease a behaviour, negative reinforcement increases the likelihood of a behaviour by removing an unpleasant stimulus as the reward.

To illustrate this concept, consider the scenario presented in Fig. 10.6. Who is reinforcing whom? The children have learned that if they

FIGURE 10.6 Coercion.

behave aversively when their mother says no, they can get their way; their mother has inadvertently *positively reinforced* them for whining. Their mother, in turn, has been *negatively reinforced* for giving the children what they want when they misbehave – she is rewarded by the fact that the children cease their misbehaviour.

The cartoon mother has fallen into what Patterson calls the '*reinforcement trap*': she obtains a short-term benefit at the expense of negative long-term consequences. The trap is that, by giving in, she has ended the children's immediate negative behaviour, but has inadvertently increased the likelihood that they will behave the same way in the future. Through the reinforcement trap, children are inadvertently rewarded for aggressiveness and the escalation of coercive behaviour, and parents are rewarded for giving in by the relief they experience when children cease their obstreperousness. However, the parents pay a heavy price. Not only are their socializing efforts negated, but their children's behaviour will become increasingly coercive over time.

Transactional Processes and the Dynamic Systems Perspective

Another significant aspect to Patterson's observations is that they involve *transactional* processes between parents and children, such that they affect and shape one another's behaviour. For example, Dumas and colleagues (1995) studied the interactions between mothers and their children, who were categorized as being socially competent, anxious, or aggressive. Surprisingly, they found that, overall, aggressive children and their mothers shared a positive emotional tone. However, in comparison to other dyads, aggressive children were more likely to use *aversive control techniques*, and their mothers were more likely to *respond indiscriminately* and to *fail to set limits* on their children's more extreme forms of coercion. Thus, they conclude, both parents and young children are active agents in the interaction and reciprocally influence one another.

This appreciation for the transactional nature of parent–child relations has led to an intriguing

dynamic systems perspective on the development of antisocial behaviour (Granic and Patterson, 2006). One of the central concepts of dynamic systems theory is of *attractors*: in essence, patterns of interaction, once established, tend to attract people to behave in ways that are consistent with those patterns. Thus, parents and children come to develop styles of relating that are based on their previous experiences with and expectations of one another. Through the *coupling* of their emotions, appraisals and the behaviour by which they are linked, these patterns become intricately interwoven in the thoughts, feelings and actions of each participant in the relationship. When such patterns are stable and repeated, as they are in the exchanges of parents and children locked in coercive cycles, they become like well-worn ruts in which family members are highly likely to become 'stuck' despite their best intentions. And, unfortunately, those patterns become increasingly fixed and difficult to break free of as development proceeds and earlier patterns *constrain* and limit the opportunities for new patterns to emerge. The theorists use the statistical term 'loss of degrees of freedom' to describe this effect that attractors have on constraining the possibility that history will not repeat itself and that relationships will chart a new course over the process of development. The result is a pathogenic *rigidity* in parent–child relations. Because family members fall repeatedly into a narrow set of behavioural patterns, their repertoires for responding interpersonally to one another – as well as to others outside the family – become limited. As we have seen, inflexible cognitive, emotion regulation and problem-solving strategies help to set the stage for the development of dysfunctional and antisocial behaviour.

In addition, dynamic systems theory predicts that these patterns will result in *escalation* over time: individuals' past experience with these patterns leads them to become sensitized to the slightest indication that a negative exchange is beginning (e.g., a child rolling his eyes, a parent emitting a long sigh) and thus to respond with full-blown hostility to even the mildest of provocations.

Granic and Patterson (2006, p. 108) give an example of just such a dynamic exchange between a hypothetical mother and son:

Feeling anxious, thinking about the many things she needs to get done by the end of the night, a mother presents her son with a vague request to 'Help clean the house'. The boy, busy playing a video game, feels irritated, thinking that his mother always makes him do chores rather than his brother. As these mildly negative emotions and appraisals coalesce, he abruptly refuses his mother's request (e.g., 'I'm busy!'). Her attention is now fully tuned to her son's defiance and her anxiety increases with the expectation that her son will force them into a confrontation. She also begins to feel irritated with his defiance. In an attempt to modulate her anxiety and feelings of irritation, the mother suggests that they could go out to a restaurant afterward if he would just help her. Perceiving his mother as a nag who is interfering with his goal of continuing to play his video games, the son's irritability grows into anger, which he expresses through loud complaining. In turn, his mother's irritable feelings also escalate into anger, overriding her anxiety, and combine with appraisals of her child as 'selfish and rude' and as an obstacle to her goal of finishing her chores. Her hostile emotions and appraisals motivate her to begin threatening her son with extreme consequences or to denigrate him in retaliation and her face settles into a scowl. Perceiving her wrath, the boy likewise escalates, becoming angrier while his appraisals change from mother as nuisance to mother as monster. Soon, these reciprocal interactions among appraisals, emotions and harsh words coalesce. The boy continues playing his video games, ignoring his mother pointedly and angrily, with his hostile perception of her confirmed. His mother, feeling beaten and unable to continue the fight, shifts from anger to contempt, which consolidates along with an appraisal of her child as 'useless' and 'always

bad'. Both dyad members remain in this seething state for the rest of the evening.

A Developmental Perspective on Parenting and Conduct Disorder

Shaw and Bell (1993) review the available evidence regarding how various qualities of parenting contribute to the early-starting developmental pathway to conduct disorder and construct a transactional account of how they might each come into play over the course of childhood. In particular, their model integrates *coercion theory* with research on parent–child *attachment*.

Focusing on attachment during the first phase, from birth to 2 years of age, Shaw and Bell (1993; Shaw et al., 2000) propose that the most important factor is likely to be *parental responsiveness*. Through inconsistent and neglectful caregiving, non-responsive parents may contribute to the development of irritable, impulsive and difficult infants who perceive the parent as unsupportive and unavailable to help them manage upsetting feelings. These conditions set the stage for the second year of life, when the child high in negative emotionality further stresses the parent's tolerance for the 'terrible twos' oppositionality and fits of anger. By age 3, the pattern of relationship between parent and child has coalesced into an internal working model that guides their expectations and behaviour. During this phase, *parental insistence* is hypothesized to take on greater importance. Rather than forming a goal-directed partnership based on mutual negotiation and compromise, parents and children who expect negativity from one another are more likely to initiate coercive and punitive patterns of exchange, which, in turn, contribute to children's further non-compliance and irritability. In the third phase, from 4 to 5 years, the most important factor is *parental inconsistency* in discipline. At this stage, as children's negative models of self and other are carried over into their peer relationships and school behaviour, conduct problems intensify and their ramifications become more serious, requiring increasing parental firmness and consistency. Instead, however, the parents of conduct-disordered children are likely to vacillate between ignoring misbehaviour and employing – or merely threatening – harsh punishment.

In summary, Shaw and Bell's model proposes that a poor attachment in toddlerhood sets the stage for the development of coercive transactions between parent and child, which lead to escalating harshness, conflict and emotional disharmony between the child and the social environment.

Over the past two decades, Shaw and colleagues have initiated a programme of research to test this developmental model. In an initial study, they followed a sample of children from infancy to age 5. Consistent with the model, they found that disorganized attachment was a predictor of disruptive behaviour during the first year, while from the second year onward, maternal personality problems and parent–child conflicts also contributed (Shaw et al., 1996). In a second study, they found that maternal rejection at 24 months was related to externalizing problems at 42 months. Children contributed to negative patterns of exchange, in that child non-compliance interacted with parenting style in order to produce the most powerful predictor of conduct disordered behaviour (Shaw et al., 1998). Subsequently, following these children into school age, the investigators found that risk factors identified at age 2 predicted conduct problems at age 8. Early problem behaviour, maternal depression, low social support and rejecting parenting contributed in an additive and interactive manner to the escalation of child misbehaviour, negative parenting and conflictual parent–child relationships (Shaw et al., 2000). Following these youth up to age 12, the research team found that early child non-compliance was a robust predictor of maternal depression, which in turn predicted teacher and youth reports of antisocial behaviour (Gross et al., 2009). Thus the investigators found compelling evidence for a transactional process in which mother and children affected one another reciprocally; but, in this case, for the worse, contributing as they did to

one another's downwardly spiralling mood and behaviour over time.

Specificity of Parenting Effects

Kim and colleagues (2003) conducted a rare study that addressed the question of *specificity* regarding how parenting contributes differentially to the development of conduct disorder, depression or a combination of the two. The investigators gathered a community sample of 897 African American children and assessed them in two waves, at ages 10 and 12. Results showed that children with both CD and comorbid CD/depression received *less nurturant and involved* parenting than did depressed children. In turn, children with co-occurring problems reported higher levels of *parenting hostility* than did those with depression alone. However, unique to children in the CD-only group, in contrast to those with depression, was a lower level of parental *warmth*.

Family Processes

Turning to whole-family processes, we find that family discord is fertile soil for producing antisocial acting out. In particular, children exposed to *interparental conflict and violence* are likely to develop behaviour problems (Kouros et al., 2010) and longitudinal research shows compellingly that witnessing such violence is predictive of later delinquency (Zinzow et al., 2009a). Further, the children in domestically violent homes are often the targets of their parents' aggression – e.g., youth who develop CD are more likely to have been victims of *childhood maltreatment* (Wilson et al., 2009).

Family stress also increases the likelihood of CD. Children who develop behaviour problems are more likely to come from families that have experienced high levels of negative life events, daily hassles, unemployment, financial hardship, moves and other disruptions. In addition, the family members of disruptive children have few sources of social support and engage in chronic conflict with others in the community (Boden et al., 2010). However, it may be that family stress is not a direct cause of antisocial behaviour, but rather that it acts as an amplifier of other problematic parent–child relationship processes (Dishion and Patterson, 2006).

The Social Context

Children with CD are readily identified by peers, and not for the better. As early as the preschool period, habitual child aggression is associated with subsequent *peer rejection*, which leads, in turn, to further aggressive behaviour (Dishion and Patterson, 2006). For example, Dishion and Patterson (2006) found that peer rejection in the first year of middle school was predictive of gang involvement by the end of the middle school years. Aggressive children gain a *negative reputation* with peers that continues to follow them even when their behaviour improves. Therefore, interactions between conduct disordered children and their peers can contribute to further aggression and problem behaviour.

Caprara and his colleagues in Italy (2001) present an interesting transactional perspective on peer reputation and why it is associated with such stable and unalterable effects: in short, reputations change children's *self-perceptions*. Their research suggests that children's behaviour leads them to gain a reputation among peers and teachers, but that the child's subsequent behaviour is filtered through these expectations. Whereas peers and teachers might ordinarily dismiss as accidental a child's bumping into another child on the playground, the child with a reputation as a bully is more likely to be perceived as purposeful and to receive a reprimand. This feedback from others, in turn, comes to influence the child's self-image and behaviour. Consequently, the child labelled as a bully is more likely to see himself or herself as such and to behave accordingly. In summary, the expectations of others influence the child's behaviour so that he increasingly comes to confirm those very expectations, a process they term 'shared consensus building'.

By middle childhood, whereas aggressive children may be rejected by their prosocial agemates,

Antisocial peer groups may provide youth with a sense of belonging and acceptance.
© Catherine Yeulet

they are apt to be accepted into *antisocial peer groups* that tolerate or even value problem behaviour. Antisocial youths spend most of their time in peer groups with no adult supervision, 'hanging out' on the streets and engaging in risky behaviour. Thus, antisocial youths tend to gravitate towards one another and reinforce one another's behaviour. Notably, almost all crimes committed by youth are committed as part of a peer group (Conger and Simons, 1997). Granic and Dishion (2003) empirically demonstrated the fact that antisocial youth may act as '*attractors*' for one another. Among boys, those who reinforced one another's talk about deviant behaviour during a 30-minute laboratory observation were more likely to engage in problem behaviour later in adolescence. In a subsequent study including both boys and girls, the investigators found that youth who engaged in deviant talk and were more empathically engaged with their deviant peers were the most likely to go on to commit offences (Piehler and Dishion, 2007).

Peer factors also are relevant to another variable predictive of the development of CD during late childhood and adolescence: *early sexual maturation*. Although the initial research suggested that early development was implicated specifically in girls' delinquency whereas late development was problematic for boys (Graber et al., 2004), the large body of cross-national research on this topic now shows that early development increases the risk for both genders (Negriff and Susman, 2011). For example, a study of 9342 Norwegian adolescents found that early developing boys and girls engaged in more theft and vandalism than their peers (Storvoll and Wichstrom, 2002). Although at first blush sexual maturation might be assumed to be a strictly biological factor, the development of secondary sexual characteristics attracts the attention of older deviant peers who draw the youth into risk-taking behaviours, including rule violations and sexual activity (Negriff and Trickett, 2011). Late maturers evidence similar behavioural problems after they biologically 'catch up' with their early maturing peers. However, for girls at least, early maturation is only a risk factor for those who attend mixed-sex schools (Caspi et al., 1993). Those who attend all-female schools are not exposed to the social pressures that make early maturation a predictor of conduct problems for other girls.

Not all youth are equally susceptible to peer influences, however. Vitaro and colleagues (1997) followed a sample of almost 900 boys from age 11 to age 13. Based on teacher reports, they typologized boys and their friends as moderately disruptive, highly disruptive or conforming. Moderately disruptive boys who associated with disruptive peers engaged in more delinquent behaviour as time went on. However, friends appeared to have no impact on the development of behaviour problems in highly disruptive or conforming boys. For these latter two groups of youths, *individual characteristics* seem to be steering their development – in a positive direction when comprised of prosocial traits but in a negative direction when comprised of antisocial tendencies.

In sum, research on the influence of peers indicates that they are a contributing factor but not a determining one. Two different processes seem to be at work that we might term 'pushing' versus 'pulling'. Whereas early aggression may cause a child to be pushed away by prosocial peers, positive attachments to antisocial peers may pull a youth in the direction of engaging in misbehaviour. This latter influence may be particularly important for understanding adolescent onset CD. In fact, association with antisocial peers has a direct effect on delinquency only in the *adolescent onset type*, while *parent socialization* is a more significant causal factor in the *child onset* form of the disorder. For adolescent onset conduct disordered youths, then, antisocial peer influences appear to be essential, while for early onset youths the picture is more complicated.

Finally, keeping our multifactorial developmental model in mind, it also is important to note that youths' tendency to gravitate toward antisocial peers does not come out of the blue, but rather is predicted by poor family relationships earlier in childhood and adolescence (Dishion and Piehler, 2007).

The Cultural Context
The Neighbourhood

A number of neighbourhood factors are associated with the risk of CD, in particular, *poverty, social disorganization* and *community violence* (Lynch, 2003; Tuvblad et al., 2006). For example, whereas most of the children who developed CD in Campbell and colleagues' (2000) study were exposed to multiple risk factors, one sizeable cohort experienced risk in only one domain: they lived in dangerous neighbourhoods. Impoverished inner-city children in the USA are routinely exposed to shocking degrees of violence: Finkelhor and colleagues' (2009) nationally representative survey of 4549 children in the USA found that more than 1 in 4 had been a witness to an act of violence in their neighbourhood or home, including shootings, assaults and, even, murders. Exposure to violence may disinhibit the enacting of violence. For example, in a longitudinal study of 4458 inner-city schoolchildren, Guerra and colleagues (2003) found that from ages 5 to 12, exposure to community violence was associated with increasing levels of aggressive behaviour, engagement in aggressive fantasies and beliefs that aggression is normative and justified.

Another insight into the ways in which exposure to violence may lead to antisocial behaviour is through the development of a sense of *futurelessness*. Compellingly, in a series of interviews with 'hardcore' youth offenders from the streets of Atlanta, Brezina and colleagues (2009) observed a marked lack of faith in the plausibility or even desirability of a future: 'Where I'm from you never know if you gonna live one minute to the next … People die every day'; 'Might be dead by 25, so who cares?' Their data confirmed a link between anticipated death and youth criminal behaviour, even after controlling for other factors. Similarly, in a large nationally representative sample of US adolescents, Borowsky and colleagues (2009) found

that those youth who believed that they would not live past age 35 were at the highest risk for engaging in risky behaviours including criminal activity, substance abuse, unsafe sexual activity, suicide attempts and fight-related injuries.

Also, it is in the neighbourhood that children are most likely to be exposed to *gang culture*. Youth in gang-ridden inner cities may feel that they have few alternatives or even that they must join in order to survive. Tolan and colleagues (2003) examined the relationships among community characteristics (poverty, crime, lack of available resources, absence of neighbourliness and social support), parenting, gang membership and youth violence. The investigators collected longitudinal data from 294 African American and Latino boys, who were assessed annually over a period of six years. The results showed that good parenting was able to partially buffer children from the effects of community disorganization. However, when parenting was poor, youths were more likely to become gang involved, which in turn led to escalating violence over the course of adolescence. Gangs, the authors argue, set a stage for '*deviancy training*', which is quite apart from other influences; therefore, prevention efforts for inner-city youths should concentrate on diverting adolescents from recruitment into gangs in the first place.

In sum, again we see that our model of CD must include multiple interrelated factors. By and large, the effects of the neighbourhood context are mediated by parenting practices (Dishion and Patterson, 2006). Parents who provide warmth, structure and close monitoring can protect their children from the negative influences of stressful, impoverished or violent community environments.

School Environment

The *school* is another aspect of the social environment that can contribute to antisocial behaviour. Kasen and colleagues (2004) found that a school environment characterized by a high degree of conflict (fighting, vandalism, defiant students and teachers unable to maintain order) was related to an increase in CD over a two-year period. Schools may also contribute to the development of antisocial behaviour in more subtle ways. Children quickly determine whether they are perceived by teachers as high or low achievers and develop attitudes toward school in keeping with the attitudes they believe their teachers harbour toward them (McKown and Weinstein, 2008). Those who experience school failure early in their careers develop negative self-perceptions, which lead to hostility and aggression (Stipek, 2001). Further, as they approach adolescence, youths who feel disenfranchised in school develop increasingly negative attitudes toward education and low expectations for themselves, leading them to disengage from the learning process and to leave school early, thereby limiting their prosocial opportunities for achieving success (Strambler and Weinstein, 2010). Antisocial behaviour becomes a likely option.

Media Influences

At a larger social level, the *media* may also play a role in promoting – and even glamorizing – antisocial behaviour. Violence is commonly depicted in many popular television shows and films. Further, violence is perpetrated by heroes as much as by villains and is seldom met with negative consequences (Eron, 2001). Instead, the lesson is largely communicated that violence is an effective method of solving problems and will be rewarded. Research bears out the relationship between television violence and children's behaviour. Children with strong preferences for viewing violent television programmes are more aggressive than their peers, and laboratory studies also show that increased viewing of aggressive material leads to subsequent increases in aggressive behaviour. Further, longitudinal studies also show that children who prefer violent television programmes during elementary school engage in more violent and criminal activity as adults (Huesmann et al., 2003). These effects are enhanced by children's identification with television characters and their belief that fictional television violence reflects reality; are consistent across gender, social class and intellectual ability; and are unaffected by parents' aggression, television viewing habits or attitudes.

Integrative Developmental Model

Patterson and his colleagues have been studying and theorizing about the origins of child conduct problems for over two decades. They provide an integrative developmental model based partly on research and partly on their own observations and experience. (Our presentation is based on an integration of Capaldi and Patterson, 1994; Dishion and Patterson, 2006; Dishion et al., 1995; Granic and Patterson, 2006; Patterson et al., 1989, 1992; Reid et al., 2002; Snyder et al., 2003; in press.)

The process of 'growing' a conduct disordered youth takes place in a series of hierarchical stages that build on and elaborate one another, consistent with the organizational hypothesis of developmental psychopathology. (See Fig. 10.7.) The process begins with a host of risk factors, some of which are in place before the birth of the child. These include low socio-economic status, living in a high-crime neighbourhood, family stress, antisocial parents and the parents' own history of being reared by unskilled caregivers. However, these risk factors do not directly lead to antisocial behaviour. Rather, their effect is mediated by family variables: the basic training camp for antisocial behaviour is the home.

The first stage begins in early childhood and involves *poor parental discipline strategies*, with initial coercive interactions escalating into increasingly punitive exchanges. Other poor parent management skills include little involvement and monitoring of children, inconsistent discipline, lack of positive reinforcement for prosocial behaviour and an absence of effective strategies for solving problems. The products of these dysfunctional family interactions are antisocial, socially unskilled children with low self-esteem.

The next stage occurs in middle childhood when children enter school, where their antisocial behaviour and social incompetence result in *peer rejection* and *poor academic performance*. Failures in these important developmental tasks also

FIGURE 10.7 Patterson's Model of the Development of Conduct Disorder.

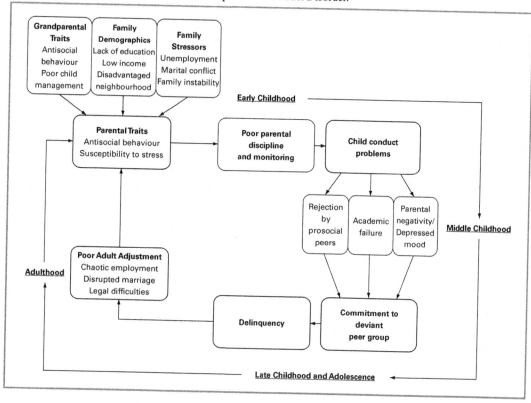

contribute to a *depressed mood*. Further, children who chronically bring home negative reports from teachers are more likely to experience *parent–child conflict* and *parental rejection*.

In adolescence, the youths are drawn to an *antisocial peer group* that has a negative attitude towards school and authority and is involved in delinquent activities, including substance abuse. These antisocial peers support further problem behaviour. As development proceeds, adolescents with an antisocial lifestyle are more likely to have similar difficulties in adulthood, including *chaotic employment* careers, *disrupted marriages* and *institutionalization* for crimes or psychiatric disorders. In late adolescence and adulthood, a process termed *assortative mating* increases the likelihood that antisocial individuals will form relationships with partners with similar personalities and conduct problems. As

stressed, unskilled and antisocial individuals form families and have children of their own, the *intergenerational cycle* is recapitulated.

Intervention

The continuity of CD from childhood to adulthood indicates that this is a psychopathology that becomes entrenched in early development and has long-lasting consequences. Further, other individuals and society pay a high price, in terms of both personal suffering and the financial costs of violence, property destruction, theft and incarceration. Thus, there is an urgent need for prevention and treatment. Yet the multiple roots of CD – cognitive and affective dysfunctions within the child, psychopathology and discord within the family, encouragement from similarly disordered peers and society at large – present major obstacles to success in both undertakings. As Eron and Huesmann (1990) state, intervention with CD 'will take all the knowledge, ingenuity, talent, and persistence we can muster' (p. 154).

Behavioural Approach: Parent Management Training

Parent management training (PMT) is one of the most successful and best documented behavioural programmes (Eyberg et al., 2008). PMT was developed by Patterson (2005) based on his model of maladaptive parent–child relationships as central to the etiology of CD. PMT focuses on altering the interactions between parent and child so that prosocial rather than coercive behaviour is reinforced. As the name implies, this is accomplished by training the parents to interact more effectively with the child, based on the principles of social learning theory. Parents learn to implement a number of behaviour modification techniques, including the use of *positive reinforcement* for prosocial behaviour and the use of *mild punishment* such as the use of a 'time-out' chair. This is a technique with a large body of empirical research behind it, and we will describe it in more detail when we discuss intervention in Chapter 17.

Cognitive Behavioural Intervention: Anger Coping Programme

Larson and Lochman (2002) developed a group intervention for schoolchildren that has demonstrated effectiveness in reducing anger and aggression in a series of investigations. Following from the empirical literature on the developmental psychopathology of aggression, the groups are designed to address core issues such as anger management, perspective-taking, social problem solving, awareness of emotions, relaxation training, social skills, dealing with peer pressure and self-regulation (Lochman et al., 2003). For example, in the groups, children learn self-control techniques, such as calming self-talk, and practise them *in vivo* while other children in the group attempt to taunt and tease them into losing their

cool. The intervention takes place in the school setting and involves both teachers and parents so that they can reinforce children's use of these new skills outside of the groups. Follow-up studies show that the intervention is effective in reducing aggression and disruptive behaviour at both home and school, increasing ontask behaviour and perceived self-competence. Gains have been maintained for as long as three years after children attended the groups.

Systemic Family Treatment
Functional Family Therapy

Functional family therapy (FFT) has garnered an impressive amount of empirical support for the treatment of problem behaviour among young people across clinical settings in Belgium, the UK, the Netherlands, Norway, Sweden, New Zealand and almost all 50 US states (Alexander et al., 1998; in press). The FFT treatment process is structured around five distinct phases. One of the most distinctive characteristics of FFT is the first phase, *Engagement*, in which the therapist uses creative techniques to meet the family 'where it is' and to dissolve barriers to the formation of a therapeutic alliance. The second stage is *Motivation*, in which family strengths are harnessed in order to increase their desire for change and confidence in their ability to affect those changes. The third phase, *Relational assessment*, focuses on understanding the relational functions that family members' behaviour serve, such as whether a youth's misbehaviour is intended to pull a parent towards increased closeness or to achieve a measure of independence. The fourth phase, *Behaviour change*, involves the implementation of an individualized treatment plan to match the unique relational styles and needs of the family. The fifth phase, *Generalization*, fosters the goal of preventing relapse by helping the family to practise the skills they have learned in therapy in relationships outside the family system, to connect with relevant available resources to support the changes they have made, and to connect with new resources in order to facilitate further positive change.

Multisystemic Therapy

Multisystemic therapy (MST) is a well-supported intervention for conduct disorder and has produced an impressive rate of success with some of the most seriously disturbed antisocial youths (Henggeler et al., 2009). MST takes to heart the lesson learned by previous investigators – namely, that there are multiple roots of antisocial behaviour. Although focused on the family system and grounded in family systems theory, the treatment is individualized and flexible, offering a variety of interventions depending on the special needs of the particular youths. Thus, treatment may focus on family disharmony and school underachievement in one case and lack of social skills and parental unemployment in another. The therapist models an active, practical and solution-focused approach: 'You say you didn't understand the teacher's feedback on Casey's school report? Let's give him a call right now and ask for more information.'

Empirical studies show the efficacy of the multisystemic approach with severely conduct disordered youths, including chronically violent adolescents (e.g., Glisson et al., 2010) and sex offenders (e.g., Letourneau et al., 2009). Family communication is improved, with a reduction in family patterns of triangulation and lower levels of conflict between parents and children and between parents themselves. Follow-ups in these treatment studies have shown that for as long as five years following the intervention, youth who receive MST have lower arrest rates than those who receive other forms of treatment.

Culturally Informed Intervention

In keeping with the origins of structural family therapy, which Minuchin developed in his work with inner-city African American families, systemic approaches have been featured in a number of interventions designed to address the specific needs of ethnically diverse populations. An example of a culturally sensitive approach to family therapy is *Familias Unidas*, which was developed to reduce the risk for problem behaviour among Hispanic immigrant youth in the US (Pantin et al., 2007). The intervention is directed towards engaging parents in a participatory process that will assist them in overcoming the stresses of immigration and acculturation to a new society, increase their understanding of risk and protective factors in their child's social world, and help them to develop skills needed to cope effectively with their new cultural environment. In order to address feelings of marginalization and to empower parents, the primary intervention is implemented in small, supportive multi-parent groups, called Parent Support Networks. One of the goals for these groups is 'Bicultural Effectiveness Training', which promotes and honours the home culture's strengths while educating parents about mainstream culture in order to help them better understand and cope with the social contexts their children will encounter. In working with the family as a system, the clinicians strive to reduce conflict, increase cohesion and improve both structure and warmth in the parent–child relationships. Parents are encouraged to become actively involved in their youth's school, to monitor peer activities and to model prosocial skills for their children. Initial investigations of the intervention's effectiveness are promising, with increased parental involvement and decreased behaviour problems over a one-year period.

Prevention

As Kazdin (1997) notes, prevention efforts need to be as multifaceted and broad based as are the risk factors for CD. In a meta-analysis of prevention efforts to date, Piquero and colleagues (2009) found that early family/parent management training has been used to good effect in aggression prevention programmes for kindergarteners and at-risk school-age children conducted in the USA, Canada, the UK, New Zealand, Australia, Hong Kong and the Netherlands. Five, and even 10 years later, those who had undergone these programmes were achieving better in school and demonstrating less antisocial behaviour than untreated youths.

Prevention of School Violence

A particular area of great concern for prevention efforts is the prevention of school violence – not only of the horrific massacres such as the one at the beginning of this chapter, but also of the ordinary, run-of-the-mill bullying that might provoke such outbursts. Over the course of the past two decades, large-scale anti-bullying programmes have been implemented in Norway, Finland, the UK, Ireland and the Netherlands. One of the most impressive efforts is the national anti-bullying programme launched in Finland called KiVa, an acronym for Kiusaamista Vastaan, which means 'against bullying' (Salmivalli et al., 2010). As of 2011, 82 per cent of all public schools in Finland were participants in the programme. One of the unique aspects of the intervention is its focus on encouraging the 'silent majority' of non-involved children to stand up against bullies and to provide support for the victims. The programme takes place on multiple levels, including universal strategies such as psychoeducation against bullying provided in every classroom as well as an anti-bullying computer game for younger children and a virtual reality environment for older children designed to increase their knowledge, skills and motivation to change their behaviour related to bullying. In addition, targeted interventions are provided when cases of bullying are uncovered, including small group discussions with the bullies, victims and bystanders that are conducted by 'school teams' comprised of children and teachers. A parent guide also is provided with information about bullying and suggestions for ways that parents can prevent the problem. The evaluation of the effectiveness of the KiVa programme is ongoing (Salmavalli et al., 2011). It currently involves more than 30 000 students from more than 1000 classrooms in 234 schools who were randomly assigned to either the treatment or a control condition. Results to date are promising, showing that after nine months of implementation, in comparison to the control children, students who receive the intervention report lower levels of both self- and peer-reported victimization and self-reported bullying, are less likely to assist and reinforce the bully, feel better able to defend themselves, and experience higher overall levels of well-being at school (Kärnä et al., 2011).

In the previous five chapters, we have been concerned with disorders whose symptoms lie somewhere along the continuum between normal and abnormal. Depressed feelings, misconduct, anxiety, oppositionality and inattentiveness can all be seen in well-functioning individuals across the lifespan. Our next chapter concerns a disorder that, like autism, lies at the extreme end of the continuum. The pervasive and erratic symptoms of schizophrenia lie far beyond the pale of normal development and thus present a major challenge to our ability to understand and treat the disorder.

CHAPTER 11

Severe Deviation in Late Childhood and Adolescence: Schizophrenia

Chapter contents

Like autism, schizophrenia is a severe, pervasive psychopathology that, in its extreme form, is incapacitating. However, in many other ways the two disorders differ. Historically, poor outcome has often been considered as an integral part of the concept of schizophrenia. Thus, 'schizophrenia' illness has become synonymous with a 'chronic, debilitating mental illness' and according to the World Health Organization (2001) is the seventh most disabling disease in the world. The overall cost of schizophrenia in the USA in 2002 was estimated to be $63 billion (Wu et al., 2005). In this chapter we present schizophrenia's descriptive characteristics and reconstruct its developmental pathway, including both risk and protective factors.

Definition and Characteristics

Definition

During the first third of the twentieth century, schizophrenia in children and adults was seen as essentially the same disorder with a broadly similar clinical presentation. In the 1930s, however, an alternative 'unitary' view of childhood psychoses was proposed which intertwined the present day concepts of autism, schizophrenia, schizotypal and borderline personality disorder (Fish and Rivito, 1979; Potter, 1933). From the mid-1930s until the 1970s the concepts of autism and childhood schizophrenia were synonymous, with autism and other developmental disorders viewed as early manifestations of adult schizophrenia. This perspective was featured by DSM-II and ICD-8 which grouped all childhood onset psychoses, including autism, under a separate category of 'childhood schizophrenia'. However, the 'unitary' view of childhood psychoses was challenged in the 1970s, following the landmark studies of Kolvin (1971) and Rutter (1972) who demonstrated that autism and childhood onset schizophrenia could be distinguished in terms of age at onset, phenomenology and family history. This led to the differentiation of adult-type schizophrenia with childhood onset from autism. Hence, in the last third of the twentieth century, the pendulum swung back to the view that schizophrenia in children and adolescents should be defined using unmodified adult diagnostic criteria. This view was endorsed by DSM-III (American Psychiatric Association, 1980) and ICD-9 (World Health Organization, 1978), and has been maintained in DSM-IV (American Psychiatric Association, 1994) and ICD-10 (World Health Organization, 1992), with the removal of the separate category of 'childhood schizophrenia' and the application of the same diagnostic criteria at all ages.

The relevant DSM-IV-TR criteria for schizophrenia are presented in Table 11.1. The symptoms of schizophrenia have been clustered into three groups: positive, negative and disorganized. *Positive symptoms* involve the presence of thought disorders, delusions and hallucinations. *Negative symptoms* involve the absence of sociability, pleasure, energy and affect. A third cluster of symptoms, *disorganized behaviour*, includes disorganized speech, bizarre behaviour and poor attention. It is important to note that the requirements that need to be fulfilled for a diagnosis of schizophrenia are not the same in the different diagnostic classification systems; for example, ICD-10 required characteristic symptoms to have been present for at least one month, and the DSM-IV for at least six continuous months, raising questions about the validity of each system. However, both classification systems allow non-specific prodromal and residual symptoms to be included in the duration of symptoms. In addition, the diagnostic process must confirm social and occupational dysfunction and it must exclude mood disorders, substance abuse and general medical conditions. If a primary diagnosis of autism spectrum disorder exists, the diagnosis of schizophrenia must include clear hallucinations or delusions.

Hallucinations are sensory perceptions occurring in the absence of any appropriate external stimuli. They are a common phenomena in traditional as well as in modern societies, occurring in approximately 80 per cent of cases. However, prevalence and notions concerning etiology, course and the need for treatment differ to a larger extent. Non-western cultures often attribute altered states of perception like hallucinations to possession by spirits or an attempt to establish a contact with a spirit, whereas modern western societies often regard these phenomena as symptoms of mental illness. Auditory hallucinations, such as hearing a voice saying 'You are evil and should die', are more frequent than visual hallucinations, such as seeing a ghost with a burned and scarred face. In fact, auditory hallucinations are considered by many as being pathogenic to the disorder and are similarly observed in both adult and children populations.

TABLE 11.1 DSM-IV-TR Criteria for Schizophrenia

A. *Characteristic symptoms*: Two (or more) of the following, each present for a significant portion of time during a 1-month period:
   (1) Delusions
   (2) Hallucinations
   (3) Disorganized speech (e.g., frequent derailment or incoherence)
   (4) Grossly disorganized or catatonic behavior
   (5) Negative symptoms (i.e., affective flattening, alogia, or avolition)
B. *Social/occupational dysfunction*: When the onset is in childhood, failure to achieve expected level of interpersonal, academic, or occupational achievement.
C. *Duration*: Continuous signs of disturbance persist for at least 6 months.
D. *Relationship to a pervasive developmental disorder*: If there is a history of autism or other PDD, the diagnosis of schizophrenia is added only if prominent delusions or hallucinations are present for at least a month.

Source: Adapted with permission from the *Diagnostic and Statistical Manual of Mental Disorders*, Fourth Edition Text Revision. Copyright 2000 by the American Psychiatric Association.

The structure of hallucinations increases in complexity with age, while the content reflects age-appropriate concerns; for example, younger children have hallucinations about monsters and pets, while older children's hallucinations may involve sex. (See Russell et al., 1989.) Parents may have reason for concern if a child of 7 years or older hears voices saying derogatory things about him or her, or voices conversing with one another, talks to himself or herself, or even stares at scary things, snakes, spiders or shadows that are not really there. While hallucinations seem to be evident in children, they are relatively less well formed than in adult onset cases.

Hallucinations are not unique to schizophrenia. They may occur in response to drugs, but also are found in a number of other psychiatric disorders. For example, Altman et al. (1997) found that 33 per cent of psychiatrically disturbed but non-schizophrenic individuals reported hallucinations. They were particularly frequent in individuals with Posttraumatic stress disorder. Hallucinations also can be found in typically developing populations. Preschoolers, for example, can have transient hallucinations in response to acute situational stress; for example, they may feel bugs crawling over their skin or see bugs in their beds (Volkmar et al., 1995).

Delusions are firmly held irrational beliefs that run counter to reality. (See Table 11.2.) Delusions are a very prominent symptom but are less frequent in children and adolescents, particularly under the age of 10 (Remschmidt et al., 2007). Approximately 50 per cent of those with childhood onset will have delusions. As with hallucinations, delusions become more complex over the course of development, while their content reflects age-appropriate concerns; for example, a younger boy might believe his stepfather wants to poison him, while an older girl might think children at school are plotting to kidnap and molest her. These two examples illustrate delusions of *persecution*. There are *somatic*

TABLE 11.2 Frequency of Children's Self-reported Psychotic Symptoms

Psychotic Symptoms	No. (percentage) of 2127 children	
	Probable Symptom	Definite Symptom
Hallucinations		
Have you heard voices that other people cannot hear?	169 (7.9)	90 (4.2)
Have you ever seen something or someone that other people could not see?	168 (7.9)	42 (2.0)
Delusions		
Have you ever thought you were spied on?	54 (2.5)	15 (0.7)
Have you ever felt like you were under the control of some special power?	41 (1.9)	16 (0.8)
Have you ever known what another person was thinking, even though that person wasn't speaking, like read their mind?	14 (0.7)	5 (0.2)
Have you ever believed that you were sent special messages through television or radio?	26 (1.2)	3 (0.1)
Have other people ever read your thoughts?	9 (0.4)	0

Source: Adapted from Polanczyk et al., 2010.

delusions, such as believing the body is emitting a foul odour or faeces will come out of the mouth if the child speaks, and there are also delusions of *grandeur*, as in the example of a boy flipping through the pages of a book he has never seen before and claiming he knows everything the books says. Like hallucinations, delusions can also be found in disturbed but non-schizophrenic populations. For example, Altman et al. (1997) found that 24 per cent of disturbed, non-schizophrenic individuals had delusional ideas. Bizarre delusional content is considered a sufficient diagnostic feature of schizophrenia in the DSM-IV-TR as long as course and social dysfunction criteria are met. However, it is often argued that bizarreness is difficult to quantify and thereby exists limited reliability of assigning bizarreness to delusions (Cermolacce et al., 2010).

Disorganized speech often involves loose associations and illogical reasoning in which the child's language may be fragmented, dissociated and bizarre. For example:

> It's open in front but closed behind. I'm open in front but closed behind. Did you see me today? I think I was here, but Mommy wasn't. They don't take it away from Mommy. My dolly won't mind. I won't mind. [Enumerates all the family members who won't mind.] I was here yesterday. Was I here today?

The primary irregularities in the speech of those with schizophrenia involve: *pragmatics*, or the social use of language; *prosody*, or the melody of speech; *auditory processing*, or attending to what others say while ignoring irrelevant information; and *abstract language*. However, it is important to note that these peculiarities are seen in autism as well as in children with schizophrenia. (See Baltaxe and Simmons, 1995.)

Disorganized behaviour would be taking all the puzzle pieces out of a box then putting them back a hundred times. It may be expressed by facial grimaces; odd postures and movements, such as persistent rocking while standing or sitting; dishevelled or bizarre dress, such as wearing multiple coats, scarves and hats on a hot day; unpredictable

agitation; or bizarre, repetitive actions such as incessantly rubbing the forehead or slapping the wrist or scratching the skin to the point of producing bleeding sores. *Catatonic behaviour* involves a marked lack of reactivity to the environment, which may include long periods of immobility (catatonic stupor); assuming inappropriate and bizarre poses (catatonic posturing); or purposeless excessive motor activity (catatonic excitement).

Social dysfunction may take a number of forms. Withdrawal is common, with children with schizophrenia often being oblivious to others, excessively preoccupied with their own thoughts, or puzzled by things happening around them. Lack of social skills may contribute to social isolation, particularly in regard to peers.

Negative symptoms like flattening, alogia or avolition (Mash and Wolfe, 2002). Affective flattening is when someone shows no emotions. Alogia is when someone does not speak very much. Finally, avolition is when someone cannot start or complete a job.

Subtypes of Schizophrenia

Subtypes are based on the prominent symptoms that are displayed. The *paranoid* type is characterized by the presence of significant delusions and sometimes auditory hallucinations of a persecutory or grandiose nature. This is the type with the best prognosis (Walker et al., 2004), but is rarely seen in childhood. The *disorganized* type, in contrast, has the worst prognosis and is the one that is most commonly observed in children. It is characterized by flat affect or emotions that are not appropriate to the content of the child's speech (e.g., silly laughter while talking about a lost pet); and disorganized behaviour and disorganized speech that is odd, tangential and not goal oriented. The *catatonic* type mainly displays psychomotor disturbances, including excessive rigidity, immobility, mutism, echolalia (parrot-like repetition of the words just spoken by another) or echopraxia (repetitive imitation of another's movements). The *undifferentiated* type includes none of the above features. In the *residual* type, the individual has undergone at least one psychotic episode in the past, but at present is not actively psychotic but shows some symptoms of the disturbance (e.g., flat affect, disorganized speech, odd beliefs).

While subtypes attempt to address the heterogeneity of the illness, subtypes are based upon the combination of several clinical features none of which is unique to the subtype (e.g., disorganized can be observed within the catatonic subtype). Importantly, defining symptoms of subtypes are also not unique to schizophrenia, such that catatonia may in fact be more common in certain mood disorders and in other medical conditions (Rosebush and Mazurek, 2010). To date the importance placed upon different symptoms and course types associated with schizophrenia has been found to be as heteregenous as the disorder itself.

Characteristics
Age of Onset
For our purposes the most important descriptive characteristic of schizophrenia is that it has two ages of onset: early onset (or childhood onset),

which means it occurs prior to 14 to 15 years of age, and adolescent onset, which occurs between 14 to 15 years and young adulthood.

Prevalence
Childhood onset schizophrenia is very rare and the incidence of schizophrenia rises steadily through adolescence before peaking in early adult life. In fact it is estimated that only 1 child in 40 000 will become schizophrenic compared to 1 in every 100 adults. Because this diagnosis is so rare in children, it is also difficult to study, which prevents us from drawing firm conclusions from the research. After childhood the number of cases of schizophrenia rises dramatically, with one study showing an approximately tenfold increase in children between 12 and 15 years of age. This dramatic increase seems specific to schizophrenia, since it is not found in the other childhood psychotic reactions, such as those that occur in severe major depression or manic episodes (Häfner and Nowotny, 1995). (See Fig. 11.1.) An estimated 39 per cent of males and 23 per cent of females

FIGURE 11.1 Increase in Schizophrenia in Adolescence.

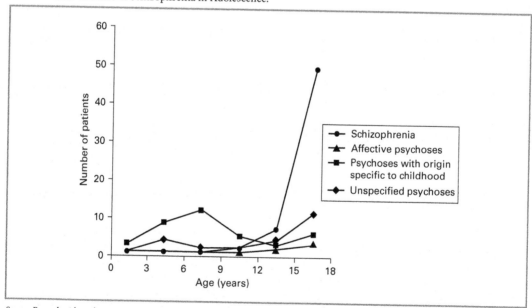

Source: Remschmidt et al., 1994.

with schizophrenia will develop the illness by the age of 19, with the average age of onset being 18 years in men and 25 years in women.

Gender Differences

There is substantial evidence to suggest that males appear to be more susceptible to developing schizophrenia than females and often show a more severe form of the disorder with a more malignant course. There is also an interesting gender shift with age: males predominate in early onset cases, with a male-to-female ratio between 2 to 1 and 5 to 1, while the rates for males and females are more even in adolescence (Asarnow and Asarnow, 2003). The reasons for this shift are not known, but might reflect differences in etiology across gender or else the unfolding of normative maturational changes that emerge earlier for boys (Spauwen et al., 2003). It has been suggested that the later onset among women may be related to a protective effect of oestrogens during puberty. Others have argued that it is the higher social skills attributed to females that provide protection to developing the disorder. We will return to this suggestion later in the chapter.

Socio-economic Status, Ethnicity and Culture

While studies of adults with schizophrenia show an excess of cases from *socio-economically underprivileged* groups, studies of children and adolescents have yielded equivocal findings (Asarnow and Asarnow, 2003). No evidence exists for different prevalence for children and adolescents from different *ethnic* groups (Yee and Sigman, 1998). Symptoms and incidence of schizophrenia in adults are highly similar across countries and cultures, although attitudes to care and resources devoted to mental health care differ between countries (Papageorgioua et al., 2011). Comparable data on children are not available.

Comorbidity

Taking child and adolescent onset schizophrenia together, there is evidence of a high rate of comorbidity. Russell et al. (1989), for example, found that 68 per cent of cases had another diagnosis, with *depression* being the most frequent (37 per cent) followed closely by *conduct disorder* or *oppositional defiant disorder* (31 per cent).

Obsessive compulsive disorder (OCD) appears to commonly co-occur in adolescents. Nechmad and colleagues (2003) found that in a sample of 50 adolescents with schizophrenia, 26 per cent met DSM-IV criteria for OCD.

In addition, youths with schizophrenia also often show *suicidal* ideation and behaviour (Shoval et al., 2011). The highest risk for suicide appears to be in the two years following the first psychotic episode. Suicide during this period is predicted by a history of self-harming behaviour, prolonged duration of psychosis, a deteriorating course and substance abuse. For example, Verdoux and colleagues (2001) found that youths who abused substances during the first two years after a psychotic break were seven times more likely to attempt suicide. Aguilar and colleagues (2003) found that among adolescents and adults with schizophrenia who attempted suicide, two distinct clinical types could be differentiated based upon the reasons that predominated: *psychotic* (e.g., rationales derived from delusional thinking) and *depressive*. To understand how psychosis might lead to suicide, it is important to recognize how terrifying and bewildering a psychotic episode can be, and how devastating to confront the fact that one has a chronic mental illness in which such episodes are likely to recur. (See Box 11.1.)

Previous studies using clinical scales – such as the Schedule for Affective Disorders and Schizophrenia for School-Age Children (K-SADS) and the Social Adjustment Inventory for Children and Adolescents (SAICA) in which the parents report on behavioural problems in childhood or different interviews – have reported extensive symptomatology in children thought to be at high risk (HR) for developing schizophrenia. More specifically, studies based on the DSM have shown high rates (54–60 per cent) of axis 1 disorders in HR children (Keshaven et al., 2008) compared to 10–22 per cent found in the general population. In addition, elevated rates of comorbidity (30 per cent) have been reported with the most frequent

---

Box 11.1 Case Study: A First-Person Account of Adolescent Onset Schizophrenia

'During the second semester of my senior year, I had only a three-hour carpentry course at South Side High School, so in the afternoon I took a job at the pizzeria as a cook. One day at the pizzeria, when I started doing the cooking and the prep work, Pat, Kelly, and the boss started talking around in circles. It seemed as though the devil was taking over their bodies when they talked to me. Kelly started talking on the phone, and it seemed he was using a voice other than his own. That confused me. I was even more confused when he told me that I didn't have to work for the rest of the day.

I drove home and found no one there. I tried to sleep on the couch, but I couldn't. I got up and went to my car. I started it up and drove to my high school. I met Scott, a friend, there and tried to tell him what was bothering me, but he was between classes and didn't have much time to talk. I went to the school library where I found Bill. But he wasn't much help either. Then I walked over to the school office where I decided to call the police and tell them of my problem of hearing strange voices. I asked if the Police Chief would come and listen to what I had to say.

He did. He picked me up at school, drove me around, and listened to me. Finally, he had me drive my car to the police station where I talked with another police officer. The police officer called my parents. Soon the four of us were in a room. My father seemed to understand me. My mother and the police officer were talking with me, but it seemed my father was playing with them with his thoughts... At home, my brother Alex and our pets appeared different, as though my father was using them with his brain. My father could take over people's minds and bodies with his brain waves. My father and I would watch television together and communicate without saying a word. My father's friends from work had a club of people who practiced brainwashing different people. They wanted to practice on me. They took over the entire household except for me and my father. My father and I would think of different people or objects. We did this to block out minds so they couldn't capture our minds or bodies. They gave up the next day.

My parents took me to the Lake City Hospital to find out what was happening to me. At the hospital we met my family doctor and a couple of other people, none of whom could figure out what was happening to me. They asked questions, took my blood pressure, and took blood samples. I tried to leave that night. I was urged on by a song from ABBA, but two big guys in white coats took me back to my room. The next morning when I was served my breakfast, I tasted and smelled my food a little before I ate it all.'

Source: Emmons et al. 1997.

---

being ADHD (10–40 per cent), anxiety disorders (13–39 per cent) and affective disorders including depression and bipolar disorders (10–17 per cent) (Hans et al., 2004).

Differential Diagnosis

As we mentioned at the outset of this chapter, schizophrenia must be differentiated from *autism*. In the past, it was believed that both schizophrenia and autism should be regarded as two manifestations of the same underlying psychopathology. The data, however, have not supported this assumption. While it is true that some children with autism later develop schizophrenia, they do so at no higher rate than children in the general population (Klinger et al., 1996). The clinical picture of the two is different also in that autism lacks the delusions and hallucinations, the loose associations and the mood disturbances that characterize schizophrenia. The age of onset and developmental course are also different. Children with childhood onset schizophrenia have a later age of onset than autistic children such that autism appears in the first 30 months of life, whereas schizophrenia begins in later childhood or adolescence. Schizophrenia also is marked by progressive declines in functioning; autism is highly stable. (See Table 11.3 for further detail.) Schizophrenics also show less intellectual impairment, display less severe social and language deficits, develop hallucinations and delusions as they get older and experience periods of remission and relapse (Mash and Wolfe, 2010).

TABLE 11.3 Summary of Pre-morbid Developmental Predictors of Schizophrenia

Developmental Deviations	Developmental Periods			
	Infancy	Toddler-Preschool	Middle Childhood	Adolescence
Motor and Sensory	Lags in gross and fine co-ordination; movement abnormalities	Lags in gross and fine co-ordination	Deviant but not specific to or predictive of schizophrenia	Clumsy but no longer deviant
Passivity	Underaroused and unresponsive; poor muscle tone	Low energy level		
Speech	Little babbling and imitation	Delayed; poor communication	Vague, confused, unclear	
Social Adjustment	Socially odd, unresponsive, flat affect, poor eye contact	'Loner', 'hyper'; anxious and hostile with peers	Increased disturbance in boys only	
Attention			Attention deficits	Distractible
Cognitive and Achievement Scores			Below average	Significant declines

Schizophrenia is not the only disorder in which psychotic symptoms are seen. Therefore, it is important to distinguish between schizophrenia and severe mood disorders, including *major depression with psychotic features* and *bipolar disorder* (see Chapter 9), both of which involve the acute onset of psychotic symptoms consequent to a dramatic shift in mood state. However, there appear to be relationships among these disorders in that longitudinal research shows that some youths who initially present with schizophrenia go on to develop bipolar illness (McClellan et al., 2001).

DSM-IV-TR also includes a diagnosis of *schizoaffective disorder*, which stands at the boundary between mood disorder and psychosis, including some but not all of the characteristics of each. The prognosis for schizoaffective disorder also lies on the middle of the continuum, better than schizophrenia but worse than a simple mood disorder (Walker et al., 2004).

Another identified group of children are diagnosed with atypical psychosis or *multidimensionally impaired disorder* (MDI) (Jacobsen and Rapoport, 1998). These children do not meet the full criteria for schizophrenia, but exhibit symptoms in the spectrum such as delusions, hallucinations, affect dysregulation, poor impulse control and inattention. Longitudinal research shows that children with MDI have an earlier age of onset and more severe cognitive and behavioural difficulties than do children with schizophrenia. Further, results of a long-term follow-up showed that half of the children with MDI later developed severe mood disorders, with or without psychotic symptoms, while the other half went on to develop disruptive behaviour disorders with no signs of psychosis. These findings have suggested to investigators in the field that MDI is a separate diagnostic entity from schizophrenia, with different precursors and consequences.

The Developmental Dimension

Is all schizophrenia one? Evidence to date suggests that child onset schizophrenia and adolescent onset schizophrenia share essentially the same features with the adult disorder and can be diagnosed with the same criteria (Asarnow et al., 2004). The similarities include not only the symptoms that characterize the disorder but also the findings concerning genetic transmission, autonomic functioning, and brain structure and function. Compared to patients with adult onset schizophrenia, early onset schizophrenia appears to be associated with higher rates of pre-morbid abnormalities, poorer cognitive performance and is associated with worse functional outcomes. Developmental delays in reaching crucial milestones are frequently reported and impairments are found in language (23 per cent), motor (31 per cent) and social functioning (36 per cent) (Hollis, 1995). Additionally, Kyriakopoulos and Frangou (2007) believe that rather than being a distinct form of schizophrenia, the early onset (prior to the age of 18) or childhood onset schizophrenia (COS) is a rarer and possibly a more severe form of adult onset schizophrenia with poorer long-term outcome expected. Early onset schizophrenia also shows high diagnostic stability over time.

While the data regarding childhood schizophrenia are limited, however, a number of developmental differences have emerged. (Here we follow Asarnow and Asarnow, 2003.)

Onset

First, childhood schizophrenia typically has a slow, insidious onset rather than an acute one. Therefore, children show a course of chronic impairment preceding the diagnosis of the disorder, complicating the delineation of the precise age of onset of the disorder as well as making it difficult to differentiate pre-morbid (pre-existing) or comorbid symptoms. For example, children often present with symptoms of ADHD prior to and during psychotic episodes. Does this mean that ADHD is a developmental precursor to schizophrenia, an earlier manifestation of the illness, a comorbid disorder, or merely a mislabelling of the disorganized thinking and behaviour characteristic of schizophrenia? As yet, we do not know and further prospective longitudinal research will be essential to answering these questions.

Symptoms

In regard to clinical manifestations, there are differences between the symptoms of child onset and adult schizophrenia. Delusions, hallucinations and formal thought disorder are rarely seen prior to age 7. Delusions in particular are less frequent in children than in adults. While all subtypes of schizophrenia may be seen in adolescence, young people are more likely to present with the disorganized or undifferentiated subtypes and more rarely with the paranoid subtype. Initial symptoms in early stages include difficulty concentrating, sleeping or doing schoolwork and may include starting to avoid friends. As the illness progresses, incoherent speech may occur, as well as beginning to see or hear things that no one else does. Illogical thinking lapses, hallucinations, paranoia, delusions, grandiose ideas, violence and suicide ideation can occur. While schizophrenia sometimes begins as an acute psychotic episode in young adults, it emerges gradually in children, often preceded by developmental disturbances, such as lags in motor and speech/language development.

The symptoms and social impairment are also more severe in children than they are in adults, while the outcome is less favourable. In regard to sex differences, the shift to a comparable number of males and females in adolescence is not typical of adults, for which males outnumber females.

However, because the signs and symptoms differ across development, there is concern that diagnosticians may overlook children who are beginning to show early signs of the disorder but do not meet the full adult criteria. Ideally, the diagnostic criteria would be adjusted to account for such developmental trends in clinical presentation. As childhood onset schizophrenia may be expressed differently at different ages, it is important to adjust the diagnostic criteria for developmental changes, to overcome issues such as distinguishing between pathological symptoms and rich imaginative fantasies of childhood, or disorganised speech during language skills development (Mash and Wolfe, 2010).

Normative Developmental Processes

The diagnosis of schizophrenia in young children also is complicated by immaturities in language and cognitive skills. Children's inability to describe their inner experiences makes it difficult for the clinician to evaluate their internal states and perceptions. Further, as we know, young children are in the pre-operational stage of development, during which magical beliefs abound and the boundary between reality and fantasy is diffuse. (For example, consider the third scenario presented in the opening to Chapter 1.) Misdiagnosis of schizophrenia in children is all too common. It is distinguished from autism by the persistence of hallucinations and delusions for at least six months, and a later age of onset – 7 years or older. Autism is usually diagnosed by age 3. Schizophrenia is also distinguished from a type of brief psychosis sometimes seen in affective, personality and dissociative disorders in children. Adolescents with bipolar disorder sometimes have acute onset of manic episodes that may be mistaken for schizophrenia. Children who have been victims of abuse may sometimes claim to hear voices of, or see visions of, the abuser. Symptoms of schizophrenia characteristically pervade the child's life, and are not limited to just certain situations, such as at school. If children show any interest in friendships, even if they fail at maintaining them, it is unlikely that they have schizophrenia. Consequently, careful

thought must be given to discriminating between psychotic thinking or delusional ideas and the normative magical thought processes of early childhood. Similarly, children lagging in language development may communicate in ways that strike the listener as illogical and disorganized, but that should not be confused with true thought disorder.

Developmental Pathways to Schizophrenia

Identifying Precursors to Schizophrenia

The developmental unfolding of schizophrenia is divided into three phases: the *pre-morbid* phase, prior to the onset of the disorder; the *prodromal* phase, during which the early signs of the disorder begin to emerge; and the *acute* phase, in which the full-blown syndrome is evident. Subsequently, phases of recovery, residual and/or chronic symptomatology may be seen. (See Fig. 11.2.) Discovering precursors to the disorder is important both to understanding the nature of the psychopathology and to developing programmes aimed at preventing its occurrence. While prospective longitudinal data provide the best evidence for isolating causal factors, gathering such

FIGURE 11.2 Natural Course of Schizophrenia Showing the Time Frame for Critical Phases of the Schizophrenic Illness.

The horizontal line represents the time dimension; the vertical dimension represents functional decline.

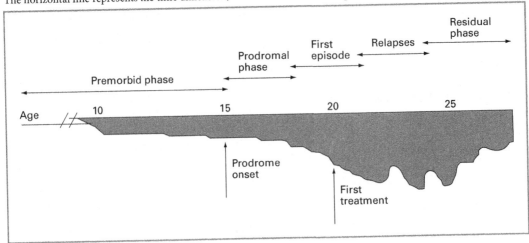

Source: Keshaven, 2003.

data is a difficult undertaking in the case of schizophrenia. Let us consider why.

Methodological Challenges

For one thing, longitudinal data that follow children from their earliest years to the onset of the disorder are few and far between – and for good reason, given the daunting methodological difficulties of locating cases in such a rare disturbance. With schizophrenia occurring in less than 1 per cent of the population, one would have to follow 10 000 randomly selected infants in order to obtain approximately 10 adolescents who will develop the disorder. While such a study is extremely rare, we will in fact encounter some impressive examples. For example, the National Child Development Study (NCDS) included 98 per cent of all births in England, Scotland and Wales registered from 3 March to 9 March 1958, and evaluated the participants again when they were 7, 11, 16 and 23 years of age (Crow et al., 1995). But consider the effort and cost involved. Of the 12 537 individuals in the final sample, the investigators identified 57 with schizophrenia.

Even with such impressive prospective longitudinal data, the pre-morbid and prodromal stages are difficult to distinguish. The onset of the disorder is preceded by a long period of behavioural deviations, some of them subtle and some of them with origins in the very early stages of life. To what extent are these deviations in early childhood truly pre-morbid, and to what extent do they represent a prodrome of the full disorder? This remains a matter for debate and further research.

Diversity in Schizophrenia

The nature of schizophrenia itself further complicates matters, given that the disorder is not a single entity but rather is a family of disturbances with a number of subtypes. Virtually no two patients present the same constellation of symptoms. Moreover, even in the same patient, symptoms can show dramatic change over time and there appears to be significant interplay between different sets of symptoms. For example, secondary negative symptoms might be ameliorated with resolution of positive symptoms, while core 'deficit' negative symptoms are more enduring but can worsen over the longitudinal course of the illness. This complexity gives rise to a research dilemma: either study subtypes, thereby reducing the typically small number of cases even further, or combine the data from the entire group and risk obscuring findings concerning subtypes. Further, both the symptom picture and the definition of schizophrenia itself change over time, presenting the researcher with a moving target. The problem of attrition, although common to all longitudinal studies, is even more acute in severely disturbed populations who are the most likely to drop out of the research as time goes on, either because of uncooperativeness or because they have drifted on to other locations without leaving a way to be reached.

Last, there is evidence that not all children who will become schizophrenic travel the same path; on the contrary, they may take distinctly different routes. Therefore, we will also need to examine these differences among pathways.

With these challenges and limitations in mind, we now review the available evidence.

Pre-morbid Development
Infancy
Motor and Sensory Deviations

Deviations in motor and sensory development along with passivity and deviant speech characterize infants at risk for becoming schizophrenic (Gooding and Iacono, 1995). More specifically, there is a lag in motor and sensory development and deficiencies in gross and fine motor co-ordination. Walker et al. (1994) also found in at-risk children limb position and movement abnormalities, including choreoathetoid movements (i.e., involuntary twisting and slow, irregular, snakelike movements). All of these motor abnormalities are at their height in the first two years of life and subsequently diminish. *Passivity* is evidenced by the at-risk infant's being underaroused and unresponsive to external stimuli, by poor alertness and orientation, and by poor muscle tone. There is some evidence that passivity may be predictive of adult schizophrenia (Gooding and Iacono, 1995).

Speech Delay

Finally, there is deviant speech development evidenced by the paucity of babbling and slowness in imitating sounds (Watkins et al., 1988).

Attachment Disturbances

Only two studies concern attachment, and their findings are inconclusive. A special subgroup of at-risk neonates were found to be less cuddly and consolable, but this did not characterize the group as a whole (Watt et al., 1984). There is evidence that separation from the caregiver in the first year increases the risk for schizophrenia, but only in infants already at genetic risk (i.e., whose mothers are also schizophrenic) (Olin and Mednick, 1996).

Toddlerhood Through Preschool
Motor and Language Deficits

Many of the deviations in infancy continue into the toddler preschool period: the abnormality in gross and fine motor co-ordination, the passivity and low energy level, seriously delayed speech, and poor communication. The most significant impairments are seen in children who have an early onset of psychosis; for example, Nicholson and colleagues (2000) found pre-morbid deficits in speech and language and motor development in 50 per cent of those who developed schizophrenia by 12 years of age.

Socio-emotional Deviations

Cantor (1988) and Watkins et al. (1988) found social oddities, including a preference for being alone, perseverative play and being 'hyper' with peers, along with bizarre responses to the social environment. The children may be anxious and hostile with others and yet be affectively flat, withdrawn and isolated in their relationship with their mothers. The meagre data on parenting by mothers who are schizophrenic suggest that they are less affectionately involved, more hostile and less stimulating than mothers in control groups.

In an ingenious study, Walker and Lewine (1990) obtained home movies of five adult onset schizophrenic patients and their healthy siblings taken during infancy and early childhood. The films were viewed by 19 judges who were blind to the psychiatric outcome of the participants. Although none of the participants had any identified psychiatric disorders in childhood, those who went on to develop schizophrenia were reliably identified by virtue of their lack of responsiveness, poor eye contact, flat affect, and poor fine and gross motor co-ordination.

Middle Childhood
Motoric Deficits

As is found in the toddler years, children at increased risk for schizophrenia display more neuromotoric deficits, particularly those reflecting motoric 'overflow' (e.g., tremors, involuntary repetitive movements). Further, in their study of 6-year-olds at risk for schizophrenia, McNeil and colleagues (2003) found that children with neuromotoric deficits were more likely than their peers to display a host of other psychiatric diagnoses, anxiety proneness, interpersonal difficulties and poor general functioning. Thus, motor difficulties potentially identify a subgroup that is particularly vulnerable to the development of schizophrenia and other disorders.

Attention Deficits

Attention deficits are both temporally stable and predictive of future development of schizophrenia. These deficits are evidenced on a number of tasks: the ability to repeat numbers forward and backward, letter cancellation and the ability to detect a given letter in an array of other letters presented at a very brief interval (Gooding and Iacono, 1995).

Social Deficits

The social deficits in child and adolescent onset schizophrenia are pervasive and significant, more so than in the adult onset version of the disorder (Hollis, 2003). As a matter of fact, many of these children demonstrate symptoms consistent with Asperger syndrome, autism, or other forms of pervasive developmental disorder during the pre-morbid phase.

Pre-morbid social withdrawal, poor interpersonal relationships and social skills deficits are specifically predictive of negative symptoms in early onset schizophrenia, including affective flattening, asociability and poverty of speech (McClellan et al.,

2003). The evidence concerning positive symptoms of schizophrenia is inconsistent, with one study finding schizophrenia to be related to excitability, aggression and disruptive behaviours in childhood and two other studies finding no relation. Thus, negative symptoms may reflect enduring predispositions and have roots in the pre-morbid phase of the disturbance, while positive symptoms may not have such roots (Walker et al., 1996).

Cognitive and Achievement Deficits
In regard to general intelligence and academic achievement, Crow et al.'s (1995) NCDS found widespread impairment in children who went on to develop schizophrenia. Not only was a measure of general intelligence below that of all other groups, but reading and arithmetic achievement also significantly lagged. Further, studies show that pre-morbid intelligence, language, reading and spelling are more negatively affected in those with early onset schizophrenia than those with the adult onset form of the disorder (Hollis, 2004; Vourdas et al., 2003). When we describe studies of brain development in children with schizophrenia later in this chapter, the likely reason will become clear.

General Psychopathology
Children destined to develop schizophrenia stand out from their peers in ways that often will call them to the attention of mental health professionals. Roff and Fultz (2003) conducted a study of 148 boys who were seen in mental health clinics prior to the onset of schizophrenia. Those who later went on to receive the diagnosis were distinguished from other clinic boys by virtue of having more problems in the areas of attention, memory and motor co-ordination. They were also more generally disturbed than the other boys. The authors suggest a developmental pathway by which poor motor co-ordination and attention are associated with impulsive, inappropriate behaviour, which results in peer rejection and increasing seclusiveness in adolescence.

Using data from the New York High-Risk Project, a longitudinal study of the children of schizophrenic parents, Ott and colleagues (2002) analysed videotapes made when the children were about age 9 to determine whether subtle signs of schizophrenia-related disturbances could be seen. Among those who went on to receive a schizophrenia diagnosis, raters observed significantly more signs of thought disorder and positive and negative symptoms. Here again, we see the fuzziness of the boundaries between the pre-morbid and prodromal stages. Long before the signs and symptoms are clear enough to warrant a diagnosis, children destined for schizophrenia have taken an aberrant path through development.

Adolescence
The largest predictors of schizophrenia reported are in fact those in memory, learning, attention and executive function.

Inattention
Distractibility, or a deficit in selective attention, emerges as a strong precursor to schizophrenia in adolescence. It also may be an important prognostic indicator (Harvey, 1991). However, recent studies have failed to show deficits across measures of sustained attention in those with early onset schizophrenia.

Motor Difficulties
In regard to motor development, Crow et al.'s (1995) NCDS found that prior signs of deviant development were no longer present in adolescence and motor co-ordination was age appropriate. However, the at-risk group was rated as clumsy when compared with the other groups.

Cognitive Deficits
Finally, there is a decline in IQ scores that is greater than the decline found in the test scores of children whose mothers are depressed. Achievement test scores of adolescents destined for a schizophrenia diagnosis also decline significantly between 13 and 16 years of age (Fuller et al., 2002). In Vourdas and colleagues' (2003) study comparing early and late onset schizophrenia, the investigators found increasing declines in functioning across the board during adolescence, particularly in boys. Intelligence scores in early onset schizophrenia (EOS) often range between 80 and 90 (around 0.7 to 1.3 standard

deviations below the normative mean) and are lower than those found in adults. In fact almost one-third of EOS will show IQ levels below 70, which is the cut-off for mild learning disability. The general consensus is that psychosis onset may be more marked in the two years before and two years after onset. General intellectual function appears to remain stable thereafter (Vyas et al. 2011).

Memory Deficits

Selective memory impairments appear to be in evidence against a background of generalized cognitive deficits. A meta-analysis of adult onset schizophrenia studies have reported a mean effect size of approximately 0.74 for memory deficits, although variability appeared across studies (Heinrichs and Zakzanis, 1998). Memory deficits appear to be more pronounced in long-term memory, in delayed free recall and delayed cue recall conditions. Importantly, this pattern has been found to be apparent regardless of the age of onset or chronicity.

Summary of the Pre-morbid Stage

As the available evidence shows, when schizophrenia begins in childhood, it has a profound effect on emerging competencies in all spheres of development, including the emotional, cognitive, social and academic. Further, pre-morbid childhood and adolescent onset schizophrenia are characterized by more pervasive and severe developmental impairments than is adult onset schizophrenia (Hollis, 2004). Motor deviations are present from infancy on but tend to be 'outgrown' by adolescence, while deviations in speech and communication seem to be important throughout the entire developmental period. Passivity (a possible precursor of the negative symptoms of schizophrenia) has been documented in the infancy through preschool period, but its subsequent fate has not been charted. Problems in social adjustment are present as early as the toddler period and continue through middle childhood, particularly for boys. Deviations in attention, which are predictive of schizophrenia, have been found from middle childhood on, as have cognitive deficits. In addition to widespread developmental delays, poor general adjustment and the presence of schizophrenia spectrum traits characterize children who will go on to earn a schizophrenia diagnosis.

Are these pre-morbid variables risk factors for, or precursors to, the development of schizophrenia? Studies appear to suggest that pre-morbid impairments are associated with developmental and/or genetic liability of schizophrenia. The fact that some individuals develop schizophrenia in the absence of these early cognitive and social deficits suggests that the developmental impairments accompany but are not causally related to or necessary to the emergence of the disorder (Hollis, 2004).

Prodromal Phase

Childhood onset schizophrenia is typically prefaced by a gradual and insidious deterioration in functioning prior to the onset of psychosis. Changes may include social isolation, bizarre preoccupations, deteriorating self-care skills, dysphoria, and alterations in sleep and appetite (McClellan et al., 2001). This prodromal phase may last from days and weeks to months and years.

For example, Hollis (2000) describes the Maudsley study of adolescent psychosis, in which approximately 100 youths ranging from 10 to 17 years were assessed over the course of 11 years. Retrospectively examining case notes at the time of the first psychotic break, the investigators identified a prodromal phase averaging a year in length previous to the onset of positive symptoms. During the prodromal phase, the youths evidenced increasing social withdrawal, declining school performance and uncharacteristically odd behaviour, which in hindsight were recognized by the investigators as early negative symptoms of schizophrenia. Because the prodromal phase is ushered in by these relatively more subtle negative symptoms, which only later shade into more overt psychotic behaviour such as hallucinations and delusions, early recognition of the disorder is made exceedingly difficult.

Moreover – and complicating the diagnostician's task further – positive psychotic symptoms in children are not necessarily predictive of schizophrenia, but rather are associated with the development of a number of disorders. In contrast, negative symptoms are associated specifically with schizophrenia as well as mood disorder-related psychotic reactions. Negative symptoms also are predicted by more severe developmental impairments, predict a more pathological course of illness and are related to the familial risk of schizophrenia, suggesting an underlying genetic and developmental mechanism (Hollis, 2004).

Acute Phase

As we know, while the acute phase is characterized by overtly psychotic behaviour and symptoms, child and adolescent onset schizophrenia presents differently than the adult onset version of the disorder. Child onset schizophrenia is characterized by more evident negative symptoms (e.g., flattened or inappropriate affect, withdrawal, odd mannerisms) and more disorganized behaviour. Well-formed delusions, such as persecutory beliefs, are rarer in young people, although other features of thought disorder (loose associations, illogical thinking) are generally present (McClellan et al., 2001). The acute phase generally lasts from one to six months, or longer depending on the youth's response to treatment.

Recovery Phase

For the next several months following the acute phase, there usually is a period of continued but less severe impairment, characterized by negative symptoms such as lack of energy and social withdrawal (McClellan et al., 2001). Some will develop a post-schizophrenic depression in which they display dysphoria and flat affect.

Residual or Chronic Phase

At this stage of the disorder, we see a divergence of pathways. Although still affected by negative symptoms, many youths will experience periods of several months or longer during which they are not acutely psychotic. In contrast, other youths will be unresponsive to treatment and will remain chronically symptomatic. Generally, chronic schizophrenia follows a pattern of cycling through the above phases, with a further deterioration in functioning following each acute episode (McClellan et al., 2001).

Multiple Pathways to Schizophrenia

So far we have raised the question, what are the precursors of child and adolescent onset schizophrenia? The best answers come from research designed to compare populations at risk for schizophrenia with populations at risk for affective psychosis, as well as with a normal control group. But there is a further question: do all at-risk children follow the same path to the ultimate psychopathology, or are there different ways of arriving at the same end point? Answering this question requires a *within-group* analysis of data obtained on at-risk children.

Walker and colleagues (1996) provide such a within-group analysis using a statistical technique called cluster analysis. They found that their followback data clustered in two groups. Cluster I children showed more behavioural and attentional problems and more rapid escalation of problems than did Cluster II children. For example, Cluster I children were both more withdrawn and delinquent and had more social problems than children in Cluster II. Moreover, Cluster I children were significantly different from their healthy siblings on all behavioural and attentional problems, whereas Cluster II children were not.

Cluster I children had more motor abnormalities and a higher rate of obstetrical complications. This latter finding helps explain why some investigators, such as Crow et al. (1995), found no difference in obstetrical complications while others did – namely, the data depend on what proportion of Cluster I and Cluster II children one happens to capture in the population.

Walker and colleagues (1996) conclude that there are two pre-morbid subtypes, one showing early, persistent and escalating deviations, and the other showing no difference from healthy children. These groups correspond to two different kinds of anecdotal information from parents, some saying that the child with schizophrenia was 'different from the beginning', and others saying they were particularly dismayed by the onset because their child had been 'perfectly normal'. Both may be right. Incidentally, this finding is important for clinical child psychologists to know so that they will not suspect parents of covering up deviations when they paint a picture of a well-adjusted childhood for a child who has been diagnosed with schizophrenia.

Next Walker and colleagues (1996) analysed their data on precursors in terms of gender differences, with equally important findings. As have other investigators, they found that males had a predominance of both externalizing problems (i.e., acting out, disruptive behaviour) *and* internalizing problems (i.e., social isolation), while the females had predominately internalizing problems (i.e., anxiety and depression). Thus, only girls conform to the stereotype of the pre-schizophrenic as being withdrawn; boys are more apt to be described as being emotionally unstable and having a 'stormy' time.

Summary
In sum, there is no single path to schizophrenia; rather, there are different routes to the same outcome. Some children will be disturbed in many areas of functioning from an early age and become increasingly so, while others will be essentially normal before schizophrenia makes its appearance. In a like manner, the route will be different for males than for females – the former having both externalizing and internalizing problems; the latter having primarily internalizing ones. The finding that different disturbances can lead to the same outcome is an example of **equifinality**.

Etiology
The prevailing theories of the etiology of schizophrenia rely on a **diathesis-stress** model. 'Diathesis' is another term for a vulnerability or a predisposition to develop schizophrenia. Stressors increase the likelihood that schizophrenia will actually appear. At present, more than 100 combinations of symptoms can lead to a diagnosis of schizophrenia, according to the DSM-IV. Among the diatheses, biological factors are most prominent.

The Biological Context
There are four sources of evidence concerning the organic etiology of schizophrenia: genetic studies, neurobiological studies (including studies of the brain, autonomic nervous system and neurochemistry), studies of neuropsychological variables such as inattention and poor executive functioning, and studies of prenatal and birth complications.

Genetic Factors
Familial Transmission
There is little doubt that genetic factors play an etiologic role in schizophrenia. More than 40 family studies spanning several decades of research show that risk to different relatives of individuals who are schizophrenic is considerably greater than the general population risk. Moreover, risk varies as a function of the degree of genetic relatedness to the affected individual. Thus, the highest concordance is between monozygotic twins, who have 100 per cent of their genes in common. The specific risk in this case is 48 per cent, which is approximately three times the 14 per cent concordance rate for dizygotic twins (Moldin and Gottesman, 1997).

For example, the University of California Los Angeles (UCLA) Family Study (Asarnow et al., 2001) compared the likelihood of schizophrenic spectrum disorders in the first-degree relatives of 148 children with schizophrenia as compared to 368 children with ADHD and 206 community controls. The investigators used careful methodology, utilizing structured diagnostic interviews conducted by clinicians who were blind to the diagnoses of the proband. The results showed a significantly higher prevalence of schizophrenia among the parents of children with the disorder, and these parents generally had an early age of onset. The relative risk (the ratio of risk for parents of children with schizophrenia versus parents of community children) was 17, considerably higher than the threefold to sixfold increase seen in families of adults with schizophrenia. Similarly, Nicolson and colleagues (2003) found that 24.74 per cent of parents of patients with childhood onset schizophrenia had disorders in the schizophrenia spectrum, in contrast to 11.35 per cent of those with adult onset schizophrenia and 1.55 per cent of parents of typically developing children.

FIGURE 11.3 Familiar Risk of Developing Schizophrenia.

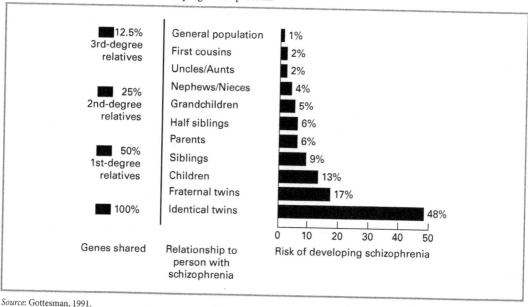

Source: Gottesman, 1991.

Taken together, these findings suggest that childhood onset schizophrenia may be an even more familial, genetically driven version of the disorder than the adult onset type. (See Fig. 11.3.)

Mechanism of Transmission

Exactly which genes are involved in the transmission of schizophrenia is not known at present. The strongest current evidence implicates microdeletions on chromosomes 22q11, which occur more frequently among individuals with schizophrenia, especially childhood onset schizophrenia (Usiskin et al., 1999). Sex chromosomes have also been identified at a greater rate in young onset cases compared to that of adult populations (see Rapoport et al., 2005, for a review).

However, the challenge of detecting and isolating a disease gene is considerable; for example, the time between establishment of linkage to identification of the precise disease gene for Huntington's disease was 10 years (Moldin and Gottesman, 1997). Moreover, genetic influences likely reflect the impact of 'many genes of small probabilistic effect rather than the sledge hammer effect of single deterministic genes' (Rende and Plomin, 1995,

p. 302). Rende and Plomin also caution that symptoms influenced by genes do not necessarily coincide with symptoms used to define a disorder. Genetic influences can cut across different disorders, such as depression and anxiety, or can influence areas of functioning not considered as core symptoms, such as attention. This lack of a nice correspondence between genes that transmit the psychopathology and the defining clinical manifestations of the psychopathology itself adds just one more complication to research on genetic etiology.

Gene–Environment Interaction

The genetic loading still allows for environmental factors to play a major role in the final production of schizophrenia. One example of the interaction of genetic and environmental factors is a classic Finnish study (Tienari et al., 1983) in which 92 children of mothers who were schizophrenic and mothers who were not were adopted into healthy or disturbed family environments. All the children who subsequently became schizophrenic were in the schizophrenic-mother, disturbed-family group. Schizophrenia did not develop when children of mothers who were not schizophrenic were adopted into disturbed families. Thus, the psychopathology was the result of the combination of a genetically vulnerable child being raised in a disturbed family environment. Equally important, the non-disturbed family protected the at-risk child from becoming schizophrenic.

Another example of gene–environment interaction is the finding that the incidence of schizophrenia increased sevenfold in African-Caribbean children whose parents had immigrated to London (Hutchinson et al., 1996). Possible environmental risks include prenatal rubella infection, drug abuse and factors associated with assimilation. However, pinpointing which variables in the environment are critical stressors for schizophrenia is as daunting a task as discovering which genes are crucial for its production.

More recent technological advances have shown that duplications or deletions, also known as copy number variation (CMV), are structural genomic variation important to the development of the disorder. A recent study showed an overabundance of rare CNVs impacting on known genes in childhood onset cases compared with adult onset schizophrenia (Walsh et al., 2008) and strong evidence has been identified for neurexin 1, a locus implicated in schizophrenia, autism and mental retardation, which has been reported to be involved in early neurodevelopmental deviance.

Central Nervous System Dysfunctions

The lion's share of research on central nervous system (CNS) dysfunctions has been conducted on adults with schizophrenia. A number of areas of the brain have been implicated, particularly the hippocampus, frontal cortex and selected left hemisphere structures. However, in spite of vigorous research efforts, one specific pathogenic brain mechanism has not yet been identified. No single brain lesion is found in all individuals with schizophrenia, and those that have been found are not unique to schizophrenia (Asarnow and Asarnow, 2003). Further, in contrast to the research on adults, research on children with schizophrenia is meagre, consisting at times of

the study of a single individual (Jacobsen and Rapoport, 1998).

Cerebral Volume

One highly consistent finding in the research to date points to a smaller total *cerebral volume* in children and adults with schizophrenia. This reduction is greater than that found in adults, and the reduction is strongly correlated with negative symptoms in the children. The reduction appears to be accounted for by loss of *grey matter*, particularly in the cerebellar and frontal areas. For example, Thompson and colleagues (2001) conducted a longitudinal study in which they obtained MRI scans from youths with early onset schizophrenia and compared them to typically developing adolescents. Repeat scans were conducted at three time points, separated by two-year intervals. The results showed that over the five-year period, there was a dynamic wave to the loss of grey matter in the early onset youths, which progressed toward the anterior of the brain into the temporal lobes, engulfing the sensorimotor and prefrontal cortical areas, and the frontal visual areas. While the temporal lobes were virtually unaffected at the time of onset of the disorder, loss of grey matter in this area became pervasive over the five-year period. (See Fig. 11.4.) The patterns of change were associated with the severity of psychotic symptoms and mirrored the neuropsychological impairments shown by the youths in auditory, visual and executive functions. Loss of grey matter appears to be specific to schizophrenia, given that it is not seen in children with multidimensional impairment or atypical psychosis (Gogtay et al., 2004).

As grey matter shrinks, there is a concomitant increase in the size of the *ventricles*, the fluid-filled cavities in the brain (Kumra et al., 2000; Sowell et al., 2000). For example, over a two-year period, one study documented that the ventricular volume increased more rapidly in children with schizophrenia than in typically developing children (Sporn et al., 2003).

Recent data suggest that there are *gender differences* in grey matter loss. Collinson and colleagues (2003) found that females with early onset

FIGURE 11.4 Rate of Grey Matter Loss in Early Onset Schizophrenia versus Typical Adolescence.

Source: Thompson et al., 2001.

schizophrenia tended to have smaller right hemispheres than did typically developing females, whereas males with early onset schizophrenia had asymmetry of the left hemisphere. Further, a provocative recent study by Sporn and colleagues (2003) discovered that smaller cerebral volumes and loss of grey matter are also found in the healthy siblings of patients with childhood onset schizophrenia. Thus, these brain abnormalities may be an important genetic marker for the disorder.

Are these changes in grey matter causes or consequences of schizophrenia? An important longitudinal study by Pantelis and colleagues (2003) provides some insight. Individuals displaying prodromal symptoms underwent MRI scans and were followed up 12 months later. At the initial assessment, those who went on to develop schizophrenia differed from their peers by virtue of having less grey matter in the right medial temporal, lateral temporal, inferior frontal and cingulate cortex. At the follow-up evaluation, those who had developed schizophrenia evidenced a loss of grey matter in the left

parahippocampal, fusiform, orbitofrontal and cerebellar cortices, as well as the cingulate gyrus. These data suggest that some of the changes in grey matter associated with schizophrenia pre-date the disorder, while others emerge at the time of its onset and progressively worsen over the course of the disorder.

Jacobsen and Rapoport (1998) conclude that the progressive changes in the brain after the onset of schizophrenia, coupled with the evidence of continued intellectual deterioration both before and after the appearance of schizophrenia, suggest that the pathological underpinnings of childhood schizophrenia do not consist of a single static lesion or event but rather a continuous or multi-event process of neurodegeneration. These massive CNS changes provide a convincing explanation for the declines in cognitive and academic performance over the course of early onset schizophrenia.

Longitudinal investigations on EOS have also demonstrated striking progressive structural brain changes. Grey matter volume appears to increase in late childhood and decrease during puberty (e.g. Gogtay et al., 2004). Such studies addressing cortical development suggest that such volumetric changes may be a reflection of a selective elimination and structural alterations of dendrite synapse during early development.

Brain Morphology

In another MRI study, White and colleagues (2003) examined the brain surface of 42 children and adolescents with schizophrenia and compared them with those of 24 healthy controls. The investigators found a reduction in cortical thickness in those with schizophrenia, particularly in the tissue underlying the sulci, the furrows of the cortex. In addition, the sulci were more flattened, while the gyri, the areas of raised surface of the brain, were more steeply curved in the young people with schizophrenia. The authors suggest that these abnormalities in brain morphology may affect communication and interconnectivity within the parts of the brain.

Corpus Collosum

Another developmental brain scan study documents progressive changes in the corpus collosum, the structure that interconnects the two hemi-spheres of the brain, in individuals with childhood onset schizophrenia. Keller and colleagues (2003) obtained MRI scans from 55 children at the time of diagnosis and at two-year intervals throughout ado-lescence and young adulthood. These scans were compared to those of 113 typically developing chil-dren matched for age and gender. While there were no differences at the time of the initial scan, longitu-dinal data showed a significant difference in the developmental trajectory of the splenium, which became progressively smaller in those with child-hood onset schizophrenia, even after adjusting for the overall decrease in total cerebral volume.

Subgroups

There is little dispute that one of the most robust biological markers of pathology in schizophrenia is alterations in brain structure as detected with mag-netic resonance imaging (MRI). However, none of the single regional alterations on its own is either sensitive or specific enough to distinguish patients from controls. It has been argued that research focusing on linking distinct brain morphological patterns to subsyndromes of schizophrenia may provide important clues to the distinct biological markers underlying the disorder. To date, few stud-ies have addressed the issue of subtypes or subsyn-dromes within schizophrenia, even despite the availability of the subtyping according to DSM-III or DSM-IV diagnostic criteria. Those that have, found more pronounced abnormalities in cortical folding in the disorganized subtype of schizophre-nia (Sallet et al., 2003a), while another study divid-ing patients into paranoid versus non-paranoid schizophrenia provide some evidence for the nega-tive symptom dimension to be related to increased structural asymmetry (Sallet et al., 2003b).

Neurochemistry

Neurotransmitters

Because of its proven efficacy in treatment, *dopa-mine*, a monoamine neurotransmitter ('chemical messenger') essential to normal nerve activity, plays a prominent role in neurochemical research con-cerning the etiology of schizophrenia. Specifically,

drugs that block the transmission of dopamine con-trol psychotic symptoms, while those that produce excessive release of dopamine are associated with the intensification of psychotic symptoms. However, the effect is not specific to schizophrenia but applies to a number of psychoses. Moreover, therapeutic effectiveness in controlling symptoms cannot be taken as proof of an etiological hypothesis because cures are not necessarily related to causes (Häfner and Nowotny, 1995). Recent research has begun to examine other neurochemicals, including gluta-mate, an excitatory neurotransmitter, and GABA, an inhibitory neurotransmitter (Walker et al., 2004).

Neurohormones

Walker and Walder (2003) outline research on the role of cortisol and the hypothalamo-pituitary-adrenal (HPA) system in the development of schiz-ophrenia. They argue that stress results in heightened release of cortisol, which exacerbates psychotic symptoms by increasing dopamine activ-ity. Hormonal changes associated with adolescence might act on the vulnerable brain to intensify the risk of schizophrenia. Interestingly, they suggest that the chronic stress inherent in having a psy-chotic illness itself might further contribute to brain degeneration.

Neuropsychological Deficits

While brain-imaging techniques help us to discern changes in the structure of the brain, neuropsycho-logical assessment allows us to determine whether the brain functions differently in children with schizophrenia. Evidence consistently points to such differences. When asked to complete neurocognitive tasks, adolescents with schizophrenia generally are found to function more poorly across the board than their typically developing peers (Kravariti et al., 2003). The findings can be summarized as follows.

Attention

The most robust research finding on schizophrenia in children, adolescents and adults is that they share a dysfunction in selective and sustained attention. This dysfunction is evidenced by studies of span of apprehension in which participants have to identify a target letter (a T or an F) embedded in an array of other letters and displayed for 50 milliseconds. When the number of letters to be identified is large – specifically five to ten rather than one to three – the performance of schizophrenic children is worse than that of typical children or ones with ADHD. Thus, the dysfunction is evidenced in those with schizophrenia when the task involves a significant burden for processing information. Finally, direct evaluation of the participants' brain activity while performing the task showed a comparable deviation in event-related potential, a measure of the brain's electrical activity (Asarnow et al., 1994).

Speed of Processing

Consistent findings show that young persons with schizophrenia have difficulty processing information in a speedy and efficient manner (Asarnow et al., 1994).

Visual-Motor and Motor Functions

Both visual-motor co-ordination and fine motor speed are impaired in individuals with schizophrenia (Niendam et al., 2003). There is also evidence that, while performance in these areas improves over the course of development in typical children, it does not do so in children with schizophrenia. This lack of improvement suggests either a delay in or failure of normal brain maturation (Jacobsen and Rapoport, 1998).

Executive Functions

As with adults, executive functions (those responsible for planned, flexible, goal-directed behaviour) are impaired in children and adolescents with schizophrenia. (See Chapter 7 for a more detailed presentation of executive functions.) For example, individuals with schizophrenia are perseverative in their thinking, a deficit that is related to damage to the frontal lobes, where higher-level executive processing takes place. A number of the findings detailed previously also suggest deficits in the executive function of *working memory*, the ability to hold information in mind while performing an operation on it. In fact, Niendam and colleagues (2003) compared the childhood test scores of indi-

viduals who did or did not go on to develop schizophrenia and found that working memory problems were one of the few deficits that were unique to those who developed the disorder.

In line with the idea of a dysfunction in processing complex information is the paradoxical finding that providing strategies for or information about performing a task to individuals with schizophrenia can interfere with their performance at times. Instead of being helpful, the added information is too much to be assimilated. In regard to relating this finding to brain functioning, it suggests that children and adolescents with schizophrenia have difficulty with processing complex information regardless of the hemisphere involved in the function assessed by the task. In other words, the dysfunction is not localized in one hemisphere or the other.

Key differences in executive functions have been observed between early and adult onset disorder. For example in the Maudsley early onset schizophrenia study, Kravariti et al. (2003) found that EOS patients showed impairments in planning accuracy and perceptual motor processing. In contrast to adult onset schizophrenia, EOS showed reduced subsequent planning time which may be related to increasing impulsivity and signs of abnormal self-monitoring. They also found deficits in spatial working memory. Inability to form effective strategies was a core feature of impairment, while maintenance of information was the least impaired.

Prenatal and Birth Complications

Studies regarding the impact of prenatal and birth complications are inconsistent and opinions in the field vary. Some investigators conclude that pregnancy and birth complications are strongly associated with schizophrenia, but only of the childhood onset type (Rosso and Cannon, 2003). Evidence also points to an increase in prenatal difficulties in high-risk children (e.g., children of schizophrenic mothers) who went on to develop the disorder (Brown and Susser, 2003). Several endogenous (internal) and exogenous (external) non-genetic factors of pregnancy and birth have been related to an increased risk for schizophrenia in later life. These factors have included maternal diabetes, low birth weight, older paternal age, winter birth and prenatal maternal stress with the chances increasing when these factors are combined (King et al., 2010). Prenatal exposure to viral infection also has been implicated. For example, Mednick and colleagues (1988) found that adults with schizophrenia were more likely to have been exposed to influenza during the second trimester of gestation, but not during the first and third trimesters, suggesting that the virus interferes with neural developments that are specific to that critical period. However, other large-scale studies have reported that the links to prenatal and birth complications are weak or even non-existent (Nicholson et al., 1999). Moreover, the direction of effects might be reversed: abnormal neurodevelopment in the foetus may be the *cause* rather than the consequence of prenatal and birth complications in schizophrenia (Hollis, 2004).

Puberty

The start of puberty marks the beginning of increasingly divergent psychosocial pathways that separate women and men at critical points in their lives. Although the convergence between the onset of puberty and the upsurge in the incidence of schizophrenia has led some to suspect a causal connection, research has failed to make such a link. In a large-scale study conducted by NIMH, no relation was found between childhood onset schizophrenia and the advent of puberty (Frazier et al., 1997). Recent research, showing puberty to delay onset of schizophrenia in women and hasten it in men, has suggested a relationship between puberty and the development of the disorder (Riecher-Rössler et al., 2010). One suggestion is that if hormones are involved then oestrogen may be crucial in delaying schizophrenia in females whereas the surge of puberty testosterone would appear to have the opposite effect in males. However, this fails to take into consideration confounding factors such as puberty being a relatively stressful time. Importantly, very few empirical studies exist to connect the two events.

Substance Abuse

Approximately half of individuals with schizophrenia have a history of substance abuse or dependence, including alcoholism, a rate which is three times higher than seen in the average population. Alcohol, marijuana and cocaine (in that order) are the substances most commonly involved. Although youths with schizophrenia may abuse substances, evidence of a hypothesized causal relationship between schizophrenia and substance abuse is elusive. Phillips and colleagues (2002) followed a group of high-risk youths (those who showed subthreshold psychotic symptoms or were relatives of someone with psychosis and recently showed a decline in functioning) over a period of 12 months. Thirty-two per cent of the youths developed an acute psychotic episode over the year, but the likelihood of psychosis was not predicted by cannabis use. Similarly, Arseneault and colleagues (2002) conducted a prospected longitudinal study of the relationship between adolescent cannabis use and schizophrenia and found that those who used cannabis by age 15 were four times as likely to develop psychosis in adulthood, but this effect was no longer significant once psychotic symptoms in childhood were accounted for. Thus, it may be the case that youths with early onset symptoms utilize substances in an attempt to self-medicate, but that these substances do not in fact precipitate psychosis. Yet these results appear to be equivocal as other studies have shown cannabis use in schizophrenia to be associated with worse clinical outcomes. For example, a recent magnetic resonance imaging study concluded that the loss of grey matter, commonly seen in the brains of schizophrenic patients, proceeds nearly twice as fast in patients who also used cannabis over a five-year follow-up (Eggan et al., 2008). In addition, common psychosocial factors (e.g., limited education, poverty, unemployment, peer influence and the structure of the mental health treatment system) may account for a portion of the increased comorbidity. Both disorders are associated with a greater exposure to stressors, which on one hand increase drug taking and on the other exacerbate psychotic symptoms in schizophrenia patients.

Integration of Biological Factors

We have presented the variables in the biological context in isolation from one another, although it is more likely that they are interconnected. For example, an influence model that guides much of the thinking is Weinberger's (1987) neurodevelopmental model of schizophrenia. Weinberger proposes that a brain legion in the limbic system and prefrontal cortex occurs early in life, but remains 'clinically silent' until the brain matures and the neural systems involved in schizophrenia have adequately developed. In particular, Weinberger suspects that schizophrenia involves deficits in the mechanisms involving the neurotransmitter dopamine, which has a major role in the response to stress.

A number of research findings to date indirectly support the *neurodevelopmental hypothesis* (McGrath et al., 2003). For example, long before the disorder reveals itself, retrospective data indicate that development of expressive language, motor skills and interpersonal relationships – all skills mediated by the frontal cortex – are negatively affected in children who go on to develop schizophrenia, consistent with the idea of a fundamental deficit whose true nature only later reveals itself. Support for the dopamine-stress connection is supported by research showing that stress often brings on an exacerbation of psychotic symptoms in individuals with schizophrenia, as well as the fact that medications that target dopamine result in dramatic alleviation of psychosis. The involvement of brain dopaminergic pathways is also likely to be a shared feature in the comorbidity of schizophrenia, both positive and negative symptoms, and drugs abuse.

Rather than being static entities, abnormal brain development and neuropsychological deficits interact with behaviour and environment in early onset schizophrenia. For example, Hollis (2004) notes the importance of executive functions during the pre-adolescent period (approximately age 8 to 15), the developmental period during which pre-schizophrenic symptoms begin to emerge. At this stage of life, executive functions are central to many important developmental capacities. For example, social relatedness requires the youth to integrate different sources of information, comprehend others' perspectives, inhibit inappropriate responses, and shift attention and mental set in order to respond to changing circumstances. The young person whose development is impaired in these areas will be unprepared for the increasing social and academic demands of adolescence. And when the youth in question is one who is genetically vulnerable to the development of schizophrenia, the stress of these social and academic failures may be the catalyst that pushes him or her over the threshold. This *executive functioning risk model* predicts that the greater the deficits in executive functioning, the earlier the onset of psychotic symptoms. Thus, we see interactions between risk factors, vulnerabilities and potentiating factors in the development of schizophrenia.

Familial Links

A fascinating line of research shows that the parents of children with schizophrenia, who are themselves without a diagnosis, share some of the same neuropsychological deficits as their children. In comparison to parents of children with ADHD or controls, Asarnow and colleagues (2002) found that parents of children with schizophrenia performed significantly worse on tests of attention and executive functions. By a similar token, unaffected *siblings* of children with schizophrenia show similar, albeit not as severe, patterns of deficit on neurocognitive tasks (Niendam et al., 2003), as well as showing similar patterns of reduction in grey matter (Gogtay et al., 2003). Once again, these findings suggest an underlying genetic liability to schizophrenia that is expressed in gross or subtle ways in different family members.

The Individual Context
Thought Disorder

The disorganized speech that characterizes schizophrenia is a reflection of disorders in thinking. Thought disorders are not only diagnostic indices of schizophrenia, but they have ominous implications for prognosis as well. However, certain of these disorders can be found in the typically developing population of younger children. Loose associations, for example, can be observed up to the age of 7 years, after which time they are infrequent. Illogical thinking also decreases markedly after that time. Therefore, the appearance of loose associations and illogical thinking in schizophrenia may be due to a developmental delay, fixation or regression, although this possible etiology is only speculation. (See Volkmar et al., 1996, which also contains a detailed summary of the literature on delusions, hallucinations and other thought disorders.)

Controlled studies have been conducted on loose and illogical thinking underlying disorganized speech. Loose thinking is defined as an unpredictable change of topics, such as answering the question 'Why do you like Tim?' with 'I call my mother Sweetie'. Illogical thinking is defined as contradictions or inappropriate causal relations, such as 'I left my hat at home because her name is Mary'. These thinking disorders may be specific to schizophrenia since they are not found in children diagnosed with ADHD, conduct disorder or oppositional disorder.

The two kinds of thought disturbances are not correlated. Loose thinking is related to distractibility, while illogical thinking is related to a short attention span (Caplan and Sherman, 1990). This latter attention deficit may underlie schizophrenic children's digressive speech, since they are deficient in the short-term attentional processes required for coherent conversation. In sum, we have two hypotheses concerning the etiology of loose and illogical thinking: fixation or regression, on the one hand, and an attentional deficit, on the other.

The Family Context

While poor family relations were at one time considered to be a causal factor in schizophrenia, the evidence clearly shows that family dysfunction constitutes a stressor that increases the probability of schizophrenia in an already vulnerable individual. There is no evidence that a dysfunctional family can produce schizophrenia in a non-vulnerable child. Three aspects of family relationships have been studied: communication deviance, affective quality and caregiving disruptions.

Communication Deviance

Communication deviance concerns the degree to which relatives' communication lacks clarity as measured by the number of unclear, amorphous, disruptive or fragmented statements they make in response to projective tests. The construct derives from the work of Lyman Wynne (1984), who regards schizophrenia as the result of a diffuse or fragmented family structure. In a *diffuse* structure, patterns of interaction are marked by vague ideas, by blurring of meaning and by irrelevancies. Thus, the drifting or scattered thinking of individuals who are schizophrenic represents the internalization of such a family structure. As an example of amorphous thinking, note the following responses of a mother being interviewed for the developmental history of her child who has schizophrenia:

Psychologist: Was it a difficult delivery or did everything go OK?

Mother: I know just what you mean. And I can say for certain that I'm not one of those women you read about where they are so brave and natural childbirth is just the greatest thing in their life (laughs). Believe me, when the time comes, I want the works when it comes to pain.

Psychologist: But did everything go OK?

Mother:Well, there was this Dr Wisekoff that I never liked and he said all kinds of doom and gloom things, but I told my husband I was the one that had the baby and I was the one that ought to know, so my husband got into this big fight and didn't pay the bill for a whole year and the doctor threatened to hire one of these collection agencies, and what that was all about don't ask me – just don't ask me.

Psychologist: I see, but I'm still not sure …

Mother (interrupting): That's just what I mean.

Later the psychologist, who was just beginning his clinical internship, told his supervisor that he wanted to shake the mother and yell at the top of his lungs, 'But was the delivery difficult or easy?' One can only imagine how difficult it would be for a child to grow up surrounded by such diffuseness, accompanied by an obliviousness to the diffuseness itself.

Just as the child's amorphous thinking derives from a diffuse family structure, *fragmented* family communication leads to fragmented thinking in Wynne's perspective. In this case communication is marked by digression from topic to topic, non sequitur reasoning, and extraneous, illogical or contradictory comments. While attention can be focused for brief moments, bits and pieces of memories become intermixed with the current train of thought. The technical term for this abrupt shift from one topic to another is overinclusive thinking, or **overinclusiveness**.

Wynne delineates other faults in the family structure. The family members cannot maintain appropriate psychological **boundaries**, and thus detached impersonality unpredictably alternates with highly personal remarks and confrontations. However, there is a concerted effort to act as if there were a strong sense of unity, resulting in what Wynne calls *pseudo-mutuality*. There is a great pressure to maintain a façade of harmony, and the child is not allowed to deviate from or question his or her prescribed role. Beneath this façade lie pervasive feelings of futility and meaninglessness.

Objective studies have confirmed that communication deviance reliably differentiates parents of individuals with schizophrenia from parents of persons without schizophrenia but not from those with bipolar (manic depressive) disorders (Miklowitz, 1994). Communication deviance also predicts the adult onset of schizophrenia spectrum disorders. For example, a 15-year follow-up study of 64 families with mild to moderately disturbed adolescents found that the incidence of schizophrenia or schizophrenia spectrum disorders was highest in families initially classified as having high communication deviance. Moreover, there were no cases of schizophrenia in families with low communication deviance, and adding measures of negative affect increased the predictive power (Goldstein, 1990). These results suggest that, for vulnerable children, disturbance in the family climate in the form of unclear or negative communication presages the appearance of schizophrenia and related disorders in adulthood.

Next, there is evidence supporting Wynne's clinical observation that communication deviance in parents interferes with the development of attention and logical thinking in their children. Mothers with high communication deviance and their offspring with schizophrenia perform poorly on measures of attention and vigilance, as well as on tasks evaluating the ability to integrate and organize complex social information into a coherent whole. Finally, there is evidence that communication deviance in parents is associated with the severity of the psychopathology. While communication deviance is also found in some parents of children with depression, it is not associated either with attentional problems or severity of disturbance in depression, suggesting that it is particularly important for the development of schizophrenic disorders (Asarnow and Asarnow, 2003).

Affective Quality

One of the most extensively studied aspects of shared affect in family interaction is *expressed emotion* (EE), which involves dimensions of *criticism* and *overinvolvement*. Research on adults shows that high EE is a good predictor of relapse after a schizophrenic episode; for example, for hospitalized adults with schizophrenia who return to a high-EE family, relapse within nine months to a year is two to three times higher than for those who return to a low EE family (Miklowitz, 1994). Evidence is somewhat mixed for the role of family EE for children with schizophrenia, but is stronger for the effects of criticism as opposed to overinvolvement (Asarnow et al., 1994). In observed interactions, parents of children with schizophrenia spectrum disorders are more likely to express harsh criticism toward their child and to respond to the child's negative verbal behaviour with a reciprocal negative response. Further, observed EE during adolescence predicts an increased risk of developing schizophrenia-related disorders in young adulthood (Goldstein, 1987). However, high EE also is found among parents of children with depression or other non-schizophrenic spectrum disorders and thus is not specific to schizophrenia (Asarnow et al., 1994).

A study of over 1000 people found that those whose interaction with their mothers when 3 years old was characterized by 'harshness towards the child: no effort to help the child' were, as adults, significantly more likely to be diagnosed with a schizophreniform disorder, but not mania, anxiety or depression (Cannon et al., 2002).

Child Trauma

The term childhood trauma has been used to capture a range of severe adverse experiences including sexual, physical and emotional abuse and neglect. A recent survey in the UK estimated prevalence of childhood sexual and physical abuse at around 11 per cent and physical abuse at 24 per cent (May-Chahal and Cawson, 2005) whereas in the USA the estimates tend to be higher. There is substantial evidence linking child sexual abuse (CSA) and child physical abuse (CPA) to a range of mental health problems with a particularly strong relationship to schizophrenia. In a study of over 500 child guidance clinic attendees, 35 per cent of those diagnosed 'schizophrenic' as adults had been removed from home because of neglect; double any other diagnosis (Robins, 1996). In another study of adult outpatients diagnosed as schizophrenic 85 per cent had suffered some form of childhood abuse or neglect (CSA 50 per cent) (Holowka et al., 2003).

Disruptions in Caregiving

There is some suggestive evidence that children who develop schizophrenia have experienced more disruptions in the caregiving environment, including loss and separation from the primary caregiver (Niemi et al., 2003). Whether this constitutes a stressor that precipitates the disorder, or whether the link is a genetic one – with the caregiving disruptions being consequences of the poor functioning of a parent who also has traits of the disorder – is not known.

Transactions

It is difficult in family interactional research to disentangle precursors from consequences. For example, in observed family interactions, children with schizophrenia or schizotypical disorders evidence a higher level of thought disorders and attentional drift (difficulty in maintaining attention to a task) than do children with major depression (Asarnow et al., 1994). This finding raises these questions: are the harsh critical comments of high EE parents one of the factors *responsible* for their children's disturbance or do they arise in *response to* the frustration of having such a child? Or do both processes occur in a *transactional* model of reciprocal effects? These questions can best be answered by the kind of longitudinal data that are not presently available.

However, King and colleagues (2003) offer one attempt to investigate family relationships in schizophrenia in a more transactional way. Although the patients were largely adults (41 outpatients with a mean age of 31 years), the results are suggestive for our understanding of family relationships in child and adolescent schizophrenia. The investigators set out to determine the extent to which mothers' EE was associated with characteristics of her schizophrenic child, versus those she brought to the situation. The investigators found that mothers' critical comments were predicted by increased symptoms of excitability in the child and lower levels of neurotic symptoms and greater feelings of subjective burden in the mother. Maternal overinvolvement, in turn, was predicted by greater conscientiousness and burden in the mother and, indirectly, by her child's level of depression. Thus, it appears that characteristics of the child interact with those of the mother in order to produce negative affect in the family.

The fact that parenting a severely mentally ill child is challenging would be hard to deny. Schizophrenia is a chronic and debilitating disorder that taxes the emotional and economic resources of the family, increasing the risk of *caregiver burden*. Parents of youths with schizophrenia report that negative symptoms (apathy, asociability, lack of affect) are the most difficult to cope with. Moreover, schizophrenia is a socially stigmatized disorder, a factor that may add to the caregivers' burden. For example, parents report that they often experience an absence of support from their social networks in addition to receiving inadequate help from the mental health system (Knudson and Coyle, 2002).

The Cultural Context
Environmental Stress

As we noted earlier when we discussed prevalence, the association between low SES and adult schizophrenia has not been clearly established for children. Should this finding hold in future research, it would not be surprising. The myriad emotional and instrumental stressors that accompany poverty might well act as precipitants to the disorder in an already vulnerable individual. While it is known that increased life stress precedes the onset of psychotic symptoms and precipitates relapse in adults with schizophrenia (Walker et al., 2004), the corresponding research in child onset samples has yet to be conducted.

Stress is defined as a relationship between the person and the environment which exceeds coping resources, thereby endangering well-being. Any situation is stressful if the individual interprets the situation as such. Little is known about the mechanisms involved in stress processing in schizophrenia. However it has been demonstrated that stress can trigger or exacerbate symptoms of schizophrenia. There is no evidence to date that schizophrenics experience greater numbers of stressful life events, yet their own perception is they have greater stress in their lives. They appear to be particularly sensitive to life events and this has been reported to be an important predictor of relapse rates in schizophrenia (Myin-Germeys and van Os, 2007). Excessive reactions to stress are also found in first degree relatives (Castro et al. 2009). Under a stress vulnerability model, stress activates the hypothalmic-pituitary-adrenal (HPA) axis and the sympatheic nervous system (SNS), which results in increased secretion of cortisol and epinephrine/noneoinephrine respectively. HPA activation and cortisol release, induced by persistent stress, activate the dopamine system, which results in symptoms onset and exacerbation in schizophrenia.

Increased cortisol may also lead to cell loss in the hippocampus causing subsequent memory loss and lack of emotion. Subsequent stress can lead to behavioural dysfunction and precipitate psychotic symptoms. Adolescents are thought to be especially vulnerable to stress as heightened stress sensitivity and a gradual increase in cortisol levels begin in early adolescence (Spear, 2009). Arousal and motivation developed in puberty occur prior to the development of regulatory competence (Forbes and Dahl, 2010). Therefore adolescents may have difficulties in controlling behaviour and emotions and are likely to handle and react badly to even minor stress.

Stigma

Also as noted in the previous section, schizophrenia appears to occur in every nation around the globe. Nevertheless, there are cultural differences in the way in which the disorder is perceived and the extent to which a negative *stigma* is attached to those who suffer from it. For example, in some traditional societies, the bizarre behaviour of the individual with schizophrenia is tolerated or even honoured as a sign that the individual has been 'touched' by a benevolent spirit. (For more on cross-cultural differences in perceptions of schizophrenia, see Jenkins et al., 2004.) Perhaps the issue of stigma versus cultural tolerance explains the results of a WHO study that discovered that individuals with schizophrenia have a more favourable outcome in developing countries than they do in the more highly industrialized nations (Jablensky et al., 1992). In Japan, the name schizophrenia was changed in 2002, at the request of patient families, in order to reduce stigma (Sato, 2006). Subsequent research suggests that changing the name resulted in an uptake of the new name in 78 per cent of the cases.

Integrative Developmental Model

Asarnow and Asarnow (2003) outline a multifactorial, transactional model of the developmental psychopathology of schizophrenia. (See Fig. 11.5.) The model specifies three etiological factors – vulnerabilities, stressors and protective factors – and the dynamic relations among them.

In this model, the roots of schizophrenia lie in genetic risk factors that lead to central nervous system dysfunctions and the accompanying impairments in attention and information processing. These deficits interact with environmental stressors, which potentiate the disorder, and protective factors, which mitigate against its development. Acting in concert, these factors influence the likelihood that an individual will develop schizophrenia over the course of development.

Vulnerabilities for schizophrenia are enduring characteristics of individuals that predispose them to the development of the disorder. Current research implicates both constitutional and environmental factors, including genetic markers; CNS abnormalities, either caused by or concomitant with prenatal and birth complications; and disturbed family patterns of affect and communication. While certain vulnerabilities may be specific to the development of schizophrenia, such as a genetic loading for the disorder, other vulnerabilities, such as family discord, may be predictive of an increased likelihood of psychopathology in general.

Stressors involve internal and environmental demands that exceed the capacity of the individual. These may include traumatic life events, such as the death of a parent, as well as more chronic stresses and strains, such as those associated with living in poverty. Furthermore, stresses interact with vulnerabilities so that events that are manageable for one child are experienced as debilitating by the child at risk for schizophrenia. For example, consider the youth whose CNS deficits interfere with the development of executive functions, who consequently will be unprepared for and stressed by the normative social and academic demands of adolescence.

Protective factors, in turn, comprise characteristics of the environment or the person that reduce the risk of schizophrenia. Those suggested in the literature include intelligence, social competence, social support and healthy patterns of family communication. One of the challenges to identifying protective factors is that if an individual does not develop a disorder, how will we know that they were protected from doing so? On the other hand,

the benefits to identifying protective factors are great in that they can lead to the development of preventative and intervention programmes.

As we have come to expect from a *transactional* developmental psychopathology model, these vulnerabilities, stressors and protective factors interact with one another over the course of development. While a predisposition to schizophrenia is genetically transmitted, the disorder is hypothesized to occur only in those individuals who are exposed to threshold levels of stress. In turn, the interaction between biological vulnerability and environmental stress is moderated by competencies in the individual (e.g., intelligence and social skills) and family responses (e.g., support and positive emotion).

Asarnow and Asarnow (2003) acknowledge that the state of knowledge in the field is not sufficiently well developed to identify with confidence protective and vulnerability factors that are specifically linked to schizophrenia. Rather than providing a precise theory of the origins of schizophrenia, therefore, this model is proposed as a helpful heuristic with which to integrate and organize the existing research findings.

Developmental Course

Short-Term Outcome

In the short term, the prognosis for a first psychotic episode is not good; in fact, the expected outcome is worse for children and adolescents than it is for adults. In the Maudsley study (Hollis, 2000), only 12 per cent of the youths achieved full remission at discharge from the hospital, in contrast with 50 per cent of those with mood-disorder related psychosis. For youths with schizophrenia, the likelihood of full recovery was greatest within the first three months following the onset of symptoms. After six months, those who were still symptomatic had only a 15 per cent chance of full recovery.

Long-Term Outcome

The longitudinal data are consistent in indicating a high degree of continuity and a poor prognosis for

FIGURE 11.5 Vulnerability-Stress Model of Childhood Onset of Schizophrenia.

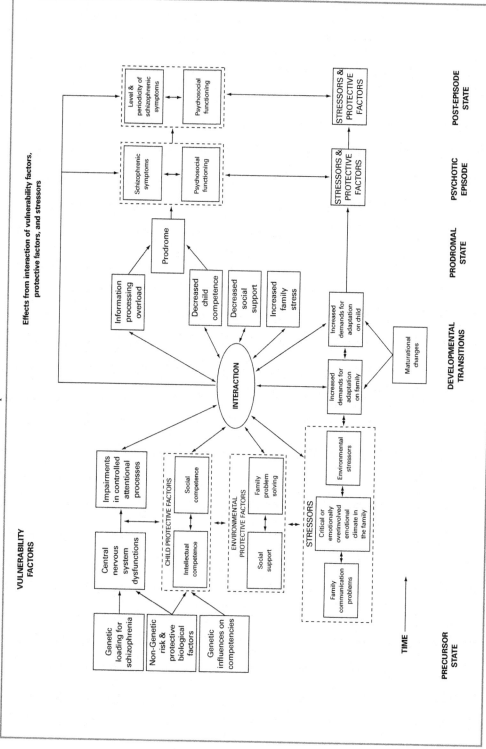

Source: Asarnow and Asarnow, 1996.

childhood onset schizophrenia. Remission rates range from 3 to 27 per cent depending on the particular study, while 61 to 90 per cent of the youths develop chronic schizophrenia with recurring episodes. In the Maudsley study, Hollis (2000) also found a high level of stability in children and adolescents diagnosed with schizophrenia, with 80 per cent retaining the diagnosis into adulthood. Further, those who had been diagnosed with schizophrenia in adolescence displayed the most impairments in adult social relationships, independent living skills, educational achievement and occupational functioning. Eggers et al. (2002) followed up 57 patients who had been diagnosed with schizophrenia prior to age 14. Approximately 16 years later, 27 per cent were in remission, 24 per cent were slightly remitted and 49 per cent were doing poorly. Similar results were found in a 3- to 7-year follow-up of children first diagnosed with schizophrenia between the ages of 7 and 14, 67 per cent of whom continued to display a disorder in the schizophrenic spectrum in adolescence (Asarnow et al., 1994). On a measure of global functioning, 56 per cent showed improvement over time, while 44 per cent either showed minimal improvement or deterioration.

Later in development, there is evidence that child and adolescent onset schizophrenia adversely affect employment, independent living and intimate relationships (Häfner and Nowotny, 1995). For example, at follow-up 42 years after the initial assessment, Eggers et al. (2002) found that about one-third of those with early onset schizophrenia were floridly psychotic and many were severely impaired in the social and occupational realms: 27 per cent were unable to work, 59 per cent were unmarried and lived alone, and only 7 per cent were in stable relationships. Considering the fact that social roles in regard to independent living and intimate partnership are in the process of being formed during childhood and adolescence, it is easy to see why these roles are particularly vulnerable to disruption by the insidious effects of early onset schizophrenia. In a more recent 15-year follow-up of patients diagnosed with schizophrenia in adolescence, only those with very early onset schizophrenia had very poor outcomes as opposed to those with child onset schizophrenia (Röpcke and Eggers, 2005)

Finally, there is an increased risk of mortality from various causes, including violent death, adverse medication-related reactions such as seizures (Hollis, 2004) and suicide, which occurs at a rate of approximately 10 per cent among those with early onset schizophrenia (McClellan et al., 2001).

Protective Factors

Protective factors identified in the literature include higher pre-morbid social and cognitive functioning, early intervention, short duration of the first psychotic episode and fewer negative symptoms of psychosis (Hollis, 2004). As with adults, later age of onset and rapid development of the disorder also are associated with a better outcome. For example, Eggers and Bunk (1997), in their 42-year follow-up study, found that none of the patients with a slow, insidious onset experienced a complete remission, whereas 33 per cent of those with an acute onset remitted completely. (See Fig. 11.6.) Acute onset was significantly more likely in youths aged 12 and older; younger children were more likely to have a chronic onset and thus a more negative outcome. Nonetheless, it is important to recognize that, with early treatment and positive prognostic signs, a young person with schizophrenia may go on to lead a productive and creative life. (See Fig. 11.7.)

Intervention

Prognosis in early onset appears to be substantively worse than in adult onset schizophrenia. The significant personal and societal costs of the disorder, its frequently deteriorating course, and the consistent negative prognosis associated with untreated illness highlight the importance of early applications of evidence-based interventions (Eack, 2009). Safe and effective treatments are therefore needed for these vulnerable youth. The lack of well-designed objective studies that has hampered our understanding of the nature and origins of childhood and adolescent schizophrenia continues to characterize the literature on intervention. For

FIGURE 11.6 Distribution of Outcome Categories of Chronic and Acute Onset Psychotic Patients.

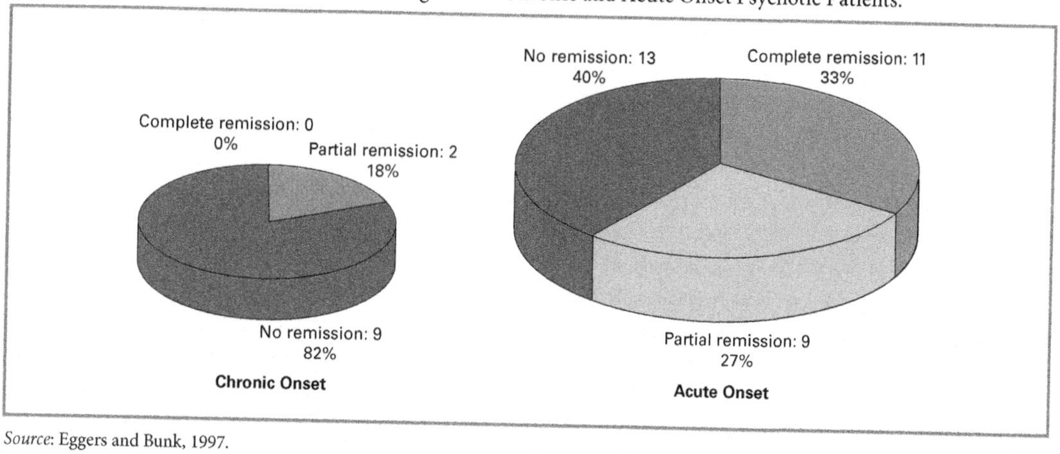

No remission: 13
40%

Complete remission: 11
33%

Complete remission: 0
0%

Partial remission: 2
18%

No remission: 9
82%

Chronic Onset

Partial remission: 9
27%

Acute Onset

Source: Eggers and Bunk, 1997.

example, in spite of the widespread use of neuroleptics (dopamine receptor blockers) in the treatment of children with schizophrenia, and in spite of the serious and sometimes toxic side effects that

FIGURE 11.7 Artwork by a Young Person with Schizophrenia.

M. Ramell, a painter and aspiring musician, was recently a featured artist in the Brushes with Life: Art, Artists and Mental Illness gallery developed by the Schizophrenia Treatment and Evaluation Program (STEP) at the University of North Carolina Department of Psychiatry.

can develop, there are few controlled studies of drug treatment. The literature on psychosocial interventions with children consists largely of clinical reports, with a dearth of controlled studies (Asarnow and Asarnow, 2003).

Psychopharmacology

Antipsychotic medication is the therapy of choice with adults, although there is limited carefully controlled research concerning the effectiveness of neuroleptics with children (McClellan et al., 2001). First-generation antipsychotics, such as haloperidol and loxapine, have shown efficacy. For example, two randomized double-blind studies report that haloperidol (Haldol) alleviated symptoms better than placebo in children and adolescents with schizophrenia (Hollis, 2004). However, younger children are may be at higher risk for extra-pyramidal side effects. Physical symptoms include tremor, slurred speech, akathisia, dystonia, anxiety, distress, paranoia and bradyphrenia, which are primarily associated with improper dosing of or unusual reactions to neuroleptic (antipsychotic) medications. Other studies have supported the use of the atypical antipsychotic clozapine (Clozaril) with children, but few are methodologically sound. However, preliminary results suggest that clozapine may be more effective than haloperidol while also being safer and avoiding its negative side effects, such as sedation, parkinsonism and seizures (Jacobsen and Rapoport, 1998). Most clinicians prescribe atypical (second-generation) antipsychotics, based on the assumption of superior efficacy and tolerability. Among second-generation antipsychotics, recent randomized control trials found that Olanzapine, Risperidone and Aripiprazole (Haas et al., 2009) have acute efficacy in the acute treatment of adolescents with schizophrenia. In fact Risperidone and Aripiprazole have been approved by the US Food and Drug Administration (FDA) for the treatment of adolescents with schizophrenia. Yet second-generation antipsychotics carry additional health implications. In the long term, the metabolic side effects of Olanzapine and Risperidone may place many youths at risk for diabetes and cardiovascular problems. Thus the balance between potential therapeutic benefits and risk of adverse events needs to be carefully monitored.

Individual Psychotherapy

Because schizophrenia may have such widespread effects on the individual as well as on the family, pharmacological treatment must be supplemented by various other kinds of remedial and rehabilitative measures. Weiner (1992) describes a programme of *individual psychotherapy* aimed at counteracting the social isolation and impaired reality contact found in schizophrenia through relationship building and reality testing. The former involves a combination of warmth and nurturance for those who have been deprived of love, and firmness without anger or punitiveness for those who cannot control their aggressive acting-out. To correct delusions and hallucinations, the therapist must point out that, while they are real to the patient, they are not real to the therapist. The next step involves identifying the needs giving rise to the cognitive distortions and dealing constructively with them. At a more practical level, the therapist helps the patient develop more effective social skills to counter social isolation.

Recent approaches to treating individuals with schizophrenia rely on *cognitive behavioural models*.

Essential features of treatment include using cognitive strategies to cope with symptoms and counter irrational beliefs, as well as social skills training to normalize interpersonal relationships.

The majority of research establishing the effectiveness of cognitive behavioural treatments has been conducted with adults (Bustillo et al., 2001). A notable exception is Power and colleagues' (2003) LifeSPAN, a cognitively oriented treatment specifically designed to prevent suicide among youths with early onset psychosis. The programme is initiated by a collaborative risk assessment in which the youth and clinician work together to formulate an understanding of the factors involved in the youth's suicidality. Subsequent treatment modules explore the rationale for suicide, hopelessness and reasons for living. Following this, the youth is helped to develop specific skills to counter the belief that suicide is the only option, including problem-solving training, strategies for tolerating emotional pain, stress management, self-esteem, help-seeking, social skills and psychoeducation regarding psychosis. To assess the effectiveness of the intervention, the investigators randomly assigned 21 youths to the treatment group and an equal number to standard clinical care. While both groups improved over the course of the study, those in the treatment group improved more on measures of hopelessness and suicidal ideation. Tragically, two participants in the study were lost to suicide, one of whom was from the treatment group.

Family Therapy

While there is extensive clinical literature regarding *family treatment* in schizophrenia – indeed, the early family systems models arose in the context of treating 'schizophrenogenic families' (e.g., Bateson et al., 1956) – randomized, controlled empirical research with children and adolescents is sparse (Wright et al. 2004). Nevertheless, it is easy to perceive how involving the family in the treatment process would help family members correct the communication and affective patterns that can precipitate a relapse. There is evidence from studies of

Box 11.2 A Comprehensive Approach to the Treatment of Schizophrenia

Given the progressive and cascading effect of schizophrenia on all areas of functioning, clinicians involved in treating the disorder urge that early detection and intervention are essential (McGorry and Yung, 2003). Malla and colleagues (2003) describe a model programme developed in Canada that uses an assertive model for the identification, treatment, retention and follow-up of young people who are undergoing a first psychotic break.

The first stage of the programme strives to reduce delays in treatment by launching a community-wide informational campaign regarding the signs and symptoms of psychosis. Once a youth is identified, treatment consists of a comprehensive array of services, including assessment, medication management, individual supportive therapy, family support and liaison with the community. In addition, youths are engaged in psychosocial group interventions geared to their stage of recovery.

Initially, youths still experiencing psychotic symptoms attend Recovery through Activity and Participation (RAP) groups that involve normalizing activities such as cooking, games, sports, art and community field trips. In the next stage of recovery, youths are involved in Youth Education and Support (YES) groups, a more intensive

intervention focused on psychoeducation about psychosis, self-identity, coping with peer relations, medication compliance, social skills and strategies for dealing with stigma. Finally, Cognitively Oriented Skills Training (COST) addresses cognitive deficits that interfere with functioning in schizophrenia, such as attention, concentration, memory and study strategies. Individual cognitive behavioural therapy is offered when indicated, such as to youths who exhibit anxiety or depression during their recovery. Ultimately, the goal is to normalize the youth's functioning by returning him or her to the community, re-establishing peer relations and re-engaging in occupational or academic activities as soon as possible.

Initial results of the first two and a half years of the programme are promising. The number of cases treated increased significantly over time, just as the delay in seeking treatment declined 50 per cent, indicating that the outreach efforts were successful. Most of the youths were treated with low doses of atypical antipsychotic medications, and retention and treatment adherence were good. At follow-up, three-quarters of the youths treated were in remission and the majority of the remaining youths had only moderate symptomatology.

---

adults that family-based interventions for adults help to prevent relapse and lead to improved adherence to medication treatment (Pilling et al., 2002). Linszen and colleagues (1996) investigated whether adding a family component would boost the effectiveness of intensive medication and individual treatment in an adolescent treatment facility. Results were highly promising for the first year, with only 16 per cent of the youths relapsing, but the effects appeared to erode in the years to follow, with 64 per cent relapsing between 17 and 55 months later. The major predictors of relapse were high EE in the family and heavy cannabis use, both of which indicate the necessity of ongoing family intervention and parental guidance for young people with schizophrenia.

Cognitive Rehabilitation Therapy

Cognitive impairments, in particular, are promising targets for early intervention because of their

early emergence, persistence and contribution to functional outcome. Unfortunately, few successful efforts have been directed toward the early treatment of cognitive deficits in schizophrenia. The only two published randomized controlled trials of cognitive rehabilitation among patients with early-course schizophrenia have yielded mixed results (Ueland and Rund, 2005; Wykes et al., 2008). Further, these trials were conducted exclusively with patients with early or childhood onset illness and used relatively short-term (three-month) interventions that focused primarily on the remediation of neurocognitive deficits in attention, memory and executive function. Long-term trials of cognitive rehabilitation approaches for patients with early course schizophrenia are noticeably absent, and most approaches place little to no emphasis on the remediation of social cognition, which may be key to improving functional outcome.

Prevention

Efforts to prevent schizophrenia are hampered by the fact that it is difficult to identify children who are at risk for the disorder before the onset of florid psychotic symptoms. For example, to date, efforts to identify prodromal youths have found that only one-fifth of those suspected of early onset schizophrenia go on to develop the disorder (Hollis, 2004). Early detection and early intervention in the acute phase, therefore, appear to be more achievable goals. Early intervention also prevents the occurrence of a long duration of untreated psychosis, and thus leads to a much better prognosis. (For a model early intervention programme, see Box 11.2.)

An alternative approach to prevention focuses on reducing the negative stigma associated with schizophrenia. Schulze and colleagues (2003) initiated a project with secondary school students aged 14 to 18 that was designed to reduce the negative stigma associated with schizophrenia by providing opportunities for personal contact between students and youths with the

disorder. Attitudes towards individuals with schizophrenia were assessed before and after the programme for 90 students and were compared with the attitudes expressed by 60 controls who did not undergo the intervention. The investigators found that the intervention significantly reduced negative stereotypes and the effects were still present at a one-month follow-up. The title of their study sums up the change in attitude nicely: 'Crazy? So what!' Currently, the World Psychiatric Association is developing plans to initiate a worldwide initiative to counter the negative stigma regarding schizophrenia (see Thompson et al., 2002).

As we have noted, research on child and adolescent schizophrenia is sparse, and many questions remain unresolved regarding the developmental dimension. By contrast, the psychopathologies we will discuss next – substance abuse and eating disorders – have been well researched and are closely tied to the developments characterizing the adolescent period.

Psychopathologies of the Adolescent Transition: Eating Disorders and Substance Abuse

Chapter Contents

Normative Adolescent Development

Adolescence marks a major life change. The transition between childhood and adulthood is accompanied by changes in every aspect of individual development and every social context. In addition, adolescence is unique in that it involves two distinct phases: into the stage as one moves from childhood to adolescence, and out of the stage as the adolescent enters adulthood (Kerig and Schulz, 2011). Thus, the developmental picture is a complex one.

The *body* itself sets the stage with physical changes more rapid than those of any other developmental period except infancy, including the attainment of a mature size and body shape, hormonal changes associated with puberty, and the advent of adult sexuality. *Society* follows suit by requiring the youth to master more complex tasks,

relinquish dependence on the family and assume responsibility for making decisions regarding the two major tasks of adulthood, love and work. This transition is facilitated by the increasingly important role *peer relations* play and by the new-found cognitive sophistication that enables the adolescent both to think abstractly and to envision future possibilities, expanding the situation-specific self-perception of childhood into the overarching question, Who am I?

Adolescence gives special meaning to many of the personality variables we have been discussing. *Self-regulation* allows for experimenting with new experiences while avoiding the extremes of inhibition and impulsivity. The intimacy of *attachment* merges with burgeoning *sexuality*, and *social relations* with peers take on a new importance. Because of physiological changes, the psychological representation of the body, or the *body image*, is more salient than it has been since the early years. Increased *cognitive* complexity allows the adolescent both to entertain hypothetical possibilities and to ask abstract questions concerning the self and the future. Cognitive development also allows the adolescent a more sophisticated level of self-exploration and a more realistic grasp of the options that society offers. Finally, the *family context* is changing, as parents must readjust their expectations and parenting styles to allow for the youth's needs for increasing independence and autonomy.

Psychopathology in Adolescence

Western society has traditionally viewed the adolescent transition as one of turmoil, the inherent instability of the period being epitomized by the phrase 'storm and stress'. Psychoanalysts characterize the period as marking the return of primitive impulses and unresolved conflicts from the early stages of psychosexual development whereas, according to Erikson's ego psychology, a weakened ego struggles to master an identity crisis and role diffusion. However, it is becoming increasingly clear that the image of adolescence as a time of turmoil is applicable primarily to a minority of troubled teens. Most adolescents make the transition without significant emotional problems. Parent–adolescent relationships are generally harmonious, and for most teenagers the search for identity goes on unaccompanied by crises.

The revised picture should not be taken to mean that adolescence is uniformly serene. Moodiness, self-depreciation and depression reach a peak in adolescence; and other psychopathologies also show a sharp rise, including suicide, schizophrenia, substance abuse and eating disorders. The overall rate of psychopathology increases only slightly, since other disturbances are on the decline; however, the new disturbances are far more serious than the ones they replace, making the picture an ominous one.

As Ebata et al. (1990) point out, a developmental psychopathology perspective on adolescence needs to attend to (1) the *normative developmental capacities* that can serve as either risk or protective mechanisms for the individual, (2) the *social context* in which individual development takes place, and (3) the dynamic and *transactional processes* that characterize the relationship between the individual and the social context. For example, whereas peer relations and academic expectations might become more challenging in adolescence, adding sources of stress that can undermine adjustment, adolescents are increasingly able to choose and influence their social contexts and in this way to have more control over their own development. In addition, adolescents have an expanded ability to draw on their own inner resources, as well as those in the environment, in order to adapt and cope.

Erikson's concept of **identity** integrates many of the diverse strands of adolescent development as well as provides leads to potential sources of protection and vulnerability. Identity involves both inner continuity and interpersonal mutuality; it is a process of coming to terms with oneself and finding one's place in society. Adolescence is marked by an identity crisis because it is a 'turning point, a crucial moment' (Erikson, 1968, p. 16) in which the adolescent must master the challenges of finding a fulfilling vocation, sexual role and ideology in order to avoid stagnation and regression. Youths approach the task of achieving an identity in ways that are influenced by how they have resolved previous stages of psychosocial development. Trust, autonomy, initiative and industry act as protective factors, while mistrust, shame, doubt, guilt and inferiority act as vulnerabilities.

The two psychopathologies we will discuss represent different ways in which developmental processes can go awry. In some youths' relentless pursuit of thinness associated with eating disorders, the body image becomes a destructive tyrant, while the self-defeating need for autonomy is reminiscent of the oppositional behaviour of the toddler period. In substance abuse, precocity propels the adolescent into assuming adult roles and freedoms for which he or she is ill prepared.

Eating Disorders: Anorexia Nervosa

Definition and Characteristics

Anorexia nervosa involves at least a 15 per cent loss of body weight through purging and/or voluntary restriction, as well as an active pursuit of thinness. DSM-IV differentiates two types based on the different means used to achieve thinness. The first

relies solely on strict dieting and is called the *restricting type*. The second, the *binge-eating/purging type*, alternates between dieting and binge eating, followed by self-induced vomiting or purging (Table 12.1).

ICD-10 (WHO, 1997) defines anorexia similarly as:

A disorder characterized by deliberate weight loss, induced and sustained by the patient. It occurs most commonly in adolescent girls and

TABLE 12.1 DSM-IV-TR Criteria for Eating Disorders

Anorexia Nervosa

A. Refusal to maintain body weight at or above a minimally normal weight for age and height (e.g., weight loss leading to maintenance of body weight less than 85 percent of that expected; or failure to make expected weight gain during period of growth, leading to body weight less than 85 percent of that expected).

B. Intense fear of gaining weight or becoming fat, even though underweight.

C. Disturbance in the way in which one's body weight or shape is experienced, undue influence of body weight or shape on self-evaluation, or denial of the seriousness of the current low body weight.

D. In postmenarcheal females, amenorrhea (i.e., the absence of at least three consecutive menstrual cycles).

Specify Type:

> **Restricting Type:** During the current episode of Anorexia Nervosa, the person has not regularly engaged in binge-eating Or purging behavior (i.e., self-induced vomiting or the misuse of laxatives, diuretics, or enemas).

> **Binge-Eating/Purging Type:** During the current episode of Anorexia Nervosa, the person has regularly engaged in binge-eating or purging behavior.

Bulimia Nervosa

A. Recurrent episodes of binge eating, characterized by both of the following:

> (1) Eating, in a discrete period of time (e.g., within any 2-hour period), an amount of food that is definitely larger than most people would eat during a similar period of time and under similar circumstances.

> (2) A sense of lack of control over eating during the episode (e.g., a feeling that one cannot stop eating or control what or how much one is eating).

B. Recurrent inappropriate compensatory behavior in order to prevent weight gain, such as self-induced vomiting; misuse of laxatives, diuretics, enemas; fasting; or excessive exercise.

C. The binge eating and inappropriate compensatory behaviors both occur, on average, at least twice a week for 3 months.

D. Self-evaluation is unduly influenced by body shape and weight.

E. The disturbance does not occur exclusively during episodes of Anorexia Nervosa.

Specify Type:

> **Purging Type:** During the current episode of Bulimia Nervosa, the person has regularly engaged in self-induced vomiting Or the misuse of laxatives, diuretics, or enemas.

> **Nonpurging Type:** During the current episode of Bulimia Nervosa, the person has used other inappropriate compensatory behaviors, such as fasting or excessive exercise, but has not regularly engaged in self-induced vomiting or the misuse of laxatives, diuretics, or enemas.

Source: Adapted with permission from the *Diagnostic and Statistical Manual of Mental Disorders*, Fourth Edition Text Revision, Copyright 2000, by the American Psychiatric Association.

young women, but adolescent boys and young men may also be affected, as may children approaching puberty and older women up to the menopause. The disorder is associated with a specific psychopathology whereby a dread of fatness and flabbiness of body contour persists as an intrusive overvalued idea, and the patients impose a low weight threshold on themselves. There is usually undernutrition of varying severity with secondary endocrine and metabolic changes and disturbances of bodily function. The symptoms include restricted dietary choice, excessive exercise, induced vomiting and purgation, and use of appetite suppressants and diuretics.

Youth with anorexia have a normal awareness of hunger but are terrified of giving in to the impulse to eat. As a consequence, the individual wastes away to a dangerous state of emaciation in pursuit of an ideal image of thinness. As the condition advances, diets become increasingly restrictive. For example, clinical case reports describe self-starvation as extreme as a youth going a year with eating only celery sticks and chewing gum. Youth who have anorexia often take extreme pride in the control they demonstrate over their food intake.

Among the secondary symptoms of anorexia, *excessive activity* is one of the most common. (Our review follows Stice and Bulik, 2008, except where noted.) At times the intensity of the activity is masked by a socially acceptable form, such as participation in sports. *Amenorrhea* (lack of menstruation) is another common secondary symptom, with menstruation often ceasing prior to weight loss. Other physical symptoms associated with self-starvation include skin discolouration (hypercarotenemia), the growth of fine, downy hair all over the body (lanugo), hypersensitivity to cold, low blood pressure (hypotension), slow heart rate (bradycardia) and other cardiovascular problems.

Anorexia is one of the few psychopathologies that can lead to death. Studies suggest mortality rates from 3 to 10 per cent, with almost half of those accounted for by suicide and the rest by medical complications secondary to the disorder (Lock and le Grange, 2006). Semi-starvation can affect most major organ systems, resulting in anaemia, renal system impairments, cardiovascular problems, osteoporosis and an irreversible shortness of stature. Chronic dehydration and depletions in serum potassium lead to imbalances in the electrolyte system that is crucial to heart functioning; cardiac arrhythmia and sudden death may ensue. As Lock and le Grange (2006) note, the likelihood of mortality increases 1 per cent for every year the youth suffers with the disorder: 'No other psychiatric illness is so lethal in its chronic form' (p. 488).

Prevalence and Onset

Data on *prevalence rates* tend to be based on clinical and convenience samples rather than the kind of population-based epidemiological studies that would provide us with definitive information. In addition, the diagnostic criteria tend to lead us to overlook younger suffers, whose weight is naturally fluctuating and menstrual periods erratic, as well as males, who cannot by definition meet the criterion of amenorrhea (Lock and le Grange, 2006). Thus, our existing statistics may be underestimates of the true rates.

Halmi (2009) summarizes the available prevalence rates from studies conducted cross-nationally. One large-scale study of patients seeking care from general practitioners in the UK found overall prevalence rates per 100 000 of 8.6 for females and 0.7 for males, with dramatic differences across age groups: by far the highest incidence rate, of 34.6 per 100 000, was found among girls ages 10–19 years (Currin et al., 2005). However, the prevalence appears to be much higher in studies that include youth who do not seek medical attention for the disorder. For example, another large-scale study conducted telephone interviews with women from a birth cohort of 2881 Finnish twins and found a lifetime prevalence of 2.2 per cent, with an incidence for females between the ages of 15 and 19 of a huge 270 per 100 000 persons (Keski-Rahkonen et al., 2007). This is a markedly higher rate than found in other studies. To explain this, the investigators point to the fact that over half of the cases in their study had never reported their symptoms to a professional and therefore would not have been detected by the typical review of medical records. In turn, the large-scale National Comorbidity Study (Merikangas et al., 2010) of adolescents in the USA did not enquire about anorexia specifically, but found eating disorders of all types among 3.8 per cent of girls and 1.5 per cent of boys.

As these data suggest, there is a significant *gender difference*, with gender ratios of males to females of about 1:12 (Halmi, 2009). In addition, tellingly, there are two peak periods of *onset*, ages 14 and 18 (APA, 2000), which correspond to the transitions into and out of the adolescence phase. Figure 12.1 presents data on age of onset from an international sample of 4139 adults from six European nations, and shows the relatively early onset of anorexia in comparison to bulimia, binge-eating disorder or simple bingeing (Preti et al., 2009).

Cross-national data also confirm that the prevalence of anorexia has been rising in developed countries, including the UK, Singapore and Australia, especially among younger girls (Halmi, 2009). Increasing rates may be accounted for by the growing awareness of eating disorders and availability of treatment, but also may reflect other pressures towards a 'relentless pursuit of thinness'. A hopeful note, however, comes from the most recent Youth Risk Behavior Survey (CDC, 2009) in the USA, which found a decrease in the proportion of youth reporting attempting to lose weight through starving themselves (10.6 per cent) or using laxatives or self-purging (4.0 per cent) over the course of the past decade.

Ethnicity and Social Class

Early stereotypes suggested that anorexia was disproportionately prevalent among youths from the middle and upper social classes (Stice and Bulik, 2008). However, it is important to keep in mind that prevalence data often come from clinical samples, and more privileged members of society may

FIGURE 12.1 Age of Onset of Eating Disorders in a Large Cross-National Sample.

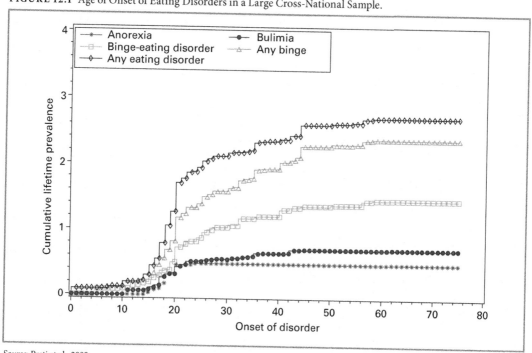

Source: Preti et al., 2009.

have better access to treatment facilities. Studies of normative samples of children in the UK, Norway and the USA fail to find an association between social class and the development of eating disorders (Doyle and Bryant-Waugh, 2000). Nonetheless, among higher SES youth, those who participate in certain 'subcultures', such as sporting teams or dance groups that place extreme emphasize on weight or appearance, may be at heightened risk for the development of eating disorders (Wilson et al., 2003).

Although there is a dearth of studies including *ethnic minority* populations, evidence is growing that eating disorders are found across racial and ethnic lines (Shaw et al., 2004). However, there are subcultural differences. While US youths from Hispanic backgrounds have rates equivalent to those of European American youths, Asian American and African American youths are less likely to develop disordered eating (Striegel-Moore et al., 2003).

Cross-culturally, the role of Westernization has been implicated in the rise of eating disorders among developing nations. The prevalence of eating disorders increases as a function of exposure to Western ideals of thinness and the importance of physical appearance (Lake et al., 2000).

Comorbidity

Depression is often present in adolescents with anorexia, with one German study reporting a comorbidity rate of 60.4 per cent (Salbach-Andrae et al., 2008). Such high comorbidity has led to the speculation that anorexia and depression share a common etiology (Wade et al., 2000). However, subsequent research has indicated that, while they occur together, they are independent disturbances. For example, improvement in the eating disorder does not necessarily relieve the depression. Also, depressed mood tends to accompany any form of starvation. In addition, longitudinal research suggests that depression pre-dates and predicts the onset of disturbed eating (Measelle et al., 2006). Moreover, following their participants over time, the investigators found that eating disorders them-

selves increased the risk of another set of disorders that are often comorbid with anorexia, namely *substance abuse* disorders. Substance disorders are most likely to occur in the binge-eating/purging subtype of anorexia (Wilson et al., 2003).

Anxiety disorders also commonly occur with anorexia, particularly obsessive-compulsive disorder (Jordan et al., 2008). Longitudinal research suggests that anxiety precedes the development of anorexic symptoms. For example, in a genetic study of over 600 women, Raney and colleagues (2008) found that 39 per cent of women with anorexia had a history of anxiety and, of those women, 94 per cent met criteria for a diagnosis of anxiety disorder prior to the onset of their eating disorder. Moreover, comorbidity of anxiety and anorexia made for a more pernicious, severe and long-lasting course. *Personality disorders* are often seen, particularly among those who binge and purge (Jordan et al., 2008).

Etiology
The Biological Context
Genetics

Anorexia tends to run in families. For example, Strober and colleagues (2000) found that individuals with anorexia were 11.3 times more likely to have a family member with anorexia and 4.2 times more likely to have a family member with bulimia when compared with normative controls. More specifically, there is an increased risk of 3–10 per cent among siblings, 27 per cent for mothers, 16 per cent for fathers and 29 per cent in first-degree relatives. Twin studies reveal some evidence of a *genetic component* in anorexia. For example, the concordance rate for monozygotic twins has been found to be approximately 10 times greater than for dizygotic twins (Wade, 2010). However, the results of twin studies are highly inconsistent, with heritability estimates ranging from 33 per cent to 84 per cent (Stice and Bulik, 2008).

Studies attempting to identify the specific genetic mechanism involved have focused on those associated with the *serotonin* system, given its relationship to appetite, mood and weight regulation, but the small sample sizes available to date have hampered the effort (Slof-O'pt et al., 2005). International collaborations among researchers also have suggested a susceptibility localized on chromosome 1 (Grice et al., 2002).

Neurochemistry

Speculation has implicated in anorexia an endocrine disorder that affects the hypothalamic-pituitary-gonadal axis. However, many of the biological correlates of anorexia appear to be secondary to weight loss and are reversible with weight gain. Therefore, it is unclear whether these abnormalities are causal or are secondary to starvation, dieting, bingeing and/or purging (Lask, 2000).

Kaye and colleagues (2003) have focused attention on *serotonergic* functioning in anorexia nervosa. These authors speculate that premorbid imbalances in serotonin precipitate dysphoric mood, which is accompanied by anxiety, obsessional thinking and perfectionism. Self-starvation, as those with anorexia subsequently discover, reduces brain serotonin overactivity and lifts dysphoric mood, thus making this behaviour highly reinforcing. As Duvvuri and colleagues (2010) state:

> Individuals with anorexia ... enter a vicious cycle, because caloric restriction results in a brief respite from dysphoric mood. However, malnutrition and weight loss, in turn, produce alterations in many neuropeptides and monoamine function, which also exaggerates dysphoric mood. Thus, those with anorexia pursue starvation in an attempt to avoid the dysphoric consequences of eating. (p. 715)

Another piece of evidence in favour of the serotonin pathway comes from long-term studies of patients who have recovered from their eating disorder and are now at normal weight. Levels of 5-hydroxyindolacetic acid (5-HIAA), a metabolite of serotonin, were found to be elevated among these women in comparison to non-eating disordered controls (Kaye et al., 1998). The authors speculate that hyperserotonic activity not only predisposes youth to disordered eating, but also

contributes to the associated personality attributes of perfectionism, obsessiveness and rigidity.

Brain-Imaging Studies

Although a number of abnormalities in brain structure and function have been found in individuals with eating disorders, these also generally appear to be consequences of self-starvation and reverse when normal weight returns (Wagner et al., 2006). An exception to this may be the finding of elevated activity in the 5-HT receptor in the frontal-limbic regions of the brain (Kaye et al., 2005). This region is associated with impulse control and behavioural inhibition, and deficits in these capacities are not only seen in youth with anorexia but are detectable before the onset of the disorder and tend to persist even after recovery (Stice and Bulik, 2008).

The Individual Context
The Body Image

Along with menstruation and breast development, females undergo a 'fat spurt' during puberty, an accumulation of large quantities of subcutaneous fat that adds an average of 24 pounds of weight. The physical changes associated with puberty force the adolescent to make a fundamental reorganization of her body image, which – coupled with her increased capacity for self-reflection – may result in a preoccupation with her body and with the responses of others to it. There is evidence that these pubertal changes are linked to the onset of preoccupation with weight and disordered eating (Culbert et al., 2009). In addition, *early maturing* girls are more likely to develop eating disorders than those who begin to physically develop later, as was confirmed recently by a group of British researchers (Day et al., 2011). This is particularly the case when early-maturing girls are victimized by peer teasing and relational aggression (Compian et al., 2009) or, as was shown in a study in the Netherlands, when they at least *perceive* themselves to be the victims of peer bullying (Giletta et al., 2010).

Studies of individuals with anorexia have suggested a developmental sequence in which body dissatisfaction leads to typical dieting attempts, which give way to preoccupation with food and weight and the use of increasingly more maladaptive methods of weight control. Therefore, *ordinary dieting*, in the context of other psychological risk factors, may be the first step in a trajectory toward pathological eating (Lock and le Grange, 2006).

Hilde Bruch's (1973) pioneering clinical observations suggested to her that girls with anorexia have *inaccurate perceptions* of their bodies. They literally did not seem to perceive how thin their bodies have become. One of her patients had difficulty discriminating between two photographs of herself even though there was a 70-pound difference in her weight. Another said she could see how emaciated her body was when looking in a mirror, but when she looked away, she reverted to her belief that she was larger. Thus, the anorexic pursuit of self-respect through food refusal is expressed in the vain pursuit of a body that literally is never perceived as sufficiently thin. More recent research from a multi-site international team confirms the relationship between eating disorder symptomatology and distortions in body image (Hrabosky et al., 2009).

Bruch (1973) also proposed that anorexic girls are unable to accurately identify and discriminate between *proprioceptive* (internal body) states, such as hunger, satiety, anger and sadness. Therefore, they are likely to mislabel their feelings or to confuse emotions such as anger with the desire to eat. Measurement of poor proprioceptive awareness is included in screening assessments for anorexia and has been found to be associated with increased risk for the development of the disorder (Lyon et al., 1997). Intriguingly, a team of Japanese researchers finds that, with weight gain and recovery from anorexia, single photon emission computed tomography (SPECT) scans show an observable increase in cerebral blood to areas of the brain – the right thalamus, right parietal lobe and right cerebellum – that are associated with proprioceptive awareness (Komatsu et al., 2010).

Personality Characteristics

Low self-esteem is commonly seen in youth with anorexia, who describe themselves in such terms as bad and unworthy (see Box 12.1). *Anxiety, obsessionality, rigidity* and *perfectionism* are particularly salient characteristics of those with anorexia and, moreover, seem to pre-date the onset of the eating disorder and persist even after recovery. (Here we follow Stice and Bulik, 2008, except where noted.)

Whereas both types of anorexia are characterized by their pursuit of thinness, those who *restrict* tend to be higher in neuroticism, including being rigid and conforming, socially insecure, obsessional and lacking in insight (Bulik et al., 2006). Those who *binge-purge*, who make up about half the population of those with anorexia, are more extroverted and sociable but are more emotionally dysregulated and alternate between rigid overcontrol and undercontrol. They also tend to have problems with *impulsivity* and *negativity* and are prone to using maladaptive strategies to cope with unpleasant emotions, such as substance abuse or self-harming behaviour (Stice, 2002). Overall, those who binge-purge have more extreme and overt psychopathology. For example, in their study of 50 young women hospitalized for anorexia, Casper and colleagues (1992) found that restricters were higher in self-control, inhibition of emotion and conscientiousness. By contrast, binge-purgers were more impulsive; and while they shared the restricters' belief in moral family values, they were emotionally more adventurous and had more characterological problems.

In one of the few studies to focus on *males*, Carlat and colleagues (1997) investigated the records of all males who had been treated for eating disorders at Massachusetts General Hospital over a 14-year period. Of the 135 identified, 22 per cent were anorexic. Over half of these suffered from major depression, and personality disorders and substance abuse were also common.

Cognition

Fairburn and colleagues in the UK (Fairburn and Harrison, 2003; Fairburn et al., 2003) give cognitions a central role in their theory of the origins of anorexia, particularly an *excessive need for control*. Control over food intake and weight become essential to escape from intolerable underlying

---

Box 12.1 A Case Study in Anorexia

'At 5 years of age I began to suffer from compulsive behaviour. That meant that I would take my socks on and off up to four or five times before I was satisfied. When walking along the pavement it was imperative that I avoided the cracks. This obsession with ordinary habits meant that I was late for everything and my parents would leave me behind as a punishment. Psychiatrists advised my mother to ignore my "negative behaviour" and reward only "good behaviour". As a result I felt rejected and loved only for the "good" me.

When I was 8 we visited my grandfather in Tuscany, and a chance remark deeply affected me. I shall never forget sitting on the grass and looking out at the glistening ocean as I experienced the last few moments of childhood innocence. My grandfather strolled past with my father and remarked, "Tara is a cute little girl, but when she loses her puppy fat she will be really beautiful!" Presumably my grandfather meant well, but he was unaware of the power his poisonous words were to have. I was sensitive and remember desperately wanting to be perfect in every way.

Before reaching my ninth birthday I had begun dieting. Along with a drastic reduction in my food intake were some rather unusual habits. I started drinking from a baby bottle and using a baby knife and fork. I found clothes from my early childhood in the attic and began wearing them. This baby syndrome was a desire to be a lovable baby again, like my brother who was a year old and loved by everyone...

In school during lunch a child in my class tormented me: "Every bite of food you eat is making you fatter," he teased. Dieting fads filtered all the way down to the playground. Parents who slimmed passed a "thin is best" message to their children, encouraged by the media. It is no coincidence that I obtained the starring role in my school play in the midst of my weight loss. The more I suffered from anorexia nervosa the more determined I became to be the best...

I was convinced that the thinner I was the more lovable I would be to the rest of the world. Fashion spreads filled the walls of my bedroom and the emaciated figure of the average fashion model became the god I worshipped... I insisted I was eating – it just happened when no one was around. When the school doctor weighed me I stole some kilogram weights and hid them in my pocket...

The way forward only emerged when I entered... long-term treatment and lived there for 10 months. My parents came in for meals and family therapy. During these meals my parents practised working as a team. This was a major change from previous meals, which were filled with arguments and anxiety. They learned how to listen and communicate when there was tension. Weekends were spent at home where the skills we learned during the week were practised... The goal treatment was particularly effective. If I behaved and ate properly I would achieve my goal in the form of a special treatment... From the beginning of my hospitalization I had individual therapy sessions... Therapy became a constant and stable part of my life...

So, what does cause anorexia nervosa in children? It seems to me that there are a variety of contributing factors: parental relations, school pressures – including academic expectations and relationships with other children, media images that are often absorbed unconsciously and an extremely negative self-image. As an anorexic child I struggled daily with intense feelings of negativity that seemed to confirm my unworthiness. In my mind I was not valuable enough to be fed properly. From personal experience I believe that one of the greatest needs during anorexia is reassurance and the continual confirmation that the sufferer is lovable and worthy.'

Source: Haggiag, 2000.

---

perceptions of the self as ineffective and inadequate. However, the intense urge to eat that follows from self-starvation threatens to reinstate perceived powerlessness, thus motivating further dietary restriction. Other *cognitive distortions*, such as perfectionism, 'catastrophizing', overgeneralizing and personalizing, have been found in those with anorexia to a much greater degree than in controls, as have dysfunctional cognitive styles such as obsessional thinking and negative self-judgements.

The fact that cognitive factors are also important in regulating eating behaviour has been demonstrated in studies of normative dieters.

Adherence to a diet is cognitively controlled, often in the form of quotas on food intake, carefully counting of calories and assiduous self-monitoring. However, chronic dieters are vulnerable to black-and-white thinking that can lead to *counter-regulatory eating*, or binge eating on high-calorie food; for example, the belief that one has transgressed one's diet can break the dieter's resolve and trigger increased food consumption (Foreyt and Mikhail, 1997). Such findings on normative populations are relevant to understanding the binge-purge cycle.

One of the cognitive factors that makes anorexia difficult to treat is that the disorder is *ego syntonic*; that is, those with anorexia view the symptoms as consistent with their self-image and personal goals. Unlike other disorders, in which youths are unhappy with their symptoms and desire to free themselves of them, those with anorexia view achieving an extremely low weight as 'a triumph of self-discipline, upon which their self-esteem depends' (Wilson et al., 2003). Consequently, the motivation to change may be weak or completely absent.

The Family Context
Parental Attitudes
Parental attitudes towards weight and dieting also appear to play a role in disordered eating in samples drawn from the USA, the UK and Europe. As early as 5 years of age, maternal concern about the daughter's weight and restricting her access to food are associated with lower perceived competence in girls (Davison and Birch, 2001), and by age 7 with body dissatisfaction and restrained eating (Anschutz et al., 2009). Consequently, eating disorders are more prevalent among girls whose parents make critical comments about their daughters' weight, body shape or eating habits and those of parents who themselves diet (Fairburn et al., 1997). These findings were confirmed in a Spanish study which found that mothers' own body dissatisfaction, drive for thinness, social insecurity and lack of interoceptive awareness were predictive of the development of eating disorders in their daughters (Canals et al., 2009). In turn, fathers' perfectionism also contributed to daughters' disordered eating.

Family Systems Theory
Minuchin and colleagues' (1978) observations of 'anorexic families' provided the basis for much of their early theorizing about the influence of the family system on psychopathology. They describe four characteristic patterns of interaction in families of adolescents with anorexia:

1 *Enmeshment.* Members of the pathologically enmeshed family are highly involved and responsive to one another but in an intrusive way. As we saw in Chapter 1, enmeshed families have poorly differentiated perceptions of each other, and roles and lines of authority are diffuse (e.g., children may assume parental roles).

2 *Overprotectiveness.* Family members of psychosomatically ill children are overly concerned for each other's welfare. A sneeze can set off 'a flurry of handkerchief offers', and criticism must be cushioned by pacifying behaviour. The family's overprotectiveness and exaggerated concern for the child retard the development of autonomy, and the child, in turn, feels responsible for protecting the family from distress.

3 *Rigidity.* Pathological families resist change. Particularly during periods of normal growth, such as adolescence, they intensify their efforts to retain their customary patterns. One consequence of rigidity is that the child's illness is used as an excuse for avoiding problems accompanying change.

4 *Lack of conflict resolution.* Some families deny conflict; others bicker in a diffuse, scattered, ineffectual way; and yet others have a parent who is conflict-avoidant, such as a father who leaves the house every time a confrontation threatens.

Minuchin and colleagues (1978) describe the anorexic family as overly concerned with diet, appearance and control. The family's intrusiveness undermines the child's autonomy, and both her psychological and bodily functions are continually subject to scrutiny. Adolescence is a particularly stressful time for the enmeshed family, which is unable to cope with the developmental task of separation. The youth, sensing the stress, responds with troubled behaviour such as self-starvation. Perhaps even more important, being symptomatic helps to maintain the youth in an ostensibly dependent role in relation to her parents, while at the same time her refusal to eat allows her a covert form of rebellion.

Some empirical support can be found for the family model. For example, Rowa and colleagues (2001) found high levels of enmeshment in families of both anorexic and bulimic patients. Similarly, Humphrey (1989) compared the observed interactions of the families of typically developing female adolescents and girls with eating disorders. In support of Minuchin's ideas, parents of daughters with anorexia tended to communicate a double message of nurturance and affection and to discount the daughter's expressions of her own thoughts and feelings. Further support comes from a multinational collaboration among researchers from the UK, Italy, Spain, Austria and Slovenia, in which investigators found that the factors most systematically associated with disordered eating were young women's use of food as a means of individualization from the family, and perceptions of parental excessive control and rules about food (Krug et al., 2009).

However, other studies suggest that these problematic patterns are seen in families of youth with many other forms of psychopathology rather than their being specific to anorexia (Casper and Troiani, 2001). In addition, the lack of prospective longitudinal research makes it unclear whether these family interactional styles are predictors or consequences of the disorder and parents' attempts to battle with an obstinate youth's refusal to eat sufficiently so as to sustain her life.

Parent–Child Attachment

Another perspective on how problematic parent–child relationships might contribute to anorexia comes from studies of adolescent *attachment*. The British researchers Ward and colleagues (2001)

conducted Adult Attachment Interviews with anorexia patients and their mothers and found that a dismissive attachment style, in which the importance of relationships is defensively downplayed, was common among both members of the dyad. In addition, interviews with the mothers frequently revealed themes of unresolved loss and trauma. The investigators speculate that a difficulty in processing emotions may be passed down from mother to daughter and thus increase the risk for the development of anorexia. Detached attitudes towards parents also were implicated in Cunha and colleagues' (2009) study of patients with anorexia in Portugal.

Child Maltreatment

Looking beyond relational qualities, researchers have investigated whether other factors in the parent–child relationship are related to the development of anorexia. For example, studies of the prevalence of *sexual abuse* in those with eating disorders range from 34 per cent to 85 per cent, depending on the definitions and methods used (Perez et al., 2002). However, these studies are generally drawn from clinical populations where maltreatment rates are likely to be high. More carefully designed longitudinal research has not tended to find that sexual abuse is a specific risk factor for anorexia (Sanci et al., 2008) but rather that it increases the likelihood of psychopathology in general (Fairburn et al., 2003).

A well-conceived study by Romans and colleagues (2001) investigated the factors that differentiated between women with a history of childhood sexual abuse who did and did not go on to develop an eating disorder. Those who developed disordered eating were likely to be younger, to have started menstruation early and to describe their fathers as overcontrolling. No variables associated with sexual abuse per se (e.g., its frequency, duration and type) contributed to the prediction of eating disordered behaviour.

The Social Context

Recall that in our review of research on comorbidity we learned that girls with anorexia often experience pre-morbid anxiety and depression, both of which are known to be associated with withdrawal from the peer group, problematic social relationships and hypersensitivity (see Chapters 8 and 9). In addition, we know that early development in the context of peer teasing is a risk factor for anorexia (Compian et al., 2009). Thus, this toxic combination – an inherent sensitivity to slights, a visible difference that inspires comments from peers and a social context of relational aggression – may potentiate the risk for vulnerable girls.

Romantic relationships in particular may be a source of stress for those individuals who are prone to disordered eating. Ferriter and colleagues (2010) followed a sample of 140 adolescents over a period of five years and found that those with symptoms of depression were at higher risk of eating pathology when they also experienced poor functioning in romantic domains. Avoidance of sexuality also may be seen. For example, Carlat and colleagues (1997) found that 58 per cent of males with anorexia were described as 'asexual' in that they eschewed any interest in sexual activity. Over time, anxiety about their appearance, lack of pleasure derived from romantic relationships and the social isolation associated with self-starvation lead youth to withdraw from peer relations entirely.

However, research on anorexia is complicated by the fact that starvation per se significantly affects behaviour, producing depression, irritability, social isolation and decreased sexual interest. Starvation can also alter relationships with family members and friends, who are helpless to intervene in eating patterns that produce striking emaciation and might result in death. Thus, the problem of distinguishing causes from consequences is a knotty one.

The Cultural Context
Femininity and Body Ideals
In Western societies the ideal of feminine beauty has changed from the curvaceous figure epitomized by such icons as Marilyn Monroe to the lean and svelte look admired today. For example, contestants in Miss Universe pageants have steadily decreased in weight over the past decades. In fact, the average

weight of beauty pageant contestants is 13 to 19 per cent below normal – the 'ideal' woman, in other words, meets the first criterion for an eating disorder diagnosis (Ohring et al., 2002).

Few young women are able to achieve the exaggeratedly tall and thin proportions exemplified by pageant contestants and high-fashion models. But cultural norms dictate that thin is beautiful and what is beautiful is good. Moreover, the message is more powerful in certain settings; for example, activities such as dancing and modelling, and certain sports which dictate certain body weights, are breeding grounds for anorexia (Lock and le Grange, 2006).

Further, there is evidence that *physical attractiveness* is more central to the female sex-role stereotype than to the masculine sex role, which may account for the fact that far fewer boys become anorexic. There are two exceptions to this. First, boys who endorse feminine sex-role characteristics appear to be as vulnerable as females to developing disordered attitudes toward eating (Meyer et al., 2001). Another exception may be found in the sexual minority community, where heightened attention to physical appearance is believed to act as a risk factor for eating disorders among homosexual males (Russell and Keel, 2002).

Ethnicity and Culture
Some evidence suggests that cultural attitudes might provide a protective factor against eating disorders. For example, in the USA, African Americans and Hispanics express less dissatisfaction with their bodies than do European Americans and endorse ideals of body shape that are both more generous and more flexible (Smolak and Striegel-Moore, 2001). On the other hand, when viewed cross-culturally, eating disorders are increasingly found across social strata and ethnicities as Western values exert their influence (Levine and Smolak, 2010) as well as among immigrants to Western societies from other cultures (Gunewardene et al., 2001).

A contrasting view is offered by Doyle and Bryant-Waugh (2000), who report that in their clinical work the ethnic minority youths most likely to develop eating disorders are not those who are more exposed to Westernization, but rather those who experience more conflict between the values of their families and the wider culture. Children whose parents rigidly maintain traditional cultural practices and socialize exclusively with members of their own group are more likely to have difficulty reconciling the disparities between their home lives and the norms and expectations of their peers and schools. These internal conflicts, the authors suggest, may represent a risk factor for the development of eating disorders.

Developmental Course

Follow-up studies show that from 50 to 70 per cent of those with anorexia recover, 20 per cent improve but have residual symptoms and 10 to 20 per cent develop chronic difficulties (Commission on Adolescent Eating Disorders, 2005). Strober and colleagues' (1997) longitudinal research found that the average length of time youth struggle with active symptoms was 10 years, and relapse was common. Even among those who received treatment, depression, low weight, disturbed eating, poor body image, anxiety, obsessive-compulsive disorders and substance abuse tended to persist. Anorexia may also be a precursor to *bulimia* for some; almost a third of Strober and colleagues' (1997) sample of 95 adolescents with anorexia went on to develop binge eating within a five-year period.

Considering the stage-salient issues of adolescence, long-term follow-ups show that educational and occupational achievement generally are unaffected, whereas social relationships outside of the family – particularly with other-sex peers – remain problematic for adolescents recovering from anorexia. Individuation from the family is a particular area of conflict and concern for these youth (Neiderman, 2000).

Resilience and Protective Factors

Although an early onset is associated with a more serious form and protracted course in other psychopathologies, such as conduct disorder (see Chapter 10), in the case of anorexia, *early onset* (i.e., before 16 years of age) may be associated with a less negative prognosis in that the disorder has yet to become an entrenched pattern of behaviour (Lock et al., 2002). Other *protective factors* that increase the likelihood of recovery include good family functioning and early, intensive intervention (Neiderman, 2000).

Eating Disorders: Bulimia Nervosa
Definition and Characteristics

Bulimia nervosa is characterized by recurrent episodes of binge eating, or the rapid consumption of large quantities of food in a brief period of time. Binge eating is followed by attempts to prevent weight gain, such as through self-induced vomiting and the misuse of laxatives or diuretics (the *purging type*) or by fasting and excessive exercise (the *non-purging type*). Although individuals with bulimia may be either underweight or overweight, their weight is usually within the average range. (See Table 12.1 on p. 417.)

A *binge* should be distinguished from normal overeating. True bingeing involves ingestion of food irrespective of actual hunger, consuming to the point of discomfort or even pain, and subsequent feelings of self-disgust or depression. Whereas it was once thought that a binge involved eating a large quantity of food, and this misconception remains in the DSM-IV-TR criteria, subsequent research has disconfirmed this (Guertin, 1999). Instead, individuals with bulimia are terrified of losing control over their eating, and this feeling of loss of control, rather than the amount of food consumed, differentiates a binge from ordinary overindulgence. In their all-or-none way of thinking, youth with bulimia fear that even eating a small amount of a forbidden food could result in catastrophic intake. In a less extreme form, they also share the anorexic fear of becoming obese and perceive themselves as fat even when their body weight is normal. Thus, the desire to gorge traps the

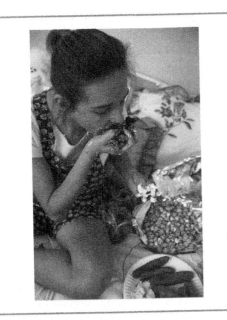

Binge eating

adolescent between anxiety over anticipated loss of control and obesity on the one hand and guilt, shame and self-contempt following a binge on the other hand.

The ICD-10 (WHO, 2007) similarly describes bulimia nervosa as: 'A syndrome characterized by repeated bouts of overeating and an excessive pre-occupation with the control of body weight, leading to a pattern of overeating followed by vomiting or use of purgatives. This disorder shares many psychological features with anorexia nervosa, including an overconcern with body shape and weight.'

Although less often associated with death than self-starvation, purging also represents a serious risk to *physical health*. Bingeing and vomiting can harm the stomach and oesophagus, and the repeated wash of stomach acids can erode the enamel of the teeth, causing permanent damage (Stice and Bulik, 2008). (See Box 12.2.) Overuse of laxatives can result in dependence and severe constipation upon withdrawal as well as permanent colon damage. Frequent purging causes electrolyte and fluid imbalances, leading to weakness, lethargy and depression, as well as kidney problems,

irregular heartbeat and sudden death. Habitual vomiting is also associated with broken blood vessels in the face, blotchy skin, excessive water retention, esophageal tears and enlargement of the salivary glands, producing a "chipmunk cheek" appearance; also, the odour of vomitus may linger on the purger. Thus, the goal of being physically attractive is defeated by the maladaptive strategies used to pursue it.

Prevalence and Onset

Bulimia has a later age of *onset* than anorexia. With a mean age of onset of 18, bulimia may begin in the adolescent or early adult years (Lock and le Grange, 2006). The lifetime *prevalence* rate of bulimia is estimated at 1.5 per cent of females and 0.5 per cent of men, with an increased risk over time found for successive birth cohorts (Hudson et al., 2007).

As with anorexia, however, these statistics may represent underestimates of the actual prevalence rates. A particular concern is that data on prevalence, as well as the characteristics and correlates of bulimia, are often drawn from clinical populations. However, youth who engage in bulimic behaviour may not be represented among those in clinical settings. For example, a carefully designed series of studies conducted by a group at Oxford University (Fairburn et al., 1999) utilized a case-control design to recruit a representative sample of 102 bulimic patients, 204 matched controls and 102 psychiatric controls, and uncovered the fact that 75 per cent of those with bulimia had never sought treatment for their disorder. Although the Youth Risk Behavior Survey (CDC, 2009) in the USA did not ask sufficient questions to determine how many youth actually met criteria for a diagnosis of bulimia, 4 per cent of adolescents in this nationally representative survey reported vomiting or using laxatives to lose weight.

In addition, the diagnostic criteria may underestimate the prevalence of bulimia through their imposition of developmentally insensitive criteria. An international workgroup of experts on the diagnosis and treatment of eating disorders in

Box 12.2 A Case Study in Bulimia

'I no longer clearly remember the first time I forced myself to throw up. What I do remember is how inexpert I was and how long it took before I succeeded in actually vomiting instead of just gagging and retching… In my mid-teens I was too young to believe I was anything but immortal. It didn't occur to me that what I was doing was dangerous – instead, it seemed a smart and practical way of coping with things. I went through months of throwing up once or twice a day, then brief periods when I did not throw up at all, when I seemed to have broken the pattern. Surely this meant I was in control. But by the time I turned 18, the months of not throwing up had diminished to weeks, and when I was vomiting I was doing it four, five, six times a day. I had become addicted to the sensation. It was no longer a penance I had to perform after eating, but the reward at the end of a binge. I loved the feeling I had after purging, of being clean and shiny inside like a scrubbed machine, superhuman. I would rise from the bathroom floor, splash my face with cold water, vigorously brush the acid from my mouth. I would take a wet cloth, wipe off the vomit that had spattered my arms, and feel as energized as someone who had just woken from a nap or returned from an invigorating jog around the block. I felt as if everything inside me had been displaced so that it was now outside myself. Not only all the food I had eaten, but my entire past. No one could tell me to stop, not even my friends, who eventually knew what I was doing. They could not control this part of my life or any other. This was mine alone.…

'I finally stopped being bulimic nearly two years ago, when I was 22. It ended not because of willpower or therapy… It ended because the pain from throwing up rendered the pleasure slight by comparison. It ended when my softened teeth cringed at every mouthful and when I woke several times each night with cramps wracking my stomach… It ended when I arrived at the point where I could no longer feel my feet. Months later, when I went to the doctor, he would diagnose it as an electrolyte imbalance caused by the vomiting up of so many vitamins and minerals… By then I had also developed a hiatal hernia – a portion of my stomach protruded through my esophagus – and my teeth became so compromised that one day one of them simply disintegrated under pressure…

'The last time I forced myself to throw up, it felt like internal surgery. Grief, love, rage, pain – it all came pouring out, yet afterwards it was still there inside me. I had been bulimic off and on for eight years, and in all that vomiting I had not purged myself of any of the things that were making me sick.'

Source: Lau, 1995.

---

children and adolescents points out that DSM-5 would do well to lower the thresholds for the frequency of behaviours such as purging and to include behavioural and psychological indicators of disordered eating even in the absence of direct self-report in order to make the diagnosis more appropriate for young people (Bravender et al., 2010).

The *gender differences* for bulimia are not as extreme as those in anorexia. Whereas most bulimia is seen in females, it is estimated that 10 to 15 per cent of those with bulimia are male (APA, 2000). Evidence suggests that, in comparison to females, males show a later onset (between ages 18 and 26), a higher prevalence of childhood obesity and less involvement with dieting (Carlat et al., 1997; Russell and Keel, 2002). However, here also there is speculation that the diagnostic criteria are sex-biased and lead us to underestimate bulimia in males, due to their predilection for using non-purging methods to lower their body weight, such as excessive exercise (Anderson and Bulik, 2004).

Although there is no evidence for *social class* differences in bulimia there are *ethnic disparities* in prevalence rates (Lock and le Grange, 2006). As with anorexia, bulimia is more often diagnosed in girls of European descent than in those from other ethnic groups in the USA. *Cross-culturally*, bulimia is most prevalent in highly industrialized societies, such as the USA, Canada, Europe, Australia and Japan (American Psychiatric Association, 2000).

Comorbidity

Among the disorders that overlap with bulimia, one of the most common are the *substance abuse* disorders, which are found in 30 to 50 per cent of individuals seeking treatment for bulimia (Stice and Peterson, 2007). These disorders also share in common particular predisposing personality factors, including the inability to regulate negative feelings and impulsivity. *Anxiety* disorders are found in as many as 70 per cent of youth with bulimia in the clinical population and in 58 per cent of those in community samples (Kaye et al., 2004). These include obsessive-compulsive disorder, social phobia, generalized anxiety and post-traumatic stress disorder. Symptoms of *depression* are frequently seen (Stice and Peterson, 2007): between 25 and 80 per cent meet criteria for an affective disorder at some point in their illness, including dysthymia, major depression and bipolar. *Conduct disorder* also is frequently comorbid (Stice and Peterson, 2007). Data on the comorbidity between bulimia and *personality disorders* is highly inconsistent. For example, the most common comorbid diagnosis noted is borderline personality disorder (see Chapter 15), but prevalence rates found vary from 2 per cent to 50 per cent (Pérez et al., 2008).

Differential Diagnosis

Both bulimia and anorexia may involve bingeing and purging. However, bulimia is differentiated from anorexia by virtue of the fact that only in anorexia does the individual maintain an extremely low body weight.

While binge eating is a hallmark of bulimia, not all who binge meet criteria for the bulimia diagnosis. The DSM-IV-TR includes another category, *binge eating disorder* (BED), which is listed among the diagnoses proposed for further study and possible inclusion in future editions of DSM. BED is characterized by the consumption of large amounts of food in a short time, accompanied by a feeling of lack of control over eating as well as subjective distress and self-disgust. Unlike bulimia, however, those with BED do not use inappropriate compensatory mechanisms (e.g., vomiting, laxatives, excessive exercise) to rid themselves of the calories they have consumed.

Bingeing, whether or not it is accompanied by purging, may result in weight gain and even *obesity*. However, despite the popular conception that obesity is a sign of psychological problems, it is important to note that obesity per se is not considered to be a form of psychopathology nor an eating disorder (Wilson et al., 2003). Troubled people may overeat in an attempt to soothe themselves and obese persons may develop eating disorders, but obesity itself is best considered to be a metabolic problem.

Etiology
The Biological Context
Genetics

As with anorexia, bulimia tends to run in families. For example, Strober and colleagues (2000) found that rates of bulimia were about 10 times higher in female relatives of those with an eating disorder as compared to normative controls. Genetic studies comparing concordance rates between monozygotic and dizygotic twins reveal inconsistent findings, with heritability estimates ranging from 28 to 83 per cent (Bulik et al., 2006).

There is likely to be a history of *overweight* in the families of adolescents diagnosed with bulimia and the youth themselves (Stice and Presnell, 2010). Therefore, there is speculation that a constitutional predisposition makes weight loss difficult for these individuals. The tendency towards being overweight increases the likelihood that they will be dissatisfied with their body shape and that they will attempt excessive weight-loss strategies such as purging. However, extreme dieting strategies tend to backfire, resulting in weight gain rather than loss, further perpetuating the problem.

Neurochemistry

Bulimia is associated with disturbances in both the *noradrenergic* and *serotonergic* systems. Serotonin is a particularly likely prospect, given its important role in eating and satiety. Whereas serotonin agonists tend to produce feelings of satiety and reduce food intake, serotonin antagonists lead to increased eating (Wilson et al., 2003). A number of studies have found that individuals with bulimia have low serotonergic activity (Steiger et al., 2001). Although it is unclear whether these imbalances are causes or consequences of disordered eating, studies have found persistent serotonin abnormalities even after recovery from bulimia, suggesting that there may be inherent differences in neurochemistry among youth at risk for the disorder (Duvvuri et al., 2010).

As we know from our discussion of depression in Chapter 9, serotonin is clearly implicated in the development of mood disorders. One supposition is that underlying bingeing, purging and restricted food intake is an attempt to regulate mood associated with depleted serotonin (Ferguson and Pigott, 2000; Kaye et al., 1998). (See Box 12.3.)

It is important to remember that *dieting* has both psychological and physiological effects that increase the likelihood of food cravings and binge eating (Stice and Bulik, 2008). Food restrictions lead to a decrease in plasma tryptophan, which directly affects brain serotonin levels, mood and perceived satiety (Duvvuri et al., 2010). Restricting food intake thus contributes to both further weight gain and disordered eating. Prospective research clearly links dieting to the development of bulimia. Indeed, in almost all cases, the onset of the disorder follows a period of dieting (Wilson, 2002). For example, in a population-based study in Australia, Patton and colleagues (1999) found that over a period of six months those who were 'severe dieters' were 18 times more likely to develop an eating disorder than those who did not diet, and even moderate dieting increased the risk.

Taken together, these studies suggest a biological underpinning to bulimia, such that dieting decreases serotonergic activity in vulnerable individuals, which in turn leads to disordered eating in an attempt to correct the imbalance.

The Individual Context
Personality Characteristics
Although there is no clear 'bulimic personality', among the intra-personal factors associated with

bulimia are *perfectionism*, a *need for approval, self-criticism* and *low self-esteem*, with self-worth contingent on being satisfied with their appearance (Lock and le Grange, 2006). Feelings of inadequacy and low self-worth are associated with disordered eating as early as in the sixth and seventh grades (Killen et al., 1994), and are observed among young women with bulimia even after their recovery from the disorder (Daley et al., 2008). Consistent with such self-consciousness and self-deprecation, *anxiety* is also a common feature of bulimia, and some studies have shown that anxiety precedes the onset of bulimia and may precipitate eating problems (Kaye et al., 2004).

Further, adolescents with bulimia are described as being high in *rejection sensitivity*. Studies show that this kind of interpersonal thin-skin is associated with difficulty managing emotions, which leads in turn to disordered eating as a way to attempt to cope with these negative affects (Selby et al., 2010).

As we noted when we discussed comorbidity, *borderline personality* traits have been found to be prevalent among bulimic patients in some studies. These include characteristics such as impulsivity, unstable relationships, identity disturbance and self-harming (see Chapter 15). For example, the Spanish researchers Pérez and colleagues (2008) found clinically significant levels of borderline pathology in 45.2 per cent of young women undergoing treatment for bulimia.

Emotion Regulation
In many ways the behaviour of those with bulimia, like their eating pattern, suggests a basic difficulty in *self-regulation*. Research has begun to point towards emotion regulation as a motivator for disordered-eating behaviour, particularly purging.

For example, in order to study the psychological processes associated with binge-purging, Smyth and colleagues (2007) came up with an ingenious strategy. They asked patients with bulimia to carry a palmtop computer over a period of two weeks and to record their moods, stress levels and episodes of bingeing or vomiting at six

Box 12.3 Dysregulation as Excess Versus Insufficiency: The Role of Serotonin in Eating Disorders

The serotonin (5-HT) neurotransmitter system is familiar to us as a suspect in the developmental psychopathology of depression (see Chapter 9). In addition, serotonin plays an important role in the modulation of appetite, which makes it a prime candidate in the search for factors leading to eating disorders. If there are problems with the modulation of serotonin in eating disorders, are they a matter of excess or insufficiency?

On the excess side of the equation, Kaye and colleagues (2003; Duvvuri et al., 2010) propose the theory that individuals with anorexia have increased activity of brain serotonergic systems. Typically, increased brain serotonin activity leads to a feeling of satiety and cessation of eating, which might account for the anorexic avoidance of food consumption. However, excessive serotonin can lead to dysphoric mood states, particularly anxiety, which is commonly seen in individuals with anorexia even prior to the onset of their eating disorder. Noting that starvation is associated with reduced levels of 5-HT activity, Kaye and colleagues propose that extreme dieting in anorexia serves the function of reducing anxiety and dysphoric mood by lowering levels of serotonin in the brain. To test this theory, the investigators depleted brain levels of serotonin by administering to research participants an amino acid mixture that was free of tryptophan (a precursor to serotonin that directly affects serotonergic functioning). In support of their hypotheses, the investigators found that both women with acute anorexia and those who had recovered from the disorder reported a significant decline in anxiety after undergoing the tryptophan depletion procedure, whereas this was not true of a sample of non-anorexic controls. Thus, the authors of the study suggest that, due to an innate disturbance of serotonin, those with anorexia turn to restricted eating in an attempt to regulate dysphoric mood. The effects are only fleeting, however, as compensatory mechanisms in the brain attempt to right the imbalance and dysphoria resumes with the onset of eating.

In sum, for anorexia, the equation might look as follows:

Innate excessive serotonin → Anxiety → Dieting → Lowered serotonin → Temporary reduction in dysphoria

The case of bulimia is quite a different story, one that leans towards the insufficiency side of the equation. Lowered levels of serotonin have been shown experimentally to lead to excessive eating and dysfunction of satiety mechanisms as well as to depressed mood. Further, dieting itself lowers plasma tryptophan, and in the vast majority of cases, dieting is a precursor to bulimia. Noting these facts, Smith and colleagues (1999) proposed that insufficient serotonin levels might play a role in bulimia. Their test of this theory involved the same tryptophan depletion procedure used by Kaye and colleagues (2003) in order to lower plasma levels of serotonin in a sample of women who had recovered from bulimia and a comparison group of non-clinical controls. Women who had previously suffered from bulimia were more likely than controls to respond to tryptophan depletion by an increase in reported depressive symptoms, concerns about body image (i.e., feeling fat) and fear of losing control over their eating. The authors also noted that the greatest increases in depression were seen in those participants with bulimia who had a history of comorbid major depression, suggesting that this subgroup may be particularly vulnerable to relapse when serotonin neurotransmission is lowered.

In sum, for bulimia the equation might look as follows:

Dieting → Insufficient Serotonin → Depressed Mood and Urge to Overeat → Binge/Purging

---

time points during the day. Analyses across days revealed that days on which participants binged and purged were characterized by higher levels of negative affect, anger and stress, and lower levels of positive emotions. Within the day, decreasing positive affect and increasing negative affect and hostility reliably predicted the onset of bulimic behaviour. Most intriguingly, after the binge-purge event, participants reported an increase in positive affect and a decrease in negative affect and hostility. These findings are consistent with those earlier reported by Johnson and Larson

(1982) in which binges were associated with feelings of depression, disgust and self-deprecation, but purges led to a re-establishment of a sense of calm, self-control and adequacy – described by patients in terms such as being 'clean', 'empty', 'spaced out' and 'ready to sleep'. See Box 12.1 for an illustration of this in author Evelyn Lau's description of her own eight-year battle with bulimia.

Purging, therefore, seems to have certain reinforcing properties in itself. In fact, some researchers have speculated that individuals with bulimia binge so they will be able to purge (Heatherton and Baumeister, 1991). Purging seems to act as a form of *self-sedation*, allowing the adolescent to escape from negative affects and regulate her mood.

Stice and colleagues (2004) also implicate emotion dysregulation in their prospective study examining the associations between bulimia and depression among 496 girls followed over a period of two years. The investigators found that depressive symptoms predicted the onset of bulimia but that bulimia, in turn, also increased the risk of depression. The investigators propose that whereas bulimic behaviour begins as an attempt to self-soothe and regulate negative emotions, the biological changes (e.g., serotonin depletion) and psychological consequences (e.g., shame, guilt, poor self-image) associated with bingeing and purging ultimately only serve to exacerbate dysphoric mood.

Cognition

Like those with anorexia, young women with bulimia tend to have a *rigid* cognitive style marked by black-or-white, all-or-none thinking (Stice and Bulik, 2008). Thus, they view themselves as completely in control or helpless, absolutely virtuous or slovenly.

Further, girls who develop bulimia, like those with anorexia, are more likely to buy into cultural ideals regarding thinness and to view their own body shapes as dissatisfactory (Stice, 2002). Cognitive conceptualizations of bulimia identify rigid and maladaptive beliefs in three domains: *unrealistic expectations* for her body weight and shape (e.g., the belief that weight loss will result in a

figure of supermodel proportions); *distorted outcome beliefs* about body weight and shape (e.g., the belief that obtaining the desired weight is crucial to achieving success in life and will earn her the self-esteem she seeks); and *inaccurate conceptualizations of food and eating* (e.g., erroneous ideas about the digestive system, the caloric values of certain foods and the biological mechanisms underlying weight loss) (Spangler, 2002). These distorted cognitions, along with a poor body image and perceived pressure to be thin, inspire her to utilize extreme efforts at weight control, which, in turn, set in motion the maladaptive physiological and psychological processes associated with bulimia.

Unlike anorexia, however, bulimia tends to be more *ego-dystonic*, or inconsistent with one's goals and self-perceptions. Those with bulimia are more likely than those with anorexia to recognize that they suffer from a disorder and, despite some fear or ambivalence about giving up their maladaptive eating patterns, are more willing to try to change their behaviour (Wilson et al., 2003).

The Social Context

One way in which peer influences play a role is in terms of *initiating* the adolescent into bulimic behaviour. Many adolescents are introduced to vomiting or use of laxatives as a weight-control technique by friends. (One young woman stopped giving inspirational talks about her own recovery from bulimia when she found that the high school girls who attended were only interested in learning the techniques she'd used for purging herself of food!) For example, Hutchinson and colleagues (2010) found in a large community sample of Australian girls that the eating behaviours of those in their social 'clique' contributed significantly to the development of pathological eating. Whereas most young women ultimately abstain from these maladaptive techniques, others become caught in the repetitive cycle of binge-purging.

Qualities of peer relationships also differentiate anorexia and bulimia. In addition to being normal weight or overweight, and thus not standing out in terms of their appearance, adolescents with bulimia tend to be more *sociable* are thus more likely than those with anorexia to appear on the surface to be functioning adequately in their academic and social worlds. In addition, adolescents with bulimia tend to be more *sexually active* than those with anorexia, perhaps related to their general tendency towards impulsivity and risk-taking (Pinheiro et al., 2010). However, clinical observations suggest that they enjoy sex less than do other youths. Rather than seeking out sex for self-gratification, adolescents with bulimia are overly compliant with pressure to engage in sexual activities because of their strong need for social approval and difficulty identifying and asserting their own needs.

Peer relationships also come into play in other ways, in complex transactions among self-image, *social status* and disordered eating. For example, Rancourt and Prinstein (2010) followed a sample of 576 adolescents ages 10 to 14 over a period of a year. The investigators found that higher levels of body dissatisfaction were associated with lower levels of popularity over time. Surprisingly, both the most popular and the least liked youth showed increases in negative cognitions about their bodies. For boys, higher levels of popularity were associated with extreme weight management strategies, although in their case directed toward building bulk and muscle. These findings suggest that those youth who are self-conscious about their appearance are particularly sensitive to the opinions of others, even when those are positive, and are consequently more likely to feel that they do not 'measure up' to some ideal of physical perfection.

In the longer term, when the binge-purge cycle is well established, the shame and secretiveness associated with these activities tends to foster *social isolation* from peers (Lock and le Grange, 2006). The adolescent with advanced bulimia is preoccupied with thoughts of food, eating and purging, to the point that all other matters fall by the wayside. Such adolescents spend less time socializing and more time alone than other youths. Many describe spending most of their time and energy planning and amassing food for their binges, as well as seeking seclusion in order to purge. As one remarked,

'Food has become my closest companion' (Johnson and Larson, 1982). The increased irritability and depressed affect resulting from disordered eating also interferes with social relationships.

The Family Context

In contrast to the family members of the adolescent diagnosed with anorexia, who may present themselves as untroubled except for the problems of the 'identified patient', the family members of youths with bulimia are more likely to be overtly disturbed. *Parental psychopathology* is often observed, particularly depression and substance abuse (Fairburn et al., 1997).

As with anorexia, family relationships of those with bulimia have been described as enmeshed and rigid; however, more characteristic of bulimia is *family discord*, including parent–child conflict and overt hostility (Fairburn et al., 2003). Other family characteristics that act as specific risk factors for bulimia include frequent parental absence, uninvolvement, high expectations, criticism and interparental discord (Fairburn et al., 1997).

Childhood maltreatment, particularly in the form of *sexual abuse*, does appear to act as a specific risk factor for bulimia. For example, in the Victoria Adolescent Health Cohort Study of 999 Australian schoolgirls followed from ages 14 to 24, Sanci and colleagues (2008) found that bulimia was 2.5 times higher among those who reported a single episode of childhood sexual abuse and 4.9 times higher among those who reported two or more sexual abuse experience.

The Cultural Context

The same societal influences that contribute to the development of anorexia have been implicated in the development of bulimia, including Western culture's emphasis on slenderness and the tendency to judge females on the basis of their physical appearance (Striegel-Moore and Bulik, 2007).

Empirical evidence in support of these ideas is available. Much more so than for males, the self-esteem of female children and adults is based on body image and is influenced by the opinions of others. Dissatisfaction with body weight and maladaptive eating habits are endemic among young females in industrialized nations, even in the preadolescent years. Strikingly, as early as 5 years of age, girls whose weight is above average have a more negative self-image – not only of their bodies but of their cognitive abilities (Davison and Birch, 2001). (See Fig. 12.2.)

Further, a large body of experimental research has shown that exposure to media representations of the thin ideal is associated with increased body dissatisfaction and negative affect among youth (Grabe et al., 2008). However, not all individuals exposed to these social forces go on to develop eating disorders. Therefore, there must be an *interaction* between sociocultural and individual factors. For example, youth with bulimia report greater perceived pressure from their peers and parents to be thin, and they are more likely to believe that

society in general requires them to be slender (Stice et al., 1996). In this way, they seem to have internalized these larger social dictates more than other youth.

Developmental Course

The peak developmental period of risk for the onset of bulimia is 14 to 19 years of age. When compared with anorexia, rates of *recovery* from an episode of bulimia are relatively high (Steinhausen and Weber, 2009), although the recovery may be far from full. Like anorexia, bulimia tends to be a chronic disorder with periods of recovery punctuated by episodes of *relapse*. Illustrating this, Fairburn and colleagues (2000) in the UK followed a group of 102 young women with bulimia over the course of five years. The participants, ranging in age from 16 to 35, underwent an assessment every 15 months. At the first 15-month follow-up, the

FIGURE 12.2 Concern about Weight and Dieting Begins Early in Female Development.

group as a whole showed improvement in their bulimic symptoms, and this was followed by continued gradual improvement in subsequent years. However, there was marked instability in their symptom picture, with each year approximately one-third remitting and one-third relapsing. At the final assessment five years later, 15 per cent continued to meet criteria for a diagnosis of bulimia, 2 per cent met criteria for anorexia and 35 per cent met criteria for a non-specific eating disorder. Strikingly, 41 per cent of the participants now also met criteria for a major depressive disorder. Further, over the course of each year, approximately one-third showed symptom remission and another third relapsed.

Thus, even when the symptoms of bulimia remit, disordered eating and body dissatisfaction in early adolescence may persist and increase the risk

for depression. The attempt to solve life problems via the attainment of slimness is doomed to fail.

A Comparison of Eating Disorders

Table 12.2 compares the diagnostic criteria and empirical findings concerning anorexia and bulimia. When compared with those who restrict their food intake, those with anorexia who binge and purge are more likely to have family or personal histories of obesity and experience more emotion dysregulation and substance abuse, characteristics that are also descriptive of bulimia. However, while families of adolescents with anorexia are characterized by rigidity and enmeshment, families of those with bulimia are more openly hostile, non-cohesive and non-nurturing.

In general, bulimia and the binge-purging type of anorexia may have more in common with each

TABLE 12.2 Comparison of Eating Disorders

Anorexia: Restricting Type	Anorexia: Binge-Purging Type	Bulimia
Typical onset age 14		Typical onset age 18
Excessive thinness		Average or overweight
Intense fear of gaining weight		Fear of losing control over eating
Disturbance of body image (self-perception as fat)		Self-evaluation unduly influenced by weight
Amenorrhoea		Normal menstruation
Voluntary food restrictions	Binge eating and purging	
Family enmeshed, overprotective, rigid, poor conflict resolution		Family history of psychological problems, substance abuse; family discord and overt hostility
Socially isolated	Socially insecure	Low self-esteem; rejection-sensitive
Disinterested in sex		Sexually active with little enjoyment
Overcontrolled	Emotionally labile	
Comorbid with depression, anxiety disorders, including social phobia and obsessive-compulsiveness	Comorbid with depression, anxiety, substance abuse, personality disorder	
Maternal history of anorexia	Family history and predisposition to overweight	
Ego syntonic (disinterested in treatment)		Ego dystonic (motivated to change)

other than either does with restricting-type anorexia. In fact, it has been suggested that it might be preferable to regard binge-purging anorexia as a special subgroup of bulimia rather than as a special subgroup of anorexia. However, more comparative studies must be done before the issue of classification can be resolved.

Integrative Developmental Models

One of the more comprehensive accounts of the developmental psychopathology of eating disorders is offered by Striegel-Moore and colleagues (Rodin et al., 1990; Striegel-Moore and Bulik, 2007; Striegel-Moore and Smolak, 2001). Although appreciating the importance of the overarching *sociocultural* context, including society's emphasis on thinness as a mark of beauty and beauty as essential to the feminine ideal, clearly not all females exposed to these pressures develop eating disorders. Therefore, a number of predisposing, precipitating and sustaining factors come into play in the various domains of development, interacting with one another in significant ways.

In addition, as we have learned, eating disorders, although more prevalent among girls, are not the exclusive purview of females. Disordered eating also is found among boys, albeit more often in the service of increasing muscularity rather than slenderizing. Of particular importance to our model is the fact that the factors predicted of eating disorders among boys are highly similar to those found among girls, including negative affect, self-esteem, perfectionism, substance abuse, perceived pressure to attain a physical ideal and participation in sports that emphasize leanness (Ricciardelli and McCabe, 2004).

First, in the *biological* domain, a *temperament* characterized by a tendency toward obsessional thinking, rigidity and poor adaptability to change may, in turn, leave the young person poorly equipped to cope with the *stresses* of adolescence. Further, girls on the pathway to eating disorders typically begin *puberty* earlier than their peers (Fairburn and Brownell, 2002), leading to increased unhappiness with their bodies because

of the weight gain that naturally occurs at menarche. Whether late maturation is a similar risk factor for boys has received only inconsistent support (McCabe et al., 2010). In addition, particularly in the case of bulimia, young people at risk may be genetically programmed to be heavier than the svelte ideal. Thus, the young people predisposed to eating disorders are more vulnerable to societal pressures for thinness because they find it physically difficult to achieve the ideal body shape. Moreover, the teenagers headed towards disordered eating also are more likely to have internalized the belief that their appearance will determine how successful they will be in life, and so their natural form is unacceptable.

In addition, in the case of bulimia particularly, Stice and Bulik (2008) emphasize the interrelations among body dissatisfaction, dieting, negative affect and disordered eating. As they point out, youth with a higher than ideal body mass may turn to severely restricting their diets, which increases the likelihood of intermittent binge eating. Dieting also involves a shift in the normal reliance on physiological cues to determine when one is hungry or sated, and instead to focus on cognitive control processes which, when disrupted, also leave the individual prone to disordered eating. Further, both body dissatisfaction and restricted eating contribute to *negative affect*, which in turn increases the risk of turning to food as a way of seeking comfort and managing uncomfortable emotional states.

In the *family* domain, the parents are likely to be conflicted and insecure. In the case of anorexia, they are perfectionistic and judgemental, while, in the case of bulimia, they are emotionally disturbed and impulsive. Their care of the infant, therefore, while on the surface devoted and attentive, is marred by insensitivity, taking the form of intrusive overprotectiveness or excessive control. Because feeling states are given the labels acceptable to parents – rather than those accurate for the child – poor recognition of feelings, and difficulty regulating and expressing them, develops.

In addition, the family models we have reviewed suggest that these family interactions undermine the daughter's development of a sense of *self-efficacy* and interfere with her development of strategies for coping with negative emotions. Thus, the parents over-control their children and ignore and negate their self-expression, which undermines the child's efforts to individuate and keeps her in a dependent state. When the normal development of healthy initiative and self-assertiveness is blocked, the only alternative is self-destructive opposition. Also included in the individual domain are factors such as a *lack of autonomy* and sense of mastery, which contribute to a fear of maturation and impending adulthood. Other personality characteristics may include a strong need for social approval and immediate need for gratification, poor impulse control, rigid thinking, obsessionality, depression and a fragile sense of self.

As Lask (2000) articulates, the issue of *dieting* comes into play because it offers one aspect of their lives and their bodies over which an adolescent can exert control. However, while rigid control over eating restores a sense of control, achievement and self-esteem, the results are only temporary and fuel ever more desperate and extreme dieting behaviours. (See Fig. 12.3.)

Development is implicated in specific ways. As we noted at the outset of this chapter, eating disorders tend to occur at two developmental transitions: at entry into adolescence and at the boundary between adolescence and young adulthood. The *stage-salient tasks* of adolescence, then, present a number of challenges. Tasks of early adolescence involve establishing a stable self-structure and regulating emotions, impulses and self-esteem; resolving identity issues; developing sexual relationships and coping with the implications of reproductive capacity; renegotiating relationships with parents in order to develop autonomy while still remaining connected; and establishing achievement goals and a meaningful life trajectory. During the transition to adulthood, tasks include establishing intimate relationships, determining and pursuing one's own values and goals, and developing an independent identity.

However, for females especially, a number of factors conspire against the easy resolution of issues related to sexuality, identity and achievement. By middle childhood, a girl's self-esteem begins to depend on others' opinions of her. In addition, a girl's perception of her own attractiveness, popularity and success is often related to a thin body image. However, the pubertal fat spurt, coupled with increasing social sensitivity and the equating of self-worth with physical appearance image, may well cause distress and lead to preoccupation with weight and dieting.

Because of her prior history and psychological make-up, the young woman vulnerable to eating disorders is particularly ill-equipped to cope with the normative demands of adolescence. Although she cannot halt the changes occurring in her body or in her interpersonal world, food becomes one realm in which she can exert some control. Disordered eating is thus a distorted attempt to resolve the conflict between the uncontrollable and rapid changes associated with the onset of puberty on the one hand, and the need for order and predictability on the other.

Intervention

Adolescents with eating disorders are difficult to treat successfully. Half of those treated continue to have eating difficulties and psychological problems. Even recovered patients continue to have distorted attitudes toward eating and weight, along with depression and unsatisfactory social relations. Thus, there is a tendency toward chronicity even with long and intensive treatment. Many different interventions have been tested and the available research base regarding their effectiveness is reviewed by Keel and Haedt (2008) and Hay and Claudino (2010). (See Miller and Mizes, 2000, for a fascinating comparison of how various treatment approaches would be applied to a single case.)

Behaviour Modification

Owing to the life-threatening dangers associated with anorexia, behaviour modification is often the first line of treatment in order to save the patient's life by restoring her body weight. When anorexia is severe, the treatment takes place in an inpatient

FIGURE 12.3 Developmental Model of Eating Disorders.

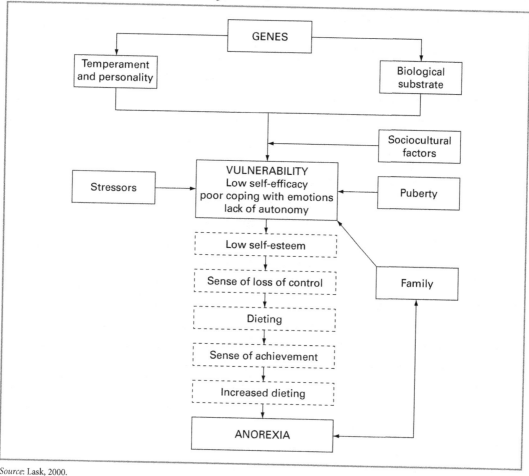

Source: Lask, 2000.

setting where careful monitoring can be provided of the patient's behaviour and medical status (Lock, 2010). *Operant conditioning* techniques include rewarding eating through such individualized reinforcers as permission to watch a favourite television show or receive visits from friends, and withholding rewards when there is non-compliance. For bulimia, *behaviour modification* focuses on discontinuing the dieting behaviour that contributes to food cravings and disordered eating, as well as encouraging more adaptive strategies for mood regulation, such as physical exercise. However, there is evidence that the inpatient treatment, while effective in achieving the goal of immediate weight

gain in anorexia, does not have long-lasting effects and that the costs might outweigh the benefits (Crow and Smiley, 2010). Further, behavioural treatment alone does not address faulty notions concerning eating, nor does it help the adolescent improve personality and interpersonal problems. These may be addressed by cognitive therapy.

Cognitive Therapy

Cognitive therapy aims at changing cognitive distortions, overgeneralizations, negative self-perceptions and erroneous beliefs about eating and about the self, such as 'If only I were thin, I would be perfect'. Techniques include engaging the adolescent in treatment as a 'scientist' who will collaborate with the therapist in the process of uncovering and disputing automatic thoughts and irrational beliefs (Wilson, 2010). Among the techniques, *self-monitoring* is used to increase awareness of the situations, thoughts and emotions that trigger disordered eating. *Behavioural contracting* is used to monitor and reinforce small steps toward larger goals of normalizing eating behaviour. *Cognitive restructuring* goes beyond thoughts about eating and extends into more general maladaptive schema the youth harbours in regard to the self, relationships with others and the need to be perfect. For example, Wonderlich and colleagues (2008) developed a cognitively based intervention specifically for bulimia called integrative cognitive-affective therapy, which focuses treatment on three targets: poor self-concept, negative affect and problematic coping strategies. In an intriguing innovation, the investigators demonstrated that the therapy could be delivered via telemedicine to participants in rural areas who otherwise might have difficulty accessing high-quality, evidence-based treatments (Mitchell et al., 2008).

Research in general shows that cognitive approaches for bulimia are successful, with full recovery reported in 50 to 90 per cent of cases and low rates of relapse (Keel and Haedt, 2008). In addition, whereas other approaches may reduce binge eating and enhance general psychological well-being, the cognitive approach is more effective in changing attitudes about the body and maladaptive dieting behaviour as well as being more successful in preventing relapse.

Interpersonal Psychotherapy

Another individual therapy approach for the treatment of eating disorders that has received empirical support is interpersonal psychotherapy (IPT), which we first encountered in our review of treatments for adolescent depression (see Chapter 9). IPT focuses specifically on the way in which symptoms arise from problematic relationships and, in turn, compromise interpersonal functioning. A version of IPT adapted specifically for bulimia by Fairburn and colleagues (1993) has shown beneficial effects that

have lasted as long as six years (Tanofsky-Kraff and Wilfley, 2010). Although results of a multisite clinical trial involving clinical investigators in the UK and the USA found that CBT was associated with a larger proportion of patients with bulimia showing improvement at the end of therapy, by the 8- to 12-month follow-up, both treatments evidenced equal effectiveness (Agras et al., 2000). Thus, IPT may exert its effects more slowly than CBT but still manages to achieve its goals.

Family Therapy

One of the most well-regarded family-based approaches for anorexia is the Maudsley model, which was originally developed at the Maudsley Hospital in the UK (Dare and Eisler, 1997; Lock et al., 2002) and subsequently has been transported to other locations in a series of clinical trials. Inspired by classical family systems models of the origins of anorexia (Minuchin et al., 1978), the Maudsley approach views the disorder as arising from ways in which troubled family relations interfere with normative adolescent development. The initial focus of the therapy, paradoxically, is to help parents to take charge of their youth's eating given that the youth's thoughts and behaviour are so compromised around food that her health is endangered. As a life-sustaining weight is regained, the treatment then turns to helping the parents to support the adolescent's gaining self-sufficiency and taking over control of her life functions herself. In the last stages of therapy, the intervention turns its attention to assisting the youth with the normative adolescent processes of separation-individuation from parents, appropriate family boundaries, development of autonomy and reinvestment in social relations with peers.

Further adaptations of the Maudsley model have included holding separate sessions for parents and youth, particularly among families in which levels of negative expressed emotion run high and threaten to undermine the treatment (Eisler et al., 2000). In particular, Eisler and colleagues found that, in families in which parents expressed high levels of criticism, youth were more likely to recover when seen separately from their parents. In another study, Le Grange and colleagues (2008) found that a short-term version of the treatment (10 sessions over six months) was as effective as a longer-term (20 sessions over 12 months) version.

Le Grange and Hoste (2010) review the available research evidence in support of the Maudsley model and find that overall, this family treatment is more effective than individual psychodynamic or supportive therapies, and between 63 and 94 per cent of cases treated show significant benefit.

Pharmacological Intervention

Some promising results in the treatment of bulimia have been found with *antidepressants*, particularly the newer type of SSRIs (see Chapter 9), although the research investigating their effectiveness and safety remains limited (McElroy et al., 2010). However, while medications may be helpful in alleviating comorbid psychopathologies such as anxiety or depression, they have little effect on eating behaviour or weight gain (Lock et al., 2002). Therefore, medications are generally used as an adjunct to, rather than as a replacement for, other forms of therapy. A major caveat is that careful clinical trials involving adolescents are sorely lacking (Lock and le Grange, 2006).

Prevention of Eating Disorders

Given the pernicious physical and psychological effects of self-starvation or purging, and the difficulty of turning a young person off this course once he or she has set upon it, prevention would be well worthwhile. Stice and Shaw (2004) provide an exhaustive meta-analysis of eating disorder prevention programmes, which overall is encouraging in showing that these efforts do pay off. The most successful prevention programmes, they found, were those that were *targeted* to at-risk youth rather than being universal to the entire school, those that were *interactive* rather than being didactic and impersonal, those that involved *multiple sessions* rather than a single intervention, programmes that were directed specifically to *girls* and to those *over 15 years* of age, and those that avoided 'preaching' to youth through focusing on psychoeducational con-

tent. Instead, the most effective strategies appeared to include *cognitive interventions* designed to counter maladaptive attitudes such as the internalization of a thin ideal and body dissatisfaction, and behavioural interventions targeting maladaptive eating patterns such as fasting and overeating.

Substance Abuse and Dependence

We turn next to a very different psychopathology that emerges during adolescence; however, there are some parallels between this and our previous topic. Whereas eating disorders represent problems with the regulation of food intake, substance abuse and dependence involve problems with modulating the consumption of alcohol and drugs.

Viewed in a historical context, we know that substance use has been a part of human society throughout time. Most cultures have used alcohol: mead was possibly used around 8000 BC, the biblical Noah became drunk, and the indigenous people who met the European explorers of the American continent made their own home brew. Drugs long have been used in religious ceremonies, to medicate, to counteract fatigue, to increase fierceness in battle, as well as for recreation. Over time, societies also have applied different sanctions to various drugs; one drug may be perfectly acceptable, while another is strongly prohibited.

An additional important source of cultural diversity concerns the attitudes that societies hold toward drug and alcohol use. Possession of a substance such as cannabis is legal in some nations, is decriminalized if held in small amounts in others and is considered to be a criminal offence in yet other countries. Within some nations, like the USA, these attitudes vary enormously even from one state to another. Similarly, whereas in some subcultures parents would respond with alarm to their children's even tasting a forbidden substance such as alcohol, in others parents routinely share with children sips of watered wine at the dinner table in order to model for them restraint and moderation in enjoying this normal part of daily life. Moreover, the age at which youth are considered capable of making their own decisions regarding alcohol use vary widely, such that crossing the border from one municipality to another changes the purchase of liquor from a status offence to a completely legal act.

However, even among jurisdictions, countries and subcultures in which substance use is tolerated and legal, there are those individuals who fall into habits of misuse and, in more extreme cases, of addiction and dependence. It is those youth who will concern us in this chapter as we consider the developmental pathways leading to alcohol and substance disorders.

Definition and Characteristics

DSM-IV defines **substance abuse** by the presence of one or more symptoms indicating the excessive use of a substance to the extent that it interferes with work or school and interpersonal relationships (see Table 12.3). **Substance dependence**, in turn, is characterized by abuse in the presence of *tolerance* for the drug, leading to the need for ever-increasing doses in order to achieve the desired effect; *withdrawal* in its absence; *inability to desist using*, despite the desire or attempt to do so; and *preoccupation* with obtaining the substance such that little time or energy is available for other pursuits. (See Box 12.4.)

The ICD-10 (WHO, 2007) includes a similar category of Mental and Behavioural Disorders due to Psychoactive Substance Use. Each diagnosis includes codes for the substance involved as well as the clinical state of the user, ranging from acute intoxication to harmful use, dependence, withdrawal, delirium or substance induced.

The Developmental Dimension

Concern has been expressed that the official diagnostic criteria do not accurately reflect the nature of substance abuse disorders in adolescence (Brown, 2008). For example, many studies report a large proportion of 'diagnostic orphans' (Chassin et al., 2003): youth who endorse only some symptoms of substance abuse or dependence and therefore do not meet criteria for a diagnosis despite problematic usage.

There are a number of reasons why the diagnostic criteria might not do an adequate job of capturing problematic substance use in adolescence. First, adolescents in general are more likely than adults to exhibit difficulties in occupational functioning and romantic relationships, which may be independent of substance abuse. Second, there is evidence that youth are less likely than adults to evidence physiological dependence, with its accompanying symptoms of tolerance, withdrawal and physical ill effects. Further, adolescents, especially girls, are less likely than adults to encounter legal difficulties in connection with illicit drugs. However, it may also be the case that it is just a matter of time: with continued long-term use, the physical and legal ramifications may catch up with substance-abusing youths.

The symptoms that are more commonly and reliably seen in youth, particularly in the realm of alcohol abuse, include *blackouts, mood problems, reduced activity level, cravings* and engagement in *risky sexual behaviour.*

Prevalence and Onset

International data on the prevalence of use were gathered by the European School Survey Project on Alcohol and Other Drugs (ESPAD; Hibell et al., 2009), which queried over 100 000 15- to 16-year-olds from 35 nations. As displayed in Table 12.4, results vary widely across countries but notable is the fact that overall two-thirds of the youth surveyed had consumed alcohol and half had been drunk to the point of staggering, having slurred speech or throwing up. Fifteen per cent admitted to problems related to their alcohol use, including serious conflicts with parents or friends, poor schoolwork, or getting into physical fights. Further, on average 23 per cent of the boys and 17 per cent of the girls had tried an illicit drug in their lifetime, including amphetamines, cocaine, crack, ecstasy, LSD or heroin, but most commonly cannabis. Use of cannabis in the past 12 months was reported by 14 per cent of all youth while use in the past 30 days was acknowledged by 9 per cent of the boys and 6 per cent of the girls. In the two countries in which

TABLE 12.3 DSM-IV-TR Criteria for Substance Disorders

Substance Abuse

A maladaptive pattern of substance use, leading to clinically significant impairment or distress, as manifested by one (or more) of the following, occurring within a 12-month period:

(1) Recurrent substance use resulting in a failure to fulfil major role obligations at work, school, or home (e.g., repeated absences or poor work performance related to substance use; substance-related absences, suspensions, or expulsions from school; neglect of children or household).

(2) Recurrent substance use in situations in which it is physically hazardous (e.g., driving an automobile or operating a machine when impaired by substance use).

(3) Recurrent substance-related legal problems (e.g., arrests for substance-related disorderly conduct).

(4) Continued substance use despite having persistent or recurrent social or interpersonal problems caused or exacerbated by the effects of the substance (e.g., arguments with spouse about consequences of intoxication, physical fights).

Substance Dependence

A maladaptive pattern of substance use, leading to clinically significant impairment or distress, as manifested by three (or more) of the following, occurring at any time within the same 12-month period:

(1) Tolerance, as defined by either of the following:

  a. A need for markedly increased amounts of the substance to achieve intoxication or desired effect

  b. Markedly diminished effect with continued use of the same amount of the substance

(2) Withdrawal, as manifested by either of the following:

  a. The characteristic withdrawal syndrome for the substance

  b. The same (or closely related) substance is taken to relieve or avoid withdrawal symptoms

(3) The substance is often taken in larger amounts or over a longer period than was intended.

(4) There is a persistent desire or unsuccessful efforts to cut down or control substance use.

(5) A great deal of time is spent in activities necessary to obtain the substance (e.g., visiting multiple doctors or driving long distance), to use the substance (e.g., chain smoking), or to recover from its effects.

(6) Important social, occupational, or recreational activities are given up or reduced because of substance use.

(7) The substance use is continued despite knowledge of having a persistent or recurrent physical or psychological problem that is likely to have been caused or exacerbated by the substance (e.g., continued cocaine use despite cocaine-induced depression; continued drinking despite alcohol-aggravated ulcer).

Specify Type:

With Physiological Dependence: Evidence of tolerance or withdrawal.
With Psychological Dependence: No evidence of tolerance or withdrawal.

Source: Adapted with permission from the *Diagnostic and Statistical Manual of Mental Disorders*, Fourth Edition Text Revision. Copyright 2000 by the American Psychiatric Association.

cannabis use was the most prevalent (the Czech Republic and the Isle of Man) one in six youth had used in the past 30 days.

In comparison, data on the prevalence of the use of various substances in the USA were compiled by the Monitoring the Future (MTF) study (Johnston et al., 2011), a survey distributed to over 46 500 children in eighth, tenth and twelfth grades in 396 schools across the USA. (Note that while the inclusiveness of the study is impressive, it fails to capture students who have dropped out of school or are in detention, youths who might be disproportionately representative of those heavily involved with substances.) The latest published data from 2011 reveal that 71 per cent of youths had consumed alcohol by the end of high school,

Box 12.4 A Case Study in Substance Dependence

Robert was born in 1965, the son of a filmmaker and an actress. Raised in Greenwich Village with his older sister, Robert made his film debut at the age of 5 playing a puppy in a film *Pound*, directed by his father, in which actors played dogs. His parents divorced when he was 13, and Robert ended up living in Los Angeles with his father. He dropped out of high school to pursue acting, and at the age of 16 moved back to New York to live with his mother.

Robert started off with good roles in several feature films and spent a year as a regular cast member of the popular comedy programme *Saturday Night Live*. He then began being cast in leading roles in movies that attracted a great deal of popular and critical acclaim. His breakthrough performance was a starring role as a cocaine addict.

However, life was imitating art. By the time he played this role, Robert had developed a serious drug problem himself. The actor reportedly began using substances at age 6, when his father introduced him to marijuana. He completed a drug-rehabilitation programme in 1987 but continued to struggle with his addictions. After several forgettable movies during the late 1980s, his acting career took wing as he turned in a number of well-received performances in films by famous directors. In 1992, Robert received an Academy Award nomination for Best Actor for his starring role in *Chaplin*. That year he also married his wife Deborah, after dating her for only six weeks, and a year later they had a son, Indio.

By this time, the 27-year-old Robert had come to be seen as one of the most gifted actors of his generation, but had also earned a reputation as a troubled and controversial figure in Hollywood. Although the actor was enjoying steady work, his off-screen life was becoming increasingly troubled.

In April 1996, Robert separated from Deborah. In June of that year, he was stopped for speeding and a police search of his car uncovered heroin, crack and cocaine, along with an unloaded gun. He was arrested again a month later when, under the influence of a controlled substance, he passed out on a neighbour's lawn. He was rearrested just three days after the second arrest after he walked out of a drug treatment centre where he had been ordered to stay. In November 1996, a judge sentenced Robert to three years' probation. His probation was revoked in December 1997, however, after he was found to have used drugs again, and the judge sentenced him to six months in prison.

While in prison, Robert was allowed to leave several times to complete work on his film projects. He entered another drug rehabilitation programme, but in June of 1999 admitted he was using drugs again. 'It's like I have a shotgun in my mouth, and I've got my finger on the trigger, and I like the taste of the gunmetal,' he told the judge. Unmoved by this testimony, the judge sentenced Robert to three years in state prison. By that time, the actor had been in and out of seven rehabilitation programmes since late 1996 and had repeatedly missed mandatory drug tests.

In jail Robert suffered from deep depression and was diagnosed with bipolar disorder, leading many of his friends and colleagues to publicly give voice to the opinion that he belonged in a psychological treatment facility, not in prison. Robert was released from prison in August of 2000 and immediately entered a residential drug rehabilitation facility. His career seemed to be back on track, as he began a guest-starring stint on a popular television show and managed to make a few screen appearances, winning praise for his work.

In November of 2000, however, Robert was again arrested, this time in a Palm Springs hotel room, and charged with felony drug possession after police allegedly found cocaine, Valium and methamphetamine in his room. The highs and lows continued for Robert, when Deborah sued him for divorce the same week that the actor picked up a Golden Globe and Screen Actors' Guild award for his work.

While awaiting trial, Robert was arrested for being under the influence of a stimulant. Officials later confined him to six months in drug rehabilitation for violating his parole. He was then fired from his television acting job. Robert's lawyers reached an agreement with prosecutors that required Robert to plead no contest to cocaine-related charges. He was sentenced to three years' probation, but the ruling allowed him to continue live-in drug treatment instead of returning to prison.

In 2003, Robert became engaged to a producer he met on the set of his new movie *Gothica*. He went on to star in a series of hit movies, including *Sherlock Holmes*, *Iron Man* and its sequels, and art films such as the avant garde *Fur*, and continues to receive accolades for his work. He wears his newfound sobriety well. 'Once I finally got committed [to sobriety],' he said, 'I discovered all sorts of hidden talents ... it's like a revelation to me.'

TABLE 12.4 International Data on Substance Use from the ESPAD Study

Summary Table. Selected key results by country. (Percentages if not otherwise indicated.) ESPAD 2007.									
	Cigarette use past 30 days	Alcohol use past 12 months	Drunk past 12 months	Alcohol volume (cl 100%) latest drinking day	Cannabis lifetime use	Any illicit drug other than cannabis lifetime use[a]	Inhalants lifetime use[b]	Tranq/ sedatives non-prescr. use lifetime	Alcohol together with pills lifetime[c]
Armenia	7	66	8	1.6	3	2	5	0	1
Austria	45	92	56	5.5	17	11	14	2	12
Belgium (Flanders)	23	83	29	4.3	24	9	8	9	4
Bulgaria	40	83	45	3.5	22	9	3	3	3
Croatia	38	84	43	5.2	18	4	11	5	8
Cyprus	23	79	18	2.1	5	5	16	7	3
Czech Republic	41	93	48	4.5	45	9	7	9	18
Estonia	29	87	42	5.1	26	9	9	7	5
Faroe Islands	33	...	41	..	6	1	8	3	6
Finland	30	77	45	5.7	8	3	10	7	9
France	30	81	36	3.6	31	11	12	15	6
Germany (7 Bundesl.)	33	91	50	5.1	20	8	11	3	7
Greece	22	87	26	3.1	6	5	9	4	3
Hungary	33	84	42	4.0	13	7	8	9	12
Iceland	16	56	...	4.1	9	5	4	7	4
Ireland	23	78	47	..	20	10	15	3	7
Isle of Man	24	93	61	7.3	34	16	17	7	12
Italy	37	81	27	3.6	23	9	5	10	4
Latvia	41	89	45	..	18	11	13	4	8
Lithuania	34	87	43	4.0	18	7	3	16	5
Malta	26	87	38	3.9	13	9	16	5	11
Monaco	25	87	35	2.5	28	10	8	12	5
Netherlands	30	84	36	4.9	28	7	6	7	4
Norway	19	66	40	5.9	6	3	7	4	4
Poland	21	78	31	3.9	16	7	6	18	5
Portugal	19	79	26	..	13	6	4	6	3
Romania	25	74	26	2.5	4	3	4	4	4
Russia	35	77	40	2.8	19	5	7	2	4
Slovak Republic	37	88	50	4.2	32	9	13	5	12
Slovenia	29	87	43	4.5	22	8	16	5	4
Sweden	21	71	37	5.2	7	4	9	7	7
Switzerland	29	85	41	3.9	33	7	9	8	6
Ukraine	31	83	32	2.8	14	4	3	4	1
United Kingdom	22	88	57	6.2	29	9	9	2	7
Average (unw.)	**29**	**82**	**39**	**4.2**	**19**	**7**	**9**	**6**	**6**
Denmark[d]	32	94	73	7.5	25	10	6	5	6

[a]'Any illicit drug other than cannabis' includes ecstasy, amphetamines, LSD or other hallucinogens, crack, cocaine and heroin.

[b]Inhalants: '... (glue etc) in order to get high'.

[c]'In order to get high' except for Cyprus('to feel differently') and Romania ('to feel better').

[d]Denmark: limited comparability.

and almost 36 per cent have done so by the eighth grade. Further, 54 per cent of twelfth-graders and 16 per cent of eighth graders had been drunk at least once in their lives. Marijuana was the most common of the substances used with daily use reported by 1.2 per cent of eighth graders, 3.3 per cent of tenth graders and 6.1 per cent of twelfth graders. Youth also reported decreasing levels of concern with marijuana's risks, decreasing disapproval of its use, and rather high ratings of its easy availability in contrast to previous decades (see Fig. 12.4).

Data reflecting diagnosable clinical levels of *abuse and dependence* come from the National Comorbidity Study in the US (Merikangas et al., 2010). These investigators found the overall

FIGURE 12.4 Prevalence of Daily Use and Attitudes Towards Marijuana in the US Monitoring the Future Study.

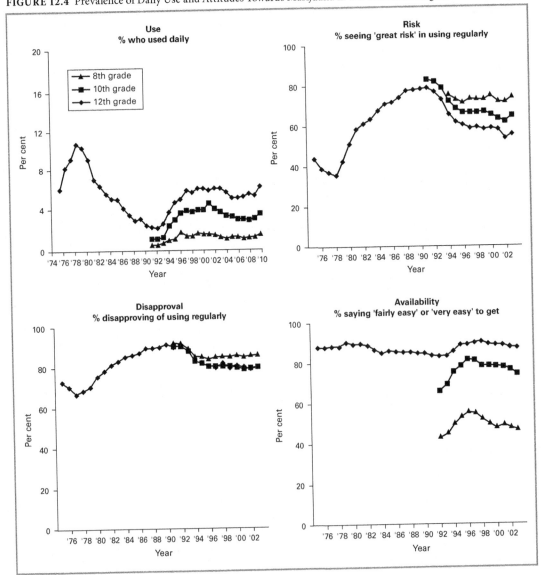

Source: Johnston et al., 2011.

prevalence of clinically significant alcohol abuse/ dependence to be 5.8 per cent among adolescent girls and 7.0 per cent among boys. In turn, drug abuse/dependence was found among 8.0 per cent of girls and 9.8 per cent of boys, and the prevalence of any substance use disorder was 10.2 per cent for girls and 12.5 per cent for boys.

Age of Onset

First, regarding substance *use*, studies in Europe and the UK indicate that the average age at which young people begin to drink is 12 years 6 months, and during the last decade, the quantity of alcohol consumed by younger adolescents has increased (Moore et al., 2010). For example, in a study of 6628 secondary-school children in Wales, Moore and colleagues found that almost three out of every four youth had tried alcohol, most of whom did so for the first time prior to age 12. Overall age trends show that most significant escalation in substance use occurs between 12 and 15 years of age, whereas late adolescence ushers in the highest levels of involvement in alcohol and drug abuse (Brown et al., 2008).

Regarding diagnosed *substance abuse and dependence*, as we might expect, rates vary with age. For example, Costello and associates (2003) conducted diagnostic interviews with a representative sample of 1420 youth in North Carolina. Virtually no substance-abuse disorders were found among children 12 years of age or younger. The prevalence began increasing in mid-adolescence with rates of 1.4 per cent at age 14, 5.3 per cent at age 15, and 7.6 per cent at age 16.

Gender

Prevalence data from international and US studies reveal a consistent *gender difference* in that boys have higher rates of substance use, particularly frequent use (Hibell et al., 2009; Johnston et al., 2011). However, girls seem to be catching up in some areas. US data show that although boys engage in more binge drinking, among tenth graders, girls are on par with boys regarding alcohol use in the past 30 days and, among eighth graders, girls now have higher rates than boys.

Further, although in the international ESPAD study (Hibell et al., 2009) overall gender differences were consistent across cultures, with boys showing more use of all substances than girls, there was one exception: in countries in which abuse of prescription drugs was prevalent, girls were twice as likely as boys to make illicit use of medications that were not prescribed for them. Similarly, in the USA, girls in the younger grades surpass boys in the use of tranquilizers and amphetamines (Johnston et al., 2011).

Ethnicity

Within US samples, youth of African descent have lower usage rates for all substances than do youth of European American or Hispanic heritage (Johnston et al., 2011). Whereas rates for European American youths are the highest among the three largest ethnic groups identified, Hispanic youth are a close second. Further, Hispanic youth are the most heavily involved with substances early in life. In turn, Asian American adolescents display the lowest rates of substance use, and this is particularly the case for Asian American girls (Luczak et al., 2006).

Rates of substance use also are high among Native American youth in the USA (Wallace et al., 2003). For example, Plunkett and Mitchell (2000) compared the rates of substance abuse among 407 high school seniors from several American Indian communities to those obtained by the MTF study. Further, these authors improved on the MTF methodology by sampling youths in the community in order to capture in their net those who might have dropped out of school. Overall, Native American youths in Plunkett and Mitchell's sample were more likely than youths in the MTF database to have used illicit substances in the past 30 days. However, the authors point out that the rates vary widely across geographic region and tribal group of origin.

Social Class

There is a trend towards a rise in binge drinking among youth whose parents have lower levels of education, whereas young children from educated families are the least likely to initiate cigarette smoking (Johnston et al., 2011). Overall, however, the influence of social class on drug use is not strong and sometimes even is reversed, with higher rates exhibited by *affluent* youths in some studies (Luthar and Becker, 2002). However, some of these findings are accounted for by use of the expensive drug cocaine, which has been supplanted in the USA by its much cheaper and easily accessed version, crack. It is likely that the links between social class and substance-abuse disorders emerge only in tandem with other risk factors.

Sexual Orientation

A meta-analysis of the available research evidence derived from multiple nations indicates that sexual-minority youths are at substantially increased risk for substance abuse (Marshal et al., 2008). Overall, the odds of substance use for sexual minority youth are 190 per cent higher than for heterosexual youth but there are differences across subpopulations: for example, the odds are 340 per cent higher for bisexual youth and 400 per cent higher for sexual minority girls. We will consider the possible reasons for this as we construct our developmental model later in this chapter.

Comorbidity

Studies also show that the majority of substance-abusing youth meet criteria for another psychological disorder. In particular, among youth in substance abuse treatment, the rates of comorbidity are 68 to 82 per cent, whereas, looked at the other way around, among youth in treatment for other psychiatric disorders, 33 to 50 per cent also meet criteria for a diagnosis of substance abuse (Brown, 2008). By far the highest level of comorbidity is between substance abuse and *conduct disorder*, especially among boys (Stein et al., 2008). Such a link is inevitable, given that use of illicit substances is the very kind of norm-violating and illegal behaviour required for the diagnosis of conduct disorder. In general, research suggests that the onset of CD generally precedes or coincides with the onset of substance use, and that a history of early onset CD in particular doubles the

risk for the development of substance problems (Sung et al., 2004). In turn, substance use and delinquency may have reciprocal influences on one another, each increasing the risk for the other disorder. For example, Mason and Windle (2002) found in their longitudinal study that, among boys, the effect of delinquency on substance use was present but small, whereas the effect of substance use on delinquency was much larger. For girls, there was no such bidirectional effect, suggesting instead the presence of a third variable that increases the risk of both problem behaviours.

Attention deficit disorder is also frequently seen in youths who abuse substances, but may be accounted for by the links among conduct disorder, substance abuse and ADHD (Wilens, 2008). (See Box 12.5.)

Disorders in the internalizing spectrum also are commonly comorbid with substance abuse, including *anxiety* (Clark et al., 2008), *depression* (Cornelius and Clark, 2008) and *posttraumatic stress disorder* (Hawke et al., 2008). For example, Giaconia and colleagues (2000) found that, among a sample of 384 adolescents, those who were substance dependent were significantly more likely than their peers to have experienced a traumatic event and were three to four times more likely to meet criteria for a diagnosis of PTSD.

Finally, youth who abuse one substance also are highly likely to engage in abuse of other substances, behaviour termed *polydrug abuse* (Kaminer and Bukstein, 2008).

Depression (Cornelius and Clark, 2008) also is a common correlate of substance abuse. The sequential relationship between these disorders does not seem clear, with some cross-national data suggesting that early onset substance use is associated with later depression (de Graaf et al., 2010) whereas other studies show that internalizing problems predate the onset of drug-taking (Hahesy et al., 2002). Nonetheless, the combination of drugs and depression may be a particularly toxic one: Windle and Windle (1997) followed a group of 975 adolescents and found that the combination

Box 12.5 Do Prescription Medications in Childhood Increase the Risk of Substance Abuse in Adolescence?

One of the concerns with prescribing psychotropic medications to children is that it might be communicating a problematic message, one that suggests that taking pills is the way to solve one's psychological problems. If this is true, it would suggest that those who take psychoactive medications in childhood are at increased risk for developing a substance-abuse problem in adolescence. The concern has emerged particularly concerning the stimulant medications used to treat ADHD (see Chapter 7), given their close links to illegal substances such as methamphetamines. The *sensitization hypothesis* suggests a possible biological underlay in that exposure to prescribed stimulants in childhood might increase sensitivity to the reinforcing effects of the drug, thus motivating illicit use and abuse. Three longitudinal studies have investigated this theory.

Mannuzza and colleagues (2003) report an investigation of school-aged children with developmental reading disorders and no other psychiatric diagnosis, who were randomly assigned to receive methylphenidate treatment or an inert placebo for 12 to 18 weeks. Sixteen years later, the participants and a sample of non-clinical controls were interviewed by clinicians blind to their group and treatment status. There were no significant differences among the groups on ratings of the prevalence, incidence, age of onset, or duration of substance abuse or dependence. Further, significantly more of the non-clinical controls had used stimulants at any time in their lives (60 per cent) when compared to those in the methylphenidate or placebo conditions (46 per cent and 41 per cent, respec-

tively). Shortcomings of this study include that the participants were not diagnosed with ADHD, as are most children who are prescribed stimulants, and they received a very short course of stimulant exposure in comparison to the years of treatment that children with ADHD typically undergo.

However, more naturalistic prospective longitudinal studies have recently been reported as well. For example, Fischer and Barkley (2003) followed into adulthood 147 individuals who were diagnosed with ADHD in early childhood and interviewed the participants about their use of substances in both adolescence and adulthood. The authors found that stimulant treatment in childhood was not associated with an increase in experimentation with substances, frequency of use or the risk of abuse. In fact, stimulants prescribed in the high school years appeared to have a protective effect against the abuse of hallucinogens in adulthood. Similar results were reported by Biederman (2003) from a longitudinal study comparing 140 adolescents with ADHD to 120 non-ADHD controls. Not only did those treated with stimulants fail to evidence higher rates of substance disorders, but youths with ADHD who did not receive stimulant medication were three to four times *more* likely to develop a substance-abuse problem than those who were prescribed stimulants in childhood.

In short, it appears that receiving appropriate medication for psychological disorders may buffer youths from engagement in maladaptive forms of self-medication, such as substance abuse.

---

of substance abuse and depression leads to an increased risk for *suicide* over time. As many as 42 per cent of suicide attempters report having problems with drugs, particularly those who make lethal attempts (Mehlenbeck et al., 2003). It may be that, like purging in bulimia, substance use is an attempt to 'self-medicate' against other sources of emotional distress. Intriguingly, the link between substance abuse and depression appears to be stronger for girls than boys (Tarter et al., 1997; Zilberman et al., 2003).

Etiology

In many Western societies, by the age of 18 the typical adolescent has had the opportunity to experiment with drugs or alcohol. Since substance use is common, perhaps even normative in some cultures, our first questions about etiology are 'What sets some adolescents on the pathway from use to abuse?' and 'Why does it occur in adolescence?' In seeking answers we will reintroduce the psychopathology of conduct disorder (see Chapter 10), which can occur with substance use and can play a determining role in escalation. We will then round out our developmental picture by describing the effect of adolescent drug abuse on adjustment in early adulthood.

The Biological Context

Genetics

Behavioural genetics studies have confirmed the link between alcohol and substance abuse in parents and their offspring (Beauchaine et al., 2008). For example, a family history of substance problems increases the risk fourfold to ninefold in boys and twofold to threefold in girls (Brown, 2008). Therefore *genetics* may play a predisposing role. This link may be explained by the presence of underlying vulnerabilities that increase the risk. For example, youth with a family history positive for alcoholism display, in comparison to their peers, more impulsivity, poorer performance on neuropsychological tests of executive functioning and response inhibition, and greater subjective and objectively rated tolerance to the effects of alcohol (Brown, 2008).

Twin studies offer the best evidence of heritability and suggest that the influence of genetics varies with the type of substance under investigation. For example, McGue and colleagues (2000) studied a sample of 626 17-year-old twins and found that heritability estimates ranged from 10 to 25 per cent for illegal drugs to 40 to 60 per cent for tobacco use and nicotine dependence. *Shared environment effects* (living in a household where drugs are available, having the same circle of friends as those who indulge in substance use) had the most significant effect on adolescent substance-related behaviour, explaining 41 to 66 per cent of the variance. However, the investigators note that as the participants grow into adulthood, the heritability estimates appear to increase in size: for males in their sample, the heritability of illicit drug dependence rose to 52 per cent in adulthood.

Molecular genetics research attempting to find the responsible candidate gene has focused on those related to liver enzyme activity, dopamine pathways in the limbic system that governs the response to reward, and the 5-HTTLPR polymorphism in the *serotonin transmission gene* (Brown, 2008). For example, in a sample of non-regular drinking youth from the Netherlands assessed annually over five years, van der Zwaluw and colleagues (2010) found that possession of the 5-HTTLPR short allele predicted larger increases in alcohol consumption over time.

In turn, in keeping with the concept of epigenetics, genetic vulnerabilities may be *potentiated* by particular environments. Van der Zwaluw and colleagues (2010) found just such an effect in their study of Dutch adolescents, for whom possession of a dopamine receptor genotype with a DRD2-A allele interacted with the effects of parental permissive attitudes in order to generate the highest levels of alcohol use over a period of three years.

Prenatal Exposure

Prenatal exposure to alcohol and tobacco also increases the risk of adolescent abuse of those substances. The mechanism of effect is not yet known. One hypothesis is that brain receptors may become sensitized by exposure, which in turn causes the child to be more reactive to the substance and to crave its effects. Alternatively, prenatal exposure may precipitate irritability and dysregulation which, in turn, increase the risk for substance abuse (Chassin et al., 2003).

Temperament

A predisposition to general *biobehavioural dysregulation*, under particular environmental circumstances, might move an individual along the pathway to substance abuse (Dawes et al., 2000). One index of dysregulation is *difficult temperament*, which involves poor adaptation to change, negative mood, social withdrawal and high intensity of emotional reactions (see Chapter 2). Longitudinal studies have confirmed that facets of difficult temperament, such as negative affectivity, behavioural undercontrol, impulsivity and aggression are predictive of adolescent substance abuse, as are other temperamental characteristics such as trait anxiety (Brown, 2008).

Evidence for a *brain mechanism* involved in behavioural dysregulation comes from brain wave studies of the P3 component in event-related potentials. (Here we follow Chassin et al., 2003.) When exposed to a novel or task-relevant stimulus, individuals with a variety of disorders involving behavioural undercontrol – including aggression, ADHD and substance abuse – evidence reduced P3 amplitude in comparison with controls. This diminished P3 reaction also is seen in young children of alcoholic parents and predicts the likelihood of the children to engage later in alcohol abuse.

Thus, biobehavioural dysregulation might underlie individuals' likelihood to develop a drug habit, their attraction to trying drugs in the first place, or their ability to engage in good decision-making about substance use in high-pressure situations. However, exposure to an environment that allows or encourages substance abuse is necessary to turning the propensity into a reality.

The Family Context
Parenting Style

Low levels of *parental support, discipline and monitoring* of children are predictive of adolescent substance abuse, as are high levels of *family conflict and disorganization* (Brown, 2008; Reid et al., 2002). In addition, parental *attitudes* towards substance use are important. For example, Moore and colleagues (2010) investigated the role of parenting in a sample of 6628 Welsh schoolchildren aged 11–16 years. Youth reports of family violence and conflict, permissive parental attitudes towards substance use and a family history of substance abuse were related to higher levels of youth alcohol use, whereas perceptions of family closeness and parental monitoring were associated with a lower likelihood of drinking.

Parental Substance Abuse

Parental *modelling* and children's direct *involvement* in their parents' drug use are robust predictors of substance abuse. Thus, the more adult family members use alcohol or drugs, the more likely it is that children will use them. However, evidence across cultures suggests that parental influences change over the course of development. For example, in a study of early adolescents (ages 12 to 16) in the Netherlands, Koning and colleagues (2010) found that parental expressions of tolerant attitudes

towards drinking were associated with early onset of youth alcohol use whereas parents' own heavy drinking was not. In contrast, Poelen and colleagues (2009) found that parent drinking was a strong predictor of late adolescent alcohol use in data drawn from the Netherlands Twin registry, just as Latendresse and associates (2008) found that parental modelling increased youth substance use in their study of a Finnish birth cohort of 4731 youth followed to age 17. Moreover, Lantendresse and colleagues found that the effects of modelling were moderated by the quality of parenting. Youth who perceived their parents as attentive to monitoring their behaviour and more consistent in discipline were less likely to engage in substance use. However, the overall effect of parenting quality decreased over time, even as the parents' modelling of substance use exerted increasing influence on their children's behaviour. It may be the case that, with increasing

Parental modelling of substance use.

cognitive complexity, youth become more sceptical of the seemingly hypocritical message from substance-abusing parents of 'do as I say and not as I do'. These findings also may reflect the growing role that peers play in teens' behavioural choices over the course of adolescence – 'often', as Latendresse and colleagues note, 'at the expense of their parents' efforts'.

In addition to modelling the use of drugs or alcohol, substance-abusing parents expose children to a number of other stressors and adversities, the effects of which are difficult to untangle. Substance-involved parents also engage in more *antisocial activity* in general, are more physically and emotionally *abusive* to their partners and children, are less *involved* and attentive parents, have more *economic problems* and engage in more *interparental conflict* and divorce (Keller et al., 2003). Thus, children exposed to substance abuse are being raised by parents who function poorly in a variety of ways, all of which increase the risk for disorder through their negative effects on multiple child developmental capacities. Ohannessian and Hesselbrock (2008), for example, followed a group of 200 youths into early adulthood and found a negative chain of events leading from paternal alcoholism to youth hostility, to risk-taking behaviour, to substance abuse.

Parental Depression

In general, parent psychopathology increases the risk for substance abuse in offspring (Mowbray and Oyserman, 2003). Interestingly, Luthar and Sexton (2007) have demonstrated that *maternal depression*, but not maternal alcoholism, is predictive of youth substance abuse. Because mothers are most often the primary caregivers, the negative effects associated with her emotionally unavailable and negative parenting may play a disproportionate role in the development of problem behaviour. On the other hand, as Ramchandani and Psychogiou (2009) point out in a review in the *Lancet*, fathers have been overlooked in much of this research; evidence suggests that paternal depression, even though half as prevalent as that in mothers, has equivalent effects on children's emotional well-being.

Child Maltreatment and Trauma

A large multi-site study of 803 adolescents undergoing substance abuse treatment found that 59 per cent of girls and 39 per cent of boys reported having experienced childhood *maltreatment* (Grella and Joshi, 2003). There were gender differences in the kinds of abuse experienced, however. Among the boys, 34 per cent had been physically abused, 0.9 per cent had been sexually abused and 4.3 per cent had experienced both. In contrast, among the girls, 17.5 per cent had been physically abused, 15.8 per cent had been sexually abused and 25.4 per cent had experienced both. These findings reflect a gender difference similar to that found by Ballon and colleagues (2001) in clinical interviews with 287 youth in treatment for substance-abuse problems, in which 64.7 per cent of the girls reported that they used drugs to help them cope with the trauma of abuse, whereas this was true for only 37.9 per cent of the boys.

Prospective longitudinal research also confirms a gender difference in the relationship between maltreatment and substance use. Lansford and colleagues (2010) found that, among a sample of 585 families followed from age five to young adulthood, physical abuse in the first five years of life predicted subsequent early onset and chronic substance use for girls but not boys.

Andersen and Teicher (2009) review the ways that traumatic life experiences negatively affect the developing brain and propose that these specifically increase the risk of substance abuse. In particular, they point to the ways in which trauma sensitizes the stress response system and ill-equips the youth to cope with the developmental challenges of adolescence. The result, they conclude, is a youth who is 'desperately driven [but with] no brakes'. This sensitized stress response system also can be understood through the construct of *PTSD* (see Chapter 8). As Hawke and colleagues (2008) state, maltreatment and other traumatic experiences increase the risk of the development of comorbid PTSD and substance abuse.

It is important to note, however, that family variables tend to be weaker predictors of teenage drug use than are peer influences in the studies that include both sources of influence. Therefore, it behoves us to turn next to the important variable of peer relations.

The Social Context
Peer Relationships

According to Brown (2008), 'the initiation or refusal to use alcohol and other drugs typically involves a social decision' (p. 431). Therefore, it is not surprising that *peer relationships* have emerged as one of the most powerful predictors of adolescent drug involvement in both longitudinal and cross-sectional studies. Heavy drinkers, for example, are more likely to have friends – especially best friends – who also drink. In addition to *modelling* substance use behaviour, peers who drink or use drugs also encourage one another to adopt *beliefs and values* supportive of substance use as well as increasing one another's *access* (Brown, 2008). In addition, peer relations may interact with other variables and risk factors. For example, adolescents are more vulnerable to deviant peer influences when their family lives are problematic. An illustration of this comes from Fergusson and Horwood's (1999) longitudinal research in New Zealand, in which they found that associations with substance-using and rule-violating peers mediated the relation between family dysfunction (parental alcoholism, economic strain and family conflict) and the development of substance use in adolescence.

Longitudinal data also show that there are two mechanisms by which peer relationships contribute to substance use (Monahan et al., 2009). One is *peer influence*, in which friends introduce peers to drugs, normalize substance use and provide models and opportunities for continued use. The other is *peer selection*, in which youths who abuse substances seek out friends and romantic partners with a similar lifestyle (van der Zwaluw et al., 2009). The idea of peer selection is related to Scarr's (1992) concept of *niche picking*: as youth enter adolescence, they act as increasingly active agents in their own development, choosing and influencing their environments by gravitating towards contexts that are compatible with their personal characteristics.

Using data from a longitudinal study of 1354 antisocial youth followed from middle adolescence into young adulthood, Monahan and colleagues (2009) found that these two processes exerted their influence differently in different developmental periods. In middle adolescence, both selection and peer influence appeared to influence substance use, as antisocial peers gravitated towards and reinforced one another's behaviour, but from ages 16 to 20 years only peer influence appeared to be operational. In turn, from age 20 onwards, the impact of peers on antisocial behaviour disappeared as participants became increasingly resistant to peer influence, just as normative social and emotional maturation processes would predict. In turn, data from the Oregon Youth Study, in which Dishion and Owen (2002) followed a sample of 206 youths from early adolescence

Peer modelling is a risk factor for substance use.

to young adulthood, shows evidence of *bidirectional* effects: substance use appeared to influence friendship selection in that youths increasingly associated with peers who fostered and reinforced activities and conversations related to drugs.

Sexual Maturation

Another interpersonal variable linked to substance use is *sexual maturation.* As with the data we reviewed related to conduct disorder (see Chapter 10), drinking and drug abuse are two forms of problem behaviour seen more often in early-maturing youth. Data from the Great Smoky Mountains longitudinal study (Costello et al., 2007) indicate that these effects hold for both boys and girls. Early pubertal maturation predicted alcohol use in both sexes, and alcohol abuse in girls. However, these effects were exacerbated when youth also evidenced conduct disorder and associated with deviant peers. In addition, early maturation also was more strongly associated with alcohol use among girls whose parents provided lax supervision and among boys exposed to poverty and family discord.

The Individual Context
Conduct Problems

With the majority of drug use beginning in middle school, we must seek its precursors during the elementary school period. Among variables within the person, early childhood *conduct problems* and *aggression* are strong predictors of adolescent experimentation with drugs, escalation in use and graduation to a full-blown substance-abuse disorder (Stein et al., 2008). The early onset conduct-disordered child we encountered in Chapter 10 is particularly vulnerable to the development of substance dependence in adulthood (Moffitt et al., 2002). Impressively, Block and colleagues' (1988) longitudinal sample identified predictors of teenage substance abuse that were present as early as three years of age. These personality attributes included antisocial behaviour, rebelliousness, poor frustration tolerance, lack of motivation and goal-directedness, lack of concern for others and unconventionality.

There are some indications of *gender differences* in these effects. Whereas childhood behaviour problems increase the likelihood of adolescence substance use, as was found in Hops and colleague's (2000) four-year prospective study, the effects are stronger for girls. Because aggression is less prevalent and less socially acceptable for girls, those who violate social norms may be at risk for escalating behaviour problems with increasingly serious consequences, such as substance abuse.

Do conduct problems lead to substance abuse, or does substance abuse lead to misbehaviour? Involvement with illicit substances is inherently an illegal activity, whereas substance use may have a disinhibiting effect on the behaviour and judgement of the young person and thus lead to conduct problems. As noted previously, the effects likely are bidirectional. Early onset conduct problems predict substance abuse; however, evidence for the other direction of effect can be found as well. The National Center on Addiction and Substance Abuse (2010) reports that 52.4 per cent of juvenile offenders incarcerated in the US meet clinical criteria for alcohol or other substance abuse disorders and that four out of every five youths currently in the US juvenile justice system had a prior history of substance offences or were under the influence of drugs or alcohol while committing their crimes.. Further, only 11 per cent of these youth are receiving any form of treatment.

Cognitive Skills and Executive Functions

Cognitive and educational skill deficits are proposed to increase the risk of substance abuse in many theoretical models. There are several mechanisms by which this effect might take place. For example, school failure may increase stress and negative affect, increase alienation from mainstream social institutions and increase the tendency to affiliate with antisocial peers, all of which are associated with substance use (Chassin et al., 2003).

Many factors are associated with poor school performance, however, so it would behove us to look at more specific cognitive skills that might be associated with substance abuse. In keeping with the theory that underlying substance abuse is a tendency toward behavioural dysregulation, youths with substance problems might be expected to evidence poorer skills on cognitive tasks assessing self-regulatory processes such as inhibitory control, planning, flexibility, set-shifting – in other words, *executive functions*. Indeed, poor executive functioning predicts earlier onset of problem drinking, greater frequency of drinking to excess and reduced ability to appreciate the negative consequences of abusing substances (Brown, 2008).

In addition, executive function deficits are seen in children of alcoholics prior to the onset of drinking and predict the extent of alcohol abuse. For example, Atyaclar and colleagues (1999) assessed executive functioning and behavioural activity levels in a sample of 10- to 12-year-olds at high risk (those whose fathers had a substance-abuse disorder) and low risk (those whose fathers had no psychiatric diagnosis) and followed them over a period of two years. High-risk children had higher initial levels of behaviour problems and executive functioning deficits and, by early adolescence, had become more involved with drugs than those at low risk. What was striking however, is that the executive function deficits, over and above behavioural problems or paternal substance use, predicted tobacco and marijuana use, number of drugs sampled and substance abuse in adolescence.

Cognitive Schemas: Expectations and Motivations

Teenagers' impulse to abuse substances may be driven by their *expectations* of the positive results that will ensue (Zucker et al., 2006). Motives or expectations that might underlie adult alcohol use include: (1) *enhancement* (i.e., to stimulate positive mood or feelings of general well-being); (2) *social* (i.e., to obtain positive social rewards such as being the 'life of the party'); (3) *coping* (i.e., to reduce or regulate negative emotions); and (4) *conformity* (i.e., to avoid peer pressure or social rejection). Cooper (1994) tested the influence of these cognitions among a sample of 2544 adolescents, approximately half of whom were African American. The results showed that enhancement, coping and social motives were strong predictors of the quantity and frequency of alcohol consumption among

adolescents, regardless of gender or race. Coping and enhancement motives, in turn, were the best predictors of alcohol abuse and problem drinking.

In a subsequent study, Cooper and colleagues (1995) further refined the model by demonstrating the different predictors and consequences of enhancement and coping motives. Youths' expectations that drinking would enhance their pleasure were related to a measure of sensation-seeking, while expectations that drinking would help them cope with negative emotions were related to measures of depression and maladaptive coping. Further, while both cognitions predicted alcohol use, coping motivations were more strongly predictive of problem drinking.

In short, the adolescents most at risk for developing a substance-abuse problem are those who believe that substances will relieve them of uncomfortable feelings or emotional pain. The youths who take substances for social reasons may be better able to confine their use to specific social contexts and to be less likely to rely on drinking or drugs to get them through an ordinary day.

Intriguingly, functional magnetic resonance imaging (fMRI) data show that youth with positive expectancies regarding substances evidence lower levels of *response inhibition* overall when compared to their peers. Anderson and colleagues (2005a) found that, during an inhibition task, youth with positive expectancies showed lower activation levels in the right inferior parietal, right middle frontal, and left superior and temporal regions of the brain. These regions are associated with capacities with clear implications for substance use, including attention, inhibitory control, and decision-making under conditions of risk.

Emotion Regulation

Whereas the self-medicating properties of bingeing and purging we discussed previously may not have been immediately apparent, this function is more intuitively obvious in the case of substance use. It is easy to see how an illicit substance might be used as a stand-in for psychoactive medication. But why would youths feel the need to self-medicate? One theory of the developmental psychopathology of substance abuse is that it arises from an attempt to escape and/or to regulate negative emotional states.

For example, Zucker and colleagues (2000) propose that the troubled family environments of future substance abusers – marked as they are by parental substance abuse and psychopathology, family discord and dysfunction – have their effects through interfering with the development of the youth's capacity to manage negative emotions and to inhibit problem behaviours. This underlying *deficit in emotion regulation* also may help to explain the comorbidity of substance abuse with so many other disorders in which problems in emotion management have been implicated.

One such disorder and negative affect is *anxiety*, which as we have seen is frequently comorbid with substance-abuse disorders among adolescents and predates their onset (Clark et al., 2008). In an intriguing study, Kendall and colleagues (2004) reported that successful treatment of anxiety disorders in children was associated with decreased risk for their abusing substances in adolescence.

Depression, on the other hand, appears to have a more complex relationship with substance abuse. For example, Stice and colleagues (2004) followed 496 adolescent girls over a period of two years. The hypothesis that depressive symptoms would predict the onset of substance abuse was confirmed in univariate tests, but not in the more stringent multivariate tests they conducted, thus providing only mixed support. In contrast, there was strong support for the hypothesis that substance abuse was a predictor of increased depression. Further, data from the World Health Organization involving 85 088 participants from 17 countries shows a modest but consistent relationship between early onset cannabis use and the risk of later depression (de Graaf et al., 2010). Thus, just like disordered eating, drug abuse may defeat its purpose by exacerbating the very negative mood states it is intended to reduce.

However, it may be that the relationship between emotion dysregulation and substance abuse holds true for only a *subset* of youth (Chassin et al., 2003). Negative emotional states may prompt

ingestion of drugs or alcohol for those who have difficulty regulating physiological and psychological distress, and, as our review of research on cognitions suggests, for those who also harbour the belief that substances will relieve them of these feelings. Other youth may gravitate toward substance use for very different reasons, such as the expectation of increased peer status, thrill-seeking, or simply because 'everyone is doing it'.

Moreover, there may be important *gender differences* in the relationship between mood and substance abuse. As noted earlier, child maltreatment and trauma, both of which are known precipitants of dysphoric affect, feature as predictors of substance abuse more often for girls than for boys (Lansford et al., 2010). Further, some data suggest that the relationship between substance use and dysphoric mood is significant for teenage girls but not boys (National Center on Addiction and Substance Abuse, 2003). Whereas boys appear to initiate smoking, drinking and substance use for the thrill of it, girls may ingest substances to relieve stress and depression.

Sensation-Seeking

Another personality variable that has been proposed to account for substance use, especially in the early years, is *sensation seeking* (Zimmerman et al., 2011). Youths who are high on sensation seeking are more likely to engage in risky behaviour such as substance abuse because they are attracted to the thrill and stimulation it provides.

Behavioural Disinhibition

A construct that is related to many of those we have reviewed above – conduct problems, executive functioning deficits, emotion dysregulation and sensation seeking – is *behavioural disinhibition*. The opposite of the self-regulation that we know is a source of resilience for youth (see Chapter 2), impulsivity and poor control over behaviour are associated with many psychopathologies, including substance abuse. Longitudinal research shows that behavioural disinhibition predicts the development of substance problems in late adolescence and emerging adulthood (Bardo et al., 2011; Windle et al., 2008). For example, in a study of 428 adolescents followed over five years in the Netherlands, Otten and colleagues (2010) found that poor self-control was related to the development of concomitant depression and cannabis use. Inability to self-regulate impulses becomes an increasing liability for youth as they progress through the adolescent stage, given the many new social and environmental contexts in which they are exposed to models and opportunities for engaging in drug and alcohol use (Brown, 2008).

More complex multidimensional models also invite us to attend to the origins of the poor self-regulation that leads to substance use. For example, Brody and Ge (2001) report results of a longitudinal study of 120 12-year-olds followed over a period of three years. Their data showed that harsh and conflictual parent–child relationships contributed to youths' increased difficulty with self-regulation, which in turn predicted increases in the use of alcohol. As usual, we are reminded of **equifinality** and that no single factor can account for the development of any psychopathology.

The Cultural Context
Social Class

One stereotype of the adolescent substance abuser is an economically disadvantaged youth who lives in a crime-ridden inner-city neighbourhood. While such negative neighbourhood and sociological variables predict delinquency and other forms of problem behaviour, however, when differences are found, the opposite seems to hold for the relationship between SES and substance abuse. As we have noted, some studies find higher rates of substance use and abuse among *affluent* youths (Luthar and Becker, 2002). Factors that appear to be related to drug use among affluent youths are *achievement pressure* and *alienation from parents* (Luthar and Latendresse, 2002).

Nonetheless, features of *low SES*, including poverty, prejudice, unemployment, deviant role models and gang influence, might contribute to one risk factor that follows from involvement in drugs, and that is participation in *drug dealing*. Dealing may appear to be the easiest – and perhaps the only – way out of poverty to disadvantaged youth (Dunlap et al., 2010). Negative consequences of dealing are

profound and include exposure to violence, legal entanglements and incarceration.

Sexual Orientation

Although sexual orientation might well be thought of as an intra-personal variable, attempts to explain the dramatically increased risk of substance abuse among *sexual minority* youth have implicated cultural factors. Recall that in our review of prevalence rates we found that odds of substance use are almost twice as high among sexual minority youth overall when compared to their peers, and four times higher among lesbian girls (Marshal et al., 2008). Unfortunately, none of the research to date has investigated mediators or moderators of these effects, and so the findings of Marshal and colleagues' meta-analysis leave us in the dark about what the underlying mechanisms are that account for this large effect. The minority stress model (Meyer, 2003; see also Chapter 2) would suggest that coming out in the context of a family, peer group and culture that is not accepting of their orientation is a source of strain for these youth, as are the hostility, discrimination and violence that they may face in a homophobic society. Two studies provide evidence in support of this hypothesis, including a multisite study involving over 9000 US high school students which found that gay, lesbian and bisexual youth reported experiencing higher levels of victimization at school (e.g., being threatened or having their personal property vandalized); in addition, there was a relationship between sexual minority status and substance use that was significantly stronger for those youth who had experienced victimization at the hands of schoolmates (Bontempo and D'Augelli, 2002). (See Fig. 12.5.) In turn, Birkett and colleagues (2009) found in their study of 7376 middle school students that a positive school climate and lack of homophobic victimization buffered sexual minority youth from the increased risk for substance abuse.

The Media

The media and the larger social context also influence young people's attitudes by conveying permissive attitudes, presenting glamorous models of

FIGURE 12.5 Relations among Sexual Minority Status, Victimization and Substance Use.

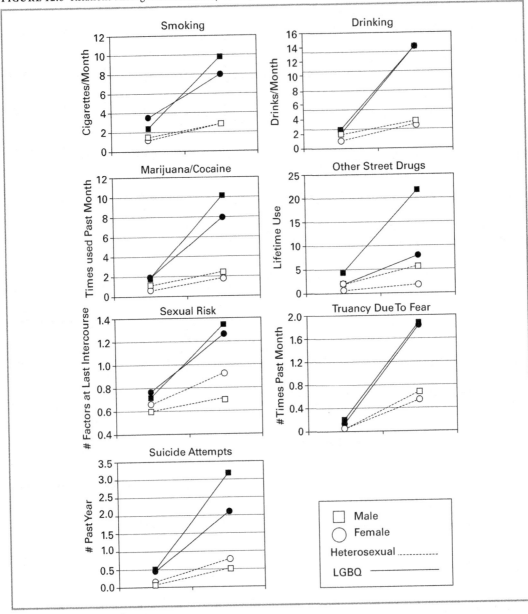

Source: Bontempo and D'Augelli, 2002.

substance use, or promoting its beneficial effects. Consequently, communitywide efforts have been recommended to reduce substance abuse among teens by restricting advertising for and access to cigarettes and alcohol (Strasburger and The Council on Communications and Media, 2010).

Cross-Cultural and Ethnic Differences

Cross-cultural studies show that the developmental psychopathology of substance abuse is similar in widely discrepant societies. For example, Pilgrim and colleagues (1999) examined the influences of personality characteristics, parenting and peer relationships on drug use among adolescents in the USA and mainland China. Across cultures, the adolescents most likely to engage in using substances over a period of a year were those high in *sensation-seeking* and whose parents were low in *authoritativeness*. One ethnic difference that did emerge was that, while *friendships* with substance-abusing friends were associated with more drug use among Chinese and European American youths, African American youths were less influenced by the behaviour of their peers. A similar finding is reported by Weaver and colleagues (2011) in their study of 680 youth involved in a substance abuse prevention programme in which they found that peer norms favouring substance use were associated with an increased propensity to consume alcohol for European American youth but not for African American adolescents.

In turn, Bray and associates (2001) report similar results across ethnic groups in their three-year study of 6522 European American, Mexican American and African American adolescents. In all ethnic groups, *family conflict* and lack of cohesion were related to increases in alcohol use, whereas ratings of adolescents' *individuation* and achievement of a developmentally appropriate sense of identity acted as a protective factor.

On the other hand, there are certain risk factors for substance abuse which are unique to minority groups, particularly recent immigrants. For example *acculturation stress* – distress resulting from a perceived clash between the values of the family of origin and the dominant culture – has been found to be associated with increased drug use in Hispanic adolescents (Saint-Jean et al., 2008).

Resilience and Protective Factors

Our review has uncovered a number of sources of resilience among youth at risk for substance abuse. On the protective side, we have learned that positive parent–child relationships can decrease the risk of substance abuse in young people, including *authoritative* parenting (Baumrind, 1991a, 1991b; see also Chapter 2), which includes warmth as well as structure, and *monitoring* of children's behaviour.

Similarly, lower substance use is found when parent–youth relationships are emotionally supportive and warm and allow children to participate in decision making – and when parents themselves are abstainers (Gutman et al., 2011).

Moreover, parental socialization practices *specifically* in regard to substance use might protect youths against involvement with drugs. For example, youths are less likely to use tobacco when parents discuss with their children reasons not to smoke, establish rules about the use of tobacco and other substances, and enforce these rules by levying consequences for misbehaviour (Chassin and Hussong, 2009).

Among individual youth characteristics that are protective against substance use are *intelligence*, *religiosity*, *low risk-taking*, *high competence* and psychological wellness, whereas *positive peer influences* include social support and conventionality rather than deviance (Brown, 2008). *Genetics* also can provide a buffer. A deficiency in the aldehyde dehydrogenase isoenzyme causes highly adverse reactions to alcohol, including flushing, racing heartbeat, hypotension and nausea, which negate any possible recreational enjoyment (Luczak et al., 2006). This condition is most prevalent among persons from northern Asia.

Developmental Course

Involvement in alcohol and drug use in the early years represents a risk for the development of later substance use disorders. Further, these disorders develop more rapidly among youth than adults, as well as being associated with significant negative consequences such as academic failure, family discord, interpersonal problems, physical health problems, risky sexual behaviour and mental health disorders (Brown, 2008). Of particular concern is the heightened risk for suicidal ideation, attempts and completions among those who abuse substances, as we noted in Chapter 9. Evidence also is emerging that alcohol and other substances have an especially pernicious effect on the adolescent developing brain (Brown et al., 2009).

However, longitudinal research suggests that there are substantially different patterns shown by youth who engage in substance use. These include *long-term moderate use, flings* (short-term heavy use, followed by abstention), *excess use* that diminishes over time, *chronic problematic use* and *late-onset heavy use* (Brown, 2008). Clearly these are different trajectories, and not all youth who experiment with substances in their younger years go on to become dependent on them. For example, approximately 10 per cent of youth in the USA engage in heavy drinking in mid-adolescence but subside to non-problematic levels by age 18, and approximately 30 per cent engage in stable moderate consumption that is associated with time-limited intermittent problems during adolescence. Among those who become ensnared in abuse and dependence, however, there also are different pathways, which we turn to next.

The Early Years: The Early-Starter, Early-Escalating Pathway

As with the other problem behaviours we have discussed (see Chapter 10), early onset of substance use is predictive of a more negative developmental course. Early initiation into substance use (i.e., before age 14) is associated with a steep escalation in use and more problematic outcomes, including substance abuse and dependence disorders (Brown, 2008). The long-term consequences of the early-starter pathway are clear. In longitudinal studies spanning adolescence and adulthood, Hops and colleagues (2000) found that early starters were the most likely to become cigarette, alcohol and marijuana users in adulthood. Further, the early-starting youths were likely to have more health problems and to experience aggression and conflict in their relationships with partners and friends.

The early starters are more typically *male*, demonstrate more *antisocial behaviour* and are more likely than other youths to come from families with a *history of substance problems* (Chassin et al., 2002).

Developmental Pathways in Early Adolescence: Risk and Protection

Jessor and colleagues (1995) tested a multidimensional model of the factors predictive of drug and alcohol abuse during the transition to adolescence. The investigators followed almost 2000 students in grades 7, 8 and 9 over a period of three years. Risk and protective factors were identified in three systems of development: personality, environment and behaviour.

Among the *risk factors* identified were *intra-individual* characteristics including low expectations of success, poor self-esteem, hopelessness and alienation. In the *environmental* realm, risk factors included peer models for problem behaviour and orientation towards peers rather than parents as guides for behaviour and life choices. Risks in the *behavioural* realm included poor school performance. However, the single most powerful predictor of substance use was the presence of *antisocial peer models*, followed by the personality variables of low expectations of success, poor self-esteem and hopelessness.

In regard to *protective factors*, in the *intra-individual* domain, the investigators targeted positive orientation towards school, concern about personal health and intolerance towards deviance. In the *environmental* domain, protective factors assessed included positive relationships with adults, regulatory controls imposed by adults on youth behaviour and peer models for prosocial behaviour. Protection in the *behavioural* domain was represented by engagement in prosocial activities.

Ultimately, the results showed that the protective factors that had the greatest impact on reducing youth substance abuse were an attitude of *intolerance towards deviance* and a *positive orientation towards school*. Further, over the three-year period, those whose problem behaviour diminished over time were not those who were exposed to fewer risk factors, but rather those who had available to them more protective factors at early stages in development. Thus, the authors conclude that 'antecedent protection has a stronger relation to change...than antecedent risk' (Jessor et al., 1995, p. 931). This suggests that prevention efforts directed at bolstering resistance to the temptations of drug use may be the most effective, a thread we will pick up later when we discuss intervention.

Developmental Pathways in Mid-Adolescence

Van Der Vorst and colleagues' (2009) four-year prospective study of 428 adolescents in the Netherlands provides information about the transition between early- to mid-adolescence. The researchers identified four categories of early adolescence in regard to their alcohol consumption – abstainers, light drinkers, increasers and heavy drinkers – and added a fifth group in mid-adolescence, termed stable drinkers. Among the *risk factors* for youth to embark on the more heavy drinking trajectories were being a boy, having a best friend or father who drinks heavily, and having parents who were permissive towards adolescents' alcohol.

In turn, Galaif and associates (2007) compiled an impressive database to examine risk and protective factors among a sample of US-born Latino ($N = 837$), foreign-born Latino ($N = 447$), White ($N = 632$) and African American ($N = 618$) adolescent boys. *Risk factors* included psychological distress and peer drug use, whereas positive relations with family and school, law abidance and guilt appeared to act as *protective factors*.

The Transition to Late Adolescence: From Use to Abuse

Newcomb and Bentler's (1988) classic nine-year prospective study of 654 adolescents provides information about the transition to the late adolescent period. The authors summarize the results in terms of the following developmental tasks faced in the transition to adulthood:

1 *Social integration*. Drug use interferes with this development by reducing social support and increasing loneliness.

2 *Occupation*. As youth involved with drugs abandon traditional educational pursuits, teenage drug use accelerates involvement in the job market while impeding successful functioning at work. This association of adolescent substance use with school dropout and lower occupational expectations has been confirmed in international data drawn from 16 countries participating in the World Health Organization Mental Health Survey (Lee et al., 2009).

3 *Sexual relations and childbearing*. Drug use has both an accelerating and detrimental impact, leading to risky sexual activity and childbearing on the one hand and relationship instability and divorce on the other.

4 *Criminal behaviour*. Youthful drug use is predictive of involvement in criminal behaviour, including stealing and violation of laws, such as driving while intoxicated or selling drugs.

5 *Mental health*. Multiple drug use is related to a small but significant increase in psychosis and a decreased ability to plan, organize and direct behaviour. Hard-drug use increases suicidal ideation in young adulthood, and alcohol increases depression.

Newcomb and Bentler (1988) conceptualize their findings in terms of *precocious development*. While precocity is generally viewed positively – in a child with musical talents, athletic abilities or intellectual capabilities beyond his or her age level, for example – a significant discrepancy between developmental level and aspirations may also jeopardize healthy development. By taking on adult functions for which they are poorly prepared, adolescent drug abusers push themselves toward a maturity that they are incapable of assuming effectively because they have not given themselves time to accumulate the needed skills and experience. In short, substance use diverts the adolescent from mastering developmental tasks that are critical to healthy adjustment in adulthood.

The Transition to Young Adulthood: The Late-Starter Pathway

Finally, a subgroup of late starters has been identified whose substance use begins only after the end of high school (Chassin et al., 2002). The transition to college or the work world provides a new level of independence and freedom from adult supervision to which drinking and drugs might be used as a 'rite of passage'. For the majority of young adults this time of experimentation is followed by a decline in substance use, commensurate with the increase in adult responsibilities associated with work, marriage and parenthood (Chassin et al., 2003). Thus, for most young people 'partying' is a developmentally limited phenomenon.

In fact, those who successfully make the transitions to these adult roles are the least likely to develop a substance problem. In contrast, the late starters who go on to become substance dependent demonstrate more overall psychopathology and negative affectivity and have difficulties functioning at work and maintaining satisfying relationships with partners. Once again, we encounter the issue of developmental preparedness but in a different guise: whereas some adolescents might push themselves to take on adult roles *precociously*, and in doing so increase the risk for substance abuse, also at risk are the young adults who are developmentally *unprepared* for the stage-salient issues of their age so as to be equipped to forge happy marriages, raise children, and launch productive careers.

Integrative Developmental Model

Illustrating the complexity of the factors involved in predicting substance abuse, Zucker and colleagues (2000, 2003, 2009) have compiled a list of risks derived from various studies. (See Fig. 12.6.) As these authors note, substance abuse is best conceptualized as a lifespan problem, with origins spanning as far back as the preschool years. They conceptualize the risks as falling within five domains, which map nicely onto our own dimensions: *intra-individual, inter-individual, family, peer* and those in the larger context such as *school* and *culture*. Thus, drug use is not due to any single cause but to a number of variables. In addition, many of these factors interact with one another, thus contributing in complex ways to the development of substance-related problems.

An important question that remains is one we posed at the beginning of this chapter: *why adolescence?* Jessor and Jessor (1977; Jessor et al., 1995) provide a classic developmental framework that addresses this issue. Their model regards behaviour as a result of interactions between personality and the perceived environment. According to the

Jessors, the transition to adolescence takes place in a societal context that affects individuals differently. While prized roles and rewards come with age in our society, the adolescent, especially the early adolescent, has limited access to the valued goals of adulthood, such as autonomy, prestige, sex and mobility. In addition, societal expectations and rules are based on chronological age alone, which ignores individual differences in adolescents' desire or readiness to pursue adult goals. While some 'late bloomers' may feel pushed to take on responsibilities for which they are not prepared, other adolescents who are ready to make the transition may feel frustrated and tantalized by the unattainable attractiveness of mature status. The result is *precocious* engagement in adult-oriented activities – a constellation including alcohol use, cigarette smoking, substance use, sexual intercourse and delinquency.

The transition from a less mature to a more mature adult status, the Jessors state, is often marked by problem behaviour. Adolescence is just such a time of transition in which stage-salient issues related to identity formation and the assumption of adult roles come to the fore. Adolescence is also a time of increasing experimentation, exploration and risk-taking. Some experimentation with drugs, therefore, is relatively expectable. 'Problem behaviour may be viewed, at least in part, as an aspect of growing up' (Jessor and Jessor, 1977, p. 238). In general, Jessor and colleagues (1991) argue, as development proceeds from adolescence into early adulthood, these kinds of problem activities will decline in most young people.

What about those for whom substance abuse and dependence result? When rebellion, defiance and antisocial behaviours become ends in themselves rather than means for promoting autonomy, adolescents may be in a state not of transition but of stagnation. Erikson's (1968) writings on *identity* are useful at this point. He states that youths often go to extremes in order to test the 'rock bottom of some truth' (p. 236) before committing themselves to a particular way of life. These extremes may include not only rebelliousness but also deviant and

FIGURE 12.6 Antecedents of Adolescent Substance Abuse.

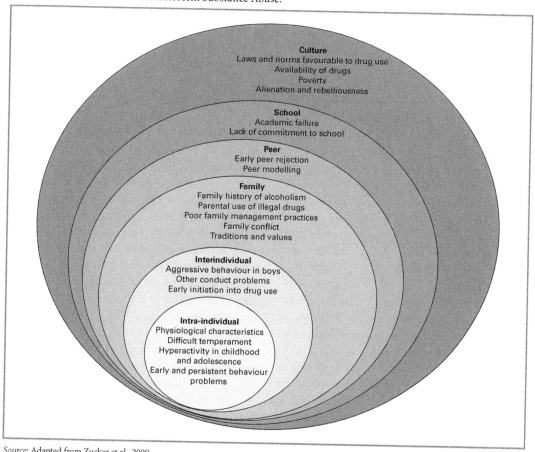

Source: Adapted from Zucker et al., 2009.

delinquent behaviours. Only when such tendencies defeat the purpose of experimentation by fixating the adolescent in this behaviour do they become psychopathological. Take, for example, a *negative identity*, in which the adolescent perversely identifies with all the roles that have been presented as undesirable or dangerous by others. Despairing of ever realizing the unattainable positive roles, the adolescents become the last thing in the world the parents would want them to be. Thus, the psychopathology underlying substance abuse may represent not only an extreme form of adolescent rebellion, but a retreat from the struggle to establish an identity rather than a progression along the way toward reaching that goal.

Further, as substance abuse becomes consolidated as part of an adolescent's behavioural repertoire and preferred method of coping, Caspi and Elder's (1988) concept of *cumulative continuity* is useful. Essentially, this concept posits that actions or events are maintained by the very consequences that they bring about. In the case of substance abuse, we see a cascading series of effects and life choices that close down opportunities to shift life to a more healthy developmental pathway. For example, the substance-abusing youth is increasingly likely to have difficulties succeeding in work or school, to be involved with deviant social networks that are defined by or revolve around substance use, to experience conflict and dissatisfaction in intimate relationships, and to encounter legal difficulties (e.g., charges for possession, driving under the influence, etc.), all of which act as stressors that are likely to serve to increase substance use.

A Different Model for Girls?

As we have noted, substance-abuse disorders are more common in males than females, which may explain why attention to girls as a unique group is quite rare. However, some evidence suggests that girls are beginning to catch up to their male peers when it comes to initiation into substance abuse. Therefore, more attention to females is warranted. Recent data suggest that there may be important gender differences in the precipitants and consequences of substance abuse. The National Center on Addiction and Substance Abuse (2004) conducted a three-year study including 1200 females aged 8 to 22. Compared with their male peers, girls who abused substances were more likely to *enter puberty early*, to suffer from *depression*, to have an *eating disorder* and to have a history of *sexual or physical abuse*. In addition, girls fell into addiction more quickly than boys, even when ingesting the same amount of substances; and girls suffered more adverse consequences, including smoking-related lung damage and alcohol-induced brain and liver damage. Significantly, boys and girls appeared to initiate smoking, drinking and substance use for different reasons: boys for the *thrills or enhanced peer status*, and girls to *relieve stress and alleviate depression*.

These data suggest that different models might be needed for the developmental psychopathology of substance abuse in males and females. In particular, models that focus on *emotion regulation*, while equivocal in mixed-gender samples, may be particularly applicable to girls. Furthermore, once a girl has become involved with illicit substances, the consequences for her physical and emotional health are particularly serious. Consequently, models of causality and treatment need to be better informed by recognition of gender differences.

For example, an intriguing finding from a sample of 2051 high school students in the Netherlands ties together the topics of this chapter in a compelling way. Larsen and colleagues (2009) found that for girls, but not for boys, the relationship between depression and substance use was accounted for by concerns about weight and dieting behaviour. Thus the precipitants of substance use may be markedly different for boys and girls and may require the development of quite different predictive models.

Intervention

Despite the pressing need for effective treatments for adolescent substance abuse, they have tended to be elusive. Surveys suggest that only about 10 per cent of adolescents who admit to substance problems actually receive treatment, and of those who do, approximately 50 per cent relapse within three months (Brown and Abrantes, 2006). In addition, although many treatments have been developed as downward extensions of adult models, developmental differences in the patterns, precursors, co-occurring problems and interpersonal contexts of adolescent substance abuse must be taken into account when designing interventions that have any hope of success. However, on a more encouraging note, as Waldron and Turner (2008) observe, the research base regarding effective interventions for adolescent substance abuse has grown considerably over the past decade and is of much higher quality than that conducted previously.

Family Systems Approaches

Intervention with adolescents also needs to take into account the family context in which substance abuse develops. Indeed, *family therapy* has been recommended as a treatment of choice for adolescence substance abuse. Empirical research bears this out: across a wide variety of studies, manualized family therapy approaches have been found to be effective in reducing substance use (Waldron and Turner, 2008). Participants are also more likely to engage in family therapy and to remain in treatment longer than those assigned to other interventions.

For example, Santisteban and his colleagues (2003) have empirically demonstrated the effectiveness of brief strategic family therapy (BSFT) for reducing substance use and other problem behaviours among Hispanic adolescents. Derived from Minuchin's structural family therapy, the focus of BSFT is on restructuring maladaptive patterns of interaction between parents and children. The investigators obtained youths' self-reports of substance use and substantiated them by urine toxicology screens after treatment. Youths were randomly assigned either to the family therapy condition or to a youth-only group therapy condition modelled after the prevention programmes that are commonly offered to adolescents in the school setting. Following treatment, which ranged between four and 20 weekly therapy sessions, depending on the severity of the presenting problem, the results showed that marijuana use reduced significantly more for those youths who received BSFT, although the effects on alcohol use were not significant. In the BSFT condition, 41 per cent were no longer using substances at termination of treatment, whereas this was true for only 13 per cent of those who received group therapy.

Multisystemic therapy (Henggeler et al., 2009), which we encountered in Chapter 10, expands treatment beyond the family to include the school and community contexts in which substance abuse develops. This is an intervention with proven success with even the most difficult to treat substance-abusing and -dependent youths.

Self-Help Groups

Another form of intervention is the *self-help group*. Twelve-step programmes such as Alcoholics Anonymous, Alateen, Cocaine Anonymous and Narcotics Anonymous are widely accepted by adolescents. In addition to steps involving admitting one's addiction, conducting a personal inventory and making amends for any harm done to others by one's substance abuse-related behaviours, an important part of this model is linking the youth with a sponsor, a recovered substance abuser who acts as a mentor, role model and source of support (SAMHSA, 2008).

Despite their popularity, there is a dearth of evidence from controlled studies to document the effectiveness of 12-step groups. In one non-controlled study, Kelly and colleagues (2000) found that 12-step meetings were associated with an increase in motivation for abstinence, which in turn predicted reduced drug use among teens. A more rigorously designed intervention study included 245 adolescents referred to drug clinics (Winters et al., 2007). Among the 179 youth who followed through on the recommendation that they participate in treatment, 54 per cent reported abstinence or only minor lapses (using a substance once or twice) in the six months following treatment, and 44 per cent retained these gains for a full year. In contrast, only 15 per cent of those who dropped out of treatment and 27 per cent who never started treatment evidenced such effects. Interestingly, outcomes tended to be somewhat better for girls than for boys.

Cognitive Behavioural Interventions

Cognitive behavioural therapies for substance abuse take a *social learning perspective*, viewing problematic substance use as a behaviour that is learned in the context of social interactions (e.g., with peers, parents and the media) and is sustained as a function of contingencies in the environment (e.g., rewards and punishments) (Brown and Abrantes, 2006). The focus is on altering those associations through cognitive strategies (e.g., identifying *distorted thinking patterns*, such as 'using drugs will make me more popular') and *behavioural interventions* (e.g., coping with cravings to use, learning substance refusal skills, and developing strategies for avoiding high-risk environments that might contribute to relapse). These interventions may be implemented in an individual therapy or a group therapy context.

Waldron and Turner's (2008) meta-analysis provides strong support for the effectiveness of CBT in the treatment of adolescent substance abuse. Although earlier reports had evoked concern that group treatments have unwanted negative effects through exposing youth to models of peer misbehaviour that reinforce their own, a process termed 'deviancy training' (Dishion and Dodge, 2005), the weight of the evidence suggests that such effects only emerge for the most at-risk youth.

Although youths with the severe problem behaviour do appear to benefit from joining a group that includes prosocial peers, there is no evidence that the more deviant youth inspire higher levels of problem behaviour in their less troubled peers (Burleson and Kaminer, 2005).

In addition, recent advances have led to integrated treatments that combine family and cognitive behavioural techniques. One such intervention is an enhanced version of Functional Family Therapy specifically designed for substance-abusing adolescents and their parents, which is amassing a strong evidence base in well-designed clinical trials (Waldron and Brody, 2010).

Prevention
School-Based Efforts

Prevention is generally less costly than treatment and may be particularly important in the case of substance abuse. As our review of the research has shown, providing protection early in development is more effective than reducing risk factors later: once established, substance use may become increasing difficult to reverse, as lifestyle changes, expectancies and physical dependence are ushered in. For example, using longitudinal data from the 30-year Dunedin, New Zealand longitudinal study, Odgers and colleagues (2008) found that approximately 50 per cent of adolescents exposed to alcohol and illicit drugs prior to age 15 had no conduct-problem history, yet were still at an increased risk for the development of substance dependence and its accompanying negative outcomes. Further, if youths typically undergo a stepwise progression from less to more serious involvement in drugs, efforts at preventing substance use in the first place are well worthwhile.

On such universal prevention effort is the Healthy School and Drugs (HSD) programme (Cuijpers et al., 2002), which is implemented in almost 60 per cent of all secondary schools in the Netherlands. The HSD programme is a multifaceted, school-based prevention programme aimed at reducing early onset and excessive substance use. The programme consists of four components.

First, *psychoeducation* takes place in the form of electronic modules developed specifically to connect with the experience of adolescents, with the inclusion of small films, cartoons and various kinds of interactive tasks. The modules teach students about the risks related to substance use, as well as preparing them to cope with peer pressure by training them in refusal skills. Youth also are given the opportunity to discuss relevant topics or to share their opinions through chat rooms and forums. Students are exposed to modules on alcohol in the first grade, on tobacco in the second grade, and on cannabis in the third grade.

Second, *parental participation* is facilitated by inviting parents to an informational meeting in which they learn about the HSD prevention programme as well as about the characteristics of and risks associated with youth substance use and the role that parents can play in discouraging it. Parents also are involved in an ongoing way through regular mailings of informational brochures and the school newsletter.

Third, the *school climate* is addressed through the setting of standards and rules concerning substance use behaviours that are designed to set firm boundaries and increase clarity. For schools that do not already have such regulations established, a special team is set up to create them including all relevant stakeholders (e.g., parents, students, teachers and the school administration).

Fourth, to provide *monitoring and ongoing counselling*, teachers, mentors, guidance counsellors and other school staff receive training regarding how to recognize and respond to signs of problematic use among students.

Evaluations of the effectiveness of school-based prevention programmes such as this indicate that they have promise. For example, Skara and Sussman (2003) evaluated the results of 25 programmes designed to prevent substance use in the middle school and high school period. Overall, the majority of studies yielded significant effects for their target goals of reducing substance use. In some studies, effects were maintained as long as 15 years. 'Booster shots', periodic refreshers of the programme curricula, appeared to be particularly helpful to maintain long-term benefits. However, the reviewers note a number of methodological problems with the studies that were conducted that limited their confidence in the results. For example, the Dutch HSD programme has to date been evaluated only through a quasi-experimental design which indicated that the intervention's strongest effects are on changing cognitions (knowledge and attitudes about drugs) and less so on changing behaviour. Acknowledging the limitations of their data, the developers have recently launched a rigorous large-scale randomized controlled trial which is still in progress (Malmberg et al., 2010).

Moving Prevention into the Larger Social Context

Comprehensive prevention programmes are informed by the research implicating multiple risk factors in the etiology of substance abuse and consequently target a number of different domains for intervention. Most importantly, these go beyond the school and family in order to address sources of risk in the larger social context of the community. One particularly influential risk factor that is targeted by such efforts is the media, through the creation of public service announcements that counter youth's beliefs that substance use is normative, benign and difficult to resist. A prime example is the Midwestern Prevention Project, a comprehensive programme that includes interventions at the level of the school, parents, community, public health and media, and which has demonstrated more beneficial effects than school-based efforts only (Riggs and Pentz, 2009).

Culturally Informed Prevention

Preventive efforts are most successful when they are culturally informed and competent (Loue, 2003).

For example, skills training needs to be adapted to reflect the life situations in which ethnic minority youths live and the *bicultural competencies* that they need to develop (Hawkins et al., 2004). One of these competencies is the ability to cope with the realities of racial oppression without succumbing to a sense of despair and hopelessness, which in turn contributes to the development of substance abuse disorders (Gibbons et al., 2004). For this reason, Brody and colleagues (2004) included *adaptive racial socialization* among the parenting variables addressed by their Strong African American Families Program for the prevention of substance use in rural African American families.

Community involvement in the programme also is essential to its acceptance and ultimate success. For example, Hawkins and colleagues (2004) describe their work partnering with Pacific Northwest tribes to develop an intervention based on the principles of the Canoe Family. The Canoe Family is a traditional rite of passage in which, over the course of a year, tribal elders prepare youths to act as representatives of their tribe during canoe trips to neighbouring Native communities, a privilege for which the youths must commit to remaining clean and sober. Like the Canoe Family, the prevention programme provides youths with strategies to cope with life challenges, both through individual effort and drawing on the strengths of the community, so that the tribe as a whole can arrive safely at its destination.

Discussions of psychopathology usually assume that the developing child is not deviant either intellectually or physiologically. The assumption has not always proved correct; in the instance of autism, for example, both mental retardation and organic brain pathology are present. This assumption is absent with our next two topics: brain injury and chronic illness.

CHAPTER 13

The Developmental Consequences of Brain Injury and Chronic Illness

In our discussion of mental retardation in the previous chapter, we learned that there are many ways in which the brain might be damaged, resulting in various kinds of cognitive deficits and psychopathologies. In this chapter, we will consider more specifically the ways in which brain injury affects development. We also will explore the field of paediatric psychology, which is concerned with the effects of chronic medical illness on child development and psychopathology.

Brain Damage

Definition

Brain damage can be defined in three different ways. A strictly *neurological* definition concerns itself with the nature, site and size of damage to the brain. A *behavioural* definition is concerned with the functions impaired by the damage: motor and communication disorders, sensory and perceptual deficits, intellectual impairment, and so on. Brain damage can also be conceptualized in terms of a wide array of *etiological factors*, such as

traumatic injury, anoxia, encephalitis, epilepsy, cerebral palsy and lead poisoning, to name a few. Each approach is valid, but the complex interrelations among them have yet to be worked out. Therefore, it is important for us to realize at the outset that the 'brain-damaged' child is an abstraction that glosses over crucial distinctions among children.

Assessment

While *autopsy* is the surest technique for establishing brain damage, it is, of course, no help in diagnosing a living child. Diagnosis of brain damage frequently relies on the child's *history*, covering factors such as pregnancy and delivery complications; developmental milestones such as sitting up, walking and speaking; and illnesses. Not only is there evidence that such information is often unreliable, but there is also no direct relation between the information and brain damage. Paradoxically, developmental histories are the least useful yet most frequently used of all diagnostic procedures.

Neurological Examination

The *neurological* examination covers such classic signs as failure of the reflexes, restriction of the visual field, and loss of sensation and function in any part of the body. An important part of the neurological exam is the assessment of the sensory and motor functioning of the 12 sets of cranial nerves (Kolb and Whishaw, 2003). Generally, all the muscles of the body are assessed from the head to the foot and the status of each recorded on a chart. Motor tone and strength are assessed on both sides of the body, as are tremors or other involuntary movements. The examiner tests co-ordination by asking the child to walk heel to toe in a straight line, touch his or her fingers to his or her nose, and so on. The intactness of the sensory system is assessed by asking the child to smell or taste substances, identify the location of stimulation such as a pinprick on the arm and identify objects that are placed in the hand while the child's eyes are closed. While valuable for identifying gross neurological deficits, the examination may not be sensitive enough to detect more subtle anomalies in children with head injuries or other forms of brain damage.

Neuroimaging Techniques

Remarkable progress has recently been made in techniques for *visualizing* brain structure and functioning. (See Kolb and Whishaw, 2003.) The traditional **electroencephalogram** (**EEG**), which measures electrical activity of the brain, can detect gross damage, but is not specific and is prone to error. In fact, 10 to 20 per cent of normal children also display abnormal records.

However, two advances in electroencephalographic techniques have resulted in increased sensitivity to brain damage. The first is the **event-related potential** (**ERP**). When a stimulus such as a light or sound is presented, the brain produces a characteristic response, or ERP. Knowing the ERP in the intact brain allows diagnosticians to detect malfunctions such as visual disorders and deafness in very young or mentally retarded children who cannot be tested by the usual techniques. Next, developments in *computer analysis* and *computer graphics* have made it possible to use many recording leads simultaneously rather than using just the few recording leads of traditional EEGs. Consequently, a detailed computer-drawn picture of the brain is now available.

There have also been advances in imaging techniques for visualizing brain structure deriving from the *X-ray* technique. Traditional X rays were limited by the fact that they could detect only gross abnormalities. **Computerized axial tomography** (**CAT**) **scans** – also called computer-assisted tomography (CT) scans – use computer-driven X-ray machines to produce exceptionally detailed images both of the brain's surface and of the levels below, making it possible to localize lesions at any level of the brain. An imaging method called **magnetic resonance imaging** (**MRI**) produces even clearer images. Use of images from successive layers of the brain makes it possible to generate an MRI-based three-dimensional image of various brain structures.

Functional magnetic resonance imaging (**fMRI**) is one of the most rapidly growing methods for imaging the living brain. It tracks subtle increases and decreases in oxygen on a moment-to-moment basis as a person performs a given task, such as attending to a visual stimulus. Then, by taking consecutive slices of the brain in various orientations, the MRI scanner reconstructs where in the brain the greatest areas of activation occur. For example, fMRI has been used to map areas of the brain used for the visual system, working memory, learning and problem solving. *Diffusions tensor imaging (DTI)* is a fairly new MRI technique which measures the diffusion properties of water molecules in tissue. This technique can measure in three dimensions, mapped and reconstructed into images that closely correspond to the underlying tissue anatomy. Also this technique provides a quantitative assessment of the integrity of white matter tissue. DTI is thought to lead to more accurate delineation of the extent of white matter injury than clinical MRI and thus may be more sensitive to changes in normal brain development. It has been shown to be particularly susceptible to long-term changes in working memory (Wozniak et al., 2007).

Positron-emission tomography (PET) scans, unlike imaging techniques, which produce static pictures of the brain and reveal only structural or anatomical deficits, can detect abnormal functioning in brains that might look structurally intact. Because brain cells metabolize glucose, radioactive glucose is introduced into the cerebral artery and the rate at which it is metabolized in various parts of the brain is recorded. The resulting PET images can then be compared with those of a normally functioning brain. Figure 13.1 contrasts the images obtained by these different techniques.

Neuropsychological Testing

Neuropsychological tests are used to pinpoint and describe the specific cognitive deficits in children with brain damage. Two of the more commonly used comprehensive test batteries for children include the NEPSY Developmental Neuropsychological Assessment (Korkman et al., 1998) and the Woodcock-Johnson-III Tests of Cognitive Ability (Woodcock et al., 2001b). While based on different models of cognitive functioning, both of these tests assess important cognitive processes that may be disrupted by brain damage, including attention, memory, speed and fluency, processing of visual or auditory information and **executive functions** such

as organization, planning, self-monitoring and cognitive flexibility.

Typically, a neuropsychological battery is administered to the child in tandem with a standardized intelligence test, which assesses the child's overall level of ability, and an educational test battery, which assesses the child's mastery of school-related tasks. Testing is repeated at regular intervals over the course of childhood in order to track changes in functioning and to adjust interventions in order to better meet the needs of the child at each stage of development. (See Box 13.1 for a case example involving comprehensive assessment of brain damage.)

Psychopathology in Brain Damage

There is evidence that brain damage increases the risk for psychological disturbances. In one of his classic studies, Rutter (1977, 1981) compared 99 children aged 5 to 14 who had cerebral palsy, epilepsy or other clearly established brain disorders with 189 children from the general population of 10- and 11-year-olds, and with 139 children ages 10 to 12 who had physical disorders not involving the brain, such as asthma, diabetes, heart disease and orthopaedic injuries. The rate of psychological disturbance in the brain-damaged group was 34.3 per cent of the population, while the rate of

FIGURE 13.1 Views of the Brain Obtained with Various Imaging Techniques.

The CT, PET and MRI scans shown here were created by three different techniques for imaging a slice of the brain. The fourth image is a photograph of a brain removed from a cadaver. (After Posner and Raichle, 1994.)

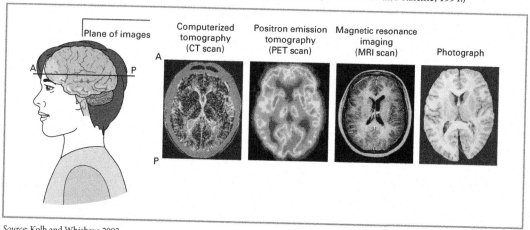

Source: Kolb and Whishaw, 2003.

Box 13.1 Case Study: Traumatic Brain Injury (TBI)

Gordon was a 9-year-old boy who received a severe traumatic brain injury when he was involved in a serious car accident. Upon his admission to the emergency room, the medical team noted that he had a large laceration on his scalp and his right pupil was dilated and unresponsive. He underwent emergency surgery for a depressed skull fracture and injury to the left side of his head. His stay in the hospital was lengthy, lasting several weeks. During his hospitalization he received a series of CT scans, which revealed multiple fractures of the skull and contusions, especially of the frontal lobes. The bleeding from the injuries placed pressure on his brain, encased as it is in the rigid skull with nowhere for this excess fluid to go. As a consequence of this pressure, over time enlargement of the ventricles was seen, indicating some atrophy of brain tissue. Gordon also had a series of EEGs with abnormal results, suggesting seizure activity, and he began taking medication for seizure control.

While Gordon had previously been described as a happy, bright-eyed, sociable child, his behaviour was markedly different post-injury. Both his parents described him as a 'different child' and said that they felt like they needed to get to know him all over again. Now, they reported, Gordon was sullen, irritable, easily frustrated and quick to anger. Gordon's social and emotional functioning was formally assessed, using behavioural observations and rating scales completed by his parents and teachers. His parents were asked to fill out the rating scales twice – once for his current functioning and once for his behaviour prior to the injury. Both his mother and his father rated his behaviour in the average range pre-injury, and both also rated his behaviour post-injury in the clinically elevated range on scales assessing conduct problems, overactivity, disorganization and psychosomatic complaints. Consistent with his parents' reports, teachers also rated Gordon as showing hyperactivity, conduct problems and poorly regulated emotions in the classroom.

In terms of his cognitive development, Gordon's early developmental history had also been normal, and his parents described him as a healthy child with no academic problems. Because Gordon's overall functioning was good, therefore, he had never before been referred for an evaluation and no pre-injury IQ scores were available for comparison. However, six months post-injury, his cognitive test scores suggested that his overall intellectual abilities were in the low average range. While he demonstrated relatively intact skills on tasks assessing his verbal reasoning, he demonstrated weakness in a number of areas,

psychological disturbance in the group with other physical handicaps was 11.5 per cent – which still was almost twice that of the normal population.

Rutter's findings do not mean that all children with brain damage are at risk, however; on the contrary, only when biological factors result in major brain disorders is the risk of psychopathology significantly increased, although, even in this case, it is not inevitable. Aside from this special group, the risk of psychopathology is minimal and difficult to detect. The functions most powerfully affected by brain damage are cognition, sensory and motor functions, and seizure thresholds (Max et al., 1997).

In light of the importance of the brain, many of the findings mentioned may seem unexpectedly mild. However, it is important to remember the remarkable recuperative powers of the brain – for example, from injuries, strokes or infections. Two

mechanisms aiding recuperation are sprouting and vicarious functioning. In *sprouting*, an undamaged neuron makes synaptic contact with neurons beyond the damaged area (lesion), while in *vicarious* functioning another area of the brain takes over the functions served by the damaged area (such as the transfer of speech from the left to the right hemisphere). Also, as we will soon see, the ameliorating potential of the social environment has been underestimated until relatively recently.

It is important to note that there is no evidence that brain damage leads to a characteristic clinical picture that can be labelled 'the brain-damaged child'. Effects tend to be non-specific, with psychopathologies ranging widely as they do in other disturbed populations.

Studies addressing consequences of brain injury have largely been drawn for six sources:

including attention and concentration, organization of visually presented information, and expressive language. His performance on educational testing also showed a strength in reading, but poor mathematics and written expression. Further neuropsychological testing of his memory showed that his ability to recall previously learned information was intact, but his ability to remember new information was significantly low. Tests of executive functions revealed that he had severe difficulties with flexibility, planning and speed of mental processing. Because it is unlikely that a child with these deficits would have been performing as well in school as Gordon had been prior to his injury, the clinicians suspected that they were related to his TBI. Further, his profile was not only consistent with a generalized pattern of brain injury, but pointed to specific location of damage: the frontal lobes.

The clinicians also evaluated the family as a whole and found that they all were greatly traumatized by the accident, even though Gordon was the only one who was physically injured. His older brother had begun showing some behaviour problems recently, and his mother was seeking individual therapy to help her with an acute depression.

Over time, as Gordon healed from his injuries, he evidenced recovery of his general cognitive abilities and remote memory. However, he continued to show prob-lems with learning and remembering new information, attention and concentration, processing visual informa-tion, organizing and problem solving. He also continued to show poor self-control and had behaviour problems at home and at school.

The treatment team made a number of recommenda-tions to ease Gordon's transition back into the regular school day. They suggested that teachers use compensa-tory strategies to help Gordon deal with his difficulties with memory, learning new material and processing vis-ual information. These included such strategies as pro-viding him with all directions both verbally and in writing, keeping instructions short and visible through-out the task, and being willing to repeat directions to Gordon as many times as necessary. To cope with his lack of mental flexibility and poor organizational skill, teachers were advised to provide Gordon with warm-up time before any new activity and to provide him with organizational tools, such as an outline of daily activities. To help with his behavioural and emotional problems, the treatment recommended parent training in behaviour management strategies, as well as family therapy to help all family members to adjust to the trauma and the pres-ence of this 'new child' in the home.

Source: Adapted from Snow and Hooper, 1994.

1 prospective studies of consecutive hospital admissions

2 retrospective cross-sectional psychiatric studies of consecutive hospital admissions

3 prospective study of referred sample of TBI children in rehabilitation centres

4 retrospective cross-sectional psychiatric studies using psychiatric assessments of child psychiatric patients

5 case reports of adults who acquired injuries during childhood

6 post-injury changes reported by parents and teachers.

We will now turn to the specific kind of brain dam-age called traumatic brain injury.

Traumatic Brain Injury
Definition and Characteristics
Traumatic brain injury is defined as 'an acquired injury to the brain caused by external physical force, resulting in total or partial functional disability or psychosocial impairment' (US Office of Education, 1992, p. 44842). TBI in children results in high rates of mortality and morbidity and therefore is a major public health concern. The majority of cases are mild in nature, but long-term outcomes of mild TBI in children are still poorly understood. While most chil-dren will make a full recovery, a proportion of them will go on to suffer from a range of post-concussive symptoms (PCS) which can persist for months. These are thought to include headaches, dizziness, fatigue and nausea as well as a variety of cognitive difficulties including poor concentration and memory

(Prigatano et al., 2010). The outcomes of TBI in children are historically controversial, with research debating whether or not PCS occurs in children. However, criteria for post-concussional disorder are included in both the ICD-10 and the DSM-IV.

There are two kinds of TBI: penetrating head injury and closed head injury. *Penetrating (open) head injury* involves penetration of the skull, dura matter (the protective layer beneath the skull) and the actual brain tissue. Penetration can be produced by a small object moving rapidly, such as a bullet, or a large, dull object such as a baseball bat. *Closed (non-penetrating, or blunt) head injury* is the more common of the two and occurs when a blow to the head does not penetrate the dura and therefore the brain is not exposed – for example, when a child is propelled violently forward in an automobile accident and the head strikes a solid object. In general, over 90 per cent of child TBIs involve closed head injuries (Snow and Hooper, 1994).

The two kinds of injuries have different effects on the brain. Penetrating head injuries produce specific and focal deficits at the point of impact, whereas closed head injuries of equal severity produce more extensive neurologic disruption and consequently are more serious. This widespread damage is generally due to tearing, twisting or shearing of fibres in the brain. Another common characteristic of closed head injury is that there is damage on the opposite side of the brain from the blow, when violent movement of the head causes the child's brain to be thrown against the skull as it moves in the direction of the blow – this is termed a *contra coup* injury. The frontal lobes are particularly vulnerable during closed head injuries because the inside of the skull in the front of the brain contains a number of bony protrusions that cause damage when the brain is thrown against them. (See Fig. 13.2.)

The seriousness of head injury is directly proportional to the extent of unconsciousness (coma) and loss of memory (amnesia) suffered by the child. The Pediatric Coma Scale (Simpson and Reilly, 1982) is a commonly used measure that assesses three aspects of consciousness: eye opening in response to stimulation, verbal responsiveness and motoric responses. As one might expect, a deeper and long-lasting coma is an indicator of more severe head injury. In regards to amnesia, severe post-traumatic amnesia (difficulty learning and retaining new information) for a week or longer is a predictor of poor outcome.

There are several systems which are used to classify types of TBI, the most common being by levels of severity (mild, moderate, severe), and by pathological feature. The Glasglow Coma scale

FIGURE 13.2 Illustration of Coup Causing the Primary Impact and the Secondary Impact or Contra Coup Injury.

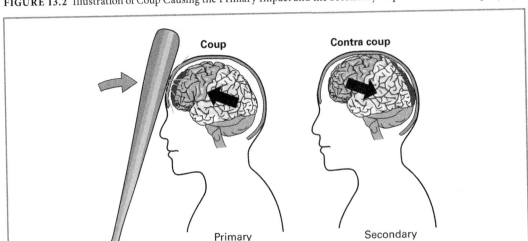

Coup

Contra coup

Primary
Impact

Secondary
Impact

TABLE 13.1 Severity of Traumatic Brain Injury

	GCS	PTA	LOC
Mild	13–14	<1day	0–30 minutes
Moderate	9–12	>1 to <7 days	>30min to <24 hours
Severe	3–8	>7 days	>24 hours

(GCS) is a widely used system for classifying the severity level of TBI (see Table 13.1). It grades a person's level of consciousness on a scale of 3–15 based on verbal, motor and eye-opening reactions to stimuli. The GCS scores range from mild (GCS 13–15), moderate (GCS 9–12) and severe (GCS <8) (Andriessen et al., 2010). However a major limitation to the GCS is that it has limited ability to predict later outcomes. Therefore GCS is often considered alongside measures of memory and consciousness: post-traumatic amnesia (PTA) and loss of consciousness (LOC). Table 13.1 shows how TBI can be classified by these measures.

In addition, TBI can also be classified by its pathological features. For example, lesions can be extra-axial (occurring within the skull but outside of the brain) or intra-axial (occurring within the brain tissue). Damage from TBI can also be focal or diffuse, confined to specific areas or distributed in a more general manner. Majority of cases involve both. Focal injuries often produce symptoms related to the functions of the damaged area. Research shows that the most common areas to have focal lesions in non-penetrating traumatic brain injury are the orbitofrontal cortex (the lower surface of the frontal lobes) and the anterior temporal lobes, areas that are involved in social behaviour, emotion regulation, olfaction and decision making. Hence the high frequency of social/emotional and judgement deficits often reported in individuals following moderate-severe TBI.

The majority of the TBIs (over 75 per cent) are classified as mild (Langlois et al., 2006). However, while the literature provides ample evidence of long-term cognitive and behavioural changes following moderate and severe TBI, the consequences of mild TBI are less clear.

Prevalence

The Centers for Disease Control and Prevention estimate that there are more than 1 million new paediatric traumatic brain injuries (TBIs) each year, resulting in 435 000 emergency room visits. In fact TBI is known to be the most common neurological condition in children (Centers for Disease Control and Prevention, 2006) as well as the leading cause of death or permanent disability for children and adolescents. However, it is likely these data are grossly underestimated because the majority of injuries may go unreported. TBI is considered a major health concern, particularly as an early insult to the brain may interrupt normal development (Catroppa and Anderson, 2007).

Gender, Race and Socio-economic Status

Males with head injuries outnumber females more than 2 to 1, and the gender difference is even more marked in the adolescent years. Males also are disproportionately likely to suffer fatalities. The little information available concerning the role of race and social class suggests that minority and low SES children are more vulnerable to TBI (Anderson et al., 2005b). Also children who develop more challenging changes in their behaviour following TBIs show greater family social disadvantage than children without new problems.

Age

It used to be assumed that infants and young children who had suffered a brain injury would eventually 'grow out of it'. Known as the Kennard principle in medical terms (Kennard, 1936), this approach holds that children, owing to their brain's neuronal plasticity (the ability of their nerve cells to change or adapt), have a greater capacity for neuronal organization than adults do. Therefore the principle holds that the younger the child at the time of injury, the better the outcome. (For a recent review see Dennis, 2010.) As a result of the 'Kennard Principle' the 'crowding hypothesis' was also formed. According to this idea, when damaged, the young brain reorganizes the best way it can at the time, without regard to any future development. Since language abilities are acquired before visuospatial ones, language recovery goes reasonably well but leaves visuospatial processing permanently retarded. In other words, when a lot of damage is done, earlier developing forms of processing 'crowd out' later developing ones. One corollary to the crowding hypothesis is that it is not the damage location that matters during early development, but instead the extent of the damage decides how much overall brain power will be lost.

However, while the crowding principle is heavily debated, it is now widely accepted that children, especially infants and preschoolers up to age 7, have a substantially higher vulnerability to neurological trauma than do adults. Thus, the opposite of the Kennard principle is considered true: the younger the child, the more vulnerable they are. Researchers have speculated that younger children display poorer outcome because they are more susceptible to the diffuse brain injury that accompanies severe TBI and its effects of post-injury are often still in development (Ewing-Cobbs et al., 2004). Recent studies have also shown that children's skulls are only one-eighth as strong as that of adults. Thus, children are much more vulnerable to injury through deformation and fracture of the skull, which can injure the brain.

Research suggests that the brain is undergoing its most marked developmental changes prior to age 5, especially in terms of the prefrontal cortex and cerebral myelination (Giedd et al., 1999). Many skills have yet to mature, or are undergoing rapid development during this period. In fact the literature surrounding TBI indicates that the timing of brain injury is one of the most important factors to future prognosis, with younger age being associated with more severe outcomes.

The two age groups which are at highest risk for TBIs are the 0 to 4s and 15- to 19-year-olds. A dramatic increase is thought to occur between 15 to 16 years of age, probably because at this age youths are allowed to drive or ride with other young drivers. Falls are the predominant injury for younger children. For school-age children, the most prevalent risks are being hit by a car while walking or riding a bicycle, or being hurt during a sports activity.

Motor vehicle accidents are the principal cause of TBI in adolescents over the age of 16.

Pre- and Post-TBI Behaviour

Certain aspects of brain injury are unique to children. For example, it is more difficult to determine the measure of loss of brain function in a child. In adults there are prior academic records, IQ scores and job listings to rely on. In children some neurologic deficits after head trauma may not manifest for many years. Frontal lobe functions, for example, develop relatively late in a child's growth, so that injury to the frontal lobes may not become apparent until the child reaches adolescence as higher-level reasoning develops. Since the frontal lobes control our social interactions and interpersonal skills, early childhood brain damage may not manifest until such frontal lobe skills are needed in their development. Similarly, injury to certain cognitive skills may not become apparent until the child reaches school age and shows signs of delayed reading and writing skills.

TBI and Psychopathology
Pre-injury Functioning

Traumatic brain injury does not occur randomly in the population. Therefore, we must look at characteristics of the child and family that precede the injury (also termed *pre-morbid functioning*).

Children at risk for brain injury are those who are active and risk-taking, tend to have academic difficulties and are experiencing other life stresses. Further, there is a high rate of pre-existing psychopathology: as many as 50 per cent of children meet criteria for a psychiatric disorder prior to suffering brain injury, with ADHD being one of those most frequently seen. However pre-existing disorders often go unaccounted for which makes it difficult to ascertain which psychiatric and behavioural disorders develop after a TBI (Prigatano et al., 2010).

In older children, pre-injury environmental factors have been shown to account for variability in outcomes following TBI, over and above injury severity (Yeates et al., 2010). For example, the families of children at risk for TBI tend to be poorly functioning and the parents often fail to provide adequate supervision. Severe head injuries often happen when the children are not being monitored by caregivers either because the caregivers are absent or are negligent. Other family factors shown to increase the rate of TBI included the number of adverse life events experienced by the family per year and mother punitiveness (McKinlay et al., 2010).

Lastly, a significant risk factor for TBI is a *previous* TBI. Probably because of the negative effects of the brain injury on judgement and functioning, children who sustain a TBI are at a threefold risk for sustaining another head injury (Snow and Hooper, 1994).

Knowing what we do about psychopathology, we could infer that such children are at risk for developing some kind of psychiatric disorder *regardless* of whether there was brain injury. In fact, research has shown a high correlation between children's pre-injury behaviour and their subsequent psychiatric difficulties. Therefore, the blow to the head is not the only factor involved in determining the outcome of TBI; all the contexts of development, including individual and interpersonal factors, still come into play.

Psychopathology Post-injury

Studies also show a high rate of *new* psychiatric diagnosis following child TBI. Psychopathology is related to the *severity* of injury: a new psychiatric diagnosis is three times more likely in children with severe head injury (62 to 69 per cent of cases) than those with mild head injury (20 to 24 per cent of cases). Max et al. (1997) examined rates of new post-injury psychiatric problems, defined in terms of psychiatric diagnoses not present prior to injury. By the second year following the TBI, 15 out of 42 (36 per cent) met criteria for a new disorder, 11 of whom (26 per cent) had a disorder beyond the 12-month period. Table 13.2 shows some of the more frequent behaviours found after a TBI.

Depression and ADHD are among the most common new diagnoses given (Bloom et al., 2001), and these disorders are likely to persist over time. In addition, a high prevalence of disrupted behaviour disorders, such as oppositional defiant disor-

TABLE 13.2 Comorbid Behaviours in Children with a History of TBI

> *Commonly observed behavioural problems in school-age children with history of traumatic brain injury*
> - Attentional difficulties
> - Disinhibited, impulsive and socially inappropriate
> - Oppositional defiant disorder
> - Aggressive/rage reactions
> - Absence of guilt following misbehaviour
> - Failure to develop empathy for others' needs and situation
> - Apathetic
> - Emotional lability and irritability
> - Depression and anxiety with associated somatic disturbances
> - Limited/if not reduced awareness of behavioural and/or cognitive disturbances

Source: Adapted from Prigatano et al., 2010.

der and conduct disorder, after paediatric TBI have been confirmed through a variety of studies. Multiple risk factors predict the development of disruptive disorders in children without TBI, including poverty, maternal depression and history of criminality in biological parents. Importantly, risk factors for these post-injury disturbances have been shown to be similar to those without post-injury disturbances (Gerring et al., 2009).

Children are also at risk from developing anxiety disorders (Max et al., 2011) and may suffer symptoms of posttraumatic stress disorder by re-experiencing the trauma event or increase avoidance of trauma-related stimuli (Hajek et al., 2010). In a recent study Zatzick and Grossman (2011) carried out a three-year prospective cohort study and found that in 10- to 19-year-olds, traumatic brain injury was associated with increased risk of receiving a full spectrum of anxiety, depressive and substance abuse diagnoses.

Personality change (PC) due to traumatic brain injury is also commonly reported and is currently listed in the DSM-IV. PC is characterized by a persistent personality disturbance thought to be related to the direct physiological effects of traumatic brain injury. In children this condition can be manifested as a marked deviation from normal development (lasting at least one year) rather than a change in stable personality pattern. Diagnosis is only given if no other identifiable mental disorder is present. Five major subtypes of PC have been described: labile, aggressive, disinhibited, apathetic and paranoid. PC is a frequent diagnosis following severe TBI in children and adolescents, but is much less common in those with mild to moderate cases of TBI (Max et al., 2000).

Childhood TBI outcome studies consistently identify three major risk factors for psychopathology: greater injury severity, psychosocial adversity and pre-injury psychopathology. However, these are not exclusively the only risk factors, as will now be addressed.

The Biological Context

There are three primary physical forces by which TBI exerts its negative effects: *tension* (tearing apart of tissues), *compression* (pushing together of tissue) and *shearing* (rubbing and abrasion of tissues against one another). Another dimension concerns whether the injury results from *acceleration* (the moving head hitting a stationary object, such as a head hitting the windshield in an auto accident), *deceleration* (the stationary head being hit by a moving object, such as a baseball bat), *rotation* (the head being twisted around) or *crushing*. Surprisingly, the latter type of injury is the most rare and least severe, given that skull fracture does not necessarily result in injury to the brain. Of more concern is the diffuse damage that is caused by twisting, tearing or breaking of the connecting fibres of the nerve cells, which is termed *diffuse axonal injury*.

In addition, certain areas of the brain appear to be more sensitive to damage regardless of the point of impact or severity of injury. Thus, there is a *selective vulnerability* among areas of the brain. One such sensitive area is the hippocampal formation, the most critical limbic system structure for memory functions. This would help explain why one of the most common symptoms of traumatic brain injury is a disturbance of memory functions.

Trauma also may bring about *biochemical changes* such as an excessive release of potassium (an ion critical for neural transmission) in the intracellular fluid. Excessive release, in turn, may lead to prolonged overexcitation that impairs metabolic cell functions and may eventuate in cell death.

Finally, *secondary brain-damaging* effects may contribute to the initial injury. These secondary effects include cerebral edema (swelling) and brain haemorrhaging (bleeding), both of which can put pressure on the brain by pressing it against the skull, thereby causing further damage. Hypoxia (poorly oxygenated blood) or ischemia (obstructed blood flow) may also damage the brain by depriving the cells of essential nutrients. Cerebral atrophy may occur when brain tissue dies, leaving a telltale enlargement of the ventricular system (the fluid-filled cavities of the brain). In addition, children are particularly vulnerable to the development of post-injury seizures, which interfere with functioning.

The Individual Context

Severe brain injury can have widespread effects on all areas of intra-personal functioning.

Cognitive Development
Intelligence

Generally children with head injuries show *declines* in their performance on intelligence tests that are commensurate with the seriousness of the injury. There also is a specific pattern of deficits, with *non-verbal skills* being more affected than verbal skills. The likely explanation for this fact is that the *verbal* scales of intelligence tests assess older, well-rehearsed knowledge (crystallized intelligence), while the non-verbal subtests tend to require speed and accuracy in the solving of novel problems (fluid intelligence). It is this new learning that is most disrupted by TBI. Children with TBI also tend to show a slow rate of mental processing, which will negatively impact their ability to accomplish timed tasks on intelligence scales. This slow processing ability has been shown in a recent study by D.N. Allen et al., 2010. Here they found in a sample of 61 children with TBI that, while all exhibited relative deficits on all subtests of the WISC-IV (Weschler, 2003c), the greatest deficits were shown in the processing speed index and coding subtests.

Although IQ scores may improve over time, they rarely return to pre-injury levels. In fact children continue to show deficits as long as five years after the injury. There is inconsistent evidence as to whether children's post-injury cognitive function is able to predict new behaviours from developing; some researchers have found a relationship, whereas others have yet to establish whether a relationship exists.

Attention

Many studies have found that children have difficulties sustaining attention and concentration post-injury. These deficits also have been found to persist for years after the injury and can contribute to significant difficulties in school. Although there are indicators in the literature that children with TBI have higher rates of pre-morbid attention, there is substantial evidence that it is also associated with the onset of new attentional problems. Children with severe TBI have been found to show signs of generalized attention deficits as long as 10 years post-TBI (Catroppa et al., 2011).

Language

Children who suffer TBI often show global difficulties with speech and language, but specific effects are commonly seen. These include problems with naming objects, verbal fluency, word and sentence repetition and written production. The developmental dimension comes into play, in that the type of language impairment is related to the skills that are emergent in the child's language development at the time of the injury.

Memory

Memory problems are one of the most common effects of TBI, particularly in regard to memory for recently learned information. Poor attention may interfere with children's initial encoding of information into memory. In a longitudinal study, Levin and colleagues demonstrated persistent working memory deficits as far out as two years post-injury (Levin et al., 2004). A range of verbal memory deficits have also been reported, and these tend to be associated with more severe injuries around the frontal and temporal regions.

Motor and Sensory Effects

Effects of TBI can include fatigue, reductions in gross and fine motor co-ordination, visual and tactile problems, and headaches, all of which may impact problem solving, school performance and mood. Deterioration of motor function is one of the most common clinical manifestations following traumatic brain injury in children and adolescents and can lead to problems with balance, manual dexterity and ball skills. A recent study has suggested that there is evidence for structural alteration of motor pathways and regions in children and adolescents with TBI that are correlated with motor functioning (Caeyenberghs et al., 2011).

Executive Function

Deficits in organization, judgement, decision making, planning and impulse control are often seen in children who have suffered TBI and are often the result of damage to the frontal lobes.

All of the cognitive changes we have just described may adversely affect schooling. Impaired ability to learn new information, concrete thinking, and language disturbances all impede academic progress, while the increased distractibility and poor impulse control and judgement may make the child more of a behaviour problem in the classroom (Mangeot et al., 2002).

Emotional Development

Even a mild TBI is typically followed by a change in the child's emotions. Frequently, irritability and poor frustration tolerance are seen in children following head injury. Severely injured children are likely to demonstrate longer-lasting and more significant negative emotions and behavioural problems, which may warrant a diagnosis such as conduct disorder. Very severely injured children may exhibit grossly disinhibited emotions and behaviour, associated with damage to the frontal lobes, which are critical to self-monitoring and the exercise of good judgement.

Children who have suffered TBI also frequently show depressed affect, withdrawal and apathy.

While this negative mood might be related to their awareness of the deficits caused by the injury, it also may be related to the location of the injury itself. Children with right hemispheric damage are the most likely to develop post-injury depression (Walker, 1997).

The Self

Children's insight into the injury and its effect on their sense of self varies as a function of age. While younger children typically deny the injury and express a lack of concern about its effects on their functioning, children ages 9 and older report a more negative self-concept and awareness of the way in which their lives and their ability to function have been affected by the injury.

The Family Context

The family may experience increased stress as it struggles to respond to the new and difficult challenges of coping with the child's deviant behaviour. It may have to alter its previous lifestyle – for example, by devoting financial resources to medical treatments rather than to vacations or by turning part of the home into a rehabilitation environment rather than a playroom. Families that are adaptable and loving can take these stresses in stride. Those that are rigid and resentful are at risk for becoming increasingly dysfunctional while at the same time impeding the child's recovery and rehabilitation. Yeates et al. (2010) found family environment to moderate the psychosocial outcomes of TBI in young children, with a loving and supportive family acting as a buffer.

The Social Context

Traumatic brain injury in children has previously been associated with theory of mind deficits and social problem-solving difficulties, potentially interfering with psychosocial development and friendships. The children's increased impulsivity, irritability and aggressiveness may also jeopardize peer relations. Old friends may become impatient, while new friendships may be difficult to make. Thus, there is an increased risk of social isolation. This can impact on long-term social outcomes, such that McKinlay et al. (2010) found that in pre-school children, mild TBI was associated with negative effects on psychosocial development in adolescence. Further, TBI may interfere with cognitive functions that are key to social interactions, such as pragmatic communication. For example, one study found that, following moderate to severe head injuries, adolescents had difficulty recognizing emotions and understanding social cues, which leads to difficulties in social relationships (Kersel et al., 2001). They are more likely to exhibit externalizing behaviours (e.g. aggression, hyperactivity, sexual acting out) than internalizing behaviours (e.g. withdrawal) and this also leaves them vulnerable to making friends.

Developmental Course

There are many sources of variability in the outcome of brain injury. We have already discussed two of them: type and severity of injury. In regard to *type* of injury, penetrating injuries have effects different from closed head injuries, as we have seen. In addition, the prognosis of recovery from head injury is directly related to the *severity* of the injury. As we know, the duration of coma is an important index of severity; the shorter the duration, the more complete the recovery. However, the effects of a milder case of TBI are highly controversial, with some studies finding evidence of deficits whereas others do not (see Fay et al., 2010, for review). Most previous studies have examined potential consequences <5 after injury, long before the developmental process is completed, and thus mild TBI may have equally long-lasting effects than is currently being reported. However, there are a number of other sources of variability, some organic and others psychological.

Age of the child at the time of injury is another important factor. Preschoolers and infants in particular are at risk for severe and long-lasting effects. Why might this be? Recall that TBI disproportionately affects *new* learning, and the learning of the child in the earliest stages of development is virtually *all* new. Older children may be able to fall back on some old learning to compensate for deficits as well as having a broader cognitive and adaptive repertoire to help them to evolve alternative strategies for coping with challenges that arise due to TBI. In children injured in the early or middle childhood years, the persisting behavioural and psychosocial problems negatively influence quality of adult life far more than the intellectual and physical problems. The *developmental status* of affected skills matters as well. Skills that are in the process of being acquired are more vulnerable to damage than are fully developed ones.

Another factor to consider is *rate of recovery*. Most recovery that is going to take place emerges in the first year post-injury; therefore, the more rapidly a function begins to improve, the more hope that it will return to a level close to that existing pre-injury. It is also dependent on the characteristics of the event and type of injury sustained.

Lastly, *intra-personal and interpersonal variables* must be considered. The individual characteristics of the children and their interpersonal relations with family and peers serve to individualize the effects of brain injury. Thus, the adjustment of the child and the family has a significant impact on the effectiveness of coping with the effects of the injury.

A number of *risk and protective factors* have been identified. For example, while denial of the injury may do the child a disservice, children are also poorly served when they or others focus unduly on the injury and make unfavourable comparisons to the child's previous level of functioning. Lack of information is another critical factor. Often, children and their families do not have a good understanding of TBI or the normal recovery process – in fact, many report that they have never had their injury explained to them and do not know what is realistic to expect in terms of recovery of function. Without accurate information, families are vulnerable to unrealistically high – or pessimistic – expectations. Teachers and school personnel also often lack understanding of the TBI and its sequelae, contributing to the child's frustration, poor self-image and misbehaviour.

Further, it is common for social support networks to rally around in the crisis stage immediately following an injury, but to drift away over time, leaving the family alone and unsupported. Peer relationships particularly may suffer when the injury is severe and has significantly changed the child's appearance, personality and cognitive level, resulting in a child who truly seems to have become a different person.

Finally, youths who have suffered TBI are at significant risk for substance abuse. It is possible that in some cases the substance abuse pre-dated the injury: for example, the adolescent whose TBI was a result of driving while intoxicated. However, the after-effects of TBI also may include impairment in judgement and impulse control, leaving the youth vulnerable to the influence of negative peer models. Further, some TBI survivors use illicit substances to self-medicate their depression and low self-esteem.

In a review of perceived quality of life (QOL) by adult survivors of childhood brain injury, contrary to what might be expected, of the 130 included in their sample, only a small proportion of 17 per cent reported dissatisfaction with quality of life (Anderson et al., 2010). Poorer quality of life was associated with low levels of perceived independence, severe TBI, younger age of injury and failure to complete school. Importantly, it was level of perceived independence that was the most consistent predictor of overall QOL rating.

Intervention

Interventions with youth survivors of traumatic brain injury must be as diverse and multifaceted as are the effects of the injury. Intervention begins with a careful assessment, which documents the child's strengths, deficits and special needs. Intervention with the school is particularly important, in order to ease the child's transition back into the classroom and to help the teachers to design compensatory learning strategies in order to insure the child's continued success and positive attitude about the educational process. (See Cave, 2004, for a review.) Psychoeducation, counselling, and social services support for parents and the whole family often are advised. Individual work with children might focus on helping them to come to terms with the injury emotionally or to learn practical strategies for coping with the changes it has wrought (Hooper et al., 2001b). For example, *cognitive rehabilitation* may involve (1) analysing and restructuring the child's daily routine in order to minimize frustrations and failures; (2) providing visual clues, such as photographs of activities, to help the child stay organized and on task; and (3) rehearsing prior to each step in the routine and reviewing the child's performance. With such supports in place, clinicians have found that they can significantly improve children's task performance at the same time that they decrease aggression and other maladaptive behaviours (Feeney and Ylvisaker, 1995).

Behavioural interventions such as contingency management procedures and traditional applied behavioural analysis (ABA) have also been found to be effective. ABA addresses the management and modification of behaviours by deliberately manipulating the consequences. In contrast, contingency management is based on the operant principle that behaviours increase or decrease in frequency as a result of positive and negative consequences.

Chronic Illness

It is estimated that there are approximately 10 million children with chronic illnesses in the USA, with 10 per cent of children in the population affected (Melamed, 2002). The sources of stress for severely ill children and their families are numerous: the pain of the illness and of medical procedures; hospitalization; and the disruption of family life, peer relations and schooling, to name only a few. In the past the focus was on such negative aspects and the toll they were expected to take on the child's psychological well-being. The fact that such expectations often were not realized forced researchers to turn attention to protective factors such as the resilience of children, the resources and adaptability of family members, and the support of health care professionals.

The study of the effects of chronic illness on youths is under the purview of the field of **paediatric psychology** (which is also known as *behavioural*

medicine). (See Ammerman and Campo, 1998; Ollendick and Schroeder, 2003.) Paediatric psychology views both sickness and health as resulting from the interplay among biological factors on the one hand and psychological, social and cultural factors on the other. Thus, paediatric psychology conforms to our now familiar *transactional model*. This interplay among factors is present at every stage of the disease process, from etiology to course to treatment, although at different points one or another factor may predominate. In addition, the field includes the psychological and social variables involved in *prevention* and *health maintenance*. Finally, paediatric psychology is primarily concerned with chronically ill children, as the lifespans of children with once-lethal illnesses increasingly are being expanded.

Definition and Characteristics
Dimensions of Chronic Illness
Generally, an illness (disease, disorder, disability or medical condition) is considered to be *chronic* when it persists for three months or more. (Here we follow Fritz and McQuaid, 2000.) Chronic illnesses differ from those that are acute in a number of ways. While an acute illness may be curable, a chronic illness will need to be managed over a period of months, years or, even, the life course. Further, while medical personnel often take over the care of the child with an acute illness, the parents of a chronically ill child – and, increasingly with age, the children themselves – usually bear a large part of the responsibility for the management of the condition.

Chronic illnesses comprise a very diverse group of disorders, which have a variety of implications for the child's psychological development. Table 13.3 presents a number of dimensions on which medical illnesses can be categorized, each of which might differentially affect the child. For example, consider the boy whose cerebral palsy creates a visible disfigurement that announces itself every time he walks into the classroom versus the boy whose physical appearance is unaffected by his illness; or the girl with a highly stigmatized disorder such as AIDS

TABLE 13.3 Dimensions of Chronic Medical Conditions in Children

Duration	Brief	....	Lengthy
Age of Onset	Congenital	....	Acquired
Limitation of Activities	None	....	Disabled
Visibility	Not Visible	....	Highly Visible
Expected Survival	Usual Lifespan	....	Immediate Life Threat
Mobility	Unimpaired	....	Extremely Impaired
Physiological Functioning	Unimpaired	....	Extremely Impaired
Cognition	Unaffected	....	Extremely Affected
Emotional/Social	Unaffected	....	Extremely Affected
Sensory Functioning	Unimpaired	....	Extremely Impaired
Communication	Unimpaired	....	Extremely Impaired
Course	Stable	....	Progressive
Uncertainty	Episodic	....	Predictable
Stigma	None	....	Extremely Stigmatized
Pain	Painless	....	Extremely Painful

Source: Adapted from Perrin et al., 1993.

that leads peers to shy from her versus the girl with cancer whose peers respond with an outpouring of sympathy and support.

Prevalence of Chronic Illness

The prevalence of chronic illness in childhood varies widely depending on whether samples are drawn from the community or the clinical setting, based on parents' reports or medical records, and how they are defined. Because of these methodological differences, prevalence rates range from 5 to 30 per cent. However, it is important to note that prevalence rates of chronic illnesses are rising, ironically because better medical care is increasing the lifespan of medically ill children who, in an earlier age, might not have survived. In fact it is estimated that more than 90 per cent of children born with a chronic condition will now survive to age of 20 years (Pinzon, 2006). This includes the rising prevalence in the increasing survival rate of

extremely premature infants, who are more likely than infants brought to term to demonstrate congenital defects.

Chronic illness is also on the rise due to an increase in childhood obesity and its consequent effects of health. The WHO estimated that nearly 43 million of the world's children under the age of 5 were overweight in 2010. Obesity is more prevalent in industrialized countries as compared to non-industrialized countries and prevalence is highest in North America, Europe and the Western Pacific at rates as high as 30 per cent in children.

A large-scale national health survey conducted in the USA provides us with an overview of the prevalence of many chronic medical disorders of childhood (Bethell et al., 2011). Data from 91 642 children under age 18 produced an estimated prevalence rate of 43 per cent of US children (32 million) currently have at least 1 of 20 chronic health conditions assessed, increasing to 54.1 per cent when overweight, obesity or being at risk for developmental delays are included; 19.2 per cent (14.2 million) have conditions resulting in a special health care need, a 1.6 point increase since 2003.

Common Chronic Illnesses of Childhood
Asthma
Asthma, a disorder of the respiratory system, is the most prevalent childhood chronic illness in the USA. In 2007, 5.6 million school-aged children and youth (5–17 years old) were reported to currently have asthma; and 2.9 million had an asthma episode or attack within the previous year (ALA, 2009). On average, it is thought that in a classroom of 30 children, about three are likely to have asthma. Asthma is the most frequent cause of emergency room visits and hospitalizations, and is the leading cause of school absences among children (DeFrances et al., 2008). In asthma, hyper-responsiveness or hypersensitivity of the trachea, bronchi and bronchiole produces a narrowing of air passages and reduction of lung function. The result may be intermittent episodes of wheezing and shortness of breath called *dyspnea*. Severe prolonged attacks, known as *status asmaticus*, can be life-threatening and may require emergency medical treatment.

Cystic Fibrosis
Cystic fibrosis (CF) is a genetic disease common among Caucasians; one in 25 people of European descent carry one allele for CF. Ireland has the highest incidence of CF in the world: 2.98 per 10 000. In the European Union, 1 in 2000–3000 newborns is found to be affected by CF whereas in the USA the incidence of CF is reported to be 1 in every 3500 births. An individual must inherit two defective cystic fibrosis genes, one from each parent, to have the disease. Each time two carriers of the disease conceive, there is a 25 per cent chance of passing cystic fibrosis to their children; a 50 per cent chance that the child will be a carrier of the cystic fibrosis gene; and a 25 per cent chance that the child will be a non-carrier. Most children with CF are diagnosed by age 2. Cystic fibrosis is caused by a defective gene which causes the body to

produce abnormally thick and sticky fluid, called mucus. This mucus builds up in the breathing passages of the lungs and in the pancreas, the organ that helps to break down and absorb food. This collection of sticky mucus results in life-threatening lung infections and serious digestion problems. CF is a devastating disease, cutting short the child's life expectancy due to pulmonary and gastrointestinal dysfunctions. However, as treatment has improved, so have survival rates, and many children with CF can expect to live into their adult years. Maintenance of the child with CF places heavy demands on the family, which must carefully monitor the child's food intake and ensure compliance with medications, particularly enzyme replacement. A particularly challenging task for parents is to engage the child's co-operation with intensive daily physical treatment that involves percussion to the chest to loosen and expel excessive fluid.

Cerebral Palsy
Cerebral palsy (CP) involves a group of disorders caused by damage to the developing brain, generally *in utero* or during the birth process. Affected children have awkward and poorly controlled movements, difficulty making voluntary movements or they suffer from rigidity. Speech often is impaired, and some, but not all, may suffer mental retardation. The prevalence of CP has increased 15 per cent over the past 20 years, coinciding with the increased survival rate of extremely premature infants. Among babies born weighing less than 1500 g, the rate of CP was more than 70 times higher compared with those weighing 2500 g or more at birth (Johnson, 2002). Results of some studies have shown that up to 99 per cent of children with mild cerebral palsy survive to adulthood (Strauss et al., 1998). The challenges presented by the disorder vary with the degree of impairment. Some individuals will require a wheelchair while others will be able to navigate on their own, just as some individuals will be able to communicate orally while others will require the use of electronic devices such as speech synthesizers. Cerebral palsy is not a progressive condition, meaning it will not get worse as the child gets older. However, it can

put a great deal of strain on their body, which can cause problems in later life.

Diabetes Mellitus

Type I (insulin-dependent) diabetes is the most common endocrine disorder in childhood, affecting 1 in 800 children under the age of 18 years in the USA. While it can appear at any age, the peak incidence occurs around puberty. Diabetes is a chronic, lifelong disorder that results when the pancreas does not produce sufficient *insulin*, which is essential for metabolizing carbohydrates. The destruction of insulin-producing cells within the pancreas appears to be an autoimmune process; however, the mechanism that triggers this autoimmune process is unknown. The results can be devastating: individuals with poorly managed diabetes are at risk for blindness, kidney dysfunction, nerve damage, heart disease and gangrene, resulting in the need for amputation of the lower extremities and even coma and death. Thus, the stakes are high in regard to compliance with medical regimens.

Treatment of the child requires heavy parental involvement. Blood glucose must be monitored daily to prevent hypoglycaemia (too little blood sugar) or hyperglycaemia (too much blood sugar). Insulin dosages must be adjusted accordingly. Monitoring is accomplished by obtaining a small sample of blood from a finger stick, placing it on a strip that changes colour, and comparing the colour with colours on a chart showing the glucose levels. Children who are insulin-dependent must take injections three or more times a day and observe a careful diet and programme of physical activity.

Sickle Cell Disease

Sickle cell disease (SCD), also known as sickle cell anaemia, is an autosomal recessive disorder that causes a number of aberrations in the blood, including the irregularly shaped platelets that give the disorder its name. It is a genetic condition that is present at birth. It is inherited when a child receives two sickle cell genes – one from each parent. The prevalence of the disease in the USA is approximately 1 in 5000. However, SCD disproportionately strikes African Americans with about 1 in 500 being affected. SCD is usually detected early in life, and the course of the disorder involves a vulnerability to infection and recurrent episodes of intense pain in the bones and joints due to vasoocclusion (blockages) of the small blood vessels. People with SCD start to have symptoms during the first year of life, usually around five months of age. Symptoms and complications of SCD are different for each person and can range from mild to severe.

Juvenile Rheumatoid Arthritis (JRA)

Juvenile arthritis is another disorder that involves chronic pain. The child may experience swelling, tenderness, warmth or acute pain at the joints. It is a highly heritable disorder. The onset is 16 years of age or younger and can have a profound effect on development, including school, peers and family relationships. While JRA is seldom life threatening, children who have many joints involved or who have a positive rheumatoid factor are more likely to have chronic pain and poor school attendance, and to be disabled. Long periods with no symptoms are more common in those who have only a small number of joints involved. Many patients with JRA eventually go into remission with very little loss of function and deformity.

Cancer

Cancer includes a heterogeneous group of conditions, the common characteristic being a *proliferation of malignant cells*. Haematological malignancies involving the blood-forming tissues (i.e., leukaemia and lymphoma) account for approximately half of the cancer diagnoses; tumours of the brain and central nervous system make up the second-largest group; and tumours affecting specific tissues and organ systems, such as bone or kidney, come in third. Acute lymphoblastic leukaemia (ALL) is the most commonly seen in children and accounts for 39 per cent of all childhood cancers. Despite its overall low prevalence rate, cancer accounts for a large number of disease-related deaths in persons under 16 years of age. However, a heartening increase in the survival rate is expected to accelerate as more effective treatments are developed.

However, treatment of cancer is often painful, invasive and prolonged. For example, treatment of ALL is a heroic undertaking involving four phases. The first phase is designed to eliminate all evidence of leukaemic cells. This phase is followed by radiation therapy to prevent the spread of the disease to the central nervous system. Next comes a consolidation phase designed to eliminate leukaemic cells that may have developed drug resistance, and, finally, a maintenance phase lasting two to three years. Many of the procedures involved are painful, involving finger sticks, intramuscular intravenous (IV) injections, lumbar punctures (spinal tap) and bone marrow aspirations (a procedure in which a large needle is inserted into the hip and bone marrow is withdrawn). Moreover, the side effects of treatment are themselves noxious (e.g., vomiting, diarrhoea, pain) or socially embarrassing (e.g., loss of hair, weight gain).

Obesity

While not present from birth, obesity is viewed as a chronic health condition. It is associated with a higher chance of premature death and disability in adulthood. In addition to increased future risks, obese children experience breathing difficulties, increased risk of fractures, hypertension, early markers of cardiovascular disease, insulin resistance and psychological effects. (See Sanderson et al., 2011, for a review.) Children in low- and middle-income countries are more vulnerable to inadequate pre-natal, infant and young child nutrition. At the same time, they are exposed to high-fat, high-sugar, high-salt, energy-dense, micronutrient-poor foods, which tend to be lower in cost. These dietary patterns, in conjunction with low levels of physical activity, result in sharp increases in childhood obesity while under-nutrition issues remain unsolved. Overweight and obesity, as well as their related non-communicable diseases, are largely preventable. Supportive environments and communities are fundamental in shaping people's choices, making the healthier choice of foods and regular physical activity the easiest choice, and therefore preventing obesity.

Ethnic and Social Differences

For chronic health conditions, treatment is not evenly distributed. Among US children, children of racial or ethnic minorities have greater health burden and experience poorer outcomes than white children. These differences may be in some cases innate or genetic and affect one population more than another (e.g., CF and sickle cell disease). In other situations the prevalence variation may be related to potentially modifiable external factors. For example, poverty has been shown to increase the likelihood that children will develop asthma (Nikiéma et al., 2010). This is illustrated in Table 13.4 which shows the discrepancies in chronic health conditions in children.

Risk for Psychopathology

A number of population-based studies show that children with chronic illnesses are at increased risk for developing psychopathology (Fritz and McQuaid, 2000). Reviews of the available research indicate that the range of psychopathologies covers the entire spectrum, from internalizing to externalizing disorders. Depression and anxiety are particularly common. In addition, children with chronic illness are more likely than their physically healthy peers to develop social and academic problems and to have a poor self-concept, placing them at further risk for more serious psychopathology over the course of development.

Although many young people adjust well to the challenge of a chronic condition, psychological comorbidity in US samples is estimated at around 20 per cent, twice that of a healthy young person (D.N. Allen et al., 2010). A good example is given by Caplan et al. (2004) addressing this issue in epilepsy. They used structured diagnostic interviews for 60 children with complex partial epilepsy and 40 children with generalized epilepsy (defined by 3 cps spike and wave discharges on EEG). They found psychopathology in 63 per cent of children with partial seizures and in 55 per cent of the children with generalized seizures. Disruptive disorders were found in 25–26 per cent, anxiety and/or affective disorders in 13 per cent, and comorbid

TABLE 13.4 Health Inequalities for Children with Chronic Health Conditions in the USA

Better Health and Health Care	
White Children • Have lower rates of cerebral palsy, HIV/AIDS, and spina bifida • Have fewer emergency department visits and hospitalizations for asthma	• Have better glycaemic control with type 1 diabetes • Die less often from asthma and diabetes • Survive longer with tetralogy of Fallot, transposition of great arteries, Down syndrome, type 1 diabetes, and TBI and acute leukaemia
Worse Health and Health Care	
Black Children • Have higher rates of cerebral palsy • Survive less often with tetralogy of Fallot, transposition of great arteries, Down syndrome, type 1 diabetes and TBI	Hispanic Children • Have higher rates of spina bifida when born to Mexico-born mothers • Have higher rates of HIV/AIDS and depression • Have poorer glycaemic control with type 1 diabetes • Survive less often with acute leukaemia

Source: Adapted from Berry et al., 2010.

disruptive and anxiety/affective disorders in 14–16 per cent of the children with seizures. Children with epilepsy have also been shown to have higher rates of behavioural difficulties (Dunn et al., 2010).

Less is known about illness-specific representations of emotional and behavioural problems. However, a study by Hysing et al. (2009) suggests that different illnesses are associated with illness-specific problems. For example, children with asthma tend to show a high frequency of internalizing disorders, while the risk of externalizing disorders is similar to their healthy peers. Psychological maladjustment has been reported to be higher in children with neurological disorders than in children with any other chronic illness, and specific patterns of emotional and behavioural problems. In support of this, children with epilepsy have been shown to have a higher rate of social interaction problems and attentions than other chronic illnesses (Rodenburg et al., 2005).

Cross-referencing is strikingly uncommon between studies of different disorders and groups of disorders. For example, remarkably little cross-referencing has taken place between publications on diabetes and cystic fibrosis, even though both are severe, lifelong disorders that necessitate daily medication, regular personal monitoring and medical review.

DSM-IV-TR Diagnosis

While not all chronically ill children will develop a psychopathological disturbance, the risk is there. When a medically ill child does come to the attention of a mental health professional, DSM's multiaxial system allows the clinician three ways to consider the interplay between the medical condition and psychopathology.

First, the illness itself is documented on Axis III as a *general medical condition*, which reminds the clinician to consider how the child's psychological functioning and response to treatment might be affected.

Second, the clinician must evaluate whether the child meets criteria for a *comorbid clinical disorder*, above and beyond the effects of the physical illness. In some cases, the psychopathology precedes the illness: for example, the conduct disordered child who develops arthritis. In other cases, the onset of the psychopathology follows the medical condition and may even be causally related to it. For example, has sadness over a shortened life expectancy in CF developed into a major depression? Has fear of needle sticks in the child with cancer transformed into a full-blown phobia? Has the non-compliance of the diabetic child generalized into an oppositional defiant disorder? In each case, the clinician must decide whether the child's behaviour meets all of the criteria for the comorbid psychiatric diagnosis, including that it interferes with the child's functioning to a clinically significant degree.

Third, the clinician may consider whether to give an Axis I diagnosis of *psychological factor affecting medical condition* (see Table 13.5). This diagnosis reflects the presence of psychological or behavioural factors that have a significant adverse effect on the course or outcome of a medical illness. For example, a comorbid emotional problem, such as depression or anxiety, might exacerbate the negative effects of the medical condition or interfere with the child's compliance with treatment. The psychological problems may take the form of full-blown Axis I or Axis II diagnoses or may represent subclinical symptoms, personality traits, maladaptive coping strategies or susceptibility to emotional stress that complicates the medical illness. The diagnosis also allows the clinician to indicate whether sociocultural factors, such as ethnicity or religion, affect the course or treatment of a child's medical condition.

Developmental Course of Psychopathology in Chronic Illness

The few longitudinal studies that have been done suggest that overall rate of psychological maladjustment is moderately stable in children with chronic illnesses. The exception to this generalization is disturbances involving the central nervous system, which tend to be very stable over time. Chronic illness also may have different effects during the various stages of the life course, as challenges of the illness interact with stage-salient issues of development (Fritz and McQuaid, 2000). A shortage of age-specific epidemiological data is one factor limiting more focused policy and planning considerations for children with chronic conditions, particularly those in adolescence. Many surveys and reports of chronic disease fail to recognize adolescence as a developmental stage by grouping adolescents with children (0–14) or with adults (15–34 years).

TABLE 13.5 DSM-IV-TR Criteria for Psychological Factor Affecting Medical Condition

---

A. A general medical condition (coded on Axis III) is present.
B. Psychological factors adversely affect the general medical condition in one of the following ways:

    (1) The factors have influenced the course of the general medical condition as shown by a close temporal association between the psychological factors and the development or exacerbation of, or delayed recovery from, the general medical condition.
    (2) The factors interfere with the treatment of the general medical condition.
    (3) The factors constitute additional health risks for the individual.
    (4) Stress-related physiological responses precipitate or exacerbate symptoms of the general medical condition.

Choose name based on the nature of the psychological factors:

Mental Disorder Affecting [the General Medical Condition] (e.g., an Axis I disorder such as major depressive disorder delaying recovery from episodic pain in sickle cell disease).

Psychological Symptoms Affecting [the General Medical Condition] (e.g., depressive symptoms delaying recovery from surgery; anxiety exacerbating asthma).

Personality Traits or Coping Styles Affecting [the General Medical Condition] (e.g., pathological denial of the need to take insulin in diabetes).

Maladaptive Health Behaviors Affecting [the General Medical Condition] (e.g., overeating, lack of exercise, risk-taking behaviors).

Stress-Related Physiological Response Affecting [the General Medical Condition] (e.g., stress-related exacerbations of hypertension, arrhythmia or tension headache).

Other or Unspecified Psychological Factors Affecting [the General Medical Condition] (e.g., interpersonal, cultural or religious factors).

Source: Adapted from DSM-IV-TR, copyright 2000 by the American Psychiatric Association.

The Developmental Dimension

Clinical child psychologists who became interested in helping paediatric patients tended to ask the clinician's questions: how is physical illness related to traditional disturbances such as anxiety disorder, depression and conduct disorders? What traditional treatments would benefit such children? While these are legitimate questions, they are too narrow to capture essential features of physical illness in children. Our preference is to ask the developmental psychopathologist's questions: what is the child's experience and understanding of illness at various developmental levels? How do these affect the intra-personal and interpersonal variables (particularly the family) that have concerned us all along? In short, what we are searching for is a *developmental psychopathology of illness*.

For example, go back to Fig. 1.2 and, instead of visualizing a healthy child in the centre, substitute a physically ill one. How would physical illness reverberate throughout all of the contexts? In the individual context, how would it be understood and coped with, and how would it affect the child's personality and adjustment? In the interpersonal context, in what ways would illness alter parental and peer relations? At the sociocultural level, how would the ill child fare in school and in occupations, and how would cultural values shape the perception of illness and its management? To the familiar list of interpersonal variables we must add *health care professionals*, such as paediatricians, nurses and therapists, just as we must add the *hospital* to the list of social institutions.

Finally, and most important of all, we must ask, How do all of these variables change with time? In addition we should know what risk factors are pressing to divert development from its normal course and what protective factors can counter such a diversion.

Pre-Infancy

Medically fragile infants have life threatening problems during the early months of life as the result of prematurity, birth defect and/or a complex chronic disease. They are often dependent on medical devices for treatment and experience long periods of hospitalization. Parents are stressed as they deal with becoming parents within the context of their child's serious illness, critical medical events and loss of uncertainty about their child's future. These challenges occur during the critical period for establishing the maternal role and parent–child relationship. Given how important attachment and parenting is to the child's subsequent health and development, learning more about the effect of chronic health conditions on children's early attachments is vitally important. However, few studies have addressed the role of chronic illness in attachment with the father. Studies which have focused on maternal role attainment (MRA) have established that mothers of pre-term infants experience maternal role identity diffusion and severe delays in achieving parenting competence (Miles et al., 2011).

Infancy and Toddlerhood

Medical management of chronic illness frequently involves separations from parents and invasive, painful medical procedures that may interfere with the development of secure attachment, interpersonal trust and self-regulation in infancy. (Here we follow Fritz and McQuaid, 2000.) Children between the ages of 1 and 4 show the most severe reactions to hospitalization, including inconsolable crying, apprehension, somatic complaints and regression in the form of loss of previously attained developmental accomplishments such as toilet training.

As children enter toddlerhood, chronic illness may interfere with socialization outside the family. Restrictions of children's activities and repeated hospitalizations might limit their opportunities to develop the skills and experiences needed to negotiate early peer relations. As negativism increases during the famous 'terrible twos', children may become increasingly non-compliant with necessary medical procedures. A challenge for parents at this stage is to resist perceiving the child as fragile or too sick for appropriate limit-setting.

Middle Childhood

Chronically ill school-age children are particularly vulnerable to negative effects in the academic and peer contexts. While the majority of medically ill children do not have intellectual disabilities, with the exception of those with disorders involving the central nervous system, there may be subtle neuropsychological effects related to their illness. Further, some treatments, such as radiation, may have enduring effects on cognitive processing and learning.

Frequent absences from school due to the illness or its treatment can interfere with the development of social and academic competence. Children may be unable to participate in routine peer activities; for example, consider the diabetic child who cannot have cake at a friend's birthday party or eat the spoils of an evening's trick or treating. However, an important variable in this period is the response to peers of the medically ill child. When peers are supportive and accepting, chronically ill children may experience no lack of friends.

Cognitive developmental level may provide an intriguing protective factor for the school-age child. The concrete, rule-oriented thinking of middle childhood fosters a belief that recovery results from strict adherence to medical regimens, and this belief promotes compliance with treatment.

Adolescence

Chronic illness presents a challenge to the teenager who is concerned with stage-salient tasks of the developing autonomy, a positive self-image, and peer and romantic relationships. Self-consciousness about physical appearance and being different from peers also arise for the adolescent with chronic illness, and body image concerns may interfere with the development of dating relationships.

There is growing evidence suggesting that adolescents with chronic conditions are likely to engage in risky behaviours (e.g. smoking, drinking and drugs) to at least similar if not higher rates as healthy peers. However, such behaviours in chronic illness have the increased potential for adverse health outcomes. Tobacco use is at least as common in young people with asthma and diabetes as it is in healthy peers, whereas alcohol is thought to be the substance most frequently used by young people

with chronic conditions, with little variation by diagnosis (Sawyer et al., 2007).

At particular risk is the adolescent whose attempts to assert his or her independence take the form of denial of the disease and resistance to the medical regimen. For example, research on diabetes shows that parents generally begin to give responsibility to their teenagers for management of their illness, but that teenagers fail to respond accordingly by accepting the responsibility. An increase in non-compliance during the adolescent years is found in many other chronic illnesses as well, including cancer and asthma. Murphy et al. (1997) found that poor compliance among adolescents with diabetes was related to (1) a negative perception of their bodies, (2) a perception that what they did would not alter their health status, and (3) the belief that negative events were due to external forces rather than being of their own making.

On the side of protective factors, cognitive development in adolescence can provide more effective and sophisticated strategies for coping with chronic illness. For example, teenagers are more likely than younger children to understand the distinction between controllable and uncontrollable stressors and to use the appropriate kind of strategy (i.e., attempting to change the situation versus adjusting to circumstances as they are) in order to adapt to their illness.

The Biological Context
Characteristics of the Illness

Generally speaking, there is no consistent relation between type of illness and psychological adjustment. One exception to this concerns conditions involving central nervous system disorders or brain damage, in which case children show more behaviour problems as well as poor peer relations and school difficulties.

Surprisingly, severity of illness also is not usually associated with an increase in behaviour problems; however, there are exceptions. Severity of central nervous system disorders does adversely affect peer relations regardless of how severity is operationalized – in terms of degree of medical intervention required, functional impairment such as being ambulatory versus non-ambulatory, neuropsychological impairment, or school placement in a regular or mainstreamed classroom. Moreover, adolescents with three or more severe impairments are likely to have very restricted social lives, with the combination of an IQ below 85, walking problems and obesity being particularly detrimental. (See Nassau and Drotar, 1997.) In addition, there is some evidence of a relation between duration of illness and adjustment in that the longer children are ill, the more adjustment problems they are apt to have.

The Individual Context

Children's response to their illness can have a significant impact on its course. Children's *perception* of illness is more strongly related to adjustment than are the characteristics of the illnesses themselves. Perceived stressfulness of the illness predicts increased anxiety and depression, as well as lower self-esteem. Low self-esteem further contributes to poor adjustment, increasing depression and behaviour problems. The child's level of anxiety is particularly important. Anxiety and stress might exacerbate the symptoms of certain disorders, for example, by increasing the frequency or intensity of asthma attacks.

The child's developmental level also has a major impact on the child's understanding of and reactions to illness. We will explore cognitive factors in two aspects of chronic illness: understanding of the nature of illness itself and comprehension of pain.

Cognitive Development: Children's Understanding of Illness

A child's adaptation to an illness is likely to be affected by his or her comprehension of the disease, what caused it, and how it is that the sometimes painful and unpleasant treatments are in fact helpful. As we know, children's cognitive development changes with age. With some exceptions, research shows that the understanding and explanation of illness follows the Piagetian stages of cognitive development. (Our presentation is based on Harbeck-Weber and Peterson, 1993, and on Thompson and Gustafson, 1996, unless otherwise noted.)

The Preoperational Period

Recall that, in this period, thinking is based on naive perception – in a literal sense, seeing is believing. Thus, the perceived cause of illness tends to be *external* events, objects or persons that the preschooler has associated with the illness through experience. These causes may be remote from the child ('A cold is caused by trees') or in physical proximity ('You get a cold when somebody stands near you'). As seen in the latter instance, preschoolers may begin to grasp the idea of *contagion*, but their thinking is still at an unsophisticated level, since they do not understand the reasons why proximity is related to illness.

Finally, in this period *causes* can be confused with *consequences*; for example, preschoolers may think that a bowel movement is caused by going to the toilet or you get a stomach ache through vomiting.

The Concrete Operations Period

While children in middle childhood still focus on external events, they now can grasp the idea of *contamination* in that there is something harmful that causes the illness; for example, you get a cold from playing with a dirty toy. Later in this period children explain illness in terms of *internalization*, such as swallowing or breathing something that affects the inside of the body. In sum, the children can now make inferences: it is not the perceived object per se but an inferred quality of the object (its harmfulness) that causes illness. Moreover, invisible objects (germs and internal organs) play a role in sickness.

The Formal Operations Period

Adolescents can grasp *internal* causes at two levels. First, they can understand *physiological* causation in terms of the functioning of body organs. Next, they can also understand *psychological* states such as fearfulness as causes. Thus, illness is now *multidetermined*, with a number of external and internal factors playing a role. Finally, adolescents can grasp *abstract* causes such as 'poor nutrition'.

However, it would be a mistake to assume that, because formal operations tends to appear in adolescence, all adolescents have a sophisticated, abstract concept of the causes of illness. Such is not the case. Crisp and colleagues (1996), for example, were interested in the effect of experience on the level of understanding the causes of illness. They called children with little experience with illness 'Novices' and those with a good deal of experience 'Experts'. They then compared a younger group (ages 7 to 10) of Novices and Experts with an older group (ages 10.7 to 14) of Novices and Experts in terms of whether their explanations of causation fell in the preoperational, concrete operations, or formal operations stage of development. Analysis of their data showed that experience did affect level of understanding. However, what interests us is that there is *not* a total shift from concrete to formal operations in adolescence. While there is a statistically significant increase in such thinking, concrete operations thinking still predominates. When we discuss compliance with medical treatment, we will examine the danger of assuming that adolescents are more sophisticated about illness than they really are.

Cognitive Development: Children's Understanding of Pain

The Infant and Toddler Periods

At one time paediatricians widely held the view that newborns could not experience pain; consequently, procedures such as circumcision often were performed without anaesthetic. However, that assumption is erroneous. The healthy infant announces pain with loud crying, dramatic facial grimaces, tightly clenched fists, limb thrashing and torso rigidity. (Our presentation follows Craig and Grunau, 1991, unless otherwise indicated.)

The infant's response to painful stimuli – for example, to a hypodermic injection – is global, diffuse and prolonged. Moreover, the infant neither localizes the region of distress nor engages in self-protective behaviour. Cognitive elements soon enter the picture, between 6 and 8 months, when the infant begins to display anticipatory fear – for example, at the sight of a hypodermic needle. Thus, learning and memory add anticipation to the painful response itself. In addition, the infant engages in rudimentary behaviour designed to ward off the threatening stimulus.

During the second year of life, toddlers become more competent in their response to pain. They scream for a shorter period, orient toward the site of the injection, attempt to protect themselves or pull away, and use language to communicate their feelings. They also visually scan their mother's face, indicating an integration of the pain experience into the social environment. As the period progresses, the response to pain becomes more localized and efforts to relieve pain become more purposeful and versatile, while expressions of anger and verbal demands for aid increase.

The Preschool Period

As was the case with the understanding of illness, research on children's understanding of pain has been heavily influenced by Piaget's theory of cognitive development. (Our presentation follows Thompson and Gustafson, 1996, unless otherwise noted.) In the preschool period pain is viewed more as an unpleasant physical entity, a *thing* that hurts or is sore. Pain is caused by external events such as having an accident. In coping with pain children are passive in that they rely on concrete methods of relief such as medicine or food, or they turn to parents to care for them.

Middle Childhood

In middle childhood pain is viewed as a feeling rather than as a thing one has. Children's understanding is more differentiated in two respects. First, pain itself is differentiated in terms of intensity, quality and duration. Second, localization of pain within the body is more differentiated. Physical and psychological causes are now recognized, although the children refer to one or the other, rather than to both. Finally, children take more initiative in coping with pain, such as diverting themselves by exercising or talking with friends. Level of understanding, however, is dependent on the kind of pain; for example, children have the least understanding of the cause of headaches and the most advanced and precise understanding of pain caused by injections.

Adolescence

Cognitively, adolescents are capable of giving sophisticated descriptions of pain and of its causes. (Our presentation of the adolescent period follows McGrath and Pisterman, 1991.) Descriptions can involve the use of physical analogies, such as 'It's like a sharp knife slicing my insides'. Causation includes both physiological and psychological factors, and adolescents are aware that psychological factors such as anxiety may intensify the purely physical reaction. Finally, adolescents are capable of understanding the adaptive purpose of pain, such as signalling the presence of disease. Table 13.6 reflects the thoughts of some adolescents about their chronic conditions.

Summary

The *concept of pain* goes from its being a physical entity in the preschool period to its being a feeling differentiated as to components and localization in middle childhood to sophisticated descriptions in adolescence. The *understanding of the cause of pain* goes from external events in the preschool period to either physical or psychological causes in middle childhood to both physical and psychological causes in adolescence. *Coping with pain* goes from passive reliance on pills or parents in the preschool period to taking initiative, such as diverting the self

TABLE 13.6 Young People's Description of the Effect of a Chronic Condition in Adolescence

- 'When I had epileptic fits, I would get angry all the time, frustrated' (16-year-old boy).
- 'My management is probably medium right now. Not the best it could be but not the lowest either. I get sick of doing all the things I have to do' (15-year-old boy).
- 'I really only have one friend that I can talk to as he has the same thing as me' (17-year-old girl).
- 'I'm managing well, but I feel that I don't have a social life at all' (17-year-old girl).
- 'I feel confident I can do what I want' (15-year-old girl).

Source: Adapted from Sawyer et al. (2007).

in middle childhood. The adaptive purpose of pain is not grasped until adolescence.

The Family Context

Chronic illness confronts families with a host of challenges and problems. (Our presentation follows Melamed, 2002.) Parents are responsible for interacting with the sometimes daunting medical system, processing complex information concerning the nature and treatment of the illness, and implementing the medical regimens. Family routines must accommodate to changes ranging from such minor ones as providing special diets, to major ones such as having to be with the child during lengthy hospital stays. Parents must strike the proper balance between sympathizing with the child's distress and encouraging healthy coping strategies and age-appropriate behaviour. Parents must also find ways of dealing with added financial burdens as well as with their own anxieties, frustrations and heartaches.

Most families, like most children, do meet such challenges successfully. Some even find the experience brings a new sense of closeness; yet, again, as with children, families do not emerge unscathed (Kazak et al., 1995).

While there are relatively few studies on the association between pain and the parent–child relationship, those that have been carried out indicate parents to have a particularly strong influence on the children's experience of pain. For example, higher levels of parental psychological distress and reduced family functioning have been associated with greater pain-related disability. Higher levels of child-related pain have also been found when mothers express emotional distress (Palermo and Eccleston, 2009).

In addition to child's perception of pain, parents have also been shown to indirectly influence their children's perceptions of their life. Young people often report a higher quality of life for themselves than their parents would rate (Britto et al., 2004). Importantly, the mother's health in particular seems to affect her rating of her child's health. The worse the mother reports her own health the lower her assessment of her child's health and consequently the child may not be encouraged to engage in as many life opportunities.

Parental Contributions to Children's Adjustment

Asthma provides a good case in point of how parental responses may help to either alleviate or exacerbate the disorder. Asthmatic children often feel anxious during an attack, or even in anticipation that one might occur, and the natural concern of parents may become exaggerated anxiety and overprotection. These parental behaviours may in turn lead to age-inappropriate dependency on the parents, isolation from peers and an increase in behaviour problems. The causal loop is completed when overdependence or social isolation negatively affects the child's emotional adjustment and becomes yet another trigger mechanism for an asthmatic attack. Figure 13.3 depicts this complex interaction of the biological, intra-personal and interpersonal contexts in asthma.

Parenting Stress

Meeting the needs of a child with chronic health condition creates added challenges for most families. When coupled with normative challenges faced by families in general, it is understandable

FIGURE 13.3 Transactional Effects in the Development of Asthma.

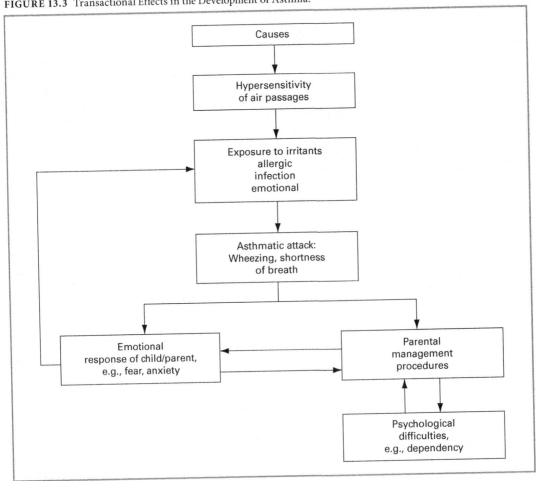

Source: Wicks-Nelson and Israel, 1997.

that many families can be overwhelmed. Many parents live with a protracted burden and have symptoms of listlessness and fatigue, a condition commonly referred to as burnout, which can consequently lead to physical and psychological fatigue (Lindström et al., 2010). Therefore the importance of parenting stress should not be overlooked, because not only the parent's well-being but the child's is affected. Prospective longitudinal research shows that parenting stress in families of chronically ill children is a better predictor of the development of child behaviour problems than many variables, including the severity of the illness or the quality of the parent–child relationship. Coping with a medical illness makes a lot of demands on the parent, and the parent who is stressed and overwhelmed will find it hard to meet those challenges (Melamed, 2002).

There appear to be some common stressors amongst parents, specifically stress related to child's treatment, medical adverse effects, changes in daily activities and disruption of social and family roles. There also exists wide variability within the family as to how they cope and this variance may be attributed to characteristics of the condition, such as age of onset, prognosis, course or type of incapacitation rather than diagnosis per se (Perrin et al., 1993).

Parental Adjustment

Generally few differences exist between families with a child who is chronically ill and comparison families in regard to parental adjustment. An exception to this is maternal adjustment. Probably because they take on the majority of child care responsibilities, mothers of medically ill children are likely to experience a high degree of stress, be prone to feelings of depression, and feel a lack of emotional and practical support (Kazak et al., 1995).

In regard to risk factors, maternal adjustment is adversely affected by disability-related stresses such as hospitalization and by daily hassles of coping with the child's illness. As for protective factors, these include the mother's perception of herself as competent in solving problems, the amount of

social support she receives from family and friends, and the degree to which she remains hopeful (Wallander and Varni, 1998). Studies exploring the maternal effects of having a child with cystic fibrosis consistently show them to have higher rates of maternal depression and emotional distress. Mothers seem to be particularly more vulnerable to the more internalizing mental problems.

Social Support

There is evidence that, in general, social isolation increases the risk of psychological disturbance in families of children with chronic illnesses. Social support, on the other hand, functions as a protective factor (Kazak et al., 2002).

Unfortunately, well-meaning relations and friends may not provide support when it is most needed in the process. When a chronic illness is diagnosed, families often receive an outpouring of sympathy and assistance. However, the amount of support provided is likely to dwindle as time goes on, even as the family's anxiety, stress and practical difficulties increase over the course of the chronic illness (Melamed, 2002).

There also are intriguing ethnic differences in the way that social support contributes to family adjustment. For example, Williams and colleagues (1993) found that social support was helpful to families coping with a child's cancer. However, African American families valued the provision of *instrumental* support (e.g., help with practical matters such as picking up a sibling from school while the parent attends a medical appointment), while European American parents valued *emotional* support from others. Interestingly, although the European American families described their social support networks as twice as large, African American families perceived their networks as more supportive.

The Social Context

Chronic illness may adversely affect peer relations. Severe illness may disrupt the child's life and limit opportunities for social interaction; for example, frequent hospitalizations may be associated with loneliness, sensitivity and isolation. Boys may be at greater risk than girls in regard to negative effects on peer relations. On the positive side, family cohesiveness, support and expressiveness serve as protective factors. Having friends, both with and without chronic conditions, can play an important role in the minimization of problems (Blum, 1992).

Intervention

Psychotherapeutic interventions for children with chronic illness will be as various as the effects of the disorder and the comorbid psychopathologies that accompany it. As we have seen, these encompass the full spectrum from internalizing disorders (anxiety, depression) to externalizing (conduct disorder, oppositional defiance). Some interventions focus on the child, while others involve parents, the whole family system and, even, the medical staff. Because in other chapters we discuss treatments for the comorbid psychopathologies, here we will focus on two interventions that are specific to children and families facing chronic illness: family systems paediatric treatment and pain management skills training. (For a more extensive presentation, see Varni et al., 2000.)

Family Systems Paediatric Interventions

Kazak et al. (2002) developed a model for intervening in the family system based on their work with children with cancer. Treatment is aimed at helping families to master three major tasks: to manage upsetting feelings in the face of the challenges the disease presents, to develop trusting relationships that allow for collaboration over the course of treatment and to manage conflict among family members and between the family and the medical staff.

The first step in the process is *joining*, which requires that the clinician empathize with the family and strive to understand their perspective with an attitude of respect, curiosity and honesty. Second, the clinician will *focus* the work on solving a specific problem that is collaboratively identified with the family. Third, the intervention emphasizes a *competence-based* approach, which views symptoms as misguided but understandable attempts to meet

developmental needs when more adaptive avenues for doing so have been thwarted. The task then is to harness the child's and family's strengths in order to develop a more adaptive response. Last, the model is *collaborative*, including not only the child, the family and the clinician, but also the other members of the medical team. (See Box 13.2 for an example of this approach in action.)

Coping with Pain

Pain often is significant for children faced with chronic illness. There are two sources of pain. One is the illness itself: for example, the sometimes debilitating joint pain that accompanies rheumatoid arthritis. The other source of pain may be the treatment: for example the repeated bone marrow aspirations (BMAs) that children with leukaemia must undergo. Consider what the BMA procedure entails. A needle is inserted deep into the child's hipbone and marrow is suctioned out with a syringe. The marrow is then examined to determine whether prior treatment has successfully destroyed the cancer cells. While lasting only a few minutes, BMA is a painful and anxiety-provoking procedure. Anticipatory anxiety can cause nausea, vomiting, insomnia and crying days before the procedures are scheduled. Young children in particular often kick, scream and physically resist to the point of having to be carried into the treatment room and strapped in a 'papoose' to keep them still during the procedure. Because of the traumatic nature of the procedure, it may take as long as two to three years for some children to learn to cope with it.

Procedure-Related Pain

Powers (1999) reviewed the literature on treatments for procedure-related pain in paediatric psychology. Many different cognitive behavioural techniques (CBT) have been tried with great success. Common strategies include *breathing exercises*, such as teaching the child to pretend to be a leaky tyre filling with air on the inbreath, and then slowly breathing out with a hissing sound as the air leaked out. For younger children, practising deep breathing by blowing into a party blower adds a bit of enjoyment. *Relaxation training* typically includes

---

Box 13.2 Case Study: Family Systems Paediatric Intervention in Chronic Illness

Kwame is an 11-year-old African American boy whose recurrent leukaemia has left him with chronic fatigue and a small stature in comparison to his peers. During a visit to the oncologist, his mother expressed concern about his increasing aggressiveness, culminating in two arrests at school for physically assaulting peers. The paediatric psychology consulting team considered how best to understand Kwame's behaviour. Unlike a traditional orientation, which tends to view behaviour through a lens of psychopathology, their competence-based approach led them to assume that Kwame's symptoms represented an attempt at adaptive functioning that was being thwarted by his illness. Their sensitivity to developmental issues suggested that they should consider the challenges faced by a boy entering adolescence, just as their awareness of social ecology suggested that they should consider neighbourhood and ethnic issues. When they asked about the family's life situation, Kwame's mother explained that they lived in a tough, inner-city neighbourhood where violence was prevalent and males earned respect through displaying physical power.

The clinician's formulation focused on the stage-salient tasks associated with becoming an adolescent male in a culture of violence. They surmised that Kwame's physical limitations were presenting him with significant developmental challenges to meeting the goal of asserting a positive masculine identity in a context that prized size and power. Consequently, Kwame was left to solve this developmental problem in the best way he knew how: with his fists.

Using the techniques of ARCH (acceptance, respect, curiosity and honesty), the clinicians conveyed *acceptance* by showing an interest and appreciation for Kwame and his mother, and by communicating their belief that Kwame was using the best strategies he had available to manage his distress about his small stature. They communicated *respect* by identifying Kwame's strengths, including his willingness to work hard to find solutions to his problems. They evidenced *curiosity* by inquiring about the neighbourhood and how the mother had attempted to help Kwame to deal with difficulties in the past. *Honesty* was conveyed by their openly sharing with the family their reactions and feelings, including their concern about Kwame's behaviour and their sincere commitment and belief that they could help him to find more adaptive strategies for asserting his masculine identity.

Source: Adapted from Kazak et al., 2002.

---

breathing combined with progressive muscle relaxation. An example of *imagery* is to invite the child to come up with a story about a favourite superhero or cartoon character using special powers to help the child cope with the medical procedure. Alternatively, imagery can be used to come up with a pleasant image that is incompatible with anxiety and pain (such as walking on a beach or going to an amusement park) and have the child hold that image in mind while breathing slowly and deeply. To be most effective, the imagery should be highly individualized such that each child chooses a unique image that is associated in his or her mind with relaxation. The results can be surprising. While adults might tend toward passive scenarios such as lying on a beach, children's images of relaxation may involve waking up on Christmas morning, attending an exciting football game, or swimming with the dolphins at Sea World.

Other CBT techniques include *distraction*, such as having children play games or do puzzles, or use humour to take their mind off their anticipatory anxiety. Sometimes *coping models* are used, such as films depicting a child explaining each step of the procedure to be done and modelling adaptive coping. *Cognitive coping skills* include making positive self-statements ('I can do this'; 'I'm a brave boy'; 'It will be over with soon'). *Reinforcement for compliance* may include presenting the child with a trophy on which his or her name is engraved as a reward for having the courage to lie still and use deep-breathing skills during the procedure. The child's ability to master and utilize the coping skills taught is enhanced by *behavioural rehearsal and role-play* prior to the procedure, and by *direct coaching* by the clinician or parent during the procedure itself.

Well-designed, controlled studies of treatment packages including several of these procedures show that CBT is generally superior to medication alone in reducing reported pain, observed distress and physiological indicators of anxiety.

Illness-Related Pain

Unlike medical procedures, which are generally time limited and planned, allowing the child to prepare and practise pain management strategies, the pain associated with illness is often unpredictable and recurrent. Further, because the pain is not limited to the doctor's office, the child and family have even more need of tools that they can take home with them and pull out of their toolbox when needed. Sickle cell disease provides a good example of this kind of pain. Although children's experience varies, on average a child with SCD can expect to experience pain episodes once or twice a month, and these episodes become severe enough to require hospitalization once or twice a year (Powers et al., 2002). Such pain may interfere with school and social activities and be associated with symptoms of depression and anxiety.

Cognitive behavioural pain management interventions have been established with some success, but none have been developed to specifically target pain management with adolescents with SCD (see Chen et al., 2004, for a review of related interventions). For example, one of the earliest studies by Gil and colleagues (2001) developed a CBT intervention for pain in children with SCD and assessed its effectiveness with a group of school-age African American children. First, children were brought into the laboratory and trained to use three coping strategies: deep breathing/counting relaxation, calming self-statements and pleasant imagery. Each strategy was explained, modelled and rehearsed by the child. The child then practised the use of the strategies in two trials that simulated a pain episode by placing a light weight on the child for up to 2 minutes. To help the child to generalize the coping strategies outside of the laboratory, each child was provided with audiotaped instruction, a tape player and homework assignments for daily practice. As an encouragement to compliance, the investigators telephoned the children at home each week to remind them to practise. A booster review session was provided a week after the initial training session.

Results showed significant reductions from before treatment to after treatment in children's use of negative coping strategies and sensitivity to pain. Four weeks after the treatment had ended, comparisons to an untreated control group showed that children who underwent CBT training used more active coping attempts, had fewer school absences and health care contacts, and were more involved in daily activities even on those days when they were experiencing pain. Schwartz et al. (2007) have recently developed a more culturally sensitive pain management intervention for African American adolescents with SCD, with promising levels of success.

Inclusion of the Parents

As we have seen, chronic illness takes a toll on the entire family system, and parents' ability to cope with the stress has a major impact on their child's behavioural, emotional and even physical well-being (see Vrijmoet-Wiersma et al., 2008, for a review). Stress reactions can take different forms in fathers and mothers and it may be relevant to identify these differences in order to deliver specific interventions. With regard to PTSS and PTSD, mothers have been reported to display more symptoms than fathers when their children are suffering from cancer (Alderfer et al., 2005).

Cognitive behavioural intervention programmes that focus on teaching the active use of coping strategies may prevent children with a chronic illness from developing psychosocial problems. However, involvement of parents may enhance coping strategies of the children in daily life. For example, Scholten et al. (2011) have been looking at the effectiveness of CBT intervention for SCD by including family members in the treatment. Children are randomly allocated to one of

FIGURE 13.4 Factors Influencing Child Coping and Distress During Painful Medical Procedures.

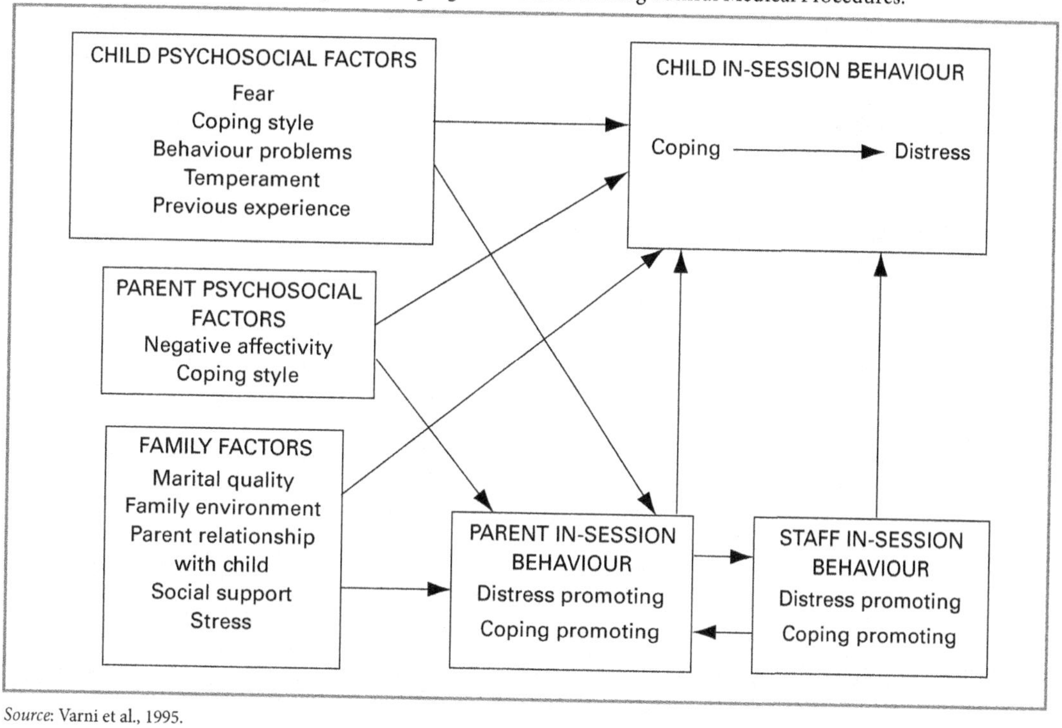

Source: Varni et al., 1995.

two intervention groups (children only and children intervention group combined with parent intervention groups) and a wait list control. Primary outcomes include child psychosocial functioning, well-being and disease relating coping skills. Among the secondary outcomes measures are child quality of life, child self-perception, parental stress, quality of parent–child interactions and parental perceived vulnerability. Outcomes are evaluated at baseline, six weeks after treatment and 6- and 12-month follow-up. If the programme proves effective, it will be implemented into clinical practice.

Figure 13.4 displays a comprehensive model of the ways in which characteristics of the child, parent and family might promote distress or adaptive coping in children undergoing painful medical procedures. With this in mind, a number of clinicians have emphasized the importance of working with the whole family in order to prevent the development of psychological problems.

Peer support

There has been a growing interest in the use of peer support to provide chronically ill young people with opportunities to meet and talk with other young people who are likely to understand their particular concerns. Peer support programmes have several benefits: they create opportunities for individuals to support one another through shared activities and discussions, and peers can also perform a unique role in empathy and support (Olsson et al., 2005).

We will now shift our focus from the body to the interpersonal context and examine two risk conditions arising from family interactions – child maltreatment and interparental violence.

CHAPTER 14

Risks in the Family Context: Child Maltreatment and Domestic Violence

Chapter contents

According to the United Nations Convention on the Rights of the Child (United Nations, 1989; Blanchfield, 2009), each child the world over is entitled to 'a standard of living adequate for the child's physical, mental, spiritual, moral, and social development' (p. 6). In the developmental psychopathology literature, these basic necessities for well-being are referred to as the *average expectable environment* (Cicchetti and Valentino, 2006). Perhaps the most profound failure of the interpersonal environment to provide these growth-promoting opportunities occurs when the child's home is a source of fear rather than a place of solace. Abuse that takes place at the hands of parents – the very people that children turn to for comfort and protection – has the most pervasive and long-lasting effects on development. Therefore, in this chapter we will focus on maltreatment in the family context.

The 'discovery' of child **maltreatment** (also called child abuse) also represents one of the most sensational chapters in the history of child psychology (Myers, 2011). The very existence of physical and sexual abuse of children was largely denied until early in the 1960s when C. Henry Kempe and colleagues (1962) brought the problem of the 'battered child syndrome' to the nation's attention. Kempe found that, while most physicians and mental health professionals honestly believed that they had never encountered a case of child abuse, this was because they simply could not bring themselves to acknowledge that such a thing took place.

The gradual uncovering of the prevalence of child maltreatment sent shock waves throughout the mental health community. Professionals were galvanized into seeking ways of protecting the child from further abuse, as well as searching for causes that could serve as the basis for intervention and prevention. The search has proved difficult. The initial assumption that abusing parents must be psychologically deviant was overly simplistic and ultimately erroneous. Child maltreatment came to be viewed as multi-determined, involving the interaction among variables from all of the contexts with which we have been concerned.

As our understanding of the determinants of child maltreatment has become more complex and multi-dimensional, so has our view of what constitutes maltreatment. Maltreatment occurs in a variety of forms, not all of which leave signs as blatant as bruises or broken bones. Along with this broader definition has come a growing recognition of the importance of developmental, interpersonal and sociocultural variables that determine the effects of a particular abusive act on a child.

Defining Maltreatment

One of the first hurdles we have to overcome is the problem of defining maltreatment. Unfortunately, no universally accepted definition exists. In actual practice, most professionals base their definitions on the laws governing mandated reporting of child abuse in their jurisdiction. However, since local laws vary significantly from place to place, such laws do not provide a satisfactory definition. Further, whereas some forms of maltreatment may be overt, with immediately detectable effects (e.g., a physical blow resulting in a red, angry welt), other forms are more subtle, with effects emerging only after some time (e.g., chronic parental indifference resulting in a lack of self-esteem). Additionally, cultural differences in childrearing attitudes and norms make it possible for one parent's 'tough love' to be another's 'abuse'.

The World Health Organization Consultation on Child Abuse Prevention (WHO, 2006) drafted the following definition:

Child abuse or maltreatment constitutes all forms of physical and/or emotional ill-treatment, sexual abuse, neglect or negligent treatment or commer-

cial or other exploitation, resulting in actual or potential harm to the child's health, survival, development or dignity in the context of a relationship of responsibility, trust, or power. (p. 9)

Types of Maltreatment

Another complication with defining maltreatment is that there are various kinds of abuse that may have different effects on children's development. It is unlikely that the child who is emotionally rejected by a parent is affected in exactly the same way as the one who is habitually beaten. Therefore, much attention has been paid to the need to distinguish among types of maltreatment.

One of the most widely accepted typologies of maltreatment is the one proposed by Barnett and colleagues (1993). These authors distinguish between *physical* abuse (e.g., beating, scalding, slapping, punching, kicking) and *sexual* abuse (e.g., fondling, intercourse, exposure to sexual acts, involvement in pornography). Another category is *neglect*, which may take such form as failure to provide basic necessities (e.g., not ensuring that adequate food, medical care or shelter is available) or lack of supervision (e.g., leaving a young child unattended or in the care of an unreliable person). The fourth category is *psychological* or emotional abuse (e.g., failing to meet a child's needs for emotional security, acceptance or autonomy, such as by ridiculing, terrorizing or excessively controlling the child).

Further research has suggested that we need to add a fifth category to this typology: *exposure to domestic violence* (Graham-Bermann and Howell, 2011). Children do not have to receive a blow in order to be traumatized by violence in the home, especially when the violence they witness is perpetrated on a parent whom they love and depend on. Further, as Hamby and colleagues (2010) found in their nationally representative sample, exposure to violence in the home is associated with substantially higher risk for all other forms of maltreatment. Specifically, the odds of experiencing maltreatment were over four times higher among children who witnessed interparental violence than among children living in non-interparentally violent homes.

In addition, the World Health Organization (2006) includes under its definition of child abuse the category of *exploitation*. Exploitation includes the use of children to fulfil adult roles in ways that violate their developmental capacities and deprive them of the shelter, care and protection that their status as children should provide: examples of exploitation include child labour, indentured servitude and enlistment of children as soldiers.

Although typologies of child maltreatment are useful, the task of identifying the kind of maltreatment children have experienced – for example, physical versus sexual abuse – is complicated by the fact that these different forms of abuse often co-occur. This is known as *polyvictimization*. For example, Finkelhor and colleagues (2010) found in their nationally representative telephone survey in the USA that almost 66 per cent of youth had been exposed to more than one form of maltreatment. Among these polyvictimized youth, 30 per cent of had experienced five or more types of victimization and 10 per cent had experienced 11 or more different forms of victimization over the course of their lifetimes. Similarly, Mennen and colleagues (2010) report that 54 per cent of their maltreated sample had experienced multiple types of abuse, and that the average child had been involved in five separate reports to child welfare agencies. In sum, multiple victimization may be the norm for maltreated children.

Assessing Maltreatment

Because definitions of maltreatment vary from jurisdiction to jurisdiction, it is difficult to compile accurate statistics that allow comparisons to be made across states and across countries. In addition, as we describe the prevalence data, we will need to keep in mind that it comes from a number of different sources: cases *reported* to child protection agencies; cases *substantiated* by authorities, which generally amount to a third or fewer of those reported; and *self-reports* of parents or children, which are often based on small and idiosyncratic samples. The strongest data come from nationally representative samples, and so we will rely on these whenever possible. Only recently have national and international databases been established in the USA and Europe which provide comprehensive information about both reported and substantiated cases.

The Developmental Dimension

Cicchetti and Toth (2005) remind us that in order to define maltreatment it is necessary to place it in a developmental context. A developmental psychopathology perspective focuses our attention on the needs children have at each stage of development, as well as the potential for harm inherent in a parent's failure to meet those needs. As Barnett and colleagues (1993) state:

> The parental acts that are judged to be unacceptable by society change as a function of the child's age. Moreover, the types of parental acts that can enhance development, or that can result in psychological harm to children, also change over the course of development. Thus, acts that might be maltreatment for a toddler would not be for an adolescent, and acts that are maltreatment for an adolescent might not be for a preschooler. (p. 24)

For example, because young children are utterly dependent on caregivers for their physical and emotional well-being, inattentive, lax or indifferent parenting might have the most severe consequences in infancy. In contrast, the opposite – overprotective, intrusive or controlling parenting – would be more disruptive for adolescent development. Therefore, a developmental perspective alerts us to the need to define maltreatment in terms of the potential impact of parental behaviour on the adjustment of a child at a particular age and stage.

Further, perhaps the most significant aspect of child maltreatment is that it often takes place in the context of the family, perpetrated by the very adults on whom children rely for protection. Consequently, the literature focuses on the major developmental capacities that emerge in the context of the parent–child relationship – emotion regulation, interpersonal trust and self-esteem – that might interfere with the child's ability to master stage-salient issues and move forward in development.

Prevalence of Maltreatment

Data on Prevalence in the US

The most recent national data in the USA, compiled from all 50 states by the National Child Abuse and Neglect Data System, indicate that, in 2010, 6 million children were reported due to suspected abuse and 826 000 (22.1 per cent) of these cases were substantiated (US Department of Health and Human Services, Administration for Children and Families, 2010): 78.3 percent had been neglected, 17.8 per cent had suffered physical abuse, 9.5 per cent had been sexually abused and 7.6 per cent had experienced psychological maltreatment. The mortality rate was 2.3 children per 100 000 and was largely accounted for by infants suffering from severe neglect.

Rates of unreported abuse are much higher. In a nationally representative telephone survey involving 4549 youth aged 0–17, Finkelhor and colleagues (2010) found that 60.6 per cent of children reported experiencing some form of victimization in the previous year. Almost half (46.3 per cent) had been physically assaulted, 24.6 per cent had been a victim of crime, 10.2 per cent had experienced child maltreatment, 6.1 per cent had been sexually victimized, and 9.8 per cent had witnessed violence among the members of their own family.

Who are the abusers? In the vast majority (80.9 per cent) of cases, the perpetrators of child maltreatment are parents, and in most cases are the biological parents of the child. Statistics further reveal that mothers are more often implicated in abuse than fathers (53.8 per cent of cases versus 44.4 per cent). (See Fig. 14.1.)

There also appear to be developmental trends in the prevalence and types of victimization to which children are exposed. (See Fig. 14.2.) For example, in Finkelhor and colleagues' (2010) US telephone survey, children were most vulnerable to experiencing physical assaults and property

FIGURE 14.1 Perpetrators of Child Maltreatment.

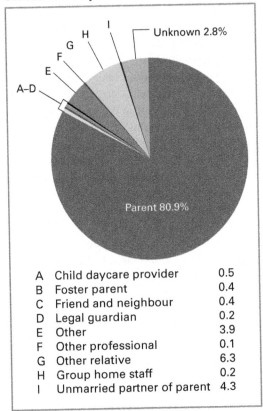

A	Child daycare provider	0.5
B	Foster parent	0.4
C	Friend and neighbour	0.4
D	Legal guardian	0.2
E	Other	3.9
F	Other professional	0.1
G	Other relative	6.3
H	Group home staff	0.2
I	Unmarried partner of parent	4.3

Source: US Department of Health and Human Services, Administration for Children and Families, Administration on Children, Youth and Families, Children's Bureau, 2010.

crimes in the 5- to 9-year-old age range, whereas witnessing violence increased dramatically after age 10. Child maltreatment, in turn, begins to rise after the age of 12 and sexual victimization peaks at the age of 15.

The Global Perspective

Efforts to compile international data regarding child abuse are complicated by the fact that there are major cross-cultural differences in how abuse is defined and perceived in various parts of the world. For example, corporal punishment (e.g., spanking), while defined as physical abuse in 16 European countries, is not so defined in the USA and Canada. In fact, corporal punishment is allowed in the

FIGURE 14.2 Developmental Trends in Child Victimization.

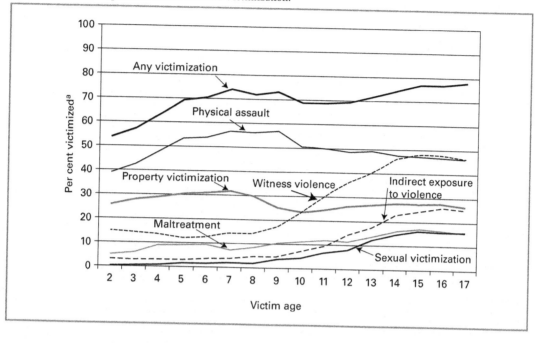

public school systems of 23 US states and 106 countries (Global Initiative to End All Corporal Punishment of Children, 2010). Beatings are accepted as a form of child discipline in many countries, including Sri Lanka, Kenya, Romania and India (Schwartz-Kenney and McCauley, 2003). On the other hand, behaviours considered normative in Western cultures might be considered abusive in other societies. For example, the expectation that young children sleep alone in a separate room might be considered a form of emotional maltreatment in societies that practise use of a family bed.

The World Health Organization (WHO, 2010) has called for worldwide data collection regarding child abuse and has begun compiling statistics from the countries for which they are available. Estimates are that as many as 53 000 children worldwide die each year as a result of homicide and that from 80 to 98 per cent experience physical punishment in their homes, including a third or more who are hit by hard objects (UNICEF, 2003). A further estimated 150 million girls and 73 million boys under the age of 18 have experienced sexual violence and

between 100 and 140 million girls have undergone genital mutilation. Although advances have been made in decreasing child labour, still as many as 218 million children are involved in the labour force, of whom 126 million are doing hazardous work. Further estimates regarding child exploitation include an estimated 5.7 million children in forced or bonded labour, 1.8 million in prostitution or pornography and 1.2 million as victims of human trafficking.

Further data from the United Nations International Children's Emergency Fund (UNICEF, 2003) report on child *fatalities* due to maltreatment in the industrialized world reports rates ranging from 0.1 per 100 000 children in Spain to 2.2 per 100 000 children in Mexico and the USA. According to their estimates, two children die from abuse and neglect every week in Germany and the UK, four a week in Japan, and 27 a week in the USA. Rates are two to three times higher among low-income versus high-income countries. Strikingly, the mortality rates in the USA are higher than those of any other developed Western society (see Fig. 14.3): for

FIGURE 14.3 Child Abuse Fatalities in Western Nations.

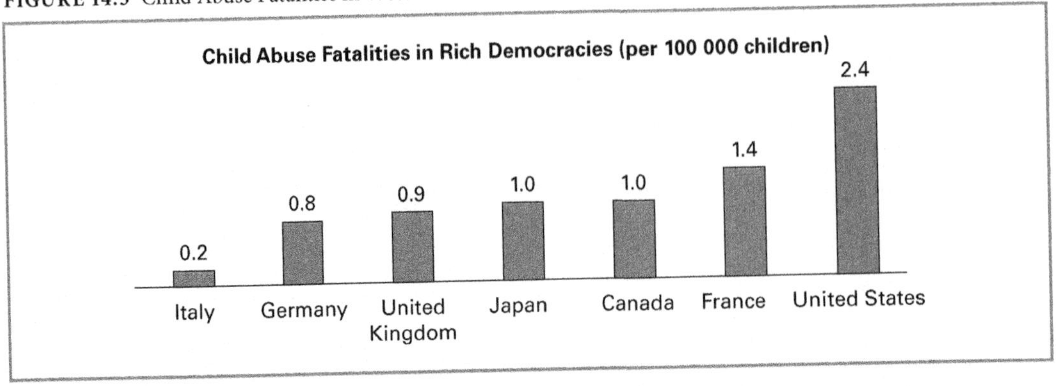

Child Abuse Fatalities in Rich Democracies (per 100 000 children)

Source: UNICEF, 2003.

example, the US child abuse death rate is three times higher than Canada's, Japan's or the UK's, and 11 times higher than Italy's (Every Child Matters Education Fund, 2010).

What accounts for these differences among nations? Among the countries with the lowest rates of child abuse fatalities are also found the lowest rates of violent crime, imprisonment and poverty (Every Child Matters Education Fund, 2010). In addition, countries with the lowest fatalities rates also invest the most in social policies that support families and mitigate against child abuse, including child care, universal health insurance, paid parental leave and visiting nurses to ensure the health and well-being of new parents and their infants.

Another important consideration is that cultural practices may influence whether child abuse is reported in the first place. For example, in cultures that emphasize obedience to adults, children may be inhibited from coming forward, whereas in cultures that emphasize family privacy, a report to authorities might be seen as an act of disloyalty (Malley-Morrison and Hines, 2004). In some cases, the consequences of reporting abuse may be so prohibitive that for the child's sake no mention of the experience is ever made. Sexually abused girls may fear ostracism – or even death, in some societies – because of the irrevocable shame their violation brings to the family (Pence, 2011).

Therefore, reliance on officially reported incidents may give a misleading picture of what actually goes on in the homes of children. Although parent and child self-reports are not free of bias, they may shed a different light on the subject. Runyan and colleagues (2010) gathered surveys on parental discipline in an international sample of 14 239 women drawn from Brazil, Chile, Egypt, India, Philippines and the USA. (See Table 14.1). A particular strength of this study is that the investigators presented the items neutrally, without labelling them as 'abusive'. Although overall 55 per cent of mothers reported that physical punishment was used in their families, rates of spanking ranged from a low of 15 per cent in an educated community in India to a high of 76 per cent in an underprivileged community in the Philippines. Wide ranges also were found in the proportion of children hit with objects or beaten by parents. Of particular concern was that, in more than nine nations, at least 20 per cent of parents admitted to shaking children younger than 2 years of age.

Further, Gilbert and colleagues' (2009) review of international prevalence statistics revealed rates of child- or parent-reported physical abuse ranging from 3.7 to 16.3 per cent of children per year in the UK, USA, New Zealand, Finland, Italy and Portugal, 12.2 to 29.7 per cent in Macedonia, Moldova, Latvia and Lithuania, and 24–29 per cent in Siberia, Russia and Romania.

TABLE 14.1 Parental Discipline Practices in International Context

Community	N	Moderate Physical Discipline %								Harsh Physical Punishment %				
		Spanked Buttocks	Hit With an Object	Slapped Face	Pulled Hair	Pinched	Twisted Ear	Put Hot Pepper in Child's Mouth	Shook Child (≤2 yrs old)	Burned	Beat-up	Choked	Smothered	Kicked
Chennai (NS)	400	58	7.4	13	2.0	16	17	0.3	0	0.3	1.0	1.0	0.0	1.0
United States	1435	44	3.6	6	—	5.7	—	0.3	2.6	0.1	0.3	—	—	0.3
Delhi (NS)	850	16	5.4	72	5.7	1.4	13	0.1	12	0.0	0.1	0.1	0.0	1.1
Philippines	1000	76	20	21	23	58	30	0.9	19	0.3	2.7	1.0	0.2	5.8
Thiruvananthapuram (NS)	700	55	48	5.1	2.8	61	19	1.8	22	0.4	0.9	0.6	0.6	2.5
Chile	422	53	4.5	13	25	3.1	29	0.0	24	0.0	0.7	0.2	0.0	0.7
Egypt	631	29	27	42	28	45	32	2.9	12	2.2	24	0.8	0.6	5.4
Thiruvananthapuram (R)	765	72	52	4.3	1.7	66	25	3.5	17	0.9	2.5	0.4	0.7	2.1
Lucknow (NS)	506	34	25	64	20	22	34	2.3	53	0.2	9.8	1.7	0.4	7.8
Chennai (S)	1000	71	35	27	17	348	31	1.2	13	2.6	12	4.1	0.0	9.7
Brazil	813	55	4.7	4.8	8.1	13	20	0.6	10	0.0	0.3	0.5	0.0	0.7
Nagpur (S)	905	57	27	76	21	13	18	6.7	37	4.5	10	0.6	0.4	6.5
Vellore (NS)	716	29	31	40	7.2	18	14	1.3	9.7	1.0	8.7	1.4	0.0	6.2
Vellore (R)	714	26	32	38	8.1	14	11	0.9	12	0.9	11	1.0	0.1	5.4
Nagpur (R)	526	60	29	77	21	5.3	13	2.2	31	2.9	10	0.8	1.0	5.1
Bhopal (S)	700	68	25	80	21	26	40	3.6	49	2.0	19	2.5	0.2	11
Lucknow (R)	906	48	39	69	24	15	28	1.4	63	0.3	14	0.7	0.5	5.8
Bhopal (R)	700	68	29	77	28	33	48	4.3	61	1.8	29	3.3	0.3	12
Delhi (S)	550	30	19	79	19	8.8	22	0.6	23	0.2	3.0	1.1	0.0	11

Note: Indian communities were classified according to official designation as rural (R), urban slum (S), or urban non-slum (NS). — indicates that the data were not collected.

Source: Adapted from Runyan et al., 2010.

Ethnic Differences

Within each nation, there also exist subcultural differences related to *ethnicity*. For example, in the USA, reports to Child Protective Services range from a low of 4.4 per 1000 Asian American children to a high of 25.2 per 1000 African American children (Malley-Morrison and Hines, 2004). The correspondence between social class and race may account for the ethnic differences in the prevalence of abuse. *Poverty* and its correlates – single parenting, parental youth and lack of education, life stress, limited resources, and a large number of young children in the home – all increase the likelihood of maltreatment. And these are just the circumstances in which many ethnic minority families live in the USA. Among African American families, for example, 30 per cent fall into the lowest income bracket in which the maltreatment prevalence rates are highest (47 per 1000). Further, 52 per cent of African American children are living only with their mothers as compared to 18 per cent of European American children (Malley-Morrison and Hines, 2004), another risk factor for abuse. Therefore, statistics on ethnicity always must be interpreted in the context of social class and economic disparity.

Disproportionate rates of abuse in ethnic minority samples also may be a product of differential reporting. In a classic experiment, Zellman (1992) presented hypothetical vignettes to almost 2000 professionals who are legally required to report suspected abuse, and altered the ethnicity and social class of the families described. The results showed that professionals were more likely to report the case and to believe that the family would benefit from a report when the families were described as African American and low SES.

Another explanation for these discrepancies is that culturally derived preconceptions might lead investigators to define as abusive tactics that are sanctioned and even adaptive when understood in context. Parenting styles that are judged negatively by white middle-class psychologists might be conceived as functional in disadvantaged communities. For example, it may be that in low SES African American families, parenting that emphasizes control over warmth is appropriate for children growing up in dangerous, high-risk environments and might even have the function of helping to 'steel' children for the harshness of the world in which they must live. To take another example, parenting in Native American communities tends to be permissive and loosely structured, allowing for multiple caregivers to assume physical custody of the child. While this may be perceived as neglectful by observers from the dominant culture, to Natives such parenting reflects cultural values of respect for the child's autonomy and reliance on the extended family (Malley-Morrison and Hines, 2004). Therefore, it is essential that investigators be culturally competent in order to accurately judge the intent and impact on the child of various parenting practices (Pence, 2011).

Empirical evidence in support of a *cultural relativism* argument comes from research by Deater-Deckard and Podge (1997), who found that physical punishment was associated with increased child aggression in European American samples but not in African American samples. The authors interpret their results as suggesting the importance of the culturally derived *meaning* of parental behaviour to the child. In particular, they argue, the emotional context of punishment is imperative, with the effects depending on whether discipline is carried out in an emotionally charged or controlled fashion. As the authors state, 'among European American families, the presence of harsh discipline may imply an out-of-control, parent-centred household for some, whereas a lack of discipline among African American parents may indicate an abdication of the parenting role to others' (p. 170). Therefore, it may be that the parent who routinely metes out physical punishment in a controlled and matter-of-fact manner affects the child less negatively than the one who use such techniques in a fit of rage. To test this hypothesis, the research team subsequently investigated attitudes towards physical punishment among mothers and children in China, India, Kenya, the Philippines and Thailand (Lansford et al., 2005). As the investigators hypothesized, the relationship between physical discipline and children's adjustment was moderated by culturally derived beliefs concerning the normativeness of corporal punishment. The use of physical discipline was less strongly associated with negative child outcomes when such discipline techniques were perceived by mothers and children as normative, expectable and benign. However, the authors take care to note that the buffering effect of this perceived normativeness was only relative: in all countries, the use of physical discipline was associated with higher rates of child aggression and anxiety.

Next we review each of the types of maltreatment and describe their effects on child development.

Physical Abuse

Definition and Characteristics

Definition

Physical abuse involves acts that result in actual or potential physical harm to a child and that are perpetrated by a caregiver who reasonably could be expected to be in control of those actions (World Health Organization, 2006). Physical abuse can range widely in terms of severity and potential to cause lasting physical harm. Injuries may be relatively minor, such as bruises or cuts, or major, such as brain damage, internal injuries, burns and lacerations. A rare form of physical abuse is *Munchausen by proxy syndrome*, in which a parent fabricates or even creates physical illness in a child, causing psychological or physical harm through subjecting the child to repeated and unnecessary medical procedures (Stirling and the Committee on Child Abuse and Neglect, 2007). (See Box 14.1.)

Prevalence

Prevalence rates vary widely from study to study because of the different definitions and measures used. A telephone survey of a nationally representative sample of 4549 US children aged 2 to 17 discovered that over the lifetime, approximately 9.8 per cent of children had been subjected to physical abuse at the hands of a caregiver and 4.4 per cent had been abused within the past year (Finkelhor et al., 2010). Physical abuse accounts for 16.1 per cent of all cases of *substantiated* maltreatment in the USA (US Department of Health and Human Services, 2010). However, it is believed that the *actual* rates are probably much higher, with the wounds and bruises children display misattributed to 'accidents' (Reece, 2011).

Child Characteristics

The incidence of physical abuse varies by *age*. Among substantiated cases, the majority of abused children are young: 51 per cent are 7 years of age or younger, whereas 26 per cent are 3 or younger. Adolescents account for 20 per cent of the sample, the third-largest group. Serious injuries are more common among the older children, but most child fatalities occur in those under the age of 2. In addition, age interacts with *gender*. Boys between the ages of 4 and 8 are the most likely to be physically abused, whereas girls are more likely to be abused between the ages of 12 and 15 (US Department of Health and Human Services, 2010).

Children at greater risk for abuse are those who are difficult or have special needs, including those who are premature or developmentally delayed. For example, a recent review of the available literature by a team of investigators in the UK found that *disabled* children are almost twice as likely to be maltreated as their peers (Stalker and McArthur, 2010). Children with *behaviour disorders*, such as oppositional-defiant disorder, also are at increased risk for physical abuse (Haskett et al., 2010). Behaviourally or developmentally challenging children may overtax the resources of the parent, who then parents poorly, thus increasing child difficulty – which in turn further stresses the parent, with the downward spiral ultimately leading to violence.

Developmental Course

As we conduct our review of the developmental consequences of physical abuse, we will need to keep in mind that the majority of the research has grouped together children who have experienced

Box 14.1 Case Study: Munchausen by Proxy Syndrome

Munchausen syndrome was named for Baron von Munchausen, a seventeenth-century nobleman famous for concocting wild tales. This is a disorder in which adults repeatedly seek medical attention for fictitious illnesses. *Munchausen by proxy syndrome* involves a parent's simulating illness in a child in order to attract the attention of medical professionals (Stirling and the Committee on Child Abuse and Neglect, 2007). The effects of this are far from benign. The child may undergo painful and invasive medical procedures and suffer the emotional stress of repeated hospitalizations. Also, in the most extreme form, the parent may intentionally subject the child to injury in order to bring about an actual illness.

One case involved an 8-year-old girl whose mother repeatedly sought help for a string of vague physical problems. While the physicians sought in vain to find a cause, the girl's health rapidly deteriorated. Although previously a slender and vivacious child, she became enormously obese and apathetic. Examination showed that her bones were under such severe stress that hairline fractures were developing throughout her body. Clearly, something was terribly wrong, and she was brought into the hospital. With more opportunity to observe mother and child, the staff began to notice other peculiarities. While previous reports indicated that this child had been progressing well in development, she now behaved immaturely and had no interest in school or peer relationships. She and her mother were inseparable, spending long periods gazing adoringly into one another's eyes in a way that the staff found unnerving. The mother was initially unwilling to co-operate with the clinical psychologists brought in to consult on the case, but slowly her trust was won. As she began to reveal more information about herself, the psychologists learned a number of peculiar facts. For example, the mother believed that her milk was the only proper sustenance for her child,

and therefore years ago, when breast-feeding her younger child, she froze a large supply of breast milk 'popsicles'. These were now a part of her school-age child's regular diet. Curious about the younger child, the psychologists inquired further about him and learned that he had died of undiagnosed causes two years before, following prolonged treatment at the very same hospital.

The solution to the mystery came when a staff member observed the mother's giving the child some tablets during visiting hours. Her purse was searched, and steroids were found. Through administering massive doses of steroids to her child, this mother had created a severe and debilitating illness.

What could cause a parent to mistreat a child in such a way? Little research has been done in this area, although interest is increasing as we come to recognize that the syndrome might not be as rare as originally thought. Sheridan (2003) uncovered 451 cases described in the empirical literature. Of the children affected, 7 per cent suffered long-term disability; a further 6 per cent had died. Victims were most likely to be infants and toddlers, but these were equally likely to be girls or boys. On average, 21 months passed between the onset of symptoms and diagnosis, and in over 60 per cent of cases siblings also had suspicious symptoms. While the perpetrating parent is usually the mother (76 per cent of cases), fathers are sometimes described as playing an enabling role. In terms of perpetrator psychopathology, 29 per cent had characteristics suggestive of Munchausen syndrome, 22 per cent had another psychiatric diagnosis, usually of depression or personality disorder, and another 22 per cent had suffered abuse themselves in childhood. Sometimes older victims are coached to participate in the deception and falsify their own symptoms, further contributing to the difficulty in detecting and treating the disorder (Parnell, 2002).

---

diverse forms of maltreatment. Therefore, some of the findings are not specific to physical abuse and are relevant to our discussions of other forms of abuse that follow. Our review integrates information from exhaustive overviews by Cichetti and Toth (2005), Cicchetti and Valentino (2006), Kolko

(2002), Perry (2008), Trickett et al. (2011a) and Wolfe et al. (2006), unless otherwise noted.

The Biological Context

Recent research in neurodevelopment confirms that child abuse has significant and adverse effects on the developing brain (Perry, 2008). Magnetic resonance imaging has uncovered negative consequences of maltreatment-related trauma, including smaller hippocampal volume, a smaller corpus collosum and amydala, and less white matter in the prefrontal cortex (Beers and De Bellis, 2002; Perry, 2008). These deficits are likely to affect executive functions and efficient communication between the parts of the brain, interfering with such important developmental capacities as emotion regulation, impulse control and reasoning. Moreover, these structural differences are related to the *age of onset* of abuse: trauma is associated with the most negative consequences when it occurs early in development (Perry, 2008).

A proposed explanation for these effects is that prolonged traumatic stress stimulates the production of *catecholamines* – neurotransmitters, including norepinephrine, epinephrine and dopamine – and activates the limbic-hypothalamic-pituitary-adrenal (LHPA) axis of the brain. These events lead to the hypersecretion of *cortisol* from the adrenal gland and stimulate the sympathetic nervous system, causing behaviour activation and intense arousal. When this activation continues unabated for long periods of time, excessive cortisol essentially has toxic effects on brain development (De Bellis, 2001). (See Fig. 14.4.) On an encouraging note, evidence also suggests that children who are rescued from abusive environments also are able to

FIGURE 14.4 Effects of Trauma on the Developing Brain.

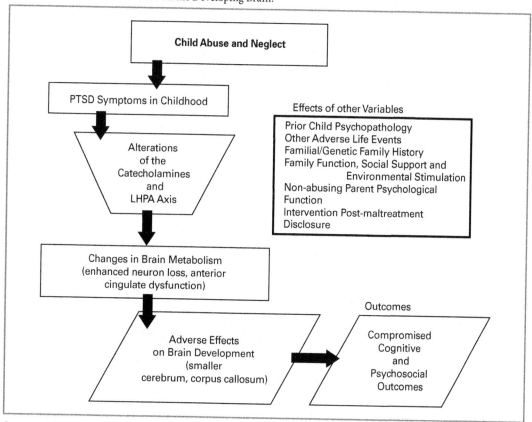

Source: De Bellis, 2001.

show recovery and normalization of their cognitive processes.

Recent research also has implicated maltreatment in an interruption of the connections among the systems involved in the psychophysiological response to stress, particularly between the sympathetic nervous system and the HPA axis. Specifically, Gordis et al. (2008) found that youth who had been maltreated exhibited greater asymmetry in cortisol and alpha amylase than non-maltreated youth when confronted with a laboratory-based stress test. In addition, abused youth show lower levels of autonomic nervous system activity, as indicated by skin conductance reactivity and respiratory sinus arrhythmia, in comparison to non-maltreated youth (Gordis et al., 2010).

Cognitive Development
Young maltreated children show significant delays in *cognitive* and *language* development, particularly expressive language (Cicchetti and Toth, 2005). As they enter middle childhood, physically abused children continue to demonstrate cognitive delays in all areas, scoring 20 points lower than non-abused children on standardized IQ tests. Similarly, school achievement tests show that physically abused children perform two years below grade level in verbal and mathematical abilities, with one-third of them requiring special education. They are also over-represented among those with learning disorders. In adolescence, lower achievement and more grade retention is seen.

In addition, the experience of physical abuse is associated with deficits in theory of mind, the ability to understand mental states in others (Pears and Fisher, 2005). In the context of a maltreating environment, children may learn that it is unacceptable or even dangerous to discuss feelings, emotions and the internal experiences of the self or others.

Emotional Development
The intra-personal and interpersonal contexts intersect in the major stage-salient task of infancy – the formation of a secure attachment relationship – which is necessary for providing the child with a sense of security, mutuality and self-esteem.

Significantly, from as many as 95 per cent of maltreated infants demonstrate insecure attachments with their caregivers (Cicchetti and Toth, 2005). Physically abused children often show a pattern of *avoidant attachment*, in which they refrain from seeking attention or contact when under stress. As we learned in Chapter 2, this behaviour may be adaptive in that it reduces the likelihood of maternal anger by keeping bids for attention minimal and low-key. However, because avoidant children's needs for security and comforting are not met, their future development is negatively affected.

As we also know, a primary function of a secure attachment relationship is to assist the child with developing the capacity to regulate affect. Consequently, it is no surprise that abused children show deficits in many aspects of emotion processing, including the recognition, expression, understanding and regulation of emotions. Regarding *emotion recognition*, children who have been physically abused demonstrate a bias toward perceiving anger in the facial expressions of others. Pollak and Sinha (2003) demonstrated this phenomenon by displaying to children computer images of faces in which the expressions of emotions gradually morphed into one another. (See Fig. 14.5.) Physically abused children were highly sensitive to the slightest expressions of anger and detected them at a much lower signal strength than did other children. The authors point out the adaptiveness of such hypersensitivity to a parent's rising anger in a household in which such signals indicate a risk of harm to the child.

Regarding emotion understanding, Beeghly and Cicchetti (1994) found that maltreated toddlers had a poor *internal state lexicon*, also termed alexithymia – that is, that they have fewer words for describing emotional states, particularly regarding negative emotions. The long-term consequences are a lack of access to emotions and the ability to regulate them.

Regarding *emotion regulation*, studies show that physically abused children have difficulty regulating affect, resulting in either over-control or under-control of emotions. For example, in a sample of 325 Chinese children and their families, Chang and

FIGURE 14.5 Computer-Morphed Facial Expressions Used to Assess Maltreated Children's Sensitivity to Angry Expressions.

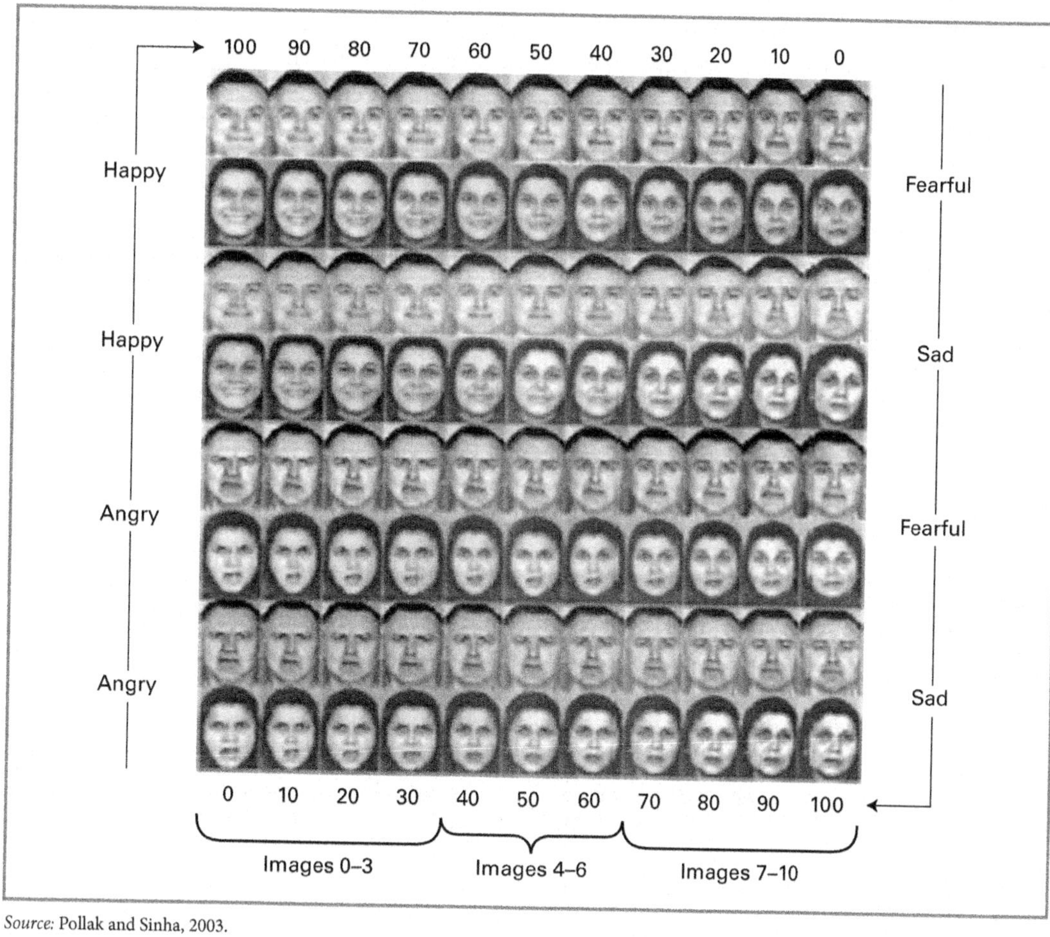

Source: Pollak and Sinha, 2003.

colleagues (2003) found that the relationship between parenting and child peer aggression was mediated by emotion dysregulation. Parental anger, the authors of the study argue, is a form of affective communication that both socializes children into negative patterns of emotion exchange and disrupts their ability to manage upsetting feelings. 'The expression of anger, coldness, or hatred that accompanies the physical act of parental aggression could well be more detrimental than the act itself' (Chang et al., 2003, p. 603).

There also is evidence that physical abuse interferes with the normal development of the *self* in the early years (Cicchetti and Toth, 2005). One of the tests of the early development of the self as an independent entity is toddlers' ability to recognize their reflection in a mirror. Such visual self-recognition is delayed in maltreated toddlers. Moreover, they react with neutral or negative affect when they do inspect their faces in the mirror, rather than with the positive affect that non-abused children show. While deficits in self-esteem most often take the form of the maltreated children's underestimating their capacities, some maltreated children also demonstrate unrealistically *inflated self-esteem*. This emphatic assertion that 'I am the best at everything!' may serve as a primitive defence against deeper feelings of powerlessness and inadequacy. However, because it is not based on actual competence, this defensive overestimation of self is brittle and easily shattered. Thus, overestimation of self serves not as a protective mechanism but rather as a new source of vulnerability (Cicchetti and Howes, 1991).

Far from abating, the emotional and behavioural problems of abused children intensify in adolescence. Childhood abuse is a significant predictor of adolescent *depression, low self-esteem, conduct disorder*, and *antisocial behaviour* (Wolfe et al., 2006). A depressive cognitive style is particularly likely to develop if maltreatment begins in early childhood, when young children depend on their parents to provide them with a sense of interpersonal trust and personal efficacy.

Social Development

Abused toddlers respond to peers in ways that parallel the behaviour of their own parents. For example, when exposed to a peer in distress, abused toddlers are less likely to respond with sympathy or concern than are other toddlers and are more likely to react with *fear* and *physical aggression*. Similarly, longitudinal research showed that physically abused children were more aggressive in preschool when compared to neglected, psychologically abused and non-abused children (Cicchetti and Toth, 2005).

Peer relationships become of increasing importance in the school-age years; therefore, it is significant that one of the most consistent consequences of physical abuse is *hostility* and *aggression* against others. Like conduct-disordered children (see Chapter 10) maltreated children have poor *interpersonal problem-solving skills* and demonstrate a *hostile attribution bias*. Abused children assume that others harbour negative intentions towards them and thus deserve the same in kind. The problem behaviour of abused children contributes to the development of a negative reputation in the peer group, including being rated as disliked, verbally and physically aggressive, and less prosocial than

other children (Anthonysamy and Zimmer-Gembeck, 2007). Consequently, they are more likely to experience *peer rejection* and, as we saw in Chapter 10, peer rejection fuels further aggression. For example, Kim and Cicchetti (2006) followed a sample of 215 maltreated and 206 non-maltreated children age 6–12 years of age over a period of a year. The investigators found a pernicious chain of effects: maltreatment contributed to emotion dysregulation, which was associated with higher levels of externalizing problems at time 1. In turn, externalizing problems were associated with peer rejection at time 2, which was related to yet further increases in externalizing over the course of childhood. On the positive side, higher levels of emotion regulation were associated with increased peer acceptance over time, and lower levels of internalizing symptoms.

In adolescence, the friendships of physically abused youth are marked by less positive affect, higher levels of conflict, and peer ratings of aggression (Trickett et al., 2011a). As we saw in Chapter 10 with the development of conduct disorder, youth with problematic peer relations tend to gravitate towards antisocial networks and research shows that physically abused youth are the most vulnerable to the negative influences of delinquent friends (Salzinger et al., 2007).

In general, the link between childhood maltreatment and adolescent *delinquency* is strongly confirmed by a host of longitudinal studies (Kerig and Becker, 2010). Some research suggests that the developmental timing of the abuse matters, in that abuse that starts or extends into adolescence is the most predictive of delinquency (Stewart et al., 2008). A number of potential *mediators* of this relationship have been found: a negative school climate, poor attachment to parents, association with antisocial peers, attitudes accepting of violence and running away from home have been implicated as factors helping to explain the association between maltreatment and delinquency (Trickett et al., 2011a).

In addition, adolescence is a time when young people begin to develop significant romantic relationships, and often their family provides them with the blueprint for intimacy. A large body of literature attests to the fact that childhood abuse has negative effects on adolescents' *dating relationships*. Maltreated children are more likely than their peers to report feeling uncomfortable with emotional intimacy and to have more relationship problems (DiLillo et al., 2007). In particular, youth who experienced abuse at the hands of their own parents are more likely to both perpetrate and to be victimized by verbal and physical *dating violence* (Jouriles et al., 2006; Kerig, 2010). The imitation of their parents' behaviour occurs despite the fact that those who were physically abused hold negative attitudes about their parents and blame them for the abuse (Wolfe et al., 1998). Victimization in childhood, therefore, appears to set the stage for violence in later intimate relationships and thus for the inter-generational transmission of abuse.

Summary

Recasting the findings concerning physical abuse in terms of the personality variables we have been using in this text, we have found that attachment, emotional development, cognition and interpersonal relationships are all adversely affected. Avoidant *attachment* sets the stage by denying the child the opportunity to have needs for security met and to develop a positive working model of self and other. Physical abuse is a particular risk factor for the development of poor emotion regulation, which reveals itself in such varied forms as *aggression* with peers and family members and *internalizing* problems such as withdrawal and depression. Cognitively, abused children evidence a depressive cognitive style and hostile attribution bias. In terms of interpersonal development, abused children have *poor social skills*, fewer friends and a lack of emotional sensitivity to others.

Resilience among Maltreated Children

Despite all the odds, research also shows the capacity for resilience among children who have experienced physical abuse. (See Box 14.2 for an example of such resilience.) Within the intra-individual context, research suggests that there are biological markers that protect some children from developing psychopathology in the context of an abusive family. For example, among twins with low *genetic risk* for conduct disorder, maltreatment is associated with a 2 per cent increase in the development of problem behaviour, whereas the risk is increased 24 per cent among children at high genetic risk (Jaffee et al., 2004). Similarly, maltreated children with a polymorphism in the *MAOA gene* that confers a high level of MAOA expression are less likely than those with a genotype that confers a low level of MAOA activity to develop antisocial behaviour (Caspi et al., 2002).

Cicchetti and Valentino (2006) review the research on other intra-individual variables that have emerged as particularly important; these include an *internal locus of control*, a *positive sense of self*, and *ego resilience* and *ego control*. Within the interpersonal context, resilience may be fostered by the presence of a relationship with someone who confers upon them a *positive sense of self*, including warm and supportive peers, other family members, or adults who play a mentorship role in the abused child's life. However, in studies of diverse samples including European American, African American, and Latino children, studies tend to find that the contributions of relationships are weaker than are personal qualities in predicting resilience among maltreated children. Indeed, it may be adaptive for children whose most important relationships are unrewarding to turn inward and to rely less on others than on their own personal strengths in their struggles against adversity. (See a case example of this phenomenon in Box 14.2.)

Nevertheless, we must keep in mind that resilience is a dynamic construct and one that changes across the course of development: for example, in one study only 62 per cent of maltreated children who were rated as resilient during the school-age years continued to show resilient qualities during adolescence (Herrenkohl et al., 1994). What benefits a child at one point in the lifespan, and allows him or her to successfully 'get through' an ordeal, may have hidden costs that only arise at later times in life to take their toll. For example, it is possible that excessive self-reliance is one of those

---

Box 14.2 Dave Pelzer: A Case Study in Resilience in the Face of Severe Maltreatment

In the case histories we have studied throughout this book, we frequently have seen inspiring examples of the capacity of children to rise above even the most adverse experiences and challenging environments. Few stories are more remarkable than that Dave Pelzer tells in the autobiographies *A Child Called It* (1995), *The Lost Boy* (1997) and *A Man Called Dave* (2000). Dave was raised in a seemingly normal middle-class American family, spending his early years happily with his parents and two brothers. However, around the age of 4, Dave began experiencing a very different kind of childhood as his mother began systematically to isolate him from his siblings, deny him food, and force him to swallow soap, ammonia and Clorox as punishments for his many inexplicable 'misbehaviours'. She ceased to use his name, referring to Dave as 'It', or 'the boy', and subjected him to increasingly serious forms of physical and psychological abuse, including beatings, stabbings, forcing him to eat faeces, and holding his arm over the flames of a gas stove. For reasons as hard for Dave to understand as the change in his mother's behaviour, his father and siblings stood by quietly and failed to intervene.

In his books, Dave writes of the strategies he used to hold on to a place inside himself which his mother could not touch and could not overcome. In his mind, he transformed the torture into a test of wills in which he took silent pride in outwitting his mother by finding surreptitious sources of food, anticipating her 'games' in order to thwart her, exaggerating his reactions so that she would think him hurt more seriously than he was, and counting in his head to make the time go faster when he was locked in confinement. Of the day he defied his mother's attempt to make him swallow soap by holding it in his mouth until he could spew it into the trashcan at the end of his long list of menial chores, he writes, 'After I finished, I felt as though I had won the Olympic marathon. I was so proud for beating Mother at her own game' (1995, p. 48). And of the time Dave defeated starvation by locating a cache of frozen food in the family garage, he writes, 'In the darkness of the garage I closed my eyes, dreaming I was a king dressed the finest robes, eating the best food mankind had to offer. As I held a piece of frozen pumpkin pie crust or a bit of a taco shell, I was the king, and like a king on his throne, I gazed down on my food and smiled' (1995, p. 49).

Intervention finally came in the form of a school nurse who, concerned about a swelling lump over Dave's eye, which had been caused by his mother slamming his head against a mirror, asked Dave to remove his shirt and then discovered the many bruises, scars and burn marks all over his malnourished body. Dave was taken into foster care at age 12, with his experience described by prosecutors as one of the worst cases of physical and emotional abuse in California history. Dave went on to a highly successful career as a bestselling author of award-winning books, including his autobiographies and a self-help book for teenagers facing adversities, and is himself now a husband and father.

---

double-edged strategies – one that helps the young child to cope with a maltreating family but which later in development interferes with other positive outcomes, such as the capacity for satisfying intimate relationships in adolescence.

Etiology: The Physically Abusive Parent

Parents perpetrate 80.9 per cent of child maltreatment, while other family members account for another 12 per cent (US Department of Health and Human Services, Administration for Children and Families, Children's Bureau, 2010). Because they are the primary providers of child care, *mothers* are the most frequent perpetrators of abuse; however, fathers and male caregivers are responsible for the majority of child fatalities (National Center on Child Abuse and Neglect, 2010). Child deaths are caused by extreme forms of assault, such as beating children about the head or violently shaking, suffocating or scalding them.

The Individual Context

Who would abuse a child? A simple explanation might be that these parents are mentally ill; however, the facts are not so simple. Almost nothing is known about male abusers; however, what can be said about the typical abusing mother is that she is *young*, having usually had her first child while still in her teens. Her *life stress* is high: she often has *many young children* in the home, enjoys few advantages, has *little social support* and lives in *poverty*. She may struggle with depression or substance abuse and be irritable and quick to anger (Runyon and Urquiza, 2011).

In addition, there are many ways in which abusing mothers appear to be ill equipped for the parenting role. Dukewich and colleagues (1996) found that lack of *preparation for parenting* – knowledge about child development, child-centredness and appropriate expectations for the parenting role – was the strongest predictor of abusiveness among adolescent mothers. Physical abusers also tend to have low *impulse control* and *frustration tolerance*. These parents may be unable to tolerate even the run-of-the-mill demands of child rearing; further, they are rigid in their choice of childrearing strategies and have few alternatives to physical punishment in their repertoire (Black et al., 2001).

The abusive parents' cognitive processing of child behaviour also appears to be problematic. For example, abusive parents engage in *cognitive distortions* regarding their children. These might take the form of misattributing behaviour problems to the child's *intentionality* (e.g., 'He *knew* it would get to me') or to *internal and stable* negative traits (e.g., 'She's a sneak'), or of *discrimination failures* when the parent allows negative feelings towards others to colour perceptions of the child (e.g., 'He's just like his father – no good!') (Azar and Weinzierl, 2005). The parent who perceives child misbehaviour as wilful and wicked is more distressed by it, and these negative attributions provide a self-justification for responding in a highly punitive way.

In addition, parental *depression* may play a role in these distorted attributions by reducing the parent's tolerance for stress and increasing the tendency to appraise events in negative ways, just as parental *executive functioning deficits* may contribute to a lack of flexible problem-solving, self-monitoring

and self-control. Azar and Weinzierl (2005) give an example of these cognitive processes in action in the scenario presented in Fig. 14.6.

The Cultural Context

Although found at all levels of society, abusive families on average are considerably below national norms on several socio-economic indicators such as income and employment. *Poverty*, *family disorganization*, *crowded housing* and frequent *disruptions* in living arrangements increase the likelihood of parent-to-child violence, with the risk increasing as the number of indicators increases (Begle et al., 2010). Abuse also tends to co-occur with many sources of *family dysfunction*, including parental substance abuse, divorce and separation, frequent moves and marital violence. The fact that there are so many negative influences operating at the same time in these families makes it difficult to isolate the specific effects associated with abuse. As noted earlier, while abuse rates vary with ethnicity, these findings are difficult to disentangle from the effects of social class and their interpretation is controversial (Malley-Morrison and Hines, 2004).

An Integrative Model

As with so many of the psychopathologies we study, the most likely scenario is one of **multideterminism** such that the risks in various contexts accumulate and interact with one another. Support for such a cumulative risk model is provided by Begle and colleagues' (2010) investigation of 610 caregivers of a child between the ages of 3 and 6 years. Risk markers were assessed in several domains, including characteristics of the parent (e.g., having experienced maltreatment as a child, parental distress, perceived control), the child (e.g., child age, health status and disruptive behaviour), the family (e.g., home disorganization, family size, household space) and the community (e.g., neighbourhood quality, availability of resources, family involvement in the neighbourhood). As the investigators expected, it was the *accumulation* of risk markers rather than those in any one sphere that acted as a significant predictor of child abuse potential.

FIGURE 14.6 Azar and Weinzierl's Cognitive Model of Abusive Parenting.

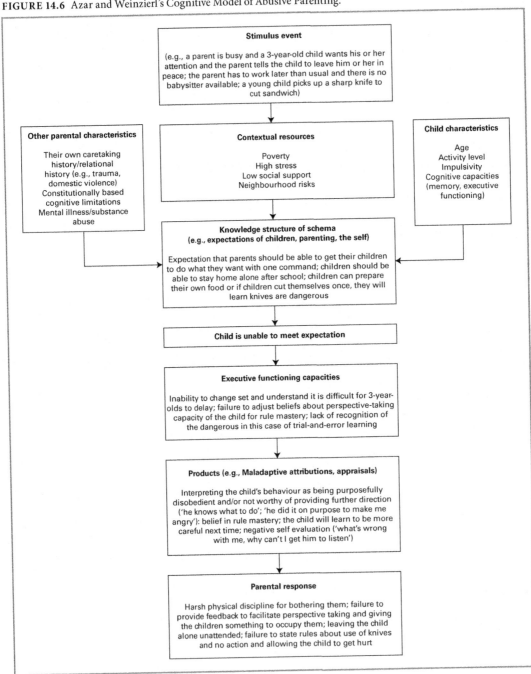

Source: Azar and Weinzierl, 2005.

Protective Factors and Resilience

Much has been made of the statement that abusing parents were themselves abused as children. Although it is true that abusers often were abused, those maltreated as children are not 'doomed to repeat'. Rough estimates of the *intergenerational transmission* of abuse are that around 30 per cent of children will go on to repeat the cycle of maltreatment in adulthood, although the state of the literature on which these estimates are based suggest that they are very rough indeed (Belsky et al., 2009). However, many parents are resilient and research has begun to identify the *protective factors* that account for such resilience. Studies have shown that high-risk parents who do not become abusers are likely to have had a supportive relation with the non-abusing parent while growing up. They also are apt to have a supportive adult relationship currently and to be experiencing fewer stressful events. Additionally, they are more openly angry about the abuse they received and more explicit in recounting not only the events of their past but the feelings their abuse elicited – this access to their own childhood emotions may help parents to empathize with their own children's distress and thus inhibit parents from being the cause of such distress (Egeland et al., 2000).

Neglect

Definition and Characteristics
Definition

The definition of **neglect** includes the failure to provide for a child's physical or mental health, education, nutrition, shelter or safe living conditions that the caregiver has the resources to provide (WHO, 2006). Erickson and Egeland (2011) describe five subtypes of neglect: *physical* (e.g., failure to protect a child from harm or to provide the basic necessities of food and shelter), *medical* (e.g., denying the child essential medical care), *mental health* (e.g., refusal to provide needed therapeutic interventions for a child with serious emotional or behavioural problems), *educational* (e.g., depriving the child of schooling) and *psychological* (e.g.,

failure to respond to a child's pleas for comfort, a category that overlaps with that of psychological maltreatment, which we consider separately later in this chapter).

As these definitions indicate, neglect is an act of *omission* rather than *commission* and thus it may be difficult to detect. For example, many 'accidental' deaths and injuries occur because children are left unsupervised, which may be a consequence of neglect. In addition, extreme emotional neglect itself may be fatal. Non-organic *failure to thrive* syndrome involves a failure of the child to grow, or even to survive, despite receiving adequate nutrition (Erickson and Egeland, 2011). Parental warmth and caring are so important to the developing young child that it may be impossible to thrive without them. As the international team of Gilbert and colleagues (2009) state, 'neglect is at least as damaging as physical or sexual abuse in the long term, but has received the least scientific and public attention' (p. 373).

Neglect may be more devastating to development than physical abuse.
© David Woo/Stock Boston

Prevalence and Child Characteristics

Although prevalence rates are complicated by the fact that neglect is defined vaguely and variously from location to location (Trickett et al., 2011a), the statistics available indicate that neglect is the most prevalent form of maltreatment, accounting for 71 per cent of all reported cases and 40 per cent of child abuse-related fatalities in the USA (US Department of Health and Human Services, 2010). In a recent national telephone survey, Finkelhor and colleagues (2010) found that about 1.5 per cent of children in the USA had experienced neglect in the past year and 3.6 per cent over their lifetime. Although previous research suggested *age differences* such that neglect was most prevalent in the infant and toddler period, more recent surveys of the literature suggest that school-age children and adolescents are equally at risk (see Fig. 14.7), as are children of both genders (Trickett et al., 2011b). *Social class* plays a role, with neglected children disproportionately likely to come from households living in poverty and in which parents have low levels of income and education.

In turn, Gilbert and colleagues' (2009) review of international prevalence rates found parent- and child-reports of neglect compiled only for the USA and the UK, where the range was from 6 to 11.8 per cent for lifetime prevalence.

Developmental Course

As with so many forms of child maltreatment, the study of the effects of neglect is complicated by polyvictimization. For example, Mennen and colleagues (2010) found that in their sample of 303 maltreated children, neglect co-occurred with emotional abuse among 61 per cent of youth and with physical abuse among 50 per cent. Therefore, as we noted in our review of research on physical abuse, most studies combine children who have experienced other kinds of maltreatment along with neglect. Nevertheless, there are data available to allow us to construct a developmental model that is specific to neglect in some if not all respects.

The Biological Context

The majority of the research cited earlier on biological dysfunctions in maltreated children includes those who have been neglected as well, and therefore

FIGURE 14.7 Incidence Rates for Child Maltreatment, Abuse and Neglect in the USA.

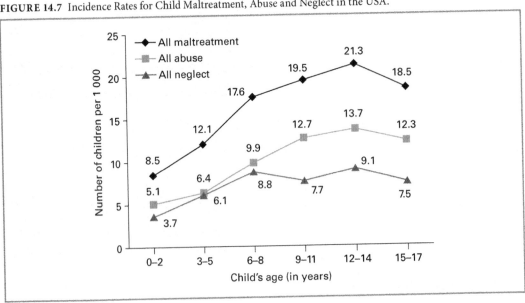

Source: Trickett et al., 2011.

provides a good summary of the neurodevelopmental effects of neglect (De Bellis, 2001; Perry, 2008). One finding that appears to be specific to neglect is its differential association with reductions in the *corpus collosum* in comparison to other kinds of abuse (Teicher et al., 2004).

Cognitive Development

Cognitive development and *language* development are more severely affected by neglect than by other forms of maltreatment (Erickson and Egeland, 2011). This is not surprising, because neglect generally occurs in an environment that is low in stimulation and responsiveness from the earliest years, with parents who show little interest in the child's achievements. Deficits in cognitive ability persist from early childhood to school age, with neglected children demonstrating more deleterious effects when compared to other abused children or controls. Neglected children have fewer basic skills at school entry and perform as much as two years below grade level on measures of language, reading and mathematics throughout their school years. Similarly, neglected adolescents achieve the lowest school grades of all abused children and are the most likely to repeat a grade (Veltman and Browne, 2001). As neglected children approach adolescence, adverse effects on achievement motivation and initiative are seen. For example, Steinberg and colleagues (1994) found that over the period of a year neglected adolescents evidenced decreasing interest in work and school and increasing involvement with delinquency and substance abuse.

Emotional Development

Neglected children demonstrate deficits in the *processing of emotion-related information*. They are less accurate in discriminating between emotional expressions (e.g., a happy versus sad face) perhaps because of the limited affective range they have been exposed to in the parent–child relationship (Pollak et al., 2000).

Insecure attachment also is a major consequence of neglect (Erickson and Egeland, 2011). Neglected infants relate to their mothers in ways that articulate clearly their sense of insecurity and their view of their mothers as unreliable and unavailable. They are less able to tolerate the stress of separation, to modulate their own affect and distress, and to cope with new situations. Whereas their *passivity* toward their mother differentiates neglected children from those who have been physically abused, increasing *anger and resistance* are seen through the toddler years.

Compared to other maltreated children, neglected preschoolers and school-age children demonstrate relatively more difficulties with *internalizing* problems, such as anxiety, sadness and social withdrawal (Manly et al., 2001).

Social Development

Neglected children's *passivity* with mothers extends to their peer relationships in the preschool years. They are generally described as avoidant, withdrawn, unassertive, lacking in social competence and unable to cope with challenging interpersonal situations. Observations of neglected preschoolers show that they *lack persistence* and enthusiasm, demonstrate *negative affect* and are highly *dependent* on caregivers and teachers for support and nurturance. As with preschoolers, neglected school-age children are more likely than either non-maltreated or physically abused children to remain *isolated* and passive with peers, to withdraw from social interactions, and to make fewer initiations for play (Erickson and Egeland, 2011).

A Longitudinal Perspective

Data from the Minnesota Mother–Child project provide an integrative summary of the findings reported in the previous section. The investigators identified a group of 267 at-risk pregnant women and followed their children into adulthood. (See Sroufe et al., 2005.) In infancy, two-thirds of neglected children demonstrated an *avoidantly anxious* attachment to their mothers. At 2 years of age, they showed a lack of enthusiasm, poor frustration tolerance, and non-compliance during a problem-solving task. At age 4, they were observed to have low impulse control, rigidity and negative affect. In their first year, they exhibited poor self-control, dependence on their teachers and general poor adjustment in the classroom. Neglect during the preschool years had a more pernicious effect than other forms of maltreatment and was associated with inattention, withdrawal from learning, anxiety, aggression, peer rejection, and poorer scores on tests of intellectual functioning and academic achievement.

Follow-up of these children in grades 1, 2, 3 and 6 showed that children neglected in their first two years were rated lower than other children in overall emotional health. Teachers described them as more socially withdrawn and unpopular than normative peers, and more withdrawn and inattentive than children who had been physically abused. Neglected children also were rated high in both internalizing and externalizing problems, and their achievement scores were lower than those of their peers. For example, only 1 neglected child out of 13 was not receiving some kind of special education in the first three grades of school.

In adolescence, those neglected in early childhood demonstrated a myriad of academic, social, behavioural and emotional problems. They had low scores on achievement tests, rated high in delinquent behaviours, substance abuse and school dropout, and were more aggressive and more likely to have made a suicide attempt than their peers. Whereas maltreated children as a whole were more likely than non-maltreated peers to meet criteria for a psychiatric disorder at age 17, the highest rate was for children whose parents were emotionally neglectful, all but one of whom received a psychiatric diagnosis.

Summary

The domains of development affected by neglect parallel those affected by physical abuse in many ways. However, *attachment* takes an avoidant form, and *emotional development* and *interpersonal* development are characterized by passivity and avoidance. *Cognitive development* is more negatively affected by neglect than by any other form of maltreatment. As Erickson and Egeland (2011) note it, neglected children do not expect to have their needs met in relationships, and so they do not even try to solicit care or affection; they do not expect to

be effective, and so they do not even try to succeed. Significantly, the effects of neglect do not appear to be moderated by the presence or absence of physical abuse; neglect derails children's development regardless. While the drama of overt violence receives the most attention, the effects of indifferent parenting are insidious yet devastating.

Etiology: The Neglecting Parent

Despite the prevalence and adverse effects of neglect, it is one of the least well-studied forms of child maltreatment. Therefore, less is known about the perpetrators of neglect than of other forms of abuse (Schumacher et al., 2001). Further, perhaps because women are more likely than fathers to be the primary caregivers of young children, the available research focuses exclusively on neglecting mothers.

The Individual Context

As with physical abuse, mothers are the most frequent perpetrators due to their role as primary caregivers to children. Like physical abusers, neglectful parents are characterized by high rates of stress, low social support, difficulties with substance abuse and impulsivity. However, there are a number of ways in which parents who neglect their children differ from those who are physically abusive. Neglecting parents tend to have a greater degree of *global distress*, as indicated by the presence of multiple psychiatric symptoms. Also, in contrast to the impulsive and intermittent nature of physical abuse, neglect occurs in the context of *chronic inadequacy*. Neglecting mothers experience more stress, failure, unmet needs, loneliness and discontent in all aspects of their lives. They tend to have few friends and to lack *social support*. In addition, neglecting mothers may have a general coping style that relies on such unhelpful strategies as *withdrawal, passivity* and *mental disengagement* to cope with life problems (Schumacher et al., 2001).

Neglecting mothers are likely to have *negative views about relationships* and to dismiss the importance of them. Thus, they see little significance in their parenting behaviour and have little motivation to change it. Further, these mothers are also likely to have personality characteristics – such as *low self-efficacy, self-preoccupation, depression* and developmentally *inappropriate expectations* regarding children – that interfere with their sensitivity to the child's signals or emotional distress (Crittenden, 1993). One explanation for this may lie in the histories of these parents, many of whom were maltreated in childhood. Those who were powerless to elicit care from others may be ill-equipped to provide it. They may even defensively block awareness of the child's distress just as they had to inure themselves to their own childhood unhappiness.

The Sociocultural Context

Although *poverty* is associated with increased risk for all forms of maltreatment, neglect is the *most* strongly predicted by economic distress (Erickson and Egeland, 2011). Neglectful parents are disproportionately likely to be living in households with incomes below the poverty line and to have low levels of education. As noted earlier, the overlap with poverty must be considered when we evaluate *ethnic differences* in rates of neglect. Some data suggest that, among children reported to Child Protective Services, 70 per cent of African American children are reported for neglect as opposed to 58 per cent of European American children (Office of Juvenile Justice, 2000).

Psychological Abuse
Definition and Characteristics
Definition

A widely cited definition of **psychological abuse** (also termed emotional abuse) is the one proposed by Hart and colleagues (1987):

> Acts of commission and omission which are judged on a basis of a combination of community standards and professional expertise to be psychologically damaging. Such acts are committed by individuals. . . in a position of differential power that renders a child vulnerable. Such acts damage immediately or ultimately the

behavioural, cognitive, affective, or physical functioning of the child. (p. 6)

Psychologically damaging acts are those that convey the message that the child is worthless, inadequate, unloved, endangered or only valuable in so far as he or she meets someone else's needs (Hart et al., 2011). Such acts might include *spurning* (e.g., rejecting, belittling, ridiculing or humiliating a child); *terrorizing* (e.g., threatening violence against a child or the child's loved ones, placing a child in dangerous situations); *isolating* (e.g., confining a child to the home, refusing to allow a child to interact with others outside the family); *exploiting or corrupting* (e.g., modelling or encouraging criminal or developmentally inappropriate behaviour, treating a child as a servant, coercing a child into playing a parentified role and meeting the parent's emotional needs at the expense of the child's own); and *denying emotional responsiveness* (e.g., interacting with a child only when necessary and failing to express affection, caring and love). Examples of each are provided in Box 14.3.

Prevalence and Characteristics

Because psychological maltreatment is the most difficult form of abuse to detect and to substantiate, rates are relatively low, accounting for approximately 7 per cent of substantiated cases (US Department of Health and Human Services, 2010). However, it is worth noting that the category of 'Other Abuse', which accounted for more than a third of the reports in the National Center on Child Abuse and Neglect's database, includes acts such as 'abandonment' and 'threats of harm' that would fit under Hart and colleagues' (2011) definition of psychological maltreatment. In Finkelhor et al.'s (2010) national survey in the USA, psychological abuse was experienced by 6.4 per cent of children in the past year and 11.9 per cent over the lifetime.

Moreover, it has been argued that psychological maltreatment is intrinsic to all forms of abuse. Physical abuse, neglect and sexual molestation all constitute major disruptions in the parent–child relationship that deprive the child of emotional

Box 14.3 Case Examples of Psychological Maltreatment

Spurning. Marcia's mother ridiculed her for showing normal emotions such as anger or sadness. The mother videotaped her when Marcia was upset and forced her and her siblings to watch the videotapes, pointing out how ridiculous Marcia looked when she was angry or sad.

Terrorizing. Frank's father secretly installed tape recorders and surveillance cameras throughout the house. The father reported to Frank and his siblings when they had gone to the bathroom, who they had talked to on the phone that day and any 'bad things' they said about him while he was at work. The children believe their father was omniscient and were terrified of him.

Isolating. Detia's family home-schooled her and would not allow her to play with the neighbourhood children. She could only leave the house with her parents or older sister, and she was strictly forbidden to converse with any adults or children who were not family members. She was told that other people didn't share the family's beliefs and were 'in league with the devil'.

Exploiting/corrupting. Tito's mother kept him out of school one to two days every week because she was lonely and wanted someone to keep her company while she drank. Tito would make sure that his mother always had a cold beer at her side, would laugh at her drunken jokes, would rub her shoulders and would make sure she had a comfortable cushion to support her bad back. Over time, Tito's mother encouraged him to drink beer to keep her company.

Denying emotional responsiveness. After her parents' divorce, Carolyn's mother accepted an overseas assignment and left her in the care of her father and her father's new girlfriend. The girlfriend repeatedly 'accidentally' locked Carolyn out of the house and once dropped her off at an amusement park and failed to pick her up at the end of the day. When a tearful Carolyn was brought to the police station, the father berated her and blamed her for not being where she was supposed to be at the appointed time. Although Carolyn's mother expressed anger to her ex-husband about how her daughter was being treated in the father's home, she refused to cut short her work assignment and care for the child herself. When children's services attempted to intervene, the father responded to their concerns by sending Carolyn away to a summer camp.

Source: Adapted from Hart et al., 2011.

security and thus involve psychological harm. However, despite the fact that psychological maltreatment *co-occurs* with other forms of abuse, evidence suggests that it has *specific* and *independent* consequences over and above those associated with its comorbid forms of maltreatment (Hart et al., 2011).

Developmental Course

Our review is based upon Hart and colleagues (2011) unless otherwise noted.

Cognitive Development

There is a correlation between psychological maltreatment and *cognitive delays* in young children. For example, Erickson and Egeland (2011) found that cognitive skills declined from ages 9 to 24 months for children of psychologically unavailable mothers. In addition, just as with children maltreated in other ways, psychologically abused school-age children demonstrate lower scores on achievement tests and poorer school performance when compared to non-abused children.

Emotional Development

Egeland's (1991) longitudinal study assessed two parenting styles that fall under the heading of psychological maltreatment: *verbal abuse* and *psychological unavailability*. These forms of psychological maltreatment in the toddler and preschool period had different effects from physical abuse and neglect. Whereas all maltreated children were noncompliant, had low self-control and lacked persistence and enthusiasm for tasks, psychologically unavailable mothering was associated with the most devastating developmental consequences throughout the early years. These included declines in *competence* and increases in *self-abusive behaviour* as well as other serious forms of psychopathology.

Not surprisingly, young children who are psychologically maltreated by their caregivers are disproportionately likely to develop insecure attachments, particularly the *disorganized* type (Finzi et al., 2001) which, as we know, is predictive of later severe psychopathology.

A number of studies have suggested that psychological abuse is related to the development of the cognitive style associated with *depression* in middle childhood, including low self-esteem, hopelessness, external locus of control and a pessimistic view of life, as well as self-harming thoughts and behaviours. Further, some studies find that depression is more strongly associated with psychological abuse than with other forms of maltreatment. *Externalizing* problems may also result. Herrenkohl and colleagues (1997) found that children subjected to parental criticism, rejection and terrorization demonstrated both *low self-esteem* and heightened *aggressiveness* during the school-age period.

Similarly, in adolescence, psychologically maltreated youths are at risk for *internalizing problems* such as depression, learned helplessness and low self-esteem. In addition, *emotional instability* has emerged as a consequence of psychological maltreatment. Thus, it is not surprising that other disorders of impulse control and emotion regulation, such as *substance abuse* and *eating disorders*, are seen in psychologically maltreated adolescents. In late adolescence, psychologically abused girls report frequent hospitalizations, somatic complaints and poor overall sense of well-being. Emotional maltreatment in childhood also predicts the development of eating disorders and personality disorders in the college years.

Social Development

Psychologically maltreated children demonstrate *poor social competence*. They are likely to withdraw from social interaction or to respond with hostility toward others. For example, data from a longitudinal study found that psychologically abused pre-schoolers were more aggressive than peers in elementary school and were more likely to engage in assaultive behaviour and delinquency in adolescence (Herrenkohl et al., 1997). In addition, Kim and Cicchetti (2006) compared the effects of various forms of maltreatment and found that only emotional maltreatment, and not physical abuse, sexual abuse or neglect, was related to increased rates of peer rejection.

Summary

Although frequently overlooked by child protection agents and psychological investigators alike, psychological maltreatment is embedded in the experience of all other forms of abuse and may even account for many of their effects (Hart et al., 2011). However, psychological maltreatment has *unique effects*, with pervasive and insidious consequences for development. While aggression is seen increasingly over the course of development, *depression* and *internalizing disorders* appear to be most strongly related to psychological maltreatment. The resulting negative views of self and others – feelings of worthlessness, self-loathing and insecurity – compromise the ability to get emotional needs met in current or future relationships.

Sexual Abuse

Definition and Characteristics

Definition

Sexual abuse is defined as the involvement of a child in sexual activity that the child does not comprehend, is unable to give informed consent to or is not developmentally prepared for; or that violates the laws and social norms of the community (WHO, 2010). The perpetrator may be an adult or an older child, typically when there is an age difference of five years or more. The sexual act itself may range from actual penetration to acts that involve no physical contact with the child, such as viewing pornography. The context may be sudden and violent, as in the case of rape, or may involve a long period of seduction and 'grooming'. The abuse may be acute or chronic over a period of years and the perpetrator may be a stranger or a family member, in which case the abuse is labelled *incest*. What constitutes sexual abuse varies from locality to locality, depending on the age at which laws specify that a young person is able to give consent. Thus, in many ways, sexual abuse differs from the other forms of maltreatment we have studied: the perpetrator may be any person, including an older child, and thus the abuse may not occur within the family context – in fact, most sexual abuse is perpetrated by *extra-familial adults* (Berliner, 2011).

One of the more recently uncovered forms of sexual victimization is via the *Internet*. Approximately 13 per cent of children report receiving unwanted online sexual solicitations, 9 per cent report sexual harassment and 35 per cent report unwanted exposure to pornography (Wolak et al., 2007).

Prevalence and Child Characteristics

Sexual abuse accounts for 9.5 per cent of substantiated child maltreatment cases in the USA (US Department of Health and Human Services, 2010). However, once again, evidence is strong that these rates underestimate the *actual* prevalence rates. In particular, reports to child abuse agencies compiled by the National Child Abuse and Neglect Data System (NCANDS) for this statistic involve only sexual abuse perpetrated by parents or caregivers, which comprise a minority of cases (Finkelhor et al., 2010). In a national telephone survey of 6000 adults, Tjaden and Thoennes (2000) found that 9 per cent of the women and 2 per cent of the men reported a history of a completed rape prior to the age of 18. In a similar study including only women, Saunders and colleagues (1999) found that among the 8.5 per cent of women reporting a childhood rape, the average age of first assault was 10.8 years and 60 per cent of the rapes occurred prior to the age of 13. The most common perpetrator (39 per cent of cases) was a non-familial person known to the victim (family friend, neighbour, co-worker, peer), whereas other adult relatives represented 20 per cent, fathers or stepfathers 16 per cent, boyfriends 9 per cent, and brothers 5 per cent of the perpetrators. In their most

recent telephone survey, Finkelhor and colleagues (2010) found that 0.3 per cent of US children acknowledged experiencing a sexual assault by an adult in the past year and 1.2 per cent did over their lifetime. The lifetime rates for boys were 0.3 per cent and for girls were 2.1 per cent.

The likelihood that official prevalence rates provide substantial underestimates is further underscored by the finding that, in retrospective surveys of adults, a striking 42 per cent of male victims and 33 per cent of female victims state that they never disclosed their childhood abuse to anyone. Similarly, in a study of children, MacMillan and colleagues (2003) found that only 8 per cent of those who had been sexually abused had had contact with child protection services.

As the data presented above suggest, there is a significant difference between sexual abuse and all other forms of maltreatment: the striking *gender ratio*. Overall, girls are three times more likely than boys to be victims of sexual abuse (Sedlak, 2010). *Age-related* differences reveal that older children and adolescents are most at risk, and the ratio of girls to boys also increases with age: 2:1 for infants, 3:1 for school-age children and 6:1 for adolescents.

International statistics reveal a similar story. Pereda and colleagues (2009) compared child sexual abuse prevalence rates in epidemiological data drawn from 21 different countries: Australia, Canada, China, El Salvador, Finland, France, Great Britain, Israel, Jordan, Malaysia, Morocco, New Zealand, Norway, Portugal, Singapore, South Africa, Spain, Sweden, Switzerland, Turkey and the USA. With some notable exceptions, such as China in which no sexual abuse was reported, and Portugal in which equal rates were reported for both boys and girls, both the prevalence and gender ratio were similar to those found by Finkelhor et al. (2010) in the USA. In turn, a compilation of population-based statistics from high-income countries around the world, including the USA, the UK, Europe, Canada, New Zealand and Australia, finds a cumulative prevalence of sexual abuse of 15–30 per cent for girls and 5–15 per cent for boys (Gilbert et al., 2009).

With regards to *ethnicity*, in the USA it appears that Latino adolescents report higher rates of sexual abuse compared to European American youth (Newcomb et al., 2009), whereas other studies suggest that children in the Native American community are disproportionately at risk (Malley-Morrison and Hines, 2004).

Other risk factors for sexual victimization include physical and cognitive vulnerabilities: for example, the incidence of sexual abuse among children with *disabilities* is 1.75 times higher than for their peers (National Center on Child Abuse and Neglect, 2010).

Developmental Course

Our discussion of sexual abuse is complicated by a number of factors that make this form of maltreatment unique. One is that the experience ranges widely from case to case: what is documented as 'sexual abuse' for one child may comprise a single incident of exposure to pornography, whereas for another it might involve repeated violent sexual assaults. It would be expected that these experiences would be associated with different kinds of outcomes. Sexual abuse that is repeated has more pernicious effects, as is that accompanied by violence or injury, as well as the terror that oneself or a loved one might be at risk of death or serious harm (Berliner, 2011). In addition, the stigma and shame surrounding childhood sexual abuse, especially when it occurs within the family, carries repercussions that echo more loudly when a child is silenced, not believed or is ostracized by others. Keeping these caveats in mind, we can summarize the available literature on the consequences of child sexual abuse. (For our discussion we integrate information from Berliner, 2011; Gilbert et al., 2009; Trickett et al., 2011b; and Wolfe et al., 2006, unless otherwise noted.)

Biological Development

Many of the acute symptoms of sexual abuse resemble general *stress reactions*. Particularly in the immediate aftermath of the abuse, signs include headaches, stomach aches, loss of appetite, enuresis, vomiting, sensitivity to touch and hypersecre-

tion of cortisol. However, a prospective longitudinal study by Trickett and colleagues (2010) found that sexually abused girls showed a pattern of attenuated cortisol response over time: although following the abuse, their cortisol levels were higher than those of non-sexually abused girls, over the course of adolescence and into adulthood, sexually abused females' cortisol levels dropped below those of the comparison group. In addition, asymmetry between indicators of sympathetic nervous system and HPA axis activity (e.g., cortisol reactivity and vagal tone) is implicated in the development of depression and antisocial behaviour among sexually abused girls in the transition from childhood to late adolescence (Trickett et al., 2011b).

A particular risk for sexually abused girls is the hastening of the onset of menarche. For example, Costello and colleagues (2007) found that, among a sample of 1420 adolescents, maltreated girls developed on average eight months earlier than those who were not maltreated, whereas no such relation between sexual abuse and puberty was found for boys. This finding also was replicated in the National Longitudinal Study of Adolescent Health (Foster et al., 2008).

Cognitive Development

Children who have been sexually abused are rated by teachers as having poor overall *academic competence*, including low task orientation, school avoidance and distractibility. Sexually abused teenagers demonstrate lower academic performance as well as more learning disorders (Trickett et al., 2011b).

The *cognitive attributions* children make about the sexual abuse have important implications for development. The abused children face the difficult task of processing the experience in such a way that they can make sense of it and integrate it into their developing schemata about themselves and others. Assimilating the experience can be further complicated by the distorted rationales given by the abuser: sexual violation is 'love'; abuse is 'normal'; a painful and degrading act is 'pleasurable'; betraying the secret makes the child 'bad'. The resulting attributions of *powerlessness, external locus of control,* and *self-blame* predict the severity of symptoms in sexually abused girls (Cohen et al., 2000).

Another set of attributions that contribute to the development of psychological and behavioural problems are those associated with *stigma* and *shame*. Feiring and colleagues (2007) demonstrated that, among 160 youth with histories of traumatic sexual abuse, stigma and shame following from the abuse were related to increased delinquent behaviour over the course of six years, and this relationship was mediated by internalizing, anger and affiliation with deviant peers. In turn, Stuewig and McCloskey (2005) found that parental rejection in the context of childhood maltreatment predicted increased shame-proneness over the course of eight years. In turn, shame-proneness was associated with adolescent depression.

Emotional Development

Most studies find that sexually abused children have *internalizing* problems, including fears, anxiety, depression, low self-esteem and excessive shyness. In the preschool years, the most frequent symptoms are anxiety and withdrawal. In young children, other emotional problems may include regression and loss of developmental achievements (e.g., bed-wetting, clinging, tantrums, fearfulness) and sleep disturbances (Berliner, 2011).

Further, one-third or more of sexually abused children meet the criteria for *posttraumatic stress disorder* (Cohen et al., 2000; see also Chapter 8), and PTSD is more prevalent among sexually abused children than among those who have suffered other forms of maltreatment (Finkelhor, 2008). One of the features associated with PTSD is utilization of the defence mechanism of *dissociation* to shut out awareness of upsetting thoughts and feelings related to sexual abuse (MacFie et al., 2001). The resulting fragmentation of self has negative implications for all domains of development (Cicchetti and Toth, 2005).

By middle childhood, many sexually abused children meet criteria for a diagnosis of *depression*. In adolescence, other signs of severe disturbance linked to sexual abuse include *eating disorders* and

substance abuse (see Chapter 12) and *running away*. In addition, childhood sexual abuse is a significant risk factor for *suicidal ideation*, suicide attempts and self-harming (Brodsky et al., 2008).

Social Development

A behavioural sign highly specific to sexual abuse is *inappropriate sexual behaviour*, including excessive masturbation, compulsive sexual play, seductive behaviour towards adults and victimization of other children (Berliner, 2011). Inappropriate sexual behaviour is most common in the *preschool period* and declines somewhat in middle childhood. Sexually inappropriate behaviour re-emerges in adolescence in the form of *promiscuity* in girls, *sexual coercion* in boys, and increased likelihood to engage in unprotected and risky sex. Sexually abused girls in particular are at increased risk for engaging in risky sexual behaviours, including a young age at first intercourse, failure to use birth control, engaging with a large number of partners and harbouring unhealthy attitudes about sexuality (Mosack et al., 2010; Negriff et al., 2010). In addition, a meta-analysis of 21 different studies indicates that childhood sexual abuse doubles the odds of teenage pregnancy among girls (Noll et al., 2009).

One of the dynamics of a sexually abusive relationship is that it is a psychologically controlling one in which the child is coerced to participate through manipulation or fear. Thus, sexually abused children are likely to develop an *internal working model* of others as untrustworthy and the self as shameful and bad. For example, victims of sexual abuse tend to believe that such abuse is pervasive and that adults are generally exploitative of children (Wolfe, 1998). This has negative implications for their self-esteem and capacity for forming satisfying relationships.

In addition, the sense that such abuse is inevitable increases the likelihood that sexually abused children will not be able to correctly identify or respond to risky situations in the future and that they will feel that they have no right to defend themselves against unwanted sexual attention. This is borne out by the fact that sexually abused children are highly likely to be *revictimized* over the course of development (Barnes et al., 2009). Particularly unfortunate is the fact that many of those sexually victimized in childhood will be victimized by the romantic partners they turn to for affection and affirmation: a child abuse history is a powerful predictor of adolescent *dating violence*. For example, Cyr and colleagues (2006) found that 45 per cent of the sexually abused girls in their sample had experienced physical aggression from a dating partner.

Long-Term Course

No one symptom characterizes the entire population and there is no pattern of symptoms that can define a 'sexual abuse syndrome'. In general, approximately one-third of child victims are *asymptomatic* over the long term. The number of children who either show no symptoms or recover may seem surprisingly high in light of the inferred traumatic nature of the experience. Remarkably, Rind and colleagues (1998) conducted a meta-analysis that showed that once all other variables were accounted for, university students who had been sexually abused in childhood looked little different from their peers. An important caveat to this meta-analysis is that it was based solely on studies of university students, who likely are a specific subset with more economic resources and better functioning overall than the general population of abuse survivors.

On the one hand, much of the variation in outcome may be related to the variation in the kinds of experiences that fall under the heading of sexual abuse, which range from a one-time experience of fondling to repeated violent sexual assaults. As might be expected, the factors that lead to the greatest number of symptoms are a *high frequency* and *long duration* of sexual contacts, the use of *force*, a close *relationship to the perpetrator* and oral, anal or vaginal *penetration* (Berliner, 2011).

In addition, there is a phenomenon called the '*sleeper effect*' in which the impact of an event occurs sometime later rather than immediately after an experience (Beitchman et al., 1992). For example, the effects of sexual abuse in early childhood may not emerge until adolescence when the youth attempts to cope with the stage-salient issues of sexuality and intimate relationships.

On the other hand, there is evidence for long-lasting effects of sexual abuse. Between 10 and 24 per cent of sexually abused children either do not improve or get worse with time (Berliner, 2011). One prospective study that followed sexually abused children over a five-year period found that, overall, there were no changes in symptoms of depression, low self-esteem and behaviour problems (Tebbutt et al., 1997). However, a closer inspection of the data revealed that this average was misleading. In fact, an equal number of children had deteriorated as had improved. Further, retrospective studies of adult women sexually abused as children show significantly higher lifetime and current episodes of *suicide, anxiety* and *conduct disorders*, as well as *depression, substance abuse* and *posttraumatic stress disorder* (Berliner, 2011; Trickett et al., 2011b). By the same token, by the time they reach manhood, boys sexually abused in childhood are at risk for *substance abuse, conduct problems* and *suicidal behaviour* (Garnefski and Arends, 1998).

Integrative Model

Finkelhor and Browne (1988) conceptualize the effects of sexual abuse in terms of four trauma-causing or *traumagenic dynamics*.

1 *Traumatic sexualization.* Sexual abuse shapes the child's sexuality in a developmentally inappropriate and interpersonally dysfunctional manner. The child may be repeatedly rewarded by affection, privileges and gifts for sexual behaviour and may also learn that sex is a means of manipulating others into meeting inappropriate needs. Traumatic sexualization may occur when certain parts of the child's body are given distorted importance and when the offender transmits misconceptions about sexual behaviour and sexual morality to the child.

The psychological impact of traumatic sexualization includes an increased salience of sexual issues, a confusion of sex with care and negative associations concerning sex or intimacy. The behavioural consequences might include sexual preoccupations, precocious or aggressive sexual behaviour, or promiscuity, on the one hand, and sexual dysfunctions and avoidance of sexual intimacy on the other.

2 *Betrayal.* Betrayal concerns the children's discovery that a trusted person on whom they depend has done them harm. During or after abuse, for example, children can come to realize that they have been manipulated through lies or misrepresentations about proper standards of behaviour, or they can realize that a loved adult treated them with callous disregard. Children can also feel betrayed by other family members who are unwilling to protect or believe them or who withdraw support after the disclosure. Betrayal can lead to a number of diverse affective reactions, such as depression and grief or anger and hostility. Young children in particular can become clingy because of an intense need to regain a sense of trust and security. Betrayal can produce a mistrust of others and subsequently can impair the adult's ability to judge the trustworthiness of others.

3 *Powerlessness.* When a child's will, desires and initiative are constantly opposed, disregarded or undermined, the result is a feeling of powerlessness. In sexual abuse, this can result when a child's body is repeatedly invaded against the child's will and when the process of abuse involves coercion and manipulation on the part of the offender. Powerlessness is strongly reinforced when the child's attempts to halt the abuse are frustrated and when efforts to make adults understand what is happening are ignored. Finally, a child's inevitable dependence on the very adults who

abuse and ignore them produces a feeling of being trapped.

Powerlessness can have two opposite effects. Children may feel anxious or helpless and perceive themselves as victims. As a protection against such terrifying feelings, they may go to the opposite extreme of identifying with the aggressive abuser or, less dramatically, may have an exaggerated need to dominate and be in control of every situation. The behavioural manifestations of powerlessness may include a number of symptoms such as nightmares, phobias and eating disorders, along with running away from home and truancy. There may also be learning and employment difficulties because victims feel unable to cope with the usual demands of life. At the other extreme, children might attempt to manage anxiety by 'turning passive into active', taking on the role of abuser themselves through aggressive and antisocial behaviour and even the perpetration of sexual abuse on other children.

4 *Stigmatization.* Stigmatization refers to the negative connotations such as badness, shame and guilt that are communicated to the child and then become incorporated into the child's self-image. Such negative meanings can come directly from the abuser, who may blame or denigrate the victim, or they may be implicit in the pressure for secrecy with its implication of having done something shameful. Positive feelings attached to the abuse (enjoyment of special attention and rewards, sexual stimulation) may further contribute to the child's feelings of being bad and blameworthy. Stigmatization may result from the child's prior knowledge that the sexual activity is deviant and taboo, and it may result from the reaction of others who hold the child responsible or regard the child as 'damaged goods' because of the molestation.

The psychological impact on the child consists of guilt, shame and lowered self-esteem. Behaviourally, stigmatization may be manifested by isolation and, in extreme cases, suicide. The child may gravitate to various stigmatized levels of society and become involved in drug abuse, criminal activity or prostitution. Stigmatization may result in a sense of being different from everyone else and a constant concern over being rejected if the truth were discovered.

Protective Factors and Resilience

The most consistently identified protective factor for sexually abused children is a *supportive relationship with the non-offending mother* (Deblinger et al., 2011). Contrast the experience of a child whose revelation is greeted with empathy and concern to the child who is disbelieved, held responsible, or criticized for getting the family in trouble. Accordingly, perceived support from the mother is found to be the most important mediator of the effects of sexual abuse on children's adjustment over time.

Etiology: The Sexual Abuser

As noted previously, the overwhelming majority of sexual abusers are *male* (82 percent of substantiated cases), in contrast to perpetrators of other forms of abuse. However, as was true of physical abuse, there is no specific type of person who sexually abuses children, nor is there a simple cause. To begin with, child sexual abuse might be just one manifestation of a more general state of being sexually aroused by children, or **paedophilia**. Paedophiles may experience sexual excitement only in relationship to children; some become sexual predators, while others may confine themselves to masturbating to magazine advertisements of children. Other sexual abusers also engage in relations with adult women.

A little-recognized fact is that a significant proportion of perpetrators are other *youths.* Juvenile offenders also perpetrate their crimes on the youngest children – 43 per cent of molestations of children under the age of 6 are perpetrated by adolescents. (A general guideline used to distinguish sexual abuse from normal childhood sexual exploration is an age difference of five years between the perpetrator and the victim.) In many cases – in some studies more than half – the victim is a sibling. The ratio of male to female adolescent sex offenders is about 20 to 1.

The Individual Context

Sexual offenders, both adults and juveniles, are a heterogeneous population (Chaffin et al., 2002). To date, no one psychiatric profile has been established that reliably characterizes the sexual abuser; however, there are a number of key risk factors, including psychological, family, peer and school problems. They are more likely than their non-offending peers to have *poor social skills* and *low impulse control. Language and learning problems* are prevalent, perhaps contributing to their social isolation. Many evidence significant *depression*, often related to their own histories of *sexual or physical abuse* witnessing interparental violence. In addition, they are characteristically exposed to antisocial male role models, and tend to exhibit compulsive sexual behaviour (Kirsch et al., 2011). Although child molesters are not necessarily likely to have higher levels of psychopathic traits (see Chapter 10) than others in the criminal justice system, those high in *psychopathy* are more likely to reoffend.

The Family Context

Characteristics of the families of sexually abused children include a more *distant* mother–child relationship, presence of *a non-biological parent* in the home, *lack of cohesion* and general *dysfunction* (Berliner, 2011). Madonna and colleagues (1991) conducted an observational study of families in which father–daughter incest had taken place. Family characteristics included a *weak parental coalition, enmeshment* and the discouragement of autonomy, and a *rigid* family belief system. Parents were described as being *emotionally unavailable* and showing an inability to appreciate the child's needs apart from their own. *Exposure to violence* in the home is prevalent, whether in the form of victimization or witnessing (Daversa and Knight, 2007).

Integrative Model

Finkelhor (2008) identifies four predictors that increase the potential for an adult to sexually assault a child, integrating the intra-personal, inter-personal, and sociocultural contexts:

1 *Motivation to sexually abuse.* Adults more likely to offend are those who are sexually aroused by children and are blocked from other, more appropriate sexual outlets. In addition, their emotional needs are sexualized, such that they seek love, care and attention solely through sexual gratification. Other emotional needs may include the need for power and control over another person, as well as the need to re-enact their own experiences of abuse and trauma. At the sociocultural level, the availability of erotic portrayals of children in advertising and pornography can foster these impulses.

2 *Disinhibition of internal constraints.* Characteristics of perpetrators that can overcome internal constraints include cognitive impairments, impulsivity, lack of empathy, use of alcohol and a family belief system that legitimizes incest or the use of children for sexual purposes. Further, the abuser may cognitively distort cause and effect in order to self-servingly rationalize the abuse as a response to the child's initiation. Superordinate factors might include weak legal sanctions against sex offenders and an ideology that supports adults' absolute rights over children.

3 *Disinhibition of external constraints.* The major factor here is the accessibility of a child to the abuser. Children most vulnerable to sexual assault are those who receive inadequate supervision, whether through parental stress, illness or intentional indifference. Living situations that provide opportunities for the abuser to be alone with the child contribute (e.g., children left unattended, sleeping arrangements that place an adult in a child's room). Superordinate

contributions include the erosion of social support networks for single mothers.

Overcoming the child's resistance. Although an adult is physically capable of forcing a child to engage in sexual activity, many abusers avoid physical force, instead using patience and sophisticated psychological strategies to overcome the child's will to resist. Often the abuse takes place only after a prolonged period of 'grooming' and gradual indoctrination. The abuser's power over the victim is enhanced when he is in a position of trust and responsibility – for example, as a coach, babysitter or step-parent – with which the child has been socialized to comply.

Exposure to Domestic Violence

As we noted earlier, a child does not have to receive a physical blow in order to be negatively affected by violence in the family. Witnessing domestic abuse, especially when it is perpetrated against the mother, in itself is a traumatic experience and investigators are increasingly coming to recognize its deleterious effects on child development (Graham-Bermann and Howell, 2011).

Definition and Characteristics
Definition

There is as yet no universally accepted definition of exposure to domestic violence, and different terms and typologies are used from study to study (Graham-Bermann and Howell, 2011). In addition, unlike other types of child maltreatment, exposure to domestic violence is as yet not universally recognized as a form of child abuse. Some states in the USA, such as Utah, classify as a separate crime domestic assault that occurs in the presence of a child.

Just as child abuse takes many forms, domestic violence may involve physical aggression, verbal threats, sexual assault and psychological abuse, all of which may be witnessed by the child in the home. The child need not be a visual witness to the violence in order to be affected by it. Hearing the cries – or even, in the case of a deaf child, feeling the thuds of the mother's body as she is thrown against the door of the room in which the child is hiding – is sufficient to inspire terror (Kerig, 2003).

Prevalence and Child Characteristics

In terms of *prevalence*, rates appear to be high worldwide. The World Health Organization (Garcia-Moreno et al., 2005) reports global data on rates of physical assault against women by their intimate male partners, which range from an astonishing 61 per cent in Peru to 6 per cent in Japan (see Fig. 14.8). Moreover, when women did seek help to end the abuse, concern for the welfare of their children was one of the most important reasons.

Although these data do not indicate directly whether children were present as witnesses during the assaults, other statistics indicate that this is highly likely. Whereas Gilbert and colleagues (2009) could not find international data on witnessing family violence for their review, Finkelhor and colleagues' (2010) nationally representative telephone survey in the USA found that 70.2 per cent of older children and 37.8 per cent of their sample as a whole had witnessed violence within their families. This included 6.2 per cent who had witnessed one parent assault the other in the past year and 16.3 per cent who had seen interparental violence in their lifetimes. Again, rates were even higher for 14- to 17-year-olds, 34.6 of whom had witnessed an interparental assault at some point in their lives. Rates of child witnessing are even higher in clinical

FIGURE 14.8 International Lifetime Prevalence of Women's Experience of Physical and Sexual Violence by an Intimate Partner.

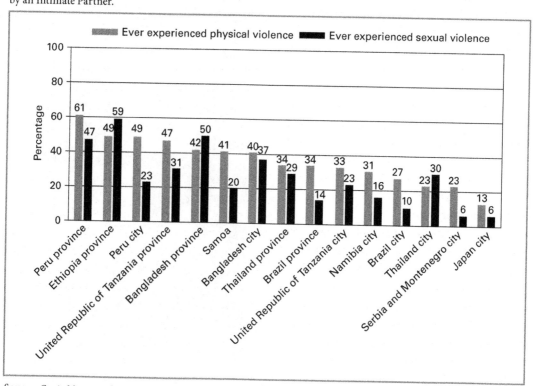

Source: Garcia-Moreno et al., 2005.

than in community samples. For example, battered women in one study reported that their children witnessed 78 per cent of all episodes of severe violence and 100 per cent of all episodes of mild violence between themselves and their partners (Graham-Bermann et al., 2009).

Ethnic differences also are found within the USA. A nationally representative survey of almost half a million households found that European American and Hispanic women were abused by intimate partners at a rate of approximately 8 per 1000 while rates for African American women were 35 per cent higher (11.1 per 1000). Native American women experienced the highest rates of all (23 per 1000) while reported woman abuse in Asian American families was the lowest (2 per 1000) (Rennison, 2001).

There is substantial *comorbidity* between exposure to domestic violence and other forms of maltreatment, with 30 per cent to 60 per cent of interparentally violent families also involving child abuse (Daro et al., 2004). Not surprisingly, those children who both observe and are the victims of violence in the home are the most negatively affected (Wolfe et al., 2003a). In addition to ways in which the physical abuse of partners might actively spill over on to children, children might be injured by accident during interparental quarrelling or used by batterers to manipulate the partner during a violent episode, such as by threatening to harm or to abduct the child in order to control the partner's behaviour (Jaffe et al., 2002).

Developmental Course

Our overview integrates information from extensive literature reviews by Graham-Bermann and Howell (2011) and Rossman et al. (1999).

Cognitive Development

Although children growing up in violent homes do not consistently show cognitive deficits, they often display academic problems. Distractibility and inattention in school may occur as a result of the trauma that is associated with exposure to violence.

Children's cognitive processing of the violence also plays a role in how they are affected by it. Studies of children's *appraisals* show that children who perceive the violence between their parents as frequent, intense and threatening are most likely to become distressed, as are those who engage in self-blame (Grych et al., 2003). Similarly, children may develop unrealistic expectations of their own ability to control their parents' quarrelling. Dangers of *perceived control* include that children may put themselves in harm's way by attempting to physically intervene in the fight, or that children may be left with feelings of guilt and inadequacy when they find they are unable to actually control the situation (Kerig, 2003).

Emotional Development

Research suggests that children exposed to domestic violence show a range of emotional and

Exposure to interparental conflict.
© *Sturti*

behavioural problems. In younger children, these include poor physical and mental health and *insecure attachment;* in the school years from 40 per cent to 60 per cent of children are rated in the clinical range on *externalizing* and *internalizing* problems, including aggression, depression, anxiety and low self-esteem (Wolfe et al., 2003a). Children from violent homes show also symptoms of *PTSD,* including nightmares, exaggerated startle response, intrusive thoughts and dissociation; and as many as 50 per cent meet full criteria for a PTSD diagnosis (Rossman and Ho, 2000). In adolescence, these behavioural problems intensify and are combined with *delinquent behaviour* and *suicidal thoughts.* One of the most sophisticated studies to date was conducted by Yates and colleagues (2003), who examined whether exposure to domestic violence had effects on children over and above any effects related to physical abuse, neglect, socio-economic status and general life stress. Using data from a prospective, longitudinal study of a sample of 155 children followed from birth through adolescence, they found that exposure to violence in the home was an independent predictor of *externalizing* problems in *boys* and *internalizing* problems in *girls.* The *timing* of the experience mattered as well. Whereas exposure to violence during the preschool years was the best predictor of maladjustment in adolescent boys and girls, the misbehaviour of boys during middle childhood was best predicted by *contemporaneous* violence in the home.

Not surprisingly, when children are exposed to uncontrolled anger and distress in the very figures they would turn to for soothing and solace, deficits in *emotion regulation* also are observed (Martinez-Torteya et al., 2009).

Social Development
Across the course of development, violence exposure has negative effects on children's *interpersonal relationships.* Preschoolers exposed to violence in the home display aggression and negative affect in interaction with others (Graham-Bermann and Howell, 2011). In the school-age years, they report more interpersonal distrust and poorer social skills

than other children and are more likely to endorse the belief that violence against women is normal and justified (Kerig, 1999). Consequently, in the adolescent years, it is not surprising that teenagers from violent homes are the most likely to become involved in *violent dating relationships,* thereby replicating the very abusive patterns they witnessed in the home (Kerig, 2010).

Resilience and Protective Factors
Although the research shows that children overall are adversely affected by exposure to domestic violence, there is a great deal of heterogeneity in their response. For example, Grych and his colleagues (2000) obtained parents' and children's reports of children's internalizing and externalizing symptoms. The investigators found that, of 228 children living in a shelter, 31 per cent could be labelled '*no problems reported*', in that they exhibited no significant behavioural or emotional difficulties. A further 18 per cent were termed '*mild distress*' in that they demonstrated low self-esteem, a few acting-out problems and mild depression and anxiety. Another 21 per cent were characterized as '*externalizing*', evidenced by clinically high levels of acting-out behaviours but no problems with self-esteem or internalizing disorders. Another group, comprising 19 per cent of the sample, was labelled '*multi-problem-externalizing*'. These children were characterized by severe conduct problems as well as some depression, anxiety and low self-esteem. In contrast, the 11 per cent termed '*multi-problem-internalizing*' evidenced high levels of depressive symptoms, low self-esteem and some conduct problems.

What *protective factors* account for the significant proportion of children who are resilient in the face of interparental violence? Grych and colleagues (2000) found that the children who demonstrated no or few measurable symptoms were distinguished from their peers by virtue of having been exposed to *less-severe* interparental violence, *less child abuse* at the hands of the father and less child abuse at the hands of the mother. Children's *appraisals* of the interparental conflict also differentiated among the groups but in complex ways. While children in the 'mild distress' or 'multi-problem-internalizing' groups perceived the fighting between their parents as more *threatening* than did the other children, children in the 'no problem' and 'externalizing' groups were the least likely to *blame themselves* for the violence. It appears that, whereas the absence of self-blame might protect children from violent homes from developing internalizing disorders, it does not protect them from developing externalizing problems.

Another important protective factor for children exposed to domestic violence is the quality of their *relationship with the mother* and her ability to provide structure, warmth and a prosocial model of relationships in the face of trauma and family disruption (Kerig, 2003). In addition, the mothers of resilient children demonstrate better overall mental health and more effective parenting skills (Howell et al., 2010).

Etiology: The Batterer

Dutton (2000) has noted that the clinical profile of the abusive man is remarkably similar to that of the victim of *childhood trauma*. Men who abuse their intimate partners evidence many of the symptoms of PTSD and have childhood histories that are marked by physical abuse, parental shaming and psychological abuse, and – significantly for our present discussion – exposure to domestic violence. Consequently, as we would expect, given our review of the literature on developmental psychopathology and child abuse, these men have difficulties with affect regulation, interpersonal problem solving, maladaptive appraisals and expectations, and aggression.

The underlying mechanism linking childhood maltreatment to adult intimate violence, Dutton (2000) proposes, is that of *insecure attachment*. Children who lack secure attachments are unable to soothe themselves in the face of threat, which may lead to unregulated emotion and, ultimately, to aggression. Consistent with this model, a specific attachment related risk factor for spousal violence is *rejection sensitivity*, the anxious expectation that others will fail to fulfil one's needs for acceptance and belonging (Downey et al., 2000). Downey and colleagues (2000) have found that men who are high in rejection sensitivity are more likely to misperceive the actions of others as rejecting and are more likely to respond to perceived rejection with hostility and physical aggression towards their intimate partners.

Emery and Laumann-Billings (1998) suggest we expand the frame of reference further, considering individual factors as only one of four interacting sets of variables that increase the risk of domestic violence. Their model suggests that violence is best conceptualized as a product of (1) individual *personality characteristics*, such as internal working models of attachment; (2) the immediate *social context*, including family structure and acute stressors, such as job loss or death in the family; (3) *community characteristics*, including poverty, inadequate housing, social isolation and neighbourhood violence; and (4) *societal factors*, including cultural beliefs such as those promoting the use of aggression in intimate relationships, and the prevalence of violence in the media.

Comparison of Maltreatment Types

Two kinds of data are available to allow us to distinguish the effects of different types of maltreatment. Most of the studies cited so far are *non-comparative* – that is, they are based on samples of children who experienced one or another form of abuse. A significant weakness of this research, however, is that frequently it asks only about a particular form of abuse. The children may have experienced multiple forms of maltreatment, but we do not know because the investigators failed to ask. This might muddy the waters if, for example, a sample of children identified as sexually abused actually comprises several subgroups, some of whom have also been neglected or physically abused. Our ability to observe whether any observed outcomes are specific to the effects of sexual abuse, therefore, will be clouded.

Despite these limitations, as the summary of this research presented in Table 14.2 suggests, trends can be found suggesting unique effects of specific forms of maltreatment. While *physical abuse* is associated with *aggression*, *neglect* is most likely to be linked to *social withdrawal*. Neglected children also show the most serious *developmental and cognitive delays*. *Sexual abuse*, in turn, is associated with *sexualized behaviour* and internalizing disorders, particularly *depression*. In general, the symptoms linked to sexual abuse centre around trauma-related emotional and behavioural problems rather than the cognitive and interpersonal problems that follow from physical abuse and neglect. In turn, *psychological maltreatment* is associated with the most significant levels of *depression*, as well as increasing *aggression* over the course of development. Lastly, *exposure to domestic violence* is related to the *intergenerational transmission* of violence in relationships with intimate partners.

Comparative studies, which directly assess the degree to which children have been exposed to various forms of maltreatment, are rare. Moreover, such research is often based on small samples and idiosyncratic measures; therefore, it is not surprising that the findings are not always consistent. In one of the most comprehensive studies, McGee and colleagues (1997) compared the effects of neglect, physical abuse, sexual abuse, psychological abuse and exposure to domestic violence on adolescents' functioning. The investigators found that *psychological abuse* overall had more pernicious effects on adolescents' mental health than neglect, sexual abuse, physical abuse or exposure to domestic violence. Moreover, psychological abuse exacerbated the effects of all other forms of maltreatment. Their study also shed light on developmental and gender differences in the effects of maltreatment. For boys, current adjustment was predicted by the interaction of physical and psychological abuse, and the interaction of neglect and witnessing domestic violence, when those experiences occurred in early childhood. Instead, for girls, adolescent well-being was most affected by an increase in neglect or psychological abuse from early to middle childhood.

Whereas boys appeared to be affected more by concrete manifestations of maltreatment, such as physical abuse and violence in the home, girls appeared to be more affected by damage to the parent–child relationship, such as non-nurturing or psychological abusive parenting.

In another study, Pears and colleagues (2008) compared the links between the functioning of preschool children in foster care and their histories of physical abuse, sexual abuse, physical neglect, supervisory neglect or emotional maltreatment. The results showed that children who had experienced *neglect or physical abuse* exhibited the lowest levels of *cognitive functioning*. In contrast, children who had experienced *physical or sexual abuse* were the highest in *internalizing problems*, whereas the children who had experienced all forms of maltreatment simultaneously had the highest levels of *externalizing*. In turn, a longitudinal study by Herronkohl and Herronkohl (2007) found that, whereas all forms of maltreatment assessed (neglect, physical abuse, sexual abuse and exposure to interparental violence) were associated with increased maladjustment from preschool to adolescence, the experience of *physical abuse* was the most strongly related to *externalizing* whereas *sexual abuse* was the most potent predictor of both *internalizing and externalizing*. As we can see, the fact that investigators select different dimensions of maltreatment to study, rather than being comprehensive in their approach, makes it difficult to summarize across the results of various studies.

Intervention and Prevention
Physical Abuse, Neglect and Psychological Abuse
Interventions for Abused and Neglected Children

Friedrich (2002) has developed an integrative model for intervening in individual therapy with maltreated children, focusing on three developmental domains affected by abuse: attachment, emotion regulation and self-perception. In the domain of *attachment*, targets for intervention include poor

TABLE 14.2 Developmental Summary of the Effects of Different Forms of Maltreatment

	Physical Abuse	Neglect	Psychological Abuse	Sexual Abuse	Exposure to Domestic Violence
Infancy and Early Childhood					
Cognitive	Cognitive delays	Most severe cognitive and language delays	Cognitive delays	Cognitive delays	Cognitive delays
Emotional	Avoidant attachment, limited understanding of emotions	Ambivalent attachment	Anger and avoidance, serious psychopathology	Anxiety, withdrawal	Anxiety, separation fears
Social	Fearfulness, aggression	Avoidance, dependence	Withdrawal, aggression	Inappropriate sexual behaviour	Aggression
Middle Childhood					
Cognitive	Cognitive, language delays, learning disorder	Most severe cognitive deficits	Low achievement and IQ, poor school performance	School avoidance, learning problems	Poor academic performance
Emotional	Poor affect recognition, externalizing (boys), internalizing (esp. girls)	Dependence, lowest self-esteem	Depression most likely, aggression	PTSD, fears, low self-esteem, depression, regression	Depression, anxiety, externalizing, PTSD
Social	Aggression, peer rejection	Isolation, passivity	Poor social competence, aggression, withdrawal	Inappropriate sexual behaviour, revictimization	Aggression
Adolescence					
Cognitive	Low academic achievement	Lowest grades, most likely to be retained	Low achievement	Poor academic performance	Truancy, poor performance in school
Emotional	Depression, low self-esteem, conduct disorder, violence	Internalizing, externalizing, low initiative	Delinquency, depression, poor emotion regulation, eating disorders, personality disorder	Depression, suicide, substance abuse, running away	Depression, suicidal thoughts, delinquency
Social	Aggression	Poor social skills	Pessimism	Revictimization	Violence in dating relationships

differentiation of self and other, the tendency to recapitulate the role of victim or victimizer, distrust and distorted perceptions of others. These issues can be addressed in therapy through establishing clear and appropriate boundaries between the child and therapist, as well as the therapist's consistent kindness and trustworthiness.

Emotion regulation is hampered by the experience of overwhelming negative emotions without the benefit of a soothing caregiver. Consequently, children who cannot tolerate strong emotions are likely to veer away from uncovering thoughts and feelings related to their abuse – just what is required of them in therapy. Techniques for addressing this problem include giving children control over the process, such as scheduling when and for how long they will talk about the abuse, or utilizing anxiety-reduction strategies such as relaxation training.

Lastly, abuse is a threat to the child's development of an accurate perception of *self*. Strategies for addressing this include fostering the child's development of an understanding of his or her own inner world. This may require refraining from rushing to offer blanket reassurances or offering effusive praise – although well meaning, these may ring false to a child who does not experience himself or herself as good-looking, smart or fun to be with. At the same time, the child can be encouraged to take progressive steps away from an 'all bad' view of self and to develop authentic realms of competence and mastery.

Interventions for Abusive Parents

Most intervention efforts involve the physically abusive parent rather than focusing solely on the abused child. For example, Azar and Weinzeirl (2005) describes a promising *cognitive behavioural* approach aimed at restructuring the distorted cognitions that lead parents to abuse. The intervention was highly successful. At a one-year follow-up, none of the parents in the cognitive behavioural group had abused their children, while 21 per cent of those treated with insight-oriented therapy had done so.

Parent–Child Interventions

Parent–Child Interaction Therapy (PCIT) is emerging as one of the leading evidence-based interventions for families in which parents maltreat children. Originally developed as a treatment for a broad range of behaviour problems, PCIT uses social learning principles to teach parents how to interact more positively with their children and how to elicit and reward good behaviour (Eyberg and Boggs, 1998). A unique aspect is the live coaching in which the therapist observes and provides feedback to parents through a 'bug in the ear' while they interact with the child. The first phase is child-directed and focuses on creating a more positive relational climate by helping parents to follow the child's lead and to describe, imitate and praise good behaviour during play. The second phase is parent-directed and focuses on giving parents more effective, non-coercive parenting strategies such as giving clear, direct commands, using praise for compliance, and providing consistent, appropriate consequences for misbehaviour (e.g., time out).

The effectiveness of PCIT for maltreating parents has been demonstrated in a number of studies. For example, Chaffin and colleagues (2004) randomly assigned abusive parents to PCIT or a community parenting group and found that parents who received PCIT had significantly fewer subsequent reports of physical abuse and more positive parent–child interactions. The intervention also has been expanded to include maltreated children removed from the home and their foster parents (Timmer et al., 2006).

Another promising family-wide intervention is Alternatives for Families – a Cognitive Behavioural Therapy (AF–CBT), which also includes child-only and parent-only components, as well as family-focused sessions (Kolko and Swenson, 2002). In both the child- and parent-focused sessions, attention is paid to the cognitions that result from, and contribute to, abusive behaviour. For example, children are helped to cognitive process their abuse experiences, and parents are assisted in examining their beliefs about violence and their unrealistic developmental expectations of children. In family sessions, parents and children work on communication skills and non-violent problem solving.

Results of controlled clinical trials indicate that parents who undergo AF-CBT are six times less likely to be subsequently reported for physically abusing their children than those who attend community-based 'treatment as usual' (Kolko et al., 2011). In addition, the AF-CBT materials have been adapted to incorporate suggestions from the African-American community for making them more culturally relevant (Kolko and Swenson, 2002).

Prevention of Abuse

Prevention programmes are the most promising of all in that their goal is to keep abuse from ever occurring. *Primary prevention* programmes might target at-risk parents either during the mother's pregnancy or at the time of birth and provide them with assistance at a number of levels: meeting concrete needs such as obtaining food, diapers, childcare or job skills training; enhancing parenting skills and efficacy through parenting education and support; increasing the quality of parent–child interaction through relationship-oriented interventions; and, in some cases, providing cognitive stimulation for the infant or individual therapy for the mother.

The most successful programmes are those that offer *home-based interventions*. A premier example is the Prenatal and Infancy Home Visitors Program (Olds, 1997). Four hundred low-income, adolescent and single mothers were contacted when pregnant with their first child. Home-based support was carried out by a nurse practitioner, who provided parent education regarding child development, involved the family and friends of the mother in providing an extended network of help and support, and linked the family to other medical and social services. Follow-up two years and even 10 to 15 years later showed that, in comparison to control group mothers, those who received home visits were 75 per cent less likely to be reported to child protection agencies, had fewer subsequent children,

spent less time on welfare and were less likely to be arrested or engage in substance abuse (Olds et al., 2007). The programme also is being adapted, developed and tested in five countries outside the USA: the Netherlands, Germany, England, Australia and Canada (Olds, 2008).

Parent–Child Interaction Therapy, which we described above, also has emerged as a promising preventative intervention for at-risk families. In an Australian sample, Thomas and Zimmer-Gembeck (2011) targeted 150 mothers who had a history of or were at high risk for maltreating their children. In comparison to a wait-list control, mothers who received 12 weeks of PCIT had more positive observed interactions with their children, and reported improved child behaviour and lower levels of stress. After the completion of treatment, mothers in the PCIT condition rated lower on a measure of child abuse potential, were higher in maternal sensitivity, and were less likely to be reported to child welfare authorities than those in the control group.

Sexual Abuse
Interventions with Sexually Abused Children

Meta-analytic studies confirm that treatments for sexually abused children are helpful in reducing symptoms, with the strongest evidence in favour of cognitive behavioural treatments (CBT) that target specific abuse-related appraisals such as self-blame and powerlessness (Harvey and Taylor, 2010).

As was true of the interventions for physical abuse we describe above, the most promising treatments for sexual abused children include a parent – although, in the case of child sexual abuse, specifically a non-offending parent. Trauma-Focused Cognitive Behavioural Therapy (TF-CBT) is a treatment that was originally developed specifically for sexually abused children but since then has been expanded for use with children exposed to a wide variety of traumatic events in childhood (Cohen et al., 2006). TF-CBT is grounded in cognitive behavioural theory but also incorporates principles from attachment theory, family systems and humanistic perspectives in order to best help parents to provide the kind of caregiving environment that will best help the child to heal. The treatment proceeds as a series of modules focusing on psychoeducation regarding trauma, sexual abuse and the PTSD response; emotion recognition and regulation; understanding the connections between thoughts, feelings and behaviour; and learning cognitive coping strategies. With these 'tools in their toolboxes' (Kerig et al., 2010a), children are then engaged in creating a narrative of the traumatic experience that helps to desensitize them from trauma reminders and allows them to uncover unhelpful thoughts and feelings – such as guilt and self-blame – that are keeping them 'stuck' in the trauma. Parents are actively involved in all phases of treatment. Specific components focused on parenting include providing parents with psychoeducation about trauma, increasing parents' adaptive skills for responding to challenging child behaviours, improving parent–child communication, supporting the child's practice of new cognitive and behavioural skills, assisting parents to manage their own post-traumatic reactions and coaching parents to respond in helpful ways to the child's trauma narrative.

A significant body of research exists to support the efficacy of TF-CBT for sexually abused children. For example, in one controlled trial, Deblinger and colleagues (2006) randomly assigned sexually abused children 8 to 14 years of age and their caregivers to either TF-CBT or to a child-centred therapy like those most typically offered in community mental health settings. Evaluations six and 12 months after the completion of therapy showed that children in the TF-CBT condition had fewer symptoms of PTSD and reported lower levels of shame, and their parents reported lower levels of distress regarding their child's abuse.

Interventions with Sexual Abusers

Kirsch and colleagues (2011) review the available research on interventions with sexual abuse perpetrators. Many different types of intervention have been implemented: one survey revealed that 338 different therapies were being used in various correctional institutions throughout the USA (Chaffin et al., 2002). Some unifying themes in the goals of treatment can be identified: (1) confronting denial, (2) identifying risk factors, (3) decreasing cognitive distortions, (4) increasing empathy for the victim, (5) increasing social competence, (6) decreasing deviant arousal and, when appropriate, (7) addressing the perpetrator's own history of victimization. Most use a group format under the assumption that confrontations are more powerful when voiced by a chorus of peers; however, the relative effectiveness of group versus individual treatment has not been established.

Reviews of the intervention research literature paint a mixed picture of the effectiveness of treatments for adult sexual offenders. The best that can be said, it seems, is that the likelihood of reoffending is decreased for *some* child molesters who complete the treatment programme. Overall, meta-analysis shows that recidivism rates for treated child molesters average about 12.3 per cent as opposed to 16 per cent for those without treatment (Hanson and Morton-Bourgon, 2005). However, effectiveness rates are higher among treatment studies that use CBT approaches (e.g., 9.9 per cent of those treated versus 17.4 per cent untreated).

Meta-analyses focusing on adolescent sex offenders report even better results, however, with 7.4 per cent of those treated recidivating versus 18.9 per cent of those untreated (Reitzel and Carbonell, 2006). Although most of the early attempts to intervene with teen sex offenders consisted of applying adult models directly to them, more recent efforts have been more developmentally informed. One promising intervention is MultiSystemic Therapy (MST), which we encountered in Chapter 10 as an intervention for conduct disorder. MST targets multiple aspects of the adolescent's social ecology, including school, family and peer relationships. Results of three randomized, controlled trials, some with a follow-up as long as 10 years, show the effectiveness of MST in reducing sexual and general recidivism as well as self-reported delinquency and risky sexual behaviours (Letourneau et al., 2009).

Prevention of Sexual Abuse

Most preventive programmes involve children and are aimed at teaching certain key concepts and skills. Among these are that children own their bodies and can control access to them; there is a continuum from good to bad touching; and trusted adults should be informed if someone makes a child feel uncomfortable or strange. Children are also informed that potential abusers are apt to be familiar individuals rather than strangers and are taught ways of coping with attempted molestation such as saying no or running away (Finkelhor, 2009).

Prevention programmes have been shown to be effective in increasing children's knowledge of sexual abuse and self-protection concepts. Younger children, such as those under age 5, are particularly likely to benefit, as are those who receive programmes that involve multiple sessions and actively engage children. However, evidence that such knowledge is effective in preventing sexual abuse or increasing children's disclosures is still lacking (Topping and Baron, 2009). Further, critics of these prevention efforts have pointed out that children who participate become more worried and fearful about the possibility of abuse, and indeed some school-based programmes do report such negative effects (Topping and Barron, 2009). On the positive side, there is evidence that sexual abusers are deterred by children who indicate that they would tell a specific adult about an assault. Thus, there may be significant benefits to teaching children, especially those who are passive, lonely or troubled, the simple strategy of telling an adult about attempted abuse.

An innovative programme developed in Germany used a theatre-based intervention to engage first-and second-graders in learning skills for distinguishing between good and bad touch, getting help, and defending themselves. Results showed beneficial effects of the intervention for children who attended the live performance or saw a DVD recording of it, and that those effects were sustained over 30 weeks afterward (Krahé and Knappert, 2009).

Exposure to Domestic Violence
Interventions with Battered Women and their Children

Developmentally sensitive and empirically supported interventions have been developed for children from violent homes (Graham-Bermann and Howell, 2011). A well-supported programme for school-age children is the Kids Club (Graham-Bermann et al., 2011), which provides parallel interventions for children and their mothers. The child groups provide children with information about family violence; address maladaptive beliefs and attitudes; and provide prosocial strategies for coping with emotional, behavioural and interpersonal problems. The intervention for mothers includes education about the effects of violence on children's development, parenting skills, and provision of support to increase empowerment and self-esteem. The investigators put their programme to a vigorous empirical test, randomly assigning participants to child-only, mother-plus-child, or comparison 'treatment-as-usual' conditions. Data from a sample of over 200 families showed that children who participated in the 10-week Kids Club improved more than those in the comparison treatment on such variables as social skills, safety planning, emotion regulation, and internalizing and externalizing symptoms; and these gains were enhanced by participation of the mother in the parent group.

Prevention of Domestic Violence

Group treatments have proven to be powerful tools in the prevention of interpersonal violence (Kerig et al., 2010b). For example, Wolfe and colleagues (1997) developed the Youth Relationships Project to prevent the development of violent dating relationships among at-risk teenagers. Peer groups are used to address the history of exposure to family violence that characterizes so many of the teens who go on to abuse their partners and attempt to counter the maladaptive beliefs that justify the use of force in intimate relationships. An evaluation of the programme was conducted with teenagers aged 14 to 17 years who were referred from social service agencies due to their exposure to violence in the home. Following participation in the groups, the investigators saw positive changes in the youths' attitudes, knowledge and endorsement of the use of violence in relationships with girlfriends or boyfriends (Wolfe et al., 2003b).

Having explored factors in the biological, intrapersonal and interpersonal contexts that place children and adolescents at risk for developing problem behaviour, we now move onward in our developmental time line and begin to explore the late adolescent transition into adulthood. In Chapter 15 our concern will be with extreme disturbances in the development of self, namely, the emergence of personality disorders.

Late Adolescence to Early Adulthood: The Emergence of Borderline Personality Disorder

Chapter contents

Our next topic marks a dramatic shift. Whereas substance use may be a part of normative adolescent exploration, and substance abuse the extreme end of a continuum, **personality disorders** represent profound deviations from normal self-development. DSM-IV-TR (2000) defines a personality disorder as 'an enduring pattern of inner experience and behavior that deviates markedly from the expectations of the individual's culture' (p. 686). The disorder must be manifested in at least two of the following areas: *cognition, affectivity, interpersonal functioning* or *impulse control*. Further, this pattern is *inflexible and pervasive across a broad range of personal and social situations, leads to significant distress and functional impairment, is stable and of long duration*, and has an *onset in adolescence or early adulthood*.

In DSM-IV-TR, the personality diagnoses are grouped into three clusters, based upon their common characteristics. Cluster A comprises disorders in which individuals appear odd or eccentric, including: *paranoid*, characterized by pervasive distrust and suspiciousness of others; *schizoid*, in which the person is detached from social relationships and expresses limited emotion; and *schizotypal*, involving pervasive interpersonal deficits, social discomfort, cognitive and perceptual distortions, and eccentric behaviour. Cluster B comprises disorders in which individuals appear dramatic and emotional, including: *histrionic*, which features excessive emotionality and attention-seeking behaviour; *narcissistic*, involving grandiosity, a need for admiration and a lack of empathy; *antisocial*, which, as we encountered in Chapter 10, involves a pervasive pattern of disregard for the rights of others; and *borderline*, marked by instability in self-image, emotions and relationships. Cluster C comprises disorders in which individuals appear anxious or fearful, and includes: *obsessive-compulsive*, featuring a preoccupation with orderliness, perfectionism and personal control; *avoidant*, characterized by social inhibition, feelings of inadequacy and hypersensitivity to criticism; and *dependent*, distinguished by a pattern of clinging submissive behaviour and fear of separation.

To focus our discussion in this chapter, however, we will target the only personality psychopathology that to date has gleaned extensive developmental theory and research, and that is *borderline personality disorder*.

Should Personality Disorder Diagnoses Be Applied to Youth?

Before we proceed, given the emphasis on 'enduring patterns', 'stability', and 'inflexibility' in the DSM criteria described in the previous section, our knowledge of development requires that we stop to ask: *can* and *should* youth be described as having personality disorders? Children and adolescents, as we have seen, change dramatically over the course of normal development, their levels of functioning waxing and waning over time. Some personality traits that might be regarded as pathological in adulthood are developmentally appropriate at earlier stages (Johnson et al., 2006). Adolescence in particular is a developmental period marked by inconsistency, volatile emotions and deviant behaviour, which might lead to an excess of 'false positives' in the diagnosis of personality disorder (Geiger and Crick, 2010). Moreover, over the course of childhood, many factors might intervene to change the trajectory of a child's developmental path; therefore, considerable hesitation is warranted before we conclude that a child's personality is a fixed or immutable 'type'. For example, one study found that among adolescents diagnosed with personality disorders, less than half retained the diagnosis over the course of two years (Bernstein et al., 1993). Given the

negative stigma and pessimistic prognosis associated with a diagnosis of personality disorder, there is concern among some clinicians that the diagnosis might do more harm than good.

Therefore, only under exceptional circumstances may a person under age 18 be given a diagnosis of personality disorder. DSM-IV-TR specifies that personality disorders may be applied to children and adolescents in *unusual instances* in which the maladaptive personality traits are *pervasive and long lasting* (at least one year) and are *likely to persist across developmental periods*.

Keeping these cautions in mind, there are a number of reasons why it is appropriate for us to explore the topic of personality disorder in our discussion of the emerging adulthood transition. First, over the course of adolescence there is an increasing coherence and predictability in emotions, attitudes and behaviour, and thus stability in personality. Second, one of the stage-salient issues of adolescence is the development of a sense of identity. Thus, we should consider the plight of those who fail to develop a coherent sense of self, as is the case in borderline personality. Third, personality disorders generally are recognizable by adolescence or even earlier in development (Johnson et al., 2006). Thus, as theory proposes and research confirms, the roots of personality disorder can be traced to childhood experiences. Therefore it is in childhood that must seek those roots.

Lastly, and for all of the reasons enumerated above, the field of developmental psychopathology recently has begun looking closely at the phenomenon of personality disorders in childhood and adolescence (Cicchetti and Crick, 2009a, 2009b) – but only very recently. After a period of long neglect, the study of personality disorder development is beginning to come to the fore.

One of the features of recent thinking that has helped child and adolescent personality research to burgeon is investigators' willingness to eschew the DSM categorical model in favour of looking at *dimensions* of personality (Tacket et al., 2009). In particular, a number of laboratories in the USA and Europe have been studying the downward extension of the adult 'Big Five' five-factor model of personality, termed the 'Little Five' (Widiger et al., 2009). The most robust typology identifies these dimensions as neuroticism, extraversion, openness, agreeableness and conscientiousness. (See Table 15.1). Just as with adults, the research indicates that these are valid and reliable dimensions of personality that can be detected in children and adolescents and that are predictive of later functioning (De Clercq et al., 2009). The research is too new to yield the fruits of longitudinal data, but a plausible argument is made that these personality features might predict and underlie the development of later personality disorders.

Borderline Personality Disorder: Definition and Characteristics

DSM-IV-TR Criteria

A common thread running through all of the characteristics associated with borderline personality disorder (BPD) is *inconsistency*: in interpersonal relationships, emotions, behaviour and self-image. Nine specific criteria are listed in DSM-IV-TR (see Table 15.2). For example, those with BPD evidence an *unstable sense of self*, with pervasive feelings of being empty, damaged or less than human. *Impulsivity* and *self-destructiveness* are often seen, including such extreme behaviour as *self-mutilation*. In addition, the relationships of individuals with BPD are marked by excessive *fear of abandonment* and extreme shifts between the opposite poles of *idealization* and *devaluation* of other people. Affects are *intense and unregulated*, and therefore the experience of strong emotions, particularly anxiety and anger, can be highly disruptive to functioning. Anxiety quickly escalates to panic and anger to unmodulated rage.

This description makes apparent why BPD is called a disorder of the *self*. Such dramatic and rapid shifts in mood, and in perceptions of self and others, interfere with the individual's ability to maintain a consistent sense of identity. A description of an adolescent diagnosed with BPD is presented in Box 15.1.

ICD-10 Criteria

In the ICD-10 (WHO, 2007), the category associated with BPD is Emotionally Unstable Personality Disorder (F60.3), Borderline type. This is defined as:

A personality disorder characterized by a definite tendency to act impulsively and without consideration of the consequences; the mood is unpredictable and capricious. There is a liability to outbursts of emotion and an incapacity to control the behavioural explosions. There is a tendency to quarrelsome behaviour and to conflicts with others, especially when impulsive acts are thwarted or censored. Two types may be distinguished: the impulsive type, characterized predominantly by emotional instability and lack of impulse control, and the borderline type, characterized in addition by disturbances in self-image, aims, and internal preferences, by chronic feelings of emptiness, by intense and unstable interpersonal relationships, and by a tendency to self-destructive behaviour, including suicide gestures and attempts.

The ICD and DSM criteria clearly are consistent and appear to be describing the same disorder, with emotion dysregulation and instability at its core. The ICD description is more fine-tuned, however, with the differentiation of primarily behaviourally disordered (impulsive) and self-disordered (borderline) subtypes.

Big Five Personality Dimensions

When viewed within the dimensional framework of the Big Five personality model, research conducted in Belgium and the Netherlands shows that adolescents who meet criteria for BPD are high on *neuroticism*, and low on *agreeableness* and *conscientiousness* (De Clercq et al., 2006; Tromp and Koot, 2009). Future longitudinal research will be needed to tell us whether

TABLE 15.1 Five Factor Model of Personality

	Maladaptively High	Normal High	Normal Low	Maladaptively Low
Neuroticism				
Anxiousness	Fearful, anxious	Vigilant, worrisome, wary	Relaxed, calm	Oblivious to signs of threat
Angry hostility	Rageful	Brooding, resentful, defiant	Even tempered	Will not even protest exploitation
Depressiveness	Depressed, suicidal	Pessimistic, discouraged	Not easily discouraged	Unrealistic, overly optimistic
Self-consciousness	Uncertain of self or identity	Self-conscious, embarrassed	Self-assured, charming	Glib, shameless
Impulsivity	Unable to resist impulses	Self-indulgent	Restrained	Overly restrained
Vulnerability	Helpless, emotionally unstable	Vulnerable	Resilient	Fearless, feels invincible
Extraversion				
Warmth	Intense attachments	Affectionate, warm	Formal, reserved	Cold, distant
Gregariousness	Attention seeking	Sociable, outgoing, personable	Independent	Isolated
Assertiveness	Dominant, pushy	Assertive, forceful	Passive	Resigned, uninfluential
Activity	Frantic	Energetic	Slow paced	Lethargic, sedentary
Excitement seeking	Reckless, foolhardy	Adventurous	Cautious	Dull, listless
Positive emotions	Melodramatic, manic	High spirited, cheerful, joyful	Placid, sober, serious	Grim, anhedonic
Openness				
Fantasy	Unrealistic, lives in fantasy	Imaginative	Practical, realistic	Concrete
Aesthetics	Bizarre interests	Aesthetic interests	Minimal aesthetic interests	Disinterested
Feelings	Intense, in turmoil	Self-aware, expressive	Constricted, blunted	Alexithymic
Actions	Eccentric	Unconventional	Predictable	Mechanized, stuck in routine
Ideas	Peculiar, weird	Creative, curious	Pragmatic	Closed minded
Values	Radical	Open, flexible	Traditional	Dogmatic, moralistically intolerant
Agreeableness				
Trust	Gullible	Trusting	Cautious, sceptical	Cynical, suspicious
Straightforwardness	Guileless	Honest, forthright	Savvy, cunning, shrewd	Deceptive, dishonest, manipulative
Altruism	Self-sacrificial, selfless	Giving, generous	Frugal, withholding	Greedy, exploitative
Compliance	Yielding, docile, meek	Co-operative, obedient, deferential	Critical, contrary	Combative, aggressive

TABLE 15.1 (Continued)

	Maladaptively High	Normal High	Normal Low	Maladaptively Low
Modesty	Self-effacing, self-denigrating	Humble, modest, unassuming	Confident, self-assured	Boastful, pretentious, arrogant
Tender-mindedness	Overly soft-hearted	Empathic, sympathetic, gentle	Strong, tough	Callous, merciless, ruthless
Conscientiousness				
Competence	Perfectionistic	Efficient, resourceful	Casual	Disinclined, lax
Order	Preoccupied with organization	Organized, methodical	Disorganized	Careless, sloppy, haphazard
Dutifulness	Rigidly principled	Dependable, reliable, responsible	Easygoing, capricious	Irresponsible, undependable, immoral
Achievement	Workaholic	Purposeful, diligent, ambitious	Carefree, content	Aimless, shiftless, desultory
Self-discipline	Single minded doggedness	Self-disciplined, willpower	Leisurely	Negligent, hedonistic
Deliberation	Ruminative, indecisive	Thoughtful, reflective, circumspect	Quick to make decisions	Hasty, rash

Source: Widiger et al., 2009.

the presence of these personality dimensions preceded, and thus led to, borderline pathology.

Prevalence

A series of large-scale prevalence studies conducted in Australia, the UK, Norway and the USA is reviewed by Distel and colleagues (2009). Overall, BPD is estimated to be present in about 2 per cent of the general population, 10 per cent of outpatients in mental health centres and 20 per cent of psychiatric inpatients. Among those diagnosed with personality disorder, 30 to 60 per cent carry the borderline label. The disorder is diagnosed predominantly in *females* (about 75 per cent). Few prevalence studies of BPD have focused on children or adolescents specifically, and few epidemiological studies involving children and adolescence inquire about personality disorders. There are two exceptions, both conducted in the USA. In a randomly selected community sample of 733 youths in upstate New York, Bernstein and colleagues (1993) found surprisingly high prevalence rates of 11 per cent among 9- to 19-year-olds, with prevalence

rates of 7.8 per cent among those same youth at a follow-up two years later. More girls than boys met criteria for the diagnosis at each time point.

Another notable exception is the Collaborative Personality Disorders Study, which followed a group of 658 youth drawn from the general population in New York over a period of nine years (Johnson et al., 2000; Skodol et al., 2007b). BPD traits were present among 1.7 per cent of youths 9–12 years of age, 1.5 per cent of those 13–16 years of age, 1.1 per cent of those 17–20 years of age, 1.0 of those 21–24 years of age and 0.7 of those ages 25–28. Thus there was a 59 per cent decline in symptoms of BPD across the span of the study. However, those youth who were high in BPD traits in early adolescence also had significant levels of BPD traits in emergent adulthood.

Criteria Specific to Children and Adolescents

Although clinicians only apply the label of BPD to young people with great caution, those who have observed extremely disturbed children in clinical

TABLE 15.2 DSM-IV-TR Criteria for Borderline Personality Disorder

A pervasive pattern of instability of interpersonal relationships, self-image, and affects, and marked impulsivity beginning by early adulthood and present in a variety of contexts, as indicated by five or more of the following:

(1) Frantic efforts to avoid real or imagined abandonment.

(2) A pattern of unstable and intense interpersonal relationships characterized by alternating between extremes of idealization and devaluation.

(3) Identity disturbance: Markedly and persistently unstable self-image or sense of self.

(4) Impulsivity in at least two areas that are potentially self-damaging (e.g., spending, sex, substance abuse, reckless driving, binge eating).

(5) Recurrent suicidal behavior, gestures, or threats, or self-mutilating behavior.

(6) Affective instability due to a marked reactivity of mood (e.g., intense episodic dysphoria, irritability, or anxiety usually lasting a few hours and only rarely more than a few days).

(7) Chronic feelings of emptiness.

(8) Inappropriate, intense anger or difficulty controlling anger (e.g., frequent displays of temper, constant anger, recurrent physical fights).

(9) Transient, stress-related paranoid ideation or severe dissociative symptoms.

Source: Adapted from DSM-IV-TR, 2000.

settings have argued that some of them do show characteristics consistent with the adult diagnosis. However, because the DSM criteria are adult oriented, others have proposed specific criteria to help us identify children with borderline pathology.

For example, Bemporad and colleagues (1982) describe five features common to children with borderline pathology. The first of these is *rapid shifts in levels of functioning*. The developmental level of children with BPD is uneven and unpredictable, sometimes age appropriate, and at other times immature or even primitive. Secondly, there is a *chronic presence of anxiety* as well as an inability to regulate affect. These children appear to be in a state of constant distress and may develop obsessions, rituals, phobias and other so-called 'neurotic' behaviours in an attempt to manage their emotions. However, they lack effective defence mechanisms and coping strategies with which to calm themselves. Therefore, they are vulnerable to being overwhelmed by their negative feelings and may experience episodes of panic and disorganization that look almost psychotic. Thirdly, their thought content and processes show excessive *fluidity between reality and fantasy*. Although children with BPD are not schizophrenic, their fantasies intrude on their reality testing to an extent that is disrup-

tive. One reason borderline children may find it difficult to avoid preoccupation with their internal worlds is that their fantasies tend to be extremely anxiety-arousing, concerned with disturbing images of self-annihilation, body mutilation and catastrophe. Fourth, their relationships with others show an *excessive need for support* and reassurance that is sought in all interactions, not only from attachment figures. Bemporad and colleagues (1982) describe these children as having an 'as-if' personality in which they over-identify with the other person, as though they are trying to merge with the other in order to avoid feeling separate and alone. Fifth, children with BPD demonstrate a *lack of control over impulses*. They find it difficult to delay gratification and tolerate frustration, which may lead to extreme rage and temper tantrums inappropriate for their developmental level.

An early attempt to validate these criteria met with some success given that they were able to distinguish between children diagnosed as borderline and those in a control group (Bentivegna et al., 1985). However, the field generally continues to utilize the standard DSM criteria. Despite concerns about the appropriateness of the DSM diagnosis for young people, evidence is accumulating that BPD can be reliably and validly detected, at

Box 15.1 Case Study in Borderline Personality Disorder

Wendy was described as a charming and coy 17-year-old upon her admission to Chestnut Lodge Hospital. She had been transferred from another private psychiatric institution after attempting to choke her latest therapist. Hospitalized the prior three years for cutting herself and assaulting others, Wendy had exhausted numerous therapists and defeated all treatment interventions. Having fired one doctor after another, Wendy set personnel against one another and displayed a genius for finding the sensitive areas of staff members' psyches and exploiting them. In defeat, the institution recommended a transfer to Chestnut Lodge, a long-term residential treatment centre.

Wendy's developmental history was a troubled one. She was the third of four siblings born to a wealthy family. Although the father was trained as an engineer, he never worked because Wendy's mother demanded that he stay home with her. However, their married life was coloured by quarrelling, heavy drinking, physical fights often culminating in bloodshed, and sexual promiscuity with others. When drunk, the father was physically and emotionally abusive while the mother retreated to her bed – cared for by a private nurse – and left the children to fend for themselves. Whereas the mother frequently was emotionally unavailable, when present she was disapproving, mean and frightening, behaving in a sexually seductive and inappropriate manner with Wendy and her brothers.

From age 4 onwards, Wendy was frequently sent away to camp, where she inevitably became ill and was extremely accident prone. Wendy's behavioural problems emerged in grade school and took the form of temper tantrums and holding her breath when upset. Despite her behaviour problems, however, she managed to make good grades and score in the average to above-average range on achievement tests. After school, her main playmate was her elder brother Eric, whose favourite game took the form of strangling birds to the edge of death and then attempting resuscitation. The neighbouring families forbade their children to play with Wendy and her brother.

By the age of 10 Wendy was cutting herself in reaction to anger and humiliation. As she approached puberty, her father's friends made sexual advances to her at drunken parties on the family compound. When Wendy was 13, what little family life existed was shattered by her mother's death in a fire that resulted from a lit cigarette the mother held while passed out in a drunken stupor. Wendy's behaviour became increasingly disorganized and unmanageable after her mother's funeral. She rampaged through the house breaking furniture, refused to attend school and assaulted playmates. Her father arranged treatment with a psychoanalyst, who quickly recommended boarding school. Once there, Wendy beat up the younger children at the slightest provocation and any form of reprimand from her teachers further inflamed her rage. After a year in the school, Wendy pleaded successfully to be allowed to return to live with her newly remarried father. Within weeks, however, Wendy decided that she hated her step-family and hit her step-sisters at every opportunity.

At this time, when Wendy was 14, her father placed her in a home for emotionally disturbed children. Upon entering the home, Wendy purposefully cut her leg, a wound that became infected and led to a long period of time in traction. Once recuperated, Wendy jumped across the net while playing tennis, fell and broke her wrist. Her father visited and accused her of breaking her wrist on purpose. In response, Wendy cut the bottoms of her feet. After only two months in the home, the headmistress informed Wendy that the staff were incapable of providing further care for her and the first of Wendy's many psychiatric hospitalizations was arranged.

Source: Adapted from Judd and McGlashan, 2003.

least among adolescents (Becker et al., 2002; Miller et al., 2008).

Comorbidity and Differential Diagnosis

Many youths diagnosed with borderline personality first present to the clinic with problems related to aggression and *conduct disorder* and the two disorders frequently co-occur (Becker et al., 2006; Zelkowitz et al., 2007). A link to the psychopathic subtype of conduct disorder also is suggested (see Chapter 10). For example, in a non-clinical sample of French youth, Chabrol and Leichsenring (2006) found that borderline personality features were significantly related to a measure of callous-unemotional traits. Symptoms consistent with *anxiety disorders* also are often found in those diagnosed with BPD, particularly posttraumatic stress disorder (*PTSD*). However, the symptom picture is dissimilar enough that it does not appear that BPD in children can be subsumed within a diagnosis of either conduct disorder or PTSD (Paris, 2003).

Mood disorders are often seen in those with BPD. While the disorders may be truly comorbid, the self-dramatizing quality of 'parasuicidal' self-harming behaviour (Linehan et al., 1991; see also Chapter 9) differs from the typical suicidal ideation seen in simple depression. Similarly, while BPD and bipolar disorder may co-occur, the recklessness and impulsive behaviour seen in BPD is of a more habitual and chronic nature than the short-lived episodes seen in mania. *ADHD* also has been found to co-occur with BPD in young persons (Lincoln et al., 1998). Borderline personality also has been found in *eating disorders*. (See Chapter 12.) This is not surprising, given that binge eating is one example of impulsive behaviour included in the DSM-IV criteria for the diagnosis of BPD. In addition, the two disorders share etiological factors such as disturbed parent–child relationships, as well as common symptoms including distorted self-perceptions and self-abusive behaviour. However, BPD is distinguished by its pervasive effect on all aspects of functioning, particularly interpersonal relationships, and is not limited to, or generally focused on, issues of eating and weight.

On the other hand, some developmental phenomena that might give the appearance of borderline pathology need to be distinguished from true borderline personality disorder. DSM-IV-TR cautions that adolescents and young adults struggling with *identity formation*, especially when involved with *substance use*, may show transient symptoms consistent with BPD, including emotional instability, anxiety, identity confusion and 'existential dilemmas'. We are reminded here of the second criterion necessary to the diagnosis of a personality disorder listed previously, that the symptom is unlikely to be limited to a particular developmental period – one such developmental phase involves the search for self and meaning associated with adolescence.

Gender Differences

In addition to the preponderance of females diagnosed with BPD, other important *gender differences* have emerged. Female children with BPD have more severe symptoms than males, and their symptoms are more likely to persist over time. Consequently, there is greater continuity of BPD in females during the transitions from childhood to adolescence and from adolescence to adulthood (Paris, 2003).

Boys who display similar symptoms, in contrast, are more likely to end up on a trajectory towards *antisocial personality disorder* (Paris, 2003). Indeed, Beauchaine and colleagues (2009) argue that the two disorders arise from the same root causes and represent a clear example of the developmental psychopathology concept of **multifinality**. This multifinality, the authors propose, results from gender differences in the trajectories that are associated with the two disorders. Whereas girls with the same underlying developmental vulnerabilities express them through mood dysregulation and *impulsive injury* to themselves, and thus come to be labelled BPD, boys do so through mood dysregulation and *impulsive aggression* towards others, and thus come to be labelled antisocial. Research confirms that those girls who do develop serious conduct problems are significantly more likely than their conduct disordered male peers to evidence symptoms of BPD (Miller et al., 2008).

Gender differences in adolescent BPD symptoms were further examined by Bradley and colleagues (2005). The investigators identified 81 youths ages 14 to 18 who had been diagnosed with BPD (55 females and 26 males) and asked the youths' clinicians to rate the patients on 200 statements describing personality characteristics associated with psychological disturbance in adolescents (e.g., 'tends to fear she will be rejected or abandoned by those who are emotionally significant';

'expresses emotion in exaggerated and theatrical ways'; 'tends to feel life has no meaning'; 'tends to become irrational when strong emotions are stirred up'). After analysing the clusters of symptoms, Bradley and colleagues found that they could identify four distinct subtypes of BPD in adolescent females. The first category, termed *high-functioning internalizing*, included tendencies to be self-critical, anxious, guilty, self-blaming and self-punishing, while still demonstrating creativity and insightfulness. The second grouping, termed *histrionic*, showed tendencies towards provocative, overly dramatic, manipulative and attention-seeking behaviour, as well as idealized and unrealistic expectations of relationships. The third category, termed *depressive internalizing*, was characterized by loneliness, feelings of being an outcast, lack of pleasure and meaning in life, and expectations of abusiveness from others. The fourth category, *angry externalizing*, included such characteristics as defiance, oppositionality, projection of unacceptable impulses and feelings onto others, sensation seeking and explosive anger.

Although the sample of boys was too small to allow for such a fine-grained analysis of subtypes, Bradley and colleagues found that the cluster of symptoms on which males scored highest was strikingly different from those of females – and strikingly different from the DSM-IV criteria for BPD, even those criteria which were the ones used to identify the patients. Whereas the male and female profiles had in common symptoms of emotion dysregulation and unstable identity, males with BPD were considerably more *aggressive, disruptive and antisocial* than their female counterparts. For example, males but not females were ranked high on gaining pleasure from being aggressive, sadistic behaviour, bullying, taking advantage of others, and having a sense of entitlement and exaggerated self-importance. Bradley and colleagues suggest that future research explore the question of whether the gendered characteristics of BPD represent two manifestations of the same underlying disorder versus whether the DSM-IV criteria for BPD are inaccurate and thus

lead to an erroneous diagnosis of males who would be placed more appropriately in the antisocial spectrum. One source for misdiagnosis of BPD in males may be the tendency of clinicians to assume that all intentional self-injury is driven by borderline pathology. In fact, adolescents self-harm for a variety of reasons, which may include demonstrating their own 'toughness' or bonding with peers who engage in similar behaviour (Klonsky and Glenn, 2009).

In either case, the identification of distinct subtypes of BPD in females has important implications for treatment, in that interventions might be more effective if they are modified to address the particular vulnerabilities and needs of each borderline personality disorder style.

Etiology

How has development gone awry in this extreme deviation from the normal sense of self – what is, in other words, the 'basic fault' (Balint, 1968)? As we will see, theorists from different perspectives characterize the disorder somewhat differently, focusing on some features among those listed in DSM as opposed to others. Whereas interest in this disorder has a long history in the psychodynamic tradition, cognitive behavioural models recently have come to the fore.

In order to build our developmental model of BPD, we will depart from our usual practice of starting with the individual context in order to lay the foundation upon which almost all of the research and theory on this topic agrees – that the roots of the disorder are in extreme disturbances in the family context.

The Family Context

Childhood Trauma and Maltreatment
Troubled parent–child relationships are the major risk factor for borderline personality disorder. A number of studies have confirmed that *child maltreatment* is implicated in the development of BPD. Looking retrospectively, as many as 91 per cent of adults diagnosed as borderline report having been

maltreated in childhood, particularly in the form of *sexual abuse* (Zanarini, 2000).

In recent years, new data-sets have begun to emerge that speak to the significance of childhood maltreatment in the developmental psychopathology of BPD. The Collaborative Longitudinal Personality Disorders Study (Johnson et al., 2006) is a multisite project that, since 1996, has been studying 668 adults aged 18 to 45 who carry diagnoses of avoidant, obsessive-compulsive, schizotypal or borderline personality disorder. In one study published by the group, retrospective interview data regarding childhood trauma revealed that the severity of personality disorder symptoms was related to the frequency and severity of childhood trauma in general (Yen et al., 2002). The findings were particularly striking for those with BPD, who reported the highest rates of traumatic experiences, the earliest ages of exposure, and the most symptoms of PTSD. A full 92 per cent of those with BPD had a significant trauma history; 55 per cent had undergone some form of sexual abuse in their early years and 37 per cent had been raped.

Looking concurrently, data from the Montreal Research Project on Children with Borderline Pathology also indicate the significance of maltreatment in childhood BDP (Paris, 2003). In comparison to those with other psychiatric disorders, school-age children with BPD symptoms have higher rates of physical abuse, sexual abuse, severe neglect and parent dysfunction, including substance abuse and criminality. The maltreatment experienced by these children tends to have an onset very early on in life and to be cumulative over the course of childhood.

Of course, one of the limitations of retrospective and concurrent data is that they cannot speak to whether the personality disorder emerged as a consequence of maltreatment; it is even possible that the direction of effects is reversed, such that characterological problems make the young people vulnerable to becoming the victims of abuse. However, the New York longitudinal data provide us with some prospective evidence. In an initial study, Johnson and colleagues (1999) found that children with documented evidence of maltreatment were more than four times more likely than others to develop a personality disorder by early adulthood. In a subsequent study, now including a sample size of 793 families, the investigators focused on *psychological abuse* – whether the mother had screamed at the child, said she did not love the child, or threatened to send the child away. Children who experienced such psychological maltreatment in childhood were three times more likely than others to develop a personality disorder. The effects of psychological abuse remained significant even when the contributions of child temperament, physical abuse, sexual abuse, neglect, parent psychopathology and comorbid disorders were taken into account.

In addition to physical, sexual and psychological abuse, data from the Montreal study show that youths with BPD are disproportionately likely to have undergone other forms of traumatic family experiences. These include *chaotic, unstable* and *violent* family environments, *separations* and *disrupted attachments* in early childhood, and parental *rejection* (Guzder et al., 1999). Paris (2003) also describes a pattern of 'grossly inappropriate' boundary violations among parents of youths with BPD: for example, one father and daughter double-dated and watched one another's sexual activities; other parents threatened to maim the family pet; and one mother handed her daughter a loaded gun, saying, 'Shoot me if you hate me that much'.

The importance of family risk factors was confirmed in Zanarini and colleagues' (1997) large-scale study of 358 adults diagnosed with BPD. Four risk factors were identified, the first of which was *female gender*. In addition, three significant childhood experiences distinguished those with BPD from individuals with other personality disorder diagnoses: *sexual abuse, emotional neglect* by a male caregiver and *inconsistent parenting* by a female caregiver. Participants with borderline diagnoses were also more likely to describe having had a caregiver withdraw from them emotionally, negate their thoughts and feelings, place them in a parenting role, and fail to provide for their safety and security.

Parent Psychopathology

Consistent evidence emerges that the parents of children with BPD demonstrate higher rates of *severe psychopathology* in general (Paris, 2003). For example, Goldman and colleagues (1993) found that 71 per cent of children with BPD had a parent who met DSM criteria for a psychiatric disorder, including substance abuse, depression and antisocial personality disorder (curiously, the authors did not document the prevalence of BPD among family members).

Looking at the question from the other direction, the Montreal research group wondered about the risks for children being raised by mothers with BPD. These investigators found that the children of mothers with borderline pathology demonstrated significantly more *psychiatric diagnoses*, more *impulse control* disorders and higher levels of *borderline symptoms* than peers raised by mothers with other kinds of personality disorders (Paris, 2003). Other researchers find that the children of mothers with borderline traits are at high risk for attention problems, disruptive behaviour disorders, aggression, anxiety and depression, even in comparison to children of mothers with other personality disorders (Barnow et al., 2006; Weiss et al., 1996).

The effects of borderline pathology on parenting are clearly evident (MacFie, 2009). For example, the Montreal group finds that children of borderline parents are exposed to highly distressing events such as parent *drug and alcohol abuse* and maternal *suicide* attempts, as well as frequent changes in household and removals from the home (Feldman et al., 1995). Studies in the UK find that when children are infants, mothers with BPD are observed to be more intrusive and insensitive than other mothers (Crandell et al., 2003) and, not surprisingly, at one year of age, 80 per cent of these children are classified in the disorganized attachment category (see Chapter 2) (Hobson et al., 2005). Clinical observations also suggest that mothers with BPD engage in *role-reversal behaviour*, which further stresses and confuses the children by placing on them expectations that they provide for parental emotional needs beyond the capabilities of their years (MacFie, 2009). (See Table 15.3.) For example, MacFie and Swan (2009) studied the children's narratives that children of BPD mothers created during a story-telling task, and found that these were characterized by themes involving parent–child role-reversal, fear of abandonment, poor emotion regulation and shameful representations of the self. All of these findings are suggestive of the possibility that being raised by a parent with BPD increases the risk for future psychopathology in general, and perhaps even BPD in particular.

The Family System

Turning to the whole family system, we are reminded that, like object relations theory, the structural family model emphasizes the importance of

TABLE 15.3 Interactions between Children and Mothers with Borderline Personality

Girl age 5, whose mother has borderline personality disorder (BPD):
> An examiner begins a story about a birthday party using family dolls, a table and a cake, then asks the girl: 'Show me and tell me what happens now.' The girl tells how the family open presents and eat cake. She then adds: *And then Mom takes off her clothes and gets drunk.*

Adolescent girl age 15, and her mother who has BPD:
> Adolescent: *Now you're acting even younger. You're giggly and weird.*
> Mother: *Oh well, that's just because I'm being rebellious at the moment. I want to try to have fun.*
> Adolescent: *I'm the teenager that's supposed to do that.*
> Mother: *It has been so long since I've had fun and done the things that I want to do. Yeah, I miss being a teenager. It'd be nice if we could have that little bit of experience together and have fun.*
> Adolescent: *No. You're supposed to be my Mom.*
> Mother: *Well, maybe some day I can be your Mom again.*
> Adolescent: *By the time you're my Mom, I'll be an adult, so it won't even matter.*

Source: MacFie (2009), pp. 1–2.

maintaining healthy psychological boundaries between individuals in the family. Therefore, we might expect that the family relationships associated with BPD would be those that interfere with the child's attainment of a separate and cohesive identity. Systemic family hypotheses were tested by Shapiro and colleagues (1975), who observed the family interactions of children diagnosed with BPD. Consistent with both family systems and object relations theories, the investigators found that children's assertions of independence were met by *emotional withdrawal* by other members of the family.

The Individual Context

Splitting and the Self System: Psychodynamic Perspectives on BPD

Mahler's (1971) *separation-individuation* theory (see Chapter 1) provides a bedrock for much of psychodynamic thinking about the origins of BPD. Mahler focuses on the first three years of life, during which time children develop their identity through their experiences with their caregivers (Mahler et al., 1975). Children who experience warm and sensitive care internalize an image of the loving parent – the 'good object' – and therefore of themselves as lovable. In contrast, children who experience poor parenting internalize an image of their caregiver as angry and rejecting and come to see themselves as unworthy and incapable of inspiring love.

All children sometimes feel anger or frustration with their caregivers, and all parents are sometimes 'bad objects' who disappoint their children. Therefore, some negative feelings are inevitable during development. However, the magical thinking of preoperational children leads them to mistakenly believe that their negative thoughts and feelings can have real consequences. For example, young children are likely to believe that their anger can actually harm someone, destroying the loving mother or transforming her into the bad object of their fears. Because the child has trouble holding on to a sense of security about the mother when she is absent, rage at the mother can be frightening. A child who thinks 'I wish she'd go away' might worry

'What if she does go away?' In such a case, angry feelings towards the mother interfere with the ability to sustain a positive image of her in the child's mind, threatening the internal image of the good mother and with it the child's positive self-image and sense of security.

In order to protect positive internal representations from these strong negative feelings, Mahler proposes that during rapprochement children defensively split their experience of the caregiver into good and bad images, as if there were two caregivers in the child's emotional world – the one who is the source of comfort and good feelings and the one who is frustrating and depriving. Similarly, the sense of self is split in two – the child who is good and lovable and the child who is bad and evokes the caregiver's ire. Thus, **splitting** is a defence mechanism that protects the infant's positive internal representations from feelings of anger and aggression. Thoughts of the loved and loving caregiver – and the lovable self – are safely locked away from negative emotions. (See Fig. 15.1.)

Whereas splitting is a normal part of the young child's development, it is a primitive defence that does not allow us to experience ourselves and others as fully fleshed, complete persons. Therefore, the final stage of separation-individuation requires that we overcome it in order to achieve emotional **object constancy**: the ability to integrate both positive and negative feelings into a single representation. Thus, it is possible to be angry with the caregiver and yet still love her or him, to be disappointed with oneself and yet still believe one is a worthwhile human being. Like Piaget's concept of object permanence, object constancy depends on the *cognitive* capacity to recognize that an object out of sight still exists. However, object constancy requires the recognition that the *emotion* we are not currently experiencing – for example, affection for someone who has just enraged us – still exists.

As Mahler theorizes, young children use the defence mechanism of splitting to protect their internal image of their loving parent – and lovable self – from their negative feelings. Over the course of development, most children can overcome

FIGURE 15.1 Splitting – Perceiving Others as 'All Good' or 'All Bad' – Keeps Us from Seeing Them as They Really Are.

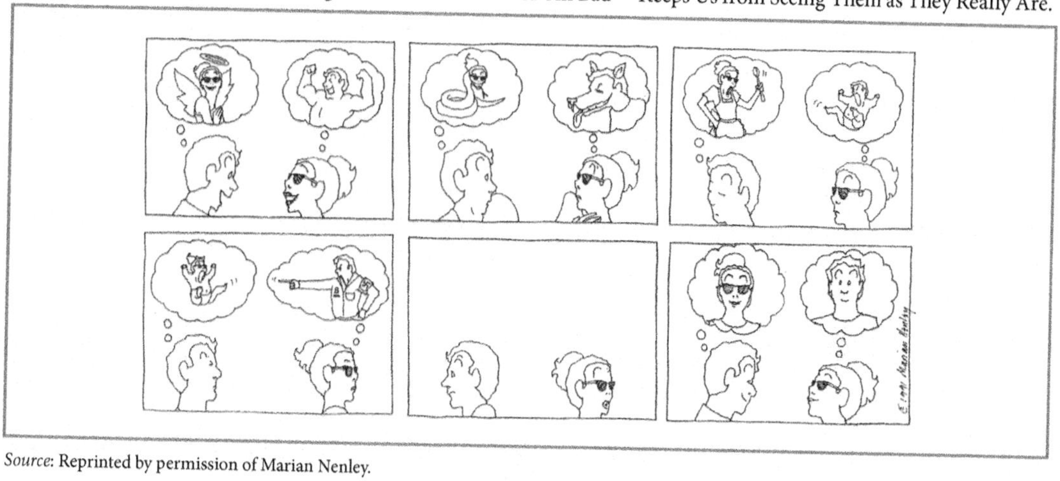

Source: Reprinted by permission of Marian Nenley.

the need to compartmentalize their positive and negative experiences in order to achieve emotional object constancy and to be able to integrate both loving and hostile feelings towards themselves and others. However, psychodynamic theorists believe that the development of children with BPD is arrested during this process. Children with BPD fail to develop emotional object constancy, and are unable to overcome the need to use the defence mechanism of splitting when dealing with difficult emotions (Mahler, 1971).

Why is this process arrested in children with BPD? The reason that some children find it difficult to achieve emotional object constancy, Kernberg (1967) believes, is that they are temperamentally prone to experiencing *excessive rage*. These intense emotional experiences interfere with the development of a stable internal world; because their negative emotions are so violent, it is more difficult for these children to hold on to positive internal images in the face of them. In their rage, they lose all sense of the positive self and loving caregiver that is so important to their sense of security. To lessen the anxiety engendered by such threatening feelings, therefore, these children rely on the defence mechanism of splitting to pathological extent.

Pine (1974) has a somewhat different perspective on BPD, which emphasizes particular defining features of the disorder: failures in ego functions, such as the ability to *modulate anxiety*; and failures in object relations, such as poor differentiation of the *boundary between self and other*. Like Kernberg, Pine believes that splitting plays a role in borderline pathology; however, Pine emphasizes anxiety as its precipitant more than rage. Because of neglectful parenting, children with BPD are often left alone with their emotional distress. Thus, they fail to develop effective defence mechanisms for coping with feelings of anxiety, which they experience as overwhelming panic. These intense and unregulated emotions, in turn, interfere with their ability to integrate positive and negative experiences, and to maintain stable internal representations of themselves and their caregivers (Pine, 1986). Therefore, they cannot tolerate being separated from their caregivers, or acknowledging negative feelings toward them, because they cannot hold onto a sense of being loved and cared for when distressed or alone.

However, in Pine's (1974) view, not only do these children 'stand still' in development, utilizing the defence mechanism of splitting long past the point at which it is developmentally appropriate, but when panicked they regress even further back in development, to an early state of merger or enmeshment with their caregiver. Therefore, Pine believes that children with BPD are arrested at a very early stage in the separation-individuation process, when self and other are not clearly differentiated. Pine sees borderline personality not just as failure to integrate positive and negative internal experiences, but as a fundamental problem in maintaining the distinction between self and other.

In addition, according to Pine (1979), relationships with others are perceived as being fraught with terrifying consequences. Although borderline children find separation anxiety-arousing, the experience of merging with the other and losing their sense of individual selfhood is also frightening. Therefore, Pine presents the child with BPD as being caught in a double-bind, vacillating fear of *abandonment* and unbearable aloneness on the one hand, while also struggling against *enmeshment* with the other and the loss of a sense of self.

What might happen during development to account for these distorted perceptions of self and other? Object relations theorists such as Pine believe that children with borderline personality BPD are the product of abusive and traumatic caregiving that interferes with the development of healthy object relations. More specifically, Masterson and Rinsley (1975) hypothesize that children with BPD are parented by caregivers who are unable to tolerate their children's development of an autonomous self. Rather than continuing to be *emotionally available* to the toddler who is aggressive, frustrating and wilful in the course of normal development, these parents turn away; they are emotionally rejecting when their children express negative feelings or independent-mindedness. According to object relations theory, this is the worst fear of the preoperational child, who believes that angry feelings might actually destroy the loving parent: 'If I get mad at you, you will go away.'

According to this theory, the parents of children with BPD demand that their children mirror them and strive to meet the parents' needs at all times. It is as if the parent conveys to the child, 'If you are not what I need you to be, you don't exist for me' (Ogden, 1982, p. 16). Masterson (1976) believes that the reason for this is that these caregivers have difficulty tolerating separation themselves, and thus

desperately need their children to provide them with a sense of security and to calm their *own* abandonment fears. The picture we are presented is one of adults who interpret their children's growing up as an abandonment of themselves, and thus have difficulty tolerating their children's attempts at individuation. Not surprisingly, Masterson's own clinical observations suggest to him that the parents of children with BPD have borderline features themselves.

Psychodynamic theorists are often purely speculative and have been faulted for neglecting the need for corroborating research. However, an interesting series of studies conducted by Westen and his colleagues (Westen and Cohen, 1993; Westen et al., 1990) lends some validation to the picture of borderline personality presented to us by object relations theory. Based on their review of psychoanalytic and cognitive perspectives on the development of the self, they devised a coding system to analyse the responses made by adolescents with BPD to projective tests (see Chapter 16). For example, they noted that the phenomenon of splitting was evident in the 'all-good' or 'all-bad' responses of these youths (e.g., 'I was always a person who could do anything and now I can't do nothing'). The researchers also found these adolescents' representations of themselves to be unstable, severely negative and lacking in clear differentiation of self and other. They were also described as losing their sense of self and becoming caught up in the emotions and drama of the moment. Again consistent with object relations theories, relationships with others were represented as malevolent, victimizing and unempathic.

Trauma and Disorganized Internal Working Models of Attachment

As we have learned, through their early attachment relationships, children develop a number of capacities fundamental to good adaptation: self-soothing and emotion regulation, positive self-evaluation, and the ability to communicate needs in a relationship and to trust that those needs will be met (see Chapter 2). However, pathological family relationships interfere with the attainment of a secure sense of self, as well as the ability to regulate emotions and to perceive others in ways not distorted by distrust. In the case of the child with BPD, the caregiving environment is terrifying and unpredictable; the child's source of security is also the source of the threat. The result is an impossible paradox, which the child can only resolve by retaining two separate schemas of relationship: one in which the parent is safe and another in which the parent is frightening and abusive. The result is a *disorganized attachment*, which has been conceptualized as a breakdown of any coherent strategy for maintaining proximity under conditions of threat.

Evidence for the link between BPD and disorganized attachment has emerged in concurrent (Agrawal et al., 2004) and longitudinal (Carlson et al., 2009) research. The association between disorganized attachment and BPD is further suggested by fact that the two are predicted by many of the very same dysfunctions, including extreme forms of *child maltreatment* and trauma; *boundary violations* in the parent–child relationship, such as parent–child role reversal; and the use of *dissociation* as a defence in times of stress (Carlson et al., 2009; Weinfield et al., 1999). The development of such insecure, disorganized and poorly integrated internal working models of self and other in turn leads to unstable interpersonal relationships, identity confusion and deviations in cognitive, emotional and behavioural development.

Judd and McGlashan (2003) further develop the idea that trauma disrupts the development of the attachment and self systems in BPD. These authors liken BPD to a form of '*developmental internalized PTSD*'. Unlike other forms of PTSD, in which trauma is linked to a memory of a specific incident, the trauma of the child with BPD is associated with the entire caregiving relationship. Because of the child's experience of overt abuse and covert forms of grossly inappropriate parenting, closeness to another person brings with it the perceived or actual threat of emotional neglect, abuse or abandonment. This trauma is not one the child recalls when exposed to a specific traumatic cue,

but rather an experience that the child lives with every moment of the day.

In Judd and McGlashan's view, the chronic psychological and physiological state of stress becomes part of the child's characteristic response to others and forms a core feature of his or her personality. Further, traumatic stress interferes with cognitive and emotional development, leading to significant informational processing deficits. These deficits arise particularly when the individual is required to process complex emotional, sensory and motor information; translate non-verbal cues into verbal codes; and discriminate and prioritize divergent visual and verbal interpersonal responses. These cognitive skills are central to the ability to develop stable and coherent representational schemas of relationships. Instead, however, characteristics of borderline thinking are odd and fragmented, resulting in developmentally immature forms of reasoning such as magical thinking, superstition, absolutist (black-and-white) thinking, dissociation and transient psychotic states.

Dissociation

Implicit in the description of the impact of trauma on the self just presented is a specific mechanism by which trauma leads to borderline pathology, and that is the defence mechanism of *dissociation*. One of the ways that children might attempt to cope with overwhelming stress is to withdraw awareness from what is going on around them, via retreating into fantasy, 'spacing out', and inducing a trance-like state of disconnection from reality. Dissociation therefore represents an attempt to protect the psyche by blocking traumatic experiences from awareness (Nader, 2008). Mild forms and brief intervals of dissociation are not uncommon in normative development (Putnam, 2006); for example, think of the last time you came alert during a lecture and realized that several moments had passed during which you were not paying attention to the speaker. However, dissociation that persists and becomes a habitual means of coping is strongly related to psychopathology in adolescence (Silberg, 2004).

Dissociative states also have been linked specifically to features of borderline pathology, including *self-harming*. Youth who self-injure may report feeling emotionally numb, detached from themselves and their surroundings, unable to feel pain, unreal or 'dead inside' and may experience feeling 'more real' or 'more alive' after engaging in self-harm (Klonsky, 2009). Others engage in self-harming behaviour while in a state of dissociation and therefore are not be able to remember having done so.

Particularly vulnerable to the development of dissociation are those children with *weak ego defences* and a poorly integrated *sense of self* (Ogawa et al., 1997). This, as we have seen, is the child who has a *disorganized* internal working model of relationships. Longitudinal research shows that disorganized attachment in infancy is a powerful predictor of dissociation in childhood, adolescence and into young adulthood, and that dissociation is predictive of borderline pathology (Carlson et al., 2009; Weinfeld et al., 1999). Here again, it is parental behaviour that is believed to provide the mechanism of effect. By presenting the child with confusing and conflicting messages – remember, for example the prototypical disorganizing parent who approaches the child with angry words but a smiling face (see Chapter 2) – the child is prevented from developing a cohesive sense of self that can span these dramatic shifts in emotional states and external realities. Moreover, the parent plays an active role in promoting this failure of integration through not only the inconsistency of his or her behaviour, but also through denial of the child's reality and refusal to acnowledge the child's inner experience. Although it certainly is a painful experience for a child to cope with an angry and abusive parent, it is an even more bewildering task to be confronted with an erratic parent who denies being angry and insists that the child deny the evidence of her own eyes and ears as well. As Ogawa and colleagues (1997) describe it, 'When salient experiences must be unnoticed, disallowed, unacknowledged, or forgotten, the result is incoherence of the self structure. Interconnections among experiences cannot be made, and the resulting gaps in personal history compromise both the complexity and the integrity of the self' (p. 871). Dissociation, therefore, suggests a fundamental failure in the integration and coherency of the self (Haugaard, 2004).

Emotion Regulation and Deliberate Self-Harm

The inability to tolerate and modulate emotions is one of the key features of borderline personality disorder. Research confirms that, just as with adults, *emotion regulation deficits* are related to BPD symptoms among children (Gratz et al., 2009). Although the effects of an abusive, traumatic and pathological home environment generally are suspected as the cause of children's failure to develop adaptive emotion regulation strategies, it also is proposed that children who are vulnerable to BPD may be temperamentally more emotionally unstable, intense and reactive than the average child (Cole et al., 2009).

Emotion dysregulation also may play a role in the development of one of the most prevalent and disturbing symptoms of the disorder, deliberate *self-harming*. In one study of adolescent inpatients, Nock and colleagues (2006a) found that 51.7 per cent of youth diagnosed with BPD engaged in non-suicidal self-injury, far more than those with any other personality disorder diagnosis. Unlike a simple suicidal 'gesture', the self-injurious behaviour of parasuicidal youths with BPD can be quite serious and disfiguring. It is not uncommon for cutting of the body to become habitual, with cuts repeatedly made in the same areas of the arms or legs so that permanent scars are left. Adolescents and adults with BPD often report that cutting themselves is a way of relieving tension, indeed the only way they know to achieve relief. In studies of adolescent inpatients who self-injure, Nock and Prinstein (2005) have found that the most frequently endorsed reasons for self-harming among psychiatrically hospitalized adolescents are to stop bad feelings, to generate feelings or to communicate distress to others.

Research also suggests that self-harming behaviour has its roots in trauma and the development of maladaptive strategies to cope with post-traumatic stress (Prinstein, 2008). A widely replicated finding is that self-injury is predicted by a history of maltreatment – primarily sexual abuse (Glassman et al., 2007; Nock and Kessler, 2006) but also peer victimization (Hilt et al., 2008). Moreover, the relationship between childhood abuse and self-injury among adolescents is mediated by symptoms of posttraumatic stress disorder (see Chapter 8). Thus, a primary goal of self-harming appears to be to regulate emotions in the face of overwhelming distress. However, the youth who self-harms is one who has not developed adaptive strategies to cope with that distress (Lloyd-Richardson et al., 2009). For example, Nock and Mendes (2008) found that, in comparison to their peers, youth with a history of self-injury evidenced lower distress tolerance and poorer problem-solving skills when faced with a laboratory-based stressor. In sum, because their emotions and coping abilities have been overwhelmed by trauma, youth with BPD resort to desperate measures in order to regulate their distress.

Some clinicians have observed that once a youth begins to self-mutilate as a way of coping with upsetting feelings, this behaviour comes to have addictive qualities. Nixon and colleagues (2002) set out to empirically test this hypothesis in a sample of 42 self-injurious adolescents admitted to a hospital over a four-month period. Almost 79 per cent of adolescents reported the urge to engage in self-injury on a daily basis, and 83 per cent gave in to the urge more than once a week. Cutting, scratching, hitting oneself, hair-pulling, biting, and interfering with the healing of wounds were among the most common forms of self-injury. The two primary reasons given for harming themselves were 'to cope with feelings of depression' and 'to release unbearable tension'. Moreover, among the adolescents in this sample, almost 98 per cent endorsed three or more symptoms consistent with addictive behaviour in relationship to their self-injury, as defined by DSM (e.g., the individual continues despite knowledge the behaviour is harmful, uncomfortable symptoms arise when the individual attempts to discontinue, the behaviour causes social problems, the frequency or intensity must be increased to achieve desired effect and the behaviour is time-consuming and disrupts normal activities). In sum, just as substance abuse or binge-purging might be used as a method of regulating emotions by some adolescents, as we learned in Chapter 12, so might self-injury become a pathological addiction.

The impulsive and addiction-prone behaviour of youth with BPD also suggests an underlying deficit in self-regulation more generally. Such a deficit is suggested by the strong association between BPD and aggression and antisocial behaviour (Beauchaine et al., 2009). In keeping with this idea, research provides direct evidence of a relationship between BPD symptoms and lack of ego control among children (Gratz et al., 2009).

In sum, emotion dysregulation is a core feature of BPD and permeates all areas of functioning. Having lacked the experience of the kind of parental empathic attunement that helps children to develop an understanding of emotions and the ability to self-regulate, the emotional and behavioural development of the child with BPD is early on set off course in fundamental ways. Due to the lack of coherence, integration and stability in their internal worlds, individuals with BPD are unable to progress in emotional development. They do not develop the ability to differentiate among emotions or to experience complex and blended emotions as part of a single experience, nor are they able to modulate or cope with strong emotions without yielding to the impulse to act on them. They lack skills to read subtle emotional cues accurately and to react adaptively in emotion-laden situations. In short, 'they face adult situations with a child's emotional repertoire' (Judd and McGlashan, 2003, p. 30).

Cognitive Dysfunctions

A number of studies of children with BPD have indicated the presence of cognitive deficits. These include problems in the areas of executive functioning, motor planning and attentional control, with BPD children scoring more poorly on these tests than children with other psychiatric diagnoses (Lincoln et al., 1998; Paris et al., 1999; Rogosch and Cicchetti, 2005). It has been proposed that impaired executive functions underlie many of the symptoms associated with BPD, including difficulty coping adaptively with anxiety, poor impulse control, poor recognition of and ability to verbalize internal states, and the tendency to decompensate under stress (Lincoln et al., 1998).

In addition, the British researchers Fonagy and Luyten (2009) hypothesize that the core features of BPD can all best understood as reflecting an impairment in *mentalization*, the ability to 'perceive and interpret human behaviour in terms of intentional mental states (e.g., needs, desires, feelings, and goals)' (p. 1357). This is a concept closely related to that of theory of mind, which was introduced in Chapter 5. In particular, Fonagy and Luyten propose that the traumatic childrearing of children who develop BPD interferes with their ability to truly understand their own inner states and to differentiate their own thoughts and emotions from those of others. The results are a confused and disorganized identity, failures in self-other differentiation, and a profound lack of social understanding. Judd and McGlashan (2003) posit a similar theory, which proposes that the essential developmental failure is a lack of metacognitive monitoring in interpersonal relationships. *Metacognitive monitoring*, also termed reflective functioning, is the ability to observe oneself, to detect errors in one's thinking or inconsistencies in one's speech, and to understand that things may look different from another's perspective – in other words, to 'think about thinking'. Without metacognition and the ability to integrate thoughts, feelings and perspectives in relationship with others, individuals with BPD are left to fall back on more developmentally primitive cognitive processes, such as denial, splitting and projection – defences that are reality distorting and fragmenting.

The Social Context

Youths with borderline personality are difficult to engage socially – they engender uncomfortable feelings in others because of their high anxiety, extreme mood changes, fluctuations between good reality-testing and disorganization, and erratic shifts in positive or negative attitudes towards others. Because this unpredictable and extreme behaviour is difficult for others to tolerate, their interpersonal relationships are often volatile and transient.

In an attempt to better understand these interpersonal deficits, some theorists have proposed that individuals with BPD characteristically engage others in a process of **projective identification** (Ogden, 1982; see also Chapter 2). Projective identification is a complex defence mechanism that involves an interaction between two people. The process takes place in three steps (Lieberman, 1992). First, unwanted thoughts and feelings are attributed to, or *projected* onto, the other person. For example, someone who defends against acknowledging his or her own angry feelings might project those onto another person. Second, the other person is *pressured to comply* with the projection (e.g., by behaving in ways that are subtly irritating and anger-arousing, one might begin to make the other person begin to feel irritable and angry). Lastly, *identification* takes place when the recipient of the projection comes to feel that these thoughts and feelings actually *are* his or her own. Through the process of projective identification, individuals with BPD can engender in others their most intolerable and distressing emotions – worthlessness, unreality, terror, rage and desolation. (See Box 15.2.)

Therefore, viewed *transactionally*, the way in which youths with borderline pathology relate to others increases the likelihood that they will experience the very rejection and abandonment they fear. In turn, poor communication with peers and peer victimization exacerbate vulnerable youths' engagement in maladaptive behaviours such as self-harming, which may further alienate the

Box 15.2 Projective Identification in Borderline Personality Disorder

In a revealing essay, psychotherapist Mark Rhine (Adler and Rhine, 1988) writes about his long-term work with a young woman with borderline personality disorder:

> Many times in the following years I wondered why I had chosen to work with this patient, questioned my ability to help her, wondered if she were treatable, and dreaded seeing her during the lengthy treatment that often left both of us confused, angry, hurt, bewildered, despairing, and feeling as if each of us was going stark raving mad because of the other. (p. 476)

The patient was a 22-year-old college graduate, working as a file clerk, who came for therapy because of chronic feelings of being less than human, lack of pleasure in life, fear of rejection and suicidal thoughts. She formed a very hostile attachment to her therapist, referring to him as 'the Gestapo' (particularly hurtful to the therapist, given that he was Jewish), criticizing his interpretations and complaining that he was a lousy therapist because she was not getting better.

Dr Rhine felt guilty about the anger and negative feelings he experienced toward his patient and made every effort to repress them. When she insulted him, he would respond mildly, offering a platitude such as, 'I am sorry that you hold me in such contempt'. In fact, he felt quite hurt, but tried to forbear to remain 'therapeutic' and to be accepting of the patient's need to express this negative transference. When she threatened to quit therapy, he would be as neutral as possible, stating, 'Although I would like you to continue, I'll respect your decision', and so forth. In response, she pressed him, asking, 'How does it *really* make you feel?'

Her attacks escalated until one day Dr Rhine succumbed to exasperation and finally let his true feelings show. He complained that the patient was unfair to him and that it was quite painful to him to be berated constantly. Her reaction surprised him. In a calm and sober voice, she stated, 'It isn't you I am berating; it is myself. I need to know what a human being would feel and do under an attack like that'. Together, they went on to discover the fact that she needed the therapist to speak for a part of herself 'that had never spoken up, that was terrified and didn't know how to be human' (p. 479) – the part of herself that suffered in silence the beatings and humiliation she received from her parents. In short, through projective identification, the patient was engendering in her therapist her own feeling state, provoking him to experience a part of her that she needed to learn more about and to master.

Projective identification is a process that can occur in any relationship. What distinguishes it in healthier people is their capacity to reality-test and recognize when they are projecting onto others. At its most adaptive level, projective identification may even be related to empathy and the capacity to feel for and with another person.

adolescent from his or her peers (Hilt et al., 2008). Further, because of their inability to cope with the demands of the normal school environment, youths with BPD are likely to be placed in inpatient settings or day treatment programmes, further isolating them from opportunities to engage in normative peer relationships.

Further, as Judd and McGlashan (2003) point out, all of the factors described in the previous sections – disorganized internal working models of relationships, cognitive dysfunctions, and emotional and behavioural instability – understandably wreak havoc with the ability to form stable intimate relationships. The shifting states of mind of individuals with BPD are extreme and absolute; Judd and McGlashan believe that these individuals are dimly if at all consciously aware of the fact that their emotions and perceptions dramatically shift from one moment to the next. Their experience of the world and of themselves is fragmented and compartmentalized. Each state of mind is all the reality there is, in the present moment, and memory is mood-dependent and cannot be retrieved when the person's state of mind changes again. Not only are experiences of others shifting, disorganized and incoherent, but so is the individual's experience of self – there is no 'me' that is consistent across situations and social contexts. Thus, there is a lack of a continuous self with which to engage others in a relationship.

The cumulative effect of these multiple developmental deficits, Judd and McGlashan state, is an *inability to sustain meaningful relationships* with others. The ability to form a truly intimate and deep attachment to a life partner, which requires a mutually reciprocal, empathic relationship, is impeded by all of the developmental failures that have gone before.

The Biological Context

As noted previously, many theorists, including those from the psychoanalytic perspective, believe that there is biological predisposition towards borderline personality disorder. The exact nature of the biological underlay is a matter of speculation, although suggestive data are beginning to emerge.

Temperament

As we noted previously, some theorists believe that the child who will develop BPD comes into the world with a genetically derived *temperamental vulnerability*. These temperamental traits, such as impulsivity and affective instability, equip children poorly to cope with stress and cause children to be overreactive, attention-seeking and dysregulated. Zanarini and Frankenburg (1997) term this temperament 'hyperbolic'. Whether such a temperament precedes or is a consequence of exposure to trauma, stress and maladaptive parenting continues to be a matter of debate.

Brain structure and function

Ceballos and colleagues (2006) conducted a series of studies of adolescent girls diagnosed with BPD and found differences in brain function that could be detected via electroencephalography. In contrast to controls and youth diagnoses with conduct disorder, those diagnosed with BPD showed patterns that were associated with lower levels of brain maturation. Other brain abnormalities among youth with BPD were observed by Whittle and colleagues (2009) in Australia. The investigators performed magnetic resonance imaging (MRI) scans on adolescent girls diagnosed with BPD and healthy controls, and found the girls with borderline pathology had decreased volume of the left anterior cingulate cortex, an area of the brain that is involved in higher-level cognitive and affective functions including problem solving, decision making and modulation of emotions. In addition, the investigators found that the extent of the volume reduction was related to the degree to which the girls with BPD demonstrated parasuicidal behaviour, impulsivity and fear of abandonment.

Investigators in Germany similarly have found reduced volume of prefrontal and orbitofrontal grey matter in adolescent girls diagnosed with BPD when compared to health controls (Brunner et al., 2010) and research conducted in Australia also finds right-sided grey matter loss in the orbitofrontal cortex of teenagers with BPD (Chanen et al., 2008b).

Genetics

Distel and colleagues' (2009) team of international researchers review the burgeoning research in support of a genetic component to the development of BPD. One of the largest twin studies compiled data from 5496 adults in the Netherlands, Belgium and Australia (Distel et al., 2008). The results indicated that *genetic influences* explained 42 per cent of the variation in BPD features overall. The correlations for monozygotic twins were twice as high as those for dizygotic twins in all three countries. In a subsequent study, the authors found that around 50 per cent of the variation in BPD could be attributed to genetic influences, with the correlation between monozygotic twins (.45) higher than that between dizygotic twins (.18) or between parents and their offspring (.13).

Among the very few studies that have estimated heritability among children, Coolidge and colleagues (2001) report a heritability estimate of 76 per cent in a small sample of pre-adolescents. In contrast, Bornovalova and colleagues (2009) collected data on a large sample of over 1000 14-year-old twin girls from the Minnesota Twin Family Study and followed them for 10 years. Their results showed that BPD traits were moderately heritable at all ages (.30 to .50). There also was evidence of strong effects of non-shared environments, which likely were attributable to individual experiences such as child abuse, differential parental treatment or adverse life events. The results also indicated that the heritability of BPD increased from ages 14 to 24. The investigators propose that this increased genetic influence over time may be due to transactions between genes and environments such that adolescents and adults gain increasing opportunities to choose environments in which their genetic vulnerabilities are likely to be expressed.

The search for a candidate gene to carry the mechanism of effect has focused on those that are related to serotonergic functioning, as we discuss in more detail next, given that serotonin is implicated in the regulation of anger, aggression, suicidal behaviour, impulsivity and emotional lability, all of which are deficient in BPD. The two most well-studied genes are tryptophan hydroxylase (TPH) and the serotonin transporter gene 5-HTT (Distel et al., 2009).

Neurochemistry

Crowell and colleagues (2009) review the available research on biological correlates of BPD, almost all of which to date has focused on adult samples. In keeping with the biological structures that have drawn the attention of genetic researchers, investigators assessing neurochemistry have focused on the central serotonin (5-HT) system. Deficits in the *5-HT system* are associated with impulsivity, aggression, affective instability, mood disorders and self-harming behaviours, all of which are features of BPD. The neurotransmitter dopamine also has been implicated, given its relationship to impulsivity and negative affectivity. Other researchers have focused on the possible roles of vasopressin, a neurotransmitter that is involved in the expression of aggression, and monoamine oxidase, an enzyme that is involved in the chemical breakdown of other neurotransmitters.

A second biologically mediated borderline trait, hyper-reactivity to the environment, is associated with irregularities in the *hypothalamic-pituitary-adrenal* (HPA) system. This system is associated with the 'flight or fight' response and is involved in the development of stress-related disorders, particularly PTSD. Research has shown persuasively that exposure to chronic stress leads to overreactive HPA responding and that the HPA axis is involved in suicidal behaviour. One of the markers of HPA axis reactivity is the failure to suppress cortisol, which can be assessed by exposing research participants to the dexamethasone suppression test.

Once again, however, the lack of prospective developmental studies confounds our ability to determine whether these differences in the neurochemistry of individuals with BPD are inherent or whether they are the consequence of other factors. As Crowell and colleagues (2009) note, all of these biological systems are highly susceptible to environmental influences. For example, deficits in the serotonergic and HPA systems are known to be related to the trauma of child maltreatment (Beers and DeBellis, 2002; Cicchetti and Rogosch, 2001).

Crowell and colleagues (2008a) also demonstrated a direct link between serotonin levels, self-injury and stressful family interactions. In their study, the investigators recruited adolescent girls who were being psychiatrically treated for self-injury and measured peripheral serotonin levels following a mother–daughter discussion of common areas of conflict (e.g., curfew or chores). Results showed that the family interactions of girls who self-injured were characterized by high levels of negative affect, and that the combination of mother–daughter negativity and low serotonin highly predicted the likelihood of self-injurious behaviour. Thus, the investigators conclude, adolescents with low levels of serotonin may be at particularly high risk for self-injury in the context of negative and conflictual family relationships.

Integrative Developmental Models

Developmental Precursors of BPD

An innovative approach to thinking about the developmental psychopathology of borderline personality features is offered by Geiger and Crick (2010). Instead of being limited by DSM-IV criteria's lack of sensitivity to the signs of BPD phenomena in young people, they propose instead focusing on the developmental precursors that lay the foundation for the emergence of maladaptive ways of thinking, feeling and behaving. Among the childhood personality features they identify as being related to, and potentially predictive of, BPD are the following: a hostile, paranoid world view, affective instability, impulsivity, excessive concern with relationships and lack of sense of self.

Hostile, Paranoid World View

Geiger and Crick (2010) propose that the origins of a distrustful attitude towards others can be found in the development of poor social information processing skills in childhood. As we have seen, some children have a bias towards interpreting others' behaviour as having hostile intent towards them (see Chapter 2) and this hostile attribution bias fuels a tendency to react negatively and even aggressively towards others.

Affective Instability

The intense, unstable and inappropriate expression of emotions that is the hallmark of BPD suggest a failure to develop emotion regulation capacities that likely result from a combination of inadequate parenting and biological vulnerability. Geiger and Crick (2010) remind us of the essential role that the secure attachment relationship plays in providing children with the kinds of soothing experiences that help them learn how to self-soothe. In contrast, the family lives of children who develop BPD are marked by insecure attachment, negativity, violence and emotional chaos, thereby disrupting the development of emotion regulation capacities. In addition, they note the research that suggests some children may have a temperamental vulnerability to affect dysregulation. This underlying hypersensitivity makes children even more stressed by environmental instability and perhaps even leads vulnerable children to experience as traumatic events that other children are able to cope with successfully.

Impulsivity

The impulsivity associated with BPD clearly is related to emotion dysregulation, but also to poor self-regulatory skills in general. Children in the BPD spectrum are characterized by low levels of effortful control. There may be a neurological underlay to these deficits, given the research that has emerged showing that children with borderline features have difficulty with executive functioning skills, such as regulating attention, planning and cognitive flexibility (e.g., Rogosch and Cicchetti, 2005). Transactional effects also might ensue when children who are impulsive, inattentive and difficult to manage arouse negative reactions in others which further exacerbate their emotional and behavioural difficulties.

Excessive Concern with Relationships

Geiger and Crick (2010) propose that one pathway to the development of relationship insecurity is relational aggression. Children who are relationally aggressive use manipulative tactics to hurt and control others (e.g., threatening to withdraw friendship, spreading rumours, encouraging others to reject a peer; see Chapter 10). However, they also appear to be anxious about and preoccupied with their relationships and consequently are possessive, jealous and easily made angry by perceived slights. As confirmed by Crick and colleagues (2005), increases in features of BPD were seen across the transition from fourth to sixth grade in children who evidenced sensitivity to relational slights, a heightened emotional response to hypothetical peer provocations, the desire for exclusivity with their close friends, and high levels of relational aggression.

Lack of a Coherent Sense of Self

It is a feature of early childhood that children have difficulty integrating opposite characteristics and thus they tend to engage in all-or-none thinking in which the self or others are viewed as all 'good' and 'bad'. Therefore, the extreme vacillations of self-image in BPD suggest a youth who is stuck at an earlier point in development. In addition, over the course of development children generally shift from a focus on external judgements as the yardstick for their own value as persons and instead come to rely on their own internal standards. Here, too, the adolescent who continues to attribute the self-image to external events evidences an immaturity in the self-system and a consequent vulnerability to the development of a self-disorder. The culprit here in the development of BPD is clearly suggested by research on the interactions of maltreatment, trauma and dissociation in the development of an incoherent sense of self.

Linehan's Biosocial Model of BPD

An important contribution to our understanding of BPD is provided by Marsha Linehan's biosocial model, recently expanded and placed in a developmental psychopathology context by Crowell and colleagues (2009).

Linehan (1993a) began her work by focusing attention on a particular subset of those who come to be diagnosed with borderline personality disorder, 'those with histories of multiple attempts to injure, mutilate, or kill themselves' (p. 10), behaviour she terms *parasuicidal*. The core characteristics she perceives in these individuals are outlined in Table 15.4 and include (1) *emotional vulnerability*,

including high emotional intensity, reactivity and poor affect regulation; (2) *self-invalidation*; (3) *perpetual crises*; (4) *inability to tolerate grief and loss*; (5) *passivity* in the face of life problems; and (6) an *appearance of competence* that belies the functional deficits under the surface.

The biosocial model of BPD posits that there are three major processes involved in the developmental unfolding of the disorder: (1) *an inherent biological vulnerability*; (2) *an invalidating environment*; and (3) *reciprocal transactions* between the inherent vulnerability and environmental risk that potentiate the disorder. We next take a closer look at each of these links in the chain. (See Fig. 15.2.)

First, based on the emerging research evidence, the biosocial model of BPD posits that there is an underlying vulnerability to borderline pathology that is biologically mediated. As the theorists note, BPD is associated with impulse control and emotion dysregulation and research suggests that both of these characteristics are highly heritable. However, Crowell and colleagues (2009) also suggest that the essential inherited trait may be one of *impulsivity*. Deficits in emotion regulation, in turn, may develop out of this temperamental vulnerability as a consequence of

TABLE 15.4 Behavioural Patterns in BPD

1. *Emotional vulnerability*: A pattern of pervasive difficulties in regulating negative emotions, including high sensitivity to negative emotional stimuli, high emotional intensity, and slow return to emotional baseline, as well as awareness and experience of emotional vulnerability. May include a tendency to blame the social environment for unrealistic expectations and demands.

2. *Self-invalidation*: Tendency to invalidate or fail to recognize one's own emotional responses, thoughts, beliefs, and behaviours. Unrealistically high standards and expectations for self. May include intense shame, self-hate, and self-directed anger.

3. *Unrelenting crises*: Pattern of frequent, stressful, negative environmental events, disruptions and roadblocks – some caused by the individual's dysfunctional lifestyle, others by an inadequate social milieu and many by fate or chance.

4. *Inhibited grieving*: Tendency to inhibit and overcontrol negative emotional responses, especially those associated with grief and loss, including sadness, anger, guilt, shame, anxiety and panic.

5. *Active passivity*: Tendency to passive interpersonal problem-solving style, involving failure to engage actively in solving of own life problems, often together with active attempts to solicit problem solving from others in the environment; learned helplessness, hopelessness.

6. *Apparent competence*: Tendency for the individual to appear deceptively more competent than she actually is; usually due to failure of competencies to generalize across expected moods, situations and time, and to failure to display adequate non-verbal cues of emotional distress.

Source: Linehan, 1993a.

FIGURE 15.2 Integrative Model of Borderline Personality Disorder.

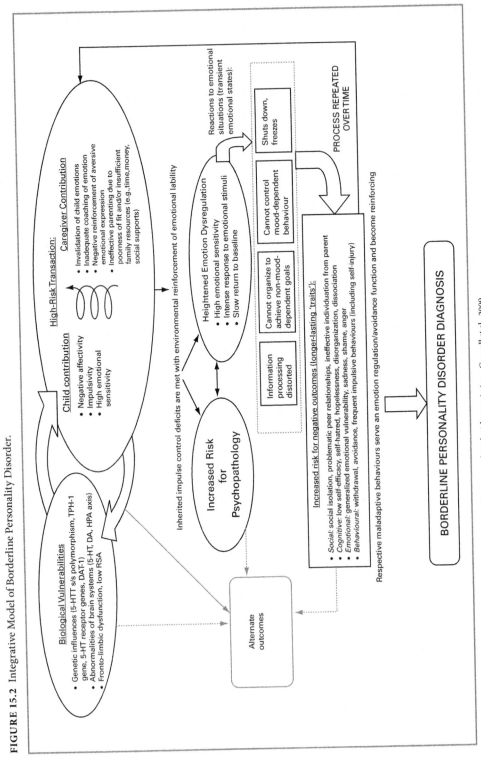

exposure to environmental risk. The theory suggests that *chronic stress* in early development affects neurotransmitter and endocrine functioning in ways that heighten the child's sensitivity, reactivity and inability to cope with environmental challenges, and thus increases the likelihood of the disorder.

The second premise of the biosocial model is that the child who develops BPD is one who is exposed to significant *environmental challenges*, specifically in the form of a high-risk family environment. Similarly to object relations theorists, BPD is theorized to arise within the context of pathological parent–child relationships. The key deficit in caregiving Linehan (1993a) identifies is an *invalidating environment*, 'one in which communication of private experiences is met by erratic, inappropriate, and extreme responses' (p. 49). Linehan believes that the parents of children destined for BPD are unable to tolerate the expression of negative emotions such as fear or anxiety and therefore invalidate, ignore or trivialize their children's emotional experiences. Although invalidation may take place in the context of overt maltreatment, it also takes subtle forms that might be seen in families without overt psychopathology. For example, a family member might express impatience that the individual with BPD 'just can't control herself'.

A key consequence of an invalidating environment is that the children do not learn to recognize or understand their internal states. In addition, because their parents do not help to comfort or soothe them, these young people do not internalize the capacity to soothe themselves, and therefore do not develop the ability to regulate their emotions and tolerate stress. Moreover, when the usual emotional displays are met with indifference, children learn that intense emotions may be the only way to evoke a response from the caregiver; thus, extreme emotional responses are reinforced. Lastly, an invalidating environment fails to teach the children to trust their own emotional and cognitive reactions. Instead, children learn to invalidate their own experiences and to

look to the social surroundings to provide cues about how to think, feel and behave. No matter how aversive the invalidating environment, the child is its prisoner – the child does not have the capacity to leave the family. Unable to change his or her environment, the child cannot do anything other than try to change his or her inner experience to meet its demands.

At the heart of the matter in borderline pathology, Linehan argues, is a failure of *dialectics* – the ability to tolerate and participate in the normal give and take of relationships and to achieve a sense of wholeness and balance that incorporates all of the rich distinctions and contradictions of reality. Individuals with BPD vacillate between rigidly held points of view, polarizing reality and relationships into 'either-or' categories, without the ability to synthesize them into a realistic and well-rounded whole.

The third phase in the biosocial model of BPD involves the way in which parent and child reciprocally influence one another. As we learned in Chapter 2, some children come into this world with a difficult temperament but whether this presages the development of psychopathology depends on the goodness of fit between the child and the caregiver. In the case of BPD, the theory suggests that there is the unfortunate combination of three toxic ingredients: a *temperamentally difficult* child; a parent who fosters *poor emotion regulation* by invalidating the child's emotions, modelling dysfunctional affective expression and negatively reinforcing extreme emotional arousal; and, third, a parent whose parenting style provides a *poor fit* for the child's temperament. Just as goodness of fit can protect a vulnerable child from developing psychopathology, poorness of fit may potentiate it. Linehan (1993a) proposes that three kinds of family dynamics increase the likelihood of borderline pathology: the 'disorganized' family in which neglect or maltreatment are pervasive; the 'perfect' family in which emotions are belittled, invalidated or disallowed expression; and the 'normal' family in which the main dysfunction is merely a poorness of fit with the child's temperament.

The biosocial model is a highly promising one, particularly because it integrates so much of what is known about the biological, family and psychological systems that are involved in BPD and places them in a developmental context. The model also presents researchers with a set of clear and testable hypotheses that certainly will inform future work devoted to uncovering the origins of borderline personality disorder.

In summary, borderline personality organization represents an extreme source of vulnerability during adolescence. The challenges that arise during this developmental period – separation from the family, achievement of a sense of individual identity and autonomous functioning – may precipitate a crisis for those youths whose psychological make-up ill equips them to cope with even the normal stresses of development.

Developmental Course

Evidence is accumulating that childhood BPD constitutes a severe deviation in development that presages poor functioning to come. Wenning (1990) conducted follow-up interviews with 28 children who had been treated for BPD on an inpatient unit. Approximately 10 years later, many continued to show signs consistent with a diagnosis of BPD, although diagnoses of *antisocial* and *schizotypal* personality also were common. One third fit criteria for generalized *anxiety disorder*, while two-thirds showed symptoms of *depression*, half having undergone a major depressive episode. Lofgren and colleagues (1991) followed 19 children diagnosed as borderline. In a follow-up 10 to 20 years later, the researchers found that five met criteria for a BPD diagnosis in adulthood, whereas 13 met criteria for other personality disorders and three were diagnosis-free. Similarly, Thomsen (1996) reports that children given the borderline label are likely to develop serious disorders in adulthood, but that more often involve antisocial personality disorder and *schizophrenia* than BPD. The Montreal group used a follow-back design to assess the adolescent functioning of children who had been diagnosed with BPD five years earlier. Compared to non-BPD

peers, those with a history of BPD exhibited higher levels of internalizing and externalizing behaviour problems and were functioning more poorly in general (Zelkowitz et al., 2007).

In contrast to the majority of studies that have focused on clinical samples, Winograd and colleagues (2008) examined the relationship between symptoms of BPD at age 14 and adult functioning at age 33 among community youth in the Collaborative Personality Disorders Study. The investigators found that, on average, higher levels of adolescent borderline symptoms in adolescence were associated with poorer functioning in work and relationships, and lower life satisfaction in adulthood. Those who had borderline symptoms in adolescence demonstrated lower academic and occupational attainment, less involvement with romantic partners, and attained fewer adult developmental milestones. Even though the absolute level of borderline symptoms decreased from adolescence to adulthood, adolescent borderline symptoms predicted adult BPD, general impairment and involvement with psychiatric services.

Perhaps the richest longitudinal data come from the Chestnut Lodge Follow-up Study, which tracked the outcomes of patients treated at the Chestnut Lodge Hospital, a renowned psychoanalytically oriented long-term treatment centre (Judd and McGlashan, 2003). Among the 81 patients who had been diagnosed with BPD, most were single and female. The onset of their disorder was usually in late adolescence, with first treatment contact in their twenties; however, there was generally a long-standing history of dysfunction in all spheres of adaptation. Treatment at the hospital was as brief as two years or as prolonged as 32 years. Fifteen years after discharge, follow-up interviews were conducted, most consisting of telephone interviews about two hours in length. The majority of those with BPD were rated as having a positive outcome, with most achieving a score of 'good', indicating that they were unimpaired by symptoms most of the time, had been seldom and only briefly rehospitalized since discharge from Chestnut Lodge, and were employed and socially active. Their outcomes compared favourably with those achieved by patients who were treated for schizophrenia or unipolar depression (see Fig. 15.3). Therefore, it appears that, at least for those on a late-starter pathway to BPD and those who receive long-term, intensive treatment, the outcome is far from dire.

However, there was evidence of persisting clinical symptoms in those who had been treated for BPD, particularly in the form of depression and substance abuse. Moreover, given the centrality of unstable relationships in the psychopathology of BPD, the investigators took a closer look at the interpersonal functioning of the individuals in the study. One group was described as having managed to form and maintain meaningful relationships over time: some with friends only, others with intimate partners but no children, and some with spouses and families of their own. However, another large proportion handled the problem of interpersonal relationships by studiously avoiding them. No longer were their relationships stormy and intense, but they had achieved that emotional equilibrium by remaining superficial, isolated, or avoidant.

Resilience and BPD

The data from both the Chestnut Lodge and Collaborative Personality Disorders Study suggest that there is a fair amount of recovery from symptoms of BPD, at least among a subgroup of youth who fit the label for the disorder. The process of maturation itself may help children to 'outgrow' personality disorders as they go through the transition from adolescence to emerging adulthood and achieve a more stable sense of self, better impulse control and interpersonal skills, and a more effective repertoire of coping strategies (Skodol et al., 2007a). In fact, perhaps it is those who do not show this shift during adolescence who are revealing that they are at risk and should be targeted for a preventative early intervention. Skodol and colleagues (2007a) also took a closer look at the children followed in the Collaborative Personality Disorders Study to determine whether there were specific factors that predict remission in adulthood. Although *positive achievement, relationships with friends, caretaker competence* and *absence of maltreatment* predicted remission from other personality disorders, surprisingly, none

FIGURE 15.3 Fifteen-Year Outcomes of the Chestnut Lodge Follow-up Study.

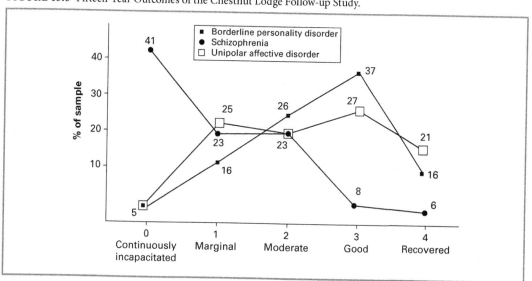

Note: Frequency distribution of clinical global functioning scale scores since discharge for patients with borderline personality disorder and comparison groups.

Source: Judd and McGlashan, 2003.

of these positive childhood variables predicted recovery from BPD. Only male gender, White ethnicity, and fewer comorbid Axis II disorders were related to resilience in children diagnosed with BPD.

Intervention

Psychodynamic Perspectives

Psychodynamic psychotherapy with borderline children and adolescents focuses on providing them with a different kind of relationship than the one that brought about the disorder – a '*corrective emotional experience*' (Freud, 1964). In particular, the therapist encourages the child to overcome the need for splitting by maintaining a consistent level of positive engagement that is not disrupted by the child's anger, projective identification and acting out. Pine (1983) writes that this approach requires the therapist to 'absorb the child's rage attacks and "hold" them within the affectionate working relationship' (p. 97). In addition, the therapist helps the child to establish better *interpersonal boundaries* by assisting the child to recognize and express his or her own thoughts and feelings, and to differentiate them from the therapist's. At the same time that expression of feelings is encouraged, *emotion regulation* also is fostered so that children will not be overwhelmed by their intense emotions. (See also Bleiberg, 2001.)

To this end, there has been much interest in integrating psychodynamic treatment with more structured interventions for BPD (Westen, 1991a). For example, the British clinician Ryle (2004) developed Cognitive Analytic Therapy (CAT), an integration of object relations theory and cognitive psychology that targets the underlying self disorder in BPD. CAT is a brief (16-session), highly structured intervention in which the patient and therapist collaborate on identifying and characterizing shifts in self-states and together create written narratives, drawings and diagrams that allow for self-reflection, communication and integration of the fragmented self. True to the psychoanalytic tradition, the goal of the therapy is to understand the origins of the patient's patterns of maladaptive

behaviour in his or her childhood experiences and in doing so to free the patient from their grip. In a randomized controlled trial conducted in Australia, Chanen and colleagues (2008a) assigned 86 adolescents who met criteria for BPD to either CAT or 'treatment as usual' in a public health service clinic. Although both sets of youth evidenced equal levels of improvement in internalizing, externalizing and self-harming behaviour, there was some evidence that those assigned to CAT improved more quickly.

Cognitive-Behavioural Approaches

A systematic cognitive behavioural approach to treating BPD has been developed by Linehan (1993b), based on her theory of etiology. Dialectical Behaviour Therapy (DBT) combines cognitive behavioural techniques with those derived from Zen philosophy and meditation practices. DBT requires the therapist to maintain an accepting attitude towards the erratic behaviour and distorted beliefs of the patient with borderline pathology, responding matter of factly to suicidal gestures and other bizarre behaviours, while supporting and modelling healthy behaviours. The focus is on changing behaviour through helping individuals to trust and *validate their own inner experiences*, *modulate their emotions* and learn more *adaptive ways of solving interpersonal problems*. Weekly individual treatment is supplemented by group therapy, in which behavioural skills are taught in the areas of interpersonal problem solving, distress tolerance, acceptance of reality, and emotion regulation. A key to these strategies is the practice of *mindfulness*, the cultivation of the ability to be engaged but dispassionately present with what *is*, in the here and now.

The success of Linehan's approach has been documented in several carefully controlled empirical studies with adults (Koerner and Linehan, 2000; see Matusiewicz et al., 2010, for a review). In addition, a team of clinicians have extended DBT to work with parasuicidal adolescents. Miller and colleagues (2006) note that the key issues targeted by DBT – emotion regulation, interpersonal effectiveness, impulse control, self-validation and identity – correspond to key developmental tasks of the adolescent period, thus making this intervention an eminently appropriate one. However, the authors adapted Linehan's intervention in two key ways to further meet the developmental needs of adolescents. First, while the therapy retains its focus on the four skills of mindfulness, distress tolerance, emotion regulation and interpersonal effectiveness, the language and the content of the DBT modules are simplified and made more developmentally appropriate. Second, in recognition that teens are living in the context of the very problematic parent–child relationships implicated in the etiology of the disorder, an important innovation is that a parent or other family member is included in the treatment. In addition to the individual therapy, the adolescent and family member participate in a multifamily skills training group.

In their work with the parents of parasuicidal adolescents, Rathus and Miller (2000) identified four 'dialectical dilemmas' that need to be addressed in the family treatment. (See Table 15.5.)

The first is a dilemma between *excessive leniency versus authoritarian control.* Just as with Patterson's (Reid et al., 2002) model of antisocial behaviour (see Chapter 10), many parents of parasuicidal children report feeling coercively controlled by the child, whose extreme emotional reactions to limit-setting tempt the parent to relinquish authority and adopt a permissive, laissez-faire style of parenting. However, the youth's uncontrolled and self-destructive behaviour subsequently compels the parent to overreact and impose restrictive limits, such as by imposing overly strict rules or unrealistic standards.

> The parents' dialectical dilemma here involves vacillating between the extremes of being overly permissive with their adolescent and feeling ineffectual, coerced, and partly responsible for their adolescent's continued difficulties on the one hand, and setting unreasonable, overly restrictive limits on the other, often to compensate for a period of perceived overpermissiveness. (Rathus and Miller, 2000, p. 428)

The therapist's dialectical dilemma, in turn, is to find a balance between supporting the parent in appropriate limit-setting while allowing the youth a reasonable level of freedom.

The second dilemma concerns *normalizing the pathological versus pathologizing the normative.* Parents of parasuicidal youths may become so desensitized to high-risk behaviours that they fail to recognize when they are truly dangerous, to overlook them out of relief that the adolescent is not engaging in even more destructive activities, or to ignore such behaviour out of the parent's own anxiety and guilt. While the parent's perspective on what is truly dangerous may become jaded by their experiences with multiple suicide attempts, hospitalizations and self-mutilation, the parent's job is made more difficult by virtue of the fact that

TABLE 15.5 Dialectical Dilemmas in DBT for Adolescents and their Families

Dilemma	Targets
Excessive leniency versus authoritarian control	Increasing authoritative discipline; decreasing excessive leniency
	Increasing adolescent self-determination; decreasing authoritarian control
Normalizing pathological behaviours versus pathologizing normative behaviours	Increasing identification of pathological behaviours; decreasing normalization of pathological behaviours
	Increasing recognition of normative behaviours; decreasing pathologizing of normative behaviours
Forcing autonomy versus fostering dependence	Increasing effective reliance on others; decreasing excessive autonomy
	Increasing individuation; decreasing excessive dependence

Source: Rathus and Miller, 2000.

normative adolescent development includes such features as unstable identity, experimentation with risky behaviours and emotional lability. 'In this case, the dialectical dilemma for the parent involves identifying those behaviors that are linked to severe negative consequences so as to properly address them, while at the same time, recognizing normal adolescent behavior so as to not impart unrealistic expectations and limitations' (Rathus and Miller, 2000, p. 429). The therapist shares the same dilemma as the parent and must help both parent and youth to discriminate where behaviours lie on the continuum between the normative and pathological.

The third dilemma concerns *forcing autonomy versus fostering dependence* and involves regulating emotional distance with the adolescent in order to allow for both connection and independent functioning. Parents of adolescents with borderline characteristics frequently forge overly close, dependent relationships with the child that are characterized by an intense, special bond. Ambivalence about separation and confusion about how to foster it in a healthy way may lead the parent to erratically push the adolescent toward independence, sometimes by inappropriately thrusting upon the youth responsibilities that are beyond his or her developmental capacities. 'For the parent, the dialectical dilemma here necessitates finding the middle way between pushing away or letting go precipitously, and clinging or caretaking to the point of stifling the adolescent's separation and individuation process' (Rathus and Miller, 2000, p. 430). For the therapist, the dilemma is to help both parent and child achieve a balance between autonomy and relatedness.

Rathus and Miller (2002) empirically tested the effectiveness of their intervention in a study of 110 consecutive admissions to an inpatient treatment programme for parasuicidal youths.

Twenty-nine adolescents were provided with 12 weeks of DBT, including weekly individual sessions and a weekly multifamily skills group, while 82 received 12 weeks of supportive-psychodynamic 'treatment as usual'. Despite the fact that the adolescents in the DBT condition had higher pretreatment symptom levels, following treatment they underwent fewer psychiatric hospitalizations and were more likely to have completed treatment than youths in the other condition. Further, youths who received DBT evidenced significant reductions in suicidal ideation, symptoms of borderline personality and general psychiatric symptoms at the end of treatment.

Family Therapy

Techniques also have been developed for working with borderline pathology in the family system. For example, Slipp's (1991) object relations family systems approach involves working with the entire family in order to reinforce the boundaries between family members and increase their differentiation from one another, striving to change the family dynamics that interfere with the youth's development of an autonomous sense of self. In particular, work with the parents focuses on helping them to get their own emotional needs met in ways that do not compromise their children's individuation.

We have now explored psychopathologies as they emerge over the lifespan, from infancy to early adulthood. Now that we know the characteristics and consequences of these disorders, our next concerns will be, How will the clinical child psychologist know that a given child has a disorder, and how will the clinician help to remediate it? These are the issues that will concern us next as we turn to in-depth discussions of assessment and intervention.

Psychological Assessment

Chapter contents

Up to this point our goal has been the scientific one of investigating the factors that help us to understand the development of psychopathology. Clinical assessment, while guided by scientific principles, has a practical focus somewhat different from that of empirical inquiry. The clinician's primary role is that of a help-giver. Therefore, the ultimate goal of child assessment is to develop an effective treatment plan to improve the child's overall ability to function in daily life.

We will take the point of view of a clinician who seeks a comprehensive understanding of the child's psychopathology, noting how different theoretical orientations, such as psychodynamic or behavioural, might influence the assessment process. In addition, in order to bring these concepts alive, we will follow a hypothetical assessment of a boy named Rudy. Coverage of specific techniques will be selective. We will assume that readers have an understanding of test construction, reliability and validity commensurate with that gained in an introductory course in psychology (For more detailed coverage, see Bailey and Gross, 2010).

Assessment from a Developmental Psychopathology Perspective

When conducting an assessment, the clinician looks for data that will confirm or rule out various hypotheses about the nature of the child's problems and the processes that account for their development. Therefore, assessment cannot be divorced from theory. The *theoretical perspective* of the clinician influences which hypotheses come most readily to mind and which kind of data will be useful for testing them. For example, *behaviourally* oriented clinicians believe that psychopathology can be understood in terms of social learning principles. Therefore, they tend to study the antecedents and consequences of children's problem behaviour in order to determine what in the environment might be reinforcing and or maintaining it. *Cognitively* oriented clinicians are more interested in children's reasoning processes and the appraisals that lead them to respond maladaptively. *Psychoanalytically* oriented clinicians focus on the unconscious determinants of children's symptoms, which cannot be observed directly but must be inferred from children's projections and fantasies. Clinicians with a *systemic* orientation believe that children's problems arise within the context of the family system and thus want to assess the ways that all the members of the family interact with one another in the here and now. In contrast, *humanistic* clinicians do not want to interfere with self-discovery by imposing their interpretations on children, and therefore they reduce assessment to a bare minimum.

However, developmental psychopathologists argue that each of these clinicians is only obtaining a piece of the puzzle. The *organizational perspective* (see Chapter 1) suggests that a complete assessment of a child needs to *integrate* information from a number of domains, including the behavioural, cognitive, emotional, psychodynamic, interpersonal and systemic (Lahey et al., 2011). Moreover, developmental psychopathologists view children not as a sum of these separate parts, but as integrated, organized and dynamic systems.

For example, even when children are working on what is ostensibly a cognitive task, such as solving a mathematical problem, they are also engaged at the emotional, behavioural and interpersonal level. Is the child happy to be challenged, anxious to please the examiner, crushed by failure, irritated at the task's difficulty? Is the child bright but oppositional, determined to fail as a way of 'getting the goat' of the examiner? Is the child striving to compete with peers or, quite the reverse, to underachieve in order to be perceived as 'one of the gang'? And there is a family context: is the child worried about parental reaction should the child fail, or about upsetting the balance in the family if the child succeeds too well? There are also situational factors to address: is the child tired, does performance reflect fatigue, are there too many distractions for the child to concentrate?

Yet another way in which an assessment needs to be integrative is in terms of the need to obtain reports on children's behaviour from a number of different perspectives. As we discussed in Chapter 3, multiple sources of information may help us obtain a more accurate picture of the child, 'triangulating' perspectives much the way a surveyor does (Cowan, 1978). To assess behavioural and emotional problems, clinicians need information from individuals who see children in their everyday contexts. Teachers are especially important sources of information when children's functioning in school is relevant, such as when ADHD is suspected. Teachers have unique knowledge of the child's classroom behaviour. In contrast, parents are often the primary sources of such information for most children. They also have a long-span view of their child that is invaluable. And only children have access to their own innermost thoughts and feelings. Therefore, each perspective may have something to contribute. Parents and teachers might be particularly good informants in regard to observable behaviour, such as hyperactivity and conduct problems, while children's reports may be more informative about subjective symptoms such as anxiety and depression (Hourigan et al., 2011).

Lastly, because our goal is to understand the child as a whole person, we must identify not only deficits, but also strengths and *competencies* that can be used to help the child overcome any areas of disadvantage. Therefore a comprehensive assessment of many different aspects of functioning is required.

The *developmental dimension* plays an important role in child assessment. Both treatment and assessment should be compatible with the developmental abilities of the child at the time of clinical presentation (Day, 2008). First, there are the challenges to developing rapport and communicating clearly with children of different ages, which we will discuss next. Further, standardized tests incorporate development into the assessment technique itself. Such tests define the age of the population for which they are used, such as tests of infant cognition or high school achievement. Only age-appropriate items are included and items progress in difficulty according to age. Consequently, the clinician can compare the developmental status of a given child with the norms established on a population of children his or her age. Even non-standardized tests, such as projective techniques, are scored in terms of normative information about what is appropriate for children at different ages. In sum, results of any assessment measure always carry the implicit proviso, 'for a child at this developmental level'.

The Assessment Process

Assessment is like a hypothesis-testing enterprise. In attempting to *assimilate*, *integrate* and *interpret* the massive amount of data they collect, clinicians implicitly proceed just like any other scientist (Logan et al., 2011). Detailed documentation is needed to *pinpoint* the specific areas in which the child's behaviour deviates from norms for age and gender. No single bit of behaviour is definitive, but each is *suggestive*. As these bits accumulate, certain initial hunches are *confirmed* and others *discarded*. By the end of the assessment process, the clinician can make some statements concerning the child's problem with a reasonable degree of assurance; other statements will be tentative and qualified, and a number of questions will remain unanswered.

Clinicians never assume that within the space of a few hours they will be able to fully apprehend the *nature* and *origin* of the problems that bring a particular child to their attention. They realize they are viewing parent and child under special circumstances that both limit and bias the data they will obtain. The child who is frightened by a clinic waiting room may not be a generally fearful child, just as one who is hyperactive in school may be a model of co-operation when taking an intelligence test. Parents may have their own misperceptions and blind spots in regard to their child's behaviour, along with varying degrees of willingness to reveal information about themselves. It is also important to recognize that here exist various motivations as to why a parent may/may not want a child to obtain an official diagnosis. Sadly, gaining both financial assistance and extra support for a child's behaviour both inside and outside school settings is often dependent upon an official diagnosis. This has been found to be one of the key factors in parents seeking a formal diagnosis in the first place. *Standardized tests* also have limitations in terms of *reliability*, *validity* or *appropriateness* for different populations. Thus, as much as clinicians strive towards achieving an understanding of the child and family, they also must be duly mindful about the limitations of the assessment techniques they use and their appropriateness for different groups of children (American Psychological Association, 2002).

Purposes of Assessment

While the medical model might strive towards the end product of a static, one-dimensional diagnosis (see Chapter 3), the goal of assessment from a developmental psychopathology perspective is a **case formulation**. A case formulation is a succinct, dynamic description of the child that incorporates the clinician's interpretation of how the problem came about and how it might be remediated (Carey and Pilgrim, 2010). In essence, the case formulation is a *hypothesis* about potential underlying influences that *precipitate* (cause) and *maintain* the behaviour, including child and environmental (family, peers, community) factors. Case formulation will typically involve a process of three stages: (1) problem identification, (2) problem explanation and (3) treatment planning. When a diagnosis is made, a wealth of clinical knowledge about the disorder is already readily available. The case formulation helps to *synthesize* all of the information the clinician obtained, such as what is the problem, what is causing the problem, why is the problem persisting, and to put it into a form that will be useful to those who requested the assessment. An effective assessment report helps its reader to understand the child and generates ideas about how to *intervene* effectively. (We will have more to say about how the case formulation informs treatment in Chapter 17.) Table 16.1 displays the elements that might be included in a comprehensive case formulation. While the case formulation helps the clinician to find a path through the forest of information collected during the assessment, it should not be a rigid one. Like all hypotheses, the

TABLE 16.1 Components of the Case Formulation

1. Presenting problem: Define in a way that reflects unique situation of this child and family
   a. Physiological
   b. Mood
   c. Behavioural
   d. Cognitive
   e. Interpersonal
2. Testing data
3. Cultural context variables
   a. Racial identity
   b. Level of acculturation
   c. Ethnocultural beliefs, values and practices
   d. Experiences of prejudice or marginalization
4. History and developmental milestones
   a. Temperament; emotional and behavioural dysregulation
   b. Developmental delays and deviations
   c. Family relationships and attachment processes
      i. Interparental relationship: conflict, co-parenting co-operation
      ii. Dyadic parent–child relationships: closeness, role clarity, boundary dissolution
      iii. Individual parenting styles: warmth, structure, over-protectiveness, demandingness, perceived parenting competence/anxiety, parenting stress
      iv. Attachment
      v. Whole-family processes: enmeshment-distance, triangulation; coalitions; scapegoating
   d. Functioning in extra-familial environments (e.g., school, peer relationships)
   e. Strengths, skills and competencies
5. Cognitive variables
   a. Automatic thoughts
   b. Schemata
   c. Cognitive distortions
6. Behavioural antecedents and consequences
7. Provisional formulation
   a. Co-ordinates the components in a dynamic and interrelated way
   b. Paints a portrait of the child's environment and inner world
   c. Relates pathogenic processes that led to disorder to change processes that will be used to intervene
8. Treatment plan
9. Expected obstacles and impediments to treatment

Source: Adapted from Friedberg and McClure, 2002.

case formulation is open to new information and can be revised in the face of disconfirming data.

In order to help *identify the nature of the problem* underlying the child's condition, clinicians will have a wealth of knowledge about specific disorders based on their understanding of *normative expectations*, awareness of *etiology* of disorders and familiarity of empirical *research*. It is at this stage in which they also have access to a wide variety of assessments from multiple sources (parent, teachers, child). In cases where multiple problems have been identified in the child there may be a need to prioritize specific problem behaviours. However, pinpointing the problem is not an easy task. In some cases the problem which is identified as the main problem may turn out to be the secondary and the case will then have to be reformulated. The second stage in the case formulation involves *interpreting the actual problem*. Developmental and family history both provide important information regarding potential genetic (family pathology) or event based causes (family or school history, traumatic events, etc.). Here the assessment process requires knowledge of the appropriate interview and observational techniques as well as broad assessment strategies (behavioural, emotional) and syndrome-specific tests (detecting anxiety or depression). These assessment methods can be pivotal in *identifying and ruling* out potential diagnoses. Knowledge of risks and protective factors can also assist in a better understanding of what might *exacerbate or moderate* the problem. *The final stage* of the case formulation involves the monitoring and evaluating treatment effectiveness. This is important in identifying changes in symptoms and behaviours during the child's development in order to increase a better understanding of the etiology of the disorder and to gain maximum benefit from intervention. It is important to note that at each stage of the case formulation an assortment of theoretical perspectives may aid in increasing our understanding. Common theoretical frameworks include biological, behavioural, cognitive (social cognitive), psychodynamic, attachment, parenting and family systems. This will be addressed throughout the coming chapter

Initial Sources of Data

Referrals

The first data concerning the child comes from the *referring person* – teacher, parent, physician, and so on – who can provide information about the problem as perceived by concerned adults, its duration and onset, its effects on the child and on others, and what measures, if any, have been taken

to remedy it. Parents and teachers are the major sources of referrals.

In contrast to adults, children rarely refer themselves to treatment, a fact that has important psychological implications. *Seeking help* is very different than being told one needs help. Children may not feel the need to change and may not understand why they are being brought for an evaluation. Sometimes parents give children reasons the children disagree with, or even fail to tell them why they are being brought to the clinic. Therefore, during the first telephone contact, it can be helpful to discuss with parents how they might introduce the topic of the assessment with their children.

You are a clinical child psychologist who has been asked to assess Rudy, an 8-year-old boy. His teacher suggested an evaluation because of academic and behavioural problems in the classroom. Specifically, his mother tells you that Rudy is failing reading and arithmetic and that his teacher describes him as 'lazy', withdrawn and uncooperative in class. A neighbour suggested that Rudy sounded just like her own boy, who was diagnosed with ADHD. The first questions in the back of your mind concern the reasons for this referral and the constructions being placed on this problem by the mother, the teacher and Rudy himself. Is this a learning problem, a conduct problem, attention-deficit related or the consequence of a negative interaction between this family and the school? Are the teacher and the parents going to be supportive of Rudy during the assessment process, or have they taken a blaming attitude that will complicate your work? Is Rudy willing to come to the clinic or will he be angry and oppositional with you? As your consultants, we will follow the evaluation of Rudy throughout this chapter in order to see how an assessment like this might play out.

In relation to assessment of the child's mental health, for example, children traditionally have been required to 'go along for the ride' as adults gather parametric data, such as physical measures and behavioural observations with adult caregivers as the primary source of information. Children have often been *excluded* from direct participation in the assessment process. Further, the assessment tools used with children have often been *simplified versions* of tools designed for adults, despite the obvious developmental differences that exist between adults and children (Day, 2008). Contemporary practice guidelines recommend that child assessments are multi-modal or include a range of different tests and measures, and multi-informant or include interviews with the parent, child and teacher (Holmbeck et al., 2004). Central to this process is the child interview, as it allows an insight to how the child views the problem and to gain a unique view into the child's internal world (Carr, 2006).

Both researchers and clinicians have emphasized the need to obtain a first-hand account of the child's experiences because psychological processes, such as *thoughts* and *feelings* and *experiences* must be conveyed to others via communication. Failure to interview the child directly can lead to difficulty in ascertaining the degree of adversity or suffering that a child is experiencing or, conversely, whether the child is experiencing any difficulty at all. Research also suggests that parents do not always report accurately on the child's psychological processes and affective experiences. In one particular study conducted in a child mental health outpatient setting, a large sample of children and patients were interviewed (Hawley and Weisz, 2003). After the assessment was complete the parents, children and therapists were asked to identify the target symptoms and their responses were compared. Only one-quarter of the sample commenced therapy with consensus between parent, child and therapist regarding the problem. Adults were dominant within the assessment process despite children's perspective having more predictive value. There has also been shown to be a clear discrepancy between parent's and children's view of the presenting problems and of the child internal state. Parents commonly report more externalizing

symptoms and behaviours, which directly increase levels of parenting burden, whereas children were more likely to report internalizing symptoms such as anxiety or depressed mood.

An example of the benefit of gaining multi-informant information can be shown using the Child Behaviour Checklist (CBCL). The CBCL is a standardized form that parents fill out to describe their children's behavioural and emotional problems. The teachers may be asked to complete the Caregiver–Teacher Report Form which has many of the same items. If one of the informants, albeit the parent or teacher, reports higher levels of particular problems such as aggressive behaviour, this does not necessarily mean that the informant is either inaccurate or the cause of the child's problem. A major benefit of using parallel assessment forms is that they explicitly document both inconsistencies and consistencies in how children's functioning is seen across a variety of situations and interaction partners. The informant-specific aspects may be as valuable as those that are consistent. For example, if a father reports a child as showing more aggressive behaviour, it would be exceedingly helpful to ask about the circumstances in which the child shows these aggressive outbursts and how these circumstances differ from what the teacher would see.

Comparisons of parents' reports with reports of others, such as teachers and adolescents, are especially helpful for assessing the *cross-informant consistency* of problems on syndromes such as anxious, somatic complaints, and attention problems, to document the need for further medical assessment or referral for mental health services. To facilitate comparisons among scores from multiple informants, cross-informant software is now available. This produces a profile scored from each form and side by side comparisons of the scores obtained from each informant on each item and each syndrome. As an example, side by side comparisons of problem items may reveal a youth reporting suicidal ideation and behaviour on the Youth Self-Report (YSR), which can be filled out by 11- to 18-year-olds to describe their own problems that neither parent or teacher report. This would indicate a possible risk for suicide that was not evident to the youth's parent and teachers.

Parent Interviews

Information concerning the child and the family usually comes first from an interview with the parents. Parents play an important role as (1) children under-report disruptive behaviour, (2) children are often more guarded about their emotions, (3) younger children have more difficulty reporting symptoms, and (4) parents are key stakeholders in the therapeutic process, and it is important to know if they believe that any progress is occurring.

Typically, the interview begins with an account of the presenting problem. It is important for the clinician to gain a list of *reasons for referral*, in the parent's own words/terms. Sometimes this can be operationalized as specific behavioural targets/objectives at a later date. Next, a detailed *developmental history* is obtained in order to explore the antecedent conditions that might have contributed to the child's present difficulties. Among the topics covered are the child's prenatal and birth history and early development. The *subsequent adjustment* of the child within the family and with peers is explored, along with social and academic performance. For teenagers, information is obtained concerning sexual development and work history, as well as possible drug and alcohol use and delinquent behaviour. The clinician also inquires about major illnesses and injuries and stresses experienced by the child and family. Information regarding any *treatment* that the child may have already been subjected to is also important to collect. To complete the picture, the parents may be asked about their own individual, marital and occupational adjustment; their specific goals, satisfactions and dissatisfactions; and the attempts they have made to deal with the problem in the past.

What about the studies showing the *unreliability* of retrospective reports? While parents may not always report accurate information concerning many aspects of the child and family, it is still important for the clinician to know the parents'

perception of the facts. Whether the child was a 'difficult' infant and a 'bad' toddler may not be as important as the parents' perception or memory of the child as difficult and bad.

In the process of interviewing, the clinician is beginning to know the parents, while the parents are also beginning to know the clinician. Since there is no hard and fast line between assessment and therapy, skilled interviewers can use this initial contact to lay the groundwork for the trust and respect that will be so crucial in the future. The establishment of *rapport* between the parent and the clinician is an important part of the process. Parents may feel shamed about bringing their child for an assessment and may have concerns either that their parenting is at fault or that the clinician will blame them for causing the problem. Thus, the interviewer wants to take care to put parents at ease, support them for their obvious concern for their child, and establish that the parents and the assessor are 'rowing on the same team'.

In addition, the parent interview provides the clinician the opportunity to gather information about the present family system of relationships, as well as the possible role that the parents' own family histories might play in their difficulties with their child. To accomplish this, Haydel and colleagues (2011) suggest asking parents to complete a family *genogram* as part of the assessment. The genogram is a pictorial representation of the relationships among the people in a family, usually spanning three generations to include the child, parents and grandparents. First, demographic information is recorded, such as birth and death dates, places of origin and career paths. Second, critical events are indicated, such as divorces, moves or traumatic experiences. Third, interaction patterns are represented by special lines connecting various family members. For example, lines can indicate relationships that are close, enmeshed, distant, conflictual, or cut off. (See Fig. 16.1.) The genogram can help the clinician to identify coalitions and triangles in the family, as well as inter-generational patterns of conflict, estrangement, role-reversal and so forth that interfere with parents' ability to respond

FIGURE 16.1 Genogram: Three Generations of Rudy's Family.

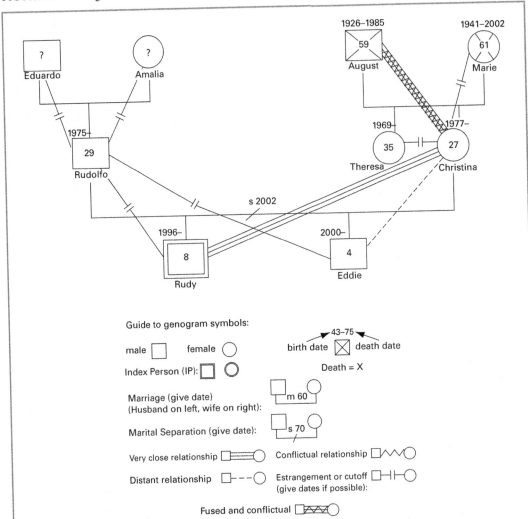

appropriately to their children's developmental needs. (See McGoldrick and Gerson, 1985, for a number of intriguing examples, including a genogram of Sigmund Freud's family.)

Rudy's mother Christina is 20 minutes late for her first meeting with you, arriving flustered and dishevelled. She explains that as a single parent she found it difficult to manage the complications of getting off work early and arranging day care for her youngest son, Eddie. She

divorced the boys' father, Rudolfo, two years ago, and they have rarely heard from him since he returned to his native Argentina. 'Everything was fine with Rudy up until then,' she says. 'Sometimes I wonder if we should've stayed together for the boys. But Rudolfo is no good – nothing but a drunken brute. Rudy is nothing like him, thank goodness. He's a terrific kid – my little man.' In contrast, she seems to have little to say about little Eddie. He is described as a 'handful', and she states she is glad to have

Rudy's help with managing her younger son's behaviour.

Christina's description of Rudy's early history includes nothing remarkable. She reports no major illnesses or deviations from expected development until the time of the divorce, which, you note, also occurred the year that Rudy entered first grade. She does not believe that there is anything 'wrong' with Rudy; she suspects that the teacher 'just can't relate to him'. She acknowledges that she and the teacher are not on particularly good terms. She explains that she herself had a lot of difficulty in school, and, with some humour, states that she looks back on her teachers as 'torturers'.

Christina is uncomfortable at first with the idea of completing a family genogram, commenting that she doesn't understand 'what this has to do with anything'. However, as your rapport improves, she agrees. What emerges is a history of broken relationships across the generations. (See Fig. 16.1.) Rudy's father cut off contact with his own parents and little is known about them. Christina also has nothing to do with her own family of origin. Her father August was a violent but charming man who died of cirrhosis of the liver when she was about Rudy's age. She was his 'favourite' when drink made him affectionate, and the special target of his abuse when he was 'mean drunk'. She says, 'I adored him and hated him in equal amounts'. Following the father's death, Christina's mother abandoned the children, leaving Christina in the care of her older sister, Theresa. The two sisters, always rivals for the little affection there was in the family, had a falling out about the disposition of their mother's will a couple of years ago and have not spoken since. When asked about current sources of support in her life, Christina pauses and then confides that she attends AA meetings. This is your first intimation that, like her father and Rudy's father, she has a problem with alcohol.

Informal Observations

The clinician's assessment begins when first seeing the child and parents. Their appearance and interactions provide clues about *family characteristics* and the relationships among its members. First impressions furnish information concerning the family's social class and general level of harmony or disharmony, as well as its stylistic characteristics – reserved, expressive, authoritarian, intellectual and so on. As always, the clinical child psychologist evaluates behaviour in terms of its age appropriateness or inappropriateness, the former providing clues about assets and resources, the latter providing clues to possible disturbances.

Once with the child, the clinician systematically gathers certain kinds of information. The overall impression of the child's *personality* is always worth noting: 'A funny, fun-loving boy'; 'he already has the worried look of an old man'; 'she has a sullen look, like she is spoiling for a fight'; 'a direct, honest, no-nonsense pre-adolescent girl, who doesn't want to be coddled'. While it is important not to prejudge children on the basis of initial impressions, these first reactions might give the clinician clues about the child's social-stimulus value, which may be a potent elicitor of positive or negative reactions from others.

The child's *manner of relating* to the clinician furnishes information concerning his or her perception of adults. It is natural for children to be reserved initially, since the clinician is a stranger. As they discover that the clinician is an interested and friendly adult, they should become more relaxed and communicative. However, certain children never warm up; they sit as far back in their chair as possible, speak in an almost inaudible monotone, either rarely look at the examiner or else watch intently, as if he or she were a kind of monster who might strike out at any minute. Provocative children 'test the limits', mischievously peeking when told to close their eyes or destroying a puzzle when asked to leave it intact.

Generally speaking, clinical observations such as these are nearer an art than a science because the procedures are not standardized and the target behaviours are so wide-ranging. It is also important that the child is observed in a variety of settings to gain a better overview of their behaviour, what they are interested in, what they can do and also any particular difficulties they have. However, observation per se is not unscientific. Behavioural clinicians, as we will see later, bring to assessment the structure and reliability that the more open-ended approach lacks.

Upon first spotting Rudy in the waiting room, you have the impression that he is a handsome and healthy-looking boy, although you are struck by the fact that he is neater and more carefully groomed than is usual for a youngster his age. When you enter the room, he is disciplining his little brother, cautioning him not to handle the magazines too roughly. He greets you brightly but checks back with his mother before he goes with you, asking her if she will be 'OK'.

Child Interviews

Structured, Semi-structured and Unstructured Interviews

The clinician wants to be able to see things from the child's-eye point of view, which can be facilitated by conducting an interview. Interviews confer a number of advantages, such as giving children a chance to present their *own perspective* on the problem, allowing the interviewer to assess areas of functioning that might not be accessible through other means, enabling the interviewer to *observe* children's behaviour and attitudes relevant to the problem, and providing an opportunity to establish the *rapport* that will be necessary if a therapeutic relationship is to develop (Frick et al., 2010). In addition, the interview gives the clinician the opportunity to clarify with children why they are there and to explain what the assessment process will be like. (For more information, see Phillips and Gross, 2010.)

Interviews can be conceptualized along a continuum based on how structured they are. In *unstructured interviews*, clinicians encourage children to put in their own words their views about the problem; the family, school and peers; interests, hopes and fears; self-concept; and, for adolescents, career aspirations, sexual relations and drug or alcohol use.

In contrast to unstructured interviews, which allow the interviewer considerable leeway for improvising and following up unexpected leads, *semi-structured interviews* consist of a series of open-ended questions followed by specific probes to help the interviewer determine the presence or absence of diagnostic symptoms. An example is the Semistructured Clinical Interview for Children and Adolescents (SCICA; McConaughy and Achenbach, 2001), which was developed for children aged 6 to 18.

A series of open-ended questions is interspersed with non-verbal tasks, such as drawings and play activities, designed to set children at ease and to encourage them to reveal their thoughts, feelings and behaviour through their interaction with the examiner. The interviewer uses both child self-reports, his or her own observations of the child and also by observers who are present in the room, watching through a one-way mirror or watching a video recording, in order to rate psychopathology.

Structured interviews also consist of a series of specific questions or statements, but the child's response is structured as well, whether as a 'yes–no' choice or as a point on a scale ranging from 'strongly agree' to 'disagree'. (For a review see Philips and Gross, 2010.) Structured interviews devised for children include the *Diagnostic Interview for Children and Adolescents* (DICA-IV; Reich, 2000); the *Schedule for Affective Disorders and Schizophrenia for School-Age Children* (K-SADS-IVR; Ambrosini and Dixon, 1996); the *Diagnostic Interview Schedule for Children and Adolescents* (DISC-IV; Shaffer et al., 2003); and the *Children's Interview for Psychiatric Syndromes* (ChIPS; Weller et al., 1999). Each of these interviews has both child and parent version, and all generate DSM diagnoses for most disorders seen in childhood. (See Frick et al., 2010, for a review.) Figure 16.2 presents excerpts from the K-SADS and

DISC illustrating the questions used to elicit information about impulsive/inattentive behaviour.

Rapport

In order for any assessment technique to be of use, the child must at least be minimally co-operative; ideally, the child should participate wholeheartedly. Therefore, essential to the assessment process is good *rapport*. The establishment of rapport requires clinical skills, sensitivity and experience. Moreover, the clinician must be prepared to deal with a variety of obstacles at different ages – a crying infant; a toddler fearful of leaving the mother; a provocative, defiant school-age child; a sullen teenager who resents all questioning by adults. But aside from such dramatic challenges, there is always the question of how one goes about establishing oneself as an interested, friendly adult to children of different ages. For example, while a preschool child might be set at ease by meeting the clinician in a playroom and using puppets or drawings to express thoughts and feelings, an adolescent might feel insulted by being interviewed in such a setting. In addition, older youths may warm more readily to an examiner who is candid and direct, treating them as a competent young person whose active participation in the assessment process is invited.

Guckian and Byrne (2011) make a few suggestions in order to establish good rapport. First, it is extremely important to first establish a connection with the child as it allows you to explore child's level of understanding. The more at ease a child feels the more information they will give (Wilson and Powell, 2001). The interviewer needs to use language appropriate to the child's developmental and cognitive ability, and needs to adopt a *warm*, *interested* and *respectful* attitude that engages the child, without being overly formal. Also where possible the clinician should attempt to match the *pace* and *interpersonal style* of the child. A shy and reticent child may be more comfortable with an examiner who talks softly and slowly, while a rough-and-tumble or streetwise child may respond best to a lively and fast-paced interviewing style. Children can also be set at ease

by some side conversations that establish common ground or mutual interests between themselves and the examiner. Other recommendations include maintaining a *supportive* and distracting free environment and *encouraging* children to talk freely. It is also essential to explain to the child your expectations of what is going to happen so they are clear as to how much information to provide. Depending on age and emotional state, parents should not be present. (For a review, see also Sattler and Hoge, 2006.)

Interview needs to be congruent with the child's developmental needs. Open-ended questions, free recall prompts, have been identified as the single most effective prompt type to increase the accuracy of information that children report about prior experiences (Lamb et al., 2007). Open-ended prompts include statements such as 'Tell me what happened' or 'Tell me everything you can about…' (Larsson and Lamb, 2009). Also allow children to give details which may seem irrelevant from an adult perspective. For optimal outcomes the interviewers usually provide a structured interview format with supportive context and interpersonal interactions (Pipe and Salmon, 2009).

Developmental Considerations

For any interview to be valid, it must be tailored to the child's level of understanding. At the very least, it is important for the interviewer to match the vocabulary level of the child in order to be understood and to help the interview go smoothly (Guckian and Byrne, 2011). However, the child's developmental level will affect many other aspects of the interview process.

During the *preschool* years, children's self-understanding is expressed primarily in terms of *physical characteristics* and *actions* ('I have brown hair'; 'I play ball'; 'I have a dog'). (Here we follow Harter, 1988; Steward et al., 1993; Stone and Lemanek, 1990.) Consequently, questions about the nature of the problem that brought them to see a psychologist are apt to elicit responses couched in terms of specific behaviours ('I hit my brother') rather than internal experiences. These, in turn,

FIGURE 16.2 Examples of Questions Used in Structured and Semi-structured Interviews.

K-SADS

Impulsivity: Refers to the child's characteristic pattern of acting before thinking about the consequences. It does not refer to 'bad' actions only but to a behavioural characteristic spanning all types of behaviour independent of moral significance.

Are you the kind of person who tends to get into trouble, or maybe even gets hurt, because you rush into things without thinking what might happen? Are you often wrong in school because you answer with the first thing that comes to your mind instead of thinking it over first? Do you get into trouble in school because you often speak out when you're supposed to be quiet? Does your teacher often have to tell you what you are supposed to do after the rest of the class has started doing it? Do you have trouble organizing your work? Do you often do things on a dare or just because the idea popped into your head or just for the heck of it?	0 No information 1 Not present 2 Slight: May occur on occasion when excited (party, etc.) but not typical and no bad consequences. 3 Mild: Definitely present. Acts impulsively at least 3 times a week in at least 2 settings. 4 Moderate: Impulsive in all settings. 5 Severe: Impulsive in all settings and has gotten into dangerous situations for lack of foresight in a few instances (more than 3 times in a year). 6 Extreme: Very impulsive; it is an almost constant characteristic of child's behaviour. Gets into danger at least once a week.

DISC			
Impulsivity	No	Sometimes	Yes
Does your teacher often tell you that you don't listen?	0		2
(if yes) Does he/she say that to you more than to most kids?	0	1	2
(if yes) How long has that been happening?	Months:		
(if yes) Have you been like that since you started school?	0		2
Does your teacher often tell you that you're not keeping your mind on your work?	0		2
(if yes) Does he/she say that to you more than to most kids?	0		2
(if yes) How long has that been happening?	Months:		
(if yes) Have you been like that since you started school?	0		2
Sometimes kids rush into things without thinking about what may happen. Do you do that?	0	1	2
(if yes) Have you always been like that?	0		2
(if yes) How long have you been like that?	Months:		
Some kids have trouble organizing their schoolwork. They can't decide what they need. They can't plan what to do first, what to do second. Are you like that?	0	1	2
(if yes) How long have you been like that?	Months:		
Do you start your schoolwork and not finish it?	0	1	2
(if yes) How long has that been happening?	Months:		
(if yes) Have you always had trouble finishing it?	0		2
(if yes) Is that because you don't know how to do it?	0	1	2

Source: K-SADS (Puig-Antich and Chambers, 1978); DISC (Costello et al., 1984).

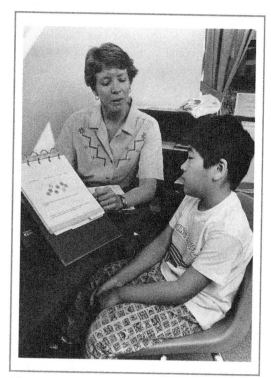

The importance of good rapport in assessment: will this child give his best performance?

probably echo what parents or other adults have said to them about being 'bad'. Recall that young children are never self-referred and often do not see themselves as having problems. In a like manner, children's view of the cause of the problem is apt to be specific and external ('I hit my brother because he takes my things').

Preschoolers' evaluations of their own emotions and those of other people are also *concrete* and *situational*; for example, being happy is having a birthday party. Consequently, interview questions must be similarly concrete and action oriented ('Do you cry?' rather than 'Do you feel sad?'). The interviewer should also expect people to be described in terms of what they do rather than what they think or how they feel.

In *middle childhood* children are able to express ideas about the self-concept that are 'psychological' and more differentiated; for example, instead of being judged 'smart' or 'dumb', the child can be

'smart' in some things and 'dumb' in others. In this period children are able to provide accurate reports of their own emotions by using *internal, psychological* cues. They also begin to attribute psychological characteristics to others and realize other people have perspectives different from their own. Along with these cognitive advances goes the ability to recognize deviance. However, even in early adolescence there is still the tendency to attribute cause to external, typically social, events, such as family quarrels and conflicts.

Cognitive development determines how the child will understand the helping relationship, including the concept of the psychologist as helper as well as the concept of being helped. The *preschooler* is apt to view the former in terms of general traits, such as being 'kind' or 'nice', along with the psychologist's specific behaviours, such as 'playing games'. In *middle childhood* references to competence begin to appear, such as 'She knows what she is doing', while the early *adolescent* recognizes the role of inner qualities of empathy and a desire to help. Being helped itself changes from denoting some form of direct action in the preschool period (for example, 'Buy me a new game to play and tell my brother to quit picking on me') to a recognition of the importance of support, validation, regard, and other kinds of indirect help in early adolescence.

Ethnic Diversity

Cultural competence, an ethical mandate for psychologists (American Psychological Association, 2003), is an important part of rapport and effective interviewing with children and families. (See also Gibbs and Huang, 2003.) Comprehension of cultural values and norms can assist the interviewer to engage with the family and appreciate rather than pathologize their differences. For example, understanding the courtesies and conventions of conversation is important. While an informal approach in which the psychologist greets the parents on a first name basis might set at ease a middle-class European American family, a traditional Asian family might perceive this friendly approach as a sign of disrespect (Ho, 1992). To take another example, Native American children prefer to wait before responding to questions, and so it is important that the clinician understands that a long lag time is not an indication of insecurity or resistance.

Being an expert in all cultural groups and their norms is not a prerequisite for becoming a clinical child psychologist. However, an awareness of one's own cultural expectations and recognizing that they are not universal norms is key to remaining open minded, receptive and non-judgemental (McIntosh, 1998). In addition, a therapist's sensitive and honestly interested inquiries into the family's cultural beliefs and practices may be quite well received. If a child's language and culture differ from those of the children he or she is being compared with, the comparisons may suggest conclusions that are not accurate. Test items may also relate to experiences that are unfamiliar to a culturally different child. For example, in some cultures children are taught to respond to adults with short answers. It is important to always include a norm-referenced assessment that is, at the most fundamental level, relevant to minority populations. (For a review see Suzuki and Ponterotto, 2008.)

Sue and Sue (2008) have identified three variables that are important when assessing ethnic minority families: *culture-bound* (e.g., cultural beliefs and practices), *language-bound* (e.g., facility with the vocabulary and linguistic conventions of the interviewer's language) and *class-bound* (e.g., the effects of socio-economic status on the family's lifestyle, community and aspirations). Issues to explore in interviews with ethnic minority children and their families include the level of *acculturation* of the family as a whole, and where there might be differences among individual family members, particularly between the generations. Acculturation is thought to be a fundamental variable that underlies the issues of cultural and linguistic diversity in assessment. According to the APA Dictionary (Vandenbos and American Psychological Association, 2007), acculturation is 'the process by which groups of individuals integrate the social and cultural values, ideas, beliefs, and behavioural

patterns of their culture of origin with those of a different culture' (p. 8) (for a review see Cormier et al., 2011). For example, immigrant children often become quickly assimilated into US culture through their exposure to peers during the school day, even when their parents continue to hold fast to traditional values derived from the home country. *Cultural strain* may also be evident when children experience conflict between meeting the demands of the old and new culture. *Ethnic identity* reflects the child's internalization of a sense of belonging to a specific cultural group. While the development of a secure sense of *bicultural identity* (e.g., identification with one's ethnic group as well as a feeling of membership in the larger culture) is believed to be linked to positive adjustment (Ogbu, 1999), many factors might interfere with its development, including prejudice, racism and experiences of marginalization. Lastly, *social class* differences among ethnic minority families are vast and belie stereotypes that automatically equate minority status with lack of privilege. Just as middle-class African American families create different contexts for child development than those who struggle with poverty, immigrants from the elite classes may have little in common with impoverished refugees from the same country.

Ho (1992) presents a transcultural framework for assessing children from diverse cultural backgrounds. (See Table 16.2.) His model integrates influences in the individual, family, school, peer and community spheres. Within each area of functioning, one of the clinician's key tasks is to determine to what extent the child's adaptation is a reflection of culturally appropriate norms that are in conflict with those of the majority norms.

Because Rudy is in middle childhood, you decide to equip the interview room with coloured pens and paper, clay, chess, and a few other games that might help to set him at ease. Your first observation is that Rudy ignores all of the toys and attends carefully to you, eager to answer all your questions. While most children are cautious initially, and rightly so, from the beginning of the

TABLE 16.2 Transcultural Guidelines for the Assessment of the Child and Family

To what extent is the individual child's adjustment a function of the following?

Individual Level of Psychosocial Adjustment

1 Physical appearance, which can be affected by malnutrition, improper diet, height, weight, skin colour and hair texture and unfavourably compared with preferred Anglo norms

2 Affect expression, which may be culturally appropriate but may be in direct conflict with the mainstream norms which emphasize directness and overt assertiveness

3 Self-concept and self-esteem, which are germane to the child's native culture and are appropriate criteria for self-evaluation but are in conflict with the mainstream criteria for self-concept and self-esteem

4 Interpersonal competence, which differs according to different sociocultural milieu

5 Definition of and attitudes towards autonomy, which may be in serious conflict with the norms of the child's school or community milieu or is adaptive within the child's overall life situation

6 Attitudes towards achievement, which are culturally appropriate but are in conflict with the traditional channels of educational achievement enforced by the public school system

7 Management of aggression and impulse control, which can enhance or impede his or her school performance and interpersonal competence

8 Coping and defence mechanisms that may be dysfunctional in certain sociocultural contexts and environments

Relationships with Family

9 Family structure that is in transition because of immigration, acculturation, or life-cycle processes

10 Roles within the family, which are in conflict with the traditional structure favouring older-age and male-gender hierarchies

11 Family communication conflict from hierarchical to egalitarian caused by acculturation and family life processes

12 Parental use of discipline, which may enhance or impede the child's performance at school or at home

13 Culturally defined dominant dyad, which is in conflict with the Anglo-American nuclear family ideals that define father–mother as the dominant dyad

14 Culturally defined autonomy, which is in conflict with the Anglo-American nuclear family ideals that define autonomy as physical departure from family of origin and financial independence

School Adjustment and Achievement

15 Psychological adjustment, which may be attributed to parental lack of education, parental negative attitudes towards the school, the child's unfamiliarity with the norms and expectations of the classroom and school environment, social-class differences and/or language difficulties

16 Social adjustment, which may require moving away from a familiar neighbourhood school to a larger school where there are greater cultural, racial and economic differences

17 Behavioural adjustment, which may be related to an unstable home situation, poor nutrition, poor physical health or the inability to handle overwhelming anxiety and stress

18 Academic achievement as measured by culturally biased achievement tests and/or verbal skills, motivation for learning, attitudes towards a particular class or towards the school in general, study habits and family support

Relationships with Peers

19 Ability to display empathy, to form friendships, to engage in co-operative and competitive activities and to manage aggressive and sexual impulses

20 Social skills to form peer relationships at school and within the child's own community and the effects of these peer relationships on overall psychosocial functioning

Adaptation to the Community

21 Quality participation in church activities, youth groups, and language- and ethnic-related classes

22 Quality participation in organized sports, arts activities, volunteer activities or part-time jobs

23 Inappropriate or excessive activities that create family conflicts or dysfunctional behaviour, such as delinquency, drug abuse or poor academic behaviour

Source: Ho, 1992.

interview Rudy is unusually open and communicative. As the interview progresses, he continues to impress you as a bright, alert, open youngster. You mentally note Rudy's behaviour and wonder what it might represent. Perhaps this is a basically well-functioning boy whose problems have been exaggerated; perhaps he has been overly close to adults at the cost of developing appropriate peer relationships; perhaps he is a charming psychopath; perhaps his social skills are a defence against some unknown fear.

Rudy offers his own perspective on the problem. 'I don't like school,' he says, and when asked what he doesn't like about it, he replies with a downcast face, 'Schoolwork is boring. And the other kids are jerks. I don't like any of them.' He spends most of his time after school helping his mother around the house and taking care of his little brother. 'I like to help out,' he says. He states that if he could have three wishes, they would be 'to stay home instead of going to school', 'to buy a big house for us to live in' and 'to have a billion dollars so that my mom wouldn't have to go to work anymore'.

When you ask Rudy about his father, his initial reaction is flat and dismissive. He describes him as 'no good', echoing his mother's words and sentiments in a way that is striking. However, as you enquire more about the father's return to his South American homeland, Rudy expresses some wistful longing to see for himself the land that his father's family hailed from. He begins to talk with animation about the things he has learned about Argentinian culture from the books he checked out of the library. Rudy seems at first taken aback and then puzzled when you ask about his own ethnic identity. 'I don't know. I never really thought about it. My dad is Argentinian,' he says, 'but I guess I'm just American like my mom.'

Psychological Tests

Of all professionals dealing with disturbed children, clinical psychologists have been the most concerned with developing assessment techniques that can be

objectively administered and scored, that have norms based on clearly defined populations and that have established reliability and validity. However, it is worth noting that a major drawback of a lot of instruments is that they are often a single narrow-band instrument and thus fail to assess comorbid conditions (Lavigne et al., 2009). While many different tests have been developed, our coverage here will focus only on a few of the more widely used tests. (For more extensive and detailed reviews of a variety of psychological tests for children, refer to Groth-Marnat, 2009; Sattler and Hoge, 2006.)

Cognitive Testing from Infancy to Adolescence
Infant Cognitive Testing
Infant testing requires that the examiner have special skills in *accommodation* in order to elicit the child's optimal performance. The examiner must know how to intrigue the infant with the test material, allow for distractions, temporarily become a comforting caretaker in response to fretting, postpone testing when distress becomes too great – in short, the good examiner must have the sensitivity, flexibility and warmth of a good parent.

One of the best constructed standardized infant tests is the *Bayley Scales of Infant Development – Third Edition* (Bayley, 2006), which evaluates cognitive, language, motor and social functioning of children 1 to 42 months of age. The Mental Scale evaluates the infant's perceptual acuity, object constancy, memory, learning, problem solving and verbal communication and yields a normalized standard score, the Mental Development Index. The Motor Scale evaluates fine and gross motor co-ordination and body control and also yields a standard score, the Psychomotor Development Index. The Behaviour Rating Scale assesses the infant's attention and arousal, social engagement with others and emotional regulation.

The Bayley can help to identify areas of development in which there are delays or impairments and can be used to design interventions to address those problems. However, while scores on the Bayley are associated with children's current developmental status, unless the scores are extremely low, they are not strong predictors of future intelligence (Kamppi and Gilmore, 2010). Therefore, unless concerns emerge very early in a child's life, such as the possibility of mental retardation, autism or developmental disability, it is more common for cognitive testing to occur in the preschool or school-age years. (For a more detailed presentation of infant assessment, see Wyly, 1997.) The assessment is often used in conjunction with the Social-Emotional Adaptive Behaviour Questionnaire. This is completed by the parent or main caregiver and establishes the range of adaptive behaviours that the child can currently achieve and enables comparisons with age norms.

The Wechsler Scales

The *Wechsler Intelligence Scale for Children – Fourth Edition* (WISC-IV; Wechsler, 2003) is the most widely used intelligence test for children aged 6 to 16. The *Wechsler Preschool and Primary Scale of Intelligence – Revised* (Wechsler, 1989) is used for children aged 3 to 7. The average IQ score is 100, and approximately 68 per cent of the population will obtain an IQ score between 85 and 115. Scores that range from 80 to 89 are considered to be within the 'low average' of intelligence, while scores above 115 but below 125 are considered to be 'high average'. Individuals who score two standard deviations below the mean would obtain an IQ of 70, which is the cut-off point for a diagnosis of mental retardation. These individuals are considered to be in the bottom 2 per cent of the population.

The WISC-IV consists of 10 core subtests and five supplemental subtests, the items in each being arranged according to increasing difficulty. (See Fig. 16.3.) The subtests are grouped into four composite indices. The *Verbal Comprehension Index*, which requires facility in using verbal symbols, consists of three basic subtests (Similarities, Vocabulary and Comprehension) and two supplemental subtests (Information and Word Reasoning). The *Perceptual Reasoning Index*, which involves concrete material such as pictures, blocks and jigsaw puzzles, consists of three basic subtests (Block Design, Picture Concepts, Matrix Reasoning) and one supplemental subtest (Picture

FIGURE 16.3 Structure of the WISC-IV.

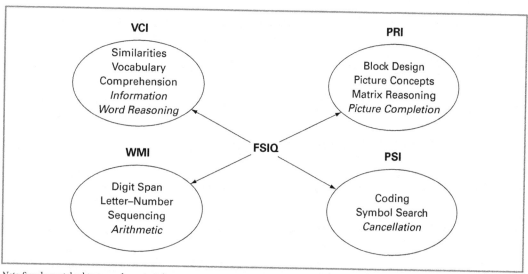

Note: Supplemental subtests are shown in italics.

Source: *Wechsler Intelligence Scale for Children—Fourth Edition*. Copyright © 2003 by Harcourt Assessment, Inc. Reproduced with permission. All rights reserved. "*Wechsler Intelligence Scale for Children*" and "*WISC*" are trademarks of Harcourt Assessment, Inc. registered in the United States of America and/or other jurisdictions.

Completion). The *Working Memory Index* comprises Digit Span and Letter–Number Sequencing with Arithmetic as a supplemental subtest. Finally, the *Processing Speed Index* consists of two basic subtests (Coding and Symbol Search) and one supplementary subtest (Cancellation). (See Fig. 16.4 for examples of WISC-IV-like items.) In addition, scoring yields a *Full-Scale IQ* with a mean score of 100 and a standard deviation of 15. For example, a child with a total score of 115 will be one standard deviation above the mean or in approximately the 84th percentile.

While the IQ score is important, it is only one of many pieces of information gained from an intelligence test. First, the assessor examines the *discrepancies* among the composite index scores on the WISC-IV to determine whether they are statistically significant. These discrepancies furnish clues about the child's differential ability to handle the various kinds of tasks. For example, the child who has a Full-Scale IQ of 100, a Verbal Comprehension Index of 120, and a Perceptual Reasoning Index of 80 is quite different from a child with the same overall IQ but with a Verbal Comprehension Index of 80 and a Perceptual Reasoning Index of 120. The second child may be particularly penalized in school, where the manipulation of verbal symbols becomes increasingly important, while being quite talented on tasks that require minimal verbal facility.

Analysis of successes and failures on individual items may provide further clues to intellectual strengths and weaknesses. A child may do well on problems involving rote learning and the accumulation of facts but do poorly on ones requiring reasoning and judgement. As another example, an otherwise bright child may be weak in visual-motor co-ordination, which might make learning to write difficult (Sattler, 2001). Below is a demonstration of a child Peter, 8 years of age, showing clear differences in performance across items (Fig. 16.5).

As shown in Fig. 16.4, results are always presented in term of standard scores. Scores will be evaluated, interpreted and integrated to formulate a more refined diagnostic impression. Anecdotal comments on test behaviours will also be presented

wherever possible to aid interpretation. For example, additional comments may include the following:

> Peter showed a rigid approach to completing block design and did not gain extra points as failed to complete in a reasonable time frame. Across other measures such as Picture Concept and Matrix Reasoning, he was exceptionally slow and was indecisive over his responses. Often gave excessive elaborations surrounding choice as if seeking reassurance that he was on the right track. Frequent requests for feedback were also noted.

Stanford-Binet Intelligence Scales, Fifth Edition

The *Stanford-Binet Intelligence Scales, Fifth Edition* (SB5) (Roid, 2003) covers the age span of 2 to 85 or more years. It consists of 10 tests, organized into five broad areas of cognitive abilities that follow from the Cattell-Horn-Carroll theory of intelligence (Carroll, 1993). Further, each factor is evaluated in Verbal and Non-verbal domains. (See Fig. 16.6.) The *Fluid Reasoning* factor involves novel tasks that are relatively free of dependence on knowledge learned in school or through previous experience. For example, the Early Reasoning subtest requires the child to observe pictures of humans in action and to deduce the underlying problem or situation by telling a story, while the Matrix subtest requires the child to determine the rules or relationships underlying a series of changes in the appearance of a visual stimulus. *Knowledge*, or Crystallized Intelligence, in contrast, involves information that is accumulated through schooling and general life experience. Subtests include Vocabulary (e.g., 'What does envelope mean?') and Procedural Understanding, which requires the child to describe the steps involved in solving an everyday problem. *Quantitative Reasoning* assesses the child's facility with numbers and numerical problem solving, using either verbally or pictorially depicted stimuli. *Visual-Spatial Processing* assesses the child's ability to comprehend patterns, spatial relationships, or the gestalt whole among separate elements. For example, the Form Board

FIGURE 16.4 WISC-IV-Like Items.

Information

How many wings does a bird have?
How many nickels make a dime?
What is steam made of?
Who wrote 'Tom Sawyer'?

Comprehension

What should you do if you see someone forget his book when he leaves a restaurant?
What is the advantage of keeping money in a bank?
Why is copper often used in electrical wires?

Arithmetic

Sam had three pieces of candy and Joe gave him four more. How many pieces of candy did Sam have altogether?
Three women divided eighteen golf balls equally among themselves. How many golf balls did each person receive?
If two buttons cost $.15, what will be the cost of a dozen buttons?

Similarities

In what way are a lion and a tiger alike?
In what way are a saw and a hammer alike?
In what way are an hour and a week alike?
In what way are a circle and a triangle alike?

Vocabulary

This test consists simply of asking, 'What is a _____ ?' or 'What does _____ mean?' The words cover a wide range of difficulty.

Digit Span

Digits Forward contains seven series of digits, 3 to 9 digits in length (Example: 1-8-9).
Digits Backward contains seven series of digits, 2 to 8 digits in length (Example: 5-8-1-9).

Picture Completion (26 items)

The task is to identify the essential missing part of the picture.
A picture of a car without a wheel.
A picture of a dog without a leg.
A picture of a telephone without numbers on the dial.
An example of a Picture Completion task is shown below.

Courtesy of The Psychological Corporation.

Picture Arrangement (12 items)

The task is to arrange a series of pictures into a meaningful sequence.

Block Design (11 items)

The task is to reproduce stimulus designs using four or nine blocks. An example of a Block Design item is shown below.

Object Assembly (4 items)

The task is to arrange pieces into a meaningful object. An example of an Object Assembly item is shown below.

Courtesy of The Psychological Corporation.

Coding

The task is to copy symbols from a key (see below).

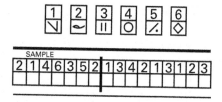

Courtesy of The Psychological Corporation.

Mazes

The task is to complete a series of mazes.

Note. The questions resemble those that appear on the WISC-IV but are not actually from the test.

FIGURE 16.5 Peter's Scores across the WISC.

Index and Scores	Standard score	Percentile
Verbal Comprehension Similarities (9) Vocabulary (11) Comprehension (11)	100 (Range 93-107) Average range	50
Perceptual Reasoning Block Design (7) Matrix Reasoning (8) Picture Concepts (8)	84 (Range 79-93) Low Average Range	14
Working Memory Digit Span (8) Letter-Number Sequence (6)	83 (Range 77-92) Low Average Range	13
Processing Speed Symbol Search (11) Coding (10)	83 (Range 76-94) Low Average Range	13
Full Scale IQ	86 (range 81-91) Low Average Range	18

requires the child to duplicate familiar patterns using puzzle pieces, and Position and Direction requires the understanding of spatial concepts such as 'behind' or 'under'. *Working Memory* involves the child's ability to store either verbal or spatial information in short-term memory while performing a cognitive operation on it.

The items in each test are arranged according to difficulty; thus, the more items children successfully complete, the higher their abilities are when compared with children their own age. Like the WISC-IV, the index factors combine to form a Full Scale IQ, with a mean of 100 and a standard deviation of 15. In addition, Verbal IQ and Non-verbal IQ scores can be derived to compare the child's functioning in these two modalities.

Observations During Cognitive Testing

The purpose of cognitive testing is not simply to derive an IQ score. The testing situation can also provide important clues about the child's *style of thinking*. Note the responses of two equally bright 8-year-olds to the question, 'What should you do when you lose a ball that belongs to someone else?' One child answered, 'I'd get him another one'. The other said, 'I'd pay money for it. I'd look for it. I'd give him another ball. I'd try to find it, but if I couldn't, I'd give him money for it because I might not have the kind of ball he wants'. Both answers receive the same high score, but one is clear, simple and to the point, while the other is needlessly cluttered.

Styles of thinking are closely related to psychological health or disturbance. Intelligence is not some kind of disembodied skill existing apart from the rest of the child's personality. On the contrary, a psychologically well-functioning child tends to think clearly, a child with poor self-control tends to think impulsively, and an obsessive child (like the one just quoted) tends to think in terms of so many possible alternatives that it becomes difficult to

FIGURE 16.6 Organization of the Stanford-Binet, Fifth Edition.

		Domains	
		Non-verbal (NV)	Verbal (V)
Factors	**Fluid Reasoning (FR)**	**Non-verbal Fluid Reasoning*** Activities: Object Series/Matrices (Routing)	**Verbal Fluid Reasoning** Activities: Early Reasoning (2–3), Verbal Absurdities (4), Verbal Analogies (5–6)
	Knowledge (KN)	**Non-verbal Knowledge** Activities: Procedural Knowledge (2–3), Picture Absurdities (4–6)	**Verbal Knowledge*** Activities: Vocabulary (Routing)
	Quantitative Reasoning (QR)	**Non-verbal Quantitative Reasoning** Activities: Quantitative Reasoning (2–6)	**Verbal Quantitative Reasoning** Activities: Quantitative Reasoning (2–6)
	Visual-Spatial Processing (VS)	**Non-verbal Visual-Spatial Processing** Activities: Form Board (1–2), Form Patterns (3–6)	**Verbal Visual-Spatial Processing** Activities: Position and Direction (2–6)
	Working Memory (WM)	**Non-verbal Working Memory** Activities: Delayed Response (1), Block Span (2–6)	**Verbal Working Memory** Activities: Memory for Sentences (2–3), Last Word (4–6)

Note: Names of the 10 subtests are in **bold italic.** Activities include the levels at which they appear.
* = *Routing subtests*
Source: Roid, 2003.

decide on one and act on it. A schizophrenic child tends to think bizarrely, as is revealed in this rambling, fantasy-saturated answer to the simple question, 'Why should one tell the truth?'

If you don't tell the truth, you get into trouble; you go to court; like teenagers who don't tell the truth; they're usually armed, guys who run around the forest and woods, the woods near the house. We go there to catch frogs, and we always have to have older people go with us because of the teenagers with guns and knives. A child drowned there not long ago. If you don't tell the truth, they start a gang and drown you.

The intelligence test also allows the clinician to evaluate the child's *work habits*. Some children are task oriented and self-motivated; they need almost no encouragement or help from the examiner. Others are uncertain and insecure, giving up readily unless encouraged or prodded, constantly seeking reassurance that they are doing well, or asking to know whether their response was right or wrong.

Finally, the tests yield information concerning the child's capacity for *self-monitoring*, which is the ability to evaluate the quality of the responses. Some children seem to be implicitly asking, 'Is that really correct?' or 'Is that the best I can do?' while others seem to have little ability to judge when they are right or wrong, an incorrect response being given with the same air of uncritical assurance as a correct one.

Strengths and Limitations of Cognitive Testing

Intelligence tests can play a useful role in child assessment. The IQ score itself is related to many aspects of the child's life – success in school, vocational choice, peer relations – and IQ is a better *predictor* of future adjustment than any score on a personality test. In addition, the test provides *data* concerning general areas of strength and weakness; the kind and degree of impairment of specific intellectual functions, such as immediate recall or abstract reasoning; the child's coping techniques, work habits and motivation; stylistic characteristics of thinking that may well be related to personality variables; and the presence of distorted thinking that might indicate either organic brain pathology or psychosis (Sattler, 2001).

Yet care must be taken that an intelligence test is used *appropriately* and that results are properly understood. For example, test motivation has been found to be a confounding factor in terms of the predictive associations between intelligence and later outcomes (Duckworth et al., 2011). As IQ became a household term, so did the misconception that the score represents an index of the child's unalterable intellectual potential existing independent of background and experience. In particular, concerns have been expressed that these tests might do more harm than good by underestimating the abilities of children from cultural groups other than the mainstream. (See Bender et al., 1995, and Kaminer and Vig, 1995, for both sides of the issue.) Flanagan et al. (2007) have asserted that 'there is an emerging body of research that suggests nonverbal tasks may actually carry as much if not more cultural content than that found in verbal tests' (p. 165). All psychometrics tests have varying degrees of cultural loading and all require some form of communication between examiner and examinee. For this reason, the ethical guidelines of the American Psychological Association (2002) require that clinicians develop *cultural competence* and demonstrate the ability to interpret test data in the light of the unique cultural and environmental factors that affect the child (see also Valencia and Suzuki, 2000).

In contrast to his friendly and open manner during the interview, Rudy's behaviour changes markedly during the WISC-IV. His brow is furrowed and he responds to the tasks as though they are stressful and even irritating to him. In addition, he tends to make self-derogatory remarks at the beginning of each new task. He says 'I don't know' too readily when items become difficult, and he quickly destroys a puzzle he had put together incorrectly, as if trying to cover up his mistake. At times he seems to use his conversational skills to divert attention away from the test material. He is willing to try the first arithmetic problems, which are easy for him and allow him to be certain about the right answer. As they get more difficult, however, he refuses even to try. He states that he 'hates' this test. When he is encouraged to respond to difficult items, it is clear that he does not know the correct answer.

The test scores add a significant bit of data: while he has high expectations for himself, Rudy has only average intelligence. In addition, there is significant scatter among his index scores. While he shows strengths on verbal comprehension tasks, he demonstrates deficits on tasks assessing working memory. You begin speculating, 'If his sociability misled me into thinking he was intellectually advanced, his mother and teachers might have also been misled into setting unrealistically high goals and pressuring him to achieve them.' This hypothesis naturally would have to be checked by interviewing the parents and teacher. Clearly there is more to be learned about Rudy's abilities to achieve in school and how they mesh with expectations that others have of him and that he has for himself.

Tests of Achievement

An assessment of academic achievement is important in deciding whether a child has a learning disability and in evaluating the effectiveness of a remedial programme. Low academic achievement may also contribute to the development of a behaviour problem. As with intelligence tests, individually administered *achievement tests* allow the clinician to make behavioural observations of the child and to analyse the nature of the child's failures. These data may provide helpful clues about motivational and academic problems; for example, a boy who gives up without trying is different from one who fails after trying his best, just as a girl who fails multiplication problems because of careless mistakes is different from another who fails because she has not grasped the basic process of multiplying. A comprehensive battery is provided by the *Woodcock-Johnson III Tests of Achievement* (WJ III; Woodcock et al., 2001a). The tests cover 10 areas, including the child's mastery of grade-level reading, mathematics, written language, oral language, and academic knowledge, skills and fluency in subjects such as social studies, science and the humanities. Clinicians are able to use the WJ III test of achievement to help assess children for learning disabilities. The Individuals with Disabilities Education Act (IDEA) is legislation that defines the terms under which students may be declared eligible for special services. The WJ III includes clusters which parallel these IDEA areas and provide procedures for determining discrepancies between a child's abilities and achievement in each area. (See Fig. 16.7.)

In order to assess the possibility that Rudy has learning problems, you administer the WJ III. Rudy's scores indicate that his achievement in most areas is about average, while his mathematics skills are far below what is expected of children at his age. Apparently, therefore, there are reasons for Rudy to report that he 'hates' mathematics. However, you note that his reading skills are at age level, and therefore the explanation for his failing reading does not seem to lie in the direction of a learning disorder. Taken together with the IQ tests results, these data also raise further questions, such as the effects of being regarded as 'lazy' on the boy's self-image. There is more to learn about Rudy the person and the ways his learning problems are affecting him emotionally.

Neuropsychological Assessment

A neuropsychological assessment usually begins with tests of intelligence and achievement. These tests not only provide information about the children's intellectual level and academic progress but, more important, they also provide clues about what psychological functions might be affected by organic brain damage. As we have seen, the manifestations of brain damage may range from a slight deficit in sensorimotor abilities to a pervasive disruption of every aspect of a child's intellectual and personality functioning. It follows that there can be no single diagnostic test for organicity.

FIGURE 16.7 IDEA Areas and WJ III Clusters.

IDEA AREA	WJ III CLUSTER
Oral Expression	Oral Expression
Listening Comprehension	Listening Comprehension
Written Expression	Written Expression
Basic Reading Skills	Basic Reading Skills
Reading Comprehension	Reading Comprehension
Mathematics Calculation	Mathematics Calculation Skills
Mathematics Reasoning	Maths Reasoning

If brain damage potentially affects a variety of functions, then a battery of tests casting a wide psychological net would seem to provide a reasonable strategy for capturing the elusive problem. One such comprehensive test is the *NEPSY*, a test specifically designed for the assessment of neuropsychological functions in children aged 3 to 12. Based on the Russian psychologist Luria's (1980) model of cognition, the NEPSY assesses functioning in five core domains: *Attention/Executive Functions, Language, Sensorimotor, Visuospatial* and *Memory/ Learning*. Each domain is assessed via a set of core subtests, while additional expanded subtests can be added to further clarify the referral question.

The diversity of the tests may be seen in the following sampling. Among the *Attention/Executive Function* tasks is the *Tower of Hanoi* (Fig. 16.8), a board with three pegs on which an array of differently coloured beads is placed. The child must move the beads to match the display represented by a model, but in no more – and no less – than a prescribed number of moves. Thus, the child is required not only to use good planning and nonverbal problem-solving skills but to inhibit the impulse to solve the problem too quickly.

In turn, the *Auditory Attention and Response Set* subtest presents the child with a box of coloured tiles and an audiotaped voice that reads off random words interspersed with the word 'red'. At first, each time the child hears the word 'red', the task is to put a red tile in a box. The second phase is more difficult in that in this pass through, each time the child hears the word 'red', the task is to put a yellow tile in the box, whereas the word 'yellow' is the signal to put in a red tile, and the word 'blue' indicates that a blue tile should be placed. The test allows for observation of errors of *commission* (false positives: that is, placing a red tile in the box when 'red' is not called) and *omission* (false negatives: that is, failing to place a tile when 'red' is called). While acts of commission generally reflect impulsivity, acts of omission are related to inattentiveness.

Among the *Language* subtests, Comprehension of Instructions requires the child to demonstrate good receptive language skills by following the examiner's directions, while Verbal Fluency assesses facility of verbal skills by asking the child to name quickly as many objects as possible that fit into a given semantic or phonemic category (e.g., types of food or words that start with the letter 'J'). Sensorimotor functions are assessed by subtests such as Imitating Hand Positions, in which the child must demonstrate good motor co-ordination and imitation, while Memory tasks include memory for

FIGURE 16.8 Tower of Hanoi.

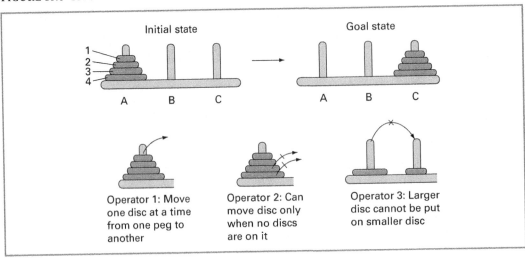

faces, names, sentences and lists. Among the *Visuospatial Processing* tasks is Route Finding, in which the child must show an understanding of directionality, orientation and spatial relationships by tracing the pathway that one would take to get from one point to another.

Another addition to the neuropsychologists' armamentarium is the Delis-Kaplan Executive Function System (*D-KEFS*) (Delis et al., 2001). It represents the first set tests exclusively designed to measure executive function. This test is designed to measure important executive functions that have been implicated in many of the psychopathologies we have discussed, such as flexibility of thinking, problem solving, planning, impulse control, inhibition, concept formation and creativity in individuals aged 8 to 89. For example, similar to the well-known Wisconsin Card Sorting Test (Heaton et al., 1993) (Fig. 16.9), the D-KEFS *Card Sort* presents the child with a set of cards with both perceptual stimuli and printed words. First, the child is invited to sort the cards into two groups using as many different concepts or rules as possible. Then, the examiner sorts the cards and the child is required to identify and describe the rules or concepts that were used.

The *Trail Making Test* assesses flexibility of thinking by asking the child to connect marks on a page according to shifting rules (e.g., by connecting just the letters, just the numbers or switching between the letters or numbers) while the *Proverb Test* assesses the child's ability to abstract the interpretation of a familiar saying. The D-KEFS also includes a *Tower Test* that parallels the NEPSY.

The *Woodcock Johnson III Tests of Cognitive Abilities* (Woodcock et al., 2001b) also assess a number of cognitive functions of interest to the neuropsychologist, including verbal comprehension, short-term memory, long-term storage and retrieval, visual-spatial thinking, auditory processing, auditory attention, fluid reasoning, processing speed, working memory, comprehension and knowledge, and executive processing.

Tests of Attention

Although tests of attention are included in most of the comprehensive neuropsychological batteries, there are several stand-alone tests of attentional processes that are frequently used by psychologists who are asked to rule out the diagnosis of ADHD. Conner's *Continuous Performance Test* (CPT II; Conners, 2000) is a computer-based instrument that assesses visual attention by asking the child to click the mouse button every time an 'X' appears on the screen. Indices are scored related to inattentiveness (e.g., omission errors, slow reaction time) impulsivity (e.g., commission errors, fast reaction time) and lack of vigilance (e.g., slowing reaction time as the test progresses). The *Test of Variables of Attention - Auditory* (Greenberg and Waldmant, 1993) is another computer-based assessment tool that also tests auditory attention by asking the child to respond every time a specific tone is heard.

FIGURE 16.9 The Wisconsin Card Sorting Test.

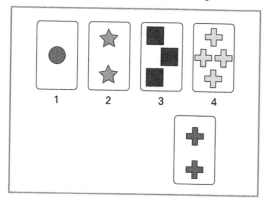

Given the discrepancies between Rudy's performance on tasks assessing different areas of intelligence on the WISC-IV, you decide to follow up with a neuropsychological screening. Given that Christina wants to know if her neighbour was correct in saying that ADHD was the explanation for his behaviour problems in the classroom, you select an instrument that will allow you to assess his attention as well. On the NEPSY, you find that his skills are in the average range overall. However, the pattern of scores is of interest. Although still in the average range,

Rudy's scores on tests of executive functions are a relative weakness for him in comparison to his strengths on language and sensorimotor tasks. His most significant deficit, however, is in the areas of auditory attention. While his ability to attend to auditory information is adequate when the stimuli presented are simple and unambiguous, his attentional efficiency markedly reduced when stimuli become more complex. His errors generally are those of commission (responding with false positives), which generally is considered a sign of impulsivity.

Socio-emotional Assessment
Parent and Teacher Report Scales

One of the most widely used adult-report inventories is the *Child Behaviour Checklist* (CBCL;

Achenbach et al., 2001), which was described in Chapter 3. There are different forms for parents (CBCL) and teachers (Teacher Report Form), and norms are provided for children from 4 to 16 years of age. Figure 16.10 presents a segment of the parent-report version of the CBCL.

The *Behaviour Assessment System for Children* (BASC-2; Reynolds and Kamphaus, 2004) similarly includes both parent- and teacher-report versions. It involves a multidimensional approach to evaluating behaviour and self-perception of children aged 2 to 21 years. It includes teachers' (TRS) and parent (PRS) rating scales, a self-report of personality (SPS), a structured developmental history (SDH). The *Self Report Scale* (SPS) has been created for children aged 6 years and over. The *Parent Rating Scale* (PRS) includes scales of

FIGURE 16.10 Excerpt from the Parent Version of the Child Behaviour Checklist.

Please print. Be sure to answer all items.

Below is a list of items that describe children and youths. For each item that describes your child **now or within the past 6 months,** please circle the **2** if the item is **very true or often true** of your child. Circle the **1** if the item is **somewhat or sometimes true** of your child. If the item is **not true** of your child, circle the **0**. Please answer all items as well as you can, even if some do not seem to apply to your child.

0 = Not True (as far as you know)   **1 = Somewhat or Sometimes True**   **2 = Very True or Often True**

0 1 2 1. Acts too young for his/her age	0 1 2 32. Feels he/she has to be perfect
0 1 2 2. Drinks alcohol without parent's approval (describe): _____	0 1 2 33. Feels or complains that no one loves him/her
	0 1 2 34. Feels others are out to get him/her
	0 1 2 35. Feels worthless or inferior
0 1 2 3. Argues a lot	
0 1 2 4. Fails to finish things he/she starts	0 1 2 36. Gets hurt a lot, accident-prone
	0 1 2 37. Gets in many fights
0 1 2 5. There is very little he/she enjoys	
0 1 2 6. Bowel movements outside toilet	0 1 2 38. Gets teased a lot
	0 1 2 39. Hangs around with others who get in trouble
0 1 2 7. Bragging, boasting	
0 1 2 8. Can't concentrate, can't pay attention for long	0 1 2 40. Hears sound or voices that aren't there (describe): _____
0 1 2 9. Can't get his/her mind off certain thoughts; obsessions (describe): _____	0 1 2 41. Impulsive or acts without thinking
	0 1 2 42. Would rather be alone than with others
0 1 2 10. Can't sit still; restless or hyperactive	0 1 2 43. Lying or cheating
0 1 2 11. Clings to adults or too dependent	0 1 2 44. Bites fingernails
0 1 2 12. Complains of loneliness	0 1 2 45. Nervous, highstrung, or tense
0 1 2 13. Confused or seems to be in a fog	0 1 2 46. Nervous movements or twitching (describe): _____
0 1 2 14. Cries a lot	

Source: Achenbach et al., 2001.

Adaptability, Anxiety, Aggression, Attention Problems, Atypicality, Conduct Problems, Depression, Hyperactivity, Leadership, Social Skills, Somatization and Withdrawal. There are separate versions for preschoolers, school-age children and adolescents. (See Table 16.3 for a description of the items loading on each scale.) The BASC Teacher Rating Scale (TRS), in turn, includes scales assessing *Externalizing Problems* (aggression, hyperactivity, conduct problems), *Internalizing Problems* (anxiety, depression, somatization), *School Problems* (inattention, learning difficulties), *Other Problems* (atypicality, withdrawal) and *Adaptive Skills* (adaptability, leadership, social skills, study skills). There are separate forms for preschool, elementary and middle/high school students, with 109, 148 and 138 items, respectively. The PRS and TRS have good psychometric properties and include indices of adaptive functioning (e.g., social skills) that are missing from many measures of children's behaviour (Kamphaus and Frick, 2005).

An alternative rating scale, which uses the same form for either teachers' or parents' reports, is the *Devereux Scales of Mental Disorders* (Naglieri et al., 1994). There are two versions, one for children ages 5 to 12 and one for ages 13 to 18; each version has 110 items. Three composite scales are derived: *Internalizing* (anxiety, depression), *Externalizing* (conduct problems, delinquency, attention problems) and *Critical Pathology* (autistic features, self-harming, substance abuse, fire-setting, hallucinations).

The *Personality Inventory for Children – Revised* (PIC-R; Wirt et al., 1990), designed for children aged 3 to 16, asks the parent to rate the presence or absence of 420 characteristics (shorter forms are also available, which include fewer items). Scales include depression and poor self-concept; worry and anxiety; reality distortion; peer relations; unsocialized aggression; conscience development; poor judgement; atypical development; distractibility, activity level and co-ordination; speech and language; somatic complaints; school adjustment; and family

TABLE 16.3 BASC-2 Parent Rating Scale

	Scales and Key Symptoms
Adaptability	Adjusts to changes in routines and plans, adjusts well to new teachers, shares toys or other possessions with others
Aggression	Argues with, bullies, teases, hits, threatens and blames others
Anxiety	Exhibits nervousness, worry, guilt, dread, fear and sensitivity to criticism
Attention Problems	Does not complete work, has difficulty concentrating and attending, forgets things and does not listen to directions
Atypicality	Has urges to hurt self, hears name when alone, cannot control thoughts and hears voices
Conduct Problems	Drinks alcohol, uses illegal drugs or chews tobacco; steals and lies, has been suspended from school, or is in trouble with police
Depression	Complains that no one listens to or understands him or her; cries, is sad, pouts, whines and complains of loneliness
Hyperactivity	Acts impulsively, interrupts others, and has tantrums: is restless, leaves seat and climbs on things
Leadership	Is creative, energetic, and good at facilitating the work of others; joins clubs and participates in extracurricular activities
Social Skills	Compliments and congratulates others, and makes suggestions tactfully; has good manners and smiles at others
Somatization	Complains about health, dizziness, heart palpitations, pain, shortness of breath and being cold; has headaches and stomach problems
Withdrawal	Avoids others and competition: is extremely shy and refuses to join group activities

Source: Adapted from Reynolds and Kamphaus, 2004.

discord. Factor analysis was used to derive four broadband scales: *Undisciplined/Poor Self-Control, Social Incompetence, Internalization/Somatic Symptoms* and *Cognitive Development.*

His mother's responses on the CBCL place Rudy well below the clinical cut-off for the disruptive behaviour scales, consistent with her description of him as a 'terrific kid'. However, what emerges on the CBCL profile that was not revealed by your interview with her are a significant number of internalizing symptoms: she indicates that Rudy often worries, feels tense and anxious, has trouble sleeping, and complains of headaches and stomach aches. The fact that the mother is aware of these problems indicates that she has the capacity to be empathic and sensitive to her son, a source of strength that you note.

His teacher's responses on the Teacher Report Form paint a very different picture of Rudy. The teacher rates him high in oppositionality and inattention and describes him as having poor interpersonal skills. Clearly, either Rudy's behaviour – or adults' perception of it – is markedly different in the classroom than at home.

Child Self-Report Scales
Syndrome-Specific Measures
Commonly used child-report measures are those that assess specific kinds of symptoms. Particularly useful are measures of internalizing symptoms, about which children's reports may be the most informative. One of the most widely used of these, the *Children's Depression Inventory* (CDI; Kovacs, 1992), is a 27-item paper-and-pencil measure for children aged 6 to 17 that assesses sadness, cognitive symptoms of depression, somatic complaints, social problems and acting out. The *Revised Children's Manifest Anxiety Scale-2* (RCMAS-2; Reynolds and Richmond, 1997) is designed to measure anxiety for children and adolescents aged 6 to 19, includes 49 yes/no items assessing academic stress, peer and family conflicts, social con-

cerns, worry and oversensitivity, as well as defensive responding. The *Multidimensional Anxiety Scale for Children* (MASC; March et al., 1997) expands the assessment of anxiety to include Physical Symptoms, Social Anxiety, Perfectionism, Separation and Panic.

Multidimensional Measures
An example of a multidimensional child self-report measure is the *Personality Inventory for Youth* (PIY; Lachar and Gruber, 1994). The PIY parallels the parent-report measure, the Personality Inventory for Children, and is designed to assess academic, emotional, behavioural and interpersonal adjustment in children 9 to 19 years of age. Four broad factors are derived: *Externalizing/ Internalizing, Cognitive Impairment, Social Withdrawal,* and *Social Skills Deficit.* In addition, three scales were developed to assess the validity of children's responses, including inattentive or provocative responses, as well as inconsistent or defensive responding. While this measure is promising, it is new on the scene and so its utility is still unknown.

The *Self-Report of Personality* (SRP) is part of the multifaceted Behaviour Assessment System for Children (BASC-2; Reynolds and Kamphaus, 2004). The SRP is designed to assess children's perceptions of school, parents, peers and self. Factor analysis was used to develop four scores. *Clinical Maladjustment* includes scales assessing anxiety, atypical feelings and behaviours, social stress, locus of control and somatization. *Personal Adjustment* includes scales assessing self-esteem, self-reliance, peer relations and positive parent–child relationships. Another scale assesses *School Maladjustment,* which includes items tapping problems that might interfere with academic functioning, such as negative attitudes towards school and teachers, and sensation-seeking for adolescents. *Emotional Symptoms* is a composite score that gives an indication of general psychopathology. A lie scale detects 'fake good' response sets by assessing whether children deny even the most ordinary, run-of-the-mill misbehaviour (e.g., 'I never get angry'). Forms are available for children aged 8 to 11, as well as adolescents aged 12 to 18. Norms are available for different age groups as well as for clinical samples.

Strengths of the SRP include a large standardization sample matched demographically to 1990 US census figures, good reliabilities, and some evidence for validity derived from comparisons between the SRP and similar scales of more established measures. Because fairly good reading ability is required, the measure might not be appropriate for mentally retarded or learning disabled youths at any age. Again, this measure has not been widely used to date.

Other measures have been developed specifically for adolescents. The *Revised Minnesota Multiphasic Personality Inventory – Adolescent* (MMPI-A; Butcher et al., 2004) is a downward extension of the well-known adult measure, the MMPI-2. Scales assess such symptoms as depression, psychopathy, paranoia, schizophrenia, anxiety, obsessiveness, conduct problems, low self-esteem, alcohol and drug abuse proneness, and school and family problems, among others. Validity scales also assess attempts to present oneself in a good or bad light, as well as defensiveness and inconsistent responding. Like the original adult version, the MMPI-A requires English literacy, and it is extremely long, preventing some youths from completing it in one sitting.

The *Youth Self-Report* (YSR; Achenbach et al., 2001) is a widely used measure of youth emotional and behavioural problems. It is used to obtain self-report ratings from adolescents aged 11 to 18 regarding *internalizing* and *externalizing* symptoms, paralleling parents' reports on the CBCL. Scales include Withdrawn, Somatic Complaints, Anxious/Depressed, Social Problems, Thought Problems, Attention Problems, Delinquent Behaviour and Aggressive Behaviour. Social Competence scales also assess participation in social activities and peer relationships. A recent study has shown that even younger youths, 7–10 years of age, are able to provide reliable reports on the YSR on the broader bands (externalising, inter-

nalizing scales), though less on the narrowband scales (Ebesutani et al., 2011).

Projective Techniques

In all the assessment instruments discussed so far, the stimulus material is as clear and unambiguous as possible. **Projective techniques** take the opposite tack by using *ambiguous* or *unstructured* material; either the stimulus has no inherent meaning, such as an inkblot, or it has a number of potential meanings, such as a picture that is to be used as the basis of a story. Theoretically, the particular *meaning* attributed to the unstructured material is a reflection of the individual's unique *personality*. The disguised nature of the responses allows the individual to express ideas that would be too threatening to talk about directly. For example, a girl who is too frightened to talk about her anger towards her mother may feel free to tell a story about a daughter being angry with and defying a parental figure. Projective tests continue to be popular, particularly projective measures such as the Draw A Person and the Kinetic Family Drawing test, which might be attributed to the *rapport-building* potential of these tests where children are concerned. Most children under 9 or 10 years of age enjoy and are familiar with drawing tasks. These tests are also very simple to administer and do not necessarily involve elaborate scoring systems. The test stimuli used in many projective methods are also less likely to be outdated than the verbal items used in many objective personality tests. Verbal self-reports of many aspects of interest that rely on introspection and abstraction, may not be very informative if they come from children younger than 12. Thus, psychological projective methods are particularly valuable in getting information about the thoughts and feelings of younger children (Björn et al., 2011).

The Rorschach

A major disadvantage of self-report questionnaires is they are based on self-report about experience and symptoms, and are therefore susceptible to changes in memory, subjectivity and intentional manipulation (Luxenberg and Levin, 2004).

Projective testing, being ambiguous and having no clear-cut 'correct' answer, may prevent these short-comings. The client has no clue as to a specific or desirable answer and thus projects bother content and processers onto the test stimuli. Unable to 'guess' what answers will serve best, he is compelled to project genuine content. The inkblot test, developed in 1921 by Hermann Rorschach, is a projective test used extensively as a diagnostic tool (Fig. 16.11). Since it consists of 10 cards, the diagnosis is not based on a single response, but rather on the analysis of all 10 or more responses. Each of the 10 inkblots are presented to the child one at a time with the question, 'What could this be?' The child's responses are recorded verbatim; and after the cards have been viewed once, the examiner asks the child to look at each card again and to explain what part of the blot was used ('Where did you see it?') and what suggested each particular response ('What made it look like that?').

Although the validity of the Rorschach has been the subject of much debate in recent years,

FIGURE 16.11 Rorschach ink blot (Plate IV).

This is a black and white card, often described as the 'father card' as this blot is supposed to identify with a person's perception of their father, or authority figures. Common good answers include bear, gorilla, or man in a heavy coat. In contrast a bad answer would be to describe the figure as menacing, i.e. a monster, or an attacking gorilla. Possible sexual imagery may include a pair of male sex organs, typically seen at the top of the image.

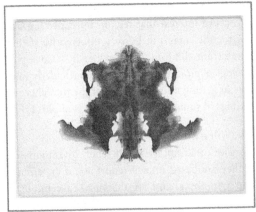

© Zmeel Photography

Exner (1993) made three important contributions to Rorschach analysis. First, he took the numerous scoring systems available and *integrated* them into a single comprehensive one. Second, he reviewed the available research and conducted a number of additional studies of the Rorschach in order to develop an *empirically based* interpretation scheme. Third, he provided separate *norms* for adults and for children 5 to 16 years of age, so that clinicians can evaluate the deviancy of a given child's responses in comparison to those of his or her peers.

Exner's system requires the examiner to code each response on seven different criteria. The first of these is *location*, or where on the blot the percept is seen. For example, it might be based on a small detail ('this little spot looks like a peephole'), or the whole blot might be used to create a complex and elaborated response ('this is an aquarium with lots of exotic plants and fish swimming around'). Second, each response is scored in terms of the *determinants*, or features that contribute to the percept described. These include such features as the form of the blot ('it is a bat because it is shaped like one') or its colour or shading ('this grey part makes it look fuzzy and furry, like a bear skin rug'). Third, *form quality* is assessed, which concerns how well the percept actually fits the blot; for example, poor form quality would be indicated by a response that in no way follows the outline or features of the blot presented. The *content* of the percept is also recorded – that is, whether the percept involves humans, animals or objects. *Popularity* is noted in terms of whether the percept is one that is commonly seen by others. *Organizational activity* concerns the degree of cognitive effort required to organize and integrate the parts of the blot into a coherent response; for example, the 'aquarium' response quoted previously would be rated as high in organization. Lastly, *special scores* are given to certain responses, such as those that include violent or morbid themes ('two cannibals eating the brains out of their victim's head').

After scoring the child's responses, the examiner first uses the norms obtained from other children of the same age in order to gauge the developmental appropriateness of the child's response. While some ways of responding to the Rorschach are indicative of psychopathology in adolescents and older children, they may appear normal for younger children. For example, young children are highly reactive to the colour of the inkblots and thus tend to use colour as a determinant of their responses rather than form. Because this reactivity to colour is believed to represent emotional liability, this is a response style that, while perhaps a sign of immaturity in an adult, is not at all surprising to find in children. In fact, a young child who does *not* give many colour-based responses might warrant concern, because this could suggest pseudomaturity and excessive control of emotions.

Exner has also constructed a number of scales that allow the assessor to gauge the likelihood that a child's Rorschach responses are indicative of a particular psychopathology, such as schizophrenia, anxiety, conduct disorder or depression. For example, characteristics of depressed children's responses include a high number of morbid responses (sad or damaged images – for example, 'an abandoned house that is falling apart because no one cares about it any more'); responses based on white space in the inkblots rather than the shaded or coloured portions; and a low ratio of responses based on colour as opposed to black and white features. Characteristics of psychotic thought processes include poor form quality, incongruous combinations ('a bird holding a basketball' or 'a man with three heads'), and bizarre or gruesome content.

It should be noted that, despite Exner's efforts, not all psychometricians are satisfied that the Rorschach has proven its validity and utility. While there have been a sufficient number of positive research findings to reassure its advocates (see Bornstein and Masling, 2005), there have also been a sufficient number of negative findings to bolster the arguments of its detractors (see Garb et al., 2005). The use of the Rorschach, therefore, is still subject to controversy.

Rudy engages readily with the Rorschach, and his responses are well elaborated and imaginative. However, he strives too hard to integrate every detail of each inkblot into his responses, sometimes at the expense of accuracy; and the themes of his percepts are not as highly sophisticated as the effort he puts into them warrants. His responses also include a significant use of white space and few responses based on colour. In addition, morbid themes emerge in many of his responses, which tend to involve helpless victims that have been 'blasted', 'knocked down' and 'squished' by sadistic monsters. You note that these responses suggest a child who is striving to accomplish beyond his abilities, and they also are consistent with the key indicators of depression.

Projective Drawings

Drawing is a popular and developmentally sensitive tool that is commonly used in clinical settings. When a drawing test is used as a projective measure, the clinician instructs the child to draw something. The clinician will then study the drawing, and make inferences about the child's psychological function. The *Draw-A-Person* (DAP) is one of the most widely used of the projective drawing techniques. According to Machover's (1949) original procedure, the child is first asked to draw a person, then to draw a person of the other sex. Next, a series of questions follows, such as 'What is the person doing?' 'How old is he or she?' 'What does the person like and dislike?' although the questions asked are not standard across clinicians. Research in experimental settings has confirmed that drawing increases the amount of verbal information that children report.

Theoretically, the child's drawing is a projection of both the self-image and the body image. Various characteristics of the drawing are interpreted in terms of psychological variables – a small figure indicating inferiority, faint lines suggesting anxiety or an amorphous identity, an overly large head indicating excessive intellectualization – while the child's answers to the assessor's questions are interpreted thematically; for example, a figure who is 'just standing there' suggests passivity, while one who is a cheerleader suggests energy and extroversion. The figure may represent either the 'real' self or the idealized self.

The *House-Tree-Person* (HTP) drawing is a variation on this theme in which the child completes three drawings – of a person, a house and a tree – in order to provide a richer source of data. In theory, the house represents the individual's home life and family situation, while the person represents the self-image and the tree represents aspects of the self-concept that are less consciously accessible (Hammer, 1958).

Yet another projective drawing task is the *Kinetic Family Drawing* (KFD; Burns, 1982). Children are instructed to draw their family 'doing something – some kind of action'. The active, or kinetic, aspect of the drawing is intended to elicit material related to the emotional quality of relationships among family members. Children's drawings are scored in terms of actions (e.g., co-operation, nurturance, tension or sadism); positions (e.g., whether figures are facing one another); physical characteristics (e.g., sizes of figures, details and facial expressions); styles (e.g., whether the figures are placed in separate 'compartments' or lined up at the top or bottom of the page); and whether there are distances separating family members or barriers blocking their access to one another. (See Fig. 16.12.)

Validity of Drawing Interpretations
While their popularity attests to their intuitive appeal, projective drawing tasks, such as the DAP, HTP and KFD, only rarely withstand empirical scrutiny. The evaluation of the effectiveness of projective drawing tests has been fraught with confounding variables and despite being popular there is little empirical evidence to support the conclusion that drawing is a valid measure of personality behaviour or intelligence (Nawal et al., 2005). There are concurring problems of misunderstanding and misinterpretation, as the scoring systems developed lack sufficient norms and have not been subjected to adequate tests of validity.

There is one point in particular on which considerable research converges. Studies of the DAP

FIGURE 16.12 An Example of a Child's Drawing from the KFD.

Source: Copyright © 2000 by the American Psychological Association. Reproduced with permission. Freidlander et al., 2000.

and KFD indicate that the *individual details* in children's drawings on which most scoring systems base their interpretations are *not* linked to specific kinds of psychopathology and are not predictive of behaviour. Therefore, glossaries to drawing features that make such interpretations as 'large eyes = suspiciousness', 'a hole in the tree signifies abuse has taken place' or 'family members placed higher on the page are more significant' have not been found to be valid.

However, scoring systems based on more *global* screenings of children's drawings have demonstrated some success in empirical research. For example, Naglieri and Pfeiffer (1992) established a scoring procedure for human figure drawings (the DAP Screening Procedure for Emotional Disturbances, or DAP SPED) that indexes a large array of possible indicators of psychopathology and successfully differentiates emotionally disturbed from normative children. Significant scores are given to such unusual features as transparencies, missing body parts, shading, vacant eyes, nude figures and aggressive symbols in the drawing.

In sum, children's drawings are probably most useful as means of generating ideas for further exploration rather than as providing definitive data in and of themselves.

In addition to its use as a projective measure, drawing has also been used as an informal assessment tool to build rapport or to facilitate children's verbal reports. Drawing is an inherently enjoyable activity, which can help the clinician to establish rapport with children who might be shy or uncommunicative. Importantly, through showing an active interest in the children's drawings (e.g., 'Tell me about your family picture. What is everyone doing?'), the clinician encourages children to describe their private worlds in a less threatening way than by direct questioning. Similarly researchers have concluded that it is the verbal report accompanying a drawing that is of greatest value (Pipe and Salmon, 2009). Hayne and her colleagues (Gross et al., 2009; Patterson and Hayne, 2011) have conducted extensive research on the use of drawing in helping children to describe their experiences. For example, Gross and Hayne (1998) asked 20 3- to 4-year-old children and 20 5- to 6-year-old children to describe a time when they were happy, sad, angry or scared. The children were assigned to either a draw-and-tell or tell-only condition. The children reported a range of emotional experiences, including negative emotion states such as loss, grief and distress related to family disharmony. Children in the draw-and-tell condition reported twice as much information compared to children in the tell-only condition, irrespective of their age group. They also showed increased accuracy irrespective of age when allowed to draw and tell. This has also been shown with older children 5 to 12 years old (Patterson and Hayne, 2009).

Using the DAP SPED procedure, you ask Rudy to create three figure drawings in turn: of a man, a woman, and of himself. Initially, Rudy is reluctant to draw a picture of a person, complaining that he's 'not a good drawer' and 'it will look stupid'. Although the quality of his drawing of a man is age-appropriate, it is somewhat sparse and lacking in detail. In addition, his picture is small and shows many erasures and hesitations. He frets over getting the man's hands right,

finally giving up and saying, 'His hands are in his pockets. He doesn't care'. His drawing of a female figure is larger and more elaborated, including many small details, such as eyelashes, jewellery and hairstyle. When asked to complete the drawing of himself, Rudy balks and protests that it is 'just too hard'. Finally, he creates an almost unrecognizable squiggle at the bottom of the page and announces, 'There!' in a defiant tone of voice. It is the first time you have seen the oppositional side of Rudy that his teachers complain about.

On a subsequent visit, during which your rapport seems stronger and Rudy appears less self-conscious, you ask him to complete a Kinetic Family Drawing. Rudy agrees but this picture too is sketchy and hesitantly drawn. Rudy depicts his little brother high on a Ferris wheel, while he and his mother stand on the ground waving at him. He wistfully describes this as representing a fun day when they went to the fair together 'a long time ago'.

Many different observations might be made of these drawings. For instance, we might remark on Rudy's attitude toward the tasks themselves. His reluctance to draw may derive from his own harsh criticism of what he will produce. A negative self-perception also is suggested by the odd and inhuman depiction of himself. Moreover, both the process and the content of his drawings reflect an incapacity to play and to be the carefree boy he wishes he could be.

Apperception Tests

Children's stories, whether they arise spontaneously during testing or in response to projective tasks, are a rich source of information when viewed with an analyst's eye toward underlying fantasies, developmental vulnerabilities and potential transferable content. The *Thematic Apperception Test* (TAT) consists of a set of 31 pictures about which the child is instructed to tell a story. Each of the pictures is intentionally ambiguous, with the assumption that in attempting to impose meaning or structure, the child will project onto the pictures his or her own needs, desires and conflicts. For example, a sketchy figure depicted leaning against a couch may be male or female, exhausted or relaxed, suicidal, in a state of bliss or merely resting. Because any of these responses is equally plausible, the only determinant of the child's own perception is his or her frame of mind. In this way, the technique is designed to allow unconscious aspects of personality to be expressed. About 10 pictures are selected for a particular child. Specific cards are designed for males or females, children, adolescents or adults. The child is instructed to make up a story about the picture, including a beginning, middle and end, and to describe what the people in the story are thinking and feeling. The examiner records the story verbatim and asks questions concerning any elements that may have been omitted.

When interpreting the TAT, most clinicians report that in actual practice they do not use a standard procedure (Rossini and Moretti, 1997). The commonly accepted assumption underlying TAT interpretation is that the protagonists of the stories represent various aspects of the individual's *self-concept*, both conscious and unconscious. Thus, special attention is paid to the protagonists' needs, interests, traits, strivings and competencies. In the *interpersonal* sphere, themes concerning parent–child and family relationships are of special interest, with the stories analysed for the extent to which others are represented as nurturing, trustworthy, hostile or unreliable. Stories are also examined for their overall *emotional tone*, along with the effectiveness of *coping strategies* used to deal with the problems generated in the stories.

Westen (1991b) has contributed an empirically validated system for TAT interpretation. The Social Cognition and Object Relations Scale (SCORS) integrates psychodynamic theory and knowledge of social-cognitive development to assess individuals' representations of interpersonal relationships. Four dimensions are rated. The first of these concerns the *complexity* of representations of people. A low score indicates a lack of differentiation between self and others while a high score indicates that others are seen in complex and multidimensional ways. Second, the *affective tone* of relationships is rated. A low score indicates that the social world is perceived as hostile and depriving, while a high score is given to responses that include a range of affects but, on balance, present others as positive and trustworthy. Third, the capacity for *emotional investment* in relationships and *moral standards* is rated. A low score indicates that people are represented as being motivated solely by self-interest, with relationships simply as means to achieving self-serving ends; a high score indicates a reciprocity and valuing of relationships with others. The fourth dimension concerns the understanding of *social causality*. A low score indicates an absence of apparent interest in interpreting the internal motivations underlying others' behaviour, while a high score indicates an understanding of the thoughts, feelings and unconscious conflicts that underlie the behaviour of people. The SCORS has fared well in reliability and validity studies and differentiates various psychopathological groups, including youths with psychosis, delinquency, borderline personality disorder and a history of sexual abuse.

An effort to adapt the apperception approach to children is the *Roberts Apperception Test for Children* (Roberts-2; McArthur and Roberts, 1982). It helps to evaluate children's social understanding by using a unique story telling format. Appropriate for children between the ages of 6 and 18, it assesses two independent dimensions: adaptive social perception (development measure) and maladaptive or atypical social perception (clinical measure). There are 16 stimulus cards depicting common situations, conflicts and stresses in children's lives – for example, interparental arguments, child misbehaviour, sibling rivalry and peer conflicts. There are three versions of the test pictures: Caucasian, African-American and Hispanic children. The Roberts-2 provides criteria and examples for scoring the stories in terms of six *adaptive scales*, including such dimensions as reliance on others, support provided to others, self-sufficiency and maturity, limit-setting by parents and authority figures, the ability to formulate concepts about the problem situation, and the child's ability to construct positive and realistic solutions to conflicts. Five *clinical scales* are rated, including anxiety, aggression, depression, rejection and lack of resolution. Critical indicators are also assessed, including atypical responses, maladaptive outcomes and card rejections. Advantages of the Roberts-2 include high agreement between assessors, and the existence of age and gender specific norms to aid the clinician in evaluating an individual child's adjustment.

You ask Rudy to respond to a TAT card that depicts a boy looking at a violin on a table in front of him, an ambiguous expression on his face. The following is Rudy's story:

Well, there is a little boy, and his teacher told him to practise the violin, and he doesn't want to practise the violin, so he just sits there staring at it. After a while he fell asleep, and he has a dream and – now I have to think up a dream. He dreamed he was the greatest violinist in the world, and fame and success brought him riches and happiness. He bought his mother beautiful things, and they like lived in luxury. Um … these are hard to figure out. He had a special violin, and he couldn't play no other violin because this was the only one that ever worked for him, because there was only one that could play the right tunes. It seemed like magic that it played all right. He kept it by his bedside because if he lost the violin, he would lose his wealth and everything. It was almost like magic. Finally, there came a time when his worst rival realized he could only play that one violin, and he sent some bandits to break up his violin and ruin his career. Just as the bandits were going to break the violin in half, he woke up.

What can we make of Rudy's story? First, it is important to keep in mind that no one story is definitive in itself; it is merely suggestive. Only as themes occur repeatedly and can be fitted together does the clinician have confidence in the interpretation of the data. Keeping that caveat in mind, it is useful to know that

this particular picture often elicits stories concerning achievement and initiative, which seem to be important themes in Rudy's life. Rudy's version contains the familiar theme of a child having to do something he does not want to do because an adult says he must. Rudy's method of coping with this conflict is to flee into a dream. Further, most striking is the contrast between the initial picture of the put-upon boy and the grandiose world-famous virtuoso in the dream. However, instead of bringing security, success is accompanied by a state of heightened vulnerability, since a competitive rival sets out to destroy him. These story themes fit with some of the formulations we have derived from other data. We might hypothesize that Rudy's strivings to meet unrealistic expectations – to achieve impossible academic goals and to act as the 'man of the house' – have generated feelings of inadequacy. In addition, Rudy seems to perceive aggression and hostile competitiveness to be an integral part of achievement. Perhaps because his actual abilities do not fit with his expectations of himself, and he fears hostility and rejection from his peers, Rudy withdraws from the whole enterprise. On the positive side, Rudy's assets include a lively imagination and an ability to express thoughts and feelings in a disguised form when they are too painful to face directly. These characteristics suggest that he might be a good candidate for psychotherapy.

Behavioural Assessment

As we have noted, a key purpose of clinical assessment is to understand the basis of the child's psychopathology sufficiently so that the clinician can design an effective intervention. A prime example of tailoring the inquiry to a therapeutic procedure is **behavioural assessment**. Since behaviour therapy concerns the current situation, assessment aims at obtaining a specific account of a child's problem behaviours along with their immediate antecedents and consequences.

Behavioural assessment utilizes many traditional diagnostic procedures, but the emphasis differs. In obtaining referral information, the clinician focuses on the question of who has seen what behaviours in which situations. Similarly, the *behavioural interview* aims primarily at obtaining behaviour-specific accounts of the problem and the environmental factors that may be eliciting and maintaining it. The behavioural clinician also inquires into attempts to change the troublesome behaviour and the results obtained. Adults directly involved with the child's problem, such as parents, teachers and relatives, are interviewed. Generally speaking, obtaining historical information is minimized, since the clinician is only incidentally interested in reconstructing etiology.

Some of the main features of the behavioural interview deserve to be presented in detail. To begin with, the interviewer *operationalizes* general descriptions of the child, such as 'uncooperative', 'withdrawn' or 'lazy', by translating them into concrete *behaviours*. Specificity is of the essence: 'Rudy misbehaves in class' is not as helpful as 'Rudy stares out the window, doesn't answer when he's called on, and gets into arguments with the other children'. Next, the interviewer inquires concerning *antecedents* (a description of the situations in which the problem behaviour occurs). Next, the clinician inquires about events that occur immediately following the problem behaviour – namely, its *consequences*. Here, as in every aspect of the interview, behavioural specificity is sought in terms of exactly who is present and what is done: 'When Rudy doesn't answer me, I call him up to the front of the class and he always says he heard something rude from the boy who sits in the second row.'

Certain ancillary information is helpful. The clinician may obtain an initial inventory of potential reinforcers to be used in therapy by asking what the child enjoys, such as favourite foods, recreational activities or pastimes. The parents or teachers may be asked what behaviour they would wish to have as a replacement for the present objectionable ones. The clinician may assess the amount of time the parent has to participate in a therapeutic programme if one were deemed desirable and may evaluate the parent's ability and willingness to do so. Finally, the child may be interviewed to obtain his or her perception of the problems as well as a list of likes and dislikes.

The interviewer's emphasis on specific behaviour in no way eliminates the problems inherent in conducting any clinical interview. Parents and teachers are personally involved rather than objective reporters; for example, in the preceding illustration, the teacher may have cited only Rudy's behaviour as an antecedent and omitted the other child's provocation out of prejudice or honest obliviousness. Thus, the behavioural clinician must be as skilled as any other in establishing rapport, constructively handling negative feelings, judging the accuracy of the information and, when it is suspect, finding ways of eliciting a realistic account without antagonizing or alienating the parent.

Behaviour Rating Scales

A number of scales have been developed for rating observed child behaviour. While they are reliable and robust, considerable time and effort is often required to train coders to use these systems.

One example is the *Behavioural Coding System* (BCS; Reid, 1978), which was designed to rate children's behaviour both at home and at school. Specific positive and negative behaviours are rated, including verbalizations (such as laughing, whining, complying and teasing) and non-verbal behaviours (such as destructiveness, ignoring or touching another person). Good inter-rater reliabilities have been demonstrated, and the BCS successfully differentiates clinical and normative samples, such as aggressive and prosocial boys, as well as revealing significant changes in rates of negative behaviour before and after behavioural treatment.

The Child Behaviour Checklist *Direct Observation Form* (DOF; Achenbach et al., 2001) has the advantage of directly paralleling the parent and teacher versions of the CBCL. Ninety-six behaviour items are rated, of which 86 overlap with the parent-report form and 73 overlap with the teacher-report form. The DOF requires the assessor to observe a child for six 10-minute sessions, during which a narrative description of the child's behaviour is recorded, including the occurrence, duration and intensity of any problem behaviours. At the end of each session, each behaviour is rated on a four-point scale. Good inter-rater reliabilities have been demonstrated, as well as correspondence between parents' and teachers', and other observers' reports. According to the DSM-IV adaptive functioning refers to how effectively individuals cope with daily life demands and how well they meet the standards of personal independence expected of someone in their particular age group, sociocultural background and community setting (p. 42). For a diagnosis of mental retardation, in addition to deficits in IQ noted previously, the child must also demonstrate impaired adaptive functioning in at least two of the following areas: communication, self-care, home living, social/interpersonal skills, use of community resources, self-direction, functional academic skills, work, leisure and health and safety.

Adaptive behaviour scales such as the Vineland Adaptive Behaviour scales (Sparrow et al., 2005) and the AAMR Adaptive Behaviour Scale-School (ABS-S:2) provide standard scores for adaptive behaviours in a number of different domains such as communication, daily living and socialization. As well as standard scores, the scales also provide scale scores ranging from 0 to 18, with the average scores being 10, which is at the 50th percentile. The Vineland Adaptive scales are in fact the leading instrument for supporting the diagnosis of intellectual and developmental disabilities. Scales are completed by the main caregiver and provide an index of adaptive functioning in three areas: Communication, Daily Living and Socialization.

Behavioural Observation

The behavioural approach has made a unique contribution by adapting the technique of naturalistic observation – previously used primarily for research purposes – to assessment goals and placing it at the heart of the process. It is easy to understand this emphasis on direct observation, since

abnormal behaviour is assumed to develop and to be maintained by environmental stimuli, while behaviour modification corrects problem behaviours by altering the environmental conditions maintaining them.

To begin with, the clinician identifies the *target behaviours* to be observed. These are derived from the information obtained from the referral, checklist and interview, but also should be behaviours for which specific treatment goals can be specified. These behaviours are, in effect, the operational definition of the child's problem. 'Uncooperative', for example, might be translated into 'not answering the teacher when called on'. Other disruptive behaviours in the classroom might include the child's being out of his or her chair without permission; touching, grabbing or destroying another child's property; vocalizing, speaking or noise-making without permission; hitting other children; and failing to do assignments.

The behavioural clinician's next task is to determine the frequency of the target behaviour in order to establish a *baseline* for its natural occurrence against which to evaluate the effectiveness of the therapeutic intervention. Observations are scheduled for the specific periods in which the problem behaviour is most likely to happen. Depending on the natural occurrence of the target behaviour, the period may last half an hour to an entire day, while observations may be made daily or only on particular days. Rudy, for example, may need to be observed for only about 30 minutes in the classroom.

There are a number of different methods for quantifying behavioural observations. *Frequency* involves counting the number of times the target behaviour occurs within a specific period. Frequency divided by time yields a measure called *response rate*; for example, a disruptive boy may leave his seat without permission five times in a 50-minute class period, and his response rate would be recorded as 5/50, or 0.10. In *interval recording* an observer has a data sheet divided into small time units, such as 20 seconds. Aided by a timing device (such as a stopwatch) attached to a clipboard, the observer indicates whether the target behaviour occurred in a given time unit. Frequently, a *time-sampling* method is used in which the observer observes the child's behaviour for 10 seconds, for example, and spends the next 5 seconds recording the target behaviours that occurred in that 15-second interval. This sequence is repeated for the duration of the observational period. Typically, only the presence or absence of this target behaviour is recorded. Some data are lost if a behaviour occurs more than once during an interval, but such losses are often unimportant. Interval recording is usually more practicable than the frequency method when the observer wishes to record a number of behaviours. Finally, *duration* consists of measuring the interval of time between the onset and termination of the target behaviour, a useful method for assessing the amount of time spent in a particular behaviour, such as head banging or socializing with peers during class time.

In addition, observation is used to carry out a *functional analysis* of the target behaviour. A common strategy for accomplishing this is the A-B-C method, which requires attending to *antecedents, behaviour* and *consequences* that might perpetuate problem behaviour (see Fig. 16.13 for an example). These data are more qualitative than quantitative, with a description of the child's behaviour provided in a narrative form. As always, the observer is aware of the situation-specific nature of the relationships observed and is alert to the possibility that the setting may significantly alter the functional meaning of behaviour. For example, a teacher's reprimand may tend to decrease provocative behaviour when teacher and child are alone, but it may increase such behaviour when other children are present, particularly if they tease or egg on the target child.

Theoretically, the baseline phase should continue until the target behaviour has become stable. Because of the variability of human behaviour, such an ideal is often difficult to achieve. The general consensus is that there should be a minimal baseline period of one week of data collection. (For a more extended presentation, see La Greca and Stone, 1992).

Reliability

In order to ensure reliability, researchers using naturalistic observation have found it necessary to train observers. Typically, two or more trainees observe, record and score the behaviour of the same child. Disagreements are discussed and reconciled. Additional observations are made and scored until agreement between observers is at least 80 to 85 per cent. Even after training is completed, it is highly desirable to 'recalibrate' the observers periodically by repeating the training procedures. Such intensive training further attests to the fact that, the emperor's new clothes notwithstanding, the untrained eye is an inaccurate observational instrument.

Behavioural clinicians rarely have the time or the personnel to train for accurate observation. Consequently, they must rely on untrained adults such as parents and teachers, whose reliability, as might be expected, is significantly lower (Solanto and Alvir, 2009). In general, a given individual is consistent with himself or herself over a period of one week to one month; even after six months, consistency is marginal but adequate. Reliability between similar observers, such as between parents or between teachers, is satisfactory but not so high as to prevent disagreements between mother and father or between teachers. Reliability plunges precipitously between adults who view the same child in different situations, such as parents and teachers, teachers and mental health workers, or even teachers who see the child in different settings. This last finding suggests that many problem behaviours may be situation specific. Thus, reliability is affected both by the implicit definitions and biases of the observers and by the different information input they have in terms of the situations in which they have observed the child.

The Developmental Dimension in Behavioural Assessment

Developmental considerations, while often neglected, need to be integrated into the behavioural assessment process (Ollendick and King, 1991). It is important to be able to compare the child's behaviour to *normative information* about

FIGURE 16.13 Hypothetical Example of Simple A-B-C Observational System of an 8-Year-Old Boy (B).

Time/Setting	Antecedent	Behaviour	Consequence
8:30 / Maths class – copying from board		B takes pencil from another child	Child ignores him
	Child ignores him	B tears paper on child's desk	Child tells teacher and teacher reprimands B
	Teacher reprimands B	B sulks	Teacher allows B to erase board
8:35 / Maths class – doing seatwork		B leaves seat to sharpen pencil	Teacher asks B to raise hand to leave seat
		B raises hand	Teacher continues to work with other student
	Teacher ignores B	B gets out of seat and pulls on teacher's shirt to get attention	Teacher scolds B for leaving seat and places name on board
	Teacher puts B's name on board	B starts to cry	Child teases B
	Child teases B	B tries to hit other child	B sent to office
8:55 / Maths class – completing seatwork	B returns to class	B sullen and refuses to work	Teacher allows B to collect assignments

Source: Kamphaus and Frick, 1996.

what can be expected of a child this age. For example, while a teacher may perceive a school-age child who does not stay in his seat as overly active and disruptive, knowledge of developmental norms will help the behavioural assessor to recognize whether it is the child's behaviour that is deviant or the adult's expectations. A second way in which developmental norms for behaviour need to be understood is in terms of *patterns of behaviour*. Behaviours associated with the same disorder might differ across gender and age. For example,

while depression in older boys is associated with 'uncommunicativeness', depressed girls are more likely to exhibit 'social withdrawal'. Similarly, older children with separation anxiety are characterized by physical complaints and school refusal, while younger children show behaviours such as sleep disturbances and excessive anxiety about their attachment figures. Therefore, behavioural assessors must be sensitive to the fact that the signs and symptoms rated change with gender and development. Finally, establishing *rapport* with children is a universal feature of assessment that requires developmentally relevant knowledge and skills.

Rudy's teacher is eager to be of help and agrees to allow your colleague to conduct a behavioural assessment by observing Rudy in the classroom. She makes note of the antecedents and consequences of Rudy's behaviour in four specific categories: on-task behaviour (doing the work assigned, raising his hand to contribute to the class discussion, asking relevant questions about the material); off-task behaviour (staring off into space, engaging in activities other than the one assigned by the teacher); oppositionality (refusing to answer the teacher when called on); and peer conflicts (negative exchanges with other children, including verbal or physical aggression, and incidents in which Rudy is the initiator or the victim). During one half hour, she observes one brief moment of on-task behaviour, six incidents of off-task behaviour, three of oppositionality, and three peer conflicts. Each off-task incident seems to occur when other students are responding to the teacher's questions, something Rudy never volunteers to do. The episodes of oppositionality occur during arithmetic lessons, and the teacher's response each time is to call him to the front of the room. As he passes one particular boy near the front, she observes subtle provocative behaviours by this other youngster, such as murmured insults, attempts to trip Rudy, and so forth. Rudy's retorts to these provocations are neither subtle nor quiet – his attempts to strike back verbally catch the teacher's attention and land Rudy in even more trouble. The other children seem to watch these little dramas with glee and even to look forward to them.

Clinical Assessment: Art and Science

While differences in assessment procedures can best be understood in terms of clinicians' different theoretical and therapeutic allegiances, there is another related source of disagreement. As scientists, psychologists strive for objectivity and precision, which require, among other things, clearly delineated procedures that are available to the scientific community. It is no accident that psychologists in the past championed the use of standardized assessment techniques over impressionistic evaluations. Nor is it by chance that behavioural assessment, with its explicit procedures for observation and avoidance of inferences about personality characteristics and motivations, is exercising a similar appeal. Concomitantly, there is a mistrust of the hypothesis-testing clinician initially described in this discussion. While utilizing theoretical and experiential guides, the process by which the clinician generates, tests, accepts and discards ideas is nearer to an art than a science. He or she may indeed come up with impressive insights but also may be seriously in error; more important – and this is what concerns the critical psychologist – there is no clearly established procedure for deciding in favour of one outcome over the other.

Certain clinicians might answer that scores are only one kind of information to be gained from a test, as we have seen in discussing intelligence tests. To limit assessment to such scores would be to eliminate the added behavioural data so vital to understanding an individual child. If such data have yet to be standardized and are of unknown reliability, their clinical utility justifies their use for the present. These clinicians rightly claim that there are a number of important areas for which no standardized, clinically useful instruments exist. Thus, they can do no more than put the pieces of assessment data together as best they can. Moreover, it is just such efforts to understand complex, heretofore unsystematized data that can ultimately serve as the basis for objective assessment techniques.

While techniques and goals may vary, all clinical assessment requires a high degree of *professional competence*. Clinicians must be skilful and sensitive in handling the many interpersonal problems inherent in dealing with troubled parents and children; they must be knowledgeable concerning the procedures they use and the problems they are called on to evaluate; they must be well acquainted with and abide by the ethical principles of their profession; and they must have received adequate academic and professional preparation, which for a clinical child psychologist typically involves a PhD or PsyD from an accredited university and at least two years of supervised experience (American Psychological Association, 2002).

Another aspect of assessment that is more art than science is the *integration* of various discrete findings into a meaningful whole. To return to the case of Rudy, the data we gathered illustrate the fact that children's emotional and behavioural problems have multiple dimensions. Therefore, there is no simple statement that will capture all the richness of the data. There is a *cognitive* component, as evidenced by Rudy's learning difficulties in the area of arithmetic; an *emotional* or psychodynamic component, as seen in his tendency to internalize his distress as well as his conflicts over achievement and aggression; a *family system* component, suggested by the caregiving role he plays with his mother; and a *behavioural* component, seen in his difficulties interacting with teachers and peers.

Which of these provides the 'right' hypothesis? Clinicians from different theoretical orientations will focus on the data that present them with the most plausible case formulation and treatment plan for a given child. However, the clinician operating from a developmental psychopathology perspective has an advantage in that no single theory dictates to him or her what evidence is to be gathered nor which data warrant attention. Instead, the developmental psychopathologist will evaluate each bit of evidence and data – regardless of what theoretical orientation it derives from or supports – in order to construct a mosaic that best depicts this most interesting and complex young person. Further, each of these orientations suggests particular avenues for intervention – for example, with Rudy, his family or the school – that might be integrated into an effective multidimensional treatment plan. Rudy's response to these different interventions, in turn, will provide the clinician with feedback about the accuracy of his or her formulation of the problem and the possible need for further psychological testing. Therefore, just as assessment informs intervention, intervention can inform assessment.

The dovetailing of assessment and psychotherapy that we have emphasized throughout this chapter will become even clearer after we explore the major intervention techniques themselves. This is the topic of our final chapter.

Intervention and Prevention

Conceptualizing and Evaluating Child Interventions

It is estimated that over 200 psychotherapies are currently in use with children and adolescents (Kazdin and Weisz, 2010). These interventions derive from different assumptions about the nature of psychopathology and different ideas about the means necessary to alleviate it. How is the clinician to choose the best course of action? Our consideration of the topic of intervention requires that we come full circle and return to the theme first introduced in Chapter 1: the various theories of psychopathology. Theory guides the clinician's understanding of what causes – and what might alleviate – children's mental health problems.

In the past, it often was the case that therapists adhered rigidly to a theoretical point of view, whether psychoanalytic, behavioural or systemic. Adherence to their 'brand' of psychotherapy led clinicians to see all cases through only one set of lenses and, in many instances, to recommend the same form of treatment for everyone (Matarazzo, 1990). Following this kind of thinking, clinical researchers set out to determine which was the overall 'best' therapy by conducting studies in which they pitted various kinds of intervention against one another. Overall, the results of these 'horse race' studies were not very discriminating. Whereas treatment was consistently associated with improvement, and treated participants fared better than those in the no-treatment group, few differences among therapies were found. As the Dodo in Lewis Carroll's *Alice in Wonderland* declared, '*Everybody* has won and *all* must have prizes' (Luborsky et al., 1975).

These earlier studies were predicated on an assumption – called the '*uniformity myth*' – that one form of therapy would be the treatment of choice for all psychopathologies. Increasingly, the movement is towards asking more complex and sophisticated questions, such as *which* therapy is most effective for *whom*, *when* (Fonagy et al., 2002). Therefore, a better approach is to find the 'best fit' for a given child, depending on his or her developmental stage, psychopathology and intra-personal and family characteristics. In the same light, another current trend in psychotherapy practice is towards developing *integrative* models that take a multifaceted approach to solving child and family problems. Integration can take place by combining individual and family treatment or by utilizing a variety of techniques drawn from biological, cognitive, social and behavioural theories (Mash, 2006.)

Finally, there is a movement afoot to promote the use of *empirically supported* (Chambless and Ollendick, 2001; Task Force on Promotion and Dissemination of Psychological Procedures, American Psychological Association, 1995) or *evidence-based* (Silverman and Hinshaw, 2008; Weisz and Kazdin, 2010) treatments. This is the case particularly in the field of clinical psychology, where the Ethical Principles of Psychologists (American Psychological Association, 2002) explicitly call for psychologists to use interventions for which there is evidence of effectiveness.

In this chapter we discuss ways in which psychopathologies of childhood can be ameliorated or even prevented. Our presentation is selective, offering examples of only a few of the 200 treatment techniques available. (For more extensive overviews, see Kazdin and Weisz, 2010; Kendall, 2011b; Mash and Barkley, 2006; and Rutter et al., 2009a.) In the realm of *intervention* we present five of the major therapeutic approaches – psychoanalytic, humanistic, behavioural, cognitive and family systemic – along with the conceptualization of psychopathology that provides the rationale for the therapeutic techniques each employs. As we consider *prevention*, we discuss programmes that target at-risk populations in order to prevent psychopathology from developing. Following the movement for evidence-based treatments, we examine the available research regarding the major forms of intervention used with children and focus our attention on those that have received empirical support. First, however, we must consider *how* we can determine whether a given treatment is effective.

Empirical Validation: Methods and Challenges

Although it might seem a simple matter to prove that an intervention 'works', there are actually a number of challenges to this endeavour (Kazdin, 2008; Weisz and Kazdin, 2010). For example, a large number of children with the same diagnosis must be recruited. The parents must be willing to allow their children to be assigned to either the treatment or control groups. The assignment to condition must be done on a random basis, and yet these groups should not differ significantly from one another in terms of such characteristics as severity of the disturbance, age, ethnicity, family constellation and social class. A number of therapists expert in the intervention of choice must be available, and the treatment protocol must be laid out specifically so that all of the therapists carry out the prescribed treatment in the same way. Careful attention must be paid to assessing *fidelity* in the way that therapists adhere to the underlying principles of the treatment manual. The outcome must be operationalized clearly, reliably and validly, and should indicate that the treatment has made a difference that is lasting and of real-world significance.

Kazdin (2008) illustrates the ways in which the majority of child therapy outcome studies have failed to hit the mark. Most of the research on child interventions consists of *analogue* studies that only approximate the way that psychotherapy is carried out in the real world. Generally, an analogue study involves the delivery of an intervention to non-clinical samples by inexperienced therapists, often graduate student research assistants. Thus, the therapies are a far cry from the actual practice of skilled professionals, and the children treated do not evidence the high *levels of disturbance* and *comorbidity* that are characteristic of real clinical samples and present significant challenges to psychotherapy. Willingness to remain in treatment is another important factor, and the more disturbed and disruptive children and families are more likely to fail to stay the course; *attrition*, or treatment dropout, is a major problem with real clinical samples. In addition, most of the studies use *narrow outcome criteria* such as symptom relief that, while statistically significant, often lack clinical significance in terms of their impact on the child's life outside of therapy. The evaluation of therapist fidelity is often lacking and *follow-up* is generally only short term, so that little evidence is presented for therapy's effectiveness over the long term.

Further, few studies have made an effort to demonstrate that the intervention *processes* themselves are what account for the change associated with therapy. Whether the intervention targets the acquisition of a skill, insight into an internal conflict, or change in maladaptive cognitions, research should establish that alterations in these particular processes are what lead to improvement. Without such evidence, intervention studies are vulnerable to the challenge that *non-specific effects*, such as attention from a caring adult – or unintended effects, such as inadvertent positive reinforcement provided by a psychoanalyst's smiles and nods – are what lead to the positive outcome. Finally, the majority of studies neglect to attend to the many *moderating factors* – for example, age, family constellation, quality of the therapeutic relationship – that might influence the impact of treatment on individual children.

Lastly, significant energy and strategizing is needed to accomplish the goal of disseminating laboratory-based treatments into real-world settings (Bearman et al., 2010; Fixsen et al., 2010). For example, much work is needed to develop the capacity of community-based mental health systems to adopt and implement evidence-based interventions, some of which might require a quite different theoretical orientation and method of delivery than 'treatment as usual' (Weisz and Chorpita, 2011). In addition, often little is known about whether and how an intervention developed in one country will 'translate' to another, although promising results are being found for some evidence-based interventions, such as functional family therapy and multisystemic therapy, which are being successfully adopted across multiple diverse cultures around the world (Scott, 2010).

Despite these challenges, the research on psychotherapy outcome in general paints an encouraging picture. Effective interventions for children have been developed, and increasing attention is being paid to the need to document their effectiveness with specific problems and across samples (Silverman and Hinshaw, 2008). The most convincing evidence for the effectiveness of child interventions comes from *meta-analysis*, which aggregates data from a number of studies. The outcome of a meta-analysis is an estimation of *effect size*: overall, in all these different samples studied in all these different settings, how much difference did treatment make?

A comprehensive meta-analysis of the child intervention research included 150 studies published between 1967 and 1993, involving children 2 to 18 years of age (Weisz et al., 1995). The effect size indicated that the average child who underwent treatment was less symptomatic at follow-up than 76 per cent of the untreated children. This is considered to be a significant effect, in the medium to large range, comparable to that found in psychotherapy outcome studies conducted with adults.

On the one hand, Weisz and colleagues found that *behaviour therapies* consistently were the most effective interventions for children, contradicting the 'Dodo verdict' reached with adults. On the other hand, only 10 per cent of the studies they reviewed involved non-behavioural interventions. Given the dearth of empirical research conducted on other forms of therapy, therefore, the jury may still be out. In general, *adolescents* tended to improve more than younger children. Curiously, *females*, especially female adolescents, gained the most from intervention. *Experienced* therapists were more effective than well-trained para-professionals in treating over-controlled problems, such as anxiety and depression, but the *para-professionals* were equally as effective in treating under-controlled problems such as conduct disorder. Further, effects were overwhelmingly stronger for *laboratory-based* interventions than for those conducted in 'real-life' settings. Finally, effects were strongest for outcome measures that were *specifically matched* to the treatment technique, arguing against the idea that the effectiveness of child therapy can be accounted for by non-specific effects.

The results of such broad meta-analyses ultimately are limited to answering a single question, as Kazdin (1997) put it: 'The basic question about whether psychotherapy "works" has been answered affirmatively and can be put to rest' (p. 115). More recent meta-analyses have been more fine-tuned and specific in attempting to understand the conditions under which *particular* therapies are effective in addressing *particular* childhood problems, such as depression (Weisz et al., 2006b), posttraumatic stress disorder (Kowalik et al., 2011), OCD (Watson and Rees, 2008), ADHD (Fabiano et al., 2009), conduct disorder (Reyno and McGrath, 2006), and the like.

The APA Division 12 Task Force Criteria

With the move towards using empirically supported interventions, APA Division 12 (Clinical Psychology) launched a task force to define, promote and disseminate psychological treatments that meet scientific standards (APA, 1995). Later refined by Chambless and Hollon (1998) and Chambless and Ollendick (2001), the criteria are presented in Table 17.1. In order to be considered empirically supported, treatments must be tested in studies that meet a number of standards of scientific inquiry. First, the experimental treatment must be compared to a *control group*, whether defined as no treatment, placebo or an alternative treatment. Second, studies must involve *random assignment* of participants to treatment conditions so that selection biases cannot colour the results. Third, the intervention must be carried out with the use of a *treatment manual* that ensures each therapist is adhering to the procedures and principles of the particular treatment under study. Fourth, there must be a *defined population* on which the study was based, with clear selection criteria that will allow the investigators to know for whom specifically the treatment was proven successful. Fifth, *outcome measures* must be reliable and valid, rather than being based on subjective or impressionistic ratings of therapist or client. Sixth, *data analyses* must be carried out in an appropriate and valid way. In short, each of these procedures is designed to assure that the study in question is carried out in an empirically sound manner, that the effects observed are due to the treatment and not some chance or confounding factor, and that it is well-enough designed and

TABLE 17.1 Summary of Criteria for Empirically Supported Psychological Therapies (EST)

1. Comparison with a no-treatment control group, alternative treatment group or placebo (a) in a randomized control trial, controlled single case experiment or equivalent time-samples design and (b) in which the EST is statistically significantly superior to no treatment, placebo or alternative treatments, or in which the EST is equivalent to a treatment already established in efficacy, and power is sufficient to detect moderate differences.
2. These studies must have been conducted with (a) a treatment manual or its logical equivalent; (b) a population, treated for specified problems, for whom inclusion criteria have been delineated in a reliable, valid manner; (c) reliable and valid outcome assessment measures, at minimum tapping the problems targeted for change; and (d) appropriate data analysis.
3. For a designation of *efficacious*, the superiority of the EST must have been shown in at least two independent research settings (sample size of 3 or more at each site in the case of single case experiments). If there is conflicting evidence, the preponderance of the well-controlled data must support the EST's efficacy.
4. For a designation of *possibly efficacious*, one study (sample size of 3 or more in the case of single case experiments) suffices in the absence of conflicting evidence.
5. For a designation of *efficacious and specific*, the EST must have been shown to be statistically significantly superior to pill or psychological placebo or to an alternative bona fide treatment in at least two independent research settings. If there is conflicting evidence, the preponderance of the well-controlled data must support the EST's efficacy and specificity.

Source: Chambless and Hollon, 1998.

described that its methods could be replicated easily by another set of investigators.

Further, the task force established three levels of empirical support: possibly efficacious, efficacious, and efficacious and specific. In order to be considered *possibly efficacious*, there must be one well-designed study evident that shows the superiority of the treatment in comparison to the control condition. To meet the higher standard of *efficacious*, the superiority of the treatment must have been demonstrated in at least two independent research laboratories. To meet the highest standard, *efficacious and specific*, the intervention must be shown to be more effective than a bona fide alternative treatment by at least two separate sets of investigators.

Is there evidence that ESTs are more effective than 'treatment as usual'? In order to address just this question, Weisz and colleagues (2006a) revisited the literature to conduct a new meta-analysis on the studies published in the decade since their previous effort. They combed the literature to find 32 randomized controlled studies in which a treatment had been included in at least one scientifically reviewed list of empirically supported interventions versus those in which a non-evidence-based intervention was provided as part of the usual care offered in a clinical setting. The results of their meta-analysis showed that whereas the overall effect size for all child therapies was modest, there were significantly stronger effects for evidence-based treatments versus usual care, and these positive effects remained constant across levels of severity of psychopathology and for youth with diverse ethnic backgrounds.

Evidence-Based Practice

In contrast to the EST movement, which focuses on the validation of specific 'name brand' treatments (Shirk and Russell, 1996), an even more recent trend in the field is toward the promotion of **evidence-based practice** (EBP) (Council for Training in Evidence-Based Behavioural Practice, 2008; Silverman and Hinshaw, 2008). The most widely cited definition of EBP is that of Dr David Sackett, a physician who founded the Centre for Evidence Based Medicine at the University of Oxford, who defines EBP as 'the conscientious, explicit and judicious use of current best evidence in making decisions about the care of the individual patient. It means integrating individual clinical expertise with the best available external clinical evidence from systematic research' (Sackett et al., 1996, p. 71).

The EBP movement acknowledges limitations of the EST approach, including the impossibility of gathering empirical data from randomized controlled trials sufficient to establish the effectiveness of every possible form of intervention with every possible combination of client characteristics in real-world clinical settings. Instead, the goal of the EBP movement is to increase our ability to develop, identify and promote the use of those techniques for which the weight of the scientific evidence indicates good results.

The EBP model espouses that best clinical practices involve integrating three components: knowledge of the best available research evidence regarding what interventions are proven effective for the problem at hand; availability of the therapist skills and competencies to carry out the interventions needed; and appreciation for the client characteristics, values and preferences that may influence which interventions are most acceptable to or effective for them. (See Fig. 17.1.) Consequently, the EBP process involves five steps:

1 Asking practical, answerable questions to determine the core issues needed to be addressed in the care of the given individual, community or population.

2 Acquiring the best available evidence regarding the question, with careful attention to the difference between primary sources of data (e.g., the results of actual empirical studies) versus secondary sources (e.g., someone else's synthesis, summary, or opinion of the primary data).

3 Critically appraising the evidence for validity and applicability to the problem at hand, with appreciation of the strengths and weaknesses of different kinds of research designs,

FIGURE 17.1 Evidence-Based Practice Model.

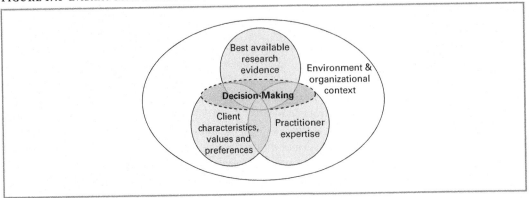

Source: Council for Training in Evidence-Based Behavioural Practice, 2008.

methodologies, and strategies for evaluating the quality and strength of evidence used in synthesized research reviews.

4 Applying the evidence by engaging in collaborative health decision-making with the affected individual(s) or group(s). Appropriate decision-making integrates the context, values and preferences of the care recipient, as well as available resources, including professional expertise.

5 Assessing the outcome and disseminating the results in ways that are collaborative with and accessible to a variety of shareholders, including clients, and devising a plan for ongoing evaluation, quality improvement and adjustment of behavioural practices as needed.

Ethnic and Cross-Cultural Diversity in Interventions with Children

Despite efforts to increase the representation of ethnic minorities in training programmes for mental health providers, it is still the case that most ethnic minority children and families will be treated by clinicians who are not members of their race. In addition, the fact that members of various cultural communities are not always included in

clinical trials leaves us without clear data as to whether those evidence-based treatments are in fact effective for those cultural groups (Huey and Polo, 2010). Therefore, training in cultural sensitivity and responsiveness is a necessity (American Psychological Association, 2003).

To this end, the effectiveness and acceptability of treatments can be increased when they are adapted to the needs and experiences of culturally diverse populations. We have encountered a number of excellent examples so far, including Robbins and colleagues' (2010) adaptation of structural family therapy for delinquent Hispanic youth (Chapter 10), Hawkins and colleagues' (2004) Canoe Family programme for preventing substance use among tribal youth in the US Pacific northwest, and Rosello and Bernal's (1999) modification of interpersonal therapy for use with depressed Puerto Rican teens (Chapter 8).

As Tharp (1991) points out, cultural issues may be relevant to child therapy on a number of levels. One of these is *cultural differences in pathology*: particular disorders may be more prevalent in particular ethnic groups, whether because of characteristic social problems, sociocultural practices or culturally specific definitions of normalcy and psychopathology. For example, hostility and prejudice associated with racism may increase the risk of conduct disorder among African American children; stresses associated with immigration may increase the risk of anxiety among Indo-Chinese refugee children; repeated losses associated with high rates of death and family dislocation may precipitate depression among Native American youth. On the other hand, parents' beliefs about socialization and proper child behaviour may lead to cultural differences in rates of disorders. For example, in Thailand, where the culture encourages inhibition, deference and peacefulness, children are more likely to be referred for internalizing problems, whereas in the USA, where independence and competitiveness are fostered, rates of child referrals for externalizing problems are more common.

Cultural differences in treatment relate both to access and effectiveness. For example, lower-income minority families may be less likely to seek help from mental health professionals, especially from unfamiliar, majority-culture dominated agencies and professional staff. In addition, research shows that, once they have entered treatment, ethnic minority families are more likely to drop out, often after the first session. Therefore, treatments that are accessible and responsive to minority clients are essential. Furthermore, techniques that are effective in one culture may not 'fit' with another. For example, behaviour therapists working with Chinese-American families report that cultural beliefs about parenting and family structure generate significant resistance from Chinese-origin parents who are asked to play with or contingently ignore their children. (A contrary point of view is expressed by Webster-Stratton and Taylor, 1998, who report good success in overcoming culturally based resistance to their parent training programme with low SES, ethnic minority families in the USA.)

Cultural differences in knowledge come into play when the clinician and client hail from different cultural backgrounds. The likelihood that such knowledge deficits will arise is a function not only of the majority status of most mental health professionals, but of the lack of attention to diverse children and families in the clinical and research literatures. Consequently, armed only with an understanding of their own cultures, therapists are highly vulnerable to misunderstanding or even pathologizing culturally normative child-rearing practices and values. For example, we encountered this problem in the study of physical discipline versus abuse in the context of African American and European American families. Obtaining such cultural knowledge, however, is complicated by the great *diversity* among and between ethnic groups. For example, the term 'Native American' comprises many different tribal groups, each with its own history and practices, just as 'Latino' families may hail from such diverse cultures as Cuba, Mexico and Puerto Rico, to name only a few.

To address the issues of cultural diversity, some clinicians advocate the development of *culturally specific* interventions that are addressed to the unique needs and perspectives of the individual culture. However, in general, the thrust is toward the development of *culturally responsive* treatments that can be modified in ways that create a better fit with the child's and family's cultural pattern (Bernal et al., 2009; Huey and Polo, 2008). Examples of such adaptations might include efforts to match the ethnicity of the clinician and the child/family, additions to the training of clinicians that focus on cultural issues, and modifications of the content of the treatment manuals to provide illustrations and examples that are more applicable to clients of various cultures (Huey and Polo, 2010). For example, McCabe and Yeh (2009) developed a culturally modified version of Parent–Child Interaction Therapy (PCIT; see Chapter 14) especially for Mexican American families. These modifications included referencing culturally related concepts throughout the programme, increasing session time spent on rapport-building, and adding representations of Latino families to the handouts. Results of a randomized controlled trial confirmed that the effects of the culturally modified treatment were superior to those of standard PCIT for this population. (For further reading about interventions for children and families from a variety of ethnic and cultural groups, see Fong, 2003; Gibbs and Huang, 2003; McGoldrick, 2008; and McGoldrick et al., 2005.)

The Developmental Psychopathology Approach

A number of clinician-scholars have suggested that an understanding of developmental psychopathology might inform our interventions with children (Fonagy and Target, 2009; Holmbeck et al., 2011; Ialongo et al., 2006; Shirk, 1999). At the most fundamental level, and consistent with the primary thesis of this text, knowledge of *normal development* is essential (Davies, 2010). First, familiarity with what is typical for children of a given age allows the clinician to *distinguish normal from pathological* behaviour. Second, an understanding of the developmental tasks the child faces may help to put the behaviour in *context* and explain its etiology. Further, the child's level of *cognitive and emotional development* must be taken into account when selecting an appropriate intervention technique. Whereas the need to adapt to the child's developmental level is obvious, few therapies have actually attended to the cognitive and linguistic differences between, for example, a preschooler or school-age child.

Other principles of developmental psychopathology also have implications for intervention. Attention to *stage-salient issues* may help tailor treatments to be maximally effective for children at particular developmental periods (Cicchetti et al., 1988; Holmbeck et al., 2011; Kerig and Schulz, 2011). For example, individuals may be more amenable to change during times of *developmental transitions*, such as first entry into school, or when poised at the cusp of adolescence. Therefore, interventions might be more effective if timed to take such transitions into account. As Sir Michael Rutter (1990) states: 'Particular attention needs to be paid to the mechanisms operating at key turning points in individual's lives, when a risk trajectory may be redirected onto a more adaptive path' (p. 210).

Finally, because problems emerge as a function of *transactional processes*, intervention in those processes provides a powerful way of inducing change (Rutter, 1990). Accordingly, interpersonal relationships are likely to provide a key to therapeutic change in the developmental psychopathology perspective.

An Integrative Developmental Psychopathology Model of Intervention

Shirk and colleagues (2011; Shirk and Russell, 1996) offer an intriguing re-conceptualization of child psychotherapy. Influenced by the developmental psychopathology perspective, they argue for therapists to relinquish adherence to 'brands' of psychotherapy and instead link intervention planning to an understanding of *pathogenic processes*. This term refers to the clinician's theoretical formulation of the developmental issues underlying the child's problems, which we encountered in Chapter 16 as the *case formulation*. The case formulation goes beyond simple diagnosis. Because there are divergent pathways to specific psychopathologies, children who share the same diagnosis may not have reached the therapist's doorway via the same road and thus may not share the same underlying pathogenic processes.

Shirk and colleagues focus on three major domains of development: cognitive, emotional and interpersonal. Within the *cognitive* realm, pathogenic processes might take the form of deficits in knowledge or skills, such as a lack of understanding of how to solve interpersonal problems, cognitive distortions and maladaptive schema about the self or others, or simply lack of insight into one's own motivations and behaviour. In the *emotional* realm, pathogenic processes might include blocked access to feelings, lack of understanding of emotions, or an inability to regulate and cope with affective states. In the *interpersonal* realm, pathogenic processes might include caregivers who fail to validate the child's self-worth, deprive the child of support and structure, or contribute to the development of insecure models of attachment relationships.

A clear understanding of the pathological processes that brought the disorder about can help the clinician to develop a treatment plan. The strategy is to match the formulation of the pathological process to the most relevant *change process*. These change processes are derived from the major theoretical orientations, with which we are familiar (see Table 17.2). For example, the formulation that an aggressive child's difficulties are a product of inadequate attachments would suggest that the therapist strive to provide a 'corrective emotional experience' via a psychodynamically nurturing relationship. In contrast, the formulation that the child's difficulties derive from a lack of social skills would suggest that the therapist play a cognitively educative function and help the child to learn those skills.

Shirk and colleagues limit their discussion to *psycho*therapies, defined as therapies directed at changing internal factors that mediate between the environment and the child's behaviour. Thus, they distinguish psychotherapies from *behaviour* therapies and *family systemic* therapies, both of which are directed towards changing the environment itself. However, their scheme can easily be expanded to include behaviourally oriented and systemic interventions; therefore, we have added these two conceptualizations to Table 17.2. For example, the

TABLE 17.2 Integrating Theories, Case Formulations and Change Processes in Child Psychotherapy

Theory	Model	Pathogenic Process	Change Process
Psychodynamic	Internal conflict	Symptoms are a compromise between an unacceptable impulse and the defence against its expression	Interpretation and insight
	Ego deficit	Developmental deficits arise as a function of failure of the environment to meet child's emotional needs	Corrective emotional experience
Humanistic	Low self-esteem	Psychopathology arises as a function of feelings of inadequacy, low self-worth, lack of self-acceptance.	Validation and emotional support
	Emotional interference	Psychopathology arises as a function of feelings that are not expressed or not accepted	Encouragement of emotional expression
Behavioural	Maladaptive conditioning	Problem behaviour occurs when a maladaptive link is made between a stimulus and a response	Classical conditioning to trigger more adaptive responses
	Inappropriate contingencies	Problem behaviour learned through reinforcement, punishment and/or modelling	Operant conditioning to change contingencies in the environment
Cognitive	Cognitive skill deficit	Psychopathology arises when child lacks necessary cognitive skills to cope with life problems	Skill development
	Cognitive distortion	Psychopathology arises due to distorted, maladaptive or irrational interpretations	Schema transformation
Systemic	Enmeshment-disengagement	Overly rigid or diffuse boundaries prevent family members from achieving closeness to or individuation from one another	Restructuring to strengthen or loosen boundaries
	Triangulation	Triangles and cross-generational coalitions have formed that place children in developmentally inappropriate roles	Detriangulating child, strengthening marital coalition

Source: Adapted from Shirk and Russell, 1996, with additions.

formulation that the child's aggression is being positively reinforced by poor parenting practices suggests that intervention should take a behavioural bent. In contrast, the formulation that the child's behaviour is an attempt to distract the parents from their marital difficulties suggests a systemic orientation.

To illustrate their approach to treatment formulation, the authors offer the case of 'Jack'. Jack was a 10-year-old boy brought to the clinician by his single mother, who was concerned about his short temper and inability to tolerate frustration. Struggles at home revolved around Jack's refusal to complete his chores, and teachers complained that despite Jack's good intelligence he seldom completed school assignments. Increasingly, Jack was coming home with bruises and scrapes that testified to his aggressive behaviour with peers. Jack showed all the signs of oppositional defiant disorder and was in danger of sliding down the slope towards more serious conduct problems.

An empirically based approach to treatment planning suggested that Jack was a prime candidate for interpersonal problem-solving skills training (see Chapter 10), one of the most effective techniques for curbing child misbehaviour. However, a trial of this kind of therapy made little headway. Jack quickly grasped the necessary concepts and demonstrated the ability to execute the requisite social problem-solving skills, but there was no apparent change in his behaviour outside of the therapy room.

Going back to the drawing board, the therapist took into consideration Jack's developmental history, which suggested an alternative formulation regarding the pathogenic processes that led to his behaviour problems. During his first two years, Jack's mother was the target of physical abuse by his father and was consequently an anxious, depressed and preoccupied parent. Jack's early life, therefore, was marked by turmoil, unpredictability and violence. Thus, he developed a set of negative expectations of others, viewing them as unreliable, self-centred and uncaring. Sensitized to this issue, the therapist began to notice other evidence of Jack's

cognitive distortions: his problems at school were due to his teachers' 'unfairness', his mother's motivation to help Jack was to 'look good to her boyfriends', the therapist met with the boy only because 'he was paid to'. A new formulation was developed that centred on the negative schemata that interfered with Jack's ability to utilize adaptive social skills. Accordingly, the target of the treatment plan shifted to the need to change his maladaptive cognitions.

Shirk and colleagues' perspective is a promising one. In the short term, they provide a useful guide to case formulation and treatment planning in child psychotherapy. For the future, their work promises to revitalize research on psychotherapy with children by contributing to the development of clear and testable hypotheses regarding the link between pathological processes and the interventions used to address them. Next, we take a closer look at how each of these formulations is put into action.

The Psychoanalytic Approach
Classical Psychoanalysis
The Conceptual Model

Psychoanalytic theory presents us with an inherently developmental model, with the *psychosexual stages* defining the pivotal conflicts to be mastered on the way to maturity. (Our presentation is based on the writings of Anna Freud, 1964.) Consequently, the focus of therapy is on the particular psychosexual stage or stages presumed to be responsible for the psychopathology (see Chapter 1).

Classical psychoanalysis grows directly out of the psychoanalytic theory of neurosis. According to this theory, psychopathology originates in the psychosexual stages, in which the child who is unable to master psychosexual anxieties defends himself or herself against them. The essence of psychoanalysis consists of reversing the *defensive process*, re-confronting the individual with the original trauma so that it can be mastered belatedly. Successful psychoanalysis is epitomized by Freud's aphorism, '*Where id was, there shall ego be*'. The once overwhelming hates, jealousies and fears of the oedipal period, for example, can now be revived

A play therapy session.
© Stockbyte/Getty

and viewed from a more mature perspective. The ensuing insight into the root of the problem exercises it. The result is a *'widening of consciousness'* in two senses: the individual can face previously unacceptable aspects of his or her personality, and the energy used for defensive manoeuvres can now be employed in growth-promoting activities.

The Therapeutic Process

A general feature of psychoanalysis is the maximizing of free expression during the psychoanalytic hour. With adult patients, this is accomplished through verbal **free association,** which involves speaking freely about whatever comes to mind. However, classical psychoanalysis with children requires major changes in procedures and techniques. In particular, because children cannot verbally free-associate, *play* is substituted.

The use of play presents special challenges to the therapist. Through verbal associations, adults provide the key to the idiosyncratic meaning of events or dreams; since children provide no such key, the analyst is left with the task of decoding the meaning of their fantasies. In order to ensure that the play is rich in the kind of material that will be useful to the analyst, the child is introduced to play material that is *projective*, such as a doll family, crayons or clay. Such play materials tap into fanta-

sies rather than skills. The analyst watches for signs that a theme is of special importance – signs such as repetition, excessive affect, regression in the form of more infantile play or speech, loss of control such as scattering the toys around or a 'they lived happily ever after' dismissal of a conflict situation.

As with adult psychoanalysis, a major goal of child psychoanalysis is the undoing of the *defence mechanisms* that inhibit self-awareness and emotional growth. One technique for overcoming defences is to analyse the **transference**. This term refers to the patient's displacing, or transferring, to the therapist his or her feelings towards the parents. The analyst calls attention to transferences so that by exploring them patients can begin to gain access to the distressing relationships that played a decisive role in their neurosis. However, children's transferences, unlike those of adults, do not involve feelings towards shadowy parental figures dating back to the distant past. Instead, the child's current relationships with parents may be acted out with the analyst in a direct and immediate way.

A second technique for dealing with defences is by analysing the *resistance*. Since defences protect the patient from anxiety, he or she will find numerous ways to retain them. The analyst gently and persistently makes **interpretations** that call attention to such manoeuvres and help the patient to focus on the threatening material that prompted them. Often this is done through the metaphor of the child's play rather than by confronting the child directly with his or her own feelings (e.g., 'I bet that family was really scared when the hurricane started coming toward their house.' 'Being locked in a closet for two years after misbehaving does seem a long time.' 'The girl doll got angry at her mommy and then suddenly ran away. I wonder if it is scary for her to feel angry'). As therapy progresses, the analyst can build bridges from the safe disguise of make-believe to the child's own feelings; for example, 'That hurricane sounds like what you told me about your mom and dad fighting'. Through such interpretations the child is led back to the original traumatic situation and is helped to recognize, re-evaluate and master it.

Correctly timed, interpretations produce *insights*; prematurely timed, they are rejected and fuel the patient's resistance. A therapeutic cure does not come in one blinding flash of insight, however. Instead, the same material has to be approached again and again from many different directions and through many different experiences in order for the insight to be firmly established – a process called *working through*. Again, however, children differ from adults in terms of their tolerance for this process. Children often lack the capacity for self-observation or self-monitoring that enables adults to participate in an intense emotional experience while at the same time observing themselves reacting. Finally, during times of developmental stress such as adolescence, children are reluctant to add to their emotional burdens by confronting their anxieties. Thus, psychoanalysis with children is a challenging enterprise.

Ego Psychology

The next stage in the development of psychoanalytic theory is *ego psychology*, associated with the work of Erik Erikson (1950). Erikson's perspective emphasizes the ego and healthy, reality-oriented aspects of development, as opposed to Freud's emphasis on the primitive drives of sex and aggression. We offer only a brief presentation of ego psychology here.

The Conceptual Model

Erikson's theory of development is familiar to us (see Chapter 1). He delineates stages of *ego development* from infancy to late adulthood, as well as the issues or crises that must be resolved at each step in order for development to proceed. (See Table 3.6.) Psychopathology results when the tasks of a given stage are not mastered and the individual cannot progress to the next stage in development, or when the individual resolves the conflict in a negative way. For example, as in the case of Jack presented earlier, a boy who experiences unreliable care in the early years may develop a sense of basic mistrust that colours his future relationships.

Erikson's model epitomizes the *stage-salient* approach recommended by developmental

psychopathology. One of the implications of this approach is that children's behaviour problems are not thought of in terms of diagnoses as much as in terms of the stage-salient issues that underlie them. Therefore, whether a school-age child is diagnosed with depression or conduct disorder, Erikson would hypothesize that underlying the behavioural problem is a struggle over feelings of inferiority and lack of industry, while an adolescent with the same diagnosis might be hypothesized to be struggling with identity confusion.

The Therapeutic Process

Consistent with his emphasis on ego functioning and adaptive strivings, Erikson sees the key to change in child therapy as the opportunity to gain *mastery* over conflicts, and the medium for this mastery is play. Play gives the child the opportunity to act out disturbing events and feelings in a safe environment with objects that are under the child's control. As Erikson (1950) states, play allows the child 'to deal with experience by creating model situations and to master reality by experiment and planning. ... To 'play it out' is the most natural self-healing measure childhood affords' (p. 222).

The therapist's role is that of a facilitator of healthy ego functioning. Sometimes this role is played by being unobtrusive and *emotionally available*, allowing the child's natural self-healing processes to unfold. The therapist's acceptance and understanding give the child the opportunity to play out secret fears or hates in order to gain internal peace. Ultimately, however, like the classical psychoanalyst, the ego psychologist strives to facilitate children's awareness of their repressed feelings through the means of *interpretation*.

Erikson made many significant contributions to the psychodynamic understanding of children through his observations of play behaviour (Erikson, 1964). For example, one of his insights had to do with the significance of *play disruptions*, those moments when children abruptly change the themes of their play or cease playing altogether (Erikson, 1964). A therapist who attends carefully to the process of the session, noting what leads up to and follows after a play disruption, gains insight into the sources of conflict in the child's internal world.

Object Relations Theory

In its third wave, psychoanalytic theory supplemented its traditional concern with the intrapsychic variables (id, ego and superego) with an emphasis on interpersonal relations. This is the realm of the British school of *object relations theory*, which we encountered in Chapter 1, and which informs the therapy process in ways we will describe briefly here.

The Conceptual Model

As we learned in Chapter 1, the object relations model posits that psychopathology results from arrests in the separation-individuation process due to negative experiences with caregivers (Mahler et al., 1975). In more severe forms of psychopathology, inadequate parenting may interfere with the development of an autonomous *self*. The child without a secure and stable sense of his or her own individual selfhood is unable to move beyond the need to use primitive defence mechanisms such as *splitting*. Further along in the separation-individuation process, after children have learned to discriminate the boundary between self and other, threats to healthy development hinge on the valence, or emotional colouring, of *internal representations* of self and other. Affectionless, abusive or inconsistent parenting may deprive the child of appropriate self-esteem as well as the capacity for interpersonal trust. The result is an internal model of others as unreliable and unloving and of the self as unlovable. The therapist's task, therefore, is to assess the point in development at which the child is arrested and to supply a *corrective emotional experience* that will help development return again to its normal course.

The Therapeutic Process

As with classical psychoanalysis, the therapist understands the children's internal world through *transference*. Children's feelings and expectations about relationships come to life in the therapy session as they are re-enacted with the therapist. However, just as the role of relationships is crucial in the etiology of psychopathology, the *therapeutic relationship* is critical to the effectiveness of object relations therapy. In contrast to the Freudian model, the psychoanalyst is more than a detached observer and interpreter. The therapist's real, human presence is an important part of object relations therapy's curative power: 'Psychoanalytic interpretation is not therapeutic *per se*, but only as it expresses a personal relationship of genuine understanding' (Guntrip, 1986, p. 448).

An object relations therapist who epitomizes this approach is the British psychoanalyst D.W. Winnicott (1975). Although much of Winnicott's work was with children, a revealing portrait of his therapeutic style was presented by one of his adult analysands, Harry Guntrip (1986), who contrasted Winnicott's warm and personable manner with the 'blank screen' presentation of his previous, more classically styled psychoanalyst. However, unlike adult object relations treatment, which relies on the verbalization of unconscious content, the child analyst's access to the child's unconscious is through the medium of play (Benedict, 2006).

For example, one of Winnicott's techniques to engage children in the therapy relationship is the 'squiggle game', in which child and therapist take turns drawing a random squiggle and then asking the other to make something out of it. The squiggles and their transformations introduce playfulness into the interaction and supply the therapist with projective material regarding children's concerns. As part of the ongoing therapy process, the squiggle game allows the therapist to work with unconscious material at a non-verbal level, more appropriate for children than the cognitively and linguistically demanding 'talking cure' of classical psychoanalysis.

Again in contrast to classical psychoanalysis, the therapist's own emotional reactions are not considered to be sources of interference in the therapeutic process but rather to be meaningful sources of data. Here the concept of *projective identification* (Chapter 15) comes into play. (See Ogden, 1979;

Silverman and Lieberman, 1999.) Children may evoke in the therapist feelings that they themselves are unable to tolerate as a way of attempting to master them. Therefore, an object relations therapist who finds herself feeling stressed and confused during a session with an anxious child, or who feels hurt and angered by the jibes and insults of a conduct-disordered child, might wonder, 'What do these feelings tell me about this child's internal world?' As therapy progresses, the therapist's ability to tolerate the child's negative emotions helps the child to overcome the need to use the defence mechanism of splitting in order to keep those feelings from consciousness.

Object Relations in the Family Context

Selma Fraiberg (1980) is another psychoanalyst who exemplifies the object relations approach. She takes to heart the idea that relationships are causal in the development of psychopathology and that they provide the key to ameliorating it. Accordingly, Fraiberg recommends treating relationships rather than individuals. Derived from Fraiberg's approach, *Child–Parent Psychotherapy* (Lieberman and Van Horn, 2008) strives to prevent psychopathology in young children through healing the breach in the parent–child attachment and banishing from the nursery the 'ghosts' of the mother's troubled childhood. Through remembering and resolving their childhood traumas, adults can avoid re-enacting them with their own children. 'In each case, when our therapy has brought the parent to remember and re-experience his childhood anxiety and suffering, the ghosts depart, and the afflicted parents become the protectors of their children against the repetition of their own conflicted past' (Fraiberg, 1980, p. 196). (See Box 17.1.)

Erickson and colleagues (Erickson and Kurz-Riemer, 2002) have continued this line of work by providing home-based interventions for at-risk mothers and young children. The *STEEP* (Steps Towards Effective, Enjoyable Parenting) programme is designed to offset the risk of an insecure attachment. The target population is mothers pregnant with their first child who are at risk for parenting problems due to poverty, youth, lack of education, social isolation and stressful life circumstances. Individual sessions are offered with the goal of helping the mother achieve insight into how her own early experiences of being inadequately cared for triggered her current feelings of sadness, loss and anger, and then to help her deal with these feelings. The therapist also serves an educative function by providing information about child care and helping the mother with issues regarding personal growth, education, work and general life management. There are also group sessions, which allow the mothers to confront their defence mechanisms, air problems and gain confidence from mutual support.

Psychodynamic Developmental Therapy

One of the most recent developments in psychoanalytic psychotherapy is Fonagy and colleagues' (Allen et al., 2008; Fonagy and Target, 2009) *psychodynamic developmental therapy for children (PDTC)*. Their work is conducted at the Anna Freud Centre in London, UK, which, as the name implies, is inspired by Anna Freud's thinking. Fonagy and colleagues were particularly interested in developing a treatment model that would lend itself to the demands of empirical investigation. Their programme of research represents a step forward in terms of its clarification of the underlying theory, its operationalization of slippery psychoanalytic concepts, and its explicit links between theory and intervention techniques.

The Conceptual Model

Influenced by the work of John Bowlby, Fonagy and colleagues consider disturbed *self-development* to lie at the heart of childhood psychopathology. Failures in the early attachment relationship with the parent deprive the child of the kind of social experiences that lead to a positive, undistorted view of self and relationships.

Further, Fonagy and colleagues utilize concepts from social cognitive theory to describe the ways children's assumptions about themselves and others

Box 17.1 A Psychoanalytic Infant–Parent Psychotherapy Session

Annie, age 16, came to the attention of the Infant Mental Health Programme when she refused to care for her baby Greg. She avoided physical contact with him and often forgot to buy milk, instead feeding him Kool-Aid and Tang. Annie herself was the product of an abusive upbringing, and while she could remember the facts of what had occurred to her, she blocked off all awareness of the emotions she suffered – just as she seemed unable to empathize with her baby's distress. The team speculated that Annie's abusive parenting arose from a defence mechanism – identification with the aggressor – that allowed her to keep from awareness her childhood feelings of anxiety and terror. Her therapist, Mrs. Shapiro, visited her at home.

Greg, 17 months old, was in his high-chair eating his breakfast. Mother kept up a stream of admonitions while he ate: 'Don't do that. Don't drop the food off.' Then suddenly, responding to some trivial mishap in the high-chair, Annie screamed, 'Stop it!' Both Greg and Mrs Shapiro jumped. Annie said to the therapist, 'I scared you, didn't I?' Mrs Shapiro, recovering from shock, decided this was the moment she was waiting for. She said, 'Sometimes, Annie, the words and sounds that come out of your mouth don't even sound like you. I wonder who they do sound like?' Annie said immediately, 'I know. They sound just like my mother. My mother used to scare me.' 'How did you feel?' Annie said, 'How would you feel if you were in with a bull in a china shop? … Besides, I don't want to talk about that. I've suffered enough. That's behind me.'

But Mrs Shapiro persisted, gently, and made the crucial interpretation. She said, 'I could imagine that as a little girl you might be so scared that, in order to make yourself less scared, you might start talking and sounding like your mother.' Annie said again, 'I don't want to talk about it right now.' But she was deeply affected by Mrs Shapiro's words.

The rest of the hour took a curious turn. Annie began to collapse before Mrs Shapiro's eyes. Instead of a tough, defiant, aggressive young woman, she became a helpless, anxious little girl. Since she could find no words to speak of the profound anxiety which had emerged in her, she began to speak of everything she could find in her contemporary life that made her feel afraid, helpless, alone.

In this way, and for many hours to come, Mrs Shapiro led Annie back into the experiences of helplessness and terror in her childhood and moved back and forth, from the present to the past, identifying for Annie the ways in which she brought her own experiences to her mothering of Greg, how identification with the feared people of her childhood was 'remembered' when she became the frightening mother to Greg. It was a moment for therapeutic rejoicing when Annie was able to say, 'I don't want my child to be afraid of me.'

Source: Fraiberg, 1980.

---

are internally represented. For example, they use the term *mentalization* to refer to the child's capacity to understand mental states in the self and others, akin to the concept of *theory of mind* which we encountered in relation to autism (see Chapter 5). This capacity is deficient in children whose parents lack empathy and emotional responsiveness. Other important mental functions that are disrupted in psychopathology include the ability to *tolerate emotions* and *control impulses* rather than being overwhelmed by them, a *reality organization* that allows the child to explore the world and take action in it, and *stable representations* of the self and others.

The Therapeutic Process

The focus of PDTC is to remove the obstacles that prevent children from progressing on a healthy developmental course. This is accomplished by providing children with *corrective experiences* that help them to develop more complete and accurate representations of self and others. The therapist strives to increase children's capacity to reflect on mental states in self and others, to bring their feelings and actions under conscious control, and to develop a 'meta-cognitive mode' — that is, to be able to think about their own thought processes. We now turn to describing how these aims are accomplished.

In order to *enhance reflective processes*, the therapist helps children to observe their own emotions, to understand and label them, and to recognize the relationship between their behaviour and their feelings. Next, in order to *strengthen impulse control* the therapist may employ a variety of techniques. One such technique involves the use of metaphor. For example, one child acted out the part of the 'most powerful train engine in the world', going so far as to threaten to jump out the window in order to prove his indestructibility. The therapist suggested that really powerful trains have good brakes and interested the child in the challenge of finding his.

Next, the psychoanalytic relationship gives the PDTC therapist the opportunity to help the child develop *awareness of others*, such as an understanding of the motivations underlying people's actions. Children who have experienced disturbed attachment relationships may find the mental states of adults to be confusing or frightening. The supportive and accepting environment of the therapy relationship provides children with a safe place to explore their ideas about interpersonal relationships and correct their faulty internal models. Lastly, PDTC aims to help children develop the *capacity to play*. The capacity to play is central to the acquisition of meta-cognitive capacities because it requires the child to hold in mind two different realities: the pretend and the actual. The therapist facilitates playfulness by exaggerating actions in order to indicate that they are 'just pretend', and by encouraging the use of play materials (e.g., wooden blocks) that do not make reference to real-world concerns.

Empirical Support

Psychoanalytically oriented psychotherapies do not lend themselves readily to empirical research. Neither the technique nor the outcome it strives to achieve is easily standardized. For example, the mechanism of change is the creation of an intense relationship between patient and therapist; interpretations must be timed just so, so that the patient is ready to receive them. The subtleties of these techniques are not easily put into a treatment manual for therapists to follow in a uniform way. Further, the outcome of a successful psychoanalysis is a change in such hypothetical constructs as defence mechanisms, ego strengths and internal representations that are difficult to observe or quantify. Thus, it comes as no surprise that efforts to empirically test the effectiveness of psychoanalysis with children are few and far between. By the same token, the difficulties inherent in research on psychoanalysis with children make the efforts that have been made all the more noteworthy.

Psychodynamic Developmental Therapy is the only psychoanalytically oriented individual child treatment to be subjected to rigorous and programmatic research. To date, Fonagy and Target (2009) have documented the success of their approach with a wide range of disorders, including depression, anxiety, phobias, posttraumatic stress disorder, oppositional-defiant disorder, conduct disorder and ADHD. Results indicate that children and adolescents with *internalizing disorders* tend to respond to psychodynamic developmental therapy better than those with externalizing disorders. For example, Target and Fonagy (1997) found that over 85 per cent of children treated for anxiety and depression were no longer diagnosable at outcome, whereas this was the case for only 69 per cent of children with conduct disorder and 30 per cent of those with obsessive-compulsive disorder. *Younger* children (less than 12 years old) benefited the most, particularly when therapy was *intensive* (four to five times per week). Similar findings emerged in a German project examining a short-term integrative model of psychodynamic treatment for children called the Heidelberg Study (Kronmüller et al., 2010).

Some empirical support also is emerging for psychoanalytically oriented parent–child treatments such as child–parent psychotherapy. Following a year of treatment, children exhibit reduced behaviour problems and mothers are less avoidant of material related to their traumatic experiences (Lieberman et al., 2006). Next, research on the *STEEP* programme (Egeland and Erickson, 2003) for preventing attachment disorders suggests, as the object relations model would predict, that enhancing new mothers' capacity to provide a secure attachment relationship enhances children's developmental outcomes. A follow-up evaluation conducted a year after the intervention ended, when the children were 2 years old, showed that the treated mothers provided a more appropriately stimulating and organized home environment for their children than did mothers in the control group. In addition, mothers had fewer symptoms of depression and anxiety and better life management skills. Attachment security was not increased in the first year, but a trend in that direction was detected in the second year. Finally, the Dutch researchers Bakermans-Kranenburg and colleagues (2005) conducted a *meta-analysis* of a number of attachment-based interventions for mothers and young children with disorganized attachment styles. Results indicated that the treatments were effective, especially when the focus of treatment was on enhancing the mother's sensitivity to her infant.

The Humanistic Approach

The **humanistic therapy** approach, also called client centred or non-directive, differs radically from the psychoanalytic and behaviour therapies. The humanistic therapist never interprets as does the analyst nor tells clients how to solve their problems as does the behaviour therapist. Instead, the therapist strives to create a non-judgemental and nurturing atmosphere in which the client can grow. While on the face of it the humanistic approach seems simple, in reality, the therapy is based on an explicit developmental model of psychopathology and is one of the most demanding for its practitioners.

The Conceptual Model

Our discussion is based on the ideas of Carl Rogers (1959), founder of humanistic therapy. Rogers stresses the primacy of the individual's *self*, the concept of who one is and of one's relations with others. As awareness of the self emerges in the tod-

dler period, the individual develops the universal need for warmth, respect, sympathy and acceptance. It is essential that the people the child loves and values foster the child's need to experience and decide things for himself or herself. This can be done only if the child receives **unconditional positive regard**. Here no aspect of the child is perceived as more or less worthy of positive regard. Children are intrinsically valued, and their experiences are not viewed judgementally as being 'good' or 'bad' by adult standards.

Normal development goes awry because of what Rogers calls **conditions of worth**. Instead of unconditional positive regard, significant adults, particularly parents, say, in essence, 'I will love you on the condition that you behave as I want you to'. Because of the strong need for positive regard, children eventually make parental values into self-values. At this point children are no longer in touch with their true selves, no longer open to experience and capable of deciding for themselves whether an experience is growth promoting. By incorporating alien values they become alienated from themselves. Because of alienation, children begin to distort experiences in order to fit the imposed model of a 'good boy' or a 'good girl': perhaps the aesthetic boy believes he has to be a competitive go-getter because this is his father's ideal, or the bright girl is hounded by feelings of inadequacy because her mother disparages intellectual achievement.

The Therapeutic Process

In light of what we have explored in our discussions, we can understand how the humanistic therapist, by offering the child unconditional positive regard, can help undo the damage of conditional love. The focus is continually on feelings because these hold the key to maturity. In addition, the process of therapy is client centred, allowing the child to take the lead in choosing the themes to be explored.

Virginia Axline (1969) is the figure most closely associated with the application of Rogers' principles to child therapy. The major change in the client-centred procedure is the introduction of *play material* for children below the pre-adolescent age range. The material is simple and conducive to self-expression – dolls, animals, clay, sand and building materials. Construction toys and games of skill are avoided as being too structured to produce varied and individualized behaviour. While the formal arrangement resembles that of psychoanalysis, the purpose is quite different. Rather than using play as the basis for interpretation, therapists limit their activity to reflecting the themes and affects the child introduces. (See Box 17.2 for an example of Axline's technique.)

The technique of *reflection* of the child's feelings is at the heart of the humanistic approach. While easily parodied in the form of mindlessly parroting back what another person says, reflection is a powerful technique, especially for working with children. Children often have the experience of talking with adults who are busy or distracted or who listen with only half an ear. The therapists' reflection of the child's own thoughts and feelings communicates that the therapist is actively listening and taking the child's concerns seriously. What is more, in the permissive atmosphere of the therapeutic session, the child begins to explore feelings that formerly had to be banished from conscious awareness. In fact, some of these feelings may never have been clearly recognized for what they were. Thus, reflection also serves a defining function rather than being a mere echo of what the child already knows.

The therapist's non-judgemental reflection also communicates *acceptance* of formerly banished feelings, which encourages the child's self-acceptance. As feelings are explicitly defined and accepted, they become congruent. For example, as the shy boy realizes his resentment for being pushed into the alien role of a go-getter, and as the studious girl can face her fear of being rejected by a non-intellectual

---

Box 17.2 A Humanistic Play Therapy Session

Joanne, age 6, comes into the playroom. She sits quietly at the table and uses clay to make the same thing she does every session: a figure of a man carrying a cane [Joanne's mother's new boyfriend also carries a cane]. Each time, after she is finished, awful things happen to him.

Therapist:	Here comes that man again.
Joanne:	Yes. (*her voice is tense, determined*)
Therapist:	The man with the cane.
Joanne:	Yes. (*she begins to punch him full of holes*)
Therapist:	You're putting holes in the clay man.
Joanne:	Stab! Stab! Stab!
Therapist:	You're stabbing him.
Joanne:	(*in a small voice*): Ouch, you hurt me. (*voice changes*) I don't care. I want to hurt you.
Therapist:	The clay man is crying because he is hurt.
Joanne:	(*interrupting*) I *want* to hurt him.
Therapist:	You want to hurt him.
Joanne:	I don't like him.

Therapist:	You don't *like* him.
Joanne:	I don't like him. I hate him. Look this hole went clear through him. It went in his front and out his back.
Therapist:	He gets holes punched clear through him. You'll fix him.
Joanne:	Yes. I'll tear his head off.
Therapist:	You'll even tear his head off.
Joanne:	I know, I know. I'll put him clear down in the bottom of the jar and then I'll put the clay in on top of him and he'll smother.
Therapist:	(*following child's actions*) You tore him into little pieces and buried him in the bottom of the jar.

Joanne nods and smiles at the therapist. Then she goes over to the baby doll, pretends to feed it, holds it tenderly in her arms, puts it to bed, and plays house very quietly.

Source: Axline, 1969.

mother, such feelings become part of the self. The once-divided self is whole again.

The therapist has complete confidence in the client's ability to solve his or her own problems with the minimum of direction – hence, the humanistic child therapist is *non-directive*. After discussing the ground rules for the therapeutic hour and describing the procedure in general terms, humanistic therapists leave the direction of the sessions up to the child. As we have seen, therapists do not interpret the meaning of the child's behaviour, nor do they introduce any material from the child's past, from the reality of the child's present situation or from previous sessions. If, for example, they learn that the child has started setting fires, they wait until the child is ready to make such behaviour part of the therapeutic session. Thus, responsibility is always on the child's shoulders. What therapists communicate implicitly is a faith in the child's ability to decide what is best for his or her own growth.

Understandably, it is demanding to be a non-directive therapist. First it means relinquishing the role of the authoritative adult who 'knows better'. Moreover, the therapist's acceptance of and respect for the child must be *genuine*. However, when children are given freedom to do what they like, many of them begin to gravitate towards destructive acting out. Not only that, but they also have a genius for finding ways of teasing, testing and provoking adults. For the therapist to maintain an attitude of acceptance and understanding rather than self-defence and retaliation requires a forbearing disposition and self-discipline.

Play Therapy

Landreth (2002) has further elaborated the client-centred approach with children in his approach to play therapy. Play has an important role in child development, providing a bridge between concrete experience and abstract thought (Piaget, 1962), allowing children a secure, self-directed means for organizing their experiences, and providing a natural means by which children express and learn about their inner worlds. For example, Landreth illustrates, following the terrorist attacks in New York City on 11 September 2001, how adults told and retold their experiences, sharing verbally their shock and anxiety. Children, however, rarely talked about their experience, but rather acted out their feelings through their play. Towers were built only to be felled by crashing airplanes, buildings burned, people were hurt and sirens wailed as the ambulances and fire trucks came to rescue them. Landreth describes a 3-year-old patient who repeatedly crashed a helicopter into a wall and said vehemently, 'I hate you, helicopter!'

In order to help children to communicate about their inner experiences, the client-centred therapist engages the child in a process of sharing that child's world. The therapist is non-directive, allowing the child to fully express and explore feelings, thoughts, behaviours and experiences through the symbolic medium of play, with the expectation that 'playing it out' in itself is a self-healing process. 'Child-centred play therapy is both a basic philosophy of the innate human capacity of children to strive toward growth and maturity and an attitude of deep and abiding belief in children's ability to be constructively self-directing' (Landreth, 2002, p. 65).

Consistent with Rogers, Landreth describes three essential conditions for therapeutic growth. The first is that the therapist is *real*; 'Genuineness is a basic and fundamental attitude that is for the therapist a way of being rather than a way of doing' (2002, p. 70). Second, the therapist must offer to the child *warm caring and acceptance*, by which the therapist communicates unconditional regard and respect for the child's worth. Third, the therapist must provide *sensitive understanding* of the child's internal world and subjective frame of reference. As the children experience this therapeutic relationship, they gradually come to feel free to be themselves and to value who they are.

One feature that sets this approach to child therapy apart from others, particularly the cognitive and behavioural approaches that we will discuss, is that the focus of attention is on the *child* rather than the 'problem'. There is no concern with diagnosis because the therapist does not vary the approach depending on the definition of the presenting problem. Instead, the conditions are set for the child to generate within himself or herself the processes that lead to growth and change. As self-healing takes effect, the behaviours or symptoms that brought the child to treatment should naturally drop away.

Empirical Support

Although Carl Rogers had an interest in assessing the effectiveness of his therapeutic approach, little programmatic research has been carried out on humanistic therapy with children. However, psychotherapy process research is consistent in showing that therapist-offered conditions, such as warmth, empathy and acceptance, are related to positive outcomes with children (Shirk and Burwell, 2010).

More systematic evidence is available regarding the efficacy of play therapy generally, although we need to keep in mind that the term 'play therapy' covers a wide variety of approaches, some of which incorporate theoretical perspectives quite disparate from humanism – for example, there are cognitive behavioural play therapies (Knell, 2000), object relations play therapies (Benedict, 2006) and integrative play therapies (Gil, 2006), to name a few, as well as diverse play therapies developed to address specific childhood problems (see Ray, 2006; Reddy et al., 2005). In a meta-analysis of the overall effectiveness of play therapies, Bratton and colleagues (2005) uncovered 93 controlled outcome studies and found an overall effect size of .80, on a par with the effectiveness demonstrated by other forms of child therapy. Moreover, the authors found that effects were more positive for humanistic-nondirective than for non-humanistic-directive treatments, and that including parents in sessions produced the greatest benefits.

Behaviour Therapies

The Conceptual Model

Behaviour therapies are characterized by attention to specific, *currently observable behaviours* of the client, by a concern with *objective measures* of the outcomes of their interventions, and by a reliance on the research laboratory to provide *general principles of behaviour change* that can be used as the basis of therapeutic intervention and as a place to put clinical findings to rigorous experimental tests (Scott and Yule, 2009). Rather than comprising a specific set of techniques, behaviour therapies are 'an *approach* to abnormal behaviour ... characterized by [an] empirical methodology' (Ross and Nelson, 1979, p. 303).

To elaborate: the goal of behaviour therapy is change, and therefore the emphasis is on current behaviours since these are most amenable to change. Behaviour therapists would not deny that such behaviours may be rooted in the past, but the past cannot be altered, whereas the present and the future can. Among ongoing behaviours, the therapists deal with three response systems: *overt-motor*, *physiological-emotional* and *cognitive-verbal*. All must be considered in a comprehensive treatment programme, since they are not necessarily correlated; for example, a boy who is constantly fighting in school may tell the therapist that 'everything is OK' and he only fights 'a little every now and then'.

In the constant interplay between the clinic and the laboratory, principles derived from research have been used to generate therapeutic procedures, just as learning theory provides the conceptual underpinnings for behaviour therapy techniques. Perhaps even more significant than the application of laboratory findings is behaviour therapy's incorporation of *experimental procedures* into psychotherapeutic practice. The behaviour therapist reasons very much like his or her experimental counterpart: if behaviour X is due to antecedent Y and consequent Z, then as Y and Z are changed, so should X. The therapeutic intervention, like an experiment, consists of testing out the hypothesis, the crucial measure being a change in the base rate of the target behaviour X in the desired direction.

The simplest design in evaluating therapeutic effectiveness is the *A-B design*, in which the dependent measure is evaluated both before intervention (baseline, or A) and during intervention

(B). If, for example, a therapist hypothesized that temper tantrums in a 3-year-old were being sustained by maternal attention, he might advise the mother to ignore them. If the base rate went down, the therapist would have evidence that the hypothesis was correct. Such a design is adequate for clinical work because it demonstrates whether change occurs. However, for a more stringent test of the hypothesis that change was caused by the intervention rather than by other variables, the reversal, the *A-B-A-B design*, is used, in which the therapeutic procedure is repeatedly applied and withdrawn. If change in the target behaviour occurs only in the presence of the intervention, then a causal relationship can be more readily assumed (see Fig. 17.2).

The Developmental Dimension

We have integrated discussion of developmental issues into our description of other forms of therapy. However, behavioural thinking is by definition *ahistorical* – current contingencies for behaviour are all that matters and the past is irrelevant. Are developmental considerations irrelevant to behav-

iour therapy? While roundly criticizing behaviourists for their insensitivity to developmental issues in their conceptualization and treatment of psychopathology, leading figures in the field have taken on the task of filling the gap. For example, Forehand and Wierson (1993) present an overview of developmental factors to be considered in designing behavioural interventions for children. They review the literature on stage-salient issues and emotional, cognitive, social and moral development, as well as considering changes in the environmental context of development from infancy to adolescence.

From their review, Forehand and Wierson derive three major areas for the behavioural therapist to consider. The first of these is the *cognitive capacity* of the child. For example, younger children require concrete, present-oriented language and cope best with non-verbal modes of interaction, such as drawings and play. With the onset of more sophisticated cognitive abilities, older children may be able to benefit from learning more sophisticated, verbally based control techniques, such as problem-solving skills.

FIGURE 17.2 A Record of Talking-Out Behaviour of an Educable Cognitively Challenged Student.

Baseline1 – before experimental conditions. Contingent Teacher Attention1 – systematic ignoring of talking out and increased teacher attention to appropriate behaviour. Baseline2 – reinstatement of teacher attention to talking-out behaviour.

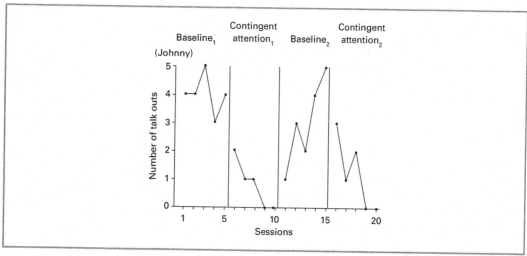

Source: Hall et al., 1971.

The second area concerns the child's *developmental tasks*. For behaviour therapy to be maximally effective, the behaviours targeted for change should be consistent with the developmental tasks the child is currently facing, such as to achieve mastery in middle childhood or to achieve individuation in adolescence. In addition, intervention must target tasks the child has failed to accomplish at previous developmental transitions. This means that the child therapist may need to go beyond the simple presenting problem in order to determine what might have gone awry in earlier developmental periods.

Third is the *developmental context*. Not only do children change over the course of development, but their environments change also, as the social world broadens from the family to include peers, school and the larger society. The individuals in each of these settings provide contingencies for children's behaviour, acting as reinforcers, punishers and models. Individuals outside the family increasingly have the capacity either to contribute to problem behaviour or to help to reduce it. Thus, over the course of development, behaviour therapists need to widen their scope of intervention from the narrow focus on parent–child relationships in order to incorporate peers and teachers into the intervention plan.

The Therapeutic Process

Principles of learning – specifically, classical conditioning, operant learning and imitation – form the bases of behaviour therapy procedures. We examine here exemplars of the application of each principle. (For an account of how behaviour therapies are applied to various childhood psychopathologies, see Akin-Little, 2009.)

Classical Conditioning

Systematic desensitization, as developed by Wolpe (1973), is a procedure for eliminating anxiety-mediated problems. In such problems, initially neutral stimuli come to elicit powerful anxiety responses as a result of classical conditioning. The bond between the conditioned stimulus and the anxiety response can be broken, however, by **reciprocal inhibition,** in which the stronger of two incompatible responses tends to inhibit the weaker. The therapist's task, therefore, becomes one of pairing anxiety-eliciting stimuli with a more powerful, incompatible response. The response Wolpe uses is deep muscle relaxation, since an individual cannot be simultaneously anxious and relaxed.

Two preliminary steps are needed to implement the therapy. First, the child must be instructed in the technique of relaxing various muscle groups throughout the body. The child is also required to make up a graduated sequence of anxiety-eliciting stimuli, going from the least to the most intense. A girl with a school phobia, for example, may feel no anxiety when she awakens and dresses, mild anxiety at breakfast, increasingly strong anxiety while waiting for the bus and approaching school, and the most intense anxiety during the free period before classes start.

In the therapy proper, the children imagine each of the steps, pairing them with the relaxation response. If the anxiety is too strong at any particular step and they cannot relax, they return to the preceding step. Over a series of sessions the children gradually are able to relax in response to even the most intense anxiety-producing stimuli. While Wolpe's rationale has been questioned and the specific variables responsible for improvement have not been satisfactorily isolated, the therapy itself has been successful in treating a host of problems. Systematic desensitization is a mainstay of many empirically supported interventions for child anxiety disorders, including phobias, social and generalized anxiety, OCD, PTSD and separation fears (Kendall et al., 2008; Piacentini et al., 2011).

Operant Conditioning

Behaviour therapists have made extensive use of the operant principle that behaviour is controlled by specific antecedent and consequent stimulus events. **Contingency management**, or the manipulation of rewards and punishments that follow or are contingent upon the response, is particularly potent in decreasing the strength of undesirable behaviours or increasing the strength of adaptive ones. There are two kinds of positive consequences: reward, or **positive reinforcement**, and removal of an aversive stimulus, or **negative reinforcement**. There are also two kinds of negative consequences: *positive punishment*, or the administering of an aversive stimulus, and *negative punishment*, or the removal of a pleasant stimulus.

Examples of the application of operant principles are legion, with some involving a therapist and others involving parents, who not only can be taught how to implement a therapeutic programme with relative ease but who also are in a position to control a wider range of behaviours than can be elicited in a therapeutic setting. For example, the language skills of 2- and 3-year-old children were enhanced when their mothers reinforced naming of objects with praise or bits of food, while the tantrums of a 21-month-old were extinguished when the mother ignored them, thereby withdrawing the attention that had been sustaining them.

Instead of direct reinforcement, a child can be given a *token*, which subsequently can be redeemed for rewards such as prizes or privileges. In one therapeutic programme children were given tokens for co-operative behaviour and doing chores but lost them for undesirable social behaviour. In **time-out**, the child receives as a consequence for negative behaviour the withdrawal of reinforcers. For example, a child who raids the cookie jar before dinner despite having been told a snack was off-limits may be required to sit for five minutes in a chair placed away from such pleasurable distractions such as the television or videogames. Parents are instructed to ignore the child's attempts to interact during the brief time-out but to immediately engage the child and praise good behaviour at the end of the interval. Time-out is a key technique taught in evidence-based parenting programmes such as *Incredible Years* (Webster-Stratton and Reid, 2010) because it is simple, non-abusive and effective.

Observational Learning
Observational learning, or **modelling**, has not been extensively employed as a primary therapeutic technique. However, having fearful children observe fearless children interacting with a phobic stimulus, such as a snake or a dog, has successfully eliminated some phobias (see Chapter 8). The model may be presented either in real life or on film. Modelling is often combined with reinforcement of the desired behaviour; for example, in teaching verbal behaviour to children with autism, the child is immediately rewarded with food upon each successful imitation of the therapist's vocalization. Another good example of this technique is the pain management modelling described in Chapter 13.

Behaviour Therapy in the Family Context
Behaviour therapists have also begun expanding their interventions to include various contexts in their treatment plan, such as the family, the school and peers. It makes little sense to change a deviant behaviour while leaving a child in a disharmonious or dysfunctional setting.

Parent Management Training (PMT), introduced in Chapter 10, is one of the most successful and best-documented programmes based on social learning principles. PMT was developed originally by Patterson (1982), who saw maladaptive parent–child relationships as central to the etiology of conduct disorder. PMT focuses on altering the interactions between parent and child so that prosocial behaviour, rather than coercive behaviour, is reinforced. As the name implies, this is accomplished by training the parents to respond more effectively to the child. The principles of operant conditioning are central to parent training therapies, primarily used for families in which children display conduct problems (Forgatch and Patterson, 2010).

First, parents learn how to think about their child-rearing problems in *behavioural terms*. They are trained to identify, define and observe problem behaviour, as well as its precipitants and consequences. In this way, they are better able to perceive their roles in perpetuating child misbehaviour and to abandon such unhelpful attributions as personalizing the problem ('I'm a lousy parent') or psychopathologizing their children ('He's a bad seed').

Second, parents learn a number of behaviour modification techniques, including the use of *positive reinforcement*. Often, parents who have become caught in repetitive cycles of coercive exchanges neglect the need to provide any sort of positive feedback to their children and seldom spend pleasurable time with them. The fundamental goals of behaviour modification are not only to reduce problem behaviour but to increase prosocial behaviour as well. Therefore, parents learn to use social praise ('Good job!') and tokens that can be exchanged for rewards when children have behaved well. Reinforcement for positive behaviour ('Try to catch the child doing something good') also counteracts the child's experience of the family as a kind of boot camp.

As a parallel to increasing positive reinforcement, parents are also trained to use *mild punishment*. Rather than using such aversive techniques as yelling, hitting or 'nattering' (repetitive nagging complaints without any follow-through) that only exacerbate the problem, parents are encouraged to provide *time out* from reinforcement or *loss of privileges* in response to misbehaviour. Typically, these skills are first applied to relatively simple, easily observed behavioural sequences. As parents become more adept, the focus shifts to more difficult and involved behaviours. As children's behaviour improves, parents learn higher-level skills such as *negotiation* and mutual problem solving with children. In this way, the overall tone of family relationships becomes more positive and collaborative, as well as being more supportive of children's increasing self-control over their own behaviour.

Empirical Support

Behaviour therapists have been the most active in documenting the effectiveness of their approach. Outcome studies report success with a wide variety of child behaviour problems, ranging from phobias to bed-wetting to conduct disorder.

For example, many outcome studies conducted over the past two decades attest to the effectiveness of Parent Management Training (PMT) (Forgatch and Patterson, 2010; Webster-Stratton and Reid, 2004). Marked improvement is shown in the behav-

iour of conduct-disordered children, which is sustained as long as 41.2 years after treatment ends. In addition, the impact of PMT is broad, with many other problem behaviours improving in addition to the specific ones targeted for treatment. Sibling behaviour also improves and ratings of maternal psychopathology, particularly depression, decrease after PMT. Overall, family members report feeling more positive emotions with one another. Thus, PMT seems to alter multiple aspects of dysfunctional family relationships.

Recently, the behavioural focus of treatments such as PMT are increasingly being augmented by interventions that also include cognitive problem-solving skills training for both parents and children (Kazdin, 2010; Sanders and Murphy-Brennan, 2010). It is to those therapies inspired by the cognitive model that we turn next.

Cognitive Therapies
The Conceptual Model

Cognitive therapies can be distinguished from behaviour therapies by their attention to the *mental processes* that mediate between stimulus and response (Lochman and Pardini, 2009). Rather than changing the environmental contingencies that reinforce child behaviour problems, cognitive therapists target the dysfunctional and maladaptive *beliefs* that guide behaviour. The basic goal is to change the way the child thinks. When this has been accomplished, behaviour will also change.

There is not actually a strict dichotomy between behaviour and cognitive therapies. Behaviour therapists employ cognitive elements as a means of achieving behavioural change; in desensitization, for example, children imagine various situations and instruct themselves to relax, both of which are cognitive activities. For their part, cognitive therapies are consistent with their behaviourist roots in that they concern themselves with changing specific observable behaviours, systematically monitor the relation between intervention and behavioural change, and retain allegiance to the scientific method. Many therapists com-bine the techniques under the rubric of 'cognitive-behavioural therapy.'

For the sake of clarity, however, we limit our discussion here to the specifically cognitive dimension of these therapies.

Cognitive therapies have been developed to address a wide variety of childhood psychopathologies, including depression, substance abuse, ADHD, anxiety, sexual abuse, conduct disorder and autism, among others. We select for presentation three treatment programmes – two for internalizing problems (anxiety and OCD), and one for an externalizing problem, conduct disorder. (For presentations of cognitive techniques applied to various disorders in children, see Kendall, 2011b, and Reinecke et al., 2003.)

The Therapeutic Process

Cognitive Therapy for Anxiety Disorders

Kendall and his colleagues (Kendall, 2011a) developed a cognitive intervention programme called Coping Cat for treating anxiety disorders in children. The core principle underlying the model is that *cognitive representations* of the environment determine children's response to it. In the case of anxiety disorders, exaggerated perceptions of *threat* – the fear of devastating loss, harsh criticism or catastrophic harm – dominate the child's reactions to events. The therapist's job is to alter these maladaptive cognitions, as well as the behavioural patterns and emotional responses that accompany them, by designing new *learning experiences* for the child.

The therapists' goals are to teach children to identify anxious feelings and to calm themselves when anxious, to modify their thoughts, to develop a plan for coping with anxiety-arousing situations, and to reward themselves for coping well. Children are taught to accomplish these goals in a series of steps identified with the acronym *FEAR*.

The first step in the FEAR sequence – *Feeling Frightened*? – focuses on helping children to recognize when they are experiencing anxiety. (See Box 17.3 for an example.) Often children do not perceive the connection between physical sensations—trembling, stomach ache, and so forth—and their emotional distress in a given situation. Recognizing that they are anxious cues them to the fact that it is time to put into place their problem-solving skills.

The second stage is *Expecting Bad Things to Happen*? Here the child is helped to identify the negative expectancies that generate the fear. For example, a child might fear riding an elevator because a 'bad man' might get on it or because her parents might disappear while she is gone. However, many young children have difficulty with this step. Their cognitive capacities are limited such that it is difficult for them to observe their own thought processes. The therapist might assist by suggesting possible expectations rather than requiring the child to come up with them (e.g., 'Some kids are afraid that the elevator will get stuck'). The therapist uses cartoons with empty 'thought bubbles' to help the child identify anxious thoughts and their alternatives in various situations (see Fig. 17.3).

The third stage is *Attitudes and Actions That Can Help*. Here the therapist assists the child to come up with more realistic attitudes about the feared event, as well as actions to cope with it. For example, the therapist might ask the child to think about the likelihood of being locked in an elevator or to conduct a poll to find how many times others have ridden in an elevator without incident. Then the child is encouraged to generate possible solutions to the problem. For example, the child might be encouraged to talk about how she could differentiate 'bad men' from harmless ones; alternatively, the child might be taught how to use the emergency phone to bring help. New coping strategies are tried out as 'experiments', a word that has a playful and non-threatening air.

The fourth stage is *Results and Rewards*. Here children evaluate the success of their problem-solving attempts and are encouraged to think of possible rewards for coping with the anxiety-arousing situation, such as having a snack, telling parents about their accomplishment, or praising themselves for doing a 'good job'.

After children have learned the FEAR steps, the next phase of treatment involves *practising* their new skills in imaginary and real-life situations. Exercises are tailored to the specific fears of

Box 17.3 A Cognitive Therapy Session for Childhood Anxiety

Allison, aged 9, was referred to treatment for separation anxiety disorder. During this session Allison and her therapist discuss how she coped with an anxiety-provoking situation one morning when she forgot to bring her homework to school. Annotations identify the FEAR steps.

Therapist:	So tell me, how did you know that you were feeling frightened? (*Feeling Frightened?*)
Allison:	My heart started pounding.
Therapist:	What else?
Allison:	Umm ... Let's see. I started biting my nails.
Therapist:	Uh-huh. That's a sign, isn't it?
Allison:	Yeah.
Therapist:	So then what did you notice? What were you thinking about? (*Expecting Bad Things to Happen?*)
Allison:	I could get in real big trouble here – get punished.
Therapist:	That's what you were thinking about. Well, what bad things were going to happen to you? What were you worried about?
Allison:	I was gonna get yelled at.
Therapist:	You were gonna get yelled at, and if you got yelled at, what?
Allison:	I would probably have to stay in for recess.
Therapist:	OK, what about your teacher? What would your teacher be thinking if you lost your health homework?
Allison:	Boy, is she forgetful. He'd say, 'Why did you take it home in the first place?'
Therapist:	He would think you were forgetful?
Allison:	Yeah, and he yells. You can hear him all the way down the hall. And when he

yells, the kids down the hall can hear him.

Therapist:	You might get yelled at, and other kids would know. What would they think?
Allison:	They'd just think I was weird.
Therapist:	They'd think you were weird. Well, no wonder you were feeling a little scared! Okay, so what did you do about that? How else could you have thought about that? (*Attitudes and Actions That Can Help*)
Allison:	Maybe he won't want to go over them today, because he didn't. I asked him at lunch, and he said he didn't want to go over them until tomorrow.
Therapist:	That was an action you took to help yourself out. Good for you, Allison; you went and asked the question! How could you have changed your scary thoughts around a little bit?
Allison:	I don't know. Maybe he'll just forget about going over them or something, and maybe if he doesn't, he won't yell at me.
Therapist:	Well, I think that you should really be congratulated for that action that you took! That's like the best idea I could have thought of – go check it out, you found out what's going to happen. (*Results and Rewards*)
Allison:	Before you start worrying your head off.
Therapist:	Before you start getting so upset and worried. Yeah, that was excellent!

Source: Levin et al., 1996.

a child and are called *Show That I Can* tasks. For example, the child who is anxious about riding an elevator might be exposed to one in increasingly proximal steps, while a child who believes he alone worries might be assigned to interview classmates and report back regarding what they worry about. *Reinforcements* are provided for children who complete their 'homework' assignments.

The completion of treatment is celebrated with a special session in which child and therapist create a videotaped commercial for the FEAR steps they have learned. Not only does this activity introduce an element of fun and creativity, but it also helps to reinforce the collaborative and positive relationship that is an important component of the therapy.

FIGURE 17.3 Identifying Anxious and Alternative Thoughts.

Self-talk 1: Seeing a big dog in the street

Self-talk 2: Mom is home late

Source: Rapee et al., 2000.

Whereas the focus on the intervention is with children, *parents* play an important role as well. Parents often inadvertently reinforce children's withdrawal from anxiety-arousing situations by giving in to their fears. The therapist works with parents to help them support their child's independence from them and to increase their capacity to tolerate the child's short-term discomfort with facing the feared situation. The therapist is also sensitive to the ways in which the parents' own concerns – such as their own anxieties or marital difficulties – might

contribute to the child's problems. Consequently, Kendall has expanded the scope of his approach in the form of cognitive behavioural family therapy (Howard et al., 2000), which controlled studies suggest has good effects (Kendall et al., 2008.)

Empirical Support

Good effects emerge in studies of the Coping Cat model. For example, Kendall and colleagues (2004) randomly assigned 94 anxiety-disordered children to cognitive treatment or a wait-list control group. Those children who underwent treatment showed significant decreases in anxiety on self-report measures, as well as on measures obtained from parents, teachers and observers. Two-thirds of the treated children were no longer diagnosable after treatment, and treatment gains were maintained at follow-ups conducted one year later, and were maintained an average of 7.4 years after treatment ended. Moreover, seven years later, children who had undergone successful cognitive treatment for their anxiety disorders were at decreased risk for substance abuse in adolescence (Kendall et al., 2004). Moreover, the programme has proven to disseminate well to other cultures, having been translated into six languages and exported to over a dozen countries, including the UK, the Netherlands, Canada (where it is called Coping Bear) and Australia (where it was renamed Coping Koala; Kendall et al., 1998).

Cognitive Therapy for Obsessive Compulsive Disorder

Cognitive techniques also are at the heart of empirically demonstrated treatments for childhood OCD (March and Mulle, 1998; Piacentini et al., 2011). After a careful assessment, treatment begins with *psychoeducation* about OCD, in which the child is helped to understand that the disorder is like a 'hiccup' in the brain – it causes unwanted things to happen, but it is a problem that can be cured. The child also is given the opportunity to make up a silly name for the disorder (e.g., 'Mr Germy'), in order to externalize it and minimize its seeming power. Next, the therapist and child work together to '*map*' *OCD*; that is, to identify the times and places when OCD 'wins', the child 'wins', or the outcome is fairly even. This third spot on the map is called the *transition zone*, and it is here that the therapist and child will concentrate their work, gradually expanding the territory that is the child's rather than the disorder's. Further, situations and stimuli are ranked on a hierarchy of anxiety so that the therapist can be guided where to begin, looking for tasks that are challenging but not too threatening.

The next step in treatment involves *cognitive training*, in which the child is taught how to 'talk back' to OCD by engaging in positive self-talk. (See Box 17.4 for an example.) For example, a boy who fears contamination by germs and is feeling the impulse to engage in ritualistic behaviour might say to himself, 'You're not the boss of me!' Humour also is a helpful strategy. For example, a boy who was obsessed with fears of the devil made up his own rhyme to use in exposure situations: 'What I once feared will become a bore; the devil is just a metaphor' (Franklin et al., 2003, p. 173).

With these coping strategies in hand, the child then begins, slowly and carefully and with the therapist's help, to move up the hierarchy of fears by engaging in exposure and response prevention. In *exposure*, the child is encouraged to remain in contact with the feared stimulus – initially, this might need to involve very distal exposure, such as being willing to hear the word 'snake', or to look at a picture of one. In *response prevention*, the children are helped to use their coping skills to refrain from engaging in the obsessional or compulsive rituals that have bound their anxiety in the past. The goal is for the child to remain in the exposure situation long enough that the anxiety subsides and, a revelation for many children with OCD, the stimulus actually becomes boring. Increasingly, exposures take place *in vivo* and *in situ*, with the therapist's taking the child on 'field trips' in which they encounter the feared stimulus in a real-life setting. The last step of the treatment is *relapse prevention*, in which the child is asked to anticipate challenges that might present themselves in the future and to describe ways in which the child might cope.

Empirical Support

A series of multisite, randomized clinical trials have established the effectiveness of CBT for paediatric OCD (Franklin et al., 2010), although the rates of recovery speak to how difficult and intractable this disorder is to treat. For example, in a study comparing the effectiveness of CBT, the specific serotonin reuptake inhibitor (SSRI) sertraline and a combined treatment, the investigators found that OCD symptoms remitted among 54 per cent of those who received the combined treatment, 39 per cent of those who received CBT alone, 21 per cent of those who receive sertraline alone, and 3 per cent who received a placebo (Pediatric OCD Treatment Study Team, 2004). Given that the most common front-line treatment offered to children with OCD is an SSRI prescription, the research group has launched a new study to investigate whether CBT can help to augment medication management for the substantial proportion of children who continue to suffer symptoms despite medication (Franklin et al., 2010).

Interpersonal Problem-Solving Skills Training (IPS)

One of the elements of Kazdin's (2010) highly successful combined parenting and child-focused model for intervening with conduct problems is Interpersonal Problem-Solving (IPS), which was developed originally by Shure and Spivack (1988). The IPS approach focuses on building competence in five skills found to be deficient in aggressive children. The first of these is to *generate alternative solutions* to a problem. Children are encouraged to brainstorm and explore different ideas without fear of censorship or premature closure. The goals are to assemble a repertoire of solutions that children can draw from and to develop the habit of thinking before acting. One of the hallmarks of IPS training is that the focus is not so much on *what* children think but on *how* they think. Rather than the children's relying on external support for their behaviour, the idea is to bring behaviour under children's control by helping them think through interpersonal problems and arrive at solutions on their own.

Box 17.4 Cognitive Therapy for Obsessive Compulsive Disorder

Kristin is a 6-year-old girl who experiences many intrusive thoughts about harm coming to herself, her family, or the planet. In order to prevent these fears from becoming actualities, she believes that she must compulsively tell her mother and repeatedly seek reassurance. To assist her in developing cognitive coping strategies, such as positive self-talk, the therapist decides to take her through an experiential exercise in the distinction between thoughts and reality.

Therapist: OK, Kristin, remember we said today we'd try to work on the scary pictures that come into your head?

Kristin: How are we going to do that?

Therapist: Well, first I want to show you a trick. Last time you were here you said that 'Tummy Tickle' (OCD) tells you that if you have one of those scary pictures in your head and you didn't tell Mommy that maybe it would happen and it would be your fault?

Kristin: I still think that.

Therapist: Well, let's see if we can mess with it a bit. First, I want you to look at that soda bottle on my desk. See it there?

Kristin: Yeah, I see it.

Therapist: Well, I want you to get a good picture of it in your head, and then close your eyes and imagine it in your head. Can you do that?

Kristin: Yeah.

Therapist: OK, good. Now I want you to move the soda bottle in your head from one side of the desk to the other.

Kristin: Do I have to move the real one too?

Therapist: No, just the one in your head.

Kristin: OK, I did it.

Therapist: Great, now make it grow wings and fly across the room like a butterfly.

Kristin: What colour should the wings be?

Therapist: Any colour you like.

Kristin: OK, it's flying now.

Therapist: Can you make it smile?

Kristin: It doesn't have a face.

Therapist: OK, give it a face and make it smile.

Kristin: It's smiling now.

Therapist: Can you see it really clearly now?

Kristin: Yes, I can see its bright blue wings and its big happy teeth.

Therapist: Great, now open your eyes. Where's the soda bottle now?

Kristin: (Laughs) It's still on your desk, silly!

Therapist: I thought it was flying around the room like a smiling butterfly?

Kristin: No, that's just the one in my head.

Therapist: So even if you see something really clearly in your head, it doesn't mean that it's real, right?

Kristin: Right.

Therapist: Let's go back to it now – close your eyes, and give the soda bottle back its mouth.

Kristin: OK.

Therapist: Can you make it bite my hand?

Kristin: That wouldn't be very nice.

Therapist: Well how about a little bite.

Kristin: OK, I guess so.

Therapist: Did it bite me?

Kristin: Yup, right on the finger.

Therapist: Which finger?

Kristin: The little finger.

Therapist: Why don't you have it bite me on the thumb now, OK?

Kristin: OK.

Therapist: OK, now open your eyes again. Do you see any teeth marks?

Kristin: No.

Therapist: How come?

Kristin: Because it was only pretend.

Therapist: And what does this say about the scary pictures that come into your head, like the one you had today while driving in with your parents?

Kristin: Well, maybe they're pretend too, and I don't have to make them go away any more.

Source: Franklin et al., 2003.

Second, children are trained to *consider the consequences* of social acts. Aggressive children do not generally think beyond the present to consider the possible negative consequences of misbehaviour or, for that matter, the positive consequences of prosocial behaviour. Therefore, children learn to consider the consequences of acts of self and others and to develop a less-impulsive response style. The third goal is to develop *means-ends thinking*, to learn to engage in the step-by-step process needed to carry out a particular solution. This may require considering several possible actions and their consequences along the way. The next stage involves the development of *social-causal thinking*, an understanding of how the people in a problem situation feel and what motivates them to act the way they do. For example, this may involve recognizing the fact that aggressive behaviour may anger other children and cause them to retaliate.

Fourth, children are helped to develop *sensitivity to interpersonal problems*. Children with poor social skills lack the sensitivity to the cues that indicate that there is a relational conflict between themselves and another person, and they often fail to recognize when a problem is an interpersonal one. Finally, at the highest level of IPS skills training, children develop a *dynamic orientation*. This refers to the ability to look beyond the surface of human behaviour and to appreciate that there may be underlying motives that arise from the unique perspective of that person, based on his or her experience in life. For example, a bully may be construed as a bad person who likes to hurt others, as someone who is insecure and trying to prove he is good enough, or as someone who is mistreated at home and is taking his frustrations out on others. The issue is not the validity of the interpretation but rather the ability to see that surface behaviour often masks underlying concerns and motivations, an understanding of which can guide a more effective response.

Another contribution to understanding the cognitive basis for children's aggression and behaviour problems is Shure and Spivack's (1988) delineation of five specific cognitive components necessary for adaptive *interpersonal problem solving*: sensitivity to human problems, the capacity to imagine alternative courses of action, the ability to conceptualize the means to achieve a given end, consideration of possible consequences and an understanding of cause and effect in human relations. (See Box 17.5.)

There is a developmental unfolding of the components related to IPS. In the preschool period, *generating alternative solutions* to problems such as 'What could you do if your sister were playing with a toy you wanted?' is the single most significant predictor of interpersonal behaviour in a classroom setting. Children who generate fewer alternatives are rated by their teachers as disruptive, disrespectful and defiant, and unable to wait to take turns. In middle childhood, alternative thinking is still related to classroom adjustment, while *means-end thinking* emerges as an equally important correlate. For instance, when presented with the problem of a boy's feeling lonely after moving to a new neighbourhood, the well-adjusted child can think not only of different solutions but also of ways to implement the solutions and overcome the obstacles involved, such as saying, 'Maybe he could find someone who liked to play Nintendo like he does, but he'd better not go to a kid's house at suppertime or his mother might get mad!' Again, impulsive and inhibited children are deficient in these cognitive skills.

The data on adolescence are meagre but suggest that means-end thinking and alternative thinking continue to be correlated with good adjustment. The new component to IPS in this developmental era involves *considering consequences* or weighing the pros and cons of potential action: 'If I do X, then someone else will do Y and that will be good (or bad).' Thus, the developing child is able to utilize progressively advanced cognitive skills to solve interpersonal problems.

Empirical Support

Kazdin's (2010) studies of cognitive problem-solving skills training have been singled out as a model of research into therapeutic effectiveness. He and his colleagues randomly assigned a sample of

---

Box 17.5 An Interpersonal Problem-Solving Skills Training Session

The following is a dialogue between a kindergarten-age child and a teacher trained in IPS. Annotations identify the IPS techniques used at each step in the process.

Teacher: What's the matter? What happened? *(eliciting child's view of problem)*

Child: Robert won't give me the clay!

Teacher: What can you do or say so he will let you have the clay? *(eliciting a problem solution)*

Child: I could ask him.

Teacher: That's one way. And what might happen next when you ask him? *(guiding means-end thinking)*

Child: He might say no.

Teacher: He might say no. What else could you try? *(guiding child to think of alternative solutions)*

Child: I could snatch it.

Teacher: That's another idea. What might happen if you do that? *(not criticizing child's solution;*

continuing to guide consequential thinking)

Child: He might hit me.

Teacher: How would that make you feel? *(encouraging social-causal thinking)*

Child: Mad.

Teacher: How would Robert feel if you grabbed the clay? *(encouraging social-causal thinking)*

Child: Mad.

Teacher: Can you think of something different you can do or say so Robert won't hit you and you both won't be mad? *(guiding child to think of further solutions)*

Child: I could say, 'You keep some and give me some'.

Teacher: That's a different idea. *(reinforcing idea as different rather than 'good', thus avoiding adult judgement)*

Source: Shure and Spivack, 1988.

---

school-age boys with conduct disorder to one of three treatments. The first group received interpersonal problem-solving skills training. The second group received the same training, but it was supplemented by *in vivo* practice; for example, they were given 'homework' involving applying what they learned in the treatment session to situations with parents, peers and teachers. The third group received relationship therapy that emphasized empathy, warmth and unconditional positive regard on the therapists' part, along with helping the boys express their feelings and discuss their interpersonal problems. The children in the two cognitive problem-solving skills training groups showed significantly greater reductions in antisocial behaviour and overall behaviour problems and greater increases in prosocial behaviour than did the children in the relationship group. The effects were present in a one-year follow-up in the home and at school. In spite of their improvement, however, the children were still outside the normal

range for antisocial behaviour. Further, gains of this kind of intervention do not always generalize beyond the treatment situation.

Using Manuals Creatively, Flexibly and Developmentally Appropriately

Having described the content of cognitive interventions, let us take a closer look at the *process* of cognitive therapy and consider how it differs – or might not differ – from more unstructured approaches. One of the advantages of cognitive behavioural therapies, and one of the reasons why they are so amenable to empirical validation, is that they are manualized. A *treatment manual* presents clear guidelines for the therapist and ensures that treatment is carried on in a standardized way across a variety of therapists and clients. However, one of the objections made by psychodynamically and humanistically oriented therapists to manualized treatments is that they run the risk of being rigid, impersonal and not individually tailored to the needs of the client. However, the 'cookbook' stereotype of manualized treatments is just that – a stereotype. Clinicians who successfully utilize treatment manuals argue that they can – and, indeed, in order to be effective they *must* – be used flexibly and creatively, with the needs, interests, culture and developmental status of the individual child in mind (Kerig et al., 2010a).

For example, Kendall and colleagues (1998) describe techniques used to bring Kendall's manualized treatment for anxiety disorders, Coping Cat, 'alive' in the USA, Netherlands, Ireland and Australia. They present a number of illustrations of how therapists bring to bear all their creativity, clinical skills and not a little humour in order to personalize the intervention for each individual child. They describe one girl who complained that the acronym FEAR, standing for the steps in the cognitive behavioural procedure, was 'boring'. Rather than run the risk of losing the child's motivation and interest, the therapist readily invited the child to rename the procedure, which she chose to call 'The Happy Helper Steps'. However, noticing that both he and the child were now having difficulty remembering what the steps were, the therapist suggested the child create definitions for the new acronym, 'THHS'. Intrigued and excited, the child created her own steps ('Thou art feeling frightened?' 'Hey! Expecting bad things to happen?' 'Happy actions and attitudes that can help' 'So? Results and rewards') and discovered a new level of excitement and mastery in teaching them to the therapist.

Maintaining the child's active interest and motivation is crucial to the success of manualized treatments, especially those like Coping Cat that challenge children to go outside of their comfort zone and face exposure to what they most fear. The therapist can assist the child by making sure that the tasks are relevant, intriguing and, whenever possible, fun. As Kendall and colleagues (1998, p. 188) state, 'being both scary and dull is a lethal combination'.

In summary, cognitive interventions, although they do not focus on the relationship as the main avenue for change, rely on the same relationship components that are attributed to the success of other therapies: warmth, engagement and a therapeutic alliance between client and therapist.

The Family Systemic Approach

Given the importance of the family system in the etiology of psychopathology, it is not surprising that therapists from most schools of psychotherapy, including behaviourists, cognitive therapists and psychoanalysts, have adapted their techniques to treating families. However, these approaches to working with individuals in the context of the family can be distinguished from approaches that specifically treat the whole family as a system. Our discussions of anorexia nervosa (Chapter 12) and schizophrenia (Chapter 11) introduced the basic premise and some of the concepts generated by the family systemic approach. Here we will examine both in greater detail.

The Conceptual Model

The basic premise is that the family is a *dynamic system*, an entity over and above the interaction of its individual members. Further, the family system has certain characteristics that define whether it is functioning adequately. As we saw in Chapter 1, Minuchin's structural approach (1974; Minuchin and Fishman, 2004) introduces two important concepts, those of boundaries and triangulation. For example, in malfunctioning families, *boundaries* may be blurred, resulting in an enmeshed system in which family members are overly involved with one another in an intrusive way; or *triangulation* may result when rigid patterns have formed in which certain family members ally with one another to the exclusion of other family members.

These patterns, once established, are difficult to change. The reason for this resistance to change, however, lies at the heart of the systemic theory of psychopathology: these troublesome patterns serve a *function* in the family system. To take a concrete example, consider the child in the *detouring-attacking* family (see Chapter 1). This is the child whose misbehaviour serves the function of distracting the parents from their marital problems. Because there is such a significant payoff for the child's symptoms – the family stays intact – there will be strong ambivalence on the part of family members about relinquishing them.

The disturbed child is merely the *identified patient* – the symptom, as it were, that something has gone wrong. The pathology itself is in the system. Consequently, treatment of one individual within the family system is not going to be effective in bringing about change, because the family will tend to reorganize in order to re-establish the old pattern. Thus, the focus of treatment must be the entire family.

The Therapeutic Process

How does the therapist facilitate change? First, in order to change the system, the therapist must become a part of it. The initial step in the process of forming a therapeutic system is *joining*. Minuchin himself joins the family through his use of self. He emphasizes aspects of his personality and life experience that are consistent with the family's, such as by sharing with an immigrant family the fact that he, too, had to struggle with adapting to life in the USA. He accepts the family's organization and style and accommodates to them, showing respect for their way of doing things. In this way, the family therapist behaves much like an anthropologist taking the role of participant-observer, accepting the way that people define their problems, using their language and openly enjoying their humour.

The next stage in the process is *enacting transactional patterns*. Here the family therapist encourages family members to show, rather than to tell, so that the therapist can observe their interactions directly. This can be informative in diagnosing the problem. For example, the therapist might note the small smile on the father's face as the conduct-disordered boy describes his pranks, or the way the mother always interrupts to qualify her anxious daughter's comments. The therapist might re-create

problematic family scenarios by instructing family members to enact them in the therapy session: for example, if a child is complaining that his father never spends time with him, Minuchin might ask him to turn to his father and talk with him about it. Enacting patterns in the therapy session not only allows the therapist to see family members in action, but also can help family members to experience their own interactions with a heightened awareness. A prototypical example of this technique is the family lunch session used in treating families of adolescents with anorexia, which was described in Chapter 12.

Once accepted into the family system, and with sufficient observation to develop a formulation of the problem, the therapist moves into action. **Restructuring techniques** are the tools of the trade used to alter family patterns of interaction. For example, the therapist acts to *re-create communication channels* among family members who resist talking directly to one another and attempt to route all their comments through the therapist. The therapist may avoid making eye contact, refuse to respond when addressed, insist that family members talk to one another, or even leave the room and observe behind a one-way mirror. Like an orchestra conductor, the therapist signals family members when to speak or be silent. The family therapist also uses *repositioning*, which involves manipulating the physical space between family members in order to alter their interactions, perhaps by moving chairs to physically separate family members who need more psychological distance from one another. For example, the therapist may sit between a mother and parentalized child in order to block the child from interfering while the mother and the identified patient talk. (See Box 17.6 for an example of Minuchin's structural techniques.)

Another restructuring technique is called *marking boundaries*. The therapist may promote clear boundaries between individuals by ensuring that family members refrain from talking for one another. In addition, the therapist encourages differentiation of individual family members by interacting differently with each of them according to their age and

Box 17.6 A Family Therapy Session

When the MacLean family sought help for an 'unmanageable' child, a terror who'd been expelled from two schools, Dr Minuchin uncovered a covert split between the parents, held in balance by not being talked about. The 10-year-old boy's misbehaviour was dramatically visible; his father had to drag him kicking and screaming into the consulting room. Meanwhile, his 7-year-old brother sat quietly, smiling engagingly. The good boy.

To broaden the focus from an 'impossible child' to issues of parental control and co-operation, Minuchin asked about 7-year-old Kevin, who misbehaved invisibly. He peed on the floor in the bathroom. According to his father, Kevin's peeing on the floor was due to 'inattentiveness'. The mother laughed when Minuchin said 'Nobody could have such poor aim'.

Minuchin talked with the boy about how wolves mark their territory, and suggested that he expand his territory by peeing in all four corners of the family room.

Minuchin: Do you have a dog?
Kevin: No.
Minuchin: Oh, so you are the family dog.

In the process of discussing the boy who peed – and his parents' response – Minuchin dramatized how the parents polarized each other.

Minuchin: Why would he do such a thing?
Father: I don't know if he did it on purpose.
Minuchin: Maybe he was in a trance?
Father: No, I think it was carelessness.
Minuchin: His aim must be terrible.

The father described the boy's behaviour as accidental; the mother considered it defiance. One of the reasons parents fall under the control of their young children is that they avoid confronting their differences. Differences are normal, but they become toxic when one parent undercuts the other's handling of the children. (It is cowardly revenge for unaddressed grievances.)

Minuchin's gentle but insistent pressure on the couple to talk about how they respond, without switching to focus on how the children behave, led to their bringing up long-held but seldom-voiced resentments.

Mother: Bob makes excuses for the children's behaviour – because he doesn't want to get in there and help me find a solution for the problem.
Father: Yes, but when I did try to help, you'd always criticize me. So after a while I gave up.

Like a photographic print in a developing tray, the spouses' conflict had become visible. Minuchin protected the parents from embarrassment (and the children from being burdened) by asking the children to leave the room. Without the preoccupation of parenting, the spouses could face each other, man and woman – and talk about their hurts and grievances. It turned out to be a sad story of lonely disengagement.

Minuchin: Do you two have areas of agreement?

He said yes; she said no. He was a minimizer; she was a critic.

Minuchin: When did you divorce Bob and marry the children?

She turned quiet; he looked off into space. She said, softly: 'Probably ten years ago.'

What followed was a painful but familiar story of how a marriage can drown in parenting and its conflicts. The conflict was never resolved because it never surfaced. And so the rift never healed; it just expanded.

With Minuchin's help, the couple took turns talking about their pain – and learning to listen. By unbalancing, Minuchin brought enormous pressure to bear to help this couple break through their differences, open up to each other, fight for what they want and, finally, begin to come together – as husband and wife, and as parents.

Source: Excerpted from Nichols and Schwartz, 2004.

developmental status. The therapist may also work to emphasize boundaries between subsystems, such as between the marital and child subsystems. For example, a boy was referred for therapy because of a dog phobia so severe he could not leave the house.

After interacting with the family, the therapist's formulation was that the mother and son were enmeshed and that the father was being excluded from their intimate twosome. The therapist decided to restructure the family interaction by increasing the affiliation between father and son. Recall that this boy had a dog phobia. As it happened, the father was a postal deliveryman and therefore an expert in dealing with dogs. Therefore, the therapist assigned the father the task of teaching his son how to cope with strange dogs. The intervention was a great success. Ultimately, the child, who was himself adopted, asked to adopt a dog; and the father and son spent time together training their new pet. As the father–son bond strengthened, a healthy separation between mother and son was promoted, and the parents embarked on marital therapy.

The therapist can also use *positive reframing* to give family members a new perspective on the problem and new lenses through which to see themselves. For instance, the therapist might praise overprotective parents for their desire to be supportive and nurturing, reframing their behaviour in positive terms. In this way, the therapist underlines the good intentions behind problematic interaction patterns, thus reducing resistance to finding new and better ways to achieve those ends.

Empirical Support

Robbins and colleagues (2010) have in progress an extensive programme of research on the effectiveness of structural family therapy in contexts of cultural diversity. In particular, their work focuses on treatment of Hispanic-American families with conduct-disordered and drug-involved adolescents. In one study, families were randomly assigned either to structural family therapy or to a control condition in which they received 'treatment as usual' as it would be delivered in an outpatient setting. Results showed that youths in both conditions improved significantly, with no differences between the types of intervention. However, there were dramatic differences in retention rates. Families in the family therapy condition were overwhelmingly more likely to complete the treatment programme: only 17 per cent dropped out of treatment as compared to 44 per cent of those in the control condition.

In another randomized controlled trial, Santisteban and colleagues (2003) compared their brief strategic family approach to a group therapy for Hispanic-American youth with externalizing problems. Overall, youth who participated in family therapy evidenced significantly lower levels of conduct disorder, delinquency and marijuana use than those who received group therapy. The effects on family functioning were particularly intriguing. Among those families whose functioning was poorest at the start of treatment, family therapy was associated with significant improvement whereas group therapy was associated with no change. Among families with relatively good functioning at baseline, however, there was no change accounted for by family therapy (in other words, the family's good functioning was maintained), whereas family functioning among the youth who received group therapy *declined*. The possibility that interventions can do harm – what are termed **iatrogenic effects** – is a startling one which has received other sources of support, particularly for group interventions that bring together troubled youth. (See Box 17.7.)

Prevention
Definition

First, we need to define **prevention**. Preventive efforts can be conceptualized along a continuum. (See Fig. 17.4.) At one end are those programmes put into place before a problem develops, designed to prevent it from occurring in the first place. This is known as *primary prevention*. An example of this is the home-based visiting programme for first-time mothers, designed to prevent child abuse, as described in Chapter 14. In contrast, *secondary prevention* efforts focus on early identification of problems in order to prevent them from blossoming into full-blown disorders. An example of this is a crisis line for stressed parents who are demonstrating poor parenting skills. Lastly, *tertiary prevention* intervenes somewhat later, in order to prevent a burgeoning problem from getting worse or reoccurring. In fact, the line between tertiary prevention and intervention is not a strict one, because most child therapies also have the goal of preventing problems from intensifying or relapsing.

Box 17.7 Can Interventions Harm?

Like the Hippocratic oath for physicians, a prevailing principle in the American Psychological Association's (2002) code of ethics is to *do no harm*. Is it possible that well-meaning therapies could actually make children worse? We have encountered one example so far, in the school-based suicide prevention programmes that were found to have the unfortunate effect of increasing distress in the students most vulnerable to suicide (see Chapter 9). Such unwanted negative outcomes of treatment are termed *iatrogenic effects*. Two examples are offered by Dishion and colleagues who uncovered iatrogenic effects of peer-group interventions designed to decrease youth problem behaviour. In the Adolescent Transitions Study, Dishion and colleagues (1999) randomly assigned 119 high-risk youths to one of four treatment conditions: parent only, teen only, parent and teen, and an attention-only condition. The teen-only treatment consisted of group sessions in which youths with behaviour problems met together to address issues such as setting prosocial goals and self-regulation. While both the parent- and teen-focused treatments initially seemed to be beneficial, longer-term outcomes were disconcerting. One year later, increases in tobacco use and teacher reports of externalizing behaviour were found for the adolescents who had been involved in the teen-focused groups. Three years later, these iatrogenic effects had persisted, with tobacco use and delinquency being consistently higher for those in the teen intervention than the other conditions, whether or not parents had been involved. Older youths were the most susceptible to the negative influences of their antisocial peers.

A similar effect was found in the Cambridge-Somerville Youth Study, in which boys at high risk for delinquency were randomly assigned to a control group or an intervention that involved a number of components, a key one of which was group activities and involvement in summer camps. Treatment, which began when the boys were about age 10 and ended when they were 16, had a disconcerting iatrogenic effect: boys who received the most attention in the treatment had the *worst* outcomes. Dishion and colleagues (1999) took a closer look at the boys' participation in the programme and found that most of the damaging effects of the intervention were accounted for by the boys who had been sent to summer camp more than once.

Like findings have emerged in studies of 'natural experiments' in which delinquent youth have been sent to residential facilities versus being assigned to diversion programmes in their communities. Among first-time offenders, the likelihood of recidivism (repeat offending) is substantially higher when youth are placed in juvenile detention centres (Shapiro et al., 2010). Through exposing them to antisocial role models, and through depriving them of opportunities to interact with prosocial youth and to engage in normative developmental adolescent experiences (Steinberg et al., 2004) such residential facilities may act as 'hot houses' for the growing of antisocial youth.

Based on these data, Dodge and colleagues (2006) urge that interventions be informed by the developmental psychopathology of the disorder under investigation. For example, association with deviant peers is a strong predictor of delinquent behaviour in youths – via the mechanism of 'deviancy training' – and interventions that prescribe just that may do more harm than good – a process termed 'peer contagion' (Dishion and Tipsord, 2011). On the other hand, the investigators point out, successful group treatments for antisocial youth have been developed but differ from those described earlier in one important way: they include a mix of prosocial and antisocial youth, which appears to have a dampening effect on problem behaviour.

Recall that when we first discussed developmental psychopathology in Chapter 1, we noted that the concepts of risk and developmental pathways could furnish guides for prevention. Developmentally oriented research has been sufficiently fruitful that some of those guides are now available. We have already discussed one prevention programme, STEEP, designed to prevent insecure attachment (Erickson and Kurz-Riemer, 2002). Here we present another preventive programme informed by the research on the developmental psychopathology of conduct disorder.

FIGURE 17.4 The Continuum of Prevention and Intervention.

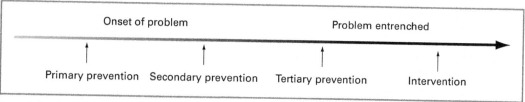

Source: Hall et al., 1971.

The Fast Track Programme

Fast Track (Conduct Problems Prevention Research Group, 2011) is based on the developmental pathway that identifies the early signs of conduct disorder and the contribution of parents, school and peers to its fruition (see Chapter 10). The target population is first-graders evidencing disruptive behaviours such as non-compliance, aggression, impulsivity and immaturity. The techniques used are ones that had been tried already with some degree of success. However, the unique feature of the programme is the integration of such techniques. In this way the separate components, such as dealing with parents and teachers, can be co-ordinated and can reinforce one another, and the chances of generalizing across settings can be maximized.

We have already presented two of the interventions: changing parents' ineffectual disciplinary practices and increasing the child's social skills in order to circumvent peer rejection (see Chapter 10). Therefore, in this discussion we concentrate on the more novel components of the programme aimed at avoiding school failure. Sessions with the family focus on setting up a structured learning environment in the home and encourage parental involvement in the child's learning as well as communication with the school. The importance of establishing a positive relation with the child's teacher is particularly emphasized. At school, teachers are trained by Fast Track staff in strategies for effective management of disruptive behaviours, such as establishing clear rules, rewarding appropriate behaviour

and not rewarding – or punishing – inappropriate behaviour. Teachers also implement special classroom programmes designed to strengthen the children's self-control, to build and maintain friendships and to enhance problem-solving abilities. Finally, children who need it are offered tutoring, especially in reading.

In the most recent evaluation of the programme, the investigators identified 891 children who were judged to be at high risk for launching on an early-starter conduct disorder pathway. The children, 69 per cent of whom were boys and 51 per cent African American, were randomly assigned to the prevention programme or a control condition. The intervention spanned 10 years and involved all components of the model: parent behaviour management training, child social cognitive skills training, tutoring in reading, home visiting, mentoring and classroom curricula. Overall, the outcomes were positive, showing that the intervention prevented children from developing conduct disorder, ODD, ADHD or any other externalizing disorder. However, there was an interesting interaction effect showing that the prevention programme prevented the lifetime prevalence of a psychiatric diagnosis only among children at the highest level of risk at the initial assessment.

Fast Track, along with recognizing the multi-determined nature of conduct disorder, is both integrated and solidly based on research. Thus, it avoids the rather piecemeal, improvisational quality of many previous attempts at prevention. As such, it is a prime example of the practical application of developmental psychopathology.

Glossary

accelerated longitudinal approach
(Also known as the longitudinal, cross-sectional approach.) A research technique in which data on the origins of a psychopathology are obtained from different age groups that are subsequently followed until the children in the younger groups are the same age as those in the next older group.

accommodation In Piaget's theory, the process of changing an existing cognitive schema in order to take into account new information from the environment.

adaptational failure A conceptualization of psychopathology in which disorder is viewed as stemming from the child's inability to adapt to the expectations of the environment.

adaptive behaviour The ability to cope with environmental demands, such as those for self-care, conventional social interactions and independent functioning in the community, at an age-appropriate level.

adjustment disorder Deviant behaviour that is a reaction to a specific event or events, such as parental death or divorce.

anaclitic depression The infant's reaction of despair following the loss of a loved and needed caregiver.

anal stage In Freud's psychosexual theory, the second stage of development, in which pleasure is derived from retaining and evacuating faeces and the toddler confronts the issue of autonomy versus compliance.

anorexia nervosa A voluntary restriction of food and/or an involvement in purging in an active pursuit of thinness that results in at least a 15 per cent loss of body weight. The *restricting* type relies solely on strict dieting to lose weight; the *binge-eating/purging* type

alternates between dieting and binge eating, followed by self-induced vomiting or purging.

anxiety disorders A group of disorders characterized by intense, chronic anxiety. Formerly called psychoneurotic disorders.

assimilation In Piaget's theory, the process of transforming information so as to make it fit with an existing cognitive schema.

asynchrony Disjointed or markedly uneven rates of progression among developmental variables.

attention deficit hyperactivity disorder Developmentally inappropriate inattention accompanied by motor restlessness and impulsivity.

attrition The loss of subjects during longitudinal studies.

authoritarian parenting Discipline requiring strict, unquestioning obedience.

authoritative parenting Discipline requiring compliance with standards for mature behaviour, accompanied by love, communication and respect for the child.

autism A severe disorder of the infancy and toddler period marked by extreme aloneness, a pathological need for sameness, and mutism or non-communicative speech.

avoidance learning A form of learning in which an organism, having experienced an aversive stimulus, behaves in order to prevent future encounters with that stimulus.

avoidant attachment A form of insecure attachment marked by precocious independence from the caregiver.

behaviour deficit or excess The behaviourists' conceptualization of psychopathology as behaviours occurring at a lower or at a higher

frequency or intensity than is expected within a given society.

behaviour therapies A group of therapies characterized by attention to specific, current behaviours, objective measurement and reliance on principles of behaviour change derived from the laboratory.

behavioural assessment Procedures designed to locate specific behaviours – along with their antecedents and consequences – that subsequently can serve as targets for modification through behavioural techniques.

behavioural inhibition A temperamental pre-disposition for children to react to novelty with avoidance or distress and to be shy and fearful.

bipolar disorder (Also known as manic-depression.) A severe form of psychopathology characterized by depression alternating with states of euphoria or over-activity.

borderline personality disorder A disorder characterized by a pervasive pattern of instability in interpersonal relationships, self-image and affect.

boundaries The separation between individuals or subsystems within the family, such as between marital and parent–child relationships.

brain damage Damage to the brain can be defined neurologically in terms of the nature, site and size of the damage, behaviourally in terms of impaired functions or etiologically in terms of the source of the damage.

brain lateralization The idea that the two halves of the brain's cerebral cortex – left and right – execute different functions.

bulimia nervosa An eating disorder characterized by recurrent episodes of binge eating (i.e., the rapid consumption of large quantities of food in a brief time), followed by attempts to prevent weight gain either through self-induced vomiting or misuse of laxatives in the purging type or through fasting or excessive exercise in the non-purging type.

bullying A pattern of behaviour in which one repeatedly perpetrates physical, verbal or relational aggression against a victim, often involving an imbalance of power or strength.

case formulation A succinct description of the child that incorporates the clinician's interpretation of how the problem came about and how it might be re-mediated.

casual attribution Beliefs concerning whether events are the result of factors within the self (internal vs external), are likely to persist (stable vs unstable), or are pervasive across situations (global vs specific).

coercion In parent–child interactions, use of negative reinforcement to influence the other's behaviour; e.g., the child who ceases to tantrum once the parents capitulate to his or her demands.

cognitive triad In Beck's cognitive theory of depression, attributions about the self involving worthlessness, helplessness and hopelessness.

cohort effect The possibility that children's behaviour might be different because they were born in different eras and therefore had different experiences.

comorbidity The co-occurrence of two or more psychopathologies.

compulsion An irrational act that an individual is compelled to do.

computerized axial tomography (CAT scan) (Also called computer-assisted tomography or CT scan.) Uses computer-driven X-ray machines to produce detailed images both of the brain's surface and of the levels below, making it possible to locate lesions at any level of the brain.

concrete-operational stage In middle childhood, the emergence of the ability to understand the world in terms of reason rather than naive perception.

conditions of worth Carl Rogers's term for conditions set by parents under which they will grant their love and respect for the child.

conduct disorders Behaviours in which children act out their feelings or impulses towards others in an antisocial or destructive fashion.

contingency management Decreases the strength of undesirable behaviours and increases the strength of adaptive ones by manipulating the rewards and punishments that follow or are contingent upon such behaviours.

continuity Consistency in the presence or absence of a disorder from one developmental period to another.

cross-sectional approach A research technique in which data from different age groups is gathered at one point in time.

defence mechanisms Unconscious strategies for reducing anxiety. See also *displacement, projection, reaction formation* and *repression*.

delusion A firmly held, irrational belief that runs counter to reality and to the individual's culture or subculture.

detouring Salvador Minuchin's term for parents' avoidance of their own conflicts by regarding their child as their sole problem.

developmental delay Development that proceeds at a significantly slower pace than normal.

developmental deviation Emergence of a behaviour that is so qualitatively different from the normative that it would be considered inappropriate at age stage of development.

developmental pathway The risk and protective factors responsible for diverting development from its normal course, maintaining the deviation or returning development to its normal course.

developmental psychopathology The study of the developmental processes that contribute to the formation of, or resistance to, psychopathology.

developmental transformation A change in the outward manifestation of a disorder due to age-related changes in individuals or their environments.

diathesis-stress model A psychological theory that explains behaviour as a result of both biological and genetic vulnerability (diathesis), and stress from life experiences. This model thus assumes that the onset of a certain disorder may result from a combination of one's biological disposition towards the given disorder and stressful events that bring about the onset to such disorder.

discontinuity Inconsistency in the presence or absence of a disorder from one developmental period to another.

discrepancy model Defining learning disability as the difference between what students should achieve in terms of their ability and their actual achievement.

disorganized or catatonic behaviour In schizophrenia, behaviour marked by extreme deviance, such as grimacing, odd posturing, long periods of immobility or self-mutilation.

disorganized speech In schizophrenia, speech characterized by loose associations, illogical reasoning, fragmentation and bizarreness.

disorganized/disoriented attachment A form of insecure attachment marked by inconsistent and odd behaviour.

displacement A mechanism of defence in which an impulse is directed towards a target that is safer than the original one.

Down syndrome A form of mental retardation caused by having three number 21 chromosomes instead of the normal two.

DSM The *Diagnostic and Statistical Manual of Mental Disorders*, published by the American Psychiatric Association, providing diagnostic criteria for mental disorders. The latest edition is DSM-IV-TR.

dynamic systems The perspective that human behaviour is part of a complex system in which relationships between individuals, and among individuals and their environments, are reciprocal and transactional in nature.

dysthymic disorder Characterized either by a depressed mood or by irritability in children, along with at least two other specific symptoms of depression. The disturbance persists for at least a year.

ego In Freud's structural theory, the psychic component responsible for learning the nature of reality in order to gratify the id's demands for maximal pleasure, on the one hand, and to avoid the painful censure of the superego, on the other hand.

ego control The extent to which individuals inhibit or give free expression to their impulses.

ego psychology Associated with Erik Erikson, an outgrowth of psychoanalytic theory that focuses on the reality-oriented, adaptive aspects of the psyche.

ego resilience The ability to adapt resourcefully to changes in the environment.

egocentrism In Jean Piaget's theory, the tendency to view the physical and social world exclusively from one's own point of view.

electroencephalogram (EEG) A device for recording the electric activity of the brain.

emotion regulation The ability to monitor, evaluate and modify one's emotional reactions in order to achieve one's goals.

encopresis Involuntary soiling with faeces in a child age 5 and older.

enmeshment An extreme form of boundary dissolution which involves a lack of recognition or acknowledgement of the psychological separateness of the self and other (see Kerig, 2005).

enuresis (Also called functional enuresis.) Involuntary urination

during the day or night in children 5 years of age or older.

equifinality Refers to how different early experiences in life (e.g., parental divorce, physical abuse, parental substance abuse) can lead to similar outcomes (e.g., schizophrenia). In other words, there are many different early experiences that can lead to the same psychological disorder.

equilibration In Piaget's theory, the balance between assimilation and accommodation.

etiology The study of the causes or of the necessary and sufficient conditions for producing various psychopathologies.

event-related potential (ERP) An electroencephalographic technique that records the brain response to a given stimulus so that one can tell whether the response is characteristic (normal) or deviant.

evidence-based practice An approach to psychological interventions that involves integrating the best available research evidence with clinician expertise and appreciation for the client's characteristics, values and preferences.

executive functions The functions underlying flexible, goal-directed behaviour; specifically, planning, working memory, set shifting and inhibition of competing behaviours.

externalizing See *internalizing-externalizing*.

extinction The gradual disappearance of a learned behaviour through the removal of reinforcements.

familial or familial cultural retardation Retardation characterized by a mild degree of retardation with no clear organic cause, a greater prevalence among minorities and individuals of low socio-economic status, and a tendency to blend in with the general population after school.

family cohesiveness A sense of strong bonding and sharing among family members.

fixation The persistence of normal behaviour beyond the point where it is developmentally appropriate. This arrest of development may be psychopathological, depending on the degree or intensity.

follow-back strategy A research technique in which the origins of a psychopathology are reconstructed by obtaining data from records made at a previous time period, such as school or court records.

follow-up strategy A research technique involving following children for a considerable period of time in order to obtain data on the antecedents of various psychopathologies.

formal-operational stage In adolescence, the ability to think in terms of general ideas and abstract concepts.

free association The basic psychoanalytic technique for uncovering unconscious material by encouraging the patient to say whatever comes to mind.

functional magnetic resonance imaging (fMRI) A brain imaging technique that tracks increases and decreases in oxygen in the brain as an individual performs a given task and subsequently can locate where the greatest areas of activation occur.

gender constancy The recognition that gender is permanent and does not change.

gender identity Self-classification as male or female.

gender identity disorder A disorder characterized by a strong and persistent desire to be, or belief that one is, a member of the other sex.

gender role Society's prescriptions for appropriate behaviours and feelings for boys and girls.

generalized anxiety disorder A disorder characterized by excessive worry and anxiety that significantly interferes with functioning across a variety of situations.

genital stage In Freud's psychosexual theory, the last stage of development, during which mature sexuality and true intimacy are achieved.

goodness of fit The optimal match between the child's temperament and the demands that the environment places on the child.

hallucination A sensory perception occurring in the absence of any appropriate external stimulus.

humanistic therapy Also termed client-centred therapy, a non-directive approach developed by Carl Rogers in which the therapist provides a non-judgemental and nurturing atmosphere in which the client can grow.

iatrogenic effects Negative effects that are caused by an intervention.

id In Freud's structural theory, the biologically based pleasure-seeking source of all psychic energy.

identity In Erik Erikson's theory, the search for inner continuity and interpersonal mutuality that begins in adolescence and is evidenced by a vocational choice.

imitation (Also called modelling.) Learning by observing the behaviour of others (models).

insecure attachment There are three types: in *resistant attachment* there is an ambivalent mixture of demands for and rejection of maternal attention; in *avoidant attachment*, the child ignores the mother; and in *disorganized/disoriented attachment* there are contradictory responses to the mother such as approaching her with depressed or flat affect.

insight In psychoanalytic psychotherapy, the patient's conscious awareness of anxiety-producing thoughts and feelings that had been in the unconscious.

intelligence quotient (IQ) A measure of intelligence derived either (1) from the relation between the child's mental age and chronological age or (2) from the deviation of a child's score from the mean score of children his or her age.

intelligence tests Standardized techniques for measuring intellectual functioning.

internal working model In attachment theory, refers to the internalization of relationships and formation of a schema regarding the self and other.

internalization The process by which behaviour that was once dependent on environmental factors for its maintenance comes to be maintained by intra-individual factors.

internalizers See *internalizing–externalizing*.

internalizing–externalizing A classification of psychopathologies based on whether the child suffers (internalizing) or the environment suffers (externalizing).

interpretation In psychoanalytic theory, interpretation consists of the therapist pointing out the meaning of material the patient is not aware of.

latency stage In Freud's psychosexual theory, the fourth stage of development, in which concerns about sexuality diminish and the child's attention is drawn to mastery of social and academic environments.

magnetic resonance imaging (MRI) A brain imaging technique that generates three-dimensional images of various brain structures by using images from successive layers of the brain.

major depression An acute, debilitating disorder characterized by five or more symptoms, one of which is depressed mood in adults or irritability in children.

maltreatment Behaviour that is outside the norms of conduct and entails a substantial risk of causing physical or emotional harm.

masked depression Underlying depression in children in middle childhood that is masked by a wide variety of deviant but non-depressive behaviours.

mastery motivation The drive to interact with the environment for the intrinsic pleasure of learning about it.

mediator A variable that accounts for the effects of one variable upon another.

mental retardation A condition characterized by subnormal intelligence, deficits in adaptive behaviour, and onset typically under the age of 18 years.

modelling See *imitation*.

moderator A variable that affects the strength or direction of the relationship between one variable and another.

multiaxial classification A diagnostic system whereby individuals are assessed in terms of a number of dimensions rather than in terms of a single classification.

multi-determinism The idea that psychopathology is determined by a number of causes rather than a single cause.

multifinality The idea that a single risk factor may have a number of different consequences depending upon contextual and intra-individual factors.

myelination The formation of an insulating sheath of white matter around the axon of the nerve cell.

negative affectivity Subsuming anxiety and depression under their shared negative affects such as fear, sadness and guilt.

negative reinforcement Increasing the probability that behaviour will occur by removing unpleasant or aversive consequences.

negative symptoms Representing a withdrawal or lack of function that you would usually expect to see in a healthy person. For example, people with schizophrenia often appear emotionless, flat and apathetic.

neglect A form of child maltreatment involving intentional withholding of physical protection; mental or physical health care; education, nutrition, shelter or safe living conditions.

neglectful parenting Parents who are indifferent to their children or uninvolved and self-centred.

neuroendocrines Processes involved in the interaction between neural and hormonal (endocrine) systems.

neurotransmitters The 'chemical messengers' responsible for communication among nerve cells.

object constancy In object relations theory, the ability to integrate both positive and negative feelings into a single representation of the self or other.

object permanence In Piaget's cognitive theory, the understanding that physical objects exist independently even when we are not in direct contact with them or observing them.

object relations In Freudian theory, the term used for an emotional attachment to another person.

obsession An irrational thought, the repeated occurrence of which is beyond the individual's conscious control.

obsessive-compulsive disorder See *obsession* and *compulsion*.

Oedipus complex In Freud's psychosexual theory, the universal desire of the preschool boy to take possession of the mother and eliminate the rivalrous father.

omnipotent thinking Belief that one can control events that, in reality, lie beyond one's power.

operant conditioning A form of conditioning in which the persistence of a response depends on its effects on the environment.

oppositional defiant disorder Purposeful defiance of adults' requests resulting in violation of minor rules.

oral stage In Freud's psychosexual theory, the first stage of development, in which pleasure is derived from sucking and biting and attachment to the caregiver is formed.

organic MR (mental retardation) Significantly below-average intellectual abilities combined with deficits in adaptive functioning prior to 18 years of age that is caused by biological factors.

overinclusiveness A thought disorder in which ideas flit from one tangential association to another.

overprotectiveness Excessive and unrealistic concern over another's welfare.

parasuicidal behaviour or non-suicidal self-injury (Also referred to as suicidal gestures.) Non-lethal self-harming behaviour such as superficial cuts to the extremities.

paediatric psychology The study of the interplay between organic factors on the one hand and psychological, social and cultural factors on the other in the etiology, course and treatment of disease. Paediatric psychology is also concerned with prevention and health maintenance.

paedophilia A state of being sexually aroused by children.

parent–child coalition Salvador Minuchin's term for a family pattern in which a child sides with one parent against the other.

parent management training (PMT) The use of social learning principles such as positive reinforcement and mild punishment to alter parent–child interactions in a prosocial direction.

permissive/indulgent parenting Parents who are undemanding, accepting and child centred but who make few attempts at control.

personality disorders Deeply ingrained, maladaptive behaviours that, while more pervasive than the anxiety disorders, still do not significantly diminish the individual's reality contact.

phallic stage In Freud's psychosexual theory, the third stage of development, in which the preschooler is expansive and assertive and wishes to be the exclusive love object of the other-sex parent.

phobia An intense, persistent, irrational fear of an animate or inanimate object or of a situation.

phonemes The sound units of speech.

phonological awareness Recognition of the fact that words are made up of separate sounds, or phonemes, an important function underlying the ability to read.

physical abuse A form of childhood maltreatment involving intentional acts that result in actual or potential physical harm.

positive reinforcement Use of rewards to increase the probability that a desired behaviour will occur.

positron-emission tomography (PET) scan A brain scan technique that detects abnormal functioning in brains that might look structurally intact by recording the rate of metabolizing radioactive glucose that has been introduced into cerebral arteries.

Posttraumatic stress disorder A disorder resulting from experiencing an event involving actual or threatened death or injury to the self or others.

potentiating factor A variable that increases the impact of a risk factor.

precocity As applied to psychopathology, precocity is an accelerated rate of development that leads to an attempt to take on adult roles and responsibilities before the child is prepared to do so successfully.

preoperational stage In the preschool period, the literal belief in what is seen so that, for example, things that look different are in fact different.

prevention Programmes initiated before a problem develops (*primary* prevention), in the early stages of a problem to forestall its development into a full-blown disorder (*secondary* prevention), or to prevent a problem from worsening or reoccurring (*tertiary* prevention).

projection A mechanism of defence in which anxiety-provoking impulses are denied in oneself and attributed to others.

projective identification A defence mechanism in which unwanted thoughts and feelings are projected onto another person and then that person is psychologically pressured to identify with those projections.

projective techniques Personality assessment methods using ambiguous or unstructured stimuli. The most popular are the *Rorschach*, consisting of a series of ink blots, the *Thematic Apperception Test (TAT)*, consisting of a series of ambiguous pictures, and human figure drawing.

protective factors Factors that promote healthy development and counteract the negative effects of risks.

protective mechanisms The underlying developmental processes that account for the positive effects of protective factors.

pruning The process of the brain ridding itself of redundant or unnecessary neural cells.

psychological abuse A form of child maltreatment involving intentionally conveying that the child is worthless, inadequate, unloved, endangered or of value only insofar as she or he meets someone else's needs.

psychopathy A psychopathology marked by callousness, egocentricity, shallow emotions, superficial charm, manipulativeness, impulsiveness and an absence of meaningful relations.

psychosexual theory Freud's developmental theory in which each stage – the oral, anal and phallic – is marked by a change in the source of erotic bodily sensations: personality development.

punishment Presentation of an aversive stimulus that decreases the probability that the response leading to it will occur.

reaction formation A mechanism of defence in which a child's thoughts and feelings are diametrically opposed to an anxiety-provoking impulse.

reactive attachment disorder A disorder characterized by disturbed social relations due to pathological caregiving in the first three years of life.

reciprocal determinism In social learning theory, the idea that both the individual and the environment influence one another rather than the individual being the passive

recipient of environmental influences.

reciprocal inhibition The inhibition of the weaker of two incompatible responses by the stronger one. Utilized in systematic desensitization.

regression The return of behaviours that once were developmentally appropriate but no longer are. Whether or not the behaviours are psychopathological depends on the degree or intensity of regression.

reinforcement An increase in the probability that a response will occur to a contiguously presented stimulus.

reliability The consistency with which an assessment instrument performs.

religiosity Strong devotion to a religious belief system.

repression The basic mechanism of defence in which anxiety-provoking impulses and ideas are banished from consciousness.

resilience A child's ability to make a good adjustment in spite of being at high risk for developing a disturbance.

resistant attachment A form of insecure attachment in which the infant is preoccupied with the caregiver while relating in an ambivalent manner.

respondent conditioning (Also called classical conditioning.) A form of conditioning in which a previously neutral stimulus takes on the properties of a stimulus that innately evokes a response.

restructuring techniques Techniques for altering faulty patterns of family interaction.

retrospective strategy A research technique involving reconstructing the origins of a psychopathology through inquiring about the past history of the disturbed child.

rigidity Excessive and unrealistic resistance to change.

risk factors Factors that increase the probability that development will be diverted from its normal path, resulting either in clinically

significant problem behaviour or psychopathology.

risk mechanisms The underlying developmental processes that account for the negative effects of risk variables.

ruminative Rumination is a response to distress that involves repetitively dwelling on thoughts and feelings regarding that distress.

savantism Also known as savant syndrome, this is a rare condition in which people with developmental disorders have one or more areas of expertise, ability or brilliance that are in contrast with the individual's overall limitations.

schema (plural, schemata) For Piaget: cognitive structures comprising children's developing understanding of their experience of the environment and of themselves. For social cognitive theories: stable mental structures incorporating perceptions of self and others and including past experiences and future expectations.

schizophrenia A severe, pervasive disorder consisting of delusions, hallucinations, disorganized speech, inappropriate affect, disorganized or bizarre behaviour, and the negative symptoms of flat affect, avolition, alogia and anhedonia.

self-constancy The sense of the self as continuous and 'going on being' despite changes in one's mood or the environment.

self-efficacy An individual's estimation of the likelihood of achieving a given outcome.

self-regulation The autonomous initiation and control over one's own behaviour.

sensorimotor stage The infant's and toddler's reliance on sensations and motor actions as vehicles for understanding the environment.

separation anxiety disorder Excessive anxiety concerning separation from those to whom the child is attached.

separation-individuation In object relations theory, the development of a sense of the self as distinct from the caregiver and the achievement of a sense of uniqueness.

sexual abuse A form of child maltreatment involving the child in sexual activity that the child cannot understand or give consent to, is not developmentally prepared for or that violates the laws and social norms of the community.

sexual orientation Attraction to same-sex or other-sex partners.

social phobia (Also known as social anxiety disorder.) A disorder characterized by excessive anxiety and avoidance of social situations.

splitting A defence mechanism that protects the internal representation of the loving parent and the lovable self from the child's feelings of anger and aggression.

stage-salient issues At each age period, the key developmental tasks that the child must accomplish in order to successfully move forward in development.

substance abuse A pattern of excessive use of a chemical substance to the extent that it interferes with work or school and interpersonal relationships.

substance dependence A pattern of continual use of a substance despite significant substance-related problems, resulting in symptoms such as tolerance, withdrawal and a lifestyle consumed with activities revolving around substance use.

substance-induced disorders The toxic effects of substances can mimic mental illness in ways that can be difficult to distinguish from mental illness. Symptoms of mental illness that are the result of substance abuse are referred to as 'substance-induced mental disorders'.

superego The moral component, or conscience, in Freud's structural theory. Initially, it is perfectionistic, requiring absolute obedience and punishing transgressions with guilt feelings.

sustained attention The ability to continue a task until it is completed.

syndrome A group of behaviours or symptoms that tend to occur together in a particular disorder.

systematic desensitization A behaviour therapy for extinguishing anxiety by pairing a graded series of anxiety stimuli with the incompatible response of relaxation.

theory of mind (ToM) A child's understanding that others have intentions, motivations, and perspectives different from one's own.

time-out In behaviour therapy, isolating the child from reinforcement for brief periods in order to extinguish undesirable behaviours.

transaction A series of dynamic, reciprocal interactions between the child, the family, and the social context.

transference In psychoanalytic therapy, the projection onto the therapist of intense feelings once directed towards significant figures, typically the parents.

triangulation Salvador Minuchin's term for a family pattern in which the child is forced to side with one parent against the other.

tripartite model of emotion A model of emotion that proposes that anxiety and depression are both related to a propensity towards negative affect, whereas in addition anxiety is related specifically to a tendency towards physiological hyperarousal and depression is related specifically to a tendency towards low positive affect.

unconditional positive regard In Carl Rogers's theory, the parents' intrinsic valuing and acceptance of the child.

validity The degree to which an instrument evaluates what it intends to evaluate.

vulnerability A factor that increases the likelihood that a child will succumb to risk.

working through In psychoanalytic theory, the process by which the patient gains insight into the many ways in which a single conflict is expressed.

References

Abela, J.R.Z. and Hankin, B.L. (2009) Cognitive vulnerability to depression in adolescents: a developmental psychopathology perspective, in S. Nolen-Hoeksema and L. M. Hilt (eds), *Handbook of Depression in Adolescents*. New York: Routledge/Taylor & Francis.

Abela, J.R.Z. and Seligman, M.E.P. (2000) The hopelessness theory of depression: a test of the diathesis-stress component in the interpersonal and achievement domains, *Cognitive Therapy & Research*, 24(4), 361–378.

Aboud, F.E. and Amato, M. (2001) Developmental and socialization influences on inter-group bias, in R. Brown and S. Gaerther (eds), *Blackwell Handbook of Social Psychology: Intergroup Process*. Oxford: Blackwell.

Achenbach, T. M. (1990) Conceptualization of developmental psychopathology, in M. Lewis and S. M. Miller (eds), *Handbook of Developmental Psychopathology*. New York: Plenum.

Achenbach, T.M. (1991) *Manual for the Child Behavior Checklist 4–18 and 1991 profile*, Deparment of Psychiatry, University of Vermont.

Achenbach, T.M. (2000) Assessment of psychopathology, in A.J. Sameroff, M. Lewis and S.M. Miller (eds), *Handbook of Developmental Psychopathology*. New York: Kluwer Academic.

Achenbach, T.M. and Rescorla, L.A. (2001) *Manual for the ASEBA School-Age: Forms & Profiles*. Burlington: University of Vermont, Research Center for Children, Youth, and Families.

Achenbach, T.M., Howell, C.T., McConaughy, S.H. and Stanger, C. (1995) Six-year predictors of problems in a national sample of children and youths: I. Cross-informant syndromes, *Journal of the American Academy of Child and Adolescent Psychiatry*, 34, 336–347.

Adler, G. and Rhine, M.W. (1988) The selfobject function of projective identification. *Bulletin of the Menninger Clinic*, 52(6), 473–491.

Afifi, T.O. Boman, J., Fleisher, W. and Sareen, J. (2009) The relationship between child abuse, parental divorce and lifetime mental disorders and suicidality in a nationally representative adult sample. *Child Abuse & Neglect*, 33(3), 139–147.

Agras, W.S., Walsh, T., Fairburn, C.G., Wilson, G.T. and Kraemer, H.C. (2000) A multicenter comparison of cognitive-behavioral therapy and interpersonal psychotherapy for bulimia nervosa, *Archives of General Psychiatry*, 57(5), 459–466.

Agrawal, H.R., Gunderson, J., Holmes, B.M. and Lyons-Ruth, K. (2004) Attachment studies with borderline patients: a review, *Harvard Review of Psychiatry*, 12(2), 94–104.

Aguilar, E.J., Leal, C., Acosta, F.J., Cejas, M.R., Fernández, L. and Gracia, R. (2003) A psychopathological study of a group of schizophrenic patients after attempting suicide. Are there two different clinical subtypes? *European Psychiatry*, 18(4), 190–192.

Aikens, N.L. and Barbarin, O. (2008) Socioeconomic differences in reading trajectories: the contribution of family, neighborhood and school contexts, *Journal of Educational Psychology*, 100(2), 235.

Ainsworth, M.D.S., Blehar, M., Waters, E. and Wall, S. (1978) *Patterns of Attachment*. Hillsdale, NJ: Erlbaum.

Akin-Little, A. (ed.) (2009) *Behavioral Interventions in the Schools: Evidence-Based Positive Strategies*. Washington, DC: American Psychological Association.

Aksan, N., Kochanska, G. and Ortmann, M.R. (2006) Mutually responsive orientation between parents and their young children: toward methodological advances in the science of realtionships. *Developmental Psychobiology*, 42, 833–848.

Albano, A.M., Chorpita, B.F. and Barlow, D.H. (1996) Childhood anxiety disorders, in E.J. Mash and R.A. Barkley (eds), *Child Psychopathology*. New York: Guilford Press.

Alderfer, M.A. et al. (2005). Patterns of posttraumatic stress symptoms in parents of childhood cancer survivors, *Journal of Family Psychology*, 19(3), 430.

Alexander, J.F., Pugh, C. and Parsons, B. (1988) *Blueprints for Violence Prevention: Book 3. Functional Family Therapy*. Denver, CO: C&M Press.

Alexander, J.F., Robbins, M., Waldron, H. and Neeb, A. (in press) *Functional Family Therapy*. Washington, DC: American Psychological Association.

Allen, D.N., Thaler, N.S. et al. (2010) WISC-IV profiles in children with traumatic brain injury: similarities to and differences from the WISC-III, *Psychological Assessment*, 22(1), 57.

Allen, J., Vessey, J.A. and Schapiro, N.A. (2010). *Primary Care of the Child with a Chronic Condition*, Elsevier Mosby.

Allen J.G., Fonagy, P. and Bateman A.W. (2008) *Mentalizing in Clinical Practice*. Arlington, VA: American Psychiatric Publishing.

Allen, J.P. and Hauser, S.T. (1996) Autonomy and relatedness in adolescent-family interactions as predictors of young adults' states of mind regarding attachment,

Development and Psychopathology, 8(4), 793–809.

Allen, J.P. and Miga, E.M. (2010) Attachment in adolescence: a move to the level of emotion regulation, *Journal of Social and Personal Relationships*, 27, 181–190.

Allen, J.P., Marsh, P., McFarland, C., McElhaney, K.B., Land, D.J., Jodl, K.M. and Peck, S. (2002) Attachment and autonomy as predictors of the development of social skills and delinquency during mid-adolescence. *Journal of Consulting and Clinical Psychology*, 70(1), 56–66.

Allen, J.P., Porter, M., McFarland, C., McElhaney, K.B. and Marsh, P. (2007) The relation of attachment security to adolescents' paternal and peer relationships, depression and externalizing behavior, *Child Development*, 78(4), 1222–1239.

Allen, L. and Astuto, J. (2009) Depression among racially, ethnically and culturally diverse adolescents, in S. Nolen-Hoeksema and L.M. Hilt (eds), *Handbook of Depression in Adolescents*. New York: Routledge/Taylor & Francis.

Alloy, L.B., Abramson, L.Y., Urosevic, S., Walshaw, P.D., Nusslock, R. and Neeren, A.M. (2005) The psychosocial context of bipolar disorder: environmental, cognitive and developmental risk factors, *Clinical Psychology Review*, 25(8), 1043–1075.

Alloy, L.B., Abramson, L.Y., Walshaw, P.D., Keyser, J. and Gerstein, R.K. (2006) A cognitive vulnerability-stress perspective on bipolar spectrum disorders in a normative adolescent brain, cognitive and emotional development context, *Development and Psychopathology*, 18(04), 1055–1103.

Althoff, R.R., Verhulst, F.C., Rettew, D.C., Hudziak, J.J. and Jan, E.van der (2010) Adult outcomes of childhood dysregulation: a 14-year follow-up study, *Journal of the American Academy of Child and Adolescent Psychiatry*, 49(11), 1105–1116.

Altman, H., Collins, M. and Mundy, P. (1997) Subclinical hallucinations and delusions in nonpsychotic adolescents, *Journal of Child Psychology and Psychiatry*, 38(4), 413–420.

Altmann, E.O. and Gotlib, I.H. (1988) The social behavior of depressed children: an observational study, *Journal of Abnormal Child Psychology*, 16(1), 29–44.

Amato, P. and Dorius, C. (2010) Fathers, children and divorce, in M.E. Lamb (ed.), *The Role of the Father in Child Development*. Hoboken, NJ: Wiley & Sons.

Amato, P. and James, S. (2010) Divorce in Europe and the United States: commonalities and differences across nations. *Family Science*, 1(1), 2–13.

Amato, P.R. and Afifi, T. (2006) Feeling caught between parents: long-term consequences for parent–child relationships and psychological well-being, *Journal of Marriage and Family*, 88, 222–235.

Amato, P.R., Booth, A., Johnson, D. and Rogers, S. (2007) *Alone Together: How Marriage in America Is Changing*. Cambridge, MA: Harvard University Press.

Amaya-Jackson, L. and March, J. (1995) Posttraumatic stress disorder, in J. March (ed.), *Anxiety Disorders in Children and Adolescents*. New York: Guilford.

Ambrosini, P. and Dixon, J.F. (1996) Schedule for affective disorders and schizophrenia for school-age children (K-SADS). Philadelphia: Allegheny University of Health Sciences.

American Academy of Child and Adolescent Psychiatry (1997) Practice parameters for the assessment and treatment of children, adolescents and adults with attention-deficit/hyperactivity disorder, *Journal of the American Academy of Child and Adolescent Psychiatry*, 36(suppl. 10), 85S–112S.

American Academy of Child and Adolescent Psychiatry (2007) Practice parameters for the assessment and treatment of children and adolescents with attention-deficit hyperactivity disorder, *Journal of the American Academy of Child and Adolescent Psychiatry*, 46, 894–921.

American Academy of Pediatrics and American College of Obstetricians and Gynecologists (2002) *Guidelines for Perinatal Care*. Elk Grove Village, IL: American Academy of Pediatrics.

American Association on Mental Retardation (AAMR) (1992) *Mental Retardation: Definition, Classification and Systems of Support*, 9th edn. Washington, DC: AAMR.

American Lung Association (ALA) (2009). *Trends in Asthma Morbidity and Mortality*. Washington, DC: American Lung Association.

American Psychiatric Association (APA) (1968) *Diagnostic and Statistical Manual of Mental Disorders*, 2nd edn. Washington, DC: APA.

American Psychiatric Association (APA) (1980) *Diagnostic and Statistical Manual of Mental Disorders*, 3rd edn. Washington, DC: APA.

American Psychiatric Association (APA) (1994) *Diagnostic and Statistical Manual of Mental Disorders*, 4th edn. Washington, DC: APA.

American Psychiatric Association (APA) (2000) *Diagnostic and Statistical Manual of Mental Disorders*, 4th edn, text revd. Washington, DC: APA.

American Psychological Association (APA) (2002a) *Criteria for evaluating treatment guidelines*. Washington, DC: APA.

American Psychological Association (APA) (2002) Ethical principles of psychologists and code of conduct, *American Psychologist*, 57, 1060–1073.

American Psychological Association (APA) (2003) Guidelines on multicultural education, training, research, practice and organizational change for psychologists, *American Psychologist*, 58(5), 377–402.

Ammerman, R.T. and Campo, J.V. (1998) *Handbook of Pediatric Psychology and Psychiatry: Disease, Injury and Illness*, London: Allyn & Bacon.

Andersen, S.L. and Teicher, M.H. (2009) Desperately driven and no brakes: developmental stress exposure and subsequent risk for substance abuse, *Neuroscience & Biobehavioral Reviews*, 33(4), 516–524.

Anderson, C.B. and Bulik, C.M. (2004) Gender differences in compensatory behaviors, weight and shape salience and drive for thinness, *Eating Behaviors*, 5(1), 1–11.

Anderson, K.G., Schweinsburg, A., Paulus, M.P., Brown, S.A. and Tapert, S. (2005a) Examining personality and alcohol expectancies using functional magnetic resonance imaging (fMRI) with adolescents, *Journal of Studies on Alcohol*, 66(3), 323–331.

Anderson, V. et al. (2005b) Functional plasticity or vulnerability after early brain injury? *Pediatrics*, 116(6), 1374–1382.

Anderson, V., Brown, S. and Newitt, H. (2010) What contributes to quality of life in adult survivors of childhood traumatic brain injury? *Journal of Neurotrauma*, 27(5), 863–870.

Andreß, H.-J., Borgloh, B., Bröckel, M., Giesselmann, M. and Hummelsheim, D. (2006) The economic consequences of partnership dissolution: a comparative analysis of panel studies from Belgium, Germany, Great Britain, Italy and Sweden, *European Sociological Review*, 22(5), 533–560.

Andriessen, T.M.J.C., Jacobs, B. and Vos, E. (2010) Clinical characteristics and pathophysiological mechanisms of focal and diffuse traumatic brain injury, *Journal of Cellular and Molecular Medicine*, 14(10), 2381–2392.

Anschutz, D.J., Kanters, L.J.A., van Strien, T., Vermulst, A.A. and Engels, R.C.M. E. (2009) Maternal behaviors and restrained eating and body dissatisfaction in young children, *International Journal of Eating Disorders*, 42(1), 54–61.

Anthonysamy, A. and Zimmer-Gembeck, M.J. (2007) Peer status and behaviors of maltreated children and their classmates in the early years of school, *Child Abuse & Neglect*, 31(9), 971–991.

Antshel, K. et al. (2011) Advances in understanding and treating ADHD, *BMC Medicine*, 9(1), 72.

Applegate, B., Lahey, B.B., Hart, E.L., Waldman, I., Biederman, J., Hynd, G.W., Barkley, R.A., Ollendick, T., Frick, P.J., Greenhill, L., McBurnett, K., Newcoren, J., Kerdyk, L., Garfinkel, B. and Shaffer, D. (1997) Validity of the age-of-onset criterion for ADHD: a report of the DSM-IV field trials, *Journal of the American Academy of Child and Adolescent Psychiatry*, 36, 1211–1221.

Apter, A. and Wasserman, D. (2003) Adolescent attempted suicide, in R.A. King and A. Apter (eds), *Suicide in Children and Adolescents*. Cambridge: Cambridge University Press.

Arns, M. et al. (2009) Efficacy of neurofeedback treatment in ADHD: the effects on inattention, impulsivity and hyperactivity: a meta-analysis, *Clinical EEG and Neuroscience Official Journal of the EEG and Clinical Neuroscience Society ENCS*, 40(3), 180–189.

Arseneault, L., Cannon, M., Poulton, R., Murray, R., Caspi, A. and Moffitt, T.E. (2002) Cannabis use in adolescence and risk for adult psychosis: longitudinal prospective study, *British Medical Journal*, 325, 1212–1213.

Asarnow, J.R. and Asarnow, R.F. (1996) Childhood-onset schizophrenia, in E.J. Marsh and R.A. Barkley (eds), *Child Psychopathology*. New York: Guilford Press.

Asarnow, J.R. and Asarnow, R.F. (2003) Childhood-onset schizophrenia, in E.J. Mash and R.A. Barkley (eds), *Child Psychopathology*, 2nd edn. New York: Guilford.

Asarnow, J.R., Carlson, G.A. and Guthrie, D. (1987) Coping strategies, self-perceptions, hopelessness and perceived family environments in depressed and suicidal children, *Journal of Consulting and Clinical Psychology*, 55(3), 361–366.

Asarnow, J.R., Goldstein, M., Carlson, G., Perdue, S., Bates, S. and Keller, J. (1988) Childhood-onset depressive disorders: a follow-up study of rates of rehospitalization and out-of-home placement among child psychiatric inpatients, *Journal of Affective Disorders*, 15, 245–253.

Asarnow, J.R., Tompson, M., Hamilton, E.B., Goldstein, M.J. and Guthrie, D. (1994) Family-expressed emotion, childhood-onset depression and childhood-onset schizophrenia spectrum disorders: is expressed emotion a nonspecific correlate of child psychopathology or a specific risk factor for depression? *Journal of Abnormal Child Psychology*, 22, 129–146.

Asarnow, J.R., Tompson, M.C. and McGrath, E.P. (2004) Annotation: childhood-onset schizophrenia: clinical and treatment issues, *Journal of Child Psychology and Psychiatry*, 45(2), 180–194.

Asarnow, R.F., Nuechterlein, K.H., Fogelson, D., Subotnik, K.L., Payne, D.A., Russell, A.T., et al. (2001) Schizophrenia and schizophrenia-spectrum personality disorders in the first-degree relatives of children with schizophrenia: the UCLA Family Study, *Archives of General Psychiatry*, 58, 581–588.

Asarnow, R.F. et al. (2002) Neurocognitive impairments in nonpsychotic parents of children with schizophrenia and attention-deficit/hyperactivity disorder: the University of California, Los Angeles Family Study, *Archives of General Psychiatry*, 59(11), 1053–1060.

Asperger, H. (1944) Die 'Autistischen Psychopathen' im Kindesalter, *European Archives of Psychiatry and Clinical Neuroscience*, 117(1), 76–136.

Attwood, A., Frith, U. and Hermelin, B. (1988) The understanding and use of interpersonal gestures by autistic and Down's syndrome children, *Journal of Autism and Developmental Disorders*, 18(2), 241–257.

Atyaclar, S., Tarter, R.E., Kirisci, L. and Lu, S. (1999) Association between hyperactivity and executive cognitive functioning in childhood and substance use in early adolescence, *Journal of the American Academy of Child and Adolescent Psychiatry*, 38, 172–178.

Aube, J., Fichman, L., Saltaris, C. and Koestner, R. (2000) Gender difference in adolescent depressive symptomatology: towards an integrated social-developmental model, *Journal of Social and Clinical Psychology*, 19(3), 297–313.

Axline, V. (1969) *Play Therapy.* New York: Ballantine.

Azar, S.T. and Weinzierl, K.M. (2005) Child maltreatment and childhood injury research: a cognitive behavioral approach, *Journal of Pediatric Psychology*, 30(7), 598–614.

Bailey, D.S. (2003) Who is learning disabled? Psychologists and educators debate over how to identify students with learning disabilities, *Monitor on Psychology*, 34, 58.

Bailey, J.R. and Gross, A.M. (2010) Cognitive assessment with children, in M. Thomas and M. Hersen (eds), *Handbook of Clinical Psychology Competencies*, vol. 2. New York: Springer.

Baird, G. et al. (2000). A screening instrument for autism at 18 months of age: a 6-year follow-up study, *Journal of the American Academy of Child & Adolescent Psychiatry*, 39(6), 694–702.

Baird, G. et al. (2006) Prevalence of disorders of the autism spectrum in a population cohort of children in South Thames: the Special Needs and Autism Project (SNAP), *The Lancet*, 368(9531), 210–215.

Bakan, D. (1966) *The Duality of Human Existence: Isolation and Communion in Western Man.* Boston, MA: Beacon Press.

Bakermans-Kranenburg, M.J., Van IJzendoorn, M.H and Juffer, F. (2003) Less is more: meta-analyses of sensitivity and attachment interventions in early childhood, *Psychological Bulletin*, 129(2), 195–215.

Bakermans-Kranenburg, M.J., van IJzendoorn, M.H. and Juffer, F. (2005) Disorganized infant attachment and preventive interventions: a review and meta-analysis, *Infant Mental Health Journal*, 26, 191–216.

Bakkaloğlu, H. (2010) A comparison of the loneliness levels of mainstreamed primary students according to their sociometric status, *Procedia-Social and Behavioral Sciences*, 2(2), 330–336.

Balint, M. (1968) *The Basic Fault: Therapeutic Aspects Of Regression.* London: Tavistock.

Ballaban-Gil, K. and Tuchman, R. (2000) Epilepsy and epileptiform EEG: association with autism and language disorders, *Mental Retardation and Developmental Disabilities Research Reviews*, 6(4), 300–308.

Ballon, B.C., Courbasson, C.M. and Smith, P.D. (2001) Physical and sexual abuse issues among youths with substance use problems, *Canadian Journal of Psychiatry*, 46(7), 617–621.

Baltaxe, C.A.M. and Simmons, J.Q. (1995) Speech and language disorders in children and adolescents with schizophrenia, *Schizophrenia Bulletin*, 21(4), 677–692.

Bandura, A. (1977) *Social Learning Theory.* New York: Holt, Rinehart & Winston.

Bandura, A. (1986) *Social Foundations of Thought and Action: A Social Cognitive Theory.* Englewood Cliffs, NJ: Prentice-Hall.

Bandura, A., Pastorelli, C., Barbaranelli, C. and Caprara, G.V. (1999) Self-efficacy pathways to childhood depression, *Journal of Personality and Social Psychology*, 76(2), 258–269.

Barber, B.K. (2002) *Intrusive Parenting: How Psychological Control Affects Children and Adolescents.* Washington, DC: American Psychological Association.

Bardo, M.T., Fishbein, D.H. and Milich, R. (eds) (2011) *Inhibitory Control and Drug Abuse Prevention: From Research to Translation.* New York: Springer Verlag.

Barkley, R.A. (1990) *Attention-Deficit Hyperactivity Disorder: A Handbook for Diagnosis and Treatment.* New York: Guilford.

Barkley, R.A. (1997) *ADHD and the Nature of Self-Control.* New York: Guilford.

Barkley, R.A. (1998) Attention-deficit/hyperactivity disorder, in E.J. Mash and R.A. Barkley (eds), *Treatment of Childhood Disorders.* New York: Guilford.

Barkley, R.A. (2003) Issues in the diagnosis of attention-deficit/hyperactivity disorder in children, *Brain and Development*, 25(2), 77–83.

Barkley, R.A. (2006) *Attention-Deficit Hyperactivity Disorder: A Handbook for Diagnosis and Treatment.* New York: Guilford Press.

Barkley, R.A. et al. (2002) International consensus statement on ADHD. January 2002, *Clinical Child and Family Psychology Review*, 5(2), 89–111.

Barnes, J.E., Noll, J.G., Putnam, F.W. and Trickett, P.K. (2009) Sexual and physical revictimization among victims of severe childhood sexual abuse, *Child Abuse & Neglect*, 33(7), 412–420.

Barnett, D., Manly, J.T. and Cicchetti, D. (1993) Defining child maltreatment: the interface between policy and research, in D. Cicchetti, S.L. Toth and I.E. Sigel (eds), *Child Abuse, Child Development and Social Policy: Advances in Applied Developmental Psychology.* Norwood, NJ: Ablex.

Barnhill, G.P. (2007) Outcomes in adults with Asperger syndrome, *Focus on Autism and Other Developmental Disabilities*, 22(2), 116–126.

Barnow, S., Spitzer, C., Grabe, H., Kessler, C. and Freyberger, H. (2006) Individual characteristics, familial experience and psychopathology in children of mothers with borderline personality disorder, *Journal of the American Academy of Child and Adolescent Psychiatry*, 45(8), 965–972.

Baron-Cohen, S. (1995) *Mindblindness*. Cambridge, MA: Bradford Book.

Baron-Cohen, S. (2000) Theory of mind and autism: a review, *International Review of Research in Mental Retardation*, 23, 169–184.

Baron-Cohen, S. (2002) The extreme male brain theory of autism, *Trends in Cognitive Sciences*, 6(6), 248–254.

Baron-Cohen, S. (2003) *The Essential Difference: The Truth about the Male and Female Brain*. New York: Basic Books.

Baron-Cohen, S. (2006) The hyper-systemizing, assortative mating theory of autism, *Progress in Neuro-Psychopharmacology and Biological Psychiatry*, 30(5), 865–872.

Baron-Cohen, S. (2008) *Autism and Asperger Syndrome*. New York: Oxford University Press.

Baron-Cohen, S., Leslie, A.M. and Frith, U. (1985) Does the autistic child have a 'theory of mind'?, *Cognition*, 21(1), 37–46.

Baron-Cohen, S., Bolton P., Wheelwright, S., Short, L., Mead, G., Smith, A. and Scahill, V. (1998) Autism occurs more often in families of physicists, engineers, and mathematicians, *Autism*, 2, 296–301.

Baron-Cohen, S., Wheelwright, S., Skinner, R. et al. (2001a) The Autism-Spectrum Quotient (AQ): evidence from Asperger syndrome/high-functioning autism, males and females, scientists and mathematicians, *Journal of Autism and Developmental Disorders*, 31(1), 5–17.

Baron-Cohen, S., Wheelwright, S., Spong, A., Scahill, V. and Lawson, J. (2001b) Are intuitive physics and intuitive psychology independent? A test with children with Asperger Syndrome, *Journal of Developmental and Learning Disorders*, 5(1), 47–78.

Barr, R., Lauricella, A., Zack, E. and Calvert, S.L. (2010) Infant and early childhood exposure to adult-directed and child-directed television programming: relations with cognitive skills at age four, *Merrill-Palmer Quarterly*, 56(1), 21–48.

Barrett, P.M., Farrell, L., Pina, A.A., Peris, T.S. and Piacentini, J. (2008) Evidence-based psychosocial treatments for child and adolescent obsessive–compulsive disorder, *Journal of Clinical Child & Adolescent Psychology*, 37(1), 131–155.

Barriga, A.Q., Sullivan-Cosetti, M. and Gibbs, J.C. (2009) Moral cognitive correlates of empathy in juvenile delinquents, *Criminal Behaviour and Mental Health*, 19(4), 253–264.

Barry, R.A., Kochanska, G. and Philibert, R.A. (2008) G × E interaction in the organization of attachment: mothers' responsiveness as a moderator of children's genotypes. *Journal of Child Psychology and Psychiatry*, 49(12), 1313–1320.

Bartels, L. and Crowder, D. (1999) Fatal friendship: How two boys traded baseball and bowling for murder and madness, *Rocky Mountain News*, http://denver.rockymountainsnews.com/shooting/0822fata1.shtm.

Bateman, B. et al. (2004) The effects of a double blind, placebo controlled, artificial food colourings and benzoate preservative challenge on hyperactivity in a general population sample of preschool children, *Archives of Disease in Childhood*, 89(6), 506–511.

Bateson, G. et al. (1956) Toward a theory of schizophrenia, *Behavioral Science*, 1(4), 251–264.

Battaglia, A. and Carey, J.C. (2003) Diagnostic evaluation of developmental delay/mental retardation: an overview, *American Journal of Medical Genetics Part C: Seminars in Medical Genetics*, 117(1), 3–14.

Baumeister, R.F., Bushman, B.J. and Campbell, W.K. (2000) Self-esteem, narcissism and aggression: does violence result from low self-esteem or threatened egotism? *Current Directions in Psychological Science*, 9(1), 26–29.

Baumrind, D. (1991a) Effective parenting during the early adolescent transition, in A. Cowan and E.M. Hetherington (eds), *Family Transitions*. Hillsdale, NJ: Erlbaum.

Baumrind, D. (1991b) The influences of parenting style on adolescent competence and substance use, *Journal of Early Adolescence*, 11, 56–95.

Bayley, N. (1969) *Bayley Scales of Infant Development: Birth to Two Years*. New York: Psychological Corporation.

Bayley, N. (1993) *Bayley Scales of Infant Development*. San Antonio, TX: Psychological Corporation.

Bayley, N. (2006) *Bayley Scales of Infant Development*. San Antonio, TX: Psychological Corporation.

Bayoumi, R.A. et al. (2006) The genetic basis of inherited primary nocturnal enuresis: A UAE study, *Journal of Psychosomatic Research*, 61(3), 317–320.

Bearman, S.K., Ugueto, A., Alleyne, A. and Weisz, J.R. (2010) Adapting cognitive-behavioral therapy: applying the deployment-focused model of treatment development and testing, in J.R. Weisz and A.E. Kazdin (eds), *Evidence-based Psychotherapies for Children and Adolescents*, 2nd edn. New York: Guilford Press.

Beauchaine, T., Klein, D., Crowell, S., Derbidge, C. and Gatzke-Kopp, L. (2009) Multifinality in the development of personality disorders: A Biology × Sex × Environment interaction model of antisocial and borderline traits, *Development and Psychopathology*, 21(03), 735–770.

Beauchaine, T.P., Hinshaw, S.P. and Gatzke-Kopp, L. (2008) Genetic and environmental influences on behavior, in T.P. Beauchaine and S.P. Hinshaw (eds), *Child and Adolescent Psychopathology*. Hoboken, NJ: John Wiley & Sons.

Beck, A.T. (2002) Cognitive models of depression, in R.L. Leahy and E.T. Dowd (eds), *Clinical Advances in Cognitive Psychotherapy: Theory and Application*. New York: Springer.

Beck, S.J. et al. (2010) A controlled trial of working memory training for children and adolescents with ADHD, *Journal of Clinical Child & Adolescent Psychology*, 39(6), 825–836.

Becker, D., McGlashan, T. and Grilo, C. (2006) Exploratory factor analysis of borderline personality disorder criteria in hospitalized adolescents, *Comprehensive Psychiatry*, 47(2), 99–105.

Becker, D.F., Grilo, C.M., Edell, W.S. and McGlashan, T.H. (2002) Diagnostic efficiency of borderline personality disorder criteria in hospitalized adolescents: comparison with hospitalized adults, *The American Journal of Psychiatry*, 159(12), 2042–2047, doi: 10.1176/appi.ajp.159.12.2042.

Bedford, H.E. and Elliman, D.A.C. (2010) MMR vaccine and autism, *British Medical Journal*, 340, c1294.

Beeghly, M. and Cicchetti, D. (1994) Child maltreatment, attachment and the self system: emergence of an internal state lexicon in toddlers at high social risk, *Development and Psychopathology*, 6(1), 5–30.

Beers, S.R. and De Bellis, M.D. (2002) Neuropsychological function in children with maltreatment-related posttraumatic stress disorder, *American Journal of Psychiatry*, 159, 483–486.

Begle, A.M., Dumas, J.E. and Hanson, R.F. (2010) Predicting child abuse potential: an empirical investigation of two theoretical frameworks, *Journal of Clinical Child and Adolescent Psychology*, 39(2), 208–219.

Behrens, K.Y., Hesse, E. and Main, M. (2007) Mothers' attachment status as determined by the Adult Attachment Interview predicts their 6-year-olds' reunion responses: a study conducted in Japan, *Developmental Psychology*, 43(6), 1553–1567.

Beidel, D.C., Turner, S.M. and Morris, T.L. (1999) The psychopathology of childhood social phobia, *Journal of the American Academy of Child and Adolescent Psychiatry*, 38, 643–650.

Beidel, D.C., Turner, S.M. and Morris, T.L. (2000) Behavioral treatment of childhood social phobia, *Journal of Consulting and Clinical Psychology*, 68, 1072–1080.

Beitchman, J.H. and Young, A.R. (1997) Learning disorders with a special emphasis on reading disorders: a review of the past 10 years, *Journal of the American Academy of Child & Adolescent Psychiatry*, 36(8), 1020–1032.

Beitchman, J.H., Zucker, K.J., Hood, J.E. and DaCosta, G.A. (1992) A review of the long-term effects of child sexual abuse, *Child Abuse & Neglect*, 16(1), 101–118.

Belsky, J., Conger, R. and Capaldi, D.M. (2009) The intergenerational transmission of parenting: introduction to the special section, *Developmental Psychology*, 45(5), 1201.

Bemporad, J.R. (1982) Management of childhood depression: developmental considerations, *Psychosomatics*, 23(3), 272–279.

Bemporad, J.R. and Schwab, M.E. (1986) The DSM-III and clinical child psychiatry, in T. Millon and G. L. Klerman (eds), *Contemporary Directions in Psychopathology: Toward the DSM-IV*. New York: Guilford.

Bemporad, J.R., Smith, H.F., Hanson, G. and Cicchetti, D. (1982) Borderline syndromes in childhood: criteria for diagnosis, *American Journal of Psychiatry*, 139(5), 596–602.

Bender, S.L. et al. (1995) For underprivileged children, standardized intelligence testing can do more harm than good: reply, *Journal of Developmental and Behavioral Pediatrics*, 16, 428–430.

Benedict, H.E. (2006) Object relations play therapy: applications to attachment problems and relational trauma, in C.E. Schaefer and H.G. Kaduson (eds), *Contemporary Play Therapy: Theory, Research and Practice*. New York: Guilford Press.

Bennett, T. et al. (2008) Differentiating autism and Asperger syndrome on the basis of language delay or impairment, *Journal of Autism and Developmental Disorders*, 38(4), 616–625.

Benoit, D. and Parker, K.C.H. (1994) Stability and transmission of attachment across three generations, *Child Development*, 65(5), 1444–1456.

Bentivegna, S.W., Ward, L.B. and Benivegna, N.P. (1985) Study of a diagnostic profile of the borderline syndrome in childhood and trends in treatment outcome, *Child Psychiatry and Human Development*, 15, 198–205.

Berlin, L., Cassidy, J. and Appleyard, K. (2008) The influence of early attachments on other relationships, in J. Cassidy and R. Shaver (eds), *Handbook of Attachment*. New York: Guilford.

Berliner, L. (2011) Child sexual abuse: definitions, prevalence and consequences, in J.F.B. Myers (ed.), *The APSAC Handbook on Child Maltreatment*. Thousand Oaks, CA: Sage.

Berman, A.L. and Jobes, D.A. (1991) *Adolescent Suicide. Assessment and Intervention*. Washington, DC: American Psychological Association.

Bernal, G., Jiménez-Chafey, M.I. and Domenech Rodríguez, M.M. (2009) Cultural adaptation of treatments: a resource for considering culture in evidence-based practice, *Professional Psychology: Research and Practice*, 40(4), 361–368.

Bernardini, L., Alesi, V., Loddo, S., et al. (2010) High-resolution SNP arrays in mental retardation diagnostics: how much do we gain & quest. *European Journal of Human Genetics*, 18(2), 178–185.

Bernstein, A.C. and Cowan, P.A. (1975) Children's concepts of how people get babies, *Child Development*, 46, 77–91.

Bernstein, D.P., Cohen, P., Velez, C.N., Schwab-Stone, M., Siever, L.J. and Shinsato, L. (1993) Prevalence and stability of the DSM-III-R personality disorders in a community-based survey of adolescents, *American Journal of Psychiatry*, 150, 1237–1243.

Berry, J.G. et al. (2010) Health inequity in children and youth with chronic health conditions, *Pediatrics*, 126(supplement), S111–S119.

Best, K.M. and Hauser, S.T. (2011) Origins of adolescent psychiatric hospitalization: using archival records to understand the lives of adolescent psychiatric patients, in P.K. Kerig, M.S. Schulz and S.T. Hauser (eds), *Adolescence and Beyond: Family Processes in Development*. New York: Oxford University Press.

Bethell, C.D. et al. (2011) A national and state profile of leading health problems and health care quality for US children: key insurance disparities and across-state variations, *Academic Pediatrics*, 11(3), S22–S33.

Bettelheim, B. (1967) *The Empty Fortress: Infantile Autism and the Birth of the Self*. Oxford: Free Press.

Bettelheim, B. (1983) *Freud and Man's Soul*. New York: Knopf.

Beyer, H.A. (1991) Litigation involving people with mental retardation, in J.L. Matson and J.A. Mulick (eds), *Handbook of Mental Retardation*. New York: Pergamon.

Biederman, J. (2003) Pharmacotherapy for attention-deficit/hyperactivity disorder (ADHD) decreases the risk for substance

abuse: findings from a longitudinal follow-up of youths with and without ADHD, *Journal of Clinical Psychiatry*, 64(supplement 11), 3–8.

Biederman, J. Monuteaux, M.C., Mick, E., Spencer, T., Wilens, T.E., Silva, J.M., Snyder, L.E., Farone, S.V. (2006) Young adult outcome of attention deficit hyperactivity disorder: a controlled 10-year follow-up study, *Psychological Medicine*, 36(2), 167–179.

Biederman, J., Santangelo, S.L., Faraone, S.V., Kiely, K., Guite, J., Mick, E., Reed, E.D., Kraus, I., Jellinek, M. and Perrin, J. (1995) Clinical correlates of enuresis in ADHD and non-ADHD children, *Journal of Child Psychology and Psychiatry*, 36(5), 865–877.

Bifulco, A. (2008) Intergenerational study of high-risk young people in London, in D. Brom, R. Pat-Horenczyk and J. Ford (eds), *Treating Traumatised Children: Risk Resilience and Recovery*. London: Routledge.

Birkett, M., Espelage, D. and Koenig, B. (2009) LGB and questioning students in schools: the moderating effects of homophobic bullying and school climate on negative outcomes, *Journal of Youth and Adolescence*, 38(7), 989–1000.

Birmaher, B., Axelson, D., Goldstein, B., Strober, M., Gill, M.K., Hunt, J. et al. (2009) Four-year longitudinal course of children and adolescents with bipolar spectrum disorders: the Course and Outcome of Bipolar Youth (COBY) study, *American Journal of Psychiatry*, 166(7), 795–804.

Birmaher, B., Axelson, D., Goldstein, B., Monk, K., Kalas, C., Obreja, M. et al. (2010) Psychiatric disorders in preschool offspring of parents with bipolar disorder: the Pittsburgh Bipolar Offspring Study (BIOS), *American Journal of Psychiatry*, 167(3), 321–330.

Bishop, D.V.M. et al. (2008) Autism and diagnostic substitution: evidence from a study of adults with a history of developmental language disorder, *Developmental Medicine & Child Neurology*, 50(5), 341–345.

Björn, G.J., Bodén, C., Sydsjö, G. and Gustafsson, P.A (2011) Psychological evaluation of refugee children: contrasting results from play diagnosis and parental interviews, *Clinical Child Psychology and Psychiatry*, 12 May, doi: 10.1177/1359104510384550.

Black, D.A., Heyman, R.E. and Smith-Slep, A.M. (2001) Risk factors for child physical abuse, *Aggression and Violent Behavior*, 6(2/3), 121–188.

Blader, J.C. and Carlson, G.A. (2007) Increased rates of bipolar disorder diagnoses among U.S. child, adolescent and adult inpatients, 1996–2004, *Biological Psychiatry*, 62(2), 107–114.

Blader, J.C. and Carlson, G.A. (2008) Bipolar disorder, in T.P. Beauchaine and S.P. Hinshaw (eds), *Child and Adolescent Psychopathology*. Hoboken, NJ: John Wiley & Sons.

Blagg, N. and Yule, W. (1994) School phobia, in T.H. Ollendick, N.J. King and W. Yule (eds), *International Handbook of Phobic and Anxiety Disorders in Children and Adolescents*. New York: Plenum Press.

Blakemore, J.E.O., Berenbaum, S.A. and Liben, L.S. (2008) *Gender Development*. New York: Psychology Press.

Blanchfield, L. (2009) *The United Nations Convention on the Rights of the Child: Background and Policy Issues*. Washington, DC: Congressional Research Service.

Blanck, R. and Blanck, G. (1992) *Ego Psychology: Theory and Practice*. New York: Columbia University Press.

Blatt, S.J. (2004) *Experiences of Depression: Theoretical, Clinical and Research Perspectives*. Washington, DC: American Psychological Association.

Blatt, S.J. and Homann, E. (1992) Parent–child interaction in the etiology of dependent and self-critical depression, *Clinical Psychology Review*, 12, 47–91.

Blatt, S.J., Zohar, A., Quinlan, D.M. and Luthar, S. (1996) Levels of relatedness within the dependency factor of the Depression Experience

Questionnaire for Adolescents, *Journal of Personality Assessment*, 67(1), 52–71.

Bleiberg, E. (2001) *Treating Personality Disorders in Children and Adolescents: A Relational Approach.* New York: Guilford.

Blinder, B.J., Cumella, E.J. and Sanathara, V.A. (2006) Psychiatric comorbidities of female inpatients with eating disorders, *Psychosomatic Medicine*, 68(3), 454–462.

Block, J., Block, J. H. and Keyes, S. (1988) Longitudinally foretelling drug usage in adolescence: Early childhood personality and environmental processes, *Child Development*, 59, 336–355.

Block, J.H. (1973) Conceptions of sex role: some cross-cultural and longitudinal perspectives, *American Psychologist*, 28, 512–526.

Block, J.H. (1983) Differential premises arising from differential socialization of the sexes: some conjectures, *Child Development*, 54, 1335–1354.

Block, J.H. and Block, J. (1980) The role of ego-control and ego-resiliency in the organization of behavior, in W.A. Collins (ed.), *Minnesota Symposia on Child Psychology.* Hillsdale, NJ: Erlbaum.

Bloom, D.R. et al. (2001) Lifetime and novel psychiatric disorders after pediatric traumatic brain injury, *Journal of the American Academy of Child & Adolescent Psychiatry*, 40(5), 572–579.

Blum, R.W. (1992) Chronic illness and disability in adolescence, *Journal of Adolescent Health*, 13, 364–368.

Boden, J.M., Fergusson, D.M. and Horwood, J.L. (2010) Risk factors for conduct disorder and oppositional/defiant disorder: evidence from a New Zealand birth cohort, *Journal of the American Academy of Child & Adolescent Psychiatry*, 49(11), 1125–1133.

Boergers, J. and Spirito, A. (2003) The outcome of suicide attempts among adolescents, in A. Spirito

and J. C. Overholser (eds), *Evaluating and Treating Adolescent Suicide Attempters: From Research to Practice.* New York: Academic Press.

Bolton, D., Luckie, M. and Steinberg, D. (1995) Long-term course of obsessive-compulsive disorder treated in adolescence, *Journal of the American Academy of Child and Adolescent Psychiatry*, 34, 1441–1450.

Bond, M. (2004) Empirical studies of defense style: relationships with psychopathology and change, *Harvard Review of Psychiatry*, 12, 263–278.

Bondy, A.S. and Frost, L.A. (1994) The picture exchange communication system, *Focus on Autism and Other Developmental Disabilities*, 9(3), 1.

Bongers, I.L., Koot, H.M., van der Ende, J. and Verhulst, F.C. (2003) The normative development of child and adolescent problem behavior, *Journal of Abnormal Psychology*, 112(2), 179–192.

Bontempo, D.E. and D'Augelli, A.R. (2002) Effects of at-school victimization and sexual orientation on lesbian, gay, or bisexual youths' health risk behavior, *Journal of Adolescent Health*, 30(5), 364–374.

Boris, N.W., Zeanah, C.H., Larrieu, J.A., Scheeringa, M.S. and Heller, S.S. (1998) Attachment disorders in infancy and early childhood: a preliminary investigation of diagnostic criteria, *American Journal of Psychiatry*, 155, 295–297.

Bornovalova, M.A., Hicks, B.M., Iacono, W.G. and McGue, M. (2009) Stability, change and heritability of borderline personality disorder traits from adolescence to adulthood: a longitudinal twin study, *Development and Psychopathology*, 21(4), 1335–1353.

Bornstein, M. and Lansford, J.E. (2010) Parenting, in M.H. Bornstein (ed.), *Handbook of Cultural Developmental Science:* New York: Psychology Press.

Bornstein, M.H. (ed.) (2010) *Handbook of Cultural Developmental Science.* New York: Psychology Press.

Bornstein, M.H. and Lamb, M.E. (eds) (2010) *Developmental Science: An Advanced Textbook.* 6th edn. New York: Taylor & Francis.

Bornstein, R.F. and Masling, J.M. (2005) The Rorschach Oral Dependency Scale, in R.F. Bornstein and J.M. Masling (eds), *Scoring the Rorschach: Seven Validated Systems.* Mahwah, NJ: Erlbaum.

Borowsky, I.W., Ireland, M. and Resnick, M.D. (2009) Health status and behavioral outcomes for youth who anticipate a high likelihood of early death, *Pediatrics*, 124(1), 81–88.

Bosmans, G., Braet, C. and Van Vlierberghe, L. (2010) Attachment and symptoms of psychopathology: early maladaptive schemas as a cognitive link? *Clinical Psychology & Psychotherapy*, 17(5), 374–385.

Bowlby, J. (1944) Forty-four juvenile thieves: their characters and home-life, *International Journal of Psychoanalysis*, 25, 19–53.

Bowlby, J. (1960) *The Psychoanalytic Study of the Child. Vol. 15: Grief and Mourning in Infancy and Early Childhood.* New York: International Universities Press.

Bowlby, J. (1982a) Attachment and loss: retrospect and prospect, *American Journal of Orthopsychiatry*, 52(4), 664–678.

Bowlby, J. (1982b) *Attachment and Loss: Vol 1. Attachment*, 2nd edn. New York: Basic Books.

Bowlby, J. (1988a) Developmental psychiatry comes of age, *American Journal of Psychiatry*, 145(1), 1–10.

Bowlby, J. (1988b) *A Secure Base: Parent–Child Attachment and Healthy Human Development.* New York: Basic Books.

Boyle, M.H., Offord, D.R., Racine, Y.A., Szatmari, P., Sanford, M. and Fleming, J.E. (1996) Interviews versus checklists: adequacy for classifying childhood psychiatric disorder based on adolescent reports, *International Journal of Methods in Psychiatric Research*, 6(4), 309–319.

Bradford, K., Barber, B.K., Olsen, J.A., Maughan, S.L., Erickson, L.D., Ward, D. and Stolz, H.E. (2003) A multi-national study of interparental conflict, parenting and adolescent functioning: South Africa, Bangladesh, China, India, Bosnia, Germany, Palestine, Columbia and the United States, *Marriage and Family Review*, 35(3/4), 107–137.

Bradley, R., Conklin, C.Z. and Westen, D. (2005) The borderline personality diagnosis in adolescents: gender differences and subtypes, *Journal of Child Psychology and Psychiatry*, 46, 1006–1019.

Bratton, S.C., Ray, D., Rhine, T. and Jones, L. (2005) The efficacy of play therapy with children: a meta-analytic review of treatment outcomes, *Professional Psychology: Research and Practice*, 36(4), 376–390.

Bravender, T., Bryant-Waugh, R., Herzog, D., Katzman, D., Kriepe, R.D., Lask, B. et al. (2010) Classification of eating disturbance in children and adolescents: proposed changes for the DSM-V, *European Eating Disorders Review*, 18(2), 79–89.

Braver, S.L., Shapiro, J.R. and Goodman, M.R. (2006) Consequences of divorce for parents, in M.A. Fine and J.H. Harvey (eds), *Handbook of Divorce and Relationship Dissolution*. Mahwah, NJ: Erlbaum.

Bray, J.H., Adams, G.J., Getz, G. and Baer, P.E. (2001) Developmental, family and ethnic influences on adolescent alcohol usage: a growth curve approach, *Journal of Family Psychology*, 15(2), 301–314.

Brennan, P.A., Hall, J.A., Bor, W., Najman, J.M. and Williams, G.M. (2003) Integrating biological and social processes in relation to early-onset persistent aggression in boys and girls, *Developmental Psychology*, 39(2), 309–323.

Brennan, P.A., Le Brocque, R. and Hammen, C. (2003a) Maternal depression, parent–child relationships and resilient outcomes in adolescence, *Journal of the American Academy of Child & Adolescent Psychiatry*, 42(12), 1469–1477.

Brent, D.A. and Mann, J.J. (2003) Familial factors in adolescent suicidal behavior, in R.A. King and A. Apter (eds), *Suicide in Children and Adolescents*. Cambridge: Cambridge University Press.

Brent, D.A., Perper, J.A., Moritz, G. and Liotus, L. (1994) Familial risk factors for adolescent suicide: a case-control study, *Acta Psychiatrica Scandinavica*, 89, 52–58.

Bretherton, I. and Munholland, K.A. (2008) Internal working models in attachment relationships, in J. Cassidy and P.R. Shaver (eds), *Handbook of Attachment*. New York: Guilford.

Brezina, T., Tekin, E. and Topalli, V. (2009) 'Might not be a tomorrow': a multimethods approach to anticipated early death and youth crime, *Criminology: An Interdisciplinary Journal*, 47(4), 1091–1129.

Brisch, K.H. (2002) *Treating Attachment Disorders: From Theory to Therapy*. New York: Guilford.

Britto, M.T. et al. (2004) Health care preferences and priorities of adolescents with chronic illnesses, *Pediatrics*, 114(5), 1272–1280.

Brodsky, B.S., Mann, J.J., Stanley, B., Tin, A., Oquendo, M., Birmaher, B. et al. (2008) Familial transmission of suicidal behavior: factors mediating the relationship between childhood abuse and offspring suicide attempts, *The Journal of Clinical Psychiatry*, 69(4), 584–596.

Brody, G.H. and Ge, X. (2001) Linking parenting processes and self-regulation to psychological functioning and alcohol use during early adolescence, *Journal of Family Psychology*, 15(1), 82–94.

Brody, G. H., Murry, V. M., Gerrard, M., Gibbons, F. X., Molgaard, V., McNair, L. et al. (2004) The Strong African American Families Program: translating research into prevention programming, *Child Development*, 75(3), 900–917.

Brody, L.R. and Hall, J. (2008) Gender and emotion in context, in M. Lewis, J. Haviland-Jones and L.F. Barrett (eds), *Handbook of Emotions*, 3rd edn. New York: Guilford Press.

Broidy, L.M., Nagin, D.S., Tremblay, R.E., Bates, J.E., Brame, B., Dodge, K.A. et al. (2003) Developmental trajectories of childhood disruptive behaviors and adolescent delinquency: a six-site, cross-national study, *Developmental Psychology*, 39(2), 222–245.

Brooks-Gunn, J. et al. (2003) The Black-White test score gap in young children: contributions of test and family characteristics, *Applied Developmental Science*, 7(4), 239–252.

Brotman, M.A., Schmajuk, M., Rich, B.A., Dickstein, D.P., Guyer, A.E., Costello, E.J. et al. (2006) Prevalence, clinical correlates and longitudinal course of severe mood dysregulation in children, *Biological Psychiatry*, 60(9), 991–997.

Brown, A.S. and Susser, E.S. (2003) Prenatal risk factors for schizophrenia, in D. Cicchetti and E. Walker (eds), *Neurodevelopmental Mechanisms in Psychopathology*. New York: Cambridge University Press.

Brown, B.B. (1999) 'You're going out with who?': Peer group influences on adolescent romantic relationships, in W. Furman, B.B. Brown and C. Feiring (eds), *The Development of Romantic Relationships in Adolescence*, 291–329. Cambridge, UK: Cambridge University Press.

Brown, L.M. (1999) *Raising their Voices: The Politics of Girls' Anger*. Cambridge, MA: Harvard University Press.

Brown, S.A. (2008) Prevalence of alcohol and drug involvement during childhood and adolescence, in T.P. Beauchaine and S.P. Hinshaw (eds), *Child and Adolescent Psychopathology*. Hoboken, NJ: Wiley.

Brown, S.A. and Abrantes, A.M. (2006) Substance use disorders, in D.A. Wolfe and E.J. Mash (eds), *Behavioral and Emotional Disorders in Adolescents: Nature, Assessment and Treatment*. New York: Guilford.

Brown, S.A., McGue, M., Maggs, J., Schulenberg, J., Hingson, R., Swartzwelder, S. et al. (2008) A developmental perspective on alcohol and youths 16 to 20 years of age, *Pediatrics*, 121(supplement 4), S290–S310.

Brown, S.A., McGue, M., Maggs, J., Schulenberg, J., Hingson, R., Swartzwelder, S. et al. (2009) Underage alcohol use: summary of developmental processes and mechanisms: ages 16–20, *Alcohol Research & Health*, 32(1), 41–52.

Brown, S.L. and Manning, W.D. (2009) Family boundary ambiguity and the measurement of family structure: the significance of cohabitation, *Demography*, 46, 85–101.

Bruch, H. (1973) Psychiatric aspects of obesity, *Psychiatric Annals*, 3(7), 6–10.

Bruffaerts, R., Demyttenaere, K., Borges, G., Haro, J.M., Chiu, W.T., Hwang, I. et al. (2010) Childhood adversities as risk factors for onset and persistence of suicidal behaviour, *British Journal of Psychiatry*, 197(1), 20–27.

Brunner, R., Henze, R., Parzer, P., Kramer, J., Feigl, N., Lutz, K., Essig, M., Resch, F. and Stieltjes, B. (2010) Reduced prefrontal and orbitofrontal gray matter in female adolescents with borderline personality disorder: is it disorder specific? *NeuroImage*, 49(1), 114–120.

Brymer, M., Jacobs, A., Layne, C., Pynoos, R., Ruzek, J., Steinberg, A., Vernberg, E. and Watson, P. (National Child Traumatic Stress Network and National Center for PTSD) (2006) Psychological first aid field operations guide. Retrieved from www.nctsn.org or www.ncptsd.va.gov.

Buckley, S.J., Bird, G., Sacks, B. (2006) Evidence that we can change the profile from a study of inclusive education, *Down syndrome Research & Practice*, 9(3), 51–53.

Bulik, C.M., Sullivan, P.F., Tozzi, F., Furberg, H., Lichtenstein, P. and Pedersen, N.L. (2006) Prevalence, heritability and prospective risk factors for anorexia nervosa, *Archives of General Psychiatry*, 63(3), 305–312.

Burke, J.D., Waldman, I. and Lahey, B.B. (2010) Predictive validity of childhood oppositional defiant disorder and conduct disorder: implications for the DSM-V, *Journal of Abnormal Psychology*, 119(4), 739–751.

Burleson, J.A. and Kaminer, Y. (2005) Self-efficacy as a predictor of treatment outcome in adolescent substance use disorders, *Addictive Behaviors*, 30(9), 1751–1764.

Burns, R.C. (1982) *Self-growth in Families: Kinetic Family Drawings (KFD) Research and Application*. New York: Brunner/Mazel.

Burt, S.A., McGue, M., Krueger, R.F. and Iacono, W.G. (2005) How are parent–child conflict and childhood externalizing symptoms related over time? Results from a genetically informative cross-lagged study, *Development and Pychopathology*, 17(1), 145–165.

Bustillo, J.R., Lauriello, J., Horan, W.P. and Keith, S.J. (2001) The psychosocial treatment of schizophrenia: an update, *American Journal of Psychiatry*, 158, 163–175.

Butcher, J.N., Atlis, M.M. and Hahn, J. (2004) The Minnesota Multiphasic Personality Inventory–2 (MMPI-2), in M. Hersen (ed.), *Comprehensive Handbook of Psychological Assessment: Personality Assessment*. Hoboken, NJ: John Wiley & Sons.

Butler, R.J. (1993) Establishing a dry run: a case study in securing bladder control, *British Psychological Society*, 32, 215–217.

Caeyenberghs, K. et al. (2011) Correlations between white matter integrity and motor function in traumatic brain injury patients, *Neurorehabilitation and Neural Repair*, 25(6), 492–502.

Cahill, B.M. and Glidden, L.M. (1996) Influence of child diagnosis on family and parental functioning: Down syndrome versus other disabilities, *American Journal on Mental Retardation*, 101(2), 149–160.

Calkins, S.D. (1994) Origins and outcomes of individual differences in emotion regulation, *Monographs of the Society for Research in Child Development*, 59, 53–72.

Calkins, S.D. and Keane, S.P. (2009) Developmental origins of early antisocial behavior, *Development and Psychopathology*, 21(4), 1095–1109.

Camp, B.W. et al. (1998) Maternal and neonatal risk factors for mental retardation: defining the 'at-risk' child, *Early Human Development*, 50(2), 159–173.

Campbell, F.A., Pungello, E.P., Miller-Johnson, S., Burchinal, M.R. and Ramey, C. (2001) The development of cognitive and academic abilities: Growth curves from an early childhood educational experiment, *Developmental Psychology*, 37(2), 231–242.

Campbell, F.A., Ramey, C.T., Pungello, E., Sparling, J. and Miller-Johnson, S. (2002) Early childhood education: young adult outcomes from the Abecedarian Project, *Applied Developmental Science*, 6(1), 42–57.

Campbell, R.L. (2006) *Jean Piaget's Genetic Epistemology: Appreciation and Critique*, http://hubcap.clemson.edu/ ~ campber/piaget.html (retrieved 25 September 2010).

Campbell, S.B. (1989) Developmental perspectives, in T.H. Ollendick and M. Hersen (eds), *Handbook of Child Psychopathology*, 2nd edn. New York: Plenum.

Campbell, S.B. (2002) *Behavior Problems in Preschool Children: Clinical and Developmental Issues*, 2nd edn. New York: Guilford.

Campbell, S.B. (2006b) *Behavior Problems in Preschool Children: Clinical and Developmental Issues*. New York: Guilford Press.

Campbell, S.B. et al. (1991) Hard-to-manage preschool boys: family context and the stability of externalizing behavior, *Journal of Abnormal Child Psychology*, 19(3), 301–318.

Campbell, S.B., Shaw, D.S. and Gilliom, M. (2000) Early externalizing behavior problems: toddlers and preschoolers at risk for later maladjustment, *Development and Psychopathology*, 12(3), 467–488.

Canals, J., Sancho, C. and Arija, M.V. (2009) Influence of parent's eating attitudes on eating disorders in school adolescents, *European Child & Adolescent Psychiatry*, 18(6), 353–359.

Canino, G. et al. (2004) The DSM-IV rates of child and adolescent disorders in Puerto Rico: prevalence, correlates, service use and the effects of impairment, *Archives of General Psychiatry*, 61(1), 85–93.

Cannon, M., Caspi, A., Moffitt, T.E., Harrington, H., Taylor, A., Murray, R.M. et al. (2002) Evidence for early-childhood, pan-developmental impairment specific to schizophreniform disorder: results from a longitudinal birth cohort, *Archives of General Psychiatry*, 59(5), 449–456.

Cantor, S. (1988) *Childhood Schizophrenia*. New York: Guilford.

Cantwell, D.P. (1996) Classification of child and adolescent psychopathology, *Journal of Child Psychology and Psychiatry*, 35, 978–987.

Capaldi, D.M. and Patterson, G.R. (1994) Interrelated influences of contextual factors on antisocial behavior in childhood and adolescence for males, in D.C. Fowles, P. Sutker and S.H. Goodman (eds), *Progress in Experimental Personality and Psychopathology Research*. New York: Springer.

Caplan, R. and Sherman, T. (1990) Thought disorder in the childhood psychoses, in B.B. Lahey and A.E. Kazdin (eds), *Advances in Clinical Child Psychology*, vol. 13. New York: Plenum.

Caplan, R. et al. (2004) Psychopathology and pediatric complex partial seizures: seizure-related, cognitive and linguistic variables, *Epilepsia*, 45(10), 1273–1281.

Cappelletty, G.G., Brown, M.M. and Shumate, S.E. (2005) Correlates of the Randolph Attachment Disorder Questionnaire (RADQ) in a sample of children in foster placement, *Child and Adolescent Social Work Journal*, 22(1), 71–84.

Capps, L., Sigman, M. and Mundy, P. (1994) Attachment security in children with autism, *Development and Psychopathology*, 6(02), 249–261.

Caprara, G.V., Barbarnelli, C. and Pastorelli, C. (2001) Prosocial behavior and aggression in childhood and pre-adolescnence, in A.C. Bohart and D.J. Stipek (eds), *Constructive and Destructive Behavior: Implications for Family, School and Society*. Washington, DC: American Psychological Association.

Carbonell, D.M., Reinherz, H.Z., Giaconia, R.M., Stashwick, C.K., Paradis, A.D. and Beardslee, W.R. (2002) Adolescent protective factors promoting resilience in young adults at risk for depression, *Child and Adolescent Social Work Journal*, 19, 393–412.

Carey, T.A. and Pilgrim, D. (2010) Diagnosis and formulation: what should we tell the students? *Clinical Psychology & Psychotherapy*, 17(6), 447–454.

Carlat, D.J., Camargo, C.A. Jr and Herzog, D.B. (1997) Eating disorders in males: a report on 135 patients, *American Journal of Psychiatry*, 154(8), 1127–1132.

Carlson, B.E. (1990) Adolescent observers of marital violence, *Journal of Family Violence*, 5, 285–299.

Carlson, C.L. and Mann, M. (2002) Sluggish cognitive tempo predicts a different pattern of impairment in the attention deficit hyperactivity disorder, predominantly inattentive type, *Journal of Clinical Child & Adolescent Psychology*, 31, 123–129.

Carlson, E. and Sroufe, L.A. (1995) Contribution of attachment theory to developmental psychopathology, in D. Cicchetti and D.J. Cohen (eds), *Developmental Psychopathology. Vol. I: Theory and Methods*. New York: Wiley.

Carlson, E.A., Egeland, B. and Sroufe, L.A. (2009) A prospective investigation of the development of borderline personality symptoms, *Development and Psychopathology*, 21(4), 1311–1334.

Carr, A. (2006) *The Handbook of Child and Adolescent Clinical Psychology: A Contextual Approach*, Philadelphia, PA: Psychology Press.

Carr, E.G., Horner, R.H., Turnbull, A.P., Marquis, J.G., McLaughlin, D.M., McAtee, M.L. et al. (1999) *Positive Behavior Support for People with Developmental Disabilities: A Research Synthesis*. Washington, DC, American Association on Mental Retardation.

Carroll, J.B. (1993) *Human Cognitive Abilities: A Survey of Factor-Analytic Studies*. Cambridge: Cambridge University Press.

Carver, C.S. and Scheier, M.F. (2010) Self-regulation of action and affect, in K.D. Vohs and R.F. Baumeister (eds), *Handbook of Self-Regulation*, 2nd edn. New York: Guilford.

Casper, R.C. and Troiani, M. (2001) Family functioning in anorexia nervosa differs by subtype, *International Journal of Eating Disorders*, 30(3), 338–342.

Casper, R.C., Hedeker, D. and McClough, J.F. (1992) Personality dimensions in eating disorders and their relevance for subtyping, *Journal of the American Academy of Child & Adolescent Psychiatry*, 31(5), 830–840.

Caspi, A. (1987) Personality in the life course, *Journal of Personality and Social Psychology*, 53(6), 1203–1213.

Caspi, A. and Elder, G.H. (1988) Emergent family patterns: the intergenerational construction of problem behavior and relationships, in R.A. Hinde and J. Stevenson-Hinde (eds), *Relationships within Families: Mutual Influences*. Oxford: Clarendon Press.

Caspi, A. and Shiner, R.L. (2007) Personality development, in W. Damon and N. Eisenberg (eds), *Handbook of Child Psychology, Vol 3: Social, Emotional and Personality Development*, 6th edn. New York: Wiley.

Caspi, A., Elder, G.H. and Bem, D.J. (1987) Moving against the world: life-course patterns of explosive children, *Developmental Psychology*, 23(2), 308–313.

Caspi, A., Elder, G.H. and Bem, D.J. (1988) Moving away from the world: life-course patterns of shy children, *Developmental Psychology*, 24(6), 824–831.

Caspi, A., Lynam, D., Moffitt, T.E. and Silva, P.A. (1993) Unraveling girls' delinquency: biological, dispositional and contextual contributions to adolescent misbehavior, *Developmental Psychology*, 29, 19–30.

Caspi, A., McClay, J., Moffitt, T.E., Mill, J., Martin, J., Craig, I.W., et al. (2002) Role of genotype in the cycle of violence in maltreated children, *Science*, 297(5582), 851–854.

Caspi, A., Moffitt, T.E., Thornton, A. and Freedman, D. (1996) The life history calendar: a research and clinical assessment method for collecting retrospective event-history data, *International Journal of Methods in Psychiatric Research*, 6(2), 101–114.

Caspi, A., Sugden, K., Moffitt, T.E., Taylor, A., Craig, I.W., Harrington, H. et al. (2003) Influence of life stress on depression: moderation by a polymorphism in the 5-HTT gene, *Science*, 301(5631), 386–389.

Cassidy, J. (2008) The nature of the child's ties, in J. Cassidy and P.R. Shaver (eds), *Handbook of Attachment*. New York: Guilford.

Cassidy, J. and Shaver, PR. (2008) *Handbook of Attachment: Theory, Research And Clinical Application*, 2nd edn. New York: Guilford.

Cassidy, S.B. and Morris, C.A. (2002) Behavioral phenotypes in genetic syndromes: genetic clues to human behavior, *Advances in Pediatrics*, 49, 59–86.

Castellanos, F.X. et al. (2008) Cingulate-precuneus interactions: a new locus of dysfunction in adult attention-deficit/hyperactivity disorder, *Biological Psychiatry*, 63(3), 332–337.

Castillo, R.J. (1997) *Culture and Mental Illness*. Pacific Grove, CA: Brooks/Cole.

Castro, M.N. et al. (2009) Heart rate variability response to mental arithmetic stress is abnormal in first-degree relatives of individuals with schizophrenia, *Schizophrenia Research*, 109(1–3), 134–140.

Catroppa, C. and Anderson, V. (2007) Recovery in memory function and its relationship to academic success, at 24 months following pediatric TBI*, *Child Neuropsychology*, 13(3), 240–261.

Catroppa, C. et al. (2011) Attentional skills 10 years post-paediatric traumatic brain injury (TBI), *Brain Injury*, 29(9), 1–12.

Cave, B.K. (2004) Brain injured students at my school? In my room? *The Clearing House*, 77(4), 169–171.

Ceballos, N., Houston, R., Hesselbrock, V. and Bauer, L. (2006) Brain maturation in conduct disorder versus borderline personality disorder, *Neuropsychobiology*, 53(2), 94–100.

Centers for Disease Control (CDC) (2009) Youth Risk Behavior Survey, http://apps.nccd.cdc.gov/youthonline/App/Default.aspx.

Centers for Disease Control (CDC) (2010) Youth Risk Behavior Survey, http://apps.nccd.cdc.gov/youthonline/App/Default.aspx.

Centers for Disease Control and Prevention (2006) *National Center for Injury Prevention and Control*, http://www.cdc.gov (retrieved 23 February 2006).

Cermolacce, M., Sass, L. and Parnas, J. (2010) What is bizarre in bizarre delusions? A critical review, *Schizophrenia Bulletin*, 36(4), 667–679.

Chabrol, H. and Leichsenring, F. (2006) Borderline personality organization and psychopathic traits in nonclinical adolescents: relationships of identity diffusion, primitive defense mechanisms and reality testing with callousness and impulsivity traits, *Bulletin of the Menninger Clinic*, 70(2), 160–170.

Chaffin, M., Letourneau, E. and Silovsky, J.F. (2002) Adults, adolescents and children who sexually abuse children: a developmental perspective, in J.E.B. Myers, L. Berliner, J. Briere, C.T. Hendrix, C. Jenny and T.A. Reid (eds), *The APSAC Handbook on Child Maltreatment*, 2nd edn. Thousand Oaks, CA: Sage.

Chaffin, M., Silovsky, J.F., Funderburk, B., Valle, L.A., Brestan, E.V., Balachova, T. et al. (2004) Parent–child interaction therapy with physically abusive parents: efficacy for reducing future abuse reports, *Journal of Consulting and Clinical Psychology*, 72(3), 500–510.

Chambless, D.L. and Hollon, S.D. (1998) Defining empirically supported therapies, *Journal of Consulting and Clinical Psychology*, 66, 7–18.

Chambless D.L. and Ollendick T.H. (2001) Empirically supported psychological interventions:

controversies and evidence, *Annual Review of Psychology*, 52, 685–716.

Chan, T.W. and Koo, A. (2010) Parenting style and youth outcomes in the UK, *European Sociological Review*, 26(5), 385–389.

Chandler, M.J., Lalonde, C.E., Sokol, B.W. and Hallett, D. (2003) *Personal Persistence, Identity Development and Suicide: A Study of Native and Non-Native North American Adolescents*, vol. 68. Oxford: Blackwell.

Chanen, A., Jackson, H., McCutcheon, L., Jovev, M., Dudgeon, P., Yuen, H. et al. (2008a) Early intervention for adolescents with borderline personality disorder using cognitive analytic therapy: randomised controlled trial, *The British Journal of Psychiatry*, 193(6), 477–484.

Chanen, A., Velakoulis, D., Carison, K., Gaunson, K., Wood, S., Yuen, H. et al. (2008b) Orbitofrontal, amygdala and hippocampal volumes in teenagers with first-presentation borderline personality disorder, *Psychiatry Research: Neuroimaging*, 163(2), 116–125.

Chang, L., Schwartz, D., Dodge, K.A. and McBride-Chang, C. (2003) Harsh parenting in relation to child emotion regulation and aggression, *Journal of Family Psychology*, 17(4), 598–606.

Chang, S. and Piacentini, J. (2002) Childhood obsessive-compulsive and tic disorders, in D.T. Marsh and M.A. Fristad (eds), *Serious Emotional Disturbance in Children and Adolescents*. New York: Wiley.

Chao, R.K. (2001) Extending research on the consequences of parenting style for Chinese Americans and European Americans, *Child Development*, 72(6), 1832–1843.

Charlop, M.H., Dennis, B., Carpenter, M.H. and Greenberg, A.L. (2010) Teaching socially expressive behaviors to children with autism through video modeling, *Education and Treatment of Children*, 33(3), 371–393.

Charlop-Christy, M.H. et al. (2002) Using the picture exchange communication system (PECS) with children with autism: assessment of PECS acquisition, speech, social-communicative behavior and problem behavior, *Journal of Applied Behavior Analysis*, 35(3), 213–231.

Charman, T. and Baron-Cohen, S. (1997) Brief report: prompted pretend play in autism, *Journal of Autism and Developmental Disorders*, 27(3), 325–332.

Charman, T. et al. (2005) Outcome at 7 years of children diagnosed with autism at age 2: predictive validity of assessments conducted at 2 and 3 years of age and pattern of symptom change over time, *Journal of Child Psychology and Psychiatry*, 46(5), 500–513.

Chassin, L. and Hussong, A. (2009) Adolescent substance use, in R.M. Lerner and R. Steinberg (eds), *Handbook of Adolescent Psychology*. New York: Wiley.

Chassin, L., Pitts, S. and Prost, J. (2002) Heavy drinking trajectories from adolescence to young adulthood in a high risk sample: predictors and substance abuse outcomes, *Journal of Consulting and Clinical Psychology*, 70, 67–78.

Chassin, L., Ritter, J., Trim, R.S. and King, K.M. (2003) Adolescent substance abuse disorders, in E.J. Mash and R.A. Barkley (eds), *Child Psychopathology*, 2nd edn. New York: Guilford.

Cheadle, J.E. (2008) Educational investment, family context and children's math and reading growth from kindergarten through the third grade, *Sociology of Education*, 81(1), 1–31.

Chen, E., Cole, S.W. and Kato, M. (2004) A review of empirically supported psychosocial interventions for pain and adherence outcomes in sickle cell disease, *Journal of Pediatric Psychology*, 29(3), 197–209.

Chen, S.X., Chan, W., Bond, M.H. and Stewart, S.M. (2006) The effects of self-efficacy and relationship harmony on depression across cultures: applying level-oriented and structure-oriented analyses, *Journal of Cross-Cultural Psychology*, 37(6), 643–658.

Chen, W., Landau, S. et al. (2004) No evidence for links between autism, MMR and measles virus, *Psychological Medicine*, 34(3), 543–553.

Chesney-Lind, M. and Belknap, J. (2004) Trends in delinquent girls' aggression and violent behavior: a review of the evidence, in M. Putallaz and K.L. Bierman (eds), *Aggression, Antisocial Behavior and Violence Among Girls*. New York: Guilford.

Chess, S. and Thomas, A. (1990) Continuities and discontinuities in temperament, in L. Robins and M. Rutter (eds), *Straight and Devious Pathways from Childhood to Adulthood*. Cambridge: Cambridge University Press.

Chess, S. and Thomas, A. (1999) *Goodness of Fit: Clinical Applications From Infancy through Adult Life*. New York: Brunner/Mazel.

Chisholm, K. C., Carter, M. C., Ames, E. W. and Morison, S. J. (1995). Attachment security and indiscriminately friendly behavior in children adopted from Romanian orphanages, *Development and Psychopathology*, 7(2), 283–294.

Chodorow, N. J. (1989) *Feminism and Psychoanalytic Theory*. New Haven, CT: Yale University Press.

Chorpita, B.F. (2002) The tripartite model and dimensions of anxiety and depression: an examination of structure in a large school sample, *Journal of Abnormal Child Psychology*, 30(2), 177–190.

Christakis, D.M., Zimmerman, F.J., DiGiuseppe, D.L. and McCarty, C.A. (2004) Early television exposure and subsequent attentional problems in children, *Pediatrics*, 113, 708–713.

Christenson, S.L. and Buerkle, K. (1999) Families as educational partners for children's school success: suggestions for school psychologists, *The Handbook of School Psychology*, 3, 709–744.

Chronis, A.M. et al. (2007) Maternal depression and early positive parenting predict future conduct problems in young children with attention-deficit/hyperactivity disorder, *Developmental Psychology*, 43(1), 70–82.

Chuang, S., Lamb, M. and Hwang, C. (2006) Personality development from childhood to adolescence: a longitudinal study of ego-control and ego-resiliency in Sweden, *International Journal of Behavioral Development*, 30(4), 338–343.

Cicchetti, D. (2006) Development and psychopathology, in D. Cicchetti and D. J. Cohen (eds), *Developmental Psychopathology, Volume I: Theory and Method*, 2nd edn. New York: Wiley.

Cicchetti, D. and Crick, N. R. (2009a) Precursors and diverse pathways to personality disorder in children and adolescents, *Development and Psychopathology*, 21(3), 683–685.

Cicchetti, D. and Crick, N. R. (2009b) Special issue: Precursors and diverse pathways to personality disorder in children and adolescents: Part 2, *Development and Psychopathology*, 21(3), 1031–1394.

Cicchetti, D. and Howes, P.W. (1991) Developmental psychopathology in the context of the family: illustrations from the study of child maltreatment, *Canadian Journal of Behavioural Science*, 23, 257–281.

Cicchetti, D. and Rogosch, F. (2009) Adaptive coping under conditions of extreme stress: multilevel influences on the determinants of resilience in maltreated children, *New Directions for Child and Adolescent Development*, 2009(124), 47–59.

Cicchetti, D. and Rogosch, F.A. (2001) The impact of child maltreatment and psychopathology on neuroendocrine functioning, *Development and Psychopathology*, 13(4), 783–804.

Cicchetti, D. and Toth, S.L. (2005) Child maltreatment, *Annual Review of Clinical Psychology*, 1(1), 409–438.

Cicchetti, D. and Toth, S.L. (2009) The past achievements and future promises of developmental psychopathology: the coming of age of a discipline, *Journal of Child Psychology and Psychiatry*, 50(1–2), 16–25.

Cicchetti, D. and Valentino, K. (2006) An ecological-transactional perspective on child maltreatment: failure of the average expectable environment and its influence on child development, in D. Cicchetti and D. J. Cohen (eds), *Developmental Psychopathology. Volume III: Risk, Disorder and Adaptation*, 2nd edn. New York: Wiley.

Cicchetti, D. and Walker, E. (2003) *Neurodevelopmental Mechanisms in Psychopathology*. New York: Cambridge.

Cicchetti, D., Toth, S.L., Bush, M.A. and Gillespie, J.F. (1988) Stage-salient issues: a transactional model of intervention, in E.D. Nannis and P.A. Cowan (eds), *Developmental Psychopathology and its Treatment*. San Francisco, CA: Jossey-Bass.

Clark, D.B., Thatcher, D.L. and Cornelius, J.R. (2008) Anxiety disorders and adolescent substance use disorders, in Y. Kaminer and O.G. Bukstein (eds), *Adolescent Substance Abuse: Psychiatric Comorbidity and High-Risk Behaviors*. New York: Routledge/Taylor & Francis Group.

Clark, D.M. (2001) A cognitive perspective on social phobia, in W. Crozier and L.E. Alden (eds), *International Handbook of Social Anxiety: Concepts, Research and Interventions Relating to the Self and Shyness*. New York: Wiley.

Clark, L.A. and Watson, D. (1991) Tripartite model of anxiety and depression: psychometric evidence and taxonomic implications, *Journal of Abnormal Psychology*, 100(3), 316–336.

Clarke, G.N., DeBar, L.L. and Lewinsohn, P.M. (2003) Cognitive-behavioral group treatment for adolescent depression, in A.E. Kazdin and J.R. Weisz (eds), *Evidence-Based Psychotherapies for Children and Adolescents*. New York: Guilford.

Cluver, L., Gardner, F. and Operario, D. (2009) Poverty and psychological health among AIDS-orphaned children in Cape Town, South Africa, *AIDS Care: Psychological and Sociomedical Aspects of AIDS/HIV*, 21(6), 732–741.

Cobham, V.E., Dadds, M.R. and Spence, S.H. (1998) The role of parental anxiety in the treatment of childhood anxiety, *Journal of Consulting and Clinical Psychology*, 66(6), 893–905.

Cohen, J. and Scheeringa, M. (2009) Post-traumatic stress disorder diagnosis in children: challenges and promises, *Translational Research*, 11, 91–99.

Cohen, J.A., Berliner, L. and Mannarino, A. (2000) Treating traumatized children: a research review and synthesis, *Trauma, Violence and Abuse: A Review Journal*, 1, 29–46.

Cohen, J.A., Mannarino, A.P. and Deblinger, E. (2006) *Treating Trauma and Traumatic Grief in Children and Adolescents*. New York: Guilford.

Cohen, J.A., Mannarino, A.P. and Dulcan, M.K. (2010) *Posttraumatic Stress Disorder Dulcan's Textbook of Child and Adolescent Psychiatry*. Arlington, VA: American Psychiatric Publishing.

Coker, T., Elliott, M., Kanouse, D., Grunbaum, J., Schwebel, D., Gilliland, M. et al. (2009) Perceived racial/ethnic discrimination among fifth-grade students and its association with mental health, *American Journal of Public Health*, 99(5), 878–884.

Cole, P.M., Llera, S.J. and Pemberton, C.K. (2009) Emotional instability, poor emotional awareness and the development of borderline personality, *Development and Psychopathology*, 21(4), 1293–1310.

Coles, E.K., Slavec, J., Bernstein, M. and Baroni, E. (2010) Exploring the gender gap in referrals for children with ADHD and other disruptive behavior disorders, *Journal of*

Attention Disorders, 13 September, doi: 10.1177/1087054710381481.

Collinson, S.L., Mackay, C.E., James, A.C., Quested, D.J., Phillips, T., Roberts, N. and Crow, T.J. (2003) Brain volume, asymmetry and intellectual impairment in relation to sex in early-onset schizophrenia, *British Journal of Psychiatry*, 183, 114–120.

Collishaw, S. et al. (2007b) Modelling the contribution of changes in family life to time trends in adolescent conduct problems, *Social Science & Medicine*, 65(12), 2576–2587.

Collishaw, S., Pickles, A., Messer, J., Rutter, M., Shearer, C. and Baughan, B. (2007a) Resilience to adult psychopathology following childhood maltreatment: evidence from a community sample, *Child Abuse & Neglect*, 31(3), 211–229.

Colonnesi, C., Stams, G.J.J.M., Van der Bruggen, C.O., Draijer, E.M., Bögels, S.M. and Noom, M.J. (2011) The relation between attachment and child anxiety: a meta-analytic review, *Journal of Clinical Child and Adolescent Psychology*, 40(4), 630–645.

Commission on Adolescent Eating Disorders (2005) Defining eating disorders, in D.L. Evans, E.B. Foa, R.E. Gur, H. Hendin, C.P.O'Brien, M.E.P. Seligman et al. (eds), *Treating and Preventing Adolescent Mental Health Disorders: What We Know and What We Don't Know*. New York: Oxford University Press.

Compas, B.E., Jaser, S.S. and Benson, M.A. (2009) Coping and emotion regulation: implications for understanding depression during adolescence, in S. Nolen-Hoeksema and L.M. Hilt (eds), *Handbook of Depression in Adolescents*. New York: Routledge/Taylor & Francis Group.

Compian, L.J., Gowen, L.K. and Hayward, C. (2009) The interactive effects of puberty and peer victimization on weight concerns and depression symptoms among early adolescent girls, *The Journal of Early Adolescence*, 29(3), 357–375.

Compton, S.N., Nelson, A.H. and March, J.S. (2000) Social phobia and separation anxiety symptoms in community and clinical samples of children and adolescents, *Journal of the American Academy of Child and Adolescent Psychiatry*, 39, 1040–1046.

Conduct Problems Prevention Research Group (2011) The effects of the Fast Track preventive intervention on the development of conduct disorder across childhood, *Child Development*, 82(1), 331–345.

Conger, R., Conger, K. and Martin, M. (2010) Socioeconomic status, family processes and individual development, *Journal of Marriage and Family*, 72(3), 685–704.

Conger, R.D. and Simons, R.L. (1997) Life-course contingencies in the development of adolescent antisocial behavior: a Matching Law approach, in T.P. Thornberry (ed.), *Developmental Theories of Crime and Delinquency*. Piscataway, NJ: Transaction Publishers.

Conley, C.S. and Rudolph, K.D. (2009) The emerging sex difference in adolescent depression: interacting contributions of puberty and peer stress, *Development and Psychopathology*, 21(2), 593–620.

Conners, C.K. (1980) *Food Additives and Hyperactive Children*. Plenum, New York.

Conners, C.K. (2000) *Conners' Continuous Performance Test II (CPT II V. 5)*. North Tonawanda, NY: Multi-Health Systems.

Consensus Statement (2002) International consensus statement on ADHD. *Clinical Child and Family Psychology Review*, 5(2), 89–111.

Cook, G.A. and Roggman, L.A. (2010) Three-generation attachment: how grandmothers and mothers contribute to children's attachment security, *Family Science*, 1(2), 112–122.

Cook, R.J. and Cusack, S. (2010) *Gender Stereotyping: Transnational Legal Perspectives*. Philadelphia, PA: University of Pennsylvania Press.

Coolidge, F., Thede, L. and Jang, K. (2001) Heritability of personality disorders in childhood: a preliminary investigation, *Journal of Personality Disorders*, 15(1), 33–40.

Cooper, M.L. (1994) Motivations for alcohol use among adolescents: development and validation of a four-factor model, *Psychological Assessment*, 6, 117–128.

Cooper, M.L., Frone, M.R., Russell, M. and Mudar, P. (1995) Drinking to regulate positive and negative emotions: a motivational model of alcohol use, *Journal of Personality and Social Psychology*, 69, 990–1005.

Copeland, W.E., Shanahan, L., Costello, J. and Angold, A. (2009) Childhood and adolescent psychiatric disorders as predictors of young adult disorders, *Archives of General Psychiatry*, 66(7), 764–772.

Corbin, J.R. (2007) Reactive attachment disorder: a biopsychosocial disturbance of attachment, *Child and Adolescent Social Work Journal*, 24(6), 539–552.

Cordero, L., Rudd, M.D., Bryan, C.J. and Corso, K.A. (2008) Accuracy of general practitioners' understanding of the FDA black box warning label, *Primary Care and Community Psychiatry*, 13, 109–114.

Cormier, D.C., McGrew, K.S. and Evans, J.J. (2011) Quantifying the 'Degree of Linguistic Demand' in spoken intelligence test directions, *Journal of Psychoeducational Assessment*, 19 May, doi: 10. 1177/0734282911405962.

Cornelius, J.R. and Clark, D.B. (2008) Depressive disorders and adolescent substance use disorders, in Y. Kaminer and O.G. Bukstein (eds), *Adolescent Substance Abuse: Psychiatric Comorbidity and High-Risk Behaviors*. New York: Routledge/Taylor & Francis Group.

Costello, E.J. et al. (1984) Testing of the NIMH Diagnostic Interview Schedule for Children (DISC) in a clinical population: final report to the Center for Epidemiological Studies, NIMH, Pittsburgh, University of Pittsburgh.

Costello, E.J., Erkanli, A., Fairbank, J.A. and Angold, A. (2002) The prevalence of potentially traumatic events in childhood and adolescence, *Journal of Traumatic Stress*, 15(2), 99–112.

Costello, E.J., Farmer, E.M.Z., Angold, A., Burns, B.J. and Erkanli, A. (1997) Psychiatric disorders among American Indian and White youth in Appalachia: the great Smoky Mountains study, *American Journal of Public Health*, 87(5), 827–832.

Costello, E.J., Loeber, R. and Stouthamer-Loeber, M. (1991) Pervasive and situational hyperactivity: confounding effect of informant, *Journal of Child Psychology and Psychiatry*, 32, 367–376.

Costello, E.J., Mustillo, S., Erklani, A., Keeler, G. and Angold, A. (2003) Prevalence and development of psychiatric disorders in childhood and adolescence, *Archives of General Psychiatry*, 60(8), 837–844.

Costello, E.J., Sung, M., Worthman, C. and Angold, A. (2007) Pubertal maturation and the development of alcohol use and abuse, *Drug and Alcohol Dependence*, 88, S50–S59.

Council for Training in Evidence-Based Behavioral Practice (2008) *Definition and Competencies for Evidence-Based Behavioral Practice (EBBP)*, http://www.behavioralinstitute.org/FreeDownloads/TIPS/EBBP_Competencies%20for%20evidence-based%20practice%205-2008.pdf (retrieved 20 July 2011).

Coutinho, M.J. and Oswald, D.P. (2005) State variation in gender disproportionality in special education, *Remedial and Special Education*, 26(1), 7–15.

Cowan, P.A. (1978) *Piaget with Feeling*. New York: Holt, Rinehart & Winston.

Craig, K.D. and Grunau, R.V.E. (1991) Developmental issues: infants and toddlers, in J.P. Bush and S.W. Harkins (eds), *Children in Pain: Clinical And Research Issues from a Developmental Perspective*. New York: Springer-Verlag.

Cramer, P. (2009) The development of defense mechanisms from pre-adolescence to early adulthood: a longitudinal study, *Journal of Research in Personality*, 43, 464–471.

Crandell, L., Patrick, M. and Hobson, R. (2003) 'Still-face' interactions between mothers with borderline personality disorder and their 2-month-old infants, *The British Journal of Psychiatry*, 183(3), 239–247.

Crick, N.R. and Dodge, K.A. (1994) A review and reformulation of social information-processing mechanisms in children's social adjustment, *Psychological Bulletin*, 115(1), 74–101.

Crick, N.R. and Rose, A.J. (2000) Toward a gender-balanced approach to the study of social-emotional development: a look at relational aggression, in P.H. Miller and E. Kofsky Scholnick (eds), *Toward a Feminist Developmental Psychology*. Florence, KY: Taylor & Frances/Routledge.

Crick, N.R., Murray-Close, D. and Woods, K. (2005) Borderline personality features in childhood: a short-term longitudinal study, *Development and Psychopathology*, 17(4), 1051–1070.

Crisp, J., Ungerer, J.A. and Goodnow, J.J. (1996) The impact of experience on children's understanding of illness, *Journal of Pediatric Psychology*, 21(1), 57–72.

Crittenden, P.M. (1988) Relationships at risk, in J. Belsky and T. Nezworski (eds), *Clinical Implications of Attachment*. Hillsdale, NJ: Erlbaum.

Crittenden, P.M. (1993) An information-processing perspective on the behavior of neglectful parents, *Criminal Justice and Behavior*, 20, 27–48.

Crockenberg, S.C., Leerkes, E.M. and Jo, P.S.B. (2008) Predicting aggressive behavior in the third year from infant reactivity and regulation as moderated by maternal behavior, *Development and Psychopathology*, 20(1), 37–54.

Croen, L.A. et al. (2007) Maternal and paternal age and risk of autism spectrum disorders, *Archives of Pediatrics and Adolescent Medicine*, 161(4), 334–340.

Crow, S.J. and Smiley, N. (2010) Costs and cost-effectiveness in eating disorders, in W.S. Agras (ed.), *The Oxford Handbook of Eating Disorders*. New York: Oxford University Press.

Crow, T.J., Done, D.J. and Sacker, A. (1995) Childhood precursors of psychosis as clues to its evolutionary origins, *European Archives of Psychiatry and Clinical Neuroscience*, 245(2), 61–69.

Crowell, J.A. and Waters, E. (1990) Separation anxiety, in M. Lewis and S.M. Miller (eds), *Handbook of Developmental Psychopathology*. New York: Plenum.

Crowell, S., Beauchaine, T. and Lenzenweger, M.F. (2008b) The development of borderline personality and self-injurious behavior, in T.P. Beauchaine and S.P. Hinshaw (eds), *Child Psychpathology*. Hoboken, NJ: John Wiley & Sons.

Crowell, S., Beauchaine, T., McCauley, E., Smith, C., Vasilev, C. and Stevens, A. (2008a) Parent–child interactions, peripheral serotonin, and self-inflicted injury in adolescents, *Journal of Consulting and Clinical Psychology*, 76(1), 15–21.

Crowell, S., Beauchaine, T. and Linehan, M. (2009) A biosocial developmental model of borderline personality: elaborating and extending Linehan's theory, *Psychological Bulletin*, 135(3), 495–510.

Cuddy-Casey, M. and Orvaschel, H. (1997) Children's understanding of death in relation to child suicidality and homicidality, *Clinical Psychology Review*, 17(1), 33–45.

Cuijpers, P., Jonkers, R., De Weerdt, I. and De Jong, A. (2002) The effects of drug abuse prevention at school: the 'Healthy school and drugs' project, *Addiction*, 97(7), 67–73.

Culbert, K.M., Burt, S.A., McGue, M., Iacono, W.G. and Klump, K.L. (2009) Puberty and the genetic diathesis of disordered eating attitudes and behaviors, *Journal of Abnormal Psychology*, 118(4), 788–796.

Cullen, D. (2004) The depressive and the psychopath: at last we know why the Columbine killers did it, *Slate*, http://slate. msn. com/id/2099203/.

Cummings, E.M. and Cummings, J.S. (2002) Parenting and attachment, in M.H. Bornstein (ed.), *Handbook of Parenting: Vol. 5: Practical Issues in Parenting*. Mahwah, NJ: Erlbaum.

Cummings, E.M. and Davies, P.T. (2010) *Marital Conflict and Children: An Emotional Security Perspective*. New York: Guilford Press.

Cunha, A.I., Relvas, A.P. and Soares, I. (2009) Anorexia nervosa and family relationships: perceived family functioning, coping strategies, beliefs and attachment to parents and peers, *International Journal of Clinical and Health Psychology*, 9(2), 229–240.

Currin, L., Schmidt, U., Treasure, J. and Jick, H. (2005) Time trends in eating disorder incidence, *British Journal of Psychiatry*, 186(2), 132–135.

Curtis, W.C. and Cicchetti, D. (2007) Emotion and resilience: a multilevel investigation of hemispheric electroencephalogram asymmetry and emotion regulation in maltreated and non-maltreated children, *Development and Psychopathology*, 19, 811–840.

Cyr, C., Euser, E., Bakermans-Kranenburg, M. and Van IJzendoorn, M. (2010) Attachment security and disorganization in maltreating and high-risk families: a series of meta-analyses, *Development and Psychopathology*, 22, 87–108.

Cyr, M., McDuff, P. and Wright, J. (2006) Prevalence and predictors of dating violence among adolescent female victims of child sexual abuse, *Journal of Interpersonal Violence*, 21(8), 1000–1017.

Dadds, M.R. and Roth, J.H. (2001) Family processes in the development of anxiety problems, in M.W. Vasey and M.R. Dadds (eds), *The Developmental Psychopathology of Anxiety*. New York: Oxford University Press.

Dadds, M.R., Ryan, S., Barrett, P.M. and Rapee, R.M. (1993) *Family Anxiety Coding Schedule Procedures Manual*. Brisbane: University of Queensland.

Dadds, M.R., Barrett, P.M. and Rapee, R.M. (1996) Family process and child anxiety and aggression: an observational analysis, *Journal of Abnormal Child Psychology*, 24(6), 715–734.

Daley, K.A., Jimerson, D.C., Heatherton, T.F., Metzger, E.D. and Wolfe, B.E. (2008) State self-esteem ratings in women with bulimia nervosa and bulimia nervosa in remission, *International Journal of Eating Disorders*, 41(2), 159–163.

Daley, T.C. (2004) From symptom recognition to diagnosis: children with autism in urban India, *Social Science & Medicine*, 58(7), 1323–1335.

Dandreaux, D.M. and Frick, P.J. (2009) Developmental pathways to conduct problems: a further test of the childhood and adolescent-onset distinction, *Journal of Abnormal Child Psychology*, 37(3), 375–385.

Dann, R. (2011) Look out! 'Looked after'! Look here! Supporting 'looked after'and adopted children in the primary classroom, *Education 3–13*, 99999(1), 1–11.

Dare, C. and Eisler, I. (1997) Family therapy for anorexia nervosa, in D.M. Garner and P.E. Garfinkel (eds), *Handbook of Treatment for Eating* Disorders, 2nd edn. New York: Guilford Press.

Daro, D., Edleson, J.L. and Pinderhughes, H. (2004) Finding common ground in the study of child maltreatment, youth violence and adult domestic violence, *Journal of Interpersonal Violence*, 19(3), 282–298.

Daversa, M.T. and Knight, R.A. (2007) A structural examination of the predictors of sexual coercion against children in adolescent sexual offenders, *Criminal Justice and Behavior*, 34(10), 1313–1333.

David-Ferdon, C. and Kaslow, N.J. (2008) Psychosocial treatments for child and adolescent depression, *Journal of Clinical Child & Adolescent Psychology*, 37(1), 62–104.

Davies, D. (2010) *Child Development: A Practitioner's Guide*, 3rd edn. New York: Guilford.

Davison, K.K. and Birch, L.L. (2001) Weight status, parent reaction and self-concept in five-year-old girls, *Pediatrics*, 107(1), 46–53.

Dawes, M.A., Antelman, S.M., Vanyukov, M.M., Giancola, P., Tarter, R.E., Susman, E.J. et al. (2000) Developmental sources of variation in liability to adolescent substance use disorders, *Drug and Alcohol Dependence*, 61(1), 3–14.

Dawson, G. (1991) A psychobiological perspective on the early socialemotional development of children with autism, in D. Cicchetti and S.L. Toth (eds), *Rochester Symposium on Developmental Psychopathology*. Rochester, NY: University of Rochester.

Dawson, G. and Osterling, J. (1997) Early intervention in autism, in M.J. Guralnick (ed.), *The Effectiveness of Early Intervention*. Baltimore, MD: Brookes.

Dawson, G. et al. (2004) Early social attention impairments in autism: social orienting, joint attention and attention to distress, *Developmental Psychology*, 40(2), 271–283.

Dawson, G., Frey, K., Panagiotides, H. and Osterling, J. (1997) Infants of depressed mothers exhibit atypical frontal brain activity: a replication and extension of previous findings, *Journal of Child Psychology and Psychiatry*, 38(2), 179–186.

Dawson, G., Webb, S. et al. (2002) Defining the broader phenotype of autism: genetic, brain and behavioral perspectives, *Development and Psychopathology*, 14(3), 581–611.

Day, C. (2008) Children's and young people's involvement and participation in mental health care, *Child and Adolescent Mental Health*, 13(1), 2–8.

Day, J., Schmidt, U., Collier, D., Perkins, S., Van den Eynde, F., Treasure, J. et al. (2011) Risk factors, correlates and markers in early-onset bulimia nervosa and EDNOS, *International Journal of Eating Disorders*, 44(4), 287–294.

De Bellis, M.D. (2001) Developmental traumatology: the psychobiological development of maltreated children and its implications for research, treatment and policy, *Development and Psychopathology*, 13(3), 539–564.

De Bruin, E.I. et al. (2007) High rates of psychiatric co-morbidity in PDD-NOS, *Journal of Autism and Developmental Disorders*, 37(5), 877–886.

De Clercq, B., De Fruyt, F., Van Leeuwen, K. and Mervielde, I. (2006) The structure of maladaptive personality traits in childhood: a step toward an integrative developmental perspective for DSM-V, *Journal of Abnormal Psychology*, 115, 639–657.

De Clercq, B., Van Leeuwen, K., Van Den Noortgate, W., De Bolle, M. and De Fruyt, F. (2009) Childhood personality pathology: dimensional stability and change, *Development and Psychopathology*, 21(3), 853–869.

De Graaf, R., Radovanovic, M., van Laar, M., Fairman, B., Degenhardt, L., Aguilar-Gaxiola, S. et al. (2010) Early cannabis use and estimated risk of later onset of depression spells: epidemiologic evidence from the population-based World Health Organization World Mental Health Survey Initiative, *American Journal of Epidemiology*, 172(2), 149–159.

De los Reyes, E.C. (2010). Autism and immunizations: separating fact from fiction, *Archives of Neurology*, 67(4), 490–492.

De Ruiter, K.P. et al. (2007) Developmental course of psychopathology in youths with and without intellectual disabilities, *Journal of Child Psychology and Psychiatry*, 48(5), 498–507.

De Wilde, E.J., Kienhorst, I.C.W.M. and Diekstra, R.F.W. (2001) Suicidal behaviour in adolescents, in I.M. Goodyer (ed.), *The Depressed Child and Adolescent*, 2nd edn. New York: Cambridge University Press.

Deater-Deckard, K. and Dodge, K.A. (1997) Externalizing behavior problems and discipline revisited: nonlinear effects and variation by culture, context and gender, *Psychological Inquiry*, 8, 161–175.

Deblinger, E., Mannarino, A.P., Cohen, J.A. and Steer, R.A. (2006) A follow-up study of a multisite, randomized, controlled trial for children with sexual abuse-related PTSD symptoms, *Journal of the American Academy of Child & Adolescent Psychiatry*, 45(12), 1474–1484.

Deblinger, E., Behl, L.E. and Glickman, A.R. (2011) Trauma-focused cognitive-behavioral therapy for children who have experienced sexual abuse, in C.K. Philip (ed.), *Child and Adolescent Therapy: Cognitive-Behavioral Procedures*, 4th edn. New York: Guilford.

DeFrances, C.J. et al. (2008) 2006 National Hospital Discharge Survey, *US Centers for Disease Control and Prevention National Health Statistics Reports*, no. 5, 30 July, 1–20.

DeKlyen, M. (1996) Disruptive behavior disorder and intergenerational attachment patterns: a comparison of clinic-referred and normally functioning preschoolers and their mothers, *Journal of Consulting and Clinical Psychology*, 64(2), 357–365.

DeKlyen, M. and Greenberg, M.T. (2008) Attachment and psychopathology in childhood, in J. Cassidy and P.R. Shaver (eds), *Handbook of Attachment: Theory, Research and Clinical Applications*, 2nd edn. New York: Guilford Press.

Delis, D.C., Kaplan, E. and Kramer, J.H. (2001). *Delis-Kaplan Executive Function System*. San Antonio, TX: Psychological Corporation.

Dennis, M. (2010) Margaret Kennard (1899–1975): Not a 'Principle'of brain plasticity but a founding mother of developmental neuropsychology, *Cortex*, 46(8), 1043–1059.

Dennis, T.A., Cole, P.M., Zahn-Waxler, C. and Mizuta, I. (2002) Self in context: autonomy and relatedness in Japanese and US mother-preschooler dyads, *Child Development*, 73(6), 1803–1817.

Department for Education and Skills (DfES) (2005) *Academies Evaluation – 2nd Annual Report*. London: The Stationery Office.

Depue, R.A., Krauss, S. and Spoont, M. (1987) A two dimensional threshold model of seasonal bipolar affective disorder, in D. Magnusson and A. Ohman (eds), *Psychopathology: An Interactions Perspective*. New York: Academic Press.

Diamond, G., Siqueland, L. and Diamond, G.M. (2003) Attachment-based family therapy for depressed adolescents: programmatic treatment development, *Clinical Child and Family Psychology Review*, 6(2), 107–127.

Diamond, G.S., Wintersteen, M.B., Brown, G.K., Diamond, G.M., Gallop, R., Shelef, K. and Levy, S. (2010) Attachment-based family therapy for adolescents with suicidal ideation: a randomized controlled trial, *Journal of the American Academy of Child and Adolescent Psychiatry*, 49(2), 122–131.

Diamond, L.M. (2008) *Sexual Fluidity: Understanding Women's Love and Desire*. New York: Harvard University Press.

Didden, R., Duker, C. and Korzilius, H. (1997) Meta-analytic study on treatment effectiveness for problem behaviors with individuals who have mental retardation, *American*

Journal on Mental Retardation, 101, 387–399.

DiGennaro Reed, F.D., Hyman, S.R. and Hirst, J.M, (2011) Applications of technology to teach social skills to children with autism, *Research in Autism Spectrum Disorders*, 5(3), 1003–1010.

Diler, R.S., Birmaher, B. and Miklowitz, D.J. (2010) Clinical presentation and longitudinal course of bipolar spectrum disorders in children and adolescents, in D.J. Miklowitz and D. Cichetti (eds), *Understanding Bipolar Disorder: A Developmental Psychopathology Perspective*. New York: Guilford Press.

DiLillo, D., Lewis, T. and Di Loreto-Colgan, A. (2007) Child maltreatment history and subsequent romantic relationships: exploring a psychological route to dyadic difficulties, *Journal of Aggression, Maltreatment & Trauma*, 15(1), 18.

Diseth, T.H. and Vandvik, I.H. (2004) Hypnotherapy in the treatment of refractory nocturnal enuresis, *Tidsskrift for den Norske laegeforening: tidsskrift for praktisk medicin, ny raekke*, 124(4), 488–491.

Dishion, T.J. and Dodge, K.A. (2005) Peer contagion in interventions for children and adolescents: moving towards an understanding of the ecology and dynamics of change, *Journal of Abnormal Child Psychology*, 33(3), 395–400.

Dishion, T.J. and Owen, L.D. (2002) A longitudinal analysis of friendships and substance use: bidirectional influence from adolescence to adulthood, *Developmental Psychology*, 35(4), 480–491.

Dishion, T.J. and Patterson, G.R. (2006) The development and ecology of antisocial behavior in children and adolescents, in D. Cichetti and D.J. Cohen (eds), *Developmental Psychopathology. Volume III: Risk, Disorder and Adaptation*, 2nd edn. New York: Wiley.

Dishion, T.J. and Piehler, T.F. (2007) Peer dynamics in the development

and change of child and adolescent problem behavior, in A.S. Masten (ed.), *Multilevel Dynamics in Developmental Psychopathology: Pathways to the Future*. New York: Taylor & Francis Group/Lawrence Erlbaum Associates.

Dishion, T. J., and Tipsord, J. M. (2011). Peer contagion in child and adolescent social and emotional development, *Annual Review of Psychology*, 62(1), 189–214

Dishion, T.J., French, D.C. and Patterson, G.R. (1995) The development and ecology of antisocial behavior, in D. Cichetti and D.J. Cohen (eds), *Developmental Psychopathology. Vol. 2: Risk, Disorder and Adaptation*. New York: Wiley.

Dishion, T.J., McCord, J. and Poulin, F. (1999) When interventions harm: peer groups and problem behavior, *American Psychologist*, 54, 755–764.

Dissanayake, C. and Sigman, M. (2001) Attachment and ER in children with autism, *International Review of Research in Mental Retardation*, 23, 239–266.

Dissanayake, E. (2001) Becoming homo aestheticus: sources of aesthetic imagination in mother-infant interactions, *Substance*, 30(1), 85–103.

Distel, M., Trull, T. and Boomsma, D. (2009) The genetic epidemiology of borderline personality disorder, in M.H. Jackson and L.F. Westbrook (eds), *Borderline Personality Disorder: New Research*. Hauppage, NY: Nova Science.

Distel, M.A., Trull, T.J., Derom, C.A., Thiery, E.W., Grimmer, M.A., Martin, N.G. et al. (2008) Heritability of borderline personality disorder features is similar across three countries, *Psychological Medicine*, 38(09), 1219–1229.

Dmitrieva, J., Chen, C., Greenberger, E. and Gil-Rivas, V. (2004) Family relationships and adolescent psychosocial outcomes: converging findings from Eastern and Western cultures, *Journal of Research on Adolescence*, 14(4), 425–447.

Dodge, K. (1993) Social-cognitive mechanisms in the development of conduct disorder and depression, *Annual Review of Psychology*, 44, 559–584.

Dodge, K.A. (2010) Social information processing patterns as mediators of the interaction between genetic factors and life experiences in the development of aggressive behavior, in M. Mikulncer and P.R. Shaver (eds), *Understanding and Reducing Aggression, Violence and their Consequences*. Washington, DC: American Psychological Association.

Dodge, K.A. and Petit, G.S. (2003) A biopsychosocial model of the development of chronic conduct problems in adolescence, *Developmental Psychology*, 39(2), 349–371.

Dodge, K.A., Bates, J.E. and Pettit, G.S. (1990) Mechanisms in the cycle of violence, *Science*, 250(4988), 1678–1683.

Dodge, K.A., Pettit, G.S., Bates, J.E. and Valente, E. (1995) Social information-processing patterns partially mediate the effect of early physical abuse on later conduct problems, *Journal of Abnormal Psychology*, 104(4), 632–643.

Dodge, K.A., Dishion, T.J. and Lansford, J.E. (2006) *Deviant Peer Influences in Programs for Youth: Problems and Solutions*. New York: Guilford Press.

Donaldson, D., Spirito, A. and Overholser, J. (2003) Treatment of adolescent suicide attempters, in A. Spirito and J. Overholser (eds), *Evaluating and Treating Adolescent Suicide Attempters: From Research to Practice*. New York: Academic Press.

Döpfner, M. et al. (2004) Effectiveness of an adaptive multimodal treatment in children with Attention-Deficit Hyperactivity Disorder – global outcome, *European Child & Adolescent Psychiatry*, 13, 117–129.

Döpfner, M., Plueck, J., Lehmkuhl, G., Huss, M., Lenz, K., Lehmkuhl, U. et al. (2009) Covariation, co-occurrence and epiphenomenal correlation of empirically based syndromes in children and adolescents, *Psychopathology*, 42(3), 177–184.

Douchette, A. (2002) Child and adolescent diagnosis: the need for a model-based approach, in L.E. Beutler and M.L. Malik (eds), *Rethinking the DSM: A Psychological Perspective*. Washington, DC: American Psychological Association.

Douglas, V.I. (1983) Attention and cognitive problems, in M. Rutter (ed.), *Developmental Neuropsychiatry*. New York: Guilford.

Douglass, H.M., Moffitt, T.E., Dar, R., McGee, R. and Silva, P. (1995) Obsessive-compulsive disorder in a birth cohort of 18-year-olds: prevalence and prediction, *Journal of the American Academy of Child and Adolescent Psychiatry*, 34(11), 1424–1430.

Doussard-Roosevelt, J.A. et al. (2003) Mother–child interaction in autistic and nonautistic children: characteristics of maternal approach behaviors and child social responses, *Development and Psychopathology*, 15(2), 277–295.

Downey, G., Feldman, S.I. and Ayduk, O. (2000) Rejection sensitivity and male violence in romantic relationships, *Personal Relationships*, 7, 45–61.

Doyle, J. and Bryant-Waugh, R. (2000) Epidemiology, in B. Lask and R. Bryant-Waugh (eds), *Anorexia Nervosa and Related Eating Disorders in Childhood and Adolescence*. Philadelphia, PA: Psychology Press.

Draaisma, D. (2009) Stereotypes of autism, *Philosophical Transactions of the Royal Society B: Biological Sciences*, 364(1522), 1475–1480.

Dray, S., Campbell, M. and Gilmore, L. (2006) Why are girls with ADHD invisible? *Connections*, 23(2), 2–7.

Dronkers, J., Kalmijn, M. and Wagner, M. (2006) Causes and consequences of divorce: cross-national and cohort differences, an introduction to this special issue,

European Sociological Review, 22(5), 479–481.

Drotar, D., Stein, R.E.K. and Perrin, E.C. (1995). Methodological issues in using the Child Behavior Checklist and its related instruments in clinical child psychology research, *Journal of Clinical Child Psychology*, 24(2), 184–192.

Duckworth, A.L. et al. (2011) Self-regulation strategies improve self-discipline in adolescents: benefits of mental contrasting and implementation intentions, *Educational Psychology*, 31(1), 17–26.

Duffy, A., Alda, M., Hajek, T. and Grof, P. (2009) Early course of bipolar disorder in high-risk offspring: prospective study, *British Journal of Psychiatry*, 195(5), 457–458.

Dukewich, T.L., Borkowski, J.G. and Whitman, T.L. (1996) Adolescent mothers and child abuse potential: an evaluation of risk factors, *Child Abuse and Neglect*, 20, 1031–1047.

Dumas, J.E., LaFreniere, P.J. and Serketich, W.J. (1995) 'Balance of power': a transactional analysis of control in mother–child dyads involving socially competent, aggressive and anxious children, *Journal of Abnormal Psychology*, 104(1), 104–113.

Dunlap, E., Johnson, B.D., Kotarba, J.A. and Fackler, J.L. (2010) Macro-level social forces and micro-level consequences: poverty, alternate occupations and drug dealing, *Journal of Ethnicity in Substance Abuse*, 9(2), 115–127.

Dunn, D.W., Johnson, S., Perkins, S.M., Fastenau, P.S., Byars, A.W., DeGrauw, T.J. and Austin, J.K. (2010) Academic problems in children with seizures: relationships with neuropsychological functioning and family variables during the 3 years after onset, *Epilepsy & Behavior*, 19(3), 455–461.

Dunn, J. (2000) Mind-reading, emotion understanding and relationships, *International Journal of Behavioral Development*, 24, 142–144.

DuPaul, G.J. and Stoner, G. (2003) *ADHD in the Schools: Assessment and Intervention Strategies*, 2nd edn. New York: Guilford Press.

DuPaul, G.J. and Volpe, R.J. (2009) ADHD and learning disabilities: research findings and clinical implications, *Current Attention Disorders Reports*, 1(4), 152–155.

DuPaul, G.J., McGoey, K.E., Eckert, T.L. and VanBrakle, J. (2001). Preschool children with attention-deficit/hyperactivity disorder: impairments in behavioral, social and school functioning, *Journal of the American Academy of Child & Adolescent Psychiatry*, 40(5), 508–515.

Dutton, D.G. (2000) Witnessing parental violence as a traumatic experience shaping the abusive personality, *Journal of Aggression, Maltreatment and Trauma*, 3, 59–67.

Duvvuri, V., Bailer, U.F. and Kaye, W.H. (2010) Altered serotonin function in anorexia and bulimia nervosa, in P.M. Christian and L.J. Barry (eds), *Handbook of Behavioral Neuroscience*. Amsterdam: Elsevier Science.

Dykens, E.M. (2007) Psychiatric and behavioral disorders in persons with Down syndrome, *Mental Retardation and Developmental Disabilities Research Reviews*, 13(3), 272–278.

Dykens, E.M., Leckman, J.F. and Cassidy, S.B. (1996) Obsessions and compulsions in Prader-Willi syndrome, *Journal of Child Psychology and Psychiatry*, 37(8), 995–1002.

Eack, S.M. (2009) Cognitive enhancement therapy for early-course schizophrenia: effects of a two-year randomized controlled trial, *Psychiatric Services*, 60, 1468–1476.

Eaves, L.J., Silberg, J.L. and Meyer, J.M. (1997) Genetics and developmental psychopathology: 2. The main effects of genes and environment on behavioral problems in the Virginia Twin Study of Adolescent Behavioral Development, *Journal of Child Psychology and Psychiatry*, 38, 965–980.

Ebata, A.T., Peterson, A.C. and Conger, J.J. (1990) The development of psychopathology in adolescence, in J. Rolf, A.S. Masten, D. Cicchetti, K.H. Nuechterlein and S. Weintraub (eds), *Risk and Protective Factors in the Development of Psychopathology*. Cambridge: Cambridge University Press.

Ebesutani, C. et al. (2011) The youth self report: applicability and validity across younger and older youths, *Journal of Clinical Child & Adolescent Psychology*, 40(2), 338–346.

Edin, K. and Kissane, R. (2010) Poverty and the American family: a decade in review, *Journal of Marriage and Family*, 72(3), 460–479.

Egeland, B. (1991) A longitudinal study of high-risk families, in R. Starr and D. Wolfe (eds), *The Effects of Child Abuse and Neglect: Issues and Research*. New York: Guilford.

Egeland, B. and Erickson M.F. (2003) Lessons from STEEP: Linking theory, research and practice for the well-being of infants and parents, in A. Sameroff, S. McDonough and K. Rosenblum (eds), *Treating Parent-Infant Relationship Problems: Strategies for Intervention*. New York: Guilford.

Egeland, B., Yates, T., Appleyard, K. and van Dulmen, M. (2002) The long-term consequences of maltreatment in the early years: a developmental pathway model to antisocial behavior, *Children's Services: Social Policy, Research & Practice*, 5(4), 249–260.

Egeland, B.R., Weinfield, N.S., Bosquet, M. and Cheng, V.K. (2000) Remembering, repeating and working through: lessons from attachment-based interventions, in J.D. Osofsky and H.E. Fitzgerald (eds), *Handbook of Infant Mental Health, Vol. 4: Infant Mental Health in Groups at High Risk*. New York: Wiley.

Eggan, S.M., Hashimoto, T. and Lewis, D.A. (2008) Reduced cortical cannabinoid 1 receptor messenger RNA and protein expression in schizophrenia, *Archives of General Psychiatry*, 65(7), 772–784.

Eggers, C. and Bunk, D. (1997) The long-term course of childhood-onset schizophrenia: a 42–year followup, *Schizophrenia Bulletin*, 23(1), 105–117.

Eggers, C., Bunk, D. and Ropcke, B. (2002) Childhood and adolescent onset schizophrenia: results from two long-term follow-up studies, *Neurology Psychiatry and Brain Research*, 9(4), 183–190.

Ein-Dor, T., Mikulincer, M. and Shaver, R. (2011) Attachment insecurities and the processing of threat-related information: studying the schemas involved in insecure people's coping strategies, *Journal of Personality and Social Psychology*, 101(1), 78–93.

Einfeld, S.L. and Aman, M. (1995) Issues in the taxonomy of psychopathology in mental retardation, *Journal of Autism and Developmental Disorders*, 25(2), 143–167.

Einfeld, S.L. and Tonge, B.J. (1996) Population prevalence of psychopathology in children and adolescents with intellectual disability: II epidemiological findings, *Journal of Intellectual Disability Research*, 40(2), 99–109.

Einfeld, S.L., Ellis, L.A. and Emerson, E. (2011) Comorbidity of intellectual disability and mental disorder in children and adolescents: a systematic review, *Journal of Intellectual and Developmental Disability*, 36(2), 137–143.

Eisenberg, N., Valiente, C., Fabes, R.A., Smith, C.L., Reiser, M., Shepard, S.A. et al. (2003) The relations of effortful control and ego control to children's resiliency and social functioning, *Developmental Psychology*, 39(4), 761–776.

Eisenberg, N., Smith, C.L. and Spinrad, T.L. (2010) Effortful control: relations with emotion regulation, adjustment and socialization in childhood, in K.D. Vohs and R.F. Baumeister (eds), *Handbook of Self-Regulation*, 2nd edn. New York: Guilford.

Eisler, I., Dare, C., Hodes, M., Russell, G., Dodge, E. and Le Grange, D. (2000) Family therapy for adolescent anorexia nervosa: the results of a controlled comparison of two family interventions, *Journal of Child Psychology and Psychiatry*, 41(6), 727–736.

Eley, T.C. (2001) Contributions of behavioral genetics research: quantifying genetic, shared environmental and nonshared environmental influences, in M.W. Vasey and M.R. Dadds (eds), *The Developmental Psychopathology of Anxiety*. New York: Oxford University Press.

Eley, T.C., Deater-Deckard, K., Fombonne, E. and Fulker, D.W. (1998) An adoption study of depressive symptoms in middle childhood, *Journal of Child Psychology and Psychiatry and Allied Disciplines*, 39(3), 337–345.

Eley, T.C., Liang, H., Plomin, R., Sham, P., Sterne, A., Williamson, R. and Purcell, S. (2004b) Parental familial vulnerability, family environment and their interactions as predictors of depressive symptoms in adolescents, *Journal of the American Academy of Child & Adolescent Psychiatry*, 43(3), 298–306.

Eley, T.C., Sugden, K., Corsico, A., Gregory, A.M., Sham, P., McGuffin, P., et al. (2004a) Gene-environment interaction analysis of serotonin system markers with adolescent depression, *Molecular Psychiatry*, 9(10), 908–915.

Elkind, D. (1981) *The Hurried Child*. Reading, MA: Addison-Wesley.

Elliott, S.N., Busse, R.T. and Shapiro, E.S. (1999) Intervention techniques for academic performance problems, *The Handbook of School Psychology*, 3rd edn. New York: Wiley.

Eme, R.F. (2007) Sex differences in child-onset, life-course persistent conduct disorder. A review of biological influences, *Clinical Psychology Review*, 27(5), 607–627.

Eme, R.F. and Kavanaugh, L. (1995) Sex differences in conduct disorder, *Journal of Clinical Child Psychology*, 24(4), 406–426.

Emerson, E. (2003) Prevalence of psychiatric disorders in children and adolescents with and without intellectual disability, *Journal of Intellectual Disability Research*, 47(1), 51–58.

Emerson, E. (2007) Poverty and people with intellectual disabilities, *Mental Retardation and Developmental Disabilities Research Reviews*, 13(2), 107–113.

Emerson, E. and Hatton, C. (2007) Mental health of children and adolescents with intellectual disabilities in Britain, *The British Journal of Psychiatry*, 191(6), 493–499.

Emerson, E., Einfeld, S. and Stancliffe, R.J. (2010) The mental health of young children with intellectual disabilities or borderline intellectual functioning, *Social Psychiatry and Psychiatric Epidemiology*, 45(5), 579–587.

Emery, N.J. (2000) The eyes have it: the neuroethology, function and evolution of social gaze, *Neuroscience and Biobehavioral Review*, 24, 581–604.

Emery, R.E. and Laumann-Billings, L. (1998) An overview of the nature, causes and consequences of abusive family relationships: toward differentiating maltreatment and violence, *American Psychologist*, 53, 121–135.

Emmons, S. et al. (1997) *Living with Schizophrenia*. New York: Taylor & Francis.

Emslie, G.J., Mayes, T.L. and Hughes, C.W. (2000) Updates in the pharmacologic treatment of childhood depression, *Psychiatric Clinics of North America*, 23(4), 813–835.

Endresen, I.M. and Olweus, D. (2001) Self-reported empathy in Norwegian adolescents: sex differences, age trends and relationship to bully-

ing, in A.C. Bohart and D.J. Stipek (eds), *Constructive and Destructive Behavior: Implications for Family, School and Society*. Washington, DC: American Psychological Association.

English, B.A., Hahn, M.K., Gizer, I.R., Mazei-Robison, M., Steele, A., Kurnik, D.M., Stein, M.A., Waldman, I.D. and Blakely, R.D. (2009) Choline transporter gene variation is associated with attention-deficit hyperactivity disorder, *Journal of Neurodevelopmental Disorders*, 1(4), 252–263.

Epstein, J.N. et al. (1998) Racial differences on the Conners Teacher Rating Scale, *Journal of Abnormal Child Psychology*, 26(2), 109–118.

Erickson, M.F. and Egeland, B.R. (2011) Child neglect, in J.F.B. Myers (ed.), *The APSAC Handbook on Child Maltreatment*. Thousand Oaks, CA: Sage.

Erickson, M.F. and Kurz-Riemer, K. (2002) *Infants, Toddlers and Families: A Framework for Support and Intervention*. New York: Guilford.

Erikson, E.H. (1950) *Childhood and Society*. New York: Norton.

Erikson, E.H. (1964) Clinical observation of play disruption in young children, in M.R. Haworth (ed.), *Child Psychotherapy*. New York: Basic Books.

Erikson, E.H. (1968) *Identity: Youth and Crisis*. New York: Norton.

Eron, L.D. (2001) Seeing is believing: how viewing violence alters attitudes and aggressive behavior, in A.C. Bohart and D.J. Stipek (eds), *Constructive & Destructive Behavior: Implications for Family, School, & Society*. Washington, DC: American Psychological Association.

Eron, L.D. and Huesmann, L.R. (1990) The stability of aggressive behavior – even unto the third generation, in M. Lewis and S.M. Miller (eds), *Handbook of Developmental Psychopathology*. New York: Plenum.

Esposito, C., Spirito, A. and Overholser, J. (2003) Behavioral factors: impulsive and aggressive behavior, in A. Spirito and J.C. Overholser (eds), *Evaluating and Treating Adolescent Suicide Attempters: From Research to Practice*. New York: Academic Press.

Essau, C.A. (2003) Comorbidity of anxiety disorders in adolescents, *Depression and Anxiety*, 18(1), 1–6.

Evans, B. and Lee, B.K. (1998) Culture and child psychopathology, in S.S. Kazarian and D.R. Evans (eds), *Cultural Clinical Psychology: Theory, Research and Practice*. New York: Oxford University Press

Evans, G.W. (2004) The environment of childhood poverty, *American Psychologist*, 59(2), 77–92.

Every Child Matters Education Fund (2010) *We Can Do Better: Child Abuse and Deaths in America*. Washington, DC: Every Child Matters Education Fund.

Ewing-Cobbs, L. et al. (2004). Modeling of longitudinal academic achievement scores after pediatric traumatic brain injury, *Childhood Head Injury: Developmental and Recovery Variables: A Special Double Issue of Developmental Neuropsychology*, 25(1 and 2), 107–133.

Exner, J. E. Jr (1993) *The Rorschach: A Comprehensive System. Vol. U.– Basic Foundations*, 3rd edn. New York: Wiley.

Eyberg, S.M. and Boggs, S.R. (1998) Parent–child interaction therapy: a psychosocial intervention for the treatment of young conduct-disordered children, in J.M. Briesmeister and C.E. Schaefer (eds), *Handbook of Parent Training*. New York: Wiley.

Eyberg, S.M., Nelson, M.M. and Boggs, S.R. (2008) Evidence-based psychosocial treatments for children and adolescents with disruptive behavior, *Journal of Clinical Child & Adolescent Psychology*, 37(1), 215–237.

Fabiano, G.A., Pelham W.E., Coles, E.K. et al. (2009) A meta-analysis of behavioral treatments for attention-deficit/hyperactivity disorder, *Clinical Psychology Review*, 29, 129–140.

Fairburn, C.G. and Brownell, K.D. (2002) *Eating Disorders And Obesity: A Comprehensive Handbook*. New York: Guilford.

Fairburn, C.G. and Harrison, P.J. (2003) Eating disorders, *The Lancet*, 361(9355), 407–416.

Fairburn, C.G., Marcus, M.D. and Wilson, G.T. (1993) Cognitive-behavioral therapy for binge eating and bulimia nervosa: a comprehensive treatment manual, in C.G. Fairburn and G.T. Wilson (eds), *Binge Eating: Nature, Assessment and Treatment*. New York: Guilford Press.

Fairburn, C.G., Welch, S.L., Doll, H.A., Davies, B.A. and O'Connor, M.E. (1997) Risk factors for bulimia nervosa: a community-based case-control study, *Archives of General Psychiatry*, 54, 509–517.

Fairburn, C.G., Cooper, Z., Welch, S.L. and Doll, H.A. (1999) Risk factors for bulimia nervosa: three integrated case-control comparisons, *Archives of General Psychiatry*, 56, 468–476.

Fairburn, C.G., Cooper, Z., Doll, H.A., Norman, P. and O'Connor, M. (2000) The natural course of bulimia nervosa and binge eating disorder in young women, *Archives of General Psychiatry*, 56, 468–476.

Fairburn, C.G., Cooper, Z. and Shafran, R. (2003) Cognitive behaviour therapy for eating disorders: a 'transdiagnostic' theory and treatment, *Behaviour Research and Therapy*, 41(5), 509–528.

Faraone, S.V, Biederman, J. and Monuteaux, M. (2000) Toward guidelines for pedigree selection in genetic studies of attention deficit hyperactivity disorder, *Genetic Epidemiology*, 18, 1–16.

Faraone, S.V., Biederman, J. and Monuteaux, M.C. (2001) Attention deficit hyperactivity disorder with bipolar disorder in girls: further evidence for a familial subtype?

Journal of Affective Disorders, 64, 19–26.

Faraone, S.V., Sergeant, J., Gillberg, C. and Biederman, J. (2003) The worldwide prevalence of ADHD: is it an American condition? *World Psychiatry*, 2(2), 104–113.

Faraone, S.V., Biederman, J. and Mick, E. (2006) The age-dependent decline of attention deficit hyperactivity disorder: a meta-analysis of follow-up studies, *Psychological Medicine*, 36(2), 159–166.

Fay, T.B. et al. (2010) Cognitive reserve as a moderator of postconcussive symptoms in children with complicated and uncomplicated mild traumatic brain injury, *Journal of the International Neuropsychological Society*, 16(1), 94–105.

Fearon, R. et al. (2010) The significance of insecure attachment and disorganization in the development of children's externalizing behavior: a meta-analytic study, *Child Development*, 81(2), 435–456.

Federal Interagency Forum on Child and Family Statistics (2010) *America's Children: Key National Indicators of Well-Being*, http://childstats.gov/index.asp.

Feeney, J.A. (2008) Adult romantic attachment, in J. Cassidy and P.R. Shaver (eds), *Handbook of Attachment*. New York: Guilford.

Feeney, T.J. and Ylvisaker, M. (1995) Choice and routine: antecedent behavioral interventions for adolescents with severe traumatic brain injury, *The Journal of Head Trauma Rehabilitation*, 10, 67–86.

Feiring, C., Miller-Johnson, S. and Cleland, C.M. (2007) Potential pathways from stigmatization and internalizing symptoms to delinquency in sexually abused youth, *Child Maltreatment*, 12(3), 220–232.

Feldman, R., Zelkowitz, P., Weiss, M., Vogel, J., Heyman, M. and Paris, J. (1995) A comparison of the families of mothers with borderline and nonborderline personality disorders, *Comprehensive Psychiatry*, 36(2), 157–163.

Felner, R.D. (2006) Poverty in childhood and adolescence, in S. Goldstein and R.B. Brooks (eds), *Handbook of Resilience in Children*. New York: Kluwer Academic/Plenum.

Ferguson, C.P. and Pigott, T.A. (2000) Anorexia and bulimia nervosa: neurobiology and pharmacotherapy, *Behavior Therapy*, 31(2), 237–263.

Fergusson, D.M. and Horwood, L.J. (1999) Prospective childhood predictors of deviant peer affiliations in adolescence, *Journal of Child Psychology and Psychiatry*, 40(4), 581–592.

Fergusson, D.M. and Horwood, L.J. (2003) Resilience to childhood adversity: results of a 12–year study, in S.S. Luthar (ed.), *Resilience and Vulnerability: Adaptation in the Context Of Childhood Adversities*. New York: Cambridge University Press.

Fergusson, D.M. and Woodward, L.J. (2000) Educational, psychosocial and sexual outcomes of girls with conduct problems in early adolescence, *Journal of Child Psychology and Psychiatry*, 41(6), 779–792.

Fergusson, D.M. et al. (1988) A longitudinal study of dentine lead levels, intelligence, school performance and behavior, *Journal of Child Psychology and Psychiatry*, 29(6), 793–809.

Fergusson, D.M., Horwood, L.J. and Beautrais, A.L. (1999) Is sexual orientation related to mental health problems and suicidality in young people? *Archives of General Psychiatry*, 56(10), 876–880.

Fergusson, D.M., Horwood, J.L. and Lynskey, M.T. (2006) The childhoods of multiple problem adolescents: a 15-year longitudinal study, *Journal of Child Psychology and Psychiatry*, 35(6), 1123-1140.

Ferriter, C., Eberhart, N.K. and Hammen, C.L. (2010) Depressive symptoms and social functioning in peer relationships as predictors of eating pathology in the transition to adulthood, *Journal of Social* *and Clinical Psychology*, 29(2), 202–227.

Filipek, A. (1999) Neuroimaging in the developmental disorders: the state of the science, *Journal of Child Psychology and Psychiatry*, 40(1), 113–128.

Filipek, P.A., Accardo, P.J., Baranek, G.T., Cook, E.H., Dawson, G., Gordon, B. et al. (1999) The screening and diagnosis of autistic spectrum disorders, *Journal of Autism and Developmental Disorders*, 29(6), 439–484.

Fincham, D.S., Altes, L.K., Stein, D.J. and Seedat, S. (2009) Posttraumatic stress disorder symptoms in adolescents: risk factors versus resilience moderation, *Comprehensive Psychiatry*, 50(3), 193–199.

Finger, E.C. et al. (2011) Disrupted reinforcement signaling in the orbitofrontal cortex and caudate in youths with conduct disorder or oppositional defiant disorder and a high level of psychopathic traits, *American Journal of Psychiatry*, 168(2), 152–162.

Finkelhor, D. (2008) *Childhood Victimization: Violence, Crime and Abuse in the Lives of Young People*. New York: Oxford University Press.

Finkelhor, D. (2009) The prevention of childhood sexual abuse, *The Future of Children*, 19(2), 169–194.

Finkelhor, D. and Browne, A. (1988) Assessing the long term impact of child sexual abuse: a review and reconceptualization, in L. Walker (ed.), *Handbook On Sexual Abuse of Children*. New York: Springer.

Finkelhor, D., Ormrod, R., Turner, H. and Hamby, S.L. (2005) The victimization of children and youth: a comprehensive, national survey, *Child Maltreatment*, 10, 5–25.

Finkelhor, D., Turner, H., Ormrod, R. and Hamby, S.L. (2009) Violence, abuse and crime exposure in a national sample of children and youth, *Pediatrics*, 124(5), 1411–1423.

Finkelhor, D., Turner, H.A., Ormrod, R.K. and Hamby, S.L. (2010) Trends in childhood violence and abuse exposure, *Archives of Pediat-*

rics & Adolescent Medicine, 164 (3): 238–242.

Finzi, R., Ram, A., Har-Even, D., Shnit, D. and Weizman, A. (2001) Attachment styles and aggression in physically abused and neglected children, *Journal of Youth and Adolescence*, 30(6), 769–786.

First, M.B. (2009) Harmonisation of ICD–11 and DSM–V: opportunities and challenges, *The British Journal of Psychiatry*, 195, 382–390.

First, M.B., Frances, A. and Pincus, H.A. (2002) *DSM-IV-TR Handbook of Differential Diagnosis*. Washington, DC: American Psychiatric Press.

Fischel, J.E. and Liebert, R.M. (2000) Disorders of elimination, in A.J. Sameroff, M. Lewis and S.M. Miller (eds), *Handbook of Developmental Psychopathology*. New York: Kluwer Academic.

Fischer, K.W. and Ayoub, C. (1994) Affective splitting and dissociation in normal and maltreated children: developmental pathways for self in relationships, in D. Cicchetti and S.L. Toth (eds), *Rochester Symposium on Developmental Psychopathology: Disorders and Dysfunctions of the Self*, vol. 5. New York: Rochester.

Fischer, M. and Barkley, R.A. (2003) Childhood stimulant treatment and risk for later substance abuse, *Journal of Clinical Psychiatry*, 64(supplement 11), 19–23.

Fischer, M., Barkley, R.A., Smallish, L. and Fletcher, K. (2002) Young adult follow-up of hyperactive children: self-reported psychiatric disorders, comorbidity and the role of childhood conduct problems and teen CD, *Journal of Abnormal Child Psychology*, 30, 463–475.

Fish, B. and Rivito, E.R. (1979) Psychoses of childhood, in D. Noshpitz (ed.), *Basic Handbook of Child Psychiatry*, vol. 2. New York: Basic Books.

Fitzgerald, M.M., Schneider, R.A., Salstrom, S., Zinzow, H.M., Jackson, J. and Fossel, R.V. (2008)

Child sexual abuse, early family risk and childhood parentification: pathways to current psychosocial adjustment, *Journal of Family Psychology*, 22(2), 320–324.

Fixsen, D.L., Blase, K.A., Duda, M.A., Naoom, S.F. and Van Dyke, M.K. (2010) Implementation of evidence-based treatments for children and adolescents: research findings and their implications for the future, in J.R. Weisz and A.E. Kazdin (eds), *Evidence-Based Psychotherapies for Children and Adolescents*, 2nd edn. New York: Guilford Press.

Flament, M.F., Whitaker, A., Rapoport, J.L. and Davies, M. (1988) Obsessive compulsive disorder in adolescence: an epidemiological study, *Journal of the American Academy of Child and Adolescent Psychiatry*, 27(6), 764–771.

Flanagan, D.P., Ortiz, S.O. and Alfonso, V.C. (2007) *Essentials of Cross-Battery Assessment*. New York: Wiley.

Fleck, D.E., Cerullo, M.A., Nandagopal, J., Adler, C.M., Patel, N.C., Strakowski, S. M. and DelBello, M.P. (2010) Neurodevelopment in bipolar disorder: a neuroimaging perspective, in D.J. Miklowitz and D. Cichetti (eds), *Understanding Bipolar Disorder: A Developmental Psychopathology Perspective*. New York: Guilford Press.

Fletcher, K. (2003) Childhood posttraumatic stress disorder, in E.J. Mash and R.A. Barkley (eds), *Child Psychopathology*. New York: Guilford.

Folstein, S.E. and Santangelo, S.L. (2000) Does Asperger syndrome aggregate in families? in A. Klin and F.R. Volkmar (eds), *Asperger Syndrome*. New York: Guilford Press.

Fombonne, E. (1999) The epidemiology of autism: a review, *Psychological Medicine*, 29(4), 769–786.

Fombonne, E. (2003) Epidemiological surveys of autism and other pervasive developmental disorders: an update, *Journal of Autism and Developmental Disorders*, 33(4), 365–382.

Fonagy, P. and Luyten, P. (2009) A developmental, mentalization-based approach to the understanding and treatment of borderline personality disorder, *Development and Psychopathology*, 21(4), 1355–1381.

Fonagy, P. and Target, M. (1996) A contemporary psychoanalytical perspective: psychodynamic developmental therapy, in E.D. Hibbs and P.S. Jensen (eds), *Psychosocial Treatments for Child and Adolescent Disorders: Empirically Based Strategies for Clinical Practice*. Washington, DC: American Psychological Association.

Fonagy, P. and Target, M. (2000) Attachment and borderline personality disorder, *Journal of the American Psychoanalytic Association*, 48(4), 1129–1146.

Fonagy, P. and Target, M. (2009) Psychodynamic treatments, in M. Rutter, D.V.M. Bishop, D.S. Pine, S. Scott, J. Stevenson, E. Taylor and A. Thapar (eds), *Rutter's Child and Adolescent Psychiatry*, 5th edn. Oxford: Blackwell.

Fonagy, P., Target, M., Cottrell, J.E., Phillips, J. and Kurtz, Z. (2002) *What Works for Whom? A Critical Review of Treatments for Children and Adolescents*. New York: Guilford.

Fonagy, P., Target, M. and Gergely, G. (2006) Psychoanalytic perspectives on developmental psychopathology, in D. Cicchetti and D.J. Cohen (eds), *Developmental Psychopathology, Vol 1: Theory and Method*, 2nd edn. Hoboken, NJ: John Wiley & Sons.

Fong, R. (2003) *Culturally Competent Practice with Immigrant and Refugee Children and Families*. New York: Guilford.

Fontaine, N., Carbonneau, R., Vitaro, F., Barker, E.D. and Tremblay, R.E. (2009) Research review: a critical review of studies on the developmental trajectories of antisocial behavior in females, *Journal of Child Psychology and Psychiatry*, 50(4), 363–385.

Foorman, B.R. et al. (1997) Early interventions for children with reading disabilities, *Components of Effective Reading Intervention: A Special Issue of Scientific Studies of Reading*, 1(3), 255–276.

Forbes, E.E. and Dahl, R.E. (2010) Pubertal development and behavior: hormonal activation of social and motivational tendencies, *Brain and Ccognition*, 72(1), 66–72.

Ford, T., Goodman, R. and Meltzer, H. (2003) The British child and adolescent mental health survey 1999: the prevalence of DSM-IV disorders, *Journal of the American Academy of Child & Adolescent Psychiatry*, 42(10), 1203–1211.

Forehand, R. and Wierson, M. (1993) The role of developmental factors in planning behavioral interventions for children: disruptive behavior as an example, *Behavior Therapy*, 24, 117–141.

Foreyt, J.P. and Mikhail, C. (1997) Anorexia nervosa and bulimia nervosa, in E.J. Mash and L.G. Terdal (eds), *Assessment of Childhood Disorders*. New York: Guilford.

Forgatch, M.S. and Patterson, G.R. (2010) Parent management training – Oregon model: an intervention for antisocial behavior in children and adolescents, in J.R. Weisz and A.E. Kazdin (eds), *Evidence-Based Psychotherapies for Children and Adolescents*, 2nd edn. New York: Guilford.

Forness, S.R. and Kavale, K.A. (1996) Treating social skill deficits in children with learning disabilities: a meta-analysis of the research, *Learning Disability Quarterly*, 19(1), 2–13.

Foster, E.M. and Watkins, S. (2010) The value of reanalysis: TV viewing and attention problems, *Child Development*, 81(1), 368–375.

Foster, H., Hagan, J. and Brooks-Gunn, J. (2008) Growing up fast: stress exposure and subjective 'weathering' in emerging adulthood, *Journal of Health and Social Behavior*, 49(2), 162–177.

Fowler, P., Tompsett, C., Braciszewski, J., Jacques-Tiura, A. and Baltes, B. (2009) Community violence: a meta-analysis on the effect of exposure and mental health outcomes of children and adolescents, *Development and Psychopathology*, 21(1), 227–259.

Fox, S.E., Levitt, P. and Nelson, C.A. III (2010) How the timing and quality of early experiences influence the development of brain architecture, *Child Development*, 81(1), 28–40.

Fraiberg, S. (1980) *Clinical Studies in Infant Mental Health: The First Year of Life*. New York: Basic Books.

Frances, A. and Pincus, H.A. (2002) *DSM-IV-TR Handbook of Differential Diagnosis*. Washington, DC: American Psychiatric Press.

Frances, C. et al. (2004) Paediatric methylphenidate (Ritalin) restrictive conditions of prescription in France, *British Journal of Clinical Pharmacology*, 57(1), 115–116.

Franklin, M.E., Rynn, M., Foa, E.B. and March, J.S. (2003) Treatment of obsessive-compulsive disorder, in M.A. Reinecke, F.M. Dattilio and A. Freeman (eds), *Cognitive Therapy with Children and Adolescents: A Casebook for Clinical Practice*, 2nd edn. New York: Guilford.

Franklin, M.E., Freeman, J. and March, J.S. (2010) Treating pediatric obsessive-compulsive disorder using exposure-based cognitive-behavioral therapy, in J.R. Weisz and A.E. Kazdin (eds), *Evidence-Based Psychotherapies for Children and Adolescents*, 2nd edn. New York: Guilford.

Frazier, J.A., Alaghband-Rad, J. and Jacobsen, L. (1997) Pubertal development and the onset of psychosis in childhood onset schizophrenia, *Psychiatry Research*, 70, 1–7.

Frederickson, N. (2010) The Gulliford Lecture: Bullying or befriending? Children's responses to classmates with special needs, *British Journal of Special Education*, 37(1), 4–12.

Freeman, S.F.N. and Alkin, M.C. (2000) Academic and social attainments of children with mental retardation in general education and special education settings, *Remedial and Special Education*, 21(1), 3–18.

Freidlander, M.L., Larney, L.C., Skau, M., Hotaling, M., Cutting, M.L. and Schwam, M. (2007) Experiences of internationally adopted children and their parents, *Journal of Counseling Psychology*, 47(2), 187–198.

Freud, A. (1964) *The Psychoanalytical Treatment Of Children*. New York: Schocken.

Freud, A. (1965) *Normality and Pathology in Childhood: Assessments of Development (The Writings of Anna Freud, Vol. 6)*. New York: International Universities Press.

Frick, P.J. (2009) Extending the contruct of psychopathy to youth: implications for understanding, diagnosing and treating antisocial children and adolescents, *The Canadian Psychiatric Association Journal / La Revue de l'Association des psychiatres du Canada*, 54(12), 803–812.

Frick, P.J. and Moffitt, T.E. (2010) *A Proposal to the DSM-V Childhood Disorders and the ADHD and Disruptive Behavior Disorders Work Groups to Include a Specifier to the Diagnosis of Conduct Disorder Based on the Presence of Callous–Unemotional Traits*. Washington, DC: American Psychiatric Association.

Frick, P.J. and Morris, A.S. (2004) Temperament and developmental pathways to conduct problems, *Journal of Clinical Child and Adolescent Psychology*, 33(1), 54–68.

Frick, P.J. and White, S.F. (2008) Research review: the importance of callous-unemotional traits for developmental models of aggressive and antisocial behavior, *Journal of Child Psychology and Psychiatry*, 49(4), 359–375.

Frick, P.J. et al. (1992). Familial risk factors to oppositional defiant disorder and conduct disorder: parental psychopathology and maternal parenting, *Journal of Consulting and Clinical Psychology*, 60(1), 49–55.

Frick, P.J., Lahey, B.B., Loeber, R., Tannenbaum, L., Van Horn, Y., Christ, M.A. et al. (1993) Oppositional defiant disorder and conduct disorder: a meta-analytic review of factor analyses and cross-validation in a clinic sample, *Clinical Psychology Review*, 13, 319–340.

Frick, P.J., Cornell, A., Bodin, D., Dane, H., Barry, C.T. and Loney, B.R. (2003) Callous-unemotional traits and developmental pathways to severe conduct problems, *Developmental Psychology*, 39(2), 246–260.

Frick, P.J., Barry, C.T. and Kamphaus, R.W. (2010) *Clinical Assessment of Child and Adolescent Personality and Behavior*, 3rd edn. New York: Springer.

Friedberg, R.D. and McClure, J.M. (2002). *Clinical practice of cognitive therapy with children and adolescents: The nuts and bolts*. New York: Guilford Press.

Friedrich, W.N. (2002) An integrated model of psychotherapy for abused children, in J.E.B. Myers, L. Berliner, J. Briere, C.T. Hendrix, C. Jenny and T.A. Reid (eds), *The APSAC Handbook on Child Maltreatment*. 2nd edn. Thousand Oaks, CA: Sage.

Friedrich, W.N., Sandfort, T.G.M., Oostveen, J. and Cohen-Kettenis, P.T. (2000) Cultural differences in sexual behavior: 2–8 year old Dutch and American children, in T.G.M. Sandfort and J. Rademakers (eds), *Childhood Sexuality: Normal Sexual Behavior and Development*. Binghamton, NY: Haworth.

Friedrich, W.N., Gerber, P.N., Koplin, B., Davis, M., Giese, J., Mykelbust, C. and Franckowiak, D. (2001) Multimodal assessment of dissociation in adolescents: inpatients and juvenile sex offenders, *Sexual Abuse: Journal of Research and Treatment*, 13(3), 167–177.

Friman, C. (2008). Evidence-based therapies for enuresis and encopresis, in R.G. Steele, T.D. Elkin and M.C. Roberts (eds), *Handbook of Evidence-Based Therapies for Children and Adolescents*. New York: Springer.

Fristad, M.A., Verducci, J.S., Walters, K. and Young, M.E. (2009) The impact of multifamily psychoeducational psychotherapy in treating children aged 8–12 with mood disorders, *Archives of General Psychiatry*, 66(9), 1013–1021.

Frith, U. (2003) Autism: explaining the enigma, *British Journal of Developmental Psychology*, 21, 465–468.

Frith, U. and Happé, F. (1995) Autism: beyond 'theory of mind', in J. Mehler and S. Franck (eds), *Cognition on Cognition*. Cambridge, MA: MIT Press.

Frith, U.E. (1991) *Autism and Asperger Syndrome*. Cambridge: Cambridge University Press.

Fritz, G. and Rockney, R. (2004) Summary of the practice parameter for the assessment and treatment of children and adolescents with enuresis, *Journal of the American Academy of Child and Adolescent Psychiatry*, 43(1), 123–125.

Fritz, G.K. and McQuaid, E.L. (2000) Chronic medical conditions: impact on development, in A.J. Sameroff, M. Lewis and S.M. Miller (eds), *Handbook of Developmental Psychopathology*. New York: Kluwer Academic.

Froehlich, T.E., Lanphear, B.P., Epstein, J.N, Barbaresi, W.J., Katusic, S.K. and Kahn, R.S. (2007) Prevalence, recognition and treatment of attention-deficit/hyperactivity disorder in a national sample of US children, *Archives of Pediatrics and Adolescent Medicine*, 161(9), 857–864.

Fuller, R., Nopoulos, P., Arndt, S., O'Leary, D., Ho, B.C. and Andreasen, N.C. (2002) Longitudinal assessment of premorbid cognitive functioning in patients with schizophrenia through examination of standardized scholastic test performance, *American Journal of Psychiatry*, 159, 1183–1189.

Furman, L.M. (2008) Attention-deficit hyperactivity disorder (ADHD): does new research support old concepts? *Journal of Child Neurology*, 23(7), 775–784.

Gabel, S. (1997) Oppositional defiant disorder, in J. Noshpitz (ed.), *Handbook of child and adolescent psychiatry*, 351–359. New York: Wiley.

Gadow, K.D. and Nolan, E.E. (2002) Differences between preschool children with ODD, ADHD and ODD+ ADHD symptoms, *Journal of Child Psychology and Psychiatry*, 43(2), 191–201.

Gadow, K.D. et al. (2000) Comparison of attention-deficit/hyperactivity disorder symptom subtypes in Ukrainian schoolchildren, *Journal of the American Academy of Child & Adolescent Psychiatry*, 39(12), 1520–1527.

Gaffney, D.A. and Roye, C. (2003) *Adolescent Sexual Development and Sexuality: Assessment and Interventions*. Kingston, NJ: Civic Research Institute.

Galaif, E.R., Newcomb, M.D., Vega, W.A. and Krell, R.D. (2007) Protective and risk influences of drug use among a multiethnic sample of adolescent boys, *Journal of Drug Education*, 37(3), 249–276.

Galambos, N.L., Leadbeater, B.J. and Barker, E.T. (2004) Gender differences in and risk factors for depression in adolescence: a 4-year longitudinal study, *International Journal of Behavioral Development*, 28(1), 16–25.

Gallo, C.L. and Pfeffer, C.R. (2003) Children and adolescents bereaved by a suicidal death: Implications for psychosocial outcomes and interventions, in R.A. King and A. Apter (eds), *Suicide in Children and Adolescents*. Cambridge: Cambridge University Press.

Garb, H.N. et al. (2005) Roots of the Rorschach controversy, *Clinical Psychology Review*, 25(1), 97–118.

Garber, J. (1984) Classification of childhood psychopathology: a developmental perspective, *Child Development*, 55, 30–48.

Garber, J., Braafladt, N. and Weiss, B. (1995) Affect regulation in depressed and nondepressed children and young adolescents, *Development and Psychopathology*, 7(1), 93–116.

Garber, J., Webb, C.A. and Horowitz, J.L. (2009) Prevention of depression in adolescents: a review of selective and indicated programs, in S. Nolen-Hoeksema and L.M. Hilt (eds), *Handbook of Depression in Adolescents*. New York: Routledge/Taylor & Francis Group.

Garcia-Moreno, C., Henrica, J., Watts, C., Ellsberg, M. and Heise, L. (2005) *WHO Multi-Country Study on Women's Health and Domestic Violence Against Women*. Geneva: WHO.

Gardner, T.W., Dishion, T.J. and Connell, A.M. (2008) Adolescent self-regulation as resilience: resistance to antisocial behavior within the deviant peer context, *Journal of Abnormal Child Psychology*, 36(2), 273–284.

Garland, E. and Weiss, M. (1996) Case study: obsessive difficult temperament and its response to serotonergic medication, *Journal of the American Academy of Child & Adolescent Psychiatry*, 35(7), 916–920.

Garnefski, N. and Arends, E. (1998) Sexual abuse and adolescent maladjustment: differences between male and female victims. *Journal of Adolescence*, 21, 99–107.

Ge, X., Natsuaki, M.N. and Conger, R.D. (2006) Trajectories of depressive symptoms and stressful life events among male and female adolescents in divorced and nondivorced families, *Development and Psychopathology*, 18(1), 153–173.

Ge, X., Natsuaki, M.N., Neiderhiser, J.M. and Reiss, D. (2009) The longitudinal effects of stressful life

events on adolescent depression are buffered by parent–child closeness, *Development and Psychopathology*, 21(2), 621–635.

Geiger, T.C. and Crick, N.R. (2010) Developmental pathways to personality disorders, in R.E. Ingram and J.M. Price (eds), *Vulnerability to psychopathology: risk across the lifespan*, 2nd edn. New York: Guilford Press.

Geller, B. and Tillman, R. (2005) Prepubertal and early adolescent bipolar disorder: Review of diagnostic validation by Robins and Guze criteria, *Journal of Clinical Psychiatry*, 66(supplement 7), 21–28.

Geller, B., Williams, M., Zimmerman, B., Frazier, J., Berringer, L. and Warner, K. (1998) Prepubertal and early adolescent bipolarity differentiated from ADHD by manic symptoms, grandiose delusions, utra-rapid or ultradian cycling, *Journal of Affective Disorders*, 51, 81–91.

Geller, B., Bolhofner, K., Craney, J.L., Williams, M., DelBello, M.P. and Gunderson, K. (2000) Psychosocial functioning in a prepubertal and early adolescent bipolar disorder phenotype, *Journal of the American Academy of Child and Adolescent Psychiatry*, 39(12), 1543–1548.

Geller, D.A., Wieland, N., Carey, K., Vivas, F., Petty, C. R., Johnson, J. et al. (2008) Perinatal factors affecting expression of obsessive compulsive disorder in children and adolescents, *Journal of Child and Adolescent Psychopharmacology*, 18(4), 373–379.

Geller, J. and Johnston, C. (1995) Predictors of mothers' responses to child noncompliance: attributions and attitudes, *Journal of Clinical Child Psychology*, 24(3), 272–278.

Gepertz, S. and Neveus, T. (2004) Imipramine for therapy resistant enuresis: a retrospective evaluation, *The Journal of Urology*, 171(6), 2607–2610.

Gerring, J.P. et al. (2009) Disruptive behaviour disorders and disruptive symptoms after severe paediatric traumatic brain injury, *Brain Injury*, 23(12), 944–955.

Gershoff, E.T., Grogan-Kaylor, A., Lansford, J.E., Chang, L., Zelli, A., Deater-Deckard, K. and Dodge, K.A. (2010) Parent discipline practices in an international sample: associations with child behaviors and moderation by perceived normativeness, *Child Development*, 81(2), 487–502.

Gershon, J. (2002) A meta-analytic review of gender differences in ADHD, *Journal of Attention Disorders*, 5(3), 143–154.

Giaconia, R.M., Reinherz, H.Z., Hauf, A.C., Paradis, A.D., Wasserman, M.S. and Langhammer, D.M. (2000) Comorbidity of substance use and post-traumatic stress disorders in a community sample of adolescents, *American Journal of Orthopsychiatry*, 70(2), 253–262.

Gibbons, F.X., Gerrard, M., Cleveland, M.J., Wills, T.A. and Brody, G. (2004) Perceived discrimination and substance use in African American parents and their children, *Journal of Personality and Social Psychology*, 86, 517–529.

Gibbons, R.D., Brown, C.H., Hur, K., Marcus, S.M., Bhaumik, D.K., Erkens, J.A. et al. (2007) Early evidence on the effects of regulators' suicidality warnings on SSRI prescriptions and suicide in children and adolescents, *American Journal of Psychiatry*, 164, 1356–1363.

Gibbs, J.T. and Huang, L.N. (2003) *Children of Color: Psychological interventions with Culturally Diverse Youth*, 2nd edn. San Francisco, CA: Jossey-Bass.

Giedd, J.N. (2003) The anatomy of mentalization: a view from developmental neuroimaging, *Bulletin of the Menninger Clinic*, 67(2), 132–142.

Giedd, J.N. et al. (1999) Brain development during childhood and adolescence: a longitudinal MRI study, *Nature Neuroscience*, 2, 861–862.

Gil, E. (2006) *Helping Abused and Traumatized Children: Integrating Directive and Nondirective Approaches.* New York: Guilford.

Gil, K.M., Anthony, K.K., Carson, J.W., Redding-Lallinger, R., Daeschner, C.W. and Ware, R.E. (2001) Daily coping practice predicts treatment effects in children with sickle cell disease, *Journal of Pediatric Psychology*, 26(3), 163–173.

Gilbert, R., Widom, C.S., Browne, K., Fergusson, D., Webb, E. and Janson, S. (2009) Burden and consequences of child maltreatment in high-income countries, *The Lancet*, 68–81.

Giletta, M., Scholte, R.H.J., Engels, R.C.M.E. and Larsen, J.K. (2010) Body mass index and victimization during adolescence: the mediation role of depressive symptoms and self-esteem, *Journal of Psychosomatic Research*, 69(6), 541–547.

Gillberg, C. (1991) Outcome in autism and autistic-like conditions, *Journal of the American Academy of Child and Adolescent Psychiatry*, 30, 375–382.

Gillberg, C. et al. (2004) Co-existing disorders in ADHD – implications for diagnosis and intervention, *European Child & Adolescent Psychiatry*, 13, 80–92.

Gillham, J.E., Brunwasser, S.M. and Freres, D.R. (2008) Preventing depression in early adolescence: the Penn Resiliency Program, in J.R.Z. Abela and B.L. Hankin (eds), *Handbook of Depression in Children and Adolescents.* New York: Guilford Press.

Glassman, L.H., Weierich, M.R., Hooley, J.M., Deliberto, T.L. and Nock, M.K. (2007) Child maltreatment, non-suicidal self-injury and the mediating role of self-criticism, *Behaviour Research and Therapy*, 45(10), 2483–2490.

Glazener, C.M. and Evans, J.H. (2002) Desmopressin for nocturnal enuresis in children, *Cochrane Database of Systematic Reviews (Online)*, (3), CD002112.

Glisson, C., Schoenwald, S.K., Hemmelgarn, A., Green, P., Dukes, D., Armstrong, K.S. and Chapman, J.E. (2010) Randomized trial of MST and ARC in a two-level evidence-based treatment implementation strategy, *Journal of Consulting and Clinical Psychology*, 78(4), 537–550.

Global Initiative to End All Corporal Punishment of Children (2010) http://www.endcorporalpunishment.org/pages/pdfs/reports/GlobalReport2010.pdf.

Godwin, G. (1994) *The Good Husband.* New York: Ballantine.

Gogtay, N., Sporn, A., Clasen, L.S., Greenstein, D., Giedd, J.N., Lenane, M. et al. (2003) Structural brain MRI abnormalities in healthy siblings of patients with child-hoodonset schizophrenia, *American Journal of Psychiatry*, 160, 569–571.

Gogtay, N. et al. (2004) Dynamic mapping of human cortical development during childhood and adolescence, *Proceedings of the National Academy of Science*, 101 (21), 8174– 8179.

Goldberg, S. (1997) Attachment and childhood behavior problems in normal, at-risk and clinical samples, in L. Atkinson and K.J. Zucker (eds), *Attachment and Psychopathology.* New York: Guilford.

Goldman, S.J., D'Angelo, E.J. and DeMaso, D.R. (1993) Psychopathology in the families of children and adolescents with borderline personality disorder, *American Journal of Psychiatry*, 150(12), 1832–1835.

Goldstein, M.J. (1987) The UCLA High-Risk Project, *Schizophrenia Bulletin*, 13, 505–514.

Goldstein, M.J. (1990) Family relations as risk factors for the onset and course of schizophrenia, in J. Rolf, A.S. Masten, D. Cicchetti, K.H. Nuechterlein and S. Weintraub (eds), *Risk and Protective Factors in the Development of Psychopathology.* Cambridge: Cambridge University Press.

Gooding, D.C. and Iacono, W.G. (1995) Schizophrenia through the lens of a developmental psychopathology perspective, in D. Cicchetti and D. J. Cohen (eds), *Developmental Psychopathology, Vol. I: Theory and Methods.* New York: Wiley.

Goodman, E., Slap, G.B. and Huang, B. (2003) The public health impact of socioeconomic status on adolescent depression and obesity, *American Journal of Public Health*, 93(11), 1844–1850.

Goodman, R., Slobodskaya, H. and Knyazev, G. (2005) Russian child mental health: a cross-sectional study of prevalence and risk factors, *European Child & Adolescent Psychiatry*, 14(1), 28–33.

Goodman, S.H. (2003) Genesis and epigenesis of psychopathology in children with depressed mothers: toward an integrative biopsychological perspective, in D. Cicchetti and E. Walker (eds), *Neurodevelopmental Mechnisms in Psychopathology.* New York: Cambridge University Press.

Goodyer, I.M. (2009) Early onset depression: meanings, mechanisms and processes, in S. Nolen-Hoeksema and L.M. Hilt (eds), *Handbook of Depression in Adolescents.* New York: Routledge/Taylor & Francis Group.

Goodyer, I.M., Bacon, A., Ban, M., Croudace, T. and Herbert, J. (2009) Serotonin transporter genotype, morning cortisol and subsequent depression in adolescents, *British Journal of Psychiatry*, 195(1), 39–45.

Gordis, E.B., Granger, D.A., Susman, E.J. and Trickett, P.K. (2008) Salivary alpha amylase-cortisol asymmetry in maltreated youth, *Hormones and Behavior*, 53(1), 96–103.

Gordis, E.B., Feres, N., Olezeski, C.L., Rabkin, A.N. and Trickett, P.K. (2010) Skin conductance reactivity and respiratory sinus arrhythmia among maltreated and comparison youth: relations with aggressive behavior, *Journal of Pediatric Psychology*, 35(5), 547.

Gorman-Smith, D. and Loeber, R. (2005) Are developmental pathways in disruptive behaviors the same for girls and boys? *Journal of Child and Family Studies*, 14(1), 15–27.

Gottesman. I.I. (1991) *Schizophrenia Genesis: The Origins of Madness.* New York: Freeman.

Gould, M.S., Shaffer, D. and Greenberg, T. (2003) The epidemiology of youth suicide, in R.A. King and A. Apter (eds), *Suicide in Children and Adolescents.* Cambridge: Cambridge University Press.

Grabe, S., Ward, L.M. and Hyde, J.S. (2008) The role of the media in body image concerns among women: a meta-analysis of experimental and correlational studies, *Psychological Bulletin*, 134(3), 460–476.

Graber, J.A., Seeley, J.R., Brooks-Gunn, J. and Lewinsohn, P.M. (2004) Is pubertal timing associated with psychopathology in young adulthood? *Journal of the American Academy of Child & Adolescent Psychiatry*, 43(6), 718–726.

Grados, M., Scahill, L. and Riddle, M.A. (1999) Pharmacotherapy in children and adolescents with obsessive-compulsive disorder, *Child and Adolescent Psychiatric Clinics of North America*, 8(3), 617–634.

Graetz, B.W. et al. (2001) Validity of DSM-IV ADHD subtypes in a nationally representative sample of Australian children and adolescents, *Journal of the American Academy of Child & Adolescent Psychiatry*, 40(12), 1410–1417.

Graf, S.C., Mullis, R.L. and Mullis, A.K. (2008) Identity formation of United States American and Asian Indian adolescents, *Adolescence*, 43, 57–69.

Graham, K.M. and Levy, J.B. (2009) Article renal, *Pediatrics in Review*, 30(5), 165–173.

Graham-Bermann, S.A. and Howell, K.H. (2011) Child maltreatment in the context of intimate partner violence, in J.F.B. Myers (ed.), *The APSAC Handbook on Child Maltreatment.* Thousand Oaks, CA: Sage.

Graham-Bermann, S.A., Gruber, G., Howell, K.H. and Girz, L. (2009) Factors discriminating among profiles of resilience and psychopathology in children exposed to intimate partner violence (IPV), *Child Abuse & Neglect*, 33(9), 648–660.

Graham-Bermann, S.A., Howell, K.H., Lilly, M. and DeVoe, E. (2011) Mediators and moderators of change in adjustment following intervention for children exposed to intimate partner violence, *Journal of Interpersonal Violence*, 26(9), 1815.

Grandin, L.D., Alloy, L.B. and Abramson, L.Y. (2007) Childhood stressful life events and bipolar spectrum disorders, *Journal of Social and Clinical Psychology*, 28(4), 460–478.

Grandin, T. (1996) *Thinking in Pictures.* New York: Vintage.

Grandin, T. (2006) *Thinking in Pictures: And other Reports from My Life with Autism.* London: Bloomsbury.

Granic, I. and Dishion, T.J. (2003) Deviant talk in adolescent friendships: a step toward measuring a pathogenic attractor process, *Social Development*, 12(3), 314–334.

Granic, I. and Patterson, G.R. (2006) Toward a comprehensive model of antisocial development: a dynamic systems approach, *Psychological Review*, 113(1), 101–131.

Gratz, K.L., Tull, M.T., Reynolds, E.K., Bagge, C.L., Latzman, R D., Daughters, S.B. and Lejuez, C.W. (2009) Extending extant models of the pathogenesis of borderline personality disorder to childhood borderline personality symptoms: the roles of affective dysfunction, disinhibition and self- and emotion-regulation deficits, *Development and Psychopathology*, 21(4), 1263–1291.

Green, J., Gilchrist, A., Burton, D. and Cox, A. (2000) Social and psychiatric functioning in adolescents with Asperger syndrome compared with conduct disorder, *Journal of Autism and Developmental Disorders*, 30, 279–293.

Greenberg, L.M. and Waldmant, I.D. (1993), Developmental normative data on the Test of Variables of Attention (TOVA™), *Journal of Child Psychology and Psychiatry*, 34(6), 1019–1030.

Greene, R.W. and Doyle, A.E. (1999) Toward a transactional conceptualization of oppositional defiant disorder: implications for assessment and treatment, *Clinical Child and Family Psychology Review*, 2(3), 129–148.

Greening, L. and Dollinger, S.J. (1989) Treatment of a child's sleep disturbance and related phobias in the family, in M.C. Roberts and C.E. Walker (eds), *Casebook of Child and Pediatric Psychology*. New York: Guilford.

Greenspan, S.I. (2003) *The Clinical Interview of the Child*, 3rd edn. Washington, DC: American Psychiatric Press.

Grella, C.E. and Joshi, V. (2003) Treatment processes and outcomes among adolescents with a history of abuse who are in drug treatment, *Child Maltreatment*, 8(1), 7–18.

Greven, C.U., Rijsdijk, F.V. and Plomin, R. (2011) A twin study of ADHD symptoms in early adolescence: hyperactivity-impulsivity and inattentiveness show substantial genetic overlap but also genetic specificity, *Journal of Abnormal Child Psychology*, 39(2), 265–275.

Grice, D.E., Halmi, K.A., Fichter, M.M., Strober, M., Woodside, D.B., Treasure, J.T. et al. (2002) Evidence for a susceptibility gene for anorexia nervosa on chromosome 1, *American Journal of Human Genetics*, 70, 787–792.

Griffith, G.M. et al. (2010) Using matched groups to explore child behavior problems and maternal well-being in children with Down syndrome and autism, *Journal of Autism and Developmental Disorders*, 40(5), 610–619.

Grigorenko, E.L. (2001) Developmental dyslexia: an update on genes, brains and environments, *Journal of Child Psychology and Psychiatry*, 42, 91–125.

Groark, C.J., McCall, R.B. and Fish, L. (2011). Characteristics of environments, caregivers and children in three Central American orphanages, *Infant Mental Health Journal*, 32(2), 232–250.

Gross, H.E., Shaw, D.S., Burwell, R.A. and Nagin, D.S. (2009) Transactional processes in child disruptive behavior and maternal depression: a longitudinal study from early childhood to adolescence, *Development and Psychopathology*, 21(1), 139–156.

Gross, J. (2010) Emotion regulation, in M. Lewis, J.M. Haviland-Jones and L.F. Barrett (eds), *Handbook of Emotions*, 2nd edn. New York: Guilford.

Gross, J. and Hayne, H. (1998) Drawing facilitates children's verbal reports of emotionally laden events, *Journal of Experimental Psychology: Applied*, 4(2), 163–179.

Gross, J., Hayne, H. and Drury, T. (2009) Drawing facilitates children's reports of factual and narrative information: implications for educational contexts, *Applied Cognitive Psychology*, 23(7), 953–971.

Groth-Marnat, G. (2009) *Handbook of Psychological Assessment*. New York: Wiley.

Group for the Advancement of Psychiatry Committee on the Family (1996) Global Assessment of Relational Functioning scale (GARF): I. Background and rationale, *Family Process*, 35(2), 155–172.

Grych, J.H., Jouriles, E.N., Swank, P.R., McDonald, R. and Norwood, W.D. (2000) Patterns of adjustment among children of battered women, *Journal of Consulting and Clinical Psychology*, 68, 84–94.

Grych, J.H., Harold, G.T. and Miles, C.J. (2003) A prospective investigation of appraisals as mediators of the link between interparental conflict and child adjustment,

Child Development, 74(4), 1176–1193.

Guckian, E. and Byrne, M. (2011) Best practice for conducting investigative interviews, *The Irish Psychologist*, 37(2), 69–77.

Guerra, N.G., Huesmann, L.R. and Spindler, A. (2003) Community violence exposure, social cognition and aggression among urban elementary-school children, *Child Development*, 74(5), 1561–1576.

Guerrero, A.P.S., Hishinuma, E.S., Andrade, N.N., Bell, C.K., Kurahar, D.K., Lee, T.G. et al. (2003) Demographic and clinical characteristics of adolescents in Hawaii with obsessive-compulsive disorder, *Archives of Pediatrics and Adolescent Medicine*, 157, 665–670.

Guertin, T.L. (1999) Eating behavior of bulimics, self-identified binge eaters and non-eating-disordered individuals: what differentiates these populations? *Clinical Psychology Review*, 19(1), 1–23.

Guiao, I. and Thompson, E.A. (2004) Ethnicity and problem behaviors among adolescent females in the United States, *Health Care for Women International*, 25(4), 296–310.

Gunewardene, A., Huon, G.F. and Zheng, R. (2001) Exposure to Westernization and dieting: a cross-cultural study, *International Journal of Eating Disorders*, 29(3), 289–293.

Gunnar, M. (2007) Stress effects on the developing brain, in D. Romer and E.F. Walker (eds), *Adolescent Psychopathology and the Developing Brain*. New York: Oxford University Press.

Gunnar, M.R., Bruce, J. and Donzella, B. (2001) Stress physiology, health and behavioral development, in A. Thornton (ed.), *The Well-Being of Children and Families: Research and Data Needs*. Ann Arbor, MI: University of Michigan Press.

Guntrip, H. (1986) My experience of analysis with Fairbairn and Winnicott (How complete a result does psychoanalytic therapy achieve?), in P. Buckley (ed.), *Essential Papers on Object Relations*, 2nd ed. New York: New York University Press.

Gustafsson, P. et al. (2000) Associations between cerebral blood-flow measured by single photon emission computed tomography (SPECT), electro-encephalogram (EEG), behaviour symptoms, cognition and neurological soft signs in children with attention-deficit hyperactivity disorder (ADHD), *Acta paediatrica*, 89(7), 830–835.

Gutierrez, P.M., Osman, A., Kopper, B.A. and Barrios, F.X. (2000) Why young people do not kill themselves: the Reasons for Living Inventory for Adolescents, *Journal of Clinical Child Psychology*, 29, 177–187.

Gutman, L.M., Eccles, J.S., Peck, S. and Malanchuk, O. (2011) The influence of family relations on trajectories of cigarette and alcohol use from early to late adolescence, *Journal of Adolescence*, 34(1), 119–128.

Guzder, J., Paris, J., Zelkowitz, P. and Feldman, R. (1999) Psychological risk factors for borderline pathology in school-age children, *Journal of the American Academy of Child & Adolescent Psychiatry*, 38(2), 206.

Haas, M. et al. (2009) A 6–week, randomized, double-blind, placebo-controlled study of the efficacy and safety of risperidone in adolescents with schizophrenia, *Journal of Child and Adolescent Psychopharmacology*, 19(6), 611–621.

Haberstick, B.C., Smolen, A. and Hewitt, J.K. (2006) Family-based association test of the 5HTTLPR and aggressive behavior in a general population sample of children, *Biological Psychiatry*, 59(9), 836–843.

Häfner, H. and Nowotny, B. (1995) Epidemiology of early-onset schizophrenia, *European archives of Psychiatry and Clinical Neuroscience*, 245(2), 80–92.

Haggerty, G.D., Siefert, C.J. and Weinberger, J. (2010) Examining the relationship between current attachment status and freely recalled autobiographical memories of childhood, *Psychoanalytic Psychology*, 27(1), 27.

Haggiag, T. (2000) The broken jigsaw: a child's perspective, in B. Lask and R. Bryant-Waugh (eds), *Anorexia Nervosa and Related Eating Disorders in Childhood and Adolescence*. Philadelphia, PA: Psychology Press.

Hahesy, A.L., Wilens, T.E., Biederman, J., Van Patten, S.L. and Spencer, T. (2002) Temporal association between childhood psychopathology and substance use disorders: findings from a sample of adults with opioid or alcohol dependency, *Psychiatry Research*, 109(3), 245–254, doi: 10.1016/s0165-1781(02)00015-x.

Hajek, C.A. et al. (2010) Agreement between parents and children on ratings of post-concussive symptoms following mild traumatic brain injury, *Child Neuropsychology*, 17(1), 17–33.

Hale, C.A. and Borkowski, J.G. (1991) Attention, memory and cognition, in J.L. Matson and J.A. Mulick (eds), *Handbook of Mental Retardation*. New York: Pergamon.

Hall, D.M. (1989) Birth asphyxia and cerebral palsy, *British Medical Journal*, 299(6694), 279.

Hall, K. (2001) *Asperger Syndrome, the Universe and Everything*. London: Jessica Kingsley.

Hall, R.V., Fox, R., Willard, D., Goldsmith, L., Emerson, M., Owen, M. et al. (1971) The teacher as observer and experimenter in the modification of disputing and talking-out behaviors, *Journal of Applied Behavioral Analysis*, 4, 141–149.

Halligan, S.L., Murray, L., Martins, C. and Cooper, P.J. (2007) Maternal depression and psychiatric outcomes in adolescent offspring: a 13-year longitudinal study, *Journal of Affective Disorders*, 97(1), 145–154.

Hallowell, E. and Ratey, J. (1994) *Driven to Distraction: Recognizing and Coping with Attention Deficit Disorder from Childhood through Adulthood*. New York: Simon & Schuster.

Halmi, K.A. (2009) Perplexities and provocations of eating disorders, *Journal of Child Psychology and Psychiatry*, 50(1–2), 163–169.

Hamby, S., Finkelhhor, D., Turner, H.A. and Ormrod, R.K. (2010) The overlap of witnessing partner violence with child maltreatment and other victimizations in a nationally representative survey of youth, *Child Abuse & Neglect*, 34, 734–741.

Hammen, C. (2009) Adolescent depression: stressful interpersonal contexts and risk for recurrence, *Current Directions in Psychological Science*, 18(4), 200–204.

Hammen, C. and Brennan, P.A. (2003) Severity, chronicity and timing of maternal depression and risk for adolescent offspring diagnoses in a community sample, *Archives of General Psychiatry*, 60(3), 253–258.

Hammen, C. and Rudolph, K.D. (1996) Childhood depression, in E.J. Mash and R.A. Barkley (eds), *Child Psychopathology*. New York: Guilford.

Hammen, C. and Rudolph, K.D. (2003) Childhood mood disorders, in E.J. Mash and R.A. Barkley (eds), *Child Psychopathology*, 2nd edn. New York: Guilford.

Hammen, C., Burge, D. and Stansbury, K. (1990) Relationship of mother and child variables to child outcomes in a high-risk sample: a causal modeling analysis, *Developmental Psychology*, 26, 24–30.

Hammer, E.F. (1958) *The Clinical Application of Projective Drawings*. Springfield, IL: Charles C. Thomas.

Hankin, B.L. and Abramson, L.Y. (2002) Measuring cognitive vulnerability to depression in adolescence: reliability, validity and gender differences, *Journal of Clinical Child and Adolescent Psychology*, 31(4), 491–504.

Hankin, B.L., Mermelstein, R. and Roesch, L. (2007) Sex differences in adolescent depression: stress exposure and reactivity, *Child Development*, 78(1), 279–295.

Hans, S.L., Auerbach, J.G., Styr, B. and Marcus, J. (2004) Offspring of parents with schizophrenia: mental disorders during childhood and adolescence, *Schizophrenia Bulletin*, 30, 303–315.

Hanson, R.F. and Spratt, E.G. (2000) Reactive attachment disorder: what we know about the disorder and implications for treatment, *Child Maltreatment*, 5(2), 137–145.

Hanson, R.K. and Morton-Bourgon, K.E. (2005) The characteristics of persistent sexual offenders: a meta-analysis of recidivism studies, *Journal of Consulting and Clinical Psychology*, 73(6), 1154.

Happé, F. (1999) Autism: cognitive deficit or cognitive style, *Trends in Cognitive Sciences*, 3(6), 216–222.

Happe, F. and Frith, U. (1996) Theory of mind and social impairment in children with conduct disorder, *British Journal of Developmental Psychology*, 14, 385–398.

Happé, F. and Frith, U. (2006) The weak coherence account: detail-focused cognitive style in autism spectrum disorders, *Journal of Autism and Developmental Disorders*, 36(1), 5–25.

Happé, F., Briskman, J. and Frith, U. (2001) Exploring the cognitive phenotype of autism: weak 'central coherence' in parents and siblings of children with autism: I. Experimental tests, *Journal of Child Psychology and Psychiatry*, 42(3), 299–307.

Happé, F.G. (1994) An advanced test of theory of mind: understanding of story characters' thoughts and feelings by able autistic, mentally handicapped and normal children and adults, *Journal of Autism and Developmental Disorders*, 24(2), 129–154.

Harbeck-Weber, C. and Peterson, L. (1993) Children's conceptions of illness and pain, *Annals of Child Development*, 9, 133–161.

Harbeck-Weber, C. and Peterson, L. (1996) Health-related disorders, in E.J. Mash and R.A. Barkley (eds), *Child Psychopathology*, New York: Guilford.

Hare, R.D. (1993) *Without Conscience: The Disturbing World of the Psychopaths among Us*. New York: Pocket Books.

Hare, R.D. (1996) Psychopathy: a clinical construct whose time has come, *Criminal Justice and Behavior*, 23(1), 25–54.

Harkness, K.L. and Lumley, M.N. (2008) Child abuse and neglect and the development of depression in children and adolescents, in J.R.Z. Abela and B.L. Hankin (eds), *Handbook of Depression in Children and Adolescents*. New York: Guilford Press.

Harlow, H.F. (1958) The nature of love, *American Psychologist*, 13, 673–685.

Harrington, R., Bredenkamp, D., Groothues, C., Rutter, M., Fudge, H. and Pickles, A. (1994) Adult outcomes of childhood and adolescent depression: III. Links with suicidal behaviours, *Journal of Child Psychology and Psychiatry*, 35(7), 1309–1319.

Harrington, R., Rutter, M. and Fombonne, E. (1996) Developmental pathways in depression: multiple meanings, antecedents and end-points, *Development and Psychopathology*, 8(4), 601–616.

Harris, M.J., Milich, R. and McAninch, C.B. (1998) When stigma becomes self-fulfilling prophecy: expectancy effects and the causes, consequences and treatment of peer rejection, in J. Brophy (ed.), *Advances in Research on Teaching: Expectations in the* Classroom, vol. 7. Greenwich, CT: JAI Press.

Harris, P.L. (2006) Social cognition, in D. Kuhn and R. Siegler (eds), *Handbook of Child Psychology*. New York: Wiley.

Hart, C. (1991) *Without Reason*. New York: Signet Book.

Hart, E.L. et al. (1995) Developmental change in attention-deficit hyperactivity disorder in boys: a four-year longitudinal study, *Journal of Abnormal Child Psychology*, 23(6), 729–749.

Hart, S.N., Germain, R. and Brassard, M. (1987) The challenge: to better understand and combat psychological maltreatment of children and youth, in M. Brassard, R. Germain and S. Hart (eds), *Psychological Maltreatment of Children and Youth*. New York: Pergamon Press.

Hart, S.N., Brassard, M.R., Davidson, H.A. Rivelis, E., Diaz, V. and Binggeli, N.J. (2011) Psychological maltreatment, in J.F.B. Myers (ed.), *The APSAC Handbook on Child Maltreatment*. Thousand Oaks, CA: Sage.

Harter, S. (1988) Developmental and dynamic changes in the nature of the selfconcept: implications for child psychotherapy, in S. Shirk (ed.), *Cognitive Development and Child Psychotherapy*. New York: Plenum.

Harter, S. (1988a) *Manual for the Self-Perception Profile for Adolescents*. Denver, CO: University of Denver.

Harter, S. (1990) Causes, correlates and the functional role of global self-worth: a life-span perspective, in R.J. Sternberg and J. Kolligian (eds), *Competence Considered*. New Haven, CT: Yale University Press.

Harter, S. (2006) Self-processes and developmental psychopathology, in D. Cicchetti and D.J. Cohen (eds), *Developmental Psychopathology. Volume I: Theory and Method*, 2nd edn. New York: Wiley.

Harter, S. (2012) *The Construction of the Self: Developmental and Sociocultural Foundations*, 2nd edn. New York: Guilford.

Harter, S. and Marold, D. (1991) A model of the determinants and mediational role of self-worth: implications for adolescent depression and suicidal ideation, in G.R. Goethals and J. Strauss (eds), *The Self: An Interdisciplinary Approach*. New York: Springer-Verlag.

Harter, S. and Marold, D.B. (1994) The directionality of the link between self-esteem and affect: beyond causal modeling, in D. Cicchetti and S.L. Toth (eds), *Rochester Symposium on Developmental Psychopathology: Disorders as Dysfunctions of the Self*, vol. 5. New York: Rochester.

Harter, S. and Whitesell, N.R. (1989) Developmental changes in children's understanding of single, multiple and blended emotion concepts, in C. Saarni and P.L. Harris (eds), *Children's Understanding of Emotion*. New York: Cambridge University Press.

Harter, S. and Whitesell, N.R. (1996) Multiple pathways to self-reported depression and psychological adjustment among adolescents, *Development and Psychopathology*, 8(4), 761–777.

Harter, S., Marold, D.B. and Whitesell, N.R. (1992) A model of psychosocial risk factors leading to suicidal ideation in young adolescents, *Development and Psychopathology*, 4(1), 167–188.

Harter, S., Bresnick, S., Bouchey, H.A. and Whitesell, N.R. (1997) The development of multiple role-related selves during adolescence, *Development and Psychopathology*, 9, 835–853.

Hartmann, T. (1997) *Attention Deficit Disorder: A New Perception*. Grass Valley, CA: Underwood Books.

Harvey, P.D. (1991) Cognitive and linguistic functions of adolescent children at risk for schizophrenia, in E.F. Walker (ed.), *Schizophrenia: A Life-course Developmental Perspective*. San Diego, CA: Academic Press.

Harvey, S.T. and Taylor, J.E. (2010) A meta-analysis of the effects of psychotherapy with sexually abused children and adolescents, *Clinical Psychology Review*, 30(5), 517–535.

Haskett, M.E., Portwood, S.G. and Lewis, K.M. (2010) Clinical and social implications of child physical abuse, in C. Ferguson (ed.), *Forensic Psychology and Violent Criminal Behavior: Clinical and Social Implications*. Thousand Oaks, CA: Sage Publications.

Haugaard, J.J. (2004) Recognizing and treating uncommon behavioral and emotional disorders in children and adolescents who have been severely maltreated: dissociative disorders, *Child Maltreatment*, 9, 146–153.

Hawk, B.N. and McCall, R.B. (2011) Specific extreme behaviors of postinstitutionalized Russian adoptees, *Developmental Psychology*, 47(3), 732.

Hawke, J.M., Albert, D. and Ford, J.D. (2008) Trauma and post-traumatic stress disorder in adolescent substance use disorders, in Y. Kaminer and O.G. Bukstein (eds), *Adolescent Substance Abuse: Psychiatric Comorbidity and High-Risk Behaviors*. New York: Routledge/Taylor & Francis Group.

Hawkins, E.H., Cummins, L.H. and Marlatt, G.A. (2004) Preventing substance abuse in American Indian and Alaska Native youth: promising strategies for healthier communities, *Psychological Bulletin*, 130(2), 304–323.

Hawley, K.M. and Weisz, J.R. (2003) Child, parent and therapist (dis)agreement on target problems in outpatient therapy: the therapist's dilemma and its implications, *Journal of Consulting and Clinical Psychology*, 71(1), 62.

Hay, P.J. and de M. Claudino, A. (2010) Evidence-based treatment for the eating disorders, in W.S. Agras (ed.), *The Oxford Handbook of Eating Disorders*. New York: Oxford University Press.

Haydel, M.E., Mercer, B.L. and Rosenblatt, E. (2011) Training assessors in therapeutic assessment, *Journal of Personality Assessment*, 93(1), 16–22.

Hayward, C., Gotlib, I.H., Schraedley, P.K. and Litt, I.F. (1999) Ethnic differences in the association between pubertal status and symptoms of depression in adolescent girls, *Journal of Adolescent Health*, 25(2), 143–149.

Hazza, I. and Tarawneh, H. (2002) Primary nocturnal enuresis among school children in Jordan, *Saudi Journal of Kidney Diseases and Transplantation*, 13(4), 478.

Heatherton, T.F. and Baumeister, R.F. (1991) Binge eating as escape from self-awareness, *Psychological Bulletin*, 110(1), 86–108.

Heaton, R.K. et al. (1993) *Wisconsin card sorting test manual: revised and expanded*. Odessa, FL: Psychological Assessment Resources.

Heinrich, H., Gevensleben, H. and Strehl, U. (2007). Annotation: neurofeedback – train your brain to train behavior, *Journal of Child Psychology and Psychiatry*, 48(1), 3–16.

Heinrichs, R.W. and Zakzanis, K.K. (1998) Neurocognitive deficit in schizophrenia: a quantitative review of the evidence, *Neuropsychology* 12(3), 426–445.

Henggeler, S.W., Schoenwald, S.K., Borduin, C.M., Rowland, M.D. and Cunningham, P.B. (2009) *Multisystemic Therapy for Antisocial Behavior in Children and Adolescents*, 2nd edn. New York: Guilford Press.

Hermelin, B. (2001) *Bright Splinters of the Mind: A Personal Story of Research with Autistic Savants*. London: Jessica Kingsley.

Herrenkohl, E.C., Herrenkohl, R.C. and Egolf, B. (1994) Resilient early school-age children from maltreating homes: outcomes in late adolescence, *American Journal of Orthopsychiatry*, 64(2), 301–309.

Herrenkohl, R.C., Egolf, B.P. and Herrenkohl, E.C. (1997) Preschool antecedents of adolescent assaultive behavior: a longitudinal study, *American Journal of Orthopsychiatry*, 67, 422–432.

Herrenkohl, T.I. and Herrenkohl, R.C. (2007) Examining the overlap and prediction of multiple forms of child maltreatment, stressors, and socioeconomic status: A longitudinal analysis of youth outcomes,

Journal of Family Violence, 22(7), 553–562.

Hess, K.L. et al. (2008) Autism treatment survey: Services received by children with autism spectrum disorders in public school classrooms, *Journal of Autism and Developmental Disorders*, 38(5), 961–971.

Hetherington, E.M. (2006) The influence of conflict, marital problem solving and parenting on children's adjustment in nondivorced, divorced and remarried families, in A. Clarke-Stewart and J. Dunn (eds), *Families Count: Effects on Child and Adolescent Development*. New York: Cambridge University Press.

Hetherington, E.M. and Elmore, A M. (2003) Risk and resilience in children coping with their parents' divorce and remarriage, in S.S. Luthar (ed.), *Resilience and Vulnerability: Adaptation in the Context of Childhood Adversities*. New York: Cambridge University Press.

Hetrick, S., Merry, S., McKenzie, J., Sindahl, P. and Proctor, M. (2007) Selective serotonin reuptake inhibitors (SSRIs) for depressive disorders in children and adolescents, *Cochrane Database of Systematic Reviews*, 18 July (3), CD004851.

Heuveline, P. and Weinshenker, M. (2008) The international child poverty gap: does demography matter? *Demography*, 45(1), 173–191.

Hewitt, J.K., Silberg, J.L. and Rutter, M. (1997) Genetics and developmental psychopathology: I. Phenotypic assessment in the Virginia Twin Study of Adolescent Behavioral Development, *Journal of Child Psychology and Psychiatry*, 38(943), 963.

Hibell, B., Ulf, G., Ahlström, S., Balakireva, O., Bjarnason, T., Kokkevi, A. and Kraus, L. (2009) *The 2007 ESPAD Report – Substance Use among Students in 35 European Countries*. Stockholm: Swedish Council for Information on Alcohol and Other Drugs (CAN).

Hillegers, M.H.J., Reichart, C.G., Wals, M., Verhulst, F.C., Ormel, J. and Nolen, W.A. (2005) Five-year prospective outcome of psychopathology in the adolescent offspring of bipolar parents, *Bipolar Disorders*, 7(4), 344–350.

Hilt, L., Cha, C. and Nolen-Hoeksema, S. (2008) Nonsuicidal self-injury in young adolescent girls: moderators of the distress-function relationship, *Journal of Consulting and Clinical Psychology*, 76(1), 63–71.

Hilt, L.M. and Nolen-Hoeksema, S. (2009) The emergence of gender differences in depression in adolescence, in S. Nolen-Hoeksema and L.M. Hilt (eds), *Handbook of Depression in Adolescents*. New York: Routledge/Taylor & Francis Group.

Hinduja, S. and Patchin, J.W. (2010) Bullying, cyberbullying and suicide, *Archives of Suicide Research*, 14(3), 206–221.

Hinshaw, S.P. (2000) Attention-deficit/hyperactivity disorder: the search for viable treatments, in P.C. Kendall (ed.), *Child and Adolescent Therapy: Cognitive-Behavioral Procedures*. New York: Guilford.

Hinshaw, S.P. (2007) Moderators and mediators of treatment outcome for youth with ADHD: understanding for whom and how interventions work, *Ambulatory Pediatrics*, 7(1), 91–100.

Hinshaw, S.P. (2010) Growing up in a family with bipolar disorder: personal experience, developmental lessons and overcoming stigma, in D.J. Miklowitz and D. Cichetti (eds), *Understanding Bipolar Disorder: A Developmental Psychopathology Perspective*. New York: Guilford Press.

Hinshaw, S.P. and Anderson, C.A. (1996) Conduct and oppositional defiant disorders, in E.J. Mash and R.A. Barkley (eds), *Child Psychopathology*. New York: Guilford.

Hinshaw, S.P. and Lee, S.S. (2003) Conduct and oppositional defiant disorders, in E.J. Mash and R.A. Barkley (eds), *Child Psychopathology*, 2nd edn. New York: Guilford.

Hinshaw, S.P., Zupan, B.A., Simmel, C., Nigg, J.T. and Melnick, S. (1997) Peer status in boys with and without attention-deficit hyperactivity disorder: predictions from overt and covert antisocial behavior, social isolation and authoritative parenting beliefs, *Child Development*, 68, 880–896.

Hirshfeld, D.R., Biederman, J., Brody, L., Faraone, S.V. and Rosenbaum, J.F. (1997) Expressed emotion toward children with behavioral inhibition: associations with maternal anxiety disorder, *Journal of the American Academy of Child and Adolescent Psychiatry*, 36, 910–917.

Ho, M.K. (1992) *Minority Children and Adolescents In Therapy*. Thousand Oaks, CA: Sage Publications.

Hobson, R., Patrick, M., Crandell, L., Garcia-Perez, R. and Lee, A. (2005) Personal relatedness and attachment in infants of mothers with borderline personality disorder, *Development and Psychopathology*, 17(2), 329–348.

Hodapp, R.M. (2002) Parenting children with mental retardation, *Children and Parenting*, 5, 355.

Hodapp, R.M. and Dykens, E.M. (2003) Mental retardation (intellectual disabilities) in E.J. Mash and R.A. Barkley (eds), *Child Psychopathology*, 2nd edn. New York: Guilford.

Hodapp, R.M. and Zigler, E. (1990) Applying the developmental perspective to individuals with Down syndrome, in D. Ciccetti and M. Beeghly (eds), *Children with Down Syndrome: A Developmental Perspective*. Cambridge: Cambridge University Press.

Hodapp, R.M. and Zigler, E. (1995) Past, present and future issues in the developmental approach to mental retardation and developmental disabilities, in D. Cicchetti and D.J. Cohen (eds), *Developmental Psychopathology: Vol. 2. Risk, disorder and adaptation*. New York: Wiley.

Hodapp, R.M., Dykens, E.M. and Masino, L.L. (1997) Families of children with Prader-Willi syndrome: stress-support and relations to child characteristics, *Journal of Autism and Developmental Disorders*, 27(1), 11–24.

Hoeve, M., Dubas, J., Eichelsheim, V., van der Laan, P., Smeenk, W. and Gerris, J. (2009) The relationship between parenting and delinquency: a meta-analysis, *Journal of Abnormal Child Psychology*, 37(6), 749–775.

Hofer, C., Eisenberg, N. and Reiser, M. (2010) The role of socialization, effortful control and ego resiliency in French adolescents' social functioning, *Journal of Research on Adolescence*, 20, 555–582.

Hoffman, M.L. (2010) Empathy and prosocial behavior, in M. Lewis, J.M. Haviland-Jones and L.F. Barrett (eds), *Handbook of Emotions*, 2nd edn. New York: Guilford.

Hollenbeck, J., Dyl, J. and Spirito, A. (2003) Social factors: family functioning, in A. Spirito and J.C. Overholser (eds), *Evaluating and Treating Adolescent Suicide Attempters: From Research to Practice*. New York: Academic Press.

Hollis, C. (1995) Child and adolescent (juvenile onset) schizophrenia. A case control study of premorbid developmental impairments, *The British Journal of Psychiatry*, 166(4), 489–495.

Hollis, C. (2000) Diagnosis and differential diagnosis, in H. Remschmidt (ed.), *Schizophrenia in Children and Adolescents*. New York: Cambridge University Press.

Hollis, C. (2003) Developmental precursors of child and adolescent-onset schizophrenia and affective psychoses: diagnostic specificity and continuity with symptom dimensions, *British Journal of Psychiatry*, 182, 37–44.

Hollis, C. (2004) Incidence of adolescent-onset psychosis in the Trent Region of the U.K., *Schizophrenia Research*, 67 (supplement), 65.

Holmbeck, G.N., Greenley, R.N. and Franks, E.A. (2004) Developmental issues in evidence-based practice, in P.M. Barrett and T.H. Ollendick (eds), *Handbook of Interventions that Work with Children and Adolescents*. Chichester: John Wiley.

Holmbeck, G.N., Devine, K.A., Wasserman, R., Schellinger, K. and Tuminello, E. (2011) Guides from developmental psychology, in C.K. Philip (ed.), *Child and Adolescent Therapy: Cognitive-Behavioral Procedures*, 4th edn. New York: Guilford.

Holowka, D.W. et al. (2003) Childhood abuse and dissociative symptoms in adult schizophrenia, *Schizophrenia Research*, 60(1), 87–90.

Honjo, H. et al. (2002) Treatment of monosymptomatic nocturnal enuresis by acupuncture: a preliminary study, *International Journal of Urology*, 9(12), 672–676.

Hooper, S.R., Baglio, C. and Hughes, J.N. (2001) Children and adolescents experiencing traumatic brain injury, in J.N. Hughes, A.M. La Greca and J.C. Conoly (eds) *Handbook of Psychological Services for Children and Adolescents*. New York: Oxford University Press.

Hooper, S.R., Walker, N.W. and Howard, C. (2001b) Training school psychologists in traumatic brain injury. The North Carolina model, *North Carolina Medical Journal*, 62, 350–354.

Hops, H., Andrews, J.A., Duncan, S.C., Duncan, T.E. and Tildesley, E. (2000) Adolescent drug use development: a social interactional and contextual perspective, in A.J. Sameroff, M. Lewis and S.M. Miller (eds), *Handbook of Developmental Psychopathology*. New York: Kluwer Academic.

Hourigan, S.E., Goodman, K.L. and Southam-Gerow, M.A., 2011. Discrepancies in parents' and children's reports of child emotion regulation, *Journal of Experimental Child Psychology*, 110(2), 198–212.

Houts, A.C. (2003) Behavioral treatment for enuresis, in A.E. Kazdin and J.R. Weisz (eds), *Evidence-Based Psychotherapies for Children and Adolescents*. New York: Guilford.

Howard, B., Chu, B.C., Krain, A.L., Marrs-Garcia, A.L. and Kendall, P.C. (2000) *Cognitive-Behavioral Family Therapy for Anxious Children: Therapist Manual*. Ardmore, PA: Workbook Publishing.

Howell, K.H., Graham-Bermann, S.A., Czyz, E. and Lilly, M. (2010) Assessing resilience in preschool children exposed to intimate partner violence, *Violence and Victims*, 25(2), 150–164.

Howlin, P. (2000) Outcome in adult life for more able individuals with autism or Asperger syndrome, *Autism*, 4(1), 63.

Howlin, P., Alcock. J., Burkin, C. (2005) An eight year follow-up of a supported employment service for high ability adults with autism or Asperger syndrome, *Autism*, 9, 533–549.

Hoza, B., Kaiser, N.M. and Hurt, E. (2008) Evidence-based treatments for attention-deficit/hyperactivity disorder (ADHD), in M. Roberts, D. Elkin and R. Steele (eds), *Handbook of Evidence-based Therapies for Childhood and Adolescents*. New York, NY: Springer.

Hrabosky, J.I., Cash, T.F., Veale, D., Neziroglu, F., Soll, E.A., Garner, D.M. et al. (2009) Multidimensional body image comparisons among patients with eating disorders, body dysmorphic disorder and clinical controls: a multisite study, *Body Image*, 6(3), 155–163.

Hudson, J.I., Hiripi, E., Pope, H.G. Jr and Kessler, R.C. (2007) The prevalence and correlates of eating disorders in the National Comorbidity Survey replication, *Biological Psychiatry*, 61(3), 348–358.

Huesmann, L.R. and Reynolds, M.A. (2001) Cognitive processes and the development of aggression, in A.C. Bohart and D.J. Stipek (eds), *Constructive and Destructive Behavior: Implications for Family, School and Society*. Washington, DC: American Psychological Association.

Huesmann, L.R., Moise-Titus, J., Podolski, C. and Eron, L.D. (2003) Longitudinal relations between children's exposure to tv violence and their aggressive and violent behavior in young adulthood, *Developmental Psychology*, 39(2), 201–221.

Huey, S.J. and Polo A.J. (2008) Evidence-based psychosocial treatments for ethnic minority youth: a review and meta-analysis, *Journal of Clinical Child and Adolescent Psychology*, 37, 262–301.

Huey, S.J. and Polo, A. (2010) Assessing the effects of evidence-based psychotherapies with ethnic minority youths, in J.R. Weisz and A.E. Kazdin (eds), *Evidence-Based Psychotherapies for Children and Adolescents*, 2nd edn. New York: Guilford Press.

Huisman, M., Araya, R., Lawlor, D., Ormel, J., Verhulst, F. and Oldehinkel, A. (2010) Cognitive ability, parental socioeconomic position and internalising and externalising problems in adolescence: findings from two European cohort studies, *European Journal of Epidemiology*, 25(8), 569–580.

Hultén, A., Jiang, G.X., Wasserman, D., Hawton, K., Hjelmeland, H., De Leo, D. et al. (2001) Repetition of attempted suicide among teenagers in Europe: frequency, timing and risk factors, *European Child & Adolescent Psychiatry*, 10(3), 161–169.

Humphrey, L. (1989) Observed family interactions among subtypes of eating disorders using structural analysis of social behavior, *Journal of Consulting and Clinical Psychology*, 57, 206–214.

Humphrey, N. (1998) Cave art, autism and the evolution of the human mind, *Cambridge Archaeological Journal*, 8(02), 165–191.

Hurlock, E.B. (1967) *Adolescent Development*. New York: McGraw-Hill.

Hutchinson, D.M., Rapee, R.M. and Taylor, A. (2010) Body dissatisfaction and eating disturbances in early adolescence: A structural modeling investigation examining negative affect and peer factors, *Journal of Early Adolescence*, 30(4), 489–517.

Hutchinson, G., Takei, N., Fahy, T.A., Bhugra, D., Gilvarry, C., Moran, P. et al. (1996) Morbid risk of schizophrenia in first-degree relatives of White and African-Caribbean patients with psychosis, *British Journal of Psychiatry*, 169, 776–780.

Hyde, J.S., Mezulis, A.H. and Abramson, L.Y. (2008) The ABCs of depression: integrating affective, biological and cognitive models to explain the emergence of the gender difference in depression, *Psychological Review*, 115(2), 291–313.

Hyman, S.W. (2001) Mood disorders in children and adolescents: an NIMH perspective, *Biological Psychiatry*, 49, 962–969.

Hysing, M. et al. (2009) Emotional and behavioural problems in subgroups of children with chronic illness: results from a large-scale population study, *Child: Care, Health and Development*, 35(4), 527–533.

Ialongo, N., Koenig-McNaught, A., Wagner, B., Pearson, J., McCreary, B., Poduska, J. and Kellam, S. (2004) African American children's reports of depressed mood, hopelessness and suicidal ideation and later suicide attempts, *Suicide and Life-Threatening Behavior*, 34(4), 395–407.

Ialongo, N.S., Rogosch, F.A., Cicchetti, D., Toth, S.L., Buckley, J., Petras, H. and Neiderhiser, J.M. (2006) A developmental psychopathology approach to the prevention of mental health disorders, in D. Cicchetti and D. J. Cohen (eds), *Developmental Psychology. Volume I: Theory and Method*, 2nd edn. New York: Wiley.

Individuals with Disabilities Education Act Amendments of 1997,

Public Law 105–17 (IDEA), 20 U. S. C. Chapter 33, Section 1415 et seq. (EDLAW, 1997).

Individuals with Disabilities Education Act Amendments of 2004, Public Law 108–446 (IDEA) (2004) The Individuals with Disabilities Education Improvement Act.

Isaksson, J., Lindqvist, R. and Bergström, E. (2010) Struggling for recognition and inclusion – parents' and pupils' experiences of special support measures in school, *International Journal of Qualitative Studies on Health and Well-Being*, 5, doi: 10.3402/qhw.v5i1.4646.

Izard, C.E., Youngstrom, E.A., Fine, S.E., Mostow, A.J. and Trentacosta, C.J. (2006) Emotions and developmental psychopathology, in D. Cicchetti and D. J. Cohen (eds), *Developmental Psychopathology. Vol I: Theory and Method*, 2nd edn. New York: Wiley.

Jablensky, A. et al. (1992) Schizophrenia: manifestations, incidence and course in different cultures: a World Health Organization ten-country study, *Psychological Medicine*, monograph supplement 20.

Jack, D.C. and Ali, A. (2010) *Silencing the Self Across Cultures: Depression and Gender in the Social World*. New York: Oxford University Press.

Jackson, L. and Attwood, T. (2003) Freaks, geeks and Asperger syndrome: a user guide to adolescence, *European Child & Adolescent Psychiatry*, 12, 50–51.

Jacobs, J. (1971) *Adolescent Suicide*. New York: Wiley.

Jacobs, J.R. and Bovasso, G.B. (2009) Re-examining the long-term effects of experiencing parental death in childhood on adult psychopathology, *Journal of Nervous and Mental Disease*, 197(1), 24–27.

Jacobsen, L.K. and Rapoport, J.L. (1998) Research update: childhood-onset schizophrenia: implications of clinical and neurobiological research, *Journal of Child Psychology and Psychiatry*, 39(1), 101–113.

Jacobson, C.M. and Gould, M. (2009) Suicide and nonsuicidal self-injurious behaviors among youth: risk and protective factors, in S. Nolen-Hoeksema and L.M. Hilt (eds), *Handbook of Depression in Adolescents*. New York: Routledge/Taylor & Francis Group.

Jacobvitz, D., Riggs, S. and Johnson, E. (1999) Cross-sex and same-sex family alliances: immediate and long-term effects on sons and daughters, in N.D. Chase (ed.), *Burdened Children*. Thousand Oaks, CA: Sage.

Jacobvitz, D., Hazen, N., Curran, M. and Hitchens, K. (2004) Observations of early triadic family interactions: boundary disturbances in the family predict depressive and anxious symptoms in middle childhood, *Development and Psychopathology*, 16(3), 577–592.

Jaffe, P.G., Lemon, N.K.D. and Poisson, S.E. (2002) *Child Custody and Domestic Violence: A Call For Safety and Accountability*. Thousand Oaks, CA: Sage.

Jaffee, S.R., Caspi, A., Moffitt, T.E., Polo-Tomas, M., Price, T.S. and Taylor, A. (2004) The limits of child effects: evidence for genetically mediated child effects on corporal punishment but not on physical maltreatment, *Developmental Psychology*, 40(6), 1047–1058.

Jaser, S.S., Champion, J.E., Reeslund, K.L., Keller, G., Merchant, M.J., Benson, M. and Compas, B.E. (2007) Cross-situational coping with peer and family stressors in adolescent offspring of depressed parents, *Journal of Adolescence*, 30(6), 917–932.

Javier, R.A., Baden, A.L., Biafora, F.A. and Camacho–Gingerich, A. (2007). *Handbook of Adoption: Implications for Researchers, Practitioners and Families*. Thousand Oaks, CA: Sage Publications.

Jenkins, J.D., Jenkins, J.H. and Barrett, R.J. (2004) *Schizophrenia, Culture and Subjectivity: The Edge of Experience*. Cambridge: Cambridge University Press.

Jensen, P.S. and Hoagwood, K. (1997) The book of names: DSM-IV in context, *Development and Psychopathology*, 9, 231–249.

Jessor, R. and Jessor, S.L. (1977) *Problem Behavior and Psychosocial Development: A Longitudinal Study of Youth*. New York: Academic Press.

Jessor, R., Donovan, J.E. and Costa, R.M. (1991) *Beyond Adolescence: Problem Behavior and Young Adult Development*. New York: Cambridge University Press.

Jessor, R., Van Den Bos, J., Vanderryn, J., Costa, F.M. and Turbin, M.S. (1995) Protective factors in adolescent problem behavior: moderator effects and developmental change, *Developmental Psychology*, 31(6), 923–933.

Jewell, J.D. and Stark, K.D. (2003) Comparing the family environments of adolescents with conduct disorder or depression, *Journal of Child and Family Studies*, 12(1), 77–89.

Johansen, E.B. et al. (2009) Origins of altered reinforcement effects in ADHD, *Behavioral and Brain Functions*, 5(1), 7.

Johnson, A. (2002) Prevalence and characteristics of children with cerebral palsy in Europe, *Developmental Medicine & Child Neurology*, 44(9), 633–640.

Johnson, C. and Larson, R. (1982) Bulimia: an analysis of moods and behavior, *Psychosomatic Medicine*, 44(4), 341–351.

Johnson, J., Cohen, P., Kasen, S., Skodol, A., Hamagami, F. and Brook, J. (2000) Age related change in personality disorder trait levels between early adolescence and adulthood: a community based longitudinal investigation, *Acta Psychiatrica Scandinavica*, 102(4), 265–275.

Johnson, J.G., Cohen, P., Brown, J., Smailes, E. et al. (1999) Childhood maltreatment increases risk for personality disorders during adulthood, *Archives of General Psychiatry*, 56(7), 600–606.

Johnson, J.G., Cohen, P., Gould, M.S., Kasen, S., Brown, J. and Brook, J.S. (2002) Childhood adversities, interpersonal difficulties and risk for suicide attempts during late adolescence and early adulthood, *Archives of General Psychiatry*, 59(8), 741–749.

Johnson, J.G., Bromley, E., Bornstein, R.F. and Sneed, J.R. (2006) Personality disorders, in D.A. Wolfe and E.J. Mash (eds), *Behavioral and Emotional Disorders in Adolescents: Nature, Assessment and Treatment*. New York: Guilford.

Johnston, C. and Jassy, J.S. (2007) Attention-deficit/hyperactivity disorder and oppositional/conduct problems: links to parent-child interactions, *Journal of the Canadian Academy of Child and Adolescent Psychiatry*, 16(2), 74–79.

Johnston, C. and Mash, E.J. (2001) Families of children with attention-deficit/hyperactivity disorder: review and recommendations for future research, *Clinical Child and Family Psychology Review*, 4(3), 183–207.

Johnston, L.D., O'Malley, P.M. and Bachman, J.G. (2011) *Monitoring the Future: National Survey Results on Adolescent Drug Use: Overview of Key Findings*. Bethesda, MD: National Institute on Drug Abuse.

Joiner, T.E., Metalsky, G.I., Katz, J. and Beach, S.R.H. (1999) Depression and excessive reassurance-seeking, *Psychological Inquiry*, 10, 269–278.

Joormann, J., Talbot, L. and Gotlib, I. H. (2007) Biased processing of emotional information in girls at risk for depression, *Journal of Abnormal Psychology*, 116(1), 135–143.

Joormann, J., Eugene, F. and Gotlib, I.H. (2009) Parental depression: impact on offspring and mechanisms underlying transmission of risk, in S. Nolen-Hoeksema and L.M. Hilt (eds), *Handbook of Depression in Adolescents*. New York: Routledge/Taylor & Francis Group.

Jordan, J., Joyce, P.R., Carter, F.A., Horn, J., McIntosh, V.V.W., Luty, S. E. et al. (2008) Specific and nonspecific comorbidity in anorexia nervosa, *International Journal of Eating Disorders*, 41(1), 47–56.

Jordan, R. and Powell, S. (1995) *Understanding and Teaching Children with Autism*. Chichester: Wiley.

Jouriles, E.N., Wolfe, D.A., Garrido, E.F. and McCarthy, A. (2006) Dating violence, in D.A. Wolfe and E.J. Mash (eds), *Behavioral and Emotional Disorders in Adolescents: Nature, Assessment and Treatment*. New York: Guilford.

Jucksch, V., Salbach-Andrae, H., Lenz, K., Goth, K., Döpfner, M., Poustka, F. et al. (2011) Severe affective and behavioural dysregulation is associated with significant psychosocial adversity and impairment, *Journal of Child Psychology and Psychiatry*, 52, 686–695.

Judd, P.H. and McGlashan, T.H. (2003) *A Developmental Model of Borderline Personality Disorder*. Washington, DC: American Psychiatric Publishing.

Jurkovic, G.J. (1997) *Lost childhoods: The Plight of the Parentified Child*. New York: Brunner/Mazel.

Kadesjö, B., Gillberg, C. and Hagberg, B. (1999) Brief report: autism and Asperger syndrome in seven-year-old children: a total population study, *Journal of Autism and Developmental Disorders*, 29(4), 327–331.

Kaffman, M. and Elizur, E. (1977) Infants who become enuretics: a longitudinal study of 161 kibbutz children, *Monographs of the Society for Research in Child Development*, 42(2), 1–89.

Kalinauskiene, L. et al. (2009) Supporting insensitive mothers: the Vilnius randomized control trial of video-feedback intervention to promote maternal sensitivity and infant attachment security, *Child: Care, Health and Development*, 35(5), 613–623.

Kameguchi, K. and Murphy-Shigetmatsu, S. (2001) Family psychology and family therapy in Japan, *American Psychologist*, 56(2), 65–70.

Kaminer, R. and Vig, S. (1995) Standardized intelligence testing: does it do more good than harm? *Journal of Developmental and Behavioral Pediatrics*, 16, 425–427.

Kaminer, Y. and Bukstein, O.G. (2008) *Adolescent Substance Abuse: Psychiatric Comorbidity and High-Risk Behaviors*. New York: Routledge/Taylor & Francis Group.

Kamphaus, R.W. and Frick, P.J. (1996) *Clinical Assessment of Child and Adolescent Personality and Behavior*. Boston, MA: Allyn & Bacon.

Kamphaus, R.W. and Frick, P.J. (2005) *Clinical Assessment of Child and Adolescent Personality and Behavior*, 2nd edn. New York: Springer Verlag.

Kamppi, D. and Gilmore, L. (2010) Assessing cognitive development in early childhood: a comparison of the Bayley-III and the Stanford-Binet, *Australian Educational and Developmental Psychologist*, 27(2), 70–75.

Kane, P. and Garber, J. (2004) The relations among depression in fathers, children's psychopathology and father-child conflict: a meta-analysis, *Clinical Psychology Review*, 24, 339–360.

Kanner, L. (1944) Early infantile autism, *The Journal of Pediatrics*, 25(3), 211–217.

Kanner, L. et al. (1943) Autistic disturbances of affective contact, *Nervous Child*, 2(1943), 217–250.

Karmiloff-Smith, A. (2009) Nativism versus neuroconstructivism: rethinking the study of developmental disorders, *Developmental Psychology*, 45(1), 56–63.

Kärnä, A., Voeten, M., Little, T.D., Poskiparta, E., Kaljonen, A. and Salmivalli, C. (2011) A large-scale evaluation of the KiVa antibullying program: grades 4–6, *Child Development*, 82(1), 311–330.

Kasari, C., Sigman, M., Baumgartner, P. and Stipek, D.J. (1993). Pride and mastery in children with autism, *Journal of Child Psychology and Psychiatry*, 34, 353–362.

Kasen, S., Berenson, K., Cohen, P. and Johnson, J.G. (2004) The effects of school climate on changes in aggressive and other behaviors related to bullying, in D.L. Espelage and S.M. Swearer (eds), *Bullying in American Schools: A Social-Ecological Perspective on Prevention and Intervention*. Mahwah, NJ: Lawrence Erlbaum.

Kasenchak, K.L. (2003) *Reconceptualizing Reactive Attachment Disorder: A Borderline Condition in Children*. Berkeley, CA: Wright Institute Graduate School of Psychology.

Kaslow, F.W. (1996) *Handbook of Relational Diagnosis and Dysfunctional Family Patterns*. New York: Wiley.

Kaslow, N.J., Broth, M.R., Arnette, N.C. and Collins, M.H. (2009) Family-based treatment for adolescent depression, in S. Nolen-Hoeksema and L.M. Hilt (eds), *Handbook of Depression in Adolescents*. New York: Routledge/Taylor & Francis Group.

Kasten, E.F. and Coury, D.L. (1991) Health policy and prevention of mental retardation, *Handbook of Mental Retardation*, 121, 336.

Katz, L.Y., Kozyrskyj, A.L., Prior, H.J., Enns, M.W., Cox, B.J. and Sareen, J.S. (2008) Effect of regulatory warnings on antidepressant prescription rates, use of health services and outcomes among children, adolescents and young adults, *Canadian Medical Association Journal*, 178, 1005–1011.

Katz, P.A. (2003) Racists or tolerant multiculturalists: how do they begin? *American Psychologist*, 58(11), 897–909.

Kaufman, B. (1981) *A Miracle to Believe in*. New York: Fawcett Crest.

Kavale, K.A. and Forness, S.R. (1996) Social skill deficits and learning disabilities: a meta-analysis, *Journal of Learning Disabilities*, 29, 226–237.

Kavale, K.A. and Forness, S.R. (2000) History, rhetoric and reality, *Remedial and Special Education*, 21(5), 279–296.

Kaye, W.H., Greeno, C.G., Moss, H., Fernstrom, J., Fernstrom, M., Lilenfeld, L.R. et al. (1998) Alterations in serotonin activity and psychiatric symptoms after recovery from bulimia nervosa, *Archives of General Psychiatry*, 55(10), 927–935.

Kaye, W.H., Barbarich, B.S., Putnam, B.S., Gendall, K.A., Fernstrom, J., Fernstrom, M. et al. (2003) Anxiolytic effects of acute tryptophan depletion (ATD) in anorexia nervosa, *International Journal of Eating Disorders*, 33, 257–267.

Kaye, W.H., Bulik, C.M., Thornton, L., Barbarich, N., Masters, K. and Price Foundation Collaborative Group (2004) Comorbidity of anxiety disorders with anorexia and bulimia nervosa, *American Journal of Psychiatry*, 161, 2215–2221.

Kaye, W.H., Bailer, U.F., Frank, G.K., Wagner, A. and Henry, S.E. (2005) Brain imaging of serotonin after recovery from anorexia and bulimia nervosa, *Physiology & Behavior*, 86(1–2), 15–17.

Kazak, A. E. (1992) The social context of coping with childhood chronic illness: Family systems and social support, in A.M. La Greca, L.J. Siegel, J.L. Wallander and C.E. Walker (eds), *Stress and Coping in Child Health*. New York: Guilford.

Kazak, A.E., Segal-Andrews, A.M. and Johnson, K. (1995) Pediatric psychology research and practice: a family/systems approach, in M.C. Roberts (ed.), *Handbook of Pediatric Psychology*, 2nd edn. New York: Guilford Press.

Kazak, A.E., Simms, S. and Rourke, M.T. (2002) Family systems practice in pediatric psychology, *Journal of Pediatric Psychology*, 27(2), 133.

Kazdin, A.E. (1997) A model for developing effective treatments: progression and interplay of theory, research and practice, *Journal of Clinical Child Psychology*, 26, 114–129.

Kazdin, A.E. (2008) Evidence-based treatment and practice: new opportunities to bridge clinical research and practice, enhance the knowledge base and improve patient care, *American Psychologist*, 63(3), 146–159.

Kazdin, A.E. (2010) Problem-solving skills training and parent management training for oppositional defiant disorder and conduct disorder, in J.R. Weisz and A.E. Kazdin (eds), *Evidence-Based Psychotherapies for Children and Adolescents*, 2nd edn. New York: Guilford Press.

Kazdin, A.E. and Weisz, J.R. (2010) Introduction: context, background and goals, in J.R. Weisz and A.E. Kazdin (eds), *Evidence-Based Psychotherapies for Children and Adolescents*, 2nd edn. New York: Guilford.

Kearney, C.A. (2009) *Casebook in Child Behavior Disorders*. Belmont, CA: Wadsworth.

Keel, P.K. and Haedt, A. (2008) Evidence-based psychosocial treatments for eating problems and eating disorders, *Journal of Clinical Child and Adolescent Psychology*, 37(1), 39–61.

Keen, D.V., Reid, F.D. and Arnone, D. (2010) Autism, ethnicity and maternal immigration, *The British Journal of Psychiatry*, 196(4), 274–281.

Keenan, K. (2000) Emotion dysregulation as a risk factor for child psychopathology, *Clinical Psychology: Science and Practice*, 7, 418–434.

Keenan, K., Loeber, R. and Green, S. (1999) Conduct disorder in girls: a review of the literature, *Clinical Child and Family Psychology Review*, 2(1), 3–19.

Keenan, K., Coyne, C. and Lahey, B.B. (2008) Should relational aggression be included in DSM-V? *Journal of the American Academy of Child & Adolescent Psychiatry*, 47(1), 86–93.

Keenan, K., Wroblewski, K., Hipwell, A., Loeber, R. and Stouthamer-Loeber, M. (2010) Age of onset, symptom threshold and expansion of the nosology of conduct disorder for girls, *Journal of Abnormal Psychology*. doi: 10.1037/a0019346

Kellam, S.G. et al. (1994) The course and malleability of aggressive behavior from early first grade into middle school: results of a developmental epidemiologically-based preventive trial, *Journal of Child Psychology and Psychiatry*, 35(2), 259–282.

Kelleher, M.J. and Chambers, D. (2003) Cross-cultural variation in child and adolescent suicide, in R.A. King and A. Apter (eds), *Suicide in Children and Adolescents*. Cambridge: Cambridge University Press.

Keller, A., Jeffries, N., Blumenthal, J., Clasen, L.S., Liu, H., Giedd, J.N. and Rapoport, J.L. (2003) Corpus callosum development in childhood-onset schizophrenia, *Schizophrenia Research*, 62, 105–114.

Kelly, J.B. (2003) Children's adjustment in conflicted marriage and divorce: a decade review of research, *Journal of the American Academy of Child and Adolescent Psychiatry*, 39(8), 963–973.

Kelly, J.F., Myers, M.G. and Brown, S.A. (2000) A multivariate process model of adolescent 12–step attendance and substance use outcome following inpatient treatment, *Psychology of Addictive Behaviors*, 14(4), 376–389.

Kempe, C.H., Silverman, F.N., Steele, B.F., Droegemueller, W. and Silver, H.K. (1962) The battered-child syndrome, *Journal of the American Medical Association*, 181(17), 17–24.

Kendall, P.C. (2000) *Cognitive-Behavioral Therapy for Anxious Children: Therapist Manual*, 2nd edn. Admore, PA: Workbook Publishing.

Kendall, P.C. (2006) *Child and Adolescent Therapy: Cognitive-Behavioral Procedures*, 3rd edn. New York: Guilford.

Kendall, P.C. (2011a) Treating anxiety disorders in youth, in P.C. Kendall (ed.), *Child and Adolescent Therapy: Cognitive-Behavioral Procedures*. 4th edn. New York: Guilford.

Kendall, P.C. (ed.) (2011b) *Child and Adolescent Therapy: Cognitive-Behavioral Procedures*, 4th edn. New York: Guilford.

Kendall, P.C., Chu, B., Gifford, A., Hayes, C. and Nauta, M. (1998) Breathing life into a manual: flexibility and creativity with manual-based treatments, *Cognitive and Behavioral Practice*, 5, 177–198.

Kendall, P.C., Aschenbrand, S.G. and Hudson, J.L. (2003) Child-focused treatment of anxiety, in A.E. Kazdin and J.R. Weisz (eds), *Evidence-Based Psychotherapies for Children and Adolescents*. New York: Guilford.

Kendall, P.C., Safford, S., Flannery-Schroeder, E. and Webb, A. (2004) Child anxiety treatment: outcomes in adolescence and impact on substance use and depression at 7.4-year follow-up, *Journal of Consulting and Clinical Psychology*, 72(2), 276–287.

Kendall, P.C., Hudson, J.L., Gosch, E., Flannery-Schroeder, E. and Suveg, C. (2008) Cognitive-behavioral therapy for anxiety disordered youth: a randomized clinical trial evaluating child and family modalities, *Journal of Consulting and Clinical Psychology*, 76, 282–297.

Kendall, P.C., Furr, J.M. and Podell, J.L. (2010) Child-focused treatment of anxiety, in J.R. Weisz and A.E. Kazdin (eds), *Evidence-Based Psychotherapy for Children and Adolescents*, 2nd edn. New York: Guilford.

Kennard, M.A. (1936) Age and other factors in motor recovery from precentral lesions in monkeys, *American Journal of Physiology – Legacy Content*, 115(1), 138–146.

Kerig, P.K. (1995) Triangles in the family circle: effects of family structure on marriage, parenting and child adjustment, *Journal of Family Psychology*, 9(1), 28–43.

Kerig, P.K. (1999) Gender issues in the effects of exposure to violence on children, *Journal of Emotional Abuse*, 1, 87–105.

Kerig, P.K. (2003) In search of protective processes for children exposed to interparental violence, *Journal of Emotional Abuse*, 3(3/4), 149–182.

Kerig, P.K. (2005) Revisiting the construct of boundary dissolution: a multidimensional perspective, in P.K. Kerig (ed.), *Implications of Parent-Child Boundary Dissolution For Developmental Psychopathology: Who Is the Parent and Who Is the Child?* New York: Haworth.

Kerig, P.K. (2010) Relational dynamics as sources of risk and resilience in adolescent dating violence, *Journal of Aggression, Maltreatment and Trauma*, 19, 585–586.

Kerig, P.K. (2012) Trauma and juvenile delinquency: dynamics and developmental mechanisms, *Journal of Child and Adolescent Trauma*.

Kerig, P.K. and Becker, S.P. (2010) From internalizing to externalizing: theoretical models of the processes linking PTSD to juvenile delinquency, in S.J. Egan (ed.), *Posttraumatic Stress Disorder (PTSD): Causes, Symptoms and Treatment*. Hauppauge, NY: Nova Science.

Kerig, P.K. and Becker, S.P. (2012) Trauma and girls' delinquency, in S. Miller, L. Leve and P.K. Kerig (eds), *Delinquent Girls: Context, Relationships and Adaptation*. New York: Springer Books.

Kerig, P.K. and Schulz, M.S. (2011) The transition from adolescence to adulthood: what lies beneath and what lies beyond, in P.K. Kerig, M.S. Schulz and S.T. Hauser (eds), *Adolescence and Beyond: Family Processes in Development*. New York: Oxford University Press.

Kerig, P.K. and Sink, H.E. (2010) The new scoundrel on the schoolyard: contributions of Machiavellianism to the understanding of youth aggression, in C.T. Barry, P.K. Kerig, K.K. Stellwagen and T.D. Barry (eds), *Narcissism and Machiavellianism in Youth: Implications for the Development of Adaptive and Maladaptive Behavior*. Washington, DC: American Psychological Association Press.

Kerig, P.K. and Stellwagen, K. (2010) Roles of callous-unemotional traits, narcissism and Machiavellianism in childhood aggression, *Journal of Psychopathology and Behavioral Assessment*, 32, 1–10.

Kerig, P.K. and Swanson, J.A. (2010) Ties that bind: triangulation, boundary dissolution and the effects of interparental conflict on child development, in M.S. Schulz, M.K. Pruett, P.K. Kerig and R.D. Parke (eds), *Strengthening Couple Relationships for Optimal Child Development: Lessons from Research and Intervention*. Washington, DC: American Psychological Association.

Kerig, P.K., Fedorowicz, A.E., Brown, C.A. and Warren, M. (2000) Assessment and intervention for PTSD in children exposed to violence, in R. Geffner, P. Jaffe and M. Sudermann (eds), *Children Exposed to Family Violence: Current Issues in Research, Intervention and Prevention and Policy Development*. Binghamton, NY: Haworth Press.

Kerig, P.K., Sink, H.E., Cuellar, R.E., Vanderzee, K.L. and Elfstrom, J.E. (2010a) Implementing trauma-focused CBT with fidelity and flexibility: a family case study, *Journal of Clinical Child and Adolescent Psychology*, 39, 713–722.

Kerig, P.K., Volz, A.R., Moeddel, M.A. and Cuellar, R.E. (2010b) Implementing the Expect Respect dating violence prevention program in diverse contexts: flexibility with fidelity, *Journal of Aggression, Maltreatment and Trauma*, 19, 661–680.

Kerig, P.K., Swanson, J.A. and Ward, R.M. (in press) Autonomy with connection: influences of parental psychological control on mutuality in emerging adults' intimate realtionships, in P.K. Kerig, M.S. Schulz and S.T. Hauser (eds), *Adolescence and Beyond: Family Processes in Development*. New York: Oxford University Press.

Kernberg, O. (1967) Borderline personality organization, *Journal of the American Psychoanalytic Association*, 15, 641–685.

Kersel, D.A. et al. (2001) Psychosocial functioning during the year following severe traumatic brain injury, *Brain Injury*, 15(8), 683–696.

Keshavan, M.S. (2003) Do disrupted sleep processes cause schizophrenia symptoms? A hypothesis, *Schizophrenia Research*, 60(1), 252–252.

Keshavan, M. et al. (2008) Psychopathology among offspring of parents with schizophrenia: relationship to premorbid impairments, *Schizophrenia research*, 103(1–3), 114–120.

Keski-Rahkonen, A., Hoek, H.W., Susser, E.S., Linna, M.S., Sihvola, E., Raevuori, A. et al. (2007) Epidemiology and course of anorexia nervosa in the community, *The American Journal of Psychiatry*, 164(8), 1259–1265.

Killen, J.D., Hayward, C., Wilson, D.M., Taylor, C.B., Hammer, L.D., Litt, I. et al. (1994) Factors associated with eating disorder symptoms in a community sample of 6th and 7th grade girls, *International Journal of Eating Disorders*, 15(4), 357–367.

Kim, E.Y. and Miklowitz, D.J. (2002) Childhood mania, attention deficit hyperactivity disorder and conduct disorder: a critical review of diagnostic dilemmas, *Bipolar Disorders*, 4(4), 215–225.

Kim, H.K., Capaldi, D.M. and Stoolmiller, M. (2003) Depressive symptoms across adolescence and young adulthood in men: predictions from parental and contextual risk factors, *Development and Psychopathology*, 15(2), 469–495.

Kim, J. and Cicchetti, D. (2006) Longitudinal trajectories of self-esteem processes and depressive symptoms among maltreated and nonmaltreated children, *Child Development*, 77(3), 624–639.

Kim, J., Cicchetti, D., Rogosch, F.A. and Manly, J.T. (2009) Child maltreatment and trajectories of personality and behavioral functioning: implications for the development of personality disorder, *Development and Psychopathology*, 21(3), 889–912.

Kim-Cohen, J., Arseneault, L., Newcombe, R., Adams, F., Bolton, H., Cant, L. et al. (2009) Five-year predictive validity of DSM-IV conduct disorder research diagnosis in 4½–5-year-old children, *European Child & Adolescent Psychiatry*, 18(5), 284–291

Kimonis, E.R. and Frick, P.J. (2010) Etiology of oppositional defiant disorder and conduct disorder: biological, familial and environmental factors identified in the development of disruptive behavior disorders, in R.C. Murrihy, A.D. Kidman, and T.H. Ollendick (eds), *Clinical Handbook of Assessing and Treating Conduct Problems in Youth*. New York: Springer.

King, B.H. et al. (1997) Mental retardation: a review of the past 10 years. Part I, *Journal of the American Academy of Child & Adolescent Psychiatry*, 36(12), 1656–1663.

King, M., Semlyen, J., Tai, S.S., Killaspy, H., Osborn, D., Popelyuk, D. and Nazareth, I. (2008) A systematic review of mental disorder, suicide and deliberate self harm in lesbian, gay and bisexual people, *BMC Psychiatry*, 8, 70–87.

King, N.J. and Ollendick, T.H. (1997) Treatment of childhood phobias, *Journal of Child Psychology and Psychiatry and Allied Disciplines*, 38(4), 389–400.

King, S., Ricard, N., Rochon, V., Steiger, H. and Nelis, S. (2003) Determinants of expressed emotion in mothers of schizophrenia patients, *Psychiatry Research*, 117, 211–222.

King, S., St-Hilaire, A. and Heidkamp, D. (2010) Prenatal factors in schizophrenia, *Current Directions in Psychological Science*, 19(4), 209–213.

Kirsch, L.G., Fanniff, A.M., Becker, J.V. (2011) Treatment of adolescent and adult sex offenders, in J.F.B. Myers (ed.), *The APSAC Handbook On Child Maltreatment*. Thousand Oaks, CA: Sage.

Kitayama, S. (2000) Collective construction of the self and social relationships: a rejoinder and some extensions, *Child Development*, 71(5), 1143–1146.

Klein, D.N., Torpey, D.C. and Bufferd, S.J. (2008) Depressive disorders, in T.P. Beauchaine and S.P. Hinshaw (eds), *Child and Adolescent Psychopathology*. Hoboken, NJ: John Wiley & Sons.

Klein, R.G. and Mannuzza, S. (1991) Long-term outcome of hyperactive children: a review, *Journal of the American Academy of Child & Adolescent Psychiatry*, 30(3), 383–387.

Klin, A. et al. (2005) Three diagnostic approaches to Asperger syndrome: implications for research, *Journal of Autism and Developmental Disorders*, 35(2), 221–234.

Kline, R.B. (2011) *Principles and Practice of Structural Equation Modeling*, 3rd edn. New York: Guilford Press.

Klinger, L.G., Dawson, G. and Renner, P. (1996) Autistic disorder, in E.J. Mash and R.A. Barkley (eds), *Child Psychopathology*. New York: Guilford.

Klinger, L.G., Dawson, G. and Renner, P. (2003) Autistic disorder, in E.J. Mash and R.A. Barkley (eds), *Child Psychopathology*, 2nd edn. New York: Guilford.

Klinnert, M.D., Campos, J.J., Sorce, J.F., Emde, R.N. and Svejda, M. (1983) Emotions as behavior regulators: social referencing in infancy, in R. Plutchik and H. Kellerman (eds), *Emotion: Theory, Research and Experience*.

Vol. 2: Emotion in Early Development. New York: Academic Press.

Klomek, A.B., Marrocco, F., Kleinman, M., Schonfeld, I.S. and Gould, M.S. (2007) Bullying, depression and suicidality in adolescents, *Journal of the American Academy of Child & Adolescent Psychiatry*, 46(1), 40–49.

Klomek, A.B., Sourander, A., Niemelä, S., Kumpulainen, K., Piha, J., Tamminen, T. et al. (2009) Childhood bullying behaviors as a risk for suicide attempts and completed suicides: a population-based birth cohort study, *Journal of the American Academy of Child & Adolescent Psychiatry*, 48(3), 254–261.

Klomek, A.B., Sourander, A. and Gould, M. (2010) The association of suicide and bullying in childhood to young adulthood: a review of cross-sectional and longitudinal research findings, *The Canadian Journal of Psychiatry*, 55(5), 282–288.

Klonsky, E.D. (2009) The functions of self-injury in young adults who cut themselves: clarifying the evidence for affect-regulation, *Psychiatry Research*, 166(2–3), 260–268.

Klonsky, E. and Glenn, C. (2009) Assessing the functions of non-suicidal self-injury: psychometric properties of the Inventory of Statements About Self-injury (ISAS), *Journal of Psychopathology and Behavioral Assessment*, 31(3), 215–219.

Knell, S.M. (2000) *Cognitive-Behavioral Play Therapy*. New York: Aronson.

Knudson, B. and Coyle, A. (2002) Parents' experiences of caring for sons and daughters with schizophrenia: a qualitative analysis of coping, *The European Journal of Psychotherapy, Counselling & Health*, 5(2), 169–183.

Kobak, R., Cassidy, J., Lyons-Ruth, K. and Ziv, Y. (2006) Attachment, stress and psychopathology: a developmental pathways model, in

D. Cicchetti and D.J. Cohen (eds), *Developmental Psychopathology. Volume I: Theory and Method*, 2nd edn. New York: Wiley.

Kobayashi, R., Murata, T. and Yoshinaga, K. (1992) A follow-up study of 201 children with autism in Kyushu and Yamaguchi areas, Japan, *Journal of Autism and Developmental Disorders*, 22(3), 395–411.

Kochanska, G. and Aksan, N. (2006) Children's conscience and self-regulation, *Journal of Personality*, 74, 1587–1617.

Kochanska, G. and Aksan, N. (2007) Conscience in childhood: past, present and future, in G.W. Ladd (ed.), *Appraising the Human Developmental Sciences: Essays in Honor of Merrill-Palmer Quarterly*. Detroit, MI: Wayne State University Press.

Kochanska, G., Barry, R.A., Aksan, N. and Boldt, L.J. (2008) A developmental model of maternal and child contributions to disruptive conduct: The first six years, *Journal of Child Psychology and Psychiatry*, 49, 1220–1227.

Kochanska, G., Barry, R.A., Jimenez, N.B., Hollatz, A.L. and Woodward, J. (2009a) Guilt and effortful control: two mechanisms that prevent disruptive developmental trajectories, *Journal of Personality and Social Psychology*, 87, 322–333.

Kochanska, G., Gross, J.N., Lin, M.H. and Nichols, K.E. (2002) Guilt in young children: development, determinants and relations with a broader system of standards, *Child Development*, 73(2), 461–482.

Kochanska, G., Philibert, R.A. and Barry, R.A. (2009b) Interplay of genes and early mother–child relationship in the development of self-regulation from toddler to preschool age, *Journal of Child Psychology and Psychiatry*, 50(11), 1331–1338.

Koerner, K. and Linehan, M.M. (2000) Borderline personality disorder: research on dialectical

behavior therapy for patients with borderline personality disorder, *Psychiatric Clinics of North America*, 23, 151–167.

Kohlberg, L. (2008) The development of children's orientations toward a moral order, *Human Development*, 51, 8–20.

Kolb, B. and Whishaw, I.Q. (2003) *Fundamentals of Human Neuropsychology*. New York: Worth.

Kolko, D.J. (2002) Child physical abuse, in J.E.B. Myers, L. Berliner, J. Briere, C.T. Hendrix, C. Jenny and T.A. Reid (eds), *The APSAC Handbook on Child Maltreatment*, 2nd edn. Thousand Oaks, CA: Sage.

Kolko, D.J. and Swenson, C.C. (2002) *Assessing and Treating Physically Abused Children and their Families: A Cognitive-Behavioral Approach*. Thousand Oaks, CA: Sage.

Kolko, D.J., Iselin, A.M.R. and Gully, K.J. (2011) Evaluation of the sustainability and clinical outcome of alternatives for families: a cognitive-behavioral therapy (af-cbt) in a child protection center, *Child Abuse & Neglect*, 35(2), 105–116.

Kolvin, I. (1971) Psychoses in childhood – a comparative study, in M. Rutter (ed.), *Infantile Autism: Concepts, Characteristics and Treatment*. London: Churchill Livingstone.

Komatsu, H., Nagamitsu, S., Ozono, S., Yamashita, Y., Ishibashi, M. and Matsuishi, T. (2010) Regional cerebral blood flow changes in early-onset anorexia nervosa before and after weight gain, *Brain and Development*, 32(8), 625–630.

Komsi, N., Räikkönen, K., Pesonen, A.-K., Heinonen, K., Keskivaara, P., Järvenpää, A.-L. and Strandberg, T. E. (2006) Continuity of temperament from infancy to middle childhood, *Infant Behavior and Development*, 29(4), 494–508.

Koning, I.M., Engels, R.C.M.E., Verdurmen, J.E.E. and Vollebergh, W.A.M. (2010) Alcohol-specific socialization practices and alcohol use in Dutch early adolescents, *Journal of Adolescence*, 33(1), 93–11.

Konrad, K. and Eickhoff, S.B. (2010) Is the ADHD brain wired differently? A review on structural and functional connectivity in attention deficit hyperactivity disorder, *Human Brain Mapping*, 31(6), 904–916.

Kooij, S. et al. (2010) European consensus statement on diagnosis and treatment of adult ADHD: the European Network Adult ADHD, *BMC Psychiatry*, 10(1), 67.

Kopp, C.B. (2002) Self-regulation in childhood, in N.J. Smelson and P.B. Baltes (eds), *International Encyclopedia of the Social and Behavioral Sciences*, vol. 3. New York: Pergamon.

Korkman, M., Kirk, U. and Kemp, S. (1998) *NEPSY: A Developmental Neuropsychological Assessment*. San Antonio, TX: Psychological Corporation.

Kouros, C.D., Cummings, E.M. and Davies, P.T. (2010) Early trajectories of interparental conflict and externalizing problems as predictors of social competence in preadolescence, *Development and Psychopathology*, 22(3), 527–537.

Kovacs, M. (1992) *Children's Depression Inventory: Manual*. Toronto: Multi-Health Systems.

Kovacs, M. and Devlin, B. (1998) Internalizing disorders in childhood, *Journal of Child Psychology and Psychiatry and Allied Disciplines*, 39(1), 47–63.

Kovacs, M., Akiskal, H.S., Gatsonis, C. and Parrone, P.L. (1994) Childhood-onset dysthymic disorder: clinical features and prospective naturalistic outcome, *Archives of General Psychiatry*, 51, 365–374.

Kovas, Y. et al. (2007) Overlap and specificity of genetic and environmental influences on mathematics and reading disability in 10-year-old twins, *Journal of Child Psychology and Psychiatry*, 48(9), 914–922.

Kowalik, J., Weller, J., Venter, J. and Drachman, D. (2011), Cognitive

behavioral therapy for the treatment of pediatric posttraumatic stress disorder: a review and meta-analysis, *Journal of Behavior Therapy and Experimental Psychiatry*, 42, 405–413.

Kowatch, R.A., Strawn, J.R. and DelBello, M.P. (2010) Developmental considerations in the pharmacological treatment of youth with bipolar disorder, in D.J. Miklowitz and D. Cichetti (eds), *Understanding Bipolar Disorder: A Developmental Psychopathology Perspective*. New York: Guilford Press.

Krahé, B. and Knappert, L. (2009) A group-randomized evaluation of a theatre-based sexual abuse prevention programme for primary school children in Germany, *Journal of Community & Applied Social Psychology*, 19(4), 321–329.

Kravariti, E., Morris, R.G., Rabe-Hesketh, S., Murray, R.M. and Frangou, S. (2003) The Maudsley Early-Onset Schizophrenia Study: cognitive function in adolescent-onset schizophrenia, *Schizophrenia Research*, 65, 95–103.

Kroger, J. (2007) *Identity Development*. Thousand Oaks, CA: Sage.

Kronmüller, K.-T., Stefini, A., Geiser-Elze, A., Horn, H., Hartmann, M. and Winkelmann, K. (2010) The Heidelberg study of psychodynamic psychotherapy for children and adolescents, in J. Tsiantis and J. Trowell (eds) *Assessing Change in Psychoanalytic Psychotherapy of Children and Adolescents: Today's Challenge*. London: Karnac Books.

Krug, I., Treasure, J., Anderluh, M., Bellodi, L., Cellini, E., Collier, D. et al. (2009) Associations of individual and family eating patterns during childhood and early adolescence: a multicentre European study of associated eating disorder factors, *British Journal of Nutrition*, 101(6), 909–918.

Kuczynski, L. and Kochanska, G. (1990) Development of children's noncompliance strategies from tod-

dlerhood to age 5, *Developmental Psychology*, 26(3), 398.

Kuhne, M., Schachar, R. and Tannock, R. (1997) Impact of comorbid oppositional or conduct problems on attention-deficit hyperactivity disorder, *Journal of the American Academy of Child & Adolescent Psychiatry*, 36(12), 1715–1725.

Kumra, S., Giedd, J.N., Vaituzis, A.C., Jacobsen, L.K., McKenna, K., Bedwell, J. et al. (2000) Childhood-onset psychotic disorders: magnetic resonance imaging of volumetric differences in brain structure, *American Journal of Psychiatry*, 157, 1467–1474.

Kung, H.C., Hoyert, D.L., Xu, J. and Murphy, S.L. (2008) Deaths: final data for 2005, *National Vital Statistics Reports*, 58 (10).

Kyriakopoulos, M. and Frangou, S. (2007) Pathophysiology of early onset schizophrenia, *International Review of Psychiatry*, 19(4), 315–324.

La Greca, A.M. and Stone, W.L. (1992) Assessing children through interviews and behavioral observations, in C.E. Walker and M.C. Roberts (eds), *Handbook of Clinical Child Psychology*. New York: Guilford.

Lachar, D. and Gruber, C.P. (1994) *The Personality Inventory for Youth*. Los Angeles, CA: Western Psychological Services.

Lahey, B.B. (2008) Oppositional defiant disorder, conduct disorder and juvenile delinquency, in T.P. Beauchaine and S.P Hinshaw (eds), *Child and Adolescent Psychopathology*. Hoboken, NJ: John Wiley & Sons.

Lahey, B.B., Miller, T.L., Gordon, R.A. and Riley, A.W. (1999) Developmental epidemiology of the disruptive behavior disorders, in H.C. Quay and A.E. Hogan (eds), *Handbook of disruptive behavior disorders*. Dordrecht: Kluwer Academic.

Lahey, B.B., McBurnett, K. and Loeber, R. (2000) Are attention-deficit/hyperactivity disorder and oppositional defiant disorder developmental precursors to conduct disorder? in A.J. Sameroff, M. Lewis and S.M. Miller (eds), *Handbook of Developmental Psychopathology*. New York: Kluwer Academic.

Lahey, B.B., Loeber, R., Burke, J. and Rathouz, P.J. (2002) Adolescent outcomes of childhood conduct disorder among clinic-referred boys: predictors of improvement, *Journal of Abnormal Child Psychology*, 30(4), 333–348.

Lahey, B.B., Moffitt, T.E. and Caspi, A. (2003) *Causes of Conduct Disorder and Juvenile Delinquency*. New York: Guilford.

Lahey, B.B., Loeber, R., Burke, J.D. and Applegate, B. (2005) Predicting future antisocial personality disorder in males from a clinical assessment in childhood, *Journal of Consulting and Clinical Psychology Review*, 73, 389–399.

Lahey, B.B. et al. (2011) Interactions between early parenting and a polymorphism of the child's dopamine transporter gene in predicting future child conduct disorder symptoms, *Journal of Abnormal Psychology*, 120(1), 33.

Lainhart, J.E. (1999) Psychiatric problems in individuals with autism, their parents and siblings, *International Review of Psychiatry*, 11(4), 278–298.

Lake, A., Staiger, P. and Glowinski, H. (2000) Effect of Western culture on women's attitudes to eating and perceptions of body shape, *International Journal of Eating Disorders*, 27, 83–89.

Lamb, M.E. (1997) *The Role of the Father in Child Development*, 3rd edn. New York: Wiley.

Lamb, M.E. (2010) *The Role of the Father in Child Development*, 5th edn. Hoboken, NJ: Wiley & Sons.

Lamb, M.E. et al. (2007) A structured forensic interview protocol improves the quality and informativeness of investigative interviews with children: a review of research using the NICHD Investigative

Interview Protocol, *Child Abuse & Neglect*, 31(11–12), 1201–1231.

Landa, R. (2000) Social language use in Asperger syndrome and high functioning autism, in A. Klin, F.R. Volkmar and S.S. Sparrow (eds), *Asperger Syndrome*. New York: Guilford.

Landreth, G.L. (2002) *Play Therapy: The Art of the Relationship*. New York: Brunner-Routledge.

Langberg, J.M. and Epstein, J.N. (2009) Non-pharmacological approaches for treating children with ADHD inattentive type, *F1000 Medicine Reports*, 1.

Langlois, J.A., Rutland-Brown, W. and Wald, M.M. (2006) The epidemiology and impact of traumatic brain injury: a brief overview, *The Journal of Head Trauma Rehabilitation*, 21(5), 375.

Langrock, A.M., Compas, B.E., Keller, G., Merchant, M.J. and Copeland, M.E. (2002) Coping with the stress of parental depression: parents' reports of children's coping, emotional and behavioral problems, *Journal of Clinical Child and Adolescent Psychology*, 31(3), 312–324.

Lansford, J.E., Chang, L., Dodge, K.A., Malone, P.S., Oburu, P., Palmerus, K. et al. (2005) Physical discipline and children's adjustment: cultural normativeness as a moderator, *Child Development*, 76(6), 1234–1246.

Lansford, J.E., Dodge, K.A., Pettit, G.S. and Bates, J.E. (2010) Does physical abuse in early childhood predict substance use in adolescence and early adulthood? *Child Maltreatment*, 15(2), 190–194.

Lara, C. et al. (2009) Childhood predictors of adult ADHD: results from the WHO World Mental Health (WMH) Survey Initiative, *Biological Psychiatry*, 65(1), 46–54.

Larsen, J.K., Otten, R. and Engels, R.C.M.E. (2009) Adolescent depressive symptoms and smoking behavior: the gender-specific role of weight concern and dieting, *Journal of Psychosomatic Research*, 66(4), 305–308.

Larson, J. and Lochman, J.E. (2002) *Helping Schoolchildren Cope with Anger: A Cognitive-Behavioral Intervention*. New York: Guilford.

Larson, R.W. and Richards, M.H. (1994) Family emotions: do young adolescents and their parents experience the same states? *Journal of Research on Adolescence*, 4(4), 567–583.

Larsson, A.S. and Lamb, M.E. (2009) Making the most of information-gathering interviews with children, *Infant and Child Development*, 18(1), 1–16.

Lask, B. (2000) Aetiology, in B. Lask and R. Bryant-Waugh (eds), *Anorexia Nervosa and Related Eating Disorders in Childhood and Adolescence*. Philadelphia, PA: Psychology Press.

Last, C.G. and Francis, G. (1988) School phobia, in B.B. Lahey and A.E. Kazdin (eds), *Advances in Clinical Child Psychology*, vol. 11. New York: Plenum.

Last, C.G. and Perrin, S. (1993) Anxiety disorders in African-American and white children, *Journal of Abnormal Child Psychology*, 21, 153–164.

Last, C.G., Perrin, S., Hersen, M. and Kazdin, A.E. (1992) DSM-III-R anxiety disorders in children: sociodemographic and clinical characteristics, *Journal of the American Academy of Child and Adolescent Psychiatry*, 31, 928–934.

Latendresse, S.J., Rose, R.J., Viken, R.J., Pulkkinen, L., Kaprio, J. and Dick, D.M. (2008) Parenting mechanisms in links between parents' and adolescents' alcohol use behaviors, *Alcoholism: Clinical and Experimental Research*, 32(2), 322–330.

Lau, E. (1995) An insatiable emptiness, *The Georgia Straight*, Vancouver, 21–28 July, 13–14.

Lau, J.Y.F. and Eley, T.C. (2008) Disentangling gene-environment correlations and interactions on adolescent depressive symptoms,

Journal of Child Psychology and Psychiatry, 49(2), 142–150.

Lau, J.Y.F. and Eley, T.C. (2009) The genetics of adolescent depression, in S. Nolen-Hoeksema and L. M. Hilt (eds), *Handbook of Depression In Adolescents*. New York: Routledge/Taylor & Francis Group.

Lavigne, J.V. et al. (2009) The child and adolescent symptom inventory-progress monitor: a brief diagnostic and statistical manual of mental disorders-referenced parent-report scale for children and adolescents, *Journal of Child and Adolescent Psychopharmacology*, 19(3), 241–252.

Le Grange, D. and Rienecke Hoste, R. (2010) Family therapy, in W.S. Agras (ed.), *The Oxford Handbook Of Eating Disorders*. New York: Oxford University Press.

Le Grange, D., Crosby, R. and Lock, J. (2008) Predictors and moderators of outcome in familybased treatment for adolescent bulimia nervosa, *Journal of the American Academy of Child and Adolescent Psychiatry*, 47, 464–470.

Leckman, J.F., Bloch, M.H. and King, R.A. (2009) Symptom dimensions and subtypes of obsessive-compulsive disorder: a developmental perspective, *Dialogues in Clinical Neuroscience*, 11(1), 21–33.

Lee, S., Tsang, A., Breslau, J., Aguilar-Gaxiola, S., Angermeyer, M., Borges, G. et al. (2009) Mental disorders and termination of education in high-income and low- and middle-income countries: epidemiological study, *British Journal of Psychiatry*, 194(5), 411–417

Lee, S.S., Lahey, B.B., Waldman, I., Van Hulle, C.A., Rathouz, P., Pelham, W. E. et al. (2007) Association of dopamine transporter genotype with disruptive behavior disorders in an eight-year longitudinal study of children and adolescents, *American Journal of Medical Genetics Part B Neuropsychiatric Genetics*, 144, 310–317.

Leffert, J.S. and Siperstein, G.N. (1996) Assessment of social-cognitive processes in children with mental retardation, *American Journal on Mental Retardation*, 100, 441–455.

Lefly, D.L. and Pennington, P.B.F. (1991) Spelling errors and reading fluency in compensated adult dyslexics, *Annals of Dyslexia*, 41, 143–162.

Lengua, L.J. and Long, A.C. (2002) The role of emotionality and self-regulation in the appraisal-coping process: tests of direct and moderating effects, *Journal of Applied Developmental Psychology*, 23(4), 471–493.

Leonard, H. et al. (2006) Maternal health in pregnancy and intellectual disability in the offspring: a population-based study, *Annals of Epidemiology*, 16(6), 448–454.

Letourneau, E.J., Henggeler, S.W., Borduin, C.M., Schewe, P.A., McCart, M.R., Chapman, J.E. and Saldana, L. (2009) Multisystemic therapy for juvenile sexual offenders: 1-year results from a randomized effectiveness trial, *Journal of Family Psychology*, 23(1), 89–102.

Leung, S.S.K., Stewart, S.M., Wong, J.P.S., Ho, D.S.Y., Fong, D.Y.T. and Lam, T.H. (2009) The association between adolescents' depressive symptoms, maternal negative affect and family relationships in Hong Kong: cross-sectional and longitudinal findings, *Journal of Family Psychology*, 23(5), 636–645.

Leve, L.D., Kerr, D.C.R., Shaw, D., Ge, X., Neiderhiser, J.M., Scaramella, L.V. et al. (2010) Infant pathways to externalizing behavior: evidence of genotype environment interaction, *Child Development*, 81(1), 340–356.

Levin, H.S. et al. (2004) Changes in working memory after traumatic brain injury in children, *Neuropsychology*, 18(2), 240.

Levin, M.R., Ashmore-Callahan, S., Kendall, P.C. and Ichii, M. (1996) Treatment of separation anxiety disorder, in M.A. Reinecke, M. Dattilio and A. Freeman (eds), *Cognitive Therapy with Children And Adolescents*. New York: Guilford.

Levine, M.P. and Smolak, L. (2010) Cultural influences on body image and the eating disorders, in W.S. Agras (ed.), *The Oxford Handbook of Eating Disorders*. New York: Oxford University Press.

Levy, F. and Hay, D.A. (2001) *Attention, Genes and ADHD*. Philadelphia, PA: Brunner-Routledge.

Levy, F., Hay, D.A., McStephen, M., Wood, C. and Waldman, I. (1997) Attention deficit hyperactivity disorder: a category or continuum? Genetic analysis of a large-scale twin study, *Journal of the American Academy of Child and Adolescent Psychiatry*, 36, 737–744.

Lewinsohn, M., Clarke, G., Seeley, J. and Rohde, P. (1994) Major depression in community adolescents: age at onset, episode duration and time to recurrence, *Journal of the American Academy of Child and Adolescent Psychiatry*, 33, 809–818.

Lewinsohn, P.M., Klein, D.N. and Seeley, J.R. (1995) Bipolar disorders in a community sample of older adolescents: prevalence, phenomenology, comorbidity and course, *Journal of the American Academy of Child and Adolescent Psychiatry*, 34(4), 454–463.

Lewinsohn, P.M., Clarke, G.N., Rohde, P., Hops, H. and Seeley, J.R. (1996) A course in coping: a cognitive-behavioral approach to the treatment of adolescent depression, in E D. Hibbs and P.S. Jensen (eds), *Psychosocial Treatments for Child and Adolescent Disorders*. Washington, DC: American Psychological Association.

Lewinsohn, P.M., Gotlib, I.H., Lewinsohn, M. and Seeley, J.R. (1998) Gender differences in anxiety disorders and anxiety symptoms in adolescents, *Journal of Abnormal Psychology*, 107(1), 109–117.

Lewinsohn, P.M., Rohde, P., Seeley, J.R., Klein, D.N. and Gotlib, I.H. (2000a) Natural course of adolescent major depressive disorder in a community sample: predictors of recurrence in young adults, *American Journal of Psychiatry*, 157, 1584–1591.

Lewinsohn, P.M., Klein, D.N. and Seeley, J.R. (2000b) Bipolar disorder during adolescence and young adulthood in a community sample, *Bipolar Disorders*, 2, 281–293.

Lewinsohn, P.M., Pettit, J.W., Joiner, T.E. and Seeley, J.R. (2003) The symptomatic expression of major depressive disorder in adolescents and young adults, *Journal of Abnormal Psychology*, 112, 244–252.

Lewis, M., Feiring, C. and Rosenthal, S. (2000) Attachment over time, *Child Development*, 71(3), 707–720.

Lieberman, A.F. (1992) Infant-parent psychotherapy with toddlers, *Development and Psychopathology*, 4(4), 559–574.

Lieberman, A.F. and Pawl, J.H. (1993) Infant–parent psychotherapy, in C.H. Zeanah (ed.), *Handbook of Infant Mental Health*. New York: Guilford.

Lieberman, A.F. and Van Horn, P. (2008) *Psychotherapy with Infants and Young Children: Repairing the Effects of Stress and Trauma on Early Attachment*. New York: Guilford.

Lieberman, A.F., Ippen, C.G. and Van Horn, P.J. (2006) Child–parent psychotherapy: 6 month follow-up of a randomized controlled trial, *Journal of the American Academy of Child and Adolescent Psychiatry*, 45, 913–918.

Lincoln, A.J. et al. (1988) A study of intellectual abilities in high-functioning people with autism, *Journal of Autism and Developmental Disorders*, 18(4), 505–524.

Lincoln, A.J., Bloom, D., Katz, M. and Boksenbaum, N. (1998) Neuropsychological and neurophysiological indices of auditory processing impairment in children with multiple complex developmental disorder, *Journal of the American Academy of Child & Adolescent Psychiatry*, 37, 100–112.

Lindblad, I., Gillberg, C. and Fernell, E. (2011) ADHD and other associated developmental problems in children with mild mental retardation. The use of the 'Five-To-Fifteen' questionnaire in a population-based sample, *Research in Developmental Disabilities*, 22 June, 1873–3379.

Lindström, C., Aman, J. and Norberg, A.L. (2010) Increased prevalence of burnout symptoms in parents of chronically ill children, *Acta Paediatrica*, 99(3), 427–432.

Linehan, M.M. (1993a) *Cognitive-Behavioral Treatment of Borderline Personality Disorder*. New York: Guilford.

Linehan, M.M. (1993b) *Skills Training Manual for Treating Borderline Personality Disorder*. New York: Guilford.

Linehan, M.M., Goodstein, J.L., Nielsen, S.L. and Chiles, J.A. (1983) Reasons for staying alive when you are thinking of killing yourself: the Reasons for Living Inventory, *Journal of Consulting and Clinical Psychology*, 51(2), 276–286.

Linehan, M.M., Armstrong, H.E., Suarez, R.A., Allmon, D. and Heard, H.L. (1991) Cognitive-behavioral treatment of chronically parasuicidal borderline patients, *Archives of General Psychiatry*, 48(12), 1060–1064.

Linszen, D., Dingemans, P., Van der Does, J.W., Nugter, A., Scholte, P., Lenoir, R. and Goldstein, M.J. (1996) Treatment, expressed emotion and relapse in recent onset schizophrenic disorders, *Psychological Medicine*, 26, 333–342.

Lloyd-Richardson, E.E., Nock, M.K. and Prinstein, M.J. (2009) Functions of adolescent nonsuicidal self-injury, in M.K. Nixon and N.L. Heath (eds), *Self-Injury in Youth: The Essential Guide to Assessment and Intervention*. New York: Routledge/Taylor & Francis Group.

Lochman, J.E. and Pardini, D.A. (2009) Cognitive-behavioral therapies, in M. Rutter, D.V. M. Bishop, D.S. Pine, S. Scott, J. Stevenson, E. Taylor and A. Thapar (eds), *Rutter's Child and Adolescent Psychiatry*, 5th edn. Oxford: Blackwell.

Lochman, J.E., Barry, T.D. and Pardini, D.A. (2003) Anger control training for aggressive youth, in A.E. Kazdin and J.R. Weisz (eds), *Evidence-Based Psychotherapies for Children and Adolescents*. New York: Guilford Press.

Lock, J. (2010) Treatment of adolescent eating disorders: progress and challenges, *Minerva Psichiatrica*, 51(3), 207–216.

Lock, J. and le Grange, D. (2006) Eating disorders, in D.A. Wolfe and E.J. Mash (eds), *Behavioral and Emotional Disorders In Adolescents: Nature, Assessment and Treatment*. New York: Guilford.

Lock, J., le Grange, D., Agras, W.S. and Dare, C. (2002) *Treatment Manual for Anorexia Nervosa: A Family-Based Approach*. New York: Guilford.

Loeber, R. and Burke, J.D. (2011) Developmental pathways in juvenile externalizing and internalizing problems, *Journal of Research on Adolescence*, 21(1), 34–46.

Loeber, R., Green, S.M., Lahey, B.B., Christ, M.A.G. and Frick, P.J. (1992) Developmental sequences in the age of onset of disruptive child behaviours, *Journal of Child and Family Studies*, 1, 21–41.

Loeber, R. et al. (2000) Findings on disruptive behavior disorders from the first decade of the Developmental Trends Study, *Clinical Child and Family Psychology Review*, 3(1), 37–60.

Loeber, R., Farrington, D.P., Stouthamer-Loeber, M. and White, H.R. (2008a) Introduction and key questions, in R. Loeber, D.P. Farrington, M. Stouthamer-Loeber and H.R. White (eds), *Violence and Serious Theft: Development and Prediction from*

Childhood to Adulthood. New York: Routledge/Taylor & Francis Group.

Loeber, R., Wim Slot, N., van der Laan, P. and Hoeve, M. (eds) (2008b) *Tomorrow's Criminals: The Development of Child Delinquency and Effective Interventions.* Ashgate: Farnham.

Loeber, R., Burke, J.D. and Pardini, D.A. (2009a) Development and etiology of disruptive and delinquent behavior, *Annual Review of Clinical Psychology,* 5, 291–310.

Loeber, R., Burke, J. and Pardini, D.A. (2009b) Perspectives on oppositional defiant disorder, conduct disorder and psychopathic features, *Journal of Child Psychology and Psychiatry,* 50(1–2), 133–142.

Lofgren, D.P., Bemporad, J., King, J., Lindem, K. and O'Driscoll, G. (1991) A prospective follow-up study of so-called borderline children, *American Journal of Psychiatry,* 148, 1541–1545.

Logan, C., Nathan, R. and Brown, A. (2011) Formulation in clinical risk assessment and management, in R. Whittington and C. Logan (eds), *Self-Harm and Violence.* Oxford: Wiley-Blackwell.

Lonigan, C.J., Carey, M.P. and Finch, A.J. (1994) Anxiety and depression in children and adolescents: negative affectivity and the utility of self-reports, *Journal of Consulting and Clinical Psychology,* 62(5), 1000–1008.

Loue, S. (2003) *Diversity Issues in Substance Abuse Treatment and Research.* New York: Kluwer.

Lovaas, O.I. (1977) *The Autistic Child: Language Development through Behavior Modification.* New York: Irvington.

Lovaas, O.I. and Smith, T. (2003) Early and intensive behavioral intervention in autism, in A.E. Kazdin and J.R. Weisz (eds), *Evidence-Based Psychotherapies for Children and Adolescents.* New York: Guilford.

Lovecky, D.V., 2004. *Different minds: Gifted children with AD/HD,*

Asperger syndrome and other learning deficits, Jessica Kingsley Pub.

Lovett, M.W., Lacerenza, L., Borden, S.L., Frijters, J.C., Steinbach, K.A. and De Palma, M. (2000) Components of effective remediation for developmental reading disabilities: combining phonological and strategy-based instruction to improve outcomes, *Journal of Educational Psychology,* 92, 263–283.

Luat, A.F. and Chugani, H.T. (2010) Positron Emission Tomography: brain glucose metabolism in pediatric epilepsy syndromes, in H. Chugani (ed.), *Neuroimaging in Epilepsy.* Oxford: Oxford Scholarship Online Monographs.

Luborsky, L., Singer, B. and Luborsky, L.I. (1975) Comparative studies of psychotherapies: is it true that 'Everyone has won and all must have prizes'? *Archives of General Psychiatry,* 32, 995–1008.

Luby, J. (2010) Preschool depression: the importance of identification of depression early in development, *Current Directions in Psychological Science,* 19(2), 91–95.

Luby, J.L., Si, X., Belden, A.C., Tandon, M. and Spitznagel, E. (2009) Preschool depression: homotypic continuity and course over 24 months, *Archives of General Psychiatry,* 66(8), 897–905.

Luby, J.L., Belden, A.C. and Tandon, M. (2010) Bipolar disorder in the preschool period: development and differential diagnosis, in D.J. Miklowitz and D. Cichetti (eds), *Understanding Bipolar Disorder: A Developmental Psychopathology Perspective.* New York: Guilford Press.

Luciano, S. and Savage, R.S. (2007) Bullying risk in children with learning difficulties in inclusive educational settings, *Canadian Journal of School Psychology,* 22(1), 14–31.

Luczak, S.E., Glatt, S.J. and Wall, T.L. (2006) Meta-analysis of ALDH2 and ADH1B with alcohol dependence in Asians, *Psychological Bulletin,* 132, 607–621.

Luman, M. et al. (2010) Impaired decision making in oppositional defiant disorder related to altered psychophysiological responses to reinforcement, *Biological Psychiatry,* 68(4), 337–344.

Luria, A. (1980) *Higher Cortical Functions in Man.* New York: Basic Books.

Luthar, S.S. (2003) *Resilience and Vulnerability: Adaptation in the Context of Childhood Adversities.* New York: Cambridge University Press.

Luthar, S.S. (2006) Resilience in development: a synthesis of research across five decades, in D. Cicchetti and D.J. Cohen (eds), *Developmental Psychopathology. Volume III: Risk, Disorder and Adaptation.* New York: Wiley.

Luthar, S.S. and Becker, B.E. (2002) Privileged but pressured? A study of affluent youth, *Child Development,* 73(5), 1593–1610.

Luthar, S.S. and Latendresse, S.J. (2002) Adolescent risk: the costs of affluence, in R. M. Lerner and C.S. Taylor (eds), *Pathways to Positive Development among Diverse Youth.* San Francisco, CA: Jossey-Bass.

Luthar, S.S. and Sexton, C.C. (2007) Maternal drug abuse versus maternal depression: vulnerability and resilience among school-age and adolescent offspring, *Development and Psychopathology,* 19(1), 205–225.

Luthar, S.S., Cicchetti, D. and Becker, B. (2000) The construct of resilience: a critical evaluation and guidelines for future work, *Child Development,* 71(3), 543–562.

Luxenberg, T. and Levin, P. (2004) The role of the Rorschach in the assessment and treatment of trauma, in J.P. Wilson and T.M. Keane (eds), *Assessing Psychological Trauma and PTSD.* New York: Guilford.

Lynch, M. (2003) Consequences of children's exposure to community violence, *Clinical Child and Family Psychology Review,* 6(4), 265–274.

Lyon, G.R., Fletcher, J.M. and Barnes, M.C. (2003a) Learning disabilities, in E.J. Mash and R.A. Barkley (eds), *Child Psychopathology*. New York: Guilford.

Lyon, G.R., Shaywitz, S.E. and Shaywitz, B.A. (2003b) A definition of dyslexia, *Annals of Dyslexia*, 53(1), 1–14.

Lyon, M., Chatoor, I., Atkins, D., Silber, T., Mosimann, J. and Gray, J. (1997) Testing the hypothesis of the multidimensional model of anorexia nervosa in adolescents, *Adolescence*, 32(125), 101–111.

Lyons-Ruth, K. (2008) Contributions of the mother-infant relationship to dissociative, borderline and conduct symptoms in young adulthood, *Infant Mental Health Journal*, 29, 203–216.

Lyons-Ruth, K. and Jacobvitz, D. (2008) Attachment disorganization: genetic factors, parenting contexts and developmental transformation from infancy to adulthood, in J. Cassidy and P.R. Shaver (eds), *Handbook of Attachment*. New York: Guilford.

Lyons-Ruth, K., Alpern, L. and Repacholi, B. (1993) Disorganized attachment classification and maternal psychosocial problems as predictors of hostile-aggressive behavior in the preschool classroom, *Child Development*, 64, 572–585.

Maccoby, E.E., Mnookin, R.H., Depner, C.E. and Peters, H.E. (1992) *Dividing the Child: Social and Legal Dilemmas of Custody*. Cambridge, MA: Harvard University Press.

MacFie, J. (2009) Development in children and adolescents whose mothers have borderline personality disorder, *Child Development Perspectives*, 3(1), 66–71.

MacFie, J. and Swan, S. (2009) Representations of the caregiver–child relationship and of the self and emotion regulation in the narratives of young children whose mothers have borderline personality disorder, *Development and Psychopathology*, 21(03), 993–1011.

MacFie, J., Cicchetti, D. and Toth, S.L. (2001) The development of dissociation in maltreated preschool-aged children, *Development and Psychopathology*, 13(2), 233–254.

MacFie, J., Houts, R.M., McElwain, N.L. and Cox, M.J. (2005) The effect of father-toddler and mother-toddler role reversal on the development of behavior problems in kindergarten, *Social Development*, 14(3), 514–531.

Machover, K. (1949) *Personality Projection in the Drawing of the Human Figure (A Method of Personality Investigation)*. Springfield, IL: Charles C. Thomas

MacKinnon, D.P. (2008) *Introduction to Statistical Mediation Analysis*. New York: Taylor & Francis.

MacMillan, H.L., Jamieson, E. and Walsh, C.A. (2003) Reported contact with child protection services among those reporting child physical and sexual abuse: results from a community survey, *Child Abuse and Neglect*, 12, 1397–1408.

MacMillan, H.L. et al. (2009) Interventions to prevent child maltreatment and associated impairment, *The Lancet*, 373(9659), 250–266.

Madonna, P.G., Van Scoyk, S. and Jones, D.P.H. (1991) Family interactions within incest and nonincest families, *American Journal of Psychiatry*, 148, 46–49.

Magnusson, P., Smari, J., Gretarsdottir, H. and Prandardottir, H. (1999) Attention-deficit/hyperactivity symptoms in Icelandic schoolchildren: assessment with the Attention Deficit/Hyperactivity Rating Scale-IV, *Scandinavian Journal of Psychology*, 40, 301–306.

Mahler, M.S. (1971) A study of the separation-individuation process and its possible application to borderline phenomena in the psychoanalytic situation, *Psychoanalytic Study of the Child*, 26, 403–424.

Mahler, M.S., Pine, F. and Bergman, A. (1975) *The Psychological Birth of the Human Infant*. New York: Basic Books.

Mahoney, A., Donnelly, W. O., Boxer, P. and Lewis, T. (2003) Marital and severe parent-to-adolescent physical aggression in clinic-referred families: mother and adolescent reports on co-occurrence and links to child behavior problems, *Journal of Family Psychology*, 17(1), 3–19.

Main, M. and Goldwyn, R. (1988) Adult attachment scoring and classification systems, unpublished manuscript, University of California at Berkeley.

Main, M. and Hesse, E. (1990) Parents' unresolved traumatic experiences are related to infant disorganized attachment status: is frightened and/or frightening parental behavior the linking mechanism? in M. Greenberg, D. Cichetti and M. Cummings (eds), *Attachment in the Preschool Years*. Chicago, IL: Chicago University Press.

Main, M. and Solomon, J. (1986) Discovery of an insecure-disorganized/disoriented attachment pattern, in T.B. Brazelton and M.W. Yogman (eds), *Affective Development in Infancy*. Westport, CT: Ablex.

Main, M. and Weston, D.R. (1982) Avoidance of the attachment figure in infancy: descriptions and interpretations, in C.M. Parkes and J. Stevenson-Hinde (eds), *The Place of Attachment in Human Behavior*. New York: Basic Books.

Majors, R., Tyler, R., Peden, B. and Hall, R.J. (1994) Cool pose: a symbolic mechanism for masculine role enactment and coping by Black males, in R. Majors and J.U. Gordon (eds), *The American Black Male: His Present Status and His Future*. Chicago, IL: Nelson-Hall.

Malla, A., Norman, R., McLean, T., Scholten, D. and Townsend, L. (2003) A Canadian programme for early intervention in nonaffective psychotic disorders, *Australian and New Zealand Journal of Psychiatry*, 37, 407–413.

Malley-Morrison, K. and Hines, D. (2004) *Family Violence in a Cultural Perspective: Defining,*

Understanding and Combating Abuse. Thousand Oaks, CA: Sage.

Malmberg, M., Overbeek, G.J., Kleinjan, M., Vermulst, A.A., Monshouwer, K., Lammers, J. et al. (2010) Effectiveness of the universal prevention program 'Healthy School and Drugs': study protocol of a randomized clustered trial, *BMC Public Health*, 10, art. no. 541.

Malphurs, J.E., Field, T.M., Larraine, C., Pickens, J., Pelaez-Nogueras, M., Yando, R. and Bendell, D. (1996) Altering withdrawn and intrusive interaction behaviors of depressed mothers, *Infant Mental Health Journal*, 17(2), 152–160.

Manassis, K. (2001) Child-parent relations: attachment and anxiety disorders, in W.K. Silverman and A. Treffers (eds), *Anxiety Disorders in Children and Adolescents: Research, Assessment and Intervention.* New York: Cambridge.

Mandell, D.S. et al. (2009) Racial/ethnic disparities in the identification of children with autism spectrum disorders, *American Journal of Public Health*, 99(3), 493–498.

Mangeot, S. et al. (2002) Long-term executive function deficits in children with traumatic brain injuries: assessment using the Behavior Rating Inventory of Executive Function (BRIEF), *Child Neuropsychology*, 8(4), 271–284.

Manly, J.T., Kim, J.E., Rogosch, F.A. and Cicchetti, D. (2001) Dimensions of child maltreatment and children's adjustment: contributions of developmental timing and subtype, *Development and Psychopathology*, 13, 759–782.

Mannuzza, S., Klein, R.G., Bessler, A., Malloy, P. and LaPadula, M. (1998) Adult psychiatric status of hyperactive boys grown up, *American Journal of Psychiatry*, 155(4), 493–498.

Mannuzza, S., Klein, R.G. and Moulton, J.L. (2003) Does stimulant treatment place children at risk for adult substance abuse? A controlled, prospective follow-up study, *Journal*

of Child and Adolescent Psychopharmacology, 13(3), 273–282.

March, J.S. and Mulle, K. (1998) *OCD in Children and Adolescents: A Cognitive-Behavioral Treatment Manual.* New York: Guilford.

March, J.S., Parker, J., Sullivan, K., Stallings, P. and Conners, C. (1997) The multidimensional anxiety scale for children (MASC): Factor structure, reliability and validity, *Journal of the American Academy of Child and Adolescent Psychiatry*, 36, 554–565.

Markon, K.E., Krueger, R., Bouchard, T.J. and Gottesman, I.I. (2002) Abnormal and normal personality traits: evidence for genetic and environmental relationships in the Minnesota Study of Twins Reared Apart, *Journal of Personality*, 70(5), 661–695.

Marks, A.K., Szalacha, L.A., Lamarre, M., Boyd, M.J. and Coll, C.G. (2007) Emerging ethnic identity and interethnic group social preferences in middle childhood: findings from the Children of Immigrants Development in Context (CIDC) study, *International Journal of Behavioral Development*, 31, 501–513.

Marmorstein, N.R., Iacono, W.G. and McGue, M. (2009) Alcohol and illicit drug dependence among parents: associations with offspring externalizing disorders, *Psychological Medicine*, 39(1), 149–155.

Marshal, M.P., Friedman, M.S., Stall, R., King, K.M., Miles, J., Gold, M.A. et al. (2008) Sexual orientation and adolescent substance use: a meta-analysis and methodological review, *Addiction*, 103(4), 546–556.

Marston, E.G., Russell, M.A., Obsuth, I. and Watson, G.K. (2012) Dealing with double jeopardy: mental health disorders among girls in the juvenile justice system, in S. Miller, L. Leve and P.K. Kerig (eds), *Delinquent Girls: Context, Relationships and Adaptation.* New York: Springer Books.

Martinez-Torteya, C., Bogat, G.A., von Eye, A. and Levendosky,

A.A. (2009) Resilience among children exposed to domestic violence: the role of risk and protective factors, *Child Development*, 80(2), 562–577.

Martins, C. and Gaffan, E.A. (2000) Effects of early maternal depression on patterns of infant–mother attachment: a meta-analytic investigation, *Journal of Child Psychology and Psychiatry*, 41(6), 737–746.

Mash, E.J. (2006) Treatment of child and family disturbance: a cognitive-developmental systems perspective, in E.J. Mash and R.A. Barkley (eds), *Treatment of Childhood Disorders*, 3rd edn. New York: Guilford.

Mash, E.J. and Barkley, R.A. (2006) *Treatment of Childhood Disorders*, 3rd edn. New York: Guilford.

Mash, E.J. and Wolfe, D.A. (2002) Autism and childhood-onset schizophrenia, in *Abnormal Child Psychology*, 2nd edn. Belmont, CA: Thomson Wadsworth.

Mash, E.J. and Wolfe, D.A. (2010) *Abnormal Child Psychology*, 4th edn. Belmont, CA: Wadsworth, Cengage Learning.

Mason, W.A. and Windle, M. (2002) Reciprocal relations between adolescent substance use and delinquency: a longitudinal latent variable analysis, *Journal of Abnormal Psychology*, 111(1), 63–76.

Masten, A.S., Hubbard, J.J., Gest, S.D., Tellegen, A., Garmezy, N. and Ramirez, M. L. (1999) Competence in the context of adversity: pathways to resilience and maladaptation from childhood to late adolescence, *Development and Psychopathology*, 11(1), 143–169.

Masten, A.S., Cutuli, J.J., Herbers, J.E. and Gabrielle-Reed, M.J. (2009) Resilience in development, in C.R. Snyder and S.J. Lopez (eds), *The Handbook of Positive Psychology*, 2nd edn. New York: Oxford University Press.

Masterson, J.F. (1976) *Psychotherapy of the Borderline Adult: A Developmental Approach.* New York: Brunner/Mazel.

Masterson, J.F. and Rinsley, D.B. (1975) The borderline syndrome: the role of the mother in the genesis and psychic structure of the borderline personality, *International Journal of Psychoanalysis*, 56, 163–177.

Matarazzo, J.D. (1990) Psychological assessment versus psychological testing: validation from Binet to the school, clinic and courtroom, *American Psychologist*, 45, 999–1017.

Matson, J.L. (2007) *Handbook of Assessment in Persons with Intellectual Disability*. New York: Academic Press.

Matson, J.L. and Boisjoli, J.A. (2007) Differential diagnosis of PDDNOS in children, *Research in Autism Spectrum Disorders*, 1(1), 75–84.

Matson, J.L. and Kozlowski, A.M. (2010) Autistic regression, *Research in Autism Spectrum Disorders*, 4(3), 340–345.

Matthys, W. et al. (2004) Response perseveration and sensitivity to reward and punishment in boys with oppositional defiant disorder, *European Child and Adolescent Psychiatry*, 13(6), 362–364.

Matusiewicz, A., Hopwood, C., Banducci, A. and Lejuez, C. (2010) The effectiveness of cognitive behavioral therapy for personality disorders, *Psychiatric Clinics of North America*, 33(3), 657–685.

Maughan, B. (1995) Annotation: long-term outcomes of developmental reading problems, *Journal of Child Psychology and Psychiatry*, 36(3), 357–371.

Maughan, B. and Rutter, M. (2001) Antisocial children grown up, in J. Hill and B. Maughan (eds), *Conduct Disorders in Childhood and Adolescence*. New York: Cambridge University Press.

Maughan, B., Pickles, A., Hagell, A., Rutter, M. and Yule, W. (1996) Reading problems and antisocial behaviour: developmental trends in comorbidity, *Journal of Child Psychology and Psychiatry*, 37, 405–418.

Maughan, B., Rowe, R., Messer, J., Goodman, R. and Meltzer, H. (2004) Conduct Disorder and Oppositional Defiant Disorder in a national sample: developmental epidemiology, *Journal of Child Psychology and Psychiatry*, 45(3), 609–621.

Maulik, K. et al. (2011) Prevalence of intellectual disability: a meta-analysis of population-based studies, *Research in Developmental Disabilities*, 32(2), 419–436.

Max, J.E. et al. (2000) Personality change disorder in children and adolescents following traumatic brain injury, *Journal of the International Neuropsychological Society*, 6(3), 279–289.

Max, J.E. et al. (2011) Anxiety disorders in children and adolescents in the first six months after traumatic brain injury, *Journal of Neuropsychiatry and Clinical Neurosciences*, 23(1), 29–39.

Max, J.E., Sharma, A. and Qurashi, M.I. (1997) Traumatic brain injury in a child psychiatry inpatient population: a controlled study, *Journal of the American Academy of Child & Adolescent Psychiatry*, 36(11), 1595–1601.

May-Chahal, C. and Cawson, P. (2005) Measuring child maltreatment in the United Kingdom: a study of the prevalence of child abuse and neglect, *Child Abuse Neglect*, 29, 969–984.

Mayes, L., Fonagy, P. and Target, M. (2007) *Developmental Science and Psychoanalysis: Integration and Innovation*. London: Karnac Books.

Maynard, A. (2008) What we thought we knew and how we came to know it: four decades of cross-cultural research from a Piagetian point of view, *Human Development*, 51, 56–65.

Mazefsky, C.A. and Oswald, D.P. (2006) The discriminative ability and diagnostic utility of the ADOS-G, ADI-R and GARS for children in a clinical setting, *Autism*, 10(6), 533.

McArdle, P., O'Brien, G. and Kolvin, I. (1995) Hyperactivity: prevalence and relationship with conduct disorder, *Journal of Child Psychology and Psychiatry*, 36(2), 279–303.

McArthur, D.S. and Roberts, G.E. (1982) *Roberts Apperception Test for Children*. Los Angeles, CA: Western Psychological Services.

McCabe, K. and Yeh, M. (2009) Parent–child interaction therapy for Mexican Americans: a randomized clinical trial, *Journal of Clinical Child & Adolescent Psychology*, 38, 753–759.

McCabe, K.M., Rodgers, C. and Yeh, M. (2004) Gender differences in childhood onset conduct disorder, *Development and Psychopathology*, 16(1), 179–192.

McCabe, M., Ricciardelli, L.A. and Holt, K. (2010) Are there different sociocultural influences on body image and body change strategies for overweight adolescent boys and girls? *Eating Behaviors*, 11(3), 156–163.

McClellan, J. et al. (2003) Premorbid functioning in early-onset psychotic disorders, *Journal of the American Academy of Child & Adolescent Psychiatry*, 42(6), 666–672.

McClellan, J.M., Werry, J.S., Bernet, W., Arnold, V., Beitchman, J.H., Benson, S., Bukestein, O., Kinlan, J., Rue, D. and Shaw, J. (2001) Practice parameters for the assessment and treatment of children and adolescents with schizophrenia, *Journal of the American Academy of Child and Adolescent Psychiatry*, 40, 4S–23S.

McClure, E.B. and Pine, D.S. (2006) Social anxiety and emotion regulation: a model for developmental psychopathology perspectives on anxiety disorders, in D. Cicchetti and D.J. Cohen (eds), *Developmental Psychopathology. Volume III: Risk, Disorder and Adaptation*, 2nd edn. New York: Wiley.

McConaughy, S.H. and Achenbach, T.M. (2001) *Manual for the Semistructured Clinical Interview for Children and Adolescents*.

Burlington, VT: University of Vermont, Research Center for Children, Youth and Families.

McEachin, J.J., Smith, T. and Lovaas, O.I. (1993) Long-term outcome for children with autism who received early intensive behavioral treatment, *Mental Retardation*, 97(4), 359–372.

McElroy, S.L., Guerdjikova, A.I., O'Melia, A.M., Mori, N. and Keck, J.P.E. (2010) Pharmacotherapy of the eating disorders, in W.S. Agras (ed.), *The Oxford Handbook of Eating Disorders*. New York: Oxford University Press.

McElwain, N.L., Cox, M., Burchinal, M. and MacFie, J. (2003) Differentiating among insecure mother-infant attachment classifications: a focus on child–friend interaction and exploration during solitary play at 36 months, *Attachment & Human Development*, 5, 136–164.

McGee, R.A., Wolfe, D.A. and Wilson, S.K. (1997) Multiple maltreatment experiences and adolescent behavior problems: adolescents' perspectives, *Development and Psychopathology*, 9, 131–150.

McGee, R.O.B. et al. (1992) DSM-III disorders from age 11 to age 15 years, *Journal of the American Academy of Child & Adolescent Psychiatry*, 31(1), 50–59.

McGoldrick, M. (2008) *Re-visioning Family Therapy: Race, Culture and Gender in Clinical Practice*, 2nd edn. New York: Guilford.

McGoldrick, M. and Carter, B. (2003) The family life cycle, in F. Walsh (ed.), *Normal Family Processes: Growing Diversity and Complexity*. New York: Guilford.

McGoldrick, M. and Gerson, R. (1985) *Genograms in Family Assessment*. New York: W.W. Norton.

McGoldrick, M., Giordano, J. and Garcia-Preto, N. (2005) *Ethnicity and Family Therapy*, 3rd edn. New York: Guilford.

McGorry, P.D. and Yung, A.R. (2003) Early intervention in psychosis: an overdue reform, *Australian and New Zealand Journal of Psychiatry*, 37, 393–398.

McGough, J.J. and Barkley, R.A. (2004) Diagnostic controversies in adult attention deficit hyperactivity disorder, *American Journal of Psychiatry*, 161, 1948–1956.

McGrath, J. and Pisterman, S. (1991) Developmental issues: adolescent pain, *Children in pain. Clinical and Research Issues from a Developmental Perspective*. New York: Springer-Verlag.

McGrath, J.J., Feron, F.P., Burne, T.H.J., Mackay-Sim, A. and Eyles, D.W. (2003) The neurodevelopmental hypothesis of schizophrenia: a review of recent developments, *Annals of Medicine*, 35, 86–93.

McGue, M., Elkins, I. and Ianoco, W.G. (2000) Genetic and environmental influences on adolescent substance use and abuse. *American Journal of Medical Genetics*, 96, 671–677.

McGuffin, P., Marušič, A. and Farmer, A. (2001) What can psychiatric genetics offer suicidology? *Crisis: The Journal of Crisis Intervention and Suicide Prevention*, 22(2), 61–65.

McIntosh, P. (1998) White privilege: unpacking the invisible knapsack, in M. McGoldrick (ed.), *Re-visioning Family Therapy: Race, Culture and Gender in Clinical Practice*. New York: Guilford.

McKinlay, A., Kyonka, E.G.E., Grace, R.C., Horwood, L.J., Fergusson, D.M. and MacFarlane, M.R. (2010) An investigation of the pre-injury risk factors associated with children who experience traumatic brain injury, *Injury Prevention*, 16(1), 31.

McKown, C. and Weinstein, R.S. (2008) Teacher expectation, classroom context and the achievement gap, *Journal of School Psychology*, 46, 235–261.

McLaughlin, K.A. (2009) Universal prevention for adolescent depression, in S. Nolen-Hoeksema and L. M. Hilt (eds), *Handbook of Depression in Adolescents*. New York: Routledge/Taylor & Francis Group.

McMahon, R.J. and Forehand, R. (2003) *Helping the Noncompliant Child: A Clinician's Guide to Effective Parent Training*, 2nd edn. New York: Guilford.

McMahon, R.J. and Frick, J. (2005) Evidence-based assessment of conduct problems in children and adolescents, *Journal of Clinical Child and Adolescent Psychology*, 34(3), 477–505.

McMahon, R.J. and Kotler, J.S. (2006) Conduct problems, in D.A. Wolfe and E.J. Mash (eds), *Behavioral and Emotional Disorders in Adolescents: Nature, Assessment and Treatment*. New York: Guilford.

McNeil, T.F., Cantor-Graae, E. and Blennow, G. (2003) Mental correlates of neuromotoric deviation in 6-year-olds at heightened risk for schizophrenia, *Schizophrenia Research*, 60(2–3), 219–228.

Mead, G.H. (1932) *Mind, Self and Society*. Chicago, IL: University of Chicago Press.

Meadows, S.O., McLanahan, S.S. and Brooks-Gunn, J. (2007) Parental depression and anxiety and early childhood behavior problems across family types, *Journal of Marriage and Family*, 69(5), 1162–1177.

Meaney, M.J. (2010) Epigenetics and the biological definition of gene x environment interactions, *Child Development*, 81(1), 41–79.

Measelle, J.R., Stice, E. and Hogansen, J.M. (2006) Developmental trajectories of co-occurring depressive, eating, antisocial and substance abuse problems in female adolescents, *Journal of Abnormal Psychology*, 115(3), 524–538.

Mednick, S.A., Machon, R.A., Huttunen, M.O. and Bonett, D. (1988) Adult schizophrenia following prenatal exposure to an influenza epidemic, *Archives of General Psychiatry*, 45, 189–192.

Mehlenbeck, R., Spirito, A., Barnett, N. and Overholser, J. (2003) Behavioral factors: substance abuse, in

A. Spirito and J.C. Overholser (eds), *Evaluating and Treating Adolescent Suicide Attempters: From Research to Practice*. New York: Academic Press.

Melamed, B.G. (2002) Parenting the ill child, in M.H. Bornstein (ed.), *Handbook of Parenting, Vol. 5: Practical Issues in Parenting*. London: Psychology Press.

Mellon, M.W. and Stern, H.P. (1998) Elmination disorders, in R.T. Ammerman and J.V. Campo, *Handbook of Pediatric Psychology and Psychiatry. Vol. 1: Psychology and Psychiatric Issues in the Pediatric Setting*. Needham Heights, MA: Allyn & Bacon.

Mennen, F.E., Kim, K., Sang, J. and Trickett, P.K. (2010) Child neglect: definition and identification of youth's experiences in official reports of child maltreatment, *Child Abuse and Neglect*, 34, 647–658.

Menzies, R.G. and Clarke, J.C. (1995) The etiology of phobias: a nonassociative account, *Clinical Psychology Review*, 15, 23–48.

Merikangas, K.R. and Knight, E. (2009) The epidemiology of depression in adolescents, in S. Nolen-Hoeksema and L.M. Hilt (eds), *Handbook of Depression in Adolescents*. New York: Routledge/Taylor & Francis Group.

Merikangas, K.R., He, J.-P., Burstein, M., Swanson, S.A., Avenevoli, S., Cui, L. et al. (2010) Lifetime prevalence of mental disorders in U.S. Adolescents: results from the National Comorbidity Survey Replication–Adolescent Supplement (NCS-A), *Journal of the American Academy of Child and Adolescent Psychiatry*, 49(10), 980–989.

Merrell, K.W. and Wolfe, T.M. (1998) The relationship of teacher-rated social skills deficits and ADHD characteristics among kindergarten-age children, *Psychology in the Schools*, 35(2), 101–110.

Merry, S., McDowell, H., Wild, C.J., Bir, J. and Cunliffe, R. (2004) A randomized placebo-controlled trial of a school-based depression prevention program, *Journal of the American Academy of Child & Adolescent Psychiatry*, 43(5), 538–547.

Mesibov, G.B., Shea, V. and Schopler, E. (2004) *The TEACCH Approach to Autism Spectrum Disorders*. New York: Springer.

Meyer, C., Blissett, J. and Oldfield, C. (2001) Sexual orientation and eating psychopathology: the role of masculinity and femininity, *International Journal of Eating Disorders*, 29, 314–318.

Meyer, I.H. (2003) Prejudice, social stress and mental health in lesbian, gay and bisexual populations: conceptual issues and research evidence, *Psychological Bulletin*, 129, 674–697.

Meyer, R.G. (1989) *Cases in Developmental Psychology and Psychopathology*. Boston, MA: Allyn & Bacon.

Meyer, S.E. and Carlson, G.A. (2010) Development, age of onset and phenomenology in bipolar disorder, in D.J. Miklowitz and D. Cichetti (eds), *Understanding Bipolar Disorder: A Developmental Psychopathology Perspective*. New York: Guilford Press.

Meyer, T.D. and Krumm-Merabet, C. (2003) Academic performance and expectations for the future in relation to a vulnerability marker for bipolar disorders: the hypomanic temperament, *Personality and Individual Differences*, 35, 785–798.

Meyer, T.D., Koßmann-Böhm, S. and Schlottke, P.F. (2004) Do child psychiatrists in Germany diagnose bipolar disorders in children and adolescents? Results from a survey, *Bipolar Disorders*, 6(5), 426–431.

Mezulis, A.H., Priess, H.A. and Hyde, J.S. (2011) Rumination mediates the relationship between infant temperament and adolescent depressive symptoms, *Depression Research and Treatment*, doi: 10.1155/2011/487873.

Miklowitz, D.J. (1994) Family risk indicators in schizophrenia, *Schizophrenia Bulletin*, 20, 137–147.

Miklowitz, D.J. and Goldstein, T.R. (2010) Family-based approaches to treating bipolar disorder in adolescence: family-focused therapy and dialectical behavior therapy, in D.J. Miklowitz and M.J. Goldstein, *Bipolar Disorder: A Family-Focused Treatment Approach*, 2nd edn, revd. New York: Guilford Publications.

Miklowitz, D.J., Axelson, D.A., Birmaher, B., George, E.L., Taylor, D.O., Schneck, C.D. et al. (2008) Family-focused treatment for adolescents with bipolar disorder: results of a 2–year randomized trial, *Archives of General Psychiatry*, 65(9), 1053–1061.

Miles, M.S. et al. (2011) Maternal role attainment with medically fragile infants: Part 1. Measurement and correlates during the first year of life, *Research in Nursing & Health*, 34(1), 20–34.

Milich, R., Balentine, A.C. and Lynam, D.R. (2001) ADHD combined type and ADHD predominantly inattentive type are distinct and unrelated disorders, *Clinical Psychology: Science and Practice*, 8(4), 463–488.

Miller, A.L., Rathus, J.H. and Linehan, M.M. (2006) *Dialectical Behavior Therapy with Suicidal Adolescents*. New York: Guilford.

Miller, A.L., Muehlenkamp, J.J. and Jacobson, C.M. (2008) Fact or fiction: diagnosing borderline personality disorder in adolescents, *Clinical Psychology Review*, 28(6), 969–981.

Miller, K. (1993) Concomitant nonpharmacologic therapy in the treatment of primary nocturnal enuresis, *Clinical Pediatrics*, 32(1 supplement), 32–37.

Miller, K.J. and Mizes, J.S. (2000) *Comparative Treatments For Eating Disorders*. New York: Springer.

Miller, S., Leve, L. and Kerig, P.K. (eds) (2012) *Delinquent Girls: Context, Relationships and Adaptation*. New York: Springer Books.

Millward, R., Kennedy, E., Towlson, K. and Minnis, H. (2006) Reactive attachment disorder in looked after children, *Emotional and Behavioural Difficulties*, 11(4), 273–279.

Milshtein, S. et al. (2010) Resolution of the diagnosis among parents of children with autism spectrum disorder: associations with child and parent characteristics, *Journal of Autism and Developmental Disorders*, 40(1), 89–99.

Minnes, P. (1988) Family stress associated with a developmentally handicapped child, *International Review of Research on Mental Retardation*, 15, 195–266.

Minnis, H. et al. (2006) Reactive attachment disorder – a theoretical model beyond attachment, *European Child & Adolescent Psychiatry*, 15(6), 336–342.

Minuchin, S. (1974) *Families and Family Therapy*. Cambridge, MA: Harvard University Press.

Minuchin, S. and Fishman, H.C. (2004) *Family Therapy Techniques*. Cambridge, MA: Harvard University Press.

Minuchin, S., Rosman, B.L. and Baker, L. (1978) *Psychosomatic Families: Anorexia Nervosa in Context*. Cambridge, MA: Harvard University Press.

Minuchin, S., Lee, W.-Y. and Simon, G. M. (2006) *Mastering family Therapy: Journeys of Growth and Transformation*, 2nd edn. Hoboken, NJ: John Wiley & Sons.

Mirenda, P. and Erickson, K.A. (2000) Augmentative communication and literacy, *Autism Spectrum Disorders: A Transactional Developmental Perspective*, 9, 333–367.

Mitchell, J., McCauley, E., Burke, P.M. and Moss, S.J. (1988) Phenomenology of depression in children and adolescents, *Journal of the American Academy of Child and Adolescent Psychiatry*, 27, 12–20.

Mitchell, J.E., Crosby, R.D., Wonderlich, S.A., Crow, S., Lancaster, K., Simonich, H. et al. (2008) A randomized trial comparing the efficacy of cognitive-behavioral therapy for bulimia

nervosa delivered via telemedicine versus face-to-face, *Behaviour Research and Therapy*, 46(5), 581–592.

Moffitt, T.E. (2003) Life-course-persistent and adolescence-limited antisocial behavior: a 10-year research review and a research agenda, in B.B. Lahey, T.E. Moffitt and A. Caspi (eds), *Causes of Conduct Disorder and Juvenile Delinquency*. New York: Guilford.

Moffit, T.E. (2005) The new look of behavioral genetics in developmental psychopathology: gene-environment interplay in antisocial behaviors, *Psychological Bulletin*, 131, 533–554.

Moffitt, T.E. (2006) Life-course-persistent versus adolescence-limited antisocial behavior, in D. Cicchetti and D.J. Cohen (eds), *Developmental Psychopathology. Volume III: Risk, Disorder and Adaptation*, 2nd edn. New York: Wiley.

Moffitt, T.E., Caspi, A., Harrington, H. and Milne, B. (2002) Males on the life-course-persistent and adolescence-limited pathways: follow-up at age 26 years, *Development and Psychopathology*, 14(1), 179–207.

Moffitt, T.E. et al. (2008) Research review: DSM-V conduct disorder: research needs for an evidence base, *Journal of Child Psychology and Psychiatry*, 49(1), 3–33.

Moldin, S.O. and Gottesman, I.J. (1997) At issue: genes, experience and chance in schizophrenia: positioning for the 21st century, *Schizophrenia Bulletin*, 23, 547–561.

Molina, B.S.G. et al. (2009) The MTA at 8 years: prospective follow-up of children treated for combined-type ADHD in a multisite study, *Journal of the American Academy of Child & Adolescent Psychiatry*, 48(5), 484–500.

Monahan, K.C., Steinberg, L. and Cauffman, E. (2009) Affiliation with antisocial peers, susceptibility to peer influence and antisocial behavior during the transition to

adulthood, *Developmental Psychology*, 45(6), 1520–1530.

Moore, G.F., Rothwell, H. and Segrott, J. (2010) An exploratory study of the relationship between parental attitudes and behaviour and young people's consumption of alcohol, *Substance Abuse Treatment, Prevention and Policy*, 5(6), doi: 10.1186/1747-597X-5-6.

Mortensen, P.B., Pedersen, C.B., Melbye, M., Mors, O. and Ewald, H. (2003) Individual and familial risk factors for bipolar affective disorders in Denmark, *Archives of General Psychiatry*, 60, 1209–1215.

Mosack, K.E., Randolph, M.E., Dickson-Gomez, J., Abbott, M., Smith, E. and Weeks, M.R. (2010) Sexual risk-taking among high-risk urban women with and without histories of childhood sexual abuse: mediating effects of contextual factors, *Journal of Child Sexual Abuse*, 19(1), 43–61.

Moskos, M., Olson, L., Halbern, S., Keller, T. and Gray, D. (2005) Utah Youth Suicide Study: Psychological autopsy, *Suicide and Life-Threatening Behavior*, 35(5), 536–546.

Mowbray, C.T. and Oyserman, D. (2003) Substance abuse in children of parents with mental illness: risks, resiliency and best prevention practices, *Journal of Primary Prevention*, 23(4), 451–482.

Mufson, L., Dorta, K.P., Moreau, D. and Weissman, M.M. (2011) *Interpersonal Psychotherapy for Depressed Adolescents*, 2nd edn. New York: Guilford Press.

Multimodal Treatment (MTA) Cooperative Group (1999) A 14-month randomized clinical trial of treatment strategies for attention-deficit/hyperactivity disorder, *Archives of General Psychiatry*, 56, 1073–1086.

Mulvey, E.P., Steinberg, L., Piquero, A.R., Besana, M., Fagan, J., Schubert, C. and Cauffman, E. (2010) Trajectories of desistance and continuity in antisocial behavior following court adjudication among serious adolescent offenders,

Development and Psychopathology, 22(2), 453–475.

Muris, P., Merckelbach, H., Gadet, B. and Moulaert, V. (2000) Fears, worries and scary dreams to 4- to 12-year-old children: their content, developmental patterns and origins, *Journal of Clinical Child Psychology*, 29, 43–52.

Murphy, L.M.B., Thompson, R.J. and Morris, M.A. (1997) Adherence behavior among adolescents with type I insulin-dependent diabetes mellitus: the role of cognitive appraisal processes, *Journal of Pediatric Psychology*, 22, 811–825.

Murray, L., Woolgar, M., Cooper, P. and Hipwell, A. (2001) Cognitive vulnerability to depression in 5-year-old children of depressed mothers, *Journal of Child Psychology and Psychiatry and Allied Disciplines*, 42(7), 891–899.

Murry, V.M., Bynum, M.S., Brody, G.H., Willert, A. and Stephens, D. (2001) African American single mothers and children in context: a review of studies of risk and resilience, *Clinical Child and Family Psychology Review*, 4(2), 133–155.

Myers, J.F.B. (2011) A short history of child protection in America, in J.F.B. Myers (ed.), *The APSAC Handbook on Child Maltreatment*. Thousand Oaks, CA: Sage.

Myin-Germeys, I. and van Os, J. (2007). Stress-reactivity in psychosis: evidence for an affective pathway to psychosis, *Clinical Psychology Review*, 27(4), 409–424.

Nabors, L. (1997) Playmate preferences of children who are typically developing for their classmates with special needs, *Mental Retardation*, 35(2), 107–113.

Nader, K. (2008) *Understanding and Assessing Trauma in Children and Adolescents*. New York: Routledge.

Naglieri, J.A. and Pfeiffer, S.I. (1992) Performance of disruptive behavior disordered and normal samples on the Draw A Person: screening procedure for emotional disturbance, *Psychological Assessment*, 4(2), 156–159.

Naglieri, J.A., LeBuffe, A. and Pfeiffer, S.I., (1994) *Manual of the Devereux Scales of Mental Disorder*. San Antonio, TX: Devereux Foundation.

Nassau, J.H. and Drotar, D. (1997) Social competence among children with central nervous system-related chronic health conditions: a review, *Journal of Pediatric Psychology*, 22(6), 771.

National Center for Health Statistics (2010) Fastats, http://www.cdc.gov/nchs/fastats/suicide.htm.

National Center on Addiction and Substance Abuse (2003) The formative years: pathways to substance abuse among girls and young women ages 8–22, http://www.casacolumbia.org/templates/publications_reports.aspx.

National Center on Addiction and Substance Abuse (2004) *Criminal Neglect: Substance Abuse, Juvenile Justice and the Children Left Behind*. New York: National Center on Addiction and Substance Abuse.

National Center on Addiction and Substance Abuse (2010) *Behind Bars II: Substance Abuse and America's Prison Population*, http://www.casacolumbia.org/templates/publications_reports.aspx.

National Center on Child Abuse and Neglect (2010) *Child Maltreatment 2009: Reports from the States to the National Center on Child Abuse and Neglect*. Washington DC: US Government Printing Office.

National Institute for Health and Clinical Excellence (NICE) (2008) *Guidance for ADHD*. London: NICE.

National Institute of Mental Health research roundtable on prepubertal bipolar disorder (2001) *Journal of the American Academy of Child and Adolescent Psychiatry*, 40(8), 871–878.

National Joint Committee on Learning Difficulties (NJCLD) (1988) Letter to NJCLD member organizations.

Nawal, S.B., Glyn, V.T. and Jolley, R.P. (2005) The use of drawing for psychological assessment in Britain: survey findings, *Psychology and Psychotherapy: Theory, Research and Practice*, 78, 205–217.

Nechmad, A. et al. (2003) Obsessive-compulsive disorder in adolescent schizophrenia patients, *American Journal of Psychiatry*, 160(5), 1002–1004.

Negriff, S. and Susman, E.J. (2011) Pubertal timing, depression and externalizing problems: a framework, review and examination of gender differences, *Journal of Research on Adolescence*, 21, doi: 10.1111/j.1532-7795.2010.00708.x.

Negriff, S., Noll, J.G., Shenk, C.E., Putnam, F.W. and Trickett, P.K. (2010) Associations between nonverbal behaviors and subsequent sexual attitudes and behaviors of sexually abused and comparison girls, *Child Maltreatment*, 15(2), 180–189.

Negriff, S., Ji, J. and Trickett, P.K. (2011) Exposure to peer delinquency as a mediator between self-report pubertal timing and delinquency: a longitudinal study of mediation, *Development and Psychopathology*, 23(1), 293–304.

Neiderman, M. (2000) Prognosis and outcome, in B. Lask and R. Bryant-Waugh (eds), *Anorexia Nervosa and Related Eating Disorders in Childhood and Adolescence*. Philadelphia, PA: Psychology Press.

Neitzel, C. and Stright, A. (2003) Mothers' scaffolding of children's problem solving: establishing a foundation of academic self-regulatory competence, *Journal of Family Psychology*, 17(1), 147–159.

Nestadt, G., Samuels, J., Riddle, M., Bienvenu, J., Liang, K.-Y., LaBuda, M. et al. (2000) A family study of obsessive-compulsive disorder, *Archives of General Psychiatry*, 57(4), 358–363.

Neveus, T. (2003) The role of sleep and arousal in nocturnal enuresis, *Acta Paediatrica*, 92(10), 1118–1123.

Newcomb, M.D. and Bentler, P.M. (1988) *Consequences of Adolescent Drug Use: Impact on the Lives of Young Adults*. Newbury Park, CA: Sage Publications.

Newcomb, M.D., Munoz, D.T. and Carmona, J.V. (2009) Child sexual abuse consequences in community samples of Latino and European American adolescents, *Child Abuse & Neglect*, 33(8), 533–544.

Newman, D.L., Caspi, A., Moffitt, T.E. and Silva, P.A. (1997) Antecedents of adult interpersonal functioning: effects of individual differences in age 3 temperament, *Developmental Psychology*, 33(2), 206–217.

Nichols, M.P. and Schwartz, R.C. (2004) *Family Therapy: Concepts and Methods*. Boston, MA: Allyn & Bacon.

Nicholson, R.M., Giedd, J.N. and Lenane, M. (1999) Clinical and neurobiological correlates of cytogenic abnormalities in childhood onset schizophrenia, *Schizophrenia Research*, 41, 55.

Nicholson, R.M., Lenane, M. and Singaracharlu, S. (2000) Premorbid speech and language impairments in childhood onset schizophrenia: association with risk factors, *Schizophrenia Research*, 41, 55.

Nicolson, R., Brookner, F.B., Lenane, M., Gochman, P., Ingraham, L.J., Egan, M.F., Kendler, K.S., Pickar, D., Weinberger, D.R. and Rapoport, J.L. (2003) Parental schizophrenia spectrum disorders in childhood-onset and adult-onset schizophrenia, *American Journal of Psychiatry*, 160, 490–495.

Niemi, L.T., Suvisaari, J.M., Tuulio-Henriksson, A. and Loennqvist, J.K. (2003) Childhood developmental abnormalities in schizophrenia: evidence from high-risk studies, *Schizophrenia Research*, 60, 239–258.

Niendam, T.A., Bearden, C.E., Rosso, I.M., Sanchez, L.E., Hadley, T., Nuechterlein, K.H. and Cannon, T.D. (2003) A prospective study of childhood neurocognitive functioning in schizophrenic patients and their siblings, *American Journal of Psychiatry*, 160, 2060–2062.

Nigg, J.T. (2006) *What Causes ADHD? Understanding What Goes Wrong And Why*. New York: Guilford.

Nihira, K. (1976) Dimensions of adaptive behavior in institutionalized mentally retarded children and adults: developmental perspective, *American Journal of Mental Deficiency*, 81, 215–226.

Nihira, K., Foster, R., Shellhaas, M. and Leland, H. (1974) *AAMD Adaptive Behavior Scale* (1974 revision). Washington, DC: American Association on Mental Deficiency.

Nikiéma, B., Spencer, N. and Séguin, L. (2010) Poverty and chronic illness in early childhood: a comparison between the United Kingdom and Quebec, *Pediatrics*, 125(3), e499.

Nikolas, M., Friderici, K., Waldman, I., Jernigan, K. and Nigg, J.T. (2010) Gene × environment interactions for ADHD: synergistic effect of 5HTTLPR genotype and youth appraisals of inter-parental conflict, *Behavioral and Brain Functions*, 6, 6–23.

Nixon, M.K., Cloutier, P.F. and Aggarwal, S. (2002) Affect regulation and addictive aspects of repetitive self-injury in hospitalized adolescents, *Journal of the American Academy of Child and Adolescent Psychiatry*, 41(11), 1333–1341.

Nock, M. and Kessler, R. (2006) Prevalence of and risk factors for suicide attempts versus suicide gestures: analysis of the National Comorbidity Survey, *Journal of Abnormal Psychology*, 115(3), 616.

Nock, M. and Prinstein, M. (2005) Contextual features and behavioral functions of self-mutilation among adolescents, *Journal of Abnormal Psychology*, 114(1), 140–146.

Nock, M.K. and Mendes, W.B. (2008) Physiological arousal, distress tolerance, and social problem-solving deficits among adolescent self-injurers, *Journal of Consulting and Clinical Psychology*, 76(1), 28–38. doi: 10.1037/0022-006x.76.1.28.

Nock, M.K., Joiner, T.E. Jr, Gordon, K.H., Lloyd-Richardson, E. and Prinstein, M.J. (2006a) Non-suicidal self-injury among adolescents: diagnostic correlates and relation to suicide attempts, *Psychiatry Research*, 144(1), 65–72.

Nock, M.K., Kazdin, A.E., Hiripi, E. and Kessler, R.C. (2006b) Prevalence, subtypes and correlates of DSM-IV conduct disorder in the National Comorbidity Survey replication, *Psychological Medicine*, 36(5), 699–710.

Nock, M.K. et al. (2007) Lifetime prevalence, correlates and persistence of oppositional defiant disorder: results from the National Comorbidity Survey Replication, *Journal of Child Psychology and Psychiatry*, 48(7), 703–713.

Nolen-Hoeksema, S. and Morrow, J. (1991) A prospective study of depression and posttraumatic stress symptoms after a natural disaster: the 1989 Loma Prieta earthquake, *Journal of Personality and Social Psychology*, 61(1), 115–121.

Noll, J.G., Shenk, C.E. and Putnam, K.T. (2009) Childhood sexual abuse and adolescent pregnancy: a meta-analytic update, *Journal of Pediatric Psychology*, 34(4), 366.

Nordahl, H.M. et al. (2010) Association between abnormal psychosocial situations in childhood, generalized anxiety disorder and oppositional defiant disorder, *Australian and New Zealand Journal of Psychiatry*, 44(9), 852–858.

Novik, T.S. et al. (2006) Influence of gender on attention-deficit/hyperactivity disorder in Europe – ADORE, *European Child & Adolescent Psychiatry*, 15, 15–24.

O'Carroll, P. and Potter, L.B. (1994) Suicide contagion and the reporting of suicide: recommendations from a national workshop, *Morbidity and Mortality Weekly Review*, 32, 9–17.

O'Connor, T.G. and Spagnola, M.E. (2009) Child and adolescent psychiatry and mental health, *Child and Adolescent Psychiatry and Mental Health*, 3, 24.

O'Connor, T.G., Deater-Deckard, K., Rutter, M. and Plomin, R. (1998) Genotype-environment correlations in late childhood and early adolescence: Antisocial behavioral problems and coercive parenting, *Developmental Psychology*, 34(5), 970–981.

Obel, C. et al. (2004) Does children's watching of television cause attention problems? Retesting the hypothesis in a Danish cohort, *Pediatrics*, 114(5), 1372.

Odgers, C.L., Caspi, A., Nagin, D.S., Piquero, A.R., Slutske, W.S., Milne, B. J. et al. (2008) Is it important to prevent early exposure to drugs and alcohol among adolescents? *Psychological Science*, 19(10), 1037–1044.

Office of Juvenile Justice (2000) *Children as Victims (1999 National Report Series, Juvenile Justice Bulletin)*, http://ncjrs. org/html/ojjdp/2000_5_2/child_09. html.

Ogawa, J.R., Sroufe, L.A., Weinfield, N.S., Carlson, E.A. and Egeland, B. (1997) Development and the fragmented self: longitudinal study of dissociative symptomatology in a nonclinical sample, *Development and Psychopathology*, 9, 855–879.

Ogbu, J.V. (1999) A cultural context of children's development, in H.E. Fitzgerald, B.M. Lister and B.S. Zuckerman (eds), *Children of Color: Research, Health and Policy Issues*. New York: Garland.

Ogden, T. (1979) On projective identification, *International Journal of Psychoanalysis*, 60(3), 357–373.

Ogden, T.H. (1982) *Projective Identification and Psychotherapeutic Technique*. New York: Academic.

Ohannessian, C.M. and Hesselbrock, V.M. (2008) Paternal alcoholism and youth substance abuse: the indirect effects of negative affect, conduct problems and risk taking, *Journal of Adolescent Health*, 42(2), 198–200.

Ohring, R., Graber, J.A. and Brooks-Gunn, J. (2002) Girls' recurrent and concurrent body dissatisfaction: correlates and consequences over 8 years, *International Journal of Eating Disorders*, 31(4), 404–415.

Olds, D.L. (1997) The prenatal early infancy project: preventing child abuse and neglect in the context of promoting maternal and child health, in D.A. Wolfe, R.J. McMahon and R.D. Peters (eds), *Child Abuse: New Directions in Prevention And Treatment across the Lifespan*. Thousand Oaks, CA: Sage.

Olds, D.L. (2008) Preventing child maltreatment and crime with prenatal and infancy support of parents: the nurse family partnership, *Journal of Scandinavian Studies in Criminology and Crime Prevention*, 9(S1), 2–24.

Olds, D.L., Kitzman, H., Hanks, C., Cole, R., Anson, E., Sidora-Arcoleo, K., Luckey, D.W., Henderson, C.R. Jr, Holmberg, J., Tutt, R.A., Stevenson, A.J. and Bondy, J. (2007) Effects of nurse home visiting on maternal and child functioning: age-9 follow-up of a randomized trial, *Pediatrics*, 120, 832–845.

Olin, S.S. and Mednick, S. (1996) Risk factors of psychosis: identifying vulnerable populations premorbidly, *Schizophrenia Bulletin*, 22(2), 223.

Ollendick, T.H. and King, N.J. (1991) Origins of childhood fears: an evaluation of Rachman's theory of fear acquisition, *Behaviour Research and Therapy*, 29(2), 117–123.

Ollendick, T.H. and Schroeder, C.S. (2003) *Encyclopedia of Clinical Child and Pediatric Psychology*. New York: Springer.

Olsson, C.A. et al. (2005) The role of peer support in facilitating psychosocial adjustment to chronic illness in adolescence, *Clinical Child Psychology and Psychiatry*, 10(1), 78–87.

Ondersma, S.J. and Walker, C.E. (1998) Elimination disorders, in T.H. Ollendick and M. Hersen (eds), *Handbook of Child Psychopathology*, 3rd edn. New York: Plenum.

Oosterlaan, J. (2001) Behavioural inhibition and the development of childhood anxiety disorders, in W.K. Silverman and A. Treffers (eds), *Anxiety Disorders in Children and Adolescents: Research, Assessment and Intervention*. New York: Cambridge.

Orbach, I. (2003) Suicide prevention for adolescents, in R.A. King and A. Apter (eds), *Suicide in Children and Adolescents*. Cambridge: Cambridge University Press.

Osterling, J. and Dawson, G. (1994) Early recognition of children with autism: a study of first birthday home videotapes, *Journal of Autism and Developmental Disorders*, 24(3), 247–257.

Osterling, J.A., Dawson, G. and Munson, J.A. (2002) Early recognition of 1–year-old infants with autism spectrum disorder versus mental retardation, *Development and Psychopathology*, 14(2), 239–251.

Ott, S.L. et al. (2002) Positive and negative thought disorder and psychopathology in childhood among subjects with adulthood schizophrenia, *Schizophrenia Research*, 58(2–3), 231–239.

Otten, R., Barker, E.D., Maughan, B., Arseneault, L. and Engels, R.C.M.E. (2010) Self-control and its relation to joint developmental trajectories of cannabis use and depressive mood symptoms, *Drug and Alcohol Dependence*, 112(3), 201–208.

Overbeek, G., Zeevalkink, H., Vermulst, A. and Scholte, R.H. (2010) Peer victimization, self-esteem and ego resilience types in adolescents: a prospective analysis of person-context interactions, *Social Development*, 19(2), 270–284.

Overholser, J. and Spirito, A. (2003) Precursors to adolescent suicide attempts, in A. Spirito and J. C. Overholser (eds), *Evaluating and Treating Adolescent Suicide Attempters: From Research to Practice.* New York: Academic Press.

Overturf, G.D. (2000) American Academy of Pediatrics. Committee on Infectious Diseases, technical report: prevention of pneumococcal infections, including the use of pneumococcal conjugate and polysaccharide vaccines and antibiotic prophylaxis, *Pediatrics*, 106(2 Pt 1), 367–376.

Ozonoff, S. and Cathcart, K. (1998) Effectiveness of a home program intervention for young children with autism, *Journal of Autism and Developmental Disorders*, 28, 25–32.

Ozonoff, S. and Griffith, E.M. (2000) Neuropsychological function and the external validity of Asperger syndrome, in A. Klin, F.R. Volkmar and S.S. Sparrow (eds), *Asperger Syndrome.* New York: Guilford.

Ozonoff, S. and McEvoy, R.E. (1994) A longitudinal study of executive function and theory of mind development in autism, *Development and Psychopathology*, 6, 415–415.

Ozonoff, S. and Miller, J.N. (1995) Teaching theory of mind: a new approach to social skills training for individuals with autism, *Journal of Autism and Developmental Disorders*, 25(4), 415–433.

Ozonoff, S. et al. (1991) Executive function deficits in high-functioning autistic individuals: relationship to theory of mind, *Journal of Child Psychology and Psychiatry*, 32(7), 1081–1105.

Pagani, L. et al. (2001) Effects of grade retention on academic performance and behavioral development, *Development and Psychopathology*, 13(2), 297–315.

Palermo, T.M. and Eccleston, C. (2009) Parents of children and adolescents with chronic pain, *Pain*, 146(1–2), 15.

Pantelis, C., Velakoulis, D., McGorry, P., Wood, S.J., Suckling, J., Phillips, L.J., Yung, A.R., Bullmore, E.T., Brewer, W., Soulsby, B., Desmond, P. and McGuire, P. (2003) Neuroanatomical abnormalities before and after onset of psychosis: a crosssectional and longitudinal MRI comparison, *Lancet*, 361, 281–288.

Pantin, H., Schwartz, S.J., Coatsworth, J.D., Sullivan, S., Briones, E. and Szapocznik, J. (2007) Familias Unidas: a systemic, parent-centered approach to preventing problem behavior in Hispanic adolescents, in P. Tolan, J. Szapocznik and S. Sambrano (eds), *Preventing Youth Substance Abuse: Science-Based Programs for Children and Adolescents.* Washington, DC: American Psychological Association.

Papageorgiou, G. et al. (2011) Country differences in patient characteristics and treatment in schizophrenia: data from a physician-based survey in Europe, *European Psychiatry*, 26(1), 17–28.

Paradies, Y. (2006) A systematic review of empirical research on self-reported racism and health, *International Journal of Epidemiology*, 35, 888–901.

Parent, A.-S., Teilmann, G., Juul, A., Skakkebaek, N.E., Toppari, J. and Bourguignon, J.-P. (2003) The timing of normal puberty and the age limits of sexual precocity: variations around the world, secular trends and changes after migration, *Endocrine Reviews*, 24(5), 668–693.

Paris, J. (2003) *Personality Disorders Over Time: Precursors, Course and Outcome.* Washington, DC: American Psychiatric. Press.

Paris, J., Zelkowitz, P., Guzder, J., Joseph, S. and Feldman, R. (1999) Neuropsychological factors associated with borderline pathology in children, *Journal of the American Academy of Child & Adolescent Psychiatry*, 38(6), 770–774.

Parker, J.G., Rubin, K.H., Erath, S.A., Wojslawowicz, J.C. and Buskirk, A.A. (2006) Peer relationships, child development and adjustment: a developmental psychopathology perspective, in D. Cicchetti and D. J. Cohen (eds), *Developmental Psychopathology. Volume I: Theory and Method*, 2nd edn. New York: Wiley.

Parnell, T.F. (2002) Munchausen by proxy syndrome, in J.E.B. Myers, L. Berliner, J. Briere, C.T. Hendrix, C. Jenny and T.A. Reid (eds), *The APSAC Handbook on Child Maltreatment*, 2nd edn. Thousand Oaks, CA: Sage.

Pastor, N. and Reuben, C.A. (2005) Racial and ethnic differences in ADHD and LD in young school-age children: parental reports in the National Health Interview Survey, *Public Health Reports*, 120(4), 383–392.

Pathela, P. and Schillinger, J.A. (2010) Sexual behaviors and sexual violence: adolescents with opposite-, same-, or both-sex partners, *Pediatrics*, 126(5), 879–86.

Pati, N.C. and Parimanik R. (1996) Social development of children with mental retardation, *Indian Journal Mental Health Disabilities*, 1996, 22–2.

Patterson, G.R. (1982) *Coercive Family Process: A Social Learning Approach.* Eugene, OR: Castalia.

Patterson, G.R. (2005) The next generation of PMTO models, *The Behavior Therapist*, 28(2), 27–33.

Patterson, G.R. and Yoerger, K. (2002) A developmental model for early- and late-onset delinquency, in J.B. Reid, G.R. Patterson and J.J. Snyder (eds), *Antisocial Behavior in Children and Adolescents: A Developmental Analysis and Model for Intervention.* Washington, DC: American Psychological Association.

Patterson, G.R., DeBaryshe, B.D. and Ramsey, E. (1989) A developmental perspective on antisocial behavior, *American Psychologist*, 44(2), 329–335.

Patterson, G.R., Reid, J.B. and Dishion, T.J. (1992) *Antisocial Boys.* Eugene, OR: Castalia.

Patterson, T. and Hayne, H. (2009). Does drawing facilitate older children's reports of emotionally laden events? *Applied Cognitive Psychology*, 23, 1–14.

Patterson, T. and Hayne, H. (2011) Does drawing facilitate older children's reports of emotionally laden events? *Applied Cognitive Psychology*, 25(1), 119–126.

Patterson, T. and Pipe, M.E.M. (2009) Exploratory assessments of child abuse: children's responses to interviewer's questions across multiple interview sessions, *Child Abuse & Neglect*, 33(8), 490–504.

Patton, G.C., Selzer, R., Coffey, C., Carlin, B. and Wolfe, R. (1999) Onset of adolescent eating disorders: Population-based cohort study over 3 years, *British Medical Journal*, 318(765), 768.

Patton, G.C., Coffey, C., Sawyer, S.M., Viner, R.M., Haller, D.M., Bose, K. et al. (2009) Global patterns of mortality in young people: a systematic analysis of population health data, *The Lancet*, 374(9693), 881–892.

Paul, P. (2010) Can preschoolers be depressed? *New York Times Magazine*, 29 August, 50–55.

Pavri, S. (2001) Loneliness in children with disabilities, *Teaching Exceptional Children*, 33(6), 52–58.

Pears, K.C. and Fisher, P.A. (2005) Emotion understanding and theory of mind among maltreated children in foster care: evidence of deficits, *Development and Psychopathology*, 17(01), 47–65.

Pears, K.C., Kim, H.K. and Fisher, P.A. (2008) Psychosocial and cognitive functioning of children with specific profiles of maltreatment, *Child Abuse & Neglect*, 32(10), 958–971.

Pediatric OCD Treatment Study Team (2004) Cognitive-behavior therapy, sertraline and their combination for children and adolescents with obsessive–compulsive disorder: the pediatric OCD treatment study (POTS) randomized controlled trial, *Journal of the American Medical Association*, 292, 1969–1976.

Peled, M. and Moretti, M.M. (2007) Rumination on anger and sadness in adolescence: fueling of fury and deepening of despair, *Journal of Clinical Child and Adolescent Psychology*, 36(1), 66–75.

Pelham, W. and Fabiano, G. (2008) Evidence-based psychosocial treatments for attention-deficit/hyperactivity disorder, *Journal of Clinical Child and Adolescent Psychology*, 37(1), 184–214.

Pelham, W.E. Jr, Wheeler, T. and Chronis, A. (1998) Empirically supported psychosocial treatments for attention deficit hyperactivity disorder, *Journal of Clinical Child Psychology*, 27, 190–205.

Pelzer, D. (1995) *A Child Called 'It'*. Deerfield Beach, FL: Health Comunications, Inc.

Pelzer, D. (1997) *The Lost Boy: A Foster Child's Search for the Love of a Family.* Deerfield Beach, FL: Health Communications, Inc.

Pelzer, D. (2000) *A Man Called Dave: A Story of Triumph and Forgiveness.* Harmondsworth: Dutton.

Pellicano, E. (2010) The development of core cognitive skills in autism: a 3-year prospective study, *Child Development*, 81(5), 1400–1416.

Pelphrey, K.A. et al. (2002) Visual scanning of faces in autism, *Journal of Autism and Developmental Disorders*, 32(4), 249–261.

Pence, D.M. (2011) Child abuse and neglect investigation, in J.F.B. Myers (ed.), *The APSAC Handbook on Child Maltreatment.* Thousand Oaks, CA: Sage.

Pennington, B.F. (2002) *The Development of Psychopathology: Nature and Nurture.* New York: Guilford Press.

Pereda, N., Guilera, G., Forns, M. and Gomez-Benito, J. (2009) The international epidemiology of child sexual abuse: a continuation of Finkelhor (1994), *Child Abuse & Neglect*, 33(6), 331–342.

Pérez, I.T., del Río Sánchez, C. and Mas, M.B. (2008) MCMI-II borderline personality disorder in anorexia and bulimia nervosa, *Psicothema*, 20(1), 138–143.

Perez, M., Voelz, Z.R., Pettit, J.W. and Joiner, T.E. Jr. (2002) The role of acculturative stress and body dissatisfaction in predicting bulimic symptomatology across ethnic groups, *International Journal of Eating Disorders*, 31(4), 442–454.

Perrin, E.C. et al. (1993) Issues involved in the definition and classification of chronic health conditions, *Pediatrics*, 91(4), 787–793.

Perry, B.D. (2008) Child maltreatment: a neurodevelopmental perspective on the role of trauma and neglect in psychopathology, in T.P. Beauchaine and S.P. Hinshaw (eds), *Child and Adolescent Psychopathology.* Hoboken NJ: Wiley.

Peterson, A.C., Compas, B.E., Brooks-Gunn, J., Stemmler, M., Ey, S. and Grant, K.E. (1993) Depression in adolescence, *American Psychologist*, 48(2), 155–168.

Pfeffer, C.R. (2007) The FDA pediatric advisories and changes in diagnosis and treatment of pediatric depression, *American Journal of Psychiatry*, 164, 843–846.

Pfeffer, C.R., Zuckerman, S., Plutchik, R. and Mizruchi, M.S. (1984) Suicidal behavior in normal school children: a comparison with child psychiatric inpatients, *Journal of the American Academy of Child Psychiatry*, 23(4), 416–423.

Pfefferbaum, B. (1997) Posttraumatic stress disorder in children: a review of the past 10 years, *Journal of the American Academy of Child and Adolescent Psychiatry*, 36(11), 1503–1511.

Pfiffner, L.J. and McBurnett, K. (1997) Social skills training with parent generalization: treatment effects for children with attention deficit disorder, *Journal of*

Consulting and Clinical Psychology, 65(5), 749–757.

Phares, V., Rojas, R., Thurston, I.B. and Hankinson, J.C. (2010) Including fathers in clinical interventions for children and adolescents, in M.E. Lamb (ed.), *The Role of the Father in Child Development.* Hoboken, NJ: Wiley.

Phillips, L.J., Curry, C., Yung, A.R., Yuen, H.P., Adlard, S. and McGorry, P.D. (2002) Cannabis use is not associated with the development of psychosis in an 'ultra' high-risk group, *Australian and New Zealand Journal of Psychiatry,* 36, 800–806.

Phillips, M.A. and Gross, A.M. (2010) Children, in D.L. Segal and M. Hersen (eds), *Diagnostic Interviewing,* 4th edn. New York, Dordrecht and London: Springer.

Phinney, J.S. (2003) Ethnic identity and acculturation, in K. Chun, P. Ball and G. Marin (eds), *Acculturation: Advances in Theory, Measurement and Applied Research.* Washington, DC: American Psychological Association.

Piacentini, T.S., March, J.S. and Franklin, M.E. (2011) Obsessive-compulsive disorder, in C.K. Philip (ed.), *Child and Adolescent Therapy: Cognitive-Behavioral Procedures,* 4th edn. New York: Guilford.

Piaget, J. (1932) *The Moral Judgment of the Child,* trans. M. Gabain. Oxford: Harcourt, Brace.

Piaget, J. (1962) *Play, Dreams and Imitation in Childhood.* New York: Norton.

Piaget, J. (1967) *Six Psychological Studies.* New York: Random House.

Piaget, J. (1981) *Intelligence and Affectivity: Their Relationship during Child Development.* Palo Alto, CA: Annual Reviews.

Pianta, R.C. (2006) Schools, schooling and developmental psychopathology, in D. Cicchetti and D.J. Cohen (eds), *Developmental Psychopathology. Volume I: Theory and Method,* 2nd edn. New York: Wiley.

Pickles, A. and Hill, J. (2006) Developmental pathways, in D. Cicchetti and D.J. Cohen (eds), *Developmental Psychopathology. Volume I: Theory and Method,* 2nd edn.New York: Wiley.

Piehler, T.F. and Dishion, T.J. (2007) Interpersonal dynamics within adolescent friendships: dyadic mutuality, deviant talk and patterns of antisocial behavior, *Child Development,* 78(5), 1611–1624.

Pilgrim, C., Luo, Q., Urberg, K.A. and Fang, X. (1999) Influence of peers, parents and individual characteristics on adolescent drug use in two cultures, *Merrill-Palmer Quarterly,* 45(1), 85–107.

Pilling, S., Bebbington, P., Kuipers, E., Garety, P., Geddes, J., Orbach, G. and Morgan, C. (2002) Psychosocial treatments in schizophrenia: I. Metaanalysis of family intervention and cognitive behaviour therapy, *Psychological Medicine,* 32, 763–782.

Pilowsky, D.J., Wickramaratne, P.J., Rush, A.J., Hughes, C.W., Garber, J., Malloy, E. et al. (2006) Children of currently depressed mothers: a STAR*D ancillary study, *Journal of Clinical Psychiatry,* 67(1), 126–136.

Pine, D., Cohen, P., Gurley, D., Brook, J. and Ma, Y. (1998) The risk for early-adulthood anxiety and depressive disorders in adolescents with anxiety and depressive disorders, *Archives of General Psychiatry,* 55(1), 56.

Pine, F. (1974) On the concept 'borderline' in children, *Psychoanalytic Study of the Child,* 29, 341–368.

Pine, F. (1979) On the pathology of the separation-individuation process as manifested in later clinical work: an attempt at delineation, *International Journal of Psychoanalysis,* 60, 225–242.

Pine, F. (1983) Borderline syndromes in childhood: a working nosology and its therapeutic implications, in K. Robson (ed.), *The Borderline Child.* New York: McGraw-Hill.

Pine, F. (1986) On the development of the 'borderline-child-to-be', *American Journal of Orthopsychiatry,* 56(3), 450–457.

Pinheiro, A.P., Raney, T.J., Thornton, L.M., Fichter, M.M., Berrettini, W.H., Goldman, D. et al. (2010) Sexual functioning in women with eating disorders, *International Journal of Eating Disorders,* 43(2), 123–129.

Pinto, A., Whisman, M.A. and Conwell, Y. (1998) Reasons for living in a clinical sample of adolescents, *Journal of Adolescence,* 21(4), 397–405.

Pinzon, J. (2006) Canadian Paediatric Society statement: care of adolescents with chronic conditions, *Paediatric Child Health (Oxf),* 11(1), 43–48.

Pipe, M.E. and Salmon, K. (2009) Dolls, drawing, body diagrams and other props: role of props in investigative interviews, in K. Kuehnle and M. Connell (eds), *The Evaluation of Child Sexual Abuse Allegations: A Comprehensive Guide to Assessment and Testimony.* Oxford: John Wiley & Sons.

Piquero, A.R., Farrington, D.P., Welsh, B.C., Tremblay, R. and Jennings, W.G. (2009) Effects of early family/parent training programs on antisocial behavior and delinquency, *Journal of Experimental Criminology,* 5(2), 83–120.

Pliszka, S.R. (2002) *Neuroscience for The Mental Health Clinician.* New York: Guilford.

Pliszka, S.R. (2004) *Neuroscience for the Mental Health Clinician.* New York: Guilford Press.

Pliszka, S.R. (2006) Subtyping ADHD based on comorbidity, *The ADHD Report,* 14(6), 1–5.

Plomin, R., DeFries, J.C., McClearn, G.E. and McGuffin, P. (2008) *Behavioral Genetics.* New York: Worth.

Plunkett, M. and Mitchell, C. (2000) Substance use rates among American Indian adolescents: regional comparisons with monitoring the future high school seniors, *Journal of Drug Issues*, 30, 593–620.

Poelen, E.A.P., Engels, R.C.M.E., Scholte, R.H.J., Boomsma, D.I. and Willemsen, G. (2009) Predictors of problem drinking in adolescence and young adulthood, *European Child & Adolescent Psychiatry*, 18(6), 345–352.

Polanczyk, G. et al. (2007) The worldwide prevalence of ADHD: a systematic review and metaregression analysis, *American Journal of Psychiatry*, 164(6), 942–948.

Polanczyk, G. et al. (2010) Etiological and clinical features of childhood psychotic symptoms: results from a birth cohort, *Archives of General Psychiatry*, 67(4), 328.

Pollak, S.D. and Sinha, P. (2003) Effects of early experience on children's recognition of facial displays of emotion, *Developmental Psychology*, 38(5), 784–791.

Pollak, S.D., Cicchetti, D., Hornung, K. and Reed, A. (2000) Recognizing emotion in faces: developmental effects of child abuse and neglect, *Developmental Psychology*, 36, 679–688.

Pomerantz, E.M. and Wang, Q. (2009) The role of parental control in children's development in western and east Asian countries, *Current Directions in Psychological Science*, 18(5), 285–289.

Posner, M.I, and Raichle, M.E. (1994) *Images of Mind*. New York: Scientific American Library.

Post, R.M. (1992) Transduction of psychosocial stress into the neurobiology of recurrent affective disorder, *American Journal of Psychiatry*, 149, 999–1010.

Potter, H.W. (1933). Schizophrenia in children, *American Journal of Psychiatry*, 89(6), 1253.

Power, P.J. R., Bell, R.J., Mills, R., Herrman-Doig, T., Davern, M., Henry, L., Yuen, H., Khademy-Deljo, A. and McGorry, P.D. (2003) Suicide prevention in first episode psychosis: the development of a randomized controlled trial of cognitive therapy for acutely suicidal patients with early psychosis, *Australian and New Zealand Journal of Psychiatry*, 37, 414–420.

Powers, S.W. (1999) Empirically supported treatments in pediatric psychology: procedure-related pain, *Journal of Pediatric Psychology*, 24(2), 131–145.

Powers, S.W., Mitchell, M.J., Gaumlich, S.E., Byars, K.C. and Kalinyak, K.A. (2002) Longitudinal assessment of pain, coping and daily functioning in children with sickle cell disease receiving pain management skills training, *Journal of Clinical Psychology in Medical Settings*, 9, 109–119.

Preti, A., de Girolamo, G., Vilagut, G., Alonso, J., de Graaf, R., Bruffaerts, R. et al. (2009) The epidemiology of eating disorders in six European countries: results of the ESEMeD-WMH project, *Journal of psychiatric research*, 43(14), 1125–1132.

Prigatano, G.P., Fulton, J. and Wethe, J. (2010) Behavioral consequences of pediatric traumatic brain injury, *Pediatric Health*, 4(4), 447–455.

Prince-Hughes, D. (2002) *Aquamarine Blue 5: Personal Stories of College Students With Autism*. Athens, OH: Ohio University Press.

Prinstein, M.J. (2003) Social factors: peer relationships, in A. Spirito and J.C. Overholser (eds), *Evaluating and Treating Adolescent Suicide Attempters: From Research to Practice*. New York: Academic Press.

Prinstein, M.J. (2008) Introduction to the special section on suicide and nonsuicidal self-injury: a review of unique challenges and important directions for self-injury science, *Journal of Consulting and Clinical Psychology*, 76(1), 1–8.

Prinstein, M.J., Boergers, J., Spirito, A., Little, T.D. and Grapentine, W.L. (2000) Peer functioning, family dysfunction and psychological symptoms in a risk factor model for adolescent inpatients' suicidal ideation severity, *Journal of Clinical Child Psychology*, 29(3), 392–405.

Prinstein, M.J., Boergers, J. and Vernberg, E.M. (2001) Overt and relational aggression in adolescents: social-psychological adjustment of aggressors and victims, *Journal of Clinical Child Psychology*, 30(4), 479–491.

Prior, M. (2003) Is there an increase in the prevalence of autism spectrum disorders? *Journal Of Paediatrics and Child Health*, 39(2), 81–82.

Puig-Antich, J. and Chambers, W. (1978) *The Schedule for Affective Disorders and Schizophrenia for School-Age Children (Kiddie-SADS)*. New York: New York State Psychiatric Institute.

Putnam, F.W. (2006) Dissociative disorders, in D. Cicchetti and D.J. Cohen (eds), *Developmental Psychopathology. Volume III: Risk, Disorder and Adaptation*, 2nd edn. New York: Wiley.

Pynoos, R.S., Steinberg, A.M. and Wraith, R. (1995) A developmental model of childhood traumatic stress, in D. Cicchetti and D.J. Cohen (eds), *Developmental Psychopathology. Vol. II: Risk, Disorder and Adaptation*. New York: Wiley.

Quinn, O. (2005) Treating adolescent girls and women with ADHD: gender-specific issues, *Journal of Clinical Psychology*, 61(5), 579–587.

Quinn, P. and Wigal, S. (2004) Perceptions of girls and ADHD: results from a national survey, *Medscape General Medicine*, 6(2), 2.

Rabiner, D.L., Murray, D.W., Rosen, L., Hardy, K., Skinner, A. and Underwood, M. (2010) Instability in teacher ratings of children's inattentive symptoms: Implications for the assessment of ADHD, *Journal of Developmental and Behavioral Pediatrics: JDBP*, 31(3), 175–180.

Radke-Yarrow, M. (1998) *Children of Depressed Mothers: From Early Childhood to Maturity*. New York: Cambridge University Press.

Radke-Yarrow, M. et al. (1995) Attachment in the context of high-risk conditions, *Development and Psychopathology*, 7(2), 247–265.

Raggi, V.L. and Chronis, A.M. (2006). Interventions to address the academic impairment of children and adolescents with ADHD, *Clinical Child and Family Psychology Review*, 9(2), 85–111.

Ramchandani, P. and Psychogiou, L. (2009) Paternal psychiatric disorders and children's psychosocial development, *The Lancet*, 374(9690), 646–653.

Ramey, C.T. and Campbell, F.A. (1991) Poverty, early childhood education and academic competence: the Abecedarian experiment, in A.C. Huston (ed.), *Children in Poverty: Child Development and Public Policy*. Cambridge: Cambridge University Press.

Rancourt, D. and Prinstein, M.J. (2010) Peer status and victimization as possible reinforcements of adolescent girls' and boys' weight-related behaviors and cognitions, *Journal of Pediatric Psychology*, 35(4), 354–367.

Raney, T.J., Thornton, L.M., Berrettini, W., Brandt, H., Crawford, S., Fichter, M. M. et al. (2008) Influence of overanxious disorder of childhood on the expression of anorexia nervosa, *International Journal of Eating Disorders*, 41(4), 326–332.

Rapee, R.M. and Sweeney, L. (2001) Social phobia in children and adolescents: nature and assessment, in W. Crozier and L.E. Alden (eds), *International Handbook of Social Anxiety: Concepts, Research and Interventions Relating to The Self and Shyness*. New York: Wiley.

Rapee, R.M., Wignall, A., Hudson, J.L. and Schniering, C.A. (2000) *Treating Anxious Children and Adolescents: An Evidence-Based Approach*. Oakland, CA: New Harbinger.

Rapoport, J., Addington, A. and Frangou, S. (2005) The neurodevelopmental model of schizophrenia: update 2005, *Molecular Psychiatry*, 10(5), 434–449.

Rapoport, J.L. and Ismond, D.R. (1996) *DSM-IV Training Guide for Diagnosis of Childhood Disorders*. New York: Routledge.

Rapoport, J.L., Inoff-Germain, G., Weissman, M.M., Greenwald, S., Narrow, W.E., Jensen, P.S. et al. (2000) Childhood obsessive-compulsive disorder in the NIMH MECA study: parent versus child identification of cases, *Journal of Anxiety Disorders*, 14, 535–548.

Rapport, M.D., Scanlan, S.W. and Denney, C.B. (1999) Attention-deficit/hyperactivity disorder and scholastic achievement: a model of dual developmental pathways, *Journal of Child Psychology and Psychiatry*, 40(8), 1169–1183.

Rasmussen, P. and Gillberg, C. (2001) Natural outcome of ADHD with developmental coordination disorder at age 22 years: a controlled, longitudinal, community-based study, *Journal of the American Academy of Child and Adolescent Psychiatry*, 39(11), 1424–1431.

Rasmussen, S.A. and Eisen, J.L. (1992) The epidemiology and clinical features of obsessive compulsive disorder, *Psychiatric Clinics of North America*, 15(4), 743–758.

Rathus, J.H. and Miller, A.L. (2000) DBT for adolescents: dialectical dilemmas and secondary treatment targets, *Cognitive and Behavioral Practice*, 7, 425–434.

Rathus, J.H. and Miller, A.L. (2002) Dialectical behavior therapy adapted for suicidal adolescents, *Suicide and Life-Threatening Behavior*, 32(3), 146–157.

Ravens-Sieberer, U., Wille, N., Erhart, M., Bettge, S., Wittchen, H.-U., Rothenberger, A. et al. (2008) Prevalence of mental health problems among children and adolescents in Germany: results of the BELLA study within the National Health Interview and Examination Survey, *European Child & Adolescent Psychiatry*, 17(supplement 1), 22–33.

Ray, D.C. (2006) Evidence-based play therapy, in C.E. Schaefer and H.G. Kaduson (eds), *Contemporary Play Therapy: Theory, Research and Practice*. New York: Guilford.

Reddy, L.A., Files-Hall, T.M. and Schaefer, C.E. (2005) *Empirically Based Play Interventions for Children*. Washington, DC: American Psychological Association.

Redfield-Jamison, R. (1995) *An Unquiet Mind*. New York: Knopf.

Reece, R.M. (2011) Medical evaluation of physical abuse, in J.F.B. Myers (ed.), *The APSAC Handbook on Child Maltreatment*. Thousand Oaks, CA: Sage.

Reef, J.P., van Meurs, I.P., Verhulst, F.C. and van der Ende, J. (2010) Children's problems predict adults' DSM-IV disorders across 24 years, *Journal of the American Academy of Child & Adolescent Psychiatry*, 49(11), 1117–1124.

Reich, W. (2000) Diagnostic interview for children and adolescents (DICA), *Journal of the American Academy of Child & Adolescent Psychiatry*, 39(1), 59–66.

Reichow, B. and Volkmar, F.R. (2010) Social skills interventions for individuals with autism: evaluation for evidence-based practices within a best evidence synthesis framework, *Journal of Autism and Developmental Disorders*, 40(2), 149–166.

Reid, D.K. and Knight, M.G. (2006) Disability justifies exclusion of minority students: a critical history grounded in disability studies, *Educational Researcher*, 35(6), 18.

Reid, J.B. (1978) *A Social Learning Approach to Family Intervention: Observations in the Home Setting*. Eugene, OR: Castalia.

Reid, J.B., Patterson, G.R. and Snyder, J.J. (2002) *Antisocial Behavior in Children and Adolescents: A Developmental Analysis and Model for Intervention*. Washington, DC: American Psychological Association.

Reinecke, M.A., Dattilio, F.M. and Freeman, A. (2003) *Cognitive Therapy with Children and Adolescents: A Casebook for Clinical Practice*, 2nd edn. New York: Guilford.

Reiss, D., Neiderhiser, J.M., Hetherington, E.M. and Plomin, R. (2000) *The Relationship Code: Deciphering Genetic and Social Influences on Adolescent Development*. Cambridge, MA: Cambridge University Press.

Reitzel, L.R. and Carbonell, J.L. (2006) The effectiveness of sexual offender treatment for juveniles as measured by recidivism: a meta-analysis, *Sexual Abuse: A Journal of Research and Treatment*, 18(4), 401–421.

Remschmidt, H. et al. (2007) Forty-two-years later: the outcome of childhood-onset schizophrenia, *Journal of Neural Transmission*, 114(4), 505–512.

Remschmidt, H.E. et al. (1994) Childhood-onset schizophrenia: history of the concept and recent studies, *Schizophrenia Bulletin*, 20(4), 727–745.

Rende, R. and Plomin, R. (1995) Nature, nurture and the development of psychopathology, in D. Cicchetti and D.J. Cohen (eds), *Developmental Psychopathology: Vol. I. Theory and Methods*. New York: Wiley.

Rende, R. and Waldman, I. (2006) Behavioral and molecular genetics and developmental psychopathology, in D. Cicchetti and D.J. Cohen (eds), *Developmental Psychopathology, Vol 2: Developmental Neuroscience*, 2nd edn. Hoboken, NJ: John Wiley & Sons.

Rende, R.D., Plomin, R., Reiss, D. and Hetherington, E.M. (1993) Genetic and environmental influences on depressive symptomatology in adolescence: individual differences and extreme scores, *Journal of Child Psychology and Psychiatry*, 8, 1387–1398.

Rennison, C.M. (2001) *Violence, Victimization and Race, 1993-1998*,

http://www.ojp.usdoj.gov/bjs/abstract/ipv.htm (retrieved 12 February 2011).

Rescorla, L., Achenbach, T.M., Ivanova, M.Y., Dumenci, L., Almqvist, F., Bilenberg, N. et al. (2007) Epidemiological comparisons of problems and positive qualities reported by adolescents in 24 countries, *Journal of Consulting and Clinical Psychology*, 75(2), 351–358.

Reyno, S.M. and McGrath, P.J. (2006) Predictors of parent training efficacy for child externalizing behavior problems – a meta-analytic review, *Journal of Child Psychology and Psychiatry*, 47, 99–111.

Reynolds, C.R. and Kamphaus, R.W. (2004) *Behavior Assessment System for Children–Parent Rating Scale (BASC-2–PRS)* Circle Pines, MN: American Guidance Service.

Reynolds, C.R. and Richmond, B.O. (1997) What I think and feel: a revised measure of children's manifest anxiety, *Journal of Abnormal Child Psychology*, 25(1), 15–20.

Rhee, S.H. and Waldman, I.D. (2002) Genetic and environmental influences on antisocial behavior: a meta-analysis of twin and adoption studies, *Psychological Bulletin*, 128(3), 490–529.

Ricciardelli, L.A. and McCabe, M.P. (2004) A biopsychosocial model of disordered eating and the pursuit of muscularity in adolescent boys, *Psychological Bulletin*, 130(2), 179–205.

Rice, F., Harold, G.T., Boivin, J., van den Bree, M., Hay, D.F. and Thapar, A. (2010) The links between prenatal stress and offspring development and psychopathology: disentangling environmental and inherited influences, *Psychological Medicine*, 40, 335–345.

Richter, L.M. and Desmond, C. (2008) Targeting AIDS orphans and child-headed households? A perspective from national surveys in South Africa, 1995–2005, *AIDS Care: Psychological and Socio-medical*

Aspects of AIDS/HIV, 20(9), 1019–1028.

Richters, J.E. and Cicchetti, D. (1993) Editorial: Toward a developmental perspective on conduct disorder, *Development and Psychopathology*, 5(1/2), 1–4.

Riecher-Rössler, A., Pflüger, M. and Borgwardt, S. (2010) Schizophrenia in women, in D. Kohen (ed.), *Oxford Textbook of Women and Mental Health*. Oxford: Oxford University Press.

Riggins-Caspers, K.M., Cadoret, R.J., Knutson, J.F. and Langbehn, D. (2003) Biology-environment interaction and evocative biology-environment correlation: contributions of harsh discipline and parental psychopathology to problem adolescent behaviors, *Behavior Genetics*, 33, 205–220.

Riggs, N.R. and Pentz, M.A. (2009) Long term effects of adolescent marijuana use prevention on adult mental health services utilization: the Midwestern prevention project, *Substance Use & Misuse*, 44(5), 616–631.

Rind, B., Tromovitch, P. and Bauserman, R. (1998) A meta-analytic examination of assumed properties of child sexual abuse using college samples, *Psychological Bulletin*, 124, 22–53.

Ritakallio, M., Koivisto, A.-M., von der Pahlen, B., Pelkonen, M., Marttunen, M. and Kaltiala-Heino, R. (2008) Continuity, comorbidity and longitudinal associations between depression and antisocial behaviour in middle adolescence: a 2-year prospective follow-up study, *Journal of Adolescence*, 31(3), 355–370.

Robbins, M.S., Horigian, V., Szapocznik, J. and Ucha, J. (2010) Treating Hispanic youths using brief strategic family therapy, in J.R. Weisz and A.E. Kazdin (eds), *Evidence-Based Psychotherapies for Children and Adolescents*, 2nd edn. New York: Guilford Press.

Roberts, R.E., Chen, Y.R. and Roberts, C.R. (1997a) Ethnocultural differences in prevalence of adolescent suicidal behaviors, *Suicide and Life-Threatening Behavior*, 27(2), 208–217.

Roberts, R.E., Roberts, C.R. and Chen, Y.R. (1997b) Ethnocultural differences in prevalence of adolescent depression, *American Journal of Community Psychology*, 25(1), 95–110.

Robertson, J. and Robertson, J. (1971) Young children in brief separation, *Psychoanalytic Study of the Child*, 26, 264–315.

Robins, L. (1996) *Deviant Children Grow Up*. London: Williams Wilkins & Ross.

Rodenburg, R. et al. (2005) Psychopathology in children with epilepsy: a meta-analysis, *Journal of Pediatric Psychology*, 30(6), 453–468.

Rodin, J., Striegel-Moore, R.H. and Silberstein, L.R. (1990) Vulnerability and resilience in the age of eating disorders: risk and protective factors for bulimia nervosa, in J. Rolf, A.S. Masten, D. Cicchetti, K.H. Nuechterlein and S. Weintraub (eds), *Risk and Protective Factors in the Development of Psychopathology*. Cambridge: Cambridge University Press.

Rodkin, C. and Berger, C. (2008) Who bullies whom? Social status asymmetries by victim gender, *International Journal of Behavioral Development*, 32(6), 473–485.

Roeyers, H., Van Oost, P. and Bothuyne, S. (1998) Immediate imitation and joint attention in young children with autism, *Development and Psychopathology*, 10(3), 441–450.

Roff, J.D. and Fultz, J.M. (2003) Childhood antecedents of schizophrenia: developmental sequencing and specificity of problem behavior, *Psychological reports*, 92(3), 793–803.

Rogers, C.R. (1959) A theory of therapy, personality and interpersonal relationships as developed in the client-centered framework, in S. Koch (ed.), *Psychology: Study of a Science: Vol. 3. Formulations of the Person and the Social Context*. New York: McGraw-Hill.

Rogers, S. and Vismara, L. (2008) Evidence-based comprehensive treatments for early autism, *Journal of Clinical Child and Adolescent Psychology*, 37, 8–38.

Rogers, S.J. (1998) Empirically supported comprehensive treatments for young children with autism, *Journal of Clinical Child Psychology*, 27(2), 168–179.

Rogosch, F.A. and Cicchetti, D. (2005) Child maltreatment, attentional networks and potential precursors to borderline personality disorder, *Development and Psychopathology*, 17(4), 1071–1089.

Rohde, L.A. et al. (2005) Attention-deficit/hyperactivity disorder in a diverse culture: do research and clinical findings support the notion of a cultural construct for the disorder? *Biological Psychiatry*, 57(11), 1436–1441.

Rohde, P. (2009) Comorbidities with adolescent depression, in S. Nolen-Hoeksema and L.M. Hilt (eds), *Handbook of Depression in Adolescents*. New York: Routledge/Taylor & Francis Group.

Rohde, P., Lewinsohn, P.M., Klein, D.N. and Seeley, J.R. (2005) Association of parental depression with psychiatric course from adolescence to young adulthood among formerly depressed individuals, *Journal of Abnormal Psychology*, 114(3), 409–420.

Roid, G.H. (2003) *Stanford-Binet Intelligence Scales (SB5)*. Itasca, IL: Riverside.

Roisman, G.I., Monahan, K.C., Campbell, S.B., Steinberg, L. and Cauffman, E. (2010) Is adolescence-onset antisocial behavior developmentally normative? *Development and Psychopathology*, 22(2), 295–311.

Romans, S.E., Gendall, K.A., Martine, J.L. and Mullen, P.E. (2001) Child sexual abuse and later disordered eating: a New Zealand epidemiological study, *International Journal of Eating Disorders*, 29, 380–392.

Romer, D. and Walker, E.F. (eds) (2007) *Adolescent Psychopathology and the Developing Brain*. New York: Oxford.

Röpcke, B. and Eggers, C. (2005) Early-onset schizophrenia, *European Child & Adolescent Psychiatry*, 14(6), 341–350.

Rorschach, H. (1921) *Psychodiagnostics*. New York: Grune and Stratton.

Rorschach, H. (1994) *Rorschach-test*. Berne: Verlag Hans Huber.

Rose, D.R. and Abramson, L.Y. (1991) Developmental predictors of depressive cognitive style: research and theory, in D. Cicchetti and S.L. Toth (eds), *Rochester Symposium on Developmental Psychopathology*, vol. 4.

Rosebush, I. and Mazurek, M.F. (2010) Catatonia and its treatment, *Schizophrenia Bulletin*, 36(2), 239.

Rosen, K.S. and Rothbaum, F. (2003) Attachment: parent–child relationships, in J.Ponzetti (ed.), *International Encyclopedia of Marriage and Family*. New York: Macmillan.

Ross, A.O. and Nelson, R.O. (1979) Behavior therapy, in H.C. Quay and J.S. Werry (eds), *Psychopathological Disorders of Childhood*, 2nd edn. New York: Wiley.

Rossello, J. and Bernal, G. (1999) Treatment of depression in Puerto Rican adolescents: the efficacy of cognitive-behavioral and interpersonal treatments, *Journal of Consulting and Clinical Psychology*, 67, 734–745.

Rossini, E.D. and Moretti, R.J. (1997) Thematic Apperception Test (TAT) interpretation: practice recommendations from a survey of clinical psychology doctoral programs accredited by the American Psychological Association, *Professional Psychology: Research and Practice*, 28(4), 393–398.

Rossman, B.B.R. and Ho, J. (2000) Posttraumatic response and children exposed to parental violence, in R. Geffner, P.G. Jaffe and

M. Sudermann (eds), *Children Exposed to Domestic Violence: Current Issues in Research, Intervention, Prevention and Policy Development*. New York: Haworth.

Rossman, B.B.R., Hughes, H.M. and Rosenberg, M.S. (1999) *Children and Interparental Violence: The Impact of Exposure*. New York: Brunner/Mazel.

Rosso, I.M. and Cannon, T. (2003) Obstetric complications and neurodevelopmental mechanisms in schizophrenia, in D. Cicchetti and E. Walker (eds), *Neurodevelopmental Mechanisms in Psychopathology*. New York: Cambridge University Press.

Rothbart, M.K. (2011) *Becoming Who We Are: Temperament and Personality in Development*. New York: Guilford.

Rothbart, M.K. and Bates, J.E. (2007) Temperament, in W. Damon and R.M. Lerner (eds), *Social, Emotional and Personality Development*, 6th edn. New York: Wiley.

Rourke, B.P. and Tsatsanis, K.D. (2000) Nonverbal learning disabilities and Asperger syndrome, in A. Klin, F.R. Volkmar and S.S. Sparrow (eds), *Asperger Syndrome*. New York: Guilford.

Rowa, K., Kerig, P.K. and Geller, J. (2001) The family and anorexia: examining parent–child boundary problems, *European Eating Disorders Review*, 9, 97–114.

Rowe, R. et al. (2005) Defining oppositional defiant disorder, *Journal of Child Psychology and Psychiatry*, 46(12), 1309–1316.

Rowe, R., Costello, E.J., Angold, A., Copeland, W.E. and Maughan, B. (2010) Developmental pathways in oppositional defiant disorder and conduct disorder, *Journal of Abnormal Psychology*, 119(4), 726–738.

Roza, S.J., Hofstra, M.B., Van der Ende, J. and Verhulst, F.C. (2003) Stable prediction of mood and anxiety disorders based on behavioral and emotional problems in childhood: a 14-year follow-up during childhood, adolescence and young adulthood, *American Journal of Psychiatry*, 160, 2116–2121.

Rubin, K.H. (1993) The Waterloo longitudinal project: correlates and consequences of social withdrawal from childhood to adolescence, in K.H. Rubin and J.B. Asendorpf (eds), *Social Withdrawal, Inhibition and Shyness*. Hillsdale, NJ: Erlbaum.

Rubin, K.H. and Mills, R.S.L. (1991) Conceptualizing developmental pathways to internalizing disorders in childhood, *Canadian Journal of Behavioural Science*, 23(3), 300–317.

Ruble, D.N., Martin, C. and Berenbaum, S.A. (2006) Gender development, in N. Eisenberg (ed.), *Handbook of Child Psychology: Vol 3 Personality and Social Development*, 6th edn. New York: John Wiley & Sons.

Ruchkin, V., Sukhodolsky, D.G., Vermeiren, R., Koposov, R.A. and Schwab-Stone, M. (2006) Depressive symptoms and associated psychopathology in urban adolescents: a cross-cultural study of three countries, *Journal of Nervous and Mental Disease*, 194(2), 106–113.

Rudd, M.D., Joiner, T. and Rajab, M.H. (2004) *Treating Suicidal Behavior: An Effective, Time-Limited Approach*. New York: Guilford.

Rudd, M.D., Mandrusiak, M. and Joiner, T.E. Jr (2006) The case against no suicide contracts: the commitment to treatment statement as a practice alternative, *Journal of Clinical Psychology*, 62(2), 243–251.

Rudd, M.D., Cordero, L. and Bryan, C.J. (2009) What every psychologist should know about the Food and Drug Administration's black box warning label for antidepressants, *Professional Psychology: Research and Practice*, 40(4), 321.

Rudolph, K.D. (2009) The interpersonal context of adolescent depression, in S. Nolen-Hoeksema and L.M. Hilt (eds), *Handbook of Depression in Adolescents*. New York: Routledge/Taylor & Francis Group.

Rudolph, K.D., Flynn, M. and Abaied, J.L. (2008) A developmental perspective on interpersonal theories of youth depression, in J.R.Z. Abela and B.L. Hankin (eds), *Handbook of Depression in Children and Adolescents*. New York: Guilford Press.

Ruiter, E.M. et al. (2007) Pure subtelomeric microduplications as a cause of mental retardation, *Clinical Genetics*, 72(4), 362–368.

Runyan, D.K., Shankar, V., Hassan, F., Hunter, W.M., Jain, D., Paula, C.S., Bangdiwala, S.I., Ramiro, L.S., Muñoz, S.R., Vizcarra, B and Bordin, I.A. (2010) International variations in harsh child discipline, *Pediatrics*, 126(3), e701–e711.

Runyon, M.K. and Urquiza, A.J. (2011) Child physical abuse: interventions for parents who engage in coercive parenting practices and their children, in J.F.B. Myers (ed.), *The APSAC Handbook on Child Maltreatment*. Thousand Oaks, CA: Sage.

Russell, A.T., Bott, L. and Sammons, C. (1989) The phenomenology of schizophrenia occurring in childhood, *Journal of the American Academy of Child & Adolescent Psychiatry*, 28(3), 399–407.

Russell, C.J. and Keel, K. (2002) Homosexuality as a specific risk factor for eating disorders in men, *International Journal of Eating Disorders*, 31(3), 300–306.

Russell, S.T. and Joyner, K. (2001) Adolescent sexual orientation and suicide risk: evidence from a national study, *American Journal of Public Health*, 91(8), 1276–1281.

Rutgers, A.H. et al. (2004) Autism and attachment: a meta-analytic review, *Journal of Child Psychology and Psychiatry*, 45(6), 1123–1134.

Rutter, M. (1972) Childhood schizophrenia reconsidered, *Journal of Autism and Developmental Disorders*, 2(3), 315–337.

Rutter, M. (1977) Brain damage syndromes in childhood: Concepts and findings, *Journal of Child Psychology and Psychiatry*, 18, 1–21.

Rutter, M. (1981) Stress, coping and development: some issues and some questions, *Journal of Child Psychology and Psychiatry*, 22(4), 323–356.

Rutter, M. (1983) Cognitive deficits in the pathogenesis of autism, *Journal of Child Psychology and Psychiatry*, 24(4), 513–531.

Rutter, M. (1990) Psychosocial resilience and protective mechanisms, in J. Rolf, A.S. Masten, D. Cicchetti, K.H. Nuechterlein and S. Weintraub (eds), *Risk and Protective Factors in the Development of Psychopathology*. Cambridge: Cambridge University Press.

Rutter, M. (2000) Psychosocial influences: critiques, findings and research needs, *Development and Psychopathology*, 12, 375–405.

Rutter, M., Silberg, J., O'Connor, T. and Simonoff, E. (1999) Genetics and child psychiatry II: empirical research findings, *Journal of Child Psychology and Psychiatry and Allied Disciplines*, 40, 19–55.

Rutter, M. et al. (2007) Effects of profound early institutional deprivation: an overview of findings from a UK longitudinal study of Romanian adoptees, *European Journal of Developmental Psychology*, 4(3), 332–350.

Rutter, M., Bishop, D.V.M., Pine, D.S., Scott, S., Stevenson, J., Taylor, E. and Thapar, A. (eds) (2009a) *Rutter's Child and Adolescent Psychiatry*. Oxford: Blackwell.

Rutter, M., Kreppner, J. and Sonuga-Barke, E. (2009b) Emanuel Miller Lecture: Attachment insecurity, disinhibited attachment and attachment disorders: where do research findings leave the concepts? *Journal of Child Psychology and Psychiatry*, 50(5), 529–543.

Rutter, M.L. (2011) Progress in understanding autism: 2007–2010, *Journal of Autism and Developmental Disorders*, doi: 10.1007/s10803-011-1184-2.

Ryan, C., Huebner, D., Diaz, R.M. and Sanchez, J. (2009) Family rejection as a predictor of negative health outcomes in white and Latino lesbian, gay and bisexual young adults, *Pediatrics*, 123, 346–352.

Ryder, A.G., Yang, J. and Heine, S.J. (2002) Somatization vs. psychologization of emotional distress: a paradigmatic example for cultural psychopathology, *Online Readings in Psychology and Culture, Unit 10*, http://scholarworks.gvsu.edu/orpc/vol10/iss2/3.

Ryle, A. (2004) The contribution of cognitive analytic therapy to the treatment of borderline personality disorder, *Journal of Personality Disorders*, 18(1), 3–35.

Saarni, C. (2006) *Emotion Regulation and Personality Development in Childhood*. Hillsdale, NJ: Erlbaum.

Sabaté, E. (2004) *Depression in the Youth and Adolescent*, archives.who.int/prioritymeds/report/background/depression.doc.

Sachs, H.T. and Barrett, R.P. (2000) Psychopathology in individuals with mental retardation, in A.J. Sameroff, M. Lewis and S.M. Miller (eds), *Handbook of Developmental Psychopathology*. New York: Kluwer Academic.

Sackett, D.L., Rosenberg, W.M.C., Gray, J.A.M., Haynes, R.B. and Richardson, W. S. (1996) Evidence-based medicine: what it is and what it isn't, *British Medical Journal*, 312, 71–72.

Sagrestano, L., Paikoff, R.L., Holmbeck, G. and Fendrich, M. (2003) A longitudinal examination of familial risk factors for depression among inner-city African American adolescents, *Journal of Family Psychology*, 17(1), 108–120.

Saigh, P.A. (1992) The behavioral treatment of child and adolescent posttraumatic stress disorder, *Advances in Behavior Research and Therapy*, 14(4), 247–275.

Saint-Jean, G., Martinez, C. and Crandall, L. (2008) Psychosocial mediators of the impact of acculturation on adolescent substance abuse, *Journal of Immigrant and Minority Health*, 10(2), 187–195.

Salbach-Andrae, H., Lenz, K., Simmendinger, N., Klinkowski, N., Lehmkuhl, U. and Pfeiffer, E. (2008) Psychiatric comorbidities among female adolescents with anorexia nervosa, *Child Psychiatry and Human Development*, 39(3), 261–272.

Salekin, R.T. and Lynam, D.R. (eds) (2010) *Handbook of Child And Adolescent Psychopathy*. New York: Guilford

Salend, S. and Duhaney, L. (2007) Inclusion: yesterday, today and tomorrow, in J.M. McLeskey (ed.) *Reflections in Inclusion: Classic Article that Shaped our Thinking*. Arlington, VA: Council for Exceptional Children.

Sallet, P.C et al. (2003a) Reduced cortical folding in schizophrenia: an MRI morphometric study, *American Journal of Psychiatry*, 160, 1606–1613.

Sallet, P.C. et al. (2003b) Rightward cerebral asymmetry in subtypes of schizophrenia according to Leonhard's classification and to DSM-IV: a structural MRI study. *Psychiatry Research: Neuroimaging*, 123, 65–79.

Salmivalli, C., Kärnä, A. and Poskiparta, E. (2010) From peer putdowns to peer support: a theoretical model and how it translated into a national anti-bullying program, in S.R. Jimerson, S.M. Swearer and D.L.Espelage (eds), *Handbook of Bullying in Schools: An International Perspective*. New York: Routledge/Taylor & Francis Group.

Salmivalli, C., Garandeau, C. and Veenstra, R. (2011) KiVa anti-bullying program: implications for school adjustment, in A.M. Ryan and G.W. Ladd (eds), *Peer Relationships and Adjustment at School*. Charlotte, NC: Information Age Publishing.

Saluja, G., Iachan, R., Scheidt, P.C, Overpeck, M., Sun, W. and Giedd, J. N. (2004) Prevalence of and risk factors for depressive symptoms among young adolescents, *Archives of Pediatric and Adolescent Medicine*, 158, 760–765.

Salzinger, S., Rosario, M. and Feldman, R.S. (2007) Physical child abuse and adolescent violent delinquency: the mediating and moderating roles of personal relationships, *Child Maltreatment*, 33(4), 208–219.

Sameroff, A. (2010) A unified theory of development: a dialectic integration of nature and nurture, *Child Development*, 81(1), 6–22.

Sameroff, A.J. (1990) Neo-environmental perspectives on developmental theory, in R.M. Hodapp, J.A. Burack and E. Zigler (eds), *Issues in the Developmental Approach to Mental Retardation*. Cambridge: Cambridge University Press.

Sameroff, A.J. (1995) General systems theories and developmental psychopathology, in D. Cicchetti and D.J. Cohen (eds), *Developmental Psychopathology. Vol. I: Theory and Methods*. New York: Wiley.

SAMHSA, *see* **Substance Abuse and Mental Health Services Administration** (2008).

Sanci, L., Coffey, C., Olsson, C., Reid, S., Carlin, J.B. and Patton, G. (2008) Childhood sexual abuse and eating disorders in females: findings from the Victorian adolescent health cohort study, *Archives of Pediatrics & Adolescent Medicine*, 162(3), 261–267.

Sanders, M.R. and Murphy-Brennan, M. (2010) The international dissemination of the Triple P Positive Parenting Program, in J.R. Weisz and A.E. Kazdin (eds), *Evidence-Based Psychotherapies for Children and Adolescents*, 2nd edn. New York: Guilford Press.

Sanderson, K., Patton, G.C., McKercher, C., Dwyer, T., Venn, A.J. (2011) Overweight and obesity in childhood and risk of mental disorder: a 20-year cohort study, *Australian and New Zealand Journal of Psychiatry*, 45(5), 384–392.

Sandfort, T.G.M. (2000) *Childhood Sexuality: Normal Sexual Behavior and Development*. Binghamton. NY: Haworth.

Sandfort, T.G.M. and Cohen-Kettenis, P. (2000) Sexual behavior in Dutch and Belgian children as observed by their mothers, in T.G.M. Sandfort and J. Rademakers (eds), *Childhood Sexuality: Normal Sexual Behavior and Development*. Binghamton. NY: Haworth.

Sanson, A., Prior, M. and Smart, D. (1996) Reading disabilities with and without behaviour problems at 7–8 years: prediction from longitudinal data from infancy to 6 years, *Journal of Child Psychology and Psychiatry*, 37(5), 529–541.

Santisteban, D.A., Coatsworth, D.J., Perez-Vidal, A., Kurtines, W., Schwartz, S., LaPerriere, A. et al. (2003) Efficacy of brief strategic family therapy in modifying Hispanic adolescent behavior problems and substance use, *Journal of Family Psychology*, 17, 121–133.

Santosh, J.P. (2000) Neuroimaging in child and adolescent psychiatric disorders, *Archives of Disease in Childhood*, 82 (5), pp 412–9.

Sarkar, J. and Adshead, G. (2006). Personality disorders as disorganisation of attachment and affect regulation, *Advances in Psychiatric Treatment*, 12(4), 297–305.

Sato, M. (2006) Renaming schizophrenia: a Japanese perspective, *World Psychiatry*, 5(1), 53.

Sattler, J.M. (1992) *Assessment of Children: Revised and Updated Third Edition*. San Diego, CA: Jerome M. Sattler.

Sattler, J.M. (2001) *Assessment of Children: Cognitive Applications*,

4th edn. San Diego, CA: Jerome M. Sattler.

Sattler, J. M. (2002) *Assessment of children: Behavioral and clinical applications*, 4th ed. San Diego, CA: Jerome M. Sattler.

Sattler, J.M and Hoge, R.D. (2006) *Assessment of Children: Behavioral, Social, and Clinical Foundations*, 5th edn. San Diego, CA: Sattler.

Saunders, B.E., Kilpatrick, D.G., Hanson, R.F., Resnick, H.S. and Walker, M.E. (1999) Prevalence, case characteristics and long-term psychological correlates of child rape among women: a national survey, *Child Maltreatment*, 4(3), 187–200.

Savin-Williams, R.C. (2001) *Mom, Dad. I'm Gay. How Families Negotiate Coming Out*. Washington, DC: American Psychological Association.

Savin-Williams, R.C. (2007) Verbal and physical abuse as stressors in the lives of lesbian, gay male and bisexual youth: associations with school problems, running away, substance abuse, prostitution and suicide, *Journal of Consulting and Clinical Psychology*, 62, 261–269.

Savin-Williams, R.C. and Ream, G.L. (2003) Suicide attempts among sexual-minority male youth, *Journal of Clinical Child and Adolescent Psychology*, 32(4), 509–522.

Savin-Williams, R.C. and Ream, G.L. (2007) Prevalence and stability of sexual orientation components during adolescence and young adulthood, *Archives of Sexual Behavior*, 36, 385–394.

Sawyer, S.M. et al. (2007) Adolescents with a chronic condition: challenges living, challenges treating, *The Lancet*, 369(9571), 1481–1489.

Sayer, L.C. (2006) Economic aspects of divorce and realtionship dissolution, in M.A. Fine and J.H. Harvey (eds), *Handbook of Divorce and Relationship Dissolution*. Mahwah, NJ: Erlbaum.

Scarr, S. (1992) Developmental theories for the 1990s: development and individual differences, *Child Development*, 64, 1333–1353.

Scarr, S. and McCartney, K. (1983) How people make their own environments: a theory of genotype -> environment effects, *Child Development*, 54, 424–435.

Schaeffer, C.M., Petras, H., Ialongo, N., Poduska, J. and Kellam, S. (2003) Modeling growth in boys' aggressive behavior across elementary school: links to later criminal involvement, conduct disorder and antisocial personality disorder, *Developmental Psychology*, 39(6), 1020–1035.

Schalock, R.L., Luckasson, R.A. and Shogren, K.A., with Borthwick-Duffy, S., Bradley, V. and Buntix, WH (2007) Perspective: the renaming of mental retardation: understanding the change to the term intellectual disability, *Intellectual and Developmental Disabilities*, 45, 116–124.

Schölmerich, A. (2007) Attachment and behvioral inhibition: two perspectives on early motivational development, *Advances in Psychology*, 131, 39–56.

Scholten, L. et al. (2011) A cognitive behavioral based group intervention for children with a chronic illness and their parents: a multicentre randomized controlled trial, *BMC Pediatrics*, 11(1), 65.

Schreibman, L. and Charlop-Christy, M.H. (1998) Autistic disorder, in T.H. Ollendick and M. Hersen (eds), *Handbook of Child Psychopathology*, 3rd edn. New York: Plenum Press.

Schuhrke, B. (2000) Young children's curiosity about other people's genitals, in T.G.M. Sandfort and J. Rademakers (eds), *Childhood Sexuality: Normal Sexual Behavior and Development*. Binghamton. NY: Haworth.

Schultz, R.T. (2005) Developmental deficits in social perception in autism: the role of the amygdala and fusiform face area, *International Journal of Developmental Neuroscience*, 23(2–3), 125–141.

Schultz, R.T., Romanski, L.M. and Tsatsanis, K.D. (2000) Neurofrontal models of autistic disorder and Asperger syndrome: clues from neuroimaging, in A. Klin, F. R. Volkmar and S.S. Sparrow (eds), *Asperger Syndrome*. New York: Guilford.

Schulze, B., Richter-Werling, M., Matschinger, H. and Angermeyer, M. C. (2003) Crazy? So what! Effects of a school project on students' attitudes towards people with schizophrenia, *Acta Psychiatrica Scandinavica*, 107, 142–150.

Schumacher, J.A., Smith-Slep, A.M. and Heyman, R.E. (2001) Risk factors for child neglect, *Aggression and Violent Behavior*, 6, 231–254.

Schwartz, J. and Steffensmeier, D. (2012) Stability and change in girls' delinquency and the gender gap: trends in violence and alcohol offending across multiple sources of evidence, in S. Miller, L. Leve and P.K. Kerig (eds), *Delinquent Girls: Context, Relationships and Adaptation*. New York: Springer Books.

Schwartz, L.A., Radcliffe, J. and Barakat, L.P. (2007) The development of a culturally sensitive pediatric pain management intervention for African American adolescents with sickle cell disease, *Children's Health Care: Journal of the Association for the Care of Children's Health*, 36(3), 267–284.

Schwartz-Kenney, B.M. and McCauley, M. (2003) Physical abuse and neglect, in J. Ponzetti, R. Hamon, Y. Kellar-Guenther, P.K. Kerig, L. Scales and J. White (eds), *International Encyclopedia of Marital and Family Relationships*. New York: Macmillan.

Scott, S. (2010) Nationwide dissemination of effective parenting interventions, in J.R. Weisz and A.E. Kazdin (eds), *Evidence-Based Psychotherapies for Children and Adolescents*, 2nd edn. New York: Guilford Press.

Scott, S. and Yule, W. (2009) Behavioral therapies, in M. Rutter, D.V.M. Bishop, D.S. Pine, S. Scott, J.

Stevenson, E. Taylor and A. Thapar (eds), *Rutter's Child and Adolescent Psychiatry*, 5th edn. Oxford: Blackwell.

Sedlak, A. (2010) *Fourth National Incidence Study of Child Abuse and Neglect (NIS-4): Report to Congress*, US Dept. of Health and Human Services, Administration for Children and Families, Administration on Children, Youth and Families, National Center on Child Abuse and Neglect.

Segerstrom, S.C., Stanton, A.L., Alden, L.E. and Shortridge, B.E. (2003) A multidimensional structure for repetitive thought: what's on your mind and how and how much? *Journal of Personality and Social Psychology*, 85, 909–921.

Seidman, L.J., Biederman, J., Faraone, S.V., Weber, W. and Ouellette, C. (1997) Toward defining a neuropsychology of attention deficit-hyperactivity disorder: performance of children and adolescents from a large clinically referred sample, *Journal of Consulting and Clinical Psychology*, 65, 150–160.

Seiner, S.H. and Gelfand, D.M. (1995) Effects of mothers' simulated withdrawal and depressed affect on mother-toddler interactions, *Child Development*, 66(5), 1519–1528.

Selby, E.A., Ward, A.C. and Joiner, T.E. Jr (2010) Dysregulated eating behaviors in borderline personality disorder: are rejection sensitivity and emotion dysregulation linking mechanisms? *International Journal of Eating Disorders*, 43(7), 667–670.

Selfe, L. (1977) *Nadia: A Case of Extraordinary Drawing Ability In An Autistic Child*. New York: Academic Press.

Seligman, M.E., Reivich, K., Jaycox, L. and Gillham, J. (2007) *The Optimistic Child: A Proven Program to Safeguard Children against Depression and Build Lifelong Resilience*. New York: Houghton Mifflin Harcourt.

Sentse, M., Veenstra, R., Lindenberg, S., Verhulst, F.C. and Ormel, J. (2009) Buffers and risks in temperament and family for early adolescent psychopathology: generic, conditional, or domain-specific effects? The trails study. *Developmental Psychology*, 45(2), 419–430.

Serafica, F.C. and Vargas, L.A. (2006) Cultural diversity in the development of child psychopathology, in D. Cicchetti and D.J. Cohen (eds), *Developmental Psychopathology. Volume I: Theory and Method*, 2nd edn. New York: Wiley.

Shaffer, A. and Sroufe, L.A. (2005) The developmental and adaptational implications of generational boundary dissolution: findings from a prospective, longitudinal study, in P.K. Kerig (ed.), *Implications of Parent–Child Boundary Dissolution For Developmental Psychopathology*. Binghamton, NY: Haworth.

Shaffer, D., Garland, A., Vieland, V., Underwood, M. and Busner, C. (1991) The impact of curriculum-based suicide prevention programs for teenagers, *Journal of the American Academy of Child and Adolescent Psychiatry*, 30, 588–596.

Shaffer, D. et al. (2003) *Scoring manual: diagnostic interview schedule for children (DISC-IV)*. New York: Columbia University.

Shapiro, C.J., Smith, B.H., Malone, P.S. and Collaro, A.L. (2010) Natural experiment in deviant peer exposure and youth recidivism, *Journal of Clinical Child and Adolescent Psychology*, 39(2), 242–251.

Shapiro, E.R., Zinner, J., Shapiro, R.L. and Berkowitz, D.A. (1975) The influence of family experience on borderline personality development, *International Review of Psycho-Analysis*, 2(4), 399–411.

Shattuck, T., (2006). The contribution of diagnostic substitution to the growing administrative prevalence of autism in US special education, *Pediatrics*, 117(4), 1028.

Shaw, D.S. and Bell, R.Q. (1993) Developmental theories of parental contributors to antisocial behavior, *Journal of Abnormal Child Psychology*, 21(5), 493–518.

Shaw, D.S., Owens, E.B., Vondra, J.I., Keenan, K. and Winslow, E.B. (1996) Early risk factors and pathways in the development of early disruptive behavior problems, *Development and Psychopathology*, 8(4), 679–699.

Shaw, D.S., Winslow, E.B., Owens, E.B. and Vondra, J.I. (1998) The development of early externalizing problems among children from low-income families: a transformational perspective, *Journal of Abnormal Child Psychology*, 26(2), 95–107.

Shaw, D.S., Bell, R.Q. and Gilliom, M. (2000) A truly early starter model of antisocial behavior revisited, *Clinical Child and Family Psychology Review*, 3(3), 155–172.

Shaw, D.S., Gilliom, M., Ingoldsby, E.M. and Nagin, D.S. (2003) Trajectories leading to school-age conduct problems, *Developmental Psychology*, 39(2), 189–200.

Shaw, H., Ramirez, L., Trost, A., Randall, P. and Stice, E. (2004) Body image and eating disturbances across ethnic groups: more similarities than differences. *Psychology of Addictive Behaviors*, 18(1), 12–18.

Shaw, S.F. et al. (1995) Operationalizing a definition of learning disabilities, *Journal of Learning Disabilities*, 28(9), 586.

Shaywitz S. (2003) *Overcoming Dyslexia: A New and Complete Science-Based Program for Reading Problems at Any Level*. New York: Knopf.

Sheeber, L., Davis, B. and Hops, H. (2002) Gender-specific vulnerability to depression in children of depressed mothers, in S.H. Goodman and I.H. Gotlib (eds), *Children of Depressed Parents: Mechanisms of Risk and Implications for Treatment*. Washington, DC: American Psychological Association.

Sheridan, M.S. (2003) The deceit continues: an updated literature review of Munchausen by proxy syndrome, *Child Abuse and Neglect*, 27, 431–451.

Shirk, S., Jungbluth, N. and Karver, M. (2011) Change processes and active components, in C.K. Philip (ed.), *Child and Adolescent Therapy: Cognitive-Behavioral Procedures*, 4th edn. New York: Guilford.

Shirk, S.R. (1999) Developmental therapy, in W.K. Silverman and T.H. Ollendick (eds), *Developmental Issues in the Clinical Treatment Of Children*. Boston, MA: Allyn & Bacon.

Shirk, S.R. and Burwell, R.A. (2010) Research on therapeutic processes in psychodynamic psychotherapy with children and adolescents, in J. Tsiantis and J. Trowell (eds), *Assessing Change in Psychodynamic Psychotherapy of Children and Adolescents*. London: Karnac Books.

Shirk, S.R. and Russell, R.L. (1996) *Change Processes in Child Psychotherapy: Revitalizing Treatment and Research*. New York: Guilford.

Shochet, I.M., Homel, R., Cockshaw, W.D. and Montgomery, D.T. (2008) How do school connectedness and attachment to parents interrelate in predicting adolescent depressive symptoms? *Journal of Clinical Child and Adolescent Psychology*, 37(3), 676–681.

Shochet, I.M., Hoge, R. and Essau, C.A. (2009) Resourceful adolescent program: a prevention and early intervention program for teenage depression, in C.A. Essau (ed.), *Treatments for Adolescent Depression: Theory and Practice*. New York: Oxford University Press.

Shorey, H.S. and Snyder, C.R. (2006) The role of adult attachment styles in psychopathology and psychotherapy outcomes, *Review of General Psychology*, 10(1), 1–20.

Shortt, J.W., Capaldi, D., Dishion, T.J., Bank, L. and Owen, L.D. (2003) The role of adolescent friends, romantic partners and siblings in the emergence of the adult antisocial lifestyle, *Journal of Family Psychology*, 17(4), 521–533.

Shoval, G. et al. (2011) Suicidal behavior and related traits among inpatient adolescents with first-episode schizophrenia, *Comprehensive Psychiatry*, March, doi.org/10.1016/j.comppsych.2011.01.005.

Shreeram, S. et al. (2009) Prevalence of enuresis and its association with attention-deficit/hyperactivity disorder among US children: results from a nationally representative study, *Journal of the American Academy of Child & Adolescent Psychiatry*, 48(1), 35–41.

Shure, M.B. and Spivack, G. (1988) Interpersonal cognitive problem-solving, in R.H. Price, E.L. Cowen, R.P. Lorion and J. Ramos-McKay (eds), *Fourteen Ounces of Prevention: A Casebook for Practitioners*. Washington, DC: American Psychological Association.

Siegler, R., DeLoache, J. and Eisenberg, N. (2003) *How Children Develop*. New York: Worth.

Sijtsema, J.J., Veenstra, R., Lindenberg, S. and Salmivalli, C. (2009) Empirical test of bullies' status goals: assessing direct goals, aggression and prestige, *Aggressive Behavior*, 35(1), 57–67.

Silberg, J., Pickles, A., Rutter, M., Hewitt, J., Simonoff, E., Maes, H. et al. (1999) The influence of genetic factors and life stress on depression among adolescent girls, *Archives of General Psychiatry*, 56(3), 225–232.

Silberg, J.L. (2004) The treatment of dissociation in sexually abused children from a family/attachment perspective, *Psychotherapy: Theory, research, practice, training*, 41(4), 487–495.

Silk, J.S. et al. (2000). Conceptualizing mental disorders in children: where have we been and where are we going? *Development and Psychopathology*, 12(4), 713–735.

Silk, J.S., Ziegler, M.L., Whalen, D.J., Dahl, R.E., Ryan, N.D., Dietz, L.J. et al. (2009) Expressed emotion in

mothers of currently depressed, remitted, high-risk and low-risk youth: links to child depression status and longitudinal course, *Journal of Clinical Child & Adolescent Psychology*, 38(1), 36–47.

Silverman, D.K. (2011) A clinical case of an avoidant attachment, *Psychoanalytic Psychology*, 28(2), 293–310.

Silverman, R.C. and Lieberman, A F. (1999) Negative maternal attributions, projective identification and the intergenerational transmission of violent relational patterns, *Psychoanalytic Dialogues*, 9, 161–186.

Silverman, W. et al. (2010) Stanford-Binet and WAIS IQ differences and their implications for adults with intellectual disability (aka mental retardation), *Intelligence*, 38(2), 242–248.

Silverman, W.K. and Ginsburg, G.S. (1998) Anxiety disorders, in T.H. Ollendick and M. Hersen (eds), *Handbook of Child Psychopathology*. New York: Plenum.

Silverman, W.K. and Hinshaw, S.P. (2008) The second special issue on evidence-based psychosocial treatments for children and adolescents: a ten year update, *Journal of Clinical Child and Adolescent Psychology*, 37, 1–7.

Silverman, W.K. and Rabian, B. (1994) Specific phobias, in T.H. Ollendick, N.J. King and W. Yule (eds), *International Handbook of Phobic and Anxiety Disorders in Children and Adolescents*. New York: Plenum.

Silverman, W.K., Pina, A.A. and Viswesvaran, C. (2008) Evidence-based psychosocial treatments for phobic and anxiety disorders in children and adolescents, *Journal of Clinical Child & Adolescent Psychology*, 37(1), 105–130.

Silverthorn, P. and Frick, P.J. (1999) Developmental pathways to antisocial behavior: the delayed-onset pathway in girls, *Development and Psychopathology*, 11(1), 101–126.

Simic, M. and Fombonne, E. (2001) Depressive conduct disorder: symp-

tom patterns and correlates in referred children and adolescents, *Journal of Affective Disorders*, 62(3), 175–185.

Simons, R.L., Murry, V., McLoyd, V., Lin, K.H., Cutrona, C. and Conger, R.D. (2002) Discrimination, crime, ethnic identity and parenting as correlates of depression symptoms among African American children: a multilevel analysis, *Development and Psychopathology*, 14(2), 371–393.

Simos, G. et al. (2000) Cerebral mechanisms involved in word reading in dyslexic children: a magnetic source imaging approach, *Cerebral Cortex*, 10(8), 809.

Simos, G. et al. (2002) Dyslexia-specific brain activation profile becomes normal following successful remedial training, *Neurology*, 58(8), 1203.

Simpson, D. and Reilly, P. (1982) Pediatric coma scale, *The Lancet*, 2(8295), 450.

Singh, A.L. and Waldman, I.D. (2010) The etiology of associations between negative emotionality and childhood externalizing disorders, *Journal of Abnormal Psychology*, 119(2), 376.

Siperstein, G.N. and Leffert, J.S. (1997) Comparison of socially accepted and rejected children with mental retardation, *American Journal on Mental Retardation*, 101, 339–351.

Siperstein, G. N., Leffert, J. S. and Wenz-Gross, M. (1997) The quality of friendships between children with and without learning problems, *American Journal of Mental Retardation*, 102, 111–125.

Sizoo, L. (2005) Swedish doctors wrote illegal ADHD prescriptions, *Local*, 5 February.

Skara, S. and Sussman, S. (2003) A review of 25 long-term adolescent tobacco and other drug use prevention program evaluations, *Preventive Medicine*, 37, 451–474.

Skodol, A., Bender, D., Pagano, M., Shea, M., Yen, S., Sanislow, C.

et al. (2007a) Positive childhood experiences: resilience and recovery from personality disorder in early adulthood, *The Journal of Clinical Psychiatry*, 68(7), 1102–1108.

Skodol, A., Johnson, J., Cohen, Sneed, J. and Crawford, T. (2007b) Personality disorder and impaired functioning from adolescence to adulthood, *The British Journal of Psychiatry*, 190(5), 415–420.

Skowyra, K.R. and Cocozza, J. (2007) *Blueprint for Change: A Comprehensive Model for the Identification and Treatment of Youth with Mental Health Needs in Contact with the Juvenile Justice System.* New York: Delmar, http://www.ncmhjj.com/Blueprint/default.shtml.

Slipp, S. (1991) *The Technique and Practice of Object Relations Family Therapy.* New York: Aronson.

Slof-Op't Landt, M.C.T., van Furth, E.F., Meulenbelt, I., Slagboom, P.E., Bartels, M., Boomsma, D.I. and Bulik, C.M. (2005) Eating disorders: from twin studies to candidate genes and beyond, *Twin Research and Human Genetics*, 8(5), 467–482.

Smart, D., Sanson, A. and Prior, M. (1996). Connections between reading disability and behavior problems: testing temporal and causal hypotheses, *Journal of Abnormal Child Psychology*, 24(3), 363–383.

Smith, K.A., Fairburn, C.G. and Cowen, P.J. (1999) Symptomatic relapse in bulimia nervosa following acute tryptophan depletion, *Archives of General Psychiatry*, 56, 171–176.

Smith, T., Scahill, L., Dawson, G., Guthrie, D., Lord, C., Odom, S., et al. (2007) Designing research studies on psychosocial interventions in autism, *Journal of Autism and Developmental Disorders*, 37, 354–366.

Smokowski, P.R., Bacallao, M. and Buchanan, R.L. (2009) Interpersonal mediators linking acculturation stressors to subsequent internalizing symptoms and self-esteem in Latino adolescents, *Journal of Community Psychology*, 37(8), 1024–1045.

Smolak, L. and Striegel-Moore, R.H. (2001) Challenging the myth of the golden girl: ethnicity and eating disorders, in R.H. Striegel-Moore and L. Smolak (eds), *Eating Disorders*. Washington, DC: American Psychological Association.

Smyth, J.M., Wonderlich, S.A., Heron, K.E., Sliwinski, M.J., Crosby, R.D., Mitchell, J.E. and Engel, S.G. (2007) Daily and momentary mood and stress are associated with binge eating and vomiting in bulimia nervosa patients in the natural environment, *Journal of Consulting and Clinical Psychology*, 75(4), 629–638.

Snow, J.H. and Hooper, S.R. (1994) *Pediatric Traumatic Brain Injury.* Newbury Park, CA: Sage Publications.

Snowling, M.J., Bishop, D.V.M., Stothard, S.E., Chipchase, B. and Kaplan, C. (2006) Psychosocial outcomes at 15 years of children with a preschool history of speech-language impairment, *Journal of Child Psychology and Psychiatry*, 47(8), 759–765.

Snyder, J., Reid, J. and Patterson, G. (2003) A social learning model of child and adolescent antisocial behavior, in B.B. Lahey, T.E. Moffitt and A. Caspi (eds), *Causes of Conduct Disorder and Juvenile Delinquency*. New York: Guilford.

Snyder, J., Schrepferman, L., McEachern, A., Barner, S., Oeser, J. and Johnson, K. (in press) Peer deviancy training and peer coercion: dual processes associated with early-onset conduct problems. *Child Development.*

So, S.A., Urbano, R.C. and Hodapp, R.M. (2007). Hospitalizations of infants and young children with Down syndrome: evidence from inpatient person-records from a statewide administrative database, *Journal of Intellectual Disability Research*, 51(12), 1030–1038.

Solantaus, T., Leinonen, J. and Punamaki, R. L. (2004) Children's mental health in times of economic recession: replication and extension of the family economic stress model in Finland, *Developmental Psychology*, 40(3), 412–429.

Solanto M. (2004) The 'quiet' form of ADHD: the inattentive subtype poses different challenges, *Behavioural Health Management*, 23(4), 38–40.

Solanto, M.V. and Alvir, J. (2009) Reliability of DSM-IV Symptom Ratings of ADHD, *Journal of Attention Disorders*, 13(2), 107.

Sonuga-Barke, E., Bitsakou, P. and Thompson, M. (2010) Beyond the dual pathway model: evidence for the dissociation of timing, inhibitory and delay-related impairments in attention-deficit/hyperactivity disorder, *Journal of the American Academy of Child & Adolescent Psychiatry*, 49(4), 345–355.

Sonuga-Barke, E.J.S. (2003) The dual pathway model of AD/HD: an elaboration of neuro-developmental characteristics, *Neuroscience & Biobehavioral Reviews*, 27(7), 593–604.

Sonuga-Barke, E.J.S. (2005) Causal models of attention-deficit/hyperactivity disorder: from common simple deficits to multiple developmental pathways, *Biological Psychiatry*, 57(11), 1231–1238.

Sonuga-Barke, E.J.S. and Castellanos, F.X. (2007) Spontaneous attentional fluctuations in impaired states and pathological conditions: a neurobiological hypothesis, *Neuroscience & Biobehavioral Reviews*, 31(7), 977–986.

Sorkhabi, N. (2005) Applicability of Baumrind's parent typology to collective cultures: analysis of cultural explanations of parent socialization effects, *International Journal of Behavioral Development*, 29(6), 552–563.

Sowell, E.R., Toga, A.W. and Asarnow, R. (2000) Brain abnormalities observed in childhood-onset schizophrenia: a review of the structural magnetic resonance imaging literature, *Mental Retardation & Developmental Disabilities Research Reviews*, 6, 180–185.

Spangler, D.L. (2002) Testing the cognitive model of eating disorders: the role of dysfunctional beliefs about appearance, *Behavior Therapy*, 33(1), 87–105.

Sparks, B.F. et al. (2002) Brain structural abnormalities in young children with autism spectrum disorder, *Neurology*, 59(2), 184.

Sparrow, S.S., Cicchetti, D.V. and Balla, D.A. (2005) *Vineland Adaptive Behavior Scales: (Vineland II), Survey Interview Form/Caregiver Rating Form*. Livonia, MN: Pearson Assessments.

Spauwen, J. et al. (2003) Sex differences in psychosis: normal or pathological? *Schizophrenia Research*, 62(1–2), 45–49.

Spear, L.P. (2009) Heightened stress responsivity and emotional reactivity during pubertal maturation: implications for psychopathology, *Developmental Psychopathology*, 21(1), 87–97.

Speltz, M.L. et al. (1995) Clinic referral for oppositional defiant disorder: relative significance of attachment and behavioral variables, *Journal of Abnormal Child Psychology*, 23(4), 487–507.

Spence, S.H., Donovan, C. and Brechman-Toussaint, M. (2000) The treatment of childhood social phobia: the effectiveness of a social skills training based cognitive behavioral intervention, with and without parental involvement, *Journal of Child Psychology and Psychiatry*, 41(6), 713–726.

Spencer, M.B., Harpalani, V., Cassidy, E., Jacobs, C.Y., Donde, S., Goss, T. N. (2006) Understanding vulnerability and resilience from a normative developmental perspective: implications for racially and ethnically diverse youth, in D. Cicchetti and D.J. Cohen (eds), *Developmental Psychopathology. Volume I: Theory and Method*, 2nd edn, New York: Wiley.

Spencer, T., Wilens, T.E., Biederman, J., Wozniak, J. and Harding-Crawford, M. (2000) Attention deficit/hyperactivity disorder with mood disorders, in T.E. Brown (ed.), *Attention Deficit Disorders and Comorbidities in Children, Adolescents and Adults*. Washington, DC: American Psychiatric Press.

Spencer, T.J. et al. (1996) Growth deficits in ADHD children revisited: evidence for disorder-associated growth delays? *Journal of the American Academy of Child & Adolescent Psychiatry*, 35(11), 1460–1469.

Spessot, A.L. and Peterson, B.S. (2006) Tourette's syndrome: a multifactorial, developmental psychopathology, in D. Cicchetti and D.J. Cohen (eds), *Developmental Pychopathology, Vol 3: Risk, Disorder and Adaptation*, 2nd edn. Hoboken, NJ: John Wiley & Sons.

Spirito, A., Kurkjian, J. and Donaldson, D. (2003) Case examples, in A. Spirito and J.C. Overholser (eds), *Evaluating and Treating Adolescent Suicide Attempters: From Research to Practice*. New York: Academic Press.

Spitz, R.A. (1946a) Anaclitic depression, *Psychoanalytic Study of the Child*, 2, 313–342.

Spitz, R.A. (1946b) Hospitalism: follow-up report on investigation described in volume I, 1945, *Psychoanalytic Study of the Child*, 2, 113–117.

Sporn, A., Greenstein, D., Gogtay, N., Jeffries, N.O., Lenane, M., Gochman, P., Clasen, L.S., Blumenthal, J., Giedd, J.N. and Rapoport, J.L. (2003) Progressive brain volume loss during adolescence in childhood-onset schizophrenia, *American Journal of Psychiatry*, 160(12), 2181–2189.

Sprafkin, J. et al. (2011). A brief DSM-IV-referenced teacher rating scale for monitoring behavioral improvement in ADHD and co-occurring symptoms, *Journal of Attention Disorders*, 15(3), 235–245.

Srinath, S. et al. (2005) Epidemiological study of child & adolescent psychiatric disorders in urban & rural areas of Bangalore, India, *Indian Journal of Medical Research*, 122(1), 67–79.

Sroufe, L.A. (1990) An organizational perspective on the self, in D. Cicchetti and M. Beeghly (eds), *The Self in Transition: Infancy to Childhood*. Chicago, IL: University of Chicago Press.

Sroufe, L.A. (1997) Psychopathology as an outcome of development, *Development and Psychopathology*, 9(2), 251–268.

Sroufe, L.A. and Rutter, M. (1984) The domain of developmental psychopathology, *Child Development*, 55, 17–29.

Sroufe, L.A., Egeland, B., Carlson, E.A. and Collins, W.A. (2005) *The Development of the Person: The Minnesota Study of Risk and Adaptation from Birth to Adulthood*. New York: Guilford.

Stadler, C., Rohrmann, S., Knopf, A. and Poustka, F. (2007) Soziomoralisches Denken bei Jungen mit einer Störung des Sozialverhaltens: Der Einfluss von Intelligenz, Erziehungsfaktoren und Psychosozialer Belastung, *Zeitschrift für Kinder- und Jugendpsychiatrie und Psychotherapie*, 35(3), 169–178.

Stalker, K. and McArthur, K. (2010) Child abuse, child protection and disabled children: a review of recent research, *Child Abuse Review*, http://dx.doi.org/10.1002/car.1154.

Stannard Gromisch, E. (2010) Neurotransmitters involved in ADHD, *Psych Central*, http://psychcentral.com/lib/2010/neurotransmitters-involved-in-adhd/ (retrieved 23 August 2011).

State, M.W., King, B.H. and Dykens, E. (1997) Mental retardation: a review of the past 10 years (Part II), *Journal of the American Academy of Child and Adolescent Psychiatry*, 36, 1664–1671.

Steele, R.G. and Forehand, R. (2003) Longitudinal correlates of depressive symptoms among urban

African American children: II. Extensive findings across 3 years, *Journal of Clinical Child and Adolescent Psychology*, 32(4), 606–612.

Stegarud, L., Solheim, B., Karlsen, M. and Kroger, J. (1999) Ego identity status in cross-cultural context: a replication study, *Psychological Reports*, 85, 457–461.

Steiger, H., Gauvin, L., Israël, M., Koerner, N., Ng Ying Kin, N.M.K., Paris, J. and Young, S.N. (2001) Association of serotonin and cortisol indices with childhood abuse in bulimia nervosa, *Archives of General Psychiatry*, 58(9), 837–843.

Stein, L.A.R., Hesselbrock, V. and Bukstein, O.G. (2008) Conduct disorder and oppositional defiant disorder and adolescent substance use disorders, in Y. Kaminer and O. G. Bukstein (eds), *Adolescent Substance Abuse: Psychiatric Comorbidity and High-Risk Behaviors*. New York: Routledge/Taylor & Francis Group.

Steinberg, L. (2009) Adolescent development and juvenile justice, *Annual Review of Clinical Psychology*, 5, 47–73.

Steinberg, L. (2010) A behavioral scientist looks at the science of adolescent brain development, *Brain and Cognition*, 72, 160–164.

Steinberg, L., Lamborn, S.D., Darling, N., Mounts, N.S. and Dornbusch, S.M. (1994) Over-time changes in adjustment and competence among adolescents from authoritative, authoritarian, indulgent and neglectful families, *Child Development*, 65, 754–770.

Steinberg, L., Chung, H.L. and Little, M. (2004) Reentry of young offenders from the justice system: a developmental perspective, *Youth Violence and Juvenile Justice*, 2, 21–38.

Steinberg, L., Graham, S., O'Brien, L., Woolard, J., Cauffman, E. and Banich, M. (2009) Age differences in future orientation and delay discounting, *Child Development*, 80, 28–44.

Steinhausen, H.C. and Weber, S. (2009) The outcome of bulimia nervosa: findings from one-quarter century of research, *American Journal of Psychiatry*, 166(12), 1331–1341.

Stern, D.N. (1985) *The Interpersonal World of the Infant*. New York: Basic Books.

Sterzer, P., Stadler, C., Poustka, F. and Kleinschmidt, A. (2007) A structural neural deficit in adolescents with conduct disorder and its association with lack of empathy, *NeuroImage*, 37(1), 335–342.

Stevens, T. and Mulsow, M. (2006) There is no meaningful relationship between television exposure and symptoms of attention-deficit/hyperactivity disorder, *Pediatrics*, 117(3), 665–672.

Steward, M.S. et al. (1993) Implications of developmental research for interviewing children, *Child Abuse & Neglect*, 17(1), 25–37.

Stewart, A., Livingston, M. and Dennison, S. (2008) Transitions and turning points: examining the links between child maltreatment and juvenile offending, *Child Abuse & Neglect*, 32(1), 51–66.

Stice, E. (2002) Risk and maintenance factors for eating pathology: a meta-analytic review, *Psychological Bulletin*, 128(5), 825–848.

Stice, E. and Bulik, C.M. (2008) Eating disorders, in T.P. Beauchaine and S.P. Hinshaw (eds), *Child and Adolescent Psychopathology*. Hoboken, NJ: John Wiley & Sons.

Stice, E. and Peterson, C.B. (2007) Eating disorders, in E.J. Mash and R.A. Barkley (eds), *Assessment of Childhood Disorders*, 4th edn. New York: Guilford Press.

Stice, E. and Presnell, K. (2010) Dieting and the eating disorders, in W.S. Agras (ed.), *The Oxford Handbook of Eating Disorders*. New York: Oxford University Press.

Stice, E. and Shaw, H. (2004) Eating disorder prevention programs: a meta-analytic review, *Psychological Bulletin*, 130(2), 206–227.

Stice, E., Ziemba, C., Margolis, J. and Flick, P. (1996) The dual pathway model differentiates bulimics, subclinical bulimics and controls: testing the continuity hypothesis, *Behavior Therapy*, 27, 531–549.

Stice, E., Burton, E.M. and Shaw, H. (2004) Prospective relations between bulimic pathology, depression and substance abuse: unpacking comorbidity in adolescent girls, *Journal of Consulting and Clinical Psychology*, 72(1), 62–71.

Stieglitz Ham, H. et al. (2008) Brief report: imitation of meaningless gestures in individuals with Asperger syndrome and high-functioning autism, *Journal of Autism and Developmental Disorders*, 38(3), 569–573.

Stipek, D.J. (2001) Pathways to constructive lives: the importance of early school success, in A.C. Bohart and D.J. Stipek (eds), *Constructive and Destructive Behavior: Implications for Family, School and Society*. Washington, DC: American Psychological Association.

Stirling, J. and the Committee on Child Abuse and Neglect. (2007) Beyond Munchausen syndrome by proxy: identification and treatment of child abuse in a medical setting, *Pediatrics*, 119(5), 1026–1030.

Stone, W.L. and Lemanek, K.L. (1990) Developmental issues in children's self-reports, in A.M. La Greca (ed.), *Through the Eyes of the Child: Obtaining Self-Reports from Children and Adolescents*. Boston, MA: Allyn & Bacon.

Storr, A. (1989) *Churchill's Black Dog*. London: HarperCollins.

Storvoll, E.E. and Wichstrøm, L. (2002) Do the risk factors associated with conduct problems in adolescents vary according to gender? *Journal of Adolescence*, 25(2), 182–202.

Strambler, M.J. and Weinstein, R.S. (2010) Psychological disengagement in elementary school among ethnic minority students,

Journal of Applied Developmental Psychology, 31(2), 155–165.

Strand, S. and Lindsay, G., (2009). Evidence of ethnic disproportionality in special education in an English population, *The Journal of Special Education*, 43(3), 174.

Strasburger, V.C. and the Council on Communications and Media (2010) Children, adolescents, substance abuse and the media, *Pediatrics*, 126, 791–799.

Straus, M. (2010) Prevalence, societal causes and trends in corporal punishment by parents in world perspective, *Law and Contemporary Problems*, 73(2), 1–30.

Straus, M., Douglas, E. and Medeiros, R. (in press) *Primordial Violence: Spanking Children and its Effect on Cognitive Development and Crime.* New York: Psychology Press.

Strauss, C.C. and Last, C.G. (1993) Social and simple phobias in children, *Journal of Anxiety Disorders*, 7, 141–152.

Strauss, D.J., Shavelle, R. and Anderson, T.W. (1998) Life expectancy of children with cerebral palsy, *Pediatric Neurology*, 18, 143–149.

Striegel-Moore, R.H. and Bulik, C.M. (2007) Risk factors for eating disorders, *American Psychologist*, 62(3), 181–198.

Striegel-Moore, R.H. and Smolak, L. (2001) *Eating Disorders: Innovative Directions in Research and Practice.* Washington, DC: APA.

Striegel-Moore, R.H., Dohm, F.A., Kraemer, H.C., Taylor, C.B., Daniels, S., Crawford, P.B. and Schreiber, G.B. (2003) Eating disorders in white and black women, *The American Journal of Psychiatry*, 160(7), 1326–1331.

Strober, M., Freeman, R. and Morrell, W. (1997) The long-term course of severe anorexia nervosa in adolescents: survival analysis of recovery, relapse and outcome predictors over 10–15 years in a prospective study, *International Journal of Eating Disorders*, 22(4), 339–360.

Strober, M., Freeman, R., Lampert, C., Diamond, J. and Kaye, W. (2000) Controlled family study of anorexia nervosa and bulimia nervosa: evidence of shared liability and transmission of partial syndromes, *American Journal of Psychiatry*, 157, 393–401.

Strohschein, L. (2005) Parental divorce and child mental health trajectories, *Journal of Marriage and Family*, 67, 1286–1300.

Stromme, P. and Hagberg, G. (2000) Aetiology in severe and mild mental retardation: a population-based study of Norwegian children, *Developmental Medicine & Child Neurology*, 42(2), 76–86.

Stuewig, J. and McCloskey, L.A. (2005) The relation of child maltreatment to shame and guilt among adolescents: psychological routes to depression and delinquency, *Child Maltreatment*, 10(4), 324.

Sturge-Apple, M.L., Davies, P.T. and Cummings, E.M. (2010) Typologies of family functioning and children's adjustment during the early school years, *Child Development*, 81(4), 1320–1335.

Substance Abuse and Mental Health Services Administration (SAMHSA) (2008) *Treatment of Adolescents with Substance Use Disorders.* Rockville, MD: US Department of Health and Human Services.

Sue, D.W. and Sue, D. (2008) *Counseling the Culturally Diverse: Theory and Practice.* Hoboken, NJ: Wiley.

Sullivan, A.E. and Miklowitz, D.J. (2010) Family functioning among adolescents with bipolar disorder, *Journal of Family Psychology*, 24(1), 60–67.

Sung, M., Erkanli, A., Angold, A. and Costello, E.J. (2004) Effects of age at first substance use and psychiatric comorbidity on the development of substance use disorders, *Drug and Alcohol Dependence*, 75(3), 287–299.

Sutton, J., Smith, P.K. and Swettenham, J. (1999) Bullying and 'theory of mind': a critique of the 'social skills deficit' view of anti-social behavior, *Social Development*, 8(1), 117–127.

Suveg, C. and Zeman, J. (2004) Emotion regulation in children with anxiety disorders, *Journal of Clinical Child and Adolescent Psychology*, 33(4), 750–759.

Suzuki, L.A. and Ponterotto, J.G. (2008) *Handbook of Multicultural Assessment: Clinical, Psychological and Educational Applications.* San Francisco, CA: Jossey-Bass.

Sweeney, L. and Rapee, R.M. (2001) Social phobia in children and adolescents: Psychological treatments, in W. Crozier and L.E. Alden (eds), *International Handbook of Social Anxiety: Concepts, Research and Interventions Relating to the Self and Shyness.* New York: Wiley.

Sweeney, M. (2010) Remarriage and stepfamilies: strategic sites for family scholarship in the 21st century, *Journal of Marriage and Family*, 72(3), 667–684.

Swettenham, J. et al. (1998) The frequency and distribution of spontaneous attention shifts between social and nonsocial stimuli in autistic, typically developing and nonautistic developmentally delayed infants, *Journal of Child Psychology and Psychiatry*, 39(5), 747–753.

Szalacha, L.A., Erkut, S., Coll, C.G., Fields, J.P., Alarcon, O. and Ceder, I. (2003) Perceived discrimination and resilience, in S.S. Luthar (ed.), *Resilience and Vulnerability: Adaptation in the Context of Childhood Adversities.* New York: Cambridge University Press.

Szatmari, P. (1992) The epidemiology of attention-deficit hyperactivity disorders, *Child and Adolescent Psychiatric Clinics of North America*, 1(2), 361–371.

Szatmari, P., Offord, D.R. and Boyle, M.H. (1989) Ontario Child Health Study: Prevalence of attention deficit disorder with hyperactivity, *Journal of Child Psychology & Psychiatry*, 30, 219–230.

Tackett, J.L., Balsis, S., Oltmanns, T.F. and Krueger, R.F. (2009) A unifying perspective on personality pathology across the life span: developmental considerations for the fifth edition of the Diagnostic and Statistical Manual of Mental Disorders, *Development and Psychopathology*, 21(3), 687–713.

TADS Team (2007) The Treatment for Adolescents with Depression Study (TADS): long-term effectiveness and safety outcomes, *Focus*, 64(10), 1132–1143.

Tager-Flusberg, H. (2000) Language and understanding minds: connections in autism, *Understanding Other Minds: Perspectives From Developmental Cognitive Neuroscience*, 2, 124–149.

Tager-Flusberg, H. (2007). Evaluating the theory-of-mind hypothesis of autism, *Current Directions in Psychological Science*, 16(6), 311–315.

Tai, H.L. et al. (2007) The epidemiology and factors associated with nocturnal enuresis and its severity in primary school children in Taiwan, *Acta paediatrica*, 96(2), 242–245.

Tannock, R. (2000) Attention-deficit/hyperactivity disorder with anxiety disorders, in T.E. Brown (ed.), *Attention Deficit Disorders and Comorbidities in Children, Adolescents, and Adults*. Washington, DC: American Psychiatric Press.

Tanofsky-Kraff, M. and Wilfley, D.E. (2010) Interpersonal psychotherapy for bulimia nervosa and binge-eating disorder, in C.M. Grilo and J.E. Mitchell (eds), *The Treatment of Eating Disorders: a Clinical Handbook*. New York: Guilford Press.

Target, M. and Fonagy, P. (1997) Research on intensive psychotherapy with children and adolescents, *Child and Adolescent Psychiatric Clinics of North America*, 6, 39–51.

Tarpey, S. et al. (2009) A systematic, large-scale resequencing screen of X-chromosome coding exons in mental retardation, *Nature Genetics*, 41(5), 535–543.

Tarter, R.E., Kirisci, L. and Mezzich, A. (1997) Multivariate typology of adolescents with alcohol use disorder, *American Journal on Addictions*, 6, 150–258.

Task Force on Promotion and Dissemination of Psychological Procedures, American Psychological Association (1995) Training in and dissemination of empirically-validated psychological treatments: report and recommendations, *The Clinical Psychologist*, 48, 3–23.

Tassone, F. et al. (2007) CGG repeat length correlates with age of onset of motor signs of the fragile X-associated tremor/ataxia syndrome (FXTAS), *American Journal of Medical Genetics Part B: Neuropsychiatric Genetics*, 144(4), 566–569.

Taylor, E. (2009) Developing ADHD, *Journal of Child Psychology and Psychiatry*, 50(1–2), 126–132.

Taylor, E. and Sandberg, S. (1984) Hyperactive behaviour in English schoolchildren: A questionnaire survey, *Journal of Abnormal Child Psychology*, 12, 143–156.

Tebbutt, J., Swanston, H., Oates, R.K. and O'Toole, B.I. (1997) Five years after child sexual abuse: persisting dysfunction and problems of prediction, *Journal of the American Academy of Child and Adolescent Psychiatry*, 36(3), 330–339.

Teicher, M.H., Dumont, N.L., Ito, Y., Vaituzis, C., Giedd, J.N. and Andersen, S.L. (2004) Childhood neglect is associated with reduced corpus callosum area, *Biological Psychiatry*, 56(2), 80–85.

Terr, L.C. (1988) What happens to early memories of trauma? A study of twenty children under age five at the time of documented traumatic events, *Journal of the American Academy of Child and Adolescent Psychiatry*, 27, 96–104.

Terr, L.C. (1991) Childhood traumas: an outline and overview, *American Journal of Psychiatry*, 148, 10–20.

Thapar, A., Langley, K., Fowler, T., Rice, F., Turic, D., Whittinger, N. et al. (2005) Catechol O-methyltransferase gene variant and birth weight predict early-onset antisocial behavior in children with attention-deficit/hyperactivity disorder, *Archives of General Psychiatry*, 62(11), 1275–1278.

Thapar, A., Langley, K., Owen, P.M.J. and O'Donovan, M.C.P. (2007) Advances in genetic findings on attention deficit hyperactivity disorder, *Psychological Medicine*, 37(12), 1681–1692.

Tharp, R.G. (1991) Cultural diversity and treatment of children, *Journal of Consulting and Clinical Psychology*, 59, 799–812.

Tharp-Taylor, S., Haviland, A. and D'Amico, E.J. (2009) Victimization from mental and physical bullying and substance use in early adolescence, *Addictive Behaviors*, 34(6–7), 561–567.

Thomas, A. and Chess, S. (1977) *Temperament and Development*. New York: Brunner/Mazel.

Thomas, R. and Zimmer-Gembeck, M.J. (2011) Accumulating evidence for parent–child interaction therapy in the prevention of child maltreatment, *Child Development*, 82(1), 177–192.

Thompson, A.H., Stuart, H., Bland, R.C., Arboleda-Florez, J., Warner, R. and Dickson, R.A. (2002) Attitudes about schizophrenia from the pilot site of the WPA worldwide campaign against the stigma of schizophrenia, *Social Psychiatry and Psychiatric Epidemiology*, 37(10), 475–482.

Thompson, P., Vidal, C., Giedd, J.N., Gochman, P., Blumenthal, J., Nicolson, R., Toga, A.W. and Rapoport, J.L. (2001) Mapping adolescent brain change reveals dynamic wave of accelerated gray matter loss in very earlyonset schizophrenia, *Proceedings of the*

National Academy of Sciences, 98, 11650–11655.

Thompson, R.J. Jr and Gustafson, K.E. (1996) *Adaptation to Chronic Childhood Illness*. Washington, DC: American Psychological Association.

Thompson, S. and Rey, J.M. (1995) Functional enuresis: is desmopressin the answer? *Journal of the American Academy of Child & Adolescent Psychiatry*, 34(3), 266–271.

Thomsen, H. (1996) Borderline conditions in childhood, *Psychopathology*, 29(6), 357–362.

Thorndike, R.L., Hagen, E.P. and Sattler, J.M. (1986) *The Stanford-Binet Intelligence Scale: Fourth Edition*. Itasca, IL: Riverside.

Tian, L. et al. (2006) Altered resting-state functional connectivity patterns of anterior cingulate cortex in adolescents with attention deficit hyperactivity disorder, *Neuroscience Letters*, 400(1–2), 39–43.

Tienari, P., Sorri, A., Naarala, M., Lahti, I. and Pohjola, J. (1983) The Finnish adoptive study: adopted-away offspring of schizophrenic mothers, in H. Stierlin, L.C. Wynne and M. Wirsching (eds), *Psychological Intervention in Schizophrenia*. Berlin: Springer-Verlag.

Tillman, R. and Geller, B. (2006) Controlled study of switching from attention-deficit/hyperactivity disorder to a prepubertal and early adolescent bipolar I disorder phenotype during 6-year prospective follow-up: rate, risk and predictors, *Development and Psychopathology*, 18(4), 1037–1053.

Timbremont, B. and Braet, C. (2004) Cognitive vulnerability in remitted depressed children and adolescents, *Behaviour Research and Therapy*, 42(4), 423–437.

Timimi, S. and Taylor, E. (2004) ADHD is best understood as a cultural construct, *British Journal of Psychiatry*, 184(1), 8–9.

Timmer, S.G., Urquiza, A.J., Herschell, A.D., McGrath, J.M., Zebell, N.M., Porter, A.L. and

Vargas, E.C. (2006) Parent–child interaction therapy: application of an empirically supported treatment to maltreated children in foster care, *Child Welfare: Journal of Policy, Practice and Program*, 85(6), 919–938.

Tjaden, P. and Thoennes, N. (2000) Prevalence and consequences of male-to-female and female-to-male intimate partner violence as measured by the National Violence Against Women Survey, *Violence Against Women*, 6(2), 142–161.

Tolan, P., Gorman-Smith, D. and Henry, D. (2003) The developmental ecology of urban males' youth violence, *Developmental Psychology*, 39(2), 274–291.

Tomchek, S.D. and Dunn, W. (2007) Sensory processing in children with and without autism: a comparative study using the short sensory profile, *The American Journal of Occupational Therapy*, 61(2), 190–200.

Tompkins, T.L., Hockett, A.R., Abraibesh, N. and Witt, J.L. (2011) A closer look at co-rumination: gender, coping, peer functioning and internalizing/externalizing problems, *Journal of Adolescence*, doi: 10.1016/j.adolescence.2011.02.005.

Topping, K.J. and Barron, I.G. (2009) School-based child sexual abuse prevention programs: a review of effectiveness, *Review of Educational Research*, 79(1), 431.

Torgesen, J.K. et al. (2001) Intensive remedial instruction for children with severe reading disabilities, *Journal of Learning Disabilities*, 34(1), 33–58.

Toth, S.L., Rogosch, F.A., Sturge-Apple, M. and Cicchetti, D. (2009) Maternal depression, children's attachment security and representational development: an organizational perspective, *Child Development*, 80(1), 192–208.

Tracy, J.L., Robins, R.W. and Tangney, J.P. (2007) *The Self-Conscious Emotions: Theory and Research*. New York: Guilford.

Treuting, J.J. and Hinshaw, S.P. (2001) Depression and self-esteem in boys with attention-deficit/hyperactivity disorder: associations with comorbid aggression and explanatory attributional mechanisms, *Journal of Abnormal Child Psychology*, 29(1), 23–39.

Trickett, P.K., Noll, J.G., Susman, E., Shenk, C.E. and Putnam, F.W. (2010) Attenuation of cortisol across development for victims of sexual abuse, *Development and Psychopathology*, 22(1), 165–175.

Trickett, P.K., Negriff, S., Ji, J. and Peckins, M. (2011a) Child maltreatment and adolescent development, *Journal of Research on Adolescence*, 21(1), 3–20.

Trickett, P.K., Noll, J.G. and Putnam, F.W. (2011b) The impact of sexual abuse on female development: lessons from a multigenerational, longitudinal research study, *Development and Psychopathology*, 23(2), 453–476.

Tromp, N.B. and Koot, H.M. (2009) Dimensions of personality pathology in adolescents: relations to DSM-IV personality disorder symptoms, *Journal of Personality Disorders*, 23, 514–527.

Tromp, N.B. and Koot, H.M. (2010) Dimensions of normal and abnormal personality: elucidating DSM-IV personality disorder symptoms in adolescents, *Journal of Personality*, 78(3), 839–864.

Tsai, L. et al. (1982) Social class distribution of fathers of children enrolled in the Iowa Autism Program, *Journal of Autism and Developmental Disorders*, 12(3), 211–221.

Tully, L.A., Arseneault, L., Caspi, A., Moffitt, T.E. and Morgan, J. (2004) Does maternal warmth moderate the effects of birth weight on twins' attentiondeficit/hyperactivity disorder (ADHD) symptoms and low IQ? *Journal of Consulting & Clinical Psychology*, 72(2), 218–226.

Turkheimer, E., Haley, A., Waldron, M., D'Onofrio, B. and Gottesman, I.I. (2003) Socioeconomic status modified heritability of IQ in young children, *Psychological Science*, 14, 623–628.

Turner, G. et al. (2008) Restoring reproductive confidence in families with X-linked mental retardation by finding the causal mutation, *Clinical Genetics*, 73(2), 188–190.

Turner, S.M., Beidel, D.C. and Wolff, P.L. (1996) Is behavioral inhibition related to the anxiety disorders? *Clinical Psychology Review*, 16, 157–172.

Tuvblad, C., Grann, M. and Lichtenstein, P. (2006) Heritability for adolescent antisocial behavior differs with socioeconomic status: gene-environment interaction, *Journal of Child Psychology and Psychiatry*, 47(7), 734–743.

Twenge, J.M. and Nolen-Hoeksema, S. (2002) Age, gender, race, socioeconomic status and birth cohort difference on the children's depression inventory: a meta-analysis, *Journal of Abnormal Psychology*, 111(4), 578–588.

Ueland, T. and Rund, B. (2005) Cognitive remediation for adolescents with early onset psychosis: a 1-year follow-up study, *Acta Psychiatrica Scandinavica*, 111(3), 193–201.

Umbarger, C.C. (1983) *Structural Family Therapy*. New York: Grune & Stratton.

Underwood, M.K. (2003) *Social Aggression among Girls*. New York: Guilford.

Ungar, M. (2008) Resilience across cultures, *British Journal of Social Work*, 38(2), 218–235.

Ungar, M. (2010) Families as navigators and negotiators: facilitating culturally and contextually specific expression of resilience, *Family Process*, 9, 421–435.

United Nations (1989) *Adoption of a Convention on the Rights of the Child (U.N. document No. A/44/736)*. New York: United Nations.

United Nations International Children's Emergency Fund (UNICEF) (2003) *A League Table of Child Maltreatment Deaths in Rich Nations*. Florence: UNICEF Innocenti Research Center.

US Census Bureau (2010) *2010 Census*. Maryland: US Census Bureau, http://2010.census.gov/2010census/data/.

US Department of Health and Human Services, Administration for Children and Families (2010) *Child Abuse and Neglect Statistics*, http://www.childwelfare.gov/systemwide/statistics/can.cfm (retrieved 20 July 2011).

US Food and Drug Administration (2004) Suicidality in children and adolescents being treated with antidepressant medications, FDA Public Health Advisory, http://www. fda. gov/cder/drug/antidepressants/SSRIPHA200410.htm.

US Office of Education (1992) Individuals with Disabilities Education Act (IDEA) *Federal Register*, 57, 44842–44843.

Usiskin, S.I., Nicolson, R., Krasnewich, D.M., Yan, W., Lenane, M. and Wudarsky, M. (1999) Velocardiofacial syndrome in childhood-onset schizophrenia, *Journal of the American Academy of Child and Adolescent Psychiatry*, 38, 1536–1543.

Valencia, R.R. and Suzuki, L.A. (2000) *Intelligence Testing and Minority Students*. Thousand Oaks, CA: Sage.

Valuck, R.J., Libby, A.M., Sills, M.R., Giese, A.A. and Allen, R.R. (2004) Antidepressant treatment and risk of suicide attempt by adolescents with major depressive disorder: A propensity-adjusted retrospective cohort study, *CNS Drugs*, 18, 1119–1132.

Van der Vorst, H., Vermulst, A.A., Meeus, W.H.J., Deković, M. and Engels, R.C.M.E. (2009) Identification and prediction of drinking trajectories in early and mid-adolescence, *Journal of Clinical Child and Adolescent Psychology*, 38(3), 329–341.

Van der Zwaluw, C.S., Scholte, R.H.J., Vermulst, A.A., Buitelaar, J., Verkes, R.J. and Engels, R.C.M.E. (2009) The crown of love: intimate relations and alcohol use in adolescence, *European Child & Adolescent Psychiatry*, 18(7), 407–417.

Van der Zwaluw, C.S., Engels, R.C.M.E., Vermulst, A.A., Rose, R.J., Verkes, R.J., Buitelaar, J.K. et al. (2010) A serotonin tranporter polymorphism (5-HTTLPR) predicts the development of adolescent alcohol use, *Drug and Alcohol Dependence*, 112(1), 134–139.

Van Grootheest, D.S., Cath, D.C., Beekman, A.T. and Boomsma, D.I. (2005) Twin studies on obsessive-compulsive disorder: a review, *Twin Research and Human Genetics*, 8(5), 450–458.

Van IJzendoorn, M. (1995) Adult attachment representations, parental responsiveness and infant attachment: a meta-analysis on the predictive validity of the Adult Attachment Interview, *Psychological Bulletin*, 117(3), 387–403.

Van IJzendoorn, M.H. and Sagi-Schwartz, A. (2008) Cross-cultural patterns of attachment: universal and contextual dimensions, in J. Cassidy and P.R. Shaver (eds), *Handbook of Attachment: Theory, Research and Clinical Applications*, 2nd edn. New York: Guilford Press.

Van Leeuwen, K.G., Van de Fruyt, F. and Mervielde, I. (2004) A longitudinal study of the utility of the resilient, overcontrolled and undercontrolled personality types as predictors of children's and adolescents' problem behavior, *International Journal of Behavioral Development*, 28, 210–220.

Van Orden, K.A., Witte, T.K., Selby, E.A., Bender, T.W. and Joiner, T.E. Jr. (2008) Suicidal behavior in youth, in J.R.Z. Abela and B.L. Hankin (eds), *Handbook of Depression in Children And Adolescents*. New York: Guilford Press.

Van Schrojenstein Lantman-de Valk, H.M.J. et al. (1997) Prevalence and incidence of health problems in people with intellectual disability, *Journal of Intellectual Disability Research*, 41(1), 42–51.

Vandenbos, G.R. and American Psychological Association (2007) *APA Dictionary of Psychology*. Washington, DC: American Psychological Association.

Vanderbilt-Adriance, E. and Shaw, D. (2008) Protective factors and the development of resilience in the context of neighborhood disadvantage, *Journal of Abnormal Child Psychology*, 36(6), 887–901.

Varela, R. and Hensley-Maloney, L. (2009) The influence of culture on anxiety in Latino youth: a review, *Clinical Child and Family Psychology Review*, 12(3), 217–233.

Vargas-Reighley, R.V. (2005) *Bicultural Competence and Academic Resilience among Immigrants*. El Paso, TX: LFB Scholarly Publishing.

Varni, J.W., Blount, R.L., Waldron, S.A. and Smith, A.J. (1995) Management of pain and distress, in M.C. Roberts (ed.), *Handbook of Pediatric Psychology*, 2nd edn. New York: Guilford.

Varni, J.W., La Greca, A.M. and Spirito, A. (2000) Cognitive-behavioral interventions for children with chronic health conditions, in P.C. Kendall (ed.), *Child and Adolescent Therapy: Cognitivebehavioral Procedures*. New York: Guilford.

Vasey, M.W. and Dadds, M.R. (2001) An introduction to the developmental psychopathology of anxiety, in M.W. Vasey and M.R. Dadds (eds), *The Developmental Psychopathology of Anxiety*. New York: Oxford University Press.

Vasey, M.W. and MacLeod, C. (2001) Information processing factors in childhood anxiety: a review and developmental perspective, in M.W. Vasey and M.R. Dadds (eds), *The Developmental Psychopathology of Anxiety*. New York: Oxford University Press.

Vasey, M.W. and Ollendick, T.H. (2001) Anxiety, in A.J. Sameroff, M.Lewis and S.M. Miller (eds), *Handbook of Developmental Psychopathology*. New York: Kluwer.

Vasey, M.W., Crnic, K.A. and Carter, W.G. (1994) Worry in childhood: a developmental perspective, *Cognitive Therapy and Research*, 18(6), 529–549.

Veenstra, R., Lindenberg, S., Verhulst, F.C. and Ormel, J. (2009) Childhood-limited versus persistent antisocial behavior: why do some recover and others do not? The TRAILS Study, *Journal of Early Adolescence*, 28(5), 718–742.

Veltman, M.W.M. and Browne, K.D. (2001) Three decades of child maltreatment research: implications for the school years, *Trauma, Violence and Abuse: A Review Journal*, 2, 215–239.

Verdine, B.N. et al. (2008) Strategies and correlates of jigsaw puzzle and visuospatial performance by persons with Prader-Willi Syndrome, *Journal Information*, 113(5), 343–355.

Verdoux, H. et al. (2001) Predictors and outcome characteristics associated with suicidal behaviour in early psychosis: a two-year follow-up of first-admitted subjects, *Acta Psychiatrica Scandinavica*, 103(5), 347–354.

Verkuyten, M. (2002) Perceptions of ethnic discrimination by minority and majority early adolescents in the Netherlands, *International Journal of Psychology*, 37(6), 321–332.

Verkuyten, M. and Thijs, J. (2006) Ethnic discrimination and global self-worth in early adolescents: the mediating role of ethnic self-esteem, *International Journal of Behavioral Development*, 30(2), 107.

Vermeiren, R., Schwab-Stone, M., Ruchkin, V.V., King, R.A., Van Heeringen, C. and Deboutte, D. (2003) Suicidal behavior and violence in male adolescents: a school-based study, *Journal of the American Academy of Child & Adolescent Psychiatry*, 42(1), 41–48.

Vitaro, F., Tremblay, R., Kerr, M., Pagani, L. and Bukowski, W.M. (1997) Disruptiveness, friends' characteristics and deliquency in early adolescence: a test of two competing models of development, *Child Development*, 68(4), 676–689.

Volbert, R. (2000) Sexual knowledge of preschool children, in T.G.M. Sandfort and J. Rademakers (eds), *Childhood Sexuality: Normal Sexual Behavior and Development*. Binghamton, NY: Haworth.

Volkmar, F.R. and Klin, A. (2000) Asperger's disorder and higher functioning autism: same or different? *International Review of Research in Mental Retardation*, 23, 83–110.

Volkmar, F.R. and Schwab-Stone, M. (1996) Annotation: childhood disorders in DSM-IV, *Journal of Child Psychology and Psychiatry and Allied Disciplines*, 37, 779–784.

Volkmar, F.R., Becker, D.F., King, R.A. and McGlashan, T.H. (1995) Psychotic processes, in D. Cicchetti and D. Cohen (eds), *Developmental Psychopathology, Vol. 2: Risk, Disorder and Adaptation*. Oxford: John Wiley & Sons.

Volkmar, F.R., Klin, A. and Cohen, D.J. (1997), Diagnosis and classification of autism and related conditions: consensus and issues, in D.J. Cohen and F.R. Volkmar (eds), *Handbook of Autism and Pervasive Developmental Disorders*, 2nd edn. New York: Wiley.

Von Soest, T., Mossige, S., Stefansen, K. and Hjemdal, O. (2010) A validation study of the Resilience Scale for Adolescents (READ), *Journal of Psychopathology and Behavioral Assessment*, 32(2), 215–225.

Vourdas, A., Pipe, R., Corrigall, R. and Frangou, S. (2003) Increased developmental deviance and premorbid dysfunction in early onset schizophrenia, *Schizophrenia Research*, 62, 13–22.

Vrijmoet-Wiersma, C.M. et al. (2008) Assessment of parental psychological stress in pediatric cancer: a review, *Journal of Pediatric Psychology*, 33(7), 694–706.

Vyas, N.S., Patel, N.H. and Puri, B.K. (2011) Neurobiology and phenotypic expression in early onset schizophrenia, *Early Intervention in Psychiatry*, 5(1), 3–14.

Vygotsky, L.S. (1978) *Mind in Society*. Cambridge, MA: Harvard University Press.

Wade, T.D. (2010) Genetic influences on eating and the eating disorders, in W.S. Agras (ed.), *The Oxford Handbook of Eating Disorders*. New York: Oxford University Press.

Wade, T.D., Bulik, C.M. and Kendler, K S. (2000) Reliability of lifetime history of bulimia nervosa: comparison with major depression, *British Journal of Psychiatry*, 177, 72–76.

Wade, T.J., Cairney, J. and Pevalin, D.J. (2002) Emergence of gender differences in depression during adolescence: national panel results from three countries, *Journal of the American Academy of Child and Adolescent Psychiatry*, 41(2), 190–198.

Wadsworth, M.E. and Santiago, C.D. (2008) Risk and resiliency processes in ethnically diverse families in poverty, *Journal of Family Psychology*, 22(3), 399–410.

Wadsworth, S.M.M. (2010) Family risk and resilience in the context of war and terrorism, *Journal of Marriage and Family*, 72(3), 537–556.

Wagner, A., Greer, P., Bailer, U.F., Frank, G.K., Henry, S.E., Putnam, K. (2006) Normal brain tissue volumes after long-term recovery in anorexia and bulimia nervosa, *Biological Psychiatry*, 59(3), 291–293.

Wagner, M. and Weiß, B. (2006) On the variation of divorce risks in Europe: findings from a meta-analysis of European longitudinal studies, *European Sociological Review*, 22(5), 483–500.

Wagner, T. (n.d.) Oppositional defiant disorder handout for professionals, www.sbbh.pitt.edu/…/WagnerODD HandoutForProfessionals%5BWiki %5D.pdf.

Waldron, H.B. and Brody, J.L. (2010) Functional family therapy for adolescent substance use disorders, in J.R. Weisz and A.E. Kazdin (eds), *Evidence-based Psychotherapies for Children and Adolescents*, 2nd edn. New York: Guilford Press.

Waldron, H.B. and Turner, C.W. (2008) Evidence-based psychosocial treatments for adolescent substance abuse, *Journal of Clinical Child and Adolescent Psychology*, 37(1), 238–261.

Walker, E. and Lewine, R.J. (1990) Prediction of adult-onset schizophrenia from childhood home movies of the patients, *American Journal of Psychiatry*, 147(8), 1052–1056.

Walker, E. et al. (2004) Schizophrenia: etiology and course, *Annual Review of Psychology*, 55, 401–430.

Walker, E.F. and Walder, D. (2003) Neurohormonal aspects of the development of psychotic disorders, in D. Cicchetti and E. Walker (eds), *Neurodevelopmental Mechanisms in Psychopathology*. New York: Cambridge University Press.

Walker, E.F., Savoie, T. and Davis, D. (1994) Neuromotor precursors of schizophrenia, *Schizophrenia Bulletin*, 20(3), 441–451.

Walker, E.F., Lewine, R.R.J. and Neumann, C. (1996) Childhood behavioral characteristics and adult brain morphology in schizophrenia, *Schizophrenia Research*, 22(2), 93–101.

Walker, J.L. et al. (1991) Anxiety, inhibition and conduct disorder in children: I. Relations to social impairment, *Journal of the American Academy of Child & Adolescent Psychiatry*, 30(2), 187–191.

Walker, N.W. (1997) *Best Practices in Assessment and Programming for Students with Traumatic Brain Injury*. Raleigh, NC: Public Schools of North Carolina.

Wallace, J.M. Jr, Bachman, J.G., O'Malley, P.M., Schulenberg, J.E., Cooper, S.M. and Johnston, L.D. (2003) Gender and ethnic differences in smoking, drinking and illicit drug use among American 8th, 10th and 12th grade students, 1976–2000, *Addiction*, 98(2), 225–234.

Wallander, J.L. and Varni, J.W. (1998) Effects of pediatric chronic physical disorders on child and family adjustment, *Journal of Child Psychology and Psychiatry*, 39(1), 29–46.

Walsh, T. et al. (2008) Rare structural variants disrupt multiple genes in neurodevelopmental pathways in schizophrenia, *Science*, 320(5875), 539–543.

Ward, A., Ramsay, R., Turnbull, S., Steele, M., Steele, H. and Treasure, J. (2001) Attachment in anorexia nervosa: a transgenerational perspective, *British Journal of Medical Psychology*, 74(4), 497–505.

Warren, S.L., Huston, L., Egeland, B. and Sroufe, L.A. (1997) Child and adolescent anxiety disorders and early attachment, *Journal of the American Academy of Child and Adolescent Psychiatry*, 36, 637–644.

Watkins, J.M., Asarnow, R.F. and Tanguay, E. (1988) Symptom development in childhood onset schizophrenia, *Journal of Child Psychology and Psychiatry*, 29(6), 865–878.

Watson, D. (2005) Rethinking the mood and anxiety disorders: a quantitative hierarchical model for DSM-V, *Journal of Abnormal Psychology*, 114(4), 522–536.

Watson, H.J. and Rees, C.S. (2008) Meta-analysis of randomized, controlled treatment trials for pediatric obsessive-compulsive disorder, *Journal of Child Psychology and Psychiatry*, 49, 489–498.

Watson, J.B. and Rayner, R. (1920) Conditioned emotional reactions, *Journal of Experimental Psychology*, 3(1), 1–14.

Watt, N.F., Anthony, E.J., Wynne, L.C. and Rolf, J.E. (eds) (1984) *Children at Risk for Schizophrenia: A Longitudinal Prospective.* New York: Cambridge University Press.

Weaver, S.R., Cheong, J., MacKinnon, D.P. and Pentz, M.A. (2011) Investigating ethnic differences in adolescent alcohol use and peer norms using semi-continuous latent growth models, *Alcohol and Alcoholism*, 46(5), 620–626.

Webster-Stratton, C. (1998) Preventing conduct problems in Head Start children: strengthening parenting competencies, *Journal of Consulting and Clinical Psychology*, 66(5), 715–730.

Webster-Stratton, C. and Hancock, L. (1998) Training for parents of young children with conduct problems: content, methods and therapeutic processes, in J.M. Briesmeister and C.E. Schaefer (eds), *Handbook of Parent Training.* New York: Wiley.

Webster-Stratton, C. and Herbert, M. (1994) *Troubled Families – Problem Children: Working with Parents: A Collaborative Process.* New York: John Wiley & Sons.

Webster-Stratton, C. and Reid, M.J. (2004) The Incredible Years parents, teachers and children training series: a multifaceted treatment approach for young children with conduct problems, in A.E. Kazdin and J.R. Weisz (eds), *Evidence-Based Psychotherapies for Children and Adolescents.* New York: Guilford.

Webster-Stratton, C.H. and Reid, M.J. (2010) The Incredible Years program for children from infancy to pre-adolescence: prevention and treatment of behavior problems, in R. Murrihy, A. Kidman and T. Ollendick (eds) *Clinical Handbook of Assessing and Treating Conduct Problems in Youth.* New York: Springer.

Webster-Stratton, C. and Taylor, T.K. (1998) Adopting and implementing empirically supported interventions: a recipe for success, in A. Buchanan (ed.), *Parenting, Schooling and Children's Behavior: Interdisciplinary Approaches.* Basingstoke: Ashgate.

Wechsler, D. (1989) *Wechsler Preschool and Primary Scale of Intelligence – Revised.* San Antonio, TX: The Psychological Corporation.

Wechsler, D. (2003) *Wechsler Intelligence Scale for Children – Fourth Edition (WISC-IV).* San Antonio, TX: The Psychological Corporation.

Wechsler, D. (2003) *WISC-IV: Administration and Scoring Manual.* San Antonio, TX: Psychological Corp.

Wechsler, D. (2003c) *Wechsler Intelligence Scale for Children – Fourth Edition: Technical and Interpretive Manual.* San Antonio, TX: Psychological Corp.

Weinberger, D.R. (1987) Implications of normal brain development for the pathogenesis of schizophrenia, *Archives of General Psychiatry*, 44, 660–669.

Weiner, I.B. (1992) *Psychological Disturbance in Adolescence*, 2nd edn. Oxford: John Wiley & Sons.

Weinfield, N.S., Sroufe, L.A., Egeland, B. and Carlson, E.A. (1999) The nature of individual differences in infant–caregiver attachment, in J. Cassidy and P.R. Shaver (eds), *Handbook of Attachment: Theory, Research and Clinical Applications.* New York: Guilford Press.

Weinfield, N.S., Sroufe, L.A. and Egeland, B. (2000) Attachment from infancy to adulthood in a high-risk sample, continuity, discontinuity and their correlates, *Developmental Psychology*, 71(3), 695–702.

Weinfield, N.S., Sroufe, L.A., Egeland, B. and Carlson, E. (2008) Individual differences in infant-caregiver attachment: conceptual and empirical aspects of security, in J. Cassidy and P.R. Shaver (eds), *Handbook of Attachment.* New York: Guilford.

Weinstein, C.S., Apfel, R.J. and Weinstein, S.R. (1998) Description of mothers with ADHD with children with ADHD, *Psychiatry*, 61(1), 12–19.

Weinstein, R.S. (2002) *Reaching Higher: The Power of Expectations in Schooling.* Cambridge, MA: Harvard University Press.

Weinstein, R.S. (2008) Schools that actualize high expectation for all youth: theory for setting change and setting creation, in B. Shinn and H. Yoshikawa (eds), *Toward Positive Youth Development: Transforming Schools and Community Programs.* New York: Oxford University Press.

Weiss, B. and Garber, J. (2003) Developmental differences in the phenomenonology of depression, *Development and Psychopathology*, 15(2), 403–430.

Weiss, D.D. and Last, C.G. (2001) Developmental variations in the prevalence and manifestation of anxiety disorders, in M.W. Vasey and M.R. Dadds (eds), *The Developmental Psychopathology of Anxiety.* New York: Oxford University Press.

Weiss, G. and Hechtman, L. (2003) *Hyperactive Children Grown up.* New York: Guildford.

Weiss, M., Zelkowitz, P., Feldman, R., Vogel, J., Heyman, M. and Paris, J. (1996) Psychopathology in offspring of mothers with borderline personality disorder: a pilot study, *Canadian Journal of Psychiatry*, 41(5), 285–290.

Weissman, M.M., Wolk, S., Goldstein, R.B., Moreau, D., Adams, P., Greenwald, S. et al. (1999) Depressed adolescents grown up, *JAMA: Journal of the American Medical Association*, 281(18), 1707–1713.

Weisz, J.R. and Chorpita, B.F. (2011) 'Mod squad' for youth psychotherapy: restructuring evidence-based treatment for clinical practice, in C.K. Philip (ed.), *Child and Adolescent Therapy: Cognitive-Behavioral*

Procedures, 4th edn. New York: Guilford.

Weisz, J.R. and Kazdin, A.E. (2010) The present and future of evidence-based psychotherapies for children and adolescents, in A.E. Kazdin and J.R. Weisz (eds), *Evidence-Based Psychotherapies for Children and Adolescents*, 2nd edn. New York: Guilford.

Weisz, J.R., Weiss, B., Han, S.S., Granger, D.A. and Morton, T. (1995) Effects of psychotherapy with children and adolescents revisited: A meta-analysis of treatment outcome studies, *Psychological Bulletin*, 117, 450–468.

Weisz, J.R., Weiss, B., Suwanlert, S. and Chaiyasit, W. (2003) Syndromal structure of psychopathology in children of Thailand and the United States, *Journal of Consulting and Clinical Psychology*, 71, 375–385.

Weisz, J.R., Jensen-Doss, A. and Hawley, K.M. (2006a) Evidence-based youth psychotherapies versus usual clinical care: a meta-analysis of direct comparisons, *American Psychologist*, 61, 671.

Weisz, J.R., McCarty, C.P. and Valeri, S.M. (2006b) Effects of psychotherapy for depression in children and adolescents: a meta-analysis, *Psychological Bulletin*, 32, 132–149.

Weller, E.B., Weller, R.A. and Fristad, M.A. (1999) *ChIPS – Children's Interview for Psychiatric Syndromes*. Washington, DC: American Psychiatric Press.

Wenar, C. et al. (1986) The development of normal and autistic children: a comparative study, *Journal of Autism and Developmental Disorders*, 16(3), 317–333.

Wenning, K. (1990) Borderline children: a closer look at diagnosis and treatment, *American Journal of Orthopsychiatry*, 60(2), 225–232.

Werner, E. et al. (2000) Brief report: recognition of autism spectrum disorder before one year of age: a retrospective study based on home videotapes, *Journal of Autism and Developmental Disorders*, 30(2), 157–162.

Werner, E.E. and Smith, R.S. (1992) *Overcoming the Odds: High Risk Children from Birth to Adulthood*. Ithaca, NY: Cornell University Press.

Westen, D. (1991a) Cognitive-behavioral interventions in the psychodynamic psychotherapy of borderline personality disorders, *Clinical Psychology Review*, 11, 211–230.

Westen, D. (1991b) Clinical assessment of object relations using the TAT, *Journal of Personality Assessment*, 56(1), 56–74.

Westen, D. (1998) The scientific legacy of Sigmund Freud: toward a psychodynamically informed psychological science, *Psychological Bulletin*, 124(3), 333–371.

Westen, D. and Cohen, R. (1993) The self in borderline personality disorder: a psychodynamic perspective, in Z.V. Segal and S.J. Blatt (eds), *The Self in Emotional Distress: Cognitive and Psychodynamic Perspectives*. New York: Guilford.

Westen, D., Barends, A., Leigh, J., Mendel, M. and Silbert, D. (1990) *Social Cognition and Object Relations Scale (SCORS): Manual for Coding Interview Data*. Department of Psychology, University of Michigan.

Westra, H.A., Boardman, C. and Moran-tynski, S. (2000) Re: The impact of providing pre-assessment information on no-show rates, *Canadian Journal of Psychiatry*, 6, 1–2.

Whalen, C.K. et al. (2002) The ADHD spectrum and everyday life: Experience sampling of adolescent moods, activities, smoking and drinking, *Child Development*, 73(1), 209–227.

White, T., Andreasen, N.C., Nopoulos, P. and Magnotta, V. (2003) Gyrification abnormalities in childhood and adolescent-onset schizophrenia, *Biological Psychiatry*, 54, 418–426.

Whittle, S., Chanen, A., Fornito, A., McGorry, P., Pantelis, C. and Yücel, M. (2009) Anterior cingulate volume in adolescents with first-presentation borderline personality disorder, *Psychiatry Research: Neuroimaging*, 172(2), 155–160.

Wicks-Nelson, R. and Israel, A. (1997) *Behaviour Disorders of Childhood*, 3rd edn. Englewood Cliffs, NJ: Prentice-Hall.

Widiger, T.A., DeClercq, B. and DeFruyt, F. (2009) Childhood antecedents of personality disorder: an alternative perspective, *Development and Psychopathology*, 21(3), 771–791.

Wilens, T.E. (2008) Attention-deficit/hyperactivity disorder and adolescent substance use disorders, in Y. Kaminer and O.G. Bukstein (eds), *Adolescent Substance Abuse: Psychiatric Comorbidity and High-Risk Behaviors*. New York: Routledge/Taylor & Francis Group.

Willcutt, E. and McQueen, M. (2010) Genetic and environmental vulnerability to bipolar spectrum disorders, in D.J. Miklowitz and D. Cichetti (eds), *Understanding Bipolar Disorder: A Developmental Psychopathology Perspective*. New York: Guilford Press.

Willcutt, E.G. and Pennington, B.F. (2000) Comorbidity of reading disability and attention-deficit/hyperactivity disorder: differences by gender and subtype, *Journal of Learning Disabilities*, 33, 179–191.

Willgerodt, M.A. (2008) Family and peer influences on adjustment among Chinese, Filipino and white youth, *Nursing Research*, 57(6), 395–405.

Williams, D., Lorenzo, F.D. and Borja, M. (1993) Pediatric chronic illness: effects on siblings and mothers, *Maternal-Child Nursing Journal*, 21, 115–121.

Williams, K.R. (2006) The Son-Rise Program® intervention for autism, *Autism*, 10(1), 86–102.

Wilson, G.T. (2002) The controversy over dieting, in C.G. Fairburn and

K.D. Brownell (eds), *Eating Disorders And Obesity: A Comprehensive Handbook*, 2nd edn. New York: Guilford.

Wilson, G.T. (2010) Cognitive behavioral therapy for eating disorders, in W.S. Agras (ed.), *The Oxford Handbook of Eating Disorders*. Oxford: Oxford University Press

Wilson, G.T., Becker, C.B. and Heffernan, K. (2003) Eating disorders, in E.J. Mash and R.A. Barkley (eds), *Child Psychopathology*. New York: Guilford.

Wilson, H.W., Stover, C.S. and Berkowitz, S.J. (2009) Research review: the relationahip between childhood violence exposure and juvenile antisocial behavior: a meta-analytic review, *Journal of Child Psychology and Psychiatry*, 50, 769–779.

Wilson, J.C. and Powell, M. (2001) *A Guide to Interviewing Children: Essential Skills for Counsellors, Police, Lawyers and Social Workers*. New York: Psychology Press.

Wimmer, J.S., Vonk, M.E. and Bordnick, (2009) A preliminary investigation of the effectiveness of attachment therapy for adopted children with reactive attachment disorder, *Child and Adolescent Social Work Journal*, 26(4), 351–360.

Windle, M., Spear, L.P., Fuligni, A.J., Angold, A., Brown, J.D., Pine, D. et al. (2008) Transitions into underage and problem drinking: developmental processes and mechanisms between 10 and 15 years of age, *Pediatrics*, 121(supplement 4), S273–S289.

Windle, R.C. and Windle, M. (1997) An investigation of adolescents' substance use behaviors, depressed affect and suicidal behaviors, *Journal of Child Psychology and Psychiatry and Allied Disciplines*, 38(8), 921–929.

Wing, L. (1980) Childhood autism and social class: a question of selection? *The British Journal of Psychiatry*, 137(5), 410–417.

Wing, L. (1981) Asperger's syndrome: a clinical account, *Psychological Medicine*, 11, 115–129.

Wing, L. (1991) The relationship between Asperger's syndrome and Kanner's autism, in U. Frith (ed.), *Autism and Asperger Syndrome*. Cambridge: Cambridge university Press.

Wing, L. (1996) Autistic spectrum disorders, *British Medical Journal*, 312(7027), 327–328.

Wing, L. and Attwood, A. (1987) Syndromes of autism and atypical development, *Handbook of Autism and Pervasive Developmental Disorders*, 1, 3–19.

Wing, L. and Gould, J. (1979) Severe impairments of social interaction and associated abnormalities in children: epidemiology and classification, *Journal of Autism and Developmental Disorders*, 9(1), 11–29.

Wing, L. and Potter, D. (2002) The epidemiology of autistic spectrum disorders: is the prevalence rising? *Mental Retardation and Developmental Disabilities Research Reviews*, 8(3), 151–161.

Winnicott, D.W. (1975) *Through Paediatrics to Psycho-Analysis*. New York: Basic Books.

Winograd, G., Cohen, P. and Chen, H. (2008) Adolescent borderline symptoms in the community: prognosis for functioning over 20 years, *Journal of Child Psychology and Psychiatry*, 49(9), 933–941.

Winters, K.C., Stinchfield, R.D., Latimer, W.W. and Lee, S. (2007) Long-term outcome of substance dependent youth following 12-step treatment, *Journal of Substance Abuse Treatment*, 33, 61–69.

Wirt, R.D., Lachar, D., Klinedinst, J.K. and Seat, P.S. (1990) *Personality Inventory for Children – 1990 Edition*. Los Angeles, CA: Western Psychological Services.

Witkin, H.A. et al. (1971) *Embedded Figures Test, Children's Embedded Figures Test, Group Embedded Figures Test: Manual*. Palo Alto, CA: Consulting Psychologists Press.

Witt, E.A., Donnellan, B. and Trzesniewski, K.H. (2010) Self-esteem, narcissism and Machiavellianism: implications for understanding antisocial behavior in adolescents and young adults, in C.T. Barry, P. Kerig, K.K. Stellwagen and T.D. Barry (eds), *Narcissism and Machiavellianism in Youth: Implications for the Development of Adaptive and Maladaptive Behavior*. Washington, DC: American Psychological Association Press.

Wolak, J., Mitchell, K. and Finkelhor, D. (2007) Unwanted and wanted exposure to online pornography in a national sample of youth Internet users, *Pediatrics*, 119(2), 247–257.

Wolak, J., Finkelhor, D., Mitchell, K.J. and Ybarra, M.L. (2008) Online 'predators' and their victims, *American Psychologist*, 63(2), 111–128.

Wolfe, D.A., Wekerle, C., Reitzel-Jaffe, D., Grasley, C., Pittman, A.L. and MacEachran, A. (1997) Interrupting the cycle of violence: empowering youth to promote healthy relationships, in D.A. Wolfe, R.J. McMahon and R.D. Peters (eds), *Child Abuse: New Directions in Prevention and Treatment across the Life Span*. Thousand Oaks, CA: Sage

Wolfe, D.A., Wekerle, C., Reitzel-Jaffe, D. and Lefebvre, L. (1998) Factors associated with abusive relationships among maltreated and nonmaltreated youth, *Development and Psychopathology*, 10, 61–85.

Wolfe, D.A., Crooks, C.V., Lee, V., McIntyre-Smith, A. and Jaffe, P.G. (2003a) The effects of children's exposure to domestic violence: A meta-analysis and critique, *Clinical Child and Family Psychology Review*, 6, 171–187.

Wolfe, D.A., Wekerle, C., Scott, K., Straatman, A.L., Grasley, C. and Reitzel-Jaffe, D. (2003b) Dating violence prevention with at-risk youth: a controlled outcome evaluation, *Journal of Consulting and Clinical Psychology*, 71(2), 279–291.

Wolfe, D.A., Rawana, J.S. and Chiodo, D. (2006) Abuse and trauma, in D.A. Wolfe and E.J. Mash (eds), *Behavioral and Emotional Disorders in Adolescents.* New York: Guilford.

Wolfe, V.V. (1998) Child sexual abuse, in E.J. Mash and R.A. Barkley (eds), *Treatment of Childhood Disorders.* New York: Guilford.

Wolfsdorf, B.A., Freeman, J., D'Eramo, K., Overholser, J. and Spirito, A. (2003) Mood states: depression, anger and anxiety, in A. Spirito and J.C. Overholser (eds), *Evaluating and Treating Adolescent Suicide Attempters: From Research to Practice.* New York: Academic Press.

Wolpe, J. (1973) *The Practice of Behavior Therapy,* 2nd edn. New York: Pergamon.

Wolraich, M.L., Felice, M.E. and Drotar, D. (1997) *The Classification of Child and Adolescent Mental Diagnoses in Primary Care: Diagnostic and Statistical Manual for Primary Care (DSM-PC) Child and Adolescent Version.* Elkgrove Village, IL: American Academy of Pediatrics.

Wonderlich, S.A., Engel, S.G., Peterson, C.B., Robinson, M.D., Crosby, R.D., Mitchell, J.E. et al. (2008) Examining the conceptual model of integrative cognitive-affective therapy for BN: Two assessment studies, *International Journal of Eating Disorders,* 41(8), 748–754.

Wong, C.A., Eccles, J.S. and Sameroff, A. (2003) The influence of ethnic discrimination and ethnic identification on African American adolescents' school and socioemotional adjustment, *Journal of Personality,* 71(6), 1197–1232.

Wood, J.J., Fujii, C. and Renno, P. (2011) Cognitive behavioral therapy in high-functioning autism: review and recommendations for treatment development, in B. Reichow, P. Doehring, D.V. Cicchetti and F.R. Volkmar (eds), *Evidence-Based Practices and Treatments for Children with Autism.* New York: Springer.

Woodcock, R.W., McGrew, K.S. and Mather, N. (2001a) *Woodcock-Johnson III Tests of Achievement.* Itasca, IL: Riverside.

Woodcock, R.W., McGrew, K.S. and Mather, N. (2001b) *Woodcock-Johnson III Tests of Cognitive Ability.* Itasca, IL: Riverside.

World Health Organization (WHO) (1978) *International Statistical Classification of Disease and Related Health Problems,* 9th revision. Geneva: World Health Organization.

World Health Organization (WHO) (1992) *International Statistical Classification of Disease and Related Health Problems,* vol. 1, 10th revision. Geneva: World Health Organization.

World Health Organization (WHO) (1996) *Multiaxial Classification of Child and Adolescent Psychiatric Disorder: The ICD-10 Classification of Mental and Behavioural Disorders in Children and Adolescents.* Cambridge: Cambridge University Press.

World Health Organization (WHO) (1997) *Multiaxial Classification of Child and Adolescent Psychiatric Disorder: The ICD-10 Classification of Mental and Behavioural Disorders in Children and Adolescents.* New York: Cambridge University Press.

World Health Organization (WHO) (2001) *International classification of functioning, disability and health: ICF.* Geneva: World Health Organization.

World Health Organization (WHO) (2006) *Report of the Consultation on Child Abuse Prevention.* Geneva: World Health Organization.

World Health Organization (WHO) (2007) *Multiaxial Classification of Child and Adolescent Psychiatric Disorder: The ICD-10 Classification of Mental and Behavioural Disorders in Children and Adolescents.* Cambridge: World Health Organization.

World Health Organization (WHO) (2010) *World Report on Violence and Health.* Geneva: World Health Organization.

Wozniak, J., Biederman, J., Faraone, S.V., Blier, H. and Monuteaux, M.C. (2001) Heterogeneity of childhood conduct disorder: further evidence of a subtype of conduct disorder linked to bipolar disorder, *Journal of Affective Disorders,* 64(2–3), 121–131.

Wozniak, J.R. et al. (2007). Neurocognitive and neuroimaging correlates of pediatric traumatic brain injury: a diffusion tensor imaging (DTI) study, *Archives of Clinical Neuropsychology,* 22(5), 555–568.

Wright, B. et al. (2004). Family work in adolescent psychosis: the need for more research, *Clinical Child Psychology and Psychiatry,* 9(1), 61–74.

Wu, E.Q. et al. (2005) The economic burden of schizophrenia in the United States in 2002, *Journal of Clinical Psychiatry,* 66, 1122–1129.

Wykes, T. et al. (2008) Cognitive behavior therapy for schizophrenia: effect sizes, clinical models and methodological rigor, *Schizophrenia Bulletin,* 34(3), 523–537.

Wyly, M.V. (1997) *Infant Assessment.* Boulder, CO: Westview Press.

Wynne, L.C. (1984) Communication patterns and family relations of children at risk for schizophrenia, in N.F. Watt, E.J. Anthony, L.C. Wynne and J.E. Rolf (eds), *Children at Risk for Schizophrenia: A Longitudinal Perspective.* Cambridge: Cambridge University Press.

Yamall, P. (2000) Current interventions in autism – a brief analysis, *The Advocate,* 33, 25–27.

Yan, L.J., Hammen, C., Cohen, A.N., Daley, S.E. and Henry, R.M. (2004) Expressed emotion versus relationship quality variables in the prediction of recurrence in bipolar patients, *Journal of Affective Disorders*, 83(2–3), 199–206.

Yates, T.M., Dodds, M.F., Sroufe, L.A. and Egeland, B. (2003) Exposure to partner violence and child behavior problems: a prospective study controlling for child physical abuse and neglect, child cognitive ability, socioeconomic status and life stress, *Development and Psychopathology*, 15, 199–218.

Yeargin-Allsopp, M. and Boyle, C. (2002) Overview: the epidemiology of neurodevelopmental disorders, *Mental Retardation and Developmental Disabilities Research Reviews*, 8(3), 113–116.

Yeargin-Allsopp, M. et al. (2003) Prevalence of autism in a US metropolitan area, *JAMA: The Journal of the American Medical Association*, 289(1), 49–55.

Yeates, K.O., Taylor, H.G., Walz, N.C., Stancin, T. and Wade, S.L. (2010) The family environment as a moderator of psychosocial outcomes following traumatic brain injury in young children, *Neuropsychology*, 24(3), 345–356.

Yee, C.M. and Sigman, M.D. (1998) Schizophrenia in children and adolescents, in T. Ollendick (ed.), *Comprehensive Clinical Psychology*. Oxford: Elsevier Science.

Yen, S., Shea, M.T., Battle, C.L., Johnson, D.M., Zlotnick, C., Dolan-Sewell, R. et al. (2002) Traumatic exposure and posttraumatic stress disorder in borderline, schizotypal, avoidant and obsessive-compulsive personality disorders: findings from the collaborative longitudinal personality disorders study, *Journal of Nervous and Mental Disease*, 190(8), 510–518.

Yingling, L.C. (2003) Family diagnosis/DSM-IV, in J. Ponzetti (ed.), *International Encyclopedia of Marriage and Family*, 2nd edn. New York: Macmillan.

Yirmiya, N., Erel, O., Shaked, M. and Solomonica-Levi, D (1998) Meta-analyses comparing theory of mind abilities of individuals with autism, individuals with mental retardation and normally developing individuals, *Psychological Bulletin*, 124(3), 283–307.

Zanarini, M.C. (2000) Childhood experiences associated with the development of borderline personality disorder, *Psychiatric Clinics of North America*, 23(1), 89–101.

Zanarini, M.C. and Frankenburg, F.R. (1997) Pathways to the development of borderline personality disorder, *Journal of Personality Disorders*, 11(1), 93–104.

Zanarini, M.C., Williams, A.A., Lewis, R.E., Reich, R.B., Vera, S.C., Marino, M.F. et al. (1997) Reported pathological childhood experiences associated with the development of borderline personality disorder, *American Journal of Psychiatry*, 154(8), 1101–1106.

Zara, G. and Farrington, D. (2009) Childhood and adolescent predictors of late onset criminal careers, *Journal of Youth and Adolescence*, 38(3), 287–300.

Zatzick, D.F. and Grossman, D.C. (2011) Association between traumatic injury and psychiatric disorders and medication prescription to youths aged 10–19, *Psychiatric Services*, 62(3), 264–271.

Zayas, L.H., Kaplan, C., Turner, S., Romano, K. and Gonzalez-Ramos, G. (2000) Understanding suicide attempts by adolescent Hispanic females, *Social Work*, 45(1), 53–63.

Zeanah, C.H. (1996) Beyond insecurity: a reconceptualization of attachment disorders in infancy, *Journal of Consulting and Clinical Psychology*, 64(1), 42–52.

Zeanah, C.H. (2000) Disturbances of attachment in young children adopted from institutions, *Journal of Developmental and Behavioral Pediatrics*, 21, 230–236.

Zeanah, C.H. and Gleason, M.M. (2010) Reactive attachment disorders: a review for DSM-V, http://www.dsm5.org/Proposed%20Revision%20Attachments/APA%20DSM-5%20Reactive%20Attachment%20Disorder%20Review.pdf (retrieved 29 December 2010).

Zeanah, C.H. and Smyke, A.T. (2008) Attachment disorders in family and social context, *Infant Mental Health Journal*, 29(3), 219–233.

Zelazo, P.R. (2001) A developmental perspective on early autism: affective, behavioral and cognitive factors, in J.A. Burack, T. Charman, N. Yirmiya and P.R. Zelazo (eds), *The Development of Autism: Perspectives from Theory and Research*. Mahwah, NJ: Erlbaum.

Zelkowitz, P., Paris, J., Guzder, J., Feldman, R., Roy, C. and Rosval, L. (2007) A five-year follow-up of patients with borderline pathology of childhood, *Journal of Personality Disorders*, 21(6), 664–674.

Zellman, G.L. (1992) The impact of case characteristics on child abuse reporting decisions, *Child Abuse and Neglect*, 16, 57–74.

Zeman, J., Shipman, K. and Suveg, C. (2002) Anger and sadness regulation: predictions to internalizing and externalizing symptoms in children, *Journal of Clinical Child and Adolescent Psychology*, 31(3), 393–398.

Zilberman, M.L., Tavares, H., Blume, S.B. and el-Guebaly, N. (2003) Substance use disorders: sex differences and psychiatric comorbidities, *Canadian Journal of Psychiatry*, 48(1), 5–13.

Zimmer-Gembeck, M.J., Hunter, T.A., Waters, A.M. and Pronk, R. (2009) Depression as a longitudinal outcome and antecedent of preadolescents' peer relationships and peer-relevant cognition, *Development and Psychopathology*, 21(2), 555–577.

Zimmerman, M.A. and Arunkumar, R. (1994) Resiliency research: implications for schools and policy, *Social Policy Report: Society for Research in Child Development*, 8(4), 1–18.

Zimmerman, R., Donohew, R., Palmgreen, P., Noar, S., Cupp, P. and Floyd, B. (2011) Designing media and classroom interventions targeting high sensation seeking or impulsive adolescents to prevent drug abuse and risky sexual behavior, in M.T. Bardo, D.H. Fishbein and R. Milich (eds), *Inhibitory Control and Drug Abuse Prevention: From Research to Translation.* New York: Springer.

Zinzow, H.M., Ruggiero, K.J., Hanson, R.F., Smith, D.W., Saunders, B.E. and Kilpatrick, D.G. (2009a) Witnessed community and parental violence in relation to substance use and delinquency in a national sample of adolescents, *Journal of Traumatic Stress*, 22(6), 535–533.

Zinzow, H., Ruggiero, K., Resnick, H., Hanson, R., Smith, D.,

Saunders, B. and Kilpatrick, D. (2009b) Prevalence and mental health correlates of witnessed parental and community violence in a national sample of adolescents, *Journal of Child Psychology and Psychiatry*, 50(4), 441–450.

Zoccolillo, M., Paquette, D. and Tremblay, R. (2005) Maternal conduct disorder and the risk for the next generation, in D. Pepler, K. Madsen, C.D. Webster and K.S. Levene (eds) *The Development and Treatment of Girlhood Aggression.* Mahwah, NJ: Lawrence Erlbaum.

Zucker, R.A., Chermack, S.T. and Curran, G.M. (2000) Alcoholism: a life span perspective on etiology and course, in A. Sameroff, M. Lewis and S.M. Miller (eds), *Handbook of Developmental Psychopathology*, 2nd edn. Dordrecht: Kluwer Academic.

Zucker, R.A., Wong, M.M., Puttler, L.I. and Fitzgerald, H.E. (2003) Resilience and vulnerability among sons of alcoholics: relationship to development outcomes between early childhood and adolescence, in S.S. Luthar (ed.), *Resilience and Vulnerability: Adaptation in the Context of Childhood Adversities.* New York: Cambridge University Press.

Zucker, R.A., Wong, M.M., Clark, D.B., Leonard, K.E., Schulenberg, J.E., Cornelius, J.R. et al. (2006) Predicting risky drinking outcomes longitudinally: what kind of advance notice can we get? *Alcoholism: Clinical and Experimental Research*, 30(2), 243–252.

Zucker, R.A., Donovan, J.E., Masten, A.S., Mattson, M.E. and Moss, H.B. (2009) Developmental processes and mechanisms: ages 0–10, *Alcohol Research & Health*, 32(1), 16–29.

Author Index

Subject Index

Developmental Psychopathology
DSM-5 Update

Developmental Psychopathology DSM-5 Update

Patricia Kerig and Amanda Ludlow

London   Boston   Burr Ridge, IL   Dubuque, IA   Madison, WI   New York   San Francisco
St. Louis   Bangkok   Bogotá   Caracas   Kuala Lumpur   Lisbon   Madrid   Mexico City
Milan   Montreal   New Delhi   Santiago   Seoul   Singapore   Sydney   Taipei   Toronto

Developmental Psychopathology DSM-5 Update

Patricia Kerig and Amanda Ludlow
ISBN-13 9780077170738
ISBN-10 0077170733

Published by McGraw-Hill Education
Shoppenhangers Road
Maidenhead
Berkshire
SL6 2QL
Telephone: 44 (0) 1628 502 500
Fax: 44 (0) 1628 770 224
Website: www.mcgraw-hill.co.uk

British Library Cataloguing in Publication Data
A catalogue record for this book is available from the British Library

Library of Congress Cataloging in Publication Data
The Library of Congress data for this book has been applied for from the Library of Congress

Head of Content and Digital Product: Natalie Jacobs
Content Product Manager: Alison Davis
Marketing Manager: Geeta Kumar

Text Design by HL Studios
Cover design by Ego Creative

Brief Table of Contents

A Note on Chapter Numbering:

The chapter numbers in this supplement directly correspond to those in Kerig, Ludlow & Wenar, *Developmental Psychology* 6th Edition. The supplement is designed to be used directly alongside the main product. Chapters 1, 2, 14, 15 and 16 do not have corresponding supplement chapters as the DSM-5 update does not impact them.

Detailed Table of Contents

CHAPTER 03

The Development and the Role of the DSM-5

This section accompanies chapter 3 in Kerig, Ludlow & Wenar (2012), *Developmental Psychopathology*, 6th Edition. McGraw-Hill Education.

Chapter contents

Brief History

The Diagnostic and Statistical Manual of Mental Disorders, in its fifth edition, was released in May 2013. Fourteen years in the writing and 20 years since it had its last big revision, the DSM-5 has seen its biggest overhaul to date of the diagnostic criteria for a range of mental disorders.

The DSM was created to enable mental health professionals to communicate using a common diagnostic language. An initial draft entitled *Statistical Manual for the Use of Institutions for the Insane* was published in 1917, primarily for gathering statistics across mental hospitals. It had just 22 diagnoses included. The first publication of the DSM was in 1952, initially as a guide to treat US service men, but also during a time when there was an increasing push against the idea of treating people in institutions. The first version had many concepts and suggestions that would be deemed shocking by today's standards. For example, homosexuality was listed as a "sociopathic personality disorder" and remained so until 1973. Autistic spectrum disorders were also thought to be a type of childhood schizophrenia. As our understanding of mental health evolves our understanding improves, therefore the DSM is periodically updated to reflect this new knowledge. In each revision, mental health conditions that are no longer considered valid are removed, while newly defined conditions are added. Table 3.1 charts some of the key changes that have occurred throughout previous versions of the DSM.

The Purpose of DSM

The DSM-5 is claimed to represent the latest scientific knowledge and this version has been praised for having more empirical evidence to test classifications than any of the previous versions. However caution is raised that there

TABLE 3.1 American Psychiatric Association's Diagnostic and Statistical Manual of Mental Disorders

1952 DSM	Featured descriptions of 106 disorders, which were referred to as "reactions." Disorders also were split into two groups based on causality.
1968 DSM-II	Only minor changes from the first edition. It increased the number of disorders to 182 and eliminated the term "reactions" because it implied causality and referred to psychoanalysis.
1980 DSM III	DSM-III saw major changes. Empiricism approach adopted instead of the previous psychodynamic perspective. Manual expanded to 494 pages with 265 diagnostic categories. Acknowledgement that biology and genetics played a key role in mental disorders.
1994 DSM-IV	There was another increase in the number of disorders (over 300). In order for disorders to be included, they had to have more empirical research to substantiate the diagnosis.
2000 DSM-IV-TR	The disorders remained unchanged from the DSM-IV. Only the background information, such as prevalence and familial patterns, was updated to reflect current research.
2013 DSM-5	A number of significant changes made in the newest version. Attempt to make the new diagnostic symptom be compatible with ICD10 (International Classification of Diseases) and ICD-11 (expected in 2015). Future revisions will be made online

are many factors that drive diagnosis aside from symptoms of the disorder. For example, changes in diagnosis criteria can be influenced by academics promoting a theory or a favourable diagnosis, clinicians wanting more predictable results, and the media (Paris, 2013).

DSM-5 Task Force

The DSM-5 task force and 13 working groups involved more than 160 leading mental health and medical professionals from 16 different countries, all renowned in their field. There were 28 task force members who over saw the entire project, whilst members of work groups brought specific expertise in their subgroup areas. The work force members between them represented 90 academic and mental health institutions and included amongst them psychiatrists, psychologists, neurologists, statisticians and even representatives from family members. Each work group's mandate (amongst which included ADHD, childhood and adolescence, neurodevelopmental, personality and eating), was to review existing literature, prepare new sets of criteria and to field test them. In addition there were 300 external advisors brought in to provide additional knowledge and expertise to the work groups. Two independent panels (a scientific review committee, and a clinical and public health committee) who were entrusted to review proposed content, open public feedback on three drafts to shape better versions, and finally thousands of clinicians who tested the proposed criteria for feasibility, clinical utility and responsiveness to change.

Despite the impressive number and range of people contributing to the creation of the DSM-5, the individuals involved have not escaped criticism. In particular, concern has been raised over conflict of interest and links between the pharmaceutical industry and the DSM-5 task force. Industry benefits financially from diagnoses that lead to wider ranges of products being obtained. For example, the relatively new category of social phobia in

DSM-IV generated billions in sales for the makers of antidepressants (Lane, 2007). Whilst over 67% of the task force were believed to have direct links to pharmaceutical companies, members of the task force have defended these links, highlighting the need for close association between researchers and industry in order to develop appropriate pharmacological treatments for mental health conditions. However in an attempt to curtail any influence from outside agencies, the DSM-5 process for the first time made it mandatory that all task force and work group members were vetted and they had to have minimal involvement with pharmaceutical companies to be able to participate.

DSM: Its importance and controversies

The DSM-5 is written for professionals to provide a clear list of mental health conditions and their symptoms. It is meant to provide a uniform set of criteria which allows clinicians and doctors to be able to give the same diagnosis to the same set of patients. Whilst the DSM has been adopted mainly in the US and the ICD is seen as its equivalent in Europe, there have been various differences identified in the diagnostic criteria between the classification systems. One of the key aims of the new edition of the DSM-5 was to harmonise more with the impending ICD-11, to make life easier for clinicians in the future and provide more consistency in disorders being diagnosed.

The new DSM is not without controversy, particularly for child and adolescent disorders. Many of the most common concerns raised are the inclusion of new disorders, criticised not only in overlapping with normal behaviours but also the minimal empirical evidence used in justifying their inclusion (Levy, 2014). In each version of DSM, criticism has been cast over softening of criteria. Whilst the relaxing of criteria succeeds in finding cases that might have been missed, it adds to the risk of diagnosing cases that would not have been otherwise diagnosed. This has been a criticism levelled at the new DSM. In contrast, others have expressed concern about the introduction of severity levels, and that those who have milder symptoms for some disorders may no longer reach the threshold required for diagnosed. The removal of the multiaxial assessment, as well as a separate section for childhood disorders, has attracted scepticism by researchers and clinicians alike.

The clinical implications of changes brought in by the DSM-5 for everyday practice remain to be seen as a lot depends on various factors, including individual's clinical training, nature of the specific disorder, setting in which the patient is diagnosed. Below we highlight some of the key changes brought in by the DSM.

Reliability and validity

The DSM-5 claims to have made substantial improvements in validity compared to previous versions and to have been based more on research studies. However the majority of this research has focused around neuroscience and genetics, and less has been based around psychological and social factors which the DSM-5 is built upon (Rodríguez-Testal, Senín-Calderón, & Perona-Garcelán, 2014).

A clear strength of the DSM-5 is its use of field trials, testing new procedures on suitable patient populations to determine reliability and validity. The trials conducted in the DSM-5 included impressively large samples, representative of practice and ratings were done by clinicians' rather than researchers. The results of field trials appeared to show good reliability, although some caution of the results are noted as trials only began in 2011 leaving limited time for replication of effects. In addition the field trials indicated that DSM-5's procedures could be followed by clinicians when treating real patients, but for many disorders reliability in field trials was only marginally acceptable of 0.5 (Kraemer, Kupfer, Clarke, Narrow & Regier, 2012).

Importantly the DSM-5 has emphasised reliability in field trials but far less has been shown for its validity. It is argued that true clinical validity should be shown by course of illness, response to treatment, and history and biomarkers (Carroll, 2014). Few formal studies have shown how clinicians use the DSM manual in daily practice; this is important as whilst clinicians may retain a general idea of criteria they may incorrectly rely on one or two specific criteria to make a diagnosis (Zimmerman & Galiane, 2010).

DSM-5

Major criterion and structural changes in DSM-5

The DSM-5 has undergone significant reordering and reorganizing of content in each of the different chapters compared to its previous

TABLE 3.2 Key changes in organization of the DSM-5

DSM-IV	DSM-5
Axis I • Clinical Disorders • Pervasive Developmental Disorders	Axes I, II, III combined
Axis II • Developmental Conditions • Personality Disorders	
Axis III • General Medical conditions	
Axis IV • Psychosocial and Environmental Problems	Axis IV discontinued
Axis V • Global Assessment of Functioning	Axis V discontinued • lack of content clarity • lack of psychometric integrity

counterpart manuals. Section I is an introduction, Section II a list of diagnoses with criteria, and Section III an appendix of proposals requiring further research. The DSM-5 has 20 chapters that have been designed for patients of all ages. Disorders of childhood and adolescence can be found throughout the manual, rather than being constrained to one specific chapter. Disorders in childhood are no longer listed as separate from those found in adults, as many conditions continue in to adulthood and many precursors start in childhood (Copeland Shanahan, Costello & Angold, 2009). Instead, disorders are arranged in a chronological fashion, with diagnoses most applicable to infancy and childhood listed first, followed by early adolescence and finally adulthood. More emphasis on the developmental nature of disorders is also listed in the DSM-5.

Chapters of related disorders are now likely to be found in the same and/or adjacent chapters. For example Anxiety Disorders has now been split in to three adjacent parts (Anxiety Disorders, Obsessive Compulsive and Related Disorders, Trauma and Stress Related Disorders) in recognition that they have distinct neurocircuitry and treatment (Table 3.3).

Elimination of the multiaxial classification system

DSM-5 has moved towards a non-axial documentation of diagnosis (collapsing of Axis I, II, III) with separate notations for important psychosocial and contextual factors, as well as for functioning (Axis IV in DSM-IV) and disability (Axis V in DSM-IV). The former axis IV of psychosocial and environment problems now falls under the chapter 'other conditions that may be a focus of clinical attention'. Also changed is the need for clinicians to complete a disability rating (Axis V Global Assessment Functioning).

Merging and renaming of disorders

A number of disorders listed as separate disorders in the DSM-IV have been merged in

TABLE 3.3 Organization of chapters in DSM-5

Neurodevelopmental disorders
Schizophrenia spectrum and other psychotic disorders
Bipolar and related disorders
Depressive disorders
Anxiety disorders
Obsessive-compulsive disorders
Trauma- and stressor-related disorders
Dissociative disorders
Somatic symptom and related disorders
Feeding and eating disorders
Elimination disorders
Sleep-wake disorders
Sexual dysfunctions
Gender dysphoria
Disruptive, impulse-control, and conduct disorders
Substance-related and addictive disorders
Neurocognitive disorders
Personality disorders
Paraphilic disorders
Other mental disorders
Medication-induced movement disorders and other adverse effects of medication
Other conditions that may be a focus of clinical attention

DSM-5. Some examples of disorders that occur as a result of merging conditions include Autism Spectrum Disorders, Specific Learning Disorder, Language Disorder and Panic Disorder. In addition some disorders have been renamed, for example DSM-IV Feeding disorder of infancy or early childhood diagnosis has changed to Avoidant/Restrictive Food Intake Disorder of Infancy or Early Development in the DSM-5.

Neurodevelopmental disorders

The Section 'Disorders usually first diagnosed in infancy, childhood and adolescence' have been replaced with 'Neurodevelopmental disorders.' This new category is further split into two: neurodevelopmental disorders with onset in the developmental period and major neurocognitive disorder (Harris, 2014). In addition to a change of labelling in this category, there are many important changes to the disorders covered under this classification. Intellectual Disability replaces the formerly known disorder of mental retardation, and its severity levels are based on adaptive behaviour rather than IQ (Salvador-Carulla et al., 2011). A new category of 'communication disorders' has been added and includes the following: language disorder; speech sound disorder; childhood onset fluency disorder; and social communication disorder. Another new category is 'specific learning disorder' encompassing reading disorder, mathematics disorder, disorder of written expression and disorder of learning disorder not otherwise specified. Additional problems in the areas of reading, maths and writing that do not meet requirements for these disorders are included as specifiers. Motor disorders, including developmental coordination disorder, Tourette's disorder and stereotypical movement disorder also fall under the category heading of neurodevelopmental disorders, with stereotypical movement disorder rewritten to show the importance of the self-injury in individuals with intellectual disability. Autism Spectrum Disorders are also classified under this category and pervasive developmental disorders and subheadings have been removed as separate conditions. ADHD is no longer regarded as a disruptive disorder and is also moved under the neurodevelopmental category.

New Diagnoses

There have also been a total of 13 new childhood diagnoses added to the manual including: Social Communication Disorder; Excoriation (Skin Picking); and Binge Eating Disorder. There has also been a new chapter added on Disruptive, Impulse-control and Conduct Disorders, characterised by problems in emotional and behavioural self–control and often co-morbid with ADHD; this includes Oppositional Defiant Disorder, Conduct Disorder, and Intermittent Explosive Disorder.

Removal of Not-Otherwise-Specified Conditions (NOS)

Not-Otherwise-Specified conditions have been replaced with other specified and unspecified diagnoses. Despite this being one of the most common diagnostic categories in the DSM-IV, its classification has been removed, as in clinical practice it was found to add little to either treatment planning or to communicating the needs of a person with this specified diagnosis.

Increasing the Dimensional approach

When the DSM-5 was in the early stages of preparation, many clinicians called for the inclusion of a dimensional component to the classification of mental disorders. It was hoped that by adopting a dimensional approach, it would highlight that not all disorders can easily be classified into one single category (Polancyzk, 2014). Whilst the DSM-5, like its predecessor, is largely based on categories and clinical judgements to dichotomous questions, there has been a shift to an increasingly dimensional approach to diagnosis. Clinicians are now required to rate a number of disorders on a continuum of severity.

Introduction of Severity Levels

The DSM-5 has introduced severity levels to be able to define the level of adaptive behaviour. DSM-5 does not list mild, moderate, severe, and profound subtypes found in the DSM-IV. Instead, it lists mild, moderate, and severe levels.

The following levels have been outlined to guide the severity levels of some conditions listed in the DSM-5:

- Level One "Requiring support": Social communication problems without supports; inflexibility of behaviour interferes with functioning in more than one setting.
- Level Two "Requiring substantial support": Marked deficits in verbal and nonverbal social communication impair functioning; inflexibility of behaviour is seen often enough to be noted by casual observer.
- Level Three "Requiring very substantial support": Severe deficits in verbal and nonverbal social communication cause severe impairments in functioning.

Reduction in the emphasis on IQ Scores

IQ testing moved to the body of the text in the DSM-5. However, DSM-5 continues to specify that standardized psychological testing must be included in the assessment of affected persons but that psychological testing should accompany clinical assessment. Emphasis is now prioritised to adaptive behaviour. This is consistent with the proposed ICD-11 criteria which do not list IQ test score requirements in the formal diagnostic criteria and instead place testing requirements in the text.

There were explicit reasons as to why less emphasis has been placed on IQ test scores in the DSM-5. For example, there has been a history of inconsistent use of IQ test scores, with a number used to define a person's overall ability and little to no consideration given to their adaptive functioning. Intelligence as defined by the AAIDD (American Association on Intellectual and Developmental Disabilities), and now in DSM-5, highlights that intelligence has multiple domains including general mental ability that involves reasoning, problem solving, planning, thinking abstractly, comprehending complex ideas, judgement, academic learning, and learning from experience. Cognitive profiles are more useful for describing intellectual abilities than a single full-scale IQ score, and clinical training and judgement are required for interpretation of test results. In addition, assessment procedures and diagnosis must take into account factors other than IDD that may limit performance (e.g., sociocultural background, native language, associated communication/language disorder, motor or sensory handicap).

More emphasis on culture

DSM-5 has placed more emphasis on the role of culture, in recognition that culture shapes mental disorders (Gone & Kirmayer, 2010). It has now included a Cultural Formation Interview, consisting of 14 questions. However it is unclear how this will be used in clinical practice.

A scale for suicide assessment

The new DSM is the first to include a scale that is not specific to diagnosis and instead addresses clinical assessment. A scale for predicting suicide is included. It has been brought in to the DSM-5 due to the demand of psychiatrists being unable to determine patients most at risk for suicide. Whilst the scale assesses standard risk factors (previous attempt, social isolation), it fails to offer scientific validity.

Future Editions

The DSM-5 represents an extensive period of work from a range of professionals and has seen some major changes to the diagnostic criteria. Some of the strengths of the DSM have been the alignment to the ICD, and it is hoped that the diagnostic criteria worldwide will be similar from this edition onwards. The DSM-5 has also seen the adoption of more appropriate terminology, particularly for disorders such as ADHD and intellectual disability, and the organization of disorders into different chapters. It is hoped that many of these changes will create a better understanding of the disorder by professionals and laypersons alike. However there remain some concerns over the new diagnostic manual. For example, the chair of the previous DSM criteria has raised caution over the new classification system, believing several of the proposed diagnoses (e.g. binge eating, mixed anxiety depression, risk of psychosis) as well as changes to some of the existing disorders (ADHD, bipolar) could lead to the creation of as many as eight new false positive epidemics of psychiatric disorder (Frances & Widiger, 2012). In contrast others have raised concern that some individuals who display milder symptoms will no longer reach the threshold for diagnosis. One thing is clear, the changes of the new diagnostic criteria will be monitored very carefully, particularly in view of prevalence rates and the success rate of individuals accessing the appropriate treatment and services they need.

CHAPTER 04

Infancy: Intellectual Disability (formerly mental retardation)

This section accompanies chapter 4 in Kerig, Ludlow & Wenar (2012), *Developmental Psychopathology,* 6th Edition. McGraw-Hill Education.

Chapter contents

The DSM category, previously known as mental retardation, has undergone a name change in the DSM-5. The new label of Intellectual Disability (also referred to as intellectual disability disorder) now aligns with the terminology used by the World Health Organisation in the International Classification of Diseases. In addition the terminology is thought to better reflect the deficits in cognitive capacity experienced in individuals with this diagnosis.

With a change of terminology, it is important to acknowledge that there are several assumptions that define intellectual disability and these differ from the term mental retardation. Firstly individual's ability to function must be considered in the context of their environment compared to what is typical of the peers and culture. Any assessment should take into consideration differences in communication, sensory, motor, and behavioural factors in addition to culture and linguistic factors. Whilst mental retardation is often defined by deficits in ability, intellectual disability is defined by both limitations and strengths. The purpose of describing an individual's limitations is to be able to develop a profile of needs to be supported. Importantly with appropriate personalized support over a sustained period, the life functioning of the person with intellectual disability generally will improve (Luckasson et al., 2002).

TABLE 4.1 DSM-5 Criteria for Intellectual Disability

Intellectual disability (intellectual developmental disorder) is a disorder with onset during the developmental period that includes both intellectual and adaptive functioning deficits in conceptual, social, and practical domains. The following three criteria must be met:

A. Deficits in intellectual functions, such as reasoning, problem solving, planning, abstract thinking, judgment, academic learning, and learning from experience, confirmed by both clinical assessment and individualized, standardized intelligence testing.

B. Deficits in adaptive functioning that result in failure to meet developmental and sociocultural standards for personal independence and social responsibility. Without ongoing support, the adaptive deficits limit functioning in one or more activities of daily life, such as communication, social participation, and independent living, across multiple environments, such as home, school, work, and community.

C. Onset of intellectual and adaptive deficits during the developmental period.

Note: The diagnostic term *intellectual disability* is the equivalent term for the ICD-11 diagnosis of *intellectual developmental disorders*. Although the term *intellectual disability* is used throughout this manual, both terms are used in the title to clarify relationships with other classification systems. Moreover, a federal statute in the United States (Public Law 111-256, Rosa's Law) replaces the term *mental retardation* with *intellectual disability*, and research journals use the term *intellectual disability*, Thus, *intellectual disability* is the term in common use by medical, educational, and other professions and by the lay public and advocacy groups.

Specify current severity:
   Mild
   Moderate
   Severe
   Profound

Source: American Psychiatric Association. (2013). *Diagnostic and statistical manual of mental disorders* (5th ed.). Arlington, VA: American Psychiatric Publishing.

Key Criteria Remains the Same

The essential criteria remain the same, and it is still characterized as a disorder of deficits in mental ability affecting adaptive functioning. Symptoms are still based on levels of severity occurring in the developmental period. It is also acknowledged as a disorder that often co-occurs with other disorders, including ADHD, autism and depression.

Name Change

Starting from its introduction in the DSM-III (1980) through to DSM-IV-TR in 2000, the classification of mental retardation (now known as intellectual disability/intellectual disability dis-order), has been based on psychiatry's guiding classification: the American Association on Mental Retardation (AAMR) formerly known as the American Association on Mental Deficiency (AAMD) and more recently American Association on Intellectual Disability (AAID). These manuals for which the DSM has been closely modelled, follows a 'disability' (numbers-based) approach more typical of psychology, rather than a 'disorder' (medical–clinical) approach more typical of psychiatry (Greenspan & Woods, 2014). The DSM-5 decision to change the name represents a shift to seeing the disorder as a more clinical and medical based condition and is more in line with the proposed changes of ICD-11 label 'Intellectual Developmental Disorder'. There is a clear consensus that the new terminology also aligns better with current professional practices that focuses on functional behaviours and contextual factors and is less offensive to a person with a disability (Schalock et al., 2007)

Adaptive Functioning

The term Intellectual Disability originally referred to impairments in intellectual disability, however, in 1959 impairments in age-appropriate day-to-day functioning (adaptive functioning) formally became part of the definition (Heber, 1959, 1961). More recent diagnostic formulations of ID have maintained the requirements for deficits in both intellectual ability and adaptive functioning, including the DSM-IV-TR and the DSM-5.

Similar to that in DSM-IV, DSM-5 diagnostic criteria for intellectual disability "general mental abilities such as reasoning, problem-solving, planning, abstract thinking, judgement, academic learning, and learning from experience," is defined as an IQ of approximately 70 +/– 5 points for error. However, whilst the intellectual ability criteria remain consistent with the previous version of the DSM, less emphasis will be placed on the IQ score and greater emphasis will be placed on the adaptive reasoning in academic, social, and practical settings.

Adaptive functioning in the DSM-IV-TR was defined by deficits as concurrent impairments (e.g., performance approximately 2 standard deviations [SD] below the mean) in at least two adaptive skill areas (i.e., communication, self-care, home living, social/interpersonal skills, use of community resources, self-direction, functional academic skills, work, leisure, health, and safety). In contrast the DSM-5 requires impairment in one or more super-ordinate domains of adaptive functioning (e.g. Conceptual, Social, Practical). The conceptual domain includes skills in language, reading, writing, maths, reasoning, knowledge, and memory. The social domain refers to empathy, social judgement, interpersonal communication skills, the ability to make and retain friendships, and similar capacities. The practical domain centres on self-management in areas such as personal care, job responsibilities, money management, recreation, and organizing school and work tasks.

Changes in Severity Levels

The four severity levels reflecting the extent of intellectual impairment: mild, moderate, severe, or profound, remain. DSM-5 has now also incorporated the use of specifiers instead of subtypes to designate the extent of adaptive dysfunction in academic, social, and practical domains. The use of specifiers enriches the clinical description of the individual's clinical course and current symptomatology, including age of onset and comorbid conditions.

IQ Criteria No Longer Part of the Formal Diagnostic Criteria

The classification of Intellectual disability/IDD in DSM-5 has intended to move away from the excessive reliance on IQ score. Various levels of severity are now defined on the basis of adaptive functioning, and not IQ scores, because it is adaptive functioning that determines the level of support required. Moreover, IQ measures are considered less valid in the lower end of the IQ range. More importance has also been placed on the need to apply clinical judgement in the interpretation of intelligence quotients (IQ) and be careful not to simply rely on standardized IQ scores. This may result in an individual with an IQ of 80 to 85 and autism spectrum disorder being diagnosed with both intellectual disability and autism spectrum disorder. In contrast, applying the DSM-IV criteria this individual would have only been diagnosed with autism.

TABLE 4.2 Key changes in criteria for Intellectual Disability: DSM-IV and DSM-5

DSM-IV	DSM-5
Mental Retardation	Intellectual Disability Disorder Term seen as less derogatory. More in line with the ICD.
Emphasis on IQ	Less Emphasis on IQ IQ is now perceived as less valid at lower end. Seen as insufficient in assessing functioning in real life.
Concurrent deficits or impairments in present adaptive functioning in at least two adaptive skill areas.	Impairment in adaptive functioning for the individual's age and sociocultural background impairment in one or more super-ordinate domains of adaptive functioning (e.g. Conceptual, Social, Practical).
The onset is before age 18 years.	All symptoms must have an onset during the developmental period. Provide more variability in the age in which symptoms can be displayed.
Severity: Mild, Moderate, Severe, Profound; based on IQ level.	Severity: Mild, Moderate, Severe; based on adaptive behaviour. Determines level of support required.

The requirement for assessment of intelligence across three domains (conceptual, social, and practical) will ensure that clinicians base their diagnosis on the impact of the deficit in general mental abilities on functioning needed for everyday life.

Age of Onset

The DSM-5 has seen minor recommendations in age at which diagnosis should occur. For example, "the developmental period" is referred rather than a specific age of onset. Symptoms are required to be present in childhood and/or adolescence. The developmental period can occur up to the age of 18, and is thought to be a better reflection in individual differences in which symptoms of intellectual disability present themselves.

A More Comprehensive Assessment in Diagnosis

Diagnosis is required though both clinical assessment and standardized testing of intelligence when now diagnosing for intellectual disability. Clinicians will be provided with more training in using assessments.

Will the Changes Hold Up to Empirical Scrutiny?

One concern that has been raised as a result of changes to adaptive criteria (adaptive skill deficits to adaptive domain deficits), is how this change will affect children with milder symptoms. Many of the psychometric measures currently used in the diagnosis of Intellectual disability, are used to quantify deficits in adaptive functioning. Papazoglou, Jacobson, McCabe, Kaufmann, & Zabel (2014) tested the effects of categorizing intellectual disability using an existing measure of adaptive functioning (ABAS-II). They found fewer children (equivalent to 9%) to qualify for a diagnosis using DSM-5 criteria relative to the DSM-IV. This was found to mainly affect children who had milder degrees of adaptive impairments.

It is also important to note that whilst less emphasis is put on the IQ, the DSM-5 still mentions IQ and IQ cut-offs. Despite the fact that the DSM includes statements to the effect that neuropsychological profiles are better than IQ scores, there is lack of a clear discussion of the possibility that someone (especially where there is a brain condition) can qualify for a diagnosis of intellectual disability/IDD even when scores are above the current ceiling number.

Remaining Concerns

The new changes bought in the DSM have been largely received as favourable by the academic and clinical community alike. The change of name is thought to be a better reflection of the disorder and is seen as less derogatory than the previous term of mental retardation. One of the changes brought by the DSM-5 that has been considered by many as being particularly positive is the move to greater reliance on adaptive functioning. Less importance is placed on IQ and instead the four severity levels of intellectual functioning, mild, moderate, severe and profound are to be based on the three domains of adaptive behaviour (social, conceptual, and practical skills). Some researchers remain concerned for those individuals with milder intellectual impairment and still caution the need for clinical judgement when interpreting scores from psychometric assessments, rather than a strict reliance upon scores from the current psychometric scale compositions.

CHAPTER 05

Infancy: Autism Spectrum Disorders

This section accompanies chapter 5 in Kerig, Ludlow & Wenar (2012), *Developmental Psychopathology*, 6th Edition. McGraw-Hill Education.

Chapter contents

Autism spectrum disorders is a term that has often been used to refer to a set of disorders listed as pervasive developmental disorders in the DSM-IV-TR, including autistic disorder and asperger's disorder. In fact, the term autism was not introduced until the DSM-III, as previously, children showing symptoms associated to autism would have been given the label Schizophrenic Reaction Disorder. Through the years, the diagnostic criteria have been continually refined and Table 5.1 outlines some of the key changes in labelling of the disorder.

DSM-5

The DSM-5 has produced a dramatic overhaul in the diagnostic criteria, choosing to combine disorders with similar symptoms rather than include them as separate disorders. In the DSM-5, autistic disorder, asperger's disorder,

childhood disintegrative disorder and pervasive developmental disorder not otherwise specified (PDD-NOS), previously distinct disorders listed in DSM-IV, are now classified into one single category called Autism spectrum disorders (ASD). This change has been made in an attempt to provide more specific and consistent criteria to these clinical disorders that share a wide variety of symptoms. Although the term ASD does not appear in DSM-IV-TR, it has already been a term popular with researchers during the last twenty years when describing PDD (inclusive of subtypes).

Table 5.2 outlines the criteria for the diagnosis of an Autism Spectrum Disorder in the DSM-5.

A single category of ASD

The most dramatic change from the DSM-IV to the DSM-5 is the removal of subtypes of ASD, such as autistic disorder, asperger's disorder,

TABLE 5.1 History of Criteria for ASD

DSM-I(1952) and DSM-II (1968)	No term for Autism and Pervasive Developmental Disorder Closest term: **Schizophrenic Reaction** (Childhood Type)
DSM-III (1980)	**Pervasive Developmental Disorders (PDD)** Childhood Onset PDD, Infantile Autism, Atypical Autism
DSM-III-R (1987)	**Pervasive Development Disorders (PDD)** PDD-NOS, Autistic Disorder
DSM-IV (1994)	**Pervasive Development Disorders (PDD)** PDD-NOS, Autistic Disorder, Asperger's Disorder, Childhood Disintegrative Disorder, Rett syndrome
DMS-IV-TR (2000)	**Pervasive Development Disorders (PDD)** PDD-NOS, Autistic Disorder, Asperger's Disorder, Childhood Disintegrative Disorder, Rett syndrome
DSM-5 (2014)	**Autism Spectrum Disorders (A single disorder)**

and pervasive developmental disorder. The rationale behind the change to a single category reflects the low inter-reliability between the subtypes of disorders. Clinicians would often diagnose the same person with different disorders and some would change their diagnosis of the same symptom from year to year (Szatmari et al., 2009). This was found to be particularly the case for children diagnosed with High Functioning Autism (HFA) and Asperger's Disorder (AD), and also for children with PDD and Asperger's. Furthermore, it was argued that autism is defined by a common set of behaviours and therefore it should be characterised by a single name according to its severity. Kamp-Becker et al. (2010)

investigated whether the difference between the autism subtypes is qualitative or quantitative. Their cluster analysis found no qualitative difference between difficulties experienced in HFA, AD and atypical autism. The lack of differentiating features supports the merger of diagnoses of AD and autism.

Deletion of Rett syndrome

Rett syndrome, a subtype of pervasive developmental disorders, thought to map on to unique and identifiable etiology factors, is no longer considered an ASD and has been removed as a separate disorder. The rationale for its removal is that very few of the salient behaviours associated with ASD are found in Rett syndrome. Whilst patients with Rett syndrome who have autistic symptoms can still be described as having an ASD, clinicians should use the specifier "with known genetic or medical condition" to indicate symptoms are related to Rett syndrome.

Introduction of coding of disorder severity

In order to differentiate across the Autism spectrum, DSM-5 has introduced a 'severity' marker based on the degree of impairment. Three severity classifications exist: Level 1 ("Requiring support"), Level 2 ("Requiring substantial support"), and Level 3 ("Requiring very substantial support"). These classifications are split across two core areas of behaviour: social communication (SC) and restricted and repetitive behaviour (RRB). Whilst qualitative differences between different impairment levels are outlined in the DSM-5 (American Psychiatric Association, 2013), actual methods for differentiating between these levels remain relatively unclear. Researchers and clinicians alike have raised concerns over resultant discrepancies between severity categorizations, and how severity should be considered according to age and developmental level. The impact of severity level on services provided also

TABLE 5.2 DSM-5 Criteria for Autism Spectrum Disorders

A. Persistent deficits in social communication and social interaction across multiple contexts, as manifested by the following, currently or by history (examples are illustrative, not exhaustive; see text):

1. Deficits in social-emotional reciprocity, ranging, for example, from abnormal social approach and failure of normal back-and-forth conversation; to reduced sharing of interests, emotions, or affect; to failure to initiate or respond to social interactions.

2. Deficits in nonverbal communicative behaviors used for social interaction, ranging, for example, from poorly integrated verbal and nonverbal communication; to abnormalities in eye contact and body language or deficits in understanding and use of gestures; to a total lack of facial expressions and nonverbal communication.

3. Deficits in developing, maintaining, and understanding relationships, ranging, for example, from difficulties adjusting behavior to suit various social contexts; to difficulties in sharing imaginative play or in making friends; to absence of interest in peers.

Specify current severity:

Severity is based on social communication impairments and restricted, repetitive patterns of behavior.

B. Restricted, repetitive patterns of behavior, interests, or activities, as manifested by at least two of the following, currently or by history (examples are illustrative, not exhaustive; see text):

1. Stereotyped or repetitive motor movements, use of objects, or speech (e.g., simple motor stereotypies, lining up toys or flipping objects, echolalia, idiosyncratic phrases).

2. Insistence on sameness, inflexible adherence to routines, or ritualized patterns of verbal or nonverbal behavior (e.g., extreme distress at small changes, difficulties with transitions, rigid thinking patterns, greeting rituals, need to take same route or eat same food every day).

3. Highly restricted, fixated interests that are abnormal in intensity or focus (e.g., strong attachment to or preoccupation with unusual objects, excessively circumscribed or perseverative interests).

4. Hyper- or hyporeactivity to sensory input or unusual interest in sensory aspects of the environment (e.g., apparent indifference to pain/temperature, adverse response to specific sounds or textures, excessive smelling or touching of objects, visual fascination with lights or movement).

Specify current severity:

Severity is based on social communication impairments and restricted, repetitive patterns of behavior.

C. Symptoms must be present in the early developmental period (but may not become fully manifest until social demands exceed limited capacities, or may be masked by learned strategies in later life).

D. Symptoms cause clinically significant impairment in social, occupational, or other important areas of current functioning.

E. These disturbances are not better explained by intellectual disability (intellectual developmental disorder) or global developmental delay. Intellectual disability and autism spectrum disorder frequently co-occur; to make comorbid diagnoses of autism spectrum disorder and intellectual disability, social communication should be below that expected for general developmental level.

Note: Individuals with a well-established DSM-IV diagnosis of autistic disorder, Asperger's disorder, or pervasive developmental disorder not otherwise specified should be given the diagnosis of autism spectrum disorder. Individuals who have marked deficits in social communication, but whose symptoms do not otherwise meet criteria for autism spectrum disorder, should be evaluated for social (pragmatic) communication disorder.

Specify if:

With or without accompanying intellectual impairment
With or without accompanying language impairment
Associated with a known medical or genetic condition or environmental factor
Associated with another neurodevelopmental, mental, or behavioural disorder
With catatonia (refer to the criteria for catatonia associated with another mental disorder, for definition)

Source: American Psychiatric Association. (2013). *Diagnostic and statistical manual of mental disorders* (5th ed.). Arlington, VA: American Psychiatric Publishing.

remains a cause for debate (Weitlauf, Gotham, Kennedy, Vehorn & Warren, 2014).

Reduction in the number of symptom domains

The triad of impairment of deficits in social interaction, communication, and repetitive and restricted behaviours, have disappeared from the new DSM. Instead the DSM-5 now recognizes only 2 domains of impairment: social communication; and restricted and repetitive patterns of behaviour, interests or activities. The decision to include communication deficits solely in relation to social contexts reflects the idea that the two are manifestations of a single set of symptoms. Merging social and communication deficits into one single domain avoids similar behaviours being counted twice under both communication and social domains, and therefore inflating the number of symptoms present. In the revised DSM, language not employed in a social context has had less importance placed upon it.

A further reason for communication to be removed as a separate symptom domain is partially due to the confusion and importance placed on using the criteria of a 'delay in language' to justify a diagnosis of asperger's disorder rather than autism. Thus, in the DSM-IV, where there was 'no clinically significant general delay in language' there would be a diagnosis of Asperger's disorder rather than autism (Lewis, Murdoch & Woodyatt, 2007). However individuals with Asperger's Disorder have consequential abnormalities, such as understanding day-to-day communication, suggesting it was misleading to say they have no clinically significant delay in language development (Kaland, 2011).

Lord and Jones (2012) reviewed the new DSM-5 criteria and summarized that all behaviours that would come under the old communication symptom domain would now fall into either the social communication domain or the restricted and repetitive behaviours domain. It is hoped then that if criteria are used as intended, that diagnosis rates will not change and that children and adolescents who already have a diagnosis will not need to be re-diagnosed.

Changes in the number of symptoms required for diagnosis in each of the domains

In addition to changes in the number of domains of symptoms, the actual number of symptoms required in each of the domains has also changed. In the DSM-IV, to reach a diagnosis, an individual must show at least 6 out of 12 symptoms divided into the three original domains: deficits in social interaction; communication; and repetitive behaviours. In the DSM-5, seven symptoms are divided into two domains: social communication; and restricted and repetitive behaviours. Social communication deficits now have three sub-criteria: problems with reciprocity; non-verbal communication; and the development and maintenance of relationships, all of which must be met for a diagnosis. There are four sub-criteria of repetitive patterns: stereotyped monitor movements; insistence on sameness; highly restricted interests; and hyper- or hypo- activity to sensory input, of which only two are needed to be met (Wing, Gould & Gillberg, 2011). Symptoms must be present in the early developmental period, but may be identified later.

Whilst the reduction of three to two domains has remained relatively unchallenged with most researchers and clinicians in agreement with this change, the reduction of symptoms across the domains has proved to be more controversial. Debate largely rests on how many criteria a patient should require for a diagnosis. Many believe the new criteria to be too strict for those who are considered high functioning and will restrict the number of these individuals meeting the requirements for diagnosis, who should actually qualify for a diagnosis. Importantly, DSM-5 criteria is seen by many researchers as being more restrictive than the DSM-IV, and it has been calculated that 12% of patients including many females will no longer reach diagnosis (Frazier et al., 2012).

Inclusion of specifiers

In addition to categorising severity levels of a patient across two domains, clinicians are also now required to include specifiers alongside their diagnosis. Some of the main specifiers include: "associated with known medical or genetic conditions or environmental factor' (e.g Fragile X syndrome); "with or without accompanying language impairment"; "with or without accompanying intellectual impairment"; and "onset with regression to be described". These co-occurring specifiers will be used to justify an individual's symptoms severity.

Subtle but important changes

There have been other more subtle changes in the criteria of ASD introduced in the DSM-5. Amongst these changes, the inclusion of stereotyped language into repetitive and restrictive behaviours, as well as the addition of sensory issues into its definition. The addition of sensory symptoms in the DSM-5 includes both hyper or hypo reactivity to sensory input or unusual interest in sensory aspects of the environment. The inclusion of sensory issues has been welcomed by many researchers, particularly as sensory abnormalities such as over reactions to loud noises or bright lights, or repetitive seeking of sensory input such as rocking, humming or watching patterns of light, are thought to be widespread in ASD. They have also been found to be pervasive across age, modality and ability range (Leekham, Nieto, Libby, Wing and Gould, 2007). Importantly in the case of diagnosis, sensory symptoms are easily observed and can be identified even before children have

access to language. These symptoms could potentially be very informative and used as early markers of an ASD.

Social (Pragmatic) Communication Disorder

For individuals who show milder symptoms in both non-verbal and verbal communication but don't reach the criteria required for ASD, a new category in the DSM has been added. This category describes children with social difficulty and pragmatic language differences that impact comprehension, production and awareness in conversation that is not caused by a delay in language or cognition. This new category remains heavily contentious with many researchers and clinicians arguing that children who fall in to this category simply reflect a milder form of ASD rather than a separate disorder (Norbury, 2014; for a review). It could be argued that an advantage of creating a new diagnostic category is that it should indicate a specific course of treatment or educational support. However, concern has been raised about children receiving a diagnosis of social (pragmatic) communication disorders rather than an ASD, due to the awareness that in the past there has existed more funding and intensive and consistent language support to children with ASD compared to those diagnosed with a language disorders (Dockrell, Ricketts, Palikara, Charman, & Lindsay, 2012).

What Will Happen to Those Who Have a Diagnosis According to the DSM-IV-TR Criteria?

Any individual who has received a diagnosis of an ASD prior to DSM-5, will not need to be revaluated for diagnosis, and should still

TABLE 5.3 Key changes in criteria for Autism Spectrum Disorders: DSM-IV and DSM-5

DSM-IV	DSM-5
Pervasive Development Disorders (PDD) PDD-NOS, Autistic Disorder, Asperger's Disorder, Childhood Disintegrative Disorder, Rett Syndrome.	**Autism Spectrum Disorders (A single disorder)**
6 out of 12 symptoms divided into the three original domains: deficits in social interaction, communication and repetitive behaviours.	**Seven symptoms are divided into two domains**; social communication and restricted and repetitive behaviours.
No official severity levels	**Three severity levels introduced:** Level 1 ("Requiring support"), Level 2 ("Requiring substantial support"), and Level 3 ("Requiring very substantial support").
No Inclusion of specifiers	**Inclusion of specifiers**

receive access to the same services and treatments. Whilst some individuals may wish to self-identify with their previous subtypes, such as Asperger's Disorder, the DSM-5 terminology of ASD will still stand as their official label. Only children given a PDD-NOS diagnosis, who would not have met sufficient DSM-IV-TR symptoms of autism, may now need to be reconsidered for a diagnostic evaluation (Hyman, 2014).

Will There be a Reduction in Prevalence?

Population reports from developed countries have shown a consistent secular increase in the diagnosis of Autism and related disorders since the mid-90s (Kim et al., 2011). Whilst some have argued that the increase in prevalence reflects a better recognition of symptoms, concern has been raised that the disorder is being over-diagnosed. The more stringent DSM-5 criteria has been seen as move towards diagnosing more classical cases of autism, as originally outlined by Kanner (1943), in order to avoid over identification. Certainly one of the key implications of a higher threshold of symptoms required for a diagnosis of ASD as listed in the new

diagnostic criteria may be a reduction in the *prevalence* of ASD diagnosis (Maenner et al., 2014).

Will the New ASD Symptoms Hold up to Empirical Scrutiny?

Although preliminary field trials suggest that DSM-5 criteria offers greater *specificity* than the previous version, this appears to be at the cost of reduced *sensitivity* for specific groups, including very young children, cognitively able individuals and individuals meeting criteria for DSM-IV PDD-NOS (Frances & Widiger, 2012; Regier et al., 2013).

There are some concerns about the new ASD criteria including the fact that more symptoms are needed to be present in a child in order for a diagnosis to be given. For example, McPartland, Reichow & Volkmar (2012) have shown in a re-analysis study that there is a significant effect on diagnosis rates for ASD with the new DSM-5. In their study they re-analysed 933 patients who were being evaluated for possible PDDs under the DSM-IV and applied the proposed DSM-5 criteria to their symptoms. They found that out of the patients who met the DSM-IV criteria, 39.4% of them would no longer meet the criteria for an ASD diagnosis under the DSM-5 criteria. There were no differences in age or gender in their re-analysis, however there was an effect of intellectual ability and an effect of what sub-group diagnosis they would have been given under the DSM-IV. Those conditions with a higher prevalence of intellectual disability were more likely to meet the DSM-5 criteria, when compared to those without.

Gibbs, Aldridge, Chandler, Witzlsperger & Smith (2012) found similar results in a re-analysis study. In their study, out of the 26 children who did not retain their DSM-IV diagnosis under the DSM-5, 14 failed to meet the new diagnosis due to insufficient repetitive behaviours present. This shows that children with communication/social difficulties and stereotypical autistic behaviours may still only meet one of the RRB criteria necessary for a diagnosis. Children who do not meet the full criteria, but still present symptoms, may therefore find it difficult to access the necessary support that they need. These studies suggests that those who would have been given an AD or PDD-NOS diagnosis will be most at risk for not meeting the DSM-5 criteria.

Remaining Concerns

Opposition to the changes incorporated in the DSM-5 have, to date, been mainly political, with many families of those affected worried about implications to treatment and schooling if the child no longer reach diagnosis. Indeed, several sources have confirmed that the DSM-5 criteria exclude individuals with mild forms of ASD and individuals who have been found to meet DSM-5 criteria have more severe disabilities than individuals that meet DSM-IV (Matson, Hattier & Williams, 2012; McPartland et al., 2012). Parents and autism support groups alike have expressed their concern

that borderline cases may be particularly at risk from getting the appropriate support such that many of the high functioning who no longer meet requirement will be prevented from accessing relevant services and treatment. High functioning individuals may appear with superficially good social skills, but will nevertheless struggle psychologically and many suffer with co-morbid mental health problems, such as depression.

Another concern is that individuals who currently hold these diagnoses from DSM-5 will likely receive a different diagnosis if re-evaluated. This has the potential to be confusing for parents of children with these diagnoses as well as children and adults who identify strongly with their diagnosis. Individuals with a diagnosis of Asperger's often embrace their label calling themselves Aspies, and strongly object to its disappearance. The loss of this label is likely to cause unnecessary anxiety and stress. In addition the stigma attached to the diagnosis of ASD for some will seem more extreme than the more favourable term Asperger's. Autism has negative connotations due to its association with mental retardation (Posey, Stigler, Erickson & McDougle 2008).

Need for Some Caution

The DSM-5 hopes to clarify the characteristics of ASD by including disorders of similar symptoms under the same category. It is hoped that the DSM-5 will change the emphasis during the process of diagnosis from giving a name to the condition to actually identifying all the needs someone has and the impact on their quality of life. The introduction of severity levels is hoped to help make explicit how one's conditions affects them. This will then help to more effectively identify the areas and support needed for each individual. It is also important to note that no changes in education or treatment have been indicated for individuals who will now receive a diagnosis of ASD according to the DSM-5.

The newly devised criterion does present some challenges, in particular, the challenge in monitoring ASD prevalence over time. With the newly brought in changes to the diagnostic criteria, it will be difficult to determine if any changes in prevalence are owing to the newly revised diagnostic criteria, better screening techniques and/or changes in risk factors. There is also the concern that some children will no longer qualify for a diagnosis of ASD and will be unable to access the support and treatment they need. Future clinical research needs to monitor the impact of DSM-5 carefully in order to establish whether any of these fears have any foundations.

CHAPTER 06

Infancy Through Preschool: Insecure Attachment, Oppositional-Defiant Disorder, and Enuresis

This section accompanies chapter 6 in Kerig, Ludlow & Wenar (2012), *Developmental Psychopathology,* 6th Edition. McGraw-Hill Education.

Attachment Disorders

There are two marked changes in the DSM-5 diagnoses related to attachment disorders. The first is that these disorders are now listed in a new category, *Trauma- and Stressor-Related Disorders*, alongside other disorders for which exposure to a traumatic or stressful event is explicitly included among the diagnostic criteria (we will return to this category when we discuss Posttraumatic Stress Disorder). The second change is that what were formerly listed as two subtypes of Reactive Attachment Disorder in DSM-IV are now distinguished as two separate diagnostic entities in DSM-5: one represented by *internalizing* symptoms and social withdrawal; and the other characterized by *externalizing* symptoms and social disinhibition.

TABLE 6.1 DSM-5 Criteria for Reactive Attachment Disorder

A. A consistent pattern of inhibited, emotionally withdrawn behavior toward adult caregivers, manifested by both of the following:

1. The child rarely or minimally seeks comfort when distressed.
2. The child rarely or minimally responds to comfort when distressed.

B. A persistent social and emotional disturbance characterized by at least two of the following:

1. Minimal social and emotional responsiveness to others.
2. Limited positive affect.
3. Episodes of unexplained irritability, sadness, or fearfulness that are evident even during nonthreatening interactions with adult caregivers.

C. The child has experienced a pattern of extremes of insufficient care as evidenced by at least one of the following:

1. Social neglect or deprivation in the form of persistent lack of having basic emotional needs for comfort, stimulation, and affection met by caregiving adults.
2. Repeated changes of primary caregivers that limit opportunities to form stable attachments (e.g., frequent changes in foster care).
3. Rearing in unusual settings that severely limit opportunities to form selective attachments (e.g., institutions with high child-to-caregiver ratios).

D. The care in Criterion C is presumed to be responsible for the disturbed behavior in Criterion A (e.g., the disturbances in Criterion A began following the lack of adequate care in Criterion C).

E. The criteria are not met for autism spectrum disorder.

F. The disturbance is evident before age 5 years.

G. The child has a developmental age of at least 9 months.

Specify if:
  Persistent: The disorder has been present for more than 12 months.

Specify current severity:
  Reactive attachment disorder is specified as **severe** when a child exhibits all symptoms of the disorder, with each symptom manifesting at relatively high levels.

Source: American Psychiatric Association. (2013). *Diagnostic and statistical manual of mental disorders* (5th ed.). Arlington, VA: American Psychiatric Publishing.

Reactive Attachment Disorder

As noted in the DSM-5 criteria (see Table 6.1) the new diagnosis for Reactive Attachment Disorder is specific to what DSM-IV previously referred to as the *inhibited type*, in which the child persistently fails to initiate and respond to social interactions. The first criterion is specific to the child's interactions with *caregivers*, and particularly notes the absence of normal attachment and security-seeking behaviours, such as seeking comfort and protection when distressed. The second criterion describes an overall *lack of social and emotional responsiveness* to others, as well as a lack of positive affect and pervasive negative emotions such as irritability, fearfulness, or sadness that are not in keeping with the child's current social environment. As with DSM-IV, the key to the diagnosis is that the relational problems are the result of severely inadequate caregiving; hence, the disorder is a *reaction* to a pathological emotional environment. Pathogenic care is evidenced by significant emotional neglect of the child, by repeated changes of caregivers, or by rearing in situations such as depriving institutions that do not allow the child opportunities to form secure, deep, and abiding attachment relationships.

Differential diagnosis

Given the potential overlap in symptoms, clinicians are advised to distinguish RAD from **autism spectrum disorder**. Although the child with ASD may exhibit dampened positive emotions and impaired social relations, the most important distinguishing feature in RAD is the child's history of severe social neglect. In addition, children with RAD do not display the kinds of restricted interests, ritualistic, and repetitive behaviours that are characteristic of ASD. Another important differential is with **intellectual developmental disorder**. Although children with RAD may exhibit developmental delays, what sets them apart is the lack of selective attachments, which

are typically seen by 7-9 months even in children with severe cognitive deficits. A third major diagnosis to be differentiated is childhood **depression**. Although depressed affect is a potential marker of RAD, again, it is the failure to seek comfort and respond to caregivers that differentiates the child with RAD from the child who is depressed.

Disinhibited Social Engagement Disorder

As noted in the DSM-5 criteria (see Table 6.2) the new diagnosis of DSED closely parallels what DSM-IV previously referred to as the RAD *disinhibited type,* in which the child interacts with non-attachment figures in a

TABLE 6.2 DSM-5 Criteria for Disinhibited Social Engagement Disorder

---

A. A pattern of behavior in which a child actively approaches and interacts with unfamiliar adults and exhibits at least two of the following:
   1. Reduced or absent reticence in approaching and interacting with unfamiliar adults.
   2. Overly familiar verbal or physical behavior (that is not consistent with culturally sanctioned and with age-appropriate social boundaries).
   3. Diminished or absent checking back with adult caregiver after venturing away, even in unfamiliar settings.
   4. Willingness to go off with an unfamiliar adult with minimal or no hesitation.
B. The behaviors in Criterion A are not limited to impulsivity (as in attention-deficit/hyperactivity disorder) but include socially disinhibited behavior.
C. The child has experienced a pattern of extremes of insufficient care as evidenced by at least one of the following:
   1. Social neglect or deprivation in the form of persistent lack of having basic emotional needs for comfort, stimulation, and affection met by caregiving adults.
   2. Repeated changes of primary caregivers that limit opportunities to form stable attachments (e.g., frequent changes in foster care).
   3. Rearing in unusual settings that severely limit opportunities to form selective attachments (e.g., institutions with high child-to-caregiver ratios).
D. The care in Criterion C is presumed to be responsible for the disturbed behavior in Criterion A (e.g., the disturbances in Criterion A began following the pathogenic care in Criterion C).
E. The child has a developmental age of at least 9 months.

Specify if:
   Persistent: The disorder has been present for more than 12 months.

Specify current severity:
   Disinhibited social engagement disorder is specified as **severe** when the child exhibits all symptoms of the disorder, with each symptom manifesting at relatively high levels.

Source: American Psychiatric Association. (2013). *Diagnostic and statistical manual of mental disorders* (5th ed.). Arlington, VA: American Psychiatric Publishing.

manner that is overly familiar. In contrast to the appropriate caution the securely attached child shows to strangers, clearly differentiating unfamiliar adults from the caregivers who provide a "safe base", the child with DSED relates to every adult in an equally friendly and incautious manner. As noted in Table 6.2, the first criterion requires the child to demonstrate this kind of behaviour in at least two of four ways, whether through a lack of appropriate reticence in approaching strangers, overly familiar behaviour (e.g., climbing into a stranger's lap, sharing highly personal information), an absence of the "checking back" behaviour that characterizes the secure child's way of modulating distance from the caregiver, and a willingness to go off with unfamiliar adults. All of these behaviours indicate a child who is not making the important distinction between attachment figures and unfamiliar adults. The second criterion emphasizes that this behaviour is not a result of impulsivity only but, as the third criterion explicitly requires, must be due to insufficient caregiving as evidenced by social deprivation, frequent changes of caregiver, or institutional rearing.

Differential diagnosis

As noted above, the main diagnosis from which DSED needs to be differentiated is **Attention-deficit/hyperactivity disorder** due to their mutual association with impulsive behaviour. However, the child with DSED will not show hyperactivity or difficulties with attention.

Will the two distinct disorders hold up to empirical scrutiny?

Internalising and externalising disorders are diametrical opposites; a child who internalises withholds and inhibits their emotional expression, whereas a child who externalises exhibits their emotions with little control. This difference in internalising and externalising behaviour is an integral dissociating

factor in the separation of the two disorders. Disinhibited social engagement disorder has similarities to Attention Deficit Hyperactivity Disorder (ADHD) whereas reactive attachment disorder seems to have more similarities with internalising disorders, such as anxiety disorders.

Importantly, they both appear to have different developmental trajectories. Whilst only a small amount of research is currently present which explores the continuation of the disorders into later childhood and adolescence, but it is suggested that disinhibited social engagement disorder is more persistent through a child's later life than reactive attachment disorder (Zeanah and Gleason, 2010). There is limited evidence present which specifically investigates which treatment options are best for the attachment disorders but there is suggestion that reactive attachment disorder can be responsive to enhanced care giving and therapies (Hanson and Spratt, 2000). Disinhibited social engagement disorder is however, less responsive to enhanced care-giving.

Oppositional-Defiant Disorder

Definition and Characteristics

In the DSM-5, the diagnosis of Oppositional-Defiant Disorder (ODD) is included in the category of *Disruptive, Impulse-Control, and Conduct Disorders*. The key criteria are not substantially changed from the previous edition of DSM but are organized into subcategories in a helpful way so as to allow the clinician to more readily identify the type of oppositional behaviour being exhibited: *angry/irritable mood; argumentative/defiant behaviour;* or *vindictiveness*. In addition, there is a specifier for severity indicating that the disorder is *mild* (symptoms are confined to a single setting), *moderate* (symptoms are present in at

TABLE 6.3 DSM-5 Criteria for Oppositional-Defiant Disorder

A. A pattern of angry/irritable mood, argumentative/defiant behavior, or vindictiveness lasting at least 6 months as evidenced by at least four symptoms from any of the following categories, and exhibited during interaction with at least one individual who is not a sibling.

Angry/Irritable Mood
1. Often loses temper.
2. Is often touchy or easily annoyed.
3. Is often angry and resentful.

Argumentative/Defiant Behavior
4. Often argues with authority figures or, for children and adolescents, with adults.
5. Often actively defies or refuses to comply with requests from authority figures or with rules.
6. Often deliberately annoys others.
7. Often blames others for his or her mistakes or misbehavior.

Vindictiveness
8. Has been spiteful or vindictive at least twice within the past 6 months.

Note: The persistence and frequency of these behaviors should be used to distinguish a behavior that is within normal limits from a behavior that is symptomatic. For children younger than 5 years, the behavior should occur on most days for a period of at least 6 months unless otherwise noted (Criterion A8). For individuals 5 years or older, the behavior should occur at least once per week for at least 6 months, unless otherwise noted (Criterion A8). While these frequency criteria provide guidance on a minimal level of frequency to define symptoms, other factors should also be considered. such as whether the frequency and intensity of the behaviors are outside a range that is normative for the individual's developmental level, gender, and culture.

B. The disturbance in behavior is associated with distress in the individual or others in his or her immediate social context (e.g., family, peer group, work colleagues), or it impacts negatively on social, educational, occupational, or other important areas of functioning.
C. The behaviors do not occur exclusively during the course of a psychotic, substance use, depressive, or bipolar disorder. Also, the criteria are not met for disruptive mood dysregulation disorder.

Specify current severity:
   Mild: Symptoms are confined to only one setting (e.g., at home, at school, at work, with peers).
   Moderate: Some symptoms are present in at least two settings.
   Severe: Some symptoms are present in three or more settings.

Source: American Psychiatric Association. (2013). *Diagnostic and statistical manual of mental disorders* (5th ed.). Arlington, VA: American Psychiatric Publishing.

least two settings) or *severe* (symptoms are present in three of more settings).

Exclusion criteria removed

In the DSM-5 the exclusion criterion for conduct disorder has been removed (Criteria D in DSM-IV). The rationale behind this change is that the diagnosis of ODD, when controlling for co-morbid CD, was still able to predict comorbidity with several mood disorders and specific behavioral outcomes (Stringaris & Goodman, 2009).

Guidelines provided on how to differentiate the condition from typically developing children

Given that many behaviors associated with symptoms of oppositional defiant disorder occur commonly in normally developing children and adolescents, a note has been added to the criteria to provide guidance on the frequency typically needed for a behavior to be considered symptomatic of the disorder. The criteria will indicate that symptoms must be present more than once a week to distinguish the diagnosis from symptoms common to normally developing children and adolescents. For children under 5 years of age, the behaviour should occur most days for a period of at least six months, with the exception of 'vindictiveness'. For individuals 5 years or older, the behaviour should occur at least once per week for at least six months, again with the exception of 'vindictiveness.'

Addition of severity ratings

A severity rating has been added to the criteria to reflect research showing that the degree of pervasiveness of symptoms across settings is an important indicator of severity (Frick & Nigg, 2012).

Current controversies

Following the release of the DSM-5, some concerns remain. As children grow and change, it is natural for them to go through periods of rebelliousness and opposition to authority. Children are expected to display labile moods, hostility, and attempts to flout the control of authorities, particularly during those times known as the terrible twos and adolescence. Research has shown that children as young as 3 or 4 can have externalizing problems that are abnormal for their age (Bates, Bayles, Bennett, Ridge & Brown, 1991). The fact that children as young as 3 or 4 can present abnormal opposition and conduct problems reveals the importance of understanding the unique presentation of these behaviors at various ages, and that these unique presentations should be accounted for in future criteria for ODD and CD.

There also needs to be more research undertaken to understand the presentation of ODD across genders, as research to date has focused too heavily around the idea that aggression is more common in males as identified by more masculine forms of aggression: physical harm, and/or threats of psychical harm (Keenan, Loeber & Green, 1999, Webster-Stratton, 1996). More understanding on aggressive behaviours in females needs to be carried out as not only are more females being found to display similar levels of aggression as males, but it is possible that lack of understanding of aggression in females is leading to under diagnosis of ODD in females. Finally whilst the DSM-5 attempts to control for effects of culture, ODD is one disorder that is particularly influenced by this factor. Different cultures can have highly contrasting expectations of children depending on the sex or age the child. For example many religiously conservative families expect their daughters to stay at home and raise children rather than continuing with further education or careers. Even different generations can add complexity to the situation. There still needs to further understanding on how culture may impact on the development of ODD.

Enuresis

Enuresis and Encopresis disorders have been reclassified and moved into a new group of disorders called Elimination Disorders. Enuresis is the persistent inability to control urination that is not consistent with one's development age. In contrast to the DSM-IV, DSM-5 recognizes the different subtypes of enuresis and their different clinical symptoms. The three main types of enuresis are nocturnal (night-time) only, diurnal (daytime) only, and nocturnal and diurnal. Nocturnal enuresis is more common in boys. Elimination often takes place in the first one third of the night, which could be caused by behavior or an underlying physical issue. Diurnal enuresis is more likely to happen in the afternoon when a child is at school or with playmates, and thus can be a source of embarrassment and teasing from peers. No other changes from the DSM-IV criteria are noted. As can be seen in Table 6.4, the criteria for the diagnosis of Enuresis remain

TABLE 6.4 DSM-5 Criteria for Enuresis

A. Repeated voiding of urine into bed or clothes, whether involuntary or intentional.
B. The behavior is clinically significant as manifested by either a frequency of at least twice a week for at least 3 consecutive months or the presence of clinically significant distress or impairment in social, academic (occupational), or other important areas of functioning.
C. Chronological age is at least 5 years (or equivalent developmental level).
D. The behavior is not attributable to the physiological effects of a substance (e.g., a diuretic, an antipsychotic medication) or another medical condition (e.g., diabetes, spina bifida, a seizure disorder).

Specify whether:
   Nocturnal only: Passage of urine only during nighttime sleep.
   Diurnal only: Passage of urine during waking hours.
   Nocturnal and diurnal: A combination of the two subtypes above.

largely unchanged in the transition from DSM-IV to DSM-5.

Potential Implications of the New DSM-5 Criteria

There have been few changes to the criteria for the diagnoses that are covered in the present section. The most marked change has been the placement of the two attachment-related disorders into a new category that emphasizes their origins in the adverse experience of grossly inadequate caregiving, and the division of the former two subtypes of RAD into two separate disorders. Given the way in which these two new disorders closely parallel the definitions of the previously-existing subtypes of RAD, this is not a change that will likely have a dramatic impact. However, given the marked difference between the two presentations—one characterized by internalizing and the other by externalizing—distinguishing them into two separate disorders may provide for increased diagnostic clarity and sharpen clinicians' ability to identify those children whose response to pathological caregiving take one of these two different forms.

CHAPTER 07

The Preschool Period: Attention Deficit/ Hyperactivity and Learning Disorders

This section accompanies chapter 7 in Kerig, Ludlow & Wenar (2012), *Developmental Psychopathology*, 6th Edition. McGraw-Hill Education.

Chapter contents

Attention Deficit/ Hyperactivity Disorder

ADHD is one of the most studied childhood disorders and yet is also one of the most controversial. Whilst the basic core symptoms of inattention, hyperactivity, and impulsivity have remained fairly consistent over time, the specific diagnostic criteria have changed to conform to the conceptual change. Key changes in the labelling are outlined in Table 7.1.

DSM-5

DSM-5 has removed the chapter with all diagnoses usually first made in infancy, childhood, or adolescence. As a result of this change, ADHD has been classified as a neuro-developmental disorder, reflecting brain developmental correlates with ADHD. Many of the

TABLE 7.1 History of Criteria for ADHD

DSM-II (1968)	**Hyper-kinetic reaction of childhood disorder** Lack of clarity over association with brain damage led to label that was behaviourally descriptive.
DSM-III (1980)	**Attention-Deficit Disorder** Inattention considered to be the primary deficit.
DSM-III-R (1987)	**Attention-Deficit/ Hyperactivity Disorder** Inattention and Hyperactivity both seen as important.
DSM-IV (1994) **DMS-IV-TR (2000)** **DSM-5 (2014)**	**Attention-Deficit/ Hyperactivity Disorder** Three types: • Hyperactive/Impulsive • Inattentive • Combined type

core criteria remain the same as in the DSM-IV and the symptoms continue to be subdivided into two categories of inattention and hyperactivity/impulsivity. Common symptoms also stay the same and include behaviours like failure to pay close attention to details, difficulty organizing tasks and activities, excessive talking, fidgeting, or an inability to remain seated in appropriate situations. However a wider understanding of the disorder has led to it now being recognized as a lifelong condition. The major changes in the DSM-5 are focused on this new awareness and have seen the diagnostic criteria adapted to allow better diagnosis of ADHD in adults to ensure they get the support they need. Table 7.2 outlines the criteria for the diagnosis of an Attention Deficit Hyperactivity Disorder in the DSM-5.

More detailed examples of criteria

Children must have at least six symptoms from either (or both) the inattention group of criteria and the hyperactivity and impulsivity criteria, while older adolescents and adults (over age 17 years) must present with five. Whilst the actual criteria have not changed from DSM-IV, examples have now been included to illustrate the types of behaviour children, older adolescents, and adults with ADHD might exhibit. For instance, one of the new examples for Criterion A, symptom (f) in the inattention category, will now read: "Often avoids, dislikes, or is reluctant to engage in tasks that require sustained mental effort (e.g., schoolwork or homework; for older adolescents and adults, preparing reports, completing forms, or reviewing lengthy papers)" (American Psychiatric

TABLE 7.2 DSM-5 Criteria for Attention Deficit Hyperactivity Disorder

A. A persistent pattern of inattention and/or hyperactivity-impulsivity that interferes with functioning or development, as characterized by (1) and/or (2):

1. **Inattention:** Six (or more) of the following symptoms have persisted for at least 6 months to a degree that is inconsistent with developmental level and that negatively impacts directly on social and academic/occupational activities:

Note: The symptoms are not solely a manifestation of oppositional behavior, defiance, hostility, or failure to understand tasks or instructions. For older adolescents and adults (age 17 and older), at least five symptoms are required.

a. Often fails to give close attention to details or makes careless mistakes in schoolwork, at work, or during other activities (e.g., overlooks or misses details, work is inaccurate).

b. Often has difficulty sustaining attention in tasks or play activities (e.g., has difficulty remaining focused during lectures, conversations, or lengthy reading).

c. Often does not seem to listen when spoken to directly (e.g., mind seems elsewhere, even in the absence of any obvious distraction).

d. Often does not follow through on instructions and fails to finish schoolwork, chores, or duties in the workplace (e.g., starts tasks but quickly loses focus and is easily sidetracked).

e. Often has difficulty organizing tasks and activities (e.g., difficulty managing sequential tasks; difficulty keeping materials and belongings in order; messy, disorganized work; has poor time management; fails to meet deadlines).

f. Often avoids, dislikes, or is reluctant to engage in tasks that require sustained mental effort (e.g., schoolwork or homework; for older adolescents and adults, preparing reports, completing forms, reviewing lengthy papers).

g. Often loses things necessary for tasks or activities (e.g., school materials, pencils, books, tools, wallets, keys, paperwork, eyeglasses, mobile telephones).

h. Is often easily distracted by extraneous stimuli (for older adolescents and adults, may include unrelated thoughts).

i. Is often forgetful in daily activities (e.g., doing chores, running errands; for older adolescents and adults, returning calls, paying bills, keeping appointments).

(Continued)

TABLE 7.2 *(Continued)* DSM-5 Criteria for Attention Deficit Hyperactivity Disorder

2. **Hyperactivity and impulsivity:** Six (or more) of the following symptoms have persisted for at least 6 months to a degree that is inconsistent with developmental level and that negatively impacts directly on social and academic/occupational activities:

   Note: The symptoms are not solely a manifestation of oppositional behavior, defiance, hostility, or a failure to understand tasks or instructions. For older adolescents and adults (age 17 and older), at least five symptoms are required.

   a. Often fidgets with or taps hands or feet or squirms in seat.
   b. Often leaves seat in situations when remaining seated is expected (e.g., leaves his or her place in the classroom, in the office or other workplace, or in other situations that require remaining in place).
   c. Often runs about or climbs in situations where it is inappropriate. (**Note:** In adolescents or adults, may be limited to feeling restless.)
   d. Often unable to play or engage in leisure activities quietly.
   e. Is often "on the go," acting as if "driven by a motor" (e.g., is unable to be or uncomfortable being still for extended time, as in restaurants, meetings; may be experienced by others as being restless or difficult to keep up with).
   f. Often talks excessively.
   g. Often blurts out an answer before a question has been completed (e.g., completes people's sentences; cannot wait for turn in conversation).
   h. Often has difficulty waiting his or her turn (e.g., while waiting in line).
   i. Often interrupts or intrudes on others (e.g., butts into conversations, games, or activities; may start using other people's things without asking or receiving permission; for adolescents and adults, may intrude into or take over what others are doing).

B. Several inattentive or hyperactive-impulsive symptoms were present prior to age 12 years.

C. Several inattentive or hyperactive-impulsive symptoms are present in two or more settings (e.g., at home, school, or work; with friends or relatives; in other activities).

D. There is clear evidence that the symptoms interfere with, or reduce the quality of, social, academic, or occupational functioning.

E. The symptoms do not occur exclusively during the course of schizophrenia or another psychotic disorder and are not better explained by another mental disorder (e.g., mood disorder, anxiety disorder, dissociative disorder, personality disorder, substance intoxication or withdrawal).

Specify whether:

Combined presentation: If both Criterion A1 (inattention) and Criterion A2 (hyperactivity-impulsivity) are met for the past 6 months.

Predominantly inattentive presentation: If Criterion A1 (inattention) is met but Criterion A2 (hyperactivity-impulsivity) is not met for the past 6 months.

Predominantly hyperactive/impulsive presentation: If Criterion A2 (hyperactivity-impulsivity) is met and Criterion A1 (inattention) is not met for the past 6 months.

Specify if:

In partial remission: When full criteria were previously met, fewer than the full criteria have been met for the past 6 months, and the symptoms still result in impairment in social, academic, or occupational functioning.

Specify current severity:

Mild: Few, if any, symptoms in excess of those required to make the diagnosis are present, and symptoms result in no more than minor impairments in social or occupational functioning.

Moderate: Symptoms or functional impairment between "mild" and "severe" are present.

Severe: Many symptoms in excess of those required to make the diagnosis, or several symptoms that are particularly severe, are present, or the symptoms result in marked impairment in social or occupational functioning.

Source: American Psychiatric Association. (2013). *Diagnostic and statistical manual of mental disorders* (5th ed.). Arlington, VA: American Psychiatric Publishing.

Association, 2013). The descriptions will help clinicians better identify typical ADHD symptoms at each stage of patients' lives (Prosser & Reid, 2013).

Change in age of onset

Using DSM-5, several of the individual's ADHD symptoms must be present prior to age 12 years, compared to 7 years as the age of onset which is listed in DSM-IV. This change is supported by substantial research published since 1994 that has found no clinical differences between children identified by 7 years versus later, in terms of course, severity, outcome, or treatment response. Barkley & Brown (2008) and Kessler et al. (2006) have shown that an age of onset of 12 years of age would capture 95% of the cases in their studies. The shift to the older age is also intended to allow for more accurate diagnosis of adolescents and adults (Bell, 2011).

Often children with ADHD are referred for clinical assessment only when their behaviour adversely affects their academic achieve-ments. This situation is more pronounced at the secondary school level (about 11 to 12 years old; Karande et al., 2007) and more often the children are diagnosed with hyperactive/impulsive type. However, inattentive type is more common in middle childhood and the age changes for the identification of ADHD (from 7 to 12 years old) will result in more children being diagnosed with predominantly inattentive form of ADHD.

Symptoms must be present in multiple settings

One of the least controversial changes is the requirement for symptoms to be present in multiple settings. This was also a specification in the DSM-IV however greater emphasis is placed in the DSM-5 on calculating symptoms across settings from reports of third parties. It has been found that in some places, such as North America, it has been common practice to rely solely on the parent's reports of a child's behaviour (Epstein, Langberg & Lichtenstein, 2009).

TABLE 7.3 Key changes in criteria for ADHD: DSM-IV and DSM-5

DSM-IV	DSM-5
Categorized under diagnoses usually first made in infancy, childhood, or adolescence.	Categorized as a Neurodevelopmental Disorder Chapter. Shared etiology with many of the disorders listed in the category. Emphasizes brain correlates of ADHD.
Symptoms from either (or both) the inattention group of criteria and hyperactivity and impulsivity criteria.	No changes in symptoms, however examples added each symptom to illustrate types of behaviour.
Onset criteria prior to 7 years of age.	Onset criteria prior to 12 years of age.
Symptoms must be present in multiple situations (e.g. school/home).	The cross-situational requirement has been strengthened to "several" symptoms in each setting.
Subtypes.	Subtypes have been replaced with presentation specifiers that map directly to the prior subtypes.
Exclusion criteria of co-morbid autism spectrum disorder.	A co-morbid diagnosis with autism spectrum disorder is now allowed.
Criteria set out only for children.	A symptom threshold change has been made for adults. Six symptoms from either (or both) the inattention group of criteria and hyperactivity and impulsivity criteria (children). Five symptoms for those 17 years +.

Exclusion criteria removed

There is a high overlap in symptoms between attention-deficit hyperactivity disorder (ADHD) and autism spectrum disorder (ASD), with many individuals meeting the diagnosis for both conditions (Rommelse, Franke, Geurts, Hartman & Buitelaar, 2010). In previous versions of the diagnostic criteria, individuals were unable to obtain a joint diagnosis of ADHD and ASD. In such cases an individual was given a diagnosis of ASD and the symptoms of ADHD were excluded (Martin, Hamshere, O'Donovan, Rutter & Thapar, 2014). An overlap of the two conditions has prompted changes to these diagnostic exclusions for the DSM-5. The DSM-5 includes no exclusion criteria for people with autism spectrum disorder, since symptoms of both disorders co-occur. However, ADHD symptoms must not occur exclusively during the course of schizophrenia or another psychotic disorder and must not be better explained by another mental disorder, such as a depressive or bipolar disorder, anxiety disorder, dissociative disorder, personality disorder, or substance intoxication or withdrawal.

Subtypes

The DSM-5 also includes modification of subtype names. What was previously known as ADHD-C (indicating ADHD combined subtype) will now be known as Combined Presentation. ADHD-I will now be Predominately Inattentive Presentation, and ADHD-H will be Predominately Hyperactive/Impulsive Presentation (APA, 2013).

Symptom threshold changed for adults

When making the diagnosis of ADHD in adults, clinicians must establish that diagnostic criteria for the disorder were met in childhood. The requirement of symptoms is reduced for adults to be able to receive a diagnosis (five instead of six). This change has been brought in to help more adults obtain the appropriate diagnosis. Cases of adults being diagnosed are reliant on retrospective diagnoses and so symptom threshold has been reduced to allow for the fact that the passage of time may make the symptoms difficult to recall. However concern has been raised that by lowering the threshold in adults there will now be an increase in the risk of false positives (Farone et al., 2006).

Will there be a reduction in prevalence?

As with most of the disorders that have undergone changes in the DSM-5, researchers have again expressed concerns regarding the possible growth in the prevalence of children with ADHD. These concerns have largely stemmed because of the changes in ages and criteria. Some researchers have raised caution over the new DSM-5 criteria which will possibility inflate the number of adolescents and adults diagnosed with ADHD, but also the number of individuals being diagnosed with inattentive type. Symptoms of inattention in schools tend to be based on difficulty and reluctance to complete schoolwork, which might easily reflect problems in learning rather than attitude and attention.

Historically, changes to the DSM criteria have resulted in increases in ADHD diagnosis, at times as much as 15% (Bastra & Frances, 2012). Therefore it is important to recognise that DSM-5 changes have the potential for similar increases in ADHD prevalence and concomitant psycho stimulant treatment (Coghill & Seth, 2011).

Implications of changes

The decision to categorise ADHD as a neurodevelopmental disorder and to separate it from being categorised with disruptive behaviour disorders, is expected to reduce the stigma often associated to this disorder. It is hoped that there will be less negative connotations of ADHD by other parents and teachers, and will also help remove the idea that ADHD is a result of familial dysfunctional factors.

This may encourage more parents in getting the appropriate support for children at risk from ADHD and will result in helping them to secure the appropriate treatment for their children (Al-Yagon et al., 2014).

Concern has also been expressed about the possible inflation of children being diagnosed with ADHD at a time when medication continues to the treatment of choice. The implications of any misdiagnosis is thought to have more extreme repercussion for ADHD, as children are likely to be offered medication rather than behavioural treatments. Given the inconsistency and confusion over diagnosis, particularly for inattentive types, the label given could have a severe impact on a child diagnosed. If more children get diagnosed then this could potentially increase the number of children using medication regularly. The issue of over-medicalization was raised by the British Psychological Society in the UK parliament in October 2011 and needs to be monitored, particularly as research has shown many side effects associated with the medication administered for ADHD symptoms.

Empirical scrutiny

Farone et al. (2006) addressed the validity of DSM-IV's age-at-onset and symptom threshold criteria by comparing four groups of adults: 127 subjects with full ADHD who met all DSM-IV criteria for childhood-onset ADHD; 79 subjects with late-onset ADHD who met all criteria except the age-at-onset criterion; 41 subjects with subthreshold ADHD who did not meet full symptom criteria for ADHD; and 123 subjects without ADHD who did not meet any criteria. Little evidence of sub-threshold ADHD was found amongst those who reported a lifetime history of some symptoms that never met DSM-IV's threshold for diagnosis. In contrast, the results suggested that late-onset adult ADHD is valid and that DSM-IV's age-at-onset criterion is too stringent.

Solanto, Wasserstein, Marks & Mitchell (2012) carried out a study to identify the appropriate symptom threshold for hyperactivity-impulsivity for diagnosis of ADHD in adults. In 88 adults meeting the criteria for ADHD combined or predominantly inattentive subtypes, they found that utilizing the strict criteria of at least six hyperactive-impulsive symptoms excludes a significant percentage (almost half) of adults who are at least $1.5\,SD$ above the population mean on a dimensional measure of hyperactivity-impulsivity. Their data provides a compelling basis for lowering the symptom threshold of hyperactivity-impulsivity for adults in the *DSM-5*.

Summary

Increasing the age of onset, combined with the requirement to show only symptoms in the past (rather than impairment), may increase levels of diagnosis (Sibley et al., 2013). However, whilst caution is noted, other researchers have argued that the effect of changes in diagnostic criteria would be minimal (eg. Polanczyk et al., 2010). Monitoring of prevalence particularly in adult samples remains a priority following the release of the new criteria, as does the number of cases of ADHD getting appropriate support and treatment.

Specific Learning Disorders

One of the categories where some of biggest changes have been made in the DSM-5 is in the category of specific learning disorders. Previously diagnosed as separate disorders, the DSM-5 has chosen to incorporate a single diagnosis of specific learning disorders characterized by deficits in academic achievement. Specific Learning Disorders (SLD) is characterized by persistent difficulties in reading, writing, arithmetic or mathematical reasoning skill during the school years. Symptoms may include slow or effortful reading, lack of clarity in written expression, problems in numeracy and memory for facts. The category of SLD includes conditions such as perceptual disabilities, brain injury, minimal brain dysfunction, dyslexia, and developmental dysphasia but excludes learning problems resulting from visual, hearing, or motor disabilities, mental retardation, emotional disturbance, or environmental, cultural, or economic disadvantage.

Terminology

An assortment of labels has been used to categories learning disorders. Four subtypes have been used in the DSM-IV: Reading Disorder; Mathematics Disorder; Written Expression Disorder; and Not Otherwise Specified (NOS). Children meeting more than one of these diagnoses are given the label NOS. The ICD-10 uses different terminology and categories. Six different categories are listed in total in the ICD (Table 7.4). The term 'specific' is used in the ICD to signify the deficit is specific to that domain. In some countries, such as the UK and Italy, subcategories of learning disabilities are commonly used and include specific language impairment, dyslexia and dyscalculia. There is lack of agreement in what these sub-categories represent amongst educational professionals. Instead, rather than using terms for subcategories, the education section in most countries adopt the broad term of specific learning difficulties/disabilities to refer to a range of learning problems.

This has led the DSM-5 to also adopt the terminology of specific learning disorders in the hope of providing more consistency between education and clinical professionals and in reducing the confusion over the terminology used.

DSM-5
Broadening the category

Compared to previous diagnostic classifications, the decision of DSM-5 was to include one single diagnosis of specific learning disorders category. The decision was made not to expand upon diagnoses of deficits in math, reading and written expression, but rather include a broader category of deficits that affect a wider range of academic skills. This decision was led by the deep dis-satisfaction of educators, clinicians, and research professionals, who felt the four subcategories did not provide enough coverage of disorders and did not map on to the education categories of special needs. It was hoped that by including one broad category that more children who needed help would be identified earlier.

Specifiers

In the DSM-5 clinicians need to identify individuals who are underperforming academically according to their age and intellectual level. After a diagnosis of a specific learning disorder, the clinician can then provide greater detail of the specific deficit using designated specifiers for each individual case. As in the DSM-IV, dyslexia will be provided in the

TABLE 7.4 Comparison of Terminology in DSM-IV and ICD-10

DSM-IV	ICD-10
• Reading Disorder • Mathematics Disorder • Written Expression Disorder • Not Otherwise Specified (NOS)	• Specific Reading Disorder • Specific Spelling Disorder • Specific Disorders of Arithmetic skill • Mixed Disorders of Scholastic skills • Other developmental disorders of scholastic skills • Developmental disorders of scholastic skills, unspecified

TABLE 7.5 DSM-5 Criteria for Specific Learning Disorders

A. Difficulties learning and using academic skills, as indicated by the presence of at least one of the following symptoms that have persisted for at least 6 months, despite the provision of interventions that target those difficulties:

1. Inaccurate or slow and effortful word reading (e.g., reads single words aloud incorrectly or slowly and hesitantly, frequently guesses words, has difficulty sounding out words).
2. Difficulty understanding the meaning of what is read (e.g., may read text accurately but not understand the sequence, relationships, inferences, or deeper meanings of what is read).
3. Difficulties with spelling (e.g., may add, omit, or substitute vowels or consonants).
4. Difficulties with written expression (e.g., makes multiple grammatical or punctuation errors within sentences; employs poor paragraph organization; written expression of ideas lacks clarity).
5. Difficulties mastering number sense, number facts, or calculation (e.g., has poor understanding of numbers, their magnitude, and relationships; counts on fingers to add single-digit numbers instead of recalling the math fact as peers do; gets lost in the midst of arithmetic computation and may switch procedures).
6. Difficulties with mathematical reasoning (e.g., has severe difficulty applying mathematical concepts, facts, or procedures to solve quantitative problems).

B. The affected academic skills are substantially and quantifiably below those expected for the individual's chronological age, and cause significant interference with academic or occupational performance, or with activities of daily living, as confirmed by individually administered standardized achievement measures and comprehensive clinical assessment. For individuals age 17 years and older, a documented history of impairing learning difficulties may be substituted for the standardized assessment.

C. The learning difficulties begin during school-age years but may not become fully manifest until the demands for those affected academic skills exceed the individual's limited capacities (e.g., as in timed tests, reading or writing lengthy complex reports for a tight deadline, excessively heavy academic loads).

D. The learning difficulties are not better accounted for by intellectual disabilities, uncorrected visual or auditory acuity, other mental or neurological disorders, psychosocial adversity, lack of proficiency in the language of academic instruction, or inadequate educational instruction.

Note: The four diagnostic criteria are to be met based on a clinical synthesis of the individual's history (developmental, medical, family, educational), school reports, and psycho-educational assessment.

Specify if:

With impairment in reading:
Word reading accuracy
Reading rate or fluency
Reading comprehension

Note: *Dyslexia* is an alternative term used to refer to a pattern of learning difficulties characterized by problems with accurate or fluent word recognition, poor decoding, and poor spelling abilities. If dyslexia is used to specify this particular pattern of difficulties, it is important also to specify any additional difficulties that are present, such as difficulties with reading comprehension or math reasoning.

With impairment in written expression:
Spelling accuracy
Grammar and punctuation accuracy
Clarity or organization of written expression

With impairment in mathematics:
Number sense
Memorization of arithmetic facts
Accurate or fluent calculation
Accurate math reasoning

(Continued)

TABLE 7.5 (*Continued*) DSM-5 Criteria for Specific Learning Disorders

Note: *Dyscalculia* is an alternative term used to refer to a pattern of difficulties characterized by problems processing numerical information, learning arithmetic facts, and performing accurate or fluent calculations. If dyscalculia is used to specify this particular pattern of mathematic difficulties, it is important also to specify any additional difficulties that are present, such as difficulties with math reasoning or word reasoning accuracy.

Specify current severity:
Mild: Some difficulties learning skills in one or two academic domains, but of mild enough severity that the individual may be able to compensate or function well when provided with appropriate accommodations or support services, especially during the school years.
Moderate: Marked difficulties learning skills in one or more academic domains, so that the individual is unlikely to become proficient without some intervals of intensive and specialized teaching during the school years. Some accommodations or supportive services at least part of the day at school, in the workplace, or at home may be needed to complete activities accurately and efficiently.
Severe: Severe difficulties learning skills, affecting several academic domains, so that the individual is unlikely to learn those skills without ongoing intensive individualized and specialized teaching for most of the school years. Even with an array of appropriate accommodations or services at home, at school, or in the workplace, the individual may not be able to complete all activities efficiently.

Source: American Psychiatric Association. (2013). *Diagnostic and statistical manual of mental disorders* (5th ed.). Arlington, VA: American Psychiatric Publishing.

descriptive text of specific learning disorder. It is hoped that this will improve more targeted interventions. The term of specific learning disorder is also seen as providing more information than dyslexia and dyscalculia would as labels by themselves.

Reduction in the reliance of standardized IQ test cut-off scores

As with other disorders listed in the DSM-5, there will be a move towards using severity specifiers in adaptive functioning rather than a reliance on IQ sores. Children's ability across different areas of an academic environment will be tested to clarify the areas in which the children are struggling. This approach focuses attention on the levels and duration of the requested support to overcome barriers to learning.

Duration of symptoms

By contrast to the requirement for persistent problems in other DSM-IV disorders, the diagnostic criteria did not specify duration of symptoms required for a diagnosis of a learning disorder or specified a need for persistent learning difficulties. Moreover, persistence of

symptoms is rarely included in the criteria for a reading disorder (Geary, 2011). The DSM-5 now requires symptoms to be present and persistent for 6 months duration (Tannock, 2013).

Empirical research

Before the DSM-5 incorporated the changes for the category specific learning disorders, the DSM-5 task force tested whether learning disorders differentiated in DSM-IV (reading disorders, mathematics disorder, writing learning disorder, learning disorder-not otherwise specified) were valid, mutually exclusive, and exhaustive, and therefore should be retained as cited in the DSM-IV; or whether they were not exhaustive and could be expanded to include other separate disorders; or not mutually exclusive or exhaustive and thus would be best "morphed" into a single overarching category of learning disorders (Tannock, 2013).

In support of a single category is the vast amount of evidence indicating both genetic and environmental overlap between the four subtypes (Haworth & Plomin, 2010; Kovas, Howarth, Dale and Plomin, 2007). There also

TABLE 7.6 Key changes in the DSM-5

DSM-IV	DSM-5
Categorized as 'Disorders First Diagnosed in Infancy, Childhood, or Adolescence'.	Categorized under 'Neurodevelopmental Disorders'.
Four subtypes of learning disorders included in the DSM-IV: • Reading Disorder • Mathematics Disorder • Written Expression Disorder • Not Otherwise Specified (NOS).	Merging of the four subtypes in a single category of specific learning disorders with unique specifiers. Lack of clarity in the boundaries of the four subtypes. Hoped to aid in more understanding of the overlap in conditions and increase in early identification.
More emphasis on IQ and cut-off scores.	Removing discrepancy between IQ and achievement. A move away from emphasis on IQ as found to be less valid at lower end.
No specific duration of symptoms.	Requirement that symptoms must be shown over a 6 month period. Reduces the number of temporary cases.

exist high rates of comorbidity across the categories of LD (Landerl & Moll, 2010). For example, 75% of a sample of children with writing disorder has been found to meet the criteria for a reading disorder (Barbaresi, Katusic, Colligan, Weaver & Jacobsen (2005)), and children with poor reading comprehension also manifest problems in mathematical reasoning (Pimperton & Nation, 2010). On the other hand it is also clear that some deficits occur in only one domain and/or one academic skill (Barbaresi et al., 2005). As the evidence is mixed as to whether the learning disorders should be considered underneath one heading or remain as they were in the DSM-IV as subgroups, the DSM-5 task force reached a compromising decision. Collapse the subgroups under one single category but preserved the developmental distinctions and continuities among the various manifestations of specific learning disorder.

Summary

The adoption in the DSM-5 of Learning Disorders as a clinical category has largely been seen by professional and researchers as a positive change. If the terminology is the same in both the education and clinical environments then this is likely to increase alignment of services. In particular, the category of learning disorders being recognized by medical authorities may aid in additional support being provided to local parent and advocacy groups. Instead of presenting the needs of several small different groups of individuals in proposed DSM-IV, they can help promote the demands and needs or a larger group to illustrate the problems they face in daily life. They may also help to secure resources for the child to be part of a more inclusive educational system. However some caution is raised in the idea of a 'one size fits all approach' which may arise as a result of categorizing a range of different disorders under this umbrella term. Therefore research must monitor the use of specifiers in ensuring a more targeted approach to intervention depending on the child's symptoms displayed.

CHAPTER 08

Middle Childhood: The Anxiety Disorders

This section accompanies chapter 8 in Kerig, Ludlow & Wenar (2012), *Developmental Psychopathology,* 6th Edition. McGraw-Hill Education.

In the move to the DSM-5, a number of disorders covered in this section have been uncoupled from the anxiety disorder spectrum. These include *obsessive-compulsive disorder*, which now is in its own section of Obsessive-Compulsive and Related Disorders, and *posttraumatic stress disorder*, which now is in a separate section entitled Trauma- and Stressor-Related Disorders. However, because these disorders are described in the present chapter of our textbook, we will retain them together here in our DSM-5 update.

Generalized Anxiety Disorder

As can be seen in Table 8.1, the criteria for the diagnosis of Generalized Anxiety Disorder (GAD) remain unchanged in the transition from DSM-IV to DSM-5.

Specific Phobias

Other than some slight reordering, the criteria for the diagnosis of Specific Phobia generally have not changed in DSM-5 from the previous criteria in DSM-IV. However, one noteworthy change for developmental psychopathologists is that, whereas previously the criteria required for the individual to recognize that the fear was excessive, and a disclaimer was needed to indicate that this might not be seen in children, that requirement has been replaced with one stating that the fear or anxiety is *out of proportion* to the actual threat the social situation might pose. Thus, rather than requir-

TABLE 8.1 DSM-5 Criteria for Generalized Anxiety Disorder

A. Excessive anxiety and worry (apprehensive expectation), occurring more days than not for at least 6 months, about a number of events or activities (such as work or school performance).
B. The individual finds it difficult to control the worry.
C. The anxiety and worry are associated with three (or more) of the following six symptoms (with at least some symptoms having been present for more days than not for the past 6 months):

Note: Only one item is required in children.

1. Restlessness or feeling keyed up or on edge.
2. Being easily fatigued.
3. Difficulty concentrating or mind going blank.
4. Irritability.
5. Muscle tension.
6. Sleep disturbance (difficulty falling or staying asleep, or restless, unsatisfying sleep).

D. The anxiety, worry, or physical symptoms cause clinically significant distress or impairment in social, occupational, or other important areas of functioning.
E. The disturbance is not attributable to the physiological effects of a substance (e.g., a drug of abuse, a medication) or another medical condition (e.g., hyperthyroidism).
F. The disturbance is not better explained by another mental disorder (e.g., anxiety or worry about having panic attacks in panic disorder, negative evaluation in social anxiety disorder [social phobia], contamination or other obsessions in obsessive compulsive disorder, separation from attachment figures in separation anxiety disorder, reminders of traumatic events in posttraumatic stress disorder, gaining weight in anorexia nervosa, physical complaints in somatic symptom disorder, perceived appearance flaws in body dysmorphic disorder, having a serious illness in illness anxiety disorder, or the content of delusional beliefs in schizophrenia of delusional disorder).

Source: American Psychiatric Association. (2013). *Diagnostic and statistical manual of mental disorders* (5th ed.). Arlington, VA: American Psychiatric Publishing.

TABLE 8.2 DSM-5 Criteria for Specific Phobia

A. Marked fear or anxiety about a specific object or situation (e.g., flying, heights, animals, receiving an injection, seeing blood).

Note: In children, the fear or anxiety may be expressed by crying, tantrums, freezing, or clinging.

B. The phobic object or situation almost always provokes immediate fear or anxiety.
C. The phobic object or situation is actively avoided or endured with intense fear or anxiety.
D. The fear or anxiety is out of proportion to the actual danger posed by the specific object or situation and to the sociocultural context.
E. The fear, anxiety, or avoidance is persistent, typically lasting for 6 months or more.
F. The fear, anxiety, or avoidance causes clinically significant distress or impairment in social, occupational, or other important areas of functioning.
G. The disturbance is not better explained by the symptoms of another mental disorder, including fear, anxiety, and avoidance of situations associated with panic-like symptoms or other incapacitating symptoms (as in agoraphobia); objects or situations related to obsessions (as in obsessive-compulsive disorder); reminders of traumatic events (as in posttraumatic stress disorder); separation from home or attachment figures (as in separation anxiety disorder); or social situations (as in social anxiety disorder).

Specify if:
Code based on the phobic stimulus:
Animal (e.g., spiders, insects, dogs).
Natural environment (e.g., heights, storms, water).
Blood-injection-injury (e.g., needles, invasive medical procedures).
Situational (e.g., airplanes, elevators, enclosed places).
Other (e.g., situations that may lead to choking or vomiting; in children, e.g., loud sounds or costumed characters).

Source: American Psychiatric Association. (2013). *Diagnostic and statistical manual of mental disorders* (5th ed.). Arlington, VA: American Psychiatric Publishing.

ing the individual to recognize that her or his reaction is inappropriate to the circumstances, the new criteria allows the diagnosing clinician to make that judgement. Another noteworthy change is that the duration of symptoms is now 6 months across all ages.

Social Anxiety Disorder (Social Phobia)

The DSM-5 criteria for the diagnosis of SAD are highly similar to those in DSM-IV, with one important exception. As with specific phobia, whereas previously the criteria required for the individual to recognize that the fear was excessive, and a disclaimer was needed to indicate that this might not be seen in children, that requirement has been replaced with one stating that the fear or anxiety is *out of proportion* to the actual threat the social situation might pose. The duration of symptoms also is now 6 months across all ages.

Separation Anxiety Disorder

As a review of Table 8.5 will indicate, there have been no substantial revisions to the diagnostic criteria for Separation Anxiety Disorder in DSM-5, other than the deletion of the specifier for the early-onset subtype.

Obsessive-Compulsive Disorder

In the DSM-5, a new category of *Obsessive-Compulsive and Related Disorders* separates OCD from the other anxiety disorders discussed in this chapter. Whereas DSM-5 still recognizes the close association between OCD and anxiety, there is increasing recognition of a separate class of disorders involving developmentally inappropriate preoccupations or rituals which frequently co-occur with one another. In addition to OCD, this new category includes *body dysmorphic disorder* (extreme preoccupation with perceived deficits or flaws in one's physical appearance) and *hoarding disorder* (persistent difficulty discarding possessions, irrespective of their actual value, resulting in accumulations of objects so significant that they interfere with functioning); both are characterized by cognitive distortions, regarding either perceived defects in the self or a need to hang on to possessions. Additional diagnoses in this spectrum include *trichotillomania* (hair-pulling) and *excoriation* (skin-picking), both of which involve repetitive behaviours focused on the body; as well as obsessive-compulsive behaviours that are due to substances, medications, or are secondary to other medical conditions.

The DSM-5 criteria for the diagnosis of OCD are listed in Table 8.6, which reveals a number of relatively small changes from DSM-IV. One is that the definition of obsessions is simplified and now includes only two features, reduced from the previous four, which are the *presence of intrusive thoughts* and *efforts to ignore, suppress, or neutralize those thoughts*. As is true with the new definition of Social Phobia, the criterion that the individual recognize that these thoughts are the product of his or her own mind is no longer included, which allows for deletion of the previous disclaimer that children cannot be expected to show such insight. However, the DSM-5 definition of compulsions does include the statement that the repetitive behaviours or mental acts have the aim of preventing or reducing anxiety, and that children may not be able to articulate such a purpose to their behaviours. The clinician also has the opportunity to specify whether the individual exhibits *good, fair, poor, or absent/delusional insight* into any obsessive beliefs.

As we have discussed, tic disorders are highly comorbid with OCD, and the DSM-5 allows the clinician to specify whether the diagnosis of OCD is *tic-related*.

TABLE 8.3 DSM-5 Criteria for Social Phobia (Social Anxiety Disorder)

A. Marked fear or anxiety about one or more social situations in which the individuals is exposed to possible scrutiny by others. Examples include social interactions (e.g., having a conversation, meeting unfamiliar people), being observed (e.g., eating or drinking), and performing in front of others (e.g., giving a speech). **Note:** In children, the anxiety must occur in peer settings and not just during interactions with adults.

B. The individuals fears that he or she will act in a way or show anxiety symptoms that will be negatively evaluated (i.e., will be humiliating or embarrassing; will lead to rejection or offend others).

C. The social situations almost always provoke fear or anxiety. **Note:** In children, the fear or anxiety may be expressed by crying, trantrums, freezing, clinging, shrinking, or failing to speak in social situations.

D. The social situations are avoided or endured with intense fear or anxiety.

E. The fear or anxiety is out of proportion to the actual threat posed by the social situation and to the sociocultural context.

F. The fear, anxiety, or avoidance is persistent, typically lasting for 6 months or more.

G. The fear, anxiety, or avoidance causes clinically significant distress or impairment in social, occupational, or other important areas of functioning.

H. The fear, anxiety, or avoidance is not attributable to the physiological effects of a substance (e.g., a drug of abuse, a medication) or another medical condition.

I. The fear, anxiety, or avoidance is not better explained by the symptoms of another mental disorder, such as panic disorder, body dysmorphic disorder, or autism spectrum disorder.

J. If another medical condition (e.g., Parkinson's disease, obesity, disfigurement from burns or injury) is present, the fear, anxiety, or avoidance is clearly unrelated or is excessive.

Specify if:
Performance only: If the fear is restricted to speaking or performing in public.

Source: American Psychiatric Association. (2013). *Diagnostic and statistical manual of mental disorders* (5th ed.). Arlington, VA: American Psychiatric Publishing.

TABLE 8.4 DSM-5 Criteria for Separation Anxiety Disorder

A. Developmentally inappropriate and excessive fear or anxiety concerning separation from those to whom the individual is attached, as evidenced by at least three of the following:

1. Recurrent excessive distress when anticipating or experiencing separation from home or from major attachment figures.

2. Persistent and excessive worry about losing major attachment figures or about possible harm to them, such as illness, injury, disasters, or death.

3. Persistent and excessive worry about experiencing an untoward event (e.g., getting lost, being kidnapped, having an accident, becoming ill) that causes separation from a major attachment figure.

4. Persistent reluctance or refusal to go out, away from home, to school, to work, or elsewhere because of fear of separation.

5. Persistent and excessive fear of or reluctance about being alone or without major attachment figures at home or in other settings.

6. Persistent reluctance or refusal to sleep away from home or to go to sleep without being near a major attachment figure.

7. Repeated nightmares involving the theme of separation.

8. Repeated complaints of physical symptoms (e.g., headaches, stomachaches, nausea, vomiting) when separation from major attachment figures occurs or is anticipated.

B. The fear, anxiety, or avoidance is persistant, lasting at least 4 weeks in children and adolescents and typically 6 months or more in adults.

C. The disturbance causes clinically significant distress or impairment in social, academic, occupational, or other important areas of functioning.

(Continued)

TABLE 8.4 (*Continued*) DSM-5 Criteria for Separation Anxiety Disorder

D. The disturbance is not better explained by another mental disorder, such as refusing to leave home because of excessive resistance to change in autism spectrum disorder; delusions or hallucinations concerning separation in psychotic disorders; refusal to go outside without a trusted companion in agoraphobia; worries about ill health or other harm befalling significant others in generalized anxiety disorder, or concerns about having an illness in illness anxiety disorder.

Source: American Psychiatric Association. (2013). *Diagnostic and statistical manual of mental disorders* (5th ed.). Arlington, VA: American Psychiatric Publishing.

TABLE 8.5 DSM-5 Criteria for Obsessive-Compulsive Disorder

A. Presence of obsessions, compulsions, or both:
   Obsessions are defined by (1) and (2):

   1. Recurrent and persistent thoughts, urges, or images that are experienced, at some time during the disturbance, as intrusive and unwanted, and that in most individuals cause marked anxiety or distress.
   2. The individual attempts to ignore or suppress such thoughts, urges, or images, or to neutralize them with some other thought or action (i.e., by performing a compulsion).

   Compulsions are defined by (1) and (2):

   1. Repetitive behaviors (e.g., hand washing, ordering, checking) or mental acts (e.g., praying, counting, repeating words silently) that the individual feels driven to perform in response to an obsession or according to rules that must be applied rigidly.
   2. The behaviors or mental acts are aimed at preventing or reducing anxiety or distress, or preventing some dreaded event or situation; however, these behaviors or mental acts are not connected in a realistic way with what they are designed to neutralize or prevent, or are clearly excessive.
      Note: Young children may not be able to articulate the aims of these behaviors or mental acts.

B. The obsessions or compulsions are time-consuming (e.g., take more than 1 hour per day) or cause clinically significant distress or impairment in social, occupational, or other important areas of functioning.

C. The obsessive-compulsive symptoms are not attributable to the physiological effects of a substance (e.g., a drug of abuse, a medication) or another medical condition.

D. The disturbance is not better explained by the symptoms of another mental disorder (e.g., excessive worries, as in generalized anxiety disorder; preoccupation with appearance, as in body dysmorphic disorder; difficulty discarding or parting with possessions, as in hoarding disorder; hair pulling, as in trichotillomania [hair-pulling disorder]; skin picking, as in excoriation [skin-picking] disorder; stereotypies, as in stereotypic movement disorder; ritualized eating behavior, as in eating disorders; preoccupation with substances or gambling, as in substance-related and addictive disorders; preoccupation with having an illness, as in illness anxiety disorder; sexual urges or fantasies, as in paraphilic disorders; impulses, as in disruptive, impulse-control, and conduct disorders; guilty ruminations, as in major depressive disorder; thought insertion or delusional preoccupations, as in schizophrenia spectrum and other psychotic disorders; or repetitive patterns of behavior, as in autism spectrum disorder).

Specify if:
With good or fair insight: The individual recognizes that obsessive-compulsive disorder beliefs are definitely or probably not true or that they may or may not be true.
With poor insight: The individual thinks obsessive-compulsive disorder beliefs are probably true.
With absent insight/delusional beliefs: The individual is completely convinced that obsessive-compulsive disorder beliefs are true.

Specify if:
Tic-related: The individual has a current or past history of a tic disorder.

Source: American Psychiatric Association. (2013). *Diagnostic and statistical manual of mental disorders* (5th ed.). Arlington, VA: American Psychiatric Publishing.

Posttraumatic Stress Disorder

Although many of the disorders in this chapter remain virtually unchanged in the transition from DSM-IV to DSM-5, that is not true of the criteria for **Posttraumatic Stress Disorder** (PTSD). First, the diagnosis of PTSD is no longer in the category of anxiety disorders, but instead is now included in a new grouping entitled *Trauma- and Stressor-Related Disorders*. All of the disorders in this cluster have in common the fact that the precipitating factor is the experience of an adverse event: in the case of *reactive attachment disorder* and *disinhibited social engagement disorder* (see chapter 4), the adversity is grossly inadequate caregiving; in *adjustment disorder* there is an identifiable distressing event that may result in a variety of stress-response reactions (e.g., depression, anxiety, disturbances in conduct); and in *PTSD* and *acute distress disorder*, the child has experienced a traumatic event.

Overview of Major DSM-5 Changes

New definition of trauma

The definition of what comprises a "traumatic event" is another one of the major changes to the diagnosis of PTSD in DSM-5. The definition has become specific to three classes of events: *actual or threatened death*; *serious injury*; or *sexual violence* (see Table 8.8). The criteria are also more specific about what comprises "exposure" to a trauma in an effort to avoid allowing the definition to expand beyond the real-life experience of adversity (e.g., seeing an event on television). Instead, the criteria specify that exposure to the event must take place in one of four ways: it was *experienced directly* (e.g., the child was the victim); the event was *witnessed* (e.g., the child saw it with his or her own eyes); the child *learned about a traumatic event occurring to a loved one*, whether a family member or close friend; or the individual has experienced repeated or extreme *exposure to aversive details* of a traumatic event (e.g., child protection workers who repeatedly interview children about the details of sexual abuse).

Perhaps the most dramatic change is that no longer included in the definition of trauma is the second part of the DSM-IV's version of Criterion A, which required that the individual's reaction to the event be one involving intense fear, helplessness, horror, or, in children, agitation or disorganized behaviour. The DSM-5's removal of the appraisal of the event from the definition was controversial, with some clinicians and researchers arguing that what is traumatic is "in the eye of the beholder" and that children especially may perceive as traumatic experiences (e.g., separation from a caregiver) that do not fall in the three categories of events listed in DSM-5. However, the PTSD committee determined that the weight of the evidence argued against the utility of this criterion for increasing the accuracy, sensitivity or specificity of the diagnosis (Friedman, 2013).

New symptom clusters

Although newly named, Cluster B is comprised of *intrusive symptoms* that will be familiar to those acquainted with the re-experiencing cluster in DSM-IV. Cluster C includes the *avoidant symptoms* that were present in the previous diagnostic criteria, but differentiates these from other symptoms that used to be included in the cluster, such as emotional numbing. Cluster D is new to the DSM-5 criteria and includes seven symptoms related to *negative alterations in cognition and mood*. These symptoms describe a variety of ways in which an individual may demonstrate changes in

TABLE 8.6 DSM-5 Criteria for Posttraumatic Stress Disorder

Posttraumatic Stress Disorder

Note: The following criteria apply to adults, adolescents, and children older than 6 years. For children 6 years and younger, see corresponding criteria below.

A. Exposure to actual or threatened death, serious injury, or sexual violence in one (or more) of the following ways:

1. Directly experiencing the traumatic event(s).
2. Witnessing, in person, the event(s) as it occurred to others.
3. Learning that the traumatic event(s) occurred to a close family member or close friend. In cases of actual or threatened death of a family member or friend, the event(s) must have been violent or accidental.
4. Experiencing repeated or extreme exposure to aversive details of the traumatic event(s) (e.g., first responders collecting human remains; police officers repeatedly exposed to details of child abuse).

   Note: Criterion A4 does not apply to exposure through electronic media, television, movies, or pictures, unless this exposure is work related.

B. Presence of one (or more) of the following intrusion symptoms associated with the traumatic event(s), beginning after the traumatic event(s) occurred:

1. Recurrent, involuntary, and intrusive distressing memories of the traumatic event(s).

   Note: In children older than 6 years, repetitive play may occur in which themes or aspects of the traumatic event(s) are expressed.

2. Recurrent distressing dreams in which the content and/or affect of the dream are related to the traumatic event(s).

   Note: In children, there may be frightening dreams without recognizable content.

3. Dissociative reactions (e.g., flashbacks) in which the individual feels or acts as if the traumatic event(s) were recurring. (Such reactions may occur on a continuum, with the most extreme expression being a complete loss of awareness of present surroundings.)

   Note: In children, trauma-specific reenactment may occur in play.

4. Intense or prolonged psychological distress at exposure to internal or external cues that symbolize or resemble an aspect of the traumatic event(s).
5. Marked physiological reactions to internal or external cues that symbolize or resemble an aspect of the traumatic event(s).

C. Persistent avoidance of stimuli associated with the traumatic event(s), beginning after the traumatic event(s) occurred, as evidenced by one or both of the following:

1. Avoidance of or efforts to avoid distressing memories, thoughts, or feelings about or closely associated with the traumatic event(s).
2. Avoidance of or efforts to avoid external reminders (people, places, conversations, activities, objects, situations) that arouse distressing memories, thoughts, or feelings about or closely associated with the traumatic event(s).

D. Negative alterations in cognitions and mood associated with the traumatic event(s), beginning or worsening after the traumatic event(s) occurred, as evidenced by two (or more) of the following:

1. Inability to remember an important aspect of the traumatic event(s) (typically due to dissociative amnesia and not to other factors such as head injury, alcohol, or drugs).
2. Persistent and exaggerated negative beliefs or expectations about oneself, others, or the world (e.g., "I am bad," "No one can be trusted," "The world is completely dangerous," "My whole nervous system is permanently ruined").
3. Persistent, distorted cognitions about the cause or consequences of the traumatic event(s) that lead the individual to blame himself/herself or others.
4. Persistent negative emotional state (e.g., fear, horror, anger, guilt, or shame).

5. Markedly diminished interest or participation in significant activities.
6. Feelings of detachment or estrangement from others.
7. Persistent inability to experience positive emotions (e.g., inability to experience happiness, satisfaction, or loving feelings).

E. Marked alterations in arousal and reactivity associated with the traumatic event(s), beginning or worsening after the traumatic event(s) occurred, as evidenced by two (or more) of the following:

1. Irritable behavior and angry outbursts (with little or no provocation) typically expressed as verbal or physical aggression toward people or objects.
2. Reckless or self-destructive behavior.
3. Hypervigilance.
4. Exaggerated startle response.
5. Problems with concentration.
6. Sleep disturbance (e.g., difficulty falling or staying asleep or restless sleep).

F. Duration of the disturbance (Criteria B, C, D, and E) is more than 1 month.
G. The disturbance causes clinically significant distress or impairment in social, occupational, or other important areas of functioning.
H. The disturbance is not attributable to the physiological effects of a substance (e.g., medication, alcohol) or another medical condition.

Specify whether:

With dissociative symptoms: The individual's symptoms meet the criteria for posttraumatic stress disorder, and in addition, in response to the stressor, the individual experiences persistent or recurrent symptoms of either of the following:

1. **Depersonalization:** Persistent or recurrent experiences of feeling detached from, and as if one were an outside observer of, one's mental processes or body (e.g., feeling as though one were in a dream; feeling a sense of unreality of self or body or of time moving slowly).
2. **Derealization:** Persistent or recurrent experiences of unreality of surroundings (e.g., the world around the individual is experienced as unreal, dreamlike, distant, or distorted).

Note: To use this subtype, the dissociative symptoms must not be attributable to the physiological effects of a substance (e.g., blackouts, behavior during alcohol intoxication) or another medical condition (e.g., complex partial seizures).

Specify if:

With delayed expression: If the full diagnostic criteria are not met until at least 6 months after the event (although the onset and expression of some symptoms may be immediate).

Source: American Psychiatric Association. (2013). *Diagnostic and statistical manual of mental disorders* (5th ed.). Arlington, VA: American Psychiatric Publishing.

feeling states or beliefs—about the self, others, or the world—consequent to a traumatic event. Some of these symptoms were previously included in other clusters (e.g., emotional numbing, which is now defined in DSM-5 as the inability to experience positive emotions) and others were described in the text of DSM-IV as "associated symptoms" of PTSD (e.g., self-blame). Cluster E, in turn, maintains the indices of *arousal and reactivity* that were present in DSM-IV but adds to these two new symptoms: *irritability or anger*, and *reckless or self-destructive behaviour*. An interesting note for developmental psychopathologists is that these two new symptoms arose initially from clinical observations of adolescents who had experienced posttraumatic stress and whose aggression toward the self or others was not adequately captured in the previous DSM criteria (Pynoos et al., 2009).

TABLE 8.7 DSM-5 Criteria for Posttraumatic Stress Disorder for Children 6 Years and Younger

A. In children 6 years and younger, exposure to actual or threatened death, serious injury, or sexual violence in one (or more) of the following ways:

   1. Directly experiencing the traumatic event(s).

   2. Witnessing, in person, the event(s) as it occurred to others, especially primary caregivers.

      Note: Witnessing does not include events that are witnessed only in electronic media, television, movies, or pictures.

   3. Learning that the traumatic event(s) occurred to a parent or caregiving figure.

B. Presence of one (or more) of the following intrusion symptoms associated with the traumatic event(s), beginning after the traumatic event(s) occurred:

   1. Recurrent, involuntary, and intrusive distressing memories of the traumatic event(s).

      Note: Spontaneous and intrusive memories may not necessarily appear distressing and may be expressed as play reenactment.

   2. Recurrent distressing dreams in which the content and/or affect of the dream are related to the traumatic event.

      Note: It may not be possible to ascertain that the frightening content is related to the traumatic event.

   3. Dissociative reactions (e.g., flashbacks) in which the child feels or acts as if the traumatic event(s) were recurring. (Such reactions may occur on a continuum, with the most extreme expression being a complete loss of awareness of present surroundings.) Such trauma-specific reenactment may occur in play.

   4. Intense or prolonged psychological distress at exposure to internal or external cues that symbolize or resemble an aspect of the traumatic event(s).

   5. Marked physiological reactions to reminders of the traumatic event(s).

C. One (or more) of the following symptoms, representing either persistent avoidance of stimuli associated with the traumatic event(s) or negative alterations in cognitions and mood associated with the traumatic event(s), must be present, beginning after the event(s) or worsening after the event(s):

Persistent Avoidance of Stimuli

   1. Avoidance of or efforts to avoids activities, places, or physical reminders that arouse recollections of the traumatic event(s).

   2. Avoidance of or efforts to avoid people, conversations, or interpersonal situations that arouse recollections of the traumatic event(s).

Negative Alterations in Cognitions

   3. Substantially increased frequency of negative emotional states (e.g., fear, guilt, sadness, shame, confusion).

   4. Markedly diminished interest or participation in significant activities, including constriction of play.

   5. Socially withdrawn behavior.

   6. Persistent reduction in expression of positive emotions.

D. Alterations in arousal and reactivity associated with the traumatic event(s), beginning or worsening after the traumatic event(s) occurred, as evidenced by two (or more) of the following:

   1. Irritable behavior and angry outbursts (with little or no provocation) typically expressed as verbal or physical aggression toward people or objects (including extreme temper tantrums).

   2. Hypervigilance.

   3. Exaggerated startle response.

   4. Problems with concentration.

   5. Sleep disturbance (e.g., difficulty falling or staying asleep or restless sleep).

E. The duration of the disturbance is more than 1 month.

F. The disturbance causes clinically significant distress or impairment in relationships with parents, siblings, peers, or other caregivers or with school behavior.

G. The disturbance is not attributable to the physiological effects of a substance (e.g., medication or alcohol) or another medical condition.

Specify whether:

With dissociative symptoms: The individual's symptoms meet the criteria for posttraumatic stress disorder, and the individual experiences persistent or recurrent symptoms of either of the following:

1. **Depersonalization:** Persistent or recurrent experiences of feeling detached from, and as if one were an outside observer of, one's mental processes or body (e.g., feeling as though one were in a dream; feeling a sense of unreality of self or body or of time moving slowly).
2. **Derealization:** Persistent or recurrent experiences of unreality of surroundings (e.g., the world around the individual is experienced as unreal, dreamlike, distant, or distorted).

Note: To use this subtype, the dissociative symptoms must not be attributable to the physiological effects of a substance (e.g., blackouts) or another medical condition (e.g., complex partial seizures).

Specify if:

With delayed expression: If the full diagnostic criteria are not met until at least 6 months after the event (although the onset and expression of some symptoms may be immediate).

Source: American Psychiatric Association. (2013). *Diagnostic and statistical manual of mental disorders* (5th ed.). Arlington, VA: American Psychiatric Publishing.

The dissociative subtype

Another new feature of the DSM-5 diagnosis of PTSD is the inclusion of a specifier that indicates whether the other symptoms are also accompanied by the presence of dissociation. Dissociation is described as presenting in two ways: as *depersonalization*, the experience of feeling like the self is not real or present in reality; and *derealisation*, the sense that the world surrounding the self is not real or like a dream.

A separate diagnosis for young children

Another major change to the DSM-5 is the inclusion of a separate set of criteria for children 6 years of age or younger. As displayed in Table 8.9, these criteria include a number of developmentally sensitive adaptations. First, the definition of a traumatic event is expanded to include *learning about an adverse event happening to a caregiver*. Second, while the *intrusive symptoms* and *arousal* clusters remain intact (with the deletion of the developmentally inappropriate "reckless or self-destructive behaviour" symptom), the other two clusters are combined into one and the number of symptoms reduced to include only those associated with *avoidance and negative alterations in cognitions*.

Potential Implications of the New DSM-5 Criteria for PTSD

Will there be a reduction in prevalence?

One potential implication of the narrowing of the definition of traumatic events in the new diagnostic criteria may be a reduction in the *prevalence* of the PTSD diagnosis. Kilpatrick, et al. (2013) directly compared the two diagnostic systems in a national sample of 2,593 US adults and found that estimates of "caseness"—that is, of individuals meeting the criteria for a diagnosis—were lower when the DSM-5 criteria were used as compared to the DSM-IV criteria. The researchers noted that one of the main reasons that individuals met DSM-IV but not DSM-5 criteria was the exclusion of non-accidental, nonviolent deaths from the definition of traumatic events in the new Criterion A. The other reason for the difference in prevalence was that DSM-5 now requires every person with the disorder to exhibit at least one symptom of active avoidance, whereas in DSM-IV the criterion for this symptom cluster could be met by the presence of either a symptom associated with avoidance or by one involving emotional numbing.

TABLE 8.8 Summary of Key Changes in Criteria For Posttraumatic Stress Disorder In DSM-5

Criterion A: Exposure to a traumatic event	Stricter criteria regarding what comprises a traumatic event (i.e., *actual or threatened death, serious injury,* or *sexual violence*). More specific definition regarding what comprises "exposure" to that event (i.e., *experienced directly, witnessed, learning the event has occurred to a loved one, repeated or extreme exposure to aversive details about the event*). Removal of the requirement that the individual's response include subjective reactions of "fear, helpless or horror" or "disorganized behaviour" in young children.
Criterion B: Intrusion symptoms	The term *intrusion* replaces the former term "re-experiencing".
Criterion C: Avoidance	Only two avoidance symptoms are included in this cluster (*avoidance of internal reminders, avoidance of external reminders*); symptoms related to emotional numbing are moved to Criterion D.
Criterion D: Negative alterations in cognition and mood	A new cluster of symptoms is added, which includes symptoms of *emotional numbing* that were previously in Criterion C, and adds several new symptoms including *amnesia, negative beliefs, distorted cognitions,* and *negative emotional states*.
Criterion E: Arousal and reactivity	Retains symptoms of hyperarousal and reactivity in the previous Criterion D; adds two new symptoms of *irritability* and *reckless or self-destructive* behaviour.
Dissociative subtype	A new dissociative subtype is added.
Separate diagnosis for children 6 years and younger	A separate diagnosis is provided for young children that lowers the diagnostic threshold for the number of symptoms required and excludes developmentally inappropriate criteria.

Of particular concern to child and adolescent clinicians is the possibility that the restricted definition of Criterion A also might be insensitive to the kinds of experiences that are traumatic to young people. For example, although separation from a caregiver does not meet the criteria for trauma in the new definition, attachment theorists would argue that threatened loss of a parent is potentially traumatic over the lifespan (Bowlby, 1973). Research by Taylor & Weems (2009) confirms that, when asked about what in their lives they have found to be most distressing, children and adolescents frequently list separations from loved ones. In addition, these researchers also found that young people often identify as traumatic, and have post-traumatic symptoms in response to other events that would not meet the DSM-5 definition, such as exposure to media violence or bad experiences involving the use of illicit substances.

Will models of trauma no longer consider peritraumatic reactions?

As noted above, one of the most controversial decisions made in devising the DSM-5 criteria was the exclusion of the second part of the DSM-IV Criterion A, which required that the individual subjectively appraise the event as distressing. These appraisals, termed *peritraumatic* reactions, were specified in DSM-IV as being indicated by one of three specific reactions—fear, helplessness, or horror—but which could be inferred by disorganized behaviour in young children. A significant body of research has demonstrated that subjective appraisals are associated with whether individuals find events upsetting and whether they develop symptoms of PTSD in the aftermath of those events, and this is as true of children and adolescents as it is of adults (Bovin & Marx, 2011; Kerig & Bennett, 2013; Taylor & Weems, 2009). Further, research suggests that it is the specific emotions identified by DSM-IV—fear, helplessness, and horror—that fail to predict of PTSD, whereas other peritraumatic reactions *do* help us to discriminate those youth who will develop the disorder. In particular, reactions during an event that are characterized by guilt, shame, anger, disgust, or peritraumatic dissociation have been found to play an important role in the development of PTSD in young people (Bui et al., 2010; Coyle, Karatzias, Summers & Power, 2014; Kerig & Bennett, 2013). The exclusion from the DSM-5 of this subjective appraisal dimension of the traumatic experience might result in a drop-off in research regarding peritraumatic reactions, which possibly could hamper efforts to understand how better to intervene so as to prevent the development of childhood PTSD.

Will the new clusters of PTSD symptoms hold up to empirical scrutiny?

Although preliminary field trials of the new set of symptoms has shown them to fit the scheme devised by the developers of DSM-5 in samples of adults (Miller et al., 2013), some research is emerging with child and adolescent samples that suggests this factor structure might not hold up well (Hafstad et al., 2014). Therefore, continued research will be needed to determine whether we are doing an adequate job of catching the phenomenon of childhood PTSD in our diagnostic net.

CHAPTER 09

Middle Childhood to Adolescence: Depression and Suicide

This section accompanies chapter 9 in Kerig, Ludlow & Wenar (2012), *Developmental Psychopathology*, 6th Edition. McGraw-Hill Education.

Adjustment Disorder with Depressed Mood

DSM-5 retains the DSM-IV diagnosis of **adjustment disorder with depressed mood** with no revisions or additions to the diagnostic criteria (see Table 9.1); however, a new feature is that the disorder is placed in the category of *Trauma- and Stressor-Related Disorders*.

For the remainder of the depressive spectrum disorders, the most marked change from DSM-IV is their separation into their own category, *Depressive Disorders*, which is now distinguished from the category that includes *Bipolar and Related Disorders*.

Disruptive Mood Dysregulation Disorder

Of particular note for developmental psychopathologists is that DSM-5 introduces a new disorder specifically for children under the age of 12, **disruptive mood dysregulation disorder** (DMDD), which is specifically designed to prevent young children from being mistakenly diagnosed with bipolar disorder. As can be seen in Table 9.2, the hallmark of the DMDD diagnosis is chronic, severe, persistent *irritability*, which may take the form of temper outbursts or angry mood. What differentiates this presentation

TABLE 9.1 DSM-IV-TR Criteria for Adjustment Disorder with Depressed Mood

> A. The development of emotional or behavioral symptoms in response to an identifiable stressor(s) occurring within 3 months of the onset of the stressor(s).
> B. These symptoms or behaviors are clinically significant, as evidenced by one are both of the following:
>   1. Marked distress that is out of proportion to the severity or intensify of the stressor, taking into account the external context and the cultural factors that might influence symptom severity and presentation.
>   2. Significant impairment in social, occupational, or other important areas of functioning.
> C. The stress-related disturbance does not meet the criteria for another mental disorder and is not merely an exacerbation of a preexisting mental disorder.
> D. The symptoms do not represent normal bereavement.
> E. Once the stressor or its consequences have terminated, the symptoms do not persist for more than an additional 6 months.
>
> *Specify* whether:
>   **With depressed mood:** Low mood, tearfulness, or feelings of hopelessness are predominant.
>   **With anxiety:** Nervousness, worry, jitteriness, or separation anxiety is predominant.
>   **With mixed anxiety and depressed mood:** A combination of depression and anxiety is predominant.
>   **With disturbance of conduct:** Disturbance of conduct in predominant.
>   **With mixed disturbance of emotions and conduct:** Both emotional symptoms (e.g., depression, anxiety) and a disturbance of conduct are predominant.
>   **Unspecified:** For maladaptive reactions that are not classifiable as one of the specific subtypes of adjustment disorder.

Source: American Psychiatric Association. (2013). *Diagnostic and statistical manual of mental disorders* (5th ed.). Arlington, VA: American Psychiatric Publishing.

from the irritability that frequently is seen in children with bipolar disorder is that it is chronic and persistent and not limited to discrete *episodes* as would be the case in bipolar disorder. In addition, the DSM-5 notes that irritability in children, although believed by many clinicians to be a hallmark of bipolar disorder, more often predicts the development of unipolar depression or anxiety as children mature into adolescence and adulthood.

Prevalence and developmental course

Because this is a new disorder, firm information is not yet available about its *prevalence*, but it is estimated to occur in 2 to 5 per cent of youth and is expected to be more often seen among school-age children than adolescents, and more often among boys than girls. Regarding the *age of onset*, the diagnosis is restricted to children who are at least 6 years of age and the age of onset must begin before age 10. Information about the *developmental course* is still being gathered, but it is believed that the disorder is most common prior to adolescence, with symptoms fading as children mature into adulthood.

Risks

Risk factors that increase the likelihood of the disorder include *difficult temperament*, which often is accompanied by irritability, oppositionality, attention deficits, and depressive symptoms. Family histories suggest *genetic links* to anxiety, depressive, and substance abuse disorders but not to bipolar disorder. Research also suggests underlying *neurocognitive dysfunctions* that are unique to the disorder, particularly those related to a deficient ability to attend to emotional stimuli.

TABLE 9.2 DSM-5 Criteria for Disruptive Mood Dysregulation Disorder

---

A. Severe recurrent temper outbursts manifested verbally (e.g., verbal rages) and/or behaviorally (e.g., physical aggression toward people or property) that are grossly out of proportion in intensity or duration to the situation or provocation.

B. The temper outbursts are inconsistent with developmental level.

C. The temper outbursts occur, on average, three or more times per week.

D. The mood between temper outbursts is persistently irritable or angry most of the day, nearly every day, and is observable by others (e.g., parents, teachers, peers).

E. Criteria A–D have been present for 12 or more months. Throughout that time, the individual has not had a period lasting 3 or more consecutive months without all of the symptoms in Criteria A–D.

F. Criteria A and D are present in at least two of three settings (i.e., at home, at school, with peers) and are severe in at least one of these.

G. The diagnosis should not be made for the first time before age 6 years of after age 18 years.

H. By history or observation, the age at onset of Criteria A–E is before 10 years.

I. There has never been a distinct period lasting more than 1 day during which the full symptom criteria, except duration, for a manic or hypomanic episode have been met.

   Note: Developmentally appropriate mood elevation, such as occurs in the context of a highly positive event or its anticipation, should not be considered as a symptom of mania or hypomania.

J. The behaviors do not occur exclusively during an episode of major depressive disorder and are not better explained by another mental disorder (e.g., autism spectrum disorder, posttraumatic stress disorder, separation anxiety disorder, persistent depressive disorder [dysthymia]).

   Note: This diagnosis cannot coexist with oppositional defiant disorder, intermittent explosive disorder, or bipolar disorder, though it can coexist with others, including major depressive disorder, attention-deficit/hyperactivity disorder, conduct disorder, and substance use disorders. Individuals whose symptoms meet criteria for both disruptive mood dysregulation disorder and oppositional defiant disorder should only be given the diagnosis of disruptive mood dysregulation disorder. If an individual has ever experienced a manic or hypomanic episode, the diagnosis of disruptive mood dysregulation disorder should not be assigned.

K. The symptoms are not attributable to the physiological effects of a substance or to another medical or neurological condition.

Source: American Psychiatric Association. (2013). *Diagnostic and statistical manual of mental disorders* (5th ed.). Arlington, VA: American Psychiatric Publishing.

Comorbidity and differential diagnosis

With symptoms associated with so many other disorders indicated as risks for DDMD, *comorbidity* is likely to be extremely high and *differential diagnosis* challenging. As noted above, the key distinction between DDMD and *bipolar disorder* is that, in the former, irritable mood is persistent rather than being episodic. In turn, DDMD is differentiated from Oppositional Defiant Disorder by the presence of not mere oppositionality, but severe and frequent temper outbursts and persistent negative mood in between those outbursts; in addition, children with DDMD must show impairments in at least two settings to meet criteria for the diagnosis. Thus, many children with DDMD might meet the criteria for ODD, but rarely—in an estimated 15 per cent of cases—will the child with ODD also meet criteria for DDMD.

DDMD can also be differentiated from a host of disorders in which negative mood or temper outbursts are present—such as *depression, anxiety,* or *autism*—by the fact that the irritability is chronic and does not ebb and flow with moods or exacerbating events (e.g., being confronted with a feared stimulus in the case of anxiety disorders, or having routines disrupted in the case of autism). Finally, DMDD can be differentiated from *intermittent explosive*

TABLE 9.3 DSM-5 Criteria for Persistent Depressive Disorder

This disorder represents a consolidation of DSM-IV-defined chronic major depressive disorder and dysthymic disorder.

A. Depressed mood for most of the day, for more days than not, as indicated by either subjective account or observation by others, for at least 2 years.

   Note: In children and adolescents, mood can be irritable and duration must be at least 1 year.

B. Presence, while depressed, of two (or more) of the following:
   1. Poor appetite or overeating.
   2. Insomnia or hypersomnia.
   3. Low energy or fatigue.
   4. Low self-esteem.
   5. Poor concentration or difficulty making decisions.
   6. Feelings of hopelessness.

C. During the 2-year period (1 year for children or adolescents) of the disturbance, the individual has never been without the symptoms in Criteria A and B for more than 2 months at a time.

D. Criteria for a major depressive disorder may be continuously present for 2 years.

E. There has never been a manic episode or a hypomanic episode, and criteria have never been met for cyclothymic disorder.

F. The disturbance is not better explained by a persistent schizoaffective disorder, schizophrenia, delusional disorder, or other specified or unspecified schizophrenia spectrum and other psychotic disorder.

G. The symptoms are not attributable to the physiological effects of a substance (e.g., a drug of abuse, a medication) or another medical condition (e.g. hypothyroidism).

H. The symptoms cause clinically significant distress or impairment in social, occupational, or other important areas of functioning.

Note: Because the criteria for a major depressive episode include four symptoms that are absent from the symptom list for persistent depressive disorder (dysthymia), a very limited number of individuals will have depressive symptoms that have persisted longer than 2 years but will not meet criteria for persistent depressive disorder. If full criteria for a major depressive episode have been met at some point during the current episode of illness, they should be given a diagnosis of major depressive disorder. Otherwise, a diagnosis of other specified depressive disorder or unspecified depressive disorder is warranted.

Specify if:
   With anxious distress
   With mixed features
   With melancholic features
   With atypical features
   With mood-congruent psychotic features
   With mood-incongruent psychotic features
   With peripartum onset

Specify if:
   In partial remission
   In full remission

Specify if:
   Early onset: If onset is before age 21 years.
   Late onset: If onset is at age 21 years or older.

Specify if (for most recent 2 years of persistent depressive disorder):
   With pure dysthymic syndrome: Full criteria for a major depressive episode have not been met in at least the preceding 2 years.
   With persistent major depressive episode: Full criteria for a major depressive episode have been met throughout the preceding 2-year period.

(Continued)

TABLE 9.3 (*Continued*) DSM-5 Criteria for Persistent Depressive Disorder

> **With intermittent major depressive episodes, with current episode:** Full criteria for a major depressive episode arc currently met, but there have been periods of at least 8 weeks in at least the preceding 2 years with symptoms below the threshold for a full major depressive episode.
> **With intermittent major depressive episodes, without current episode:** Full criteria for a major depressive episode are not currently met, but there has been one or more major depressive episodes in at least the preceding 2 years.
>
> *Specify* current severity:
> **Mild**
> **Moderate**
> **Severe**

Source: American Psychiatric Association. (2013). *Diagnostic and statistical manual of mental disorders* (5th ed.). Arlington, VA: American Psychiatric Publishing.

disorder by virtue of the fact that there is persistent negative mood in between outbursts.

Persistent Depressive Disorder (Dysthymia)

Another change from the DSM-IV is that the DSM-5 now consolidates two disorders that were previously separate, chronic major depression and dysthymic disorder, into one category, **persistent depressive disorder**. As can be seen in Table 9.3, the criteria for this disorder map onto the previous symptoms described for dysthymia. However, there is the opportunity to specify a number of characteristics that might better describe the presentation of an individual, for example: the presence of anxious distress or psychotic features; early or late onset; with or without major depressive episodes. As before, DSM-5 specifies that in children and adolescents the key feature of negative mood may take the form of *irritability* rather than depression.

Major Depressive Disorder

The diagnostic criteria for **major depressive disorder** remain little changed from DSM-IV with one major exception: DSM-5 no longer lists bereavement as a "rule out" for the diagnosis. Instead, a note is provided that guides clinicians to consider whether depression might in fact co-occur in the context of grief over a major loss. Clinical judgement, the individual's history, and cultural norms regarding reactions to loss should be considered in determining whether major depression is present.

In order to differentiate grief-related major depression from normal grieving, DSM-5 notes that the predominant emotional state in the case of grief is one of *sadness and loss*, which ebbs and flows with thoughts about the deceased. In contrast, during a major depressive episode, there is persistent *negative mood, anhedonia* (inability to feel pleasure), and *self-loathing*. In keeping with this new perspective on grief as potentially accompanying, rather than ruling out, a disorder, the DSM-5 also includes in the appendix of conditions for further study a proposed new diagnosis of *persistent complex bereavement disorder*. In this proposed disorder, following the death of a loved one, the individual's functioning is severely disrupted (for a period of 12 months for adults and 6 months for children) by symptoms including persistent yearning for and preoccupation with the deceased, marked difficulty accepting the death, feeling that life is empty and meaningless, and the desire to cease living oneself.

Premenstrual Dysphoric Disorder

Another disorder that is new to the DSM-5 is **premenstrual dysphoric disorder**, which

TABLE 9.4 DSM-5 Criteria for Major Depressive Disorder

A. Five (or more) of the following symptoms have been present during the same 2-week period and represent a change from previous functioning; at least one of the symptoms is either (1) depressed mood or (2) loss of interest or pleasure.

Note: Do not include symptoms that are clearly attributable to another medical conditions.

1. Depressed mood must of the day, nearly every day, as indicated by either subjective report (e.g., feels sad, empty, hopeless) or observation made by other (e.g., appears tearful). (**Note:** In children and adolescents, can be irritable mood.)
2. Markedly diminished interest or pleasure in all, or almost all, activities most of the day, nearly every day (as indicated by either subjective account or observation).
3. Significant weight loss when not dieting or weight gain (e.g., a change of more than 5% of body weight in a month), or decrease or increase in appetite nearly every day. (**Note:** In children, consider failure to make expected weight gain.)
4. Insomnia or hypersomnia nearly every day.
5. Psychomotor agitation or retardation nearly every day (observable by others, not merely subjective feelings of restlessness or being slowed down).
6. Fatigue or loss of energy nearly every day.
7. Feelings of worthlessness or excessive or inappropriate guilt (which may be delusional) nearly every day (not merely self-reproach or guilt about being sick).
8. Diminished ability to think or concentrate, or indecisiveness, nearly every day (either by subjective account or as observed by others).
9. Recurrent thoughts of death (not just fear of dying), recurrent suicidal ideation without a specific plan, or a suicide attempt or a specific plan for committing suicide.

B. The symptoms cause clinically significant distress or impairment in social, occupational, or other important areas of functioning.

C. The episode is not attributable to the physiological effects of a substance or to another medical condition.

Note: Criteria A–C represent a major depressive episode.

Note: Responses to a significant loss (e.g., bereavement, financial ruin, losses from a natural disaster, a serious medical illness or disability) may include the feelings of intense sadness, rumination about the loss, insomnia, poor appetite, and weight loss noted in Criterion A, which may resemble a depressive episode. Although such symptoms may be understandable or considered appropriate to the loss, the presence of a major depressive episode in addition to the normal response to a significant loss should also be carefully considered. This decision inevitably requires the exercise of clinical judgment based on the individual's history and the cultural norms for the expression of distress in the context of loss.

D. The occurrence of the major depressive episode is not better explained by schizoaffective disorder, schizophrenia, schizophreniform disorder, delusional disorder, or other specified and unspecified schizophrenia spectrum and other psychotic disorders.

E. There has never been a manic episode or a hypomanic episode.

Note: This exclusion does not apply if all of the manic-like or hypomanic-like episodes are substance-induced or are attributable to the physiological effects of another medical condition.

Source: American Psychiatric Association. (2013). *Diagnostic and statistical manual of mental disorders* (5th ed.). Arlington, VA: American Psychiatric Publishing.

previously was one of the potential disorders listed as worthy of further study in an appendix of the DSM-IV. As noted in Table 9.5, the main features of this disorder are changes in mood—irritability, dysphoria, anxiety, and emotional lability (mood swings)—during the premenstrual phase of a girl's cycle. There must be a clear distinction between her prevailing mood during other phases of her cycle, and she must show a succession of symptoms once the menstrual cycle has begun.

Prevalence and age of onset

Prevalence of the disorder is estimated at between 1.8 and 5.8 of females who have reached the age of menstruation, although no

TABLE 9.5 DSM-5 Criteria for Premenstrual Dysphoric Disorder

A. In the majority of menstrual cycles, at least five symptoms must be present in the final week before the onset of menses, star to *improve* within a few days after the onset of menses, and become *minimal* or absent in the week postmenses.

B. One (or more) of the following symptoms must be present:
   1. Marked affective lability (e.g., mood swings; feeling suddenly sad or tearful, or increased sensitivity to rejection).
   2. Marked irritability or anger or increased interpersonal conflicts.
   3. Marked depressed mood, feelings of hopelessness, or self-deprecating thoughts.
   4. Marked anxiety, tension, and/or feelings of being keyed up or on edge.

C. One (or more) of the following symptoms must additionally be present, to reach a total of *five* symptoms when combined with symptoms from Criterion B above.
   1. Decreased interest in usual activities (e.g., work, school, friends, hobbies).
   2. Subjective difficulty in concentration.
   3. Lethargy, easy fatigability, or marked lack of energy.
   4. Marked change in appetite; overeating; or specific food cravings.
   5. Hypersomnia or insomnia.
   6. A sense of being overwhelmed or out of control.
   7. Physical symptoms such as breast tenderness or swelling, joint or muscle pain, a sensation of "bloating," or weight gain.

   Note: The symptoms in Criteria A–C must have been met for most menstrual, cycles that occurred in the preceding year.

D. The symptoms are associated with clinically significant distress or interference with work, school, usual social activities, or relationships with others (e.g., avoidance of social activities; decreased productivity and efficiency at work, school, or home).

E. The disturbance is not merely an exacerbation of the symptoms of another disorder, such as major depressive disorder, panic disorder, persistent depressive disorder (dysthymia), or a personality disorder (although it may co-occur with any of these disorders).

F. Criterion A should be confirmed by prospective daily ratings during at least two symptomatic cycles. (**Note:** The diagnosis may be made provisionally prior to this confirmation.)

G. The symptoms are not attributable to the physiological effects of a substance (e.g., a drug of abuse, a medication, other treatment) or another medical condition (e.g., hyperthyroidism).

Source: American Psychiatric Association. (2013). *Diagnostic and statistical manual of mental disorders* (5th ed.). Arlington, VA: American Psychiatric Publishing.

information is provided about whether these data are based on adult samples or include girls. As we have noted in this chapter in the book, the age of onset of menstruation has been decreasing in Westernized societies, and it is no longer unusual to see girls as young as 11 who have begun their cycles—thus, this is a disorder that will be relevant to understanding developmental psychopathology in the later school-age and adolescent years.

Risks

Risk factors for the disorder include environmental factors such as *stress*, a history of interpersonal *trauma*, and *sociocultural* expectations for the feminine role. Estimates of *heritability* are rough, with little data yet available, but range from 30 to 50 per cent.

Comorbidity and differential diagnosis

PDD is often comorbid with other *mood disorders*, particularly major depressive episodes but differential diagnosis is suggested by the cyclical nature of the symptoms, which clearly follow the phases of the menstrual cycle. Particularly important to the diagnosis is the gathering of prospective daily ratings of mood. The DSM-5 notes that many women with mood disorders believe that they suffer from PDD but, when asked to keep a daily diary, find that their retrospective recollections of the timing of their moods don't actually correspond to their menstrual cycles.

Bipolar Disorder

As noted above, a major change in DSM-5 is the separation of *Bipolar and Related Disorders* into their own category. In addition, this category is intentionally placed in between the depressive and psychotic disorders in recognition of way bipolar disorder acts a bridge between them in regards to symptom expression, family history, and genetics. Except for some small changes in wording, the criteria for a **manic episode** remain appreciably unchanged (see Table 9.6) as do the differentiation between types, which include *bipolar I* (presence of a manic episode), *bipolar II* (intermittent hypomanic and major depressive episodes), and *cyclothymic disorder* (cycling between hypomanic and depressive episodes). The most notable change in the diagnoses is that now both *changes in mood* and *changes in activity or energy level* are included as criteria.

Potential Implications of the New DSM-5 Criteria

The addition to DSM-5 of two new diagnoses covered in this chapter, DMDD and PDD, has in both cases been accompanied by

TABLE 9.6 DSM-5 Criteria for Manic Episode

A. A distinct period of abnormally and persistently elevated, expansive, or irritable mood and abnormally and persistently increased goal-directed activity or energy, lasting at least 1 week and present most of the day, nearly every day (or any duration if hospitalization is necessary).

B. During the period of mood disturbance and increased energy or activity, three (or more) of the following symptoms (four if the mood is only irritable) are present to a significant degree and represent a noticeable change from usual behavior:

  1. Inflated self-esteem or grandiosity.
  2. Decreased need for sleep (e.g., feels rested after only 3 hours of sleep).
  3. More talkative than usual or pressure to keep talking.
  4. Flight of ideas or subjective experience that thoughts are racing.
  5. Distractibility (i.e., attention too easily drawn to unimportant or irrelevant external stimuli), as reported or observed.
  6. Increase in goal-directed activity (either socially, at work or school, or sexually) or psychomotor agitation (i.e., purposeless non-goal-directed activity).
  7. Excessive involvement in activities that have a high potential for painful consequences (e.g., engaging in unrestrained buying sprees, sexual indiscretions, or foolish business investments).

C. The mood disturbance is sufficiently severe to cause marked impairment in social or occupational functioning or to necessitate hospitalization to prevent harm to self or others, or there are psychotic features.

D. The episode is not attributable to the physiological effects of a substance (e.g., a drug of abuse, a medication, other treatment) or to another medical condition.
  Note: A full manic episode that emerges during antidepressant treatment (e.g., medication, electroconvulsive therapy) but persists at a fully syndromal level beyond the physiological effect of that treatment is sufficient evidence for a manic episode and, therefore, a bipolar I diagnosis.

Note: Criteria A–D constitute a manic episode. At least one lifetime manic episode is required for the diagnosis of bipolar I disorder.

Source: American Psychiatric Association. (2013). *Diagnostic and statistical manual of mental disorders* (5th ed.). Arlington, VA: American Psychiatric Publishing.

controversy and debate. In the case of DMDD, proponents of the diagnosis concur with the rationale provided by the DSM-5 developers, that the new category is necessary to decrease the overdiagnosis and mistreatment of inappropriately-labelled bipolar disorder in young children. On the other hand, critics of the DMDD diagnosis argue that it has too much overlap with other disorders to be reliably discriminated, particularly given that irritability is such a prevalent accompaniment to childhood emotional problems and spans the entire spectrum from internalizing to externalizing disorders. Such disruptions in children's mood and behaviour also might signal the presence of environmental adversities—such as family stress or maltreatment in the home—rather than a psychiatric disorder residing within the individual child.

Some research appears to reinforce the concerns over whether DMDD can be reliably discriminated from other disorders and whether it makes an independent contribution to our understanding of childhood psychopathology. For example, in a clinical sample of over 700 US children, Axelson et al. (2012) found that DMDD could not be delimited from oppositional defiant disorder or conduct disorder, that the diagnosis had limited stability over time, and was not associated with the child's or parents' mood or anxiety disorders. The authors suggest that these findings raise concerns about the diagnostic utility of the DMDD diagnosis. Similar findings have emerged in a study involving over 3,000 US children, in which Copeland, Angold, Costello & Egger (2013) found that DMDD co-occurred with another disorder in 32 per cent to 92 per cent of cases. The highest odds of co-occurrence were with depressive disorders (between 9.9 to 23.5 of the time) and oppositional defiant disorder (between 52.9 and 100 per cent of the time). Children growing up in poverty were more likely than their more privileged peers to earn the diagnosis. However, children who met criteria for the diagnosis clearly

exhibited significant psychopathology, including elevated levels of social impairment, school suspensions, and referrals for mental health and educational services.

In turn, concerns about including a PDD diagnosis in the DSM have long centred on the question of whether a normative biological function is being pathologized and whether the ramifications of terming this a mental disorder will be beneficial or stigmatizing for girls and women (Caplan, McCurdy-Myers & Gans, 1992). However, proponents of the diagnosis note the strong evidence base that has accumulated in support of its validity, the human suffering that can be attributed to the disorder, and the potential benefits of the diagnosis for spurring research into effective treatments and routing girls and women who otherwise might have their symptoms ignored or misdiagnosed to appropriate interventions (Epperson et al., 2012).

Regarding diagnoses in the depressive spectrum, the deletion of bereavement as an exclusionary "rule out" for the diagnosis of depression has also been controversial. Opponents have expressed concern that the diagnosis will pathologize a normal process of grief and, moreover, have questioned the scientific evidence in support of the claim that the bereavement exclusion is not valid (Wakefield & First, 2013). Nonetheless, as the DSM-5 argues, the loss of a loved one may in fact precipitate an episode of major depression in an individual with vulnerabilities and, without treatment, may increase the risk for negative outcomes such as suicidal thoughts, poor self-care, and emotional suffering. Research in support of the idea that bereavement may occur along with—and not instead of—depression is emerging with increasing study of the newly proposed diagnosis for future consideration, *persistent complex bereavement disorder*, including studies focused specifically on children and adolescents (Kaplow, Howell & Layne, 2014; Kaplow, Layne, Pynoos, Cohen & Lieberman, 2012).

CHAPTER 10

Middle Childhood to Adolescence: Conduct Disorder

This section accompanies chapter 10 in Kerig, Ludlow & Wenar (2012), *Developmental Psychopathology*, 6th Edition. McGraw-Hill Education.

Chapter contents

Conduct Disorder

In the DSM-5, **conduct disorder** appears in the category of *Disruptive, Impulse-Control, and Conduct Disorders*, along with **oppositional defiant disorder** (see Chapter 6 in primary text). Other disruptive disorders listed in this spectrum include: intermittent explosive disorder; antisocial personality disorder; pyromania (fire-setting); and kleptomania (compulsive thieving). What all of these disorders have in common are underlying problems with the regulation of emotions or behaviour. Given that they frequently co-occur, it is believed that these disorders also stem from a common personality dimension termed *disinhibition* as well as, to a lesser extent, *negative emotionality*. The disorders in this category also stand apart in that the associated behaviours violate the rights of others (e.g., through aggression, destruction of property, or theft) or bring the person into conflict with the norms and laws of society.

Just as DSM-IV, DSM-5 defines **Conduct Disorder** (CD) as "a repetitive and persistent pattern of behavior in which either the basic rights of others or major age-appropriate societal norms or rules are violated" (See Table 10.1.) in the four categories of *aggression to people and animals, destruction of property, deceitfulness or theft,* and *serious violations of rules*.

In addition to the specifications for *severity* (mild, moderate, or severe) and for *onset* (child or adolescent) that were present in DSM-IV, DSM-5 adds a new specifier, *with limited prosocial emotions*. The description of this subtype will be familiar to readers of the main textbook. As we have reviewed, evidence supports that an important distinction should be made regarding whether youth demonstrate the

TABLE 10.1 DSM-5 Criteria for the Diagnosis of Conduct Disorder

A. A repetitive and persistent pattern of behavior in which the basic rights of others or major age-appropriate societal norms or rules are violated, as manifested by the presence of at least three of the following 15 criteria in the past 12 months from any of the categories below, with at least one criterion present in the past 6 months:

Aggression to People and Animals
1. Often bullies, threatens, or intimidates others.
2. Often initiates physical fights.
3. Has used a weapon that can cause serious physical harm to others (e.g., a bat, brick, broken bottle, knife, gun).
4. Has been physically cruel to people.
5. Has been physically cruel to animals.
6. Has stolen while confronting a victim (e.g., mugging, purse snatching, extortion, armed robbery).
7. Has forced someone into sexual activity.

Destruction of Property
8. Has deliberately engaged in fire setting with the intention of causing serious damage.
9. Has deliberately destroyed others' property (other than by fire setting).

Deceitfulness or Theft
10. Has broken into someone else's house, building or car.
11. Often lies to obtain goods or favors or to avoid obligations (i.e., "cons" others).
12. Has stolen items of nontrivial value without confronting a victim (e.g., shoplifting, but without breaking and entering; forgery).

Serious Violations of Rules
13. Often stays out at night despite parental prohibitions, beginning before age 13 years.
14. Has run away from home overnight at least twice while living in the parental or parental surrogate home, or once without returning for a length period.
15. Is often truant from school, beginning before age 13 years.

B. The disturbance in behavior causes clinically significant impairment in social, academic or occupational functioning.

C. If the individual is 18 years or older, criteria are not met for antisocial personality disorder.

Specify whether:
   Childhood-onset type: Individuals show at least one symptom characteristic of conduct disorder prior to age 10 years.
   Adolescent-onset type: Individuals show no symptoms characteristic of conduct disorder prior to age 10 years.
   Unspecified-onset type: Criteria for a diagnosis of conduct disorder are met, but there is not enough information available to determine whether the onset of the first symptom was before or after age 10 years.

Specify if:
   With limited prosocial emptions: To qualify for this specifier, an individual must have displayed at least two of the following characteristics persistently over at least 12 months and in multiple relationships and settings. These characteristics reflect the individual's typical pattern of interpersonal and emotional functioning over this period and not just occasional occurrences in some situations. Thus, to assess the criteria for the specifier, multiple information sources are necessary. In addition to the individual's self-report, it is necessary to consider reports by others who have known the individual for extended periods of time (e.g., parents, teachers, co-workers, extended family members, peers).
   Lack of remorse or guilt: Does not feel bad or guilty when he or she does something wrong (exclude remorse when expressed only when caught and/or facing punishment). The individual shows a general lack of concern about the negative consequences of his or her actions. For example, the individual is not remorseful after hurting someone or does not care about the consequences of breaking rules.

Callous – lack of empathy: Disregards and is unconcerned about the feelings of others. The individual is described as cold and uncaring. The person appears more concerned about the effects of his or her actions on himself or herself, rather than their effects on others, even when they result in substantial harm to others.

Unconcerned about performance: Does not show concern about poor/problematic performance at school, at work, or in other important activities. The individual does not put forth the effort necessary to perform well, even when expectations are clear, and typically blames others for his or her poor performance.

Shallow or deficient affect: Does not express feelings or show emotions to others, except in ways that seem shallow, insincere, or superficial (e.g., actions contradict the emotion displayed; can turn emotions "on" or "off" quickly) or when emotional expressions are used for gain (e.g., emotions displayed to manipulate or intimidate others).

Specify current severity:

Mild: Few if any conduct problems in excess of those required to make the diagnosis are present, and conduct problems cause relatively minor harm to others (e.g., lying, truancy, staying out after dark without permissions, other rule breaking).

Moderate: The number of conduct problems and the effect on others are intermediate between those specified in "mild" and those in "severe" (e.g., stealing without confronting a victim, vandalism).

Severe: Many conduct problems in excess of those required to make the diagnosis are present, or conduct problems cause considerable hard to others (e.g., forced sex, physical cruelty, use of a weapon, stealing while confronting a victim, breaking and entering).

Source: American Psychiatric Association. (2013). *Diagnostic and statistical manual of mental disorders* (5th ed.). Arlington, VA: American Psychiatric Publishing.

presence of characteristics associated with juvenile psychopathy, or **callous-unemotional** (CU) traits. The characteristics listed in DSM-5 follow directly from those identified in research on CU traits in children and adolescents (Frick, Ray, Thornton & Kahn, 2013), including *lack of remorse or guilt, callousness* toward others and *lack of empathy, lack of concern* about performing to meet other's expectations, and *shallow or superficial emotions*.

Potential Implications of the New DSM-5 Criteria for Conduct Disorder

Although the research evidence in regard to the callous-unemotional subtype of conduct disorder has been accumulating for many years, it is notable that only in this most recent edition of the DSM is it acknowledged in the diagnostic criteria. One reason for this long hesitation has been concern about the possible negative effects of saddling a child with a label – such as "psychopathic" – that has such negative connotations (Kahn, Frick, Youngstrom, Findling & Youngstrom, 2012). In particular, there is a widely-held belief that individuals with these features are "born, not made" and thus are not amenable to intervention. Recent work, however, has shown that the assumption that high-CU youth can't be treated is based on an overgeneralization (Hawes, Price, & Dadds, 2014). Although youth with CU features might not respond well to the typical treatments employed for conduct disorder, they are shown to be amenable to interventions that are designed especially for them, which address their underlying deficits in impulse control, motivation, and responsiveness to others (Salekin, Tippey & Allen, 2012).

Moreover, as we have seen, the research evidence makes clear that only a subset of youth who exhibit behaviour problems have

CU characteristics and that these traits are predictive of the most serious, persistent and violent offenses. Therefore the DSM-5 committee found good reason to distinguish children with these traits from those with "garden variety" conduct problems. However, in recognition of the concerns about labelling, you will note the care that DSM-5 takes to avoid using potentially pejorative terms such as "psychopathy" in the definition of the subtype.

As a side comment, and a bit of a puzzle, it is noteworthy that no such subtype is included in the new DSM-5 criteria for the diagnosis of adult antisocial personality disorder. This is the case even though the research base demonstrating differences between antisocial adults with and without psychopathic traits is even more long-standing and well-established than that involving children (Hare, 1996).

Severe Deviation in Late Childhood and Adolescence: Schizophrenia Spectrum and Other Psychotic Disorders

This section accompanies chapter 11 in Kerig, Ludlow & Wenar (2012), *Developmental Psychopathology*, 6th Edition. McGraw-Hill Education.

Chapter contents

Overview

The overall diagnosis of schizophrenia has not greatly changed from the DSM-IV. The same basic diagnoses are still available in the DSM-5 with schizophrenia characterized by delusions, hallucinations, disorganized speech and behaviour, and other symptoms that cause social or occupational dysfunction. For a diagnosis, symptoms must have been present for six months and include at least one month of active symptoms.

The reason for retaining the core diagnostic criteria of the DSM-IV is that it has been found to be clinically useful and have both high reliability and validity (Haahr et al., 2008). For example 90% found to retain their diagnosis after 1-10 years. However, DSM-5 has added the word, "spectrum" to the title to reflect the continuum of symptoms. Schizotypal personality disorder, schizophreniform disorder, brief psychotic disorder and delusional disorder whilst still considered separate disorders in the DSM-5 are now categorized under the term schizophrenia spectrum. In addition some symptom criteria have been changed to make diagnosis more accurate and precise. Table 11.1 lists the new DSM-5 criteria.

Changes between DSM-IV and DSM-5

A rise in symptom threshold

The DSM-IV required individuals to exhibit at least one specified symptom to be eligible for a diagnosis. The DSM-5 has increased the requirement to at least two specified symptoms from five of criteria A. At least one of these two symptoms must be a core positive symptom (delusions, hallucinations, disorganized speech) due the high reliability of these symptoms in diagnosing schizophrenia. These proposed changes are unlikely to affect prevalence rates as already there is at least one of these symptoms present in all cases of schizophrenia diagnosed with the DSM-IV.

Removal of subtypes

Individuals were previously identified by one of five sub-types (paranoid; disorganized; catatonic; undifferentiated; residual), determined by their prominent symptoms at the time of diagnosis. DSM-5 decided to remove the subtypes as there was not a clear distinction between the different subtypes and symptoms could often vary over time between the subtypes (Rey, 2010). Some of the subtypes are now used as specifiers instead. Because the catatonic, disorganised and residual subtypes are rarely used, this change is predicted to have minimum impact on routine clinical practice.

Negative symptoms of schizophrenia

The DSM-5 has seen a number of changes in its classification of schizophrenia in its diagnosis of negative symptoms compared to the DSM-IV. The negative symptoms included in the diagnostic criteria will now include diminished emotional expression and avolition. In DSM-5 the deficits in emotional expression are defined by flat affect, diminished expression whereas avolition is categorised by volition, asociality and anhedonia. Previously in the DSM-IV these symptoms were considered to have significant overlap with each other, but they are now separated in the DSM-5 based on the evidence that the two subdomains not only differ in their clinical presentation but can also have a different impact on functional outcome (Barch et al., 2013). In addition, the way negative symptoms are diagnosed has changed. The DSM-IV listed negative symptoms to be noted 'such as affective flattening, alogia & avolition;' in contrast the DSM-5 includes more directive specifiers to diagnose negative symptoms. For example emotional expression is to be diagnosed based on expressivity (gestures, facial expressions and prosody) during the actual clinical interview whereas avolition is instructed to be based on patient self-initiated behaviours outside of the clinical setting (Malaspina et al., 2014).

No clear distinction between bizarre and non-bizarre delusions

Previous diagnostic criteria have given weight to bizarre delusions or Schnederian hallucinations. However these criteria have been removed, as there is little evidence that they are exclusive to this disorder and the distinction between bizarre and non-bizarre delusions has been found to have poor reliability (Tandon et al., 2013). According to DSM-5, evidence of symptoms of delusion would simply be a delusional disorder.

Catatonic specifiers and new Catatonic Disorders

Historically, catatonia has been associated with schizophrenia and is listed as a subtype of

TABLE 11.1 DSM-5 Criteria for Schizophrenia and other psychotic disorders

A. Two (or more) of the following, each present for a significant portion of time during a 1-month period (or less if successfully treated). At least one of these must be (1), (2), or (3):

1. Delusions.
2. Hallucinations.
3. Disorganized speech (e.g., frequent derailment or incoherence).
4. Grossly disorganized or catatonic behavior.
5. Negative symptoms (i.e., diminished emotional expression or avolition).

B. For a significant portion of the time since the onset of the disturbance, level of functioning in one or more major areas, such as work, interpersonal relations, or self-care, is markedly below the level achieved prior to the onset (or when the onset is in childhood or adolescence, there is failure to achieve expected level of interpersonal, academic, or occupational functioning).

C. Continuous signs of the disturbance persist for at least 6 months. This 6-month period must include at least 1 month of symptoms (or less if successfully treated) that meet Criterion A (i.e., active-phase symptoms) and may include periods of prodromal or residual symptoms. During these prodromal or residual periods, the signs of the disturbance may be manifested by only negative symptoms or by two or more symptoms listed in Criterion A present in an attenuated form (e.g., odd beliefs, unusual perceptual experiences).

D. Schizoaffective disorder and depressive or bipolar disorder with psychotic features have been ruled out because either 1) no major depressive or manic episodes have occurred concurrently with the active-phase symptoms, or 2) if mood episodes have occurred during active-phase symptoms, they have been present for a minority of the total duration of the active and residual periods of the illness.

E. The disturbance is not attributable to the physiological effects of a substance (e.g., a drug of abuse, a medication) or another medical condition.

F. If there is a history of autism spectrum disorder or a communication disorder of childhood onset, the additional diagnosis of schizophrenia is made only if prominent delusions or hallucinations, in addition to the other required symptoms of schizophrenia, are also present for at least 1 month (or less if successfully treated).

Specify if:

The following course specifiers are only to be used after a 1-year duration of the disorder and if they are not in contradiction to the diagnostic course criteria.

First episode, currently in acute episode: First manifestation of the disorder meeting the defining diagnostic symptom and time criteria. An *acute episode* is a time period in which the symptom criteria are fulfilled.

First episode, currently in partial remission: *Partial remission* is a period of time during which an improvement after a previous episode is maintained and in which the defining criteria of the disorder are only partially fulfilled.

First episode, currently in full remission: *Full remission* is a period of time after a previous episode during which no disorder-specific symptoms are present.

Multiple episodes, currently in acute episode: Multiple episodes may be determined after a minimum of two episodes (i.e., after a first episode, a remission and a minimum of one relapse).

Multiple episodes, currently in partial remission

Multiple episodes, currently in full remission

Continuous: Symptoms fulfilling the diagnostic symptom criteria of the disorder are remaining for the majority of the illness course, with subthreshold symptom periods being very brief relative to the overall course.

Unspecified

Specify if:

With catatonia (refer to the criteria for catatonia associated with another mental disorder for definition).

(Continued)

TABLE 11.1 *(Continued)* DSM-5 Criteria for Schizophrenia and other psychotic disorders

> *Specify* current severity:
>   Severity is rated by a quantitative assessment of the primary symptoms of psychosis, including delusions, hallucinations, disorganized speech, abnormal psychomotor behavior, and negative symptoms. Each of these symptoms may be rated for its current severity (most severe in the last 7 days) on a 5-point scale ranging from 0 (not present) to 4 (present and severe). (See Clinician-Rated Dimensions of Psychosis Symptom Severity in the chapter "Assessment Measures.")
>
>   **Note:** Diagnosis of schizophrenia can be made without using this severity specifier.

Source: American Psychiatric Association. (2013). *Diagnostic and statistical manual of mental disorders* (5th ed.). Arlington, VA: American Psychiatric Publishing.

the disorder; it can occur in patients with a primary mood disorder and in association with neurological diseases and other general medical conditions (Weder, Muralee, Penland & Tampi, 2008). In recognition of its co-morbidity with other medical conditions, a new condition of catatonia secondary to a general medical conditionwas added to the DSM-IV, as well as catatonia being added as an episode specifier of major mood disorders (Tandon et al., 2013). However the diagnosis of catatonia has often proved problematic as the diagnosis of catatonia has been found to be difficult to recognize by clinicians and therefore often goes undiagnosed. Furthermore it is comorbid with many other disorders not found to be associated with schizophrenia. This has led to some changes in the DSM-5.

In the DSM-5 catatonia is diagnosed by single set of criteria and will appear the same throughout the manual. It is treated as specifiers to a range of disorders including schizophrenia and major mood disorders, but also for other psychotic disorders. In a further attempt to increase recognition, a new residual category of catatonia not otherwise specified will be used for cases for severely ill patients who do not meet diagnosis. These changes are hoped to help individual cases to be better identified and also to improve chances of individuals suffering with catatonia getting treatment.

TABLE 11.2 Key changes in DSM-5 criteria

DSM-IV	DSM-5
Criterion A allowed for just one symptom if delusions were "bizarre" or hallucinations included "running commentary" or "two or more voices."	Eliminated these special attributions.
	Requires two criterion A symptoms.
	Plus, must have one of the following core positive symptoms: • Delusions • Hallucinations • Disorganized speech
Subtypes: • Paranoid • Disorganized • Catatonic • Undifferentiated • Residual	Subtypes eliminated due to: • Limited diagnostic stability • Low reliability • Poor validity • Not clearly related to differential treatment

Disorders that lie on this spectrum are now listed

Schizotypal personality disorder, schizophreniform disorder, brief psychotic disorder and delusional disorder are all included under the heading of Schizophrenia Spectrum and Other Psychotic Disorders in the DSM-5. These conditions all have similar symptoms, such as a severely limited ability to make social connections along with a lack of emotional expression. However, unlike schizotypal personality disorder and schizophrenia, people with schizoid personality disorder are, in touch with reality; they're unlikely to experience paranoia or hallucinations; and they make sense when they speak, although the tone may not be animated; in contrast to conversational patterns of someone with schizotypal personality disorder or schizophrenia, which are typically strange and hard to follow and may/may not be animated in tone.

The primary change to schizoaffective disorder is the requirement that a major mood episode be present for a majority of the disorder's total duration after Criterion A has been met. This change makes schizoaffective disorder a longitudinal instead of a cross sectional diagnosis more comparable to schizophrenia, bipolar disorder, and major depressive disorder, which are bridged by this condition.

Attenuated psychosis syndrome not included

Attenuated psychosis syndrome is not yet considered a formal disorder. A person who does not have full blown psychotic disorder but shows minor versions of relevant symptoms could potentially fall into this category. It is included in Section III of the new manual: conditions listed which require future research.

Summary

Some of the key changes adopted by the DSM-5 include modification of criterion A, removal of subtypes, and inclusion of specifiers allowing for more descriptive criteria to aid in diagnosis. A major criticism of the new criteria is the failure to include any neurobiological criteria for a schizophrenia spectrum disorder. Whilst it was purposefully left out of the latest edition of the DSM due to a lack of consistency of evidence, it is suggested that future editions will become more reliant on neurobiological criteria to understand and more accurately diagnosis individuals showing a schizophrenia disorder (Cho & Lee, 2014).

Psychopathologies of the Adolescent Transition: Eating Disorders and Substance Use

This section accompanies chapter 12 in Kerig, Ludlow & Wenar (2012), *Developmental Psychology*, 6th Edition. McGraw-Hill Education.

Chapter contents

Eating Disorders: Anorexia Nervosa

The two changes in the first criteria for **anorexia nervosa** in DSM-5 are: the elimination of amenorrhea as a criterion; and exclusion from the first requirement that the individual exhibit a minimum 15 per cent loss of body weight (see Table 12.1). Instead, the disorder is now defined by a restriction of nutritional intake that leads to a significantly lower body weight than is appropriate given the individual's personal characteristics. This new criterion acknowledges that there are vast individual differences in what comprises a healthy weight across body types and developmental stages. Per cent loss of body weight comes into play in the assessment of the severity of the disorder as *mild, moderate, severe,* or *extreme,* and is based on the calculation of the individual's *body mass index* (BMI) (see Table 12.2).

TABLE 12.1 DSM-5 Criteria for Anorexia Nervosa

A. Restriction of energy intake relative to requirements, leading to a significantly low body weight in the context of age, sex, developmental trajectory, and physical health. *Significantly low weight* is defined as a weight that is less than minimally normal or, for children and adolescents, less than that minimally expected.

B. Intense fear of gaining weight or of becoming fat, or persistent behavior that interferes with weight gain, even though at a significantly low weight.

C. Disturbance in the way in which one's body weight or shape is experienced, undue influence of body weight or shape on self-evaluation, or persistent lack of recognition of the seriousness of the current low body weight.

Specify whether:

Restricting type: During the last 3 months, the individual has not engaged in recurrent episodes of binge eating or purging behavior (i.e., self-induced vomiting or the misuse of laxatives, diuretics, or enemas). This subtype describes presentations in which weight loss is accomplished primarily through dieting, fasting, and/or excessive exercise.

Binge-eating/purging type: During the last 3 months, the individual has engaged in recurrent episodes of binge eating or purging behavior (i.e., self-induced vomiting or the misuse of laxatives, diuretics, or enemas).

Specify if:

In partial remission: After full criteria for anorexia nervosa were previously met, Criterion A (low body weight) has not been met for a sustained period, but either Criterion B (intense fear of gaining weight or becoming fat or behavior that interferes with weight gain) or Criterion C (disturbances in self-perception of weight and shape) is still met.

In full remission: After full criteria for anorexia nervosa were previously met, none of the criteria have been met for a sustained period of time.

Specify current severity:

The minimum level of severity is based, for adults, on current body mass index (BMI) (see below) or, for children and adolescents, on BMI percentile. The ranges below are derived from World Health Organization categories for thinness in adults; for children and adolescents, corresponding BMI percentiles should be used. The level of severity may be increased to reflect clinical symptoms, the degree of functional disability, and the need for supervision.

Mild: BMI $\geq$ 17 kg/m^2
Moderate: BMI 16–16.99 kg/m^2
Severe: BMI 15–15.99 kg/m^2
Extreme: BMI < 15 kg/m^2

Source: American Psychiatric Association. (2013). Diagnostic and statistical manual of mental disorders (5th ed.). Arlington, VA: American Psychiatric Publishing.

The only other change of note is to Criterion B, which now includes not only *fear of weight gain* but the taking of *actions that interfere with putting on weight*. The rest of the criteria for the diagnosis of anorexia nervosa remain unchanged, including the differentiation of the two types based on the different means used to achieve thinness—*restricting* versus *binge-eating/purging* (Table 12.1).

Eating Disorders: Bulimia Nervosa

As a review of the criteria listed in Table 12.3 will show, there are two significant changes to the diagnosis of **bulimia nervosa** in DSM-5 (see Table 12.3). One is that the frequency of binges required is reduced to an average of once a week, from the prior requirement of twice a week, over the course of 3 months. The second major change is the omission of the two subtypes of *purging* versus *non-purging* that were listed in DSM-5. Instead, the use of any form of compensatory behaviours (e.g., self-induced vomiting, laxatives, excessive exercise) may be seen in the disorder.

Eating Disorders: Binge-Eating Disorder

As we noted when the main text was published prior to the release of DSM-5, DSM-IV included **Binge-Eating Disorder** in the appendix of disorders for future consideration. In DSM-5,

---

FIGURE 12.1 Calculating and Interpreting the Body Mass Index for Children and Teens.

1. Obtain accurate height and weight measurements.
2. Calculate the BMI and percentile using the Child and Teen BMI Calculator. (http://apps.nccd.cdc.gov/dnpabmi). The BMI number is calculated using the following formulas:

Measurement Units	Formula and Calculation
Kilograms and metres (or centimetres)	Formula: weight (kg)/[height (m)]^2 With the metric system, the formula for BMI is weight in kilograms divided by height in meters squared. Since height is commonly measured in centimetres, divide height in centimetres by 100 to obtain height in meters. Example: Weight = 68 kg, Height = 165 cm (1.65 m) Calculation: $68 \div (1.65)^2 = 24.98$
Pounds and inches	Formula: weight (lb)/[height (in)]^2 × 703 Calculate BMI by dividing weight in pounds (lbs) by height in inches (in) squared and multiplying by a conversion factor of 703. Example: Weight = 150 lbs, Height = 5′5″ (65″) Calculation: $[150 \div (65)^2] \times 703 = 24.96$

3. Obtain the BMI-for-age percentile. The BMI-for-age percentile is used to interpret the BMI number because BMI is both age- and sex-specific for children and teens due to the fact that (a) the amount of body fat changes with age and (b) the amount of body fat differs between girls and boys. The CDC BMI-for-age growth charts for girls and boys (http://www.cdc.gov/growthcharts) take into account these differences and allow translation of a BMI number into a percentile for a youth's sex and age.
4. Find the weight status category for the calculated BMI-for-age percentile.

Weight Status Category	Percentile Range
Underweight	Less than the 5th percentile
Healthy weight	5th percentile to less than the 85th percentile
Overweight	85th to less than the 95th percentile
Obese	Equal to or greater than the 95th percentile

BED has "graduated" to becoming its own fully fledged disorder (see Table 12.3). Just like bulimia, the main feature of BED is recurrent episodes of excessive food intake within a discrete period of time, accompanied by a sense of lack of control. However, the important distinction is that binge-eating is not followed by attempts at compensating for the excessive consumption (e.g., purging, laxatives, exercise). Instead, it is the binge itself that is the focus of the pathology, as defined by a number of abnormal characteris-

See the following example of how BMI numbers would be interpreted for a 10-year-old boy:

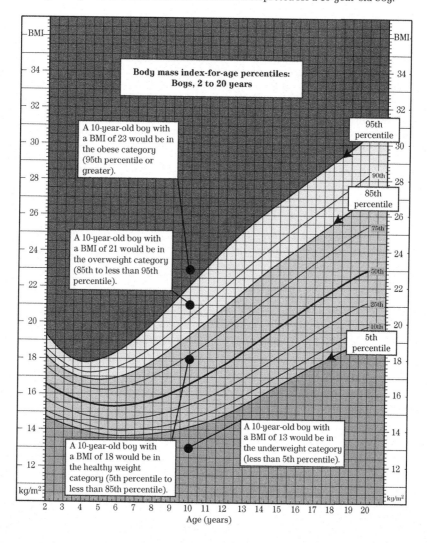

Source: Adapted from the Centers for Disease Control website (http://www.cdc.gov/healthyweight/assessing/bmi/childrens_bmi/about_childrens_bmi.html).

TABLE 12.2 DSM-5 Criteria for the Diagnosis of Bulimia Nervosa

A. Recurrent episodes of binge eating. An episode of binge eating is characterized by both of the following:
   1. Eating, in a discrete period of time (e.g., within any 2-hour period), an amount of food that is definitely larger than what most individuals would eat in a similar period of time under similar circumstances.
   2. A sense of lack of control ever eating during the episode (e.g., a feeling that one cannot stop eating or control what or how much one is eating).
B. Recurrent inappropriate compensatory behaviors in order to prevent weight gain, such as self-induced vomiting; misuse of laxatives, diuretics, or other medications; fasting; or excessive exercise.
C. The binge eating and inappropriate compensatory behaviors both occur, on average, at least once a week for 3 months.
D. Self-evaluation is unduly influenced by body shape and weight.
E. The disturbance does not occur exclusively during episodes of anorexia nervosa.

Specify if:
   In partial remission: After full criteria for bulimia nervosa were previously met, some, but not all, of the criteria have been met for a sustained period of time.
   In full remission: After full criteria for bulimia nervosa were previously met, none of the criteria have been met for a sustained period of time.

Specify current severity:
The minimum level of severity is based on the frequency of inappropriate compensatory behaviors (see below). The level of severity may be increased to reflect other symptoms and the degree of functional disability.
   Mild: An average of 1–3 episodes of inappropriate compensatory behaviors per week.
   Moderate: An average of 4–7 episodes of inappropriate compensatory behaviors per week.
   Severe: An average of 8–13 episodes of inappropriate compensatory behaviors per week.
   Extreme: An average of 14 or more episodes of inappropriate compensatory behaviors per week.

Source: American Psychiatric Association. (2013). *Diagnostic and statistical manual of mental disorders* (5th ed.). Arlington, VA: American Psychiatric Publishing.

tics of the eating behaviour, including that it is rapid, not associated with actual hunger, not responsive to physical sensations that one is full, and accompanied by feelings of embarrassment or disgust. Another requirement is that, unlike someone who merely enjoys eating too well, the individual with BED experiences marked distress regarding the binge eating. Severity is defined by the frequency of binge episodes, ranging from *mild* (1 to 3 per week) to *extreme* (14 or more per week).

Characteristics
Prevalence
International data from the World Health Organization's survey of over 24,000 adults in 14 mostly high-income countries indicates lifetime prevalence rates ranging from .8 to 1.9 per cent, with an average of 1.4% (Kessler et al., 2013). Estimates among adults in the US are 1.6 per cent for women and 0.8 per cent for men. No information is available currently about prevalence among children or adolescents.

Development and course
As this is a newly-defined disorder, little is known about its development or course. However, as with other eating disorders, increases in body fat and weight gain may provoke disordered eating. Thus, it is no surprise that the onset is most typically during adolescence or emerging adulthood. In contrast to bulimia nervosa, in which dysfunctional dieting is the beginning of the vicious cycle,

TABLE 12.3 DSM-5 Criteria for the Diagnosis of Binge-Eating Disorder

---

A. Recurrent episodes of binge eating. An episode of binge eating is characterized by both of the following:

    1. Eating, in a discrete period of time (e.g. within any 2-hour period) an amount of food that is definitely larger than what most people would eat in a similar period of time under similar circumstances.

    2. A sense of lack of control over eating during the episode (e.g., a feeling that one cannot stop eating or control what or how much one is eating).

B. The binge-eating episodes are associated with three (or more) of the following:

    1. Eating much more rapidly than normal.

    2. Eating until feeling uncomfortably full.

    3. Eating large amounts of food when not feeling physically hungry.

    4. Eating alone because of feeling embarrassed by how much one is eating.

    5. Feeling disgusted with oneself, depressed, or very guilty afterward.

C. Marked distress regarding binge eating is present.

D. The binge eating occurs, on average, at least one a week for 3 months.

E. The binge eating is not associated with the recurrent use of inappropriate compensatory behavior as in bulimia nervosa and does not occur exclusively during the course of bulimia nervosa or anorexia nervosa.

Specify if:

In partial remission: After full criteria for binge-eating disorder were previously met, binge eating occurs at an average frequency of less than one episode per week for a sustained period of time.

In full remission: After full criteria for binge-eating were previously met, none of the criteria have been met for a sustained period of time.

Specify current severity:

The minimum level of severity is based on the frequency of episodes of binge eating (see below). The level of severity may be increased to reflect other symptoms and the degree of functional disability.

    Mild: 1–3 binge-eating episodes per week.

    Moderate: 4–7 binge-eating episodes per week.

    Severe: 8–13 binge-eating episodes per week.

    Extreme: 14 or more binge-eating episodes per week.

Source: American Psychiatric Association. (2013). *Diagnostic and statistical manual of mental disorders* (5th ed.). Arlington, VA: American Psychiatric Publishing.

excessive dieting more typically follows after the development of BED.

Risk factors

BED appears to run in families and so a genetic component is suspected.

Differential diagnosis and comorbidity

As the definition of the disorder makes clear, the major distinction with *bulimia nervosa* is the absence of compensatory behaviours in BED. Although those with BED may diet, their food restrictions or attempts to reduce body weight are not as severe, sustained, and all-consuming. Overeating also may occur in the context of *depression* but only if there is an accompanying sense of loss of control would a diagnosis of BED also be considered. Similarly, BED may be present in those with *borderline personality disorder* (see Chapter 15 of the main text) given the way the two disorders are linked to deficits in impulse control. Finally, although many who seek treatment for BED are overweight, the disorder can occur in normal-weight individuals and is not synonymous with *obesity*. It is rare for obese individuals to engage in recurrent binge eating in which so many excessive calories are consumed in a short period of time, and obesity itself is not associated with the same kinds of functional impairments, psychological distress, and comorbid mental health problems as BED. Other common comorbidities include *bipolar, anxiety,* and *substance abuse disorders.*

Eating Disorders: Avoidant/ Restrictive Food Intake Disorder

Another new disorder added to DSM-5 is *avoidant/restrictive food intake disorder,* which replaces and extends a previous category of *feeding disorder of infancy/early childhood.* No longer restricted to young children, this diagnosis is applied to those who avoid eating, not because of a fear of gaining weight, as in anorexia nervosa, but because food or the process of eating are perceived as unpleasant or aversive (see Table 12.3). For some individuals, the aversion is related to the sensory characteristics of food – intense dislike of its colour, smell, texture or taste – and may result in highly "picky" eating in which only certain brands, shapes, or types of food can be tolerated. For others, the aversion is related to concerns about possible negative consequences of eating. These concerns may in fact comprise a conditioned reaction following from a negative experience the individual has undergone, such as choking on food, undergoing an invasive medical examination of the throat, or enduring an episode of vomiting.

Frequently, children and adolescents with the disorder fail to eat enough to keep a healthy body weight and trajectory of growth and consequently may be low in energy, irritable, and withdrawn. In the later school-age and adolescent years, low energy and malnutrition may interfere with the child's development and ability to learn in school as well as to participate in normative social activities. (An illustrative case example involving a 13 year-old boy is provided by Bryant-Waugh, 2013).

TABLE 12.4 DSM-5 Criteria for Avoidant/Restrictive Food Intake Disorder

A. An eating or feeding disturbance (e.g. apparent lack of interest in eating or food; avoidance based on the sensory characteristics of food; concern about aversive consequences of eating) as manifested by persistent failure to meet appropriate nutritional and/or energy needs associated with one (or more) of the following:

   1. Significant weight loss (or failure to achieve expected weight gain or faltering growth in children).
   2. Significant nutritional deficiency.
   3. Dependence on enteral feeding or oral nutritional supplements.
   4. Marked interference with psychosocial functioning.

B. The disturbance is not better explained by lack of available food or by an associated culturally sanctioned practice.

C. The eating disturbance does not occur exclusively during the course of anorexia nervosa or bulimia nervosa, and there is no evidence of a disturbance in the way in which one's body weight or shape is experienced.

D. The eating disturbance is not attributable to a concurrent medical condition or not better explained by another mental disorder. When the eating disturbance occurs in the context of another condition or disorder, the severity of the eating disturbance exceeds that routinely associated with the condition or disorder and warrants additional clinical attention.

Specify if:

   In remission: After full criteria for avoidant/restrictive food intake disorder were previously met, the criteria have not been met for a sustained period of time.

Source: American Psychiatric Association. (2013). *Diagnostic and statistical manual of mental disorders* (5th ed.). Arlington, VA: American Psychiatric Publishing.

Age of onset and developmental course

Although avoidance of food because of unpleasant sensory sensations tends to begin during early childhood, avoidance related to unpleasant consequences of eating may arise at any point in development. Problematic parent-child relationships might contribute the development of the disorder, particularly if parents present food in ways that are aversive to children or get into "battles" over feeding. Should a change in caregivers result in improved eating, DSM-5 suggests that child maltreatment might be involved. Difficult infant temperament might be a precipitating factor, although this may be a transactional association, in that the irritability following from poor eating might also contribute to difficult temperament. Although little data are available about long-term outcomes, it appears that when sensory-related aversion to food persists into adulthood, the disorder can be associated with otherwise normal functioning.

Differential diagnosis and comorbidity

Given the many and widely divergent reasons why a child may experience feeding difficulties – including some that involve not child psychopathology, but a maltreating environment – DSM-5 discusses a long list of differential diagnoses that should be made. For example, children with *reactive attachment disorder* often experience problems in the parent-child relationship that might interfere with feeding but only in ARFID is the feeding the primary target of treatment. Similarly, children with *autism spectrum disorder* often have rigid eating behaviours and sensory sensitivities but rarely restrict eating so severely that they fail to thrive physically. The differential with *specific phobia*, the DSM-5 acknowledges, is more difficult, especially when ARFID arises as a reaction to a negative experience, but is the recommended diagnosis when severely restricting eating, rather

than simply a fear of eating, is the primary concern. ARFID also shares a number of characteristics with *anorexia nervosa*, but is differentiated by the absence of a fear of gaining weight or engaging in behaviours (e.g., over-exercise, purging) that are designed to rid the body of unwanted food. Similarly, *obsessive-compulsive disorder* also may involve rituals and restrictions related to food and *depression* may severely suppress appetite; thus, both may be difficult to distinguish from ARFID, but also may co-occur, or even lead to, ARFID.

Substance Use Disorders

A major change from the DSM-IV criteria is that DSM-5 no longer separates diagnoses for substance abuse and dependence, but instead provides criteria for various **substance use disorders**, which include reference to the specific substance (e.g., cannabis, opioids, alcohol, tobacco), each of which also is accompanied by criteria for **substance intoxication, substance withdrawal**, and **substance-induced disorder** (e.g., *alcohol-induced depressive disorder* or *opioid-induced anxiety disorder*). The previous criterion involving legal problems has been replaced by a new symptom, of *craving or having a strong urge to use* the substance. The threshold for the diagnosis is lowered, with the requirement that only two or more of the criteria be met.

As all the diagnoses for disorders follow the same format, with the distinguishing feature only the name of the substance being used, an example is provided of **cannabis use disorder** in Table 12.4. The first criterion for the disorder focuses on a pathological pattern of behaviours related to use of the substance, which can be grouped into the following categories: *impaired control* (e.g., habitual overuse, inability to cut down, craving the substance); *social impairment* (e.g., the substance use interferes with functioning at

TABLE 12.5 DSM-5 Criteria for Alcohol Use Disorder

A. A problematic pattern of alcohol use leading to clinically significant impairment or distress, as manifested by at least two of the following, occurring within a 12-month period:

1. Alcohol is often taken in larger amounts or over a longer period than was intended.
2. There is a persistent desire or unsuccessful efforts to cut down or control alcohol use.
3. A great deal of time is spent in activities necessary to obtain alcohol, use alcohol, or recover from its effects.
4. Craving, or a strong desire or urge to use alcohol.
5. Recurrent alcohol use resulting in a failure to fulfill major role obligations at work, school, or home.
6. Continued alcohol use despite having persistent or recurrent social or interpersonal problems caused or exacerbated by the effects of alcohol.
7. Important social, occupational, or recreational activities are given up or reduced because of alcohol use.
8. Recurrent alcohol use in situations in which it is physically hazardous.
9. Alcohol use is continued despite knowledge of having a persistent or recurrent physical or psychological problem that is likely to have been caused or exacerbated by alcohol.
10. Tolerance, as defined by either of the following:
    a. A need for markedly increased amounts of alcohol to achieve intoxication or desired effect.
    b. A markedly diminished effect with continued use of the same amount of alcohol.
11. Withdrawal, as manifested by either of the following:
    a. The characteristic withdrawal syndrome for alcohol.
    b. Alcohol (or a closely related substance, such as a benzodiazepine) is taken to relieve or avoid withdrawal symptoms.

Specify if:
In early remission: After full criteria for alcohol use disorder were previously met, none of the criteria for alcohol use disorder have been met for at least 3 months but for less than 12 months (with the exception that Criterion A4, "Craving, or a strong desire or urge to use alcohol," may be met).
In sustained remission: After full criteria for alcohol use disorder were previously met, none of the criteria for alcohol use disorder have been met at any time during a period of 12 months or longer (with the exception that Criterion A4, "Craving, or a strong desire or urge to use alcohol," may be met).

Specify if:
In a controlled environment: This additional specifier is used if the individual is in an environment where access to alcohol is restricted.

Specify current severity:
Mild: Presence of 2–3 symptoms.
Moderate: Presence of 4–5 symptoms.
Severe: Presence of 6 or more symptoms.

Source: American Psychiatric Association. (2013). Diagnostic and statistical manual of mental disorders (5th ed.). Arlington, VA: American Psychiatric Publishing.

home, school or work, or with important relationships), *risky use* (e.g., pursuing the substance in dangerous situations or despite known risks to one's health); and *pharmacological criteria* (e.g., demonstrated biological changes that accompanying chronic substance use, including increased tolerance and symptoms of withdrawal).

Potential Implications of the New DSM-5 Criteria

Among the eating disorders, the inclusion of BMI in the evaluation of anorexia seems likely to make an important improvement to diagnostic accuracy, especially for children and adolescents, who may fluctuate widely in body weight across development while still remaining healthy and in the normative range. The addition of the criterion that the individual must be involved in taking drastic actions to reduce weight, rather than merely exhibiting a fear of gaining weight, also may help to differentiate true anorexia nervosa from the compulsion to be thin that is so prevalent amongst teenagers.

Overall, data indicate that using the DSM-5 criteria may increase the prevalence of disorders in the eating disorder spectrum. In a study of 215 children and adolescents presenting for eating problems at an adolescent medicine clinic, Ornstein et al. (2013) found that using the DSM-5 criteria resulted in an increase over DSM-IV in the prevalence of anorexia (from 30.0% to 40.0%) and bulimia (from 7.3% to 11.8%); 14 per cent of youth met criteria for the AFRID diagnosis. In addition, there also was a reduction in the number of youth diagnosed in the non-specific "not otherwise specified" category,

FIGURE 12.2 Percentage of Children and Adolescents Meeting Criteria for Eating Disorder Diagnoses Using DSM-IV and DSM-5 criteria

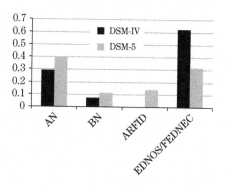

Note: AN = anorexia nervosa; ARFID = avoidant/restrictive food intake disorder; BN = bulimia nervosa; DSM-IV =Diagnostic and Statistical Manual, fourth edition; DSM-5 = Diagnostic and Statistical Manual, fifth edition; EDNOS = eating disorder not otherwise specified; FEDNEC = feeding or eating disorder not elsewhere classified.

Source: Data from Ornstein et al., 2013

which may be an indication of increased diagnostic accuracy.

In turn, the inclusion of BED in the eating disorders spectrum has been under consideration for some time and a fair amount of empirical support for its existence has accumulated. Data gathered by the World Health Organization Mental Health Surveys (Kessler, et al. 2013) involving over 24,000 adults across 14 countries shows that BED is more prevalent than bulimia, more persistent, and equally likely to be associated with functional impairments. Also, as might be expected, the addition of this category in itself is likely to increase the prevalence of eating disorder diagnoses. For example, Hudson, Coit, Lalonde & Pope (2012) found that, in a sample of 888 relatives of participants in a family study of disordered eating, the increase in lifetime prevalence of eating disorders when including the new DSM-5 criteria for BED was 2.9 per cent for women and 3.0 per cent for men.

As the other new disorder added to this spectrum, ARFID, is so recent, less research is available. However, accumulating evidence suggests it too is capturing a clinically significant subset of young people who otherwise might have been overlooked. As Kenny and Walsh (2013) point out, this classification replaces an older diagnosis, "feeding disorder of infancy or early childhood," which was seldom used and has not appeared in the empirical literature in over a decade. With the new diagnostic criteria for ARFID available in DSM-5, Fisher et al. (2014) assessed a sample of over 700 children and adolescents who presented to an eating disorders clinic and found that, among the almost 14 per cent who met criteria for ARFID, these young people were younger, more likely to be male, had a longer duration of symptoms, and were more likely to have a comorbid anxiety disorder or medical condition when compared to those who met criteria for a diagnosis of anorexia or bulimia.

Regarding substance use disorders, as we have noted, the key distinction is a removal of the distinction between substance *use* and substance *abuse*. This seems mostly like a matter of increasing accuracy and relieving clinicians of the need to make distinctions that were not actually useful. Research to date is supportive of the new criteria, with excellent correspondence to the DSM-IV diagnoses for substance dependence shown in a nationally representative study involving over 42,000 US adults (Compton, Dawson, Goldstein & Grant, 2013). As Winters, Martin, and Chung (2011) point out, the diagnostic changes also appear to be developmentally appropriate for adolescents. Adolescence is a time of increased normative experimentation with drugs and alcohol, as well as substance use problems, and these appear to be better differentiated by the DSM-5 criteria than they were by the older criteria. The removal of the "legal problems" criterion in the DSM-5 also seems wise, particularly for younger adolescents and girls, who do not necessarily have run-ins with the law in the context of substance use.

The Developmental Consequences of Brain Injury and Chronic Illness: Acquired Brain Injury & Neurocognitive Disorder

This section accompanies chapter 13 in Kerig, Ludlow &Wenar (2012), *Developmental Psychopathology*, 6th Edition. McGraw-Hill Education.

Acquired Brain Injury (ABI) refers to any type of brain damage or neurological disruption occurring after birth. The term 'Neurocognitive Disorder' (NCD) has been adopted by the DSM-5 to categorise the same spectrum of impairments as 'Acquired Brain Injury' with causes including trauma, vascular disease, Alzheimer's disease and infection. The term Neurocognitive Disorder also provides a diagnosis for people experiencing cognitive symptoms alone, without memory or physical impairments. This means that many individuals who are not currently receiving recognition or services (due to the lack of memory or physical impairments) will have the opportunity to be diagnosed (Simpson, 2014).

In DSM-5, not all brain injuries can be considered potentially causative of Neurocognitive Disorder (NCD). The diagnostic criteria for NCD due to Traumatic Brain Injury (TBI) require that the TBI be associated with at least one of four features: loss of consciousness; posttraumatic amnesia; disorientation and confusion; or neurological signs, such as neuroimaging findings, seizures, visual field cuts, anosmia, or hemiparesis. In addition, the NCD must have its onset either immediately after the TBI or after recovery of consciousness and must persist past the acute post-injury period. Importantly in cases where there is no immediate cognitive or neurological change following the trauma, the individual will not be diagnosed with a NCD.

It is important to note that many of the disorders that feature in the neurocognitive disorder chapter of the DSM are related to adulthood, and hence neurocognitive disorders feature as one of the later chapters in the manual. The lack of focus on childhood conditions means that here we will only consider briefly the key changes brought in to this category in the DSM-5.

Major and Minor Neurocognitive Disorder

Minor neurocognitive disorder was not included in previous editions of the DSM. In order to be given a diagnosis of a minor neurocognitive disorder, an individual must show a modest cognitive decline from a previous level of performance in one or more cognitive domains-such as complex attention, executive function, learning, memory. The Diagnostic Criteria for major and minor neurocognitive disorder are outlined in Table 13.2 and 13.3.

The addition of a mild degree of cognitive impairment has been bought in due to extensive amount of research suggesting that treatments for declining cognition may be phase-specific, with certain medications and approaches possibly only working early in the development of the disorder. In the DSM-5, the use of standardized neuropsychological testing is discussed in the context of distinguishing between major and mild NCDs.

Mild neurocognitive disorder requires "modest" cognitive decline which does not interfere with "capacity for independence in everyday activities" like paying bills or taking medications correctly. Cognitive decline meets the "major" criteria when "significant" impairment is evident or reported and when it does interfere with a patient's independence to the point that assistance is required. In other words, the diagnostic distinction relies heavily on observable behaviours.

New Descriptors Added

New descriptions of the cognitive domains affected by NCDs are introduced in DMS-5. In DSM-IV, the cognitive disturbances that could be seen in dementia (in addition to memory impairment) were all cognitive including aphasia, apraxia, agnosia, and impaired executive

TABLE 13.1 DSM-5 Criteria for Traumatic Brain Injury

A. The criteria are met for major or mild neurocognitive disorder.
B. There is evidence of a traumatic brain injury—that is, an impact to the head or other mechanisms of rapid movement or displacement of the brain within the skull, with one or more of the following: 1. Loss of consciousness. 2. Posttraumatic amnesia. 3. Disorientation and confusion. 4. Neurological signs (e.g., neuroimaging demonstrating injury; a new onset of seizures; a marked worsening of a preexisting seizure disorder; visual field cuts; anosmia; hemiparesis).
C. The neurocognitive disorder presents immediately after the occurrence of the traumatic brain injury or immediately after recovery of consciousness and persists past the acute post-injury period.

Source: American Psychiatric Association. (2013). *Diagnostic and statistical manual of mental disorders* (5th ed.). Arlington, VA: American Psychiatric Publishing.

TABLE 13.2 DSM-5 Criteria for Major Neurocognitive Disorder

A. Evidence of significant cognitive decline from a previous level of performance in one or more cognitive domains (complex attention, executive function, learning and memory, language, perceptual-motor, or social cognition) based on:

1. Concern of the individual, a knowledgeable informant, or the clinician that there has been a significant decline in cognitive function; and
2. A substantial impairment in cognitive performance, preferably documented by standardized neuropsychological testing or, in its absence, another quantified clinical assessment.

B. The cognitive deficits interfere with independence in everyday activities (i.e., at a minimum, requiring assistance with complex instrumental activities of daily living such as paying bills or managing medications).
C. The cognitive deficits do not occur exclusively in the context of a delirium.
D. The cognitive deficits are not better explained by another mental disorder (e.g., major depressive disorder, schizophrenia).

Specify whether due to:
   Alzheimer's disease
   Frontotemporal lobar degeneration
   Lewy body disease
   Vascular disease
   Traumatic brain injury
   Substance/medication use
   HIV infection
   Prion disease
   Parkinson's disease
   Huntington's disease
   Another medical condition
   Multiple etiologies
   Unspecified

Specify:
   Without behavioral disturbance: If the cognitive disturbance is not accompanied by any clinically significant behavioral disturbance.
   With behavioral disturbance *(specify disturbance)*: If the cognitive disturbance is accompanied by a clinically significant behavioral disturbance (e.g., psychotic symptom mood disturbance, agitation, apathy, or other behavioral symptoms).

Specify current severity:
   Mild: Difficulties with instrumental activities of daily living (e.g., housework, managing money).
   Moderate: Difficulties with basic activities of daily living (e.g., feeding, dressing).
   Severe: Fully dependent.

Source: American Psychiatric Association. (2013). *Diagnostic and statistical manual of mental disorders* (5th ed.). Arlington, VA: American Psychiatric Publishing.

functioning. DSM-5 has reworded some of these concepts, and adds the domain of social cognition. The six new cognitive domains are titled as follows: complex attention; executive function; learning and memory; language; perceptual motor; and social cognition. The DSM-5 also lists examples of signs and symptoms and possible methods of assessment.

TABLE 13.3 DSM-5 Criteria for Minor Neurocognitive Disorder

A. Evidence of modest cognitive decline from a previous level of performance in one or more cognitive domains (complex attention, executive function, learning and memory, language, perceptual motor, or social cognition) based on:

 1. Concern of the individual, a knowledgeable informant, or the clinician that there has been a mild decline in cognitive function; and
 2. A modest impairment in cognitive performance, preferably documented by standardized neuropsychological testing or, in its absence, another quantified clinical assessment.

B. The cognitive deficits do not interfere with capacity for independence in everyday activities (i.e., complex instrumental activities of daily living such as paying bills or managing medications are preserved, but greater effort, compensatory strategies, or accommodation may be required).

C. The cognitive deficits do not occur exclusively in the context of a delirium.

D. The cognitive deficits are not better explained by another mental disorder (e.g., major depressive disorder, schizophrenia).

Specify whether due to:
 Alzheimer's disease
 Frontotemporal lobar degeneration
 Lewy body disease
 Vascular disease
 Traumatic brain injury
 Substance/medication use
 HIV infection
 Prion disease
 Parkinson's disease
 Huntington's disease
 Another medical condition
 Multiple etiologies
 Unspecified

Specify:
 Without behavioral disturbance: If the cognitive disturbance is not accompanied by any clinically significant behavioral disturbance.
 With behavioral disturbance *(specify disturbance)*: If the cognitive disturbance is accompanied by a clinically significant behavioral disturbance (e.g., psychotic symptoms, mood disturbance, agitation, apathy, or other behavioral symptoms).

Source: American Psychiatric Association. (2013). *Diagnostic and statistical manual of mental disorders* (5th ed.). Arlington, VA: American Psychiatric Publishing.

CHAPTER 15

Late Adolescence to Early Adulthood: Borderline Personality Disorder

This section accompanies chapter 15 in Kerig, Ludlow &Wenar (2012), *Developmental Psychopathology*, 6th Edition. McGraw-Hill Education.

The Personality Disorders section of DSM-5 remains appreciably unchanged from DSM-IV, as do the criteria for the diagnosis of **borderline personality disorder** specifically (see Table 15.1).

Potential Implications of the DSM-5 Criteria for the Diagnosis of Borderline Personality Disorder

As we have noted, there are no changes in the standard criteria for the diagnosis of BPD in DSM-5. However, the story may not be such a simple one. As an indication of the wide variety of expert opinion represented by the working group concerned with the personality disorder criteria, DSM-5 also contains an appendix describing an alternative *Multidimensional Personality and Trait Model* for the assessment and diagnosis of personality disorders. The alternative model focuses on two underlying dimensions: *impairments in personality functioning*; and the presence of *pathological personality traits*. These traits are conceptualized as being related to the five underlying negative characteristics that have emerged in a large body of research in the psychology of personality: *negative affectivity; detachment; antagonism; disinhibition; and psychoticism*.

In this alternative model, the functional impairments noted for BPD specifically

TABLE 15.1 DSM-5 Criteria for Borderline Personality Disorder

A pervasive pattern of instability of interpersonal relationships, self-image, and affects, and marked impulsivity, beginning by early adulthood and present in a variety of contexts, as indicated by five (or more) of the following:

1. Frantic efforts to avoid real or imagined abandonment. (**Note:** Do not include suicidal or self-mutilating behavior covered in Criterion 5.)
2. A pattern of unstable and intense interpersonal relationships characterized by alternating between extremes of idealization and devaluation.
3. Identity disturbance: markedly and persistently unstable self-image or sense of self.
4. Impulsivity in at least two areas that are potentially self-damaging (e.g., spending, sex, substance abuse, reckless driving, binge eating). (**Note:** Do not include suicidal or self-mutilating behavior covered in Criterion 5.)
5. Recurrent suicidal behavior, gestures, or threats, or self-mutilating behavior.
6. Affective instability due to a marked reactivity of mood (e.g., intense episodic dysphoria, irritability, or anxiety usually lasting a few hours and only rarely more than a few days).
7. Chronic feelings of emptiness.
8. Inappropriate, intense anger or difficulty controlling anger (e.g., frequent displays of temper, constant anger, recurrent physical fights).
9. Transient, stress-related paranoid ideation or severe dissociative symptoms.

Source: American Psychiatric Association. (2013). *Diagnostic and statistical manual of mental disorders* (5th ed.). Arlington, VA: American Psychiatric Publishing.

include difficulties with *identity, self-direction, empathy,* and *intimacy.* In turn, pathological traits associated with BPD include *emotional lability, anxiousness, separation insecurity, depressivity, impulsivity, risk-taking,* and *hostility.*

This is an intriguing model, particularly so given its grounding in a long line of empirical research. How well it will be utilized or incorporated into research and clinical practice is unclear, however, given its sequestration into an appendix in the nether regions of the DSM-5.

References

Al-Yagon, M., Cavendish, W., Cornoldi, C., Fawcett, A. J., Grünke, M., Hung, L. Y., ... & Vio, C. (2013). The Proposed Changes for DSM-5 for SLD and ADHD International Perspectives—Australia, Germany, Greece, India, Israel, Italy, Spain, Taiwan, United Kingdom, and United States. *Journal of learning disabilities, 46*(1), 58–72.

American Psychiatric Association. (2013). *Diagnostic and statistical manual of mental disorders.* (5th ed.). Arlington, VA: American Psychiatric Publishing.

Axelson, D., Findling, R. L., Fristad, M. A., Kowatch, R. A., Youngstrom, E. A., Horwitz, S. M., ... & Birmaher, B. (2012). Examining the proposed disruptive mood dysregulation disorder diagnosis in children in the Longitudinal Assessment of Manic Symptoms study. *Journal of Clinical Psychiatry, 73*(10), 1342.

Barbaresi, W. J., Katusic, S. K., Colligan, R. C., Weaver, A. L., & Jacobsen, S. J. (2005). Math learning disorder: Incidence in a population-based birth cohort, 1976–82, Rochester, Minn. *Ambulatory Pediatrics, 5*(5), 281–289.

Barch, D. M., Bustillo, J., Gaebel, W., Gur, R., Heckers, S., Malaspina, D., ... & Carpenter, W. (2013). Logic and justification for dimensional assessment of symptoms and related clinical phenomena in psychosis: relevance to DSM-5. *Schizophrenia research, 150*(1), 15–20.

Barkley, R. A., & Brown, T. E. (2008). Unrecognized attention-deficit/hyperactivity disorder in adults presenting with other psychiatric disorders. *CNS Spectrums, 13*(11), 977–984.

Bastra, L. & Frances, M.D. (2012) DSM-5 further inflates attention deficit hyperactivity disorder. *The Journal of Nervous and Mental Disease, 200,* 486–488.

Bates, J. E., Bayles, K., Bennett, D. S., Ridge, B., & Brown, M. M. (1991). Origins of externalizing behavior problems at eight years of age. *The development and treatment of childhood aggression, 17,* 93–120.

Bell, A. S. (2011) A critical review of ADHD diagnostic criteria: what to address in the DSM-V. *Journal of Attention Disorders, 15,* 3–10.

Bovin, M. J., & Marx, B. P. (2011). The importance of the peritraumatic experience in defining traumatic stress. *Psychological Bulletin, 137,* 47–67. doi:10.1037/a0021353

Bowlby, J. (1973). *Attachment and loss: Vol. II. Separation.* London, UK: Pimlico.

British Psychological Society. (2011). Response to the American Psychiatric Association: DSM-5 development. Retrieved from: http://apps.bps.org.uk/_publicationfiles/consultation-responses/DSM-5%20 2011%20-%20BPS%20response.pdf

Bryant-Waugh, R. (2013). Avoidant restrictive food intake disorder: An illustrative case example. *International Journal of Eating Disorders, 46*(5), 420–423.

Bui, E., Brunet, A., Allenou, C., Camassel, C., Raynaud, J. P., Claudet, I., ... & Birmes, P. (2010). Peritraumatic reactions and posttraumatic stress symptoms in school-aged children victims of road traffic accident. *General Hospital Psychiatry, 32*(3), 330–333.

Caplan, P. J, McCurdy-Myers, J., & Gans, M. (1992). Should premenstrual syndrome be called a psychiatric abnormality? *Feminism & Psychology, 2*(1), 27–44.

Carroll, B. J. (2014). Lessons for ICD-11 coming after DSM-5. *Australian and New Zealand journal of psychiatry, 48*(1), 90–91.

Cho, C. H., & Lee, H. J. (2014). Schizophrenia Spectrum Disorder in DSM-5: Is this a New Change? *Korean Journal of Schizophrenia Research, 17*(1), 5–11.

Coghill, D., & Seth, S. (2011) Do the diagnostic criteria for ADHD need to change? Comments on the preliminary proposals of the DSM-5 ADHD and Disruptive Behavior Disorders Committee. *European Journal of Child and Adolescent Psychiatry, 20,* 75–81.

Compton, W. M., Dawson, D. A., Goldstein, R. B., & Grant, B. F. (2013). Crosswalk between DSM-IV dependence and DSM-5 substance use disorders for opioids, cannabis, cocaine and alcohol. *Drug and alcohol dependence, 132*(1), 387–390.

Copeland, W. E., Angold, A., Costello, E. J., & Egger, H. (2013). Prevalence, comorbidity, and correlates of DSM-5 proposed disruptive mood dysregulation disorder.

American Journal of Psychiatry, 170(2), 173–179.

Copeland, W. E., Shanahan, L., Costello, E. J., & Angold, A. (2009). Childhood and adolescent psychiatric disorders as predictors of young adult disorders. *Archives of general psychiatry, 66*(7), 764–772.

Coyle, E., Karatzias, T., Summers, A., & Power, M. (2014). Emotions and emotion regulation in survivors of childhood sexual abuse: The importance of "disgust" in traumatic stress and psychopathology. *European Journal of Psychotraumatology, 5.*

Dockrell, J., Ricketts, J., Palikara, O., Charman, T., & Lindsay, G. (2012). Profiles of need and provision for children with language impairments and autism spectrum disorders in mainstream schools: A prospective study. Research Report DFE-RR247-BCRP9. London: Department for Education.

Eapen, V., & Črnčec, R. (2014). DSM 5 and child psychiatric disorders: What is new? What has changed? *Asian Journal of Psychiatry.*

Epperson, C. N., Steiner, M., Hartlage, S. A., Eriksson, E., Schmidt, P. J., Jones, I., & Yonkers, K. A. (2012). Premenstrual dysphoric disorder: Evidence for a new category for DSM-5. *American Journal of Psychiatry, 169*(5), 465–475.

Epstein, J.N., Langberg, J.M., Lichtenstein, P.K., et al. (2009) Community-wide intervention to improve the attention-deficit/hyperactivity disorder assessment and treatment practices of community physicians. *Pediatrics, 122,* 19–27.

Faraone, S., Biederman, J., Spencer, T., Mick, E., Murray, K., Petty, C., ... & Monuteaux, M. (2006). Diagnosing adult attention deficit hyperactivity disorder: are late onset and sub-

threshold diagnoses valid? *American Journal of Psychiatry, 163*(10), 1720–1729.

Fisher, M. M., Rosen, D. S., Ornstein, R. M., Mammel, K. A., Katzman, D. K., Rome, E. S., ... & Walsh, B. T. (2014). Characteristics of Avoidant/Restrictive Food Intake Disorder in children and adolescents: A "new disorder" in DSM-5. *Journal of Adolescent Health, 55*(1), 49–52.

Frances, A.J., & Widiger, T. (2012). Psychiatric diagnosis: Lessons from the DSM-5 past and cautions from the DSM-5 future. *Annual Review of Clinical Psychology, 8,* 109–130.

Frazier, T. W., Youngstrom, E. A., Speer, L., Embacher, R., Law, P., Constantino, J., Findling, R.L., Hardan, A.Y., & Eng, C. (2012). Validation of Proposed DSM-5 Criteria for Autism Spectrum Disorder. *Journal of the American Academy of Child & Adolescent Psychiatry, 51*(1), 28–40.

Frick, P. J., & Nigg, J. T. (2012). Current issues in the diagnosis of attention deficit hyperactivity disorder, oppositional defiant disorder, and conduct disorder. *Annual Review of Clinical Psychology, 8,* 77–107.

Frick, P. J., Ray, J. V., Thornton, L. C., & Kahn, R. E. (2013). Can callous-unemotional traits enhance the understanding, diagnosis, and treatment of serious conduct problems in children and adolescents? A comprehensive review. *Psychological Bulletin.*

Friedman, Matthew J. (2013). Finalizing PTSD in DSM-5: Getting here from there and where to go next. *Journal of Traumatic Stress, 26*(5), 548–556.

Geary, D. C. (2011). Characteristics, and causes of mathematical learning disabilities and persistent low achievement in mathematics. *Journal of*

Developmental and Behavioral Pediatrics, 32(3), 250–263.

Gibbs, V., Aldridge, F., Chandler, F., Witzlsperger, E., & Smith, K. (2012). Brief report: an exploratory study comparing diagnostic outcomes for autism spectrum disorders under DSM-IV-TR with the proposed DSM-5 revision. *Journal of Autism and Developmental Disorders, 42*(8), 1750–1756.

Gone, J.P., & Kirmayer, L.J. (2010). On the wisdom of considering culture and context in psychopathology. In Millon, T, Krueger, R, Simonsen, E. (Eds.), *Contemporary Directions in Psychopathology: Scientific foundations of the DSM-V and ICD-11.* New York: Guildford Press pp. 72–96.

Greenspan, S., & Woods, G. W. (2014). Intellectual disability as a disorder of reasoning and judgement: the gradual move away from intelligence quotient-ceilings. *Current opinion in psychiatry, 27*(2), 110–116.

Haahr, U., Friis, S., Larsen, T. K., Melle, I., Johannessen, J. O., Opjordsmoen, S., ... & McGlashan, T. (2008). First-episode psychosis: diagnostic stability over one and two years. *Psychopathology, 41*(5), 322–329.

Hafstad, G., Dyb, G., & Thoresen, S. (2014). *PTSD in ICD-11: a comparison of the proposed ICD-11 and DSM5 diagnostic criteria in a sample of young survivors of a catastrophic shooting.* Paper presented at the 30th Annual Meeting of the International Society for Traumatic Stress Studies, Miami, FL.

Hanson, R. F., & Spratt, E. G. (2000). Reactive attachment disorder: What we know about the disorder and implications for treatment. *Child Maltreatment, 5*(2), 137–145.

Hare, R. D. (1996). Psychopathy: A clinical construct whose time has come. *Criminal Justice and Behavior, 23*(1), 25–54.

Harris, J. C. (2014). New classification for neurodevelopmental disorders in DSM-5. *Current opinion in psychiatry, 27*(2), 95–97.

Hawes, D. J, Price, M. J., & Dadds, M. R. (2014). Callous-unemotional traits and the treatment of conduct problems in childhood and adolescence: A comprehensive review. *Clinical Child and Family Psychology Review*, 1–20.

Haworth, C., & Plomin, R. (2010). Quantitative genetics in the era of molecular genetics: Learning abilities and disabilities as an example. *Journal of the American Academy of Child & Adolescent Psychiatry, 49*(8), 783–793.

Heber, R. (1959) 'A manual on terminology and classification in mental retardation', American Journal Of Mental Deficiency, 64(Monograph Supplement)

Hudson, J. I., Coit, C. E., Lalonde, J. K., & Pope, H. G. (2012). By how much will the proposed new DSM-5 criteria increase the prevalence of binge eating disorder? *International Journal of Eating Disorders, 45*(1), 139–141.

Huerta, M., Bishop, S. L., Duncan, A., Hus, V., & Lord, C. (2012). Application of DSM-5 criteria for autism spectrum disorder to three samples of children with DSM-IV diagnoses of pervasive developmental disorders. *American Journal of Psychiatry, 169*(10), 1056–1064.

Hyman, S. L. (2014). New DSM-5 includes changes to autism criteria. AAP News.

Kahn, R. E., Frick, P. J., Youngstrom, E., Findling, R. L., & Youngstrom, J. K. (2012). The effects of including a callous–unemotional specifier for the diagnosis of conduct disorder.

Journal of Child Psychology and Psychiatry, 53(3), 271–282.

Kaland, N. (2011). Should Asperger syndrome be excluded from the forthcoming DSM-V? *Research in Autism Spectrum Disorders, 5*(3), 984–999.

Kamp-Becker, I., Smidt, J., Ghahreman, M., Heinzel-Gutenbrunner, M., Becker, K., & Remschmidt, H. (2010). Categorical and dimensional structure of autism spectrum disorders: the nosologic validity of Asperger syndrome. *Journal of autism and developmental disorders, 40*(8), 921–929.

Kanner, L. (1943). Autistic disturbances of affective contact. *Nervous Child, 2,* 217–250.

Kaplow, J B., Layne, C. M., Pynoos, R. S., Cohen, J. A., & Lieberman, A. (2012). DSM-V diagnostic criteria for bereavement-related disorders in children and adolescents: Developmental considerations. *Psychiatry: Interpersonal and Biological Processes, 75*(3), 243–266.

Kaplow, J. B., Howell, K. H., & Layne, C. M. (2014). Do circumstances of the death matter? Identifying socioenvironmental risks for grief-related psychopathology in bereaved youth. *Journal of Traumatic Stress, 27*(1), 42–49.

Karande, S. (2008). Current challenges in managing specific learning disability in Indian children [Editorial]. *Journal of Postgraduate Medicine, 54* (2), 75–77.

Karande, S., Mehta, V., & Kulkarni, M. (2007). Impact of an education program on parental knowledge of specific learning disability. *Indian Journal of Medical Sciences, 61*(7), 398–406.

Keenan, K., Loeber, R., & Green, S. (1999). Conduct disorder in girls: A review of the literature. *Clinical child and*

family psychology review, 2(1), 3–19.

Kenney, L., & Walsh, B. T. (2013). Avoidant/Restrictive Food Intake Disorder (ARFID). *Eating Disorders Review, 24*(3), 1–4.

Kerig, P. K., & Bennett, D. C. (2013). Beyond fear, helplessness, and horror: Peritraumatic reactions associated with post-traumatic stress disorder among traumatized delinquent youth. *Psychological Trauma, 5*(5), 431–438.

Kessler, R. C., Berglund, P. A., Chiu, W. T., Deitz, A. C., Hudson, J. I., Shahly, V., ... & Xavier, M. (2013). The prevalence and correlates of binge eating disorder in the World Health Organization World Mental Health Surveys. *Biological Psychiatry, 73*(9), 904–914.

Kessler, R., Adler, L., Barkley, R., Biederman, J., Conners, C., Demler, O., ... & Zaslavsky, A. (2006). The prevalence and correlates of adult ADHD in the United States: results from the National Comorbidity Survey Replication. *American Journal of Psychiatry, 163*(4), 716–723.

Kilpatrick, D. G., Resnick, H. S., Milanak, M. E., Miller, M. W., Keyes, K. M., & Friedman, M. J. (2013). National estimates of exposure to traumatic events and PTSD prevalence using DSM-IV and DSM-5 criteria. *Journal of Traumatic Stress, 26*(5), 537–547.

Kim, Y. S., Leventhal, B. L., Koh, Y. J., Fombonne, E., Laska, E., Lim, E. C., ... & Grinker, R. R. (2011). Prevalence of autism spectrum disorders in a total population sample. *American Journal of Psychiatry, 168*(9), 904–912.

Kovas, Y., Haworth, C. M., Dale, P. S., Plomin, R., Weinberg, R. A., Thomson, J. M., & Fischer, K. W. (2007). The genetic and environmental origins of learning abilities and disabilities in the early school years. *Monographs of the Society for research in Child Development*, i-156.

Kraemer, H. C., Kupfer, D. J., Clarke, D. E., Narrow, W. E., & Regier, D. A. (2012). DSM-5: how reliable is reliable enough? *American Journal of Psychiatry*, *169*(1), 13–15.

Landerl, K., & Moll, K. (2010). Comorbidity of learning disorders: prevalence and familial transmission. *Journal of Child Psychology and Psychiatry*, *51*(3), 287–294.

Lane, C. (2007). Shyness. *New Haven, CT: Yale University*.

Leekam, S. R., Nieto, C., Libby, S. J., Wing, L., & Gould, J. (2007). Describing the sensory abnormalities of children and adults with autism. *Journal of autism and developmental disorders*, *37*(5), 894–910.

Levy, F. (2014). Child and adolescent changes to DSM-5. *Asian Journal of Psychiatry*.

Lewis, F.M., Murdoch, B.E., & Woodyatt, G.C. (2007). Communicative competence and metalinguistic ability: performance by children and adults with autism spectrum disorder. *Journal of Autism and Developmental Disorders*, *37*(8), 1525–38

Lord, C., & Jones, R. M. (2012). Annual Research Review: Re-thinking the classification of autism spectrum disorders. *Journal of Child Psychology and Psychiatry*, *53*(5), 490–509.

Luckasson, R., Borthwick-Duffy, S., Buntinx, W. H., Coulter, D. L., Craig, E. M. P., Reeve, A., ... & Tasse, M. J. (2002). *Mental retardation: Definition, classification, and systems of supports*. **American Association on Mental Retardation**.

Maenner, M.J., Rice, C.E., Arneson, C.L., Cunniff, C.,

Schieve, L.A., Carpenter, L.A., Van Naarden Braun, K., Kirby, R.S., Bakian, A.V., & Durkin, M.S. (2014). Potential Impact of DSM-5 Criteria on Autism Spectrum Disorder (ASD) Prevalence Estimates. *JAMA Psychiatry* (in press)

Malaspina, D., Walsh-Messinger, J., Gaebel, W., Smith, L. M., Gorun, A., Prudent, V., ... & Trémeau, F. (2014). Negative symptoms, past and present: A historical perspective and moving to DSM-5. *European Neuropsychopharmacology*, *24*(5), 710–724.

Martin, J., Hamshere, M. L., O'Donovan, M. C., Rutter, M., & Thapar, A. (2014). Factor structure of autistic traits in children with ADHD. *Journal of autism and developmental disorders*, *44*(1), 204–215.

Matson, J. L., Hattier, M. A., & Williams, L. W. (2012). How does relaxing the algorithm for autism affect DSM-V prevalence rates? *Journal of Autism and Developmental Disorders*, *42*(8), 1549–1556.

McPartland, J. C., Reichow, B., & Volkmar, F. R. (2012). Sensitivity and Specificity of Proposed DSM-5: Diagnostic Criteria for Autism Spectrum Disorder. *Journal of the American Academy of Child & Adolescent Psychiatry*, *51*(4), 368–383.

Miller, M.W., Wolf, E.J., Kilpatrick, D., Resnick, H., Marx, B.P., Holowka, D.W., ... & Friedman, M.J. (2013). The prevalence and latent structure of proposed DSM-5 posttraumatic stress disorder symptoms in US national and veteran samples. *Psychological Trauma*, *5*(6), 501.

Norbury, C. F. (2014). Practitioner Review: Social (pragmatic) communication disorder conceptualization, evidence and clinical implications. *Journal of Child Psychology and Psychiatry*, *55*(3), 204–216.

Ornstein, R. M., Rosen, D. S., Mammel, K. A., Callahan, S. T., Forman, S., Jay, M. S., ... & Walsh, B. T. (2013). Distribution of eating disorders in children and adolescents using the proposed DSM-5 criteria for feeding and eating disorders. *Journal of Adolescent Health*, *53*(2), 303–305.

Papazoglou, A., Jacobson, L. A., McCabe, M., Kaufmann, W., & Zabel, T. A. (2014). To ID or Not to ID? Changes in Classification Rates of Intellectual Disability Using DSM-5. *Mental Retardation*, *52*(3), 165–174.

Paris, J. (2013). *The Intelligent Clinician's Guide to the DSM-5RG.*Oxford University Press.

Pimperton, H., & Nation, K. (2010). Suppressing irrelevant information from working memory: Evidence for domain-specific deficits in poor comprehenders. *Journal of Memory and Language*, *62*(4), 380–391.

Polanczyk, G. V. (2014). Dimensionality of childhood psychopathology and the challenge of integration into clinical practice. *European child & adolescent psychiatry*, *23*(4), 183–185.

Polanczyk, G., Caspi, A., Houts, R., Kollins, S. H., Rohde, L. A., & Moffitt, T. E. (2010). Implications of extending the ADHD age-of-onset criterion to age 12: results from a prospectively studied birth cohort. *Journal of the American Academy of Child and Adolescent Psychiatry*, *49*(3), 210–216.

Posey, D. J., Stigler, K. A., Erickson, C. A., & McDougle, C. J. (2008). Antipsychotics in the treatment of autism. *The Journal of clinical investigation*, *118*(1), 6–14.

Prosser, B., & Reid, R. (2013). The DSM-5 changes and ADHD: More than a tweak of terms. *Australian and New Zealand Journal of Psychiatry*, *47*(12), 1196–1197.

Pynoos, R. S., Steinberg, A. M., Layne, C. M., Briggs, E. C., Ostrowski, S. A., & Fairbank, J. A. (2009). DSM-V PTSD diagnostic criteria for children and adolescents: A developmental perspective and recommendations. *Journal of Traumatic Stress, 22*(5), 391–398.

Regier, D.A., Kuhl, E.A., & Kupfer, D.J. (2013). The DSM-5: Classification and criteria changes. *World Psychiatry, 12*(2), 92–98.

Rey, J. (2010). Proposed changes to the psychiatric classification: towards DSM5. *Australian Psychiatry, 18*(4), 309–313.

Rodríguez-Testal, J. F., Senín-Calderón, C., & Perona-Garcelán, S. (2014). From DSM-IV-TR to DSM-5: analysis of some changes. *International Journal of Clinical and Health Psychology.* 221–231.

Rommelse, N. N. J., Franke, B., Geurts, H. M., Hartman, C. A., & Buitelaar, J. K. (2010). Shared heritability of attention-deficit/hyperactivity disorder and autism spectrum disorder. *European Child and Adolescent Psychiatry, 19*(3), 281–29.

Salekin, R. T., Tippey, J. G., & Allen, A. D. (2012). Treatment of conduct problem youth with interpersonal callous traits using mental models: Measurement of risk and change. *Behavioral Sciences & the Law, 30*(4), 470–486.

Salvador Carulla, L. S., Reed, G. M., Vaez-Azizi, L. M., Cooper, S. A., Leal, R., Bertelli, M., ... & Saxena, S. (2011). Intellectual developmental disorders: towards a new name, definition and framework for "mental retardation/intellectual disability" in ICD-11. *World Psychiatry, 10*(3), 175–180.

Schalock, R. L., Luckasson, R. A., & Shogren, K. A. (2007). The renaming of mental retardation: Understanding the change to the term intellectual disability. *Journal Information, 45*(2), 116–124.

Sibley, M.H., Waxmonsky, J.G., Robb, J.A., & Pelham, W.E. (2013). Implications of Changes for the Field ADHD. *Journal of Learning Disabilities, 46*(1), 34–42.

Simpson, J. (2014). DSM-5 and Neurocognitive Disorders. *Journal of the American Academy of Psychiatry and the Law, 42*(2), 159–164.

Solanto, M. V., Wasserstein, J., Marks, D. J., & Mitchell, K. J. (2012). Diagnosis of ADHD in Adults What Is the Appropriate DSM-5 Symptom Threshold for Hyperactivity-Impulsivity? *Journal of attention disorders, 16*(8), 631–634.

Stringaris, A., & Goodman, R. (2009). Three dimensions of oppositionality in youth. *Journal of Child Psychology and Psychiatry, 50*(3), 216–223.

Szatmari, P., Bryson, S., Duku, E., Vaccarella, L., Zwaigenbaum, L., Bennett, T., & Boyle, M. H. (2009). Similar developmental trajectories in autism and Asperger syndrome: from early childhood to adolescence. *Journal of Child Psychology and Psychiatry, 50*(12), 1459–1467.

Tandon, R., Heckers, S., Bustillo, J., Barch, D. M., Gaebel, W., Gur, R. E., ... & Carpenter, W. (2013). Catatonia in DSM-5. *Schizophrenia research, 150*(1), 26–30.

Tannock, R. (2013). Rethinking ADHD and LD in DSM-5 Proposed Changes in Diagnostic Criteria. *Journal of learning disabilities, 46*(1), 5–25.

Taylor, L. K., & Weems, C. F. (2009). What do youth report as a traumatic event? Toward a developmentally informed classifaction of traumatic stressors. *Psychological Trauma, 1*(2), 91–106.

Wakefield, J. C., & First, M. B. (2013). Validity of the bereavement exclusion to major depression: Does the empirical evidence support the proposal to eliminate the exclusion in DSM-5? *World Psychiatry, 11*(1), 3–10.

Webster-Stratton, C. (1996). Early onset conduct problems: Does gender make a difference? *Journal of Consulting and Clinical Psychology, 64*(3), 540–551.

Weder, N. D., Muralee, S., Penland, H., & Tampi, R. R. (2008). Catatonia: a review. *Annals of Clinical Psychiatry, 20*(2), 97–107.

Weitlauf, A. S., Gotham, K. O., Vehorn, A. C., & Warren, Z. E. (2014). Brief Report: DSM-5 "Levels of Support:" A Comment on Discrepant Conceptualizations of Severity in ASD. *Journal of autism and developmental disorders, 44*(2), 471–476.

Wing, L., Gould, J., & Gillberg, C. (2011). Autism spectrum disorders in the DSM-V: better or worse than the DSM-IV? *Research in developmental disabilities, 32*(2), 768–773.

Winters, K. C., Martin, C. S., & Chung, T. (2011). Substance use disorders in DSM-V when applied to adolescents. *Addiction, 106*(5), 882–884.

Zeanah, C. H., & Gleason, M. M. (2010). Reactive attachment disorder: a review for DSM-V. Report presented to the *American Psychiatric Association.*

Zimmerman, M., & Galione, J. (2010). Psychiatrists' and nonpsychiatrist physicians' reported use of the DSM-IV criteria for major depressive disorder. *The Journal of clinical psychiatry, 71*(3), 235–238.

Zupanick, C. E. (2013). The New DSM-5: Schizophrenia Spectrum and Other Psychotic Disorders. *AMHC,* 207.